The Korean Wave in a Post-Pandemic World

Geon-Cheol Shin · Mark D. Whitaker

The Korean Wave in a Post-Pandemic World

BTS, Cosmax and Squid Game

Springer

Geon-Cheol Shin
School of Management
Kyung Hee University
Seoul, Korea (Republic of)

Mark D. Whitaker
Department of Technology and Society
Stony Brook University
The State University of New York, Korea
(SUNY Korea)
Incheon, Korea (Republic of)

ISBN 978-981-99-3682-3 ISBN 978-981-99-3683-0 (eBook)
https://doi.org/10.1007/978-981-99-3683-0

This work was supported by grant from Kyung Hee University in 2023 (KHU-20231230)

This Springer imprint is published by the registered company Springer Nature Singapore Pte Ltd.
The registered company address is: 152 Beach Road, #21-01/04 Gateway East, Singapore 189721, Singapore

To my daughter, Hyein

—Geon-Cheol Shin

Preface

We two co-authors seek to illuminate the successes of Korea and the Korean Wave to the best of our combined abilities by showing different insights on the same topic. One author is a Korean professor of Marketing and International Business. His research interests are in the areas of competitive strategies in international markets and in global strategic management, particularly on dynamic competitive strategies in the cross-cultural perspectives on the global entertainment industry. From his MBA and Ph.D. in the 1980's in the U.S., he observed how Korea has successfully transformed itself from a developing country to a developed economy and most recently to a global leader in innovation and technology. Earlier from only its manufacturing sector, now Korea spreads its contemporary culture across wide and diverse societies around the world. Emanating from Korean culture, the Korean Wave has marked South Korea as a soft power leader. Serving as the country director of Korea for the Academy of International Business, he believes that Korean Wave and its global diffusion can be understood effectively in terms of the production and distribution processes of each cultural industry. The other author is an American professor of Sociology, interested in comparative world development and particularly Information Communication Technology for Development (ICT4D). He has lived fully in Korea since 2007. Thus, even he has seen personally the rise of a more digital Korea and the rise of the global Korean Wave over the years. While many remain puzzled about the digital success of the simultaneous harbinger and outlier of Korea, he has been driven to think about Korea in comparison with other developing countries on many more factors than digital ones. He seeks to explain Korea's stunning cultural, political, and economic successes in comparison with other developing nations—and even in comparison with declines in other already developed nations with their less stellar, faltering, or even stalled development now. He brings more comparative lenses to bear on what explains Korean success for what could be transferred to other countries, whether with ease or with difficulty.

Both co-authors' contributions give insights into success factors of Korea as the world's *best* case so far of a durable fast development drive and the world's *only* case so far of a durably successful global cultural wave from a non-Western country. Plus, we want to know how Korea got to this digital future before anyone else while remaining intact and even improved instead of smashed by the growing 'triple global storm' of a digital global economy, a digital global culture, and a digital and decentralized global media. Korea gives us a mentor of general developmental excellence and digital developmental excellence—whether in economics, in multi-party democratic politics, in a growing insistence on universal civil rights, or in a stable culture under a digital onslaught. Other developing countries give us mostly cautionary tales of horror as they are pulled apart by their earlier development drives or by their own fresh digital cultures as they are turned into unrepresentative digital police states or are unable nimbly to adapt economically to a global digital economy.

We hope everyone in the world is the audience of this book. This is because regardless of many different countries of origin, many different cultures, and many different development levels, we have to start thinking of our national choices in this common digital future more seriously, as all past nations' non-digital economics and non-digital past cultures burn brightly behind us as we go through a digital bottleneck. Korea, like a tenacious calm eye in this digital firestorm, has taken advantage of successful global digital development and created a globally digital cultural wave while remaining culturally intact and while becoming improved culturally, economically, and politically instead of being pulled apart.

In short, this is a book about the uniquely successful Korean fast development drive leading into the now uniquely successful global cultural Korean Wave. It is equally a comparative book about world development and the history of communications viewed respectively through the lens of the world's best success so far of an (ex-) developing country that is now a developed country, and viewed through the lens of the world's earliest and still most 'digitally saturated' larger nation. In conclusion, Korea has important and even unique lessons to teach about its fast development drive and cultural wave for how to have a better digital future compared to what other countries are inventing now, if we listen.

Seoul, Korea (Republic of) Geon-Cheol Shin
Incheon, Korea (Republic of) Mark D. Whitaker

"Lamp of the East"

In the golden age of Asia,
Korea was one of its lamp bearers,
And that lamp is waiting to be lit once again,
For the illumination of the East.

—Rabindranath Tagore, 1929

(Nobel Prize in Literature, 1913)

Contents

About the Authors

Dr. Geon-Cheol Shin (Georgia State University, 1992) is Professor of the School of Management and Executive Director of the Management Research Institute at Kyung Hee University in Seoul, Korea. He currently serves as Country Director of Korea for the Academy of International Business and is hosting the 66th annual meeting of the AIB in Seoul, Korea. Professor Shin also served as President of both the Korean Academy of International Business and the Association of APEC Studies. He has authored a dozen books among which include *Global Business and Marketing Principles in the Era of Market 4.0*. He has published over 100 articles in journals such as Korean Management Review, Industrial Marketing Management, Journal of Business Research, International Marketing Review, Journal of Product Innovation Management, and International Business Review. He serves on the editorial board of the Asia Pacific Business Review and is Guest Editor of its special issue entitled "Post-pandemic business opportunities in East Asia".

Dr. Mark D. Whitaker (U. of Wisconsin-Madison, 2008) is an American Sociology Professor and Author at Stony Brook University's Department of Technology and Society, at the State University of New York, Korea (SUNY Korea). He has lived and worked in South Korea since 2007, studying Korean culture and its digital economy. His research involves comparative-historical human, environmental, and technical interactions in world economic development and civil development. His other books include *Ecological Revolution* and *Toward a Bioregional State*. In his teaching and curricular development in Information Communication Technology for Development (ICT4D), he is interested in how media regime changes altered cultural forms, patterns of daily life, and economic development. He has been invited to present at the United Nations Secretariat in New York and at the Asia Development Bank in Manila, Philippines on ICT4D strategies for sustainability. He is the recipient of awards from the U.S. National Research Foundation and grants from the Korean National Research Foundation—the latter being a rare honor for a foreign national in Korea.

List of Figures

List of Tables

Chapter 1
Introduction

There was a declared pandemic called officially "COVID-19" by the World Health Organization in December 2019. Throughout early 2020, many national governments took China's historically untried totalitarian policies of quarantine control and tried to copy them in their own nations, worldwide. As a result, a group of invasive policies with a lot of national variation developed—around face masks, 'social distancing,' technocratic digital tracking of all individuals via ostensibly illegal public use of their private data from their mobile phones and their private medical decisions, emergency-authorized PCR testing or rapid antigen testing, emergency authorized experimental mRNA genetic injections, single nationally standardized treatment protocols, forced injections, digital 'vaccine passports' and denial of much public social life via denial of organizational access to public accommodations without them, and of course 'lockdowns.' The latter term is a euphemism for a quarantine martial law policy that totally closed or partially limited the 'in-person' indoor crowd size of various business, restaurants, schools, gyms, hospitals, and even totally closed or partially limited open air public facilities like parks, playgrounds, and concert venues for what became an ever-extending indefinite period, thus banning free assembly until further notice. Some countries even locked or welded people in their homes (like respectively Italy or China), limited citizens' freedoms of travel around their own country (like in Australia), or, if they wanted to visit hospitals and doctor's offices, would deny medical care unless they gave up their civil rights of voluntary informed consent and their right to refuse medical treatments. Governments went so far as to deny visits to loved ones in hospitals and denied public funerals. Governments blocked in-person celebrations like graduation ceremonies and marriages.

For many it was a traumatic time of sorrow, loss, panic, and bankruptcy. Equally, it was a time of great wealth transfer to digitalization in the 'non-face-to-face economy.' Global workers lost an estimated $3.7 trillion in earnings, an 8.3% decline. Nationally, American workers saw the largest losses in earnings, with a 10.3% decline. Globally, 114 million people lost employment, called an "unprecedented" level, with global women losing 5% of their jobs compared to men losing only 3.9% of their jobs. Plus, the global youth of "Generation Z" (age 15 to 24) saw the largest losses of

G.-C. Shin and M. D. Whitaker, *The Korean Wave in a Post-Pandemic World*,
https://doi.org/10.1007/978-981-99-3683-0_1

8.7% of their jobs (Kaplan, 2021). Meanwhile the world's billionaires instantly got richer by $3.9 trillion—*in merely the first ten months* of the first year between March 2020 to December 2020. Thus the world's 2,365 billionaires got a nearly "$4 trillion boost to their wealth during the first year of the pandemic, increasing their fortunes by 54%..." By 2023, the top 1% had gained $26 trillion for their asset portfolios (Elliott, 2023). Meanwhile, "people living in poverty globally doubled to more than 500 million during the first nine months" (Picchi, 2021). Approximately 150 million more people were living in hunger and starvation in 2021 compared to 2019 (WHO, 2022).

As the in-person economy was closed or made so irregular, capricious, and unpredictable in its changing rules and regulations that it became expensive or impossible for many businesses to remain open and profitable, the only predictable regular markets and medium of life with stability became the world's online digital economy. Digital by default became a surrogate totalizing real world experience. Many different kinds of social relationships started to look homogeneously the same and be delivered the same, by being mediated through an Internet-connected computer screen and a slew of online platform accounts.

Obviously the world of performing arts was particularly affected. However, much of the Korean Wave already was involved in a deep digitalization of its entertainment. Therefore, the Korean Wave adjusted well, and even brilliantly, to these externally-forced conditions. How did all of this occur? How did Korea and the Korean Wave find itself so much more prepared digitally as a nation and a culture in its past? In the present, what were this lockdown period's effects on the Korean Wave and the Korean economy? What are the implications for Korea and the world of this increasingly digital global culture into the future?

Thus, one focus of this book becomes these three questions about the past, present, and future of Korea and the Korean Wave. Korea has adapted well to our increasingly global digital economy, our global digital culture, and our global decentralized media. Korea seems the world's most brilliant example of success so far in durably interfacing with and durably profiting in this global digital world without so far losing its culture or without losing its multi-party democracy and civil rights. However, a second focus of this book is on world development: how might the world learn from Korea to transfer its development prowess and its successful strategies of a cultural wave to their own nations? A third focus of this book is the history of communications, given we are in the middle of a massive global 'regime change' of media into cultures dominated by decentralized wireless telecommunications of mobile multimedia—with over five billion mobile phones worldwide by 2022, in a world of over eight billion people by 2022. South Korea from the 1990s to the present became the earliest most 'saturated' digital culture and digital economy in world history (See Appendix 1). What is that media change doing to us, to cultures, to nations, and to world development itself? What is the connection of this media regime change to South Korea's stunning developmental prowess? What is the connection of this media regime change to world development in general?

In Part I, about the past, one success factor of the more digital Korean Wave is the economic Korean Miracle from the 1960s to the present. Korea's fast development drive has been so much more successful than other developing countries. Plus, Korea chose digital telecommunications from the 1980s as an export-led economic sector and has continued to prioritize it. This helps explain the rise of a digital economy and then a digital cultural wave in Korea so much earlier and so much more thoroughly than other developing nations so far. Thus, Korea was more prepared to move more of the Korean Wave online from 2020 through 2023. However, Korean success is so much more than just a digital economic sector. There is something to learn for world development here around the preservation of the Korean culture and around Korea's national policies of greater consensus that help explain this nation's greater abilities of innovation and durability in crisis. Other developing nations can learn much that is useful for their own development by analyzing Korea.

Korea of course experienced its own traumas of the past: colonial experiences, poverty, civil war, ideological division, military coups, dictatorial politics, bad side effects of compressed growth, and a rising gap between rich and the poor. Korea was once so infrastructurally destroyed and so deeply dependent on foreign aid, it could not even feed itself in the late 1950s. However, Korea has transcended its past. Korea entered the OECD in 1997, the 'country club' of the world's most advanced and globally-interlinked national economies. Korea remains a unique outlier in being *the only non-Western ex-colonized nation in the OECD today*, and recently it got the honor of being the only country in the world *ever* to be removed from the developing country category and put into the United Nations' fully developed country category in 2021. By 2022, Korea is the tenth largest national economy in the world, the eighth largest generator of electricity, the sixth largest importer of energy, and the seventh largest entertainment industry in the world. Korea is now one of the more generous foreign aid *donors* to the world as well. Plus, Korea has achieved dozens of 'world firsts' in its digital readiness (as noted in Appendix 1). From the late 1990s, Korea built for itself one of the world's best-equipped, most updated, and most culturally saturated culture of telecommunication networks in use in the world today. This gave Korea an earlier advantage and earlier business expertise in disseminating its cultural contents to a digital world through its information and communications infrastructure to itself and to the world in the Korean Wave.

In short, no other country in the world *so far* except Korea has conquered *so many* of the bad conditions of their economic and political past *so fast*, while achieving *so much,* despite still conserving and respecting the cultural past *so deeply,* while becoming *so digital.*

Thus, Korea built its own future, and yet this future was hardly a full break with its ancient past. After its fast development drive started from 1961 to the present, Korea has relied on export-led development increasingly merged with enhancing other parts of its rural and traditional ancient culture even as it demoted its ancient aristocracy from power for good by the 1960s. This proud Korean cultural continuity is arguably a resource that supercharged the economic Korean Miracle and still supercharges the Korean Wave today. Koreans spend much time, effort, and loving attention to detail in their stylish historical movie dramas as they spend in training modern K-pop idols, in innovating cosmetics, or in designing digital technology like smartphones or metaverse applications. Koreans are ancient culturally yet modern innovators just the same.

Korea's *durable*, modern, multi-sector economic successes combined with *durable* cultural preservation instead of cultural self-destruction is the envy today of developing or developed nations alike. Korea and the Korean Wave have become beacons to the world that made billions of people in much larger or smaller countries curious about how a once very poor 'mid-sized' nation built itself into a highly-developed and culturally-acclaimed nation. Korea has had this double success that is hard to build in any nation whether it is a developing country or an already developed nation. So, even already developed nations are puzzled at Korea's odd combination of great modern technical innovation in digital technology quickly invented and implemented that nonetheless are invented in a mostly very conservative and homogenous culture that dislikes cultural innovation. Thus, it is useful to understand how or why Korea's technological changes are so innovative while its culture is so traditional, particularly when compared to developed countries with their rising cultural problems or lesser technical innovation in a more competitive multi-polar global economy. Therefore even people living in developed countries can learn from analyzing Korean successes instead of the interested audience being only developing countries. Plus, this book is written for the audience of Koreans themselves—who debate about the causes of their own tremendous success. In short, this book attempts to provide a more comparative and analytical attempt at an explanation of success factors of both the economic Korean Miracle and the global cultural Korean Wave.

In Part II, about the present, a timeline and analysis follow about the rising Korean Wave along with the fresh Korean digital innovations during the multi-year duration of lockdown policies between 2020 to 2023.

First, the rising Korean Wave has played a leading role in exporting Korea's cultural content to the world in the past 30 years. It started to accelerate only in the past five years with the first 'simultaneous successes' of the global Korean Wave from 2018, described later. After 2020, the Korean Wave is clearly a big cultural weapon helping 'mid-sized' Korea form a much larger global digital fandom for Korean culture and products. By increasing the number of consumers of Korean culture who are friendly to Korea around the world, the Korean Wave has catalyzed a virtuous cycle that enhances Korea's status as a cultural and economic powerhouse. The Korean International Exchange Foundation estimates that as of 2021, there are 105 million Korean Wave fan club members in more than 100 countries. Other estimates put this closer to 150 million. The Korean Wave is now a universally attractive 'brand' or craze that appears as chic and valuable to the whole world across a variety of Korean products, material or cultural. The Korean Wave has not only upgraded Korea's national image, but also enhances export competitiveness of Korean consumer goods and service industries by their association with it.

Culturally, there is a uniquely *modern* and *universal* quality to the Korean Wave. The true global popularity of the Korean Wave indicates there is something sublime, transcendent, and universal found by people worldwide in the themes of the Korean Wave beyond being just a distant echoing of this one nation's culture around the world. This modern and universal quality of the Korean Wave may seem odd, because

Korea's unique cultural features of the past are that it has been *ancient, stable,* and *isolated instead of* modern, dynamic, and universal. It is argued later that ancient Korea historically is a true outlier to many shared themes of world history defined more by the common transfers of ideas, peoples, and technologies across and through different cultures. However, in modern Korea, the rapid digitalization of this more isolated Korean culture has made them quickly cosmopolitan in their export-led economy while remaining very closed to cultural assimilation themselves. Instead of it fading away, this homogeneous culture at home remains a major motivating cultural strength in the Korean Wave. Honing their skills over decades, artists in the Korean Wave have become good at expressing the universality of our human condition yet in the guise of their own Korean culture. They can express this universality whether themes are taken from the daily life of sophisticated contemporary Korea or taken from ancient historical personalities in costume dramas. Universal themes like social inequality, the desperate gaps between rich and poor, people torn by competing or double loyalties between personal love or love of nation, shy innocent romances, school dramas, coming-of-age family struggles, patriotism, national and community betrayal, etc., are timeless global cultural phenomena not limited to one country. Particularly in the past few years of tragic lockdowns, as people worldwide were suffering from economic anxiety, mental and physical exhaustion, and dark future prospects, the energy and messages of the Korean Wave inspired positive thinking to young and old people around the world. The Korean Wave additionally got very good at creating ironic comedic satire that was cathartic to watch about the world's rising inequalities and desperation.

Second, fresh Korean digital innovations in global Korean Wave accelerated further due to many countries' lockdown conditions worldwide between 2020 and 2023 providing an entrepreneurial market in Korea being forced to adapt to this. Plus, it is testament to Korea's uncanny cultural ability to have a quicker collective innovation on tasks they set their minds to do, seemingly faster in response compared than other nations. By 2023, Korea has emerged stronger, fleeter, more beautiful, more popular, and more digital than ever in its offerings to the global culture. These fresh digital innovations brought about a turning point in the entertainment industry of the Korean Wave toward a more totalizing digital transformation that will affect both Korea and the world for years to come. In these inventions, the Korean economy particularly, and the whole world less so, got an artificial global-scale boost to go further ahead into a scenario of what a total digital future would look like. Once more on this theme of where world development is going, we can glimpse one scenario of this global digital future within the Korea of today.

In Part III, the future of Korea, the Korean Wave, and the world is analyzed in terms of several scenarios of what it will mean for all nations to have access to or potentially to be wrecked by a more thoroughly global digital economy, a global digital culture, and a global decentralized media. What will this do to Korea and the Korean Wave over time? What will this do to other countries' economies and cultural productions? What will it do to enhance or harm viability of different kinds of nations? Which kinds of nations' economies and cultures will thrive in this triple digital storm even as other kinds of nations will be unable to adapt, and thus find collapse and breakdown?

On the one hand, in *learning from Korea for world development*, Korea can be treated as a good *harbinger* and good model to emulate. It is a particularly well-balanced digital future, since Korea digitized without losing its culture and while keeping its democracy and civil rights intact and even improved. Plus, Korea blossoms worldwide now by showing its culture in the global Korean Wave. However, the same digital future may work out very differently and unrepresentatively in other nations. Already other nations show a great difficulty in adapting to this global digital economy and culture. This has put Korea further ahead in digital competition as well.

Thus, on the other hand, Korea can be treated as a *global outlier*. Korea was already very far ahead in its digital economy and digital culture compared to other nations before 2019. So, after 2020, and through 2023, Korea has only rocketed further ahead in its digital prowess and digital readiness to take on the whole world.

How has it been done? To what extent are Korea's successes transferrable to other countries? Korea is a harbinger foreshadowing a more common digital future for us all, based on what it has done to Korea first. Equally, to what extent are Korea's successes the product of unique conditions as a true outlier—easy to learn from though hard to follow? Regardless of whether the reader considers Korea as digital harbinger or digital outlier, the world can learn from Korea's superlatively successful case of non-Western development and its equally successful global cultural wave for what it means to live on the cusp of the twenty-first century as different options of the digital future are in the offing. Countries are now competing within a dawning more multi-polar world culture and within a revolutionary change of media toward two-way viral mass media. This media regime change is compounded by the fact that there already over 3 billion smartphones (and over 5 billion mobile phones in general) rather evenly distributed around the world, instead of mobile phones suffering from a great deal of 'digital divide' in this technology unlike previous communications technologies. This means Korea and all countries are riding within the same decentralized and global digital networked communication. Easy global cultural production, distribution, and reception are now possible for the first time all over the world, all the time, from the palm of nearly everyone's hand.

As Korea and the whole world is in the beginning of this global digital media change, it will continue to alter or even to collapse past economies and even past national cultures in which we have lived before. This global digital media change is like a burning bridge behind our backs, lighting the way ahead while forcing us to focus more deeply on only the path ahead. Korea is one version of this digital future, already there on the other side of this burning bridge, welcoming us. We can see Korea surprisingly is unburnt and intact despite already crossing this burning bridge. For another analogy, Korea has already passed through this 'digital bottleneck' through which not all countries will survive to look the same on the other side.

For instance, in the midst of national and generally global lockdowns that destroyed cultures and economies worldwide, on July 6, 2021, the status of the Republic of Korea (South Korea) was changed to a 'developed country' at the 68th United Nations Conference on Trade and Development (UNCTAD). This made Korea the first case so far of a status change from a 'developing country' to a 'developed country' since the establishment of UNCTAD in 1964. Earlier, in 2018, Korea's global economic ranking became so strong that it became the 10th largest national economy, a status it still holds in 2022 (Global PEO Services, 2022). Plus, Korea is generous: it is the sixth largest aid-for-trade donor in the Organization for Economic Cooperation and Development (OECD). South Korea's status now as a leading nation in the world shows it definitely changed its position more than any other country in the past 75 years.

Like a phoenix from the flame and ashes of the twentieth century has been modern twenty-first century Korea. The country transcended its short colonial period (1910–1945) and the Korean War (1950–1953) via its economic Korean Miracle (1961 to the present) and by its increasing cultural Korean Wave that is spreading its wings worldwide now. The Republic of Korea's massive success as an (ex-)developing country becoming a developed country makes it a true outlier because it has comparatively been harder for every other developing country to do—except Korea. So we can learn from this outlier of Korea how to approach that excellence. Plus, Korea is additionally a harbinger of what is to come for the rest of the world if we can learn to transfer, to the rest of the world, its *internal* recipes for earlier fast development success and its ongoing uncanny ability to surf and ride well three *external* global trends: a global digital decentralized economy, a global digital culture, and a modern globally digital decentralized media.

In the twenty-first century, South Korea via its culture and export-led economy now makes a large contribution to the international cultural community and to the technical and material development of the world. Thus, in a unique and innovative way, it exports facets of both its durable ancient culture and its hypermodern technical and entertainment products synergistically that has captured the admiration and curiosity of the world. South Korea's successful economic revolution took the country from one of the poorest in the world after World War II to now one of the wealthiest by the twenty-first century. However, Korea mostly avoided a more typical leftist ideological motivation in state-led economic development itself or a leftist/class-based cultural revolution outcome typical of many modern urban industrial economic successes. This has provided a deep cultural continuity in South Korea, arguably one of its ongoing resources in its fast development drive and now the Korean Wave. While the Korean Wave is the country's claim to fame globally, both regarded at home and abroad as the height of the country's success, much of the cultural content in this modern Korean Wave comes from very traditionalist and non-modern themes in the culture despite high-tech savvy producing and exporting it profitably to an appreciative world. How did this interesting hybrid phenomenon come about? To answer this question, this book explores Korea's interesting durable homogeneous culture and its modern technological export by comparatively analyzing development factors and trends of the economic Korean Miracle into the cultural Korean Wave, along with detailed case studies of particular sectors of the Korean Wave in K-pop music, cosmetics, and online movies.

Comparatively, South Korean successful economic development and later cultural projection can be explained by having access to many unique historical conditions by happenstance that were useful later *and* by choosing well in many of its developmental choices over time. First, it is argued many hybrid developmental policy *good choices* in *politics* and in *economics* (described later) contributed to South Korea fortunately missing much of the arrested or stalled development that plagues many other developing countries. Plus, South Korea by its *good choices* of its hybrid *cultural* settlement mostly missed tragic and violent cultural revolutions seen in the world throughout the twentieth century that in retrospect plagued or set back other developing countries. Second, it is argued South Korea's fast development *aggregated many more background factors as 'good accidents,' meaning good happenstance historical factors* that encouraged durable good choices for fast-paced development in a globalizing world in South Korea far more than other countries. Many of these have been conceptualized already in the development literature yet they are assembled here for the first time to show how many 'good accidents' Korea actually had available compared to other less developed countries with far less. Both these points in South Korea, good choices and good accidents, led to immense national and global success later in a slow way—economically, politically, and culturally. From both points, it is argued that many parts of this Korean success story are accessible and transferrable to other countries.

However, do other countries really want it as bad as the Koreans did? Third, it is argued it is more than good choices and good accidents. South Koreans have deep *cultural resources in a more homogeneous culture* that many other more heterogeneous cultures in our modern world lack. A more homogeneous culture is argued to encourage a greater 'collective innovation' than other countries, defined as a faster ability to form and to work in teams on common goals, to accept durable leaderships, and to keep together as teams durably on challenging projects until they are successful instead of to pare off in individual dissent or disagreement. On the one hand, a more homogeneous culture is able to have more capacity for collective innovation than other cultural demographics because of two main mechanisms. The first is having an easier established common future or ethos, and holding together in making something true without much dissention. The second is a common past, leading to an easier established or accepted leadership authority married in mentorship and sponsorship to followers less likely to disagree though to follow—for better or for worse, for richer or for poorer.

On the other hand, more heterogeneous cultures to their credit can have more cultural innovations or individual innovations, though can have much less collective innovation. For instance, the *New York Times* reports in "The Downside of Diversity" that "[i]t has become increasingly popular to speak of racial and ethnic diversity as a civic strength. From multicultural festivals to pronouncements from political leaders, the message is the same, our differences make us strong....But a massive new study, based on detailed interviews of nearly 30,000 people across America, has concluded just the opposite. Harvard political scientist Robert Putnam—famous for *Bowling Alone*—his 2000 book on declining civic engagement—has found that the greater the diversity in a community the fewer people vote and the less they volunteer, the less they give to charity and work on [collective] community projects. In the most diverse communities, neighbors trust one another about half as much as they do in the most homogeneous settings. The study, the largest ever on civic engagement in America, found that virtually all measures of civic health are lower in more diverse settings." "The extent of the effect is shocking," says Scott Page, a University of Michigan political scientist" (Jonas, 2007).

So, it is argued that nothing has succeeded better, so far in the world's many examples of attempted fast development, than having access to a more homogeneous culture or common ethos, defined as something that can hold a people and their national government together on durable collective projects to succeed. Thus, it is a mistake to think a stable, homogeneous culture 'lacks innovation.' It is a mistake to think so because Korea actually is ranked at the top of the Bloomberg Innovation Index for seven out of the last nine years (Jamrisko et al., 2021). Therefore, it is useful to be specific about what kinds of innovation we are talking about, and to try to classify the different kinds of innovation that the world has in three kinds. It will be proposed that there are three kinds of basic innovation: collective, individual, and cultural. These are discussed momentarily. Plus, it is useful to analyze more than just the specific developmental policies or background factors of South Korea for its secret recipe. It is argued that South Korea's chosen policies, when animated by a more homogeneous culture with its capacity of this collective innovation, created an ongoing historical dynamic. It is this ongoing historical dynamic between a more homogeneous culture, its policy choices, and its background factors that has created two kinds of ongoing virtuous cycles in economic and political development. These two ongoing virtuous cycles in South Korea succeeded brilliantly in aggregating development over time without interruption due to both faster and easier policy changes to adjust to a global economy with innovation, as well as easier policy durability more than many other heterogeneous cultural nations. In other words, it is argued that there are useful 'transferrable' political and economic policies of South Korea after 1961 that provided an uncannily good framework, yet it was their interaction with the Korean more homogeneous culture that created great virtuous cycles of development, both politically and economically, instead of only the policies themselves being magic. Thus, it is argued that the durable creation of a more homogeneous culture is something much less transferrable, despite this particular kind of culture and its collective innovations being key to actions undertaken over time in South Korea that led to success in economic development and success in cultural projection. However, we may learn someday how to create that shared ethos for development even in other places as well.

For two caveats before we begin, first, it is hardly argued that there is a simple "necessary and sufficient" causality between a more homogeneous culture causing more collective innovation. This is because in the case of South Korea its culture's capacity has been supercharged by its mediating policy choices, particularly in the politics of a multi-party republic with individual civil rights and in a hybrid economics that merged an export-led economy with national protection and grass roots development. This avoided economic policies that destroyed the culture in the process of such collective innovation on the chosen tasks of an urban industrial economy. Both these political and economic hybrid policies left the ancient culture intact or even enhanced and protected like it was in the eye in the storm. It is argued that since innovation is multifaceted and with a regional dynamic, recognized as long ago as the 1890s (Tarde), that there are more complex causalities and interactions at play instead of only one factor focused on here in the greater collective innovation potentials of a more homogeneous culture mediated by particular policy choices. Plus, even this one factor is a hypothesis about a tendency or likelihood of a particular kind of more homogeneous or more heterogeneous culture being more capable by default toward one or more of these three kinds of innovation. It is the peculiar dynamics of South Korea that combined its historical more homogeneous culture with the double hybrid choice of a multi-party republic and an export-led economy and yet regional grass-roots development. Both supercharged such collective innovation durably well into ongoing virtuous cycles that failed to destroy the culture in the process. Plus, by South Korea's own record, it takes a lot of other factors like financial aid, technical and cultural, toward creating more export events and more technological innovation by having more funding per capita on such research and development than any other nation in the world as well. So, what is argued here is hardly only a culturally-driven model, though instead it is the historical dynamic of development that is of interest here and whether virtuous cycles of growth or vicious cycles of decline are created by such plural factors creating durable dynamics over time. Plus, as noted later, particularly South Koreans lacked many other options and were closer to being painted into a corner by a lack of other kinds of raw material wealth. Therefore, with this background context as a 'good accident' they were more likely to make good choices to utilize collective innovation and their brainpower instead of to take economic rent off raw materials mindlessly—as North Korea is able to do in mining coal or minerals exports to China for instance to its long term chagrin, creating more vicious cycles of diminishing returns and failure to innovate or update modernistic development.

A second caveat is the way that Korean politics and politicians are judged and described throughout this book. Fairness instead of hagiography is key here. Most political scientists judge South Korea as having a very polarized and combative politics, so, in turn, Korean history readers tend to expect very polarized hagiography or condemnation. Three criteria of judgment are mostly used which were thought fair: how well or how poorly leaderships, organization, policies, or background factors (1) contribute over time to modern urban-industrial economic development, (2) contribute to solving instead of ignoring its human and environmental externalities, and (3) contribute to modern republican ideals of multi-party democratic dynamics of transparent open elections and common universal civil and human rights whether in politics, economics, or culture. Sometimes one factor is judged well in one context in one year or in one discrete sector and later may decline. Sometimes one factor is judged poorly originally and yet comes later to shine. Please keep this in mind particularly as reversals (and thus the origins of this ambivalence) happen regularly in modern Korean history, year by year, around the mixed results over time of different Korean presidential leaderships particularly like Syngman Rhee (1948–1960), Park Chung-hee (1961–1979), Chun Doo-hwan (1979/1980–1988), and Roh Tae-woo (1988–1993). Note judgments and preferences about culture or political party preference itself are unimportant here and thus kept to a minimum. The main theme is how politics, economics, and cultural policies encouraged (or disencouraged) fast developmental drives as durable, because the durability is judged as useful for both the long-term economic Korean Miracle and the global Korean Wave instead of judged as being interrupted or regressive to these three development goals.

Thus, two great unsung arts of the modern world should get more appreciation than they do because they are the background arts for everything modern: economic development policy and political constitutional engineering. They are the background arts of our world because our modern world is self-created by will and by design as future-oriented projects. Sometimes the art is beautiful and sticks on the canvas available (different nations and different cultures) very well, and sometimes the art itself is poor and only destroys the canvas available. On the one hand, we can see something unique in Korea as these modern Korean political artists have changed the Korean constitution six times by now, as Koreans are on their Sixth Republic (1987 to present) in a mere 75 years (1948–2023). On the other hand, we can see something else unique in Korea in contrast to their changing political constitutions: Korean economic policies have kept to the same development policy since 1961 and only buckled to buttress it over time with more consensus support every time it was critiqued, by adding ancillary economic policies as wider economic policies. This was like protecting and subsidizing traditional artisans from 1963, like grass roots development being added from 1970, and like widening the welfare state over time starting from a strong economic support for only those aiding the executive branch around the President into a wider and increasingly universal welfare state more akin to Scandinavian countries. Equally throughout, to maintain support for export-led development, the Korean state had a very strong national economic protectionism tweaked in many domestic sectors over time, despite the export-led orientation, because national economic protection in some sectors aimed to widen support for the export-led orientation in other sectors. Over time in both politics and economics it will be argued that via these ongoing adjusting ways, Koreans made what will be called more ‘hybrid’ policies, defined as less based on ideological principles and more based on increasing procedures of consensus from addressing conflict directly instead of only choosing to address it indirectly via repression. States and development policies are only human creations. The increasing consensus artistry that Koreans have made is worth analyzing.

Koreans by choice, hard work, cultural solidarity, and even luck, combined their national energies better and more durably than others to make their previously ‘developing’ country into one of the most developed countries in the world in the single lifetime of many modern Koreans. As a result, South Korea durably worked hard and built many ‘world firsts’ in its development, one after another in a series so far, without end in sight. This is particularly clear in its series of successes in telecommunication-based digital development that started from the 1980s, discussed later (See Appendix 1). However, this Korean drive of innovation started well before its telecommunications sector. It can be seen even earlier in the durable successes from the very beginning of its Economic Miracle from 1961 onward. It can be seen even earlier in older ancient Korean history in many technical innovations without par for their time in world history, in many cases (Korean Spirit & Culture Promotion Project,

2007, 2008). This is why it is argued that Korean development seems deeply rooted in dynamics around how having access to a more homogeneous culture has greater developmental benefits than a more heterogeneous culture since it is seen in the past or the modern present as already more prone to more durable collective innovation. Now that innovative dynamic has only been 'supercharged' by its modern choices of political and economic policy that created virtuous cycles of durable development between culture and policies from 1961 onward.

Economically, South Korea has been in the OECD from 1996. The OECD is the world's top 'country club' of global leaders in industry. South Korea and Japan are the only two 'non-European-heritage' nations in this mostly Eurocentric OECD. Uniquely, unlike Japan, South Korea is the additionally the only *non-European* OECD member that has transcended a colonial past, so far. Currently, only 38 wealthy industrial nations (out of 206 sovereign nations) are in this globally developed 'country club,' by invitation only. The OECD as a club globalizes each others' economies further by extending to each other perks in their respective national markets. So their rising tide raises only their own boats, mostly. However, in our world of an estimated 8 billion people by November 2022, there are only 1.4 billion people in these 38 wealthy countries of the OECD combined. Plus, only 2 of these 38 wealthy countries are non-European: South Korea and Japan.

Therefore, the vast majority of our world lives in undeveloped or less developed nations. These nations are the vast majority of the world's population and are keenly interested in South Korea's recipes for such economic and cultural success. As of 2022, South Korea is only the 27th most populous country in the world with 51.8 million people (near the population scale of Italy, Myanmar, Colombia, and Spain), and yet according to the most recent data from the World Bank, South Korea in 2022 is the 10th largest economy in the world by Gross Domestic Product (GDP), placed between Canada and Russia. South Korea's export-led economy (and now its digital fandom in the global Korean Wave) encourages the country to 'punch above its size' in the global economy. This fast development drive started from the beginning of its modern economic policies from 1961 and has not stopped. This is unlike many other developing countries that have stalled or fallen behind after succeeding for a time, or they never succeeded at all (Collier, 2007; De Rivero, 2013).

Therefore, all developing countries and even the whole world can learn from this book. First, South Korea was not so unique *earlier* when comparing its common original problems in the 1960s to other currently-developing countries with still many of the same problems. Korea itself in the 1950s was once on the economic level that Papua New Guinea is today. In the 1960s, it was similar to the economic level of the Philippines today. By the late 1970s, South Korea began to surpass the socialist state of North Korea for the first time, and North Korea kept falling behind after that as well. Therefore, the mediating policies themselves are argued to matter as much as the more homogeneous culture. All developing countries can learn how to create such durable virtuous cycles between cultures and policies as seen in the ongoing economic Korean Miracle and its later cultural Korean Wave. The more we analyze how South Korea has succeeded, the more likely we may transfer Korean choices to other countries, if they wish. Plus, on top of this, the world can learn that a lot of the success of Korea is argued to be durability in policies: keeping one or a few ongoing aggregated policies for decades without changing incessantly the fast development drive. The world as a whole—including the already developed world—can learn in this book about both the durable export-led economy that started from 1961 and another durable policy of cultural exports that started as early as the 1980s that has become tremendous by the second decade of the twenty-first century. This combined digital economic and cultural tsunami of the Korean Wave portents at least one scenario of our collective future as an ever more immersive, more global, and more multi-polar digital popular culture for us all.

Two books were reflected upon in crafting the arguments that follow. First, a similar book was written almost 200 years ago about the early pre-industrial and pre-telecommunicative United States. French author Alexis de Tocqueville wrote *De La Démocratie en Amérique* (*Democracy in America*), published in two volumes between 1835 and 1840. The book was de Toqueville's attempt to explore the United States as a case of "democracy." He wondered what the future of culture and scientific-technical worlds would look like when increasingly created under "democratic (more homogeneous) conditions" that he felt were better exemplified at the time by the United States than any other country. Thus, he felt that the United States could be analyzed as a case of what a more homogeneous democratization was creating in culture and development that could soon change the whole world—and within one hundred years was doing just that. However, this book attempts to be the "de Tocqueville" for South Korea as a case of what a more homogeneous and 'saturated' *digital culture* does to culture and development, in order to peer into the future to document a similar, budding, outsized, global influence from South Korea for what it may increasingly mean for the whole world. This outsized global influence of South Korea has its origins in its 'saturated' (deep, even, and homogeneous) digital extremes, its cultural homogeneousness, its long history of high technological innovation, its fast economic development, and even its political uniqueness (See Appendix 1). The authors explore how what is happening in digitally saturated South Korea will increasingly influence the whole world either as a model of what to be or as something to react against. The unique dynamics of Korea's ancient factors, in its older pre-conditions and homogeneous culture, started to merge with its modern development choices after 1961. This soon made South Korea a supercharged world leader in economics, technology, and digital cultural reach in its Korean Wave by the early twenty-first century. What global lessons may be learned about such successes? To what extent are the successes reproducible elsewhere, or are they unique? What cautionary tales may be told as well? We ask, similar to de Tocqueville on what will happen to culture and development under more *democratic* conditions in the future, what will happen to future culture and development under more saturated *digital* conditions? Currently, the best place to analyze for this theme is South Korea and its Korean Wave globally now. Thus, the best place to look for what may happen to other cultures and development *nationally* under digital conditions is in South Korea right now, given the information in Appendix 1. So we can legitimately ask, what does Korea's irresistible digital revolution portend *for the whole world's future* of *global* culture, development, and technology as we enter the twenty-first century?

The second book reflected upon was Adam Smith's *The Wealth of Nations* (1776). Instead, this book attempts to be an exploration of the "Wealth of K-Nations." This means, loosely, what are the recipes of digital global economic and cultural success for all *non-European* developing countries taken from an analysis of the most successful case so far, the Republic of Korea? A "K-Nation" is first defined as doing two kinds of digital development durably over time in the same country: digital hardware production and digital cultural production. Second, this neologism "K-Nation" stands for one of three possible futures for all developing countries. First, it can stand for *only* South Korea if you consider it an outlier, and yet we can learn from an outlier for its brilliant successes for other developing countries. Following from that, on the other hand, second, the term can stand for how Korea could be *only the first* in group of non-European and ex-colonial nations that have chosen well internally and have chosen well externally in riding the three main global trends of our era and succeeded in doing it well: taking advantage of the global digital economy, the global digital culture, and the global decentralized media. Thus, it is argued that key characteristics of fast-development "K-Nations" like South Korea create their global economic stature relatively quickly in a digital development (Oh & Larson, 2019) by riding these three external trends well, and yet have many internal choices and background factors that have helped as well. South Korea is currently the *only* one, though it may be just the *first* one. Third, the term can stand for how these three global trends of distributed economics, culture, and media are reformatting demographically or geographically smaller or larger and more heterogeneous cultural nations into more division and seeming oblivion. In other words, are both smaller and larger nations breaking up and reformatting into "K-Nations"? Are "K-Nations" *selected for* by the three global digital trends to be more viable than other kinds of nations that are *selected against?* Thus, are larger, older, and heterogeneous cultures and their nation states *unviable* in an increasingly 'saturated' digital world unless they reformat upon "digital development with Korean characteristics?" Given we find continuing global and human intrinsic value in individual innovation and cultural innovation, that comes regularly only from more heterogeneous countries despite their problems, can we learn from South Korea for how to create solutions to maintain more heterogeneous nations from the global digital onslaught of cultural and developmental change, or potential political and economic breakup as well? Are we finally seeing what Kohr talked about in the 1940s onward as the breakdown of nations (Kohr, 2001), delivered not only by sheer problems with material scale or scale of violence that creates poor quality of life, though now how poor quality of life is delivered by problems and selection factors within globally large digital scale, i.e., showing only more homogeneous 'mid-sized' nations to the contrary become more durable and viable within a global digital cultural onslaught and a globally digital fast-changing developmental condition?

Our world is now replete with South Korea's global digital and material cultural exports, as this country is the first K-Nation on the scene. This is slowly upending past Eurocentric hegemonic relationships around the world in economics, culture, and media technological leadership upheld for hundreds of years until the early twenty-first century. This aspect of the book reflects on the following questions around what catalyzes the wealth of K-Nations. The wider term of the "wealth of K-Nations" means what has created this large and durable mould-breaking wealth, economically and culturally, beyond Eurocentric standards or comparisons and transcending past ex-colonial status that is part of a more multi-polar world? The global Korean Wave is something few Westerners (or non-Westerners, for that matter) had expected to find displacing the top ranks of Americanized youth culture and world youth culture just five years before. However, South Korea keeps showing our world durable and repeated strong successes, with higher global spectacles of cultural polish and more trend-setting digital technology starting to outclass and put even 'developed' Americans and Europeans to shame.

To outside observers, who it is assumed are mostly unaware of the first fifty years of 'brandless' South Korean developmental history, South Koreans and their commercial, financial, and cultural capital and 'global city' of Seoul seem to have appeared on the world scene only about a decade ago like a lightning bolt. For some, it is as if the Emerald City of the Wizard of Oz had been built on the Han River in the Korean Peninsula quickly. For popular world culture, Seoul and its culture was revealed to the world dramatically as the backdrop and content of Psy's "Gangnam Style" video, song, and dance of 2012. It was like a series of frenetic images or postcards sent to the world from a country few even knew beyond old black-and-white images of the Korean War (1950–1953). People start to wonder, '*when* did once marginalized Koreans build *that* and *how*?' However, the first fifty years of this story was long and slow. Koreans quietly without fanfare were building their national economic Korean Miracle for many decades before the Korean Wave. One of the rationales why South Korea appeared suddenly illuminated like under a lightning bolt in the night is because the world (and even Korea itself only a decade or more ago) failed to consider the country as having a modern 'brand' image at all. Only later has the Korean Wave emerged increasingly as the brand of Korea, even though it was first formed within regional East Asia from 1992 to around 1999 (the latter date when the term "Hallyu" started to be used), and later and more globally only after 2012 in "the year of Psy". Koreans started to shock with beauty, style, sass, innovative technical skills, colorful artistry, and cultural energy that spread around the world. Koreans themselves started to point to the cultural Korean Wave as their long-desired brand image for all other material exports they already had been selling globally for decades. To the world and even to Koreans, it truly seemed like some South Korean utopia was finally in the offing.

Of course, these self-generated images of the Korean Wave nowadays are in stark contrast to the previously projected dark images that the Eurocentric media had been repeating in the world mind about the Korean Peninsula. One of those earlier dark media images that were kept 'on file' to be used as an archetype to think about Korea was the dystopia of North Korea. This cloistered totalitarian state bans most international travel by its citizens and tries to rule them by censorship and fear. It additionally attempts to rule by brainwashing its citizens with love of a national leadership 'cult of personality' around a now-third generation of the dictatorial Kim family. This non-developmental stasis makes North Korea akin to the world's largest religious cult with nuclear warheads instead of a viable nation. A second dark archetype kept 'on file' in the Eurocentric media about the Korean Peninsula was the stark black-and-white images of the tragic Korean War (1950–1953), presumed to continue there like a still-life portrait. This repeated past image made South Korea seem frozen in time, in poverty and stillness, as if that 1950s war was still the only big event of consequence there and as if nothing happened after that. For many undeveloped countries, 'poverty and stillness' is indeed what happens, or indeed does not happen, in many lands of the world to this day—akin to living in a purgatory of development, poised just above hell though far from heaven.

Therefore, the sudden, well-orchestrated, and world-class visibility of a futuristic South Korean culture of optimism, joy, and polish was surprising to many, given only these negative archetypes they had to work with in the past about the Korean Peninsula. Even more surprising, as will be explained, is how durable the Korean Wave has been for over thirty years or more. Its first real success was in 1992 in Hong Kong (Hong, 2014). This makes it difficult to interpret or dismiss it as only a fad worthy of ignoring with a lack of analysis. Instead, we should be analyzing it. It is the first durable non-Eurocentric modern cultural wave in world history. We should be spending time analyzing how a durable and digitized Korean Wave started and continued. We should be spending time analyzing how it is now, ever so slightly, displacing or at least de-centering centuries older Western hegemony over global economics, cultural standards, and media hardware and cultural production. People worldwide require fresh interpretive lenses to analyze South Korea properly for how its well-developed cultural products, artistry, events, and material products are all highly desired globally now due to their durable high quality and cultural panache instead of simply desired as a temporary substitute by short-term hype or cheapness. This book seeks to give people such a reference book of useful comparative ideas, metrics, and case studies of certain sectors to understand what has been happening in South Korea and what has been happening to the world because of South Korea.

What is happening in South Korea is a big global challenge to everyone. Much of the West, we think, still prefers to interpret South Korea in terms of Western categories as a permanent bit player in *their* global economy and culture. However, it would be a mistake to turn our collective head and pretend South Korea is just a 'flash in the pan' and will go away soon as if there is nothing to worry about. Or, as the argument runs, even if there were something to worry about, the global West may still prefer the interpretation that it is still not yet at any scale of world level importance. One can argue that either of these kinds of ratiocinations is based on past projected images of dismissive and condescending gazes that hamper analysis of what is actually happening. It hampers analysis of the truly amazing economic Korean Miracle and the durable cultural Korean Wave, both (unfortunately) without any peer in the world that are not going away and which have already achieved world level importance. The Korean economic development has been happening for over 60 years, and the Korean Wave has been developing for at least 30 years, and both are only getting stronger. Thus an elitist global West leans upon fading laurels and looks with hubris down upon South Korea, and tries to dodge the economic and cultural worry of seeing their own youth cultures and cultural industries start to be unable to complete at the level of quality, adaptability, innovation, and sheer desirability of products that South Koreans create for themselves and the world.

By contrast, now even a Eurocentric and unipolar media starts to showcase bright colorful images from South Korea. This obviously fails to fit past interpretive frameworks relegating Korea to the global sidelines. These are seen in higher relief because they are truly a revolutionary departure into a more colorful multi-polar cultural world instead of a unipolar and polarized world of only a few powerful European-heritage nations, past or present, ruling over a static colorless and less developed world. Instead a more colorful future and multi-polar world has been slowly developed by South Koreans since 1961, accelerating from the 1980s. From around the year 2000 onward, in less than twenty years, images of the Korean Wave started to displace past tragic images of the despair of the Korean War, and yet they are only slightly displacing durable fear of the poor and belligerent North Korea.

Unlike Western-inspired *full economic revolutions and full cultural revolutions into 'modernity' that Communist China exemplifies or Soviet Russia exemplified,* Korea shows this is hardly the only path toward modernity. Instead, this first 'K-Nation' of South Korea has had an economic half-revolution and was without any cultural revolution—showing it is possible. Moreover, it is argued to be so innovative because of this retained deep cultural capital. It is argued without irony that *because* South Korea luckily lacked both a cultural revolution and a fully top-down revolutionary developmental state that it has been able to have a better modern economic revolution than others and then have a more durable cultural Korean Wave longer than others. This is because both were built Koreans' deep cultural capital as a vast resource of collective innovation. This resource of a more homogeneous culture for collective innovation is argued to be the keystone, the secret to catalyzing South Korea's national wealth (in league with great background factors and good mediating choices of policy) as a *durable* development and a *durable* Korean Wave. However, a more homogeneous culture is a resource many modern nations lack. This is because almost all other paths of modernity took countries on one of three other paths in the past 200 years that led them to miss awareness of the charms and innovation that can come from such a homogenous culture. Some went modern by intentional policy to destroy any ancient homogeneous culture in a fit of cultural revolution like France, Turkey, China, or Russia/Soviet Union. Some were lacking a homogeneous culture in the first place by being more heterogeneous ancient empires by default like much of Central Europe. Some once did have a more homogeneous cultural nation that helped their economic success like Germany, England (only after the 1660s), Denmark, Sweden, or New England in the United States, yet because of that economic success or later policies, now find themselves more divided and culturally heterogeneous with a less common root culture since it is increasingly censored, muted, shattered, or lost in the heterogeneous din.

However, the South Koreans' more homogeneous culture and its greater capacities for collective innovation is argued to be a major factor (though hardly the only factor) responsible keeping up a *durable* economic Korean Miracle leading into a *durable* cultural Korean Wave. So, while people look for singular or easily-transferrable 'secrets' of Korean economic and cultural projection, what they are attempting to understand are hardly only policies. They are attempting to understand and copy *durable* successful development as a process. In this case, it is argued they have to understand the *uniquely strong cultural energy of membership in a more homogeneous culture, and the strong shared ethos and images of a past or future that can animate it* (Polak, 1954/1973). A homogeneous culture and its collective innovation are deeply responsible for the national energy seen in the economic Korean Miracle and the cultural Korean Wave.

Other questions arise about this "K-Nation." Is South Korea reflective of global trends or only is an outlier? If South Korea is an outlier, does it have factors from which we can learn, regardless, to transfer economic and cultural successes to other countries? From this point, what will be discussed is the assortment of unique factors, that when combined, helped avoid arrested development and which accelerated chances of fast-paced economic development being more durable. Later what is described is a common problem of all developing countries: they have to generate *facilitating dynamics* of durable virtuous cycles of development between their cultures and their policies, yes, though they equally have to run a 'development gauntlet' of many different *self-disrupting factors* coming out of success of those virtuous cycles that all developing countries have to pass that can easily hurt, arrest, or kill any development drive on its journey. First, South Korea was already fortunate to create two durable virtuous cycles of development, economically and politically, by its hybrid policies in league with its homogeneous culture. This supercharged its development drive with positive aspects of collective innovation as well as checked and balanced against other negative aspects of a homogeneous culture, as discussed later. Second, South Korea equally and successfully ran the 'development gauntlet' of many common problematic factors that stand ready to destroy and to disrupt any virtuous cycles, including factors that in retrospect are regularly more like easy temptations and distractions from the development path, like a recourse to political violence, changing policies, cultural revolution, or raw material exports. South Korea has uniquely almost avoided dozens of these factors of arrested development, endless setbacks, and bad choices that plague many less developed and underdeveloped countries (See Appendix 2 and 3). The development gauntlet's many problems overlap particularly badly in the 'bottom billion,' meaning, the poorest countries of the world. As Collier argues, the poorest of the world are so badly off because they are in overlapping 'traps' of factors that have created vicious cycles of underdevelopment that damage their ability even to make virtuous cycles to escape into development (Collier, 2007). Of course South Korea would have been classed in this category of the 'bottom billion' if you had looked at it in the 1950s, so it is hardly only a more homogeneous culture that is required to spark fast-paced development. South Korea chose well to create virtuous cycles of development, and equally ran the 'development gauntlet' successfully. The levels of this common development gauntlet are discussed in a later chapter.

Second, once South Korea got out of the bottom billion, it avoided further problems of a hypothesized 'middle income trap' (Gill & Kharas, 2006) that plagues other developing countries with a record of diminishing returns of slowed growth, reverses, and policy dead ends. One recommendation the originating authors of this concept have is choosing a specialized sector with a high-growth potential to escape the diminishing returns of the middle-income trap. South Korea by the late 1970s was indeed already slowing economically in its original sectoral development until it chose digital telecommunications by the early 1980s. Digital telecommunications arguably helped Korea stop from stalling in its own 'middle income trap,' among other sectors simultaneously developed for global export from 1986 like what was once only its own domestic automobile industry, Hyundai. The United States itself industrialized on automobiles and that industry's many synergistic industrial labor, material, and service requirements. The United States as well pioneered digital telecommunications as well, however, interestingly, Korean national rollout of telecommunication improvements was without triage of marginalized areas in Korea that you see regularly in 'digital divides' in many countries including the United States. Telecommunications in South Korea was a true nationwide rollout, filtered down even to the many hundreds of marginal islands off the coast of South Korea given its more hybrid economic policy of regional grass roots development mixed with its export-led economics. Thus, it is the particular collective and national inclusion in South Korean policies of digital telecommunications that kept aggregation potentials at their peak, instead of only 'choosing telecommunications in the abstract.' These equitable and 'saturated' policies around digital telecommunications kept the whole nation growing together (in virtuous cycles) to try to displace unrest (a self-generated issue of harm coming out of the success down the development gauntlet) from areas outside of Seoul that disliked the increasing power of the economy around the primate city of Seoul. This kind of political tension attempting to stifle grounds for unrest was less regularly chosen by violence after 1980 (though not after a state massacre in Gwangju in 1980, that was blocked from being followed up with other massacres in other cities out of fear it would cause a true cultural revolution and by its American ally's opposition). Instead, the political tension of an urban development zone and a rural underdeveloped zone was solved better by keeping national development as geographically inclusive as possible. In turn, this national enfranchisement in development kept up pressure on Korea's developmental model to be ever more inclusive. This kind of dynamic was behind what pushed the many earlier land reforms from 1948 through 1953. It later pushed the traditional artisan protections from 1963 and the grass roots development from 1970 onward that instead of impinging on export-led development was paired to support it as a model of development. This is what will be later referred to as Korea's more 'hybrid' and consensus approach to development that developed out of this political, economic and geographic tension in rural areas around the primate city of Seoul.

Third, South Korea has had many 'good choices' in policy and many 'good accidents' at the same time. This gathered many catalysts for rapid development in one country. It will be argued we can learn from this outlier status of South Korea in global development about all these good choices and good accidents for transfer to other countries in this way (See Appendices 2 and 3).

On the other hand, South Korean success can be framed as an external question, of global contexts successfully used, instead of only an internal question of good choices and good accidents. This can be framed as how this first K-Nation came to surf three major global trends of distributed digital *economics*, digital *culture*, and increasingly distributed digital *media.* Korea 'seized the chance' in a world-system of competitive national development by luring global capital to seek investment in South Korea while luring the world to buy its value-added products and cultural productions. It is argued we can learn from this first K-Nation on how to do this, as this is even more transferrable and replicable for other countries—at least for some kinds of countries as argued in Part III. What will be discussed is how South Korea utilized these three trends (global export-led economic development opportunities from the 1960s, and a digital media change starting from the 1980s, that started to facilitate participation in a global digital culture by the 1990s) to its advantage so well that it appears as an outlier so far ahead of other countries. In short, South Korea is an outlier by successfully running the development gauntlet with many good choices and good accidents internally, as well as because other countries in sharp relief to it were *unable* to ride all three of these external global waves as *consecutively, as simultaneously, or as durably* as South Korea.

Regardless, South Korea continues to be the first major outlier "K-Nation," a rare example of a non-Western country achieving global-levels of economic wealth, development, and cultural power. Korea has started, even if so slightly, to displace top spots of economic and cultural production even against competitors of the global West. Hopefully, South Korea is only to be the first "K-Nation," instead of the last. We can learn many internal and external factors that helped this development along in South Korea, to make sure it is hardly the only or hardly the last.

So, why have such K-Nations been so rare before? What does it mean that South Korea remains the only major success story despite 80 years of supposed 'development advice'? First, it means that both the West (including funding patterns of the World Bank, Asia Development Bank, the U.N., or even Soviet Union advice) equally were outrageously wrong. Were they even gaslighting and lying to the world about what really developed or hampered them in the first place? (Chang, 2011; De Rivero, 2013; Perkins, 2005; Wendler, 2014) Dozens of countries that failed to develop under such '(in)expert advice' should be outraged that such advice rarely worked. Thus, to what degree are *external* wealthy countries advice, programs, and funding patterns at fault in keeping other developing countries down or wrecked? (Hancock, 1989) What did South Korea do? It is should be equally outrageous to other less developed countries that South Korea is one of those few countries that rarely took any global advice on how to develop. South Koreans created their own path of many 'hybrid' policies described later, many unique in the world as unique as their success is today. However, on the other hand, to what degree are bad *internal* decisions and other *internal* contexts in poorer countries to blame autonomously as well? As said, South Korea has an amazing number of good choices and even 'good accidents' on its side that we can learn from—as well as how its choices fitted to external contexts and opportunities.

So, given combined internal and external factors that intersected well in South Korea, will K-Nations continue in other non-Western countries or will South Korea remain a unique outlier because so many tumblers have to be aligned for Korean keys of development to be turned to unlock it? What can we learn by thinking of

South Korea as a *harbinger*, as only the first K-Nation, in its well-oriented internal and external factors? What can be learned by thinking of South Korea as an *outlier* by having a unique historical settlement, or even unique geographical and geological contexts that helped force its 'good choices' along a narrower path and a durable path of development which as well helped create a very durable transmission of a more homogeneous culture?

Other questions about this K-Nation can be about why was it left to relatively small South Korea to have the first durable non-Western cultural wave? This is because Japan was and is so much more populous and economically developed even from the 1700s. For instance, Edo (now Tokyo) was one of the world's largest cities by the 1720s, with over 1 million people in an era when Europe was without any cities of that size until London around 1815. Plus, Japan in the 1700s had the world's *first* formalized stock markets, futures contracts, regularly published urban restaurant guides, theater guides, etc. Thus, Japan already had an internal large scale urban and commercial development long before Western contact. Japan equally has a strong and proud domestic culture, thus, with equal resources for collective innovation in a more homogenous culture. However, the Japanese have rarely pushed their culture durably for export or cared about global views of their culture as deeply in the way Koreans do durably push their culture into the world and indeed do care deeply about world opinion of their country as key to the status they feel about themselves. Instead, the Japanese with their homogeneous culture have more often pushed their military durably in conquest, or rather have been pushed by their aristocratic militarists into conquest. Japan has been led for centuries by an unbroken and durable royal house and aristocracy deeply embedded as the motivating force of Japanese militarism. However, Korea is instead pushing a more homogeneous culture *without* a military engagement. However, military conquest and extension was something historically missing even in the ancient history of Korea as well. Korea did have a strong aristocracy in the past, and a regularly strong defense against many invasions, though its own aristocracy rarely led the defense and instead historically interfered jealously with each other for leadership perks of such a national defense, making unified national action of defense difficult. Japan in the 1590s in its attempted invasion of Korea in the Imjin War had a similar self-defeating dynamic as the Korean aristocracy: having a hubristic aristocracy that enjoyed war as status among itself and yet were divided for the spoils and honor of that war even to the point of undercutting each other in the Korean invasion.

However, a different factor between Japan and Korea is that despite both having similar homogeneous cultures and strong aristocracies in the past, Korea now lacks its ancient aristocracy while Japan still has it as cultural, economic, and political leadership. Thus, Korea experienced by the mid-twentieth century one of the few and rare world-historical cleansings of a conserved aristocratic clique, yet without a cultural revolution that catalyzed it, since it started to occur under the Japanese Empire that ended the Joseon Dynasty by 1910 which started to displace the power of the native Korean aristocrats economically through 1945. However, the Korean aristocracy did try to return to cultural and political leadership from 1948 to 1960 under President Syngman Rhee, himself descended from early Joseon dynasty King

Taejong (r. 1400–1418), father of King Sejong (r., 1418–1450), which made Rhee a relative of that famous cultural hero of modern Koreans, King Sejong. Plus, Rhee's first Prime Minister was Lee Beom-seok (1900–1972), previously Chief of Staff General of the Korean Liberation Army and himself a descendant equally of King Sejong's fifth son Gwangpyeong Daegun (1425–1444). President Rhee even adopted two of his own far-distant royal blood relatives in the 1950s and 1960s, trying to set up the first as the next President after him. Since Rhee lost his only biological son Rhee Bong-su in 1908, and since his first wife divorced him in 1910 (since his whole life was busy at this time getting U.S. academic degrees (Master of Arts, Harvard University (1908); Doctorate, Princeton University (1910)) and in revolutionary Korean nationalist plots against the Japanese Empire, Rhee adopted three different sons over the years. Soon after Rhee became Korean President, Rhee ended the adoption of his first (now adult) and non-royalist son Rhee Un-soo, in 1949. Rhee then made Lee Kang-seok into his second adopted son, who was the eldest son of Rhee's own Vice President Lee-Ki-poong, who himself was a descendant of Prince Hyoryeong, the second son of King Taejong, and thus a distant cousin of President Rhee himself who was descended from the first son of King Taejong. However, on April 26, 1960, in the midst of protests against President Rhee, Rhee was encouraged to resign to stop the protests. However, protestors kept converging on his Presidential Palace on April 28, 1960, so the U.S. Central Intelligence Agency evacuated Rhee via helicopter on this day, leading to his eventual exile in Hawaii. On April 28, 1960, left in Rhee's mansion and surrounded by protestors, and presumably abandoned by Rhee, his adopted son Lee Kang-seok first shot and killed his real father Lee Ki-poong, then killed Lee's whole family, and then killed himself in a combination of patricide and suicide. After Rhee was evacuated in 1960 and while in exile in Hawaii, Rhee created his third adopted son, Rhee In-soo, who was descended from Prince Yangnyeong, the first son of King Taejong, just like Rhee. However, despite these royalist pretentions of Rhee's First Republic, the Korean aristocracy during Rhee was losing even more of its landed estates by the 1950s by many kinds of land distributions between 1948 to 1952—the first by U.S. military administrative acts, and the later ones by Korean governmental acts or combined with massive voluntary privatization as large landlords wanted to sell early to locals under threat of losing the Korean War or instead of have the state nationalize and buy their land at a potential lower price for later land redistribution. After 1960, with this further decline in the traditional Korean aristocratic economic power, there is a power vacuum from the end of the First Republic (1948–1960) into the Second Republic (1960–1961), making the Military Revolutionary Committee around later President Park (1961–1963) find an easy toppling of that Second Republic. Thus, from 1961, the older Korean resurgent aristocrats were decisively jettisoned from Korean modern political leadership by a modernizing military coup increasingly solely around Park, whose personal military networks of loyalty to all three main modern Korean military academies became more key to political power after that instead of bloodline issues. As argued later, this ongoing political vacuum and the lack of a durable aristocracy in modern Korea is a modern benefit, i.e., a good accident. This is another unique factor of the fast-development outlier of South Korea. The country by default was left on the one hand with the strong cultural capital of a more homogeneous culture in a land distribution with its collective innovation, without in the future being led by the 'dead hand' of an older aristocracy into modern wars, economically-destructive national projects, or pet hubristic projects. Equally Korea avoided being led into choosing cultural revolution against its older aristocracy either. For instance, Rhee did his best to try to continue the Korean War after 1953, even refusing to sign the armistice and trying to create a casus belli for more war in Korea by releasing thousands of North Korean prisoners within South Korea. Thus, all of Korea likely dodged a bullet, no pun intended, by leaving its hubristic, arrogant, and faction-prone aristocracy in the past. It is an odd hybrid cultural settlement of a missing aristocracy, in a durable homogeneous culture, where that hybrid situation was derived because of a lack of an internal cultural revolution to get to this point where other countries choose one. This is another rare 'hybrid' phenomenon in the modern world's development as well.

In short, will South Korea remain the only K-Nation, or just one of many in the future? Can other countries learn something transferrable from South Korea to catalyze better development for themselves by its good example or will South Korea retain its beautiful and unobtainable outlier status in the world into the foreseeable future? Plus, is South Korea simply so much further along on development projects than other nations, that even if other nations were to attempt to catch up, would they be incapable of competing with ongoing other innovations in South Korea?

Another related series of questions revolves around how does or how can the 'global West' respond to K-Nations like South Korea instead of only how do other less developed countries respond to or learn from South Korea? This is because, as argued later, South Korea will likely remain at least ten years ahead of *all* other nations (developed or less developed alike) in its governmental and business expertise in merging digital technology and culture into a world-class global entertainment culture. Plus, South Korea will likely remain top in the world in scale of government financial aid to export-oriented cultural projects and in scale of governmental financial research and development grants for technological innovation. Few other countries invest so much of their finances in creating their own collective innovations of culture and technology for the future as does South Korea. Only Israel and South Korea are anywhere near the same scale of money per capita spent on research and development for the technical future they want, though of course we fail to see any equal amount of interest in expanding, funding, or coordinating an "Israeli Wave," and Israel has never ranked higher than South Korea on the Bloomberg Innovation Index despite spending comparably to South Korea (See Appendix 1). Thus, it is argued that countries *that fund and coordinate both the cultural and technical future that they want* more than other countries generally build the future they want by force of will, simply by having more resource mobilization for more successes and more mistakes to learn from than others on both projects. It is interesting for the thesis of this book that the top two spenders on research and development per capita, South Korea and Israel, are somewhat both "K-Nations" with similar homogeneous cultures which exhibit their collective innovation by working hard for the future they want in a digital economy of export-led development. Equally, both exhibit a motivation by a deep fear of traumas of the past that they want to avoid—seemingly far more than other countries do. However, like Japan, Israel never conceived of exporting its culture in an "Israeli Wave". Only South Korea so far has durably done cultural exports in parallel with technical exports.

1.1 Three World-Unique Issues in the First K-Nation: Hybrid Policies in a Homogeneous Culture Transcending a Colonial Past

To introduce a few themes that follow, as South Korea grew steadily from 1961 to the present, three world-unique issues have been developed from comparative analysis that describe it well, as well as seem causally linked to it being the first K-Nation and hopefully not the last. As said earlier, South Korea is the only example of a country moved fully by the United Nations from the 'undeveloped' to the 'developing' column after World War II. The fact that it is the only example should be admired, as it should make us curious about what if any were its unique policies, cultural characteristics, or historical contexts. South Korea can be summarized as a once peripheral nation now with an outsized economic and cultural prowess as core nation, and even competing well against core European-heritage nations worldwide. However, four themes in South Korea had been happening almost entirely out of mind (and out of the gaze of development theory models) until the happy shock of the global Korean Wave.

In no particular order, the first point shows how most past policies supposedly designed to 'aid world development' suggested by the United States, the United Nations, or the Soviet Union were in retrospect nothing of the kind: in retrospect, they all been economically useless for national development and may have been intentionally useless to gain clients in the ongoing Cold War environment between the superpowers of the United States and the Soviet Union. First, we can state that South Korea is currently the *only* successful wealthy nation that rose from nearly nothing after 1960 to join the OECD by 1996 or even afterward to 2022. That itself should give us pause because South Korea was a country that rejected by the 1960s all advice of powerful nations and international organizations for how to develop itself, and even rejected many American allied overtures and ideas, while other nations kept taking advice from the currently powerful and came up with far less. Countries that did take economic or cultural advice from the United States, United Nations, or Soviet Union are mostly still in underdeveloped stasis, or they keep undergoing repeating crises of growth then its halt with requisite hyperinflations, coups, and civil wars. In the worst cases of Soviet-aligned Cuba and North Korea, when they lost their model, sponsor, and subsidizer when the Soviet Union collapsed in 1991, both countries soon went into famine. Equally many nations whether as clients of the United States or the Soviet Union remained in such clientelistic relationships with powerful global states and organizations similar to relationships with an ex-colonial master.

Instead, first, South Koreans created in retrospect many examples of their own 'hybrid economic developmental models' and even backed into creating an interesting flexible 'hybrid political system'. For the former, this was and remains a world-unique mix of export-led development for the urban industrial sectors and yet with decentralized land tenures, subsidies for traditional artisans, and even later grass-roots village-based development in its agricultural sectors. Typically most countries using grass roots development are failed industrializers or have weak states unable to do so in the first place like India (earlier), Sri Lanka, or some Central American countries. Second, typically most urban industrialization drives are connected to agricultural industrialization, which starts to create a cultural revolution and cultural erosion as many farmers are displaced. However, in South Korea, consolidation and capital intensity was promoted in urban industrial sectors and yet avoided in agricultural sectors. It is rarely commented upon that South Korea was almost food secure in itself (though increasingly scarce at the time with less rice) throughout the 1970s because it was not industrializing the rural landscape though intensifying and sponsoring village-based communities at the same moment it was building its first domestic automobile industries around the car named the Hyundai Pony, not sold overseas until 1986 (with the Hyundai Excel as well). Both these points are discussed later as respectively supercharging the homogeneous culture on a common project of export-led urban industrialization while maintaining cultural transmission of a home culture that continued the economic drive instead of destroying that culture in the process of urban industrialization. There are other hybrid policy ideas created in Korea by happenstance as well in politics and economics, discussed later. All these hybrid ideas are transferrable to other countries.

However, third, one of the keys seemingly to South Korean success *with these policies*, are perhaps less transferrable because it is about how these policies supercharged the collective innovation of a very homogeneous culture in a unique way, unlike other countries. In other words, the less transferrable aspects of the Korean hybrid development model are based on how South Korea has access to vast continuities in its homogenous culture to animate it. The cultural capital of having a durable homogeneous culture, still capable of vast collective innovation and national and/or patriotic self-sacrifice is a useful starting point for fast-paced development. Alternatively, a culture of more individualistic or ethically divisive situations in more heterogeneous cultures may find such hybrid policies intolerable as exclusionary to some and beneficial to others. However, a culturally homogeneous situation in a globalized world is one regularly demoted in practice instead of maintained as part of the development drive itself. For many poor countries' people interested in economic revolution, particularly Maoists, a past homogeneous culture regularly is tried to be demoted by intentional cultural revolution like in the bloody and self-genocidal Cambodia's Khmer Rouge, many examples of African or South American Maoist socialist movements in the 1960s, Mao's destruction of urban Chinese intelligencias and Confucian heritages, the rural Maoists in Nepal, or the Soviet Russia's rural collectivization, intentional starvations, and intentional ethnic-religious genocides or population mixing of areas it invaded and wanted to dominate, as in the

Ukrainian Christian Holodomor. To list all such tragedies of state-led cultural revolution and intentional internal genocide (called by Rommel a 'democide') would make depressing reading. On the other hand, *a policy* to maintain a homogeneous culture is a check and balance against tragic extremes of cultural revolution. Plus, sometimes afterwards an unintentional cultural revolution takes places after economic successes by diffusion of heterogeneous immigrants coming into a once more homogenous area, simply by developing 'successful' class conflict in an urban industrial economy and other nations' immigrants wishing to join in one of the rare successes of urban industrial development in another country—as well as being let into the country by urban industrialists or rural plantation owners alike interested in divide and conquer against native homogeneous cultural solidarity of labor movements. Thus whether by top down revolutionary intent, or by bottom up sharing in the economic success itself later, or by a combination of both, a mash of heterogeneity can develop. A durable resource of cultural homogeneity can be lost forever that seems to be a key to economic development in the first place, in South Korea as well as in other places that you can see, that have avoided tragedies and economic setbacks of cultural revolution in the twentieth century.

A fourth secret of this first K-Nation is that it has conquered and transcended its past colonial heritage. This is rarely done in the modern world. It is argued transcendence of a colonial past has a great deal to do with the virtuous cycles set up between the hybrid policies and the homogeneous culture, that maintained the culture and expanding the economy outside of the nation instead of nationalized itself to ever diminishing returns and increasing scapegoating or middle-income traps. It is sadly rare that South Korea remains an *outlier five times over in transcending its colonial heritage,* succinctly described below.

To describe the first two aspects of this unique outlier status, South Korea is the world's only example of a "*non-Western ex-colony*" in the 'country club' of the world, the OECD. There is only one other *non-Western* nation as well in the OECD. It is Japan. However, Japan historically was not really colonized by Westerners despite limited extraterritoriality treaties in the late 1800s, and Japan is more on the model at the time of a Western-funded proxy imperial power in itself, geopolitically expanded by American or European capital funding Japan's empire to harm Imperial Russia or other quiet agreements between American President Theodore Roosevelt who agreed to allow Japan free reign to conquer Korea after 1905 without American interference (Bradley, 2009).

Thus, the OECD by how it remains a club of mostly European heritage states in 36 of its 38 countries by 2023, shows how Eurocentric cultural heritage and Eurocentric economic global power work in tandem in the modern world similar to hundreds of years ago in the era of formal European empires. However, Japan had it easier. Japan avoided the hardship of any formal colonialism in its past even though multi-nation extraterritoriality was imposed upon it (just like China) for a time in the late 1800s. However, Japan was with a large domestic industry and large urban economy long before European pressures upon it, so Japan did more of a material and technical retooling of its already urban industrial economy to face outside military pressures from coal-fired steel military ships at the time. Plus, despite Japan being decimated economically and starving after losing World War II, it was able to recover its earlier industrial development by aid and sponsorship by the Americans interested in building up Japan as a check against a rising Communist China allowed to be consolidated after 1949 since Americans blocked Nationalist Chinese from leaving Taiwan to reinvade Mao-led China. Thus in this complicated geopolitics, the scale of industrial Tokyo was relatively quick to join the entirely European OECD in a process starting from 1962 to 1964. There are indeed other ex-colonies in the OECD nowadays, yet they are European/Spanish cultural heritage states like Colombia, Costa Rica, and Chile—with common colonial culture, language, and religion softening the differences of integration with Europeans. Plus, Turkey (in the OECD from 1961) has a softened integration by its deep modern revolutionary European heritage. Some might consider Turkey to be an exception or outlier as well, yet Turkey had an equally modern European cultural revolutionary heritage far more than its deeper Ottoman Islamic heritage. This is because the state of modern Turkey is a revolutionary state pushing dual modern economic revolutions and cultural revolutions against a past homogenous Islamic religious empire of the Ottomans. Thus, Turkey's modernity is a European-inspired revolution. Plus, even Turkey has a close deep European heritage for thousands of years before by being in the Greco-Roman Mediterranean. Greek and Roman cities and ruins are part of Turkey's proud heritage instead of more deeply only a part of the Islamic, Middle Eastern, and Persian heritage. Thus, to repeat, South Korea is the only outlier in two categories as the only *non-Western ex-colony* to be economically successful, that makes it unlike Japan. Japan experienced less hardships compared to Korea in the twentieth century as well as Japan's economic growth has been over centuries itself which makes it different. Korea is unlike *European-heritage* ex-colonies that seldom have cultural and language barriers with existing European core states that makes it easier for these ex-colonies to trade with and to (re)join a European-dominated world-system as a peer or ally instead of as an outlier.

Plus, South Korea is an *outlier a third time by the scale of its success even among other Asian ex-colonies* that did developed economically yet were never invited into the OECD so far. By the 1980s, South Korea was classed as "one of the Four 'Asian Tigers'" of fast-economic development that were Singapore, Hong Kong, Taiwan, and South Korea. All four of these are Asian cultural heritage states with strong colonial British or colonial Japanese pasts, and all had strong modern economic development after World War II—some developing first after their colonial period (Singapore, Taiwan, and Korea) and some developing first still within a colonial period (like Hong Kong under British rule until 1997). However, only the ex-colony of South Korea quickly outgrew its association with this litter of Tiger Cubs by becoming the only Adult Tiger since South Korea's economy is many times larger than the also-ran of Taiwan and far larger economically than city-states of Singapore or Hong Kong. The Three Tiger Cubs are not developed enough now to be in the OECD, and may never have what it requires to compete durably in scale or across time in the way that South Korea does in the world-system.

Plus, South Korea is an outlier a fourth time *by being an ex-colony that was colonized by another Asian country*, Japan, in a short period between 1910 to 1945. Thus,

South Korea was quite isolated even in the early twentieth century by being colonized by the Japanese Empire instead of by Europeans unlike other Asian ex-colonies that experienced a European empire of racial displacement and land displacement for sometimes hundreds of violent years, massacres, and exploitations. Plus, Japan only started in the 1930s its short-lived attempt at cultural destruction of Korea, starting first with the policy of blocking Koreans from taking Japanese names and then later changing its mind and giving Koreans all Japanese names along with the banning the teaching of Korean. This attempt at cultural extirpation of Koreans was only close to the end of the Japanese Empire in Korea (by 1945) instead of part of an originating intent from 1910 when it annexed Korea.

For a fifth outlier experience that takes us to the twenty-first century topic of this book, South Korea is *the only example of a durable non-Western cultural wave* in the modern world-system. Japan had a slight expansion of a Japanese Wave by the 1980s economically and culturally around the world. However, the Japanese Wave was demoted in the sudden economic downturn in Japan in the 1990s. Meanwhile, South Korea experienced its own sudden economic downturn from 1997 in the more global financial crisis of that year. However, South Korea made the decision to accelerate Korean cultural exports instead of to cut back, choosing differently than Japan did in the same situation in the early 1990s. Instead, South Korea now starts to have such an outsized influence on world culture durably because, first, it is due to the 'push' of its state export drives and, second, it is because of the 'pull' of global market desires combined. This is the inverse sequence from the earlier and shorter Japanese wave where the faddish pull of others seemed more crucial than state-orchestration or 'push' of the Japanese Wave itself. Plus, Korea's cultural Korean Wave has continued for thirty years or more against a long global European leadership trend. Korea has become the first example of a non-European state capable of expanding its own cultural wave against the European tide, so to speak, to continue oceanic metaphors. Other non-Western states like Japan generated their own cultural waves, yet in retrospect, these became of much shorter duration and are remembered as closer to international fads that relied more on the pull of other East Asian or Western desires instead of depended on the 'push' of the Japanese economy or its export strategies as much as Korea does push and organize its global Korean Wave.

Of course our current world-system remains to this day dominated mostly by European-heritage core nations' economic, cultural and material products stemming from their original massive industrialization and inventive exports of the 1800s that changed the world and built colonial plantation economies worldwide of raw material production and extraction for those central European (and later American) markets. Even though the development of China is slightly upending this, the development of China is due to massive global infusions of capital and industrial investment into China from the early twenty-first century, so the world is interpreted to be 'developing itself in China' instead of China developing itself per se. For example, China has a huge number of many dozens of global city sites that are key to its 'national' development that make Chinese development very dependent upon the agreement of many others urban industrial core nations to stop investing in themselves to keep investing in China to develop China. However, a unique factor in South

Korea is a successful economic Korean Miracle that is a kind of true Korean-centric globalization since the 1960s, because it was an export-led economy. In the case studies in Part Two, an added "Korean Wave" starts to look more like Korean global cultural conquest on top of already achieved many material exports to the world—particularly to the eyes of worried Westerners unused to real challenges to global cultural production and cultural leadership.

Thus, from these themes above, it is evident that the rise of K-Nations begins. However, it remains to be seen whether South Korea is harbinger of a growing trend or remains the beautiful outlier that got it right, and then kept getting it right durably. This book is written *to help the world learn from this outlier so we can treat it as a harbinger* by understanding what Koreans got right that can be transferred potentially to other countries. Thus, the wealth of K-Nations like South Korea is both miraculous and encouraging, yet disappointing and confusing to other ex-colonial countries across Asia and European areas. They have tried for many generations or even more than a century (like the Philippines or Brazil) to achieve what South Korea did. However, South Korea did it within less than one generation's lifetime from 1961 to the present.

Therefore, it is of world historical importance to explore where these South Korean development trends and their successful dynamics came from, to explore the unique alliances that created them, and to ponder what future culture may come from Korean Wave's digital advances not only for South Korea though for the rest of the world's digitally-mediated global culture and entertainment. It is also a kind of reckoning for "what the Korean Wave may be doing to Korea itself," domestically, by simplifying and regimenting its culture for the purposes of an export trade, and in the process ignoring a priority on policies to fix a growing national unhappiness and loss of a higher quality of life for many Koreans due to addictive focus on making the Korean Wave become more successful, beautiful, polished, desired—and perhaps exotically unobtainable. This development story should be interesting to more people than those fascinated only by the cultural products of the Korean Wave. South Korea as a culture and as a well-oiled machine of global development is interesting for both what may be transferrable to other countries' development as well as for an analysis of the untoward effects upon the country itself by its own economic Korean Miracle or its own cultural Korean Wave. The whole world is now being asked tacitly or forced to respond to South Korea's synergistic expertise and insanely high standards in cultural productions under Internet conditions. Should other countries just satisfy themselves to enjoy the view, while their own cultural industries are outclassed? Should they take South Korea as a model of what they should do, or of what they should not do? What are the benefits and what are the costs of the Korean Wave?

1.2 Two Methods and Three Global Trends in the Book

More is mentioned now on how a global digital economy, a global digital culture, and a global digital media are changing the world from the late 20th into the early twenty-first century. The Korean Wave shows South Korea is powerful because it is the first country to successfully ride all three of these current larger waves of world history simultaneously. In short, South Koreans are doing it better than other countries so far. Will South Korea's success remain an outlier in a Eurocentric world, or will the country become a harbinger of a completely changed multi-polar world, culturally and economically?

There are two methods of our analysis to understand the Korean Wave. On the one hand, our analysis focuses on actual case studies in the spread of the Korean Wave in specific Korean cultural industries that have developed a global presence: Korean popular music (BTS), cosmetics (Cosmax), and digital TV production (*Squid Game*). General issues across all sectors are mentioned in the case studies as well. This method focuses on creating a timeline in history of the Korean Wave: understanding its precursors, understanding its original mere regionality (like so many other developing countries by the 1980s that had their own cultural waves that were very similar), and then understanding its increasingly unique global qualities.

On the other hand, our analysis is comparative and historical on the general question of why did South Korea become the world's first global-level 'K-Nation' in the first place? This means an exploration of the precursors of the economic Korean Miracle into the cultural Korean Wave compared to the failures or lesser successes of other countries in the same. South Korea has created such an outsized economic and cultural success that it is associated with many 'world firsts' in statistics as the country most dedicated to its export economy as a percentage of GNP than any other nation so far, as well as having fifty 'world first' benchmarks in digital development as noted in Appendix 1. This makes it hard to compare analytically South Korea directly with other countries or to truly understand dynamics of what has happened here because South Korea has placed itself in a case by itself. Therefore, other kinds of comparisons are used, noted in Appendix 2. For the whole world's sake, it is important to understand what happened in South Korea to 'supercharge' the country's economic development into the world's first long-term 'non-Western' cultural wave and projection on the global stage as well. This is commendable for Koreans, yet the lack of true good comparisons hampers understanding the truly outsized economic success and the unique policy path that took root in South Korean culture so well that it now flowers into the Korean Wave.

Since there is a lack of true comparative cases to currently peerless South Korea, three kinds of basic comparisons are used: internal, external and combined internal/external. Sometimes these are comparisons across different times as well. Lists of many comparative factors considered in thinking about everything that has come together to make South Korea's virtuous cycles work as it went down a dangerous development gauntlet that might demote it, are in Appendix 2 and Appendix 3.

First, *internal* national conditions, pre-cursors, and facilitators in South Korea are explored in comparison with other nations' sometimes equal internal desires for such projections of economics or culture, and yet with the latter countries experiencing more problems or failures in doing so effectively compared to South Korea. Comparisons are with a range of lesser *internal* outcomes compared to South Korea, with some countries either succeeding somewhat, failing outright, or starting and then stalling in attempts at similar fast-paced economic development and/or cultural projection. Equally, we ask what are the comparative national internal pre-conditions of any "K-Nation," of which South Korea is we hope only the first instead of the last, both in terms of economic development and cultural projection? What political, economic, and cultural forces in South Korea explain the development of the Korean Wave? For other kinds of internal comparisons, what explains why other countries are failing at fast-economic development or global cultural export particularly when you consider given South Korea started far behind almost all of other developing countries, and yet South Korea became the first "K-Nation" to transcend past problems to shine globally now? Ideas of second-generation modernization theory that take into account a traditional culture's importance as modern developmental resource have influenced this analysis (So, 1990).

Next, what are global *external* preconditions that helped the rise of South Korea as well, that were taken advantage of well in this country and less so in other countries? The general methodological model of global development considered here derives from Wallerstein's 'world-system theory' and its three-fold classification of countries in economic development shared or exploited across periphery, semi-periphery, and core countries that have made an open-ended dynamic in a world system of global capital flows, raw material flows, and value-added product flows. Wallerstein argued this world-system developed uniquely after 1945, starting to replace other more imperial models of world-system before it (So, 1990).

Third, other comparative combined '*internal and external*' analysis comes from thinking about economically stagnant countries of the 'bottom billion' in our modern world (Collier, 2007). South Korea once would have surely been classed within this category. However, its rare fast-paced developmental success showed that it has escaped, fully or partially, all four 'traps' theorized by Collier. South Korea even escaped the other 'fifth trap' of 'missing the boat' (i.e., failing to 'seize the chance' of global development), defined as being late to some novel sector of globally-desired products that led investment to go elsewhere even if a country has escaped the four traps (Collier, 2007). For South Korea, it has 'seized the chance' at least twice—first in the digital telecommunications revolution by the 1980s around various digital telephone networking equipment, and second, being the first by the early twenty-first century to make cheaper smartphones and cheaper semiconductor circuitry for related digital products (Oh & Larson, 2019). It is argued that South Korea, more than most countries, tries to keep finding and innovating other global products to seize the chance with, and it has been very successful in doing so many times and rarely has failed.

Equally for these combined 'internal/external' comparisons, other methods came from thinking about the importance of having 'global cities' in certain countries in our world economy. Ideas from Sassen's model of the 'global city' are adopted, yet for how such a globalized urban telecommunications site in a country can be developmental to less developed countries instead of only underdevelopmental of already developed countries (Sassen, 2001). So, even though Sassen's view of a global city is of literally one global telecommunications city with pieces of it in many countries, and a view that thus a global city infrastructure underdevelops all national economies, instead, to the contrary, particularly after her book was last updated in 2001, an access to a global city of capital formation and international financial services is important in thinking about *how capital is drawn to developing countries' telecommunication networks instead of only drawn away from already developed national economies.* Instead of seeing global city infrastructure as only undermining national development as Sassen argues, having a place like the digital megalopolis of Seoul instead of lacking such a place (like many other stagnant or less developed countries of the world), is very important to South Korean economic development. So, instead of undermining the South Korean national success, Seoul is a global city in a then-developing country that aided South Korean national development. Many other factors are involved in South Korea of course that made this more equitable that Sassen assumes, likely because of the aforementioned hybrid economic policies that maintain more national policies of equity, as well as other factors like a strong semi-peripheral state and the singularity of this primate city of Seoul that helps consolidate development wins in the country in one economic agglomeration instead of having multiple peer cities in a country that can lead to regionalized elite infighting over where fast-paced development or digital development should occur (Sandbrook et al., 2007).

Thus, by combining national and global structural pre-conditions and Korean cultural analysis, we show a unique developmental pathway and unique cultural and media situation that was both 'nationally and internally emerging' and 'globally and externally triangulating' in South Korea from the 1960s.

In short, Korea has demonstrated the only, or only the first, example of a durable and self-sustaining fast-paced development via the economic Korean Miracle from 1961 to the present. This now extends into cultural production and cultural projection in the Korean Wave. Comparisons help us explain factors involved in how South Korea did this economic and cultural projection *far earlier, more durably, more flexibly, and at greater magnitude* than all other newly developed countries. In contrast, other freed nations or even newly invented nations after World War II failed outright in being unable to start, or they started and then stalled, or they developed such projection and then withdrew it.

Plus, the Korean Wave has been fortunate to surf successfully on three large global trends and to do it well: (1) the trend of globally-competitive and distributed economic development after World War II; (2) the globalization of a digital culture; and (3), a globally-competitive telecommunications sector and the rise of more decentralized, digitally distributed, and multi-media communications. South Korea is one of the few countries that surfed all three global trends well and durably for decades without either failing originally or faltering later like other nations did in the global software industry (Arora & Gambardella, 2005; Paus, 2005) or in digital hardware production (like Hong Kong and somewhat Japan).

For the development of this *first* trend of more decentralized development possibilities in a multi-polar world, it came from the dissolution of many world empires as they lost their imperial economic models and colonies beginning after World War II. This was a slow process after 1945 that continued as late as 1991, if you consider the collapse of the Soviet Union as the collapse of a Russia-centric empire as well. This global decolonization process has not completely ended yet, if you consider Communist China as a Chinese-centric empire in Central Asia that is equally of course very jingoistic toward Taiwan as well as entirely destroying past cultural and political principles of Hong Kong's greater civil and political freedoms that helped develop the city state in the first place.

The *second* trend is the building ever more miniaturized and cheapened technologies of the Internet into mobile smartphones other mobile internet-connected multi-media technologies. This trend started to spread around the world from the 1970s onward as the first 'brick' mobile phones were developed and as ever-smaller personal computers were developed that became linked to the Internet. These separate telecommunication products (mobile phones, personal computers, and the Internet) have further miniaturized and merged into one medium, evolving into the first flat glass and lightweight networkable smartphones from 2007. The first of these was LG Prada phone from South Korea (see Appendix 1), soon followed by the iPhone introduced by Apple Computer of the United States. It was joined within two years by many other competitive Korean smartphones as well (Oh & Larson, 2019).

In short, with these two methods of analysis—using case studies of the Korean Wave along with comparative analysis of the unique developmental path of South Korea and how three global waves triangulated well in South Korea—the book distills how South Korean development combined all of this very well. Details follow in later chapters.

1.3 Accelerated Digitalization and Globalization of the Korean Wave in Lockdown after 2020

Instead of the cultural wave of South Korea slowing down, a further digitalization and globalization occurred in South Korea in the last three years of state-mandated lockdowns over pandemic fears of Corona-19 in many countries of the world. However, instead of this being an economic setback for cultural production in Korea like it was for many other nations, the already deeply-digitalized national culture in Korea and in the global Korean Wave (Appendix 1) in retrospect will remember this as a further boom time, instead of a decline. It was a time for growth into wider global entertainment markets readied for massive simultaneous online spectacles of digital entertainment in millions of homes and millions of smartphones. This was due to various lockdown conditions as many of the world's governments shut down other market-competitive venues of public entertainment almost entirely.

The Korean government adopted questionable lockdowns as many European and North American countries did: only based on projections, future scenarios, and most of all the questionable PCR test data (revoked of its emergency use by the United States in December 2021, because in retrospect it was unable to differentiate between "Covid-19" and the regular flu—thus all data of 'case positives' was faulty and inflated upon which previous lockdown policies were based from the beginning.) Now lockdowns in retrospect are seen more clearly as the totalitarian overreaction that it was—giving more damage and deaths from externalities of the policy in economics, in high business bankruptcies of millions of small businesses, lowered child development markers, lowered schooling outcomes, closed hospitals, postponed doctors visits, rising addictions, government debt, stolen and defrauded subsidies, growing poverty, depression, and raised suicidal tendencies. There was much of this in countries that chose to do this, and less of this in countries that refused to inflict the self-harm of lockdowns on themselves like Sweden, Belarus, the U.S. State of Florida, or in a handful of African nations or in the Caribbean like Haiti.

However, regardless, in the South Korean context by being a country highly dependent upon its export-led economy, lockdowns were experienced as an external *global* context of Korean entertainment markets in various nations at the same time. However, this catapulted the Korean Wave even further ahead of other nations in digital offerings of entertainment. Korea quickly developed *digital technical innovations* in online distribution and participation and developed *digital business model innovations* and sector restructurings.

So, between 2020 to 2023, South Korea and the Korean Wave was adaptable instead of static or declining. For decades already, however, South Korea as a culture and a development model already had shown an uncommonly quick ability to reverse national economic downturn—like it did before in national economic crises of 1979, in the global financial crisis of 1997, or in the global financial crisis of 2008. In times of economic crisis and downturn, the Korean actions taken commonly have always been a further expansion and a retooling of their previous export-led economy into fresh sectors to make up for losses in other sectors. In essence, Korea keeps building other ways to escape the middle income trap repeatedly more than other countries, as it is more of an export-led economy finding it easier to do so. So, just like the past, from the year 2020 and over the past three years, South Korea escaped bad economic downturns in the Korean Wave by further innovative digitalization. The economic sector of the global Korean Wave grew during this time in ever more digital ways even while there were devastating economic and cultural policies of lockdown, social distancing, closed public venues, and real businesses suffering damage and bankruptcies cascading through the rest of the Korean national economy and laboring population and worldwide.

In many countries, such lockdown situations were the beginning of an economic shock treatment of a Great Reset (Klein, 2008; Schwab & Malleret, 2020) that deeply hurt in-person economies and cultural industries dependent on physical venues and live events while forcing innovation toward a more purely digital economy. Perhaps unsurprisingly, Korea, by already being a very digital national culture, and by the Korean Wave already being a more global digital phenomenon, transcended its own national and cross-national lockdown policy constraints by launching more into cyberspace. The Korean Wave leaned to take market advantage of Korean or any aggregate global level lockdowns to export more digitally-mediated entertainment to a wider captive audience.

For only two introductory examples of many discussed later about the innovations in Korea in the past three years during the developed world's general lockdown, the Korean Wave hosted the largest 'online concert' in world history by the K-pop boy group BTS. This online concert was seen concurrently by millions of people over three days, globally. This could happen because Korea was already deeply a digital culture. It is argued that Korea is an estimated 10 years into the world's digital future before other countries due to its earlier digital saturations of scale, and remains an outlier far ahead for decades (See Appendix 1). The Korean Wave already helped catalyze *domestically* in Korea the world's best saturated digital culture by 2013 at the earliest. Thus, domestically Korea and its Korean Wave by 2020 could take advantage of an unparalleled digital expertise and experience in national and global virtual marketing and related business plans, synergies, and technologies more than other country's cultural productions before and during this period between 2020 and 2023. The already supremely digital Korea took advantage of adversity and grew its Korean Wave into a cultural void to innovate more digitally than before.

Second, if the Korean Wave had always aimed at global conquest, now it aimed at global *online* conquest via fresh inventions: artificial-intelligence-based global platforms, metaverse-technologies of augmented reality, business plans, and global empires of digital content ownership around them. All of this was amazingly set into motion in less than two short years between 2020 and 2022. Such digital innovations under lockdown will ripple in influence for likely the next decade in global popular culture. Korea has set a very high bar for what other countries (already behind) have to compete with for all future global online entertainment.

So, while many nations' in-person cultural production declined from 2020 through 2022, the digital quality of the Korean Wave already more decentralized, online, virtual, and viral than any other national culture innovated technically to be able to survive at larger global scales. The rest of the world literally is now trying to catch up to Korean levels of digital saturation achieved after 2013 and accelerated since then. Plus, after 2020, Korea rocketed further ahead as other nations, already behind digitally, started to fall behind further in their own 'raw' cultural production as well. Thus, many countries experienced the past three years between 2020 to 2023 as a cultural and economic death rattle caused by an overzealous 'treatment' worse than a disease, inflicted by their own government. However, instead of market death in Korea for entertainment and the Korean Wave, lockdowns were market acceleration under artificial state-forced conditions.

Comparatively speaking, the only other earlier comparable modern time of such global cultural disruption that was remotely like 2020 to 2023 was in the destroyed economic conditions and cultural shock in Europe after World War II. After this, much of Europe succumbed to the entertainments of the 'American Wave' even more deeply. It was only in the wrecked economies and cultures after World War II in which a global expansion of Americanization occurred. This Americanization is defined as the global commercialization of an already internally-invented American 'teen culture' complex of one-way mass media entertainment recordings and other American consumer products, along with American concerts and American cultural mores (Savage, 2008). Similarly, the digital Korean Wave equally developed internally for a long time, and then started to extend even further internationally across the Internet and distributed mobile phone participation particularly. The world experienced a similar global cultural wasteland between 2020 and 2023 into which Korean digital entertainment products and Korean mores expanded as well.

After World War II, American teen culture and American media entertainment products expanded worldwide. The rest of the world had to respond or see the death of their own cultural industries (Mattelart, 2000). A similar situation is occurring now in the expansion of the Korean Wave increasingly from 2018. There is already a beginning of a global reactionary response to try to close cultural borders or to try to match cultural and technical capacities of Korea—or simply go under. Nations after World War II's destabilizations soon saw more destabilizations from Soviet or American cultural and/or military invasions. With all of that, many nations after World War II had great difficulties in surviving independently in culture. Therefore now by 2023, many nations are expected similarly to have great difficulties in surviving independently in culture in the face of a global digital culture, currently dominated by the Korean Wave. This 'short, sharp shock' of the lockdown period electrified the Korean Wave into higher success while serving as a shock treatment (Klein, 2008) on lockdown nations that faltered under the same condition.

1.4 Three Long Term Trends in the Korean Wave: Globally Distributed Economic Development, Culture, and Media

For a long-term view of this digital Koreanization, hopefully, the twenty-first century will be remembered as the century of the development of much more distributed economic development and thus a more shared global culture. This is because we stand at a unique point in world history due to three trends, if we are fortunate to continue on this path.

The first unique trend is that we have wider and more evenly-distributed global economic development potential than ever before. This trend began in the years after World War II as European, Japanese, and then Soviet empires began to collapse worldwide. Approximately one hundred nations were freed or born for the first time. Early in the 1940s into the 1960s, this was a very optimistic time in world history because many of this 'first run' of fresh countries had not failed at modern development yet. This was a time when wide optimistic and futurist debate existed on what were the proper paths for economic, political, and cultural development. This first global trend of decolonization was despite a growing Cold War between polarized blocks of the United States and Soviet Union that encouraged a dueling and renewed 'double neo-colonialism.' On one side was America's recommended idea of 'slow modernization theory' requiring open borders, global trade, and deep cultural links to the United States as required for modern development. On the other side were the Soviet-aligned states encouraging more top-down socialist and revolutionary models. They argued, in what was soon called 'dependency theory,' that only guerilla revolutionary actions combined with severing global trade connections (despite ironically allowing Soviet state assistance, trade, and cultural programs) can help remove old or new 'modernizing' foreign colonizers' and heritages of colonial wealth extraction to the colonizer's home country. Thus both the United States and the Soviet Union by their geopolitical conflicts wanted to curtail the autonomy of developmental freedom of these fresh nations by convincing them to see only two models of development against each other. However, a widening non-aligned movement existed, led at the time by India. Regardless, all of this geopolitical ferment meant true open chances existed for more equitable world development for more nations and peoples than ever before, if you could balance between two warring superpowers' desires to capture your country to one or another side.

However, by the 1970s into the 1990s, despite some American-inspired successes and despite some Soviet-model successes, greater pessimism existed because it was now seen as very hard to craft any fast-development national policies, particularly ones that created durable economic growth and cultural stability. By the 1970s, given the continued rise of some countries into development out of fading colonialism, and given even ex-dominating core states like Portugal or Spain losing empires and becoming mere raw material peripheral exporters mostly, or given the U.K. losing the world's largest empire ever, a view of Wallerstein's 'world-system' theory of rises and falls of many different countries dynamically together was developed. World-system theory argues different stages of peripheral, semi-peripheral, or core nations are linked to each other's development in one system. In some ways, South Korea is a classic example of Wallerstein's rising semi-periphery that experiences a dictatorial period of state-directed growth and repression of labor movements while aligned to global capital flows, that later 'matures' into more core state status of a high-value industrial economy, political democracy, and its own capital exports to other countries—while repeating the same cycle of underdevelopment of peripheries and development of semi-peripheries elsewhere by getting peripheral clients of its own to get its raw materials. However, in other ways, to be described later, South Korea had unique conditions. It never was a big periphery in Wallerstein's sense at all, as it was without raw materials of any scale that anyone wanted. Japan was in a similar situation. By the 1950s, Prebisch and others were calling raw material export dedication a 'trap' against development in the first place (Collier, 2007; So, 1990), instead of a key to beginning modernistic growth. Only a very few raw material exporters have ever been able to use that wealth to actually develop. It typically has to be a seller's market in very rare and lucrative items like precious metals, diamonds, or even meats. However, it should be "not too much wealth" like seen in oil exporting nations that leave them underdeveloped and unstable even despite their wealth (Karl, 1997). This is because most raw materials can come from many countries, so most commodity chains generally become a buyer's market of easily substitutable or cheaper agricultural or energy mass commodity production that means little stability of export scale or pricing for selling countries, since bulk commodities can come from or be expanded from a number of countries. So, by lacking raw material wealth to fall back upon, South Korea escaped being trapped and unstable in a globally-dominated peripheral raw material economy. However, this escape of course is more by default than by choice. North Korea on the other and had all the raw materials. North Korea had a sudden burst of development from raw material exports, imported Soviet technologies, and a residual use of a very modern infrastructure built during the Japanese Empire before 1945. However, by the 1970s, North Korea started to fall behind as expected on such an economic dedication of the export of raw materials and had an inability to update its older Japanese physical plant with modern technology of an innovation-based economy. By the 1990s, it even lost the Soviet Union as a sponsor, as that state collapsed. Then, in the mid 1990s, North Korea started to fall into famine.

Thus, as we learn from South Korea as the most successful developing nation yet, we can learn from the spectacular failure of North Korea so far as well—particularly as both countries start with the same historical conditions and culture and yet have incredibly divergent outcomes by different background conditions and by their different good choices and bad choices.

Nonetheless, despite many nations' setbacks and uneven further development in our modern world, there has been great distributed global economic development. More people have been pulled out of poverty in the midst of economic globalization in the past 30 years than all other past ideas combined (Collier, 2007). However, as Collier knows, this has typically meant a decline in the jurisdictional strength of their states to set their own courses in a decline in democratic meaningfulness except for rare exceptions like Costa Rica, Chile, Mauritius, Kerala (in India), and South Korea that combined economic globalization with a strengthening democratic state and a growing welfare state (Sandbrook et al., 2007). From the 1960s onward, distributed global development was highest among the 'Asian Tigers' (Hong Kong, Singapore, Taiwan, and South Korea) and nowadays continues with additions of many newly developed "BRICS" nations (Brazil, Russia, Indonesia, China, and South Africa) with many others wanting to join that group after 2022 like Saudi Arabia and Iran. Meanwhile, the residual mostly Western European/Atlantacist 'G7' states (United States, Canada, U.K, France, Germany, Italy, and Japan) by 2019 controlled only 46.3% of the world economy if measured by global GDP. If measured by purchasing power parity (PPP) in 2021, the G7 has even less economic power with only 32% of global PPP (Calcea, 2021).

The second trend is a global digital culture impinging on various local national cultures. One the one hand, "Koreanization" is a Korean version of past globalized Americanization of the world's youth culture, though centered off Korea's versions of youth culture and this nations' wider entertainment, material, and cultural products. However, there are three main differences. First, what is different now from past Americanization is that the Korean Wave is more than a youth culture of products, shared events, fads, and aesthetics being popularized. What is being popularized are ancient Korean cultural hierarchies and propriety, in narratives and different cultural behaviors in a more collectivist Korean Wave instead of a rebellious individualization in Americanization. Plus, what is being popularized is a more granulated and viral digital world instead of an American one-way mass media world. As said earlier, the greater collective innovations and a conservative, polite mindset of South Korean culture in the Korean Wave are powerfully different *coordinated* cultural principles than an *uncoordinated* American-style individual or cultural innovation. Third, the expansion of the Korean Wave is different this time from past Americanization because even a still-dominant United States, to remain relevant and competitive, feels forced to adapt its own media and cultural production to online strategies, standards, tactics increasingly pioneered in Korea—and even hiring the same Korean idols for American movies by 2022. For example, a Korean actor who was a star of the world-popular Netflix drama *Squid Game* was hired in 2022 to try to make Disney's failing Star Wars franchise strike back in a planned show called *The Apprentice*. Equally, the American pop star Ariana Grande's management tried to do a copy of online concerts made popular by the Korean K-pop group BTS for her own digital exposure in online concerts later. Thus, it is useful to take a long-term and comparative view for how the wider 'digital Koreanization' of global culture began to compete with past 'one-way mass-media and individualist Americanization' in global culture. In short, the Korean Wave's online production, digital distribution, as well as Korean cultural mores and even Korean idols and actors start to show themselves as the global standard to beat for online entertainment for the foreseeable future.

Therefore, despite mostly Atlantacist powers still hegemonically dominating much of global finance and almost all international institutions, they are losing their control due to a wider distributed development and a wider distributed global culture. Thus, we see a past where almost all global industrial development and major cultural trends were focused around what happens in 'core' European and American culture. Now, there is increasingly more multi-polar global cultural interest in what happens in the developing global periphery of billions of people escaping poverty and participating in the global digital culture whether as producers or consumers for the first time. So, on the one hand, we witness a potential conclusion or at least a major dent in over 500 years of unchallenged Western European/Atlantacist economic hegemony over the world economy, at the same moment there is a declining and waning Euro-American global cultural supremacy in the minds of the world in terms of aesthetic standards, arts, political systems, cultural trends, and tourism.

This third unique trend in world history is the media regime change, in this case, toward more distributed peer-to-peer telecommunications replacing the past hegemony of one-way mass media. This is creating a "network society" defined as a social world mediated by electronic networks. There have always been networks in social relations, though rarely have such a wide array of electronically mediated networks defined the basics of socialization in politics, education, religious adherence, consumption, market participation, and even finance (Castells, 1996). Except for pioneers of communication history and economic history like Harold Innis, many historians or development economists ignore media changes or think media change is only an epiphenomenon, or merely an economic sector among larger economic trends they want to analyze. However, media changes can have very deep and profound effects as 'first movers' on culture and economic development itself. Such media changes have mostly come upon the world unaware because analysts rarely think of historical changes of 'media regimes' as important as economic policy changes.

However, regardless of how most analysts have ignored it, from around 2007 to 2019, we have now a more equitably-distributed access to peer-to-peer communication for more people than in the past five thousand years of world history. Since smartphones were only invented in 2007, this has happened very fast. By 2019, in a world then of 7.7 billion people, there were already over 5 billion mobile phones and smartphones (We are Social/Hootsuite, 2019a) allowing more peer-to-peer communication and its endlessly reorganized and unpredictably viral ways. By 2021, the number of smartphones (not unique users) was estimated by Ericsson and the Radicati Group to be 6.37 billion (Bank my Cell, 2023), and Hootsuite data from 2022 estimated 5.31 billion unique smartphone users (We are Social, 2022). These mobile phones are very evenly distributed given even the center of Africa had over 50% of its population with access to smartphones by 2019—and that was the lowest regional average in the whole world at the time. This means everyone from 2019 across the whole planet lived in regions in which 50% or more of the people there had access to peer-to-peer mobile phone telecommunications access (We are Social/Hootsuite, 2019b). In other words, we are starting to live in "smart regions" (Whitaker & Pawar, 2020) that can coordinate their own real geographic community parallel to their regional virtual dynamics, with this itself linked in parallel to the whole virtual world. This is undermining both older national/regionalized cultures and older centralized economic and political organizations alike (Castells, 2004). It is undermining the economic viability of many different kinds of past centralized, one-way, mass-media cultural production as well: movie theaters, newspapers, classified ads, book publishing, the recording industry, the film industry, broadcast television, etc. For instance, the majority of the world's Internet browsing which is increasingly our cultural production took place on smartphones as early as 2017 (We are Social/Hootsuite, 2017). This was only a mere decade after the first smartphones were shipped by Apple in 2007 and other companies thereafter. This was preparatory and only one year before the first "simultaneously successes" of the global Korean Wave in 2018, as noted in later chapters. It is argued that these issues are entirely connected instead of separate.

South Korea's innovation in selling its cultural and technological prowess around the world has happened so fast, it helps to put this country's successes in terms of these three longer-term global trends that the Koreans have successfully used. Koreans have used the distributed spread of modernization-based development in their export-led economic choices, and they have a global digital culture to their advantage in the Korean Wave, and they have used 'media development' in digital telecommunications based development from the 1980s to the present. Academically, this is called ICT4D (Information Communication Technologies for Development).

Are more serious changes to occur in the still dominant Euro-American world culture? Particularly clear from cases like South Korea, do changes in communication technologies foreshadow or even causally lead a sea change in later global economics and later global cultural trends? This is argued to be so in South Korea once its Korean culture and Korean digital telecommunications development got connected to its earlier ongoing economic development. This took advantage of these three global trends that externally set the stage for a durable Korean Wave.

These three global trends have changed South Korea more than other states so far. Next, South Koreans now change the world after these three trends triangulated more in their country than others' nations so far. So on the one hand, this book analyzes this interaction of these three external macro-trends at play in the "Korean Wave" for where it came from as well as what kind of more digital future is to come from all three for the whole world.

South Korea's domestic, internal preconditions were a fertile ground for these three global trends to focus in the country, more than other countries. Uniquely, South Korea is a fast developmental success because it has embraced all three global trends well, while other developing countries either joined one trend only, or had fewer prowess in either trend, or were stagnant after awhile in one or the other trend due to being unable to keep up with the rigorous global competition required in both of them. Other secrets for why the economic "Korean Miracle" of its fast development drive flowed well into the cultural Korean Wave are suggested by South Korea's unique cultural, economic, and political policies and internal settlements that created a more moderating modern 'hybrid development' after 1961 that no other countries concocted. Since South Korea has been a successful outlier far ahead of others in massive economic and cultural projection, and since the country invented unique hybrid models of development and used them exclusively to focus an export-led economy to seize the chance in these three external global trends while keeping itself culturally stable at home, then it is worth entertaining the hypothesis that the latter helped cause the former. Data for this thesis is given throughout this book. Korean good choices (and even Korean background conditions suitably understood) can be copied elsewhere for others' development success. Plus, South Korea's modern hybrid developmental policy decisions were important pre-cursors of the later synergies and virtuous cycles seen in the economic Korean Miracle and the cultural Korean Wave for how *durable* they have remained compared to other countries' lesser successes at a fast development drive and a cultural wave.

Since South Korea's innovation in selling its cultural and technological prowess around the world has happened so fast, it helps to put this country's successes in terms of the three longer-term global trends that the country has successfully used. These are the distributed spread of modernization-based development and the growth of media development particularly more distributed and participatory telecommunications. Literally the majority of the world's population for many years now accesses information mostly via portable smartphones in the billions that failed to exist as recently as 2007. Looking over the past 15 years, the smartphone is unlike other communications technologies that have regularly created "digital divides" as they diffused worldwide. "Digital divides" are defined as situations where technological diffusion creates different levels of inequitable technological use, in this case, access to communication. Instead, smartphones have experienced a quick global "digital parity." This neologism "digital parity" means a technology more equitably distributed around the world. In the case of smartphones, they are found in the hands of the well-connected rich and marginalized poor alike. They are owned alike by isolated elderly and evanescent youth. This is contrary to digital divides of the past that saw communication and media technology diffusion mostly within a few wealthy countries' or their youth demographics per se. In some countries, like the United States, smartphone ownership even exhibits a "digital surplus," defined as a situation where previously culturally and economically marginalized groups are more 'connected' than past hegemonic groups over them. For instance, smartphone diffusion per capita has quickly become more saturated in the generally poorer Black American minority (Pew Research Center, 2015a). Plus, surveys of elderly tend to show they love the "freedoms" granted to their ailing bodies by their smartphones even more than the demographics of youth that find them more of a "leash" and constraining (Pew Research Center, 2014).

However, smartphone networks have a '*triple digital parity*': being found in a nation's rich and poor, in its elderly and its youth, and even in a global distribution among wealthy and poor countries alike. Plus, its digital *surplus* is hardly unique to a few countries. Actually nowadays, the poorer a country is, the more likely there is a digital parity in smartphone ownership. Class inequalities and generation gaps fade away in this fresh communication regime as everyone more equitably owns or has access to smartphones and social media, even the poorer a country is (Pew Research Center, 2015b). As said above, the truly revolutionary potential of this media regime change was that by 2019, all zones of the world reached 50% or more in "digital saturation" around mobile phones even in the center of Africa (We Are Social/Hootsuite, 2019b).

This digital parity in smartphones is astounding and unexpected in the rapidity of its technical diffusion. It gives hope for a wider world civil and cultural participation and representation than ever before. Later, we will see how crucial this global digital backdrop is for the Korean Wave's strategies of cheaper and opportunistic expansion through it that helped give South Korea a truly outsized cultural influence in the world to match its already outsized economic influence and throughput in the world. However, as a precursor of this, South Korea was additionally the first digitally "saturated" nation of any scale (see Appendix 1), far deeper and earlier by 2013 than any other nation in the world at the time. This gave South Korea, alone in the world, at least ten years of extra time and experience over other nations to learn how to perfect marketing and business plans that built a *primary* digital-based cultural sphere and made *secondary* any one-way mass media campaigns or advertising. Meanwhile, other countries despite having some digital development were seldom at Korean scales of digital saturation. Thus, other countries had a more pragmatic interest in maintaining many different kinds of 'heritage' one-way media empires like separated TV channel production from cinema houses *because* such countries were less saturated with mobile phones than South Korea. So the point is South Korea built this saturated digital future internally in its own country first. When it was perfected enough, and when global conditions were ripe in the demographics of moving such virtual marketing and sharing overseas, Koreans were the only ones with pragmatic experience and practice in what no one else could have first, which was how to arrange marketing and business organization for a *primary* digital sphere. The base of this was expanding worldwide before 2020, and has only accelerated after 2020 via artificial governmental lockdowns in many countries. Therefore, South Koreans could more readily than others parlay their own primary, digitally-saturated culture into a more global-scale export economy in the Korean Wave across the distributed global Internet and particularly across billions of smartphones by that point. By 2017, the global networks of smartphones were already over 50% ownership. This indicated how more people accessed the Internet more from mobiles than any other arrangement from this date globally. Therefore, Koreans had the world's first potential audience of simultaneous billions of digital customers and patrons starting simultaneously to be the majority in each of their respective countries as well, if you knew how to tap it properly. After 2020 in the midst of many nations' governmental lockdowns, the digital culture became more of a life or death issue to all nations' cultural and economic production for whether you could tap it. If a nation was unable to tap it, both were dispersing to other countries that could like South Korea. However, South Korea was already 'world first' in digital far better than others by that point for many years (See Appendix 1).

In retrospect, the 'media regime' change that we are in the midst of now globally is a very rare occurrence in world history. Taking a longer historical view of networked smartphones as a media regime, it is argued that there have been only seven true media regime changes in the past 5,000 years (See Appendix 4.) We have entered rapidly this "Regime #7" of networked smartphones faster than any other media regime before it. Other media regime changes typically took hundreds of years to gain their traction and to "saturate" their economies, politics, and cultures to such an extent before it changed the basic character of information flows enough to marginalize older 'mismatched' political and economic institutional dynamics that can be stranded and empty of purpose by the reoriented flow of information toward the fresh media regime. In turn, the fresh hegemonic media regime starts to see people invent own fresh institutions using it whether political, economic, cultural, or financial. However, a very rapid media change in networked smartphones is almost dissolving, within only a few years, past economics, cultural dynamics, media empires, and older institutional forms in the four basic positions of social life: political power, economics/market access, education/knowledge transmission, and even financial currencies. Distributed smartphones as a media regime in the billions globally has created a truly global world, and all four once separate positions of social life are merging even into the same institutions and platforms in the digital convergence. However, while a digital convergence blends a platform-based world with the older institutional based world, cultural production remains decentralized. This is creating a huge friction between expanded potentials for totalitarian censorship and centralized control in the digital convergence at the same moment the same medium encourages a decentralized cultural production and decentralized economic production. This means there is a big conflict coming up for what human values will be spread through these linked networks.

This media regime change is a challenge to economies, cultures, and even national stability or national democracy alike. It undermines past scaled production and distribution. It reconstructs and helps selects what kinds of social organizations are more optimal economically and socially. It may even alter or select for *what sizes and qualities of countries are more optimal* economically and socially, for surviving amidst such an ever-changing global digital dynamics in which technological change requires expensive retooling repeatedly. It is involved in how online cultural onslaughts challenge older cultural transmissions. It is argued South Korea may be in a triple 'sweet spot': of the required 'mid-sized' scale of geography and demography in countries, and having a more homogeneous culture that can handle such a global digital culture and still survive intact. Korea seems to be doing very well in the middle of this globally changing digital economy, as "not too small geographically or demographically" to be unable to fund such technological changes, and yet "not too big geographically or demographically" to find it exorbitantly expensive to do so. South Korea as well is "not too heterogeneous" as to find it hard to come to policies to maintain a common cultural transmission over time, to survive as a culture in a globally digital age. Thus, there may be a selection factor for what qualities of nation and culture are more successful in such a fast-paced digital economy and culture as "not too individualistic" or divided that it creates difficulties in fast-paced coordination required and "not too collectivist" that creates problems of slower centralized response as well. There may even be a selection factor for what kinds of governments we will have in the future in a global digital economy, as the leadership that can organize and subsidize such extensive technical retooling (like South Korea or like Taiwan is willing to do) would be selected for against other kinds of laissez-faire governments (like Hong Kong) that become unable to manage such logistics, coordination, updates, research, development, or expenses over time. Such latter places may fall by the wayside politically and culturally as a consequence just as laissez faire Hong Kong did leaving them to be captive of other countries' technological digital hardware productions and digital cultural productions.

Global networks of smartphones and their viral content will continue to smash and to dissolve past mass-media institutional arrangements and cultures, since older institutions and larger countries may be now 'mismatched' and selected against in two ways. First, they are mismatched since they are built on the premises of previous communication technologies that are now rapidly bypassed and outclassed. Second, they are mismatched because this media change is occurring in larger culturally heterogeneous geographic empires or cultural zones that will find it harder to adapt, to fund technical updates, to produce a common digital culture people want to buy. Thus, they may culturally implode or explode, resolving themselves down to several different "K-Nation"-sized pieces. Many heterogeneous cultures are really plural regionalized homogeneous cultures already (Fischer, 1989; Garreau, 1982; Woodward, 2012). So, will culture under current conditions of networked globalization create greater frictions in all regions of more heterogeneous cultures over time in reaction to it, as has happened in earlier globalizations? (Jennings, 2010).

In such changing times, past cultural impediments may become cultural boons. Korea's 'mid-size' and its ancient cultural homogeneity that still has resources for collective innovation may be selected for in such a media regime. It is argued that such kinds of cultures may be selected for and survive better under onslaught of global digitalization, surviving as transmissible more *homogenous cultures* into the future, and surviving as more 'mid-sized' *political economies* capable of handling creation, recreation, and retooling required of such a fast-paced technological innovations as a digital economy and its infrastructures. Such "Korean sized" nations and a "Korean quality" of a more homogeneous culture may be selected for, since such nations will handle these ongoing issues far better than larger more heterogeneous states already fracturing widely under digitalization without past cultural resources or capacity for having a common image of the future—or now without the ability to hide or ignore their ongoing lack of it.

The media regime change of networked smartphones that we experience now can be summarized succinctly as *a move away from* our past one-way, top-down, expensive and centralized mass-communication technologies *toward* more two-way, peer-to-peer, cheap, and decentralized ad hoc and viral communication technologies. Centralized institutions, large states, and empires used to be the required 'expensive communication architectures' that processed information at scale at a singular source node of gathering and then decision-making. However, a network society renders (in all senses of that word) the rotting waste of many of these kinds of central institutions as unimportant, by processing information more cheaply and more quickly globally in ever-changing networks without an economic advantage to those past central hierarchies (Castells, 2004).

This particular media regime change of Regime #7 is doubly rare. This is because it has increased communication parity even among the most marginalized peoples of the world in hundreds of various nations simultaneously instead of how most communicative changes of the past enhanced or reformatted a durable inequality of urban-based communication, publication, and participation against different excluded rural peripheries whether geographic or cultural (Innis, 1950, 1986). Now, with smartphone networks equitably distributed across the world's landscapes, we enter a world of 'smart regions' instead of only 'smart cities'. These 'smart regions' are worldwide, so even rural areas and less developed areas have equal communication and coordination capacities similar to major cities (Whitaker & Pawar, 2020). Of course inequalities still exist in bandwidth and cost (Ang, 2020), though that digital parity of access is already solving its own economic distribution problems in virtuous cycles even in Central Africa (Park, 2019).

All media regime changes are revolutionary. However, most academics keep ignoring media changes in history, yet they do this now at their peril by continuing to think the only changes of importance are always material and economic instead of equally communicative, symbolic, and informational. As presciently written by Marshall McLuhan in the 1960s,

> "Wedded as [we are mentally] to nineteenth-century industrial technology as the basis of class liberation, nothing could be more subversive of the Marxian dialectic than the idea that linguistic media shape social development, *as much as* do the means of production." (McLuhan, 1964, 1994, p. 49) [italics added]

Note McLuhan failed to say economic changes are unimportant. He argued media shaped our societies "as much as" economics. However, this book takes this idea a bit further: how much more impactful are the world's few eras of *media regime changes* in being primary factors causally explaining later wider and long-lasting *changes* in social and economic development? How do once peripheral countries like South Korea, once they are embedded or saturated more in fresh media, become unexpected quick leaders? How do larger, older, and more heterogeneous countries with more mismatched institutions and outdated media get challenged and bypassed in information management under such changes, or suffer more internal cultural conflicts because they are finally sharing in a participative media that reveals old divisions instead of hides them anymore? The latter situation is seen in heterogeneous states like the United States, India, and Ethiopia where saturated digitalization is hardly rejoining the country, though is exposing previously unvoiced deep divisions that a previous centralized and one-way media regime could hide more effectively. All three of these countries are increasingly resorting to strategies of massive censorship of their internet public, in different tactical ways. All three of these nations have older mismatched institutional elites seeking to keep the past inequalities of their power going that was much easier to do when the only media was a one-way mass media that centralized both production and censorship seamlessly at once, since past media production could be media censorship at the same moment. However, our fresh media regime daily exposes censorship and cultural production as two separate acts given a more decentralized sphere of cultural production can recognize it and comment upon it now.

Considering this point, on the one hand, would not more homogenous cultures like South Korea, Japan, or China have a greater chance to rise to the economic top under this situation as countries more selected to successfully keep transmitting their culture to survive despite the global media onslaught? On the other hand, would not the larger, culturally dissonant, and more regionally inequitable countries with pluralistic different religions, regions, and peoples suddenly see themselves culturally start falling apart like the United States, Indonesia, the Philippines, Ethiopia, China, or India? Which heritage nations are really capable of riding this media wave of the future, which nations will collapse, and what future kinds of nations may be invented to handle it as well? There are many cross-cutting issues here: what sizes of nations (both geographically and demographically), what levels and regionality of wealth of nations (more equitable economically to many regional inequalities), what quality of governments (from collectivist to laissez faire), and what kinds of cultures (more homogeneous or more heterogeneous) will be selected for to survive together to transmit themselves into the future?

As early as the 1930s, Fritz Machlup argued that the areas of the U.S. economy and society that had greater, faster, or more accurate information could act upon it faster, so better and more accurate applied information was theorized as key to economic development in various leading sectors. Castells found the same point when analyzing how by the 1990s the 'network society' was creating leading sub-sectors depending on how more 'digital' these were becoming (Castells, 1996). Innis in the 1950s was theorizing how different media innately had a bias on current socialization. However, neither Machlup, Innis, nor Castells spent much time on *the thesis of media regime change and the institutional mismatch that it creates* in the overlap period where past principles of a previous media regime try to stay paramount culturally even though institutionally they are failing. This thesis of institutional mismatch argues that older once-powerful institutional leaderships regularly are arrogant, and thus ignorant, and thus laggard, in adapting to what happens in their periphery. Therefore some peripheries may seize the chance if they are 'doing media better' (defined as handing information processing with more efficient costs and/or at larger scale capacities and flexibility) than past core zones. Thus past core zones of information processing may become bypassed and become a fresh hollowed out periphery themselves, if they fail in their own media regime change adaptation and reorganization.

As an example of this current media mismatch, it is argued that much about the older American and European institutional and cultural leaderships are now out of phase with how the world is sharing information, and they lag against our modern daily digital culture globally. This has given an opening to once peripheral countries like South Korea or unique digital and culturally homogeneous zones of India like Bangalore or Kerala, or similar digital and more homogenous cultural countries like Mauritius, Estonia, or Poland. Institutional mismatch equally helps to understand why the world was blindsided by development of the economic Korean Miracle and the cultural Korean Wave as well. For a quote that captures succinctly this idea of media change, institutional mismatch, and the revolutionary potential these situations have in history for dissolving past powerful aggregated social systems of information, culture, and political power all at once, ponder the somewhat threatening words of decentralized computer programmer Pia Mancini: "We are 21st-century citizens, doing our very best to interact with nineteenth century-designed institutions that are based on an information technology of the fifteenth century" (Mancini, 2014). So, mobile electronic networks of communication in the hands of over 5 to 6 billion people employ ever-shifting peer-oriented information flows. This was estimated to be 2.5 to 3.3 billion smartphones out of the 5 billion mobile phones in our world of 7.7 billion people as of 2019, and up to a total of 6.37 billion total mobiles in use in 2021. By 2022, this was around 5.31 billion unique users of mobile phones for a 67.1% coverage of the world's population (Bank my Cell, 2023; Kemp, 2019; We are Social, 2022). This networked world of smartphones has greater economic capacity and greater peer-cultural communication, sharing, and creation for all.

The media change will likely be remembered as the more profound since such media changes happen less often, and since this is the first media change reversing a pattern of media that is thousands of years old: millennia of bias toward more hierarchical transmission of power, culture, and media. However, any technologies including media hardly determine social relations. For instance, decentralized communication networks can be used to make decentralized societies and maximize individual freedoms with intentional data fragmentation policies, or they can be used to make more authoritarian-minded surveillance states with data convergence policies. There are dystopian options like the social credit systems of Communist China where the whole country has already been converted into an open-air jail based on surveillance cameras with facial recognition combined with smartphone monitoring and notifications with digitally-delivered messages about access or denials based on lifelong logged behaviors, comments, and even state-based judgments on friendship circles. Therefore, past media changes and particularly our fresh digital media regime change are underdetermined: media changes are open to systemic possibilities for how the same media may be used in many different orientations whether in the past or now in these troubled times.

Regardless, South Korea has moved first and best on making us into the first daily audience of five billion or more together. Such media changes, instead of only freeing individual creators who jump for the chance, see others who get 'pushed' into obsolescence at the same time as their previous jobs and stable institutions dissolve into cyberspace (Standing, 2011). Plus, this world trend of networked smartphones changes international dynamics in our world-system and shows once-marginal yet more homogeneous smaller countries like Estonia, Poland, or South Korea have had the power of quick collective innovation to leap at the chance. Other geographically larger and/or heterogeneous countries seem now to stall in division and indecision or get 'pushed' into adapting by self-interested actors toward more surveillance states as their only response like older powerful countries of the United States, Russia, India, or other nations.

On the whole, it is argued that this media regime change has made more mid-size homogeneous nations into more optimal and durable creators far more than geographically and demographically larger (or smaller) and more heterogeneous countries that have wider cultural differences and more expensive fixed costs in past technical systems. On both points, this makes it more expensive for larger countries to maintain technology at that scale and cultural content in these conditions. Such nations in the media regime change may find it difficult to adapt, to innovate, to retool, and to produce profitable culture as fast as more mid-sized homogeneous nations in the same media regime change that get selected for instead. Smaller size nations may be able to adapt and retool faster than anyone, yet the issue is their ability to compete as well in the world digital economy as more 'mid-sized' nations in a variety of other ways dealing with their smaller labor pools, investment capital, or real estate expansion possibilities.

There are three caveats to this thesis. First, from looking at cases, sometimes small city states may be selected for whether they are homogeneous or heterogeneous, it seems, since they have been successful in keeping up such digital globalization by reducing fixed costs to a tiny areas of retooling. This is particularly clear in multi-ethnic 'micronations' like Singapore or more homogeneous cultures like Dubai. However, for slightly geographically-larger or demographically-larger territorial nations, they tend to be more successful in digital globalization the more they have a homogeneous culture. This is like South Korea, Taiwan, Japan, Poland, Finland, Sweden, or Estonia. Second, *it may be possible* that even geographically larger and more heterogeneous states can be successful in digital globalization, *though it has yet to happen.* It may have to do with lacking a dominant ethnic culture or at least dominant ethnic elite culture, since in a heterogeneous cultural state, elites can be very split along with the wider culture of the state. Plus, even in a larger more homogeneous state, a digital triage starts to exist like in China or Russia for instance where digital hardware production and digital cultural production takes place in certain zones that innately is versus the rest of the country. Therefore, future collaboration is more difficult to coordinate. Meanwhile, *future digital collaboration instead of digital division is more likely to occur in the more homogeneous 'mid-sized' cultural nations that already have been collaborating well for a long time* in such collective innovation. Third, the caveat is that the so-called 'problem of heterogeneity' of culture in a digital economy may only be in situations in which a large minority exists within a larger hegemonic culture (Collier, 2007) seen in some very poor countries as well as very rich ones like the United States with generally poorer Black Americans within more middle class European-heritage dominated cultures. In other words, *heterogeneity* per se *may hardly be a problem when it is taken to its extreme in large scales of actual heterogeneity where no one is the majority,* because that may encourage greater collective innovation instead of being a problem itself. There is some evidence of this kind of extreme heterogeneity encouraging similar collective innovation and collaboration seen in Rwanda, Singapore, or Mauritius (Sandbrook et al., 2007). Note the large collective ethos and common national identity created in Singapore from the 1960s out of once a very ethnically-divided city without any common past identity, as they were forced to be their own country once jettisoned from the Malaysian confederation. It is interesting that more heterogeneous cultural nations of Rwanda, Mauritius, and Singapore have had larger success than most other moderately more heterogeneous nations in their collective policies toward a digital economy, for instance.

Thus our fresh 'network society' as it moves into networked smartphones in the billions seems particularly to challenge and undermine past dominant, geographically large, and heterogeneous nations. Three of the largest demographic countries in our world are very heterogeneous cultures: India, the United States, and Indonesia. China is demographically large of course yet in China well over 90% are Han ethnicity, and yet there are many dozens of official minorities. Meanwhile, the top four countries *by geographic area* alone in the world are Russia, China, the United States, and Canada—and only smaller or specific zones of these have any scale of digital saturation. However, the more *digitally saturated* places in the world in this 'mobile revolution' of networked smartphones are small 'global cities' that are small countries in themselves (Sassen, 2001) like Dubai, Singapore, Estonia, or Hong Kong and some of the world's 'mid-sized' and more homogeneous cultures like Estonia, Sweden, Finland, Poland, and South Korea. Thus, the homogeneous tribes may inherit the digital Earth (Kotkin, 1994).

Throughout almost all past world history, smaller more homogeneous and 'meek' nations or territorial zones were at best passive 'watchers' or 'absorbers' of what a handful of big countries' cultural industries were creating for the world stage. "Culture" with a capital 'C' meant the products of world imperial capitals that exported Culture and Civilization upon the world (and violent imperialism and slavery), willingly or unwillingly. Such large states were ignoring or simply enthralling the entire world's other cultures to think that they only had culture with a lower case 'c'. However, the current media regime is quickly developing a reversal of thousands of years of this cultural flow. This is because countries that handle quicker digital and technical innovations can retool faster to capture global technical and cultural markets, whether in materials or in ideas. These are more often now mid-sized homogenous countries that have a less difficult internal economic, political, organizational, or cultural inequality to solve first to act on such plans.

So unless we want a future cultural world of *only* traditional, derivative, collective innovation and homogeneous cultures in a digital economy, finding digital solutions for 'rescuing' geographically larger, demographically larger, and more heterogeneous cultural nations from their two mounting technical and cultural problems under network conditions is very important. Of course cultural divisions hardly are caused by only one factor of 'media regime change' that can be blamed for all such divisions arising, as if mere exposure to fresh media like fresh air sets them all afire. Instead, cultures either completely collapse or dissolve into multiple regions for a variety of different rationales in a variety of different cases. The only concern discussed here is the suddenly-revealed impermanence, thinness, and dissention in many large geographic or demographic countries in how their more heterogeneous cultures' have a declining economic competitiveness in a digital economy, and how their economic decline is associated with the decline of their common identities over time in a digital culture. This may be due to either their greater costs in retooling fixed capital for digital globalization and due likely to being more indecisive of what kinds of digital culture extension they should focus upon at all. The main point here is that if we care deeply about the greater individual and cultural innovation that comes from geographically-larger and more heterogeneous cultures, finding ways for such 'heritage' big states and heterogeneous cultures to participate more successfully in digital globalization to continue to give us their individual and cultural innovations is of paramount concern. This is because at present it seems that more heterogeneous cultures of geographically larger and demographically larger nations are falling apart, resolving into multiple, hostile, and competing mid-size regional more homogeneous cultures within them when such past nations are placed under digital globalization.

If the leadership of Earth in this media change is now going to be under global digitalization, it may be under a kind of unfortunate neo-feudalism under more homogenous 'tribal' groups that network very well with or without smartphones (Kotkin, 1994, 2020). Thus, when we add a nation's ability to maintain, service, and retool such smartphone networks, the world's more mid-sized, homogeneous, and once peripheral nations we may find jumping faster to participate electronically as peer digital states in digital hardware production and in digital global cultural production. South Korea is the rare country that has done both (See Appendix 1). The future global leadership may come literally to be found in 'mid-size' homogenous cultural locations that rule a larger fragmented heterogeneous world. Meanwhile, larger more heterogeneous countries may have potentially larger internal markets, yet they additionally have larger and older organizations, more fixed costs, and more divisive, slow, and lugubrious politics. All of this combined perhaps means they will be unable to adapt politically or economically as fast or as nimbly as smaller city-states or mid-sized homogeneous nations that have greater access to the pleasures of fast-moving collective innovation in better ratios of capital formation to digital technical rollout or digital cultural production. Meanwhile, more heterogeneous nations indeed may have greater access to only the pleasures of individual innovation or cultural innovation, yet they have greater tragedies of politically-hamstrung decision making in planning for their collective future. Therefore, we live in a world increasingly in which mid-sized more homogeneous cultures like South Korea are filling up the minds and hopes of billions of other people in larger heterogeneous nations, with their own mid-sized nations' conservative and homogeneous content.

It has been only ten years or less that the Korean Wave truly has spread around the world from its early 'nest' within regional East Asia in the early 1990s and beyond. It is argued that it is not a coincidence that the last ten years or less was equally the first decade of global smartphone networks at any saturated scale. This created an institutionally mismatched world everywhere within other country's older national one-way media—everywhere almost, except in South Korea. This Korean primacy in telecommunications can be said on many levels. Even today, it is argued South Korea remains a decade ahead of in innovative business plans and marketing strategies for such a saturated digital world before other countries reached such levels. This has only accelerated in South Korea after 2020 due to artificial lockdown contexts across many global nations, while those other global nations mostly 'decelerated' at the same time—making an even larger digital gap between South Korea's digital prowess and other nations in cultural production. Plus, South Koreans' own national culture was easily conquered first by a version of its own digitally distributed Korean Wave itself, instead of only seeing this as an international push on the world as well. These points are mentioned later in more detail.

1.5 Conclusion: Three Themes in this Review

By reviewing the national and global dynamics that led to the Korean Wave, this is not meant as a boosterish pro-Korean document trying to advertise the Korean Wave to the world or trying to wallow in national self-pride, however well deserved. Those kinds of books are shallow and quickly forgotten. Instead, there are three sections of this book: past, present, and future. Part One is the past, about the precursors of the Korean Wave and how unique has been the Korean fast development drive compared to other nations. Part Two is the present, which includes timelines of the Korean Wave, analysis of its different segmented periods of it over time in comparison to other nations' cultural waves and their characteristics, and three case studies of particularly strong successes in the Korean Wave. Part Three is about the future. It is a review of current trends and future scenarios about Korea, the Korean Wave, and world development in general if these trends continue and what may happen increasingly once all past nations are within a global digital economy, a global digital culture, and a global decentralized digital media.

Within these three sections, there are three running themes. First, there is a discussion of trends in world development that Korea has taken advantage of well, and how we might learn from this for other countries. In this wider analysis of the world, this book tries to be a calm, comparative, exploratory, and even precautionary hypothesis of what the whole world may face in the rise of *external* pressures from digital globalization, economically, culturally, and in media technology, when in competition with other nations for who succeeds in technical rollout and cultural reproduction over time when facing a mostly immoral or amoral digital onslaught. This mobile revolution in development seems a selection factor on what kinds of 'mid-sized' and more homogeneous cultural nations may survive, thrive, or be (re)invented out of the scrap wreckage of larger and more heterogeneous nations after a bad crash.

Second, this review is an *internal* case study of how the economic Korean Miracle blossomed into the currently unique and peerless cultural Korean Wave since it is the only durable example of a non-Western cultural wave so far. It is argued that it is hardly an accident that this happens to occur in the best example of a mid-sized more homogeneous cultural nation that seems selected for globally by the media regime change. This helped South Korea capitalize on its demographic, geographic and more homogeneous cultural context best. However, beyond these happenstance issues, Koreans were choosing well in hybrid developmental policies that made their country grow faster and more durably than any other nation in the past 70 years. Plus, Koreans have seized these now global digital conditions best by starting very early from the 1980s. Surely, there is much to learn for the world here as well, since most of the world has had very different failed or less successful developmental policies. Can they copy South Korean choices?

Third, there is a theme of cultural critique and sympathy to Koreans. Their success has been awfully stressful. There is much to learn about just what high costs the Koreans have suffered in this fast development, and now just what are the added higher costs to participate even in their own national culture when what passes for national success is judged immediately on whether it is good enough to be globally competitive in the Korean Wave. Is simply enjoying Korean national culture as a collective pleasure passé without the modern stressful basis of cultural judgment in Korea of whether it can survive global capitalistic competition? Has the Korean Wave outmoded or commoditized the Korean culture itself? If a national culture gets hitched to define its own success on global acceptance instead of just national pleasure, this may become a very thin and stereotypical content and a very stressful order of affairs.

Thus a winnowing of Korean cultural complexity has happened to cut away some aspects of treasured cultural forms that may atrophy in service to fey and changing global markets or to current political leaders' like or dislike (and thus subsidy or blacklisting) of particular acts. Koreans have built a Procrustean bed for themselves in the Korean Wave, and now find they regularly have to stretch or to cut their culture and themselves to fit a global market, instead of simply enjoying the cold comfort of their own culture. Despite being culturally homogeneous, mostly conservative, and mostly against global heterogeneity, South Korea has let its government and entertainment companies make their country into a ground zero of global cultural production anyway. However, is the only purpose of a Korean national culture now to serve global markets or to serve Koreans? They are seeing the ultimate globalist gentrification of their own culture.

Plus, it is a Sisyphean task to keep central in a global digital economy. So, while other countries and mass publics may look at the Korean Miracle or the Korean Wave in admiration, and be entertained by the Korean Wave, *they are looking at it from a distance*. Up close, an analysis of both the economic Korean Miracle and the cultural Korean Wave is full of a more durable hardship of years of disciplined market research, practice, tears, and pain. There are only small interludes for resting on their laurels or enjoying an ever-ephemeral fragile glory of economic or global cultural success seen in the short flash bulb of the global paparazzi. In other words, it would be the worst irony if the aftereffects of the Korean Wave were to create a cultural revolution against this that Koreans avoided in the past, that would now destroy the durable more homogeneous Korean culture that set up the virtuous cycles that made their durable development possible in the first place.

After understanding the Korean Miracle into the Korean Wave in these three ways, other countries may want to find what is transferrable to themselves, while others may wonder whether they are better off not being likely to succeed or better off not wanting to complete in triple ways that South Korea does now—in the global digital economy, the global digital culture, and in decentralized media technological production. Plus, to transfer ideas from South Korea to other countries desirous of its models of fast-economic development or cultural projection may mean many countries would have to winnow and to change entirely their cultures or even their constitutions to a more authoritarian vein to have the equal stable leadership or collective culture that has animated the Korean Miracle and the Korean Wave. Everyone wants the glory of South Korea instantly transferred to their countries. Few want to go through the same pain, hard work, and dedication that it has taken for this country to get there.

As much as people admire how beautiful is the result, it should equally be admired and respected for how difficult and against all odds it was for Koreans to walk such a 'development gauntlet' successfully while other nations were failing on similar projects all around them from the 1960s onward. Collier argued two points that are germane here. First, he stated "[s]tarting from being a failing state, a country was more likely to achieve a sustained turnaround the larger its population, the greater the proportion of its population that had secondary education, and—perhaps more surprisingly—if it had recently emerged from civil war" (Collier, 2007, p. 70). These three points are uncannily exactly the preconditions of South Korea by the late 1950s after the Korean War, inclusive of the main development policy of President Rhee (1948–1960) that was educational expansion instead of economic development. President Rhee additionally founded the National Academy of Sciences of the Republic of Korea. The second germane point from Collier is his calculation about statistical likelihood and then length of time on average that it would take to escape all the interactive 'traps' of being a poor country or a failed state: "Overall, we find that the probability of a sustained turnaround starting in any year is very low: a mere 1.6 percent. Countries are therefore likely to stay as failing states for a long time. Indeed, from this annual probability…the average length of time it takes to get out of being a failing state…comes out as fifty-nine years" (Collier, 2007, p. 71). This was judged from the current crop of the poorest one billion people and their countries. Given it took Korea's fast development drive from 1961 to 1997 to enter the OECD, Korea seemed to have done in about half that expected time. Thus, Korea walked the development gauntlet and became that "1.6%" that has created a sustained development turnaround. So, as we admire the Korean nation's accomplishments, good choices, and even good accidents of historical happenstance, we may learn how to help that 98.4% left behind trapped in their vicious cycles of lack of development.

To summarize the three trends that South Korea has ridden well, if the decline of 500 years of an Atlantacist economic hegemony was "not enough" of one revolution to live through as one radical change, the current global multi-polar digital culture is another revolution to live through, and a third revolution to live through is the media regime change itself toward networked smartphones in the billions worldwide. This is changing the cultural and informational dynamics within all countries and making past cultural hierarchies inside as well as cultural boundaries on borders unlikely to be maintained. Digital globalization may create a multipolar world, yet it may mean the destruction of many different kinds of more heterogeneous nations that reduce our access to individual innovation and cultural innovation. Plus, digital globalization may be jury-rigged into a global totalitarian world that may snuff out potential of small regions and smaller countries' participation economically or culturally forever—or for as long as we live in globally mobile-phone-saturated society. In short, there are other futures attempting to play out instead of only "more K-Nations" as the only clear option.

However, we hope South Korea and the early twenty-first century may be remembered a century later as like the winged god Mercury, as the first harbinger of this triple change in long term trends toward "distributed development, culture, and media" that were triangulated well in this first K-Nation of South Korea. We hope South Korea at the turn of the twenty-first century may be remembered as the start of a global regime change that began to upend more inequitable past rules of world history that bigger states always win and smaller states always suffer what they must. Instead, under global digitalization now rising everywhere, perhaps the smaller and more homogenous will inherit the Earth while the prideful larger and/or heterogeneous areas may dissolve into conflict and break up into their own kinds of 'component' homogenous zones under the onslaught of these three global trends? Instead of with glee at this destruction, we write to help all nations try to make a better future with better developmental choices modeled from learning from South Korea as a case and as a comparative analysis of world development. Therefore, South Korea may provide more than entertainment in the Korean Wave to the world. South Korea may provide a better developmental model if people can handle its rigors. Equally, it may show how to maintain more peer-oriented and inclusive political and cultural uses of digital technology instead of falling into hierarchical 'social credit' models, durable exclusions, and developmental triages.

For one point about what is to come, it will be argued that South Korea was for decades and remains now well positioned to rise via these three global trends via its own political and economic choices, via its own background history, and via its own more homogeneous culture that has a fast-paced collective innovation that took advantage of these trends' situations well. The governmental imposed lockdowns after 2020 in many countries of the world only further elevated the digital Korean Wave even more in the cultural vacuum.

For another point of what is to come, the more revolutionary argument is South Korea is a harbinger of what successful states 'might *have to* look like' in the future if nations are to survive the massive changes of informational flows in our global network society. If we get blessed with several more stable generations of culture and economic globalization, despite this onslaught of organizational mismatch that the network society is causing, many other countries' cultures may come to develop more equitably and to participate more equitably in the global culture, as South Korea has. Within 50 years, we may know which path the world is taking right now. However, from understanding these options, we will plan better versions of the future now that we want to achieve later. We will only know later if South Korea in retrospect was an outlier that got it right that is more unapproachable by others as a model, or was something we can learn from as a true harbinger of three global trends. Regardless, these three global digital trends have started to upend both the past's larger heterogeneous or larger homogeneous nations. This will perhaps leave the global playing field to many more mid-sized and more homogeneous K-Nations to be sculpted out of the digital cultural wreckage. It helps to learn from and about South Korea's culture, its good choices, and its good accidents in attempts to apply its development ideas to other countries as all countries are going through the same digital bottleneck.

References

Ang, C. (2020, July 3). What does 1GB of mobile data cost in every country? *Visual Capitalist*. https://www.visualcapitalist.com/cost-of-mobile-data-worldwide/

Arora, A., & Gambardella, A. (2005). *From underdogs to tigers: The rise and growth of the software industry in Brazil, China, India, Ireland, and Israel*. Oxford University Press.

Bank My Cell. (2023). Number of mobile phone and smartphone users. https://www.bankmycell.com/blog/how-many-hones-are-in-the-world

Bradley, J. (2009). *The imperial cruise: A secret history of empire and war*. Little, Brown and Company.

Calcea, N. (2021, June 11). How the G7's economic power has diminished. *The New Stateman*. https://www.newstatesman.com/business/economics/2021/06/how-g7-s-economic-power-has-diminished

Castells, M. (1996). *The rise of the network society: The information age: Economy, society, and culture* (Volume 1). Blackwell Publishers.

Castells, M. (2004). Chapter one: Informationalism, networks, and the network society: A theoretical blueprint. *The network society: A cross-cultural perspective*. Edward Elgar.

Chang, H.-J. (2011). *23 Things they don't tell you about capitalism*. Bloomsbury Press.

Collier, P. (2007). *The bottom billion: Why the poorest countries are failing and what can be done about it*. Oxford University Press.

De Rivero, O. (2013). *The myth of development: Non-viable economies and the crisis of civilization*, 2nd Edition. Zed Books.

Elliott, L. (2023, January 16). Call for new taxes on super-rich after 1% pocket two-thirds of all new wealth; $26 trillion of new wealth created since start of pandemic went to richest, Oxfam report reveals. *UK Guardian.* https://www.theguardian.com/inequality/2023/jan/16/oxfam-calls-for-new-taxes-on-super-rich-pocket-dollar-26tn-start-of-pandemic-davos

Fischer, D. H. (1989). *Albion's seed: Four British folkways in America* (America: A cultural history, Volume I). Oxford University Press.

Garreau, J. (1982). *The nine nations of North America.* Avon Books.

Gill, I., & Kharas, H. (2006). An East Asian renaissance: Ideas for economic growth. *The World Bank.* https://openknowledge.worldbank.org/bitstream/handle/10986/6798/399860REPLACEM1601OFFICAL0USE0ONLY1.pdf

Global PEO Services. (2022). Top 15 countries by GDP in 2022. https://globalpeoservices.com/top-15-countries-by-gdp-in-2022/

Hancock, G. (1989). *The lords of poverty: The power, prestige, and corruption of the international aid business.* Atlantic Monthly Press.

Hong, E. (2014). *The birth of Korean cool: How one nation is conquering the world through pop culture.* Picador.

Innis, H. A. (1950/1986). *Empire and communications*, D. Godfrey (Ed.). Press Porcepic.

Jamrisko, M., Lu, W., & Tanzi, A. (2021, February 3). South Korea leads world in innovation as U.S. exits top ten. *Bloomberg.*

Jennings, J. (2010). *Globalizations and the ancient world.* Cambridge University Press.

Jonas, M. (2007, August 5). The downside of diversity. *New York Times.*

Kaplan, J. (2021, January 26). Workers lost $3.7 trillion in earnings during the pandemic. Women and Gen Z saw the biggest losses. *Business Insider*. https://www.businessinsider.com/workers-lost-37-trillion-in-earnings-during-the-pandemic-2021-1

Karl, T. L. (1997). *The paradox of plenty: Oil booms and petrol-states.* University of California Press.

Kemp, S. (2019). Digital 2019: Global digital overview. *Datareportal.* https://datareportal.com/reports/digital-2019-global-digital-overview

Klein, N. (2008). *The shock doctrine: The rise of disaster capitalism.* Picador.

Kohr, L. (2001). *The breakdown of nations* (Originally published, 1954). Green Books, an imprint of UIT Cambridge, Ltd.

Korean Spirit & Culture Promotion Project. (Ed.). (2007). *Fifty wonders of Korea, Volume 1. Culture and art.* Samjung Munhwasa. http://www.kscpp.net

Korean Spirit & Culture Promotion Project. (Ed.). (2008). *Fifty wonders of Korea, Volume 2. Science and technology.* Samjung Munhwasa. http://www.kscpp.net.

Kotkin, J. (1994). *Tribes: How race, religion and identity determine success in the new global economy.* Random House.

Kotkin, J. (2020). *The coming of neo-feudalism: A warning to the global middle class.* Encounter Books.

McLuhan, M. (1994). *Understanding media: The extensions of man* (Originally published, 1964) L. H. Lapham, Introduction. MIT Press.

Mancini, P. (2014). How to upgrade democracy for the Internet era. *TEDGlobal 2014.* https://www.ted.com/talks/pia_mancini_how_to_upgrade_democracy_for_the_internet_era

Mattelart, A. (2000). *Networking the world, 1794–2000.* University of Minnesota Press.

Oh, M., & Larson, J. F. (2019). *Digital development in Korea: Lessons for a sustainable world*, 2nd Edition. Routledge Advances in Korean Studies. Routlege.

Park, G. (2019). *Rethinking mobile diffusion: Explanatory analysis of factors affecting mobile diffusion in African countries in the Sub-Saharan region.* Paper for the Completion of "'Part A' Exam" in the Graduate School of Stony Brook University, Department of Technology and Society, The State University of New York, Korea.

Paus, E. (2005). *Foreign investment, development, and globalization: Can Costa Rica become Ireland?* Palgrave Macmillan.

Perkins, J. (2005). *Confessions of an economic hit man.* Penguin Group (USA), Inc.

Pew Research Center. (2014, October 3–27). Older adults most likely age group to describe their smartphone as 'Freeing,' 'Connecting.' *American Trends Panel Survey* (2014). https://www.pewresearch.org/american-trends-panel-datasets/.

Pew Research Center. (2015a). Several groups are shifting their home internet connectivity away from broadband and toward smartphones. *Home Broadband 2015*. https://www.pewresearch.org/wp-content/uploads/sites/9/2015/12/Broadband-adoption-full.pdf

Pew Research Center. (2015b). The social media age gap. *Spring 2015 Global Attitudes Survey*. https://www.pewresearch.org/global/dataset/spring-2015-survey-data/.

Picchi, A. (2021, March 31). Billionaires got 54% richer during pandemic, sparking calls for "wealth tax". *CBS News*. https://www.cbsnews.com/news/billionaire-wealth-covid-pandemic-12-trillion-jeff-bezos-wealth-tax/

Polak, F. (1973). *The image of the future*. Originally published in Dutch as *Die Toekomst Is Verleden Tijd* (1954). Translated and Abridged by Elise Boulding. The Jossey-Bass/Elsevier International Series. Jossey-Bass, Inc., Publishers.

Sandbrook, R., Edelman, M., Heller, P., & Teichman, J. (2007). *Social democracy in the global periphery: Origins, challenges*. Cambridge University Press.

Sassen, S. (2001). *The global city: New York, London, Tokyo* (2nd ed.). Princeton University Press.

Savage, J. (2008). *Teenage: The prehistory of youth culture: 1875–1945*. Penguin.

Schwab, K., & Malleret, T. (2020). *COVID-19: The great reset*. World Economic Forum.

So, A. Y. (1990). *Social change and development: Modernization, dependency, and world-systems theories*. Sage Publications, Inc.

Standing, G. (2011). *The precariat: The new dangerous class*. Bloomsbury.

Tarde, G. D. (1903). *The laws of imitation*. E. W. C. Parsons, trans. H. Holt and Company.

We Are Social. (2022). Digital 2022: Another year of bumper growth. *We Are Social*. www.wearesocial.com/uk/blog/2022/digital-2022-another-year-of-bumper-growth-2/

We Are Social/Hootsuite. (2017). January 2017: Mobile's share of web traffic. https://datareportal.com/reports/digital-2017-global-digital-overview.

We Are Social/Hootsuite. (2019a). Digital 2019: Global internet use accelerates. https://wearesocial.com/blog/2019/01/digital-2019-global-internet-use-accelerates.

We Are Social/Hootsuite. (2019b). Global social media users pass 3.5 billion. *We Are Social*. https://wearesocial.com/blog/2019b/07/global-social-media-users-pass-3-5-billion

Wendler, E. (2014). *Friedrich List (1789–1846): A visionary economist with social responsibility* (The European heritage in economics and the social sciences, Book #16). Springer.

Whitaker, M. D., & Pawar, P. (2020). Commodity ecology: From smart cities to smart regions via a blockchain-based virtual community platform for ecological design in choosing all materials and wastes. *Blockchain Technology for Smart Cities (Blockchain Technologies)*. Springer.

WION News. (2021, January 26). World's billionaires get richer by 3.9 trillion during pandemic. *WION News*. https://www.wionews.com/videos/worlds-billionaires-get-richer-by-39-trillion-during-pandemic-359360

Woodward, C. (2012). *American nations: A history of the eleven rival regional cultures of North America*. Penguin Books, Reprint Edition.

World Health Organization (WHO). (2022, July 6). UN report: Global hunger numbers rose to as many as 828 million in 2021. *World Health Organization*. https://www.who.int/news/item/06-07-2022-un-report--global-hunger-numbers-rose-to-as-many-as-828-million-in-2021

Part I
Out of the Past: Cultural and Organizational Success Factors of the Korean Wave

Chapter 2
The Development of Hallyu: Cultural Success Factors that Made the Korean Miracle and the Korean Wave

2.1 Two Chapters to Disaggregate the Background of the Korean Wave

There are two chapters in Part I. They disaggregate respectively the ancient cultural and then the modern organizational developmental factors in the Korean Wave. The Korean Wave is an interaction between earlier and ancient cultural themes and history, and then, modern economic and political policies and decisions from 1961 onward that led to the development of the economic Korean Miracle and later the cultural Korean Wave. As a growing part of this wider economic Korean Miracle, the cultural Korean Wave is best conceptualized as just another an economic export sector. This is different than almost all other nation's cultural waves in the modern world that are entangled with larger issues of military imperialism, jingoism, and senses of cultural supremacy. These factors are absent in the Korean cultural wave. A 'proto-Korean Wave' was attempted as early as the mid-1980s without it being conceptualized as such by producing Korean dramas with foreign language dubbing in mind from the beginning, yet such Korean cultural exports would only begin with the first singular success in Hong Kong TV by 1992 for a Korean drama called "What is Love?" that had a great deal of synergistic state and corporate support to make it happen. This is still in a 'nameless' period of Korean cultural exports. The Korean Wave proper was only desperately expanded with greater state support after 1997, along with many other fresh digital sectors in that year, due to an interactive domestic Korean economic crisis within the wider global financial liquidity crisis of that year. By two years later, in 1999, the Korean cultural wave was given its first official name, as regional "Hallyu."

The first chapter of Part I is *mostly* about *the homogeneous Korean culture* as a background to this cultural wave and its cultural interactions with the organizational choices of Korean development that made two virtuous cycles of politics and economics with the homogeneous culture toward greater consensus and greater innovation, respectively. Plus, regarding this culture, it is argued that there are five comparative causes of greater cultural homogeneity in world history, and Korea has all five:

G.-C. Shin and M. D. Whitaker, *The Korean Wave in a Post-Pandemic World*,
https://doi.org/10.1007/978-981-99-3683-0_2

linguistic isolation, geographic isolation, geopolitical isolation, and how geopolitical isolation combined to maintain long-lasting, stable, cultural hierarchies, and then how that encouraged ongoing conserved information transmission and conserved infrastructures for ongoing technical innovation as well. Next, to describe the culture of Korea, six case studies of durable ancient cultural forms are described that developed in this cultural homogeneity that are proudly still seen in the Korean Wave today. These are singing, archery, martial arts as performance and dance, a concern of body beauty, fashion, and formal public style, the durable character of Korean public festival events, and even Korea's extreme technological innovation. All of these six cultural forms are seen in the deep Korean cultural past as well as in the present.

Plus, instead of this chapter being only about Korean culture, it was felt that a prefatory discussion of the whole Part I was required for how this more ancient homogeneous culture interacts with modern organizational and developmental choices in modern Korea. This section touches upon this 'supercharging' organizational context of this homogeneous culture due to three unique modern historical contexts that started to interact. The first organizational context of this culture was the loss of power and wealth of Korea's hereditary aristocracy from 1910 to 1961 despite a still strong rural homogeneous culture. This led to what will be called the hybrid cultural settlement after 1961. The second and third organizational contexts of this culture are the later increasingly consensus-oriented hybrid political and economic settlements within such an elite political, cultural, and economic vacuum that interacted with this durable homogeneous culture.

These three 'hybrid' situations (of culture, politics, and economics), particularly the unique 'hybrid' political and economic policies described later, interfaced with this 'hybrid' organizational context of this homogeneous culture to create two ongoing virtuous cycles in Korean politics and economics, each influenced by the 'hybrid' cultural settlement mentioned above. These two virtuous cycles are argued to have made possible the ongoing pressures for widening consensus and thus durability for both political support and flexibility of inventive economic action in the economic Korean Miracle and the cultural Korean Wave. These policy choices in these virtuous cycles, in turn, enhanced the durability of the remaining homogeneous culture as part of the fast development drive instead of opposed to it. Instead of a fast development drive eroding the ancient culture, the cultural-developmental alliance kept the ancient culture as an increasing pressure of representativeness against top down revolutionary dictatorship both in politics and in economic policy after 1961 in retrospect. This growing representation has been maintained despite attempts by Korean political elites to be less representative between 1971 to 1987, attempts that failed to hold due to unrelenting cultural pressure against it. In other words, these Korean modern developmental elite attempts to be less representative implies only the latter half of President Park's period in power (fully 1963–1979, yet here referencing only 1971 to 1979), and it implies fully the period in power of President Chun (1979/1980 to 1987), despite his constitutional changes for greater civil rights protections in his Fifth Republic (1981-1987) in desperation to make people more ambivalent to his military coup that happened within months after the assassination of President Park in 1979. It was President Chun who eventually relented in 1987 after slowly losing his own power in the National Assembly elections by the mid-1980s despite continuing to give himself, like President Park before him from 1972 through 1979, the right to nominate up to one third of the National Assembly without elections. However, exactly like Park by the late 1970s, the same loss of power in the National Assembly started to occur for Chun by the mid-1980s. Even appointing one-third of the National Assembly was hardly enough for Chun to pass laws. Later, on top of that, the June Democratic Struggle between June 10th to 29th, 1987, saw daily protests seeking a whole list of other democratic reforms against Chun, including open multi-party Presidential elections next time that went against Chun's announced wish to continue a militarized Presidency without elections. After Chun relented, equally the first labor unions were allowed to form in 1987, and many more Koreans were allowed to start to travel outside the country for the first time. Most South Koreans were blocked from leaving the country without state permission between 1948 to 1987. Before 1987, this policy in South Korea was very similar to North Korean rules about holding its own citizens captive. Thus, the reader can see how many modern organizational factors kept a more homogeneous culture preserved well into the 1980s instead of only the culture as an issue of habit from the ancient past.

However, both these increasing representative hybrid political and economic policies that supported the more homogeneous culture are argued to be the secrets of holding together the nation. Korea has been held in a singular, durable, yet flexible process of long-term Korean economic and cultural extension that seldom faltered from the design set out in 1961, and it only expanded its representativeness over time (despite attempted setbacks between 1971 to 1987) instead of being altered or blocked. That flexibility and ongoing pressure for greater representativeness and consensus in state policy was served well by an absence of interfering older aristocratic families, by the loss of their land tenures, by the loss of their political and military control, and importantly an absence of a cultural revolution to get to this point. That flexibility and great representativeness over time in retrospect was encouraged equally by the first low-legitimacy military coup of the Revolutionary Military Committee (1961–1963) overthrowing the Second Republic (1960–1961). The military leader Park Chung-hee was only one of several military leaders at this point. However, this military coup by committee started the revolutionary state development drive from 1961 onward. The military coup, in turn, found itself in an accommodating battle with the culture itself that disliked the unrepresentative top-down policies though wanted economic development. Thus, this pressure from the homogeneous culture upon the top-down developmental state, in such an elite cultural power vacuum, made the grassroots cultural pressure very powerful. State developmental policies around the later elected President Park Chung-hee from 1963 at the start of the Third Republic (1963–1971) increasingly became less ideological, more plural, more flexible, and thus more durable as a policy settlement with wider consensus. The military coup that created the developmental state after 1961 felt it had to keep adding other parallel development policies that made the Korean fast development drive more representative despite itself, including returning to open elections in 1963 in order that militarists around Park, and later the barely-elected President Park, could stay in power legitimately over the long term to implement their development policies durably over time.

In short, Korea has a unique modern continuity in its ancient homogeneous culture that has survived its foreign colonial period (1910–1945), survived the decline of its native Korean aristocracy and royalty (1910–1960), and *survived its own fast development drive* after 1961 to the present. Any of these three quite historically abrupt changes could have destroyed the homogeneous culture, its cultural teamwork, and its collective innovation still seen strongly in the Korean Miracle and the Korean Wave today. South Korea has remained at the top of the Bloomberg Innovation Index for years, though the rationale why is how the Korean culture is responsible for this result only when interlinked with the above two main political and economic organizational factors. These earlier accommodations kept buckling to create a wider and growing consensus of support in order to try to achieve greater political legitimacy or to achieve at least greater cultural ambivalence. The same culture in North Korea under different organizational choices is like peering through a glass darkly for what greater tragedies could have happened in South Korea given the same homogeneous culture under different organizational arrangements. As the ancient cultural forms remain durable in modern Korean culture, these cultural forms feature widely as recognizable content of the Korean Wave today.

2.2 Culture and Different Organizational Development Choices

2.2.1 Setting the Stage: The Developmental Split between North and South Korea in the Same Homogeneous Culture

To begin this first section about Korean culture, similar to Dickens' *A Tale of Two Cities*, Korea is a tale of two countries. The same culture in both countries has been in long-term interaction with very different modern political and economic organizational choices. In the North, there has been the same culture under conditions of full socialist revolution in a one-party state after 1948, where everything came to be owned by the state increasingly after 1953. In the South, there has been the same culture under conditions of only a half-revolutionary development, with a heritage of a Western-style constitution guaranteeing individual liberties, property rights, multiple parties, and checks and balances on power from 1948, yet by 1961, finding itself within a culturally conservative yet politically ambivalent revolutionary military coup for economic development despite its best attempts to stay in power earlier by land distributions to small-scale rural landholders repeatedly between 1948 and 1953. However, in the South, this half-revolutionary and half-traditionalist model became a more hybrid accommodation making the state-led fast development drive more consensus-oriented and gradualist for being in league with the priorities of a traditional culture now with wide land distribution instead of attempting to destroy both in an active cultural revolution like in the North or instead of attempting to passively destroy it with neglect from 1961 as seemingly originally conceived—until rural pushback against that as well by 1963 onward. Thus, a short historical comparison between North Korea and South Korea sets the stage for the theoretical and comparative discussion of how this stable and old Korean homogenous culture is an independent development factor in the modern era in both countries. However, only in South Korea has its culture become 'supercharged' into very virtuous cycles of development. In North Korea the same homogeneous culture connected to different organizational choices has created more self-defeating vicious cycles.

In the first republican system of Korea's First Republic (1948–1960), the homogeneous culture in South Korea, run by restored conservative aristocratic families from the destroyed Joseon dynasty, avoided a political, economic, and cultural revolution of land nationalization under a totalitarian state that was being done in North Korea after 1953. Northern Korea under Soviet occupation after World War II started first with 'the tyranny of a good example' on March 5, 1946 with its own decentralized land distribution in the Land Reform Law after the end of the Japanese Empire. It was implemented by the North Korean Provisional People's Committee, led by Kim Il Sung (who was soon to be the first dictatorial leader of North Korea, 1948–1994). "Japanese and Korean landlords who possessed more than 50,000 square meters of land were to have it expropriated and distributed to existing tenant farmers for free, whilst the existing tenant farming system was to be abolished. [This was]...expropriation without compensation and land distribution for free to former peasant tenants...[yet]...those owning more than 50,000 square meters of land but without tenant peasants were excluded....However, post-distribution use of the land was restricted [prohibiting]...using land as collateral in lending, the selling of land[,] or subletting to tenants" (Yoo, 2010).

Southern Koreans seethed and wanted the same, yet it was held off there by a still powerful aristocracy and by policy decisions under American occupation after World War II. However, Southern Koreans started to see the Northern Koreans as a political leadership. So, in the South, to avoid communist revolution equally in South Korea, as a government had yet to be formed either in the North or the South, citizens in the southern half of Korea belatedly yet equally benefitted from land *distribution* from 1948 done under the U.S. military authority. Later, land distribution was done once more in the South between 1950 to 1953 under the First Republic (1948–1960). In this way, a relict Korean aristocracy self-sponsored the dissolution of its own *economic* landholding power out of existence in the South in the attempt to survive and to accommodate *politically* in its First Republic. These many land distributions economically weakened an already culturally-weak legitimation of family lines of the older Korean aristocracy attempting to run the First Republic. The old Korean aristocracy was culturally weak because none of the Korean aristocracy were historically nationalists wanting equal rights for all. Koreans as a whole in the late Joseon dynasty before 1910 saw instead most of their Joseon aristocratic groups fighting to preserve a heritage of large landed estates and nearly 1,000 years of slavery on their own Korean citizens (Palais, 1995) upon which was built an aristocracy's easier lives and privileges. Plus, even the old Joseon royal court was hardly an ally to national renewal against the aristocracy, since the Joseon royal court had supported foreign modernized Chinese Qing dynasty troops under Yuan Shikai in 1893–1894 to invade their own Joseon dynasty to repress the widely popular Korean nationalist, democratic, and religious Tonghak rebellions (Whitaker, 2012). This only catalyzed Japanese invasions of Korea as well, with the Japanese winning against the Chinese in Korea within six weeks (stunning the world) and then the Japanese repressed the Korean anti-foreigner, democratic, religious rebellion of Tonghak as well. The late Joseon dynasty's attempts from the 1880s at technical and organizational modernization aimed only to create a stronger central king instead of any senses of national civic equalities under that king. Plus, the renamed "Korean Empire" from 1897–1910 was frustrated as well by the old Korean aristocracy during this period that disliked any such development attempt by a powerful royal central state at all as well as a rising Japanese power in the region more sponsored at the time by the United States' President Theodore Roosevelt who wanted Japan to have a greater 'free hand' in Korea and China (Bradley, 2009). Meanwhile, the Korean aristocracy preferred to undermine the Joseon kings with factional collaborations of their own with Russia, China, or Japan (Lankov, 2007). Thus the divided Joseon royal and aristocratic elite were a power vacuum that made the Japanese Empire in Korea (1910–1945) easier to accomplish formally. It had started after the 1890s, yet accelerated in 1905 after a Japanese ninja team assassinated a queen of the Korean royal family in their own palace, to Joseon dynasty embarrassment. The Joseon king was forced to flee his own palace, and he took up residence for protection in the Russian Embassy in Seoul. By 1910, the annexation of Korea to the Japanese Empire was the formal ending of the Joseon royal house. This Joseon royal line soon married into the conquering Japanese imperial dynasty itself. Thus, the ignominious decline of the late Joseon dynasty took place without any elite, secular, nationalist, democratic, cross-class support for reform. Instead, Korean democratic and anti-Japanese empire pressures were confined within more theocratic movements of nationalism like Tonghak. In the first major Korean nationalist revolt against the Japanese on March 1, 1919, the largest religious affiliation of those Korean nationalists arrested by the Japanese were Tonghak believers (Whitaker, 2012). However, after 1919, there was increasing more secular nationalist collaboration yet still a secular nationalism mostly between different religious movements like Christianity and Tonghak. Plus, at the time, many Koreans thought Japan was a modernization force as well, crippling Koreans own nationalist capacities of change. For example, laws were made by the Japanese Empire in Korea first to stop Koreans from adopting Japanese names, long before the law was reversed very late in 1939 (six years before the end of the Japanese Empire) to try to forcibly encourage Koreans to adopt Japanese family names. This was additionally the period that the expensive and modern physical plant of Korean industry was built in North Korea replete with electrical systems, hydroelectric dams, and along with other modern factory and industrial projects around mining there as well. On the other hand, South Korea was without minerals, and so remained more economically and culturally isolated from the Japanese colonial urban and mining industrialization of the northern half of Korea.

However, at the end of the Japanese Empire in 1945, as Japan lost World War II, the Russian Soviets took up the Japanese power vacuum—and took over and the Japanese industrial infrastructure in North Korea. The Soviets propped up Kim Il Sung as leader, and Kim Il-Sung propped himself up as leader with a land distribution that helped him win popular elections to the Provisional Government. "The farming committee members were instrumental in carrying out the land reform, mostly by aiding in distribution and record keeping. Committee members subsequently became Communist party members and supported the regime at the regional and local level. Consequently, the number of party members rose from 4,530 in December 1945, to 26,000 in April 1946 [a month after the North Korean land distribution] and 356,000 by June 1946. The success of the land reform consolidated the authority of the North Korean Provisional People's Committee, and resulted in successful elections for the North Korean Provisional People's Committee in February 1947 at the local level" (Yoo, 2010).

Meanwhile, in the South, the Americans as equal victors in World War II took up the Japanese power vacuum in 'South Korea.' At the time the terms north and south were just geographical, instead of political. In the northern part of Soviet-occupied Korea, in response to a more socialist party cadre and land distribution developing in occupied North Korea from 1946, in turn, the Americans chose to sponsor the ancient Korean aristocracy in South Korea and so tried to postpone land distributions. However, the Americans did conduct their own managed land distribution in 1948—yet two years after North Korea did the same. As early as October 1945, before the end of World War II, General MacArthur had American-sponsored Protestant Syngman Rhee flown into Seoul, using MacArthur's personal airplane. Rhee had been living in the United States and had been involved in anti-Japanese movements for Korean independence for decades. Rhee had attended George Washington University, then Harvard, and then got a doctorate from Princeton University. As an aristocrat descended from Joseon dynasty kings, Rhee was trying to reemerge as the default cultural aristocratic leadership for Korea yet under a Western-inspired constitutional convention that had much resistance about this idea from Koreans there:

> The United States pushed for the establishment of a separate government in South Korea via a general election. The election was opposed by students, leftists, farmers, and labor organizers, who led general strikes and protests. Nearly 1.5 million participated; the USAMGIK's response resulted in fifty-seven deaths and 10,584 arrests. (Yoo, 2010)

Rhee assumed many hats: the Presidency of the Independence Promotion Central Committee, Chairmanship of the Korean People's Representative Democratic Legislature, and President of the Headquarters for Unification. Rhee was even the first head of this Korean Constitutional Convention and then the first and only President of the First Republic as well (1948–1960). From the beginning he disliked the shared American and Soviet idea of a trusteeship for Korea, written at the Moscow Conference of December 16–26, 1945, with its desired collaboration between all left-wing and right-wing parties.

Therefore, under Rhee in South Korea, his economic policies after the destructions of the Korean War were a strategy to try to expand agricultural production once more as well as to do it in a way that would keep this rather illegitimate ruling group of older aristocratic families in power in republican institutions, strengthened by support from economically small-scale agriculturalists and their traditional rural Confucian culture. The First Republic from 1948 was equally trying to consolidate its national power against a continued strong history of regional people's committees and autonomous grass roots development throughout its territory, and against a strong Soviet-inspired social movement that saw North Korea as a better model. So both the U.S. military autonomously from 1948 and the First Republic of Korea (1948–1960) even in the midst of the Korean War (1950–1953) in 1950 and 1952 tried to shore up support for themselves as political leaderships by many land distributions in the attempt to demote support for the 'other models' of decentralized grass roots development throughout South Korea already, and against more centralized development like North Korea during the war. In North Korea, a political, economic and cultural revolution happened toward a one-party state. It even already had a land distribution from 1946. However, after the Korean War (1950–1953), North Korea reversed itself between 1954 to 1958 and renationalized all land to the present day (Yoo, 2010). As said, during the Korean War, South Korea desperately had several land distributions both public and private between 1950 and 1953.

For more detail, these land distributions were first done in the area of later South Korea even before the First Republic existed from 1948. As said, they were first done by U.S. military authority in 1948 in reaction to three events: (1) the North Korean Land Reform Law that started to do a land distribution in the North from March 5, 1946; (2) the Korean Communist Party-led Korean General Strike of September 1946 in which around 250,000 laborers participated throughout Korea; and (3) the U.S. attempt to shore up support for itself in Southern areas of the Korean Peninsula after the Daegu Uprising of October 1946 (officially called the Daegu October Incident, in Korean parlance) that occurred only after the U.S. military tried to ban the very strong regional people's committees throughout Korea in 1945 through 1946 that had autonomously formed to run Korea after the collapse of the Japanese Empire in 1945.

Land distributions were continued later by the conservative Rhee government in the uncertain times of the Korean War (1950–1953), that itself ended in a stalemate and only a temporary armistice instead of a peace treaty. There were attempts by Rhee to shore up his own support in the Korean War with land distributions announced and conceptualized in 1950 right before war broke out and even undertaken by 1952 in the middle of the war. This two year period saw both state-facilitated land distributions and even larger pre-emptive private land distributions and sales, with large landholders worried about any future lower prices they would get if conquered by North Korea or a forced sale to the government later. Thus, three types of land distributions occurred either from 1948 or from 1950–1953. They were all motivated by the two fearful examples of decentralized grass roots development without any support for any kind of state leadership, or the example of potential communist cultural revolution after 1945 in South Korea. The United States attempted to repress those people's committees throughout the South Korean zone. The left-aligned party in South Korea and its social movements rejected the U.N.-brokered Korean partition, the U.S. military government, and the later government of Rhee's South Korea. Even right-wing Rhee in the South disliked the next idea of a partition of Korea as much as he disliked the first idea of a combined U.S/Soviet trusteeship over Korea. Just like right-wing Rhee, the equal left-wing dislike of U.N./U.S./Soviet partition of Korea was exemplified at the time by (1) the Korean Communist Party-organized Korean General Strike in September 1946 (with Korean left-leaning national strikers attacked by U.S. military forces), (2) by the multi-left-party-sponsored Workers' Party of South Korea (WPSK) that had infiltrated an already stable, peaceful, and autonomous, community-based government in Jeju Island. The WPSK recruited it for their more militarized, left-aligned Jeju Uprising after April 1948—an uprising taken in protest after the U.S.-requested and U.N.-authorized partition of Korea into North and South Korea at the 38th parallel. This was the Jeju April 3rd Incident, in South Korean parlance, from April 1948 to May 1949. Next, (3) there was the simultaneously occurring Yeosu-Suncheon rebellion in Jeolla-do (known as the Yeo-Sun Rebellion) from October 1948 to November 1948 by left-leaning military companies of the First Republic itself that disliked being shock troops for President Rhee's crackdown on WPSK-organized Jeju Island. All three rebellious and even leftist-revolutionary events in South Korea, meeting escalating repression by the First Republic's military, led into the more global-allied Cold War between the Soviet Union/China versus U.N. troops (led greatly by the United States) soon descending on the Korean Peninsula, known as the Korean War (1950–1953). So, the "Korean War" was just an ongoing more international escalation of these internal battles in Korea between the U.S. block of nations in the United Nations that wanted to shore up a right-wing Rhee's military crackdowns in South Korea versus the block of Chinese Communists and Soviet Russian Communists in military support of northern invasions into South Korea to aid several different struggling left-led oppositional rebellions in the southernmost areas of South Korea.

Thus, the land distributions from 1948 onward to 1952 were an accommodating reaction to much internal unrest that wanted political and cultural revolution in South Korea and were trying to have it by joining with North Korea and rejecting the U.S./U.N.'s partition of South Korea and rejecting the Soviet Union's sponsoring of the partition of North Korea as well. This dynamic led into a brutal global Cold War that was simultaneously an internal Korean ideological civil war. However, surprisingly, by the Korean War armistice of 1953, there had been little cultural changes, border changes, or governmental changes—only huge death, mutual recriminations, ongoing ideological battle, vast infrastructural destruction of all cities, agricultural collapse, and starvation. Thus, by the later enforced poverty of the aftermath of the Korean War after 1953, this wider homogeneous culture in South Korea had avoided cultural revolution and yet was only deeper in post-war poverty amidst destroyed cities and amidst a still decentralized land ownership culture developing in South Korea. Next to occur was a North Korean communist land *nationalization* from 1953 (You, 2014) leading into state-sponsored collectivized farms in the North (1954–1958), and an ongoing communist/left-aligned national strikes and strong regional-community-aligned rejection of continuing U.S. administration and occupation after 1953 in South Korea.

Thus, land distributions in South Korea from 1948 through 1952 were attempts to keep facing off renewed calls for cultural revolution and even were just pragmatically after 1953 used to simply raise agricultural production to survive after the Korean War's destruction of land and labor. North Korea had reversed its land distributions after 1953, and conducted a land nationalization to raise agricultural production. South Korea had the same aim of raising agricultural production, yet chose more decentralized agricultural land distribution to achieve it along with crony chaebol connections in a plan of import substitution industrialization that failed to make much success. In retrospect, despite South Koreans by 1960 being now war-weakened and even poorer than before, they had become a practiced independent cultural/political force, a regional community force, and a decentralized economic force within South Korea's ongoing republican governments. Most rural zones from this point would be now more supportive for later culturally conservative yet revolutionarily developmental military coups. This homogeneous culture carried on its ideals of local rural people's committees as well. So, land distribution policies and the Korean War itself was an attempt to avoid a cultural revolution and political revolution in South Korea similar to North Korea in the 1940s into the 1950s. Plus, it was a return to the U.S.'s desired territorial stalemate at the end of the Korean War (1950–1953).

So, instead of any clear win at the end of the Korean War, the armistice only confirmed the earlier U.S.-desired and U.N.-adjudicated split after 1947 in the territory of the Korean Peninsula. However, at the time, North Korea and South Korea were hardly split culturally or politically on unification. Both North and South Korea still wanted to end the externally imposed division and reach reunification. They just disagreed on who would rule the unified Korea. The first South Korean President Syngman Rhee refused to sign the armistice, unlike all other international allies, as he wanted to keep the war going to conquer North Korea and disagreed with regularizing or recognizing the U.N. partition of 1947. Rhee repeatedly tried to get South Korea involved in further military consolidation toward North Korea—not considering it a legitimate separate state, politically or culturally.

However, under Rhee's policy priority of more war and more conquest, there was little pragmatic concern for further economic development throughout the 1950s in South Korea for improving lives of people after the Korean War in the South. The priority that the aristocratic-heritage Rhee had was a war of unification. However, he was unable to find allies to initiate it. Instead, in this impasse, Rhee concentrated on creating a national educational system and ignored ideas for economic development except preferring to keep peasants as peasants, and aristocrats as aristocrats connected to large state-supported private enterprises. Rhee was never popularly elected in the first place. Instead, the First Republic elected its own President (Rhee) out of the National Assembly itself, and the First Republic's constitution was changed in the middle of the Korean War in 1952 to allow for direct presidential elections for the first time, to try to be more legitimate during the Korean War. However, becoming less democratic, Rhee changed the constitution once more in 1954 removing his term limits so that he could run for more than two terms as president—a tactic that Park Chung-hee would later do as well in 1972.

Simultaneous to this earlier period of the formative 1950s in South Korea, there was a top-down dictatorial model and a political, cultural, and economic revolution in North Korea as a developmental model. However, in response, another economic development model developed in South Korea after 1948 toward decentralized agriculture, and after 1961, a complete change from the more laissez-faire developmentalism in South Korea around crony chaebol families tied to Rhee personally, toward instead under Park a top-down military revolutionary development state against a slow or non-existent economic development policy of import substitution based on modernization theory in the First Republic (1948–1960) or the short-lived Second Republic (1960–1961). The aristocratic yet left-wing government of the Second Republic was overthrown so quickly that its own fresh state-led policies of economic development had little time to be implemented. The more conservative and anti-communist Third Republic worked once more with the same few large private enterprises yet within a top-down military revolutionary development state that mostly adopted the left-wing Second Republic's statist development ideas like a five year state plan.

The story of the political vacuum after the First Republic and then a military coup against the Second Republic makes fascinating history. A military coup of development-minded militarists had been organized for many months behind the scenes by Park Chung-hee and others by 1961, and they moved against the short-lived parliamentarian structure of the Second Republic that barely lasted over one year. The First Republic had fallen when Rhee resigned under his own military's pressure on April 26, 1960, and then quickly fled two days later to Hawaii after a left-party and student street uprising still continued that had claimed massive election fraud by Rhee's party for his named successor (and his royalist bloodline in-law) Lee Ki-poong in 1960. Rhee's military was sent to murder and brutalize the left-wing protestors, yet the military under General Song refused to arm the police with bullets and saw itself as a peacekeeping force. In some interpretations this catalyzed only durable street violence in 1960 and in other interpretations this kept a leftist revolution from occurring by General Song refusing to allow Rhee's military to escalate bloodshed. General Song encouraged Rhee to resign, and then when protestors were still surrounding the Presidential Palace two days later, encouraged Rhee to flee as well. As Rhee resigned then fled, a Second Republic (lasting only from April 1960 to May 1961) was created. However, it was still like the previous First Republic in being an 'authoritarian parliamentarian' arrangement without open Presidential elections despite in reaction to the authoritarian Rhee who had already escaped the country. The First Republic was without public elections for President, as the President was just elected by the National Assembly. This was the same for the Second Republic, ruled by a figurehead President Yun Posun (1897–1990) for only a little more than a year, and who was to be the first and the only President of the Second Republic, elected by the parliament. The Second Republic was really ruled by a more powerful administrator as Prime Minister, named Chang Myon (1899–1966), himself to be the first and only Prime Minister of the very unstable Second Republic.

Both Yun and Chang were 'elected without national elections' by the pre-existing National Assembly, just like Rhee's first election in the First Republic. This is why it is called a more authoritarian parliamentary system. Chang Myon was once a sponsored ally of Rhee's First Republic, becoming Rhee's fourth Vice President in the late 1950s. However, Chang grew disgusted by Rhee's authoritarian methods and lack of economic development policy. Chang became an internal opposition to Rhee, and seems lucky to have survived presumed assassination in Rhee's First Republic in the last years of the 1950s.

However, before the greater economic development policies of Chang's Second Republic could have time to be tried, a coup was being planned against this arrangement. The coup kept continuing to be planned despite being postponed and despite even found out several times. The fact that a coup kept being plotted, despite being reported to the Second Republic's military itself, is interpreted to show a great deal of military disgust in its own Second Republic and in conditions from the 1950s into 1961. Park Chung-hee was earlier involved in the Yeo-Sun left-wing military rebellion, and he had barely escaped with his life for participation. He allegedly survived because he turned on his leftist military compatriots and helped capture them for being involved in that leftist military rebellion. Whether this is selfishness or ideological change of heart can be debated by others. However, after the military coup of May 16, 1961 (planned earlier yet postponed several times), the politically ambiguous Park now received popular military and civil support for his Supreme Council of National Reconstruction, the now public and formal title of the Military Revolutionary Committee that had secretly conducted the earlier coup. This military coup attempted to legitimate itself in media pronouncements by focusing on right-wing announcements of anti-communism and on political revolution against the bloatedness, cronyness, and incompetence of Chang's government—despite Chang being in power only a little over a year at that point. In retrospect, the year 1961 would be the end of nearly 2,000 years of Korean aristocratic precedence. That is far more important than normally commented upon as a precursor to the eventual success of the fast development drive (Palais, 1995).

Park announced that the Military Revolutionary Committee aimed for the long-delayed top-down economic revolution that the earlier aristocratic Rhee was uninterested in facilitating, and which the aristocratic yet Catholic humanist Chang Myon had little time to start. After the successful military coup against Chang's Second Republic, given very little blood that was shed in defense for it or against it, Chang emerged after hiding a few days. He and his whole cabinet agreed to resign on May 20, 1961. Soon, even the main global military ally of the United States under President Kennedy supported Park's government, with Park visiting President Kennedy in the United States in November 1961. The Military Revolutionary Committee seems unsure as of what to do with Chang at first. He was free throughout 1961, yet was arrested and prohibited from further politics on March 30, 1962, and threatened with death. However, by August 1962, he was allowed to go free once more. Chang Myon survived, yet never ran as a Presidential candidate against Park in the 1960s as he had been banned from direct public politics under the Third Republic. He instead likely supported his erstwhile proxy ex-President of the Second Republic

Yun Posun in the Presidential open elections of 1963, as the two-year military coup of 1961 to 1963 became a return to constitutional rule in the Third Republic (1963–1971). Chang Myon died in 1966 of hepatitis. In this way, and in many ways, further bloodshed and recriminations were avoided from both sides (of Chang and of Park) in retrospect that could have happened to make everything worse.

Despite Park in the Korean collective way having truly worked within a team-based authority of a Revolutionary Military Committee (1961–1963) before the democratic restoration of a Third Republic (1963–1972), Park increasingly was the only top military officer consolidating many once-separate military leadership and policy positions in the Committee between 1961 to 1963. Plus, Park was the only military officer with experience, mentors, or clients within all three different Korean military academies of the time, which he attended in his military career so far. Thus, Park increasingly was the topmost leader trusted by all military factions during the military coup, even if he at first operated within the collective Revolutionary Military Committee that suspended the Korean constitution during the period 1961 to 1963.

How did this military coup in 1961 develop? In 1948, the First Republic was created, and Protestant Syngman Rhee was elected as its first (and only) President. In 1960, Rhee's right-wing government of the First Republic collapsed (1948–1960) as he resigned after widely-considered corrupt election results to keep his faction in power over the years as well as many presumed assassination attempts and massive vote fraud against opposition candidates (including Chang Myon himself). However, Rhee only resigned under duress from Chief of Staff of the Republic of Korea Army, Song Yo-chan, who on Rhee's command earlier did declare martial law in Seoul in March 1960 against the protestors struggling against Rhee, yet General Song later refused to provide the bullets and army that the police were calling for to murder the protestors. General Song saw his role as peacekeeping among factions instead of contributing to one side in more violence. These protests, without an escalation of a military crackdown thanks to General Song Yo-chan, became known as the April Revolution of 1960. So the April Revolution itself was already a kind of soft military coup of non-support of Rhee by the military, combined with street protests against Rhee. After Rhee's forced resignation, with his own military head General Song pushing his resignation, Rhee fled the country secretly on a U.S. C.I.A. plane to Hawaii, where he died in 1965. After 1960, to pick up the pieces, a more left-wing Second Republic was started in April 1960 by Rhee's fourth ex-Vice President, the Catholic humanist Chang Myon—who disliked Rhee's authoritarian bent and wanted more economic development. General Song resigned from his top Republic of Korea (ROK) military position in May 1960, and went to the United States to study for year. However, by May 1961, a military coup against Chang's government was successful. Very few troops defended Chang's Second Republic. An anti-communist Revolutionary Military Committee ruled for two years cutting a bloated governmental apparatus and starting many national development projects—and even adopting left-wing Chang's ideas of a socialist five-year plan starting in 1962 without many changes at all.

Since this military committee was full of its own problems, jealousies, and factions, it was increasingly led by Park. He and his wife were devout Buddhists.

In Korea, this is the centuries-old 'establishment' conservative and wealthy temple-based institutional religion. General Song soon returned to Korea upon invitation to be a member of the Supreme Council for National Reconstruction after the military coup of May 1961, then General Song became Minister of Foreign Affairs, and then acting Prime Minister. However, disagreeing over economic policy differences, General Song resigned. He publicly in print encouraged Park to return to civilian rule. President Kennedy of the United States encouraged Park to return to civilian rule as well. After the return to civilian rule in 1963 in the Third Republic (1963–1972), General Song later ran in 1963 for a time as the Presidential candidate for the freshly formed opposition political party, the Liberal Democratic Party, though Song resigned from that run to have a unified opposition candidate merged into the Civil Rule Party that tried to elect the ex-Second Republic's President Yun Posun in 1963, who ran against Park in that first crucial year of a return to civilian rule. Park was barely elected in 1963 with 46.65% of the vote for him and 45.10% of the vote for Yun Posun. In the next Presidential election it was a re-run of the first, though Park was reelected in 1967 with an even higher 51.4% of the vote against Yun Posun once more, with this time Yun receiving only 40.9% of the vote. Park thus became the first and only President of the Third Republic. Park both shepherded a transition away from this faction-prone military committee to the Third Republic (1963–1972), as well as was a continuing martial force within the Presidential executive of the Third Republic itself. As he was banned from running for president more than twice under the Third Republic, and as he saw the growing power of left-wing Catholic Kim Dae-jung winning the metropolis of Seoul out from under him in the elections, Park would eventually conduct an autocoup against his own Third Republic in 1971 to create a more dictatorial constitution of the Fourth Republic (1972–1981) where he could be President for life to guide his development ideas of Korea into the future with less oppositional force—or so he thought. In this way, Park started to gain public power, first democratically by 1963 and then by 1971 ever more autocratically. Though Park's 'restored' Third Republic (1963–1972) was the Second Korean republic to have public elections for the Korean Presidency, Park barely won the Presidency each time, and total wins are always only slight, and he overthrew it as well by 1971. In 1963 and 1967, the election map results of the two Presidential elections of the Third Republic show a very fluxing and unstable base of support for Park. Plus, in Park's first two Presidential elections, he was challenged strongly by Yun Posun both the first and second time—who was of course the displaced President of the short lived Second Republic that the military junta overthrew in May 1961.

'Peaceful oddities' like this are used to argue that Korean politics have been mistakenly described as a stereotypical 'developmental dictatorship' during this period. Park was authoritarian, yes, yet unrepresentative he was not. Korea was innately divided. Even the Second Republic of Chang Myon that was overthrown went through three cabinets in five months, while street protests were a daily occurrence in the political vacuum. Plus, it should be known more widely how little blood was spilled in the power vacuum at the end of the Second Republic, how divided was the Military Revolutionary Committee itself, how weak and fluxing was Park's election support, *and as a result, how much consensus was attempted by Park once he was President to keep adding different hybrid development ideas* instead of sticking to any ideological program of development at all. Thus, while we still accept that the term 'developmental dictatorship' describes Korea of the 1960s and 1970s very well, the Korean version leaned more toward a representative 'authoritarian parliamentarianism' that tried to stay in power by representing *a managed consensus of development* through Park, instead of an *unrepresentative* dictatorship through Park at this time. This analysis stresses a more representative authoritarian developmentalism model by pluralistic consensus of factions under Park from 1963–1972, instead of an unrepresentative 'dictatorship of development' under Park at this time. After 1972, it would change to the latter—being more of a 'dictatorship of development' that was even attempting its own repressive right-wing cultural revolution as well. After 1972, Park as well was the only president under his Fourth Republic (1972–1981) as he was 'elected' in 1971 to a six year term and then 'reelected' (without opposition or popular elections) in 1978 to another six year term. Park introduced the Fourth Republic as a more authoritarian model after 1972 without any open elections for president since it had an appointed electoral college that almost unanimously elected Park each time, twice. The constitution of the Fourth Republic additionally allowed Park to appoint one-third of the National Assembly, and outlawed criticism of the fresh constitution and outlawed criticism of President Park as well. Park survived a *public* assassination attempt via gunshot in 1974 that accidentally killed his wife sharing the stage, yet he was eventually *more privately* assassinated with a shot to the head and chest in 1979 in a Seoul safe house by his erstwhile military compatriot who had supported Park's military coup from 1961 onward. The gun was fired by his own long-term ally, Kim Jae-gyu, the head of his Korean Central Intelligence Agency.

Four factors are important to understand the context of Park's assassination in 1979, and only the last one is a more hypothetical factor of importance. First, even though Park was 're-elected' as President for a second six-year term in 1978 (despite a lack of open Presidential elections since 1971), the more open legislative elections of the National Assembly now were dominated by the plurality of the opposition party, the New Democratic Party (1967–1980) with 32.82% of the seats, and only then Park's own party, the Democratic Republican Party (1963–1980) with 31.70% of the seats. In other words, Park already had exhausted the scale of his one-third appointee power of the National Assembly even under his own Fourth Republic's constitution—and he was still losing power and support. Second, on the one hand, Park's assassination in 1979 was motivated by seeming personal jealousies by once-loyal ally Kim Jae-gyu, who was increasingly angered and embarrassed publicly by Park, as Kim was being passed over for other sponsored favorites of Park at the time, instead of interpreting Kim as having any deep loyalties to Korean republicanism as his motivation. On the other hand, giving Kim the benefit of the doubt, third, Park's assassination did happen on October 26, 1979, just six days after Park had used the regular army to arrest 400 students and to crush student protests in the "Pu-Ma" Struggle of October 16–20, 1979, the Korean abbreviation for the Pusan and Masan university students protests calling for the end of Park's dictatorship and the end of his Fourth Republic. Park declared martial law in these two cities on

October 18, 1979. On October 20, 1979, Park sent the professional army to attack and end the student protests, and many dozens were put under military trial as well. So, Park was assassinated eight days after he had declared martial law and six days after he had used the regular army to attack university students to stop the "Pu-Ma" Struggle. One interpretation is that Kim's assassination of Park was a crime of passion *blended with* many contextual factors that were attempted to be used by Kim as false alibis.

For another fourth contextual factor as a hypothesis about global nuclear geopolitics that may have influenced Park's assassination, Park by the late 1970s started to want more war for reunification with North Korea once more. This could have started World War III between the Soviet Union and the United States. For evidence of this increased belligerence by Park, by September 26, 1978, his South Korea had successfully tested its first designed major missile, the Nike Hercules Korea-1 missile, given its first successful launch on this day. This missile was designed to target only Pyongyang, the capital of North Korea. Plus, Park had started his own nuclear weapons development with a target date of 1983. However, after Park's assassination in 1979, which was just barely over a year from the first launch of the Nike Hercules missile, Park's missile program and Park's nuclear weapons program both were halted by the next military dictator-to-President, Chun Doo-hwan. The United States from 1969 through 1979 had been coordinating SALT I and SALT II treaties (strategic arms limitation talks) reducing the risk of nuclear warfare between the United States and the Soviet Union with a de-escalation policy of more frank talking instead of saber rattling then called 'détente.' However, from the late 1970s, Park's brandishing of more missiles at the Soviet Bloc that included North Korea, was against this U.S. policy at the time. Even U.S. President Ronald Reagan, elected on anti-détente policy, was by 1983 ready for détente once more as he wanted to 'start' more strategic arms reduction treaties with the Soviet Union under what would be known as the more formal START treaty (strategic arms reduction treaty) rejoining the 'détente' policies and the de-escalation policies with the Soviet Union. After Park's assassination in 1979, General-to-President Chun of the Fifth Republic of Korea (1979/1980–1988) was the first foreign head of state to visit President Reagan of the United States. This is interpreted to show how it was recognized that the ongoing division of Korea in global geopolitics was a dangerously volatile global touchpoint that could lead to escalation of nuclear war. Chun's desired support of Reagan from 1981 may have come with de-escalation promises to stop these missile programs and nuclear warhead programs from the Park administration earlier. Chun did stop both programs. Reagan as well would later encourage de-escalation in 1987 by Chun against street protests against his regime in Korea as well.

However, throughout Park or Chun, something important had happened. The informal economic policy consensus of a fast development drive around export-led development from 1961 was kept in this homogeneous culture, and a buttressing consensus of both political and economic policies around it would keep expanding to keep it untouched. Even Chun's constitution of the Fifth Republic started to be more consensus-oriented and include greater protections of privacy of correspondence, civil rights, and a legal rejection of torture for forced confessions, despite his dictatorial model. The argument is that this growing pressure for consensus and buckling to it was the only means of political and economic stability since 1961. This came from the power vacuum once Park cleansed the hereditary aristocratic families from power in 1961—something that would become permanent over decades. So, despite large formal institutional changes of politics, the ongoing same economic policies were maintained from the Third (1963–1972) through the present Sixth Republic (1987 to the present), and the end of Korean aristocratic privilege was maintained as well. Starting from the Revolutionary Military Committee (1961–1963), and then continuing into the Third Republic (1963–1971), and into the Fourth Republic (1972–1981), the authoritarian administrations of Park and Chun both failed to grant special reserved places for past aristocratic precedence as the First and Second Republics did in practice. Instead, mentor/sponsor links of graduates in the modern Korean military educational institutes under Park or Chun became more important in getting to Korean political power after 1961. This militarized meritocratic hazing to get into high Korean politics exists well into the present as well in South Korea. It is hardly odd. As long ago as the Roman Republic, a militarized meritocratic hazing was that republic's very stable and established 'developmental' principle in the Cursus Honorum. All future Roman leaders had to test themselves as to show themselves capable to other Romans by establishing both military leadership and political leadership in this cycle of appointments to hone their skills, trusts, loyalties and abilities. The Cursus Honorum was used to recognize and to discover the best state leadership that Rome had to offer. It lasted hundreds of years successfully. Plus, the Roman Republic only began to dissolve into an Empire and a Emperor when this Cursus Honorum was corrupted in the last 100 years of the Roman Republic by ending the meritocratic and leadership discovery aspects of it while keeping the political and military perks of it increasingly monopolized by faction-prone aristocratic lines of much fewer Senatorial families instead.

Let us summarize how themes of this Korean 'hybrid development' are argued to be the secret to ongoing, stable, aggregating, fast development. First, there is an economic consensus trying to be developed by the processes of land distribution. The Korean aristocracy was trying to keep itself in political power within early republican institutions, yet in retrospect, they gave Korea "a land reform without a cultural revolution or a political revolution." This led to their sudden eclipse after 1961 despite nearly 2,000 years of the same families of ongoing power conserved in the Korean Peninsula across multiple dynasties. This long continuity is rare in world history, and this sudden lost of aristocratic preferment in a more peaceful and default way is even rarer in ancient or modern world history. Thus, this dynamic turn of events seems an important factor in South Korea's secret to a durable development and to a durable rural culture—with the latter as a further resource in development and greater consensus pressures in the political vacuum without an aristocratic violent reaction and without their political veto against urban industrial development itself. Second, political consensus was encouraged as well. A second strong challenger to Park Chung-hee, after Yun Posun retired from politics by the 1970s, was the left-wing Kim Dae-jung who, started out in an opposition party to Park developing in the

1960s. Plus, showing the importance of personal and religious connections in Korean politics, Catholic Chang Myon was the Catholic godfather of Catholic convert Kim Dae-jung. Chang-connected Kim Dae-jung ran as the next 'dubbed' unified opposition party candidate in 1971, after Yun Posun refused to keep losing publicly. Even though Park Chung-hee won (his third) 1971 Presidential election with 53.20% to Kim Dae-jung's 45.26%, Kim carried the most urban industrial developed area of Gyeongi-do and the capital city of Seoul as well as his home base of the southwestern province of Jeolla-do. Like Chang Myon and Yun Posun, Kim Dae-jung would survive Park's administration. Chang and Yun would survive by Park's desire to avoid recatalyzing militarized street battles or cultural revolution in the 1960s, while Kim would survive only by happenstance and U.S. intervention to keep him alive instead of murdered by the KCIA (presumably known to Park). One month after losing the 1971 Presidential election, Kim was helping out opposition candidates in the upcoming legislative elections. While driving, a truck turned directly into his path. He and two aides in the car were seriously injured, and Kim walked with a limp from that 'accident' for the rest of his life. Afraid for his life, Kim left for Japan. Soon after Kim left Korea, Park seemed emboldened to conduct his autocoup and overthrew his own Third Republic so he could run unchallenged as President thereafter for life, as well as allowing himself to rig one-third of the National Assembly seats from 1972 onward in his updated Yushin ("Restoration") Constitution of the Fourth Republic (1972–1981). In 1973, while still overseas, unified leftist opposition leader Kim Dae-jung was kidnapped by the KCIA from his Japanese hotel. He was put on a Japanese boat that sped out into the ocean. He was to be thrown into the ocean to die. The U.S. Ambassador to South Korea Philip Habib learned of this and intervened with the Korean government. Kim later recounted: "Just when they were about to throw me overboard, Jesus Christ appeared before me with such clarity. I clung to him and begged him to save me. At that very moment, an airplane was sent down from Heaven by the almighty God Himself to rescue me from the moment of death" (Kim, 2000). That plane was a divine wind from the Japanese Maritime Self-Defense Force that had been tracking and watching the kidnapping without intervening. However, it soon did intervene upon a message from Habib and the Korean government to stop the execution. However, instead of returning Kim to Japan, Kim was returned to South Korea and arrested. He was banned from participating in politics. However, Kim did participate in a public announcement of an anti-government/Park manifesto, he was sentenced to five years in jail from 1976, commuted to house arrest in 1978. The assassination of President Park on October 26, 1979 by his own KCIA head, temporarily freed Kim back to civilian life by order of acting President Choi Kyu-hah. However, very quickly afterwards, a military coup by General Chun on December 12, 1979 rearrested Kim on the charge of sedition with a sentence of death by claiming Kim had instigated the Gwangju Uprising from May 18–27, 1980. Kim was to be executed in September 1980. However, staff from the incoming U.S. Reagan Presidential Administration in 1981 made it known that they did not want the execution, and they wanted it commuted. Chun agreed yet on condition that he would be the first foreign head of state to visit President Reagan in the White House in 1981, and he was. However, Kim's sentence of death was commuted only to twenty years in prison. However, by 1982, Kim Dae-jung was granted exile in the United States, and by December 1982, he was in Boston teaching at Harvard University in the Center for International Affairs and getting an Honorary Doctorate from Emory University. Kim returned to South Korea with a large entourage in 1985. He and his wife were immediately seized and put under house arrest once more. However, in attempts to make consensus once more, Kim and his wife were released after Chun's Democratic Justice Party barely won the plurality in the 1985 parliamentary election seats. However, Kim was still banned from running for election in politics. Chun's ruling party in 1985 had retained only 148 seats of the total 276 in the National Assembly, yet faced future legislative failure and minority party cultural support due to both the united opposition of three leftwing parties that could almost overrule any of his laws (with 67, 35, and 20 seats apiece), and given these three parties received 29.26%, 19.68%, and 9.16% of the vote—which was well above the mere 35.25% of the national voters who supported Chun's party. However, given the Fourth Republic's constitution said the President could only serve one term (which was a seven year term at the time), Chun in 1987 announced that his party had chosen the next President without an election, President Roh, who was an ex-military officer loyal to Chun. This catalyzed the June Struggle of 1987, which lasted for nearly three weeks of protests throughout Korea daily. Two of the many demands were open presidential elections and the releasing of Kim Dae-jung back into politics. Chun relented to almost all demands after learning President Reagan would not support further crackdowns by Chun on street protests against him. Chun thus was forced to allow the first competitive presidential election since the early 1970s. Kim Dae-jung had almost won against Park in the early 1970s by carrying the Seoul metropolis instead of Park. However, in the 1987 open Presidential election, the left was split in its support between two left-wing candidates, Kim Young-sam and Kim Dae-jung. Therefore, the military's candidate of President Roh was elected anyway on a low plurality of only 35.64%, with Kim Young-Sam receiving 28.04% and Kim Dae-jung receiving 27.05% as both were unable to decide on a united front. Founder of the KCIA Kim Jong-pil ran as well and received 8.07% of the votes. After the next President Roh (1988–1993), first, Kim Young-sam would be the next Korean President (1993–1998), and then Kim Dae-jung would live to become the Korean president as well (1998–2003). President Kim Young-sam would start treason proceedings against both previous Presidents Chun and Roh who would be sentenced for their part played in the Gwangju Massacre of 1980, yet President Kim Young-sam would equally pardon both later after the sentence was announced, upon advice of Kim Dae-jung. Even recycled Kim Jong-pil would become the Prime Minister of Kim Dae-jung in a power sharing agreement with his party. These three together are known as the 'three Kims' in Korean modern politics.

Why was this detail recounted? Once more, it was to note the odd 'hybrid' cultural outcome and the odd 'hybrid' political system developing here of military coups yet without much violence or deep recriminations, or with two military coup leaders (Park and Chun) both later running for President in a very competitive party system for President that they or their preferred candidate both barely win. Plus, note creative ways that both right-wing and left-wing stop their opposition from catalyzing a polarizing cultural revolutionary situation by mutual pardons from the 1980 onward through the 1990s. Note even dictatorial constitutions of the Fifth Republic (1981–1987) had large civil rights improvements, even as Chun banned all existing political parties from 1980 and curtailed and consolidated the public media to state control. Chun's constitution sponsored greater individual human rights protections than before. By 1985, even Chun's 'dictatorial' Fifth Republic and its ruling party was nearly losing the open legislative elections just like Park's 'dictatorial' Yushin Constitution by 1978 still saw it barely winning a plurality against more voters of the opposition parties. Plus, Chun despite being 'dictator' failed to keep power in 1987 despite ostensibly having a dictatorship, and even the founder of the KCIA Kim Jong-pil ran against presumably his faction's choice for President, Roh Tae-woo. That is the hybrid political settlement of Korea.

Plus, there were more 'hybrid' economic policies, mixing socialist five-year plans inherited from Chang's government of the Second Republic yet added to the Third Republic's capitalist, profit-based development. By the early 1970s, more 'hybrid' economic policies were added in the New Village Movement (Korean, "Saemaul Undong") for decentralized, village-based, grass roots development in South Korea.

The main theme here is the ever widening desires for basing consensus in these 'hybrid' political policies. This is seen with the widening civil rights protections granted by 'dictatorships' despite themselves. This is seen with the widening 'hybrid' economic policies to shore up support for export-led urban industrial development by adding recognition and subsidies for traditional artisans for ongoing cultural transmission purposes from 1963, and then later adding village-based grass roots development from rural areas that felt left behind by 1970 particularly as Park's urban election support started to wane in the 1970s. All of this kept the traditional culture together along with keeping the political economic support for the fast development drive together, for even further urban industrialization in the increasing devolutionary consensus to keep Park (and later Chun) in power. As Chun's hold on power was unknown from 1980, he started to catalyze cultural subsidies of his own by using the Korean state for orchestrating an early series of distracting entertainments to try to hold onto power as well as to try to encourage color television, to revivify a freshly uncensored cinema with novel audiences, to arrange staged sports and pageant events, even to be a dictator that ended a national curfew instead of extended it. This is that odd amalgam of an 'authoritarian parliamentary' system once more. In retrospect, this in turn kept the Korean fast development drive continuing on an ever more consensus basis of economic policies by adding more state-supported entertainment policies as a growth sector in the 1980s. This is contrasted to other developing countries that start, stop, and change ideas or different programs over time. This leads to less durable economic aggregation on any path. This leads instead to an economic policy more ideologically divided against itself in policy, and thus stalling. Instead, Korea just kept adding more sectors in tandem over time in widening consensus politics.

In conclusion to the above summary, South Korea's developing odd 'hybrid' cultural, political, and economic system had broken the mould of the past Korean aristocracy and even tempered two developmental dictatorships within an ongoing multiparty Presidential and legislative election system, an ongoing National Assembly, growing institutionalization of civil rights after 1980, a state-oriented entertainment industry for filling the culture with more unifying (or distracting) non-politicized propaganda of sex appeal, dramas, and sports in entertainment. *In economic policy*, there was an increasingly non-ideological view of economic development that integrated rural traditional artisans and village based communities as well as urban industrial development for an export-led economy that included digital technologies, television programs, and cinema as attempted exports later as well. *In politics*, there were many attempts to develop consensus and avoid violent cultural revolution of right or left. *In culture*, there was a growth of a more depoliticized entertainment sphere that served state-directed cultural unification or state-directed cultural pacification as the years rolled by in Chun's weakening hold on political dictatorship. You can take your pick of which trend of that cultural wave is more important.

However by contrast North Korea had the complete opposite organization in all three, yet the same homogeneous culture. North Korea after 1953 developed land renationalization under a political, economic, and cultural revolution. However, through this choice of organization, equally, the culture of North Korea was reinventing a renewed state-based bloodline aristocracy, comprised of the first generation of Korean communist party members. They benefited from family perks of control over nationalized economic properties in a political one-party state that was the military leadership simultaneously. Thus, this more aristocratic and factional-prone North Korean politics remained unstable and full of repeated violent purges. There remain to this day many very nepotistic, neo-aristocratic battles between the Kim 'dynasty' of leaders and their married allies with and against other military-party factions that would like to unseat this family from its position in the North or just control it from behind the scenes. Early on, North Korea with this organization actually grew economically faster in the 1950s into the 1960s. However, it had an unfair head start, built as it was from Japanese industrial might inherited from the Japanese Empire. Plus, the dynamics set up in North Korea created a lack of commercial and competitive technical innovation. That stalled North Korea by the 1970s, and it increasingly failed economically and politically thereafter. North Korea started to alienate even its few European lender nations by the 1970s by refusing to pay back loans, and then it lost its main sponsor of the Soviet Union as that country collapsed in 1991. North Korea began to starve thereafter, just like Cuba did for a time in the 1990s by losing the same ally.

So if you want fast economic improvement and you only judge it for a decade, you might choose North Korean development built on a revolutionarily requisitioned head start. However, if you want to develop for the long term over 70 years or more, choose the model of South Korea without such a cultural revolution. In it was a much slower yet much steadier consensus-based and aggregated economic growth over decades, including incentives for technical innovation, a steady improving politics, and a widening consensus on economic development beyond mere export-led urban industrial development in the same period. These were accommodating alliances of the 'hybrid politics' of a dictatorial/Presidential model yet checked by a strongly decentralized regional culture of land distribution and doubly checked by ongoing multi-party elections for a National Assembly and even for a President after 1963.

There were accommodating economic policies as well that increasingly tempered the export-led urban industrialization with more traditional artisan support and then grass roots village-based development, prioritized by villages themselves—followed by the first Korean National Health Service plans in 1977. There were accommodating economic policies by the 1980s as well, as President Chun oversaw the passing of legislation in 1986 toward a Korean National Pension Service that was pre-planned to start from 1988. There were accommodating cultural policies by the 1980s as well, in the attempt to create a more neutral cultural sphere of light entertainments of 'sex, screen, and sports'—or intentionally numbing distractions depending on your point of view. Regardless of interpretation, *the 1980s are equally the origin of this durable apolitical and conservative strategy of the Korean Wave today.*

Returning to military coup leader and later President Park as the originator of the fast development drive, even though there was election support for President Park, it was never a totalizing support despite a strong conservative homogeneous culture perhaps thanks to a multi-party system. Results of South Korea election totals and election maps from the 1960s and 1970 show bare wins by Park and show endlessly fluxing support for him and for oppositional party dynamics, instead of a clear 'base' for anyone. Such competitive politics and the lack of ability to get support to create centralized national agricultural policies or nationalization policies were realities that pushed by default Park into an export-led urban and industrial development instead of an internally consolidating agricultural or industrial modernization. Many people fail to know that Korea was almost entirely food sufficient at 86% in 1970 to only 48.4% by 1985. However, this export-led policy and the increasing rural economic shakeout by these food policies led to massive rural labor displacement to the cities. This fed into the cheap labor of the industrial urban proletariat and the increasingly close run parliamentary elections in the 1970s that continued into the 1980s.

First, Park buckled to widen the economic policy ideas beyond export-led development. Thus, even after Park's military coup of 1961, and even after he was President Park after 1963, he and the more martial networks of the executive branch had to participate in *competitive* Presidential elections and *competitive* national assembly elections. They increasingly accommodated and had less ideologically pure plans for national economic development. Second, Chun even buckled after his own coup of May 17, 1980, by radically decentralizing the previous centralized Korean state, with many fresh ministries instead of everything decided by a few top people like in the 1970s. Chun saw the rise of a more technocratic bureaucracy with more power to innovate fresh economic sectors independently as well as having the power of an ongoing more segmented bureaucracy that in retrospect could keep development policies steady by institutional inertia as well.

This is what is called South Korea's odd 'hybrid dictatorship' that avoided totalizing excesses of dictatorship in a homogeneous culture that you can see through a glass darkly in North Korea under different political and economic institutional choices in the same homogeneous culture. In South Korea, first, President Park after 1963 kept winning only slightly instead of largely against half the nation that wanted to not only unseat him in the 1960s by elections, yet increasingly wanted the whole framework of this hybrid dictatorship gone by the 1970s. However, Park's hybrid dictatorship model pushed its own more dictatorial, yet still hybrid Yushin Constitution (1972–1981) at this point, removing only his own presidential elections from popular election support requirements (within an electoral college support), while keeping parliamentary elections intact, and yet giving himself the power to appoint one-third of the legislature. Of course there were tensions of the ongoing 'cold civil war' and ideological Cold War between a communist North Korea and a more democratic capitalist South Korea well into the 1990s. In the late 1960s into the early 1970s, high level assassination teams from the North stole across the border or similar teams were trained in the South to infiltrate the North, in attempts to kill each other's leadership. Later, there was ongoing North Korean Communist terrorism in South Korea itself and even with bombs placed in South Korea's national airlines and overseas missions that assassinated many South Korean officials. However after 1953, somehow a renewed hot war was averted—something it is argued that could have cursed the South Korean development drive. A hot war could have been avoided as well by the assassination of President Park in 1979 itself, since by 1978 Park had a missile program to attack Pyongyang and he was planning on having nuclear weapons by 1983. However, after the assassination in 1979, both military provocations were ended. Chun refused to continue both these military provocations on North Korea.

Avoiding war is another great way to keep your development drive durable (Collier, 2007). In the next chapter, the idea of a 'development gauntlet' is introduced that all countries should pass through if they choose modern urban industrial development. From other's comparative analysis of successes and failures in development drives among the poorest countries in the world, it is part of the 'development gauntlet' to avoid the trap of endless war (Collier, 2007). Even North and South Korea agreed publicly by 1972 that blood and their homogeneous culture would be stronger than modern politics or ideology. Both leaders announced publicly they wanted peaceable reunification without any foreign (American) military presence used in the process, even if Park may have desired continuing it alone potentially by the late 1970s.

Thus, in ongoing political compromises, and even under communist threat, the 'hybrid dictatorship' team around President Park and then President Chun crafted a more 'hybrid economic' policy both from the start as well as made it more hybrid over time well into the 1980s. The term 'hybrid' policy means here in essence an ability to craft policies without clear ideological purity or dichotomized thinking, avoiding its dangers. For instance, despite being an anti-communist military coup, Park's politics are very ambiguous both before in the leftist Yeo-Sun rebellion, or later in the rightist anti-communist military coup that he helped organize that nonetheless had as its signature policy a five-year socialist plan of national development concentrating on building modern infrastructures in public state-owned companies yet equally planning out and coordinating the future goals of a private neoliberal export-led development. Park even adapted leftist revolutionary Maoist village-based grass roots development, turning it into a conservative and traditional movement of small rural land holders who made democratic priorities on their group development by themselves, regionally. Park's ideological flexibility is similar to later Chinese leader Deng Xiaoping in the 1980s who was more of a compromising 'developmental nationalist' uninterested in ideological purity despite being leader of the Chinese Communist Party in its first economic drive from the 1980s onward. Park, despite repressing labor movements and communist sentiment, continued Prime Minister Chang's ideas of socialist five year plans from the Second Republic. This was grafted onto his own Third Republic's increasingly profit-oriented, private, corporate capitalist development. From originally working against them, Park's government even agreed to collaborate with economic family dynasties (chaebol) that were profiteers and Japanese collaborationists in the period of the Japanese Empire (1910–1945) and the First Republic (1948–1960). They avoided punishment for their Japanese collaborationist past because they were pragmatically useful in bringing their small Korean capitalist networks and expertise to the national development drive. As said above, Park's administration even grafted on itself Maoist grassroots development from 1970 onward, yet separated it from the politics of leftist cultural revolution even if attempting to build into it a rightist cultural revolution. Instead of based on ideological purity in support of Mao and a youth cultural revolution, it was based off ideological purity of support of Park and renewed traditional Korean concepts of village democracy, participation, and self-prioritization. Later in the 1980s, Chun was very flexible as well. He left much of the economic development of the 1980s to more decentralized technocrats while leaving 'cultural events planning and media control' to himself and others at the top.

So instead of only export-led urban industrial economies after 1961, after 1970 there was an increasingly village-based, regional, democratic grass roots development with priorities of plans and labor left to the village itself with government only supplying modern infrastructural materials of concrete and roofing for instance. Plus, after 1961, there were the parallel growing subsidies to increasing thousands of traditional artisans for cultural preservation and transmission, combined with national economic protectionism. Much of these policies equally had interests of trying to minimize growing political, economic and cultural disparities of rural poverty and urban wealth created by the export-led economy. Plus, pragmatically, all of these policies of cultural and regional preservation were linked to how multi-party elections were won for keeping the main export-led economy in urban industrial development in textiles, steel, chemicals, and heavy industry, and construction *in attempts to keep Catholic/left-wing urban labor parties from winning elections by appealing to more rural Buddhist/Confucian voting blocks.*

Thus, *leftist* cultural revolution was avoided even into the 1970s, and yet Park if he had lived perhaps would have tried to lead an increasing *rightist* cultural revolution combined with increasing state censorship. That could have wrecked the ongoing 'hybrid' consensus drives of his own country's development. Even the institutions of the New Village Movement were for Park having a second use as trying to avoid leftist cultural revolution while unfortunately supporting their own right-wing cultural revolutionary group that supported Park in rural areas against rural based labor movements. They started to use village meetings to do more than plan village development, though to find rural people in the area who disliked Park, and even murdering them. If this had continued after his assassination in 1979, or if he had survived his assassination after 1979, Park despite himself would have facilitated a more right-wing cultural revolution that likely would have made a more polarized politics of Korea. This may have hampered or even stalled Korea's development drive in the process or even called forth the leftist cultural revolution that he was trying to stop. Equally later, with Chun's media consolidations and licensing of journalists by the state, there was only state cultural propaganda dominating the media in the 1980s. Frankly, this stress on media propaganda and media sphere control was a sign that Chun felt that using only police and military violence to shut down attempts at a changed urban culture would be self-defeating by catalyzing a leftist cultural revolution even more. So, cultural revolution is something that the whole modern heritage of 'consensus brinksmanship' in Korea seems to have been trying its best to avoid by these ongoing more 'hybrid' solutions to political, cultural, and economic policies instead of more ideologically pure solutions of cultural revolution reminiscent of North Korea.

The short historical description above helps explain the origin of what will be called South Korea's unique hybrid cultural system, hybrid political system, and hybrid economic policies. A 'hybrid dictatorial' politics became rather stable only because it was a hybrid and accommodating dictatorship instead of because it was a dictatorship. *Politically*, this is shown in how the institutional dynamics of culture, politics, and economics remained the same and were flexible enough to handle first a military coup in 1961 without losing wider elections for Presidents or legislatures by 1963 when they returned. Then Korea handled the assassination of Park in 1979 and a second military coup of Chun by 1980 without losing wider elections either. The fact that the main political oppositions of leftist Yun Posun/Chang Myon, then leftist Kim Dae-Jung, and then leftist Cardinal Kim (who granted sanctuary for Korean labor leaders in his Myeongdong Cathedral protecting them from arrest by Park in the 1970s) survived though hardly thrived. This is further evidence that it was a more 'hybrid dictatorship' instead of a full one. A real dictatorship would have seen all three of these men dead.

To summarize further this hybrid dictatorial politics, even this can be seen in the military coup of Chun, who as said, made the most civil-rights-protecting constitution yet in the Fifth Republic (1981–1987) and decentralized the economic ministries in his government and made it illegal for himself as President to change the constitution during his term to allow extension of his rule (something done so far by both Rhee in 1954 and Park in 1972). All these checks and balances that Chun imposed on his own government was aiming to squelch opposition to himself since he was President without open elections for his position from 1980 to 1987 just like Park from 1972 to 1979. Plus, Chun buckled in passing the 1986 plan for a National Pension Service to start in 1988, and buckled further after massive civil unrest after he announced the next President would be his crony Roh in an attempt to continue his military rule and lack of Presidential elections. As said earlier, this catalyzed the June Struggle of 1987, after which Chun backed down to stop the massive protests. He even agreed to release leftist political prisoner Kim Dae-jung. This is a further example of Korea's more 'hybrid dictatorship,' that any dictator has always had a hard time dictating in such an elite power vacuum and a homogeneous cultural opposition. Both Park's and Chun's dictatorship buckled in the end—with Park buckling more economically through the 1960s and 1970s, and Chun buckling economically from 1980 and politically after 1985 that saw him only slightly winning even his own (constitutionally) rigged elections to the National Assembly while definitely losing the popular vote. So, Chun more peaceably agreed without further violence to competitive open presidential elections once more in 1987. External allies like President Ronald Reagan of the United States, who refused to support further crackdowns on the civilian population in 1987, seem crucial in brokering this more 'hybrid' and consensus based solution of the return to competitive party Presidential elections from 1987 as well.

However, in another twist, this hybrid dictatorship was still a move to 'hybrid democracy' since Chun's sponsored next military dictator of Roh was soon just another Presidential candidate—who won open elections that year, just as once-military dictator Park had won open elections in 1963. This made a smoother 'hybrid' democratic transition rarely seen in any other country. This is because this democratic transition twice now was a military transition working within a democratic election system (in 1963 and in 1987), instead of being dichotomized and starkly one or the other. As said, the outcome of 1987 with ex-military officer Roh winning as President was very similar to the earlier history of modern hybrid politics and hybrid economic policies in South Korea after the beginning of the development drive from 1961 through 1963 as the military coup of Park saw him later as President Park.

To summarize the hybrid economic policies, a similar *flexibility yet stability* is seen that continued to be maintained after 1961. The export-led economic development continued, built from using socialist five-year plans in public corporations for infrastructure yet equally coordinating large corporate-based profiteering aims yet held to state metrics on projects, as well as subsidies for increasing numbers of 'living treasures,' the Korean euphemism for individual Korean artisans who are recognized by the government as holding historical, tangible, and intangible cultural skills and techniques deemed worthy of preservation for modern transmission to the next generation. Plus, village-led democracy and grass roots political and economic development were priorities across Korea as well.

By the early 1980s, even export-led economic sectors became more flexible and plural, and thus more stable economically as a group. This was the period that saw the technocrats under Chun adding economic sectors like digital telecommunications to shore up any middle income traps that started in the late 1970s in South Korea (Gill & Kharas, 2006; Oh & Larson, 2019). Chun additionally pushed the introduction of color television broadcasting, developing cultural and sports events for it to cover as well. Chun equally aided Korean cinema with less regulations, and even started exporting the first Korean automobiles to the world by 1986 and even foreign-language dubbed Korean dramas.

To summarize the theme of this chapter, the economy as a whole could benefit from having a stable, ongoing cultural strength that created collective innovation and teamwork of the Korean people. This cultural continuity was kept sound without a truly successful left or right cultural revolution. This was a major benefit for the ongoing fast development drive. Plus, the homogeneous culture benefitted from the state avoiding internal economic consolidation on land tenure. Instead, economic development was focused on expansion outward into the global economy instead of inward into the nation, with the major profiting private companies focused abroad, while grass roots development, artisanal cultural transmission, national protectionism, and public-owned corporations remained at home, instead of having only one or the other side of this developmental ideology in place.

So the three hybrid political, cultural, and economic policies are argued to have led to a more durable and flexible Korean development drive. These ideas may be 'transferrable' to less developed countries though they do come out of systemic dynamics of odd historical, economic and political realities in South Korea mentioned above that would likely have to be transferred or created first.

To close on the comparison with the very different systemic dynamics in North Korea once more, it of course started with the same homogeneous culture yet became developed under other organizational choices of politics and economics. In this way, the same culture in North Korea chose economic autarky without world trade, economic nationalization, and political institutions of a one-party state built upon a history of a leftist cultural revolution. This encouraged a completely dictatorial model from land nationalization, all infrastructure being nationalized, and a Marxist-Leninist ideology of national political economic autonomy against the capitalist world-system, called Juche, instead of engagement with it. It resulted in originally very fast economic growth, yet later created *non-durable* diminishing economic returns and a lack of incentives for economic innovation by the 1970s, along with inflexibility in economic and political abilities to change course. Plus, the one-party-state elites of North Korea forms and culturally supports now what is tantamount to a fresh royal bloodline and many fresh aristocratic bloodlines. In North Korea, this militarized socialist party of internecine family factions has only invented plots with and against each other instead of invented an ongoing stable economic drive. However, regardless of the growing suffering, stagnation and even famine in North Korea by the late 1990s, its one-party state leadership clique continued to benefit economically.

In retrospect, the 1970s was the 'scissors point' in the Korean Peninsula in this tale of two countries. It was the decade that saw the slow fading decline of the totalitarian model of North Korea and the accelerating rapid growth in the South Korea under its hybrid political, cultural, and economic policies. So, in South Korea, under these different policy choices yet in the same homogeneous culture, the South has been able durably and flexibly to keep changing *political* course as it grew without destroying its culture, as well to keep changing *economic* course to shore off problems of economic decline in particular sectors over time to create economic growth. This was aided throughout by the collective innovation of its homogenous culture as well geared toward world markets of technological development. North Korea applies its collective innovation mostly in drill parades and national military technology. South Korea additionally kept its hybrid cultural settlement together by being unable so far to form a fresh intermarried aristocracy of wealth that has durable inherited political powers—though that may be changing. That topic is left for Part III.

It is argued that throughout all of this development in South Korea, the core homogeneous culture maintained a unique historical *stability* while its hybrid political and economic organizational choices created a unique historical *durability* and *flexibility* in its ongoing dynamics. This created two virtuous cycles of growth in political representation pressures and in economic representation pressures in South Korea without destroying the facilitating culture. Meanwhile, the same culture in North Korea under different totalitarian political and economic choices and a cultural revolution set up vicious cycles of decline in politics and in economics.

2.2.2 Four Factors that Make a Unique Conundrum in Korean Development and in the Korean Wave

The above summarized the content of this first section of Part I, around the hybrid cultural settlement and power vacuum of South Korea and how this made greater pressures for organizational consensus possible by pushing against any revolutionary developmental dictatorship. This ongoing homogeneous culture made a greater pressure for consensus, and pushed more hybrid political and economic policies that have grown the economic Korean Miracle into the cultural Korean Wave. However, there is a conundrum in this strongly homogeneous Korean culture choosing very different organizational settings for its development and extension.

From the above, you might notice how the Korean culture being so insular and homogeneous can be a paradox here since Korean organizational policies have been the opposite toward export-led economic development and an equal export sector of the Korean Wave. South Korea finds itself as a budding global leader in the cultural industries, and yet the country is not very open to outside heterogeneous cultural influences changing its culture, despite being very open to adapting others' cultural forms along with others' technical, economic, and political influences. Thus, the cultural Korean Wave is mostly "one way" aiming outward despite it being conducted in "two-way" viral media. This makes an endlessly renewed tsunami of cultural productions from South Korea to the world without much allowed heterogeneous cultural influences from that world back into homogeneous South Korea. A massive amount of people in the world now are inspired to learn about Korean cultural motifs, Korean aesthetics, and even Korean language training, yet these people outside of Korea who are enjoying the Korean Wave think they are equal participants in this exciting and snazzy Korean Wave global culture. However, South Korea dislikes a global or cosmopolitan assimilationist policy at home despite globalizing its culture to the world. Four key examples will suffice to illustrate points that touch the heart of any culture: citizenship, family reproduction, military loyalty, and the treatment of refugees, in this case, the general fate of North Korean refugees in South Korea.

Merging the first and second point, in the 1990s, foreign men were denied visas to stay in South Korea even despite having a Korean wife. Until around 2000, foreign nationals granted South Korean citizenship annually stood at only 34 per year. From after the first decade of the 2000s, men married to Korean women now easily receive a visa to stay in the country, however citizenship is still mostly by blood. Nonetheless by

2023, there are now three routes for foreign nationals being naturalized South Koreans with full citizenship rights, yet by 2015 this has been granted to only around 150,000 people. For 'generalized naturalization,' foreign nationals have to end any other citizenship they have. For 'simplified naturalization,' dual citizenship is allowed yet only if there is the required blood Korean family relationship in the foreign national, and then that is all that is required to add a Korean citizenship. A third category now is the 'special naturalization' for foreign nationals who may of course still have at least the Korean lineage, plus have done something stipulated in the Law Related to the Honorable Treatment and Support of Those Involved in Meritorious Deeds for Korea, or have desired talents like Olympic athletes or are already established sports heroes in other fields joining the Korean team, literally and figuatively. Showing a homogeneous culture's expectations of how 'simple' naturalization can be by blood, if a Korean male is born overseas without Korean citizenship, upon his arrival in Korea, there have been examples in which such males were drafted into the South Korean army if the government border officers judged the "Korean youth," even if not Korean by nationality, as trying to escape universal male Korean army service. This is because multiple citizenship status (adding Korean citizenship in addition to some other citizenship) is automatic in Korea regardless of the registration of birth, if the parents are Korean. Therefore, foreign Korean-heritage males innately have their (never used) Korean and their natal citizenship, at the time of birth. This is according to Article 11-2, paragraph 1 of the Nationality Act, which states such a person in Korea will only be legally treated as a Korean national. Merging the third and fourth point, on the topic of military loyalty, and treatment of refugees, sometimes North Korean defectors are so ostracized by South Korean culture, they die of starvation at home and are discovered weeks later. Most North Korean defectors desperately try to hide their status from South Korean 'peers' due to this kind of discrimination. Korean family and culture are mostly defined by ancient bongwan bloodline connections tied to particular regions instead of allowing cultural assimilation by simple language heritage use, residence, or naturalization changes. Bongwan is a term related to all the various regional family cultural and intermarriage taboos (even among Koreans themselves) in their very regionalized South Korean culture. Even North Koreans thus can have the wrong bongwan to intermarry into South Korean families and may be treated as innately suspicious traitors for having bongwan in North Korea.

That brings us to summarize the main four factors that combined to supercharge the economic Korean Miracle into the cultural Korean Wave: (1) Korea's ancient *homogeneous cultural continuities*, (2) truly radical, odd, and even fortunate *modern political discontinuities* including hybrid policies in *politics*, (3) in a *hybrid cultural settlement* of a durable rural traditional population only missing an ancient aristocracy, and (4) various *hybrid economic development models* without par in the world. The latter is exemplified by a particularly odd economic model of revolutionary top-down, export-led development in urban industrial and machine sectors yet merged with a more protectionist national policy for protection of artisan small businesses, public corporations, and even protection and encouragement of village-based grass roots development simultaneously. The strength of the cultural Korean Wave as an economic export sector *and as a cultural force of pride that remains durable in Korea* came from the dynamics around these four factors. These developed a dynamics that became a virtuous cycle of growth that maintained this ancient culture and even promoted it in a power vacuum that encouraged more consensus-based developmental policies from the very beginning in 1963 to the Korean Wave today, instead of attempting to demote it in 'modern revolutionary fast development.' These four factors found a way to maintain themselves in virtuous cycles from 1963 *without any course change* on these four points so far yet with instead only endless *political* organization change and *economic* sector changes as additions to the general development drive that only got more usefully synergistic and complicated in time. The synergistic economic sector changes and additions were made within an equally odd hybrid political arrangement that South Korea was fortunate to craft and was fortunate to avoid in other choices like North Korea.

Five arguments are made about these four interactive factors that have catapulted Korean scales of development higher than other developing nations. This summarizes the short capsule history in the previous section. First, less ideological and more hybrid choices of politics and economics helped South Koreans organizationally be more flexible in tactics how to achieve development goals *while keeping the same strategy* of rapid development over time. Second, in the opposite sense, these hybrid policy choices once established helped Koreans maintain further consensus strategies of widening political and economic accommodations in these four factors mentioned above without course change in these hybrid settlements themselves. Third, this *provided cultural stability yet amongst fast political and economic organizational change* that was desired. Fourth, this was an *actively facilitated* cultural continuity and *ongoing intended reproduction of the culture* seen as a resource to be harnessed and involved in the fast development changes—instead of the past culture seen as an enemy of development and thus either passively neglected or actively smashed in cultural revolution. Fifth, whenever various eventual economic crises happened, or whenever ideological political party hegemony changed, an overall dedication to the older hybrid political and hybrid economic settlements maintained course in policy, even despite drastic military coups in 1972, 1979/1980, or in the sudden return to open presidential elections in 1987. Overall, choosing to buckle toward more hybrid settlements of more consensus helped Koreans keep political, cultural, and economic policy stability that is easily lost in fast developing countries that could result in setbacks. These hybrid settlements, by keeping stability better, helped Koreans keep durable and flexible development better on one ongoing aggregation drive, instead of starting over from square one after a cultural revolution or a political revolution, or instead of seeing political policy change of direction after each economic crisis or election change as happens regularly in many developing countries. Plus, a hybrid political system's management was built from the strong continuity of personnel over generations from the same meritocratic military educational networks of sponsorship. This avoided the worst cronyisms of a dictatorial model that lacks administrative or technical expertise and avoided the worst cronyisms of relaunching powerful aristocratic inherited interests in the nation as fallback managerial talent. However, one future trend in Korea to watch and to defend against is the private chaebol dynasties increasingly and dangerously becoming such a revived inbred aristocracy of wealth, politics, and rent seeking instead of innovation and meritocracy. However, for much of the politics of Korea, a meritocratic military technocracy was begun as the leadership in the originating hybrid political settlement under Park (1961/1963–1979). This was indeed aligned with certain private chaebol families, yet Park and the military networks of state guided the economic sector decisions of the chaebol themselves by controlling their funding. This meritocratic military technocracy got even stronger from 1980 under Chun who was a strong Park loyalist from the beginning of 1961, which encouraged more policy continuity. Chun hired more technocrats to further decide upon what fresh economic sectors to create in the first place, instead of leaving such decisions to the President as leader as before (Oh & Larson, 2019). Out of the wider technocratic brain trusts under Chun in the 1980s came the decision to start digital telecommunications quickly as a priority area of development. What developed was an odd combination of durability in long-term strategic policies for export-led development of and by state-supported private corporations, yet wrapped within a stable hybrid economic and political settlement of institutional arrangements that added nationally-protected economic sectors, public corporations, protection of traditional rural artisanal transmission, and village-based grass roots development. This stability and consensus internally to the nation has encouraged export-led flexibility of the nation. This helped Koreans develop a durable additive economic aggregation over time instead of stalling or falling behind over time without any durability in development.

In summary, it is the ability in South Korea to maintain the more homogeneous culture and its collective innovations in the midst of these hybrid settlements that supercharged ongoing national and patriotic sentiment into an ethos of economic and technical innovation toward an 'economic development war' abroad instead of foreign military warfare per se. Plus, the very hybrid political and economic organizations themselves helped the homogeneous culture to avoid political and economic excesses of a homogeneous culture as well. These dynamics held the culture and country together during perhaps innate cultural destabilizations of fast development economically that could encourage further political, economic or cultural revolution. It is argued Koreans, generation after generation since 1961 in the blurring changes of their fast development drive, have had something stable to hold on to in keeping access to an ongoing past-harkening culture along with its forward-harkening goals and collective innovation in an export-led economy. So despite changes from declining or added economic sectors, both of which could be related to cultural instability, the more hybrid choices of South Korea avoided durable interruptions and kept up potentials for teamwork, trust, and collective innovation through various crises.

In combination, these four factors are argued to have made (and still make) a world-unique developmental combination in South Korea that other developing countries can learn from deeply. This overall recipe has worked because it has catalyzed a durable yet flexible 'double virtuous cycle' of political and economic development that avoided being injured by background factors or bad choices down the 'development gauntlet' (described later in Chapter 3). This can be contrasted with other nations' development drives that are incomplete, inflexible, and thus hardly durable in political and economic crises down the development gauntlet. The recipe for South

Korea's development drive supercharged cultural action and collective innovation. It has catapulted the country higher and faster than any other modern developing country.

Out of this more stable, durable, and yet flexible dynamic in South Korea after 1961 came its later international cultural projection in the Korea Wave by the late 1980s. It started to be arranged once Korean digital telecommunications and Korean cultural production both started to be developed together as added export-led economic sectors upon a vast pile of other economic sectors. Thus these many export-led policies merged with other pre-existing factors of modern historical conditions and a homogeneous culture that was far older. Plus, nowadays, Korea is further involved than any other country in a deeply 'saturated' digitalized cultural wave that takes the world and even 'underdevelops' the world's potential to compete because of the strong and multi-faceted digital skill sets that Koreans have established. (See Appendix 1 and later Chapters 5 through 8.)

To conclude this review section about these unique dynamics in South Korea, these chosen hybrid dynamics avoided the worst excesses of state-led development, the worst excesses of a homogeneous culture, and/or the worst excesses of a cultural revolution. Thus South Korea began to have a durable modern economic revolution without regularly associated political or cultural revolutions that are toxic to aggregating economic growth, toxic to cultural continuity, and toxic to processes of growing political consensus by their instability and resets. This has made South Korea the envy of other developing nations that are currently far behind. South Korean politics rejected a modern cultural revolution even though this regularly happens either alongside the state development drive whether by original intent or by cultural erosion that takes place after scaled economic change. South Korea instead has only strengthened its traditional homogeneous culture. A "Korean Wave" in a sense was part of its hybrid developmental model from the start: to preserve and enhance the traditional artisan culture from the beginning after 1963 and then do the same for village-based rural development by the 1970s. This durable cultural energy involved in Korean national development kept providing access to a durably renewed collective innovation that has served the *export-led economy* and the *cultural continuity* well after 1961. In short, the homogeneous culture and its collective innovation has served the more 'formal' economic sector of the Korean Wave instead of eroding either the culture or the economic sector over time, like how many fast development drives can alter a homogeneous culture, and in turn a loss of homogeneous culture might cause a loss of collective innovation and thus loss of economic drive.

2.2.3 Theoretical Summary: Two Virtuous Cycles in Korean Culture Helped the Economic 'Korean Miracle' Keep Growing into the Cultural Korean Wave

As said earlier, this first chapter of Part I is about Korean culture, in two main parts involving a short history of the homogeneous cultural interactions with the organizational choices of its fast development drive and then a discussion of the cultural forms of the culture itself. As a concluding section about this interaction, this section summarizes theoretical and comparative insight about how this interaction of a durable and ancient homogeneous culture and other modern policy factors created two virtuous cycles of development in interaction with the culture.

The many factors of importance identified in these global comparisons about fast development successes and failures are built on the work of giants in this field of global modern development. Many have noted important patterns for what encourages either a rise to wealth, a rise only to false starts returning to stagnation and durable poverty, or incessant failures (See Appendix 2 and 3.) To see farther than giants, it is important to stand on their shoulders in order to see further than them. It is equally important to stand on the toes of giants sometimes to see further than them—meaning, to disagree openly with them to note neglected factors of development or causes of the lack thereof that they have missed. In this process of standing on the shoulders and the toes of giants, there is a theory below about what 'full development' means and what only 'partial development' means.

Many modern nations had huge choices for a development drive after World War II in being cultures and nations freed from colonization or having their nations invented outright for the first time. However, many of these nascent nations rarely led into a development drive for many rationales (Collier, 2007; de Rivero, 2013). To the contrary, South Korea is among just a handful of non-Western newly developed countries after World War II including Taiwan, Hong Kong, and Singapore. Most other newly invented or freed nations after World War II have hardly developed at all in over 70 years. However among the handful of newly developed nations, South Korea has shone most brightly in fast development, and without burning itself up in the process. This should be analyzed more closely for its unique recipes of fast development that remained durable and flexible without showing any diminishing economic returns like in the middle income trap (described later) or without showing any diminishing cultural returns in cultural destruction that typically comes with fast development.

Based on the earlier historical analysis, this section summarizes a theoretical view of the unique interactions of a *less transferrable* ancient homogeneous culture merging well with its *transferrable* choices of modern economic and political policies. These three factors merged into historical dynamics so very well that it led to the creation of two virtuous cycles that did three important actions over time: (1) it supercharged activities of the homogeneous culture both economically and politically; (2) it avoided the act of self-destroying the culture (killing the golden goose) in the economic growth process that was geared instead toward an export-led economy and an internal national cultural reproduction simultaneously; and, (3) it even checked and balanced against downsides or dangers of a homogeneous culture. These downsides or dangers of a homogeneous culture can be seen through a glass darkly in North Korea where the same homogenous Korean culture chose different economic policies and political organizations and led into more vicious cycles of decline.

In this theoretical section about these two virtuous cycles that developed in South Korea, two main kinds of comparisons are used as data to think about choices and contexts of South Korean success: comparisons with North Korea and comparisons with all other nations. Thus we can think about choices and contexts in general for how to set up either virtuous cycles of durable development like we see in the case of South Korea or to set up vicious cycles of stagnation and diminishing returns like we see in the case of North Korea or in other less successful developing nations. Second, instead of only cultural comparisons between North and South Korea, more global comparisons are drawn from over two decades of studying factors in and case studies of success and failure in any modern rapid development. This frames the Koreas and their divergent outcomes in fast development more comparatively to all other countries at their lesser scales of success or greater scales of failure as well.

For the first comparisons they are based upon thinking about theories of development in homogeneous cultures versus more heterogeneous cultures. These are modern reflections on how a current stark North Korea versus an ebullient South Korea began from a natural experiment from 1946 onward in geopolitics that split the peninsula as both nations chose very different political organizations and economic policies despite sharing the same ancient homogeneous culture. (See Appendix 2.) Both nations start with the same cultural homogeneity and dire poverty in the beginning, though by the 1970s onward increasingly created very different modern timelines and outcomes. Only South Korea has created what will be called a *full and long-term development drive*, while North Korea has only created a *partial and short-term economic drive.*

A definition is proposed for the terms 'cycles of development' or 'development drive.' This means any countries' historical dynamics of culture, economics, and politics that can be growth-inducing and virtuous in its cycles, or self-diminishing and vicious in its cycles. 'Development drive' is defined as a combined economic and political development instead of only one or the other that will be called only the 'economic drive' or the 'political drive.' The 'cultural drive' is a term that will be used to express the hypothesis that different kinds of cultural demographics have different kinds of innovation drives, with homogeneous cultures 'driven' to create more toward collective innovations (among other factors, good and bad, while selecting against other kinds of innovation), while more heterogeneous cultures are 'driven' more toward individual innovations and cultural innovations (among other factors, good and bad, while making it more difficult to find a common shared ethos for collective innovation together). It is assumed that greater development capabilities of individuals in general (Nussbaum, 2011; Sen, 1992, 2000) are enhanced by actually functional political drives and economic drives within the wider development drive even if in the South Korea case a more homogeneous culture has masked much of the surface appearance of growing individual capabilities by preferring a history that rewards more visible team-based collective innovation instead of rewarding more visible individual or cultural innovations.

So, what has happened in the development drive in South Korea is beautiful and amazing. However, what the same homogeneous culture did in North Korea, with other choices of economics and politics, is truly horrifying and dystopian. In retrospect, the latter's choices led into an earlier and rapid industrialization in only an economic drive in North Korea, yet in the long run, led into economic self-destruction, stasis of diminishing returns, and an economic, cultural, and political inability to change course. This is because North Korea lacked a political drive, and thus lacked a true development drive. By the 1970s, North Korea was politically unable to change course (i.e., lacking a political drive) as its fading first economic drive got to watch South Korea more slowly develop economically via its different hybrid political and economic choices that were able to more flexibly politically change to move away from its first fading economic drives to avoid the middle income trap. In talking to an advisor directly on the scene in the "Blue House" (the euphemism for the South Korean Presidential residence) from the late 1970s under Park into the 1980s under Chun, who surely would like to remain anonymous in print, he argued that the only way South Korea achieved this political flexibility to change economic sectors from the 1970s into the 1980s was simply because the assassination of Park provided that political flexibility, without which a middle income trap may have commenced like so many other fast developing countries (Gill & Kharas, 2006). However, this witness's interpretation of the late 1970s and early 1980s is only a counterfactual argument, since we are without such an alternative South Korea to think about what might have happened if Park survived the assassination attempt in 1979 like he had survived a previous onc that had killed his wife by accident in 1974. However, this is just like the counterfactual argument about *removing the older Korean aristocracy yet without a cultural revolution* was very important in both the later stable, flexible and durable fast development in South Korea and the ongoing durable homogeneous culture. It is just like the counterfactual argument that an inflexible neo-aristocracy in North Korea killed the economic drive by lacking a political drive there by the 1970s. However, the latter two counterfactuals rise to greater validity potentially by being more comparative statements about all national development instead of only about South Korea per se, while any claims about 'killing the king' in South Korea in 1979 remains more nebulously counterfactual. It will be argued here that the assassination of Park in 1979 was important for beginning an opening for political change in South Korea, though by hardly any means did that assassination directly cause what happened later. Instead, other ongoing 'hybrid' political drives were already in place from 1963, and these only continued. That continued the ever widening political consensus in Korean political development. It is that ongoing virtuous political cycle which is argued to have helped the Korean ability to innovate toward more economic sectors by the 1980s to avoid a middle income trap.

However, another way to try to justify counterfactual arguments is by analyzing the direction of trends within the case itself, as another route for comparison. The question can become did the trend change at all by the interruptive power of such an event? In this case, did the assassination in 1979 avoid the actual already visible trend of Park's consolidating dictatorship after 1972 that certainly showed his preference for killing the earlier hybrid political drive? It is on this internal comparison before and after 1979 that this counterfactual seems more plausible than most counterfactuals. Killing the hybrid political settlement more over time toward pure dictatorship without the Park assassination in 1979 would have made it even more difficult to change economic sectors after 1979 to avoid the middle income trap developing in the economic decline by the late 1970s, if Park had lived past 1979.

However, Park's assassination in 1979 occurred. Therefore, after the unsettled military coup by Chun afterwards, who was trying to keep his own legitimacy, a hybrid political drive survived both the life and the death of Park, despite being shepherded into existence by him from 1961 through the 1970s and despite his desire to end it after 1972 in the Yushin Constitution (1972–1981). So, after Park's assassination of 1979, South Korea's full development drive revived and continued, both politically and economically—with its hybrid policies' greater stability, durability, and flexibility.

Into the 1980s, this 'hybrid dictatorship' settlement remained, and a hybrid economic policy continued as well. Both seem important factors why South Korea was able to switch economic sectors flexibly and durably over time into the 1980s, or even to switch political arrangements well over time by the later 1980s, without both settlements falling apart or changing course to a more pure dictatorship or a more pure republic. Collier would argue that very poor countries falling into either pure dictatorship or pure republics may be dually deadly down the development gauntlet, since durable dictatorships in very poor countries tend to stall their own *economic* advance and thus kill their own golden goose in time, while democracy in very poor countries can stall *political* stability and thus kill their own *economic* advance as well via this other indirect mechanism (Collier, 2007). Thus, these durable yet flexible hybrid policies in the political drive and the economic drive of South Korea continued. They have yet to stop even today in South Korea from the point of view of the ongoing economic Korean Miracle or the slowly growing 30-year old Korean Wave.

Ceteris paribus, back to the question of the different outcomes of North and South Korea, they are arguably mostly due to how these different economic and political choices in a homogeneous culture created either *virtuous cycles of ongoing development* in South Korea of a slower rise toward wealth and growth, with easier abilities of changing economic sectors or political arrangements. Meanwhile, the same culture under different policies in North Korea created *vicious cycles of collapsed development* toward an original faster economic drive yet missing a political drive and thus in the long term toward only a partial economic drive and a more durable self-destruction since the development drive lacked the ability of internal political self-correction or economic sector changes being politically possible. Equally, unlike South Korea, North Korea gained many other factors that distracted it or damaged its development drive while moving through the development gauntlet, like its renewed military aristocracy of communist party families, their larger tendencies to internal violent repression or external terrorism instead of compromise, and the North Korean large reliance on raw material exports for economic sectors. For the latter point, many from the 1950s argued from available evidence even then that a nation's greater dedication to raw material wealth exports is a trap instead of a boon to economic, political, or environmental benefits in the long run (So, 1990; Karl, 1997; Ascher, 1999; Collier, 2007). On the other hand, South Korea avoided this trap down the development gauntlet by lacking many raw materials in the first place. Thus, South Korea was pressed to develop growth-inducing and value-added products that bring raw materials to itself instead for making valuable products with them, instead of simply exporting mindlessly raw materials to others. This is exactly the same dynamic arranged by raw-material poor yet very developed Japan, by the way (Bunker & Ciccantell, 2005; 2007).

Thus, a comparative view of this raw material trap is available for analysis. The only two major modern non-European development successes are Japan and South Korea, and both of these nations have a similar lack of raw materials (Barham et al., 1994; Bunker & Ciccantell, 2005; 2007). This encouraged in both countries value-added products in an export-led economy, worked on by a similar more homogeneous culture with more potential for collective innovation. However, comparing the scales of their export-led economies, South Korea is a smaller nation demographically than Japan and you would expect thus that Japan would export a higher percentage than South Korea, though it does not. Thus, the argument is that while Japan can grow its economy on its large internal consumption of 124 million people, South Korea with only 51 million people is unable to depend upon expanding internal consumption. Thus, South Korea's solution has been to have an even higher percentage exports in their economic expansion, particularly in value-added products and index-measured innovation in those value-added products, above all other nations in the OECD, including Japan, Germany, Scandinavian states, and the United States. (See Appendix 1.) This is why it is argued that thinking about South Korea's 'mid-level' size, more homogeneous culture, and lack of raw materials are all important in its collective innovation and its massive scale of export-led sectors in only value-added products leading to its development success, instead of assuming its lack of raw material wealth or a 'mid-size' demographics are hampering effects on its development instead of catalysts of it.

Plus, unlike Japan, South Korea has avoided much polarizing international war or internal civil war particularly after 1953. South Korea was repeatedly pressured both by its own cultural movements and by its external allies like the United States to stop internal violent repression or to contain the then-aristocratic Korean leadership in the 1950s from continuing international war. Keeping out of internal civil wars, political purges, and external wars has let South Korea travel further down the development gauntlet, while ongoing North Korean internal political purges are argued to keep that country less developed despite it as well keeping out of external wars. Thus, South Korea by default was more greatly forced to deal with its domestic problems first by greater pressures toward political consensus instead of choosing external war, internal civil war, or political purges to try to get rid of them. This encouraged greater buckling and consensus. South Korea as well was by default more forced to choose routes of less violent political compromises and more economic development policies of export-led development that brought the world's raw materials to it, for making more lucrative value-added products with them. This facilitated the best use of its more homogeneous culture and its collective innovation. Plus, such an export-led development strategy is less easily displaced by other nations as it relies on tasks of brainpower and inventiveness that could draw upon the large collective innovation of a homogeneous culture in such a project. Comparatively speaking, as said above, Japan had the same situation of scarcity of raw materials that forced a strategy of raw material imports, then acted upon by its own homogeneous nation's deep collective innovation. However, Japan kept its aristocracy, and has a much larger domestic economy. Its aristocratic-led development policies pressured underhanded violence and political purges in politics nationally and pressured an empire overseas—two issues that were deeply responsible for its own economic setbacks later. It was this Japanese aristocratic group that encouraged the external Japanese Empire in the first place via the Genyosha group against its own growing national democracy, and this aristocratic leadership ultimately led to their own empire's collapse later after World War II at the hands of the Americans. This set Japan back well over ten years after World War II, and only opened up American imperial overlordship of Japan that still continues somewhat today (Kaplan & Dubro, 2003).

However, to the contrary, after Rhee fled South Korea's First Republic in 1960, and then after the 1961 military coup against the short-lived Second Republic, in retrospect South Korea blissfully missed after this all sorts of hubristic antics of privilege-conscious aristocratic dynasties that repeatedly and tragically wreck and warp their own national development because their private projects are always more important to them than political compromise. This regularly results in great atrocities domestically and internationally from such hubris in the process. This can be seen in Rhee's attempt to sabotage the armistice in 1953 that ended the Korean War to try to restart the Korean War. This can be seen in the racist uncompromising starvation policies in India by aristocratic Churchill in World War II that contributed to losing the British Empire entirely after the war. This can be seen in the aristocratic Junkers in Germany sponsoring the empire of the Nazi German Third Reich, in weak Italian kings pushing Ethiopian invasions, or in rogue weak Belgian monarchs like King Leopold that created an evil 'heart of darkness' zone in the Congo out of his own dark heart in the early 20th century simply because he refused to compromise in political and economic power at home with a growing Belgian democracy. The development problem of many nations has been an aristocratic hatred of political compromise at home that can be seen in the expansion of the Japanese empire abroad as well, as a similar strategy to try to regain greater repressive power at home against widening democratic procedures. Aristocracies and their oligarchies are anti-developmental and anti-democracy. Aristocracies feel they are 'born to the throne,' and thus they are bad economic business managers and bad republicans at the same time as they see budget limitations and political compromise as a personal affront instead of keys to development success. Aristocracies are power centers that are atrocities waiting to happen because they refuse to accept politically and economically representative compromises. Instead, they wreck their nations or other nations to stay in power preferring to rule over a wasteland to get there. Therefore, it is best that South Korea avoided such renewed aristocratic rule during Park in the 1960s and 1970s, or under Chun in the 1980s. It is further best that this happened without a cultural revolution that would have developed its own problems of renewed aristocracies like in North Korea. Plus, in South Korea, even if Park had survived, he would have likely tried to continue a right-wing cultural revolution that he started in the 1970s. Instead, we can have better cultural continuity and better durable modern development without parasitical aristocracies or without violent cultural revolutions against them—both paths having equally wrecking influence and instabilities on their nations.

In short, South Korean political and economic institutional choices *went against the grain of its homogeneous culture*. All of these issues have helped make all the difference in the world for slowing down tendencies of a homogeneous culture for potential excesses of dictatorial leadership and nationalistic political and economic excesses. Plus, it has supercharged this homogeneous culture's collective innovation and patriotism only economically against outside forces, instead of militarily on outside forces, and instead of arranging against internal factions of themselves as well. Equally, this is due to a drive toward an export-led economy and how internal agricultural consolidation was blocked by missing a large aristocratic landholding tenure anymore, as well as how external warfare and conquest were blocked or minimized by losing hubristic aristocrats that tend to lead imperial drives into self-destruction—with Italy, Belgium, Britain, Germany, or Japan cited as examples.

2.3 Five Comparable Factors Encouraging Cultural Homogeneity in the Korean Peninsula

The remaining sections of this chapter are about only the durable strength over the generations of this homogeneous culture itself that has been enhanced instead of demoted by the modern *organizational choices* of economic and political policy in South Korea. The cultural Korean Wave is one of the most recent Korean export sectors. It joins an earlier wide family of equally planned, state-guided, export sectors. As said above, it is argued that all ongoing economic sectors, including the modern cultural Korean Wave, are the product of these two virtuous cycles in odd hybrid economic and hybrid political organizations merged with and aided by a more homogeneous culture.

Comparatively speaking, Korea's homogenous culture seems more profoundly homogeneous compared to many other countries, and even odd in its depth of self-referential qualities compared to many other countries. However, how can we define a 'homogeneous' culture? How can such subjective judgments hope to rise to the level of objective analysis? It can do so by thinking about a list of common comparative factors in world history that both contribute to creating a homogeneous culture and in turn keep it transmitting and reproducing over time, whether due to lack of challenges, in spite of challenges, or both. How many of these comparative isolative factors does the Korean Peninsula have, compared to other areas of the world?

It is argued that the Korean culture has existed far more homogeneously over comparative time and over comparative spaces than other cultures into the late 20th century because *the geographic area has five factors that encourage cultural homogeneity*. Some are related to modern and ancient *cultural settlements* that encouraged this homogeneity, had other factors related to more *geophysical situations* as historical accidents that kept the homogeneous culture intact and uninterrupted over long term history, and had other *historically chosen factors* in time that reinforced it deeply like trade policies, unique languages, and unique writing systems.

To introduce this "general theory of cultural homogeneity and isolation *from* world history," more isolation means a lack of external interruptions on a culture. In turn, a greater lack of external interruptions means more stability. In turn, more stability means more chance of virtuous cycles of a homogeneous culture developing. Of course even internal instabilities and internal interruptions develop regardless caused by elite-inflicted environmental degradation from unrepresentative politics throughout world history (Whitaker, 2009), though that is outside the point here, even though this has surely occurred in the Korean Peninsula as well. However, it is argued that even such internal and self-generated instabilities over time in a state culture have only become more internally destabilizing by inspiration from external factors of interruption in many ways. What happens when there are less external inspirations though?

From this general theory, the corollary is there seems to be five main factors *in world history* encouraging a deeper cultural homogeneity, stability, and cultural reproduction *away from world history*. It is argued below that the Korean Peninsula has more of these five factors than other modern or ancient nations whether judging this over time, in space, or as happening in parallel more regularly or durably. The five factors are: (1) linguistic/writing systems isolation; (2) geographic isolation that can include the degree of a geography's ecological, geological, and climactic regularity (not necessarily isolation, though at least regularity and stability) in world history; (3) geopolitical isolation creating more stable states as more unchallengable 'drifting continuities or inertias' in cultural hierarchies that are hard to disperse; and for a more modern point reflecting on the odd 20th-century historical settlement and discontinuity of Korea itself, (4) the degree of cultural continuity itself as self-perpetuating noted in either (4a) a continuity of a state/aristocratic culture or (4b) its rural peasant community regional cultures both capable of self-perpetuating themselves autonomously. The latter fourth factor depends on having a state in the abstract, yet both subfactors depend on the particular state design for whether the cultural continuity has both, only one, or none. As said earlier, the modern South Korean homogeneous culture and state is now missing its past aristocratic cosmopolitan-linked moderation from aristocratic leadership. It lost this subfactor from the early 20th century into the 1960s, even as it kept and 'supercharged' the latter subfactor after 1963. The fifth factor is (5) the degree to which a culture has more access to a durable, conserved collective innovation to further protect against cross-cultural transmissions.

With cross-cultural transmissions more truly defining most of the world history of other civilizations, the Korean Peninsula's fivefold isolation has truly become "Planet

Korea." Thus, we can contrast the Korean Peninsula's fivefold isolations against the whole theme of world history. World history is a historiography developed only clearly during and after World War II starting with historians like Marshall Hodgeson (1922–1968). World history was crafted to be a historiography more about the widely-shared, cross-civilizational, historical transmissions between cultures that sometimes are key experiences of many different countries' histories. However, Korea fits poorly into a world history, because the Korean Peninsula has been more characterized by its comparative isolations on these five isolating, stabilizing, and homogenizing factors mentioned above that defined Korean cultural transmission and innovation far more than cross-civilizational transmission.

A deep aspect of modern Korean culture is this ancient mindset (and granted, somewhat the reality) that they are a culturally world apart in four main ways: linguistically, geographically, geopolitically, and culturally/ethnically. While cultures by definition may have the 'fourth source' of isolation and insularity by self-perpetuation, Koreans historically have such isolative factors four times over in synergistic effect, and that has encouraged the fifth factor reinforcing it, mentioned above. So, to think comparatively about this "Planet Korea" on Planet Earth, it is more than an outlier developmentally in the modern world. Korea is an outlier in the way cultural transmissions regularly occur in world history, past or present. Cultural transmissions regularly are at least far more balanced between isolating factors and cross-cultural transmissions in world history. Comparatively speaking, in looking at many sources of cultural homogeneity, sometimes countries have at least one or up to three of these factors of isolation that encourages stability over time into a more homogeneous culture. This can be a source of strength and pride, for instance, like in the Jewish diaspora that has three of these isolating factors that create virtuous cycles of self-reproduction: linguistically, religio-culturally/ethnically, and in self-perpetuation of an 'aristocracy' (that is additionally a theocracy) of mostly bloodline-based leadership of rabbis despite losing their formal state (and the Sanhedrin state version of the aristocracy) and losing their homogeneous peasant agricultural communities millennia ago, only refounded in modern times after World War II around the modern communal kibbutz movement reinventing a missing regional agricultural culture for later cultural self-reproduction in that way as well. However, for a culture to have *all four points, to have them longer than others, and to have them more in parallel than others that creates that fifth factor*—is rare enough to make the Korean Peninsula into "Planet Korea" for the last 1,500 years at least.

In short, this fivefold theory of fourfold isolation in (or from) the flows of world history is that this accidental or self-chosen isolation creates a lack of external interruptions, and that in turn creates regularity and stability, and that in turn encourages only a self-reinforcing homogeneity in the culture. As well, the theory argues for five major factors in world history that do encourage such a homogeneous culture. Thus, so many factors together have contributed to what others mention as the unique historical path of Koreans: bizarrely durable cultural settlements characterize Korean history that are regularly twice the temporal length of other states, and even 'inherited' stable aristocratic hierarchies across these different dynasties. (Palais, 1995) What Palais left out though is what is referred to as the fifth factor of isolation above:

the collective innovation that has been created by such durable homogeneous cultural transmissions and particularly its aristocratic transmissions instead of this cultural stability creating total 'stasis' and a lack of innovation in the Korean Peninsula. It is hypothesized that the less interrupted and more homogeneous culture in ancient Korea (Palais, 1995) or in modern Korea (Lankov, 2007) has continued a longer aggregating history of conserved knowledge and faster collective innovation than other cultures. That evidence is the many dozens of 'world firsts' in the Korean Peninsula in the world history of scientific and technical innovation before 1800, discussed in the next section (Korean Spirit and Culture Promotion Project, 2008).

On the one hand, it is theorized that Koreans having all the first four isolating factors together has contributed to what Palais mentions as the bizarrely long and durable cultural settlements and aristocratic hierarchies that characterize Korean history far more than this happens in world history in any other place in the world (Palais, 1995). On the other hand, for the fifth factor, this fails to mean Korea has been stagnant or lacking scientific or technical innovation. It is hypothesized, when viewing the world history of scientific and technical innovation, that the more homogeneous culture in ancient Korea was uniquely *more innovative* than other cultures because of its stability. This means any ongoing external military challenges, by being mostly failures, became a further source of defensive innovation and an ongoing trend of improvement technically that made it ever harder to invade Korea compared to its peer nations around it—with other nations in East Asia suffering far more interruptions in their technical innovations in world history. This equally means external *military* challenges, by being mostly failures in the Korean Peninsula, led to an ongoing *internal* conserved infrastructure and *uninterrupted* knowledge transmission in this stasis to tinker upon and with over centuries to improve as another source of growing innovation (Korean Spirit and Culture Promotion Project, 2008). Thus, Korea's lack of interruptions only helped its ongoing innovations be expressed, conserved, and thus compounded more effectively over time compared to other areas of the world with more interruptions. Of course the theme of this book is that modern Korea, in continuing this homogeneous culture historically under these first fourfold conditions, has greater resources to be more uniquely innovative—i.e., to have the fifth factor. This is expressed in being the first and only developing country so far after the 1960s to be successful in being shifted from the developing column to the developed column by international standards in 2021. Plus, this is expressed by being the first and only non-Western culture to have developed in turn a durable global cultural wave on top of this strong economic fast development. Both are signs of deep collective (and technical) innovation. So, by having cultures and states as more isolated in the Korean Peninsula, they have been more stable, and thus more homogeneous, and from that as a 'fifth factor' maintaining isolation more actively, Koreans have even more access to collective innovation further to protect against cross-cultural transmissions and trends that more truly have defined most of the world history of other civilizations.

So, the historical Korean culture exhibited a tremendous amount of its own collective innovation in its isolation and in its homogeneous culture. Particularly the scientific and technical history of the culture of Korea, some of which is summarized below, calls for a global reconsideration of the Eurocentric deduction that cultural isolation is judged always to create a technical and scientific backwater or laggardness instead of creating all of these 'world firsts' in Korea centuries ago that show an isolation from world history can be good and even more innovative. However, the caveat here is that it seems that the pressures for such collective scientific and technical innovation in ancient Korean culture came from the interaction of these isolating factors *and* external world historical pressures of other states trying to conquer it, that mostly failed by the higher levels of Korean scientific and technical innovation and sheer ingenuity on national defense organized and encouraged by their more durable culture and states. The situation was the four-fold isolations and the deep homogenous culture that resulted from it created a situation that catalyzed the fifth factor of isolation more greatly, this faster collective innovation on actions and technical inventions to save themselves repeatedly over time. These more conserved innovations that were able to be used over time, instead of forgotten or destroyed in interdynastic interims that are situations of intellectual amnesia, technological destruction, and knowledge loss that plague other areas of the world repeatedly far more often.

However, as implied above, it is hardly true that all ancient Korean innovation was only military technology based on external world historical pressures interacting with this conserved and innovative isolation. Because of Korean stability on infrastructures of the built environment as well as cultural records, collective innovation was even more greatly focused on improving domestic quality of life in housing, publishing, and scientific continuity. Koreans could draw on records of hundreds of years without fail from even previous dynasties far more regularly than other countries that regularly saw their housing stock burn in war, their artisans kidnapped or murdered, and their libraries go up in smoke. This will be described in the next section as well.

So with Korea being the geopolitical geode that it was for at least the last 1,500 years by choice and by its own technically innovative success at defending itself against external threats of larger armies and states over centuries, Korea has had all five of these isolating, stabilizing, and homogenizing factors aligned together in parallel longer than any other place in world history. Of course there were a few and very short external interruptions from 'world history' during this period, though the main theme is how Korea's fivefold isolation catalyzed technical and scientific innovations that physically kept out external interruptions of most other culture's incursions. This in turn made the culture more capable of being 'innovatively impervious' to incursions resulting in more cultural self-reproduction and in being ahead of its peer countries in East Asia in technological advancement for hundreds of years. The first four factors are described below. The fifth factor is described at the conclusion to Sect. 2.4 on 'technical innovation', as it is more truly an example of an ongoing *renewed and active cultural form* contributing to greater isolation instead of classed more as *stable background factor* contributing to greater isolation like the below four factors that facilitate the fifth factor in turn.

2.3.1 Linguistic Isolation from World History

Linguistically, the Korean language has been argued to be the largest 'language isolate' in the world or in the 'smallest language family' in the world. The term 'language isolate' means a language unable to be placed into larger language families. It means the sounds and syntax of the language in combination are without clear connections phonetically or grammatically to other current language families in the world or to other known past language families. A language isolate might be the last remaining strand of a larger language family, or it might be developed in isolation a long time away from other language families in normal linguistic drift. While the grammar of Korean is organized like Japanese in the order of 'subject, object, verb' and having postpositions like Japanese generally, many words, up to half, have historically been borrowed from Chinese phonetically. However, only a small number of the Korean root words are of Chinese origin. Thus, there is a debate whether Korean is a true language isolate or a small language family of Koreanic and Jeju languages, though either way this illustrates the point here. Whether we call the language of the Korean Peninsula the largest language isolate or the smallest language family basically points to the same linguistic isolation from all other languages. There is even a debate whether to call the Korean oral language a language isolate or not, based on various theories of some links to Siberian languages or Turkish for instance. However, it will be called an *effective language isolate* by cultural reinforcement itself. For clarity's sake, the term language isolate will be used below though whether it truly is a language isolate or a small family of two languages still means it is an isolated language.

Typically, a language isolate means a small number of speakers near extinction of the language, with only a few thousand speakers. However, Korean is doubly odd to be a language isolate with a very large body of living speakers. There are around 82 million Koreans ranging across North Korea (25 million, estimated), South Korea (approximately 51 million), and a small global Korean diaspora (7.3 million, estimated). This means Koreans are slightly over only 1% of the world's population despite South Korea being the fifth largest exporter, the ninth largest importer, and the tenth largest economy in the world in 2021. Plus, most Korean speakers are still in the Korean Peninsula instead of in a diaspora, further encouraging a homogeneous culture geographically, unlike Chinese or Jewish diasporic speakers that are around the world more prominently in a global diaspora. It is equally odd that the small Korean diaspora may now find itself at the center of attention in the 'outside world' because of the Korean Wave, however, the Korean diaspora has little influence at home in the Korean Peninsula on being a leading edge in the Korean Wave or in Korea's international cultural leadership. This is because Korean Wave is truly only manufactured in the homogeneous South Korean cultural homeland, for export, instead of the Korean global diaspora being a crucial part of its rise. If anything the Korean diaspora is only caught up now in the Korean Wave manufactured at home, and it gets to enjoy the afterglow from afar. This reverses the utility of cultural diasporas because the Korean Wave comes from mostly collective innovation at home instead of individual or cultural innovation abroad that is more likely when Koreans are in that multi-cultural context. The latter individual or cultural innovations of a cultural diaspora are more regularly seen. This makes cultural diasporas a cutting edge of such cultural innovations abroad that influences even a culture at home. However, that is hardly the case with the Korean diaspora, as cultural innovation is hardly a source of status in the more homogeneous culture of Korea.

Plus, for another level of cultural-linguistic isolation, when Koreans write their isolated language, from the 1440s they further isolated themselves by writing in a self-invented simple script now known as Hangeul. Linguists use the term 'simple script' to refer to an easy-to-learn writing system of a limited numbers of characters generally based on phonetic or syllabic principles. The whole world's simple scripts are normally split into three categories themselves with the elder script inventions mentioned first: abjads (writing only consonants as characters and assuming vowel sounds like Phoenician, Hebrew, or Arabic), alphabets (writing consonants and vowels as their own characters like Greek, Roman, or Cyrillic letters), and abugidas (writing signs only for syllables of 'consonant–vowel' blocks like Japanese, Indian Devanagari, or Pali). This term 'simple script' is meant to contrast it to the opposite term 'complex script' (See Appendix 4). All complex scripts occurred earlier in world history than all simple scripts, and the former are based less on recording sounds directly in symbols and more on recording interpreted meanings or indirectly interpreted sounds in symbols via many thousands of possible characters. Respectively, this means complex scripts are either *morphemes*, denoting blocks of meaning like Chinese characters, or they are writing down what are effectively *rebuses* in recording pictures that symbolize then-current orally spoken sounds for the picture in a language that are or were once known only to living oral speakers of the language like Egyptian hieroglyphs or ancient Sumerian. This partially explains how it was so easy to 'lose' ability to remember how to sound out what was meant by some complex scripts that were rebuses like Egyptian hieroglyphs or Sumerian because older complex scripts like this require having a living speaker to teach the current sound of the sign from their working memory of the oral language, instead of the sign carrying actual directly teachable phonetic meaning like a simple script does per se. Another partial explanation is that complex scripts historically when invented were only used by a tiny scribal elite anyway, over a mass of only oral and illiterate speakers, instead of were an effective or easy means of mass public communication. So a complex script was carried by a tiny scribal elite, and a complex script carried morphic or pictorial meaning with the sign or picture having a meaning or sound from an oral language for the picture that was recorded instead. For instance, if you saw a picture of a 'bee' and then a 'leaf', you would know to pronounce that as 'belief' to indicate an abstract meaning instead of the pictures you see. However, if people forgot what the English sounds of the image of the 'bee' or the 'leaf' were, it would be very hard to reconstruct how to sound out the word 'belief.'

So, if complex scripts regularly have thousands of characters trying to convey meaning and sounds via morphemes or via rebuses using the sounds of currently spoken languages and only have limited and difficult historical literacy among a living population, simple scripts are direct attempts to symbolize phonetic sounds and have a wide capacity for mass literacy among a living population. Simple scripts rarely have more than 30 characters for direct sounds as they follow a language's phonetic sound literally instead of indirectly in meaning or in pictures. Plus, it is a fact of world history that simple scripts are mostly built into the world history of cultural and technological diffusion between cultures since they are so much easier for foreign speakers to learn to write as well. Beginning from the first millennia BCE, simple scripts of Egyptian hieratic, then Phoenician abjads, and soon Mediterranean alphabets like Greek allowed people of different cultures for the first time quickly to learn how to communicate with each other via an easy-to-learn script and via easily-copied and shared manuscripts.

However, unlike the world history of these widely diffused simple writing scripts, Hangeul is a simple script yet it is not historically a shared simple script, similar to the unshared Japanese simple scripts of hiragana and katakana. Before the past 30 years, Korea's Hangeul has never been part of any past world historical transmissions or cross-cultural sharing despite being a simple script suitable for such purpose. So, despite being invented over 600 years ago, Hangeul in the Korean Wave is the first time it has ever been widely shared in world history. Hangeul now helps prime the Korean Wave by being a simple script that is easily learned. It is very suitable for its purpose of quicker cross-cultural communication or learning another culture's language and writing system. Imaging the difficulty of a "Chinese wave" for instance, blocked from adding millions of foreigners by the complex script of Chinese itself. China has a huge barrier in its cultural projection through still using a complex script of logographic/morphemic Chinese. However, a complex script encourages a homogeneous culture more as it would be a higher barrier for scaled cross-cultural transmissions. Hangeul may encourage this cross-cultural transmission now in the Korean Wave of course, though historically Hangeul was invented comparatively late in the 1440s after many regions of the world had their own simple scripts already, and thus Hangeul was invented with little desire or pragmatic ability to facilitate international discussion in a common language of Korean—because Korean was an uncommon language to begin with of course as said above. Thus the simple script of Hangeul never diffused and never was thought of as facilitating global cultural diffusion—even though that is what it does today in the Korean Wave.

This development of Hangeul from the 1440s is of course far later than other simple scripts of hiragana and katakana that the Japanese invented from the 600s CE onward, or the other simple scripts invented as long ago as before 1000 BCE. Most Koreans were so culturally conservative in ancient history that writing in Chinese characters was the only proper cultural expression for males, and females were banned from learning Chinese characters. However, Chinese characters rarely could be used well by Koreans to write down their own language sounds of Korean, so various other poor substitutes were invented though they were without much cultural status.

In summary, unsurprisingly in a homogeneous culture uninterested in cultural extension, Hangeul never diffused into the world widely before the Korean Wave. This is a result of three factors: its lateness on the world historical scene with already many cross-cultural simple scripts being used; how Hangeul was meant to record accurately only the uniquely odd Korean language sounds that differ from all other language families as a large language isolate; and Koreans' or others own historical lack of desire to use it to facilitate international communication. Hangeul was invented to facilitate internal communication and mass communication within Korea alone.

So, Koreans invented a simple script intended to be used by no one else except Koreans because it was explicitly meant to record Korean sounds and be used by Korean culture only. It had an inherent 'national' and centralizing politics in its attempt to displace the status of aristocratic use of Chinese in the royal court of King Sejong in the 1440s (r., 1418–1450) who oversaw and participated in the linguistic team creating it to help his nation. Hangeul was shrewdly helpful in royal power toward finding and training more lower-class clients willing to be more subservient to himself—attempting to displace aristocratic power and culture, in a sense. However, Hangeul is incredibly innovative, attaining a level of scientific phonetics in the mid-1400s that was not seen in Europe until the 1800s when the comparative study of phonetics started to be developed. Thus, Hangeul is a simple script invented in the 1440s though it is truly closer to the modern era's motivations for scientific analysis toward a universal phonetic alphabet of all human sounds possible. It is equally closer to the social context of later invented syllabaries of the nineteenth century onward for tribal groups like the Cherokee or Inuit who wanted to write down only their own language's unique sounds more accurately than other pre-existing writing systems available for them could do.

This Hangeul simple script was one of the penultimate state-led projects of the only long-lived Joseon dynasty ruler, King Sejong (r. 1418–1450). Originally, the linguistic project was named the Hunminjeong'eum (The Correct Sounds for the Instruction of the People), yet by the twentieth century the simpler name "Hangeul" (한글) was the original English spelling coined by Korean linguist Ju Si-gyeong in 1912. Hangeul literally meant 'great script' as well as has a double meaning of 'han' referring to the Korean people and thus equally meaning 'Korean people's script'. Later, in the 1950s, President Syngman Rhee invited the creators of another Yale University-based Romanization to help with formatting Korean letters for English alphabets. The Yale team used the term "hān kul" (hence the other modern spelling of the term Hangul), even if currently the Romanization recommended by the Korean Government from the year 2000 would (re)spell it in Roman letters once more as "Hangeul"—in a project to try to erase the (daily potentially dropped) diacritics that Yale's linguistic team relied upon, among other points. North Koreans further complicate the matter by having their own Romanization called Chosŏn'gŭl (조선글), after Chosŏn, the North Korean name for Korea. Regardless, Hangeul's current total of 40 letters allow recording the Korean language's 19 different consonants and fully 21 different vowel sounds with modern levels of phonetic accuracy with different letters per each sound. Hangeul is as detailed as the modern International Phonetic Alphabet (IPA) that started to be formulated from 1886, yet Hangeul was innovated in the mid-1400s in the Korean Peninsula when hardly any Europeans could write. However, the Korean state of King Sejong was popularizing an invented simple script 'for the people' at large. Plus, Koreans already were using metal typefaces to print *Chinese* characters perhaps in the early 1300s as noted in the extant document from circa 1377 called the "Jikji" which obviously shows a mature technology, so it was hardly the first year of this metal-typefaced mass print, and then metal typefaces for *Hangeul* books in the 1440s—both instances far earlier than anyone else in world history. This is centuries before the Gutenberg press of the 1450s onward, and even earlier than China which was still using wood blockprint or wood/clay typefaces at this point in the 1300s. Korea seems technically ahead even then in both the material science of metalwork for such literary printing applications and in the publishing technologies of mass print itself—a theme of long-lasting Korean precocious technical innovation, discussed later (in Sect. 2.4).

Furthermore, Hangeul is further isolated by being in its own innovative 'fourth category' of simple script design unique in the world. Hangeul is structurally different from the world's three shared solutions to simple scripts (abjads, alphabets, and abugidas) because Hangeul is written in a syllable block of consonant–vowel combinations similar to an abugida, yet Hangeul builds those syllable blocks with discrete phonetic signs as well by having separate consonants and vowels in a true alphabet. Plus, Hangeul can build syllable blocks out of more than consonant–vowel combinations. So, despite Koreans having a true alphabet, Koreans write the Korean script in syllable blocks of grouped letters, and the Korean alphabet is seldom written in isolated letters at all. However, this hybrid and innovative 'alphabetical-abugida' fits the Korean language scientifically well, as it should, since it was designed solely for writing the sounds of Korean almost exclusively. Hangeul originally had more scientific diacritics and a few more letters (both long disused now) to document some Chinese sounds in translation as well in ongoing Korean writing. However, Hangeul is further odd as it is a *pictorial alphabetical abugida, with the shapes of the letters being designed to mimic the shape of the mouth to speak the correct sounds*. After all, it was originally called The Correct Sounds for the Instruction of the People—to teach a Korean people who would have been mostly illiterate by making Hangeul letters into literal pictures so they could interpret the shapes of the mouth and tongue orientation they should use to make and write the phonetic sounds. Therefore, making all the letters into pictures for mouth shapes would help in reading and writing quickly among illiterates. Some have called this the "figural" basis of the Korean alphabet. However, no one has commented that a pictorial or figural basis of Hangeul makes it similar to how complex scripts are written, despite it being a simple script.

Thus, Hangeul's innovative hybrid solutions are truly odd because it is a writing solution for a simple script categorically unlike any used by any other country or language in world history, past or present. As said above, most world writing systems are technologies diffused in world history across cultural borders as shared solutions around the world. However, the two simple scripts of Japanese characters of hiragana and katakana have stayed in Japan, and Hangeul has stayed at home in Korea. This further isolated Koreans from other countries' older literary cultures in Chinese. That was originally partly why the royalist Hangeul innovation was resisted deeply by the aristocratic Chinese-writing literary elite of the Joseon state, and why Joseon state support for Hangeul ended very soon after the death of King Sejong. However, Hangeul had already escaped the laboratory. As it was designed, it began to spread virally among the people of all Korean economic classes. Even Korean women could at last learn to write and read as well—as even women at the royal court were solely using Hangeul after the 1440s, since even elite women were banned from learning Chinese characters. However, Hangeul began to be treated as a children's writing language in the Joseon dynasty: something all Korean children should know, though should only be a preparation for (males) learning more complicated Chinese characters of the literary elite. Thus Hangeul's status was very low for most of its early modern history, until the late 1800s when it was repopularized as a common national script of public discourse with the rise of modern nationalism and the modern lower-class religious revolution of Tonghak in the Korea of the 1890s.

In a modern era, Hangeul even isolates foreign learners' of Korean (inspired by the Korean Wave) because learning Korean/Hangeul is truly a sunk cost: you are learning a language isolate, in an isolated script, with both language and script unable to be used anywhere else in the world except in Korea. In other words, learning Hangeul is kind of the same social dedication that it takes for Islamic populations globally to pray toward Mecca—just as Seoul is the only one place in the world a global diaspora of Korean speakers or writers would ever converge in real life to be in Korea communicating in Korean or through Hangeul. However, nonetheless in being a simple script, it is easy to learn. It does encourage people inspired by the Korean Wave to learn it. However, think of the 'dead end' sunk cost of learning Korean and Hangeul to only be able to come to one place in the world, Korea, to converse and write in the language, and contrast that with the truly cosmopolitan act of learning a globally-used and cross-national script like Roman letters (used to learn Latin, English, French, Portuguese, Spanish, German, etc.) or Cyrillic (used to learn Russian, other Eastern European languages, and Mongolian) that is a useful investment in many countries' languages.

However, the Korean Wave is turning isolated Korean and isolated Hangeul into what any language or simple script always had a potential to accomplish: to be a simple script shared by millions of secondary speakers worldwide. According to the online language learning tool Duolingo, Korean is now the second fastest growing language/script being learned on that digital platform, and Korean is suddenly the seventh most popular 'second language' known. It goes well with Korea having the seventh largest cultural products industry in the world by 2022. So truly the first global diaspora of Hangeul writers and Korean speakers now start to focus on South Korea and Seoul—that Mecca of the Korean Wave, from which Korea issues cultural missives and receives global tourists as consumer penitents. However, unlike cosmopolitan Mecca in Saudi Arabia, visiting South Korea can be an experience of a deeply homogeneous culture still rarely open to outsiders even if they speak or write the language. *Koreans as people* are publicly polite and selfless in a beautiful way. They generally are happy to and take pride in politely aiding many foreign visitors that they see in their streets. However, *the Korean culture* per se is hardly open to accepting foreign nationals as cultural equals even if they learn the language and writing system, due to the other synergistic issues of isolation forming the culture, as will be discussed momentarily.

The innovation of Hangeul from the 1440s allowed even poor rural agricultural commoners whether male or female to record and to share information for centuries after that. Unlike European history which showed a high level of illiteracy until the modern nationalist era of compulsory public schooling starting in the late 1800s onward, both Korea and Japan with their simple scripts far earlier became highly saturated literate societies hundreds of years ago. Thus Japan and Korea, *for hundreds of years longer than Europeans,* have done *more collective innovation by sharing information better among themselves in such simple scripts widely used, creating deeply literate cultures based on mass communication.* Western visitors in the late 1800s to Korea were amazed that even the poorest Korean could show off some kinds of cheap mass printed books in their houses. Both Korea and Japan were the odd countries out in world history by being widely literate for hundreds of years before the modern period, in part, thanks to the invention of own simple scripts as a background culture shared by all classes, both in government and 'below' them, even though their governmental elites still preferred to write in more status-based Chinese characters. However, Japan has been publishing texts in simple scripts of hiragana and katakana for over a millennium—even before their very urbanized society of the capital at Edo (now modern Tokyo) from the early 1700s. For a comparison, Hangeul mass popularization started in the 1440s, and was a national mass media ('Regime 4' in the parlance of Appendix 4) by the 1500s. It was rekindled as the public face of some of the first 'popular' Korean newspapers in the 1890s or Tonghak revolutionary fliers of the same decade. While Japan and China have had popular gazettes in their scripts for centuries, the first Hangeul-only national newspapers were as late as the 1890s as the country was still very rural without large cities and without many merchants. The long ban in the Joseon dynasty against using Hangeul for popular public communication was hard to overcome until the first newspapers were allowed in the later 1890s after the Gabo Reform of 1894–96. This response to allow more public freedoms to create a civil sphere in Hangeul came only after the near overthrow of the Joseon dynasty by the Tonghak peasant revolution in 1892–93. The revolution was stopped only by the double invasion of first an invited Chinese army and then an uninvited Japanese army into the Korean Peninsula (Whitaker, 2012).

2.3.2 Geographic Isolation in World History

Geographically, the ancient Korean homogeneous culture has always faced oceans on three sides of the Korean Peninsula that protected it from invasion more than facilitated invasions. Koreans only really feared invasions easily across the shallow Yalu River (the current northern border of North Korea) from northern nomadic tribes or from China's empires since the river is mostly only about a meter deep and freezes solid enough to travel across in the winter. Alternatively, Japanese samurai of the late Muromachi period (after 1573) did try an invasion across the ocean from the southern coast of Korea in the 1590s, called the Imjin War. The Japanese samurai had vainglorious aristocratic dreams of using Korea as a base to conquer China. However, the Japanese invasion was divided and uncoordinated by mutual samurai jealousies for getting their personal glory first or demoting the glory of others. Thus, the Japanese samurai invasion of Korea stalled and then failed before the decade was out. Thus, Korea has been very protected by its oceans in its history from invasion, along with being protected by its own strategic and technical innovations in oceanic warships to take advantage of it. Successful invasions from the north were rare as well.

However, geography is hardly deterministic to culture. It is what a culture decides to do in relation to its geography that matters. For instance, the cultural use of the same Korean geography changed drastically back and forth over Korean history: from extreme oceanic trade to the 1200s, to strong isolation from the late 1300s until the mid-twentieth century using the same oceans differently, to now back to extreme oceanic trade after 1961.

Founded in 1392, the Joseon dynasty preferred more isolation as it was removing a partial collaboration with external Chinese/Mongols at this point that had been holding captive the previous dynasty. However, the fact of being surrounded by oceans hardly means isolation can be the only policy. Even before this Chinese/Mongol dynamic, before the 1300s, all earlier Korean dynasties voluntarily saw oceans as useful transportation routes to the world, and Koreans seem more assimilative and blurred into foreign cultures then. Only by the Joseon dynasty from 1392 did the cultural use of the oceans turn them into more of a moat than a highway. For examples of this switch, two early Korean statelets were deeply based on international trade, Gaya and Baekjae. Gaya (43 CE–532 CE) had its capital city at Gimhae, which was a short distance up the Nakdong River giving them a good harbor on the southeast coast. From Gimhae, Gaya traded with the world *as far as India.* There is still an Indian stupa in Gimhae, reassembled there due to a political marriage of a Gaya lord to an Indian princess.

For another example, Baekjae was ruled by a group of elites that could be called the 'Phoenicians of East Asia'. Baekjae/Paekchae (18 BCE-660 CE) was on the southwest coast, and it had deep 'Japanese-Korean' links. It kept multiple commercial-capital cities at Wireseong (until 475 CE), Ungjin (until 583 CE, now Gongju) and Sabi (until the state surrendered to Silla in 660 CE). Even Later Silla or 'Unified Silla' (668–935 CE) after its conquest of Baekjae continued Phoenician-like policies as it conquered Baekjae (with Chinese T'ang dynasty aid) and 'inherited' its wealthy trade routes throughout East Asia. Later, Goryeo (918–1392) was the first consolidated single-cultural state across the whole Korean Peninsula, yet it inherited and kept the international trade. It was tying together the earlier very different state cultures of its conquered foes of Baekjae, Silla, and Goguryeo (once known as the Three Kingdoms or 'Samhan').

The switch to cultural and political isolation by choice was only clear in retrospect after the start of the Joseon dynasty (1392–1897; Korean Empire, 1897–1910). For nearly six centuries, the Joseon dynasty introduced and maintained Confucian policies of culture for the first time in Korea that furthered one great national homogeneous culture economically organized against merchants and for subsistence agriculture and non-migrating populations as Confucian economic policy requires.

This Chinese-Confucian model of economic policy minimizes all 'culturally destabilizing' trade, and supports a stable agriculturally-regional subsistence economy, thus regional economic autonomy without much peasant movement in order to keep people and food in their own geographic places. Only state elites had wider travel capacities due to being administrators over all regions. Thus, the Joseon dynasty's Confucian settlement was internally and externally against merchants and trade. This policy paired with geopolitical isolation and of course less oceanic trade. Plus, by intentional design instead of a lack of forethought, Joseon was without any national roadways. This was compounded by Korea lacking easily navigable rivers or canals for trade. China had both of those features of navigable rivers or canals for millennia, despite being Confucian. Therefore, Joseon might be said to be the most Confucian state simply by how Korean geographical happenstance fit the ideal Confucian economic policy arrangements more than China ever had.

Even the Japanese Empire in Korea (1910–1945) had a policy to keep Koreans as they were and where they were. The Japanese failed to make an extensive national road system in its colony of Korea either. So well into the modern 1940s a deep regional geographic, material, and ideological isolation was preserved in most of Korean culture. The ancient Korean homogeneous culture was able to maintain itself in Joseon and even afterwards in the Japanese Empire by the same trade isolation policies being kept after Japanese formal annexation between 1910 and 1945. Joseon and then the Japanese empire curtailed travel internally and externally to Koreans. The Japanese built the first airport in Korea in 1939 at Gimpo, south of Seoul. From a U.S. Army decree of September 8, 1945, Seoul and Incheon had an imposed curfew from 10 p.m. to 4 a.m. shortly after the end of Japanese rule. This curfew was expanded nationwide under President Rhee in April 1954 after the Korean War (1950–1953). In 1961, hours were reduced to midnight through 4 a.m., yet Korea's nationwide curfew was only lifted in the cities on January 5, 1982 though still kept in many coastal areas. Even airplanes arriving late were unable to land in Korea during this curfew period, because the airport was closed, so planes had to keep flying to other countries (Kim, 2023). As you can imagine, tours into Korea had a very limited market because Korean tourists would have been under curfews as well until 1982. So, there was little relief from the cultural effects of geographic isolation due to tourists being scarce, before the Olympics in 1988. "In 1965, the entire country had only 2,648 tourist hotel rooms and only 33,464 foreigners visited it that year. Not until 1978 did visitors exceed the 1 million mark" (Jameson, 1988).

Plus, well into modern Korea from the 1940s into the 1980s, it was hard for Koreans to get passports to leave their own country, as the government was attempting instead to bring back home the Korean diaspora's 'brain drain' via huge social and economic perks instead of letting them leave (Hong, 2014), or trying to keep all Korean cash in the country instead of seeing it spent outside the country (Jameson, 1988). Plus, private foreign currency loans went through government agencies for disbursement to Korean businesses from the 1950s onward, giving both President Rhee and later President Park greater state control over economic planning respectively toward import substitution first and then later export-led economics. Thus, with the centralized capital redirection as well as citizen blocks on leaving, Korea solved another issue that let it go down the development gauntlet further, by finding policies that coordinated economic development as well as solved 'brain drain' of upwardly mobile Koreans to stay home with both carrots and sticks—offering subsidies for relocation back in South Korea and offering punishments by banning most external travel or export of capital. This was made easier by Korea being surrounded by oceans on all sides except for a hostile North Korea on the landward north. This effectively made South Korea an island in the world with all its charms, drawbacks, and isolations. This virtual island of South Korea was forced to import materials and then to finish them as value-added trade in an export-led economy to grow and to survive at home because it was without much raw material wealth to export as another option.

For other examples of spatial isolation, only as late as 1970 did South Korea get its first nationally paved road, the Gyeongbu Expressway, built by Hyundai for the Korean Government between February 1968 and July 1970. The Expressway linked the growing urban industrial capital city of Seoul in the north with the now revived international port at Pusan on the southeast coast. Under President Park, Pusan developed one of the world's first intentionally designed container ports which lowered global transshipment costs to and from South Korea's budding export-led economy (Levinson, 2006). The Port of Pusan was by 2003 the fourth largest container port in the world. Pusan is still currently ranked as fifth or sixth in the world for container throughput.

Plus, as another way to think about geographic isolation, only from 1989 under President Roh did Koreans start to be allowed to travel abroad without limitations. Overseas pleasure trips by Korean citizens were banned entirely until 1983. The last restrictions on free travel of any Koreans out of their country were removed on January 1, 1989, "opening foreign travel for Korean tourists in their 20s, the marrying age, for the first time." Thus, before 1989, most young or old Koreans lived trapped inside their country their whole life, with only rare governmental allowances to leave the country instead of it being a common freedom of Korean citizenship to leave. Travel restrictions are of course still the case for North Korean citizens. In short, Korean geographic, economic, and cultural isolation has been profound into the modern twentieth century history, lasting deeply into the 1970s, and yet from the late 1980s becoming the extreme opposite.

Equally, the homogeneous culture of Korea experienced geographic isolation and stability because of geological history and climatic patterns. The Korean Peninsula is a geologically stable crustal zone, calmly riding between earthquake fault lines more prominent throughout China and Japan. Plus, the Korean Peninsula is without many volcanic zones unlike those that cover Japan. Thus, earthquakes and volcanoes are rare. The last major volcanic episode that Koreans had to worry about was over 1,000 years ago, though it was a mega-explosion rated at VEI 7 in 946 CE at Bekdusan/Changbaishan on the northern border of current North Korea and China. The volcanic mountain straddles the modern border there, explaining why it has both Korean and Chinese names. The blasted mountaintop at Bekdusan/Changbaishan is now a beautiful caldera lake. The same kind of volcanic explosion and scale made Crater Lake in Oregon in the United States when that ex-mountain now called Mt. Mayama blew up 7,500 years ago. However, Bekdusan/Changbaishan blew up at this same scale in historical memory around 946 CE. Nonetheless, it now is of minor geological or geographic risk. Mostly small eruptions are recorded there for 1124, 1200, 1403, 1597, 1668, 1702 and 1898 with the last activity being recorded in 1903 (KMA, 2010).

Equally unlike Japan, Korea can afford blissfully to not be prepared for earthquakes. It is rare to see any Korean earthquakes at 6.0 or 7.0 on the Richter scale. In ancient Korean annals, you have to go back in time as far as 779 CE in the city of Gyeongju to have what is considered by some to be the 'most deadly' earthquake in the modern geographic area of South Korea, rated at an estimated 6 or 7. Then, we wait until 1518 CE to get the next large earthquake of scale with a speculated epicenter near Seoul. Then we wait over 100 years more until 1643 to get something comparable, at Ulsan on the southeast coast. Next, the Yangyang earthquake of 1681 is speculated to be the strongest earthquake in all of recorded Korean history, at least in the modern geographic area of South Korea. In other words, you can count all major earthquakes and volcanoes in over 1,300 years of Korean history with the fingers on one hand. Thus, only a handful of major earthquakes or volcanic explosions were large enough to be written down in Korean historical annuals spanning over one millennia. The point is that there is a lack of many geological external interruptions of the stable homogeneous culture.

Plus, Korea is a climatically stable zone, despite being connected deeply to the 'teleconnections' of climate disturbances from the now-well-known El Nino Southern Oscillation (ENSO) of the South Pacific climate system that drive regular climate disturbances of El Nino's or La Nina's worldwide. Mostly, all of the Korean Peninsula experiences a very predictable dry season throughout the winter and spring with only one rainy monsoon season in August through early September. Even annually dangerous Pacific typhoons rarely make landfall on Korea strongly or directly since they hit Japan first and are weakened even if they continue to wander further west to the Korean Peninsula. Plus, most typhoons in the Pacific have landfall in the warmer waters off China or the Philippines far to the south of the Korean Peninsula. Korea is surrounded by colder northern waters that fail to sustain strong typhoon creation. Thus, it is rare for a typhoon to sustain itself in colder northern waters around Korea. It is even rarer for a typhoon to thread itself like a needle around the southernmost Japanese island of Kyushu and then veer north for a direct hit on the south of the Korean Peninsula. It is equally rare for typhoons to thread themselves up the thin East or West Seas of Korea to hit coastal cities like Gangneung or Incheon, respectively.

Thus, the Korean Peninsula has few earthquakes, volcanoes, or typhoons to cause regular or lasting infrastructure damage. These are three natural bases in which a more homogeneous culture develops over time amongst its conserved built environment that is rarely destroyed by natural disasters or by foreign invasions for that matter. In short, many kinds of unpredictable natural disasters rarely visit to interrupt Korean history and culture as much as they do in neighboring China or Japan. Greater stability in the ancient Korean geology, geography, and climate contributes to less external interruptions and thus more stability of culture and its built environment over centuries. For instance, Korea's ancient wooden buildings and wooden cultural properties continue to exist in the modern world, like the unparalleled Koreana Tripitaka. This is a carved wood blockprint archive of the whole Buddhist canon of writings, made in the 1200s, and still publicly displayed in parades annually. Plus, Korea has many original wooden Buddhist temples over one millennia old even in the capital of Seoul. One of these 'ancient modern' examples is Bongeunsa, a Buddhist temple founded in 794 CE, once in the mountains south of historical Seoul yet now entirely surrounded by Gangnam in modern Seoul. Bongeunsa is still used today. It is a truly massive complex in the mountains, now oddly juxtaposed directly across from tall modern glass skyscrapers of a global business event venue called the Coex Mall. Plus, Bongeunsa's massive Buddhist temple complex in the mountains is only one block off the "Wall Street" of South Korea that stretches down the boulevard of Tehran-ro in Gangnam, Seoul. Another example of ancient built infrastructure as a cultural continuity in daily Korean life is Seunggasa, founded in 756 CE by the state of Silla. Equally once in the isolated mountains, it is now swallowed up by the zone of Jongno-gu, in metropolitan Seoul as well. Dozens of examples like this exist. There are many daily-seen examples of ancient continuity in the Korean culture that maintain the same cultural sites over millennia. Can you name another hypermodern country with such ancient continuity? For a comparison, earthquake prone Japan may have old cultural properties, yet it has a culture that ritually rebuilds ancient structures every generation or so. For instance, ancient (re)building skills are kept alive in Japan at the Shrine of Ise for religious purposes—and likely out of pragmatism to keep up a practice in each generation because of Japan's far more frequent earthquakes, volcanoes, and typhoons. Thus, *Korea as a culture gets to preserve original ancient buildings in wood and stone far more easily for millennia.* This stability of the physical environment contributes to the durability of the built environment, and in turn may contribute to South Koreans' an oddly lackadaisical, nonchalant attitude that it is 'normal' to interact daily with 1000-year old wooden buildings in modern urban zones. Such buildings are not treated as museums though just other daily public venues, like any other modern buildings, despite many designated as national treasures.

Because of this deep environmental stability, there is perhaps a deeper overreaction to natural disasters in the Korean public showing strong emotional shock whenever they do occur. For example, a mere 5.0 earthquake with an epicenter near Gyeongju in 2016 was shocking to Koreans nationally. It was revealed most of the nation's buildings were woefully unprepared for even the possibility of a mild earthquake. From data of 2018, only around 500,000 buildings out of 1,994,520 buildings in Seoul were designed for seismic events. Plus, only 19% of larger buildings in Seoul were designed for any earthquake-resistance in mind. The number of domestic houses rated for earthquake resistance is even lower: a mere 6.2% of detached houses met seismic performance building standards. The seismic design rate for Seoul's modern subway lines #1 through #8 was rated even lower at 5.2% (Choi, 2018).

Blissfully unprepared, with a stress on bliss instead of unprepared, Koreans lack a history of repeated tragic natural disasters like those regularly interrupt cultural stability and transmission by wrecking infrastructures, burning libraries, or flooding cities like that which more regularly occurs in the history of China, Japan, or Southeast Asia. In short, Korea's far more isolating geography, stable geology, and stable climate means an ancient Korean homogeneous culture can have few natural external interruptions.

2.3.3 Geopolitical Isolation and Stable Cultural Hierarchies

Equally, the geography of the Korean Peninsula contributes to a geopolitical isolation having few and only very short cultural disruptions from foreign invasions. Plus, the homogenous culture itself in such a geography over time has shown great alacrity in its amassed and undisturbed collective innovation in science and technology to protect itself—aided by the conservation of built infrastructure as mentioned above. From this, Koreans experience a comparatively very stable culture, for better or for worse. This has even created the linguistic evolution, the linguistic isolation, and the political evolution of Koreans toward ever more stringent hierarchies and repression all their own.

In summary, there are four natural 'defenses' of the Korean Peninsula that contribute to *geopolitical* isolation and lack of external interruption: fast and treacherous ocean currents; shallow poorly-navigable rivers of meandering flows full of ever shifting silt and sandbars rarely flushed to the ocean due to only one monsoon season annually; uniquely deep and wide tidal mudflats on the southern and western sides of the country at river terminuses seldom flushed out to sea due to the lack of many strong typhoons, surreally reminiscent of large zones of quicksand to the horizon in a tidal zone that regularly ebbs several kilometers out to sea at low tide before rushing back at high tide; and how most of the Korean Peninsula is very mountainous instead of flat or easily traversable.

Therefore, gaining ground from the north in a land invasion by horses or by beachhead for external conquest from the sea were both very difficult to sustain for very long before the 1950s—until the fresh invention of helicopters were used in war for the first time in world history in the Korean War (1950–1953). Even American General MacArthur's famous invasion at Incheon from September 15–19, 1950 was lucky to be successful instead of stuck in quicksand of the mudflats around the terminus of the Han River there, as they were originally relying on faulty Japanese maps before reconnoitering the area themselves. Mudflats always accumulate worldwide where any river meets the sea. However, Korea's tidal mudflats on the west and south are immense, like at Mokpo's Suncheon Bay, or at Saemangum on the West Sea, or at Incheon at the terminus of the Han River. These Korean tidal mudflats on the south and west coasts get immense and complex because they are rarely disturbed at their river terminuses on the coast by the low probability of oceanic storms or earthquakes, unlike other places in the world where such events disperse mudflats into the deeper ocean faster than floods can make them grow from upriver. Korea's mudflats at several river terminuses are wide hourglasses of sand extending far into the ocean at low tide for many kilometers in all directions. Time is measured here by stable centuries of many meters of deep gray silt, with the annual pulse of the monsoon season flushing downriver more silt yet without regular strong typhoons to disperse it. The immense mudflats and their fast receding and encroaching tides create a natural defense against water-based invasions upriver. For example, tides at Incheon can range from 9 to 11 meters in height. However, even if you were successfully to cross the quicksand of several kilometers of shallow mudflats to get to those rare Korean rivers, you would find that Korean river levels are high only during the short month-long pulse of the annual monsoon. So for eleven months of the year Korean rivers themselves are non-navigable and naturally blocked with ever-changing sandbars in very low levels of water. As a result, Korean rivers are poorly navigable due to lack of regular rain for the whole year that would keep any river deep, straight, and navigable.

Some argue such geological and geopolitical isolation on the Korean Peninsula contributed to Korea's unique (and almost uniquely bad) cultural and political evolution. This became a self-enforcing system of four geopolitical factors: (1) bizarrely long dynasties of 600 to 900 years (when typically a state or a dynasty rarely lasts more than 200 years on average in other places of the world), (2) resulting in very weak kings (as invasions rarely happen, so who requires a strong king) combined with very strong stable aristocracies of inherited cultural power motivated by petty divisive national politics among the same families across 2,000 years, instead of reforming with each fresh state; and (3) a growing hereditary slave underclass approaching nearly 30% of the population starting from the 700s to its height in the late 1700s yet without many religious or underclass rebellions since external interruptions from subaltern ideas to motivate them were hard to find. Thus external interruptions and internal ferment are regularly associated. Without world history regularly mixing up the pot with cultural innovation, the Korean culture became very stable for better or for worse. However, it was hardly stagnant as long-term conserved Korean collective innovation in technology was unparalleled in such a stable situation, as discussed later. World history only entered the Korean peninsula durably in the disruptions and cultural innovations from European global trading in the middle 1800s, particularly in the form of different forms of Christianity from different European national zones. This finally gave Korean peasants subaltern ideas of how to organize their lives differently and autonomously against Joseon dynasty elites and their cultural hegemony. As Palais writes:

> No other country in East Asia had a slave holding society worthy of the name…[with about]…one-third of its population as chattel slaves let alone the three-quarters registered in the extant census for a small suburban area of the capital of Seoul in 1663….Why did Buddhism, praised for its effect in ameliorating the harsh terms of punishment in Goryeo, play no role whatsoever in condemning slavery, and in fact participated in it by owning monastery slaves in abundance? Why did Neo-Confucianism, praised for its absorption with moral criteria of behavior, fail to protest the condemnation of the [hereditary] innocent children of slaves to lives of undeserved servitude? This is not the proper occasion to delve into answers to those two questions, but we must take note of the severity of status discrimination and social hierarchy in Korean society after the tenth century and the dependence of the ruling class on slave labor. (Palais, 1995, pp. 414–417)

However, to venture a quick hypothetical answer to Palais's question about the origins of this uniquely high scale of enslavement, status discrimination, and social hierarchy in a homogeneous culture, it is argued that ancient Korean cultural stability for all four of these factors allowed the culture to drift into more repressive aristocratic political economic and cultural settlements, resting upon a growing slave society without external interruptions to this trend by opportunistic historical events. Without many external interruptions, there was little call for interrupting this situation with strong royal jurisdictions that potentially could have ameliorated it in the wider national interest for defense. Thus, a lack of many kinds of external interruptions mentioned above, including invasions and cultural innovations, interact and perpetuate weak kings and a stronger aristocratic political and economic settlement. All of these four factors facilitating a homogeneous culture at Korean levels of extremes are part of the same issue of why an ever-growing aristocratic factionalism dominated the culture for two millennia and why an ever-deepening hereditary slavery dominated the culture for nearly one millennium.

Few systemic events in Korean history encouraged a strong king to exist to rally people to rigor of trying a different political alliance of common civil rules in a consolidated external defense, that would have reduced the autonomous power and wealth of the aristocracy. Invasions and external interruptions require competence in life and death situations. Finding competence regularly requires a political alliance of meritocratic, bureaucratic, and military defense and its centralized military king and more rigorous taxes. All of this hard-to-maintain competence was rarely required for Korean defense, and Korea was never interested in external offense either. Instead, taxes were accumulated and assessed in increasing corrupt ways just to benefit each region's aristocratic wealth. In short, rare examples of external war may be an odd gift to peasants and slaves, in retrospect, as only during troubled times underclasses can effectively have political autonomy to rise meritocratically or to break stable bonds to an aristocracy in fresh settlements that improve and express their material interests. So, without long external wars or long internal invasions, Korean culture had few 'freeing interruptions' against a systemic drift of growing Korean aristocratic precedence, durable cultural hierarchy, deepening slavery, and a penchant for weak (or else, murdered) kings.

Plus, even if foreign land armies were historically successful in getting a foothold in the Korean Peninsula, Korea has been more of a gravesite of empires instead of a colony for them. Much of East Asian history can be written as a series of failed invasions of Korea over millennia: whether from China in the early Qin dynasty that led to its collapse after a failed Korean invasion, or the Chinese Sui dynasty that attempted conquest of Korea later in the early 600s CE that led to its collapse and replacement by the Chinese T'ang dynasty, or the somewhat-failed Mongol conquests of the 1300s impossible to continue on horseback across mountains without modern levels of naval support and against Korean guerilla warriors like snipers, skillful at firing the bow from their safely distant mountain redoubts. Therefore, Korea even stopped the Mongols in a stalemate. Instead of a true conquest, only a Mongol military oversight was created over still-existing Korean weak kings that worked through equally sponsored Korean military families like the Choe in later Goryeo. This simply mimicked earlier domestic Korean relationships of weak kings as figureheads yet with the Choe military family as overlords of Korean kings after 1258, working with the Mongols, instead of a direct Mongol conquest winning by changing the dynasty in Korea (Palais, 1995).

Plus, since Korea is a highly mountainous terrain with only a few river valleys suitable for agriculture at any scale, it makes it difficult finding food for any potentially marauding and conquering armies—that is, if you could even get your armies across treacherous oceans, then across quicksand mudflats, then up silt-filled rivers, and then across endless mountain chains already filled with ancient well-guarded redoubts of well-practiced archers. Mountains are difficult terrain for horses, and mountains make it easy for Koreans to hide whenever threatened. In this way, a previously successful Mongol conquest and destruction of all states across the whole Eurasian continent in the late 1200s to the 1300s was stopped in the Korean Peninsula via a nearly 25-year war stalemate that ended in a frustrated marriage of Mongol royal houses and Choe martial proxies with resilient Korean Goryeo aristocrats still against them, instead of a true external conquest seeing the end of Korean state autonomy. For an apt analogy, the Korean Peninsula looks like the inflamed appendix of all Asian empires (including the Eurasian-wide Mongol Empire) rupturing their digestion and power drive, which painfully reverberates back home and leads to their death. For another analogy, Korea may look small, though it is a hard bite to swallow for the many Asian empires that repeatedly choked and died attempting more than they could chew.

For over two thousand years, only the T'ang dynasty in the 600s was successful in conquering parts of the Korean Peninsula. This was only because the T'ang was in league with (the soon Unified) Silla in a mutual military consolidation of the Korean Peninsula instead of China conquering it alone. Next, 400 years later, a few Khaitan invasions from the area of Manchuria around the 1000s were temporarily successful, yet soon left. Next, nearly 600 years later, the Japanese samurai in the Imjin War of the 1590s were (briefly) successful in conquest of small parts of Korea for a few short years, though were unable to advance temporary gains. Only in the early twentieth century's industrial warfare with steamships did the same aristocratic Japanese samurai houses as the 1590s, now in charge of a modern industrial and mass military state, return to be successful in conquering all of Korea and reducing it to Japanese colonial status. The same imperial aristocrats were arrogant uncompromising fascists at home fighting against a growing Japanese democracy and a global Communist movement. However, even Japan's colonization of Korea was very brief, from 1910 to 1945. The attempt at Korean cultural genocide started as late as 1938 by banning the Korean language in that year and as late as 1939 banning Korean family names, so that heightened Japanese cultural stress during the Korean colonial period was briefer than a decade.

Korea was freed as a result of the Japanese losing World War II instead of by large internal organized resistance and thus there was a large power vacuum. Much of the southern half of Korea started to be administered by village grass roots associations without a state after 1945—repressed by the Americans starting in 1946. This repression caused massive protests and pushed some southern Koreans to be pro-Communist allies. Equally enticing to southern zone Koreans, the northern zone administered by the Soviet Union already had a land distribution to the tillers/peasants in 1946, yet nothing similar in land distribution would happen for two more years in the southern zone of Korea until 1948. This further aggregated support from this southern zone for the Soviets in the north during this period. Equally during this period, in an echo of the Korean/Japanese past, what happened to Japan as it left Korea after World War II was a mirror to what happened to Japan as it left Korea in the early 1600s. The Japanese aristocratic samurai dynasties once more returned chastened to their islands, and once more demobilized their armies into a peaceful society that renounced elite wars. Throughout world history, only U.N.-allied and American-led armies had it lucky in modern invasions of Korea in the early 1950s in the Korean War (1950–1953). Americans landed oddly in Incheon under General MacArthur in September 1950, which can be interpreted as foolishly risky or brilliantly surprising depending on your point of view—or dangerously both. It was perhaps one of the worst locations for an invasion in modern history and yet became the most surprisingly well executed invasion in modern history. Given great dangers of being bogged down trying to reach land across kilometers of mudflats of quicksand, the invasion was practiced in other similar areas first, and the actual area was reconaissanced for weeks beforehand—finding among other points that their Japanese tidal data maps had been wrong. However, MacArthur's landing at Incheon happened at the best time, at a low tide in more stable mudflats. Plus, Communist (later North) Korea gave up this marginal area of Incheon without a fight. No one was fighting MacArthur as he landed, as the Communists thought invasion there was impossible to do. Thus, outside of the Port of Pusan, the zone of Incheon became the only beachhead for the American army simply because the Communists failed to expect such a suicidal invasion across quicksand mudflats would be contemplated much less could succeed.

In summary, Koreans lived most of the last 2,000 years in this synergistic fourfold context that made geopolitical conquest difficult and made Korea's resulting homogeneous culture hard to shift from aristocratic precedence. Most horse-riding armies of the pre-modern world lacked strong ocean going navies (much less modern air forces). However, by the early twentieth century, the Japanese Empire had steamships that could power against any fast moving tides and had industrial production. Next, the Korean War from 1950–1953 was the first war in world history to add helicopters to an industrial invasion mix that could conquer the mostly roadless mountainous Korean geography by simply flying over it and landing in any small spot available. Thus, the earlier Korean isolation against external interruption was never the same after the period from 1910 to the 1950s due to the outside world's technical advances. The modern world's combination of such invasion tactics truly started to disrupt Korean geopolitical isolation only in the early twentieth century—by removing its previously solid defense for at least 600 years. Equally, Korea's status as a linguistic isolate mentioned above is another proof of a long-term geographical isolation on the Korean Peninsula that became later an added geopolitical isolation. The odd and durable Korean language itself is a proof of the many failed or temporary foreign invasions of the peninsula.

2.3.4 Ancient Homogeneous Culture, Yet Missing an Aristocratic Leadership

From world comparisons, it was argued above that five factors contribute to a uniquely stable and ancient durable Korean culture. This section elaborates the fourth point about a homogeneous culture being socially self-replicated by two paths: a more delocalized aristocratic one and a more geographic agricultural peasant one, both in an overarching governmental arrangement. Modern Korea only maintains one level of this ancient cultural self-replication via rural village life since so much on the aristocratic cultural level and the older Joseon dynastic state was radically lost during the Japanese Empire (1910–1945) and into the First Republic of Korea (1948–1960). (Later, a fifth mechanism is discussed for a homogeneous culture being self-replicated in a more active and inventive sense by its unique and ongoing technical-oriented collective innovation to defend itself and to improve itself that helps to preserve such cultural isolation.)

Ongoing themes of the Korean homogeneous culture that are important in this section are: (1) ethnic homogeneity without historically large minority ethnic experiences, (2) ongoing deep taboos against marrying into one's 'own' extended families called bongwan localism (despite these extended families now numbering in the millions of Koreans sometimes), (3) how Confucian education has become the surrogate king in the culture, creating in the past and in the present unique overlapping networks between older mentors and younger students that last their whole lives. These client-mentor networks are a coveted and ever-gathered treasure, good or bad, conserving links durably for a Korean's whole life from elementary school, to high school, to the military, to the university, to the private business world, and even into public government. All of this creates the fourth factor of the Korean culture: (4) crony networks, equally for good and for bad. They are bad of course for the systemic corruption that can be catalyzed out of such an arrangement, found in interpersonal relationships (Kim & Whitaker, 2013), and they can be bad for the whole country's developmental paradigm (Kang, 2002). They are equally a force of good given a homogeneous culture encourages more collective innovation if there are many more cross-cutting 'weak link' networks held for life throughout the whole county (Grannovetter, 1973). This allows quick collaboration toward assembling fresh team-based or national goals from networks of trust already established.

On the other hand, deeper networks of loyalty, trust, and personal sponsorship exist for Korean interpersonal networks far more than they do to for the lesser loyalty to the abstract nation. So, when these crony networks were merged into the modern Korean military, such networks of trust have built three coups against the Korean constitution: the military coups of May 16, 1961, then December 12, 1979, and then May 17, 1980.

However, the most surprising historical loss and challenge to these Korean crony networks was losing its core coordinating crony feature: an ancient durable aristocracy. The Korean rural village cultural transmission is intact and even strengthened by policies starting from the Japanese Empire to try to demote aristocratic resurgence, and then strengthened more by the several years of direct regional grass roots autonomy by default between 1945 to 1947 throughout the Korean Peninsula when it was a stateless zone before both North Korea (1948 to present) or the South Korean First Republic (1948–1960). However, from 1948 through 1960, an aristocratic resurgence was further demoted in retrospect ironically by U.S. military allies in 1948 and then by the remaining Korean aristocrats themselves by 1953. In trying so hard to help the Korean aristocracy survive in republican political power after World War II, both the Americans and the Korean aristocrats ended their own economic kinds of power throughout South Korea by encouraging small-holders in land distributions and ended their own military kinds of power by encouraging a more meritocratic military without a return to aristocratic family oversight like that which had existed in the late Joeseon dynasty's military. The irony has been that for the older Korean aristocracy to try to survive in politics in the First Republic, it removed its own rural economic power and sold it away to agricultural smallholders to try to create wider ambivalence in the population against a socialist cultural revolution and removed itself mostly from any military oversight at all. The last Korean aristocrat to head any Korean army was Lee Beom-seok, descendant of Sejong the Great's fifth son Gwangpyeong Daegun. However, the only organization he really founded (with Ahn Ho-sang) was the Korean National Youth Association on October 9, 1946, which was a fascist, right-wing group of militarized youth. Getting funding from U.S. General MacArthur in Japan directly, the national group that was said to number about one million by 1949 was eventually dissolved by Rhee and absorbed into the unified Great Korean Young Adults Association in 1949—only after resistance was shown by Lee to Rhee's idea of absorption. At the same time as it was dissolved, Lee Beom-seok was fired from his position of Defense Minister under President Rhee. From this point, most Defense Ministers of the First Republic were non-aristocrats, until Rhee's support only for his fellow distant aristocratic relative Lee Ki-poong for the position in the late 1950s. In general, examining early biographies of the head Chief of Staff of the modern Republic of Korean Army (ROK) or the appointed civilian Defense Ministers, it shows overall both positions were filled with men of mostly humble families and presumably meritocratic origins. The irony is many modern nations *struggle against* their modern leaders for an agricultural land reform (like the Philippines, or like many Latin American states for example), or they struggle against an inherited leadership like a caste built into the military establishment. However, Koreans (as well as Taiwanese, Japanese, and Malaysians) got some of these rare agricultural land distribution reforms in a *giveaway from* their modern leaders, and their modern republican military establishment remained severed from its deeply aristocratic past as well. Koreans first got land distributions by Japanese confiscations of Korean aristocratic land and by small accommodations to rural peasants at the hands of Japanese occupiers trying to quell uprisings against them in the Korean Peninsula (yet mostly the Japanese were consolidating land tenures to themselves), then later by the U.S. military itself in 1948, and then by conservative Korean leaderships between 1950 to 1952 in the midst of the Korean War (1950–1953) afraid of leftist cultural revolution and support for North Korea in the South and thinking they had better sell land during the war just in case the North Koreans won the Korean War and took it away from them anyway.

The policy of land distribution both wrecked larger aristocratic landholdings and enhanced a rural homogeneous culture in economic influence. Later, this set the stage for the more hybrid political and economic model with a strong regional culture versus a top down political revolution and military coup around Park (1961–1963) that was trying to encourage an economic revolution toward an export-led economy while itself trying to avoid a cultural revolution. The continuing policies around militarist President Park (1963–1979) left the rural nation only culturally *improved*, instead of culturally *dismantled*, because policies for the export-led economy were increasingly mixed with greater respect for (winning votes from) small-scale artisans and agriculturalists and supporting conservative rural village-based grass roots development that was trying to counter the vote power of increasingly urban economic class conflict that was voting for Park's political opposition epitomized in Kim Dae-jung.

As noted above, the other irony is many modern nations struggle against an oligarchic crony military of wealthy families and their sponsors, while the Korean military after World War II developed a bureaucratic army training through several major academies and had a more meritocratic staffing from the First Republic onward. This means the modern Korean military lacks any ancient Korean aristocratic oversight like you might expect given other clear continuities of ancient to modern aristocratic military officer dynamics in states like Prussia into the Third German Reich, the ancient samurai dynasties into the modern Japanese Empire, or the modern British Empire. Historically, this break happened because of three main rationales.

First, the break between governmental and military aristocracies had already existed in Korea for a thousand years. This had weakened status of the military administrators compared to the civil administrators in ancient Korea. The ancient Korean aristocracy really was called the 'yangban,' literally the "two branches" of the civil service administration (munban, 문반, 文班) and the military service administration (muban, 무반, 武班). The term and administrative use of yangban is as old as Goryeo (918–1392). The design was to keep a royal position in charge by having divided administrations, instead of facing off a potentially greater power of a consolidated aristocracy. Even though both civil and military positions were means-tested and based on separate civil or military tests to achieve such an administrative position that people could fail, the same families over generations came to specialize in one or the other of the branches of the dynastic civil service. Plus, it has already been noted there was a relatively weak requirement to have a large or disciplined military in dynastic Korean history except for occasional decades.

Second, by the late 1800s the Korean military and its dynastic administrators were called on to upgrade into a strong modern army like China was attempting with its new army under Yuan Shikai. However, the Koreans ultimately failed by 1907—greatly by lack of international allies for the project at the time. The catalyst for this military modernization in the 1890s in Korea was how it was the Chinese army under General Yuan Shikai that was called upon to invade Joseon in the early 1890s, by the Joseon king himself, to crush the religious/nationalist Tonghak Rebellion, since the ancient Joseon military generally was defecting to the rebels. Another catalyst for this Korean military modernization was how the Japanese army could so easily invade Korea. The invited Chinese invasion of Korea catalyzed the uninvited modern Japanese invasion of Korea. The Japanese soon crushed the Chinese army to the shock of the world, and then the Japanese army crushed the Tonghak rebels for the Korean king (Whitaker, 2012). Fearful of growing Japanese military power, the last years of the Joseon dynasty did see it try to rebrand itself as the Korean Empire (1897–1910) with a partial modernization of ten military battalions on Western models, and other ideas of modernization in economics and education were attempted.

However, third, this native Korean military modernization was frustrated by growing U.S.-Japanese alliances as noted in the Taft-Sakura agreement of 1905 that placed Korea firmly under Japanese authority for exchange of Japan accepting the Philippines under American authority. The Russian Czar refused to intervene to protect Korean autonomy even though he disliked Japanese incursions in Korea itself. Plus, Joseon/Korean emissaries sent to the early international court in the Hague to complain about the illegal Japanese invasion were rebuffed. This was at time when the Chinese coast was already *legally* occupied by a growing Japanese Empire and its military from the Boxer Protocol of 1901, when eight different nations (including Japan) were called upon by the Qing Dynasty to put down the nationalist Chinese Boxer Rebellion. Isolated of all foreign allies, the Korean ministers in 1905 signed the Eulsa Treaty with Japan that ended diplomatic sovereignty of Korea, making Japan officially Korea's international representative. The first Japanese Resident-General of Korea, Itō Hirobumi, arrived in 1906. Another Korea-Japan Treaty of 1907 began to place Japanese legally in both civil administrative and military administrative positions in the Korean Empire. The Korean military then was disbanded on August 1, 1907. Even the elite unit of the modernized Korean army, the Jinwidae that was tasked for protecting the Korean king, was disarmed. Thus, Japanese soldiers from 1907 were defending (controlling) the Korean imperial palace itself. It was at this point that more nationalist Koreans or the residual Korean Imperial Army members started to organize their own peasant militias to fight the Japanese and to protest. The Japanese military started to repress these actions successfully in 1909. Many independence-minded Koreans fled to Chinese Manchuria (already legally occupied by Russia under the Boxer Protocol) or to China itself. By a treaty of August 22, 1910, the Korean Empire was formally ended and annexed to Japan, and it was announced on August 29, 1910.

In short, there was hardly a strong aristocratic martial culture in the Joseon dynasty anyway, and its attempts at a modern organizational military were disbanded by the Korea-Japan Treaty of 1907. All of these points are why an aristocratic military service was hardly seen as a strength in traditional Korea or was missing in modern Korea after World War II. Instead, given the successful conquest of Korea by Japan, the ideals of the Japanese military service and Japanese versions of economic modernization were paramount in Korea. Even later President Park himself was very much influenced by his own Japanese military officers training. So the Korean military aristocracy outmoded itself in institutional loss of capacities of violence and thus the leadership of violence, and then demoted itself in economics in the 1950s with land distributions while the First Republic under President Syngman Rhee was trying to bring back only the civil aristocratic families in political/cultural leadership. This included Rhee himself who had studied and passed the Joseon gwageo (the dynasty's civil service exam) just before it was ended in the 1890s. Plus, given the lack of financial capital and less priority on economic exports in the First Republic, the revanchist Korean aristocracy after World War II lacked alignments with native or international merchants that could have saved them with vast injections of subsidies to keep them in power after the Revolutionary Military Committee's developmental coup of 1961 against the short lived Second Republic (1960–1961).

Plus, after 1961, Korea maintains culturally good points of losing its civil and military aristocratic heritage. There is a lack of an imperialist and aristocratic mindset in the modern Korean military unlike typically seen in other homogeneous cultures and countries that keep arrogant aristocratic heritages as an animating drive of their imperialism and their anti-democratic politics. This is seen in Great Britain, Japan, or even in the late German Third Reich. The German Empire lost their Kaiser after World War I though failed to lose their Prussian Junker aristocratic elite. You can see a neo-aristocracy of wealth developing into an American empire abroad from the 1890s, though these corporate capitalist banking dynasties shared a common intermarriage culture (sometimes with the imperial British aristocracy) from a mostly rarified Yankee Ivy League school background or a shared Anglo-British university background like the Rhodes Scholars.

For a generalization, when such anti-democratic dreams of empire are kept alive at home or abroad by an excessively inbred culture of older or refreshed aristocratic families, they breed and brood with each other on how to strategically (re)gain more oligarchic power against modern democratic national states in which they dislike being just equals instead of unjust overlords. There are deep connections between the Japanese aristocracy hating their growing national democracy and this group seeking out greater wealth and power overseas, in development of an autonomous Japanese imperialism that they would exclusively control in the late 1800s into the early 1900s for instance (Kaplan & Dubro, 2003). This is the same dynamic that led to the worst abuses of the Belgian Congo when a relict Belgian King Leopold in a modern democracy refused to accept such a relict status and instead began to be in competition with his own growing democratization at home by expanding a personal wealth from exploitation of an expanded terrorized colony only under his personal jurisdiction in the African Congo (Hochschild, 1998).

It is argued that South Korea has thankfully lost both its older politically active and culturally active aristocracy and royalty, yet thankfully kept its homogeneous culture and its collective innovation that has been so useful in holding together fast development drives for the long term. Typically, losing your oligarchic aristocracy and royalty means only benefits, instead of drawbacks, since a nation only loses a major source of modern anti-democratic politics whether seen in the external violence of colonization or in the internal violence against political enemies. Even if some of these families still pride themselves as Korean aristocrats as Kim Jong-pil did openly (1926–2018)—he of the line of the Gimhae Kim's which is the old ruling house of Gaya and not so incidentally the founder of the Korean CIA under President Park—they have been in the background instead of in the foreground of Korean modern power since 1961. For a counterfactual argument, let us imagine if aristocratic Syngman Rhee had remained in power after 1960. Despite being the first modern Korean President, Syngman Rhee (1948–1960) attempted to arrange older aristocratic families as a renewed aristocracy. With Rhee's aristocratic lineage tracing back to the first son of King Taejong (1367–1422, r. 1400–1418), the third king of the Joseon Dynasty (1394–1895/1910), who was the father of King Sejong the Great (1397–1450, r. 1418–1450), it is perhaps understandable how Rhee was chosen as a senior elder to be the Speaker of the Assembly for the Provisional Government after World War II. Rhee oversaw the Korean National Convention that wrote the Korean constitution. It adopted his own tabled idea that the National Assembly alone should choose the President instead of having popular elections for President. Rhee soon was chosen as the first (and only) Assembly-elected President under the First Republic of Korea (1948–1960)—under undemocratic rules he tabled himself that made it into the constitutional framework. Even if from 1952 there was a sop towards wider open democratic systems of multi-party elections in attempts to legitimate the South Korean government in the middle of the Korean War (1950–1953), Rhee by 1954 ended that sop as soon as possible by changing the constitution once more to make it possible for him to be President for life, and then was trying to set up his own distant royal blood relative Lee Ki-poong as the next President by the late 1950s. Regardless of this, soon after his inauguration in 1948 with his increasing crackdowns on communist agitation and on grass roots autonomy, the previous global allies of the United States and the Soviet Union in World War II (1939–1945) split in the next Korean War (1950–1953). Both the United States (under U.N. military authority) and the Soviet Union (supporting Kim Il Sung's one-party state Communist government) descended upon the Korean Peninsula. This made the Soviets and later the Communist Chinese as the global allies of North Korea versus the United States and the United Nations as the global allies of South Korea. Both geopolitical powers were vying to have a single military consolidation over the whole Korean Peninsula. However, both failed. The Korean War decimated even more of a residual aristocratic land tenure and power as well. Rhee himself kept trying to restart the Korean War as soon as possible for conquest of North Korea after 1953. Unlike other international armies that signed the Korean War armistice in 1953, Rhee's South Korea did not sign the armistice. Only once aristocratic Rhee was out of power by 1960, a truer truce between North Korean and South Korea could be held more effectively. Rhee's aristocratic disdain on having limitations to his personal plans for more war (assisted by widely-felt rigged elections in the First Republic to maintain his power) was jettisoned after 1960. However, in the wider world, other aristocracies' dreams of empire and hatred of representative democracy are kept alive by the still excessive powers of the oligarchic British or Japanese families in their own countries. At least South Korea can stop worrying about this factor at home, though North Korea (and thus South Korea anyway) does have to worry about it with North Korea's renewed military aristocracy of oligarchic families there.

2.3.4.1 Ethnic Homogeneity Without Minority Experiences

In short, in part because of these split cultural dynamics of the loss of an aristocracy as a power of veto economically and militarily, and with a grass roots rural culture strengthened by land distributions, South Korea became a radically developed country in a short amount of time and yet remains a deeply ancient conservative nation, culturally. This split heritage of truly radical and innovative top-down political and economic revolution yet cultural conservatism is crucial to understanding the unique story of both the economic Korean Miracle and the cultural Korean Wave.

In Korea, what encourages this cultural conservatism is that there are no effective historical minorities at all to catalyze places for durable individual or cultural innovation. This only slightly began to change in the modern era after the 1950s around the interactions of Koreans durably with U.S. military personnel or around modern 'Korean Chinese' that found themselves surprisingly 'living in China' after borders were drawn for the consolidated Chinese revolution of 1949 and decades later would become guest workers in South Korea. Plus, there are small groups of refugee North Koreans in South Korea as well. By 2007, the total of all foreign nationals in South Korea reached 1 million people, and then 2 million people by 2016, and over 2.5 million people by 2021. After 2021, the scale of foreign nationals started to fall once more in South Korea however. Note the majority of 'intercultural' experiences in modern Korea are with other versions of Koreans—North Koreans or Chinese Koreans—with the latter being the largest ethnic minority in South Korea with more than 500,000 of that approximately 2.5 million people in a nation of approximately 51 million people. This is hardly very diverse now.

Historical Korea would be even less diverse and more homogeneous. Durable large subaltern underclass cultural dynamics failed to exist. There were no historically special trading groups, no large clear ethnic minorities or guest workers, and no clear religious and language differentiation. There were historically marginalized 'baekjeong' groups that took the dirty and marginal jobs, coming from captured troops from a Khitan invasion in the 1000s that were forced later to live outside agricultural settlements. However, baekjeong were hardly sizable enough to cause internal dissention in the main homogenous Korean amalgam of Buddhist, Confucian, and shamanist culture. Plus, religious underclass dynamics seen in many countries' political and culturally revolutionary events had been missing in all Korean history until the Tonghak movements of the late 1800s. This is because Korean religion became an easy mixture of an ongoing heritage of shamanism to which was added Buddhism by the 600s CE and to which was added Confucianism by the early 1400s CE. This amalgam became the background Korean religious culture making Koreans unique since none of these three religious principles became a differentiated or sizable subset of believers distinct or regionally differentiated from other Koreans.

The only kinds of ancient internal discrimination of 'Koreans upon Koreans' was threefold: hereditary Korean debt slavery upon other Koreans that disappeared from the late 1700s through the early twentieth century, occupational-based discrimination against a tiny minority of 'baekjeong' who were an 'untouchable' occupational caste of a tiny resettled ethnic minority from captured Khaitans who invaded Korea and failed in the 900s CE, and durable modern regional discriminations against the people of Jeolla-do, a province of the southwest. In its internal conquest in the late 1300s, the state of Joseon was ranged against this less-easily-conquered or integrated area of the southwest of the Korean Peninsula for a long time. The geography of this zone's ancient Koreans lived in an even more inaccessible, mountainous, and island-filled province that knew the area well enough to flee temporarily if tax gatherers or army drafts came around. As a result, the Joseon dynasty rejected representation at court from this Jeolla-do region at all. Such ancient and modern discrimination against Koreans from Jeolla-do still exists even in the urban industrial hierarchies of Korea (Yu, 1990).

In modern times, there was little religious opposition or collective sense of a religious underclass until the late 1800s. It only started when Western foreigners came to Korea with the different religious ideas of Christianity. Koreans of the 1800s, when viewing the different cultural principles of Christianity given its religious doctrine of the equality of all believers, felt this idea to be totally revolutionary against all Confucian status hierarchies with their justified inequalities instead. Thus there was mostly a peasant love of these principles of Christian equality while Korean elites felt xenophobic against Protestantism and Catholicism as attested to by the many Korean martyrs to this Catholic faith in Korea, killed by the Joseon dynasty. However, even the secret underground Tonghak movement was a deeply xenophobic reaction to Christianity and to all foreigners in Korea itself despite Tonghak taking up parts of Christian social doctrines of equality of all (Korean only) believers and a kind of economic democracy among peasants.

Regardless of Tonghak's important influence on modern Korean nationalism (Whitaker, 2012), the grander influence in modern Korea is the continuity with the Joseon dynasty's many centuries of encouragement of Confucianism from the late 1300s. Confucianism yielded a public harmony (and justified public bullying) based on strict and proper hierarchical behaviors based on age seniority and male seniority. Modern Korea's ethnic homogeneity has *supercharged this now in urban areas* as well, instead of it fading away in urban areas or only seen in rural areas at all. A second level of how ethnic homogeneity was supercharged was when this ancient culture *began to be digitally linked in modern mobile networks of telecommunication* from the 1980s through the early 2000s—with more discussion of that in the later chapters about the digital side of the Korean Wave.

Europeans of the late 1800s were fascinated by the fresh social phenomena of larger cities in their midst. It was felt by early social theorists that the development of modern urban themes of individual freedom, fresh cultural innovations, and wider cultural options were universally the same in large urban sites the world over. This is what fascinated the early social scientists of Europe like de Tonnies, Durkheim, or Simmel in the late 1800s to the early twentieth century. However, despite large urbanization, these themes of individual freedom and cultural innovation are greatly missing in both Koreas. To use de Tonnies's term, it is argued that particularly in South Korea, despite fast industrial development and urbanization, it remains more of a "Gemeinschaft" society even in modern industrial and urban areas as much as rural areas. This is defined as a society of inherited personalized relationships, honors, and ancestral family ties. This is contrasted to what generally was developing in Europe and the Atlantic states and cities, then called a "Gessellshaft" society of individual rational contracts, temporary relationships, and secular goals. European theorists liked to think that such a Gesselshaft society was created in all cases of urbanization, industrialization and modernization as simply caused by living in big cities—because that kind of outcome is what all the Atlantacist/European cases showed.

However, when we think about Korea's equal urbanization, industrialization, and modernization, it is clear that changes to Gesselschaft do not to occur unless other key factors are there like various ethnic, religious and cultural pluralities that take place within such industrialization and modernization in big cities. So the argument is that the first generations of social scientists were wrong in their attributions of 'modernism' and individual freedoms and cultural changes as merely caused by industrialization and urban living. This was because they only sampled European experiences of industrialization, modernization, and urban living. Thus with limited samples, they mispecified the origins of "Gesselschaft" as coming innately out of experience of an industrialized urban society, when instead such European relationships really came from European cultural heterogeneity in the crucible of all cases of Atlantacist/European experiences of industrialization, cultural innovation and big cities from the 1800s onward.

To the contrary, both Japan and North/South Korea show the falsity of this old sociological argument about 'effects of industrialization and big cities toward Gesselschaft' because Japan and Korea did both, yet they remain very much Gemeinschaft societies in large urban areas due to ongoing homogeneity instead of cultural plurality in such developments. Plus, the idea of three different kinds of innovation in different cultural circumstances (collective, individual, and cultural) helps avoid the morally dichotomized debate that early sociologists had about whether urban or rural cultural economies were morally better or more innovative. Gemeinshaft arrangements of rural solidarity and homogeneous cultures have more collective innovation, while Gesselschaft contexts arise out of cultural pluralism and so tend to have more individual innovation and cultural innovation—though they both have positive innovation drives in them instead of Durkheim's argument that only urban cultures and areas of pluralism do. That is clearly mistaken when looking at Japan, South Korea, or China for that matter.

For instance, to a degree widely unknown to those who admire the cosmopolitan Korean Wave, many millions of modern urban twenty-first century Koreans—the same people sporting smartphones, miniskirts, smart suits, or go to BTS concerts—keep strong family intermarriage taboos that are hundreds of years old (and sometimes thousands of years old) that curtail their choices of marriage partners. Plus, modern Koreans listening to K-pop annually renew ritualized shamanistic-inspired yet formally Confucian ancestor worship at gravesites either when they visit their home village during Chuseok every autumn season or when they visit in other rounds of events throughout their lives like in the Lunar New Year celebrations that equally renew their lifelong educational, extended family, or hometown ties. So, modern Koreans "never let go" of the past or reinvent themselves. They keep friendships from childhood through their whole life. The people that their families married or did not marry centuries earlier remains very important to many. The point of mentioning this is not to lambaste these practices, though to truly understand the cultural forms and the social relations that have made the Korean Wave and, which arguably, have made it more successful than any other countries that have regularly failed at such an export of their culture.

On the other hand, against this reputed harmony, Korea has an ancient and modern problem with a bullying culture in schools, in gender relations, in age hierarchies, and in wider civil life which seems to resonate with the same Confucian hierarchies. This is because those having the higher Confucian status—those who are male, who are older, or who have certain educational or governmental titles (or a combination of all of these like teacher over student, or boss over worker, or even modern elected representative over citizen) not only feel culturally privileged to be above people lower than them, though others are expected to be in an automatic hierarchy of deference to them. If that deference is challenged, it is their cultural hierarchical right to act decisively or dismissively without collaboration, question, or consultation and ignore any complaints. This is because legitimate authoritative leaders give both awards and punishments to those in their networks without redress or without requiring detailed justification. It is mostly the way a Confucian culture works—with required formal public awards and required public shame. So if South Korea gets both public harmony and a bullying culture out of Confucianism, North Korea gets this same negative side of a Confucian heritage blurred with Stalinism. This is what is called North Korea's culture of 'songbun,' a hereditary 'revolutionary' status hierarchy of 'loyal aristocratic' families of the revolution, then next below them, a 'wavering' peasantry group of lower status, and finally a required 'impure' group of ex-landowners and other foreign collaborators that remain the hereditarily shamed underclasses.

However, in addressing the Korean Wave, it is unfairly one-sided to concentrate only on Confucian-based bullying, callousness, hierarchy, or exploitation. This is because in Korea there is a great deal *more* of the same hierarchical sponsorship animating deep and life-long respect, admiration, self-sacrifice, and even love of achieved lifetime mentor-follower bonds as what makes a Korean happy whether they are higher or lower than another. The public/private mentorship links and sponsorships *are what you are as a Korean*, as without them you are literally nothing. This is particularly so because both sides get status and cultural fulfillment from such associations of harmonious yet hierarchical working relationships when expressed in this positive way. Thus South Korea's Confucian civil, gender, and age hierarchy has good and bad points depending how it is expressed. It will be argued that such positive sides of the Confucian hierarchies deeply animate why Koreans are happy to promote the Korean Wave nationally and overseas. While other nations may have to rely on centralized formal advertising for their cultural industries, Koreans as the original 'network society' of crony and tight relationships and mutual aid can help the Korean Wave easily as just part of a proud patriotic sense of being Korean and working with other Koreans. Cultural homogeneity is key to the Korean Wave, and it has only been further supercharged by Korea being an electronically networked society far earlier than other nations. However, for the dark side of this, you can understand how North Koreans escaping to South Korea for freedom are so totally free that sometimes individuals or whole families starve to death alone and unwanted among them. Therefore, most North Koreans refugees in South Korea try to hide the fact that they are from the North—hiding from the culture of the South instead of fear of retribution from the North.

2.3.4.2 Families, Marriage Taboos, and Bongwan Localism

That cautionary tale about North Koreans in South Korea continues into this theme about bongwan localism as the true residual king of Korea. South Korea remains unique here in two ways regarding the Korean Wave. It is uniquely odd for a culture to have a tight-regionalized identity and an exclusionary and blood-based citizenship while so strongly exporting its culture as a global cosmopolitan model for the world. Plus, second, South Korea's strong ethnic sense of identity, homogeneity, and 'connectionism' (Kim & Whitaker, 2013) creates such a strong emotion as the basis of identity of who is in the culture and who is outside of it. This deep internal cultural reference in the Korean culture, and as a consequence in the Korean Wave, hardly is possible to be shared fully by those admiring it from afar despite it being exported.

Regional family ties and its specific regional rules count for very much in modern South Korea. Even as late as 1997, it was illegal for South Koreans of the same bongwan (family/geographic designation) to marry even if they were only weak 'relatives' hundreds of years prior. That was ruled unconstitutional only in 1997. Plus, when Korean females marry, they keep their maiden name. However, this is done not out of modern respect of themselves as females, though because it would be rude to their specific regional fathers and ancestors to hide a male lineage line simply because of a marriage. Only after children are born in a marriage, does the child take up the married father's name, and never the wife doing so. Plus, the Korean census is still based on male-headed households instead of individual Koreans, and Korean females when they marry are shifted from one male-headed household to another instead of the census being a record of Korean individuals. Thus, the idea that 'Korean culture is family' is far deeper than other national cultures. The proper address by a Korean to a Korean stranger who is an older man or woman is still to call the stranger "grandfather" or "grandmother" out of respect, even if the two people have zero blood relationship. Plus, measured from the approximate full population of Korea in 2015, fully 44.4% of the Korean population have only three family names of Kim, Lee, and Park. The family name Kim itself is over 20% of the population. However, each of these three names has very different bongwan and each cannot marry each other without breaking cultural taboos. So, with many Korean clans with over 1 million members—sizable numbers in a country of only 51 million people—there are a lot of marriage rules and taboos. The five largest family clans in Korea over 1 million members of heritage actually are ancient aristocratic or royal lineages like the "Gimhae Kims" (at over 4.4 million people) which can still claim heritage of descent however tenuous to the founding King Suro of Gaya well over two thousand years ago. This results in modern marriage taboos just the same. Even only looking at the top five bongwan with over 1 million members, this is a total of 13.4 million people or fully 26.8% of the national population that would have deep intermarriage taboos of hundreds of years in their extended families. Most bongwan are not allowed to intermarry themselves and have held this 'national' principle for thousands of years. For instance, only in the twentieth century—after nearly 2,000 years of avoidance—did various branches of the 4.4 million members of the Gimhae Kims just now start to intermarry. Plus, more than six million current Koreans (like those of the Gimhae Kim, Gimhae Heo, and Gimhae Lee (Yi) clans) that associate their common bongwan ('geo-biological' lineage) at Gimhae in South Gyeongsang Province, South Korea, additionally *place restrictions on marriage with each other as well*, due to shared ancestors.

So, the modern Korean 'connectionism' animating the Korean Wave simultaneously is deeply reflective of this ancient Korean culture instead of being a separate modern culture in itself. It is built upon having a clear ancient bongwan or regional family loyalty, and a specific regional hometown with annually visited ancestral gravesites exclusively in South Korea. However, as only the first son is required to maintain the ritual gravesite, this means many extended families escape the Chuseok or Lunar New Year gravesite rituals themselves, though it equally places great stress on finding some future son from a future marriage to continue ancestor worship as well.

2.3.4.3 Confucian Education Is King: Mentors and Students for Life, Good and Bad

Plus, Korean culture is equally built on another aspect of Confucian ethics: a lifelong network of ever-growing educational peer-group friendships and teacher-student mentor hierarchies. This extends from whom you went to elementary school with, to high school, to college level, to military schools, as well as the mentor/teacher hierarchies at all levels—preserved, treasured, and kept for life. This educational-teacher status network from childhood to adulthood is added to throughout the lifespan. It is regularly renewed in ongoing annual events at all levels, for life. One of the authors of this book has seen this first hand, as he is an American who married a Korean national. At his rather large wedding in Seoul, he found out that much of the very elderly and happy friends invited as wedding guests by his Korean family were their elementary school friends of over 60 years ago.

After World War II, military school friendships became another modern yet traditionally male Confucian school network of mentors and followers, since all Korean males get hazed through the military by law for around two years from their late teens to age thirty. Only recently, more meritocratic college-level networks of friendship and occupational networks have been added, yet these ride on a deep combined ancestral, regional, and educational mix of connections. However, this deep connectionism in a positive way has been supercharged in an urban homogeneous environment and further supercharged by digital telecommunications. This makes collaboration and networking very easy among Koreans nationally in any field, particularly though hardly exclusive to the cultural industries in the Korean Wave.

2.3.4.4 Crony Networks Can Move Mountains, Good and Bad

As an effect of such deep and lifelong networks, the vast majority of Koreans openly admit to interviewers that they are willing to do illegal acts for their networks like accept bribery from other's in their networks or to give undue preference to them (Kim & Whitaker, 2013). This of course breaks modern rules of neutral meritocracy and equality. However, if they fail to help others in their networks they are really being anti-Korean and risk ostracization themselves.

The tight cronyness of Korean networks is connected with the Korean term "nunchi", which can be defined as the social situation Koreans feel when around those above them in a hierarchy that makes subordinates anticipate feelings of the superior to perform agreeable actions that they think are desired by the superior. On the one hand, nunchi is a collective loyal service instead of only public politeness, and it is expected to be returned later from the other person higher in the hierarchy. As a force of good, nunchi can create a great deal of the collective innovation and teamwork seen in Korea. On the other hand, nunchi means equally Koreans define success as the dream of escaping nunchi-servility to others, and like to be known as and enjoy acting as the highest in the hierarchy without any checks on bad behavior. When Koreans are, *or even when they just feel they are in a special short-term contextual situation*, nunchi can encourage elite deviance, personal bad behavior and thus collective bad behavior. Koreans to signify their felt high status can be brusque, curt, loud, and physically brutal to other Koreans intentionally. Therefore, the flip side of this hierarchical Confucian harmony is a superior's sense of self-justifiable bullying, abuse, and casual exploitation of people that they think are lesser than them or disposable in the hierarchy. This is because it is a power game: Koreans 'pull rank' in a hierarchy regularly to show their status and know that no one culturally (if they are Korean as well) gets any reward for challenging them on elite deviance, and only have a possibility of reward later for aiding and abetting them or at least passively serving them. Thus, when Koreans of high status see behavior in other Koreans that displeases them, they can put on melodramatic airs, scream, and assault people because no one has cultural authority to stop them except someone higher up in the pyramid. From their hierarchical sense of being an untouchable epitome of status and success, or simply age differences in this hierarchy as well, Koreans can be suddenly a lordly teacher over other Koreans, giving punishments or critiques about others' behavior or ordering certain behaviors from others who should immediately comply to confirm their subservience, instead of leaders only distributing rewards. Thus, those that feel highest in a hierarchy ignore nunchi, and act as if all other people simply exist to serve them personally—and in turn many Koreans comply as well. Koreans readily abuse these nunchi networks of expected loyal service to force compliance of individual or even group behaviors that many would think bizarre or even surreal. One author has seen personally an elder Korean grandmother hitting repeatedly a line of young male policemen in the heads and chests, to show them her disfavor with them of their attempt to block a social protest she was attending. The young male police did nothing except stand there and let the grandmother keep hitting them. The lesson here is the Korean hierarchical system and nunchi can be above the police and the law so strongly that it approaches being the main law in Korea in itself.

A now classic example of nunchi networks gone rogue was what Koreans came to know as the 'nut rage' incident. It happened at John F. Kennedy International Airport within Korean Air Flight 086 on December 5, 2014. Miss Cho Hyun-ah, the Vice President daughter of the then Chairman and CEO of Korean Airlines, was flying first class in Korean Airlines from the USA to Seoul. She got so upset with the way macadamia nuts were served in first class to her, in a plastic bag, that even though it was the regulation she was able to pull rank over even pilots to get the massive Airbus A380 plane, the world's largest passenger airliner, to return to the gate to throw off the male cabin crew chief that told her the regulation was actually to serve them in the plastic bag. According to another first class passenger witness of Cho's increasingly heated conversation and interrogation of the cabin crew chief, she physically assaulted him and other employees, threw the bag of nuts at him, and then she fired him and ordered the chief off the plane even though he was correct and his service staff was actually following procedures. Everyone else followed numbly along, including the pilots. Cho ordered the cabin crew service chief Park Chang-jin to kneel in front of her to beg forgiveness as she repeatedly struck Park's knuckles with her digital tablet—a common trope from Korean primary schools where teachers regularly physically discipline and belittle students in the classroom as admonishment to them and as a collective lesson to others watching. Then she fired Park from his job right there in the plane, and ordered the plane to return to the gate to throw him off and change crew. Pilots complied. She had just hijacked an airplane by the power of Korean culture. The plane returned to the gate, aborting its taxi to takeoff, and delaying the flight for about twenty minutes. She had the fired male cabin crew chief Park thrown off the plane and substituted for someone else. In U.S. law what she did in changing the flight path was a major crime, though it was done with the weapon of nunchi instead and thus was a *collective* Korean allowance to let her hijack their airplane, if she wished it. When Cho arrived back in Korea by the flight, nothing happened. Park originally agreed with Korean Air executives to cover up the whole event, though within a few days Vice President Cho started to spread rumors of an affair between the fired Park and the female flight attendant Kim Do-hee who served her the macadamia nuts, so Park initiated a formal complaint with Korean governmental airline regulators. Still nothing happened to Cho, and the crony hierarchy of Korean Airlines defended its own and instead increasingly tried to defame and to demonize Park in order to defend its Vice President Cho against governmental investigation. In fact Korean Airlines contacted the fired Park over a dozen times trying to pressure him to lie to Korean governmental authorities about Cho's illegal and bad behavior, trying to get him to claim that he had somehow voluntarily quit in the middle of the plane as it taxied to take off in the midst of debate over how to serve a bag of macadamia nuts. That was the implausible story that

Korean Airlines wanted Park to give to the Korean government when they questioned him as to the rationale why the plane had to return to the gate. Korean Airlines wanted it to be Park's fault. Plus, two ex-Korean Airline employees were on the Korean government's investigative committee. From upside-down antics like this, Park felt even the governmental investigation was being rigged, so he then contacted the Korean media. After this, it was soon revealed that the haywire Vice President Cho had already attacked another flight attendant in 2013 over badly cooked ramen noodles in flight, and it was revealed that the airline already had covered that up and argued nothing bad had occurred. It was additionally revealed at this point by police that a Korean Air executive illegally ordered employees to delete records about Cho's 'nut rage' incident. This compounded the first crime about endangering aviation safety or illegally altering a flight plan with another crime of destruction of evidence. However, still nothing happened to that executive and Cho. However, given large public embarrassment to Korean Air from the bad media attention of the story, Cho announced on December 10, 2014, that she would resign from all positions in the airline—though she lied and only resigned from the Vice President's position of Korean Air and stayed on as a chairperson of Korean Air, the President of KAL Hotel Network and the President of Hanjin Tour. These are the top people and networks running Korea. This is why great Korean public hostility exists against the chaebol dynasties, though to be fair, this is equally a story of the extent that normal Korean nunchi can compound and create *collective* bad behavior and bad decisions. Eventually criminal charges were filed against Cho within Korea, and Cho almost cost Korean Airlines a fine of $2 million dollars from the United States for endangering its air safety as well. It is hard to say, though there might have been a slight domestic boycott of Korean Airlines in December 2014. As news of 'nut rage' spread, Korean Airline's passenger rates on domestic flights dropped 6.6% in that month compared to the previous year.

About six weeks later, by January 19, 2015, Cho was on trial for endangering aviation safety. She bizarrely denied all charges in court, as was her right, yet this was despite in mid-December 2014 apologizing to the cabin crew by visiting their homes and leaving apology notes since they were not at home. The female flight attendant Kim Do-hee said in court that Cho pushed her and forced her to kneel as well. By February 12, 2015, Cho was found guilty of obstructing aviation safety that changed the airline route, a crime punishable by up to ten years, though she was given only a one year prison sentence. By May 22, 2015, the Seoul High Court instead found her not guilty of changing the airline route, and so the sentence was reduced to ten months, and then the sentence was suspended by the Seoul High Court. Therefore, Cho was released immediately, having only served a few months in jail for hijacking daddy's airline while lawyers tried to get her out of jail on appeal. A separate lawsuit ordered Korean Airlines to pay the flight attendant Park approximately $18,000 for attempting to coerce him to drop the case, and Park was found entitled to a further $27,000 as compensation for Cho's assault.

Imaging having the cultural power of 'nunchi' over others. A Vice Presidential daughter of the CEO can fire cabin crew when going down the runway, and can give willingly-followed orders to pilots to abort takeoff. Then your friends in the hierarchy try to get workers around you to delete information about the whole incident, and then, after being jailed, you get the Seoul High Court to void, reduce, and suspend the sentence to release you immediately. Thus, the 'nut rage' incident popularized another term for the dark side of collective nunchi, now called 'gapjil', defined as the arrogant and authoritarian abuse of underlings in a Korean hierarchy. Therefore, between nunchi and gapjil, there is this pull and push in a Korean social hierarchy to do their personal networks a favor to help them. In this way, for good or for bad, *Koreans together can move mountains*—or collectively allow 'important people' to hijack airlines or make a secret cultural blacklist, whatever the mountain may be.

Plus, Koreans deeply involved in nunchi like pushing their own people from their own hometown, schools, and extended family clans into a better kind of sponsored social or economic position. Plus, such networks can be 'pulled' into doing illegal actions to maintain good ties as well. When Koreans are asked about their penchant to offer bribes or to accept bribes, actually family nepotism by itself was rated by Koreans as the lowest facilitator for such corruption. Instead, it has been found that only the most networked Koreans, with the highest bridging capital *between* "geography, family, and alumni networks" combined, seemed the more important predictor of Koreans to be agreeable in accepting bribes for a fellow network member. In a study on self-admitted prevalence to bribery among South Korean populations compared to their participation in various personal networks:

> …[There is less likelihood of bribery [found in South Korea] if people are more deeply connected [only] to the close-knit ethics of family networks of institutions...than other arrangements of their social life….Alumni networks based on the modern education system have increased the likelihood of bribery particularly when linked to other networks despite assumptions about mass educational systems in modernization theory as being expected to replace the ethics and nepotism of traditional culture and institutions instead of, as here, to enhance geographic reach and scale of their particularistic and collective influence….The effect of the ancestral hometown tie suggests that regionalism [as well] is influential on bribery particularly when tied to alumni associations….What is distinct are patterns that show alumni networks and ancestral hometown networks are influential on bribery in combination with other ties, rather than each having isolated and independent effect. Once more it is the bridging social capital that we stress as important in network subversion instead of any particular single network to blame. When all three networks are combined in relational association, they tend to be more strongly associated with bribery….[T]he theme is that combined bridging networks are influential in network subversion…. (Kim & Whitaker, 2013)

Plus, for another piece of data on the durability of this corruption, Transparency International tracks Koreans' own opinions of themselves over the years in its survey on political corruption. Unlike many other fast developing countries, Koreans feel that the large level of their systemic 'connectionism' and corruption in their country has remained the same since the 1970s. This is despite typically more transparency, meritocracy, and less corruption happening with greater modern economic development, more wealth, and more modern democratic politics. Koreans themselves think that legality and transparency in Korean civil life has not improved despite more democracy and more economic development. This is the negative side of the deep ancestral 'connectionism' and nunchi in ancient Korean culture.

However, as said above, Korean connectionism can have positive sides as well. It will be argued in the next chapter that Korean ethnic homogeneity has been supercharged twice: first by wider urbanization from the 1960s and later by the 1980s onward with growing digital communications. This is contrary to Western theories and stereotypes that 'anonymous' cities or 'alienating' digital worlds of nomads are the main social effects of such changes. However, it is argued here that cultural homogeneity instead supercharges the connectionism possible of an ancient Korean culture when undergoing industrial urbanization or in living in networks of smartphones—as Koreans are doing both deeply at present.

2.4 Durable Ancient Cultural Forms Remain in the Modern Korean Wave

2.4.1 Singing

Some themes of the modern Korean Wave actually are cultural forms with incredibly beautiful continuities over millennia. Foreign records indicate ancient visitors to Korea regularly noted Koreans already loved music and dance more than other cultural motifs. Several still extant ancient Chinese texts give opinions about people living in the Korean peninsula over 1,500 years ago as deeply loving music, singing, and dancing in their popular festivals. This is recorded in "The Three Kingdoms" and the "Weiji Dongyijeon" (魏志東夷傳), written in 297 CE during the Jin dynasty in China (266–420 CE). Even centuries later, 'Koreans that love to sing' still was considered characteristic according to Beom-yeop (范曄) of Southern Song, writing during the Northern and Southern Song Dynasties of China (420–589 CE).

Singing continues in the present, particularly in the Korean Wave. However, the point here is that across the whole of Korean culture at any event is where people will sing, or be persuaded to sing, at almost at any occasion. Modern South Korea is full of rentable 'norae-bang' (singing rooms) for after-dinner family parties or drinking parties. However, competitive singing is the center of cultural attention instead of drinking or partying, because there are many singing rooms that avoid serving alcohol altogether. In the early 1990s, South Korea even had specialized 'norae-bang taxi cabs' you could reserve that were equipped with microphones and extra speaker systems so passengers could sing along to their destination with music accompaniment. It was considered a fad unique to Seoul at first, though spread to some countries after that. Singing is even a key aspect of modern Korean business culture. Before 2018, working hours in Korea were 'restricted' to 68 hours per week, and it was very common for formal workdays and meetings to have rounds of 'required' parties to attend afterwards. In these, business associates unwind, drink, sing, and socialize until late in the evening together. Around 2011, there were around 35,000 norae-bang rooms in South Korea generally for such purpose (Navlakha, 2019). After 2018, with the government restricting working hours to 52 hours per week, there was a slight decline in the number of norae-bang by 2019 to 33,000 rooms. However, singing itself is hardly on the decline, given K-pop revenue soared in the same year showing a growth in recorded music revenues of 44.8% from 2019 to 2020, the highest increase for any country in the world, according to the IFPI Global Music Report (Buchholz, 2021). Plus, Koreans hold many public busking events in city streets, stages in shopping malls, and at private family parties to practice and to show off singing among the public, friends, or work associates. For the total sales of the music industry in South Korea in 2020, music production earned over $2 billion, online music distribution around $1.9 billion, and norae-bang at around $824 million *in that one year alone.* In fourth place were earnings from formal concerts. This shows private and non-professional singing in Korea in norae-bangs is at third place with having more revenue than formal concert music at fourth place (Statista Research Department, 2022). The export sales of the Korean music industry in the same year was less at $679.6 million, showing even the whole global Korean Wave spent less than Koreans themselves on their own cultural music lives, domestically (Statista Research Department, 2022).

Being a good singer is widely admired as bridging 'cultural capital' in South Korea. Singing skill can breach the increasingly deep modern class inequalities in Korea. It can bridge more durable regional divisions in Korean culture. Thus, singing well is a key 'elevator' raising any Korean's status. Even poor struggling manual laborers like Choi Sung-bong, abandoned at an orphanage at age three and later experiencing bouts of homelessness, found his singing skills were a transcendent cultural success. He was 'discovered' while working as a motorcycle delivery driver. He had been forced to drop out of an arts preparatory school earlier due to lack of funds. However Choi, in true studious Confucian Korean fashion, kept practicing opera arias at the top of his lungs above the din of his motorcycle engine up and down public streets on delivery jobs for years. In short, Korean culture may be studious, serious, and bookish—yet it is equally deeply emotional and 'singing-conscious.' Koreans admire and enjoy deep public emotion without shame, both in singers and from audiences easily moved to public tears.

As European media notes "Koreans [can't] stop singing. The launch in 2009 of the TV show '*Superstar K*', Korea's version of the TV show *Britain's Got Talent*, saw more than 700,000 Koreans apply to audition. By the fourth season in 2012 that number had passed 2 million" (Adams, 2022). By 2012, *it was estimated that approximately 15–17% of the entire youth of South Korea had auditioned to sing on this one TV talent show* if we assume applications were mostly under 20 years of age at a time when a total of 12.01 million people were under 20 in that year, with them being around 24.3% of total South Koreans then (Kim, 2020). This percentage *would be closer to 35% of all South Korean youth auditioning* between 2009 and 2012 for this one TV singing talent show, if we total all earlier years and assume repeat auditions were disallowed.

In short, instead of embarrassed about singing in public, Koreans are embarrassed more about refusing to sing when encouraged, or embarrassed more at being unable to sing well. A polished, dramatic, and deeply emotional singing performance in public or private venues of daily life is key to general Korean status and pleasure.

Plus, singing excellence is appreciated and practiced by all age groups in Korea, instead of only being a youth culture. If singing was how ancient Koreans relaxed and had fun, modern Koreans continue the same cultural forms. However, Korean singing occurs now in a nationally competitive way for media status and approval beyond mere local friends and work associates. National digital social media and TV audiences can be more unforgiving, which puts great pressure upon the whole nation and yet is a crucible that creates great competitive heights, results, and skills. Like winning the lottery, the Korean Wave heightened the scale of economic and cultural success that can come from singing, so millions of Koreans work hard and train for it. It is unsurprising how many professional music entertainers there are in Korea and in the Korean Wave, given this wide pool of national amateur talent and diligent practice in the culture at large at all age groups aiding and mentoring each other in a Confucian way as well.

2.4.2 Archery

Archery is another ancient cultural form still practiced in modern Korea. It features prominently in the Korean Wave's many popular historical TV dramas and movies. Like Koreans' love of song over millennia, skill in archery is evident from records of ancient Korean history. Archery skills seem to rank even greater in the past compared to now, despite modern Koreans being recognized for an unparalleled global excellence in archery in the modern Olympic Games for decades without a true challenger whether judged in individual male, individual female, or in team archery. South Korea's unique modern global supremacy in archery is built on a national cultural pressure to excel in it just like their ancestors, and Korean archery seems to be an even higher level of modern national cultural concern than singing.

On the one hand, the culture around archery is wider and older than Korea. This culture around archery influenced all East Asia from the earlier Chinese heritage. It was one of the six skills making a Confucian gentleman: rites, music, archery, charioteering, calligraphy, and mathematics. This cultural ideal existed as early as the Chinese Zhou dynasty before 1200 BCE. However, beyond the training of Confucian gentlemen and warriors, the art of the bow was used as a practice to inculcate moral virtue across all levels of society in ancient East Asia, whether male or female alike, and regardless of age and social class. On the other hand, the story of archery in ancient Korean culture seems an even deeper, longer, and more thorough practice than China whether we look at its wider scale of application, its deeper professional status and mastery, or Korea's unique technological advancements in archery. This is because professional archers were crucial for Korean defense over many millennia of invasions. Korea was invaded many times, yet very few invasions of Korea were ever successful for long. This was in large part due to Korean's extreme skill and technological development in archery.

Historians argue that in a mostly mountainous Korean peninsula with its smaller and less financially powerful states compared to others around it like China, Japan, or various nomadic peoples to the north, over millennia Koreans specialized to become more reliant upon improving archery skills and technological innovation so that they could fire arrows upon invading enemies from safer and longer distances than other armies could achieve, similar to sniper fire today. The famous Korean bow's longer distance capacity for firing arrows put retaliation out of reach from invading nations. Invaders might be larger and more powerful nations though they were always lesser nations of archers. In this way, Koreans could defend their country more economically, instead of creating expensive massed and mounted troops for direct battles (Korean Spirit and Culture Promotion Project, 2008). Historical records show Koreans have been improving technical innovations in archery for over 2,000 years honed by these regular life-and-death competitions during invasions of Korea. As a result, ancient records show other countries' royal courts regularly asked visiting Korean dignitaries to demonstrate their superlative skill in archery, likely for entertainment and yet likely equally because kings and generals at the foreign court feared Korean archery and its unique technologies and wanted to judge Koreans in action with their unique bows and arrows, first hand.

By the Joseon dynasty (1392–1910), Korean innovations in archery reached a shorter, lighter and more portable Korean compound 'national bow,' called the 'Gukgung' that other nations lacked. Partnered with the more powerful Gukgung came a more accurate, shorter, and faster arrow called the Pyeonjeon. Koreans even added an atlatl device in the form of a half tube called the 'Tong-ah' for firing these shorter Korean arrows even faster and at longer distances toward enemies who were unable to respond at such distances or even hear these silent arrows arriving. Around Korea, no other country's military had these three technologies or likely practiced archery longer or more widely across the whole culture instead of it being only for military troops.

When launched, these Korean faster and smaller arrows could pierce metal armor. Plus, they were indeed like sniper fire as shorter arrows were like adding a 'silencer' attachment to the bow. The short Pyeonjeon was less detected in advance by being faster and almost silent due to its smaller size. There was less time, less visual cues, or less sound cues about this arrow's approach to react before it was embedded in your torso or metal armor from an unseen distance and location. In the Joseon dynasty's book Seongho Saseol, scholar Seongho Yi Ik writes the Pyeonjeon was a specialty of Joseon, feared by enemies "[b]ecause it fires off a great distance and has a strong penetrating power, [so] the enemies were afraid of pyeonjeon." Yeonryeosilgisul ("Writings by Yeonryeosil," a 59-volume series of an unofficial history of Korea), now in the Jangseogak Archives, records "Pyeonjeon is unique to our country. It came to be considered unrivaled in the world, together with the China's spears or Japan's matchlocks." However to the contrary of the mention, the Chinese bian jian(邊箭), the Byzantine solenarion, and the Turkish majra were all similar devices around short arrows. However, in the regional neighborhood of East Asia of course Koreans were the only unparalleled archers. Despite many different bows used and invented over the last 2,000 years of Korean history, by the Joseon dynasty the mainstay was this unique and unchallenged assortment of the 'national bow' called the Gukgung, firing short silent armor-piercing arrows called Pyeonjeon, and launched faster from the bow with the Tong-ah.

Comparing many bow ranges in a modern test, Koreans could indeed attack from further away since compared "to the British longbow…[that] can shoot 200 m, the Gukgung can shoot an arrow as far as 500 m with an effective range of 350 m" (Antique Alive, 2015). Keeping at a great distance that your enemies were unable to respond to, even as you were fighting them, was an unparalleled combined offense and defense for the Joseon dynasty. These technologies gave Koreans five times the firing range of even early flintlock rifles like the European Arquebus or the Japanese matchlock called the Tanegashima. The current modern distance record for using 'ancient-inspired' designs of Korean bows and arrows reputedly was reputedly set in 2011 at 428.8 meters using a Pyeonjeon fired from a 57-pound modern Gukgung. (Gunsi Workshop, unk.) The range of a Tong-ah-launched Pyeonjeon would be even greater.

Keep in mind modern Olympic archery competitions only have distances up to 70 meters (77 yards) at the most. The base requirement of every single one of the Joseon dynasty's royal guards was to pass many archery tests that are far harder than winning modern Olympic medals. One of these tests for the Joseon royal guards was to show that you could be able to fire arrows accurately at 150 meters by hitting three bull's-eyes at a minimum. Remember, this perfect score of hitting three bull's-eyes was just one of many exams to be in the Joseon royal guards, and it was testing an archer at a distance of more than twice the modern Olympics' archery competition. Thus, if we could take the Joseon dynasty's royal guards to the twenty-first century, they would be the most peerless gold medal team in Olympic history if they could represent Korea.

However, time-traveling Joseon royal guards are unrequired for Koreans to win every year at archery in the Olympics. Koreans already do it now. Modern Koreans carry on the tradition of excellence and practice in archery. Koreans regularly are the gold medal winners in archery at the Olympics ever since the archery event was reintroduced in the Olympics in 1984. From 1984 to the present, South Koreans have received fully 27 gold medals in archery out of the total possible 39 gold medals for both individual men and women over this period. Plus, stunningly, South Korea has won *every* gold medal in women's team archery since the competition was introduced at the 1988 Olympics—the first Olympic games hosted by Korea. Plus, as of 2020, all four classes of world records in archery—for individual males, for teams of males, for individual women, and for teams of women—are held only by South Koreans.

Unsurprisingly, Korean ancient archery inventions and skills are pridefully shown in modern dramas of the Korean Wave as well. They are either background events or deeply part of how a drama shows a Korean character's development or personality. Even modern Korean Wave TV historical dramas or films feature males and females in ancient Korea versed in and practicing archery. Actually, this is true to ancient Korean culture. Records show both males and females whether at royal courts or in rural villages widely practiced archery. At the ancient Goguryeo capital at Pyongyang, people of the city practiced archery regularly in mixed gender groups as part of religious and perhaps matchmaking ceremonies. This is shown in the records of the Chinese Sui dynasty in the 500s CE to the early 600s CE, where it was written that "[i]n Pyongyang, we build a seo-dang (school) next to the street, gathering unmarried people together to practice reciting religious texts and practicing archery." In the Kwongun(權近) there are other records of a deep culture of archery in Goguryeo's capital of Pyongyang. For other examples, the painting "Shooting an Arrow," featured in the book "Album of Genre Paintings" by Joseon-era artist Kim Hong-do, shows archery enjoyed by the common people. Joseon-era villages even held archery events called hyangsarye as well. Hundreds of years later, early modern Korean ethnographers like American ethnographer Stewart Culin (1858–1929) wrote in his book *Korean Games*, that Koreans practice archery under the name "Hap-sa-ha-ki" ("side shooting") in teams that split to have a contest. Old photographs by foreigners in early modernizing Korea of the late 1800s through 1910s show women learning and practicing archery instead of only men. Even kings practiced archery inside the palace. Joseon Kings Taejo and Jeongjo are well-known to be excellent archers. The Eosahwagi (Records of a King Shooting Arrows), the last and only copy of a book held in the collection of the Jangseogak Archives, documents shooting events and scores of an unnamed king. All of this offers a view of how seriously Korean kings, men and women at court, as well as the common people at large worked on mastering the bow. Thus, archery is embedded throughout ancient or modern Korean culture. Founders of various states in Korean history were known to be master archers.

Four examples of ancient archery in the modern Korean Wave will suffice. The TV drama Sungkyunkwan Scandal (2010) on KBS (Korea Broadcasting Service) featured archery throughout the storyline. The film War of the Arrows (2011), the biggest grossing film of that year in Korea and popular as a Japanese export, was set during the second Manchu invasion of Korea in 1636. It depicts the main male character fashioning a 'Tong-ah' while on the run from Manchu/Qing dynasty troops as he shot and fashioned broken arrows into shorter Pyeonjeon. The Korean drama Empress Ki (2013), anachronistically set in ancient Goguryeo when the Pyeonjeon was likely not yet invented, shows the main female character Seung Nyang as an expert with the Pyeonjeon. Fourth, Olympic stars in archery are treated as Korean TV celebrities on special shows that feature archery, like the Korean Wave show "Idol Star" that has competitions in archery. In this show, the current reigning Olympic archery teams are filmed for television twice a year, both at the regular annual autumn's festivities for Chuseok and in the celebrations of the winter Lunar New Year. In these biannual Korean Wave events of "Idol Star", K-pop stars and other Korean entertainment celebrities pair up and compete in archery with Korea's world-famous Olympic archery teams, in good fun. Plus, for just one of many examples, in 2018, Idol Star featured an archery match between K-pop girl groups themselves. At one point, Tzuyu (from the group TWICE) and Irene (from the group Red Velvet) were competing. The top voted comment at the YouTube excerpt of this competition aptly says "I can't tell if this is a game show, a beauty contest, a high school/slice of life anime or a serious sporting event" (TV-People, 2018). It seems to be all the above. Even this short 3-minute excerpt of "Tzuyu vs Irene" has received over 24 million views in the five years since it was posted.

So, for over 2,000 years, in military, general culture, and status, Korean archery has remained a deep principle of cultural continuity embedded in daily life. Archery was practiced throughout Korean ancient culture regardless of male or female, wealth or poverty, royal court or peasant village, or status as military officers or civil bureaucrat.

Nowadays, another serious 'export sector' of the Korean Wave is manufacturing gold medals in Olympic archery competitions. Just like the ubiquitous practice of regular singing, Koreans more extensively mass train more of their youth in archery than any other modern nation. Archery in Korea starts in elementary school, in order that by high school, there are always thousands of fresh excellent youth each year ready to compete for national and then Olympic medals as archery superstars. It is the same principle at the national TV talent shows mentioned earlier around Korean singing or around Korean archery. Future Korean professional archers are encouraged to practice in real competitions at earlier ages than other nations as they compete nationally among millions of amateur Koreans. In this vetting, the nation finds a dozen superstars every year that are subsidized generously if they decide to make archery their full time 'adult' job. Modern Korean individual archers or archery teams of men and women are without exaggeration the unrivaled best in the world since the 1970s. Extremely high levels of modern Korean skill in archery competitions for both men and women (whether as individuals or teams) are unmatched globally. Just like the Korean music industry is a machine that manufactures K-pop stars and teaches them how to shine from years of polishing and training long before they are famous, a Korean archery machine exists in the culture as well that makes young archers see the benefit of becoming a professional full-time archer who practices hours a day, subsidized by the state.

In conclusion, another aspect of the modern Korean Wave as ancient as singing is the culture of archery. Archery is the true national sport of South Korea, and its excellence eternally returns since male and female archery teams start training professionally in high school even for the Olympics. Korean youth train far harder and longer than any other country in this sport, and are subsidized more for specializing in these skills. Other countries seem unwilling to copy such a high level of subsidies, youth pressure, or time spent on archery. Of course by working harder as a team, the Korean nation innately keeps coming to the top of this field. This is another example of Koreans unique ability to combine their ancient cultural forms and values with modern developmental prowess instead of these being at odds with each other.

2.4.3 *Martial Arts Blending into Performance and Dance*

Like the Korean culture of mass singing or mass archery, Koreans are equally proud of their national martial arts tradition, now called 'Taekwondo'. This is translated as 'the art or way of kicking/punching'. This Korean martial art specializes in visually dramatic head-height kicks and spinning kicks. However, unlike other contents of the Korean Wave mentioned above, instead of Taekwondo being an ancient practice, it is a modern amalgam of many ancient Korean practices of martial arts.

The amalgam of Taekwondo was formalized only after the modern independence of South Korea, after 1945 into the 1950s. This modern amalgam mixes different ancient Korean martial arts techniques like Taekkyon (using hands, feet, knees, elbows, joint locks, and pressure point attacks to unbalance, trip, or throw an opponent), Subak (bare hand fighting techniques) and Gwonbeop (ancient Korean versions of Chinese quan fa/kung fu). Two of these three (Takkyon and Gwonbeop) were taught for over a thousand years at least. For instance, though Gwonbeop was formalized only in the Joseon Dynasty, it was part of an older series of martial arts developed differently under different earlier Korean kingdoms of Goguryeo, Baekjae, and Silla during the Three Kingdoms period over 1,500 years ago. Plus, Taekkyon was documented as early as the second century CE. Subak had an origin in different regions of Korea though now only two regional heritages remain in Subak. Why do only two regional practices of Subak still exist? It is because all three ancient Korean cultural martial arts were banned during the Japanese Empire in the Korean Peninsula (1910–1945). When Koreans were freed by 1945, all ancient martial arts practices were in real danger of being forgotten totally due to 35 years of banned practice. So, to conserve the knowledge of the uneven and remaining few masters, these three ancient main Korean martial arts were blended into one in modern Taekwondo by the 1950s. Reassembled, reforged, and taught together as Taekwondo, the mettle of all three Korean ancient martial arts heritages now continue today as one, stronger for being alloyed together.

Plus, in the modern music entertainment of the Korean Wave, it is not odd to see Korean concert performances in which Korean boy group members integrate their K-pop dances directly with Taekwondo, or demonstrate it separately in pauses in the concert, in order to break a few wooden boards with flying kicks dramatically to wild applause, and then seamlessly to go back into a song and dance routine as if it is normal for a pop concert to demonstrate martial arts. In Korea, it is a normal practice, and this is reflected in the Korean Wave as well. It is equally not odd how the current growing global popularity of Taekwondo is inspired from the global Korean Wave itself as more global youth see it in Korean entertainment and find the Korean martial arts forms appealing enough to learn themselves (OMR Taekwondo Academy, 2013).

As the Korean Wave's entertainment gained popularity as a regional Hallyu across East Asia from the 1990s onward, many boy bands in the Korean Wave showcased Taekwondo moves that they likely first learned in South Korea's all-male mandatory modern military service, since Taekwondo was added into every male's formal training in the 1950s. Other boy bands might have learned Taekwondo earlier than their military service, even in their elementary school days from the many 'after school academies' (hagwons) on various subjects. Youth Taekwondo is popular among very young children in Korea as an exercise, as an escape from study (that is another kind of study in itself), and as a hobby helping them gain pride from their disciplined skills. BTS is a good example of a popular boy group in the Korean Wave nowadays that employs Taekwondo in performances, particularly showcased by its member Jimin who additionally has formal professional modern dance training and even traditional Korean dance training. In short, many boy bands like BTS and even mixed boy-girl groups like the K-Tigers showcase Korean martial arts training as an added entertainment mixed into modern stage dances and performances to high international applause and acclaim.

The modern Korean Wave's version of this cultural blurring of Taekwondo as dance, acrobatics, music, and martial arts was rekindled first in the group called the "K-Tigers" from the early 1990s. The original line up of the K-Tigers was a simultaneous entertainment dance group and Taekwondo demonstration team, founded by An Hak-sun in 1990 in Seoul. It included a male team, a female team, and even a child-level team called the 'little K-Tigers.' K-Tigers are fondly remembered as the first generation merging Taekwondo in the song-and-dance entertainment complex of the Korean Wave. The K-Tigers gained popularity after their cover of a dance song "Ringa Linga" by the boy group Big Bang, sung originally by its member Taeyang. Later lineups of the K-Tigers have covered BTS's "Boys in Luv" and Big Bang's "Good Boy." By 2016, the K-Tigers were under management by CJ E&M Music Entertainment as a 9-member group with their own album called *Hero.* Updated lineups of K-Tigers still exist today, having released another EP in 2019 called "Huinoaerak" (translated as 'Happiness, Anger, Sorrow, and Tears").

Given traditional Confucian principles on strict gender segregation and gendered rules in public in Korean culture, it is oddly 'Western' for K-Tigers to be a K-pop group with male and female group members together. It is still normal in the modern Korean Wave entertainment industry to have segregated male-only and female-only dance groups or bands, echoing how traditional formal Chuseok family dining parties may exhibit segregated male-only and female-only tables for easier conviviality, i.e., a kind of a segregation helping Koreans have more freedom from public gendered rules constraining celebration and fun, instead of less freedom. Plus, in many Korean Wave entertainment contracts, female group members may be prevented by contract from dating or from keeping relationships a secret from their managers so they can focus on practice and performance. Thus, the quite gendered male martial arts training of Taekwondo and the mostly female dating restrictions on Korean 'rock n' roll stars' in contracts epitomizes this 'modern export-led yet disciplined conservative/traditionalist' Korean Wave. From 2016, more in keeping with Korean culture, even K-Tigers sometimes split into male-only and female-only performances that are the norm in acts of the Korean Wave as in the ancient Korean and modern Korean culture.

However, just like singing and archery, the modern Korean Wave 'appropriation' of Taekwondo and martial arts as public entertainment is not a strange mixture. A similar ancient performative martial arts mixed with dancing existed in ancient public festivals as a deep part of Korean culture, just like singing and archery. For instance, there was a Subak Dance routine, mixing martial arts and public dancing centuries ago though it has mostly died out today except in small zones of Mongolian-based Koreans. Plus, Taekkyon and Subak both have a 'military' version and a 'game/competition' version, with the latter used in ancient public festivals. Mentioned in the chronicle of the Joseon dynasty, it is written that in ancient Goryeo, a hand-to-hand-combat warrior elite, called 'sunbae,' met annually every year in the early spring for a public "demonstration-entertainment" festival where "people gathered….at a site of ritual, where they enjoyed a sword dance, archery, Taekkyon contests and so on." This implies that Taekkyon martial arts were already a popular public entertainment.

Plus, it shows even Goguryeo-era swordplay was both treated as martial art and an entertaining public dance (OMR Taekwondo Academy, 2013).

Taekkyon had a street fighting ‘game version’ looked down upon by the Joseon aristocracy. It was widely seen centuries ago, though missing today in the crowded, clean, and modern Seoul. Plus, instead of only a martial art, ancient Subak was a true organized spectator sport in which an audience’s gambling on who would win was a parallel wager-based entertainment in public festivals. Unsurprisingly given the deep cultural continuity that Korea has, the modern Korean love of gambling is another sign of ancient cultural durability passed forward into to the present. Modern Koreans love gambling today in person or online, wagering on wrestling, archery, or games of chance. However, the modern Korean government is strictly against gambling for the most part, even though in the past decade casinos have become part of the export-led economy itself as a draw of foreign tourist income spent there since they are regularly near major international airports like at Incheon International Airport which is now ringed by large casinos and conference hotels. In short, records of singing, archery, martial arts, gambling, and drinking run as interwoven threads through ancient stories of Korea. Ancient public entertainments in Korea *were* the martial arts, the archery competitions, and the public singing—and the gambling and drinking around them.

2.4.4 Body Beauty, Fashion Clothing, and Public Formal Style

Any discussion of ancient or modern Korean culture has to discuss the culture attempting what will be called ‘bodily perfection.’ This is defined as the desire for excellence in their formal public presentation whether intellectual, aesthetic, or in manual skill. Plus, Koreans try to show these superior skills in a competition with each other. Thus, this bodily perfection extends into a highly competitive beauty culture and competitive skill culture that animates much of the visible material culture of Korea. The result is that it raises material product quality and performance to a high tenor. This desire for bodily perfection is seen in Korean clothing, fashion, cosmetics, plastic surgery, and even performance skills and after school training in hagwons of all kinds. The high material and skill-based standards that Koreans impose upon themselves are now exported to the world in the Korean Wave.

It is more than a modern competitive economy, because in many competitive economies there is a ‘race to the bottom’ in quality or a lesser cultural concern with quality, instead of a race to the top in quality as argued in Korea. The argument is that it has a great deal to do with an ongoing ancient homogeneous culture and its cultural forms from the now defunct Korean aristocracy. So, even if aristocratic family power has dissipated to nothing in modern Korea, the same shared status markings and cultural forms survive. It is seen in the honor given to Koreans, by each other, for a deep and polished formal clothing, for bodily perfection, and nowadays extended to any 'manual' exhibition of skills in performance or presentation without errors in public. Koreans still pride themselves in exhibiting bodily perfection in important public performances, rituals, competitions, or social events.

What is the origin of this aristocratic cultural form? Despite the Korean aristocracy being known as the 'yangban' from the days of Goryeo (935–1392), literally meaning the 'two branches' of the governmental service examinations for civil and military administrators, by the Joseon dynasty (1392–1910) the term yangban included simply the whole landowning class that could buy the title and status (raising funds for the government in this way). Later, by the close of the Joseon dynasty, the yangban title was even 'forcibly given away' en masse by the king to try to raise money for the Korean state. However, the earlier Joseon state had a rigidly closed and self-perpetuating four-class system of yangban, chungin (intermediate class), sangmin (common people), and chonmin (lowborn people). The yangban were the epitome of the top class of cultural trend setters. Plus, only yangban could perpetuate themselves at the top, as they were the only group allowed to take the civil service examinations over generations, even being exempt from all 'manual or menial' military duties, state-based labor requirements and most taxations if they passed the test. The yangban could even hire slaves to serve their own terms of punishment as well (Encyclopedia Britannica, 2018).

Given such a continuous, inherited, non-manual, refined, and high political status among the same test-taking competitive families for a thousand years or more, Korean elite cultural heritage was greatly about intellectual and aesthetic competition among yangban. In the absence of much long-term war as a means of showing excellence or gaining status or power, this means cultural power was attainable mostly through greater beauty, greater emotional depth, greater projects, greater etiquette, greater polish—and greater civil or military test scores. This is unlike, for example, an aristocracy like the Japanese samurai after the 1200s based equally on aesthetics and families, and yet having nothing to do with tests yet based on material self-denial, service, sacrifice, family honor, disciplined emotionless control, or unpredictable yet expected bursts of gratuitous violence. In this way, the Korean cultural elite of the Joseon dynasty were freer individuals, if they chose, to focus on expansive, lifelong, or long-term literary, scientific, technical, and aesthetic concerns and improvements. Many of them did, given a lack of many historical conquests in the Korean Peninsula for 2,000 years except for intermittent challenges from abroad from Mongols for 50 years, or a Japanese invasion from 1592 to 1598, or Chinese invasions in the 1630s. That is an optimistic interpretation. A more pessimistic interpretation is that just as many did the opposite with such a luxury of time: making nothing of value at all. They equally created an effete and jealously-divided aristocracy that continued to waste most of their pointless lives on petty daily concerns of cultural polishing as they lorded over a slave society that took care of their material requirements, even extending to carrying them up stairs or lighting their pipes.

According to Horace Allan, the American Representative to Korea and a Western observer of the last generations of the Korean yangban in the late 1800s, he described them generally as stubborn, idle, effeminate, weak, infuriating, inconvenient, and acting with an "overpowering air of condescension." (Neff, 2020a) Yangban would act as if they are superior experts of everything yet without possessing any tangible or real knowledge. (Neff, 2020b) They had a strong hierarchical contempt for everyone lower than them, particularly women, and they "meted out disproportionate punishment for any slights—real or perceived." James Scarth Gale, a Christian missionary from Canada, echoes Allan's observations: "If he is an official of importance, he does not walk alone, but is assisted by the arms on each side. If he ventures by himself, it is with a magnificent stride that clears the street of indifferent passers, and commands only on-lookers. In one hand is a pipe three feet long [that he never personally lights though his servants do it], in the other a fan; over his eyes [are] two immense discs of dark crystal, not to assist him in seeing, but to insure his being seen" (Neff, 2020a).

A saying about the yangban was 'a gentleman never runs or looks hurried.' Running and being hurried was for slaves. Once more, this echoes the modern Korean desire for perfect bodily control of emotions and movements as a sign of higher status. There was even a special aristocratic walk of the yangban to show their status and mindset in public—legs slightly splayed, feet and toes pointed outward, and arms clasped and folded behind the back as they walked. This encouraged them to walk slowly with a relaxed and peaceful contemplation. This aristocratic walk is performed still today, though fully only in Korean historical dramas of the Korean Wave. However, partially, it still appears in the culture throughout East Asia of today of Asian elders and their walking habits. This is because the origin of this aristocratic walk is the wider elite state culture of East Asia when all the region's states were more exclusively Chinese-centric in literature, culture, and power. The Korean term for this wider East Asian aristocratic cultural form of walking is the compound term yangban-geoleum (using the two words yangban and geoleum for 'yangban walking'), or the Korean slang 'paljageoleum', which means literally 'Chinese character sign of eight (palja)-walk (geoleum)', or 'toeing out' walk. This is because the Chinese character for eight looks like human legs splayed outward. So, it is equally defined as a way of walking slowly with one's toes pointed outwards or simply 'yangban walking.' The old Joseon nobles walked in this way to show their elite status publicly and to emphasize leisureliness on purpose because they considered walking at a quick pace unbecoming of a nobleman. This was a merged sign of superiority, status, authority, strength, power, calmness, and contemplation that they exhibited and thought they were. Most modern Koreans or East Asians still ape this walk partially as an 'elder walk', with only the hands clasped behind the back as all that remains of the form. However, many modern East Asians or even elderly seem unaware of the historically aristocratic origin of this cultural form of walk, despite it continuing throughout all of East Asia in many elders still today in a partial way by only arms folded behind the back as the part remembered in quiet contemplation while strolling. However, this walk was originally an elite cultural sign of being dignified in public, instead of a sign of only being elderly. However, judging from ignorant levels of Internet discussion about this, its older symbolic meaning has been lost to many and only the form remains, interpreted as if it is a kind of health regime or a functional back stretch for Asian elderly in general. That is hardly its origin however. It was once an aristocratic sign of being dignified, calm, and self-controlled.

The yangban may have used their contemplative walk more in their gardens or properties. In cities however, when alone, they used a pushy "magnificent stride that clears the street" as noted above. Mostly the yangban would travel with a retinue of many servants, carrying them in expensive slow litters or they rode on horses or donkeys only at a leisurely walking pace. Since it was unbecoming to walk unaccompanied, most yangban if they could afford it were always in public with numerous (and violent) staff that would pre-announce the yangban's presence in the street and try to clear the street in front of them as they moved through the city. The desire to avoid such "infuriating" inconveniences of yangban in the public streets led to the Korean invention of 'pimat-gil' (the road to avoid horses), which were smaller alleys that paralleled the main thoroughfares specifically so commoners could move unbothered by status-conscious yangban whose staff announced them coming down the street and required everyone to get out of the way, dismount, stop moving, stop smoking, and stand up to honor the yangban. Refusers would be physically assaulted with long wooden paddles until they did so (Neff, 2020a).

Yangban were dissolved as a class in the Gabo Reforms by 1894, yet their cultural forms of an expected aesthetic polish and an expected strict formal status hierarchy remain powerful influences in modern Korea. Obviously, the Korean aristocracy was a very cultured and polished people born to rule, unused to having their cultural authority challenged. This made them unused to using real political violence instead of only daily petty violence to maintain status in their immediate vicinity. Their attempt to control simply by culturally overawing others shows their effete lack of ability truly to have a commanding military leadership in political crises. The Joseon dynasty even stooped to invite China to invade itself in 1893, because the court felt the foreign military of China would be more loyal than their own defecting Korean military in killing the Korean people's proto-nationalist and anti-aristocratic Tonghak rebellion that started in the same year. The Japanese then invaded as well, first beating the Chinese and then destroying the Tonghak rebellion for the Joseon court as well. In this way China lost its old control over Korean foreign policy and wider East Asia, as an increasingly urban industrial Japan started to gain hegemony on both. The Korean Joseon court in 1893 was a coterie of aristocratic elites with a strong disdain for the common people of Korea. They failed to want any modern ideas that would convert them into representatives of Korean peasants that they detested culturally. However, in the Gabo Reforms after the close-run success of destroying the Tonghak Rebellion, the whole yangban class was dismantled in 1894 by the Joseon dynasty in a last-ditch attempt to maintain itself in competition with encroaching outside forces like Japan and many inside domestic political pressures.

All of this taken together makes it easy to see how an *unloved* Korean aristocracy was so easily displaced by the early twentieth century. However, in a continuing homogenous culture of status, it is equally easy to see how their cultural forms remained *loved* regardless. So, despite aristocratic military, political, and economic power ending in the Korean Peninsula between 1910 through 1961, the deep aristocratic cultural importance remains. It focuses on style, perfectionism in clothing, and bodily perfection in formal events as a way to demonstrate excellence and superiority over others. This remains a coveted sign of an elite person in South Korea to the present. In short, Koreans dress conservatively for success, dress to be seen, and use cosmetics and even plastic surgery for similar purposes of a desire for honor and a desire for that collectively-acclaimed authority via excellence in public, instead of seeing all of this show and polish as an individual's desire or idiosyncratic showiness. It is a social desire to conform, to confirm, and to shine in the most polished and socially approved conservative ways.

So, this polished perfectionism of an aristocratic culture extends from ancient to modern Korean cultural forms. It has even been extended now into appreciating the more manual arts of singing, dance, or athletic performance in the desire to demonstrate in public a bodily perfection in beauty or in disciplined control in any way. This desire for bodily perfection is seen in desires for singing perfection, in gold medals for archery, and in martial arts blending into dance performances showcasing bodily skill and beauty in public. In short, this older pushy public aristocratic style has combined in the modern Korean world with admiration of the labor and physical discipline to achieve excellence in any chosen walk of life with calm leadership instead of visible stress. This exhibition has to be one of calm and polished excellence. This is strongly admired in modern Korean culture. Koreans love to strive for, love to watch, and most of all love to be gossipy judgmental spectators with the aesthetic awareness to analyze or critique performances of perfectly-skilled beautiful physical bodies under complete control whether in music, dance, archery, or martial arts. This why gold medals in the Olympics are considered the only true successes in Korean culture, while silver and bronze medals are considered somewhat failures.

Plus, as a result, modern Koreans from their ancient culture and from modern competitive business culture are very beauty conscious in both males and females. Modern Seoul specializes in an area of plastic surgery around Apgujeong, a section of the wealthy Gangnam zone. In Apgujeong, there are hundreds of doctors specializing in plastic surgery in a tight zone of conspicuous consumption. Apgujeong is presumed to be the largest and most dense concentration of plastic surgery clinics in the world with over 500 clinics in a 15-square-mile neighborhood (National Public Radio, 2022). The American co-author of this book lived for a time in Nonhyeon-dong, a part of Gangnam wedged between Seoul's business district of Tehran-ro and the beauty capital of Apgujeong. He can vouch that it was not odd to see mostly Korean women or some foreign women in 'medical tourism' walking around 'between surgeries' with their face or whole head covered in white bandages like a mummy with sunglasses, under their sun umbrellas. Extreme services are offered in South Korea. Korean cosmetic surgeons attack the whole skull instead of only the surface skin. There is jawbone contouring, extension, retracting, or reshaping instead of only 'eye or nose jobs.' Increasingly, modern South Korea seems to consider plastic surgery as a kind of expected 'rite of passage' done after high school yet before going to a competitive university, useful for preparing your body as much as your mind for the competitive and very judgmental Korean economy. A negative view of this, even in Korea, is called 'lookism.' It argues that Koreans are driving themselves insane over obsessively high public standards that make them more miserable than happy inside to be so beautiful outside. However, this ancient cultural expectation of bodily perfection as a sign of elite status and cultural authority, truly still honored by others, has merged with modern economic pressures for a supercharged competitive economy. Many Koreans may critique it yet they keep paying high prices for plastic surgeons and expect only the best cosmetics and clothing, or they take their business elsewhere.

Now that more relaxed cultures have globally come into contact with the material products and visuals of the Korean Wave, other non-Korean cultures may be just as overawed by Korean aesthetics, or as stressed and outclassed, as many Koreans feel about their 'lookism' and high expectations of the Korean beauty culture. Internationally, people have become interested in 'K-beauty' products generated out of these high beauty standards of the Korean culture itself. In the process, the whole world is becoming addicted to the same high Korean aesthetic standards. Foreign medical tourists already take advantage of the accrued Korean skill and aesthetic perfectionism in its plastic surgery, or take advantage of its skill at mixing beauty products. Now, even larger once dominant China is overawed by Korean aesthetics. China's market is the largest one in the world for Korean cosmetics, with about half of Korean production of cosmetics going to China.

Plus, showing that it is not only female beauty perfection that is admired by Koreans though general bodily perfection itself that is admired, by 2020 "about three quarters of South Korean men undertake a beauty or grooming treatment (from salon hair treatments to at-home facials) at least once a week" (Rapp, 2020). It is a custom of all Korean job applicants, whatever the position, to provide pictures of themselves on their application. This practice would be seen as biasing, narcissistic, or unimportant in a Western country generally. However, without a picture on the application, Koreans would think the application is incomplete, or that the candidate is second-rate immediately because they are intentionally hiding something or may be a bad public face for the company. People are judged by their looks in Korea, definitely, though this is pressured on male and female alike.

Perceptively said by Rapp, "[male] beauty is generally much more accepted as a concept in South Korea, but it doesn't relieve each gender of their traditional roles....Gender roles are still fairly rigid, sexual choices other than heterosexuality are generally not talked about, and it's a patriarchal culture" (Rapp, 2020). Thus a Korean stress on male beauty aesthetics is very different from the British/Western idea that beautiful men are homosexuals or unsatisfied with being men and so want to rebel and look like women. Instead, South Korea has pioneered "a makeup look solely for men that's completely different from women, which is what K-pop male stars subscribe to" (Rapp, 2020). As early as 2012, South Korean men bought 21% of the whole world's cosmetics made for men (Cho, 2012). This placed South Korean men as the top per capita spender on male cosmetics in the world in 2012 (DeNinno, 2012). By 2015, South Korean men were still the world's top per-capita consumers of skincare products, at four times the runner-up of the males of Denmark (Novak, 2015).

With upmost seriousness, modern Koreans explain female and male cosmetics as functional requirements in their culture, as if it was due only to modern factors like the hyper-competitive job market in South Korea with "insufficient full-time, white-collar positions to absorb a highly educated populace" (Salmon, 2019). However, other countries are just as economically competitive and yet have failed to automatically create the same kind of extreme beauty culture. Therefore, within this modern economic competition, there has always been an older competitive standard in elite body beauty in Korean culture. It now has modern economic accelerants like competitive job markets, or even media accelerants like high-definition television shows featuring K-pop stars or singing competitions daily, showing high standards of competition in beauty to the whole country—and now the whole world.

A third modern accelerant of competitive beauty in males seems to be the required two-year male military service in South Korea interacting at cross purposes with the heightened modern 'K-pop aesthetics' as a cultural standard. Nowadays more Korean males want to maintain their appearance despite several years of required outdoor military exertion.

> "AmorePacific [a Korean cosmetics company] has even launched a special military line, which features natural camouflage makeup and post-training cooling and whitening masks. According to the company, an estimated 70% of South Korea's military men use cosmetics [in the wider sense of facial applications instead of meaning 'makeup']. "Interest...in cosmetic products begins during [military service]—due to the frequent outdoor activity that requires sun protection and skin care in general," said the company. (Novak, 2015)

However, Korean use of male cosmetics daily outside of these conditions is very small. In a recent survey of 750 Korea males, only an estimated 3.9% of Korean males were wearing cosmetics daily, yet the percentage rises to 16.7% for 'special occasions' which still seems very minor (Statista, 2021). Thus, from this statistical data, it is argued that the sense of bodily perfection is deeply connected to avoiding the look of skin damage of outdoor manual labor, and thus it is motivated by public show and a competitive judgmental economic situation instead of only personal vanity. Korean males seem forced to try to get *a competitive beauty edge in life's conservative economic competitions* instead of assuming it is motivated by personal idiosyncrasies, rebellion, or rejection of such competitions. Instead, it is the Korean culture's idiosyncrasies.

With Korea's high internal cultural standards of body beauty and clothing, it is unsurprising that the wider world's women and even men start to join in the Korean Wave by buying products from "K-beauty" firms. "Tourists come from all over Asia to Seoul in order to shop, not just to shop but to see what the Korean women are wearing and what cosmetics they're using because that kind of sets the standards for all of Asia. Gangnam is very much sort of the Mecca of high consumption" (National Public Radio, 2022).

The Korean Wave's "K-cosmetics" are featured in a later case study of Cosmax. Cosmax is a 'quiet Korean brand' that is an innovative octopus of global services for the whole cosmetics industry—offering market analysis, advertising, brand-invention, cosmetics manufacturing, and general cosmetics material mixing and material innovation for other companies. Cosmax is literally the trusted research brains and the manufacturing brawn behind many dozens of very different yet equally famous global and national brands. Thus, one Korean company of Cosmax actually designs, markets, and mixes the cosmetic recipes of dozens of global brands that people buy thinking they are getting a unique company's product. They all are.

That unique company worldwide is Cosmax, the 'Costco of cosmetics innovation' for all global brands. Yes, multiple "non-Korean" cosmetic lines are really Korean already for decades. In general, Korean cosmetics are in a large category of Korean Wave aesthetic purchases toward bodily perfection ideals that now include clothing, cars, international 'medical tourism' from abroad, shopping, spas, hospital stays, and plastic surgery.

2.4.5 Public Events

Koreans past or present love boisterous public celebrations. Long before the popularity of the Korean Wave, in modern Korea, Koreans were the first to enjoy taxis doubling as singing rooms from the 1990s. Even modern buses are decked out as singing rooms for longer trips, with their flashing colored LED lights and mirror balls barreling down Korean freeways for a sing-along party to the destination. In this way, a larger party can travel together, singing and partying while passing around wireless microphones on the way to their group's final tourism destination. One of these 'pimped out' Korean party buses satirically is shown in Psy's video for "Gangnam Style." Psy's video and song of 2012 called "Gangnam Style" started the more global Korean Wave by piquing world curiosity about all of the modern Korean cultural images Psy's team packed into this rapid-fire video that feels like a short documentary of high-living in Korea as well. It showed the world a very different Korea than the Western media (or the Korean government, for that matter) had been framing. However, Psy's "singular success" of 2012 was years before the more group-based "simultaneous successes" of many different Korean Wave offerings that began to occur only from 2018.

Before the singing taxi or the disco bus, how did Koreans party? Ancient public events and ancient Korean cultural parties are mentioned in the old Korean text called the Dongijeon. According to this, it is said that there was a October festival called Mucheon (舞天) in the state of Dongye (that existed between 200s BCE–400s CE). Later, a similar October festival event called Alliance (東盟) existed during the state of Goguryeo (37 BCE–668 CE), plus another one in December called Yeonggo (迎鼓). Details about these older Korean multi-day festivals of songs and dances are lost to history. However, given the time span of these examples, it is safe to say Koreans enjoyed long multi-day public festivals of songs and dances as a common cultural motif for millennia. There are records that they ate, drank, sang, danced, and likely shopped. Ancient Korea had and modern Korea still has a long calendar of seasonal and culinary festivals the year round, particularly featuring regional produce harvests. An echo of this party experience is seen when multi-day temporary outdoor stores, singing events, and restaurants by the dozens merge together, creating a festive atmosphere. Koreans will have a party anywhere. They will set up a picnic blanket beside a busy highway. They will hold a multi-day pajeon (onion/scallion pancake) eating festival in the parking lot of the Seoul National University Hospital. From the cultural forms mentioned already in other sections, many ancient Korean cultural forms had their own calendars of annual parties or demonstrations around archery or martial arts that became singing and dancing competitions as well instead of only having one or two big parties per year.

2.4.6 Technological Innovation: Science and Civilization in Korea

Technical and scientific innovation in the Korean Peninsula is really an ancient cultural prowess as well, instead of only a modern one. However, since this technical innovation in ancient Korean culture is wrapped in a history of deep Korean political and cultural stasis, it may seem boring to most social or historical scholars. This bias of historians seems why the Korean Peninsula has less international awareness of its peculiarities in world history (Palais, 1995). One strong cultural peculiarity of the Korean 'civilizational' experience has been the long Korean history of scientific and technical advances in world history that created many world firsts in the Korean Peninsula sometimes hundreds of years before any other areas of the world exhibited the same invention. What is happening here? Why is it happening here? Why is the cultural and political stability so different than the deep and durable technical innovation?

The history of Korean inventions has many world firsts, so this point alone should be of interest to historians of science and technology far greater than it is now to people interested in the technical prowess of the culture behind the Korean Wave. Second, it should be of interest to historians of science because of what is conjectured here to be a unique "Korean-style scientific saltation," to coin a phrase. The meaning of 'saltation' in this sense of scientific saltation means any discontinuous and abrupt movement or transition in the tenor of scientific and technical advance. It has been used by Vaclav Smil's view of the world history of science and technology for describing two major discontinuous changes of rapid scientific advance in world history. He claimed that the world only had two main 'scientific saltations' in the Han dynasty's rapid expansions (221 BCE–200 CE) and the American saltation that 'invented the twentieth century' between the 1860s to the 1910s (Smil, 2005). Thus, to use the term 'Korean scientific saltation' or 'Korean saltation' may seem a misnomer, if much of Korean history is cultural and political continuity and stability. However, the history of Korean scientific and technical advance is the complete opposite of the presumed stasis that is indeed seen in Korea's long-lived states, its homogeneous aristocratic culture, or its isolated regionalized peasant cultures. So, in parallel and deep within Korea's ancient cultural and political stability is ironically a slowly moving thread of ongoing improved expertise in all kinds of technical innovations and scientific measurement tools that aggregated over time in the larger cultural stability to leave Koreans far ahead of their immediate neighbors (or even the world) in all kinds of technical innovations.

How is that a 'saltation?' You may say that slow technical and scientific improvement happens everywhere. It does, though it typically experiences many external interruptions or internal interruptions. On the other hand, Koreans had the same slow improvements as anyone, yet they lacked many great external or internal interruptions. Therefore, the 'normal' slow technical and scientific innovations and knowledge transmission could be sustained and improved over time far better in the Korean Peninsula than in other world regional areas. Plainly stated, the hypothesis is that how we can explain so many *Korean world firsts* is because of this region's relative lack of many great *breaks* in its own slow technical improvement compared to other areas of the world that have such breaks more often. This is different than the earlier hypothesis about Korean innovation about a more homogeneous culture exhibiting more capacity for collective innovation—which equally would apply here of course yet only be reinforced by this other principle of Korea equally having fewer breaks and fewer tragic losses in its common slow technical improvement than other areas of the world. Beyond that greater collective innovation in crisis, thus, there are other factors to help explain *comparative* world firsts in Korean history of science and technology. These several unique factors coming together are what is meant by the 'Korean saltation.' It is stretching the meaning of the term scientific saltation away from describing only abrupt discontinuities in science and technology to a way to characterize different kinds of ongoing priorities animating scientific and technical advance when based on different kinds of cultural, political, and economic processes under which they are facilitated. Below it is argued that there are at least eight *different* kinds of sociological contexts explaining *different* kinds of scientific saltations and how each developed their own different virtuous cycles, in different areas, and in different times in world history based on their different facilitating contexts. These eight kinds of scientific saltations can overlap and have overlapped in world history. So the slower kind of durable Korean saltation is a scientific 'evolution' instead of 'revolution' that has had even more amazing results than any scientific revolution, judged by the number of world firsts that Korea has. So, if ancient Korea as a culture and as unique sociological context created many more world firsts from slow technological evolution as the greater innovation compared to other civilizations' more abrupt scientific revolutions or technical revolutions, it is worth attempting to explain why.

A discussion of Korean 'world first' technical and scientific inventiveness could be organized in four overlapping themes: metalworking with military applications, automation with military applications, education/literature and the technologies of publishing hundreds of years before both Europe and China, and a large category of more domestic technical improvements applied to small-scale agriculture, small home design, more comfortable daily lives, and/or scientific studies of long-term ecological and climatic phenomena that can be applied to agricultural planning that only Koreans were doing as early as 500 years ago or more in world history. True, much of ancient Korean technical innovation seems to have a state military purpose or a state-agricultural improvement purpose involved in technical improvements to make both more successful, efficient, and productive. First, this is the case for many states being pushed by military technical improvements though only Koreans came up with repeated 'world firsts.' Second however, other long-term improvements were seen in the domestic sphere, in the cultural sphere of publication and knowledge sharing, and even in scientific instrumentation that were far ahead of China or Europeans. In short, the deep Korean inventiveness of the past can be seen in many world firsts in metallurgy, publishing, agriculture, shipbuilding, automation, rocketry, artillery, the most efficient bows and arrows for distance (already discussed), time-delay bombs, mass manufacture of shipbuilding, domestic home construction, stainless metal tableware, home heat recycling, heated greenhouses, mass publishing, non-acidic 'archival-grade' paper manufactures that last 1,000 years or more, and climatic scientific instrumentation. However, in the interests of space, there are other books on this topic that can be referenced instead of a discussion here (Korean Spirit and Culture Promotion Project, 2008). So, the theory about this more 'evolutionary Korean saltation' is stated clearly with a few illustrative examples only.

As a introduction to comparing these different 'scientific saltations', British historian Joseph Needham (1900–1995) spent his lifetime studying and publishing about the history of *Science and Civilization in China,* animated by the question why China was ahead globally and then stopped developing greatly in science and technology after the 1500s. However, this section is just a contribution making it more known how equally interesting has been *Science and Civilization in Korea.* Korea was further ahead in many areas than even China before the 1500s, and Koreans continued to advance afterwards as China declined. Now in the twenty-first century, Koreans maintain great technological leadership in our global world today.

First, the contention is that there are very different kinds of 'scientific saltations' in world history based on different sociological backgrounds motivating their different investigative questions and research productions. Second, the argument to explain why there are so many technical and scientific world firsts in Korea is that the area had a very unique kind of scientific saltation unseen anywhere else in world history for three rationales: (1) because Koreans experienced far less external interruption and less internal interruption; (2), because they are a more homogeneous culture with more collective innovation possible in a crisis instead of culturally splintering and falling apart; and (3), as well as how both of these together encourage a more continuous and aggregating knowledge transmission.

Putting these factors together means a political economy over a longer period of time in a particular space that can encourage a culture of conservative improvements to existing infrastructures, instead of more individualistic innovations or cultural innovations, and instead of experiencing various breaks or setbacks in that slow improvement, or instead of experiencing very rapid improvements either. The point is that the Korean saltation has so many world firsts because it is more cumulative without setbacks compared to other areas of the world. As they say, slow and steady wins the race. However, in this case it is equally 'slow and steady without taking breaks, suffering from amnesia, or running backward sometimes' wins the race. For such durable incentives of technical innovation, it has been said that "Korea's small territory with limited natural resources, spurs on the creative spirit of its people" (Korean Spirit and Culture Promotion Project, 2008, p. 71). It should more clearly be stated that Korea's small, quiet, endlessly-threatened yet rarely-invaded homogeneous culture calls up great collective innovation repeatedly in its population to survive, yet by surviving so often, they compete and prosper at a far higher advanced level compared to their geopolitical neighbors because of the lack of setbacks that do plague others whose scientific saltations are regularly interrupted more often. A technical success in avoiding external interruptions or internal challenges in turn further compounded Korean cultural isolation as well.

However, most historians of science poorly interpret the historiography of technical advance as *only* coming from those external interruptions or internal challenges instead of from ongoing conserved stasis in culture or instead argue it can only come from more pluralistic culture that shares more ideas. It is true that external or internal interruptions can create fast change, and they did in Korea as well in a few circumstances, though it is equally true that those interruptions can stop fast or slow change. Therefore, it is the greater lack of interruptions that wins the technical and scientific race for higher quality of life in the end. Plus, while pluralistic cultures do create their own kinds of innovations individually or culturally, more homogeneous cultures are argued to create faster collaborative innovations in crisis periods, the periods in which other cultures are more prone to fall apart and divide. So if Korea blended a long time, with few breaks, without forgetting, in a particular place, with deeper and faster collaboration both on conserved infrastructures and better coordination in crisis periods, this has created many world firsts in the history of Korean science and technology.

As the issue of collective innovation in a more homogeneous culture has already been discussed as one facilitator of a scientific saltation, this section discusses the other factors that are facilitators like the lack of interruptions and the cultural stability that are argued to create far more tangible material, scientific, and intellectual innovation and skilled labor conservation. This is contrary to the assumption by deduction that there are purportedly more scientific benefits from external or internal interruptions than, as argued here, really far more setbacks from them. This is because conserved knowledge and infrastructures without breaks create virtuous cycles of more durable and more accretive changes leading to many more inductively demonstrated world firsts in Korean history than would be assumed by the merely deductive theory about interruptions creating innovation only. Over time, this made trends of science and technology in Korea come out ahead of other states and cultures in other lands, scientifically and technically, since other lands did 'rely' on or just accidentally experience more innovation driven only by external interruptions or internal interruptions—and of course had more ongoing setbacks because of the same factors. In other words, the much larger setbacks from external interruptions and internal interruptions have been more ignored while people concentrated more on the innovation from them.

For an analogy, the Korean Peninsula has been like some undisturbed space inside a geode or cave, in which two factors of a quiet uninterrupted space and a slowly dripping temporal advance are dual rationales why incomparably beautiful crystals, stalactites, or stalagmites are created over thousands of years. So the Korean Peninsula was historically like some geopolitical geode, in which science and technological improvement grew slowly to great lengths in a more conserved transmission over thousands of years in the Korean Peninsula and because of a lack of major knowledge breaks, setbacks, and interruptions that other civilizations regularly experienced in the lands surrounding it. Of course Korean collective innovation in a more homogeneous culture over time mattered as well.

For the historical discussion before further theoretical statement that will help explain the later statements, Korean technical and scientific advances seem an ancient part of a wide competitive culture of material and intellectual improvement in many areas, instead of only seeing that competition in a limited sense of material bodily perfection in the culture, as described above. On the one hand, it is not right to argue that modern Korean technological innovation came entirely out of a 'modern culture' of Korea. This is because a very deep heritage exists that has worked on technical innovation as intellectual/scientific improvement as 'national service' problems trying to solve Korea's military problems, as well as equally daily domestic or agricultural problems for thousands of years. On the other hand, you can say this for any areas of the world. Every culture tries to work on material improvement of itself over time. So, why is this so different or important in Korea?

It is different and important because in world history, comparatively speaking, ongoing trends of technical innovation are amazing in ancient Korea and demand explanation. It is argued that some cultural situations allow technical improvements to become more of a virtuous cycle improved upon for generations instead of to be lost and regained later. These situations would be whenever a culture has unique stabilities, durable incentives, conserved infrastructures, or all intertwined. As said earlier, unique stabilities are found in the Korean Peninsula in the bizarrely long lengths of many Korean dynasties in the past. Some dynasties lasted approximately 1,000 years (Silla/Unified Silla (57 BCE–935 CE), or 600 years (Goguryeo, 37 BCE–668 CE; Baekjae, 18 BCE–660 CE; Kaya Confederacy, 42–562 CE; Joseon Dynasty 1392–1910 CE), or even 400 years (Goryeo, 918–1392 CE). Typically, most states in world history barely survive 200 years in other parts of the world. Apply that fact to scientific and technical transmission and improvement. Apply that fact to other places that repeatedly are set back every few hundred years. The latter is less the case in the Korean Peninsula.

Other unique stabilities are how Korean dynastic states were mostly ruled by weak kings with conserved aristocratic families even over multiple dynasties of dynastic changes (Palais, 1995). So, a deeply stable Korean aristocracy and oligarchy was only truly jettisoned by 1960, yet it has been involved in conserving its own cultural, technical, and scientific transmissions for millennia without regular interruption and loss of knowledge that are seen in deeply destructive inter-dynastic periods in other parts of the world in many cases.

On the one hand, a loss of this aristocracy is a rare occurrence in world history. Losing an aristocracy has regularly set off massive social and technical changes itself, of the kind seen in modern South Korea after 1961, or seen earlier in the Song dynasty of China after the relatively quick destruction of millennia-old conserved aristocratic families from the early Han dynasties into the T'ang dynasty (Tackett, 2014). Even at the start of the United States, framed in a wider comparative context of European culture, the United States was a European cultural colonial zone sloughing off its native British aristocracy as well as failing to ever have a stable rural peasantry either. This soon led to a large amount of urban-commercial innovation as seen similarly in the Chinese Song dynasty. This is seen as well in Korea after 1961 as Korea lost its aristocracy from the politics of the First Republic (1948–1960) after the aristocracy already lost it in economics throughout the earlier part of the twentieth century into the many land distributions from 1948 to 1952. However, after 1961 as Korea kept its stable rural peasantry with land distributions, other sociological sources of technical innovation were to come, from first, the Korean state's focus on export-led development instead, and in time, second, Korea's own problem solving around urban infrastructural issues to handle it durably.

On the other hand, an ongoing conserved aristocracy for millennia is something Koreans benefitted from instead of only suffered from over the years. This is because it can be a conserved base of cultural transmission in buildings, books, innovations, relationships, mentorship, prideful family heritage, and spare time away from daily drudgeries of life that helps to study, to think, and to invent to solve problems. The lack of long term wars and lack of many major natural disasters in the Korean Peninsula can be a conserved space in rural village life as well, providing incentives to work on slow regional improvements in the more conserved domestic housing and agricultural implements instead of worrying about such interruptions all the time that could make such an investments in time and effort pointless.

The argument is that this earlier aristocratic-side of the Korean-style saltation ended around the early twentieth century in the colonial period (1910–1945), and after 1961 was converted into a more common modern British/American-style commercial urban industrial saltation of science and technology for mass markets of consumers and for global exports at the same moment. However, given the strength of a rural culture, some aspects of the rural-side of this Korean saltation may have existed in an ongoing way in the grass roots development and regional optimization drives from 1970 onward for a time. However, concentrating only on what happens in Korea after 1961 disguises dozens of world firsts in science and technology that came from the earlier (aristocratic-side or the rural-side of the) Korean saltation long before even the European Renaissance started to organized different virtuous cycles of science.

To further theorize now from the above, while reflecting on comparative world history of science, first, there seem four common sources in world history for the loss of skills, personnel, and knowledge transmissions that create setbacks in scientific and technical innovations. These setbacks are: (1) violent and/or long interregnums between dynastic states, (2) internal coups within states and internal peasant rebellions both keen on destroying the coordinating records and personnel of the previous regime, (3) external wartime violence on a defender's infrastructures and intentional cultural heritage destruction as psychological terrorism in war beyond strategic aims of winning battles, or (4) natural disasters like earthquakes, large storms, and tsunamis associated with related fires, floods, infrastructural abandonment, loss of artisans, loss of skills, or just loss of desire in despair and loss of economic budgets to repair. These four scientific traumas are huge setbacks to scientific and technical transmission and improvement worldwide for any kind of scientific and technical advance, particularly those toward more quality of life. They are the four 'scientific horsemen of the apocalypse' that plague all civilizations' technical improvement in world history—*except for Koreans on all four points*.

Second, if we think about all different kinds of virtuous cycles of scientific saltation, we have at least eight kinds of different scientific saltations by *different kinds of sociological stability or instability*. (1) We have state facilitation by *simple territorial stability* and its security without much large urbanization, in a Han dynasty-style saltation (221 BCE to approximately 200 CE). (2) We have a public and/or underground mass publishing-based scientific saltation created when a *dissenting cultural stability in transmission* starts to exist through it, instead of being divided or isolated as before. This is the cultural and publishing architecture that facilitated the slow cross-state development of European/Renaissance-style saltation in a 'republic of letters' stemming first from the recovery of Greek scientific and occult manuscripts in Florence in the early 1400s. This rapidly expanded with Gutenberg's printing press that invented cheaper ways for spreading both these older texts and of course updated or newer knowledge. Novel individual mass-published scholars and thinkers, both scientific and religious, made a shared dissenting saltation outside the monopoly control of the publishing and teaching edifice of the Catholic Church—which was the European medieval world's version of our current Google-based censorship, monitoring, and persecution of dissenting ideas trying to be shared (Morozov, 2011; Vorhies & Heckenlively, 2021).

(3) We have an urban, commercial, and industrial-style scientific saltation facilitated by *mass market stability* in rural or urban consumers, in an American style scientific saltation (approximately from the 1860s through the 1910s (Smil, 2005). (4) For historical Korea, we have long-term aristocratic and peasant continuities in an evolutionary scientific saltation. These provide a *stability here that is long term because of lack of many external and internal interruptions*. Because of that long temporal and spatial stability, we see a Korean-style scientific saltation from over two thousand years ago to around the early twentieth century for the aristocratic/state side, and somewhat continuing in the rural side to the twenty-first century despite external and internal interruptions and depredations of World War II and the Korean War that truly wrecked cultural continuity in almost all places of North Korea and most places in South Korea. (5) We have a *state-policy stability* that can guide scientific saltations based on a very filtered priority through subsidized funding or personnel coordination toward what kind of technical futures a state wants to build and against other kinds of technical futures it wants to repress.

(6) Plus, we have scientific saltations by different *kinds of instabilities from external interruptions*, like internecine wars, mere durable fears of invasion, or long-term competitive empires all creating a scientific saltation between competitive military industrial complexes, or (7) scientific saltations by *instabilities from internal interruptions*, like after the European Great Plague or "Black Death" of the late 1300s that created a 'labor-saving saltation' with far more focus upon how to construct labor saving equipment to demote suddenly more expensive labor costs due to perhaps one-third of Europeans dying of plague in the late 1300s. Such labor-saving saltations can come from many different other kinds of saltations mentioned

above as well of course, instead of exclusive to this motivation. (8) By the late twentieth century, we globally and regionally enter another kind of *scientific saltation via either (8a) external instability from the wider ecology and internally from pollutions and from political protests* from an urban, regional, national, or international citizen base *or an economic protest base*, or (8b) *long-term and commons-based tinkering under local conditions*, both pushing us into a circular economy saltation. This has been encouraged by social pressures from a 'risk society' (Beck, 1992) toward how to design durable and flexible virtuous cycles of ecological improvement in a 'reflexive modernization' in all our institutions (whether political, economic, scientific, and/or material). This scientific saltation pushes us to attempt to minimize contributions of the past's risky ecological situations, that these institutions have created, as they equally now consider their future more ecologically-sound development.

These eight kinds of scientific saltations can of course interact, like how scientific saltations encouraged and curated by long-term aristocratic interests (into Korean-style saltations) or like in the British Empire that merged its own long-term conserved aristocratic interests with more mass market stabilities of urban industrialization, concerns about urban pollution handling of London, and with international military competition as four different yet interactive and combined saltation factors among the British Empire by the late 1800s onward. On the other hand, we have other kinds of scientific saltations that expand in the political and economic vacuum when such aristocracies die, like under Park Chung-hee from 1961 onward in South Korea leading into Korea's more state-directed scientific saltation combining with American style saltation of an urban commercial economy. This was like the dual dynamics of two scientific saltations equally seen in the Chinese Song dynasty (960 to 1279) after the death of the earlier Chinese T'ang dynasty aristocracy conserved from the Han dynasty or before, as the Song dynasty equally had something similar to South Korea after 1961 in having a state-policy led saltation in military weapons combined with its 'freed' urban commercial economy saltation as well.

Thus, these different kinds of scientific saltations can overlap of course in particular political economies like having a continuing British aristocracy's 'Korean style' saltation of scientific interests of chemists, physicists, and geographical exploration as well as its support of elite artisanal consumption in fine foods and teas, and later linked even more with London's urban commercial mass market economy, as well as a saltation trying to scientifically solve the pollution of waste treatment and water flows in London, and even linked within the wider British Empire's competitive military-industrial-complex saltation interacting with the scientific and technical inventions of other empires and European states. In other words, some cultures in some periods of time have access to multiple scientific saltations while others have access to less or even have zero.

However, it is conjectured that only the Korean style saltation, *when occurring alone*, in the lack of external or internal interruptions is one that may develop an interest in *expanding technologies of wider quality of life* and military security by *exclusively defense technologies* at low costs. This qualitative concern about increased quality of life and toward minimizing military damage and lessening military costs is different for instance to just innovating technologies around wider offensive depredation in military advance regardless of cost, and different than technologies designed only to undercut labor wages, or different than technologies or materials designed just to make short-cuts in quality in order to make greater efficiencies of scale in profit in a commercial mass economy of serviceable yet low quality items.

Back to the Korean Peninsula, in the past, such a high political cultural stability, elite autonomy, and obviously greater aristocratic free time is argued to have been a uniquely fertile situation for having a stable enough culture, information transmission, wealth, and politics for slow and long-term scientific 'evolution' of invention and technological improvement. This is not the kind of slow yet focused kind of scientific revolution that occurred from the 1500s onward in Europe as the durable incentives of shared private publishing and a growing commercial economy started to effect improvements of various technologies well into the early 1800s. It is not a kind of faster 'technical revolution' of the kind seen in the unique stabilities and durable incentives of the 'great saltation' of the Han dynasty of China after hundreds of years of war leading into this first consolidated territorial dynasty (221 BCE–220 CE). The Han dynasty was the time when improvements and scaled innovations of many Chinese technologies were invented for the first time because they were made for the first time for a large stable market arrangement in China built in the shadow of the first major stable empire of China. Equally, historical Korea is not a kind of faster technical 'urban commercial revolution' in the American style saltation seen from the 1860s through the early twentieth century from durable incentives to serve and to profit from providing technical solutions for novel large-scale mass markets of millions of rural or urban people. Such mass markets helped wealthy entrepreneurs and scientific innovators find each other regularly for the first time in world history to (re)design nearly everything about our modern life's materials in this short period to exhibit mass society characteristics. This mass society infrastructure is one we still live within globally now (Smil, 2005) that is only slightly being altered by a more circular economy saltation. Some aspects of this American style saltation can be seen in the British Empire around London's mass markets, and the circular economy saltation can be seen in the mass problems leading to ecological concerns in Liverpool and London particularly by the 1850s as well. So even the eighth scientific saltation, toward a circular economy, can be seen developing earlier in Liverpool and London than anywhere else in Europe. Liverpool was the British Isles' most important port, and thus its most diseased and dirty port. Modern water handling and urban sewer technologies were innovated there first. Next, London became the first city in world history approaching a scale of 2 million people after the 1850s. Therefore, many more circular systems of water, sewers, garbage collection, etc., were starting to be invented or elaborated as interactive infrastructures in order to stop systemic mass death from cholera and other urban ills at the time like river pollution or air pollution. Equally, In Tokugawa Japan (1600–1858), at the capital of Edo (now Tokyo) it showed another early example of this eighth kind of scientific saltation toward a circular economy. This is because Edo was a massive durable city of 1 million people from the early 1700s to the present, starting even earlier than London on trying to make urban living sustainable. Tokyo remained over 1 million for hundreds of years which is quite a social and technical accomplishment, similar to Rome's earlier record of at least 400 years into the 500s CE. Thus the structures of Edo and the people of Edo had to learn to innovate to handle pressures of 'interruption' from such urban wastes at massive scales daily for centuries, while cut off from global trade as well. Thus Edo can be said to have had its own Korean style saltation by a similar conserved aristocratic interest combined with a lack of wars or external contact at this time from the 1600s through the 1850s that merged with its circular economy saltation. Typically however, any isolated Korean-style saltation is incapable of building such larger cities without international trade.

Therefore, like most cases of the world, nothing is pure—particularly scientific saltation. The Korean saltation is blended into that other kind of scientific saltation like competitive military advance. However, the ongoing Korean saltation could concentrate on *having fewer setbacks in finding technical solutions* for more defense-based technologies at cheaper labor and material costs, instead of developing more military technologies designed for external invasion or instead of experiencing setbacks. This is because the Joseon dynasty (similar to the defensive military saltation of Constantinople for centuries) wished to maintain isolation via technical advance, instead of wished to wreck that isolation by extending conquest to other areas of the world—which though is the more common pressure in many nation's competitive military scientific saltations.

For one instance of a lack of setbacks and a world first, there are records of gunpowder recipes being used in Korea from the 600s, *far earlier than the Chinese* in the Song Dynasty after 1000 CE onward.

> Gunpowder-based weapons were in use in Korea much earlier than is commonly believed. *Prerequisites for a Military Commander*, a war manual published in the latter half of the Joseon period (1392-1910), explains the principles of explosives, and gives an account of ancient gunpowder-based weapons called chung-jon-roe and hwa-roe-po. Academics have assigned these weapons to the Three Kingdoms period (57 BC ~ AD 668). In the History of the Three Kingdoms, also, the army of Silla is said to have used 'black powder' against Goguryeo in the battle of Pukhansan Castle in 661. (Korean Spirit and Culture Promotion Project, 2008, p. 59)

For two other instances, it is unsurprising Koreans seem the first in world history from available evidence to combine bronze with zinc by the 900s CE. This is difficult to do because of zinc's low boiling (away) point compared to other metals in the alloy that are in their molten states only at the same temperature. Equally, Koreans were equally the first to have a fully-armored horse and cavalry (Korean Spirit and Culture Promotion Project, 2008, p. 61), likely given rarity and value of such cavalry in smaller Korean armies of archers. However, showing the wealth of metals they had available, ancient Korean horse cavalry were said to be "closer to full tanks on all sides" while other civilizations' horse cavalry was only partial. "The kaema musa, or armored cavalry, enabled Goguryeo to maintain the upper hand in this war with the [much larger armies of the Chinese] Sui and hold considerable influence in East Asia over a long period of time" (Korean Spirit and Culture Promotion Project, 2008, p. 48). The Chinese losing to Goguryeo Koreans in 613 and 614 CE led to the successful coup and collapse of the young Chinese Sui dynasty, after which China was then ruled by the Chinese T'ang dynasty. Where did Goguryeo get such steel manufacturing expertise? It got the expertise from its ancestors of Old Joseon, over 700 years earlier instead of as a fresh invention.

For yet another instance of world firsts, the famous Korean 'turtle ships' (Korean, 'kobukson') were the world's first plate-armored ocean warships. People generally associate their 'invention' was by Joseon Admiral Yi Sun-sin (1545–1598) in the 1590s. Actually, these kobukson were only his updates of plans of Korean armor-plated ships archived from the early 1410s, used already in war games then, and found in almost 200-year-old documents that Koreans still had the luxury to reference in order to advance further than others upon their own earlier advances, instead of starting armored ships from scratch each time (Korean Spirit and Culture Promotion Project, 2008). Therefore, even competitive military advance benefits from such Korean-style scientific saltations. Koreans had less scientific setbacks over time while they were seeking out mostly only further ways to maintain a lack of external interruptions, via defense of their peninsula instead of military innovations trying to take offensive battles to the Japanese islands for instance even though they could have. However, that latter kind of offensive military saltation, with a more costly and more competitive expansionism that takes war to other lands, is different than the more internalized Korean saltation zone and culture that instead sought how to maximize quality of life even by military technologies focused more on defense instead of seeking out the most destructive purposes they could find in the interests of offensive attacks. Thus much about the military innovations of ancient Korea are about how they can maintain their geopolitical geode more efficiently—with better defense, smarter materials, less effort, more automation/mechanization in technical skills, and less economic disruption—instead of how to maintain an external empire and instead of escalating destructive techniques as well.

Thus, even the Korean saltation was hardly exclusively acting only from one kind of internal pressure or dynamic from the lack of external or internal interruptions. Thus some parts of the Korean saltation are hardly separate from other saltations like the competitive military pressures of technical advance. However, the Korean-style saltation could keep existing because of technical success in avoiding the setbacks of invasions by others and avoiding their own costly external invasions taken to others' countries. Koreans were further ahead than others by a lack of technical setbacks—setbacks that did plague more regularly Korea's geopolitical competitors over time like the Mongols, China, and Japan. Plus, all those endless fears of invasion of Korea rarely occurred by ongoing good Korean technical developments themselves that had a lack of setbacks for centuries. This combined with the greater collective innovation in crisis that a more homogeneous culture has to utilize. Meanwhile a more heterogeneous culture arguably will more likely fall apart into subcultural parts in existential crises upon being invaded or attacked. This of course can systemically perpetuate larger crises of cultural dissolution and conquest instead of solve them with the reputed benefits of a heterogeneous culture. Thus, the drawbacks and greater difficulties of a heterogeneous culture are exposed in its existential crises, while in more peaceful times they may be judged to look as if they have only superior benefits.

Both of these issues of a greater homogeneous culture's collective innovation and thus its ability to solve existential crises under external threat have influenced the military branch of the Korean saltation's applications.

However, a competitive military purpose was hardly the only elaborated motivation for or result of the Korean saltation per se. Once such a long-term stability started to exist in the first place in the Korean Peninsula, it developed a separate logic for technical tinkering toward better quality of life for poorer people in general. Many other lands unfortunately never even get to see this kind of saltation *toward greater quality of life in particular regions* as a motivator of their scientific advance, due to their wide interruptions over time or due to their scientific saltations being more exclusively caught up in limited applications for an aristocratic elite, a competitive offensive war, or a mass market economy instead of motivated by localization and optimization. Thus in the Korean saltation many world firsts were created in expanding regional quality of life, building on that 'lack of setbacks' that poor or rich Koreans could enjoy.

So the Korean saltation is a long-term, slow, effective technological and scientific improvement of periods of uniquely long stabilities in Korean history, rarely seen anywhere in world history except in Korean history. Historical Korea was blessed to be without many dynastic, geopolitical, or geophysical external interruptions like respectively coups, wartime invasions, or major natural disasters like earthquakes, typhoons, or tsunamis. All of these regularly impact a culture in the same way by destroying a region's heritage and continuity in architecture, books, libraries, artisans, skills, market scale, factories, etc., in sudden changes that are social, psychological, and physical. In the Korean Peninsula, the strong continuity of elite groups across dynastic states and in regional peasant populations was without many serious wartime invasions and dislocation. This avoids other civilizations' double transmission losses in elites' or commoners' knowledge that regularly occur in interregnums between dynastic states or in wartime violence on the defender's infrastructures or agricultural zones.

A darker side of preconditions for such unique geopolitical and geophysical stability in the Korean saltation is that the large amount of free time that Korean aristocracies or royal houses had for scholarship or sponsoring potential innovation was surely connected to the equal loss of free time for others. In world history, Korea had a uniquely large and durable level of slavery as its darker side associated with this aristocratic stable settlement and a lack of external interruptions. Korea had domestic and hereditary enslavement of its own Korean people by these Korean aristocratic families. Even Buddhist religious institutions tolerated and kept expanding slavery upon the native Korean population, without invasions 'disrupting' the darker side of these 'unique stabilities.' In retrospect, one can argue external invasions are beneficial great resets for enslaved and repressed peasantries, so it might have been good occasionally for the Korean peasantry and its increasingly enslaved conditions if there had been more often a serious invasion threat that would have more regularly threatened the growing bad political settlement between a growing slavery and the aristocracy. Nothing seems better than a good external invasion or internal peasant rebellion to help aristocrats see their own mortality when they lack willing peasant allies, under which they may try to reframe bad political settlements among their own people to the latter's favor to try to keep them from being opportunistic rebels or willing executioners against them in such times. This large, Korean, aristocratic, royal, and temple-based slavery upon Koreans existed well into the 1890s (Palais, 1995). Many socially degrading practices like this were ended in the Gabo Reforms of 1894-96, and, to show that rule mentioned above, it was only a nearly successful Tonghak peasant religious rebellion that had its goals as killing off all Korean aristocrats and foreigners in the country had set these reforms in motion. As much of the Joeseon military sent to fight against the Tonghak rebellion instead presumably joined the rebellion instead, this peasant rebellion was only put down by external dual Chinese and Japanese invasions, the former Chinese one traitorously invited into Korea by the Joseon dynasty itself and the latter an opportunistic one by the Japanese. However, for about one thousand years before the 1890s, slaves increasingly busied themselves with work of daily life for their aristocratic owners across several dynastic changes, so aristocrats had unique stabilities and free time for such technical and scientific inventiveness and improvement, if they so chose.

However, on the other hand, unique stabilities in the Korean Peninsula seem to have served equally as a durable incentive for peasant inventiveness in improving their properties, agriculture, and general organization of village life under the long conditions without war or rebellion. This could influence how they design their houses and agriculture to be more efficient regionally over time—like how Koreans invented the first heated greenhouse about 500 years ago, known from (the last copy of) a mass published book. Plus, Koreans had the world's only example of efficient full-floor heating called kudle or ondol, based on a circular economy saltation or motif of recycling kitchen smoke and cooking heat under the raised non-flammable stone floor of the home to get floor-based heating in the winter instead of having a separate energy expense for getting that heat. This equally used a smart awareness of how certain unique natural materials, like mica stone that comes in layers and is a high heat insulator, could be used to serve as the home's layered heat insulation on the stone floors for this purpose. (Korean Spirit and Culture Promotion Project, 2008). Similarly, after the collapse of the Later Han dynasty after 220 CE, as the competitive military saltation of large-scale and centralized military spending and invasions were less prominent motivators (or destroyers) of technical change, only then did China start to popularize similar technology for higher peasant quality of life like the Chinese 'kang,' the heated bed-stove. It was invented earlier, yet only popularized in this less martial time after the collapse of the Later Han dynasty. However, the Chinese kang was only a smaller raised brick heated platform about two meters square added inside a house. Instead, only the Korean ondol was an extensive full-floor heating in the redesign of the house, and only the ondol was designed intelligently to reuse recycled kitchen heat a second time for two different purposes, for higher quality of life and less costs all around. The martial and commercial Romans did invent the hypocaust, yet it was only for state-subsidized public baths and was expanded only as a technology to install as a profitable commercial business venture in expensive aristocratic villas instead of the Romans fretting how technically to improve quality of life in individual plebeian homes. Vitruvius in his *De architectura* (approx., 15

BC) can be read to show that that the hypocaust was only part of an aristocratic and mass market commercial saltation: being designed by the wealthy merchant Gaius Sergius Orata (fl., ~95 BCE) who was only involved in technology when it served his several mass market commercial schemes like the mass production of oysters as well as exclusively designing hypocausts originally for the only private market that would bear it, the aristocratic villa.

In fact, the early twentieth century American architect Frank Lloyd Wright, on a visit to Japan, visited a Japanese hotel with a warm "Korean room." This room he remarked seemed to him to be as warm and joyful as summer with an entirely different mood, despite it being in the middle of the winter. This was due to the fully heated "Korean" floor. Subsequently, Wright copied the design of a heated Korean floor using modern electricity into some of his American suburban homes' bathrooms or even whole-home floor plans. Apple Computer's co-founder and later CEO Steve Jobs grew up in one of Wright's suburban homes that had this Korean inspired heated-floor technology. Jobs later remarked that it was in this Wright house, in which he lived with his adopted parents, where he started first to admire and to think about the importance of good design. Likely, Jobs never knew that he and Apple Computer later were inspired to think about good design in the first place by the influence of well-designed Korean technology (Isaacson, 2011). So as Steve Jobs grew up in one of these Wright suburban houses in California, he came to be inspired by the oddly good craftsmanship of his parent's house as one factor that got him interested in elegant and effective design. Ultimately, Korean material culture and its goals of good quality of life for all was inspiring Steve Jobs in his early life, whether he knew it or not.

Plus, many good 'quality of life' tinkerings happened over centuries in a conserved infrastructure in the ever greater isolation from the late 1300s onward into the Joseon dynasty. It was during the more isolated Joseon dynasty that many technologies and design ideas merged into the traditional Korean home called a 'hanok.' Since Korea has a climate of very hot summers and very cold winters, in addition to kudle (ondol) stone-heated floors for very cold winters, Koreans invented retractable external walls of a house that were opened like double doors, swung fully back and locked to another door-wall panel, then both locked pieces could pivot up from the top of the door and be 'hung' under the roof of the veranda, parallel to the floor of a veranda, from hooks in the extended roof. This allowed breezes to get into the homes in summer seasons. Later these could be unhooked, pivoted, and then twisted and locked back in place as insulated walls for the winter. In short, Korean 'hanok' houses had a difficult regional climactic design order to fulfill that was executed perfectly over the centuries likely due to ongoing conservation of infrastructures and tinkerings. In the winter, hanok had to be secure against cold drafty air to be very warm in the winter. So it had to be very energy efficient and insulated, yet without dangers of burning down or death of the occupants by smoke inhalation in such air-sealed rooms. Therefore, heated and insulated stone floors were preferred instead of internal fires in the home. In the summer, hanok simultaneously had to be the opposite of an air-tight and floor-heated winter home, and had to be converted easily into an airy house with cool floors to avoid filling the house with mold in the very humid and rainy Korean summers. Hanok, combining heated-floor kudle and louvered-panels of insulated walls, fit two very different seasonal requirements admirably in the same house. Moreover, the stone floors would remain cool in the summer as well. The stone floors were covered with special soft and thick Korean oil-preserved yellow paper, reminiscent of soft linoleum, which avoided stains as well as helped to insulate against burns from direct skin contact with the hot stone floor itself in the winter upon which Koreans slept to keep warm. So Koreans had heated beds as well in this way. Koreans cheaply papered their floors for easy cleaning and to avoid burns from the ondol, and cheaply papered their windows in a similar fashion to let in opaque light and yet maintain privacy. These paper products could be cheaply replaced when required. Plus, hanok designs over time in the Korean saltation were fitted to different regions of Korea quite well, with the 'traditional plan' of northern Korea being more closed in a square format with an open quad to the sky in the middle. The closed design of hanok was built only in the colder north, to stop cold drafts. However, in the southern part of Korea, more linear and open-plans of hanok were preferred since the warmer southern region would allow cooling breezes to flow directly through both sides of a more linear house. Many modern Korean high-rise apartment buildings still have hanok-inspired verandas in each apartment and still have hanok-inspired linear house designs since one apartment is designed to take up the whole floor of a building and thus has large windows on both sides of a modern building to enjoy any cooling breezes through one side of the building and out the other side. This is unlike many Western apartments with common windowless dark internal hallways with apartments on each side of the hallway and thus with only one wall with windows per apartment, without much cross-ventilation built into the design (Inaji & Virgilio, 1998). In short the traditional Korean house called hanok is the work of centuries of different regions' adaptations and yet always designed to be cheap to upkeep and to be efficient in materials, heating, and cooking. Hanok was and remains uniquely suitable to the ecological extremes of the Korean peninsula with its very cold winters that descend in storms directly from the tundra of northern Siberia, to the hot and humid summers of the monsoonal season from across the Pacific Ocean with lots of daily rain. Modern Koreans stereotype older hanok as drafty and cold, compared to modern dwellings. However, the real comparisons are older hanok dwellings compared to how older peasants in other cultures lived without any ongoing technical thought for improvement in their dwellings for hundreds of years at all, unlike Korea.

Equally popularized during the more isolated Joseon dynasty, good quality of life comes from the first 'bronze stainless steel' of 'bangjja yugi' (Korean bronzeware) invented in Korea. Bangjja is tableware of exactly 22% tin and 78% copper only found in Korea, because only briefly at this high percentage of tin does the bronze ratio show a pleasing whitish-golden color that no one else discovered in the world. It was not discovered elsewhere because 22% tin in bronze is very difficult to work with or to cast as it shatters easily. This 22% tin in Korean bronzes is more than double the normal amount of tin found in other brassware worldwide with their ratios generally at 9 parts copper to only 1 part tin. However, Koreans have been perfecting the artistry and foundry skill in around making and handling these more easily-shattered 'double tin' bronzes from at least the 1300s for domestic tableware. Bangjja was first used by the aristocracy and royal court, given the pleasing golden color and how such a high amount of copper of course holds heat very well when used as serving dishes. Later, in our modern world, it was realized that the high copper tableware of bangjja has an anti-biotic effect as well, killing *E. coli* bacteria in food. Europeans were using a similar tableware of pewter (tin alloy with antimony or lead) since Roman times, and pewter has even been found in ancient Egyptian tombs. However, Westerners were using a quite toxic lead tableware without bacterial sterilization capacities—except perhaps for sterilizing themselves over time. So, with Koreans using copper-tin bronzewares (that required higher heat, costs, and skills to make) instead of lead–tin wares (that required lower heat, costs, and skills to make—yet were biologically toxic to the users) shows Koreans with a long and deep familiarity with both improved health in quality of life as well as a deep skill set in metal materials to hit upon such a potentially brittle-forged 22% tin to 78% copper bronze alloy for a stainless tableware yet without brittleness only once hardened. It shows the domestic quality of life goals that Koreans were seeking that could be encouraged by default better in the Korean saltation over time. Koreans seem to have been using this bangjja metal stainless tableware since the 1300s, though pewter was used longer in the Mediterranean. Other similar modern and less toxic alloys like stainless steel for tableware and cutlery were not invented until the early twentieth century.

Thus, arguably, many interacting rationales exist for these long-term improvements in the domestic sphere instead of technical applications only caught up in a military saltation. First, this was because of unique conserved stabilities in Korean infrastructures of the past that encouraged being tinkered with over time by rich and poor alike instead of wholly replaced, because of less setbacks in knowledge transmission over time. Second, there was the Korean saltation's high shared status of education across the full Korean culture for millennia among elites seen in mass publishing with metal typefaces in Chinese characters from the 1300s—far earlier than other states in the world. Increasingly, mass publishing for public education in simple scripts of Hangeul from the 1440s developed—as a mass publishing for public education equally far earlier than other states in the world. Third, to continue about Hangeul, even in this more isolated period of the Joseon dynasty, there was stress on education and transmission of knowledge. Only within approximately fifty years of the dynasty's start, this was the time of the rise of Hangeul from the 1440s onward. It gave even peasant populations and women (the latter previously banned from being literate in Chinese characters, even at court) greater access to information sharing. Koreans moved toward more European/Renaissance style mass-publishing style saltations all their own seen in the start of a history of Korean Joseon dynasty recipe books in Hangeul, scientific record keeping in Hangeul for agricultural improvement, or medical compendiums in Hangeul that all came in some way from alliances of common elite-and-peasant cultural concerns. Plus, the invention of Hangeul itself in the more isolated Joseon dynasty sees greater invention instead of stasis. Hangeul's invention itself stems from another of these common elite-and-peasant cultural concerns. Fourth, that leads into the same argument about how such common elite-peasant cultural concerns are easier to act upon in a homogeneous culture, and that itself has greater access to that collective innovation as another factor built into the Korean saltation of the past.

These common advances in daily quality of life, in sheer human comfort, in economic efficiency of recycled cooking heat for home heating, in easily reusable and sanitary stainless table ware, and in scientific record keeping of centuries of weather phenomena, was done in a time and in an isolated country while Europeans were in open battles for centuries with each other and were hardly spending any time innovating domestic living, much less doing anything about the importance of centralized and multi-regional weather records for thinking about regional optimality. Even though Europeans innovated materials in war as much as Koreans, Koreans were equally living in innovative infrastructures with full-floor recycled heating while Europeans were living in drafty and smoky thatch homes. Even the innovation of a specialized chimney failed to develop in Europe widely until the late 1500s to early 1600s. Despite the first still-extant chimney being at Coinsbrough Castle, Yorkshire, England, dated to approximately in 1185 CE, most European aristocrats were living in 'castles' in which water froze to ice in the winter as these castles were made of cold stone without even fireplaces—while at the same time the more humanistic, energy-conserving, and regionally- and ecologically-fitted hanok were being built throughout Korea by the 1300s. There are records of even European princesses pathetically forced to clutch many small domestic dogs in bed for warmth in the winter. At the same time in Europe, peasants were sleeping eight or more to a bed as the only 'technical advance' for centuries that Europeans acted on for warmth. The hypothesis is that *because* Korean homes and constructions were more conserved infrastructures, and because the Joseon dynastic period was a period of even higher isolation than before, it was during this time Koreans were more likely than ever before to have had the incentive to tinker technically on improvements for the long term on the village level or the aristocratic level without much worry that all their home or garden improvements would be destroyed by external war or internal disruptions every twenty years or so, as would be the case for many European regions. Europeans got durable incentives for very few built infrastructural investments at such scale since they were regularly wrecking them, rebuilding, or simply fleeing them by escaping from wars, revolts, arson, and theft. Koreans in having much less worry about being killed or displaced regularly, meant they had more time to worry about how to live well instead of only how to make military technology.

Thus, this Korean saltation before the twentieth century accelerated and compounded in the isolation of the Joseon dynasty. It was a slow ongoing improvement of various kinds of technical and scientific skills catalyzed by unique stabilities, durable incentives, and conserved infrastructures over thousands of years without regular setbacks. This conserved state aristocratic elite or this conserved village-level continuity, both with very few major interruptions, *locked out* Koreans from long-term cultural changes like long military battles, ancient colonization, peasant rebellions, or natural disasters, and *locked in Koreans within* their own slow improvement. This even benefitted Koreans *competitively and militarily* within a system of larger East Asian states *that did have many more interruptions,* and thus despite being larger states with greater resources, kept falling backward repeatedly and found themselves over time behind the isolated Koreans in many military technologies. In such long term isolation, by the 1300s onward Koreans were building ecological and energy-conserving housing, building heated greenhouses for more food security, taking detailed climactic and rain records with standardized instruments and nationally assembling the data, living in a culture of mass publishing for the people at large instead of only for elites, automating artillery barrages, building time-release bombs, and inventing multi-meter long rocketry and armor-plating their oceanic warships. This was several centuries before Europeans.

This is not to argue other kinds of virtuous or vicious cycles of scientific saltations fail to exist as created from 'useful' external or internal interruptions, as said above. However, scientific and technical advances by these kinds of external competitions in war or in internal competitions in a labor market are *qualitatively* different than the Korean saltation and its lack of major external interruptions for millennia (despite external challenges of course) that made *greater* scientific and technical *nuance* and engineering *excellence* possible as something *to hone* over time due to the long-term actions exercised on such questions. This kind of Korean saltation once more makes "Planet Korea" very different place than the technical and scientific trends seen in other places in world history. Korea was far more technically advanced far earlier, even against its larger neighboring states. This is argued to be so because of Korea's greater lack of external or internal interruptions compared to its neighboring states and compared to other places of the world.

In short, modern Koreans are justifiably very proud of ancient Korean excellence of design and craftsmanship in many physical mediums whether pottery, metals, weaving, or scientific instruments like rain gauges, astronomical devices, or even massive water clocks for marking time. Even the Japanese recognized this and tried to steal Korean potters or printing technology to take back to Japan in the Imjin War of the 1590s. Plus, Japan in the 1590s stole and archived some *metal typefaces* that the Joseon dynasty had invented in the 1440s to print in the unique script Hangeul for state-supported national publication drives. This was before Gutenberg's smaller-scale and commercial-origins of metal types in Europe. Both Korean ceramic skill and publishing skill was judged by their neighboring state competitors as ahead of both China and Japan. This is argued as having to do with the unique stability of many ancient Korean dynasties compared to more systemic violence and interruptions in the history of China or Japan comparatively speaking.

It is only by the early twentieth century that Korea began to lose its earlier scientific saltation with external interruptions of colonization and internal interruption of peasant revolts, however short. Coming with this was the loss of its unique stability of conserved elite aristocracies and rural infrastructures. Much of the Korean intellectual and artistic heritage of excellence was sold cheaply or stolen by other countries during the colonial period. Then, there was another external and internal interruption of the Korean War, however short, though it was very infrastructurally destructive and deadly to artisanal skill and cultural transmission since it involved a global left-Communist versus a global right-capitalist/democratic ideological 'Cold War' war starting from 1945 though quickly turning hot in 1950 through 1953 in the Korean

Peninsula. All North Korean cities were entirely destroyed by American bombing. Most of South Korean cities were destroyed. The capital of Seoul was invaded and destroyed several times by both armies. This was the uncharacteristic 'underdeveloped' and missing infrastructural situation that the proud and civilized Koreans found themselves in by the 1950s. Between 1892 to 1953, Koreans were externally and internally interrupted in their cultural transmission more than they had ever been in millennia of history.

However, after these depredations and setbacks, and after a power vacuum of a demoted aristocracy in retrospect after 1961, Koreans started to remodel their older Korean inventive aristocratic saltation and stability-based saltation to the opposite kind of inventive saltation created as an aristocracy dies. This has regularly freed people to invent for an increasing urban-commercial economy that either was hamstrung by past aristocracies, by cheap slavery-based labor, or both. Sometimes aristocracies do survive and convert themselves into whatever is the next saltation like seen in Renaissance Florence as a city state, as well as seen in Great Britain as an empire from the 1600s onward, slowly converting royal and aristocratic groups into participants and funders of the urban-commercial-mining economy instead of the former trying to avoid it or hamper it as seen in Korean and Chinese history. The traditional Korean aristocratic and peasant saltation in isolation was prominent until the 1890s, and it suffered a major setback from that point until 1961. After 1961, the scientific and technical innovation in Korea was something closer to an American style urban commercial mass market saltation (like its inventions between 1860 to the 1910s), yet in Korea this was combined more with a state-directed saltation and yet one without a great deal of international military competition motivating it, with Korea's now large military technology exports increasingly motivated more by being a part of a commercial export-led economy instead. All of this was due to South Korea's slowly growing export-led commercial economy, centered in Seoul's growing industrial urbanization yet extending down the axis of Korea's first paved highway from Seoul to Pusan's international port. This Seoul-to-Pusan axis of development encouraged technical invention for wide mass markets and problem solving for profit, both domestically and internationally, as the basis for the Korean saltation for the first time. Modern Korea from the 1970s onward additionally did a great deal of competitive military saltation within its state-directed saltation, in research and development for its military that was for the export-led commercial economy of armament sales for other states as much as the country was involved in a commercial urban economy for mass consumers as well. Plus, Korea started to try to deal with its massive pollution by creating a more circular economy saltation pressure as well. By the twenty-first century, Korea still has innovation driven by a combined state-guided, for-profit, and export-led economy for urban industrial mass markets that we see as the market for the Korean Wave. This kind of development drive has been successful in guiding and coordinating Korean collective innovation since 1961 to the present.

2.5 Summary of Hybrid Culture and Hybrid Organizational Choices in Korean Development into the Korean Wave

This chapter has three descriptions and three arguments around the Korean culture as involved in its own economic development into its cultural wave. First was described a short history of the ongoing economic Korean Miracle from 1961 that will lead into the later cultural Korean Wave, attempting to explain why both are so durable from Korea compared to other countries that are less so. However, the goal was to start to provide a more generalized and theoretical model that might be useful for transferring ideas to other developing countries that seek to learn from Korea, the world's most successful fast development drive yet and the world's most successful non-Western cultural wave yet. This chapter's explanation of Korea's success at fast development revolves around how Korea created virtuous cycles between a *blissfully available* more homogeneous culture and its *good choices* of increasingly a consensus-based political, economic, and cultural developmental policy, despite attempted elite setbacks between 1971 to 1987. This drive preserved and enhanced that homogeneous culture via widened consensus, instead of demoted the culture or demoted a widening consensus. Korea's first developmental dictatorship under Park (1961/1963–1979) was hardly strong enough to go against this flow for long between 1971 to 1979, and the second developmental dictatorship under Chun (1979/1980–1987) felt forced to keep widening the civil rights consensus in political and economic areas despite attempting to manage the media sphere to the contrary, in retrospect, until even the latter state media control or the military-appointed Presidency was unable to be sustained.

This growing consensus pressure in a more homogeneous culture additionally provided a check and balance against the worst groupthink outcomes of that more homogeneous culture itself as well, something you can see through a glass darkly in North Korea that chose a very different non-consensus model in the same homogenous culture. As said earlier, it helped as well that these hybrid institutional arrangements of growing consensus in South Korea went *against the grain of a homogeneous culture* and checked and balanced against its own political excesses while focusing it on more constructive economic endeavors in an export-led economy, or its own traditional artisanship, or in its own village-based grass roots development. This has helped make all the difference in the world for slowing down tendencies of a homogeneous culture for potential excesses pushing more dictatorial leadership, pushing more murderous national political purges, or pushing economic nationalization. The same collective innovation and same hybrid settlements kept pushing outward in an export-led economy and animated the cultural Korean Wave. The Korean Wave has been through a nearly 30-year durable cultural, economic, and political project from the early 1990s that shows little sign of stopping in 2023. It seems to be only strengthening now.

On the one hand, this *widening* sense of consensus building in South Korea was done in both political organization and economic policy over time. This *can be seen and tracked in the ongoing formal institutional and formal policy adjustments, and in the historical events and sequence trends* of the Korean fast developmental drive. This widening political and economic policy consensus was argued to be facilitated by other factors that were *blissfully missing*, particularly like a missing durable aristocratic oligarchy and a missing cultural revolution. Meanwhile, North Korea created more of an anti-developmentalist dystopia around the same homogeneous culture with its two main bad choices being the opposite in both that worked against consensus, particularly by creating mechanisms of a neo-aristocratic oligarchy within its one party state and by having a violent cultural revolution. *In South Korea, everything merged well together* to keep a very unrepresentative First Republic and then two separate illegitimate state military coup(s) of 1961 and 1979 *still involved in an ongoing virtuous cycle of widening consensus building*, despite themselves, over decades. Meanwhile, in North Korea, everything merged badly to create vicious cycles of a lack of development from a lack of consensus building.

Second, since a more homogeneous culture seems so much more politically and economically developmental only when organizational trends check and balance it toward widening consensus, both in Korea and in many developing or already developed nations, then the next section explained why the Korean culture is so much more homogeneous than other cultures. Five factors were describing about the Korean Peninsula in world history that helped its culture maintain internal stability as well as external stability. This led toward a more homogeneous culture than most over time compared to other places in the world. This is argued to be useful for a fast development drive now, as well as for achieving conserved technical innovations of excellence in the past over time. Both are due to the particular kind of Korean innovative 'scientific saltation.' It occurred in aggregate over time in such Korean cultural homogeneity and its undisturbed isolation in the past, under external pressures and under internal conserved and stable infrastructures. Korean technical and scientific innovation occurred in the present as well built from the already-achieved cultural homogeneity yet linked this time to an export-led development that provided the same external pressures and which avoided exhausting itself by only an internal economic development policy like that seen in North Korea. Korea is especially odd by having all five factors that encourage such stability and thus homogeneity over time, whereas other cultures rarely have more than one or two.

Third, a final section discussed six durable *ancient* cultural forms of the specific Korean culture itself. These ancient cultural forms are seen still in modern Korean culture, and these six that are mentioned have been selected to be boosted as international export-led content that increasingly defines the 'brand' of the *modern* Korean Wave instead of these ancient cultural forms being distinct from Korea's modern cultural wave. The same could be said for the economic Korean Miracle. The *economic* Korean Miracle from 1961 should be seen as instrumentally developing the *cultural* Korean Wave later as just another economic sector of the fast development drive. The cultural sector of the Korean Wave is just one of many added export sectors over time of this economic Korean Miracle. So, instead of separating an earlier 'economic' drive from a later 'cultural' wave to comprehend the Korean Wave, we should equally understand the ancient Korean culture to understand the modern economic Korean Miracle, and understand both to understand the modern cultural Korean Wave. Korea is a country where deep cultural continuities have been wedded to and which still supercharge radical political and economic developmental breaks by access to the homogeneous culture's durable greater collective innovation. Korea is additionally a country having the luck of ending their ancient aristocracy without a violent cultural revolution that freed them to a more consensus-based policies as a nation. It freed Koreans from an inbred, nepotistic, hubristic, anti-democratic political faction, that comparatively speaking, regularly is the origin of much durable internal violence and external imperialist violence together that could have destroyed or hampered their fast development drive. It is good to end your aristocracy and ancient oligarchies as peaceably as possible to have a fast development drive.

In short, drawing on what was said in these three sections around the culture and its organizational choices, both together created a self-renewing and virtuous cycle over time. Thus, the Korean Wave is more than cultural evanescence. First, the Korean cultural wave is equally one in a long line of economic policy choices in a very flexible yet durable export-led economic drive of the Korean Miracle from 1961 to the present. Second, this is because the homogenous culture of South Korea has been involved in the economic Korean Miracle from the start as it repeatedly has been able to animate an economic success into different export-led sectors by working very hard and by having a large amount of collective innovation—and perhaps working harder and more durably than other countries want to work over time to make themselves successful. Thus, in the Korean Wave, it is hardly different. Selected parts of an ancient Korean culture have always filtered through and even made Korea's almost world-unique version of modern urban industrial development. In other words, if the Korean Wave is understandable as an extension sector of the wider economic Korean Miracle, then the economic Korean Miracle in turn has been an extension of the wider qualities of the Korean culture itself—under particular organizational 'good choices and good accidents' (discussed in the next chapter). Korea has been so much more successful in scale than other countries because the Korean homogeneous culture has been involved from the start instead of only freshly added to a later cultural wave. One slight difference is the filtering of that Korean culture now. While the economic Korean Miracle relied on the wider culture before, the Korean Wave has grown into a globally influential entertainment machine that literally manufactures the cultural sector to order in select issues through many pre-emptive years of corporate training programs as well as through Korean state priorities and subsidies that direct specific fields to develop in this priming of the culture, instead of recruiting random individuals who self-willed their own intrinsic talents into existence and instead of a mere process of discovering autonomous talent where it already exists (Adams, 2022). While the culture may be ancient which has helped the full development drive, it is now selected and polished by a very rationalized, modern, and future-oriented machine of for-profit capitalist cultural production and Korean state cultural priming in a more winnowed fashion. Koreans in the Korean Wave are mostly trained by companies that invest in them from an early age in the many skills that a global 'star' will require later to be successful. The Korean state as well has been increasingly priming the wider Korean culture from the 1980s, as argued below. It all started to come together by the early 1990s in the first international success in 1992 in Hong Kong, as discussed later.

What can we learn from this fast development drive to transfer to other countries as development advice? To summarize the policy recommendations from analyzing these Korean dynamics, what is transferrable and what is less transferrable? Three factors seem important. First, it is argued a 'less transferrable' homogeneous Korean culture (or at least a common development ethos and team building) is key in explaining the durability of its economic and cultural successes in the economic Korean Miracle by the late twentieth century as well as the cultural Korean Wave by the early twenty-first century. However, despite it being difficult to transfer, it is something paramount that other countries should attempt to craft more than anything else. A homogeneous culture and its easier common ethos and common image of the future has been key to holding the nation together, and that has been crucial to pressure against any unrepresentative government toward increasing consensus-based politics and economics over time. It has been crucial for the collective innovation as well. Both the increasing consensus-based politics and economics, and the collective innovation, have held together the Korean developmental state despite its own elite excesses and its own elite's regular attempts toward more unrepresentative policies. That developmental state though has remained the same since 1961 despite ongoing changes of political constitutions and economic leading sectors, since it aligns the country more with a common cultural future ethos or image of the future, together. The Korean developmental state sometimes starts on a divisive path, yet over time corrects itself in wider consensus building recovered without dividing into left-wing or right-wing cultural revolutions very long that are anti-developmental equally. Obviously North Korea is left-wing and anti-developmental, though equally Park in the 1970s started to become right-wing and anti-developmental. The completely justifiable desire of President Kim Young-sam to arrest both Chun and Roh in the mid-1990s was kind of a left-wing cultural revolution against the past, though keep in mind that consensus returned when even Kim Dae-jung encouraged President Kim Young-sam to pardon them both, even after they were the people who arrested Kim Dae-jung in the 1980s and nearly sentenced him to death in the 1970s except for U.S. intervention, or despite them being the ones that put him under house arrest and who were going to try him for treason once more in the early 1980s. In short, keeping together in wider consensus down this developmental gauntlet despite large political forces that sought to throw the country to one or the other left-wing or right-wing reactionary side is what Korea has done despite partisan attempts to the contrary. Compromise rarely makes ideologues happy, though the purpose of development is hardly to make ideologues happy. The purpose of development is development, and ideological compromise and ongoing widening consensus has allowed Koreans a more durable and more flexible fast development drive than anyone else so far. Cultural revolutions like North Korea (or like South Korea's President Park between 1971 to 1979) have only ended in tears.

Equally, second, the policy of ending the aristocracy without violence was very beneficial in retrospect. Since this was joined with keeping the wider homogeneous culture, it set what was called the 'hybrid cultural settlement.' This catalyzed a wider consensus pressure against the bad effects of dictatorial models, and removed a context in which those latter dictatorships would have been more powerful if an aristocratic oligarchy had been maintained. Thus, losing the aristocracy created a political vacuum that on the one hand created the likelihood of a military coup to maintain stability, yet at the same time, on the other hand, checked and balanced against that dictatorship in political and economic policies over time as those military coups for dictatorship could hardly consolidate themselves entirely given the lack of a large and strong culturally legitimate oligarchic group supporting it. Plus, those aristocratic groups were mostly self-destroyed by their own policies before 1961, i.e., without a violent cultural revolution demoting their power. The Revolutionary Military Committee after 1961 just formalized what mostly the Japanese Empire and then the First Republic under Rhee had done already in thoroughly destroying the Korean aristocratic basis of culture, economics, and military power. All the Korean aristocrats had left by 1961 was political power. The Revolutionary Military Committee just finalized this aristocratic removal by removing them from political power as well after May 1961. Korean aristocrats had nothing left in those other three positions of social power to fall back upon to try to regain that political power, in other words. After this, a vetted military meritocracy became the centralized way to get political power in South Korea, which still is greatly the road to politics in present day South Korea much like the ancient Roman republican Cursus Honorum.

So while the lack of a durable aristocracy was a dangerous power vacuum because it catalyzed the likelihood of a successful military coup, yet after that military coup, this became a beneficial power vacuum because the dictatorship was illegitimate and lacked elite sponsorship and knew it. Therefore, even a military coup was forced over time to create widening procedures of consensus building itself, to protect itself. That consensus process was aided by the military coup(s) being always in the midst of a more undivided and homogeneous culture, and the consensus process was aided by these military coups lacking powerful culturally legitimate and economic allies of a jettisoned aristocracy that would have helped it remain more undemocratic.

Third, in retrospect, it was useful to have a modicum of challenge and danger from ongoing alternative images of the future particularly the widely assumed better future provided from North Korean leadership. However, this was an innocent time before North Korea's true dystopian path and its anti-developmental vicious cycles between its homogeneous culture and its one-party state arrangement discredited it later. North Korea is like a mirage of an oasis ahead that leads people into the desert to die. The image drives people on, yet reality keeps receding into the future and fails to come. Earlier from the 1940s through the 1970s, this threat of another developmental model in North Korea was intriguing for many then, yet in retrospect it was a left-wing false idol and a developmental mirage to believe that a cultural revolution and a one-party totalitarian state can create development instead of only set a country backwards toward corruption and a renewed feudal-like aristocracy. However, at the time, well into the 1980s, this other image of the developmental future was equally a pressure that made the wider consensus model of South Korea work that much harder.

Even if it is easy to show the anti-developmental shortcomings of the North Korean model now, it is hard to get a policy of 'the end of an aristocracy without a cultural revolution' since that self-ending of the aristocracy's economic power depended upon the real fear of that other developmental model at the time, yet it is now very discredited. This is because very few left-wing dictatorial or martial governments have ever showed themselves fully developmental at all, and only have been partially developmental and only for a short time. However, equally, very few openly fascist and dictatorial right-wing governments have shown themselves as fully developmental for the long term either. So, even if it is hard to transfer 'self-demotion of the aristocracy' as a policy, or 'the benefits of a more homogeneous culture' as a policy, it is equally argued that you can approximate getting there by the 'more transferrable' idea of copying Korean success in the inverse. What this means is first applying South Korea's choices of hybrid economic and political policies and regional grass roots cultural promotion, that in turn, may start to demote a nation's violent power and wealth inequalities of older or newer aristocracies in their own nations. It can do this by setting up a procedural process of development that can come to find some common cultural ground through that consensus processes on politics, economics, and culture, if a country so desires.

So, both the durability of consensus and even the original pressures for the creation of it via hybrid policies, reflecting consensus and thus designed to grow more consensus, are argued to have come directly from the strong homogeneous culture and its virtuous cycle of dynamics in the midst of such 'hybrid cultural' settlements (i.e., the loss of the Korean aristocracy yet the survival and durability of the Korean culture without them regardless), instead of coming directly from any magical policies. Thus, the voluntary ending of the aristocracy without a cultural revolution that later set up the greater pressures of consensus without elite violent veto against it came from the three fears of South Korean conservative politicians in the 1940s through the 1960s, fearful of losing power in three ways: fears of a leftist communist *cultural* revolution, fears of a leftist one-party state *political* revolution, or fears of a leftist *economic* revolution of land nationalization. These three fears made conservative aristocratic-era politicians of the First and Second Republics and even later military coups after the Third Republic more willing to compromise toward consensus building in all three areas. This encouraged South Korean leaderships to build ever more hybrid political and economic policies, encouraged by that political vacuum of a hybrid cultural settlement without a cultural revolution. Otherwise, leaderships interpreted they would lose all power to a communist revolution in all three points. This was despite a lapse of this in Korea between 1972 to 1987, though a return to it after 1987.

For instance, the beginning of these *economic hybrid* policies started well before 1961 in the deciding factor as the American military government in 1948 and then South Korea in the early 1950s sponsored successful *land distribution.* The United States even sponsored and created the South Korean government, flying in Syngman Rhee for the purpose, just before the Soviet-sponsored North Korean government under Kim Il Sung. However, even by the 1950s and into two military coups of 1961 and 1979, all South Korean leaders of Rhee, Park, and Chun felt they had to maintain a *politically hybrid* multi-party *parliamentary* elections and even multi-party *presidential elections*. In other words, even later military dictators failed to get their way in the *politics* of this so-called 'developmental dictatorship,' so it is better to call it a more 'authoritarian parliamentary' arrangement, given the ongoing hybrid political and hybrid economic organizational arrangements.

We should be very analytical with words, because clearly Korea was hardly either a pure dictatorship or a pure parliamentary republic from 1948 onward to 1988 in any year that you care to analyze. Before 1960, South Korea was more authoritarian and less consensus-oriented under Rhee, even though Rhee moved toward open multi-party Presidential elections by 1952 changes to the constitution of the First Republic (1948–1960). After the military coup against the short-lived Second Republic, in May 16, 1961, South Korea can be said to have become even more authoritarian, and yet from 1963 even more consensus-oriented at the same moment given the loss of the oligarchic aristocracy and the loss of the legitimacy of the government development policies as they derived from a military coup. Therefore, the flexible and politically ambivalent Park's administration despite its anti-communist rhetoric, kept buckling to appease the politics of the traditional homogeneous culture and even leftists by using socialist five-year plans and public corporations for national infrastructural development or standardizations, merged with his desired neoliberalist (before that term even existed) private corporate fast development drive for export-led development. This merged as well from 1963 with the first protections and state subsidies for traditional artisan cultural transmissions that felt maligned or demoted, and from 1970, even adopting rural grass roots village-based development across South Korea. All three or four of these other policies are the exact 'ideological' opposites to the originally desired export-led industrial development drive. However, these other economic development policies were the important consensus buttresses added to maintain it as more representative. Plus, it is hardly a 'developmental dictatorship' if the presumed 'dictator' ends the dictatorship by 1963 and then has to participate in close won multi-party elections in 1963 and 1967 that showed hardly any clear durable stability of support for Park from any region when analyzing the resulting electoral maps of these elections. Equally, military dictators failed to get their full way in the economics of this so called 'developmental dictatorship', so it is better to note how the economic policies of Park became a wide buttressing series of nationally protecting and regionally protecting economic developmental policies for supporting and yet tempering the original policy ideas of an exclusive export-led economic drive. This has made all the difference in keeping up a wider consensus process that checked against any military coups or dictatorial desires. Maybe in developing countries or even in already developed countries the military should be allowed to run a patriotic nationalist political party, for instance, against internal divisions and against outside forces? Maybe export-led economics buttressed by national protection and grass roots regional development are transferrable as an economic model as well?

Throughout this chapter, North Korea and all stalled or declining developing countries have been used to think about what would happen or would not be able to happen if South Korea had more 'pure' dictatorships, or more 'pure' political, economic, or cultural revolutions instead of more hybrid policies and only partial revolutions in culture, politics, and economics. To elaborate, culturally, only in South Korea was there either *an avoided cultural revolution* in one interpretation, meaning the lack of a revolutionary attempt to change the culture, or a mere *partial cultural* revolution in the interpretation that the aristocracy was gone while the rural village level community organizations were strengthened as the hegemonic culture over time. Either way this is interpreted, the result was a 'hybrid cultural' settlement with huge anchoring effects of an ancient homogeneous culture against cultural change in modern Korea so much that the reader might think nothing much has been lost from the past. However, what is missing in both North and South Korea was the ancient Korean royalty or aristocracy. The argument was that this lack of an aristocracy has hardly hampered continuity in this ancient Korean culture though it did set up a power vacuum toward two true political and economic revolutions from above in both North and South Korea. These two versions of Korea got different reactions whether it was associated with further full cultural revolution in the North that reinforced it or whether it was opposed by an ongoing lack of cultural revolution and wider compromise in the South that checked against it. Since only South Korea avoided a cultural revolution, this started it successfully down a developmental gauntlet with a more accommodating hybrid political and economic development policies that has made all the difference in maintaining greater representation, and thus greater durability and flexibility, to the development drive there. However, taking the less developmental path, North Korea reinforced its political and economic revolution with a cultural revolution, and then started to develop a fresh military aristocracy soon after that became just as hereditary, faction-prone, hubristic, and selfish as the Joseon dynasty's aristocracy.

The short answer is the Korean Peninsula as a whole got rid of the dead hand or sure tiller of its deep aristocracy, and this opened both Koreas to future innovation possibilities in a development drive of politics and economics while jettisoning ancient entitlements of older elites that if they had remained could have destroyed that full development drive in South Korea for political and economic development in an originally poor country. Whenever you lose or entirely lack an aristocracy—as shown by the USA, the USSR, ancient Song China, or modern Korea—you have the ability to quickly experience amazing innovative political and economic development and political equality in such a power vacuum. That this happens so suddenly in many cases of world history shows how much aristocratic elite politics is mostly an obfuscating and distracting dead hand on the people they rule instead of a useful force for development. However, most aristocratic removals come from cultural revolution similar to North Korea. However, in South Korea, by avoiding a cultural revolution, as the aristocracy was displaced, a stronger and more durable homogeneous conservative culture began to pressure into existence its own participation as a far more consensus-based hybrid political and economic policy settlement. This led to only (thankfully) partial top-down political and economic revolutions around Park Chung-hee after 1961, because of the strong consensus pressures capable of having more pressure when merged with this elite political vacuum.

Plus, losing its old aristocracy is argued to have kept South Korea away from another major historical source of corruption and hubris: warmongering or violent anti-republican sentiment in a conservative culture. You can see what happened in the Japanese political economy in the early twentieth century if an ancient aristocracy and an ancient rural culture are both kept into a modern fast developmental drive. By the 1930s in Japan, it was clear that this results in generally highly repressive politics, anti-democratic fascist aristocracies ordering assassinations through organized crime links, and foreign imperial pressures that eventually were self-destructive of its national fast development drive given Japan lost World War II and lost its empire as well. So, in a counterfactual, if Korea had maintained its aristocracy, it is argued, this would have equally further damaged the Korean development drive just like Japan into being solely an economic drive to service the world's mass market urban economy developing after 1961 in export-led economic development with an increasingly violent and warmongering South Korean aristocratic class against North Korea, meeting their mirror image there in the recreated dynastic politics in the North. Thus, South Korea would have been without any political development drive if it had kept its durable aristocracy. This could have set up South Korea for leftist cultural revolution against it even more strongly, or even encourage war with North Korea once more that would demote the fast development drive itself with hubristic collapse. Another comparative way to think about the lack of a cultural aristocracy in South Korea is how the fresh martial and cultural aristocracy in North Korea, despite removing a past aristocracy via a cultural revolution, only became another fresh aristocracy that indeed does endlessly threaten its neighbors militarily nearly every year with rockets, hubris, and anti-republican sentiment.

This kind of aristocratic family 'clean sweep' from political power, military power, and economic power of land tenure is rare enough, yet even rarer it happened without mass death or leftist leadership in a cultural revolution. This sets South Korea apart from many other cases of fast development except Taiwan or Malaysia that did something similar in all these three positions of social power. We are so far without many cases like South Korea in which truly old aristocratic families were entirely self-removed from power without a cultural revolution while a conservative rural culture was maintained and *even economically consolidated and politically participative in very radical political and economic revolutions without being demoted later itself* by fast development drives. Plus, Koreans had access to greater collective innovation in a *more homogeneous culture for mass market export-led economies*, despite these two factors rarely ever connecting anywhere in the world outside of Japan or Taiwan in lesser scales.

To summarize, first, only in South Korea was there a *partial top-down economic revolution* in having a state managed land distribution in the midst of even larger privatized land distributions, and later a top-down *partial top-down economic revolution* that aimed for the hybrid idea of a state-directed yet export-led capitalist economy though one merged with supporting national protection, public corporations for infrastructure development, traditional artisans, traditional culture, village-based democracy and large private corporations as well. North Korea instead had a full economic revolution of a land nationalization (after 1954), a full top-down economic revolution upon itself internally in a policy of economic autonomy (and heavy subsidies from the USSR and China), and a full political revolution of establishing a one-party revolutionary state. All of those turned out to be the worst anti-developmental choices, despite at the time recommended by the highest of emotions and arguments of justice. As said by Žižek, "[t]he horror of Communism, Stalinism, is not that bad people do bad things—they always do. It's that good people do horrible things thinking they are doing something great." Thinking it was doing something great, North Korea experienced ever decreasing internal economic returns from its full economic and political revolutions and throughout was putting its political prisoners in death camps and increasing starving by the 1990s when it lost its subsidizers from the Soviet Union. North Korea has only its own bad choices to blame. Meanwhile, only in South Korea's *partial top-down economic revolution* could the cultural capital of a homogeneous traditional culture still exist to supercharge that fast developmental drive toward an export-led mass market economy for profit while keeping the internal national landscape and culture intact by avoiding any land nationalization and by avoiding some rural economic shakeout due to national agricultural protection and somewhat due to grass roots rural economic development policies after 1970 in the midst of that export-led economic development. You might call South Korea's development model the 'eye of the storm' model instead of an export-led development model because its hybrid economic qualities made it a more stable cultural, rural, and national economic core around a very innovative urban industrial export-led economy. Second, only in South Korea was there a partial top-down political revolution as well. Though a military coup did want a fuller political revolution after 1961, it soon felt forced to return to multi-party elections very quickly by 1963 to maintain itself, forced back as it was into a hybrid political system into which the militarists felt pressed to participate in multi-party elections for the Presidency to try to legitimate themselves—in elections that Park barely kept winning and feared he would lose by the early 1970s. By then, it was illegal for him in the constitution of the Third Republic (1963–1971) to have more than two terms that he had already used. This context pushed him to launch an autocoup in 1971 and to change the constitution to the Fourth Republic (1972–1981) so he could keep being president for life with more autocratic methods to stay in power like appointing one-third of the National Assembly without elections.

Meanwhile, North Korea had a full top-down political revolution and economic revolution aligned with a cultural revolution and as a result of such unrepresentative processes was unable to make political changes or economic changes over time particularly as economic downturns hit by the 1970s. Meanwhile, South Korea even despite assassination of Park in 1979 and another military coup soon in December 1979 under Chun, still remained within a multi-party parliamentary system that was more able to keep (or forced to keep making) more representative political and economic changes over time to stay in power toward expanding ever more political freedoms and more economic deliberation on policy within the government, despite itself.

Overall, the '*less-transferrable*' factor is the more homogenous culture, with its greater capacities for collective innovation. Plus, it is this ancient homogeneous culture without a cultural revolution, it is argued, that has made the more hybrid policies work, and even was a cause of these hybrid policies being invented and strengthened over time in the first place against a top-down state's desired political revolution and economic revolution that instead was forced to form a growing political compromise and accommodation in the culture's favor because of the political vacuum that left the military coup without any major systemic allies in the culture except itself. Once these factors were in place, this '*less transferrable*' pre-existing national cultural energy and collective innovation was guided and filtered against its own excesses through the '*more-transferrable*' choices of hybrid economics and hybrid politics. This kept the country in virtuous cycles of growth, and kept it away from many ideologically purist dangers as it went down the development gauntlet with its many tempting distractions, violence, and short-cut desires for less collaboration that could derail it.

It is argued these merely partial political and economic revolutions, and these hybrid political and economic policies, have made all the difference in the world for creating a more durable and flexible development drive. It has flexed one way toward dictatorship and dedication toward an export-led economy without losing its multiparty National Assembly or civil rights or losing local grass roots development. It has flexed the other way later toward more democracy and less dictatorship, yet the actual democratic transition in 1987 onward was simultaneously a hybrid military transition, since the military's candidate ex-officer Roh won the open elections, since there is still a large degree of hazed military networks involved in all Korean civil and economic spheres, and since there still is the ongoing centralized five-year plan despite the transition away from the hybrid developmental dictatorship. Thus, South Korea since 1961 has maintained these two ongoing virtuous cycles of political and economic development in more hybrid settlements that are stretched repeatedly out of shape yet have avoided a break in the settlements and in the development. Many other countries have such breaks all the time, in coups or other political violence through which they suffer huge setbacks by ongoing recriminations due to endlessly indecisive ideological resets in institutional, economic, cultural, or political settlements.

The theme has been a full development drive was created in South Korea because it was durable and flexible in creating two virtuous cycles of politics and economics with the culture for the long term. Only South Korea chose what is here called a full development drive of both a political drive and an economic drive, while North Korea only chose a partial development drive, because it is an economic drive without any political drive because the North was arrested its own political development with a one-party state dictatorship and a cultural revolution which hampered it later from being durable and flexible enough to keep developing or to address politically its own growing internal economic or cultural inequalities. Such cultural inequalities in the North were born and justified via violence, and thus could more easily justify themselves in an ongoing way with more violence. However, the ongoing virtuous cycles in South Korea toward a full development drive goes well into the next chapter for why Korea kept up its durable and flexible economic aggregation into its economic Korean Miracle and then kept it up into the cultural Korean Wave.

Thus, a more homogeneous culture is a strong resource for a fast development drive *as well as a kind of internal check and balance against cultural revolution—at least within an organizational situation that can express it like a multi-party system.* Korea has been durable in its full development drive because its left-wing or right-wing ideological politics have rarely for long got the better of the more consensus-built Korean state that seems easier in a homogeneous culture in a wide land tenure and without an interfering and polarizing aristocratic continuity. Thus, in the opposite sense, we can see how anti-developmental leftist or rightist cultural revolutions are cultural polarizations that may be more likely to erupt within more heterogeneous cultures, and how that, in turn, may hamper an ongoing economic aggregation of the fast development drive itself.

2.5.1 From Economic Miracle into the Proto-Korean Wave in the 1980s

All of these factors and the dynamics they made are important. For example, whenever Park started to develop his own rightist cultural revolution in the 1970s it failed to last long, and even his power in his own rigged parliament waned simply by the elections themselves by the late 1970s. After Park's assassination in 1979, Chun was left to pick up the pieces, and though Chun started out like Park in 1979 with a military coup and kept up rightist cultural revolution in 1980 into 1981, he quickly returned toward a wider consensus and fresh ways to animate that consensus after 1981 to stay in power.

This point about Chun after 1981 is elaborated because it is very germane to the origins of the organizational dynamics that created the later Korean Wave. To elaborate this point, when the Korean state under Park tried to end the growing consensus building of a multi-party parliamentary republic from 1971 onward by conducting an autocoup, Park himself started to try to create his own right-wing cultural revolution by the 1970s. However, this might have catalyzed a left-wing cultural revolution as well and ended the Korea development drive in mutual animosity and renewed civil and class war. That was what was occurring by the late 1970s: a decline in support for his party in his own parliament (rigged to give one-third of its seats to Park to appoint, yet it was hardly enough to keep in power soon), a decline in economic growth, growing Catholic/labor unrest and democratic unrest, and even Park's own desire to take the war to North Korea itself with his own fresh missiles targeting Pyongyang by 1978 and his plan to have nuclear weapons by 1982. After Park's assassination in September 1979, the next military coup by Chun in December 1979 seemed to carry on Park's legacy. However, by 1981, Chun in many ways went back to a closer 'authoritarian parliamentarian' model instead of trying very long to catalyze a right-wing cultural revolution anymore. Plus, instead of continuing the missile and nuclear provocations against North Korea, Chun ended them. Chun equally made it illegal for any sitting presidents (like himself) to extend their presidential rule later like both Rhee and Park had done earlier, with Chun having that rule placed in his constitution of the Fifth Republic (1981–1987). This had been a bone of contention for decades in South Korea since it was an abused tactic use by Rhee in 1956 to artificially prolong his power and was used by Park in 1972 to artificially prolong his power as well. Chun banned the practice. Plus, Chun enshrined more budding Korean civil rights in that constitution—against Rhee's and Park's abuses. Chun demoted Park's moralizing cinema censorship, another aspect of Park's right-wing cultural revolutionary attempt that was steadily killing Korean cinema with various rules and regulations on narrative and content. Chun as well stopped police from Park's era from measuring 'illegal' female short skirt lengths in the street or cutting 'illegal' male long hair in the street—both part of Park's right-wing cultural revolution of his more dictatorial 1970s that was of course attempting to stop a left-wing cultural revolution as well. Chun ended the nighttime curfew in 1982 that the American military occupation started in 1945 in Seoul and Incheon only, which Rhee had extended to the whole nation in 1954.

However, even unelected Chun after 1985 faced the same reckoning as the unelected Park did after 1972. Just like Park, Chun saw a decline in support for his party in his own parliament (still rigged to give one-third of its seats for the president to appoint, just like Park had arranged it earlier). That was hardly enough to keep Park in power in the 1970s, and the same started to happen to Chun as well after 1985. Plus, just like the 1970s, in the 1980s, there was growing Catholic/labor unrest and democratic unrest against Chun just like against Park, and yet this time in the 1980s, there was a rise in economic growth throughout the 1980s. Plus, nearly every day in Seoul there was a protest of some sort by the middle of the 1980s.

Instead of just hemmed in with more conceded rules, the continued shrinking of an unelected militarized presidency in Korea into a vanishing point can in retrospect be seen as direction Korea was taking in the 1980s. Chun still felt strong enough to announce that the idea of an unelected military dictator/president would continue, and he said it would be his "#2", Roh Tae-woo, a close member of the original coup around Chun by Roh's membership in Chun's 'Hanahoe,' a secret military officer group. However, Chun reversed himself in the attempt to try to stop daily pro-democracy and pro-freedom protests for nearly a month after that announcement, called the June Struggle of 1987. This June Struggle was aided by the refusal of Chun's main ally of the United States and President Reagan to support his anti-democratic crackdowns in the streets anymore. Chun acquiesced. Despite wanting to continue Korea's hybrid military developmental overlordship or 'authoritarian parliamentarianism', by 1987 Chun announced the end of the Korean military's direct and unelected participation in the nation's political and economic direction. Against his own wishes, he granted open presidential multi-party elections for 1987. However, in the divisive election of 1987 that was a four way race, Chun's pick of President Roh was inaugurated later anyway, though with a very low plurality win. However, it had been the first open presidential election since 1967, and it had ended the military's direct steering and direct staffing in Korean development since 1961.

However, *of interest to the future Korean Wave*, despite the odd 'liberal dictator' antics of Chun that expanded Korean political and civil freedoms and really curtailed powers of his own military executive with greater civil rights standards that had failed to exist before (in trying to legitimate his unelected powers), and despite Chun decentralizing economic decisions away from himself by expanding the bureaucratic management of the economy with technocratic experts instead of just a handful of dictatorial cronies as under Park, *Chun did consolidate the media sphere. He ended free journalism by making the profession conditional on a state license, state contracts, and state approval. He put government agents in all media organizations or was in daily telephone communication in order to direct editorial and story content. He invented state-primed cultural events to allow greater governmental content control of cultural direction as his last redoubt of dictatorial defense.* This greater media control by the government happened even while ostensibly granting more freedoms and while chaining up his own marital presidency with checks and balances on his administrative power and decentralizing his presidency's economic power of decision. Koreans were freer in actions and options under Chun, and Korean political and economic policy started to be involved with more stakeholders, yet the Korean media world and Korean cultural world was attempted to be made into a state-driven and state-vetted project.

Due to media consolidation and primed state-cultural events as the last dictatorial redoubt, in Chun's administration Koreans were increasingly brainwashed, distracted, censored, and encouraged to amuse themselves to death. This was in a *dual interest* of priming economic expansion (to a '24 hour economy,' without curfews) and of creating consumerist distractions from political revolution by the greater 'bread and circuses' that his state organizationally directed. In the interest of making the economy grow, Chun chose to expand consumer desire: there was the more lascivious cinema, the start of both national sports leagues in baseball and in soccer, the start of color television broadcasting (carrying the sports leagues and more), and the arranging of international events to be held in Chun's Korea like international beauty pageants and the international Olympics by 1988. Thus, *Chun started the context of the proto-cultural wave, which is at base a greater coordination between subsidies, priming and vetting by the Korean public state and Korean for-profit private corporations finding selected cultural themes to popularize (and others to censor or to blacklist) in the interests of economic expansion of profit, light entertainment, and political distraction combined. This deepening corporate state coordination, management, and even priming of culture in Korea from the 1980s in the background was a softer way of social control than the violent harder ways of the later decade of President Park.*

So, despite this return to multi-party presidential elections by 1987 (last seen in 1967), and despite the truly democratic watershed of the legalization of labor unions for the first time in that year and despite allowed media dissention once more after 1986, Chun is still the ghost in the machine of the Korean Wave. His Korean state management of culture and priming of cultural events as a form of soft control and economic profit remained intact beyond him, and even into the more left-wing presidents of the mid 1990s onward after Roh, regardless of fuller democratization or media freedoms after 1987. *The thread of continuity to the modern global Korean Wave is Chun's state-managed media sphere and its primed cultural events that started to take up a great portion of the wider culture itself to the present.* This was maintained even as other parts of the Korean state kept getting more consensus-oriented and democratic over time.

On the one hand, the economic Korean Miracle into the cultural Korean Wave seem almost foreordained after 1961 by supercharging the strengths of that conservative collective innovation and all the hybrid political and economic policies that maintained a durable and flexible politics and economics that allowed aggregation to keep proceeding well. However, on the other hand, nothing is foreordained. That is where Chun's media control strategies come in as a path dependent choice of the 1980s that started out as a domestic policy and yet in turn became turned toward how to create a cultural wave in export-led economic sectors later. Plus, a lot depended on other ongoing good choices and good accidents of historical happenstance before 1961 and after 1961. That is the more organizational question of the next chapter for why there is a very strong economic Korean Miracle and cultural Korean Wave and why other countries have none or lesser examples.

In conclusion of this chapter, instead of falling into either one or the other side on this argument on the transferability or lack of transferability of the Korean Miracle to other countries, it will be argued some potentially transferrable policies do exist as advice for other countries on replicating the economic Korean Miracle. These are the *good choices*. However, the Korean fast development drive is equally argued to be based on *good choices and good accidents* (the latter meaning historical happenstance) that helped South Korean development are mentioned in the next chapter. While the durability of Korean development from the 1960s is argued to be in these dual virtuous cycles involving its homogeneous culture interacting with hybrid choices of political organization and a unique hybrid economic developmental model, there are other various good decisions, policies, and lucky preconditions discussed in the next chapter, like these decisions by Chun among other ones, that lead us into the Korean Wave.

All of these good choices and good accidents together are the real basis of jealousy of other countries. Not paradoxically, less easily transferrable features like a durable homogeneous culture, the ending of an aristocracy without a cultural revolution, real land distribution, and a revolutionary right-wing military coup yet for 'leftist' political and economic development which kept being forced to widen (and kept smartly choosing to accept) a political and economic consensus are what created the supposedly 'more transferrable' hybrid developmental policies and other good economic policy ideas in the first place. This makes the hybrid political policies and hybrid economic policies perhaps easy to transfer, yet over time *difficult actually to bring to life or to keep alive over time* without the other factors mentioned above (missing aristocracies, military dictators that choose representation, more homogeneous cultures, etc.) as the good accidents of historical happenstance in dynamics with these good choices of hybrid policies.

Thus, the source of the world's admiration and jealousy may be wrongly assuming that 'secret policies' magically exist that can be transferred to other countries. It is argued that the real recipe of South Korean success is the odd and ever more consensus-based hybrid settlements that interacted with the durable and homogeneous culture itself. This dynamics was supercharged by Korean good accidents in interaction with its good choices (and how these accidental historical factors helped the country maintain such good choices).

One good accident has been this more homogenous culture, it is argued. Another has been the missing aristocracy without a cultural revolution. Another has been dictators that were hemmed in to be 'authoritarian parliamentarians' instead. All of these are less immediately transferrable, though may be a great resource to think about for transferring to any fast development drive. However, as the next chapter shows, both good choices of human agency and good accidents of historical happenstance interacted and helped Koreans by pushing them more often than otherwise into those good choices of greater consensus or an export-led economy that encouraged their durable economic aggregation over time. The next chapter explains how Korea, more than most countries, has made *many* good choices to go successfully down what will be called the 'development gauntlet.' In this sense, Korea becomes a *harbinger* with transferrable ideas. However, the next chapter equally details all the many 'good accidents' of historical happenstance that have helped Korea along far more than other countries have available. In that sense, Korea becomes an *outlier* unlikely to replicate easily at all because of very many good choices and good accidents together over time. Regardless, we can learn from these good choices and good accidents for thinking about other developing nations as well.

References

Adams, T. (2022, September 4). K-everything: The rise and rise of Korean culture. *UK Guardian*. https://www.theguardian.com/world/2022/sep/04/korea-culture-k-pop-music-film-tv-hallyu-v-and-a

Antique Alive. (2015). Korean Bow—An ancient tool reborn in modern times. *Antique alive: The provider of ancient artistic traditions*. https://www.antiquealive.com/Blogs/Korean_Bow.html

Ascher, W. (1999). *Why governments waste natural resources: Policy failures in developing countries*. The Johns Hopkins Press.

Barham, B., Bunker, S. G., & O'Hearn, D. (Eds.). (1994). *States, firms, and raw materials: The world economy and ecology of aluminum*. University of Wisconsin Press.

Beck, U. (1992). *Risk society: Towards a new modernity*. Sage Publications.

Bradley, J. (2009). *The imperial cruise: A secret history of empire and war*. Little, Brown and Company.

Buchholz, K. (2021, April 20). K-Pop boom lets music revenues soar in Korea. *Statista*. https://www.statista.com/chart/24671/recorded-music-revenues-selected-countries/

Bunker, S. G., & Ciccantell, P. S. (2005). *Globalization and the race for resources* (Themes in global social change). The Johns Hopkins University Press.

Bunker, S. G., & Ciccantell, P. S. (2007). *East Asia and the global economy: Japan's ascent, with implications for China's future* (Johns Hopkins studies in globalization). Johns Hopkins University Press.

Cho, J. (2012, September 26). Korean 'Flower men' buy 20% of the world's cosmetics for men. *ABC News*. https://abcnews.go.com/International/korean-flower-men-increasingly-turning-cosmetics-plastic-surgery/story?id=17328380

Choi, J. (2018, October 22). Only 19% earthquake-resistant design rate of buildings in Seoul. *Safetimes*. http://www.safetimes.co.kr/news/articleView.html?idxno=70726

Collier, P. (2007). *The bottom billion: Why the poorest countries are failing and what can be done about it*. Oxford University Press.

De Rivero, O. (2013). *The myth of development: Non-viable economies and the crisis of civilization (Development essentials)*, 2nd Edition. Zed Books.

DeNinno, N. (2012, September 18). The Korean men makeup fad: South Korea is largest market for men's skincare in the world. *IBTimes.com*. https://www.ibtimes.com/korean-men-makeup-fad-south-korea-largest-market-mens-skincare-world-790100

Encyclopedia Britannica. (2018). Yangban. *Encyclopedia Brittanica*. https://www.britannica.com/topic/yangban

Gill, I., & Kharas, H. (2006). *An East Asian renaissance: Ideas for economic growth*. The World Bank. https://openknowledge.worldbank.org/bitstream/handle/10986/6798/399860REPLACEM1601OFFICAL0USE0ONLY1.pdf

Granovetter, M. (1973). The strength of weak ties. *American Journal of Sociology, 78*(May), 1360–1380.

Gunsi Workshop. (unk). Gukgung. *Gunsi Workshop*. Cafe Naver. https://cafe.naver.com/thecrossbow/56388

Hochschild, A. (1998). *King Leopold's ghost: A story of greed, terror, and heroism in Colonial Africa*. Houghton Mifflin.

Hong, E. (2014). *The birth of Korean cool: How one nation is conquering the world through pop culture*. Picador.

Inaji, T., & Virgilio, P. (1998). *The garden as architecture: Form and spirit in the gardens of Japan, China, and Korea*. Kodansha America Inc.

Isaacson, W. (2011). *Steve Jobs*. Simon & Schuster.

Jameson, S. (1988, September 12). Korea opens door outward for its tourists: With business booming at home, curbs on foreign trips by own citizens ease. *Los Angeles Times*. https://www.latimes.com/archives/la-xpm-1988-09-12-fi-1381-story.html

Kang, D. C. (2002). *Crony capitalism: Corruption and development in South Korea and the Philippines* (Cambridge studies in comparative politics). Cambridge University Press.

Kaplan, D. E., & Dubro, A. (2003). *Yakuza Japan's criminal underworld*. University of California Press.

Karl, T. L. (1997). *The paradox of plenty: Oil booms and petrol-states*. University of California Press.

Kim, D.-J. (2000). Nobel Lecture. http://www.nobelprize.org/prizes/peace/2000/dae-jung/lecture/

Kim, S.-h. (2023, April 12). [Korean History] Lifting of curfew in 1982 signals exit from era of repression in daily life; Nightly restriction Cleared after 36 years to boost economy, national image ahead of Seoul Olympics. *The Korean Herald*. http://m.koreaherald.com/view.php?ud=20230412000650.

Kim, U., & Whitaker, M. D. (2013). Network subversion: The contrasting effects of multiple networks on bribery in South Korea. *International Journal of Law, Crime and Justice, 41*, 16–35.

Kim, Y.-s. (2020, June 21st). Number of Koreans aged under-20 falls 2.5 million since 2011. *Korea Herald*. http://www.koreaherald.com/view.php?ud=20200621000071

KMA. (2010). Current status of volcanic eruption on Mt. Baekdu. Korean Meterological Association. https://www.weather.go.kr/weather/earthquake_volcano/volcano_02_1.js

Korean Spirit & Culture Promotion Project. (Ed.). (2008). *Fifty wonders of Korea, Volume 2. Science and Technology*. Samjung Munhwasa. http://www.kscpp.net

Lankov, A. (2007). *The dawn of modern Korea*. EunHaeng NaMu.

Levinson, M. (2006). *The box: How the shipping container made the world smaller and the world economy bigger*. Princeton University Press.

Morozov, E. (2011). *The net delusion: The dark side of internet freedom*. Public Affairs.

National Public Radio. (2022, September 8). How Korean culture went global. *National Public Radio*. https://www.npr.org/transcripts/1121364712

Navlakha, M. (2019, August 23). South Korea is saying goodbye to classic karaoke bars and late-night hangouts with coworkers. *Vice*. https://www.vice.com/en/article/pa7b87/south-korea-is-saying-goodbye-to-classic-karaoke-bars-and-late-night-hangouts-with-co-workers

Neff, R. (2020a, March 28). The Yangban: A nuisance in the streets. *The Korea Times*. https://koreatimes.co.kr/www/opinion/2023/02/721_286903.html

Neff, R. (2020b, March 29). The Yangban: The ignoble noble. *The Korea Times*. https://www.koreatimes.co.kr/www/opinion/2020b/03/137_286904.html

Novak, K. (2015, October 4). Why South Korea's men are buying tons of cosmetics. *CNNMoney*. https://money.cnn.com/2015/10/04/news/south-korea-men-cosmetics/index.html

Nussbaum, M. C. (2011). *Creating capabilities: The human development approach*. Belknap Press of Harvard University Press.

Oh, M., & Larson, J. F. (2019). *Digital development in Korea: Lessons for a sustainable world*, 2nd Edition (Routledge Advances in Korean Studies). Routledge.

OMR Taekwondo Academy. (2013). "Popularity" and "History of Taekwondo". OMR Taekwondo Academy. http://www.taekwondoacademy.in/taekwondo-popularity.html; http://www.taekwondoacademy.in/taekwondo-in-chennai.html

Palais, J. B. (1995, December). A search for Korean Uniqueness. *Harvard Journal of Asiatic Studies, 55*(2), 409–425. http://www.jstor.org/stable/2719348

Rapp, J. (2020, March 3). South Korean men lead the world's male beauty market. Will the West ever follow suit? *CNN.com*. https://edition.cnn.com/style/article/south-korea-male-beauty-market-chanel/index.html

Salmon, A. (2019, December 31). 75% of young want to escape South Korean 'Hell': Does research reflect global middle class angst, a uniquely Korean malaise—or mere talk? *Asia Times*. https://asiatimes.com/2019/12/75-of-young-want-to-escape-south-korean-hell/

Sen, A. (1992). *Inequality reexamined*. Harvard University Press.

Sen, A. (2000). *Development as freedom*. Anchor.

Smil, V. (2005). *Creating the twentieth century: Technical innovations of 1867–1914 and their lasting impact*. Oxford University Press.

So, A. Y. (1990). *Social change and development: Modernization, dependency, and world-systems theories*. Sage Publications, Inc.

Statista. (2021). Make-up usage among male consumers in South Korea in 2021. https://www.statista.com/statistics/1113338/south-korea-make-up-usage-men/

Statista Research Department. (2022a, November 22). South Korea's music industry—Statistics & Facts. https://www.statista.com/topics/5098/music-industry-in-south-korea/

Statista Research Department. (2022b, October 5). Total sales of the music industry in South Korea in 2020, by type of business (in billion South Korean won). https://www.statista.com/statistics/941291/south-korea-music-industry-total-sales-by-business-type/

Tackett, N. (2014). *Destruction of the medieval Chinese aristocracy*. Harvard University Asia Center.

TV-People. (2018, March 12). TVPP Tzuyu(TWICE) vs Irene(Red Velvet) - Match of archery goddesses @Idol Championship 2018. *YouTube*. https://www.youtube.com/watch?v=pTWwxk06eu4

Vorhies, Z., & Heckenlively, K. (2021). *Google leaks: A whistleblower's exposé of big tech censorship*. Skyhorse.

Whitaker, M. D. (2009). *Ecological revolution: The political origins of environmental degradation and the environmental origins of axial religions; China, Japan*. LAP Lambert Academic Publishers, AG.

Whitaker, M. D. (2012). Tonghak Rebellion (Korea). *Encyclopedia of Cultural Sociology of the Middle East, Asia, and Africa; Volume 3: Cultural Sociology of East and Southeast Asia; Part 2, 1200 to 1900*. Sage Publications.

Yoo, G. H. (2010, March 5). Collective or farmer: Land ownership in North Korea. *Daily NK*. https://www.dailynk.com/english/collective-or-farmer-land-ownershi/

You, J.-s. (2014). Land reform, inequality, and corruption: A comparative historical study of Korea, Taiwan, and the Philippines. *The Korean Journal of International Studies, 12*(2), June. https://doi.org/10.14731/kjis.2014.06.12.1.191

Yu, E.-Y. (1990). Regionalism in the South Korean job market: An analysis of regional-origin inequality among migrants in Seoul. *Pacific Affairs, 63*(1), 24–39. University of British Columbia: Pacific Affairs. http://www.jstor.org/stable/2759812

Chapter 3
Organizational Success Factors of the Korean Wave: Modern Development Decisions and Conditions That Made the Korean Miracle and the Korean Wave

3.1 Development Gauntlets, Good Choices, and Good Accidents

Instead of Korea's successful fast development drive being made only by the more homogeneous culture, there are good choices of modern development decisions and what will be called 'good accidents' (happenstance background conditions) of the past that made the economic Korean Miracle and the cultural Korean Wave. The recognition that something odd was happening in Korea compared to other developing countries came in the late 1980s. People started to venture guesses as to why. Just like the last chapter of Part I, the arguments in this chapter about the many good decisions and the many more good accidents in Korea toward its successful development go far beyond simple causality models of single factors that many people claim universally and predictably create development.

For an instance of that kind of oversimplified argument, a famous article about simple causality in this vein about South Korea entitled "Making a Miracle" started to be written in 1991, and it was published in 1993. The author was Dr. Robert Lucas, a professor at the University of Chicago who soon won the Nobel Prize in economics in 1995. Lucas comparatively researched South Korean and Philippine development trends and noted the miraculous differences between these two countries despite similar starting points on many metrics in the 1960s. Lucas argued that "simply advising a society to 'follow the Korean model' is a little like advising an aspiring basketball player to 'follow the Michael Jordan model.' To make use of someone else's successful performance at any task, one needs to be able to break this performance down into its component parts so that one can see what each part contributes to the whole, which aspects of this performance are imitable and, of these, which are worth imitating. One needs, in short, a theory." Lucas has one theory of one single factor that he proposes, based on productivity expansions from human capital and technology, and he says frankly that his "viewpoint…[is]…even narrower than…neoclassical theories…" (Lucas, 1993).

G.-C. Shin and M. D. Whitaker, *The Korean Wave in a Post-Pandemic World*,
https://doi.org/10.1007/978-981-99-3683-0_3

Therefore, a more holistic theory of what happened in Korea keeps being discussed throughout this Part I. It is based on a viewpoint drawn from comparative data like Lucas, yet it is more comparative than Lucas's view of analysis of winners and lesser winners/stagnators, to include countries that stalled halfway in the 'middle income trap' (Gill & Kharas, 2006) as well as true developmental losers of the 'bottom billion' in the world that should be rescued if we are humane (Collier, 2007). Plus, the methods are both as nomothetic as Lucas in seeking general principles and yet equally ideographic in respecting case analysis of many factors of history far more than he attempts. This is because human decisions, along with the background contexts of human decisions themselves, and even the interpretations motivating such decisions are all in play for explaining how decisions are made, good or bad, toward achieving development and economic aggregation. Thus, the view here is more about the actual human agency of decisions that are influenced by the wider specific and ideographic cases of cultural dynamics already described in Chapter 2. Now in this chapter the question becomes what are those good choices and 'good accidents' of context that influences those good choices of development? What can be learned from Korea using this rubric, the world's top case of a successful fast development drive so far? First, nomothetically speaking, the result is a model of successful development itself that applies to all countries. This will be called the theory of the 'development gauntlet'. From comparative analysis, it argues there are at least four critical junctures in choices for how a nation as a historical case proceeds to handle its fast development drive, and in turn, how it handles any externalities or opposition that develops within that development drive from inside the country or from outside the country that can come from its own success that could derail its own development drive over time. Ideographically, it additionally attempts to make sense of all the various levels of development that we see in the world in this way as well, with some countries achieving all four levels, some achieving three before they are arrested and stopped, some achieving two, some achieving one, and some achieving none. It is additionally possible to fall backwards, down or 'out' of the development gauntlet, at any point as well. For instance, described later, this would be like moving from stage three back to stage one once more. In this way the general theory attempts to interface with and make sense of specific cases of cultures, states, and their own development drives for their unique background conditions, ongoing decisions, and ongoing interpretations about themselves as explaining their historical process and their scale of development.

Before dipping into that fresh theory about a development gauntlet, a more *comparative* discussion of the successes of the Korean economic 'miracle' is in order. This comparison is more *statistical* than the historical case analysis of dynamics provided in Chapter 2, in order to see why the world already for decades has wanted to learn from Korea as much as it can. Now that South Korea is capped by a cultural wave, even more global attention is being focused on trying to explain the economic Korean Miracle and the cultural Korean Wave.

Korea's economic growth since the 1960s is indeed like a miracle difficult to explain with any reductionistic economic theory—even Lucas's attempt. In fact, there are no other cases in the world that have risen to the level of advanced countries in such a short period of time. It only took 36 years for Korea to be fully developed, measuring from 1961 to 1997, respectively, the year when the fast development drive started under the Military Revolutionary Committee, to the year when a very different Korea, politically and economically (yet little altered culturally), entered the OECD. Until the 1960s, the Korean economy had a smaller national income than many poor African countries, yet rose to 13th largest economy in the world in 50 years judged by gross domestic product in 2014 compared to where Korea was in 1964. By 2021, Korea grew even more into the 10th largest economy in the world. (It actually had been 10th largest economy in the world for a short time as early as 2002.)

However, instead of only focusing on economic development, Korea had politically changed as well over this time. Korea had slowly demoted its civil rights disasters by the 1990s, like how Korean teenagers' fingernails could be pulled out by the police in the 1980s for having contraband political literature. Arrests of political opposition was common. By the 1980s, being a journalist was a government-licensed occupation with signed documents where journalists 'had to agree' to various stipulations set by the state, and even with state agents placed in all newspapers. Any 'activist' pro-democratic newspapers or radio stations (that had built the Korean democracy earlier) were shut down or consolidated with others by 1981. Only from 1982 was a nationwide nightly military curfew ended. The nightly curfew had started in 1954, running originally from 10 p.m. to 4 a.m., later 'liberalized' to be every night from midnight to 4 a.m. Only from 1986 did some media freedom return. Only from 1989 did all Koreans have rights of travel to leave their country. Thus, as described in Chapter 2, Korea only by 1987 started to end its past military leadership heritage as an 'authoritarian parliamentarian' hybrid political system that started from 1963 and slowly become a full multi-party republic. However, increasing levels of protected civil rights started earlier in the 1980s, ironically, at the height of military/governmental media control. Throughout all these changes, Korea maintained a very stable culture despite the fast economic and political developmental changes.

Back to statistics, in this authoritarian context from the 1960s onward, extreme poverty was diminished in an absolute sense faster than almost any other country in the modern world. At the time of the development-minded Military Revolutionary Committee's coup on May 16, 1961, a coup that overthrew easily the Second Republic (1960–1961), South Korea's extreme poverty was 66.9%. After nearly two decades of militarist leadership under President Park, who was in charge between 1961 and 1979, by the time of his assassination in 1979 extreme poverty in Korea was only 11.2%. This had been one of the fastest and largest reductions in poverty in human history (Gapminder, 2020). By 2022, out of its 51.3 million people, South Korean extreme poverty is now only 0.16%, with the average income level now as high as 50 dollars a day. Comparatively for Japan, out of its 126 million people, it has a similar average of only 0.56% in extreme poverty, with the average income level being the same at around 50 dollars a day. Meanwhile, North Korean extreme poverty by 2022 is estimated at 9.4%, with an average income level estimated to be around only 5 dollars a day. Out of 1.45 billion people, China is rated to have a similar low average in extreme poverty by 2022 at only 0.12%, yet with an average income level being only around 12 dollars a day. According to Gapminder Foundation, if all of the 4.63

billion people in Asia are averaged together, as a group they have a daily income only slightly higher than North Korea. Therefore, South Korea and Japan are true outliers in improved incomes.

However, South Korean achievements are both in "wealth and health", i.e., have combined *absolute* reductions in poverty with *even stronger* reductions in child morality and *even stronger* growth in life expectancy that are almost 'world firsts' for all large countries like Korea as they became economically rich. Comparatively, many other countries find it far easier to make citizens healthier, yet countries tend to stall or fail when they try to add economic aggregation to it. For example, in the same period mentioned above, about the demotion of extreme poverty between 1961 and 1979, South Korean child morality similarly declined by 64% and life expectancy expanded (Our World in Data, 2020). South Korea in this period showed the 19th largest reduction in child morality. On the one hand, South Korea is in a large clique of 29 countries all with relative declines of 60% or more between 1961 and 1979. Plus, people should know that Japanese child morality relatively declined even more during this period, by 71%. However, Korean successes have been more impressive, far stronger, and more rapid in absolute terms in both measures of health. In Japan, child morality only had to decline in an absolute change from an already low 3.62% to 1.05% to have this high relative change, while Korea's child mortality was an impressive absolute change that declined from 10.65 to 3.84%. Plus, almost all other countries that did have a faster relative or absolute decline in child mortality compared to South Korea were mostly much smaller countries and island nations.

Plus, in absolute improvement, South Korean life expectancy is a 'world first.' South Korea has recorded the largest absolute change and largest increase in life expectancy for any country in the modern world. For perspective, from OECD and World Bank data, nations with the largest relative positive changes in life expectancy over the twentieth century into the twenty-first century are a very small clique of only six nations that show over a 200% increase. These six top nations with the most improved life expectancy of over 200% are in order: Cuba (18.9 years in 1899 to 73.7 years in 2021; +290%), South Korea (23.5 years in 1908 to 83.7 years in 2021; +256%), Pakistan (20.1 years in 1920 to 66.1 years in 2021; +228%), North Korea (23.5 years in 1908 to 73.3 years in 2021; +212%), Nicaragua (24.0 years in 1920 to 73.8 years in 2021; +207%), Kuwait (26 years in 1908 to 78.7 years in 2021; +203%), and Mexico (23.3 years in 1893 to 70.2 years in 2021; +201%). Thus, from this list it is clear *that South Korea (51 million people) and Kuwait (4.3 million people) are the only two of these six to combine fast development success in both "wealth and health."* Plus, few know South Korea equally shows the largest absolute change of improved life expectancy in the world, an improvement of 60.2 years from 1908 to 2021. No other country did it better. North Korea only records the world's ninth largest absolute change in improved life expectancy over the same period, an improvement of 49.8 years (Our World in Data, 2021).

So, if the world is *truly* interested in a more multi-polar world of more distributed development, the case of South Korea or Kuwait are *supremely* important more than any other countries right now to analyze successes of improvements in combined wealth and health, for two rationales. Plus, only South Korea did better than Kuwait.

First, South Korea achieved the difficult 'development trifecta' *combining* some of the world's highest improvements in *child mortality, longevity, and wealth* in the shortest amount of time. To reiterate, Korea has some of the world's highest absolute improvements in reduction of child morality, the top absolute improvement in longevity, and one of the largest top changes in scale of economic development and per capita wealth, whether measured from 1961 to 1979 or from 1961 to 2022.

South Korea thus gives us a model of 'full development drive success in health and wealth' to reflect upon in order to achieve many similar "K-Nations", while other nations it is argued only give us models of 'partial development drive successes.' So, we should learn the historical *sequence* of Korean changes here and *develop a general theory to compare this sequence of decisions and background factors with other nations*. Comparatively speaking, one factor truly stands out in the 'Korean sequence' is that it is a *durable singular drive* in its fast development drive instead of retooling or changing development ideas or plans over time like many other developing nations. Only this seems to have encouraged the whole sequence of *ongoing economic aggregation* for fast human and economic development capped with a cultural wave. In this Korean sequence, and in other developing nations, we can see the same four steps in their drive down the 'development gauntlet', yet only South Korea among (ex-)developing nations has hardly deviated from one policy from 1961, *while other countries keep changing their policies* whether in politically reactionary movements against an earlier development policy that were disliked as unrepresentative, or given how successes in other countries tend to decline in time with diminishing returns without replacement of the declining sectors. However, Korea kept inventing other sectors to pass the economic baton to other sectors—a key factor of the ongoing collective innovation of Korea that shows strongly. All of these ideas are discussed below in this more general theory of the "development gauntlet." Equally, in this theory, we require a model that respects individual case variations, i.e., that helps us understand what particular discrete and contingent events take place down this development gauntlet, in both setbacks as well as good choices.

If this four-fold sequence can work in South Korea, it may work anywhere. This is because South Korea's sequence down the development gauntlet went from almost the worst starting point economically in the 1940s as one of the poorest underdeveloped ex-colonial countries in the world without raw material resources into one of the most durably developed and digitalized countries in the world by the 1990s to the present in the early twenty-first century (see Appendix 1). It shows us that if it was possible here, it may be as possible in other countries. Despite many places being less developed now, many are still at a better starting point economically or politically than South Korea was in the 1940s into the 1950s.

Three parsimonious terms are introduced after much comparative analysis and thought to help understand, *in the same model,* both the success factors of the Korean Wave *and* the lesser successes and even outright failures of other countries in fast development. The model is called the development gauntlet, and its three terms help us focus on: how (1) *good choices* and (2) *good accidents* help a country move down (3) *the four levels of the development gauntlet* anywhere in the world. This includes and yet is beyond the earlier argument in Chapter 2 about durable aggregation from good choices of hybrid policy beginnings and two virtuous cycles of development in Korean economics and politics, both interacting discretely with the more homogeneous culture. These three additional terms help us reflect comparatively on the sequence of development success and policy changes or interactions that considered and solved the externalities of that self-generated development of South Korea over time. This 'reflexive modernization' (Beck, 1992), a modernization that tries to solve the human and environmental externalities from its own already successful development, took place in Korea very well. This reflexive modernization takes place less well in other countries so far. These three terms all help describe the same phenomenon *of how economic aggregation proceeds* as a historical process, instead of these three terms being different terms for three different phenomena per se. If Lucas focused on trying to explain productivity expansions, this theory focuses on the wider issues of how such economic aggregation that includes productivity expansion is either held together culturally and politically in policy over time, or how economic aggregation is smashed by cultural changes or political/policy changes over time.

To start with the last term that explains the others, the *development gauntlet* is a model of both a common trajectory describing the problems of achieving a durable aggregated economic development as well as the *good choices in a series* over time that are taken to get out of this gauntlet to full development. Full development is defined as having a cultural wave like only a handful of countries like South Korea or a few other Western countries. However, in many cases, these good choices for aggregated economic development themselves are hard to disentangle from the '*good accidents*' of either beneficial historical conditions *before* the beginning of a development drive or even beneficial events *during* it that made certain decisions toward economic aggregation more likely to be possible, more by default. Plus, overlap can happen in each of these four stages down the development gauntlet instead of discretely one stage ending before the next one begins. This is because the development gauntlet is a series of kept good choices, over time. It is additive and built on previous choices instead of a series of four different autonomous periods. Thus it becomes more complicated over time to maintain a country intact down the development gauntlet by keeping up good choices over time and making them work together, and addressing one's own developing externalities from development itself, instead of falling backward down it with one mistake which is far easier. Thus a lack of good decisions in each stage can block further aggregation, yet keeping simultaneously all four levels of solutions over time is the only solution that durably keeps economic aggregation, instead of falling backward.

For the other terms, it will be argued South Korea went fully through the development gauntlet and out of it into a cultural wave by taking advantage of many more *good accidents* of its history compared to other countries, as well as very many *good choices* as well. Thus, both good accidents and good choices are defined together as how they mutually contribute toward the greater likelihood of creating decisions or situations of durable economic aggregation, and bad accidents and bad choices contribute toward respectively being unable to develop economic aggregation or how wider 'free' choice can contribute to more tangential and uncoordinated actions that self-sabotage it. However, the stress remains on good choices regardless of good or bad accidents of history, since development remains a choice and an ongoing choice to keep.

For those seeking a literature review about these theoretical propositions, the analysis below about the development gauntlet eclectically pieces together ideas from the following theories: second-generation modernization theory, dependency theory, world-systems theory (So, 1990), the 'middle income trap' (Gill & Kharas, 2006), the various 'traps' that the least developed countries exhibit in the 'bottom billion' (Collier, 2007), Beck's 'risk society' and his ideas of reflexive/ecological modernization (Beck, 1992; Whitaker, 2005, 2009), and three telecommunications-based ideas of development and/or underdevelopment: 'global cities' (Sassen, 2001), cluster-based development, and the developmental power of mobile networks autonomously themselves (Whitaker & Pawar, 2020; Whitaker & Shin, 2020; Park, 2019; Oh & Larson, 2019). It additionally relies on information gleaned from teaching over fifteen years about comparative world history, comparative world development, democratic breakdown/transitions, communications history, and the uniquely durable developmental successes of South Korea.

From this merger of ideas, it is argued that a country's development drive fails to happen randomly or drifts into existence slowly around one sector like first generation modernization theory proclaimed in the 1950s (So, 1990). To the contrary, since the 1950s all successful development drives have mostly been fast, planned, and organized from above instead of slow like American functionalists argued without much data during the Cold War.

However, for two caveats, first, hardly all development drives simply by being organized from above were by definition successes though. Plus, second, hardly all fast development drives of countries that have been successful have been as durable as South Korea either. So, from the early twenty-first century, after a lot of data in the past 75 years about global development successes and failures, twice as long as the data or literature that Lucas worked with, it is theorized that any durably fast development drive is an ongoing series of good choices aided by taking advantage of good accidents to keep economically aggregating and yet coming up against four crucial or critical junctures of decisions on policy that have to be solved to do so. These are framed as the four steps of the development gauntlet. This means the good choice is to keep innovating under four such arising challenges to escape such problems. Most of all, it means the desire to avoid falling backwards 'down' the development gauntlet once more. To do that would only render a country captive of another country's development drive in our world-system at present. A market re-colonization by others outside of a country is all that awaits a failed development drive if nation's development problems remain unsolved. The only choices of development remain two: does a country develop itself or is it developed or underdeveloped by other countries further down the development gauntlet than it is, in a form of neo-colonialization? The first trend goes toward a more multi-polar global economy and global culture. The second trend goes toward a durable globalized imperial system dominated by only a few developed countries, forever, even if those countries in those top core positions may change over time to rise up or to fall.

In short, without this additional kind of four step 'sequence analysis' about common arising problems in creating economic aggregation of development, for what starts it and then what holds it together over time given problems of maintaining it durably, a multi-polar world is unlikely because other countries require more advice beyond simply recommended good starting points. Other countries require advice on how to solve various common shared internal policy issues that keep cropping up in any case of a nation's aggregative development worldwide, in common situations like what to do whenever a nation's development stalls, has setbacks, experiences failure, has political dissolution, has political debate about what policies to start with, has political debate about ending one development drive to change policies to another, or has a potential cultural revolution on their hands against a past development drive that is interpreted as unrepresentative for what their nation wants for the future. These critical junctures in decision making around development happen everywhere. Without this kind of 'sequence advice' based on the above real world existential issues that all countries face in the history of their own cases of development drives, other counties may continue to fail, and South Korea will remain only an outlier despite many transferable pieces for the world's development to learn from whether from its starting points or its later ongoing decisions in the sequence of development itself. The development gauntlet lets us learn how even a once more innately challenged South Korea itself triumphed to solve its own bad starting conditions and even solved every one of its own later self-generated problems. Only this led South Korea to aggregate more durably than other nations for decades.

It will be argued that South Korea has passed through all four 'gauntlets' correctly, in a series. Thus, South Korea is the best place in the world right now to look for solutions from its leadership's deep thought for how to organize development choices as a series of aggregating good choices, and for their thought on how to develop solutions to any later externalities and problems that developed simply from their earlier successful development choices, that let them develop even more.

After the discussion of the four steps of the development gauntlet, there are three other sections to this chapter to help explain the unique success factors of the Korean Wave as well as somewhat all cultural waves that are the penultimate last step of the development gauntlet. These sections show why it is so rare for any country to ever have a cultural wave, even most Western developed countries being without them. All those later three sections explore success factors of how South Korea developed so long and durably enough to have a cultural wave. This entire analysis taken as a whole can help in transferring policy ideas from South Korea's successful development so we can hopefully have many more K-Nations in the future, for a more multi-polar global world, instead of a more neo-feudal and neo-imperial one (Kotkin, 2020; Moore & Lewis, 2000).

First, there is a theoretical discussion of this common phenomenon of a development gauntlet, with illustrations from comparative case examples for each of the four steps that focus on South Korea compared to other countries. The development gauntlet is defined as a four-level sequence of *good choices in development toward avoiding four bottlenecks* in development toward ever more economic aggregation that, if desired and kept to, can arrive at a global cultural wave. In each of the four subsections to this discussion, South Korea and other countries are used as cases to describe these four stages of the development gauntlet into the cultural wave. The point is to explain unique success factors in each of the four levels in South Korea that led to an ever growing aggregating and consecutive series capping with the Korean Wave, while illustrating what happens under other bad choices or bad accidents to frustrate this in other countries. In other words, in any example of a cultural wave, there is a contingent four-part path to get to a cultural wave that makes it very rare comparatively, instead of there being a singular easy recipe to get to a cultural wave 'all at once.'

This is argued inductively from evidence that the development gauntlet describes well the preconditions of all cultural waves—that exist so far at least. It is granted that there may be other innovative recipes in the future to get a cultural wave, though if we theorize from the data currently so far, the idea of a common long-term development gauntlet to get to a cultural wave is what theoretically appears when we sift the silt for gold. Thus, the model of the development gauntlet explains why it is so rare and hard to have an aggregative development durably over time or so hard to get to a durable cultural wave preconditioned upon that. Equally, the development gauntlet explains why it is so much easier to stall and to fall backward in losing aggregative development at any stage than in growing it.

Second, a select number of major good accidents and good choices that helped South Korea down the development gauntlet are discussed. These helped keep the country growing durably into its Korean wave. Only a select number is *discussed* in this chapter since the universe of all of these is very large in our world and in South Korea in particular. Perhaps before you continue reading, see Appendix 3 for an attempt at a thorough (yet surely non-exhaustive) list of all of these good accidents and good choices in South Korea toward durable economic aggregation down the development gauntlet. Many other nations have far fewer good accidents and good choices to help them down the development gauntlet.

Third, as an extension of the previous chapter's slight mention of good organizational choices, two of Korea's particularly good organizational choices of sectors down the development gauntlet feature prominently in the development of the Korean Wave and thus help explain the origins of the Korean Wave as well. This was a double choice of two fresh state-led economic sectors in the early 1980s: digital telecommunications and (originally analog yet increasingly digital) cultural entertainment productions. These two sectors were given to Korea as equally distracting 'circuses' and as expanded 'bread' of economic sectors all at once after the military coup of Chun in December 1979 onward, yet studied and arranged as a development strategy by his hired technocrats instead of personally by him. Thus both of these sectors were used doubly from the early 1980s for both export-led economic rationales and for domestic economic and even political propaganda use. Later, in the 1990s, this analog cultural entertainment sector started to be digital entertainment. It started to create the potential for a more profitable and less costly digital convergence in that digital cultural wave of exports as well as merging synergistically with Korea's digital hardware exports. As such, both these sectors of digital hardware and digital entertainment came full circle as Korean entertainment could be carried more easily and far more cheaply to the world in still state-assisted yet now easier self-perpetuating digitally viral fads, aided by increasingly larger numbers of ownership of the cheaper and more portable digital telecommunications by the late 1990s into the first decade of the twenty-first century. This viral digital fad of the Korean Wave particularly accelerated after the beginning of the first mobile Internet-accessible smartphones from 2007. Therefore, these two sectors of 'digital hardware' and 'digital culture' started to merge first domestically in South Korea and in its main regional export neighbors in East Asia like China, Taiwan, and Japan.

Equally the following section helps explain the history of the three-step order of the economic aggregation in the Korean Wave itself. First, there were the deep digital saturations of South Korea domestically that came first or at least came in tandem with (second) the East Asian region. Third, the more global Korean Wave took place only once the hardware basis of further billions of mobile smartphones was in place globally for the first time, and once at least one country (South Korea) had the world's first deep experience in marketing entertainment mainly toward that digital space domestically and internationally for over ten years. Since over half of the world's Internet access was by mobile phones for the first time in 2017, it is argued that it is hardly accidental that this neatly coincides with the first wider level of the globally viral interest in the Korean Wave for the first time only after 2017 as noted from the data in the introduction. However, that is hardly the only major factor from 2017 into 2018 in the Korean Wave, as another major factor discussed later is the ending of the cultural blacklist after 2017 that was important in the growth of the Korean Wave from 2018 (We Are Social / Hootsuite, 2017).

3.1.1 Theory: Four Levels Down the Development Gauntlet to a Cultural Wave

To adapt an idea that Dostoevsky had in his novel *Anna Karenina* (1877) about happy and sad families and to apply it to national development, successfully developed countries all look happily the same. They have all gone down the same development gauntlet. They all have had a full developmental drive. However, unsuccessfully developed countries are all sadly unique in their own way. They have only had partial development drives, or had large success and then failure in setbacks, or have seldom developed at all.

The development gauntlet can explain both. First, it explains the growing similarities of developed countries. Second, it explains the many different levels of development of less successful countries. The development gauntlet explains why so much more variety exists in the world's less developed countries that include setbacks, stalls, and a lack of cultural waves so far. These latter countries' assortments of cultural, economic and political damage combine with stagnation, upset, false starts, and general unhappiness. These problems and sorrows are the main issue of the development gauntlet. Rare countries like successfully-developed South Korea that do make it to a cultural wave can help the world blaze better similar paths down the whole development gauntlet if both successes and failures of nations' fast development drives are put under the same analysis. In short, there exists an unhappy variety in the world's less developed countries and an increasing uniformity in developed countries because the latter have gone further down the same development gauntlet while the former were mostly arrested in their development earlier at different levels by their own bad choices, bad accidents, or failing in the four major sequence challenges in economic aggregation given by the development gauntlet itself.

To frame what the very few successfully developed countries with a cultural wave have done so far in reaching that point, a theory of the development gauntlet is offered to make sense *both* the data of a few high successes of countries that have achieved a cultural wave, *and* the data about many different kinds of lesser successes or failures in development that look quite different. Respectively, the first hypothesis or idea is that *there is only one common four-level way down to a full development gauntlet, toward a cultural wave.* The second hypothesis is that there are as a result *many more ways to get off that path than to succeed on it*—either by taking detours at different levels earlier into stagnation at a certain level or even later setbacks to earlier levels.

It is called the 'development gauntlet' because successful development depends on having good choices added to each other in a series over time to maintain an ongoing aggregated development path, instead of choosing endlessly to change paths. This comparatively speaking gets more statistically rare. This phenomenon of successful urban industrial development into a cultural wave will be called 'going down the development gauntlet,' as it is a series of good decisions in an ongoing way that starts to have a *durable* development drive exemplified by both its *flexibility* and thus its *adaptation* in avoiding two common interactive gauntlet issues of economic stalling and/or politically or culturally falling apart in the face of national or global challenges and externalities called forth by the original plans of the development drive itself. Any bad choice, even a single one, might lead to a reset that erases any good aggregating trend so far, called 'exiting or being stopped in traveling further down the development gauntlet.' Thus, *repeated* good factors keeping to the *same* development path are like a 'track' down a safer middle path that can help get further toward aggregated economic development and a cultural wave. Alternatively, other wider, freer, and less disciplined choices lack ongoing synergistic coordination or stability required for economic aggregation, and thus can be interpreted as bad choices since they 'demote the helpful existence of any such guiding track' down the development gauntlet at all. The latter can encourage a country to make much wider decisions and get injured or get stopped down the development gauntlet instead of guided through it more safely without change. Wider decisions and an endlessly changing strategy can be bad for a poor country since both can lead to a less aggregated economic development. So, wider decisions, weaker plans, disagreements on plans, reversed plans, or multiple different plans from different departments of state or different parties are far more likely to demote any potential of an ongoing aggregated development.

Therefore, let us frame development problems theoretically at each of the four levels of this ongoing aggregation down the development gauntlet before describing the many good success factors that helped South Korea achieve the Korean Wave. South Korea is our model case under analysis, yet to have good comparisons we require an 'ideal type' explanation of the development gauntlet for each of these four levels to understand more than South Korea's path though to understand *any* county's fast development as a series of the same four good choices over time toward aggregation. Plus, understanding each of these four choices shows that it is an open question how to solve it since different countries with different background conditions and choices will try and should try to solve the same four issues in different ways.

Given South Korea is the first 'once-undeveloped country' now recognized by 2021 to be a fully developed country, with a successful urban industrialization and a cultural wave, and given we would like to see this happen more often toward a more multi-polar world that that can model this success, the best use of the case of South Korea is comparative. As we think about South Korea, it is important to reflect on all the countries that never succeeded, succeeded then failed, succeeded then stalled, or started a cultural wave and then failed in it. We reflect on how South Korea solved and avoided bad situations of many less developed countries so well that it has achieved a global cultural wave as the icing on its development cake. Development comparisons help us to further learn how to transfer development successes more widely.

In the development gauntlet, it is argued the four below problematic situations develop that can help or can hamper an ongoing development drive into a cultural wave. These will be called the *primary, secondary, tertiary, and quaternary* problems down the development gauntlet. Each fresh level of problems has to be solved while keeping in turn the solutions of all the former levels of problems in order to keep moving down the *same* development gauntlet. Failing to do so means a country may start to fail, then stall, or even later fall backward to the lesser levels they solved, or even fall backward further particularly if they built those previous levels poorly for later flexible adaptation. Respectively, a country can stall in the development gauntlet (1) by failing to enter it in the first place, or (2) it can enter it, yet it can later fail upon later addressing some of the early externality problems of the durable aggregation itself which is based on earlier successful settlements, or (3) it can fail in later retooling of the original successful settlements as they create diminishing returns, even if they had been addressing earlier externalities, or (4) even if achieving all of this, it can fail in a cultural wave either by failing to start one or by starting one though failing to keep it. Plus, a country can even fall backwards from higher levels to lesser ones as well, at any time. Words and analogies are important. So, instead of calling this '*achieving*' development, as if it is complete or final, it is better to think of development as only and always *kept*, i.e., always in danger of being easily lost by ongoing bad decisions, bad events, or a lack of ongoing innovations in decisions or misinterpretations about situations thereof as well.

Thus, the development gauntlet is a *series of good choices* kept to over time that (1) first contribute to successful *aggregation* in development, *in turn* forcing the country (2) to have to contribute to *successful problem solving around externalities of its own successful aggregation* itself to aggregate more if they started to achieve it in the first place, and then (3) *finding later solutions for the diminishing returns* of the earlier model regardless, and then after all this (4) to have a cultural wave later built from still having *durable homogeneous cultural energy to combine with the aggregated economic power* that generally includes *revolutionary media innovations.*

The caveat is that the development gauntlet is hardly a model that says all development has to be defined as urban industrialization capped by a cultural wave. Many other countries are just as happy or even happier with other development models that have little to do with this development gauntlet as they are based on other final goals like subjective quality of life issues like 'gross national happiness' and more ecological decisions from the beginning like Bhutan or Costa Rica for instance. However, the point is that *if the goal is understanding the success factors of the Korean Wave along with all global cultural waves*, so far all of them only have come to fruition once a nation has reached a sizable level of urban industrial development that includes some durable proud and more homogeneous culture (and markets) combined with a kind of revolutionary media innovation both for further expanding its own cultural entertainments in further economic aggregation in itself and against its global competitors, as described below. The goal of this analysis is hardly saying that this kind of development described below is universally normative or even an entirely good framework for development. It is simply a comparative analysis of how a cultural wave has occurred in all available cases so far.

3.1.1.1 Primary

The primary step down the development gauntlet comes from how to start everything: how to start *economic* aggregation, how to provide *political* stability for it as a major project that will last more than a few years, and how to develop representative *cultural* legitimacy for both the economic and political arrangements that will drastically start to change the current nation. In other words, successful development will start to upset instead of satisfy originating conditions and settlements themselves, hence, problems of development start from starting development itself. Therefore, how to keep settlements going durably and flexibly stem from good choices at the start that allow both flexible changes and ongoing aggregation of the originating settlements, instead of repeatedly smashing and reforming settlements to address future problems that would reduce capacities of ongoing economic aggregation down the development gauntlet. A country's ability in its leadership to maintain *a longer single development drive* is called a successful path down the 'development gauntlet.' Inversely, it is contrasted to countries that choose to have an ever-changing development drive, i.e., are without economic aggregation, without political stability, and without representative cultural legitimacy. Thus, a lack of economic aggregation is premised on an endlessly changing and ever-broken economic, political, and cultural settlement. That is called falling out of the development gauntlet early or never making it into the development gauntlet in the first place.

If economic development drastically changes the culture toward what is interpreted to be worse, or alters economics or politics only for what is interpreted to be worse, the fast development drive will be judged by aggregate citizens as unrepresentative, a failure, and bad. These cultural judgments can lead into reactionary cultural revolution against a development drive in time, which can arrest such a development drive's aggregation potential. At this point, a state leadership might try violently to press its older policies onto its more unwilling people, as if the state were a cookie cutter treating citizens disrespectfully as only so much Procrustean wet dough. This can be done, though it will mean the cultural legitimacy will unravel further in the development drive. A country could either suffer a cultural revolution against the development drive, or it will hardly venture down the development gauntlet at all in a dictatorship model with diminishing returns to policies and in a failing culture that mistrusts leaders and with people refusing to participate.

From comparisons, the only way beyond the primary step in the development gauntlet into the second step is in addressing the economic, political, and cultural externalities well. Thus, to save time, it is best to start step one with originating settlements of economics, politics and culture that have the ability to become more representative, with leaders increasingly listening to and flexibly adapting to complaints into the development drive itself.

South Korea in retrospect did this greater consensus attempt after 1963 despite the Military Revolutionary Committee originally attempting the opposite. This started to lead to what was called earlier Korea's almost world-unique 'triple hybrid' cultural, economic, and political design settlements that were all aligned for wider consensus over time almost from the start of 1963. Despite Park and then Chun's attempt to break this consensus pressure after 1970 through 1987, the consensus pressure returned between the National Assembly elections of 1985 (the first time ever a modern Korean ruling party—in this case Chun's party—failed to win a majority in the legislature since 1950) and June 1987. Thus, with changes already starting under Chun in 1986, and then the changes via Roh's eight-point declaration of June 29, 1987 to end the June Struggle of 1987 that announced open multi-party Presidential elections and media liberalization among other points, the ultimate stronger force in Korean culture and politics was this consensus pressure. As noted in the concluding chapters, that consensus pressure has continued into the present to keep Korea in a full development drive that has blocked and undone other more digitally dictatorial attempts from 1995 through 2020 to make Korea into a digital surveillance police state. (See some points in Appendix 1 for a summary of a few of these issues.)

From an ideological point of view, these hybrid policies after 1963 make little sense. From a point of view more akin to social impact assessment that judges and values non-ideological and pragmatic points of view of many stakeholders innately involved in the process, discussion, and flexible adjustment of development over time, Korea's sequence down the development gauntlet makes a great deal of sense as an adjustable process. However of course the ideological or regional conflicts between the state and the citizens at the time over development policy in the 1960s onward perhaps failed to see the result would be a less ideologically satisfying result than any group wanted, and yet a more successful result than anyone anticipated or even dreamed would be possible—whether leftists, rightists, regionalists, or centralists. Korea's greater starting hybrid potentials for a consensus process bested all these ideologies over time.

In the case of South Korea, framed in the development gauntlet now, these early more representative and compromising *triple hybrid settlements in culture, economics, and politics* comparatively are seen *as better starting points down the development gauntlet for any country than other countries' arrangements.* This is because choosing and having these as background conditions avoided future problems in their development sequence because of these starting conditions toward more consensus and how they created a virtuous cycle of development as well. Therefore, starting a path down the development gauntlet with a virtuous cycle of development in this triple hybrid way—in a political vacuum and in low cultural legitimacy that encouraged such widening of consensus instead of in a situation in which there were unrepresentative vetoes on development or greater representation by large private interests at the start—has been one of the secrets of South Korea's durable aggregation. This is because such a widening consensus rendered later sequences toward wider aggregation more readily achievable since the starting point was far more flexible and thus more durable than countries that lacked these settlements.

In other words, after that crucial first step, the later three steps down the development gauntlet are problems of how to maintain even more aggregation in the face of *problems that develop only because of success in solving the first problem.* Many countries solve the first step, though in retrospect if they fail to get past the other steps they show they solved the first step poorly, because how they solve the first step badly and unrepresentatively without widening consensus is how they become unable to solve any other, and thus they can stall or even fall backward because of the attempt to maintain such an unrepresentative developmental drive into the future. So this idea of the development gauntlet is a sequence of existential decisions for how to start and then how to solve growing problems of aggregation over time to maintain even more aggregation in time, typically by buckling to create greater consensus over time to hold together the development drive as judged from the case of South Korea that did just that culturally, politically, and economically in its organizational policies.

Given the above issue of more flexible and durable consensus processes of adjustment being required to get down the development gauntlet, inversely, we can argue what are bad starting choices down the development gauntlet as well. So, this would be a longer list of *what many less developed countries have to avoid at the start instead of only what they have to catalyze at the start* to make good decisions for the first step down the development gauntlet that call forth future aggregation, instead of simply to frustrate it later.

What developing countries should avoid has already been described: like avoiding a cultural revolution, avoiding pure ideological left or right politics or economics, avoiding economic nationalized oligarchies of land run by government elite families, avoiding privatized oligarchies of land run by different or similar state families, avoiding the economic policies of having only an internal autonomous development or having only an export-led economy, or avoiding having only a complete dictatorship or having only a complete republican multi-party system at the start. It is called the development gauntlet because it is easier to fall out of it, easier to fall toward one or the other side only, and easier to be injured in the gauntlet and thus to fail, instead of easier to make formative decisions from the start that are flexible enough and thus durable enough to help a country grow within one ongoing policy about its own development over time that gives it a greater chance to have an ongoing economic aggregation. Thus, what helps at the start as a shield against upcoming factors down the development gauntlet are more representative, flexible, and less ideological 'hybrid' cultural, political, and economic settlements. These were described in the last chapter as some unique ideas from the case of South Korea that are quite unlike settlements or policy ideas from other less developed countries—that *remain* less developed of course by being unable to advance down the development gauntlet because of these factors mentioned above.

Many less developed countries think they should start with a cultural revolution, nationalization, and a developmental dictatorship. However, North Korea is a great example of what happens if pure ideological settlements like that are set up from the start in culture, economics, and politics. If South Korea created a rare triple hybrid settlement toward consensus that helped get it down the development gauntlet, North Korea has an equally rare triple ideological settlement toward dystopia. Because it is ideologically pure, it is unlikely capable of allowing public discussion to figure a more consensus way out of its development stall and setbacks without culturally negating what it has done in the past to itself. Thus, fixing North Korea implies a complete cultural collapse may happen before it resets in the development gauntlet at step one, once more, on more consensus starting points. However, with North Korean complete media and religious control, that public space for discussion is unlikely to happen either. So North Korea is stuck at a certain level in the development gauntlet and will likely remain stuck timelessly there for a long time. Like North Korea, a country may grow rapidly for a while with such policies, even faster than others, though the development gauntlet comes into play as such first step decisions fail to set up clear ways to achieve the second, third, or fourth step. Meanwhile, the hybrid settlements in South Korea have been surprisingly flexible, and thus singularly durable over time in the process of fast development. This has provided a great deal more continuity in a fast development drive than other nations. This has provided a great deal more continuity as the growing aggregation can keep the first step's settlements without resetting even as the second, third, and eventually the fourth steps' settlements are achieved as well.

After 1961, South Korea did have an attempt at a more pure and unrepresentative developmental dictatorship by the Military Revolutionary Committee, yet first it avoided a potential leftist cultural revolution in the process and second, soon by 1963, it avoided a potential other cultural revolution against itself, since suspension of the constitution was ended and parliamentary politics and presidential elections returned. Thus, after 1963, the developmental dictatorship and its economic policies were itself oddly merged into the Third Republic's more hybrid cultural and political settlements. That is why earlier it was said it may be a misnomer to classify South Korea as a typical 'developmental dictatorship,' because nothing about South Korea has been typical in its great economic aggregation, and thus this grand economic aggregation over time likely has a great deal to do with the more 'authoritarian parliamentarianism' of South Korea after 1963 in its hybrid settlements than any pure 'dictatorship' per se staring in 1961 and ending rather quickly by 1963. Plus, in the hybrid economic settlements of growing consensus after 1963, a large cultural and political pressure on the originating solely export-led development drive led the Park administration to adapt to make it more economically representative and culturally legitimate, by adding first greater concern for cultural continuity and regional artisanal transmission as part of the development drive itself, and then later, adding village-based grass roots development by the 1970s as ongoing compromises in the name of consensus building toward keeping that export-led development drive itself. Other consensus mechanisms of South Korea were simultaneous combinations of socialist five-year plans, public corporations generally working on national infrastructure construction and standardizations, and private corporations typically working in the globalist export-led economic sectors. These many compromises in economic policy and in political policy, back to multi-party elections and presidential elections quickly by 1963, helped avoided growing dissent for later cultural revolutions and their larger accommodative resets of these three basic hybrid settlements of culture, politics, or economics after 1963 as described in the previous chapter. Through more flexible and accommodative settlements in the first step, South Korea avoided deep instabilities and deep inability to address externalities (step two) and avoided later stalled development (step three).

On the other hand, the way North Korea solved step one led to failures to address step two and step three that in turn has only created an unrepresentative and novel state aristocracy around a one-party military state, respectively unwilling to address externalities of its development ideals (step two) and unable to address the diminishing returns of its original development drive by the 1970s (step three). Plus, throughout there has been a failing culture in North Korea more toward a cultural revolution against the state, unwilling to participate voluntarily in the development drive and more in love with counterband pirated South Korean films and ideals. Only when facing starvation in the 1990s, did North Korea develop a few small hybrid economic policy successes. It is one of the few examples where North Korea did buckle and become more consensus oriented, yet only because of famine in the 1990s did the state dismantle parts of its ideological state-socialist model and collectivist agriculture toward a more hybrid economic settlement that allowed private land production of food yet along with continuing nationalized land and exploitative and unrepresentative state quotas of course.

In summary, judging from South Korea, how does a country make good choices in step one? What is key is having more representative hybrid settlements in culture, economics, and politics over time, and *more* hybrid settlements over time that get more representative instead of more reactionary and less representative. This shields a country down the development gauntlet. For an analogy, *more* seats at the table are far easier to arrange if hybrid settlements of such a table with already at least a few seats are already there from the start. Those three hybrid starting points remain important recommendations to make another K-Nation. However, these three recommendations are now revealed to be wider good choices because they are durable and flexible arrangements as well that allow for adaption to solve better other issues later down the development gauntlet from the first decisions, instead of having settlements change over time to address other issues that come later. That alternative path would demote ongoing aggregation. So, this view of a development gauntlet, *as a sequence of ongoing good decisions* toward more aggregation yet with possibilities of falling backward, is contrasted to merely making a checklist of starting conditions like the three development recommendations earlier based on hybrid starting conditions in culture, economic, or political arrangements, as discussed in the previous chapter.

It is argued that these three kinds of hybrid originating choices of South Korea made later stages of the common development gauntlet easier to pass through or achieve, *because* they were unsatisfying non-ideological and plural in their motivations. South Korea after 1963 was full of ongoing compromises, and ever bent toward more compromises after that. Even the *anti-communist* Military Revolutionary Committee under later President Park in the Third Republic (1963–1972) kept the Second Republic's (1960) *socialist* five-year planning model wedded to a series of *public corporations* for major infrastructure development, and yet combined it with *competitive private corporations* of a market economy staffed with financial capital and skill from 'at best the least' patriotic financial families like the Shin family of Lotte 'chaebol' (translation from the Korean, 'rich family' or 'financial clique') that owed their past wealth and connections to their collaboration with the Japanese Empire (1910–1945) in Korea. Like President Rhee before him, President Park even compromised pragmatically with the same chaebol working with Rhee earlier to pool assets and widen consensus allies for aggregative development, instead of what could have been done under Rhee or under Park—a 'denazification' of the economy as the more important ideological point, like that taken after World War II in France for instance. However, in ongoing compromise in South Korea after 1963, ideologies seem less important despite the rhetoric of anti-communism than pooling all kinds of allies' leftist or rightist ideas and all kinds of capital and cultural support from wherever it could come. In this sense of the first step in the development gauntlet, the First Republic (1948–1960) of President Rhee is seen as an unrepresentative settlement in politics despite its constitutional form (given the reinvitation of the old aristocracy back into the government, a lack of national elections for President at the beginning and then questionable practices in them in practice from 1952 onward, given Rhee had the constitution changed in 1954 to allow him to be president for life, and given his attempt to set up his own royalist blood relation Lee Ki-poong as his successor). It is seen as a very ideological settlement in economics that believed in only mostly laissez-faire large private capital collaborations with the state and an education-centric development policy only, instead of a multi-stakeholder ability to craft economic policies or more agricultural production after the destructions of the Korean War. Plus, Rhee had a very repressive cultural settlement of purges and a nightly curfew extended to the whole nation after 1954. Rhee was unable to establish a stable step one of consensus down the development gauntlet, given how he only catalyzed a more leftist cultural revolution against himself in this way by April 1960, that ended this First Republic with his resignation on April 26, 1960, and given his quick flight from the country two days later aided by the U.S. C.I.A. as protests against Rhee continued to surround his Presidential Palace and refused to stop after his resignation.

The point is that there is nothing intellectually, ideologically, or morally satisfying about compromise, though the argument is that doing something else besides consensus building is a bad way to choose to start the first step. It is better to be developmentally satisfying, i.e., to collaborate on a common image of the future. Comparing Rhee to Park, a more homogeneous culture and a growing 'authoritarian collaboration' after 1961 perhaps helped such developmental dynamics work better in South Korea than elsewhere, to paper over past historical issues within a fresh common front of national development toward this common cultural image of the future. It is equally argued that if the first step is more collaborative from the start, aided by these three kinds of hybrid originating background conditions or conscious choices, it makes later stages of the common development gauntlet easier to pass through or achieve *in any country*.

Second, how is a country helped to craft a good step one? Many (hardly just Korea's) successes in fast development have harnessed somehow and self-reproduced an already available more homogeneous culture, argued to have much more capacity for collective innovation than individual or cultural innovation toward common development goals. If holding together down the development gauntlet is important for ongoing aggregation, then more homogeneous cultures at the start aid in that greater aggregation, it is argued. The opposite situation of more heterogeneous cultures at step one, with their greater capacities for cultural innovation and individual innovation, can unravel such economic aggregation at an early stage. South Korea's solution from the start was very flexible and durable, yet was in an easier situation by fortuitous accident and good choices a path of being in a more homogeneous culture and of course good choices toward a path of maintaining a virtuous cycle of development with more consensus-based hybrid settlements that maintained and strengthened the homogeneous culture, as people are the greatest resource for innovation in the world (Simon, 1998).

So the particular virtuous cycles that South Korea developed at the start are a unique starting point in their favor. However, there are *more factors* of both good accidents and good choices that helped guide the path down the development gauntlet. Despite South Korea being 'far behind' in the 1940s and into the 1950s, it will be argued as before that the key resource in South Korea in retrospect became its people and its homogeneous culture in a particular organizational dynamic of growing consensus, that let the country hold together better in poverty and in ongoing crises than other countries as they made innovative good choices in greater solidarity to get out of such crises. Koreans innately had a culture of greater 'human capital' advancement from a Confucian heritage. The Rhee administration's earlier stress on expanding primary and secondary education was influenced by that Confucian heritage. Armed with more knowledge, any more homogeneous culture like Korea had more chances for collective innovation in this less developed situation and could innovate faster than other less developed countries that are regularly more heterogeneous or have less policy stress on education. More heterogeneous cultures handle crises more by falling apart or by individuals paring off and leaving the country after being educated, instead of staying together to innovate. Of course both South Korea and North Korea 'solved' this common 'brain drain' problem in step one for how to educate citizens in a poor country to remain: by refusing to grant permission to leave. Smarter and more intelligent citizens that receive education in a less developed country typically prefer to abandon their country, as they know enough about the world to dream of a future of leaving, instead of staying and contributing to their country's fast development drive with its less pay and rare chances of national or career success. Without a large heritage of civil rights, both North and South Korea solved the brain drain problem with the same totalitarian policy. Both Koreas soon after 1948 jailed their whole populations inside both countries, and both refused visas to leave except under very rare circumstances. Second, another more creative way South Korea solved the 'brain drain' problem of "investing in educating people until they are smart enough to want to leave," was to subsidize expatriate Koreans exorbitantly back into their national jail with free housing in Apgujeong/Gangnam, cars, paid schools, and more. President Chun's administration in the 1980s was giving huge subsidies to already educated Koreans abroad to come back to South Korea and contribute to the economy even if they had earlier refused to return, or even if they were foreign national Koreans with other citizenships at that point (Hong, 2014). It was as late as 1989 that President Roh of South Korea finally ended the totalitarian policy that denied citizens freedom of travel to leave the country, feeling by 1989 they could finally open the 'market' of travel to Koreans without much brain drain or without losing national economic power from Koreans leaving with their money, since capital flight and brain drain were both worries in the 1980s. North Korea of course still has these totalitarian policies. On reflection, beyond bongwan habits of North Koreans wanting to be near their regional ancestors, these two jail-like policies are likely the major policies holding North Korea socially and financially together at all, since they stop people and any money leaving its developmental stasis and poverty.

Third, how is a country helped in step one? As said, it helps to have a common image of the future that is desired, yet one that is flexible enough to be adaptable. This began to happen after 1963 when Park's solely export-led development drive organized by powerful corporate private capital became ideologically unrecognizable in the more hybrid economic policy soon after by being merged with a socialist five year plan, full of public state-owned corporations and many private corporations, as well as increasing hundreds of subsidies for maintaining traditional regional artisanal transmission of skills and thus material cultural durability, and even village-based regional prioritization on development policy by the 1970s. The state provided the materials, and the village provided the labor and priorities of what to do with it. Fourth, it helped that South Korea could define itself starkly against North Korea instead of having to define itself in isolation. Thus, all its hybrid settlements held together in a more homogeneous culture yet equally held together by publicly being more "anti-North Korea" (threatening others to stay in line in this way) instead of entirely "pro-South Korea" in internal in agreement in themselves.

3.1.1.2 Secondary

So your country deserves congratulations if it started its development drive and entered the development gauntlet successfully—concentrating on the goal of durable economic aggregation in one policy, and improving support for that one policy over time, which means flexibility and ever greater consensus building in mind at step one. Being more representative in economics, politics, and culture makes a country more likely in its original settlements in step one to be able to hold to these policies as you enter step two or three. Thus instead of wrecking your past culture in the process of development choices, it makes it possible that the country may still have a national culture domestically strong enough and globally enticing enough to be a proud resource if you keep aggregating your economy. If you do this long enough, your national culture may have its own strong internal mass media presence. That quadruple combination of ever growing consensus, a durable culture, economic aggregation, and media innovation can let you exploit your own nations' strengths at step four if there is a policy desire for a cultural wave on top of everything else by then.

However, hardly every country starts with such representative policies in development, particularly given some choices of development sectors can create fresh inequalities and problems that were missing earlier. Therefore, step two is defined as the first major challenge *after* starting the path of economic aggregation. This second step is *how to address externalities* that develop after, because of that earlier conditional success. These are mostly *internal* problems like greater consensus toward addressing cultural, economic, political, or environmental externalities lest the combination of a more unrepresentative repressive government in development creates a wider polarized cultural revolution against that fast development drive. There are always iterative and previously unknown problems that leaderships are pressured to address later that come out of any of their earlier successes at aggregation.

Three paired terms should be defined to understand good and bad decisions at step two, and contexts that make them. These paired terms relate to 'representativeness/unrepresentativeness' of decisions, 'full/partial' development drive decisions, and how to define 'weak/strong' states.

For the first paired terms, for defining representativeness and unrepresentativeness, passing beyond step two depends upon decisions in the fast development drive to become *a more representative* policy success domestically, thus *keeping* a country going down that development gauntlet instead of stalling and falling backward over time. These further secondary problems arise only if primary derailing factors were avoided. Therefore, to move further down this development gauntlet successfully now, a country has *to keep making added representative good decisions* defined as addressing previously unknown externalities about the first step and willing to make such compromises.

For the second paired terms, if a country makes *all* added good choices in *all* three economic, political, and cultural ways, more rarely it catalyzes what will be called *a successful full development drive*. This is characterized as a settlement that can *buffer against and handle future problems*, instabilities, and potential setbacks created later out of its own successful development drive. This *successful full development drive* has capacities of greater representation over time in all three economic, political, and cultural settlements. In short, the advice is that a country should be durable and flexible enough in its development drive to address any ongoing economic, political, or cultural crises created by their own development successes itself, that it calls forth. Integrating these secondary problems lets a country proceed in the development gauntlet further than others, yet only to the next tertiary stage of challenges—described in the next section.

In other words, only a few countries may move further down the development gauntlet in step two. More regularly in less developed countries a country either has to keep resetting decisions in step one to move on, or it treats step two in only a partial or indirect way that sets itself up for a fall later, or it deals with none or only a few of the three issues of greater representation in its culture, politics, and economic policies. Therefore, in all these ways it has only created what is defined as *an unsuccessful partial development drive.* In many cases at the second step, a country's leadership chooses badly toward what will be called *an unsuccessful partial development drive* that *only catalyzes their own other problems*, instabilities, and setbacks in their own development instead of solves them. This is a series of bad decisions taken to try to ignore externalities temporarily or permanently that creates worse problems later that may derail the whole fast development drive. For an example of this, think of a country's leadership and its particular economic solutions of step one that it dislikes changing or making more representative at all. The leadership may block against adjusting some development policy even if criticisms are aired, or they may attempt indirectly to try to distract from solving it directly by adding repressive policies designed to stop the criticism by adjusting unrelated policies in other issues entirely. An example of this is when there is a criticism in an economic development drive, and the government responds only by some slight political changes or cultural changes instead of addressing the economic issue. Or perhaps there is a political criticism, and the government only responses with an economic change. In these situations, a country could go into an unsuccessful partial development drive like an "economic drive without democratization" or a "political democratization without opening up economic development plans." It is argued theoretically that much of the world's development drives can be classed as either *both starting and failing at step one, or only in a partial development drive, in a partial step two,* that leads in time to an unsuccessful development drive overall—which makes it likely the country may fall out of the development gauntlet.

For the third paired terms, what kinds of states feel more forced to make representative adjustments? A state that is more likely to make representative accommodations directly will be defined as a 'weak state,' and the opposite term 'strong state' is defined as a state that attempts *to avoid* policies being adjusted and remade into something more representative in step two. This is done by 'indirect' policies dodging the issue (defined above) or by direct violence. So it is good to be a 'weak state' in order to have a further and ongoing full development drive.

So, what makes a country's leadership more prone to listen to feedback? It is when they feel or interpret they are 'weak' in their legitimacy. This motivates them seriously to address complaints as they are worried about being legitimately overthrown or assassinated. So, the 'good' weak state is meek and tempered to its people. A weak state is argued to listen to more feedback, just as a strong state would be less likely to be forced to listen as much as a weaker state will. However, a strong state in a sense can be equally only a sense of interpretation, in elite hubris and cultural arrogance from the past or from their own minds with little connection to current realities of strength as well. For example, this sense of a strong state in a hubristic mindset that thinks it can avoid criticism was the case in South Korea before 1960 in at least the first aristocratic-run First Republic that can be classified as a more unrepresentative, partially developing, strong state. The equally aristocratic-run Second Republic was overthrown so quickly it is hard to pass any kind of judgment on it except to say it was trying to be a more representative, partially developing, weak state—meaning a state that recognized it was a weak state with poor legitimacy, and so it had started to change both economic and political settlements toward more representation, though culturally was still the same as the First Republic by being run mostly by the traditional aristocratic family lines of ancient/modern Korea. Both these regimes failed to enter the development gauntlet, as both were overthrown by partial military coups. The First Republic (1948–1960) is said here to be overthrown by a partial military coup instead of only by street violence, given General Song in the First Republic refused instead of attempted to protect President Rhee, by refusing to arm police begging for bullets to put down civilian street protests against President Rhee, at the same time the General insisted that President Rhee resign. The Second Republic (1960–1961) was overthrown more overtly by the military, and yet it was both a direct coup through (short lived) battles on May 16, 1961 as well as an ongoing indirect coup for months prior because the future military coup was discovered many times and the military failed to arrest or even to stop the perpetrators, and the military of the Second Republic refused to pass on the information about a military coup being planned against Prime Minister Chang of the Second Republic. Interestingly, General Song was invited back into the Military Revolutionary Committee for a time after May 1961, though became equally one of the earlier military critics of Park publicly in print, encouraging him to return the country to constitutional rule very quickly.

However, ironically, with the military coup of 1961–1963, and then the beginning of the Third Republic run by the staff around (now) President Park, the militarists knew they were a legitimately weak state. They had overthrown the legitimate power, and were in a very weak cultural, political, and economic position. Therefore, in this situation after 1963, a weak state in South Korea in the Third Republic actually did start to create to a great deal of more representative and consensus-based good decisions in step two by adjusting the Military Revolutionary Committee's earlier politics, economics, and cultural ideas from 1961 to 1963 toward a wider adaption of policies over time to stay in power after 1963. A weak state making a more full development drive through more representative policies is what repeatedly happened throughout the 1960s in South Korea.

In retrospect, the true weakness of the Second Republic as a state into early 1961 before the military coup probably was despite having political legitimacy it lacked cultural legitimacy simply because of how such a military coup could even happen at all, since it seemed everyone of importance in the military knew about Park's recruitment plans and development goals long in advance yet did nothing about reporting to the elected officials about it. However, in the opposite way, weakness can simply be an interpretation or attitude that they are strong when they fail to actually be—and thus feel justified in their more unrepresentative policies. The ancient Korean aristocrats that ran the First and Second Republic were so hubristic that they thought they were entirely required for all Korean futures. It was a strength of their arrogance that made them a strong state (in the interpretive minds of the leadership) and this issue kept them from seriously adapting policies earlier or reflecting as seriously on what was desired by the Korean population. Effectively the hubris of the First Republic in refusing to enter step two is evident, and even the hubris of the Second Republic is evident given there was a widely disloyal military that set them up for the military coup months in advance and the government seemed unaware that it was coming. In their minds, an oblivious arrogance and cultural strength of the older Joseon dynasty aristocratic families that ran the First Republic (1948–1960) and the Second Republic (1960–1961) felt themselves strongly insulated culturally from having to make adjustments as quickly as they perhaps should in retrospect. Particularly the First Republic under Rhee felt totally legitimate in its lack of major economic policies and its slaughtering of citizens in the street to stay in power after assuredly many rigged elections. Rhee's First Republic was truly immune to adjusting to civil feedback in step one or step two. Rhee's main goal in step one was really more war for Korean unification after 1953, without major economic policies at all except land distribution, so, more war would have been extorted from a subsistence country already wrecked by three years of the international war that descended upon the Korean Peninsula. Few except Rhee wanted more war after the 1953 armistice that ended the Korean War, an armistice that he refused to sign. His only developmental plans for the people at large seemed to be for mass primary education and literacy, yet it is hard to imagine starving illiterate Koreans at the time clamoring that their *only* priority should be mass compulsory schooling for young children instead of economic aid and economic development after the Korean War since much of the country was subsisting on U.S. aid at this point in food materials—passed through the chaebol cronies of Rhee.

Rhee was without any economic development policies except a forced land distribution. This was done more in a reactionary desire of an indirect policy to guard against political critique instead of directly an economic policy only per se. Therefore, it is interpreted as a *partial development drive* since it is designed less as an economic policy and more as a way to keep his own political power without change instead of really addressing directly either economics or political critiques. It aimed only to divide the strength of socialist calls for land nationalization in the South, since the North was doing nationalization from 1954, instead of truly having an economic development drive by such land distribution. This is a classic kind of indirect bad decision in step two by refusing to listen to political and economic criticism in one area and so giving people indirect change in another area of economics instead. Instead, both before and after 1953, he actively attempted to repress people when they did voice complaint about any of his policies—failing entirely at step two. Rhee was the one that set up the nationwide civilian curfew in 1954 as well, from 10 p.m. to 4 a.m.—geographically extending nationwide a U.S. military curfew from 1945 that was only in Incheon and Seoul. Thus, with Rhee's bad tone-deaf decisions in step one or two, by 1960 there was a mass leftwing student street revolt catalyzed off a dead leftist student murdered by his police as well as arguments that the whole 1960 election that reseated Rhee in power was stolen. Plus, the escalating situation that overthrew him in April 1960 was facilitated by his own military's stand-down after declaring martial law and only providing peace keeping services, i.e., refusing to arm police to kill Koreans in the street to keep Rhee in power. Instead of staying, and pressured by General Song, Rhee does resign and two days later flees the country in a U.S. C.I.A. plane headed to Hawaii where he dies in a few years. The only political continuity for Korea at this moment was Rhee's once-erstwhile ally and later opposition, Chang Myon, who bravely stayed behind to pick up the pieces and tried to learn the lessons that Rhee refused to learn. However step one had to be begun all over in the Second Republic yet with a more self-aware weak state, pushed to do more representative policies, and yet still attempting only a partial development drive. It would be left for the Military Revolutionary Committee to clear the slate of the state in May 1961 in a military coup and to attempt a full development drive in an ongoing adjusted way after 1963.

So, with Rhee fleeing the country in 1960, and before the military coup of May 16, 1961, Chang Myon remained to become the main force behind the changed model of the Second Republic. What were the changed decisions in step one? Chang argued for and arranged for more politically representative settlements of a more parliamentary model of state power. This contrasted with the presidential model of state power that Rhee had promoted at the National Convention back in 1947 with the First Republic's position of the Presidency created greatly on Rhee's design in 1948. This means groups around Chang listened to the more representative concern and wanted to avoid the repeated corruptions of a presidential model of the First Republic in a poor country that was under Rhee. Therefore, in this step, the groups around Chang were *already thinking ahead* in a 'step two' decision, toward more representative political power sharing in a legislature and more democratization that in turn would decide better about economic issues and more. Equally, from the start they reflected on what was lacking in economic policies in the First Republic, so Chang as the first (and only) Prime Minister of the Second Republic readied the first South Korean five year economic plan of state-led development. In short, Chang tried to start the fast development drive. He seemed to be doing a lot right—with more representative political and economic policies. He had been listening.

In retrospect however, the Second Republic's government still had very bad cultural legitimacy. It kept collapsing and reforming the Prime Minister's Cabinet, and it only had a little more than a year in power. It only had nine months exactly under Prime Minister Chang himself. Therefore, it is hard to see what would have happened with the other two policies of politics and economics yet the Second Republic is here classified for now as only have starting a partial development drive. Given Chang's own military kept allowing a military coup to keep growing and recruiting, it showed that mere state institutional changes and improved economic policy priorities still were seen as illegitimate in being more culturally left wing as well. Thus, it is fair to say Chang made good decisions down the development gauntlet as a good 'weak state', yet there was little way to quickly integrate the priority of the military or of the masses of poor people in South Korea at the time. The latter groups seemed to want much quicker action, particularly since in most countries the rank and file of the military *are* the poorer classes. It was noted already that the hybrid cultural settlement already had removed the aristocracy's once hereditary dominance of the yangban-style *military* before 1910 and after 1953 removed the aristocracy's residual *economic* power in land as well. Aristocratic cultural families only had the political power of the government and the *ideological/cultural* power of the ancient habits of mind in Koreans at large that aristocrats should rule. So, Chang's government inherited a bloated and corrupt government style of older aristocratic Joseon dynasty families that lacked much cultural experience in being *representatives* working on economic development of anyone except their own families, with little cultural loyalties or focus or the improvement of the livelihoods of the mostly subsistence farmers of South Korea living in thatch-roofed huts on dirt roads well into the 1960s.

Prime Minister Chang Myon of the Second Republic was making good 'step one' decisions politically and economically in keeping in mind how to arrange feedback and listening to what was lacking in the First Republic, yet still he was effectively creating only an unsuccessful partial development drive in politics since there was a lack of open elections in this way still for the executive of South Korea. Regardless of whether it was President without elections appointed by the National Assembly in the First Republic between 1948 and 1952, or whether it was a Prime Minister and President without elections appointed by the National Assembly in 1960, it seems like the elites were focused on very slow kinds of change within their own levels of power. Nothing really had changed about the top executive of South Korea still being unelected per se directly. Thus the interpretation here is that this Second Republic is perhaps a political, economic, and cultural policy that was "too slow" in its changes. It was certainly very slow in "cultural" change by simply following the Joseon-dynasty aristocratic family heritage of family rule in the First Republic. Chang's government as well might be called a 'strong state' in its own mind from its cultural authority sense, and yet a 'weak state' in trying to move on more representative changes of politics and economics. In retrospect, the Second Republic was unable to move quickly on economics or politics, or to keep its military loyal. All of this seems to have contributed to it being unable to save itself from a military coup that was widely known to be coming and yet comically being covered up repeatedly to keep the military plot and its allies growing. The military plotters were already operating like a political party: they were recruiting in the military on the ideas that there would be a priority on economic development and (military) cultural participation ideas instead of what Chang Myon seemed to think was the priority: playing around with governmental formal institutional arrangements of a Prime Minister and stronger legislative power over executive power—as if that was what was being asked for by the population at large as a prioritized idea for change.

The Military Revolutionary Committee seized power on May 16, 1961 very easily, without much fighting against Chang's Second Republic. That is what happens when leaders have been judged to have made bad decisions or are judged to have made "too slow" decisions in step one: you are out, your attempt is over, and few defend you even if you are admirable. The country keeps resetting, trying to find another step one that is better. From 1961 through 1963, the Military Revolutionary Committee instead started to move more quickly on economic issues (even though these economic policies included keeping Chang Myon's first five year economic plan almost verbatim, and yet adding other policies to it). The military equally moved quickly against what they saw a bloated governmental corruption—by suspending the whole government. The adapted Korean constitution was restarted in 1963 with the elections of the Third Republic. So between 1961 and 1963, a greater meritocracy of hand-picked military leaders will rule the nation for a while. This period was a weak state military regime in legitimacy as well, and it only got weaker after 1963, as noted below. This kept up the pressure for widening consensus in step two in many areas that even leftist centralizer Chang Myon would hardly have dreamed of as policy. However, after 1963 with the ending of that martial law period (1961–1963), and with the return or reinvention of the Korean Constitution in the Third Republic in 1963, the now barely elected President Park was in a continuing weak state. It was weak because it was culturally weak because of its weakness of legitimacy. He nearly lost the election to the unseated figurehead President of the Second Republic, Christian aristocrat Yun Posun, who co-organized a political party against Rhee in the First Republic before he ran against Park in the Third Republic. Second, Park's state was weak because it was combined with a homogeneous culture that pressured such a weakly legitimate government to listen carefully to criticism instead of blithely ignore it (as in the First Republic) or delay it and desire only slower change (as in the Second Republic). A third overview factor of this weak state (that makes good decisions in step two) is the uneasy armistice (no peace treaty) between a communist North Korea and a more capitalist/democratic South Korea. As only an armistice agreement, both maintained legal right to start a war to convert the rest of the peninsula to their own pattern. North Korea at the time was attempting to destabilize the South in such a situation. In other words, any missteps of President Park in South Korea would help convert South Koreans to cultural revolution and support for North Korea if the people turned against Park's development model.

In addition to a homogeneous culture being a good check and balance for such feedbacks into better decisions of step two, a 'good enemy' is good for step two. That is one of the regular situations of history where an enemy can be the best friend of a country less by their military threats and more by keeping that country's own elites honest and far more representative and open to listening to their own population. For a counterfactual, if South Korea lacked a communist enemy in the North that was originally more developed, the South Korean leaderships would have been on far looser leash (feeling they were a 'strong state' in their minds) and would have felt they could abuse their own citizens far more than they did—perhaps abusing them enough to make very self-destructive policies without accountability that would damage their own development drive.

So, anything that helps make weak states in step one helps such states be more representative consensus oriented and toward a full development drive. All of this moves toward integrating further criticisms and feedback to make good decisions in step two. This is good for internalizing all those externalities in an ongoing development drive, that only makes the development drive more representative, durable, and flexible simultaneously—priming it for more stable economic aggregation over time. There was much about the conditions after 1963 that included reflecting on the failures of the First and Second Republics that encouraged Park and his team to make good decisions in step one in faster military-led political change and faster economic change.

Park and his team were encouraged as well in step two toward listening and adapting to any hint of criticism in their fast development drive beginning from 1963 when the programs for the 'living cultural treasures' were announced to maintain traditional artisan economic and cultural transmission, instead of only a policy of an urban industrial drive as desired before. Next, beginning in the 1970s, widening consensus of economic policies were to choosing grass roots development as well in the New Village Movement. However, by the early 1970s, Park's growing sense he was a strong state meant that he had started to create a partial development drive, by only expanding this latter grassroots development policy as a more indirect policy in economics as a distraction against the real criticism in politics at the time that he was becoming a truer political dictator. Thus, policies of indirect deflection instead of direct address of problems that are characteristic of a strong state and a partial development drive started from the 1970s into 1972. Indeed, South Korea did become a strong state dictatorship that was more unrepresentative after the autocoup by President Park against his own Third Republic that had constitutional limitations against him being president longer than two four-year terms. So he overthrew the Third Republic, and started a Fourth Republic that allowed a President to keep being elected for life on longer seven-year terms as well. These more unrepresentative changes could have thrown off the whole development drive if they had continued. However, Park was assassinated in 1979.

Even the next military coup of Chun failed to act as dictatorial as Park, and was aware it was a weak state. Therefore, it enshrined even greater representative political freedoms like greater civil rights in its Fifth Republic's constitution and made economic policy more technocratic with many more ministries in the government making economic decisions about the future. However, even the Fifth Republic (1981–1987) remained a partial development drive. This is because while improving some political and economic policies toward civil rights and representation, in other policies it was of course more unrepresentative *politically*—being born of a military coup once more and ruled by a military-Presidential dictator once more. Equally, Chun was more unrepresentative in the *cultural* sphere as his cultural policies were an indirect change, to try to distract and ignore against the direct criticisms of politics and economics with a cultural policy of 'entertainment as development' that was pushed instead. These are ideas of more indirect responses to criticism characteristic of a partial development drive as well. To set the stage for how this occurred, we should discuss what came before Chun culturally.

It has already been discussed earlier how President Park hit upon more hybrid representative policies in politics, economics, and culture. To summarize, the political representation was his refusal to continue a totally authoritarian government, and yet have his military leaderships participate in multi-party elections instead after 1963, even releasing Chang Myon in 1962 from a potential death penalty, after which he was banned from politics directly yet still supported Park's opposition candidates of the ex-President of the Second Republic Yun Posun, before Chang died in 1966. The economic and cultural representation of Park's state-led urban industrialization drive for export was soon balanced by listening to the Korean people as well, and he added the multifarious regional traditional artisan support and later village-based democratization after 1970. Plus, toward wider cultural inclusion, the older inbred aristocrats and their veto power on policy were out of power now, and a wider homogeneous culture of various regions in Korea was being listened to for the first time—except for the durable economic and cultural discrimination against the province of Jeolla-do in the southwest that exploded into open revolt in 1980 against the military coup of Chun in 1980 after President Park was assassinated in 1979. However, besides this bad regional discrimination continuing upon Jeolla-do, many kinds of good decisions on step two in other words were made under Park's government. Many kinds of good decisions on step two in other words were made under Park's government. Since Park between 1963 and 1970 touched on all three issues of later greater representation in politics, in economics, and in culture, it is judged as a successful full development drive between in this time.

However, after around 1970, as said above, Park's administration began to be a more partial development drive. It was becoming more unstable and illegitimate after 1970 by becoming less representative in politics and culture. The full development drive was only with difficulty regained by 1987. As said earlier, it is far easier to fall out of the development gauntlet than to remain within it and keep growing. South Korea has been lucky to correct itself toward more consensus based full development drives in politics, economics, and culture by 1987.

What explains these setbacks in representation in South Korea after 1970? It is theorized that choices to conquer in step two are threefold: how to make the cultural settlement, economic settlement, and political settlement *ever more representative*, to handle externalities of a successful fast development drive. In very few cases, a country hits all three at once and keeps aggregating well. *In many more cases, a country's elites, in their own nepotistic self-interest as aggregation develops, try to backslide in one or more of these three issues.* If they backslide in all three, they would soon drop out of the development gauntlet in step one and would only invite mass oppositions against them culturally, economically, and politically. This kind of policy decision in step one would hardly last long.

Therefore, elites regularly try strategies of 'divide and conquer': trying to buy civil support for their backsliding in some issues through an indirect accommodation package in other areas to compensate for other issues of greater lack of representation. This is what began to be arranged by the 1970s under President Park, with his politics starting to be less politically representative. Instead of listening to direct political criticism about that or simply following the constitution by refusing to run for the Presidency a third time, he simply tried to start buying support by other indirect cultural or economic policies instead. These are bad step two decisions. This soon after was compounded by his overthrow of his own Third Republic toward his own constitutionally-designed Fourth Republic (1972–1981) that did allow him to run for President for life on very long seven year terms as well.

Thus a full step two is very rare. This is because a culture is almost always innately divided in various factions that any unrepresentative leadership can play against each other. However, a more homogenous culture in South Korea made this kind of strategy potentially backfire into catalyzing a deep and wide solidarity against declining representativeness. Park started to try indirectly to appeal to only the rural areas from 1970 for political, cultural, and economic policy support because he started to lose the support from urban areas catalyzed by his own earlier fast development drive—and most importantly, he started to be unwilling to compromise anymore to work with these urban areas either. However, by 1981, even Chun's administration saw this intentionally governmentally driven partisan political division between rural and urban was dangerous and tried to reinstate national political civil rights and as well as wide national economic growth and even a common cultural policy—though only after changing his mind after 1980 by almost catalyzing national leftist revolution against himself by his military attack upon civilians in Gwangju, Jeolla-do (discussed later). *It is very rare to see citizen pressure in a less developed country be successful enough to see authoritarian leaderships like Chun acquiesce to it in any way,* instead of it being further repressed. However, between late 1980 through June 1987, this is what increasingly happened in South Korea in the slow return to greater representation in all three issues. Thus only from 1987 does a full development drive return in South Korea in this interpretation, after being increasingly gained between 1963 and 1970 and then lost to only partial development drives between 1970 and 1987.

Let us examine two issues of how the increasingly unsuccessful and partial development drive in step two, by the 1970s, did return by 1987 and turn into a more successful development drive in step two in South Korea. It is additionally the story of how the state engineered Korean Wave began to start later.

By 1970, South Korea was a case like many other less developed countries at this time: a case of political leadership backsliding corruptly on their more representative settlements in some areas and indirectly attempting to accommodate by expanding settlements in other sectors as a distraction to that direct criticism. South Korea is additionally one of the rare cases of a mass national civil protest leading to greater returns to more representative settlements in all three areas of step two by 1987, after much repression in politics and culture had been attempted between 1970 and 1987.

Before 1961, the country had failed twice in the development gauntlet by then and reset its 'step one,' twice: once as Rhee resigned then fled in April 1960 as the First Republic collapsed, and the other reset came soon after in the military coup of 1961 that collapsed the plans of the Second Republic. These were the two resets of step one in the development gauntlet. With the beginning of the Third Republic in

1963, a more representative and compromising 'step one' developed as a series of cultural, political, and economic policies attempting to learn from the past better in an increasingly full development drive.

Over time as externalities were aired in the 1960s, three levels of politics, economics, and culture were adjusted toward more representation. However, after 1970, *only economic policies began to be adjusted* to be more representative in the citizens' favor, while by 1972, instead the direct political complaints or cultural complaints were increasingly ignored in President Park's autocoup against his own Third Republic to become more politically authoritarian in Fourth Republic (1971-1981), and while Park started a more culturally repressive period that was indirectly included in his grassroots development drive as a substitutionary appeal for 'losing' his urban developmental appeal and urban cultural support.

With the rise of that urban industrial economy, that was desired, it was generating much class conflict in urban workers that wanted more economic input and adjustment for themselves. However, Park was uninterested. So, instead of being more representative of the people who were complaining, they turned to a Catholic-church sponsored labor movement protection at the time as a cultural and economic revolution against Park, since labor unions at the time were illegal.

Only indirectly, does Park attempt to try to be more representative of people already supportive of him, and at the same time was indirectly addressing this loss of urban support (and ignoring that he could change his mind to keep that urban support) by developing a wider rural grass roots democratization movement called the New Village Movement. This is a classic example of a bad decision in step two—ignoring the actual criticism of urban workers and instead trying to make a temporary solution indirectly against them by outflanking them and supporting rural village development instead. In this way, President Park started to have only a partial development drive. A full development drive was very difficult to return to, and it was only restored by 1987 in which economics, politics, and culture was more representative once more.

So a more indirect cultural, economic, and political accommodation was sought by Park via the New Village Movement (in Korean, "Saemaul Undong"). On the one hand, economically speaking, this was a good decision of step two to widen economic representation to more rural areas instead of only the urban economy, despite being a partial development drive. This was a good idea because it was an appeal to sponsor and expand village-level democratic prioritizations of their own infrastructural improvements, with Park's government only providing the materials for the village to provide the leadership, goals, and labor. However, at the same time, it was motivated more by an indirect policy to avoid political compromise and representation in urban areas elsewhere. This made it a partial development drive because these village based meetings were used for more than economic development. Pro-Park forces used them as a cultural revolutionary base against anti-Park citizens in rural areas, and as a political base against urban areas. Many thousands of people were targeted and killed by this movement of ostensibly grassroots development. Thus, Park himself started to break one of the main ways a country stays in the development gauntlet: avoid a cultural revolution. Park started to facilitate his own right-wing cultural revolution using the New Village Movement in these dual ways. This was occurring as he violently opposed (and thus catalyzed) another left-wing cultural revolution in urban areas around a Catholic labor movement by his state repression or even assassination attempts trying to stop legal left wing parties and their leaderships like Kim Dae-jung (a Catholic) from participating in elections against him after 1972 by ending all open Presidential elections in the Fourth Republic (1972–1981). Thus Park unfortunately chose a more unrepresentative and non-consensus path increasingly after 1970 that catalyzed two counteropposed cultural revolutions in South Korea at the time. This could have pulled South Korea apart into fresh civil war that could have been taken advantage of by North Korea. All of this war and cultural dissention could have definitely taken both South Korea and North Korea out of the development gauntlet if it had continued.

So, during this period of the late 1960s through 1987, both Park and later the coup by military leader (and later President) Chun (1979/1980–1988) were backsliding on *cultural representativeness*. President Park created various sumptuary laws against male long hair and female short skirts, amongst other rules on music publishing that attempted to stop a more Western-inspired leftist cultural revolution from taking place in South Korea. All popular music acts to be published on records had to have their songs vetted by the government as well as had to record at least one patriotic song and put it on the record as well. Only a very few stage acts were brave enough to refuse. Park continued the nighttime curfew that had been in place since 1945 in Seoul and Incheon and since 1954 nationwide to stop autonomous cultural meetings and to stop long-term conviviality after working hours. In this context, the cultural meaning of the New Village Movement ("Saemael Undong") had an ambivalent meaning. Economic positives of its grass roots development are discussed before its culturally negative manifestations. For the economic positives, the whole idea developed after devastating floods in South Korea in 1969. President Park was touring the flooded rural villages and damaged areas. However, he came across one village with a particularly strong community spirit that solved by itself its own flooding and infrastructural problems. This was the village of Sindo-ri in Cheongdo-gun, Gyeongsangbuk-do. He was impressed since instead of the villagers moping or crying over losses, this village had a local-level technological confidence in collectively fixing their own flood damage through localized prioritization and voluntary team labor of how to fix their own infrastructure of the village common areas to minimize flooding in the future. Park thought to encourage such villages as a national plan as well, so from April 22, 1970, Park announced the Saemaul Undong or New Village Movement as that national plan. In the beginning the same base amount of only 335 bags of free cement without any governmental interference was provided to approximately 33,000 villages across South Korea. It was designed to give them some material basis upon which they could exercise their own self-help, cooperative spirit, and prioritization—so they could dream of their own priorities of what to build for a better village. As the plan was announced in April 1970, half of the Korean population was rural, and 80% of those rural villages had thatched straw roofs. All had dirt roads and were without phone or most electrical service. Rural poverty and isolation was versus the "Seoul to Pusan" axis of urban industrial development for export. Even in April 1970, all of South Korea did not yet have one completed paved national highway, even though it was underway in construction from 1968. That highway would be completed in a few months later on July 7, 1970. The highway as well was inspired by another good example when Park saw the German autobahn for the first time and made it an election promise in 1967 to built one in Korea as well. When completed on July 7, 1970, this first paved highway in Korea became known as Highway 1 or the Gyeongbu Expressway. It was completed from Pusan to Seoul at this date, however discrete segments were opened earlier as they were completed. So as rural areas were beginning to be connected to and to see a national freeway system, villages were being encouraged to develop themselves as well. However, instead of a policy of helping the worst villages, Park's policy was to only further help the best villages that had shown their own ability to exercise that disciplined self-help effectively with their first concrete allotment. It was judged that about half of the villages had shown results better than the others, and only those better organized villages that got a larger amount of 500 bags of cement and one ton of steel bars. Village projects started to be more ambitious: to replace all village thatch roofs with the still-seen orange colored tiles—along with of course to make better communal infrastructure like widened roads, village bridges, community baths, and community centers. By 1973, there were three classifications of evaluated villages: 'basic' village, 'self-help' village, and 'self-reliance' village. There continued to be greater preferential aid for only the most outstanding examples, instead of helping the worst. At this time, government started to use the established village bases for agricultural outreach—providing fresh high-yield rice varieties for example. Other villages decided at this time to start growing far more specialty crops than before—like mushrooms, fruit trees, silkworms, livestock, and the start of the now ubiquitously seen greenhouse-based agricultural production. Access to electricity and telephone services began to be expanded to rural areas previously neglected—even if the service remained expensive. A Saemaul Undong Library movement developed as well—mostly geared to state-goals of expanding agricultural production. Next, Park wanted to take back the cities from the Catholic labor movement to which he had lost Seoul in the past election. This was a priority as well in the whole rural movement itself, to build a more stable political base for Park, given the loss of that urban election support in Seoul to Kim Dae-jung had led to Park's autocoup overthrowing his own the Third Republic toward a more dictatorial Fourth Republic (1972–1981). So in 1974, in the increasingly repressive and dictatorial Fourth Republic where it was illegal to even criticize Park or the Yushin (restoration) Constitution, Saemaul Undong went to the cities and their factories under the banner of 'rooting out corruption', 'promoting sound work ethics,' and 'harmonized' factories of higher quality control. There was even Saemaul education for Park's state ministers in 1974. Nationwide, approximately 680,000 joined the Saemaul camp training to raise leaders of the movement for both rural and urban areas. (Global Saemaul Undong, 2015) For the cultural negatives, Park's New Village Movement despite the encouragement to a commons-based economic localism was a national state-based cultural revolution in the suppression of local beliefs and cultural traditions. Thus the movement had equally the air of a cultural revolution and a Maoist movement against political 'deviation' opposed to the True Leader, as this movement's instruction was against divisive 'religion' (when the Catholic-based labor movements were the main organized opposition to Park) and even against Korean traditional practices like female-headed shamanism. Saemael Undong meetings were used in parallel to identify political enemies, with many hundreds up to approximately 1,700 who were killed, along with nearly 7,500 jailed after being labeled as anti-Park. The Saemael Undong movement was used spitefully to cut down thousands of massive old village meeting trees simply because of their ideological association with religious practices of shamanism. Thus it is fair to say that South Korea started to be only a partial development drive and started to catalyze two different kinds of cultural revolutions, one right wing and one left wing/Catholic. South Korea could have dropped out of the development gauntlet as many more decisions in the politics and cultural issues of step two started to be less representative. On the other hand, it was a good choice to attempt to remove the growing disparities between urban and rural development in Korea.

On the one hand, state repression of and state direction of cultural transmission escalated under Chun after 1980, as more than 60,000 citizens were arrested and put into "re-education labor camps" for challenging his coup after the assassination of President Park in 1979. Others were attacked in the streets by state-supported thugs under a 'social cleansing' policy and arrested without warrants. Chun equally closed universities, closed media publications, and stationed troops in all major cities. This event catalyzed citizens in Gwangju protesting the military occupation of their city by taking over the city hall. Equally the subtext of the protest was how the Korean state had been ignoring this Jeolla-do region of Korea in economic development since the 1960s. This led to Chun's order for the Gwangju Massacre of still unknown numbers of civilians killed in the streets and in the city hall by Chun's allowance to use tanks and helicopter fire to retake the city hall in 1980. In retrospect, it is fortunate that Chun's civil massacre failed to continue across other protesting cities. It is equally fortunate that external allies of the US Reagan Administration cautioned Chun against further violence, and were against him murdering ongoing political opposition candidates like Kim Dae-jung as well, who the KCIA under Park had already tried to kill in the 1970s. All of this state violence could have unraveled further the cultural legitimacy and dropped Korea out of the development gauntlet as it could have set off political/cultural revolution against either Park or Chun and ended the economic aggregation.

However, political and cultural repression was kept at a low simmer instead of a hard boil. In retrospect, frankly, it seems against all odds that the Korean development gauntlet remained intact given all that was happening between 1970 and 1987 against it. It was definitely a period of partial development drives only in economic aggregation that kept expanding. Park and Chun between 1970 to 1987 became the nation's worst enemies politically and culturally because they were only trying to focus indirectly on economic advance. This kind of indirect policy only supported partial development drives. Both during this period were against being more representative by increasing a widening political consensus or a widening cultural openness of the earlier times of the 1960s, and instead both mostly concentrated on indirect economic policy liberalization—particularly Chun.

After Chun seized power in a military coup in December 1979 and later once more, he ultimately became President Chun by 1981. Even though he kept greater political authoritarianism and cultural authoritarianism, Chun did start freer representative consensus processes for economic policy and for consumerism far more than Park ever did. In this vein, Chun let a bunch of foreign trained (Korean) technocrats help decide what fresh economic sectors the country should pursue. This led to a way that South Korea would solve the third step of the development gauntlet—discussed momentarily—that was becoming a problem by the economic declines in growth rates by the late 1970s under Park. Equally, despite creating a stronger dictatorship model of politics, ironically Chun as well attempted greater cultural legitimacy and political legitimacy by enshrining more political rights in the Fifth Republic's constitution, far more than Park ever did as well.

Important in our story of the coming Korean Wave, Chun's greater political authoritarianism in the 1980s failed to open up culture though. Instead, like Park before him, Chun supported far more state-directed culture. However, unlike Park's mostly negative censorship policies in the 1970s, Chun's even stronger negative censorship policies were matched with more positive state-driven cultural events that mixed propaganda, low distraction, and a priming for economic development through fresh economic sectors like electronics carrying a revived economic sector in entertainment at the same moment. This can be seen in at least four policies.

The *first* state-directed cultural direction policy was his Policy for Merger and Abolition of the Press in November 1980 taken once his coup and its martial law conditions of 1979–1980 were ended, yet with desire to formalize it other durable ways. Chun's government shrank the number of organizations involved in the Korean civil media sphere in urban and regional newspapers and broadcasters, and all remaining owners were forced to sign agreements with the government to this effect that government content control would be respected. The Christian Broadcasting System was forced to stop being a news agency and became only an apolitical and non-democratic religious radio network banned from contributing to social issues or political activism.

The *second* state-directed cultural direction was Chun's desire to catalyze and to invite cultural festivals of foreign female beauties to Korea or to show erotic cinema on the Korean screen. The world's top female beauty pageant, the 29th Miss Universe Pageant, was brought to Seoul in July 1980—held ironically in staid, stoic, and multi-columned Sejong Cultural Center almost immediately after a military coup on May 17, 1980, and then a subsequent army massacre of civilians in the Gwangju Uprising a few days afterward stemming from armed civilian protest against the military coup with their occupation of Gwangju City Hall that started on May 18, 1980. Next, by September 30, 1980, Chun's coup had secured enough votes from the international Olympic Congress to arrange the 1988 Summer Olympic Games to be held in Seoul as well. It is said to be one of the last projects of President Park (assassinated in 1979) to attempt to bring the Olympics to Seoul. Chun was able to do this with this vote in 1980. Soon after that Olympic vote in his favor, Chun organized the "Korean Breeze '81" festival, said to be under-attended. Later, in 1986, Chun arranged to host the 1986 Asian Olympic Games in Seoul as well.

Plus, a long series of sultry cinema hits began to be produced, with the most famous being called "Madam Aema," first premièred on February 6, 1982. The lascivious series of "Madam Aema" went on to have 13 titillating sequels in the 1980s, released regularly (Lankov, 2007). The plot, if it existed at all, was to show a woman's extramarital affairs while her husband was in jail. It was additionally a way to kickstart a failing Korean cinema that was suffering as more Koreans stayed at home and watched television by the 1970s, and as President Park's moralizing cinema censorship of the 1970s became extreme in his right-wing cultural revolution, trying to match the ongoing left wing/labor cultural revolution of the time: "By the late 1970s the Korean movie industry was panicking. Korean cinema was dying....In 1969, the Korean movie industry produced 229 full length features. However, the situation changed dramatically towards the late 1970s. In 1975, production fell to 94 features, and kept going down. There were two reasons for the crisis. The 1972–1979 Yushin dictatorship [i.e., the Fourth Republic (1972–1981), with its "Yushin" Constitution, meaning "restoration"] enforced strict censorship rules, and this made work difficult for many directors. However, by far the more important factor was the explosive growth of TV. Over the same period, from 1969 to 1975 [black and white] TV ownership increased almost tenfold, from to 224,000 to 2.1 million sets. People did not go to [color] cinema any more: they preferred to watch serials at home instead" (Lankov, 2007). Chun's encouragement of a more sexual cinema went hand in hand with the Korean state priming the cinema industry and priming a television-watching public with color television broadcasting as well. This dedication to pleasure afterhours connected well with the end of the nightly curfew in March 1982 that had been in place nationally since 1954. Late night lascivious cinema like "Madame Aema" was immediately on the bill as the military government lifted the curfew. "Late night shows were another invention of the military regime which was preparing to lift a decades-old curfew. [Ae]ma was screened in the Seoul Theater, in the largest hall which could sit 1,500, but the owners sold 5,000 tickets! So powerful was the allure of the recently forbidden fruits: erotic movies and the possibility of being outside the house so late into the night" (Lankov, 2007).

The *third* state-directed cultural direction was Chun's rush to create domestic sports leagues in baseball and soccer throughout South Korea in an attempt to let citizens themselves provide their own distracting and enervating circuses instead of only his state or international events providing them. The Korean Baseball Organization League was launched in 1982 simultaneous to six fresh baseball teams. President Chun threw the first ceremonial pitch at the first game. Professional soccer leagues were organized in 1983.

The *fourth* theme was the introduction of color television broadcasting in 1980 soon after Chun's first military coup of December 1979. Some argue this was only to update Korea technically, yet equally this has to be considered within Chun's whole increasingly progressive or repressive (take your pick of terms and interpretation) cultural policy to enthrall or to numb the masses better or to expand economic development—or both, which is the argument here. This can be said because the move toward color TV broadcasts was hardly alone as a technical policy. It was combined with a reduction in TV censorship against lascivious content on broadcast networks instead of only a reduction of cinema regulations. In this way, throughout the 1980s, Chun attempted a cultural reorientation by appealing to low, prurient, passive sexual urges and sports interests, and thus away from religiously high-minded, active political protest and economic protest against himself and his regime typically led culturally by traditionalist moral religious organizations and their highly religious mass media organizations. It was additionally a way to signify the moral censorship of President Park was finished as Chun attempted to appeal to making his own military coup as legitimate by doing the exact opposite—at least indirectly of course. He hoped Koreans would distract and pleasure themselves into submission, if given enough entertainment regularly. There were more state supports for such enervating and sexualized TV dramas and cinema, more passive spectator events, and color-televised sports events were broadcast across the nation for the first time. It seems that the Chun administration hoped citizens would lounge away their evenings together in conviviality if offered regular state-approved entertainments that dulled and distracted them with pleasures, instead of like Park earlier expecting all late-night conviviality would act on high minded civic or religious senses of loss of political participation or cultural direction.

All of these four themes came later to be cynically called Chun's "3S Policy" (sex, screen, sports). Of course some still living members of the Chun (or later Roh) administration in charge of such cultural policies deny they used the phrase "3S" at the time, and no documents have been found with this phrase. Yet whether there was a written document with this phrase is hardly the issue, and seeking or chasing down such a document is entirely a red herring and dodging the issue. Plus, naïve journalists who think people of Chun's administration would tell the truth is artful dodging as well. Plus, *Chun's actions are a direct link of a Korean state starting to prime all later Korean "3S" policies seen as content of much of the global content of the Korean Wave.* It is undeniable that immediately after his military coup in 1979 and after the large civil opposition to his civilian massacre in Gwangju in late May 1980, Chun had a priority on media censorship in the rural provinces while priming mass entertainment and prurient distractions. He was likely trained or encouraged to do the latter instead of only the former because both military leaders of Chun and later Roh were trained in psychological warfare in the United States. Plus, the U.S. military after World War II in Japan organized its own kind of American-centric "3S" policy to distract a Japanese public from their ongoing American occupation by similar American state-offered cultural events and distractions (Kang, 2019).

Under Chun, this nascent *state-led policy for cultural production* could be called a "Proto-Korean-Wave," *particularly as his administration equally started to encourage production of Korean TV dramas intentionally that could be dubbed into foreign languages for intentional export and profit* as well as encouraging color television and a revived Korean cinema with less moral regulation. However, in this *economic expansion* in the 1980s, Chun's Proto-Korean-Wave was mostly geared toward *domestic* audiences for *combined entertainment, distractive, and productive* purposes to prime the television industry and the cinema industry at home—particularly as Korean cinema's popularity was failing by the late 1970s in Korea due to the rise of television watching at home. Differently later, the Korean Wave's conditions were geared toward more *international* audiences for more *strictly commercial* purposes by the early 1990s.

Next, it took *partial economic collapse* in 1997, for the Korean culture to further receive greater state-led subsidization, which began to catalyze massive scales of state allotments for cultural production overseas under now left-wing governments toward more *toward international audiences for profit purposes* instead of domestic audiences for repressive or distractive purposes. However, it is hard to truly separate such domestic purposes and international purposes, or political from economic purposes when it is *the same culture involved that was increasingly being state directed as well as state censored.* This increasing state-directed cultural production became ever more a theme of the Korean Wave by the 1990s. The Korean culture by the 1990s increasingly became treated first as a commodified export-led sector and only second as an autonomous Korean cultural expression that failed to require profit making to justify its existence.

However, even as Chun's political/cultural authoritarianism was reaching its peak in the early 1980s, he did attempt to be more representative than Park in other ways. Chun for the first time made (surprisingly) confessions by torture inadmissible in a court of law in South Korea, obviously permissible before, as well as making sure in his Fifth Republic (1981–1988) that the incumbent president (himself) could not make changes to the constitution about extending his own tenure in office—something done by Rhee in 1956 and Park in 1972 to wide hostility. It is ironic that President Chun, born of a military coup himself, additionally enshrined constitutional rules in the Fifth Republic for the privacy of personal correspondence and removed laws that indicated guilt by mere association introduced under President Park. Therefore, despite Chun's *informal* political authoritarianism increasing into cultural authoritarianism, the *formal* arrangements allowed for greater democratic change for the first time as well. However, despite this modicum of political consensus building, it was still a partial development drive. In culture, this was because there was still a greater state cultural control of media expression. In economics, there was still a ban on all labor unions. In politics, opposition candidates like Kim Dae-jung were held under house arrest, and there was still a lack of national elections for president. Open presidential elections had been "self-revoked" by President Park in his autocoup against his own Third Republic (1963–1972) toward his Fourth Republic (1972–1981). This lack of multi-party open Presidential elections in Korea was continued by Chun in his Fifth Republic (1981–1987). This lack of open national multi-party presidential elections remained the case until 1987, and it took nearly a month of daily mass protests around the country among blue collar workers, students, and even increasingly white collar office workers before Chun felt pressured enough by a unified culture to acquiesce to open elections once more for the 1987 Presidential elections.

The capstone event of both the second and third points of Chun's cultural policies was the fact that the international 1988 Summer Olympics did come to Seoul. It was the first global Olympics ever held in South Korea. By 1987, in the summer before the event, this upcoming global event in Seoul began to be used as political leverage by masses of Korean citizens to challenge the political and cultural authoritarianism of Chun once South Korea was in the spotlight for these upcoming international games. Such sports were originally intended only to showcase Korea to the world, for purposes of economic development, and of course to distract Koreans culturally from their internal political, cultural, and economic authoritarianism. However, the upcoming Olympics could equally be used as a powerful lever of social movements' brinksmanship *against* Chun to embarrass South Korea on the world stage, and such embarrassment would only be worse if he attempted a military crackdown soon before the Olympics started. Thus, a year before the Olympics opening ceremony, Chun simply announced the next military leader of Roh Tae Woo as his chosen President in 1988, without any open elections once more which had been the case since 1972. This catalyzed the June Struggle of 1987 (June 10–29, 1987), a daily series of nationwide protests immediately after the announcement.

However, thankfully yet surprisingly after the June Struggle, Chun realized his weak state, and on June 19th he called out the military yet rescinded his own order within hours whether by his own design or by U.S. pressure. Throughout this period, U.S. President Reagan is telling Chun openly via the major U.S. media that the United States refuses to support his further crackdowns and wanted to see many more policy changes—particularly mentioning the release of Kim Dae-jung from a recent house re-arrest imposed by Chun. By June 29th, Roh announced promises for constitutional reform, media liberalization, open Presidential elections, and other points like freeing Kim Dae-jung. Soon labor unions were legal. Soon afterwards, returning to some kind of economic consensus and a fuller development drive, for the first time in Korean history it was legal to organize unions. Suddenly, approximately 4,000 fresh labor unions were created, unionizing approximately 700,000 industrial laborers. Nearly 3,500 labor social movement actions occurred between June 29th through September 15th. By October 28th, 1987 the fresh constitution for the Sixth Republic was accepted by 93% of voters in a national referendum. It would come into effect upon the next Presidential inauguration in February 1988. However, Korea has kept the state-directed cultural authoritarianism of Chun that is the heir to the Korean Wave later. Though Chun acquiesced to most of the protestor's demands including open elections for the later 1987 Presidential election, his preferred military candidate Roh ran as the military's candidate in the multi-party elections, yet only as one among other candidates. Soon after, in the hastily organized Presidential elections of autumn of 1987, Roh was elected anyway. This was mostly due to a deep split of a four-way result, giving Roh only a low 37% plurality win. It would have been even a five way split though the first female Korean presidential candidate Hong Sook-ja withdrew to consolidate the attempt to elect Kim Young-sam. The wider dynamics of these open Presidential elections of 1987 led the two main left-wing candidates of Kim Dae-jung (~27%) and Kim Young Sam (~28%) to split the left vote with another third powerful regional candidate Kim Jong-pil (~8%)—who founded the KCIA under Park in the early 1960s. This "third Kim" came from one of those politically displaced aristocratic families under Park who remained proud of his aristocratic heritage family in ancient Korea. Thus, Roh Tae Woo won the plurality at a mere 36.64% of the total of votes. This low plurality win for President Roh (1988–1993) ended Chun's Fifth Republic and began the still current Sixth Republic, with that constitution starting with Roh's inauguration on February 25th, 1988. This is the current constitution of South Korea to this day.

However, despite all this political change within one year before the international Summer Olympics of 1988, despite a true military candidate in Roh winning the low plurality election, despite thousands of unions formed for the first time in modern Korean history, and despite much less repression in the cultural media, surprisingly the Korean democratic reforms held even under the military's President Roh or under equally militant labor union movements. This ongoing accommodation was in retrospect good for South Korea's development gauntlet since if more right-wing military repression and/or leftist labor revolution was introduced it could have unraveled the whole development drive from this point.

Another unique factor in the great continuity that can be seen in South Korea's development drive, is that the election of military candidate Roh anyway in competitive elections of 1988 led to a rare "double transition to democracy": a *democratic transition* of power and a *military transition* of power, merged as one, instead of only one or the other against each other seen in many developing countries. Plus, in retrospect, it is argued that it was fortunate that Roh won because it was later revealed decades later that there were military plans arranged for another military coup or vote fraud if Roh had lost, according to documents revealed in the past few years that presumably were not used or implemented.

So, the 1988 Summer Olympic Games was a fine closure to a less developed dictatorial South Korea. It was a fine closure to nearly twenty years of increasingly partial development drives. It was a denouement to Korea restarting a full development drive like between 1963 and 1970, since after 1988, South Korea once more became a more complicated and yet more consensus-oriented, representative, and developed country that now looked outward and faced the world instead of only looked inward upon itself alone. The opening ceremony of the 1988 Olympics in Seoul was hosted by incoming President Roh. It saw hundreds of Korean adults and children performing synchronous Taekwondo moves—something still in the cultural repertoire of the Korean Wave today. Taekwondo today in South Korea is still seen as deeply ancient, modern, and patriotic all at once. Plus in 1988 with Koreans as the Olympic host, they introduced individual and team archery to the Olympics once more, as the sport had fallen out of favor earlier on the international scene. Archery as well remains another strong point in the current Korean Wave still. From 1988, Koreans started to win almost all Olympic competitions in archery ever since.

Therefore, close viewing of the 1988 Olympics and the whole Korean 1980s rewards us with understanding the later Korean Wave better. In the 1980s, we see the Korean state's cultural priming of events and priorities of cultural sectors as economic development taking shape. We additionally see the cultural forms of the "Proto-Korean Wave" taking shape under the Korean state of President Chun and President Roh. Chun in retrospect started a state-directed cultural wave in at least six ways: by priming international events to focus on and to come to Korea and thus for Koreans to start to consider the wider culture of the world; starting the digital telecommunications sector; encouraging the start of the color television sector domestically, as well as dubbing black-and-white films for export into foreign languages; trying policies that would revive Korean cinema in the 1980s; and by censorship and state direction trying to make the culture (for better or for worse) less morally and politically led by an earlier more decentralized *mass media of religious or civil political sentiment.* Instead, public Korean culture steered by Chun from the early 1980s attempted to make the culture more consolidated by being state-led in direction, corporate-led for profit, and *toward priming mass consumer cultural desires* toward wider and more secular purchasing pleasures. This sounds a lot like the Korean Wave later of course.

In conclusion to this section, in retrospect, good choices of South Korea held over time in three stable hybrid development settlements in culture, politics, and economics since 1963 to the late 1960s. This was a full development drive that moved into step two. However, there was a backsliding to only a partial development drive in the 1970s through the 1980s that was only with difficulty recovered after 1987. Comparatively speaking, most countries fail to recover, and they simply stall or slide out of the development gauntlet. In the South Korean case, only between 1963 to approximately around 1970, and then only once more after 1987 to the present, can it be clearly said that South Korea chose a *full development drive* as an ongoing sequence that kept getting more representative. These periods helped the country check and balance against only half-solutions in step two as mentioned above. For a counterfactual, if a fuller dictatorship over time had developed or consolidated after the 1970s, it would have surely made even more unrepresentative and self-destructive economic policy and cultural policy over time, given its destruction of political consensus in politics already evident after 1970 only formalized from Park's autocoup. Therefore, a mere partial development drive in step two in the 1970s, if it had been kept, would have likely created a more vicious cycle of decline backward down the development gauntlet, instead of a virtuous cycle further along it. Either a fuller dictatorship over time or an ever more unrepresentative and self-destructive economic policy and cultural policy over time, if left unchecked, could have destroyed the country's culture, families, economy, politics, and environment in the process of its fast development.

If the history of other less developed countries can be used a comparative judgment against South Korea, the potential was that Park's partial development drive from the 1970s that could have solidified in South Korea—turning it into a more permanent political and cultural authoritarianism. That likely would have only catalyzed three different kinds of cultural revolution in the process against the fast development attempt that became less representative. There was Park's own right-wing cultural revolution in Korea by this time in the Saemaul Undong. There was the rising Catholic Church-protected labor movement as a left-wing cultural revolution. There was the growing influence of the consumerist/cultural revolution of Americanization particularly in a 'long haired and short skirted' folk music culture in Korea that was quite popular against the Korean state in the 1970s—a whole different Korea that was very hegemonic in the 1970s' youth and consumerist culture yet it has now gone down the Orwellian 'memory hole' in most Korean's popular imaginations. Either one or the other of these state-led right or bottom-up left wing cultural revolutions that were in the offing in the 1970s could have led to calls for another political revolution or military coup that could resettle past political and economic accommodations—demoting all aggregation entirely. This, in turn, could have reset the country back to some kind of ideologically driven purity of a military coup, or a one-party political movement regardless of whether it was a reactionary rightist or more revolutionary leftist cultural revolution that would have been in power. Either result would place the country back to step one, or even before step one in terms of a path down the development gauntlet because aggregation of the past would have been called into question and even the economic policies associated with Park have been changed or shattered in their legitimacy.

Notice the sequence of the development drive in South Korea is buckling to greater representation in *economic policies* first, and then with that wider economic settlement setting up greater support and greater growth, a more political authoritarianism in a growing dictatorship tries to hold on *with more cultural authoritarianism* as well. However, it still keeps buckling toward greater grass roots *economic rural economic development.* However, despite all these indirect attempts to insulate an increasing political dictatorship, all these economically-widening and accommodating successes in the Korean case eventually 'overtopped' the dictatorial political-cultural system itself *and bent it into more multi-party open political representation* and more open cultural representation after 1987 regardless. None of the political authoritarian leaderships of Park or Chun wanted to create this growing national consensus in politics or culture. However, it was the rising externalities of protest that finally were addressed to make everything (politics, economics, and culture) more representative from 1987 onward in the Sixth Republic. Thankfully, Chun's government was a weak enough state that it realized it had to buckle and adapt in a more representative way toward a more full development drive once more. However, it was an undesired elite move toward a more democratic politics. It was like an overspilling of the earlier economic development like when water becomes high enough to make a pretty waterfall, that overspills what was once only a dam designed to hold the water back. Meanwhile, the dam equally was amassing a larger scale of water behind it over time, making it dangerous to allow it to keep building without a controlled release. However, one thread that remains is the growing state direction of the culture that we see from the 1980s under President Chun. Regardless of whether the right or the left have been in the Presidency or the National Assembly after that, what has remained unquestioned is this deeper institutionalized state direction of culture that from Chun's era has been in collaboration with large private capital for priming a consumerist Korean culture—first at home and increasingly abroad as well as another export-led economic sector.

In short, only a full development drive becomes good solution to step one or step two, because it is a check against being blocked in secondary gauntlets and in partial development drives that create their own future externalities of unrepresentative politics or unrepresentative economic policies in the process of development itself.

3.1.1.3 Tertiary

Note from above that as President Chun was being pressured toward ever more representative settlements particularly from 1985 through 1987 as a fuller solution to step two, his government was in the middle of trying to solve "step three" as well. This is defined below. Unless step two had been solved well after 1987 toward the greater consensus of a full development drive once more, the hypothesis is that the deep repression exemplified by a partial development drive in only an economic drive without greater political representation would have kept the economic success of step three from lasting very long.

For Korea, its 'step three' can be seen in the development of many fresh economic sectors under President Chun that were unknown to President Park—of course particularly due to Park's assassination in 1979. However, step three is more than economics. First, 'step three' *includes economic issues* like escaping a "middle income trap" (Gill & Kharas, 2006). These many fresh economic sectors were toward solving the problems of Park's slowing economy of the 1970s. Some of these fresh export sectors in the 1980s were like digital telecommunications, color televisions, or automobile exports. The latter export was based on an already established and successful domestic automobile production from Hyundai in the 1970s, starting with the Hyundai Pony—aided in its original success by a policy that almost totally blocked all foreign car imports in the 1970s. However, Hyundai cars were sold only domestically until 1986, when for the first time two Hyundai car models started to be exported to the world market as well. Barely thirty years later, South Korea is now the fourth largest automobile manufacturer in the world. The top five exporting countries for automobiles in the world in 2021 account for 51.2% of all automobile production, and by value they are: Germany ($139.1 billion or 19.2%), Japan ($85.6 billion or 12%), United States ($54.7 billion or 7.7%), South Korea ($44.3 billion or 6.2%), and Mexico ($39.9 billion or 5.6%). Hyundai is the eighth largest car company in the world by 2021, and the only Korean car company in the world's top ten largest automobile manufacturers (Workman, 2021).

However 'step three' is *defined as far more than economic change* as explained below. Step three implies equally the ability of a nation *culturally, psychologically, and politically to raise adults* and to have a more autonomous political organization and an open future that can move on from more childlike cults of personality or formal institutions animated by only images of the past and/or a past singular national leadership that may have started a nation's development yet in time can equally arrest a nation's cultural, political, and economic innovation and development as well.

As said earlier, at each step, the odds become statistically harder and harder down the development gauntlet. It is easy to make one good development decision or a few good development decisions. It is a difficult matter to set up a situation that encourages ongoing good choices for several generations. This means training an ongoing leadership to be flexible and thus capable intellectually and even culturally of changing the first economic sectors of the original development leadership. It is a difficult matter to set up this development culture as a politics that trains a country for several generations to make good choices more deliberatively and durably than otherwise. However, stunningly, this is exactly what South Korea has done. It should be lauded and celebrated as something very hard to do, culturally speaking, within a developing country. It means South Korea kept winning decade after decade more than otherwise despite many large changes that were mostly setbacks like in 1972, 1979, 1980, 1981, 1987. The year 1987 in retrospect of course was a leap forward to open Presidential elections instead of a setback—yet a large change that could have led to another setback in a potential third military coup in Korea for Roh as it has been revealed recently that Chun's military government was prepared for creating electoral fraud for Roh, if he lost the open Presidential elections of 1987. If that vote fraud planning had been found out in 1988 instead of over 30 years later, it could have easily caused a left-wing revolutionary scandal with a continuation of the June Struggle of 1987 merging with the ongoing thousands of labor social movement strikes from 1987 onward. Korea might have dropped out of the development gauntlet in the unrest, catalyzed by the military revealed as having a dishonest democratic support, given it was planning another military coup in 1987 if Roh lost. Other important years of decision were in 1997, 2008, and of course between 2020–2023.

Many other countries get 'stuck' somewhere after entering the development gauntlet as noted above, in the discussion for step two, because in important times they are unable to make clear or decisive decisions whether because of culture or because of the politics of their nations. However, South Korea's various setbacks were temporary or even catalyzing of the collective innovation of the Korean people's culture and government, instead of being arresting and durable. This is because of many various factors (see Appendix 3).

Thus, what really *separates the many less developed countries from the very few fully developed countries* are the tertiary or quaternary factors down the development gauntlet. The theme of both of these is the same open question of *whether a country can escape itself and its own undeveloped past* to chart the open future it wants, or, is the country captive durably to its past? This means, "is the developing country captive to what was decided long ago at the beginning of their development drive, politically or economically?" If it is captive of its past, it is unable to make it past the tertiary factors of the development gauntlet since it is unable to grow past its first decisions in politics or economics into anything beyond what was started originally. For a metaphor, is the development drive a train under control of its current drivers, or is it a mindless runaway train loyal to long dead drivers (like in North Korea, Zimbabwe, or post-apartheid South Africa) with no one alive who has the ability, training, inventiveness, or legitimacy to be future autonomous leaders who adjust what was set in motion earlier? Like a runaway train, is the country destined to stay on its first and only path until it derails, likely in a catastrophic crash or an ever slowing train, perhaps even worse and more miserable? Both can happen because modern leaders are unable to make legitimate autonomous decisions later of what do to about upcoming problems that may be *different* or more *representative* or *innovative* than before.

However, there are two levels to the third step: *domestic and international* blames or facilitations. The first half is the third stage's *domestic* problems of further moving down the development gauntlet. This half of the third step is what is known as the 'middle income trap' (Gill & Kharas, 2006) though it is more than this economic issue. It is equally a question of the social psychology of the country created by the fast development drive and how that has created different kinds of people and expectations because of the development drive. This reflects on the character of the adult leaders, their thinking styles, and their problem solving abilities. The third step implies that the earlier arrangement of the first step itself worked, and implies externalities were beginning to be fixed with that in the second step. However, the same path is unable to work forever on economic aggregation like clockwork. Novel economic sectors should be chosen to innovate away from diminishing returns of all older economic sectors in general in a globally competitive economy. Sure, a country could choose national autarky like North Korea (still today) or Ethiopia (originally, yet it has changed this policy), though from comparative analysis there are zero examples of countries making it down the development gauntlet beyond 'middle income' with only a policy of national autarky. A rough definition of 'middle income' would be those nations between $8,000 and $15,000 annual income per capita. A definition of 'high-end' begins around $20,000 annual income per capita. The United States by the way has an average of $75,180, the second highest in the world after Switzerland. "In fact, very few countries (excluding OPEC members) have ever made this leap from middle-income to high-income. The only examples in Asia are Japan, South Korea, Hong Kong, Taiwan, and Singapore. This list leaves many more countries (Malaysia, India, Thailand, Brazil, Mexico, Argentina, Russia, Chile, and others) stuck in the middle income trap with China" (Tyler, 2023).

The second half of the third stage is the *international* side: how can a fast developing country rearrange its relationships with its ex-colonial powers as now one among peer nations, or will it be captured or lulled into a novel neo-colonial relationship of financial aid, subsidized markets, and military interventions from previous powers or fresh powers, somewhat rationally or willingly, if it is unable to solve for itself the more internal side of the third stage of the development gauntlet?

In summary, the *tertiary* factors mean whether these ongoing more balanced virtuous cycles of development, in a full development drive, are themselves *further durable and flexible enough not only against externalities and change called forth by themselves if successful (i.e., solving the secondary gauntlet issues), though are they further durable and flexible in the face of three kinds of future-oriented factors* that face all developing countries if they are successful. Below, discussion ranges in those three areas: *economics, culture/politics, and the durability of initiating settlements to sudden unexpected disaster and crises.*

These three factors are, first, do they have the ability to navigate past their *first* domestic choices in *economics*? Can they evaluate, plan, and administer additional, alternative, autonomous future paths of economic sectors, steering the train legitimately onto another rail, so to speak, particularly as the first sectors surely will experience diminishing returns and find derailment or some dead end track without ongoing adjustment sooner or later? This means can a developing country later escape the 'middle income trap' that they set up themselves successfully in those first few economic sectors that soon decline as they gain greater international competition?

(Gill & Kharas, 2006) The above short list of countries has done this with the ability to create ongoing fresh economic sectors for themselves domestically.

However, second, to do this is more than a good economic idea. It has to do with leadership, culture, and politics. Does the developing country have the *ability to navigate past their first choices in politics*? Can mere later followers be brave enough to be innovative leaders themselves, to crack the political shell of their original facilitating developmental dictatorships' political models or decision making procedures, for instance? Otherwise, are later followers stuck and only ritually loyal to a missing dead driver of the train, with no one else even allowed to be a major leader whether due to mutual jealousies or simple disagreements over who should take the train onto which different rail? Is it taboo even to criticize past political dynamics or decision making procedure, as the political system would dissolve into jealousies and opportunistic attacks, and may collapse? Has the country raised leadership to do more than follow mindlessly any past fast-development leaders? Has it raised leaders and does it exist in a culture that can legitimately lay fresh track, i.e., develop other economic sectors that innately challenge previous glorified economic sectors' political and economic primacy? For another analogy, how do you tell your country or yourself that the previous national golden goose is dying, so you recommend killing it off earlier because it is dying anyway and a poor future now? How do you do this without finding yourself ousted politically? Can the country reinvent itself economically to do something beyond rent seeking on its past good choices? For another third metaphor, can a country economically 'shed its skin or shell to grow larger' and grow away from its first and smaller economic regimes in its development drive, or is the country unable to do so because they want to ignore growing problems or they want to be a pretty shell that honors past political leaders' "correctness" as the highest litmus test of success? Equally, said inversely, do ongoing leaderships have a lack of experience and thus bad planning or practice at economic transitions? Are fresh economic changes internally and intentionally sabotaged or later altered or ignored and starved for allies by other domestic groups connected to past powerful economic sectors that disagree on the whole issue of what additional economic sectors are required, particularly if it demotes earlier crony subsidies and budgets? What other bad mixed choices could be taken, like oddly-good planning and agreement that no one wants to change—yet with it aiming for clearly bad choices, in retrospect? What if there is very bad implementation of a good idea, in retrospect?

Third, for the durability of settlements, are the country's development settlements *resilient enough to be able to handle unexpected political and economic crises*, whether internal or external, that have nothing to do with the other two points above about 'outgrowing' a past economic or political choice? This third aspect of 'step three' has been aided in South Korea by its homogeneous culture both being a cultural 'buffer' to weather any random and unpredictable challenges of history as well as allowing greater collective innovation in crises, while other more heterogeneous cultures arguably are less able to do both very easily. Another aspect of South Korea that helped in earlier stages of the development gauntlet and kept helping in the third stage, domestically and economically, was its five-year plan. This regularized such economic and developmental soul-searching as a regular cycle of national politics, instead of leaving it off the agenda. Another aspect of South Korea that helped in second and third stages as well was the heritage of more consensus building from the fast development drive started by the Military Revolutionary Committee in 1961 and then by President Park between 1963 to around 1970. The political assassination of President Park in 1979 was one of those unexpected events and crises that tested these 'buffering' abilities of the culture and institutions to outside shocks—with Park and many others dying by the gunshot wounds received by the head of his own secret police itself, the KCIA, led then by a long-term developmental compatriot and friend with him from the early 1960s at that. It must have been a true moment of pathos for Park: "Et tu, Brute?" However, this assassination event was another ancillary shock that helped move South Korea into its third stage, as discussed below. It helped that in retrospect only for a short while did Chun simply want to repeat the past, though after late 1980 in the aftermath of the assassination, Chun chose a different future path of more technocrats and wide experts in consensus building about the next economic sectors instead of leaving it to another coterie of militarists to decide, as well as eventually Chun's political decision after June 19th, 1987 for a peaceable democratic and military transition in 1987 that would lead away from Chun into Roh yet under conditions of open presidential elections.

Developmental Korea survived well in retrospect, both politically and economically. Economic direction became less dictatorial and more consensus-oriented around technocrats with varied expertise instead of only a crony group around the next military coup into the next President Chun. Political direction even became in some ways more hybrid in its politics once more—with added civil rights protections and institutional provisions against future 'lifetime' informal dictatorships that were added to the constitution of the Fifth Republic by Chun's administration. However, in other ways, as said, Chun continued and even further consolidated an informal media dictatorship on information and kept the executive branch without elections to keep himself in power with his expected ability to later simply 'anoint' the next military sponsored leader as the next Presidency. That failed to happen by 1987 though by several interactive factors that helped Korea remain in stage three: massive national protests at Chun's announcement of Roh as the next President who would become it without an open election, by international pressures (particularly from the United States) refusing support for Chun's desired further domestic violent crackdowns to keep this announcement in place, and of course Chun's own autonomous decision to accommodate and rescind his own military order on June 19th, 1987, instead of be responsible for launching his country into a left-versus-right wing civil and cultural war over the next presidential election.

However, as said, the third step of the development gauntlet is hardly only an economic question, it is the social psychological ability to handle this step that separates the adults from the children, metaphorically speaking. This is because this step is politically and emotionally hard for many countries because it shows two kinds of countries develop by this third stage out of how they handle step one and step two. Some kinds of countries have actually trained or have available the next generation of patriotic adult leaders who can make such decisions. They live in a political arrangement that allows open debate at least among each other. This happened somewhat in the economic policies of the early 1980s in South Korea; it is said somewhat because many of Chun's technocrats were American-trained Koreans. Plus, this can be seen in the political constitutional changes of the 1980s in the Fifth Republic as well since of course even a presumed military dictator-become-President like Chun failed to want to repeat the past and be assassinated like Park earlier. Chun felt like a weak state enough to be pressured to enshrine ever more civil rights protections for Korean citizens even against his own dictatorship. He felt pressured enough to put into his constitution of the Fifth Republic that he would not simply reauthorize himself as a lifetime president as Rhee did in 1956 in the First Republic or Park did after 1972 in the Fourth Republic.

Other kinds of countries create more childlike followers of earlier leaderships. They live in a political arrangement of only worship of past leaders, emotional retribution, and fear. They punish open debate or see it as a taboo criticism of first leaderships or themselves. This is more like China, North Korea, or Zimbabwe. People here are more afraid than in control, and this creates captive leaderships easily pressured, threatened, or compromised by outside forces since their ambivalent people increasingly fail to support them generally. That kind of cultural revolution against such leadership of course will set them back in the development gauntlet.

At this step, many developing countries fail *internally* as they have trained more childlike followers, mistrustful of each other, and thus afraid or unable to change anything from the past even as everything collapses around them because problems now are caused by the earlier settlement of the foundational leadership itself that brought them together and kept them in power. Earlier developmental leaderships may be worshipped like China's Mao, North Korea's Kim Il Sung, or Mandela's South Africa regardless of their bad developmental records. Therefore, it is hard to gain future power in such a political system by saying the earlier lauded arrangements are now to blame for the country's declining or failing ability later. A nation that is unable to enter stage three is very close to a culture based on what Hans Christian Andersen wrote about in his short story about a naked emperor parading around in "the emperor's new clothes." Everyone is afraid of telling the emperor he really is naked and self-deluded, because their jobs depend solely on complimenting him and his bad abilities instead of being honest. Truth is explosive in such pantomimes of countries. The Ethiopian state under its last king Haile Selassie had a similar self-deluded high court system that contributed to its decline (Kapuściński, 1983).

Externally as well, foreign pressures on a country may attempt to maintain the older status quo where increasingly a 'newly developing country' is pressured to remain in its past as only a proxy or a bit-player to another country's development drive—particularly by selling cheap raw materials or cheap items to the other core. Previously once gentle sponsors can drop the mask at this stage and get violent with assassinations of leaderships who attempted to become autonomous from previous international sponsors if something threatens to alter past international clientelistic dynamics. This is because as the 'newly developed country' gains the economic power increasingly to set an autonomous future course without a potential past sponsor's approval, the only veto possible now is external violence, terrorism, and/or external bribery to threaten a country to maintain the past status quo (Perkins,

2005). Plus, if a country lacks its own internal ideas and lacks the developmental 'adulthood' for how to rescue themselves domestically in some ongoing economic decline, they may acquiesce to remain developmental children to another's empire in such a situation pragmatically. However, that is the end of their development gauntlet advance until that relationship is ended.

However, in the South Korean situation, as mentioned earlier, in the economic sense there was a lack of raw material wealth to worry about that could set off external concern of other countries about Korean economic growth or changes in its raw material export conditions because South Korea failed to have any major examples of it. Therefore, *by default twice*, internally and externally, South Korea escaped this decision point or problem that happens to many other countries as they develop an urban industrial economy: internally, its previous developmental dictator in being assassinated unexpectedly helped South Korea change after 1979 politically, psychologically, and culturally gave them a chance to be future developmental 'adults' very quickly and more easily than most developing countries; and extenally in economic issues, South Korea's lack of raw materials kept it from ever being invaded or manipulated by other countries interested in keeping the country in a subordinate raw material exporting relationship to another core country. Respectively, in both of these two default situations, South Korea could more easily escape internal problems blocking the move to step three, and more easily escape some external economic problems blocking the move to step three. However, externally in political relationships, South Korea is still firmly in the orbit of the United States military alliances globally even if in external economic and external cultural relationships South Korea has created its own relationships, re-centering the world on itself to a great extent. Plus, economically, Korea continues to have passed the third gauntlet, even despite short setbacks in keeping it after the 1997 global financial crisis, in which a damaged Korean economy took on a short term (yet large) economic debt to the International Monetary Fund. The IMF started to give all sorts of external economic and external political control conditions to received the loan. This short-term neo-colonial experience began to restructure Korean economic policy around what the global external International Monetary Fund and global external banks wanted out of Korea, more than serving the Korean economy per se. However, Korea regained the third gauntlet with large civil effort of donations of private citizen gold to the government in the first four months of 1998. It is estimated that around 3.51 million Koreans collectively donated about 227 tons of their private gold to the Korean government. Since this was worth about $2.13 billion, in this way the civil campaign helped the Korean government repay the $19.5 billion debt to the IMF by August 2001, which was three years ahead of schedule. In this way, Korea could regain greater economic independence of action once more and move once more past the third gauntlet particularly by showing it is a nation capable of addressing unexpected economic crises. Externally in cultural relationships, Korea has passed the gauntlet here as well. It has done this via the ongoing growth of the first successes of regional Hallyu from 1992 in Hong Kong, to more global successes of the Korean Wave measured only intermittently with individual singular successes from 2003 to 2012, and only more simultaneous global success from 2018 onward. However, the idea of breaking older external dependencies on another country's culture being severed and recentered in a developing country's favor is what will be called the 'quarternary' or fourth gauntlet, so it will be discussed in the next section.

To compare step two and step three, in step two externalities are *internal* only like cultural, economic, political, or environmental externalities that should be addressed lest a revolution against the development drive occurs. In step three, the externalities are *both internal and external*. This makes it more politically touchy. For a comparison, in stage two, it is politically easier simply to add more seats at the table on the same development drive to address various externalities and complaints, so this is what typically results from stage two that maintains the economic aggregation from before. However, it becomes more politically touchy, domestically or internationally, to change course later when there is regularly a failing success of the original *internal* economic recipes of success at the same moment when the country's growing relative autonomy (from previous external sponsors) may lead leadership to acquiesce to growing pressures of *external* sponsors who want to remain *eternal* sponsors that can help a country solve or subsidize its own internal pressures to create more regular development as well. In other words, failing in step three likely makes you a permanent proxy of other countries' development paths, like developmental children taken care of by overlord development adults elsewhere, forever.

As said, psychologically weak leaderships without ideas how to expand even more relative autonomy and economic aggregation at this point may simply take the easy way out internally and externally, as mentioned above. They agree it is easier to be a bit-part player of another country's economic sphere of influence forever if the more powerful country subsidizes the less powerful country in the latter's middle income trap due to its lack of decisive culture just like it was a neocolonial possession of another nation. Many 'freed' countries even if they make it down the development gauntlet somewhat can fall back into dependency even after becoming more urbanized and industrially developed. Thus they seldom move further down the development gauntlet to greater independence, since they 'solved' their tertiary problems domestically and internationally by connecting to another country's development gauntlet instead of continuing to craft their own future. If a nation is very dedicated to a raw material export economy as its developmental policy, they are already deeply connected to other countries' development drives from step one, and rarely make it to step two much less step three.

Admittedly, it seems safer that way, internally or externally, *though that is only for the short run*. However this is the end of the development gauntlet for the country. Plus, it is very dangerous what may happen from this point in such a country. First, it can be harmful or deadly in the long run if you lose that sponsor—particularly if it is lost quickly like what happened to Cuba or North Korea in the 1990s when both lost their sponsor of the Soviet Union and quickly collapsed into famine conditions for years. Second, it can be deadly in the long run as such subsidization only encourages an ongoing lack of solutions to stage three's unsolved problems of economic diminishing returns. Both Cuba and North Korea had avoided step three by relying on the Soviet Union internationally to solve their internal problems for them. However, after the collapse of the Soviet Union in 1991, only Cuba has shown itself more psychologically adult in its development capacities. Cuba has internally solved its domestic agricultural problems somewhat and moved a bit down the developmental gauntlet via its autonomous decision to undertake the world's only national permacultural transition for a more ecological agriculture so far. Cuba achieved its desired food security, and is truly trying to set its own future. This bodes well for Cuba moving down the development gauntlet. However, this Cuban situation is still a partial development drive that will come to sabotage itself, since this is only a partial economic development drive in Cuban land, since the land is still nationalized economically, and since Cuba is still without a political development drive by being a one-party state. Cubans only grow land in usufruct land tenure conditions. North Korea adapted less well and seems incapable of setting its own autonomous future different than the past. North Korea is still in a partial development drive by only allowing some kinds of private market economy in food to encourage more food production in a novel economic development drive, yet without any true change in its political drive or its economic drive. Plus, land in North Korea like Cuba is still maintained as nationalized in a similar usufruct relationship, yet North Korean food still is additionally requisitioned by the state regardless of the growth of the private market economy in agriculture slightly. Plus, North Korea is making bad economic decisions by destroying its ecology by farming ever further up the sides of mountains. This causes greater erosion and flooding—and thus self-sabotaging its own economic system of agriculture with ever diminishing economic returns. This has set North Korea even further backward down the development gauntlet—or even out of it entirely.

Dealing successfully with step three sets up even larger relative autonomy of the country's economic aggregation in urban industrial development. It sets up many self-generated plans for future innovation, a more complicated economy, and many added economic sectors if successful. Any success in stage three means a greater ability to aggregate via *setting more open-ended, consensus-based, and flexible national political and economic priorities from this point forward* instead of locked to past decisions. From a successful stage three, the country is a peer 'developed country' in the world, competing with other developed countries with the ability to craft economic futures they want and the economic and technical innovations they want via research and development budgets along with state-led coordination of that in different tactical ways.

South Korea began to enter this third stage from the early 1980s to the early 1990s after the country suffered the crisis of the assassination of President Park in 1979. This unexpected assassination released a great deal of creative thinking about fresh economic sectors and less moral censorship to escape the middle income trap, ideas that likely would have been vetoed with Park's continuing presence. From 1980, President Chun stopped trying to centralize economic decisions in the Presidency as Park had, and instead let economic future planning be promoted by many Korean 'technocrats' who had foreign-national training and degrees. Many more governmental departments in the national bureaucracy were created as well to decentralize economic planning beyond a few people. It is debatable whether South Korea could have solved the third step (at least in this delegated and collective way) if President Park were alive in 1980, though it is likely sure that South Korea depended on President Park earlier. South Korea likely would have never gotten those particular first or second steps down the development gauntlet or achieved them at such an accelerated speed without him. In retrospect, however, the main two sectors of the later Korean Wave, digital telecommunications and originally analog cultural production industries were advanced only after Park by Chun's government priorities. Originally these two fresh economic sectors were separate, though came to join by the 1990s in the history of the growing Korean Wave. Therefore, South Korea started to solve its third step in the 1980s in a way that in retrospect can be seen to later set up a potential for the fourth step, defined as a cultural wave.

For better and for worse, South Korea's fast development drive is imprinted with President Park's increasingly hybrid cultural, economic, and political settlements between 1963 and 1970. These were durable and flexible enough to be adapted to keep allowing for greater economic aggregation even after he was gone, and they were strong enough even to survive him after he started to abandon that earlier representativeness by the 1970s himself. So even as Park became disloyal to these growing consensus and hybrid settlements in which he felt 'trapped' from 1970 onward, these hybrid settlements lived on without him since a growing consensus outlasted him and outlasted Chun. In South Korea, this stable and flexible step one and step two between 1963 and 1970 with triple hybrid developmental policies (in culture, politics, and economics) encouraged more representation as a matter of course over time in each. This is the true heritage or gift to Korea from 'early Park', despite 'later Park' himself in the 1970s.

3.1.1.4 Quarternary

Next, the quaternary or fourth step is defined as a cultural wave of exports into other countries as a market. This step truly *separates developed countries from each other* in going down the development gauntlet, since only a few developed countries ever have had an international cultural wave *via their own growing media capacities* later aiding in an appreciation of and a purchase of their own cultural products by other cultures.

Six discrete penultimate factors are listed below that show whether an already developed country is economically scaled enough, culturally in content adored enough, and technically in media competent enough compared in competition with other developed countries to have a cultural wave internationally after becoming a developed country. Few developed countries ever even have these six factors together.

Comparing past and present cultural waves for common themes, the first two of these common themes for achieving a cultural wave are (1) whether a nation still has a culture that is stable, more homogeneous, hegemonic, expansive, proud, and strong enough even after going through (2) the rigors of urban industrial economic development and wider representative political and economic development.

However, on the first point, sometimes urban industrialization can alter the nation so much that it is split and more heterogeneous culturally in the process of its fast development drive, instead of maintaining a clear, proud, hegemonic culture. This may lead the nation to lose national pride or common ethos in their culture—and thus be unable to enter a cultural wave judged from how all cultural waves so far have been promulgated as part of such a cultural pride of past and present achievements. This can be alternatively argued in the inverse for what seems to stop a proud cultural wave. Judging from less developed countries with or without a cultural wave, many of them undergo 'brain drain,' a phenomenon in which their intelligencia see their home country as a cultural pariah and as one of the last places that they want to go back to or to associate themselves with proudly in the future. Therefore, that curtails the likelihood of a cultural wave later there since the developing country has raised its talented top achievers to flee the country instead of remain cultural loyalists. It is interesting that in the 1980s, South Korea crafted interesting policies to try to demote 'brain drain' by luring its well-educated, foreign-resident Koreans back to Korea with huge subsidies and living perks. Few countries have ever even conceived of this, much less succeeded somewhat in it as Korea did.

The second common issue mentioned above in cultural waves would be whether the country developed a complicated enough economy or at least one at large enough scale *to justify its own self-generated media technologies and/or media inventiveness all to themselves.* This point is argued because many developing or developed countries are hardly always large enough demographically or economically to have a cultural wave. This is connected to whether they can support mass media innovations of a developed economy from a large enough demographic within themselves first to catalyze it. Judging from all the countries with a cultural wave throughout the twentieth century, all had point #1, i.e., some kind of cultural homogeneity that survived urban industrialization and all had point #2, i.e., all were demographically large enough to be innovative and even revolutionary in media technologies. They then may parley this into their later global technical and cultural waves.

However, hardly all of past or present cultural waves have the remaining points, the first of which is (3) a cultural wave that is synergistic with many different sectors of products of cultural interest around the world instead of only one. On the third point about a cultural wave truly having multiple sectors of exports instead of only one, of the few cultural waves that do emanate from less developed or developing countries like Mexico's telenovelas (TV dramas), Brazilian pop music, or Indian movies of "Bollywood," indeed it is only in one sector pulled by global fads into international consumption.

A fourth factor of a successful cultural wave that is hardly seen in all of them is that (4) it can develop by the push or priming facilitation of the state in question, instead of only depending on the pull of global markets in cultural products that are less durable and only faddish. The fifth point is (5) whether the country in question is on the leading curve of media technological innovation in some way, that it can parley into its cultural wave before other countries utilize such a situation. The sixth big factor is a country that has a context of a slowly blooming cultural wave is that it equally (6) has to have some common image of the future desired by the world and sold to them as potentially their own future as well, so that others can participate within, assimilate, and enjoy. This has to be carried or related to some kind of innovation in media (point #5) as well that is available to many countries in question to carry both the futurist ideas and the media materials in question.

In these six criteria of a very successful step four of an international cultural wave, the three previous steps of the development gauntlet have to be maintained for a while before a cultural wave starts slowly to bloom, or rather to seep, into the global sphere of influence of such a developed country in its growing exports and cultural awareness in others.

What are some factors of greater success in a cultural wave? All six points would be best. However, at least first, a more homogeneous culture innately is better to catalyze a cultural wave, as it already has a common cultural image, and it only has to be selectively sold to others. Second of importance, a country should have domestic mass markets that are demographically large enough to encourage investments in mass media technologies for itself. These can create products that are more readily parleyed internationally as cultural artifacts to others. However, inversely, a more heterogeneous culture rarely generates such a common image, and instead generates one thousand private images out of its greater individual innovations and cultural innovations. Plus, sometimes a more heterogeneous culture or a smaller demographic culture (or both combined like in a small underdeveloped country) lack the media technological savvy to parley its culture into a large enough central market in a cultural wave as an economic sector. Equally, a country could have chosen a heterogeneous labor import over time in its economic aggregation drive, even if it has more revolutionary media technologies, and thus is without a common image of the future to sell as well. Plus, a country equally could only be a small city state, or a small demographic zone, without a large enough internal cultural market to catalyze such a culture wave within itself first even if it were a more homogeneous culture.

For one example, this point about an increasingly heterogeneous culture down the development gauntlet making a cultural wave difficult has hardly been a problem until recently within the historically more consolidated and homogeneous culture of France by the twentieth century, plus, given its strong modern heritage of industrialization in a few sectors on the coast. Equally France continues its own strong inventions of many modern media technologies from the early twentieth century—even into the 1970s in its own versions of a national Internet in Minitel long before any other country developed such a technology. This continues today as some of the most successful technology development clusters are in Paris in the world economy. Plus, culturally, France continues to be the world's premier location for global cinema screenings, at Cannes. It was cinema awards at Cannes that helped to make the world aware of the Korean Wave, particularly for the Korean Wave film *Parasite*.

The point is only a handful of countries in modern times have ever reached this fourth level of the development gauntlet by achieving or creating for themselves a global cultural stage based in the hearts, minds, and wallets in other countries. However, a cultural wave is defined differently than merely a 'pull' by a cultural fad surrounding a developed country's cultural products like sometimes seen in Swiss, German, or Italian knickknacks. Thus, a cultural wave is defined by more than the 'pull' of the world's cultural fads to support a foreign culture's products in their own. It has to have a cultural 'push' from the agreement of a state's desire or even culture's desire *to expand domestic cultural production globally* as well. Both of these can be as nebulous and revocable as the world's pull by cultural fads as well. Thus, a cultural wave depends on that virtuous cycle of re-priming that pull by others from an endlessly-renewed 'push' for it from a national political economic (re)priming of the national and global market, and of course the desired response of global 'pull' from a global public once primed. That ongoing national political economic push is built on the back of successful mass economic strengths, media technological superiority, cultural strengths, and the images of the future that others see in that cultural wave for themselves that they can participate within.

Many assume a modern cultural wave has only been done by a few countries of the wider 'Atlantacist' culture of Western Europe spread around the Atlantic (like the U.K., France, or the United States). However, in a meaningful way, Japan had a cultural fad from the 1800s in European culture, yet it only became a true cultural wave in the 1980s with the Japanese state starting to agree in this time of extreme Japanese economic exuberance that its culture could be a profitable export. However, this period of Japanese economic 'push' and exuberance was very short. It was abruptly ended with the decline of this 'push' by reprioritization on other domestic issues due to the large Japanese economic downturn starting in 1990 that has in many ways continued ever since. However, Japanese culture internationally still retains an important 'pull' as an international fad in our global culture despite losing its important 'push' factor of its domestic national political economy. Plus, Japan has always prided itself more on its cultural isolation and its different cultural trajectories, thus culturally Japan is less desirous of having a cultural wave at all. However, differently, there is something in the Korean psyche that enjoys and craves international recognition and comparison, and there is a durable great state support as well. By Part III, another factor will be discussed in the 'mid-size' of the Korean demographic scale that encourages greater export-led economies instead of only internal industrialization drives like much larger Japan that can survive better its cultural wave is only internal because the internal market is so large. Therefore, there is an ongoing 'push' factor for some aspects of the culture, the Korean state, Korean companies, and Korean demographic size combined to all contribute to a common cultural export sector.

So, in this way South Korea has all six points. It has joined this very small developed country club with their common cultural wave extensions. South Korea has remained more durable in its important 'push' factors unlike the Japanese cultural wave that has more depended upon ongoing 'pull' factors far more than 100 years really. Instead, the Korean cultural wave depended on 'push' factors, particularly since the early 1990s when it started to grow by Korean state public policies, Korean corporate private profit, and aspects of the Korean culture itself that helped to 'push' its recognition within regional East Asia first instead of only depending on the random 'pull' of international fads. This regional East Asian cultural wave increasingly kept being pushed until it reached the international level after the year of 2012 which was the 'Post-Gangnam Style' era of the Korean wave. Reaching the fourth gauntlet means the world is your oyster—though only if you can keep this rarely achieved pearl growing ever larger by an ongoing virtuous cycle of state/producer push and consumer pull in the world-system.

South Korea has been the first to develop a cultural wave almost exclusively on the back of a global *digital* cultural sphere instead of catalyzed by more tangible cultural artifacts first. That in turn came from its own domestic story of its national digital saturation in digital telecommunications starting from the 1980s and accelerating in the late 1990s. All that was prefatory. However, it is hard path to maintain supremacy in a digital cultural wave due to endlessly innovated digital technologies and cultural production now elevated to expected standards of high-definition imagery and high-fidelity sound along with increasing standards of miniaturization. However, as other chapters indicate, South Korea excels even in this push to the world for several decades in both the production of the hardware of its digital media and the 'software' of its cultural content in that digital media now.

Maintaining this combined sextuple push of a strongly confident culture, internationally desired ideals, agreeable expanding economics, and media innovations, etc., *over other developing countries* attempting the same has been a problem for the deindustrialzing zones and more heterogeneous zones of the United Kingdom and the United States when they start for the first time in world history to have competition from more homogeneous cultures with similar criteria they had in the past, yet in now a more multi-polar world. The U.K. had great global technical innovations in catalyzing the world's first global industrial-scale urban commercial revolutions from the late 1700s onward, and then innovating transport technologies in urban life and urban waste/water handling for sanitary living to keep up with and to address well the economic externalities of that urban commercial revolution, and then to keep up with and to address well the political externalities of that urban commercial revolution to make changes toward wider urban representation and widened democratic franchise and public health services. The United Kingdom even later helped pioneer the aviation sector in the early twentieth century. It even added many cultural innovations with Britain having one of the first industrial film studios, some of the first regular national television programming and broadcasting, and then the push of a "British Invasion" in culture in a British cultural wave from the early 1960s like the Beatles and other British popular music acts that overawed American teen culture at the time. This so-called push of a 'British Invasion' (as a nickname for the British cultural wave) began to make the global 1960s what they were, as a merged Anglo-American cultural wave that went around the world. Both continued strongly into the 1970s with many modern folk rock music groups, then into the 1980s with televised popular music leading the video art of early British synthpop of the New Romantics to even top the U.S. charts, along with punk, goth, ska, industrial, house, ambient, electronic, and dream pop that set the cultural forms for many other nations' cultural creations as well as copies. The Anglo side of this Anglo-American cultural wave began to decline in the later 1980s, with the decline of many internal push factors from the U.K., in an era of retrenchment under neoliberalist Thatcher and greater domestic dissent and violence. The 1980s however was a short period of many push factors from the Japanese political economy in a growing Japanese wave soon across

East Asia. This period additionally saw similar push factors from a growing Korean wave in the early 1990s onward.

Meanwhile, the United States has maintained a strong showing in its ongoing push factor of an American cultural wave along with the world's pull factor as well. It started from the early 1900s to the present around a more homogeneous culture of strength and pride, a confident image of the technological and urban consumerist future that others wanted that led it to be a site of vast immigration. Plus, other American quaternary push strengths were the many American-invented media technologies and American cultural content recorded on them that Americans mutually pioneered like the nickelodeon, the kinescope, sound and color movies joined, theater organs, radio music and its disc jockeys, and mass record production itself. Within this fresh media hardware, the more homogenous American White culture's technological effervescence at the time, and these many technical innovations blended into the growing cultural innovations coming from America's equal durable ethnic Black heterogeneity of culture. The cultural innovations were the music of ragtime, jazz, blues, swing, and rock-n-roll that went around the world. It was recorded on American media in audio and visual recordings or live radio broadcasts. This cultural push has continued from ragtime through early rock'n' roll in the 1950s, to the 1970s in heavy metal and disco, to the growing markets for American country music from the 1940s onward, up to the New York house and rap music additions from the late 1970s onward. For nearly a century, Hollywood movies and American cultural soundtracks have become the background to the world's culture. The American cultural wave has been so encompassing and pervasive it is hard to disentangle what the twentieth century would have been like, or whether it would have even existed, without many of the United States's key technical media and cultural media influences.

However even if the innovation of the United States came from both its earlier more homogeneous culture that still had major heterogeneous cultural splits, it was an urban industrial economy of huge scale. It was that as well that encouraged greater individual innovation and cultural innovations technically for mass markets. Even if there was a dominant hegemonic culture in the American wave at first related to the Protestant hegemonic culture, the increasing dominance of the Jewish minority in American cultural production encouraged a more pronounced view of lauding outsider stories of the "American dream" and a common individualism accessible to all in American cinematic culture. This openness under Hollywood was starkly against earlier American White cinema that was quite ethnically closed on who could actually participate in American culture (Halpern & Jacobovici, 1998). While earlier American cinema was one of White European-stock or Anglo-Saxon Protestant hegemony, later cinema of Hollywood, freely admitted by the Jewish acting and film production population of the United States itself (Halpern & Jacobovici, 1998), has contributed to the greater universalizing of America as an image of the future for others instead of only for the founding cultures and religion of the settlers, by selling images of freedom of religion, and freedom of individual conscience as common cultural values and individual freedoms assimilated across all immigrant populations and Black American, Hispanic American, and Indigenous American populations alike.

However, by the 1960s as immigration policies changed into the twenty-first century, there have been more cultural wars in the United States over what should be hegemonic if at all. This has started to wreck this past key large demographic/market transmission feature and a shared ideal image of the future in the American wave of a common more homogeneous culture itself. The 'woke' cultural conflicts get louder than the American cultural wave itself. U.S.'s Hollywood reported over $500 billion in losses in 2022 alone that was contributed to by massive numbers of box office flops due to 'woke' storylines (National Tribune, 2023). Thus, the United States starts to lose some of those six 'push' factors mentioned above: a strongly confident culture, internationally desired ideals, agreeable expanding economics, and media innovations.

Meanwhile, the more homogeneous conservative culture of the Korean Wave starts to fill the world's music playlists and movie followers. In Korea now, these six push factors work well together. Thus, the Korean wave is around its own different digital media innovations and a still homogeneous cultural/market transmission with a stable shared image of the future and a growing economics. These factors working together keep the global Korean Wave growing. However, many developed nations' cultural waves decline by the slow loss of some of these factors over time.

3.2 Good Accidents and Good Choices: Ancillary Factors Down the Development Gauntlet

Comparatively speaking, there are two kinds of interactive more generalizable categorical or conceptual factors that help explain success down that four-step development gauntlet: **good choices and good accidents.** Some good choices have already been featured in the discussion of the development gauntlet above in the case of South Korea. Other good choices along with the conceptual idea of 'good accidents' of historical circumstance that have an influence to help hold a country to good choices are featured in the below section. A larger suggested list of good choices and good accidents in South Korean development is in Appendix 3. Koreans seemed blessed with a huge amount of both factors far more than other less developed countries. This long list of both kinds of good factors in development helped catalyze South Korea's specific path down the developmental gauntlet (step one), helped them continue it by encouraging greater integration of externalities over time (step two), helped them institutionally and social psychologically invent wider economic sectors than their originating ones (step three) toward their economic Korean Miracle, and eventually helped them toward a cultural Korean Wave (step four).

This has made South Korea *the world's only major story of developmental success* measured by being the only poor ex-colonial and non-European nation after World War II to enter the OECD by 1996 and the only nation ever moved from the 'developing' to the 'developed' category by the United Nations Conference on Trade and Development (UNCTAD) since its beginning in 1964. That is happy for South Korea, though it is sobering or outrageous to reflect upon for how rare it is comparatively. It means almost all of the 'development trade,' including its many international organizations of NGOs and international banks with many billions of dollars spent on the project, have been mostly failures and have given bad advice. If they gave good advice, many more non-European ex-colonial nations would be developed 75 years later instead of mostly only South Korea. The first of two conclusions about that is that developed countries and international agencies unknowingly or knowingly gave bad advice and instead tried to corrupt many countries into geopolitical clientelism in the middle of the global Cold War from 1945 to 1991 between the United States and the Soviet Union, and would say and do anything to achieve that goal. However, simply making dependent clients of other freed nations after World War II in the Cold War has rarely led to a truly multi-polar world of distributed development (Perkins, 2005; So, 1990). South Korea did its best to ignore much advice in the early 'development trade' and crafted its own solutions for its fast development drive. The second of two conclusions about South Korea is that it has a plethora of what will be called these 'good choices and good accidents' that helped it stay on track down the development gauntlet instead of being distracted or falling out of it over time like many other less developed countries.

Korea is only one of those *nearly 100 fresh countries freed or created after World War II*, from the decline of most global European and Japanese empires between 1945 and the 1980s. Many of those countries were poor ex-colonial territories, freed from imperial rule that wanted to develop themselves. However, what choices should any country make to develop itself? There were many different developmental theories at the time by the 1950s into the 1960s. However, by the late twentieth century, Korea outclassed all other developing nations by becoming a truly developed nation by the late 1990s by entering the OECD in 1996. This was equally the time when the Korean cultural wave began to grow yet only throughout East Asia. Plus, this was many years before it became a global Korean Wave and still a few years before it was even called "Hallyu" from 1999.

Most people are unaware of this uniquely successful developmental context of Korea before the Korean Wave. South *Korea is only one of two non-Western countries in the world* (South Korea and Japan)—and *the only non-Western ex-colonial nation*—so far to be invited into the 'elite country club of the world,' the Organization for Economic Cooperation and Development (OECD). Obviously so far, there tends to be a European-heritage 'glass ceiling' in global development, noted by how merely two non-European-heritage nations in the OECD are Japan from 1963 and Korea from 1996. However, Japan was already massively urbanized by the early 1700s with Edo (now Tokyo) being a city of one million people for the first time around 1720. For comparison to Edo/Tokyo, London became a city of 1 million people for the first time only around 1815—the first and only European city at that scale since Rome between 100–400 CE. Thus, Japan was more easily industrialized by the late 1800s as the country already had strong internal mass markets, a deeply literate population, and even the world's first stock markets with futures contracts in the 1700s. Japan's modern urban industrialization began in the 1870s so it only had to recover after World War II, and Japan did that very quickly in the 1950s.

Differently, Korea is unique once more by only starting its fast development drive from almost nothing merely from 1961. Many Koreans lived in thatch-roofed homes at the time. Even one national paved road for automobiles failed to exist. Seoul was invaded repeatedly over the Korean War (1950–1953) and destroyed each time. The first car freeway in South Korea was the Gyeongbu Expressway, built by Hyundai for the Korean Government between February 1968 and July 1970, and the paved highway extended eventually from Seoul to Pusan. As Korea was looking for ideas to model about its development from 1961, many of them came from the good choices of Japan's quick reindustrialization in building a top-down developmental state in a synergistic collaboration between private banks and their own big private companies, national centralized financial control, low interest rates to state-planned sectors, and many other factors. All of these Japanese ideas for a fast development drive were admired and copied by the Military Revolutionary Committee between 1961–1963, and continued later as policies by President Park's administration after 1963 though Park added domestic ideas of a socialist five-year plan (from the overthrown Second Republic) into the mix along with pubic corporations for infrastructure and for material standards.

Even though all countries can make some good choices and bad choices over time, and even though all countries are unavoidably with some good background factors and some bad background factors, few countries seem to have *as many good choices as well as many good accidents (background factors)* as seen in South Korea. To reflect on the case of South Korea comparatively, it is bizarre how this country has had so *many* good choices and so *many* good accidents of history, and so few bad choices and so few bad accidents of historical context when reflecting on Appendices 1, 2, and 3. Thus, it may be a tall order for other countries to replicate South Korea if they want to truly learn from this outlier to make it a harbinger or plan for others.

To define terms, South Korea was full of many 'good choices' over time, defined as "good" in the abstract based on one major criteria of whether it created ongoing virtuous cycles of development in the culture that avoided eroding toward vicious cycles. Thus, "good" is defined equally in terms of whether it maintained or encouraged successful economic aggregation over time instead of contributed to its decline. Thus, choices can be defined as 'good' based on a judgment of whether they have contributed to ongoing virtuous cycles in development against diminishing returns, toward cultural enhancement, toward more competitive markets, toward less path dependence, toward more ability for technical innovation, and toward less political state capture.

Plus, South Korea had a tremendous number of 'good accidents' or background conditions that were dealt in its favor that encouraged the same economic aggregation. Good accidents are defined similarly as non-chosen historical contexts and happenstances helping Koreans choose such virtuous cycles of development more than others down the development gauntlet—without seeding many of their own reverses by bad choices and bad accidents of history. Thus, these two categories interact. For instance, some 'good choices' look more like forced decisions encouraged by the 'good accidents' of the Korean historical context, instead of simply the art of good choices being the free will of good or bad choices themselves. One example of a good accident from Korea is how the Third Republic under President Park avoided the 'choice' of known downsides of specializing in a raw material export economy (Collier, 2007; So, 1990)—indirectly because South Korea lacked many raw materials. Another example of good choices more directly would be how Korea in the 1960s avoided the diminishing returns and social externalities of impoverished farmers being thrown to the cities in agricultural consolidation, because Park chose to keep decentralized land tenure in agriculture instead of consolidating large agricultural farms in national production, and chose a village-based grass roots development for rural areas while keeping the urban industrial export-led economy. However, this might be said to be a good choice and a good accident simply because this was the background political settlement already set up as the Third Republic began, so to choose otherwise would probably have led to a coup or cultural revolution against President Park in South Korea for taking up a land nationalization policy like North Korea after 1954. So alternatively, this is why these two categories can be interpreted as one wide blurred category in how "good choices and good accidents" interactively matter highly in the South Korean fast development drive eventually toward the global Korean Wave.

From comparative analysis, this section summarizes only a few major 'good choices' and 'good accidents' that helped South Korea's virtuous cycles stay together down the development gauntlet toward the Korean Wave. While the earlier idea of virtuous cycles has been discussed and defined already, and while the term 'development gauntlet' is defined above as a series of four levels of problems to address for keeping on track to future successful economic aggregation, the question now focused on in this section is what actual factors encourage economic aggregation (good choices and good accidents) or lead to denigration of it (by the lack of such factors)? Down the development gauntlet, good choices and good accidents are swords raised above the head of the country to allow it to pass unscathed down a line that equally honors and yet holds it to a certain honorable path. Alternatively, bad choices and bad accidents are swords in a development gauntlet thrust randomly in any direction that impede any guiding progress toward a durable economic aggregation down the developmental line. Bad choices and bad accidents equally can be swords missing entirely, leaving the country to go aimlessly onward in any direction it chooses without being held by any honorable choice or honorable adversity to any particular path at all.

So, good choices and good accidents are hardly separate 'facilitating' factors because it is argued that the main causes or facilitators of durable development is the creation of ongoing virtuous cycles of particular arrangements of culture/ethos, economics, and politics. These two wider factors of good choices and good accidents are at best encouragements to virtuous cycles of dynamics, or, when lacking, at their worst contribute to the denigration of positive dynamics of aggregating economic growth into vicious cycles of decline. If replicating the two virtuous cycles of Korean development politically and economically in its hybrid choice seems difficult for other countries, replicating all the good choices and good accidents is a tall order if we want to replicate the current outlier of South Korea and turn it into a mere harbinger as a plan for others. In short, many good choices as policies and many fortuitous background factors (that encouraged good choices) helped South Korea's already good decisions down the development gauntlet to guide its self-generated development to aggregate and to last last long enough to blossom into the cultural Korean Wave.

The irony is that in many less developed countries freed from colonial status or invented for the first time after World War II have a great deal of free will in their choices. However, free will can yield random, changing, and thus less extreme aggregating wins over time. Thus, it is argued, it takes true 'good accidents' in the historical background of a country to help forcibly hold to *certain 'good choices' to a particular singular pattern over time* since this helps constrain total free will to push a more singular economic aggregation down the development gauntlet.

Effectively, good accidents help 'pre-rig' or 'pre-load' the development trend of a country toward economic aggregation *in three ways*. First, *good accidents train the undisciplined 'free will of choices,'* toward only the greater chance that a country will make more constrained good choices on one singular development drive toward ever more representative and ever more aggregated development on one ongoing plan. It may look like intelligent discipline, though in many cases, it is more effectively desperation by default in some way that holds a poor country to a particular developmental line. Thus good accidents sometimes mean more constrained choices for a developing country. For instance, it is a good accident of South Korea to lack many raw materials, as it held South Korea to more of an export-led development and value-added product specialization, just as it is a bad accident for North Korea to have many raw materials that allowed the country simply to gain rent by exporting non-value added materials and gain very little from it over time as so many countries can export raw materials, so the prices can be very unpredictable and make it difficult to plan the future with this kind of unstable capital inflow. For another instance, it is far easier for North Korea to take easier changing, repressive, or unrepresentative development policies. However, doing this demotes or smashes the greater potential of economic aggregation over time. Meanwhile, it is far harder for South Korea to try to keep its growing consensus-based processes intact even though doing this helps move a country down the development gauntlet well. The second and third way respectively that good accidents matter is that current conditions are regularly smashed by external variables that break up bad conditions of development and thus help people choose better ones of economic aggregation, or events are uniquely missing that can help create more constrained paths of good choices toward more undisturbed economic aggregation. To elaborate that second way that these good accidents work in history is as unplanned and contingent events themselves sometimes, which in retrospect, are good since they intervene and take out some problematic factor damaging further economic aggregation or add some useful factor that helps the other points of economic aggregation. Therefore, good accidents sometimes operate when *rogue outside or inside forces hit a country* and sometimes operate when they are *missing in the background of a country's history.*

It is important to explore how widely distributed around the world are these good accidents of historical context that interact with and encourage good choices toward development aggregation and guard against wider, easier, and more free choices that tend to demote aggregation with tangential fads over time. In other words, good accidents are hardly always recognized until later, because good accidents of history in the short run may look like curses and extra challenges that constrain or interrupt free decisions to 'force' harder yet ultimately good choices toward a more singular aggregation over time instead.

A wide discussion of all good accidents and good choices of all development aiding economic aggregation over time is not the focus of this section. Therefore, only a few highlights are noted below for how good accidents or good choices helped form the particular path of successful fast economic development into the Korean Wave. See Appendix 3 for more thinking in general on world development of how good/bad accidents or good/bad decisions help or hinder a country down the development gauntlet. The next sections only illustrates conceptually the idea of good accidents and good choices through discussion of a few factors in each category related to fast development drive success in South Korea that extended long enough to form the cultural Korean Wave.

3.2.1 Good Accidents

South Korea has good accidents *of all three kinds* mentioned above: background historical factors that exist and curtail free will of developmental policy choices to particular constrained choices that are good for economic aggregation; background historical factors or events that are missing that help in the same way in economic aggregation; and unexpected and interrupting events that help in economic aggregation. In short, good accidents can be summarized as "good factors that are there, bad factors that are missing, and interrupting events that help instead of harm." At least one kind of good accident will be discussed from each of these three sub-categories.

For the first and second category—good accidents of historical circumstance that are there and that are missing—there are many that have helped Korea to grow economically. First, South Korea has partially escaped all four of Collier's 'development traps,' many of which that he defines as the bad conditions of historical circumstance that overlap in many countries in much of sub-Saharan Africa or in the less developed areas of the world in general (Collier, 2007). Plus, South Korea is aided by its own unique natural geography that has disciplined its 'developmental free will' toward export-led developmental choices and economic aggregation on that point.

One of Collier's four suggested 'bad accidental' traps correlated with low levels of development or developmental failure is being a 'landlocked state with bad neighbors.' The meaning of 'bad neighbors' is having other failing/failed states around your country that makes it harder to be a successful state that accumulates stable economic aggregation of its own, as the state simply is full of the neighbor's damaging externalities of civil wars, coups, drug trades, and refugees over time. Many African nations have four or five bad neighbors, for instance and many of the problematic countries are landlocked around those bad neighbors (Collier, 2007).

Alternatively, South Korea is of course in a good accidental situation that is completely the opposite by escaping landlocked conditions by being ocean-facing on three sides, and by the good accident that on its remaining side it has only one bad neighbor, North Korea, though even that bad neighbor is insulated from influencing South Korea very much by refugees or invasions by a stable militarized border surrounded by a large and wide demilitarized zone. The greater good accident of the first kind in of South Korea is its ocean-based geophysical 'isolation' is really an extremely cheap transportation connectivity that forces good choices of specializing in a more export-led economic development drive that innately has greater chances of wide economic aggregation beyond satisfying a national economy's markets. It additionally is a background historical factor that helps South Korea have 'missing' bad neighbors at larger scales. South Korea is effectively an island facing the world economy after 1961, yet without the geophysical isolation or demographic smallness of island nations due to the scale of this 'mid-sized' nation and its larger demographics of around 51 million people now by 2023 that provide for such global production a large labor pool as well as a geography capable of providing larger scales of cheaper real estate, unlike most 'other islands' in the world where real estate and labor costs are dear. South Korea's modern geopolitics make it though an 'island dependent upon the world' for survival, via forced choices of only having global oceanic trade allies, routes, airlines, and increasingly now the Internet economy linking it to the whole world. Plus, the geography of this peninsular land is organized in such a way that few places in South Korea are ever very far inland. This equalizes reduced transport costs for international shipments nearly anywhere in the country, which encourages a very export-led economy to focus itself within Korea for the whole world-system.

Another one of the four main development traps from Collier's analysis that he sees across many failed states of the 'bottom billion' of the world is the bad accident of being a raw material exporter. Specifically, the more dedication a poor country has to having a high degree of non-value-added raw material exports in a country's overall economic trade, the less likely it will be developed. However, alternatively, South Korea is 'blessed' with the good accident of historical background of the second kind: being without many raw materials to (badly) choose from in the first place for a raw material export trade. Comparatively speaking, this is a good accident of geology that encouraged good choices of South Korea toward an export-led economy of more value-added products, based on raw materials that had to be imported instead. This dynamic encouraged a wider skill set toward economic aggregation in value-added products over time, as well as required applications of updated competitive education and brain power, instead of the well known unpredictable booms and busts and lack of intellectual innovation required of almost any raw material economy in competition with other raw material suppliers. From Karl's work, raw material dedication as well tends to be a bad accident connected to a greater penchant for having a more authoritarian state uninterested in developing representative political processes, culture, or economics. This works in good times of high raw material prices when central states can simply arrange loyal allies with distributionary funds, yet is a kind of distributionary politics of loyalty that quickly falls apart in bad times of low raw material prices—that remove capacities of economic aggregation and past political accommodations to leave nothing to fall back upon domestically, economically or politically, in bad times. Plus, even in times of good prices, raw material trades tend to undermine the rest of the domestic manufacturing or product economy because everything can be imported much more cheaply than developing one's own national economic aggregation at home in a country. Therefore, raw materials exports are undevelopmental even when they do bring wealth and even more undevelopmental in good times of high prices for raw materials. (Karl, 1997) Earlier, many in the 1950s thought it would be bad if freed ex-colonial countries lacked raw material wealth that they could trade with the world. However, in comparative analysis after 75 years, we see that countries lucky enough to have the 'good accident' of being without this easy route of raw material wealth and rent from it, have developed greater economic aggregation far better than others like South Korea, Japan, Taiwan, Hong Kong, or Singapore that are all without major raw material wealth. When the Netherlands discovered oil in its offshore waters after World War II, they thought it would be a boon to develop it, as an addition to their current industrial economy, yet the huge wealth from oil simply made their own national economy prices for value-added goods hard to support when value-added products could now simply be bought from overseas with oil money. This oil extraction started to decimate the Netherlands' industrial economy, and this is why this phenomenon is called "Dutch disease." So, the same point about a lack of raw materials as a good accident of history can be said for the forced good choices of all other Asian Tiger economies. This good accident of a forced choice toward an export-led economy with value-added products from the beginning helped all of them down the development gauntlet. They lacked any lazy raw material 'detours' that North Korea has relied on for instance. North Korea does have the bad accident of having a great deal of raw material wealth, particularly metals and coal, so it chose these easier bad choices to exploit that have only led to ever diminishing returns and little value-added products or economic aggregation in the country to show for it as well as a clearly more authoritarian government as well.

Another kind of good accident of the second kind in the Korean past would be how the older Korean aristocracy cleansed itself in the 1950s from its past consolidated landholding without having a cultural revolution to achieve this. A good accident of the first kind remained however, in how Korea still perpetuated a homogeneous culture regionally and rurally among common citizens regardless that was only enhanced by that self-depreciating aristocracy's land distribution to commoners at large throughout the late 1940s through early 1950s, instead of such land being bought up by major companies for instance for consolidated land ownership once more. This once more was a good accident that pushed economic development toward export-led industrialization instead of internalized agricultural industrialization that would have thrown more angry poor people toward the cities in economic shakeout of their agricultural jobs as well as would be more of a break in the more homogeneous culture because of it. So, before the mid-20th century's clean sweep of this Korean aristocracy, their proud and divisive families had mostly always put themselves before their country and only fought with each other. This contributed to strong aristocracies and weak kings, with deep internal divisions over millennia in the Korean Peninsula. However, the fear by this aristocracy in the 1950s against a communist revolution in their territory in the First Republic led toward one of the world's few successful land distributions that was mostly completed by 1952 in the midst of the Korean War (1950–1953). That land distribution helps explain how their old aristocratic corruption, divisions, and hubristic warmongering was jettisoned from governmental policy formation from 1961 onward—first by them being outside the military establishment itself in Korea for over fifty years before 1961, second by their own land distribution, and third by the coup de grace of removing them from political power as well by the Military Revolutionary Committee, and how their lack of political power only continued under the Third Republic onward for over sixty years now after 1961. The durably oligarchic Korean aristocracy could only be effectively removed from systemic power decision by the combination of the loss of their earlier military power that had already been achieved before 1910, and then by the loss of their economic power by the early 1950s in three kinds of land reforms by that time. (You, 2014) Later, after 1961, they were removed even from political power by the more nationalistic and meritocratic military coup of 1961 to 1963. This has remained the settlement of politics in modern Korea without them into the Third Republic (1963–1971) onward.

With the same aristocratic political and economic elite vacuum in both North and South Korea, both these countries developed similar kinds of top-down revolutionary authoritarian cultural leadership toward fast economic development after World War II. However, while North Korea renationalized its agricultural land from 1954 (removing a good choice of policy they had after 1948 for a land distribution), the North additionally recreated a bad choice of a modern aristocracy of a one-party militarized state. Only South Korea was blessed by avoiding neo-aristocratic militarists and avoiding a landscape of nationalized land with this non-developmental outcome, yet a good accident remained in their traditional durable ancient culture regardless of aristocratic leadership purges. As noted in the concluding chapter, the rise of cross-marriages and inheritances between Korean chaebol families in South Korea may forebode a bad choice and a less developmental future for the country and only a return to a partial developmental drive in the South if this neo-aristocracy's dominance, corruption, and path dependence slows and vetoes ongoing economic innovation of the country by reinventing a Korean digital, manufacturing, and distribution-based 'yangban' aristocracy of the twenty-first century.

Despite a lot of comparative analysis, no other modern nation was found to experience this hybrid "Korean kind" of modern political economic and cultural alliance that encouraged consensus building that is missing an aristocracy yet has a deeply stable more homogeneous culture regardless. This is an odd situation and a good accident because typically modern revolutionaries are simultaneously both economic and cultural *revolutionaries* if they get into power—and South Korea alone avoided a bad cultural revolution yet got the good aristocratic purge anyway without it. It is equally a good accident and an odd situation because typically the *reactionaries* or opposition to modern development drives were missing in South Korea as well, since such movements are led or funded by ancient rural families of wealth and prestige that oppose modern urban industrialization drives as it changes the relative weight of their economic power in a country or its culture toward urban politics instead of rural politics. You can see this in the history of coffee-exporting states for instance (Williams, 1994). Plus, this kind of durable aristocratic South Korean alliance if it had existed could have been self-destroyed by its own warmongering, exemplified by the reactionary rural Junker family-led coterie in the German Third Reich or in the Japanese aristocratic-led modern Japanese Empire (Kaplan & Dubro, 2003). However, the good accident was that Korea was without capacities for military expansion after World War II despite still having a rural aristocracy in power for a while under President Rhee until 1960s that nonetheless did have only dreams of animating more ongoing war after 1953 despite the economic collapse of his own country between 1950 and 1953 in the Korean War. However, they soon outmoded themselves in ongoing land distributions. Later in this aristocratic absence, there was a successful merging of opposite trends, of economic revolution in the service of cultural conservatism and yet without large private aristocratic drives to control it and combine it with foreign militarism like that which animated the growing Japanese Empire of the early twentieth century, run by its ancient aristocracy against its modern democracy. Thus in South Korea, as a result, the *large stable active military became used for development purposes instead* of steered by powerful aristocrats toward (self-) destructive purposes. Plus, rural cultural continuity was kept without being destroyed by rural market economic shakeout via national agricultural market protection. The rural cultural continuity was enfranchised in the Third Republic instead of creating only a pro-urban industrial politics against it. So, it is this wide and increasingly consensus-based political alliance over time that animated the export-led development of South Korea after 1961. As said above, there were setbacks in this full development drive between 1972 and 1987, though the ongoing full development drive recovered by civil pressures by the latter year. In short, removing the aristocracy yet maintaining the rural culture and a nationalized military was a doorway that opened many of these developmental hybrids to be harnessed without an aristocratic-led militarized self-destruction. The same political and cultural alliance continues to be renewed over the generations after 1961. A kind of martial patriotism still animates the Korean Wave, culturally and economically.

Another kind of good accident of the first kind is Korea's quite old odd "Western-style" religious plurality for hundreds of years as a background factor. This has existed for centuries in the Korean Peninsula despite the more homogeneous culture. Like very developed South Korea, very developed Taiwan as well has a very high religious plurality, within a more homogeneous culture. More about the developmental implications of this comparison will be discussed in Part III. This good accident of religious plurality disciplined against bad choices that would demote consensus politics. To the contrary of Korea and Taiwan, many East Asian-heritage countries are both culturally and religiously uniform like Japan or China and more authoritarian in culture and thus in politics that demotes civil rights. This makes a competitive Western-style civil sphere and principles of individual civil rights difficult to develop in any East Asian version of modern democratic institutions. However, a plurality in religious demographics in South Korea despite a more homogeneous ethnic culture is a good accident. Korea historically is the only country in the world in which the Buddhist religion and the Abramanic religions (Judaism, Christianity, and Islam) overlap to any extent in the world map of modern religion. This modern religious plurality was built on an earlier deeper layer even of common ongoing shamanism, Buddhism, and Confucianism, along with deep regionalism in identification. Thus, a large degree of modern religious plurality on top of ancient religious regional cultural plurality animates the culture of South Korea's republican institutions despite a homogeneous culture. This is a good accident that animates a double check and balance against any desires of dictatorial leanings combined with a homogeneous culture.

The origins of this early religious plurality and civil freedom of religion in the Korean Peninsula was the odd situation of the previous Confucian Joseon dynasty as an aftermath of the Imjin War against the Japanese invasion in the 1590s. When the repressed Buddhist establishment monks were seen as good fighters against the Japanese invasion as much as anyone else in the Confucian state, Buddhism was given some levels of religious freedom by the 1600s that made the Confucian-based settlement of the Joseon Dynasty less harsh. Later in the 1800s, more religious plurality from European incursions of Christianity gave Koreans a growing (small at the time) percentage of native Protestants and Catholics. This inspiration from Christianity catalyzed even more synergistic religious plurality from fresh religious creations like Tonghak that continued into the twentieth century under its more formal name as Chondogyo. It developed in reaction against Christianity yet soon operated in parallel with it in the religious diversity during the Japanese occupation as a common collaborative Korean national front. By the 1970s, more religious plurality existed because Korea's native Catholicism was expanding in many in the lower working classes of Korea that were equally joining in a Catholic-organized labor movement—led by leftist Catholics like Kim Dae-jung (adopted godson of leftist Catholic Chang Myon)—given secular labor unions were illegal until after the June Struggle of 1987.

This good accident of durable and expanding religious and regional plurality gave South Korea a competitive advantage in creating a durable public sphere and pressures for individual civil rights against their own collectivist culture. Plus, this has been useful in animating a modern multi-party democracy as real and competitive. This good accident was a check and balance against the dangers of a more homogenous culture of peer pressure to support dictatorships and self-repression.

Another kind of good accident of this first kind aiding later economic aggregation is the simple fact of having only one major primate city in South Korea, in Seoul. This has been a good accident disciplining Koreans to put all their development eggs in one basket of Seoul. Some have argued that when comparing other less developed countries, it helps economic aggregation and political cooperation in a less developed country if there is one place of such aggregation to conserve it. Korea's lack of inter-urban competition for scarce resources in the beginning of its fast development drive was helpful. On the other hand, a history of competitive capitals or different powerful regions like in Costa Rica for instance can frustrate or hamstring singular different national policies via their own boosterism by having different state elites competing with each other instead of collaborating on a national plan (Sandbrook et al., 2007).

Another good accident of the first kind is the ability of South Korea to develop within itself and its major primate city some of the global telecommunications infrastructure and international businesses of the 'global city.' This term refers to both the global digital infrastructural access as well as how that creates a regional location for branches of same organizational expertise in social, business, and technical services for the global financial sector. This has increasingly pulled much of the world's international businesses and firms to global cities like Seoul, making Seoul and thus South Korea a part of this worldwide singular global city infrastructure. In many ways, Sassen who invented the term and the analysis argues the opposite: that the global city has been a force of underdevelopment for an already developed country (Sassen, 2001). However, in South Korea as originally a less developed country, having a piece of the global city in Seoul has instead pulled a great deal of global development into South Korea. Meanwhile, many other less developed countries remain less developed globally because of many factors though one of these factors is argued to be the lack of all examples of any telecommunications-dense global cities as touch down points for a global economy within their boundaries that could encourage their own national economic aggregation and development.

For an example of good accidents of the first kind and the second kind, combined, there is the good accident of a lack of some kind of external destructive force from the climate or from geology in South Korean history. It is known environmental disasters repeatedly set back development of the poorest in the worst ways (Coppola, 2007). However, South Korea's strong geological stability and climactic predictability provides an uncannily good foundation for a fast development drive without setbacks, by encouraging good choices of ongoing economic aggregation without wasting precious capital on physical plant rebuilding after many national natural disasters like that seen far more often in places like the Philippines, Japan, or China, for examples. Korea's stable natural climate patterns and geology has been useful in creating that very stable resource of a durable culture. All of this has helped Korea's modern choices after the 1960s toward less costly big infrastructural investments over time for export-led development. South Korea could avoid costly repairs from major annual climate disasters like extreme monsoons seen in India or major geological destructions like massive earthquakes, tsunamis, or volcanoes seen in Japan or much of Southeast Asia. As said in earlier chapters, it is a good accident that Korea has been greatly free from any repeating major natural disasters of storms, earthquakes or floods—unlike many other developing nations that get repeated costly setbacks in their infrastructure over time from these environmental forces.

Another example of this second type of good accident, of a lack of an external destructive force, is how Korea avoided a long colonial period. The Korean colonial period (1910–1945) by the Japanese Empire was relatively short when compared to many other ex-colonial 'freed' nations that experienced culturally numbing centuries before being free. On the contrary for Korea, this good accident of history was the comparatively short duration of the Japanese Empire after which Korea was freed relatively quickly within one living generation from a short twentieth century colonialism, i.e., without deeply altering its homogeneous culture. As said earlier, a homogenous culture or at least a common development ethos is a major resource for development in this case. Many other nations across Latin America have suffered huge impediments in development aggregation after living for centuries under an imperial power that extracted their raw material wealth, and demoted their culture and pride. A long colonialism in Latin America increasingly divided its people into many different heterogeneous bloodline-status cultures of many different origins yet all with the same common high status full-blood Spanish or Portuguese occupiers versus others who had various levels of half-blood relations in relation to the occupiers that became a merchant class or blue collar class, and with many others without any colonial family relationships becoming shunned ethnic/cultural underclasses. Colonialism when that long steals more than economic wealth. It steals the spirit of the occupied people. It encourages their fatalism, accommodation, and dissociation about their own autonomous future, since their dreams become connected to the empire. A longer colonialism more regularly divides even a common people under the imperial sovereignty instead of unites it, making it easier for colonial conditions to continue via both clientelistic family relationships and a highly 'divided and conquered' status culture with many deeply unified with the occupiers, their culture, and their religion after hundreds of years. This creates fatalistic psychological conditions in ongoing expectations of cultural subservience, exploitation, lack of representation and regular violent repression. This rarely generates unified leaderships that can throw off an imperial power much less lead a freed nation, and can generate only desires for a cycle of retributive violence instead—perhaps understandable, yet none of which in retrospect has been very developmental (Fanon, 1961/2021).

For another example of a good accident of the second kind, the divisive yet belligerent aristocracy was removed in South Korea by 1961—militarily, economically, and then politically. In retrospect for modern Korea, it is likely that this good event contributed to both North and South Korea avoiding renewed war for consolidation after the armistice of 1953 that concluded the 'hot' Korean War. However, if aristocratic Rhee remained in power after 1960, and if you can believe his stated main goal, he wanted more war as he refused to sign the armistice to the Korean War in 1953. However, no one else wanted to keep fighting. He even sabotaged his own country by releasing thousands of North Korean prisoners within South Korea after the Korean War on their own recognizance perhaps hoping to catalyze atrocities on his own people that he could use to start the war once more. Even the sponsoring Americans felt Rhee was a reckless leader that created many problems. Since his stated goal was more war against North Korea instead of a stronger economic development of South Korea, it is fortunate that such aristocratic personalities and their prideful inbred heritage from the Joseon dynasty that had made them were slowly and *non-revolutionarily* purged from military power before 1910, *non-revolutionarily* purged from their own landowning economic power by the mid 1950s, and then more *revolutionarily* purged from South Korean political history by 1961 in a military coup against the Second Republic. Meanwhile, seen through a glass darkly, the Japanese aristocracy comparatively remains a major facet of the Japanese modern political, economic, ideological, and military power. Aristocratic politics was key to animating the overseas atrocities in Japan's push for empire in the late 1800s throughout East

Asia attempting to keep autonomy of power against greater rule-bound and representative democratic national politics at home. It was the Japanese aristocracy that ran the military rearmament by the 'zaibatsu' conglomerates, then supported the native Japanese fascist movement and its assassinations against the nation's own nascent multi-party democracy, seeking to maintain their supremacy. This right-wing cultural revolution in Japan only encouraged a wider polarization and further reactionary left wing communist movements in turn, and vice versa (Kaplan & Dubro, 2003).

Next, good accidents of the third kind are conditional events that are unexpected, yet which intervene in a good way in retrospect to maintain or to encourage greater economic aggregation. Of course many unexpected events can be quite bad in stopping economic aggregation. However, a small selection of them can be judged as good if they restart or catalyze greater economic aggregation. In this instance, the assassination of President Park in 1979 helped restart greater economic aggregation. However, it is argued the life of President Park between 1961 and 1970 was crucial in setting up step one and step two down the development gauntlet in South Korea, so it was a good accident that President Park existed. Thus it is hard to think what South Korea would have been like if he were missing. However, it is provocatively argued here that another good accident was his assassination in 1979. That counterfactual hypothesis fails to come from the authors' here per se, though from a high-level Korean governmental participant in the Chun administration itself in the early 1980s. The sudden death of Park facilitated a more abrupt shift and a faster, cleaner 'step three' down the development gauntlet both in fresh economic sectors that helped Korea get out of a potential 'middle income trap' as well as breaking social psychological subservience to Park's whole design for the future of South Korea forever. Plus, it ended Park's own attempt at a right-wing cultural revolution that in turn was contributing to more polarized left wing movements of the 1970s and was experiencing a lessened economic growth in the late 1970s. Park had developed a growing series of powers after his coup in 1972 that removed direct Presidential elections and removed limitations on him being that President for life as well.

The renewed South Korean development solutions and choices in the early 1980s seem hard to understand without this good accident of the third kind, of this sudden 'missing' element of Park himself from later 1979, just as Park was crucial before as a good accident from 1961 to around 1970, even if he became more of a veto to fresh innovation in the Korean development drive by the late 1970s. There are two kinds of data for this assertion beyond the mere weak counterfactual argument. First, in general, an idea about this is found in Collier, who statistically argued that a developmental dictatorship is good for keeping out internal violence while economic aggregation begins. However, Collier argued the data show that a lengthy developmental dictatorship is associated statistically with lesser and lesser economic development. Therefore, Collier argued it is important to make a political transition to a more open political democratic system away from a dictatorship in order to have continued economic aggregation. Park's assassination in 1979 contributed toward that. As said above, the second kind of data was eyewitness testimony. As explained to one of the authors by a Korean bureaucrat (who wishes to remain anonymous) who was hired into in the Blue House (the Korean Presidency staff) in the wake of

President Park's assassination during the early years of Chun in the 1980s, he felt that Park's assassination was the ultimate good accidental factor that opened the Korean economy to wider innovation in the 1980s since it stopped Park's increasing desire from the early 1970s to micromanage the direction of the whole economy, politics, and culture. In that sense, the bureaucrat felt it was a good accident that Park was assassinated *yet only at that point in time* instead of earlier that might have led to other worse outcomes. In short, if the life of President Park itself was a good accident and boon for South Korean development between 1961 into 1970, it is debatable whether his assassination in 1979 was a good accident as a further boon for his country's economic aggregation, in other words.

Another good accident in this third sense of unexpected events would be the near collapse of the Korean economy in 1997, where fully 15 of the top 30 chaebol (industrial family conglomerates) went bankrupt. A survey of Koreans mentions that the year 1997 was the most traumatic event of the past 50 or more years for many of them (Hong, 2014). However, without that traumatic event, it is likely the pressure toward state-led development encouraging both the cultural sector of the Korean Wave and a high speed internet economy would have postponed or even ignored at this point. However, this is a very thin reading of a 'good accident' since what was said above about disruptive events holds true: there are many more that are destabilizing instead of improving to economic aggregation. So, what seems to be a useful good accident for the history of the Korean Wave was mostly a disaster for Koreans as a whole, Korea's happiness, and its wider middle class since the nation developed far more economic polarization after 1997 and the middle class has only kept declining since 1997. Thus, it is an open question: would it be better to entirely miss the chance of the digital economy of the Korean Wave if it truly could only come at the ongoing high price of large durable unemployment and middle class decimation, and the equal ongoing high price of the beginnings of a trend of increasing hopeless generations of Koreans mired in compensatory escapism in behaviorally problematic internet use? This is the ignominious beginning of the earliest domestic digital Korean Wave: an online gaming 'cultural expertise' developed strongly in South Korea more than any other country in the late 1990s simply because the government spent large sums on making Korea a digital Internet country for the future economy just as a lot of past productive workers were out of work and went to escape their lives to play video games for hours on end in "PC-bangs" (personal computer game rooms) as unemployment tripled from 1997 to 1999 and many small and large businesses were lost. This is the world shown in the movie *Parasite* of many struggling Korean chicken restaurants and castella cake stores—of small business owners of food services desperate to try anything after their professional lifelong employment with big companies was dissolved (Park, 2020).

3.2.2 Good Choices

For examples of good choices, South Korea has been making them even before the fast development drive started in 1961. One of these major good choices before 1961 was having a thorough land distribution—three different ones in fact (You, 2014). This is an important choice. The handful of other successes in fast-paced development after World War II had similar preparatory land or wealth distribution reforms like Japan, Taiwan, and Malaysia (the latter for wealth distribution as well). Alternatively, countries with more repressive politics like the Philippines kept promising yet ultimately refused a politics of land distribution. That country continues to suffer from oligarchic economic stasis. Equally like the Philippines, many Latin American countries (and increasingly Australia) maintain and defend very inequitable land tenures, export-led raw material economies, and oligarchic and repressive politics. All of this is associated of course with very low levels of value-added products in economic development. From both categories of countries, it is argued land distribution is a universally good choice catalyzing later fast development drives. First, it helps undermine more rural oligarchic politics in a state that regularly derail a fast development drive and break the rural plantation labor clientelism complex. Plus, land distribution can maintain and strengthen civil feedback in economics and politics if it is based within a more homogeneous culture. This equitable grass roots pressure in rural areas protects the country better against a potential unrepresentative top-down cultural or political revolution, even if in some situations it may facilitate rural cultural revolution.

For a European instance of that rural cultural revolution, it seems only to occur though, if a state has a revanchist aristocracy that refuses to be dismantled. South Korea did demote its aristocracy earlier in many positions of social power even before 1961. However, for a case of the opposite from Europe, Tudor-era English land distributions in the mid 1500s under King Henry VIII and his Dissolution of the Monasteries (and their landholdings) started to make England developmentally unique in Europe given a large amount of distributed private land markets and private gentry land ownership that it generated. This helped coordinate an economic and political-cultural preservation of English Protestantism against a series of earlier and later Catholic kings and aristocrats. Thus, that wide land distribution, when combined with an oppositional Protestantism, began to be ranged against later Catholic King Charles I's or Charles II's attempts to maintain a Catholic aristocracy and royalty, as well as the attempt to keep both Catholic and Protestant religious faiths under his authority. Catholic royalist attempts like this failed partially due to a wide Protestant rural economic gentry and Protestant urban underclass opposition to such policies. This was so strong that anti-Catholic pressures became a factor that catalyzed an English Civil War and soon even the dissolution of the monarchy for a time in the 1650s through the 1660s toward a Protestant 'theocratic yet parliamentarian' commonwealth under an austere Protestant dictatorship of Cromwell as "Lord Protector." Catholic King Charles I was beheaded as a traitor to the country—showing just how much religious, rural/urban economic, and political consolidated pressures were ranged against that later Catholic line of kings. Later, with another royalist Restoration in the 1660s under another Catholic King Charles II, the same dynamic as before catalyzed another Protestant rural/urban coup that came to be called the "Glorious Revolution" against Charles II in 1688. It was really a foreign-aligned, parliamentary-organized coup and foreign invasion allowed by the national Parliament, the military, and the City of London capitalists who invited or even 'hired' the Protestant king and queen of the Netherlands, William and Mary, to take over England yet under a contract with various attempted royal limitations of parliamentary supremacy over the monarchy in the future. The ongoing revanchist Catholic royalty and aristocracy lasted well into the 1740s in the British Isles as a long term civil war between the deposed Catholic ruling house, aligned with the Pope and continental powers like France, versus this now combined English Protestant/Dutch Protestant ruling house. In these unsettled times, the land distributions in England held. Eventually after the 1740s, the less powerfully supported Catholic religious and political settlements failed. Similar to South Korean more equitable land tenures, these kinds of outcomes in England centuries earlier contributed to a growing Protestant middle class gentry's economics and politics that paralleled a mercantile Protestant/Anglican aristocracy running the corporations of the Empire. Despite England having a more equitable land tenure yet keeping a now more Protestant aristocracy and monarchy instead of dissolving it, as South Korea effectively saw the opposite happen in the dissolution of their aristocracy's military, economic, and then political powers between 1910 to 1961, this land distribution in turn regardless of that durable aristocracy set England upon a different development path compared to most other European nations' development except Sweden, as both kept a more equitable politics of aristocratic parliamentarism, kings, and a rural equitable support as well. Sweden though had an earlier similar parliamentary strength, royalist strength and weak aristocracy in a common Protestant culture, while England had a similar parliamentary strength and a strong aristocracy and weaker kings through that parliament in a common Anglican/Protestant culture. However, many European states shunned land distributions and mercantile behavior, unlike England or Sweden.

Back in East Asia and back in our modern world, the countries of South Korea, Japan, or Taiwan are somewhat following the English lead in the 1500s since land distribution arguably worked to catalyze a development drive and to preserve a durable homogeneous culture as a resource. However the Korean version was more extreme than Japan given the outcomes of Korean history were jettisoning the whole aristocracy's land tenure powers by 1952 along with the Korean military and monarchy earlier, destroyed respectively by the Japanese Empire between 1907 to 1910. In retrospect, the political and cultural demotion of the ancient Korean aristocracy is the long term combined effect of the foreign Japanese colonial period, the Korean aristocracy's own self-dismantling of land tenure ownership by 1952, and then the native military coup under the Military Revolutionary Committee of 1961. The latter substituted modern Korean military leadership for the residual political aristocrats, and created the fast development drive. So in the Korean case, the combined military, economic and political demotion of the Korean aristocracy from

1907 through 1961 broke all institutional powers of cultural transmission and path dependence of this oligarchy in the South Korean military, politics, and the economy.

However, what is mostly forgotten is that South Korea was motivated to have its land distribution by the tyranny of a good example from North Korea originally. North Korea had its own land distribution earlier, immediately in 1946 after the end of World War II in late 1945, yet South Korea avoided land distribution until 1948. At that time in 1948, in South Korea, the "richest 2.7% of rural households owned two thirds of all the cultivated lands, while 58% owned no land at all" (You, 2014). In total, three South Korea land distributions occurred between 1948 and 1952. The first was by the US occupation force in 1948… "distribut[ting] 240,000 hectares of former Japanese lands to former tenants, which accounted for 11.7% of total cultivated land" (You, 2014). The other two land distributions occurred between 1950 and 1952 with the first immediately before the Korean War, and the latter occurring during the Korean War. "Restricting the upper ceiling of landownership to three hectares, the government redistributed 330,000 hectares of farmland by 1952. In addition, about 500,000 hectares were sold directly by landlords to their tenants. Thus, 52% of total cultivated land transferred ownership, and the 'principle of land to tillers' was realized." All three land distributions were originally conducted in attempts to forestall support for communist revolution and (at the time) were copying the example of the North Korean-style decentralized land tenures to challenge the Northern cultural leadership in the South, in an era in which the split of Korea seemed less politically consolidated unlike now (You, 2014). The land distributions under President Rhee from 1950 to 1952 in South Korea were state facilitated and yet a 'fourth land distribution' was done autonomously, occurring in private sales at the same time from even larger private tranches of land sold to small proprietors—out of seeming fear that private consolidated landholders would have nothing left at all if North Korea won the war. Measuring from 1948 to 1956, a mere eight years showed a tremendous change in land tenure. In the South Korea of 1956, the top 6% owned a mere 18% of cultivated lands, when as recently as 1948 the top 2.7% owned two thirds of all cultivated land. Plus by 1956, landless "[t]enancy dropped from 49 to 7% of all farming households, and the area of cultivated land under tenancy fell from 65 to 18%." Through these four public and private land distributions, it is estimated that "the top 4% of …previous landlords…lost 80% of their income, while the bottom 80% (tenants and owner-tenants) increased their income by 20–30%…" (You, 2014).

However, after the Korean War (1950–1953), by 1954, North Korea revoked its good choice of land distribution and instituted the bad choice of nationalization and collectivization of farms in attempts to expand food production after the war. This is seen as a bad choice of ultimately diminishing returns that continue to plague North Korean agriculture now. The irony is that collectivization was slightly reversed in North Korea as a policy in the 1990s yet for the same purpose to make more food available—yet now via the opposite policy of allowing market sales and private labor on farmed food, and yet the state still requisitions from and exploits that as well.

In short, even before South Korea's other good choices of a multi-party political system and a hybrid economic development policy that balances an export-led economy with national economic protectionism, support for traditional artisan cultural production, and rural village-based grass roots development, it seems the good choice of a land distribution encouraged the good accident later of the end of the Korean aristocracy that was displaced. Instead, in the more export-led economic orientation after 1961, it was still built on a foundation on rural land distribution without a cultural revolution. It is considered a good choice because it was a pro-Korean aristocratic attempt first to keep their political leadership intact in a more unrepresentative political state in the First Republic (1948–1960), instead of the actual goal of the land distribution being the economic unseating of the Korean aristocrats themselves. This self-demolition of an aristocracy without a cultural revolution to achieve it is a recommendation that could transfer Korean economic successes to other nations, we hope.

Next, for other good choices, after 1963 South Koreans made good choices down their development gauntlet for a long time—and far more good choices than bad choices. The main good choices after 1963 were already mentioned earlier: the ways that South Korea started to adjust itself economically, politically, and culturally with more flexible, hybrid, and representative policies in all three areas. This was possible because of the above good choice of a land distribution that catalyzed the 'good accident' of the unintended political vacuum of the dissolution of the economic veto power of the Korean aristocracy itself by 1960. This created self-renewing virtuous cycles of development and growing consensus policies between 1963 to 1970 only because of the lack of aristocratic political veto, and this made step two easier because of choices like this in step one down the development gauntlet.

Plus, the military coup is seen as a good choice, defined in terms of course in economic aggregation potential, yet only a good choice because of the context. However, this military coup revealed itself as a good choice *only because of this context of a good accident that a power vacuum already existed.* Only in this context was a military coup a better 'weak state' without powerful elite allies, so it kept choosing wisely to compromise and to back down between 1963 to around 1970 with ever more hybrid and representative *economic policies* even if President Park was backsliding toward his own kind of right-wing cultural revolution of unrepresentative *political and cultural authoritarianism* between 1970 to 1979 as well.

First, to summarize these other good choices as success factors in general development, the hybrid cultural policies came first (i.e., losing the aristocracy without a cultural revolution, while keeping the regional culture within small scale agriculture due to successful land distributions) and set up a very weak cultural legitimacy of state power after the military coup of 1961. Despite attempts at stronger dictatorship from 1961, the Military Revolutionary Committee buckled in its political authoritarianism by 1963 in the return to competitive Presidential elections. After 1963, President Park (only narrowly winning election in 1963 to 1967) started to buckle in his administration's main economic policies to create very open procedures from ongoing integration of complaints and feedback. This weak legitimacy both created and equally kept the more hybrid political policies and hybrid economic policies. Both were a wider *consensus building* despite or at least coordinated from a weakly legitimate top-down fast development drive. So, it was hardly a strong military coup and dictatorship from 1961 that was the recipe for creating the consensus around

Korea's fast development drive. The secret recipe was the weakly legitimate dictatorship trying to stay in power as just one among many parties for the presidency from 1963. In 1963, in the very first election of the Third Republic, Park ran against the President of the Second Republic, Yun Posun, that had been removed in the military coup in 1961, and Park still had to face a parliamentary multi-party legislature that continued as well after 1963. This is why it is hard to call Korea after 1963 a developmental dictatorship, and why the term 'authoritarian parliamentarianism' is preferred, as said earlier. It was still a developmental authoritarian model, yet one so very insecure of its power that it felt it had to release the still alive President Yun Posun and Prime Minister Chang Myon of the Second Republic as free agents, and even see the removed President of the Second Republic Yun operate as an opposition party in the Third Republic throughout the 1960s. Only Chang Myon had limitations on his political support in public, though other than that he was alive and lived to die naturally of hepatitis in 1966, presumably as the story goes. It *was* that happy context of a weakly legitimate dynamic in the Third Republic that kept President Park making *good choices in buckling and compromising* to stay in power. This encouraged this process toward wider and ongoing consensus orientation in politics and in economic policy in the fast development drive.

Despite the earlier weakly-legitimate Korean military developmental forces trying to escape between 1971 to 1987 this growing consensus orientation, eventually the same weak legitimacy of the military forces under Park later encouraged Chun to compromise once more after 1987. Just like the odd compromises of Park between 1963 and 1970, this made the 1980s under Chun a very odd dictatorship indeed. Chun's team had a military coup, and they forced the current legal President by proxy after Park's assassination to extend martial law to the whole country on May 17th 1980. However, within one day of Chun's order for national martial law, on May 18th, many cities started militia uprisings against his illegitimate coup, particularly in Gwangju. These massive multi-city uprisings were only ended when Chun used the Korean army, with American foreknowledge and thus authorization under Ambassador William H. Gleysteen, to massacre civilians/militia at the occupied Gwangju city hall weeks later. (In July 2021, the South Korean government asked the U.S. government to declassify and share U.S. documents confirming this.) The subsequent massacre of civilians and armed civilian militias by the army escalated to even torturing to death provincial police commissioners like Ahn Byung-ha over a week later, for his refusal to give the order for civilian police to fire on civilians as well. Chun's military paratroopers even assaulted civilian police and chased others. They shot taxi cab drivers ferrying the wounded to hospitals. Helicopter gunfire from the army strafed the civilians in Gwangju, and the national media hid this fact and much else. Civilians burned down the MBC television studios there for lying about Gwangju events for Chun.

However, in the growing sense of illegitimacy of his military coup and his civilian massacre in May 1980, Chun felt boxed in, and was left only to concentrate more on the stick of national media censorship and the carrot of national cultural distractions. It was such a weak dictatorship that Chun felt boxed in and failed even to kill his main opposition candidate of Kim Dae-jung, given (yet another) American intervention to save Kim's life in 1980, this time by both President Carter and through the incoming team of President Reagan. Chun's coup had given Kim a trumped up 'treason' charge that claimed Kim instigated the Gwangju uprising in 1980—against Chun's of course already illegal military coup, so go figure. Chun even buckled back to compromise and greater civil rights promises as early as 1981 in the formal frameworks of the Fifth Republic itself—for instance enshrining in the Korean constitution for the first time correspondence privacy and rules against torture-based confessions and against group punishments, and even rules against any dictator maintaining themselves by enshrining the end to all second Presidential terms or the ability of a President to change this factor in the constitution later. Chun felt boxed in on economic policy as well, since future export-led economic policy was removed from direct dictatorial control and given to appointed technocrats. Chun was boxed in by the ongoing parliamentary system as well. Even Chun's expectation he could control politics by personally appointing one-third of the legislature in the Fifth Republic (just like Park before him, in the Fourth Republic) was found by Chun in 1985, as found by Park earlier in 1978, hardly to be enough to control the legislature. By 1985, with Chun's party's drubbing in the parliamentary elections, Chun felt boxed in even more and released 14 jailed opposition candidates, though Kim Dae-jung stayed in house arrest.

So even the "Park loyalist" of Chun, by 1981 onward, tried to stay in power partially by promising to repudiate Park's dictatorial cultural, political and economic powers of the 1970s. Thus, the secret of Korea is its combination of a *weak legitimacy in a top-down development drive*. This has been a more successful dynamic for greater consensus over time compared to other countries' dynamics that generally had stronger authoritarian governments in their fast development drives and thus less durable or less consensus-oriented fast development drives.

In comparative retrospect, South Korea chose a triple hybrid settlement earlier than most. This made its development more flexible, durable, and capable of ongoing economic aggregation more than other less developed countries at the time that instead regularly kept resetting via setbacks and failures before they move on. Even bad choices from the 1970s toward more political and cultural authoritarianism were corrected in time with other good choices, though only from a lot of good choices of wider protest and even good choices of Korea's ally the United States pushing Chun to avoid further violent reactions after the Gwangju Massacre in May 1980 and later by pushing Chun to release Kim Dae-jung and by being against further violent crackdowns in June 1987, despite secretly supporting such original crackdowns of Chun in May 1980. Thus, the United States helped Korea in the late 1980s keep being a weak state in which Chun felt ever more forced to compromise as a good choice. Otherwise, left to his own devices, and if he had further U.S. support for such crackdowns, Chun would have assuredly continued the assassinated Park's right-wing cultural revolution and used tanks and helicopters on more cities than Gwangju in 1980. He would have assuredly killed Kim Dae-Jung. He would have assuredly used violent crackdowns on the protests for democracy in 1987, perhaps sparking a wider left wing cultural revolution in the 1980s even more than there was already. All of that might have totally killed the fast development drive as well.

By the 1980s, South Korea's other good choices were toward innovating in fresh economic sectors, in the export of digital telecommunications and its automobiles. These high value goods helped the country avoid falling backward down the development gauntlet after the first chemical and heavy industrial sectors under Park that he preferred started to weaken by the late 1970s in their competitiveness at home or abroad. By the way, the United States itself became a more urban industrialized nation in the 1920s only once it developed the multi-faceted input and services requirements of the automotive industry in the previous decade, and only during and after it pioneered analog electronics and then digital electronics between the early 1900s through the 1950s. With similar good choices, South Korea avoided failure in the third step of the development gauntlet after 1979, and these good economic choices into the 1980s kept the Korean economy growing instead. Plus, as elaborated more in the last section of this chapter, Korea's digital telecommunications in the 1980s was a good choice since it would set up so much about the telecommunications mediums and markets of the Korean Wave that was to follow.

Another good choice was to maintain the traditional cultural transmission of the homogeneous rural culture of Korea with growing subsidizations of ancient skills of traditional artisans and then with village-based grass roots development policies. Both together kept alive the cultural appreciation and cultural transmission of the Korean traditional native artistry and production of its material artifacts. This may seem more of a political requirement instead of a mere good choice by the Korean government of the 1960s, unless President Park preferred political suicide between 1963 through 1970, respectively, when both policies were inaugurated by Park. However, it was a good choice nonetheless in the weak state of President Park that kept making his preferred export-led economy buttressed with many other levels of national protection, traditional artisanal cultural transmission, and later devolutionary grass roots economic development to rural villages. For contrast of what might have occurred, keep in mind what was happening in North Korea at the same time: an ultimately non-developmental and top-down leftist cultural and economic revolution, against the same traditional culture due to collectivization and via a fresh military one-party state.

Plus, comparatively speaking, a choice of modern urban industrial development is rarely associated with equally subsidizing an ancient rural cultural continuity and its skill sets or village based rural priorities on development. However all of this combined is what has happened in South Korea after 1963 into the early 1970s. Only the former happened as a good choice in Japan in the 1950s, since Japan was without any devolution to village grass roots democracy like South Korea though did have a similar 'cultural living treasures' policy taken for equal rationales that the Japanese disliked seeing their cultural radically changed even if they desired urban industrial development recovery after World War II. To the contrary of these many good choices of South Korea, other attempts at development drives in less developed nations typically involve a highly emotional cultural revolution that devalues autonomous traditional rural life and regularly entails deep destruction and reorganization of the economic and cultural life ways of rural life. Rarely do we find in the world the situation of South Korea as a left-wing inspired, top-down, state-led economic revolution that occurred *without a left-wing or right-wing cultural revolution* or reaction, and even succeeding because of Korea's state alliance with its ancient conservative regionalized culture in attempting to serve it instead of sever it. In South Korea of the early twentieth century, parts of the ancient rural Korean culture survived by happenstance ("good accidents") into the 1960s, yet it later survived by good choices as well, i.e., by intent and by active support. This was part of the political alliance after 1963 in the economic Korean Miracle itself that *aimed to maintain an ancient conservative rural culture* while radically *revolutionizing only export-led economic politics and the urban economy* on the strength of the collective innovation of this more homogeneous culture.

The authors are unaware of any other so fully hybrid developmental recipe in the modern world like South Korea—with hybrid consensus policies in culture, politics, and economics. Thus, the good choice of keeping the more homogenous culture itself helped South Korea avoid a cultural revolution, whether at the hands of its own state's top-down military/economic revolution or by North Korean military invasion. Plus, this hybrid cultural settlement has shown to help catalyze a more economically successful and durable development supercharged by loyal and traditional cultural participation far more than other countries after World War I through after World War II that took more ideologically left-wing (Turkey, USSR/Russia, Mongolia, Cambodia, China, Vietnam, etc.) oppositional stances of purges of their traditional culture, or right-wing (Germany, Iran, Columbia, Brazil, Chile, etc.) stances of aligning with their traditional culture. The odd hybrid dynamic maintained the culture and in turn kept supercharging South Koreans' collective innovation into an economic Korean Miracle. This kept the culture intact while export-led development proceeded instead of eroding the latter away from the former. This meant much of the heritage of traditional Korea was available for proud modern use in the cultural Korean Wave in a more hybrid political and multi-party settlement that kept the culture from being requisitioned for long by exclusively right-wing groups' cultural revolutions and kept it alive and intact in the political protections that blocked cultural revolutions by left-wing groups.

Part of the traditional homogeneous culture in South Korea is the very high status given to education. On the one hand, educational promotion is seen as a good choice encouraging a fast development drive, greater productivity, and greater innovation. From the First Republic, a major policy of President Rhee was toward enhancing widened literacy and education in national primary schooling. Much later by the mid 2010s, for another world first, the number of advanced tertiary degree holders in South Korea is top in the world. According to OECD data, the top educated country in the OECD is South Korea with fully 64% of Koreans aged 25–34 with a bachelor's degree. This is followed by Japan's 59% and then New Zealand's 46%. The OECD average is 39%. Plus, Korea's private spending on education is higher than all other OECD nations as well, at 2.8% of GDP. This is higher than the next runners up of Chile (2.5%), the USA (2.2%), and Canada (1.5%). Since the OECD's private educational spending average is 0.9% of GNP, it means Korea spends privately over three times the OECD average on educational attainment. Both statistics mean the South Korean political economy keeps abreast of the global competition.

However, on the other hand, the Korean attitude toward education itself is more of a culture of extrinsic certification, prestige, and status than a sense of intrinsic value for a culture of knowledge itself per se. Within Korean culture, extrinsic prestige and surface attributes of accreditation seems more than or at least as crucial as the actual internal knowledge. It seems to fail to matter for a development drive however, whether Koreans would rather attend an expensive elite school for status and be anonymous there and work hard as a team instead of be known as an intelligent maverick innovator who is top of their class in a less prestigious school. On the one hand, to show the level of status involved in Korean education and the culture's greater stress on collective innovation in teams and accreditation from the 'right institutions' instead of stress on individual or cultural innovation, there is a great deal of corruption attempting to get into top educational positions in Korea, whether as students or professors. While the following described crony acts in other cultures may seem a small peccadillo, in Korea there was mass anger at President Park Geun-hye in 2015 because she tried to get her friends' children preferred entry in student positions at the highly prestigious Ewha Womans University (founded 1886) that they failed to qualify for by their test scores. Ewha is the largest, oldest, most expensive, and most culturally prestigious female university in Korea. On the other hand, to show the difficulty Koreans have in cultivating, respecting, or rewarding individual innovation within such a group-oriented homogeneous culture, Korea despite being top in the world in tertiary degrees and despite being top in the world in private educational spending is without any scientific Nobel Prizes in any field. Korea is the *largest* garden oasis of tertiary education in the world, with a huge number of *technological* innovations in patents, yet it remains a desert of *intellectual* innovation. This is despite a huge amount of extra research and development spent by the government explicitly in special 'basic research' institutions aiming to 'manufacture' Nobel Prizes for the nation (Zastrow, 2019).

The argument is that this shows that education and collective innovation for applied knowledge problem solving is deeply a part of a culture useful for a fast development drive. Meanwhile, individualized intellectual or cultural innovations are shunned in Korea despite winning larger than anything else in the Korean Wave when they do accidentally occur against all odds. For example, the Korean Wave's largest stars are like iconoclastic figure-skating gold medalist Kim Yuna who was shunned by the Korean state since the whole category of female figure skating was ignored by the state despite Kim winning all global awards for years until her recognition and lauding—only after she won the gold medal at the Winter Olympics. The equally iconoclastic "Psy" was shunned or even censored and banned by the Korean state that concentrated on other kinds of music popularization in the Korean Wave while blocking the sales of his albums to Korean youth over very mild indecency. Kim Yuna and Psy are hardly manufactured successes, though were more intrinsic individual successes that show individual bravery and strength of character to buck the trends. Koreans generally have a bullying culture that hates both characteristics since such people seem immune to the collective social criticism that controls the culture. However, oddly, Koreans still obsess and covet the status of individually innovative scientific Nobel Prizes. The Korean state wants Nobel Prizes so much now that it is trying to find a way to 'mass manufacture' a special educational and research funding system called the Institute for Basic Research in hopes it can create some kind of individual intellectual innovation that would get a Nobel Prize. It is argued that it is easier for the Korean culture to win Gold Medals in the Olympics or win in global markets in technology or in the Korean Wave because these awards have clear extrinsic shared goals or have patents for applied knowledge solutions that solve shared explicit problems. These two categories of inventiveness have externally set standards to beat. Meanwhile, Nobel Prizes or cultural innovations like Kim Yuna or Psy depend on a tabooed and less-desired Korean individual discovery and innovation at its own pace or even for its own intrinsic sake, i.e., without clear standards or clear external motivation or profit motivation. That is why Korea is attempting to change the trend with the Institute for Basic Science, because in Korea, generally, an individual's innovative intellectual curiosity is punished as costly and unpragmatic. However, Koreans seem one of the only cultures in the world that covet a Nobel Prize simply as an extrinsic motivation of the prize itself more than they are motivated to want the knowledge or inventiveness required to achieve it.

In summary of this point, individual innovation has the implication of standing out, shattering, or going beyond current expected social or technical standards, including making one's hierarchical leadership look foolish for failing to achieve it. Therefore, Koreans regularly fail to reward and even actively punish development of personalized skill sets that make individuals shine brighter than or who disagree with leadership-driven goals for teams in which they work. Therefore, Koreans in their homogeneous culture do far better in collective innovation toward some already set extrinsic goals or applied problems, instead of doing well on inventing novel issues or problems to work on from scratch from more intrinsic motivation. Few competitive problem solving tasks that seek tangible goals and results set up an open-ended exploration that gets pure scientific Nobel Prizes. This makes South Korea an educational culture that encourages a fast development drive, and one in which even K-pop idols and Korean Olympic stars are expected to conform more than invent toward national development goals. Even Korean entertainers and managers are expected to have an undergraduate degree if not graduate or doctorate degrees. For instance, after winning the gold medal at the Olympics, Kim Yuna went to Korea University to get an undergraduate degree in Physical Education—and then by 2014 a Master's Degree in the same. For another example, the manager of K-pop boy group BTS who recruited and assembled them as a group has a degree in Aesthetics from Seoul National University. However, the culture has been unable to achieve any scientific Nobel Prizes. It has been argued this is because of the dynamics of a more homogeneous culture with more extrinsic motivations miss the point that achieving an intellectual prize like the Nobel Prize is hardly something to be 'sought for' from the beginning, like an Olympic gold medal. Intellectual prizes are rarely approved of or encouraged collectively. It should be something from intrinsic interest that ignores applied economics and ignores social approval and current opinion on some topic of frontier research from the start. Koreans lack a culture that encourages mavericks to 'waste time' on non-economic pursuits regardless that goals may encourage huge economic growth later. Koreans know this as well, and that is why they are trying to change it by throwing large money toward basic research from at least 2014 from the Presidency of Park Geun-hye (2014–2017) onward to the present.

For two predictions, perhaps a future scientific Nobel Prize for Korea is possible, yet it may come only from a well-funded collective domestic team discovering something in pure science by accident on some other applied project, and having to work secretly on this other project for a while or publishing it against their own leadership's sponsorship or awareness. Second it might happen as a collective team that is cross-culturally involved with a project like a merger of 'Korean-heritage' scientists living and working overseas together instead of generated within the domestic Korean cultural context itself. Regardless, this traditional culture with its strong extrinsic educational drive is not dying out. It is argued that the durable and homogeneous ancient Korean culture of rural areas is a key factor that made the Korean Miracle and the Korean Wave both possible. Both rely on a stable culture endlessly retooled and adapted nimbly to fast-economic development changes in a globally competitive economy instead of being hopelessly broken by the development drive itself. So, it is hardly a loss that Korea is missing Nobel Prizes. Korea has the real world prize that no one else has yet: the most speedy and uniquely successful development drive in the world, and the first ever durable non-Western cultural wave. Both of these take advantage of special cultural Korean characteristics very well.

Another good choice was to avoid getting into external war after the 1960s onward. That likely would have destroyed both the development drive and the culture. Missing a hot-headed Korean aristocracy in politics surely helped keep a military armistice between North and South Korea intact. Thus the 'good decision behind that good decision' is how a military coup overthrew a gradualist political culture of Korean aristocrats that tolerated little development yet wanted more war in the 1950s under President Rhee. However, it was left to the good choices of President Park (and Kim Il-Sung) after the 1960s to never to let North–South disagreements or even mutual assassination teams trying to kill each other's leaderships in the late 1960s to catalyze a full civil war by the 1970s that would have destroyed both their development drives entirely. For instance, the aristocratic heritage of Syngman Rhee had rejected the stalemate at the end of the Korean War and did his best to try to create war like conditions that he could use to continue the war. However, without such figures after 1961 in South Korea, the country prospered once Rhee was gone. Plus, the factional aristocracy of family nepotisms was purged from Korea's modern democratic government by the time of the Third Republic. Keeping these Korean aristocrats as modern republican leadership is hypothesized to have led to South Korean self-destruction like effects of the German Junkers in the ex-Third Reich, or like the Japanese aristocracy in the ex-Japanese Empire, or like the British aristocracy in the ex-British Empire. All durable aristocratic settlements have to their credit is their own discredit: they seem to prefer to destroy their own countries by hubristic overextension since they are mostly unable to compromise or to empathize with their own national republican trends of representativeness or their colonial subjects that they exploit and can hate equally. Aristocratic arrogance calls forth war. In short, both North and South Korea's good choice has been to avoid further war after 1953, and it is argued that was made more likely by the total purge of Korea's ancient aristocratic families from the military by 1907, from their landed wealth by the 1950s, and from political power forever in retrospect by the Military Revolutionary Committee and its coup de grace in 1961. The durable 'double avoidance' of further war between two very martial countries of North and South Korea from the 1970s is likely now connected to the purge of the aristocracy in the South only increasingly, given this peace now seems ever-challenged by novel reckless North Korean one-party state family aristocracies, internal factionalisms, and purges around the Kim clan in the North.

Another good choice in South Korea argued to hold the country together in its fast development drive has been the good use of male military hazing as a common acculturation in Korea nationally across mutually hostile different religious, ideological, class, and regional connections of this politically divided country. In this way the Third, Fourth, Fifth, and now Sixth Republic held themselves together as one ongoing stable military meritocracy from 1961 to the present. Despite networks of personal loyalties in the military creating constitutional autocoups and other military coups, the military acculturated the whole nation with an ethos of national service and military meritocracy given in South Korea how the military served as a positive developmental resource instead of only assuming it is a parasitical institution creating war, destruction, and economic setback. Of course the military can only be a developmental resource if actual war is kept from being chosen. That helps keep alive a whole generation of well disciplined sons for later national economic development. It was, and they were. The South Korean military has been very creative and developmental since 1961 in infrastructural *creation* since (aristocratic-led) war and infrastructural *destruction* was being blocked.

Most fail to know that South Korea is actually the second largest militarized state in the world per capita, with the first being North Korea, according to the United States' International Institute for Strategic Studies (IISS). South Korea is a truly militarized culture with an estimated 130/1,000 per capita in the active military, reserve military, or paramilitary. The IISS data show both North and South Korea are #1 and #2 in the world in paramilitary scale per capita, and show South Korea as #2 in the world in reserve military strength at 3,100,000 (after #1 Vietnam at 5 million), with North Korea at only a reserve military strength of 600,000 at #10. Plus, South Korea is low on the financial drain of its active military scale, with active military ranking at only #8 on the world, while North Korea is very high on the financial drain of its active military, ranking at 1,280,000 at #4 in the world. Given North Korea is only around 25 million people, this is an astounding per capita scale of a standing army in the North given the only other three largest active militaries above it are the world's largest two countries with over a billion people each (being in order China and India) and then the 330 million people of the United States. In short, overall totals of military scale of all branches together put North Korea and South Korea at respectively #1 and #2 in the world for being militarized societies. However, while the North has a high financial burden, the South has less of an active military burden yet gets a great deal of military national acculturation out of it as a good choice. So a recommendation for a less developed country or even a more heterogeneous developed country would be to have a required two-year male citizen service in the military (inclusive of male foreign refugees allowed into the country) that generates what South Korea has: a large standing or reserve army for acculturation purposes of national solidarity and group ethos, as well as many prim and fortunately disciplined teams toward national development projects. However, sending them off to war is hardly the purpose and would waste the investment in the fast development drive.

Given this deep militarized culture in South Korea, it is unsurprising that the Korean Wave embedded and emanating from this culture has a patriotic and 'martial' air in its collective national fight against all other nations to maintain autonomy. The content of the Korean Wave gets militarized since even 'artistic rebels' in Korea's cultural industries are required to undergo universal military cultural 'hazing' of the male population for around two years. The military tie binds male groups together who would otherwise be distant from each other into potentially unique synergies of collaboration that otherwise would fail to exist. However, this means Korean culture and the culture of the producers of the Korean Wave is hierarchical and group-oriented instead of rebellious or anti-hierarchical in an individual sense or in a cultural sense as you might expect from cultural producers in other countries that are mostly bohemian rebels. This is surely due to a triply compounded hierarchy: an ancient Confucian heritage of male hierarchy, in addition to a modern mass military hierarchy for all males required to go into the army at some point in their early lives, as well as due to the fact that militarized networks of friends and allies have been the main nationalist developmental engine of innovation in South Korea for most of its modern history. This has been a common stable military network behind the ever-changing Korean corporations or ever-changing republican constitutions, even if crony secretive networks of military loyalty themselves are responsible for the success of the Military Revolutionary Committee and its coup in May 1961, the autocoup of Park in 1971, and the coup of Chun in 1979/1980. As a consequence, the Korean Wave equally sees stereotypical female/familial roles of subordination prominent and accepted (whether actively or with bitterness) in almost all Korean public society. Therefore, rebellious cultural motifs where they do exist are less internally divisive, though are focused on abstract hate of fate and feelings of injustice, in the well known Korean colonial-era and post-colonial-era term 'han'. This is the Korean cultural term for a difficult-to-define melange of mixed feelings like sad hurt rage, resentful hurt pride, personal helplessness, collective loss, and yet manic hopeful energy railing against bad fate or superior powers trying to conquer anything against all odds and at all costs. It is additionally a concept popularized by the Japanese Empire's intellectual class as their projected Korean "beauty of sorrow," trying to project a very non-historic stereotype upon all of the Korean culture and its pre-colonial history as if it was defined by the same romanticized tragedy and helpless sorrow at being unjustly treated for centuries—trying to reify the modern Japanese Empire as caused by a timeless Korean lack instead a sudden Japanese might. For cross-cultural comparisons, it is kind of the way Americans in the era of "manifest destiny" in the 1800s romanticized the American Indians, whom they felt at the time were beautiful and noble suffering groups yet sadly destined to disappear in the face of American might. It is kind of the way Franz Fanon described the combined sorrow and rage of Black colonized groups under Europeans. After World

War II, Korea's version of this known as 'han' was converted into a kind of 'collectivist Promethianism' where instead of only one brave individual stealing the fire of the gods or railing against the gods who takes up wings to fly at the sun, by the era of President Park Chung-hee, it becomes the sublimated sorrow and rage of an individual or group, a rage against bad luck in life in the past that can do equal miracles in working hard together regardless of high personal costs. Thus Korean rebelliousness even now is hatred of being unjustly ignored, neglected, or spurned that becomes a motivator for its militarized team spirit working on Korean national development against other nations. This means a rebellion against other major leading countries (originally, particularly Japan in the 1990s in its various technical and cultural fields) and a reluctance to accept foreign cultural products as better products, despite this is exactly what Korea is trying to do to others in the Korean Wave. It is a feeling of 'han' when Koreans fail to want to be the best rap stars in *Korean* popular music, they work hard and want to be the best rap stars *in the world*. In the popularity of BTS, they achieved it. It is a feeling of 'han' when Koreans fail to want to make passable copies of French bread in *Korea*, they want to make the best French bread in the world *and sell it in Paris*, to Parisians. (Han et al., 2018) Given that franchises of the Korean bakery chain Paris Baguette in 2018 won the Coupe du Monde de Boulangerie, the most prestigious French baking competition, and have successful massive stores in Paris's Opera district near the Palais Garnier, shows that Koreans are indeed seamlessly integrated into Paris, without the French even noticing or caring which is testament to Korean success as well. All of this is 'han.' It is a military ethos of development as well, a conquest of fate and of other countries combined in any field of the Korean Wave or Korean economy. Behind a striving for world excellence is a lot of trauma. That is the lesson of Korean 'han.'

Another good choice is export-led development. Doing this for development innately avoids a great deal of internal dissention as well as internal domestic diminishing returns over time, both of which we can see in North Korea in their bad choice of only a more intensive internal development while trying to separate themselves from the world-system of trade. However, export-led economics has been a good choice in Korea from 1961 only when balanced with its hybrid policies of greater national economic protectionism, artisan cultural transmission, and rural grass roots development of villages. Plus, the ever increasing massive scale expansions that are possible only in an export-led economy seem key to South Korean success that is worth mentioning. Earlier, a simple internal import substitution model failed to get very far within the First Republic—because there was little to substitute for in a mostly subsistence economy without large national consumer markets.

From 1961 onward, below are a few quick facts about the massive scale of the Korean export-led economy, compared to the other 'Asian Tiger' economies of Taiwan, Hong Kong, and Singapore. Koreans are proud of their Korean economy now being the tenth largest economy in the world after 2020, though few Koreans know that Korea ranks even higher in 2021 as the fifth largest exporter in the world, the ninth largest importer, and the fourth most 'complex' economy in the world (OEC, 2023). South Korea is the eighth largest generator of electricity in 2023 as well. As mentioned earlier, compared to all nations, South Korea is one of two most militarized nations in the world, and compared to other OECD countries, South Korea is the top spender on private education and the highest holder of advanced academic degrees. Koreas' massive scale of education, energy, organization, and throughput put into its export-led development in retrospect has kept Korea's economy growing despite domestic economic shocks and declines over time that surely would be more severe if the export-led economy was a smaller percentage of national wealth, if they were less team oriented, and if the elder generation were less traumatized by the past. (However, the younger generations of Korea are going though a different context that should be solved for Korea to continue in the development gauntlet. See Chapter 11 on this point.)

As proof, comparisons of the three economic plunges from trade crises in South Korean economics are described from 1996 onward to show and how fast the country has recovered each time. This is argued to be aided by or even buffered by its strong export-led economic dedication. The GDP plunged by 6.9% in the global downturn in 1998, yet more than recovered by 9% in 1999–2000. Next, even in the severe global economic downturn in 2008, *GNP growth in South Korea still increased though slowed to 0.2% in 2009*. In third quarter of 2009, the economy surged in part due to export growth, low interest rates, and expansionary fiscal policy as growth exceeded 6% in 2010 despite much of the world in a global recession at that point (Nation Master, unk). Recently, in 2021, despite many nations of the world seeing their nations' political elites placing their countries in a coordinated global precautionary 'lockdown' of the economy and other institutions over mere projected pandemic concerns, South Korean exports actually hit a record high in 2021, showing its 13th consecutive year of trade surplus. This is despite a divergence developing in a hollowing out of the domestic economy (Salmon, 2022; Yonhap, 2017). Related to that hollowing out of the domestic economy, comparatively, between 1996 and 2015, South Korea had the 27th lowest ratio of GDP to GNP in the OECD's 35 countries, with domestic Korean demand accounting for an average of only a very low 61.9% of total GNP, according to a report from the South Korean National Assembly Budget Office. In this period, the United States had the world's highest ratio of domestic demand (GDP to GNP) at 88%, trailed by Brazil with 87.4% and Japan with 84.8%. For South Korea, it is the opposite: the country's export-led dedication is stronger than nearly any other country in the world. The proportion of the South Korean economy consumed domestically when it was then Asia's fourth largest economy dropped as low as an average of 56% between 2006–2015 (meaning 44% of everything made in South Korea was exported) compared to a still low 70.1% (meaning 29.9% exported) from 1996–2015. Equally a measure of Korea's export-led dedication is the measure of "embodied energy" per country. From 1995 to 2020, from a large sample of developed countries only, South Korea showed the fifth largest absolute change in using more energy only for "embodied energy" (meaning, using net energy imported that is only embedded in traded/exported goods as a share of domestic energy use), changing from 2.0% to -10% of the national energy used it consumed domestically. This means during this period, South Korea has strong exports as a net exporter of energy that goes into the 'embodied energy' of its exported products that it does not consume itself—since that imported energy ends up in exported products. From 1995 to 2020, in a wide sample of countries, South Korea was even the second highest relative change in having a growing amount of its total energy use in the embodied energy of its product exports, only behind Finland's export led dedication regarding its domestic energy use (Ritchie, 2021). Thus, South Korea's good choice has been to be more dedicated to an export-led economy than most other fast developing countries themselves as a class, as a buffer against economic downturn.

Choosing an extreme scale of export-led development is a good choice for a geographically 'mid-sized' nation as well. Some say that South Korea geographically is a 'small nation,' with the size of the U.S. state of Indiana only. On the other hand, it is a very demographically large nation for its size. Thus, equally it could be said that South Korea is the largest 'national entrepot/city-state' in the world. South Korea hovers between these two categories of 'mid-sized nation' and 'city-state' by having the large domestic economy and hinterlands of a territorial nation, yet equally is dependent for its fast-development drive upon the economic power of its largest metropolitan region of Seoul. Seoul's metropolitan region is approximately 25 million people, or fully almost half of the whole national population of 51 million people in one very urban industrialized region. That makes Seoul closer to the other two city-states of the other Asian Tigers, like Singapore and Hong Kong, and it makes it like the only other 'national entrepot/city-state' Taiwan with its equally gargantuan national city of Taipei. Seoul's metropolitan area of approximately 25 million is itself the size of the entire national population of Australia or North Korea. So geographically, South Korea may be small, yet economically and demographically it is huge in its throughput of the export economy and in energy as mentioned above.

Plus, Seoul has been a capital city for more than 600 years, since the 1390s. This is far longer than Taipei has been a modern capital of Taiwan. Seoul even has been a capital city for many hundreds of years longer than Edo/Tokyo has been capital of Japan since 1600. Seoul is truly an amazing ancient and modern continuity. It is amazing that Seoul still exists as a Korean political and economic capital for over 600 years despite all the changes in the twentieth century. For a European analogy, Seoul is more like Paris is to France or London is to England—an uncontested overlapping primate capital of politics, economics, and culture in the nation. This is why Seoul and its "Gangnam Style" are central to the Korean Wave's expression instead of the assumption that the Korean diaspora is important to the Korean Wave.

Comparatively, South Korea was once known as one of the four "Asian Tiger" economies in the 1970s and 1980s, yet South Korea always was different in that it was then and remains now the most populous Asian Tiger and thus more than just a city state like the others participating in the global economy. The comparative population scales of the Asian Tigers are now: Singapore (5.7M), Hong Kong (7.5M), the Taipei metropolitan area of Taiwan (7M, in a total of 23M) and the Seoul metropolitan area in South Korea (25M, in a total of 51.3M). So, unlike the other three Asian Tigers, South Korea has the largest national population of the four, has the largest 'city-state' of these four, and has approximately three times the land area of Taiwan—and has a land uniquely stable against climatic and geological natural disasters unlike Japan or Taiwan, as mentioned in the previous chapter. Thus, despite South Korea being the most populous and the geographically largest Asian Tiger, it still has an economic profile of an entrepot-style city-state that depends more stably on the common rises (and rare falls) in the global economy instead of riding only on internal domestic growth or diminishing returns. For example, as said above, in the OECD's 35 countries, South Korea has the 27th *lowest* ratio of GDP (Gross Domestic Product, what is produced/consumed internally in the country) to GNP (Gross National Product, what is produced/consumed for global markets). This larger economic aggregation over time has been encouraged by its larger demographics and geographics than other Asian Tigers.

Nowadays, South Korea has become so big in its export-led economy that it has begun to upturn global-level cultural trends of Western hegemony that have lasted hundreds of years. South Korea now has an economy nearly four times larger than the also-ran "Asian Tiger" of Taiwan. Respectively, South Korea's towering $2.75 trillion GNP in 2022 is large compared to Taiwan's moderate $841.2 billion GNP in 2022. This places the 51 million people in South Korea as the tenth largest national economy in the world—directly after Russia's over 100 million people and before Australia's 25 million people in economic scale. Seoul by itself had an economy of $895 billion in 2018, an economic production larger than the entire nation of Taiwan in 2022.

Choosing this large *economic* scale from an export-led economy has benefitted the *cultural* status of South Korea and the Korean Wave as well. Let us contrast this scale of South Korean economic and cultural power with North Korea. By 2022, North Koreans' 'passport power' was very low, measured by the number of countries that covet visitors so much they fail to require explicit visas. North Korea is not widely loved, since it ranked at 104 in the world with visa-free entry to only a mere 39 countries out of over 200 countries in the world. Meanwhile, South Korea's huge financial pull and its global connections are more coveted. From 2018, for another world first, South Korea was judged as having the topmost powerful passport in the world along with Singapore with visa-free entry to 162 countries (Esmezyan, 2018). In 2019, South Korea was tied at third with two other countries, Germany and Finland, for visa free travel to 188 countries then (Jung, 2019). Into 2022, South Korea maintained the second most 'powerful' passport in the world with its citizens welcomed visa-free to fully 190 countries worldwide in 2022 and fully 175 countries in 2023. By 2023, the United Arab Emirates ranked first with visa free travel to 180 countries, Korea ranked second with 175 countries (with ten others like Sweden, Germany, Finland, Spain, France, Italy, and the Netherlands), and the United States and Japan among other countries ranked fourth at 173 countries (Joseonilbo, 2022; Passport Index, 2023).

Plus, by 2022, South Korea was judged as sixth in the rank of global 'power,' defined as "consistently [able to] dominate news headlines, preoccupy policymakers and shape global economic patterns." This puts South Korea after the top five of the U.S., China, Russia, Germany, and the U.K., yet ahead of France (at #7)—and ahead of Japan, the United Arab Emirates, and Israel immediately thereafter (U.S. News and World Report, 2023). Therefore, when we include strong Korean economic statistics with the strong cultural pull of all the "simultaneous successes" of the Korean Wave internationally from 2018, it is not surprising that South Korea ranks so highly in passport power or cultural power compared to other countries. In the past, South Korea was once understandably classed within the other 'Asian Tigers' of fast economic growth along with Hong Kong, Singapore, and Taiwan. However, from the 1980s, South Korea started to rocket into a unique class by itself, here called the first 'K-Nation' of world importance.

For the second to the last good choice to mention, South Korea is equally one of the few countries that have chosen to take advantage of a global neoliberal economy while maintaining and even strengthening its social democratic welfare state and democratization. Typically, these two trends are stereotyped to be at odds with each other ideologically as if greater dedication to the global neoliberal economy means by definition an erosion of the national welfare state or of democratic representativeness. Certainly, the IMF and World Bank have tried to encourage that ideologically neoliberal view, yet theirs is hardly a sound policy of national development. From data from 2007, South Korea was judged as one of only five nations in the world that has chosen to maintain both development trends. The other places with such a balance in the early twenty-first century are Mauritius, Kerala in India, Costa Rica, and Chile. When we include South Korea, all five of these countries have been uniquely successful in their fast development drives while keeping their culture and nation from falling apart in such global economic competition by improving consensus building in an ever greater political democracy and by expanding consensus building in ever greater economic democracy of a universal welfare state (Sandbrook et al., 2007). This is particularly strong in Korea's medical coverage as a safety net that keeps Koreans healthier and more productive, instead of sick, unproductive, in debt, bankrupt, and dead. This choice of universal, cheaper, and more effective *physical* medical care is something to learn from in South Korea as well. However, Korea's *mental* medical care leaves much to be desired by being a place of high competition, with high rates of anxiety, depression, and suicide connected more to economic stresses than loneliness. According to the 2008 Korean National Survey of the national statistics office, the most common causes for suicidal ideation was economic difficulties (36.2%), then family trouble (15.6%) and only in third place was loneliness (14.4%) (Lee et al., 2018).

The last good choice touches on a point mentioned earlier: it is a good choice to avoid a cultural revolution. Even the content of the Korean Wave shows how conservative and apolitical it is, following traditional gender dynamics as well. In a sentence, this is because the South Korean modern economic and political revolution was without a cultural revolution. This was of course not without trying by some Koreans and by other global forces from the 1960s into the 1980s. There is still one wonderfully zany section of Seoul around Hongik University frequented by more bohemian artists and designers that attend that university. Nonetheless, Western-inspired individualist cultural rebellions or Maoist/Soviet-inspired leftist mass cultural revolutions of the 1960s and 1970s were repressed effectively by an increasingly authoritarian right-wing cultural revolution itself around President Park during the 1970s. The same cultural revolutions were occurring in Japan throughout the 1960s, though Japan saw far bloodier right-wing cultural counterrevolution starting off in 1960 with the murder of the top Japanese Communist party leader on stage by a smiling

Japanese rightist assassin with a samurai sword. However, South Korea's homogeneous culture was unlike Japan in missing a reactionary aristocratic class that loved to fund and to lead such a violent, reactionary cultural revolution. This meant South Korea's traditional elite power vacuum in politics could mostly avoid large numbers of violent reactionary leaderships that called for bloody retributionary politics and cultural wars—whether from the right or the left, whether nationalist or internationalist. In retrospect, this is why it is said that South Korea "skipped" the radical 1960s of Western-led "New Left" cultural revolutions with their ethnic diversity, gender freedoms, and sexual diversity. You might say 'skipped' though equally could say 'tripped' as there was a lot of work in policing the public against any tangible artifacts of both Western-inspired clothing, hair, music styles or Chinese Maoist-inspired or Catholic-inspired cultural labor revolution in Korea in the 1970s. There was more than policing of artifacts of religion or of leftism in the 1970s though. Rightist Koreans policed and murdered well over a thousand leftist Koreans for deviation from Park's ideological line in the 1970s, particularly in the 'double use' already mentioned before of the Saemaul Undong rural grass roots development movement that equally was a rural organization used in parallel to find "anti-Park" individuals in Korea to arrest or to murder them. South Korea until 1987 even skipped much of the "Old Left" of a secular labor movement, since secular labor unions were banned until 1987. Instead, labor movements instead saw advances in the 1970s into the 1980s only as a culturally conservative movement of working-class Korean Catholics finding ways to organize differently. Therefore, instead of the labor movement in Korea being only culturally Marxist, secular, leftist, and revolutionary, it was highly Catholic, religious, and conservative as well. Both Korean 'leftists' of Prime Minister of the Second Republic Chang Myon (died in 1966) and his godson and later Korean President Kim Dae-Jung were both Catholic activists against the Korean dictatorial movements of their day, first against Park together and then later with Kim versus Chun alone. Independent labor organizing remained illegal until after the large political opening of 1987 with a return to national multi-party elections for President at the same time. These positive democratic gains and labor gains came after nearly three weeks of mass protests nationwide called the June Struggle or June Democracy Movement in 1987 against President Chun's announced desire to simply name the next President Roh without any election. Thus, the Korean labor movement earlier was a culturally conservative Catholic-linked labor movement of Liberation Theology, protected by the Korean Cardinal Kim (the first Korean Catholic Cardinal) from his Myeongdong Cathedral in downtown Seoul. Behind the intricately designed metal doors of this cathedral that commemorate images of many Catholic martyrs of the late Joseon dynasty, Cardinal Kim provided amnesty and protection to labor leaders in the 1970s that the Park administration wanted to arrest. Thus, even a universal labor movement had a culturally traditional and religious leadership in South Korea instead of being a secular and socialist-linked labor movement.

Therefore, to close this section on this theme of the Korean avoidance of cultural revolution, instead of the ancient Korean culture fading away in modern leftist economic revolution, labor unrest, or bloody cultural revolution from the left or right, a traditional culture was supercharged in four ways. First, it was supercharged already by the hybrid approach to export-led development that by the 1970s onward included a conservative rural grass roots development and other factors. This maintained a rural culture of villages alongside an urban industrial development, instead of only displacing the former for the latter. Second, this was supercharged by being connected to thousands of individual artisan protections and subsidies for these 'living national treasures' of all kinds—people that knew and maintained traditional construction and artistry skills for the next generation. Third, the homogeneous culture was supercharged by labor unrest being a culturally conservative religious and nationalist movement originally instead of a secular socialist or internationalist leadership. Fourth, by the 1980s, the ancient culture was supercharged once more by a mass culture based on intentionally designed *conservative cultural and patriotic consumption.* This was because by the 1980s there was beginning under Chun a highly state-controlled combination of cultural exports and internal cultural production created by Chun's forced media closures, media centralizations, cultural repression and even cultural priming as well. Thus, continuing from Park's Saemaul Undong, there was an increasing Korean state intervention toward winnowing the Korean culture, into a thinness developing for what passed as public discourse by the 1980s in Korea. So in South Korea, despite how industrial, urban economic, and communications revolutions regularly break down a traditional culture that can lead to true cultural revolutions, Korean conservatism continued in politics, in economics, and increasingly in the state-consolidated and censored mass media into the Korean Wave.

In conclusion, a fuller list of Korean good choices and good accidents are in Appendix 2. It is food for thought and food for national development—for other countries. It has been argued that a very wide assortment of many *good accidents and good choices* in a series kept South Korea going down the development gauntlet further than other countries, when those other countries are compared to Korea's fast development drive. Sometimes less developed countries may have *worse choices* and *bad accidents* of their contexts, or they are capable of making some good choices yet are incapable of making good choices in a series regularly. All of this could lead less developed countries to fail to start a developmental drive as all that develops are more vicious self-destructive cycles, resets, false starts, or stagnations over time. This could equally lead a less developed country only to start their developmental drive with a few good choices, yet to see it fail by bad choices later or bad accidents later. However, South Korea received *an abundance of good accidents and good choices* that ultimately combined to keep pressuring the nation to maintain its full development drive even after it got off the track between 1972 and 1987. All these good accidents and good choices arguably helped South Korea remain more durable in ongoing economic aggregation at far larger scales than other developing nations' only partial development drives or entirely missing development drives. The result has been a massive economic aggregation in an export-led economy strong for generations with ongoing innovations to its credit creating a highly synergistic economy. This has become the global economic production background of the Korean Wave.

3.3 Digital Telecommunications: A Good Domestic National Test Bed for the Korean Wave

Another good choice in Korea that deserves its own section is the choice of digital telecommunications. In the 1980s, Korea started to move from economic 'catch up' into a potential for being a cultural 'trend setter' by choosing these communications technologies as one of the next sectors of state-assisted development. Korea found itself uniquely placed by the 1980s to have a "digital transformation" by choosing to focus on the production of communications technology. This would by the close of the twentieth century start to move Korea's analog cultural production into digital cultural production, for both itself and for the world, later.

After this digital transformation, five unique points made South Korea the only Lion of the Asian Tigers and into the first K-Nation—the main example so far of a highly successful once-less developed country that now has global levels of importance and scale of influence. First, other nations attempted both sectors of the manufacturing of the hardware of digital telecommunications and the (future digital) cultural wave of export and failed to succeed as much as Korea has digitally in either, much less approaching its national cultural wave *by synergy in both.* This has put Korea ahead by default of a lack of global competition in any other developing countries' cultural waves that *remained regional* while Korea became the only one durably to go global. Second, it is argued that this dual digital synergy is very important in the extensive scale *of the* multiple different sectors of the Korean Wave compared to other developing countries that *only had a cultural wave in one cultural product.* Third, South Korea is unique that it is the only other nation after Americanization and after World War II that ever developed the *large capacity or desire* for exporting its culture around the world even into Western nations. Fourth, the Korean Wave is further unique in that it has maintained and expanded this cultural export success for 30 years or more into the present without signs of slowing down or stopping anytime soon. This is because the first true success of regional Hallyu started in 1992 on a British Hong Kong television channel which agreed to show a Korean TV drama. This started the Korean craze in nearby mainland Communist China as well (Hong, 2014). Fifth, South Korea remains to this day the only (ex-)developing country that the United Nations has moved to the 'developed' category, which happened in 2021. It will hopefully be only the first.

Therefore, this section focuses on the other good choice of digital telecommunications as an export sector. This is explicitly the precursor how the Korean Wave flowed first in fresh ways within Korean culture domestically and later globally in the twenty-first century. This is because a digital medium was the basic technological infrastructure, the source of business expertise, and later the source of the digital synergy between Korean digital telecommunications, a Korean cultural industry of major corporations, and a peer-to-peer popular culture of digital sharing that we see today in the Korean Wave. The Proto-Korean Wave before it even had a name begins in the 1980s with the first competitive sectors of digital telecommunications equipment made in Korea. Unlike Korean automobile production since the 1970s for the closed domestic market that expanded into exports by 1986, digital technologies were export-led from the beginning as much as domestic. By the 1980s, equally, the Korean entertainment industry (still in analogue) started to produce domestic TV dramas that could be dubbed at the start for export as well, with the thought of profiting from Korean visual culture exports.

However, all countries that start digital telecommunications are unable to start it from scratch. All national examples of both success and failure in our world in digital telecommunications start this sector very far down their development gauntlet indeed. Comparatively speaking, digital telecommunications seem to start only after the second gauntlet is successfully passed. Thus, digital telecommunications start in only few select countries that already have a very developed and durable urban industrial and mass consumer marketing sphere with international links already established for many other industrial products. Some countries drop out here because it should be combined additionally with a state government keen on subsidizing the digital industry to keep its research and development afloat as well as to coordinate it—with the latter being what Japan's state did for its uncoordinated Japanese semiconductor and electronics industries in the 1980s as well as what Korea and Taiwan does. Countries that ideologically are unwilling to subsidize or aid their digital telecommunications sectors tend to fall behind, like the rise and then collapse of the computer and electronics industry in Hong Kong for example.

When digital telecommunications started in Korea, first, it was the period before any Korean cultural wave. This is a period of 'brandless' Korea. This means many Korean exports then lacked a complex synergy between each other, and lacked any connection to being sold as framed as part of Korean culture. They were just products. However, second, from the early 1990s these "normal products" were increasingly and *indirectly associated and branded with* symbolism derived from the cultural products of the Korean Wave. As said above, the key event here was the synergy involved between the Korean state and Korean corporations to get an already popular domestic Korean TV drama called "What is Love?" on Hong Kong television in 1992. This combined project was successful. Third, next, material products of digital telecommunications themselves started to share *directly* in Korean culture by carrying the culture of the Korean Wave themselves, instead of the government having to be a sole coordinator per se. This is seen how Korean digital TVs, smartphones, online platforms, artificial intelligence, and now augmented reality technologies sell the Korean cultural content and share it directly in a more distributed and viral way without governmental coordination always being the catalyst. However, this digital virality continues with regular advertising, corporate cultural production, and state assistance. Nowadays, all this digital and synergistic complexity of the Korean economy is reflected in the fact that, in a world of over 200 nations, the Korean economy which gave birth to this Korean Wave can now the fourth most 'complex' economy in the world (OEC, 2023). A digital synergy in the content of the Korean Wave could more cheaply, quickly, and easily be expanded overseas even before the rest of the world started to catch up to South Korean levels of "saturated" telecommunications particularly in smartphones and bandwidth (see Appendix 1).

The term “saturated” refers to a representative cultural hegemony in a communications medium that is roughly above 90% personal familiarity, in this case in smartphone ownership. A representative media “hegemony” starts to matter hypothetically when a culture reaches half (50%) utilization, and starts to be a “saturated” hegemony at 90%. This is contrasted to other kinds of “unsaturated”, unrepresentative, and unequal hegemonies of cultural leadership power in media like historically a tiny state bureaucratic elite using Chinese complex scripts administrating power over a mass of illiterate oral Chinese, or like early large and expensive non-commercial computers and/or the ARPANET were used only by the U.S. military over everyone else, or like when early larger commercial computers and the early Internet over phone lines were only used by militaries and large financial corporations like banks in the 1960s versus everyone else. The fresh digital saturation seen in South Korea and increasingly in the Korean Wave may be considered profound because it upends 5,000 years of ‘normal’ urban civilization. Previously, it was normal or even fated to have a very inequitable unsaturated cultural and media participation. Inequitable media participation in content has been framed by pioneering historians of communications like Harold Innis as creating a durable ‘urban core versus rural periphery’ and an innate divide in ‘civilized’ culture versus others outside the sphere of its urban civilization. These cultural and media inequalities of participation had lasted for thousands of years (Innis, 1950/1986). Thus, past media inequalities have always contributed to power and cultural inequalities: for instance, in creating a tiny literate urban elite culture easily dominating a widely illiterate or non-literate oral urban or rural culture in past states, politics, and formal culture (Goody, 1987).

However, growing mass produced personal computers from the late 1970s later joined by the World Wide Web’s hypertext technology by 1991 and the first web browsers like Netscape Navigator in 1994 and then mass produced smartphones from 2007 started to prime a later growing digital saturation worldwide. So, three ancient kinds of informational divides like inequalities in past cultural participation, power, and media participation are ending for the first time in any media regime. We have to go back to the invention of oral speech tens of thousands of years ago in “Regime #1” to see power, culture, and media as saturated and equalized as now. This means most of world history for the last 5,000 years from the invention of complex scripts to one-way mass telecommuniations (with the exception of the invention of simple scripts onward, or early two-way wireless in the 1890s through the 1910s) were very inequitable forms of power, culture, and media. The Korean Wave became the first national cultural wave to ride this global media regime change. Given the global scale of this media regime change, the Korean Wave may be the last *national* cultural wave entirely, as all national cultures including Korea’s start to be replaced with a common mélange of different layers of a globalized cultural production within themselves due to a more multi-polar digital world. Widely saturated networks of mobile phones easily send information *and allow peer participation* across urban and rural landscapes alike, and do the same across literate, less literate, or even illiterate groups alike. Instead of the heralded age of ‘smart cities’ as prognosticated in the 1990s, we now have entered the age of ‘smart regions’. In such smart regions, we have mutual deliberation and cultural phenomena at scales previously impossible to conceive of or to organize because digital technology is now far less scarce or costly than it was only twenty years ago (Whitaker & Pawar, 2020).

In retrospect, this change toward media saturation potential can be traced back to three technical communication trends developing separately that merged powerfully for the first time in 2007 in the first internet-accessible smartphones with their own tailored computer applications themselves, like the Apple iPhone or Korea's LG Prada phone (see Appendix 1). To make such a smartphone product, first, (1) it came out of the older trend of two-way radio communication from the 1890s—the first decade of wireless (radio) communication. Such equipment only started to get smaller from the 1970s. However, even then, the expense and logistics of wireless two-way personal communication became only a tool of rich elites in corporate or governmental leadership in a handful of cities by the 1980s. However, the quickening and widening of the participation in this wireless communication for the masses is due to two other trends: (2) a parallel trend of computer miniaturization beginning in 1970 and (3) the growing digital convergence across all different multiple media formats from the 1980s.

So, these three trends coalesced in a revolutionary way for communication for the masses by 2007 with the invention of the first mass manufactured 'smartphones.' The smartphone was the apotheosis of that long developing *wireless* trend merging with the more recent *miniaturization* trend of computers that started in the early 1970s and the *digitalization* trend that started in the same period with digital storage of computer information and increasingly other digital storage mediums like the CD ROM by the early 1980s. Thus a *wireless, miniaturized, digital convergence of mobile multimedia* finally merged into smartphone manufacture. It took the world by storm since 2007, so much so, that by 2019 there were over 5 billion owners of mobile phones. By 2021, there were an estimated 6.37 billion mobile phones, with an estimated 5.31 billion unique mobile phone users (Bank My Cell, 2023; We Are Social, 2022). This is only fourteen years after the smartphone's invention in 2007. As early as 2017, even the majority of Internet experience was estimated to be mediated by smartphones globally (We Are Social / Hootsuite, 2017).

The dual entries of 2007 were Korea's LG Prada phone and Apple's iPhone. These began a still-continuing global standard design for what such a communications device should look like as a flat-glass, touchscreen-based smartphone. Sixteen years later in 2023 at the time of this writing, many other companies now outsell Apple's smartphones worldwide though do so only by mimicking its design and functionality while making it cheaper, more accessible, and thus more diffused around the world. By 2019, the growth of networks of smartphones has become saturated enough to create a global 'media regime change.' From 2019, *all specific regions of the world* had 50% or more of their populations with smartphone access for the first time—including central Africa. This term 'media regime change' is defined as a historical period in which media communications, related technologies, and patterns of information exchange alter the culture of daily life—long before changes are seen in the lagged and 'mismatched' social institutions of the past based on information flows of a previous media regime. This is how the Korean Wave snuck up upon the world unaware. Given the Korean LG Prada phone and the first Apple iPhone were only invented in 2007, it is amazing that there are 5.31 billion smartphone owners around the world rather evenly distributed only 14 years later. Other communication technologies may still have a 'digital divide.' However, smartphones particularly developed what will be called a 'digital parity' and even a 'digital surplus,' i.e., the latter term defined by how in many countries, the previous marginalized underclasses and/or minorities or even marginalized majorities of various kinds (whether linguistic, class, ethnic, religious, etc.) regularly are better connected online at higher saturation rates than even previous state elite rulers and those older cultures. This is shown by how the poorer a country is worldwide, the more likely the country is to have more of its full age demographic online, from youth to elderly, compared to richer countries that only tend to have more youth online (Pew Research Center, 2014, 2015a, 2015b). Therefore, the technological diffusion and saturated media hegemony of the smartphone is unparalleled in the modern world, with it arriving at a representative "hegemonic" scale of use of over 50% of most national populations with amazing quickness and then a few select countries like South Korea being world first in being saturated.

Smartphones were adopted in the United States at a faster rate than any other communication technology in the past in that country, *yet the technical diffusion of smartphones was even faster in South Korea. That gave South Korea later a larger advantage in exporting its culture worldwide*, which we have come to know as the Korean Wave. These developments were pioneered in South Korea while the rest of the world was mostly ignorant of what was occurring there from the 1960s through the 2010s. Since South Korean innovation was a change starting in a global periphery, this is what Innis argued was a common situation of all the past (very few) media regime changes in world history that he could analyze (Innis, 1950/1986). A change in communication in a periphery comes to challenge or alter past core dominating states. This is the modern situation given how the networked smartphones of relatively small South Korea with 51 million people finds itself in a world of much larger states of hundreds of millions of people or even billions of people who hang on every word, image, or song from the Korean Wave distributed in perfect digital copies and transmissions.

Therefore, a growing international wave from South Korea could fill small segments of other international nations' markets digitally in the background. This is why the Korean Wave went international and yet failed for a decade or so to place within the older one-way mass media's 'top hits' lists of radio play or TV programs until it was almost "too late" to see what was occurring internationally. The world's youth started to participate in the earlier-mentioned two virtuous cycles of South Korean development via digital participation. Therefore, it looked like the world was faced with a 'sudden' global Koreanization because instead of rising up a nations' charts, the Korean Wave for a decade or more had increasingly gotten popular in a slow way until it was large enough internationally to start seizing top spots nationally—across many nations at once.

The Korean Wave could do this spillover across the Internet because of four main factors it is argued: the cheaper cost of international communication digitally, the viral transmission of the Korean Wave even at small scales in the beginning as a peer-to-peer forwarding and sharing that reduced costs of transmission more, the earlier extreme saturation of digital development and national digital cultural production in South Korea first, as well as after 2017 the ending of a great deal of internal censorship on the Korean Wave from within Korea that released thousands of other creative Korean minds and Korean artists on the world in 2018 for state aid in the Korean Wave after being on a secret cultural blacklist banning them from state aid for years. The earlier three factors around digital saturation in South Korea are argued to have existed at least ten years before any other developed country by the middle of the second decade of the 2000s. This led to Koreans' expertise and familiarity of producers and consumers alike in digital cultural production before others as a hegemonic medium of culture instead of just a partial medium of mass media culture. The first K-Nation in other words was the first widely saturated E-Nation. The latter factor about ending the secret cultural blacklist in Korea was exposed after 2017, and it is mentioned in the next chapter that is about the timeline of the Korean Wave itself.

So, the point is hardly it being a tall order for other national markets to catch up to Korean digital saturation levels to participate in the Korean Wave. The point is that the larger Korean digital cultural saturation, far earlier, could flow downhill into the rest of the digital world, and in this way the Korean Wave connected with many global countries' far lesser digital cultures, far earlier. This reoriented any other dawning (K-)national digital cultures into a more international and Korean orbit. This led to digital cultural 'underdevelopment' in their own countries once they became so dominated by developments of the Korean Wave. This Korean orbit has increasingly made other nations, some far larger, into cultural satellites now rotating around 'Planet Korea' and its Korean Wave. This 'digital cultural underdevelopment' is another kind of development gauntlet that other nations may now have to run against. This is something that digital South Korea never had to experience and tried very hard to avoid by many policies of digital economic protectionism in 1998 onward. This is hard to recover from because Korean content is already taking up many other nations' online cultures. It is of course possible, yet it is just as unlikely as running all the other development gauntlets mentioned in the earlier sections on this point.

This poses a conundrum for any other future K-Nations in the offing: how do you catch up or even challenge economies of scale and aggregation developed in the Korean Wave centered in South Korea that have been so strong as to colonize the whole world's digital culture? How do other nations' own attempts start now to compete with an increasingly dominant digital cultural production from South Korea, except by a similar cultural nationalism? This was what was touched on earlier in the argument that the world in an increasingly saturated digital culture is having selection effects upon what kinds of national reproduction and what kinds of cultural nations will be successful or not successful in the future. Thus, it was easier for South Koreans to export their already saturated digitized culture before the rest of the world caught up to levels of digital ownership saturation and digital participation already experienced in South Korea. Koreans could more quickly and competitively fill the bandwidth and minds of other countries with Korean digital entertainment than other countries could ever do in inverse. All of the case studies that follow in this book have this theme. This easier 'downhill' era for the Korean Wave may be coming to a close if other saturated digital countries now can take part in the global digital virality just as much as the 'world first' Koreans, though equally Koreans may remain ahead since they are already better at global level exports of their culture as well.

Preparatory for this digital telecommunications surge in the 1980s in South Korea, and distinct from the discussion about the development gauntlet or digital communications earlier, what has been key to all countries' success in the global economy in the past 500 years when looking at various economic and cultural hegemons in a series, is their success is predicated on a drive to first cheapen transportation and cheapen raw material costs, and then cheaper production costs *by further economies of scale in all three* of these *in competition with those doing the same before them* (Bunker & Ciccantell, 2005). This required South Korea to compete first via raising even higher economies of raw material scale in shipping than other hegemons before them exemplified by the United States' bulk carriers or Japan's bulk carriers in order to reduce transportation costs even more. Larger Korean ships began to recenter both global investments into South Korea by cheapening bulk material transportation into South Korea and by cheapening material flows of exported production from South Korea (Levinson, 2006). This is similar to what both Japan and China were doing concurrently to South Korea, respectively (Bunker & Ciccantell, 2005, 2007). It is hardly an accident that Korea started to specialize in making some of the largest ships in the world either for itself or for international clients in this period: "…[A]s the new vessels came on line in 1971 and 1972…[t]rade soared.…Oceanborne exports from South Korea, 2.9 million tons in 1969, reached 6 million tons in 1973. Korean exports to the United States trebled over those three years as lower shipping costs made its garments competitive in the U.S. market" (Levinson, 2006, p. 219). Plus, the privatization of global ports gave even latecomers to containerization like Pusan top billing in East Asia, simply because global shipping lines wanted to use Korea as a centralizing base between countries for many operations. By as early as 2003, the Port of Pusan was one of the top container ports in the world, truly eclipsed then by only two ports in the world, Hong Kong and Singapore, and only slightly behind Shanghai and Shenzhen. Pusan moved 2.9 million twenty-foot-equivalents in 1990 to over triple this at 10.4 million in 2003 (Levinson, 2006, p. 273). By 2021, Pusan is still one of the busiest ports in the world at seventh largest in throughput behind only five Chinese ports and Singapore in the entire world. This means all American ports and all European ports are below Pusan in throughput by 2021. Therefore, Korea's larger ship designs, more efficient 'containerized' ports, and Korea's centrality in East Asia for private container shipping lines that chose Pusan as a home base or a production base has done all three 'cheapening' points mentioned above. Korea has re-centered global ship production that became less costly to make and to base in Korea, plus materials were less costly to ship into Korea, and plus production and transport costs were less costly out of Korea. All of this is compared to more costly or less central global ports in other developing countries except for China. However, China is stuck as a 'middle income' country and increasingly going backward down the development gauntlet by becoming less representative and more authoritarian which will have an aftereffect on losing its even partial development drive later in a cultural revolution of its people against the Chinese Communist Party (CCP) leadership that is already starting its disaffection, as mentioned in the concluding chapters of Part III.

However, on top of this recentering of ever cheaper bulk transport into and out of Korea, Korea was at the same moment choosing the 'harder' telecommunications sector. This is comparatively a hard sector to catch up with or even to keep up with, in pre-existing competition. Thus when thinking about success factors of countries specializing in digital telecommunications hardware production, in comparison to the few successes of additional hegemons of telecommunications that exist beyond the U.S.'s Silicon Valley, there generally are required extreme levels of state coordination, investment, economies of scale, retooling, and technological innovation against others over time. This is seen in Finland, Taiwan, South Korea, and less so in Japan. All of these countries arranged all of these factors to make telecommunications successful more durably as a growth sector instead of a short-term success leading into a failing sector. For instance of telecommunication starts then failures, both the smaller Asian Tiger city states of Singapore or Hong Kong were unable to maintain their own attempted electronics and telecommunications drive. Only the larger Asian Tiger countries like Taiwan or South Korea with larger capital and labor pools and a culture of willing state coordination and even deep state investment could aid higher levels of costly research and development required to be internationally competitive in telecommunications durably for the long term. Japan of course was in the 1980s known for its pioneering mechanical electronics, yet Japan had an expensive conversion problem from its mechanical electronics of the 1980s into the digital 1990s at the same time it entered a long economic depression in the 1990s. That is the point: it is very hard to start or to keep up a *competitive* digital telecommunications sector for the long term. However, South Korea has succeeded for over 30 years at it, and it helped that Korea started with digital, i.e., comparatively without the costs of many digital conversions that all other previously developed countries had.

Sure, it may be somewhat easy for some massive countries to re-center global trade to themselves in the above ways, by economies of scale aided by the 'fatness' of their demographic scale instead of any exclusive ingeniousness on their part. This may be the case with China for instance, however even China's capacity to re-center global production imports, and exports into itself was kind of a hybrid political economic compromise with inventing more freedoms within 'free trade zones' like Shenzhen and other locations—buckling the purism of the socialist Maoist doctrine of separation from capitalist world trade and investment, toward Deng's compromising and less ideologically puritanical visions of a national capitalism of China and its participation within world trade and investment. However, China has failed so far on trying to re-center electronics production of semiconductors in itself beyond being an assembly house of cheap labor for other Taiwanese, Korean, or U.S. computer chip manufacturers. Plus, re-centering larger economies of raw material scale in smaller countries will certainly fail to be an option for many countries in the world, by simply being "too small" geographically or demographically as a market for labor or consumption, or being "too poor" in capacities to do so, or "too divided" to do so, or by lacking good harbors to trade globally from central locations very well. That limits modern scaled development in competition for such trades and production to a mere handful of countries with larger populations, with good ocean harbors, and which are judged as central by international shippers managing global trade lines. Second, that other issue of re-centering larger economies of scale in your country toward telecommunications on top of that may be even a smaller number of countries durably over time. For instance, China repeatedly has failed to create a durable scaled domestic semiconductor or computer chips market in innovations or capacities, despite wasting a huge amount of state-subsidized money on it so far.

That limits modern digital telecommunications production to only a few more nimble and globally competitive countries with all the above characteristics. Thus, South Korea seems more weighted to be an outlier instead of a harbinger on all these factors of general economies of raw material scale, trading throughput, and further economies of scale in digital telecommunications durably in the long term.

So, first, it is rarely possible for many countries to have the ability to re-center the global economy in their country at all as Korea has done. Second, it is even rarer to re-center the global economy on your country's digital telecommunications sector. A lot of preconditions have to happen that open the door to this kind of ongoing durable leading growth in economies of scale and in telecommunications. For instance, many countries tried out a telecommunications growth engine like India or the Soviet Union or a software industry like Ireland yet failed after a while, compared to the very few like the United States, Taiwan, or South Korea that have been able to keep it going.

So, if your country is able to recenter global raw material trade to your nation, and second, if it is then able to do the same durably in telecommunications, and third, if it is able to coordinate your own culture for export utilizing that telecommunications drive, you might be South Korea. This is because no one else has done all three vettings so far except the United States. All three vettings have to be there for the jackpot of Americanization or the Korean Wave, and this has winnowed many countries out of the running on each of these three levels over time. A few other countries may have passed one or two of these vettings, though so far only the USA and South Korea are the outliers that exhibit the durable desire and ability to maintain all three over several generations. Thus one argument that this analysis faces is that the United States itself is a very oddly successful outlier country that has re-centered the world upon itself as well—something few can compete with *because* of the large success of both Korea and the United States globally in still doing it generation after generation.

While the outlier of the United States or South Korea can be learned from for all these potentially transferrable topics, the issue is will other countries be able to apply them at all, or will the USA and Planet Korea continue to be unique in the world? The term Planet Korea is used here in two senses: in terms of the world-level oddities of its choices and other factors of development that mostly go into a positive column for having them instead of the negative column in lacking them (for instance, see Appendices 1, 2, and 3); and in terms of the resulting cultural orbits that many other 'satellite nations' and their youth find themselves within as they that increasingly revolve around South Korea as a global popular cultural mecca to visit and to learn from for taking back to their countries. In turn, however, does orbiting around this Korean Wave or Americanization really help replicate the idea to other countries for having their own cultural wave in other lands, or does it only dilute the desire or capacity of other cultures to achieve a cultural wave of their own if all they are doing is reinforcing other nations' cultural waves? May this lead them mostly "underdeveloping" their own countries' potential cultural waves and eroding their capacities instead of aiding them? Thus, the power of this "Korean Wave" may really be power vacuum based on other areas growing more powerless to keep responding over time as quickly as Korea can in digital telecommunications and digital cultural production—at least so far.

The choice of communications technology for a future development sector in South Korea was more effectively done as a durable sector compared to other countries. Others failed to keep up the global level of digital technological innovation required over time, like Japan, while South Korea started with digital telecommunications and has kept innovating within it over decades. This helped Korea in three ways toward the Korean Wave. First, Korea could avoid a costly digital conversion unlike mechanical-electrical industries of Japan from the 1980s. Second, Korea could continuously focus on one kind of ever improving technology for over 30 years—which is a difficult task for many countries. Third, *only in communications technologies in general* is there a useful "built-in" synergistic bridge to move from *marketing technical devices to marketing ideas*: from making technological infrastructures to making culture industries. The fact that it is *digital* encourages a common digital convergence in all cultural media equally that has been helpful for Korea to avoid extra costs and problems of multiple different media storages and recording mediums in international trade in the Korean Wave that Japanese cultural wave media and electronic products had to deal with in the 1980s.

However, *doing all three of these points successfully over time* around digital telecommunications has been the true Korean miracle. This is because digital telecommunications are a very globally competitive sector hard to maintain given large degrees of technological innovation happening, plus the ongoing expensive retooling of production and market expectations changing almost annually at a near constant due to trends like "Moore's Law" about ongoing miniaturization and the lowered costs of computer hardware capacities. This makes digital telecommunications which include computer chips a very expensive jewel to maintain in a country over time. It requires a great deal of research and development funding and a very long term support from governments to keep such a developmental sector competitive and subsidized over time.

For a slight comparison, there was a smaller Japanese Wave of cultural products from the 1980s into the early 1990s across East Asia mostly. Japan did well in mechanical electronics from the 1960s to the 1980s, and then similarly as argued in the ideas around the development gauntlet started to slowly explore the export of its own Japanese cultural exports by the 1980s involved in such domestically produced electronics media particularly to other East Asian countries. Japan was even letting its state-based coordination aid in the early Japanese industry for making machines for semiconductor fabrication. However, in the deep economic downturn in the 1990s in Japan, this connected with its greater insular culture and politics and its much larger national domestic consumption as a country that failed to require as large of an export market as smaller South Korea. Thus Japan could refocus its economic priorities on other easier large domestic production sectors and on equally large domestic cultural markets. Japan's comparatively smaller export market as a percentage of GNP failed to make it rational to prioritize a large state-project to get foreigners interested in Japanese cultural exports.

Despite a similar massive economic downturn in South Korea in 1997, comparable to Japan's recession that started in the early 1990s, and despite a similar insular conservative culture and politics like Japan, South Korea's economic depression was only short lived. Double digit growth returned by 1999—something that failed to happen to Japan even after a few decades. One of the rationales why is that Korea always has been more interested in expansion of its export economy regardless, both in digital hardware and in cultural issues. Korea put a fresh state-supported focus on cultural exports in its own economic downturn in 1998, a state support which has not faltered to the present day. Plus, the argument is that Korea already had a *digital* technological base instead of an outmoded mechanical technological base that made Japan famous by the 1980s. This made it harder for Japan to retool in its economic depression of the 1990s into competing in more digital telecommunications instead of mechano-electronics.

However, as you might surmise, Korean cultural content itself was shared already in the country's modern Internet and mobile networks among its increasingly digitally saturated population, yet this was sharing its own internal-looking and truly ancient Korean culture. This inward-looking culture is what makes Korea an odd candidate for global export of its culture in the Korean Wave in terms of content, yet in terms of technology and fast business abilities, the strong innovation around this homogeneous culture makes it a far easier enterprise and earlier candidate to do such exports well. In short, the cultural Korean Wave is a deep expression of an ancient Korean culture yet equally the next in a long line of ongoing modern economic products in South Korea's export-led economy from the 1960s. This is because the cultural Korean Wave *is an export-led sector and strategy:* it contains the same old goal set by the economic Korean Miracle's development strategy from the 1960s to the present, updated for stronger state support for catalyzing cultural exports after 1998. Of course it contains content desired by *domestic* Korean popular culture, *yet that domestic content market becomes filtered and shallow* to have a dual focus to appeal to ancient themes in Korean culture and to succeed in a world market of only the few factors of Korean culture with mass cultural interest in competition with other countries' cultural industries. While an ancient Korean cultural continuity makes both North and South Korea unique culturally, only South Korea's successful and durable 'Korean Miracle' of fast economic growth in export-led development and its synergy around digital telecommunications has made it unique economically. Adding the Korean cultural wave into this mix has made South Korea more unique as the only country combining some of the most massive bulk economic shipping, some of the largest and most durable digital telecommunications exports as a sector, and one of the largest and most durable non-Western global cultural waves combined.

What began this push toward these two fresh economic sectors in its export-led economy was a growing middle income trap in the late 1970s before such a comparative term even existed. In retrospect, in this export-led economy the Proto-Korean Wave began from two once separated *good choices of export sectors: telecommunications after an economic and political crisis in the late 1970s, and then after a further economic crisis in the late 1990s, and then more state assistance in cultural production.* While such state priming of cultural events began as early as 1980 under Chun, it was hardly designed as an export sector until the 1990s, and hardly given a larger budget for such purposes until after 1997. *However, as early as the 1980s we can see these two foundational sectors of the later Korean Wave starting to come together: digital telecommunications and state-led cultural production.*

Let us discuss the history of these two sectors in South Korea *before* they merged and then *when* they merged. First, the South Korean state by the early 1980s arranged policies to focus large investments and even larger reorganization of South Korean *culture* and telecommunications. However, these two sectors came together *first only for domestic markets* in President Chun's increasingly state-managed culture and repressive government of the 1980s. The focus is on the cultural sector first, and then digital telecommunications is discussed second.

Chun's regime brought in color television broadcasting updates in 1980 that had been blocked by the previous President Park, assassinated in 1979. However, this was less a cultural opening up, and was *a "more entertaining closing down,"* censorship, continued state-led consolidation of Korean culture under Chun as under Park, and yet an aid to a fresh economic sector. While Park wanted to create a seamless political, civic, ideological mental world in urban and rural *producers* by the mid-1970s, Chun wanted to create a seamless media world in national *consumers*—with a state-vetted content to control, to numb, and to distract Koreans from using media for other civil or political public purposes beyond his approval as much as it was equally for aiding economic expansion of Korean private profits in entertainment. These other civil or political purposes beyond his approval would be many, though they were mostly around transmitting politics in the mass media that reflected negatively on Chun's 'presidential dictatorship' starting with his military coup in December 1979 in the wake of the assassination of President Park, which was followed by Chun becoming the next "Korean President" without having an open election just like Park after 1972. Plus, Chun was keen on stopping anyone knowing, via the media, what actually happened following his Gwangju Massacre in May 1980. To clamp down, between August 1980 and January 1981, more than 60,000 Koreans were arrested to stop their civil and political opposition to Chun's developing regime, with many tortured and sent to "reeducation camps."

During this time, the Basic Press Act of December 1980 became the basis of Chun's media control. He was trying to turn all of Korea into an easier-managed "reeducation camp," via the mass media. Chun aimed from December 1980 to censor and to control all public media mass communications: newspapers, periodicals, and broadcast media. All news agencies were merged into a single state-run agency in

December 1980, named Yonhap News Agency. Many regional newspapers were ordered to be closed by Chun, and even central newspapers were forbidden to put correspondents in provincial cities. The heritage of early Korean democracy and its political civil sphere aided by the Christian Broadcasting System network was forbidden now to provide any news or political coverage. The existing state-run Korean Broadcasting System (KBS) absorbed and destroyed two other independent broadcasting companies. Chun's Defense Security Command, headed by his "#2" Roh Tae Woo and Chun's Ministry of Culture and Information fired hundreds of South Korean journalists and banned them from all newspaper writing or editing. How can a government fire journalists? The Basic Press Act set "professional qualifications" for journalists, as a government license to be a journalist. What if a journalist or editor refused to collaborate with Chun? Most writers and journalists revealed themselves as cowards and followed along. This was of course one of the most criticized polices of Chun by the mid 1980s, yet former Ministry of Culture and Information official told a Korean National Assembly hearing in 1988 that journalistic compliance reached 70% from 1980 to 1982. Methods to get the "fake news" Chun wanted ranged from simple telephone calls to violent interrogations and beatings by police.

Therefore, the content of this shallow public sphere was a true Orwellian state. It was a both a *state-vetted censorship* and *an artificially-generated public sphere* coordinated with intelligence officials, government agencies, and presidential staff. The "Office of Public Information Policy" within the Ministry of Culture and Information gave daily guidelines to all newspaper editors about topics to push and topics to censor. To create fresh cultural content to fill up the media time and to disguise the censorship, Chun equally began state-facilitated baseball and soccer teams in the early 1980s, for the first time. At the same time, he arranged to host international beauty pageants and invited international sports events—the most successful ones being the 1986 Asian Games and the 1988 Summer Olympics, the latter held in Seoul. At the same time, Chun lessened rules against sexual content in the cinema and in the fresh color television broadcasts.

In summary, after Chun's Basic Press Act, Chun closed many political medias of the older Korean democracy, consolidated many others, and forced them to sign 'contracts' about content they would show and content they would censor. Simultaneously as this Basic Press Act was taking hold, Chun's administration arranged the first state-sponsored cultural events and products, along with various cultural festivals of foreign beauty, the first dubbed TV dramas, the first national baseball sports teams, the first national soccer sports teams, televised songs, themes of patriotism, and of course internal censorship of oppositional political and democratic topics as noted earlier. It was the same apolitical, happy, and sexy "Korean Wave" though it was directed only toward Koreans immediately after Chun's Gwangju Massacre. Chun's dictatorial culture arguably was the start of this 'sector' of a "coordinated state-led attempt at an apolitical culture for private profit expansion" that we still see now into the more global Korean Wave.

Given the point earlier that Korea can hardly be called a full dictatorship and always was a weak state with a more hybrid political settlement, a bill was introduced in the National Assembly to end the Basic Press Act, even though it was voted down by the Chun appointed one-third of the "National" Assembly under his constitution of the Fifth Republic (which was the same scale of rigging of the National Assembly under President Park's Fourth Republic). Next, a public boycott to withhold compulsory viewers' fees (just like current protests and boycotts against the BBC in the U.K. from 2021 onward) was taken in protest against censorship by the dominating KBS government-run television network. Chun's policies started to lose parliamentary support via ongoing elections though, and even in this rigged electoral system, by the summer of 1986 his own party felt forced to respond to public opinion in an easing of restrictions on independent media. Newspapers started to found their own journalism labor unions in protest as well. This period is the origin of many uniquely democratic media organizations in Korea, like *The Hankyoreh,* founded in 1988 as a reader-funded cooperative to be independent of large capital, or like the democratic administrative changes to the *Kyunghyang Shinmun*, originally founded in 1946 by the Catholic Church yet unconnected with it now. Literally translated as 'Urbi et Orbi' Daily Newspaper (a Catholic papal phrase of blessing, meaning 'to the city and the world'), it is an independent newspaper where the CEO is elected, who can appoint an editor, yet the editor still has to be approved by majority vote of the approximately 600 journalists working at the newspaper. After nearly three weeks of daily nationwide protests in June 1987 against Chun's announcement that Roh would simply 'become' their next President without an open election, to try to end the protests, Roh released an eight-point declaration on June 29, 1987, which among other points provided for a free press, including allowing newspapers to base correspondents in provincial cities and withdrawing security officials (that were true Soviet-style political commissars, under other names) from newspaper offices. The Basic Press Act was revoked in 1987 as well. Thus, the Christian Broadcasting System's network was allowed to talk about news and politics once more in 1987, along with everyone else.

Despite President Chun's desire from December 1980 through 1987 *for a centralized* and state-managed 'apolitical' culture of only entertainment for the first time that was like a national mass media version of a "reeducation camp," there was *for the first time a more decentralized* approach to economic sector decisions unlike the past. Chun's economic technocrats were hired, and left alone. It was they who dreamed up future economic sectors with their wider and more professional expertise. Among other sectors, they recommended to forge a digital telecommunications/computerization drive, while Chun's administration itself was more involved in the attempt to host, design, and winnow content of cultural events domestically for political purposes of distraction as much as for domestic purposes of economic expansion at the time.

This may seem surprising to relate, yet as mentioned above, South Korea was a country in which color TV was not regularly broadcast until 1980, and only fully broadcast in color by 1981. Globally, the United States' television station named CBS was the first ever to broadcast in color, from 1950. Japan started to broadcast in color in 1961. Even though South Korea *manufactured* color TVs from 1975, President Park simply blocked the idea of *broadcasting* in color as he felt it would be a stark counterpoint that would show citizen inequalities of who could afford color TV compared to who could afford cheaper black and white TV. Black and white

TV, in other words, was more about goals of national cultural solidarity. Meanwhile, North Korea (and no one could say they were unconcerned about solidarity) started to broadcast regularly in color earlier, from 1974. North Korean fully color broadcasts started in 1977. In South Korea, the idea of regular color TV broadcasting had to wait until after Park's assassination in 1979.

Equally in the 1970s, South Korea under President Park failed to even have many telephones. Telecommunications was hardly Park's priority. However, after his assassination in 1979, South Korea from 1980 went from a faltering country with a *multi-year* waiting list for private telephone installation in that year (via a reigning government monopoly on telephones), to *the world first saturated country for private mobile phone ownership* soon merged with *the fastest wireless broadband speeds for a large country* by the second decade of the twenty-first century (see Appendix 1). Plus, during the 1980s, the governmental telecommunications monopoly quickly was dismantled. A very capitalist-competitive internal and external telecommunications sector took its place (Oh & Larson, 2019). Later, South Korea became known for innovating so much that it was the first place in the world with wireless color television broadcasts received by (pre-smartphone) mobile phone screens via digital radio frequencies that could equally be used to send wireless radio or other data to mobile phones, navigation systems, and other mobile devices. *This was before smartphones or LTE wireless internet/broadband as an option even existed.* Plus, nowadays Korea *is almost the only country in the world* to make flexible organic LEDs (OLEDs) for thin-screen, high-definition digital color televisions. Korea has dominated OLED from 2004, the year when Samsung Display became the world's largest OLED manufacturer by making 40% of the world's OLED displays. By 2010, Samsung Display made fully 98% of the world's more modern active-matrix OLED (AMOLED) displays. Since nearly all modern TVs, computer monitors, and smartphone screens use AMOLED technology, nearly the whole world looks at the Internet or at their favorite visual entertainment via the same Samsung screen product.

By 2022, South Korea's scale of *mass national* mobile phone ownership and fast bandwidth speed has been matched only by a handful of *tiny* global city states at best, instead of any other territorial countries being near the high levels of South Korean mobile phone saturation or bandwidth speeds. The only places in the world now with comparable broadband speeds to South Korea are tiny Hong Kong, Singapore, or Dubai, with at most 10 million people in each of these locations at best. However, South Korea has regularly done the same comparable high speeds *for 50 million people* or more as early as 2013. Plus, South Korea's earlier policies to demote rural and urban inequalities of wealth in grass roots development is related to its later equitable rural and urban mobile and wireless services, maintained even in minor inhabited islands off the coast. In the United States, there was always a greater rural triage in telecommunication diffusion, since big telecommunication companies preferred profits and rural triage was the best way to maintain profits, so American companies refused to extend telephone service to rural America. It took court battles to extend telephones to rural areas in the United States. However, there has been an easier and greater urban-to-rural telecommunications parity and equality in South Korea likely as part of the earlier state-guided yet competitive private development drive from the start and likely as part of the fast development drive's integration of rural village-based grass roots development throughout Korea as well.

This 'state-directed open competition' was spurred into action in the 1980s in telecommunications. By the late 1990s, telecommunications contributed to South Korea's domestic *digital development* that in that decade merged with its own internal digital cultural production more than other countries per se—surely influenced by the greater communication parity among other factors of course. From this point, it was easier with this durable political and cultural will and with wider market scale over decades to parlay this into even wider world-encompassing competitive exports of Korean digital cultural production. However, this could happen *globally* only once three requisite digital issues had developed and matured outside of Korea: (1) a global diffusion of the more accessible technologies of the World Wide Web from the 1990s onward, (2) multiple global digital platforms from the late 1990s onward, and (3) the global diffusion of smartphones after 2007.

By the *early* 1990s, it was found how to more clearly coordinate *analog* telecommunications and cultural sector profit first in Hong Kong in 1992. So Korea was already doing this connection in analog form in the early 1990s. State-ramped cultural productions of the 1980s, designed as pleasant distractions in politically conflicting times and as a potential domestic profit sector and even export sector really only came into their own with a key coordinating project of the Korean state with many Korean corporations to place a particular Korean drama on Hong Kong TV. This was the Korean TV drama called "What is Love?" in 1992. This is argued here to be truly the beginning of "Hallyu", before it was called "Hallyu" though. It may be one of the rationales why the earliest term for the Korean Wave was of Chinese origin in the first place, "Hallyu." There is more on this debate about Hallyu name origins in Chapter 4.

However, by the late 1990s, Korea was learning to increasingly use *digital* telecommunications and *the Internet* to profit from difficult economic times. This fresh digital medium required its own fresh yet similar cultural content industries that could fit this digital medium: online video games. This was the connection point of the digital telecommunications and the increasingly state-assisted cultural Korean Wave at the time. The digital telecommunications infrastructure made Korean online video games the largest sector of the Korean Wave in profit until well after 2010 (see Appendix 1). It is fair to say that a subtext of President Kim Dae-jung's desire from 1998 to expand the Korean Internet-based cultural wave domestically and overseas could have been that it could serve a similar "3S" strategy at the same moment for providing distraction to the suffering Korean masses as unemployment grew and as fully 15 of the top 30 chaebol collapsed into bankruptcy in a sudden financial liquidity loss that created a short and sharp economic downturn. However, as said earlier, by 1999, the Korean economy had recovered at scale, though the Korean economy and its cultural mood started to look quite different in an organizational sense and feel more pessimistic in a cultural sense.

How did this video game sector come about, as the first link between the digital hardware economy and the digital cultural economy in South Korea? One of the key fresh growth infrastructures in this economic crisis of the late 1990s was a project for a high speed internet and economic growth in online services and online business sales that might accrue from it. One of the first users of this fresh high speed internet was the business of connecting and servicing "PC-bang" video gaming rooms. These became the basis upon which millions of sometimes happy, sometimes sad, escapist, and unemployed Koreans in the economic downturn of 1998 onward could lounge away their days and take their mind off their problems by playing in the fresh industry of Korean videogame production. Second, the push to create a nationwide digital authentication regime to facilitate trust in online transactions was instituted at this time in the hopes that greater online security in transactions would provide greater financial benefits. This gave Korea another world first: *the first country in the world with a national digital authentication policy* in one sole technology of encrypted Public Key Infrastructure (PKI). However, the singular technological monopoly in digital authentication technologies, that the Korean state fostered and defended for fifteen years (before removing the mandate in 2015), actually would come to set back Korean Internet transaction security instead, and led to the country becoming the second most hacked country in the world after the United States instead of making 'online Korea' more secure in digital financial transactions as was intended (see Appendix 1).

To summarize, in the Proto-Korean Wave, a synergy was coming together. It was in two major state-facilitated sectors: export-led digital telecommunications and an increasing state-facilitated cultural production. Note the latter was originally for domestic political propaganda purposes and *domestic economic* purposes for Chun's government to create and to censor cultural content. Later, in the early 'nameless' period of the Korean Wave, in the early 1990s, the two sectors started to have more analog-based synergies overseas, in more exclusive *export economic* purposes together in order to create "Korean" cultural content designed *for overseas audiences as expanded Korean markets.* Later, the digital synergy was visible when others overseas starting buying Korean material artifacts including digital technologies through which they could more easily be hooked into Korean cultural production values and themes like Korean video games and thus pull other material sectors of exports along with the gamers in unison.

Good choices and good sequencing matter in the synergy of digital Korean Wave exports. Digital telecommunications had to come first. Upon it, South Koreans learned to market cultural content *domestically* first in *analog* culture items (TV dramas, music, etc.), then in *digital* games domestically next, and then digital games *internationally* in the same way in both. This sequence is clearly seen in the timeline of Appendix 1 in many digital items, with the earlier building of all major digital infrastructure before later mass consumer digital sectors are popularized. However, of course there is an unevenness to the world's analog and digital telecommunications, unlike Korea. That fails to change the fact that once a more digital cultural production could begin in Korea, both its digital hardware and digital content sectors could be highly linked synergistically in marketing. Around 2003, there was a 'cross over' period where the early regional Hallyu was both analog media and digital media as it spread to neighboring East Asian countries as analog music, analog TV, and digital video games. More digital capacities slowly developed in the wider world after 1998. Upon that global digital foundation, a wider digital global Korean Wave could start to take shape beyond online video games. It helped as well that Korea was starting to achieve a 'world first' in its domestic digital saturation. This created the pragmatic scale of markets and business skill in *technically making and culturally marketing* to a more completely digital and even wireless cultural sphere in Korea. These early Korean digital business skills could then be used in exports to other countries before those other countries even had their own domestic digital markets to develop such skills.

In summary, the sectors of digital telecommunications and increasingly digital cultural production synergistically came together—though only once this more national *digital* sphere began to exist after the further economic crises of 1998. This digital synergy led South Korea to start to innately work on the nation's own exclusive digital cultural production in video games and its own exclusive online digital authentication. Then, upon the skill and expertise, technically and in marketing for a more fully saturated *domestic* digital cultural and commercial sphere, Korea had the earliest 'world first' national wireless digital internet from 2006. So, South Koreans *were ahead of other nations* in marketing, selling, and in basic national wireless infrastructure by 2006, priming themselves early as a *domestic* nation for being some of the earliest digital content providers for a developing *global* digital cultural sphere. Then, due to ever cheapening and miniaturizing distributed media like cheaper televisions and smartphones from the early twenty-first century, the world itself began to allow Korea to catapult what it had already developed domestically into an even larger export-led digital cultural production.

3.4 Korean Culture: An Odd Domestic National Test Bed for the Korean Wave

However, there is an oddity of the cultural content of the Korean Wave itself. Most other nations are accustomed to creating only cultural productions for themselves, as they should. However, South Korea is in many ways the 'inside out' country with an insular culture yet with an economy deeply dedicated to export-led sectors. Therefore, it is unsurprising that Koreans eventually would attempt to turn their very homogeneous and insular culture inside out for export. However, it is surprising nonetheless that this Korean Wave content has come out of one of the world's most non-assimilative cultures in stark contrast to its export-orientation and global sales in the Korean Wave. The homogeneous culture giveth the Korean Wave out of its collective innovation, yet it taketh away as well by rendering much about the Korean cultural experience impervious to the very foreigners they are appealing to, except in a very surface fashion.

Thus, first, the cosmopolitan Korean Wave is a very filtered experience of the wider gamut of Korean culture, and, second, it is ultimately a culture foreigners are unable to share in completely if they ever visit its source in non-cosmopolitan Korea.

Third, the Korean wave would be less of this one-way tsunami without a pre-arranged network of billions of mobile smartphones distributed around the world or the billions of views on global platforms of social media or video platforms that virally magnify the reach of the Korean Wave. However, as you might surmise, the Korean content shared in its modern Internet and mobile networks among its digitally saturated population was its internal-looking and truly ancient Korean culture. So, *this culture* is an odd candidate for a global export despite how *this digital technology* makes it a far easier and earlier candidate to do and despite *Korea's export-led orientation* making it far easier to conceive of other economic synergistic rationales for doing so.

So, while the Korean Wave is part of the wider Korean export-led economy of state and economic corporate drives, the Korean culture and the Korean people themselves have little desire of exporting themselves. South Korea has a very stable, ancient, and even xenophobic culture that now finds itself strangely inverted, requisitioned, and even drafted unwillingly in the Korean Wave as a force of global cosmopolitanism. This modern 'neo-Korean cosmopolitanism' of the Korean Wave is furthest from its deep 'cold comfort' values of an ancient Korean culture. This ancient Korean culture has been brought into service of the South Korean state's export-led drive to commodify select and sponsored themes from this insular and more homogeneous culture. So, it is not without irony that cultural themes of a once-isolated ancient Korean regional culture now take the world culturally, because of the earlier state-led development drive, and because of Korea's earlier digital saturation than all other countries (see Appendix 1).

Some of this odd dynamic for how it occurred is understandable in the following comparative way. Korea has always for centuries tried to be 'innovatively impervious' in order to keep its homogeneous culture great by greater innovation *against* external incursions. This was reviewed in the previous chapter's section about 'technological innovation' and 'science and civilization in Korea' that shows unique scales of Korean innovation technically over time for various rationales discussed there, that are very different from and always 'ahead' of its neighbors in East Asia even hundreds of years ago. Plus, this goal of national protection can be still seen in the openly stated motivations for the greater state support for the Korean Wave and other fresh digital sectors in the last years of the 1990s. They were both innovative plans for further economic sectors of expansion in the export-led economy in a downturn, and yet were equally framed as a rearguard cultural and protectionist cultural and technical action similar to ancient Korean history of trying to stop military invasions, yet now were *trying to stop others' invasion via global digital culture and digital businesses from colonizing South Korea* culturally and technically before Koreans had a chance to extend themselves digitally at home and against that growing digital world outside as well. For instance, the Korean state's policy documents about digital authentication state these dual goals of building such a national digital authentication for potential exports later, though equally as a way to ban other global/American digital authentication companies from the Korean markets in the late 1990s before Korea has fielded competitors of its own (Son & Whitaker, 2020).

So, the three best modern examples from the late 1990s through the first decade of the twenty-first century of this national protectionism are the nationally exclusive digital authentication network itself in Korea from 1998, the block on foreign mobile phones for almost two years after 2007, and various Korean-only platforms like search engines or social medias throughout. All of this was to develop to serve the increasingly digitally "saturated" Korean public earlier than most, to stop foreign global digital conquests of their land, as well as to ready digital salvos later in the export-led economy. These modern desires of national production, national protection, and national exports merged into technical innovation, exactly like hundreds of years ago except for the technology exports. These are the tricks that South Korea did to protect its own domestic digital economy after 1998 from *foreign* digital authentication companies, from *foreign* web platform tools after 1998, and from *foreign* smartphone incursions after 2007 (Oh & Larson, 2019; Son and Whitaker, 2020). It is a large irony that for Koreans to keep their autonomy and homogeneous culture safe from an encroaching external global digital infiltration in the late 1990s, Koreans first set out to try to isolate themselves *digitally* from the world in the late 1990s through 2010 (Oh & Larson, 2019; Son & Whitaker, 2020) in technological standards, in exclusively national rules in the digital economy, in banning Apple iPhone/smartphone imports, and in developing their own search engines and their own social media platforms. However, at the same time, Koreans were prepping *digitally* to conquer the world in the same areas in which they were digitally isolating by choice. In retrospect, this digital national protectionism only made them better prepared for their own external digital conquest in the Korean Wave by the institutional autonomy, scale of production, and digital cultural capacities they were building. Both actions—*readying further digital economic sectors of the export-led economy* into the expansion of the Korean Wave and the expansion of Korean digital technologies and *building national digital autonomy and protections against the global digital economy*—were done even in the same policies around digital authentication or blocking the Apple iPhone from being used in Korea for almost two years as native smartphone versions were manufactured in order to save themselves from foreign digital colonization *while they were trying to set up a plan to do the same to other nations in the global market.*

It is fair to say that since the Korean Wave is competitive innately with other previous countries' cultural industries, the Korean Wave has to be understood *as built on using and competing with* past pioneering technical and mass media American innovations used in the export of American popular culture productions beginning after World War II and into the 1980s. This includes mass media music recordings, movies, radio play songs, cassettes, CD ROM, portable music players, music videos, youth fads in clothing, and even an exuberant and rebellious spirit. However, the Korean Wave is hardly a derivative of American mass culture for three rationales. First, the Korean Wave is built from Korea's quite ancient stable cultural motifs instead of a rebellious teen culture or its modern gloss. Second, the Korean Wave is built on the economic Korean Miracle's export-led economy and state-directed policies. This makes the Korean Wave mostly a continuing revolutionary economic production strategy and more of a strictly economic policy of global conquest and domestic economic survival instead of a cultural policy of global conquest or attempts at assimilation of others—something widely undesired by Koreans anyway. Plus, the Korean Wave itself as it became popular colonized and simplified South Korean culture first. Since the export-led economy is now focused on only exporting winnowed features of Korea's ancient culture, this is why the cultural colonization of the Korean Wave really is a cultural colonization of themselves first, in a replication of shallower features that stand a global market and are less politicized than the American wave, instead of representing wider features of Korean culture or politics that you might see in Americanization in many more unstructured or uncoordinated American cultural industry offerings. Third, trumping American-derived technologies, Korea came to take advantage of its own innovations in global *digital* telecommunications networks and personal digital technologies. Domestically using them first at any scale, the Koreans developed an expertise of marketing to their own culture's saturated digital networks, and are argued to be at least ten years ahead of any competition. This goes even for the Americans that remained far longer in their analog media culture (with digital television conversions only in 2018, for instance). So, Americans could hardly take advantage of any synergies between Silicon Valley's digital telecommunications and American culture so easily because of the greater power of more analog regimes of music sales and other kinds of terrestrial analog, cable television, movies, or empires of CD music production that became regimes opposed to such digital synergies and which made easy conversion difficult.

Meanwhile, Korea did its digital television conversion from 2012, and by 2013 the nation was nearly 100% saturated as a culture in smartphones through age 18—the most saturated place in the world for smartphones. By 2015, nearly 100% of the whole country below the age of 35 had a smartphone, once more a world first in such digital saturations. By 2013, the United States' population had only had around a 50% ownership in smartphones (see Appendix 1). Thus, despite pioneering many of these digital technologies, the United States lacked a digital synergy with its already popular cultural production until much later than Korea did. Despite digital Silicon Valley, the wider American cultural production itself remained analogue in a one-way mass media far longer in its business models and had less access to a saturated smartphone market for longer. Instead, in Korea, there has been a fast-paced digital telecommunications development *and* a digital cultural saturation *merging years before any other country* in the world, as noted in the review in Appendix 1. That earlier *digital synergy* domestically made all the difference in the world later in the global Korean Wave when merged with Korea's longer history of export-led synergy as well.

To summarize the points of this section and connect it with digital telecommunications, and to compare it to the United States, the stable Korean ancient culture expressed in the Korean Wave is at odds with U.S.'s modern rebellious teen culture in two main ways. First, the American teen product culture comes out of the urban industrial mass media cultural production of the United States that was servicing the earliest more heterogeneous immigrant-based urban areas. That earlier production of a 'teen culture complex,' and now its updated mostly teenage 'woke' culture of sexual, gender, and ethnic politics, has become America's latest cultural revolutionary export. It is a cultural wave stressing individual and cultural innovations as cultural content. Meanwhile, Korean 'teen culture' comes out of a sense of a more homogeneous cultural tradition and a sense of conservative national service, teamwork, age-hierarchy respect, politeness, and collective innovation instead of individual or cultural innovation. Second, modern Korean technical innovation and even its 'digital business models' of innovation are far ahead of the 'ancient' twentieth century's one-way mass media's centralized tactics widely employed still by the United States' cultural production. Korea is ahead of the United States because the whole world is entering a period of growing saturation toward a more viral and virtual digital media world in the twenty-first century. Because of South Korea's earlier drive toward digital mobile telecommunications saturation in its culture, and because of South Korea's greater cultural and political abilities for synergistic cooperation instead of only competition and conflict, Korea has learned the art of utilizing digital networks at higher levels of corporate, state, and cultural cross-coordination and uses them far more nimbly as a team compared to the divided, competitive and uncoordinated cultural production companies of the United States that have formed large vertically integrated conglomerates against each other instead. Plus, it is argued that a Korean state-led coordination in its Korean Wave yields greater cultural capacities for content and technical coordination than the United States even if something similar from the U.S. federal state does exist in cultural trend setting in the United States via the U.S. federal military and intelligence services interceding with and coordinating with Hollywood filmmakers, music producers, and digital content providers in similar yet less openly voiced kinds of state-led coordination in the Americanization of world culture (Levine, 2018; McGowan, 2014). However, given the fact that Korea is not a polarizing military empire unlike the United States or built into a Cold War ideological competition either with the outside world (beyond North Korea), the cultural result in the Korean Wave is hardly brazenly ideological-based or imperially-minded in content like that of the United States' cultural exports that developed in the 1930s against Nazi Germany or after World War II from 1945 against the Soviet Union during the global Cold War that made Americanization more militant and ideological. Korea's cultural wave successes began to occur only as the global Cold War wound down abruptly with the decline of the Soviet Union in 1991, and given the first successes of the early 'nameless' period of regional Hallyu by 1992 in Hong Kong. Even though the Korean Cold War still exists of course in microcosm, given a divided Korean Peninsula on those old ideological lines, a less ideological or militarized Korean Wave facing the world helps explain why Korea has been able to catapult this cultural wave to conquer the world steadily over three decades without alienating or polarizing any particular audiences the way the German Nazis did, Sovietization did, Maoism did, or Americanization still does.

As said above, the Korean Wave is a one-way tsunami in a two-way media, trying to keep it from flowing back into themselves. This is very different than a more two-way American cultural deluge of products and ideas in its older one-way mass media that promotes a vision of a globally shared individualized and rebellious liberty, teen culture, and happy consumption where America expected conversion to American culture and welcomed converts into itself from abroad (Savage, 2008). However, unlike the American wave, the Korean Wave is not designed as a break against all past global culture around mass markets of adolescence, or is not designed as a break against past Korean culture, or is not designed around ideas of a Korean Dream of immigrant success and assimilation in Korea. Instead, the Korean Wave is a painstakingly rational, state-planned marketing strategy of cross-industrial synergies. It is profit and loss. It is an assimilationist drive only to the extent that it exports and profits from Korean values abroad while holding foreigners and their digital products at bay at a cultural distance instead of welcoming them with open arms at home equally.

3.5 Conclusion

In summary, what kept Koreans' fast development going was its (1) good hybrid policy starting points creating durable virtuous cycles of development, aided by (2) many ongoing good choices and (3) many good accidents that helped keep them going down (4) a common 'developmental gauntlet' that can be analyzed as well. These combined issues helped keep these virtuous cycles intact down the development gauntlet. Other countries have been less lucky historically, as well as made fewer good choices as South Korea. Can all four factors be learned from and replicated as much as possible to help other countries participate in a much wider multi-polar cultural world of the future? Many less developed countries stall because they do develop somewhat, yet they are unable to solve the contextual problems of their own development to move beyond their original settlements as they start to experience diminishing returns to the original less representative settlements. However, South Korea has made it through all four levels of the development gauntlet into its global cultural wave—something only achieved by a handful of other countries.

Plus, the good choices of the export of digital telecommunications and the export of cultural production came synergistically to interact over time, yet only domestically at first. Synergistic interactions started domestically because South Korea developed a more saturated culture of digital communication earlier than any other country, and so it was economically valuable earlier in Korea to learn how to market, buy, sell, and entertain across a more hegemonic digital medium instead of the digital medium of culture being a sideline per se to an ongoing one-way analog mass media. After ten years of changed digital business practice and changed cultural expectations, Korea's earlier saturated digital culture was part of the global expansion of the Korean Wave particularly after 2012. Now, South Korea finds itself so far ahead in the digital competition with other nations that other nations may have to find other sectors to compete upon instead of being able to reach the Korean artistic and digital marketing skill that already exists.

References

Bank My Cell. (2023). *Number of mobile phone and smartphone users, 2023*. www.bankmycell.com/blog/how-many-hones-are-in-the-world

Beck, U. (1992). *Risk society: Towards a new modernity*. Sage.

Bunker, S. G., & Ciccantell, P. S. (2005). *Globalization and the race for resources* (Themes in global social change). The Johns Hopkins University Press.

Bunker, S. G., & Ciccantell, P. S. (2007). *East Asia and the global economy: Japan's ascent, with implications for China's future* (Johns Hopkins studies in globalization). Johns Hopkins University Press.

Collier, P. (2007). *The bottom billion: Why the poorest countries are failing and what can be done about it*. Oxford University Press.

Coppola, D. (2007). *Introduction to International Disaster Management*. Elsevier.

Esmezyan, T. (2018). South Korea wins most powerful passport in the world. *The Passport Index*. https://discover.passportindex.org/press-releases/south-korea-becomes-most-powerful-passport-in-the-world/

Fanon, F. (1961/2021). *The wretched of the earth, 60th anniversary edition* (R. Philcox, Trans.). Grove Press.

Gapminder. (2020). *Extreme Poverty*. https://www.gapminder.org/topics/extreme-poverty/. Gapminder Foundation.

Gill, I., & Kharas, H. (2006). *An East Asian renaissance: Ideas for economic growth*. The World Bank. https://openknowledge.worldbank.org/bitstream/handle/10986/6798/399860REPLACEM1601OFFICAL0USE0ONLY1.pdf

Global Saemaul Undong. (2015, October 2). Introduction of Saemaul Undong(Eng)_2014 *YouTube.com* https://www.youtube.com/watch?v=hkLL6u2HreM

Goody, J. (1987). Part 1: Writing and the alphabet; Chapter 1: The historical development of writing. In *The interface between the written and the oral*. Cambridge University Press.

Halpern, E., & Jacobovici, S. (Prod.). (1998). *Hollywoodism: Jews, movies, and the American dream*. Associated Producers, Ltd.; Produced in association with A&E, Channel 4 and ZDF/Arte. https://rumble.com/v2dedxw-hollywoodism-how-the-jews-invented-hollywood-1998.html

Han, J. K.; Mittal, S.; Joshi, H.; Sohn, Y. S. (2018). Paris Baguette: A Korean's brand success in France, Center for Management Practice, Singapore Management University. https://cmp.smu.edu.sg/ami/article/20181211/south-koreas-paris-baguette

Hong, E. (2014). *The birth of Korean cool: How one nation is conquering the world through pop culture*. New York: Picador.

Innis, H. A. (1950/1986). *Empire and communications* (D. Godfrey, Ed.). Press Porcepic.

Joseonilbo. (2022, January 14). S. Korea ranks 2nd in global passport power. *The Joseonilbo*. http://english.Joseon.com/site/data/html_dir/2022/01/14/2022011401012.html

Jung, M.-H. (2019, October 7). South Korea has third most powerful passport. *The Korea Times*. https://www.koreatimes.co.kr/www/culture/2019/10/141_276736.html

Kang, H.-K. (2019, October 21). Three S's in 1980s—A left-wing conspiracy? *The Korea Times*. https://www.koreatimes.co.kr/www/nation/2021/05/356_277394.html

Kaplan, D. E., & Dubro, A. (2003). *Yakuza Japan's criminal underworld*. University of California Press.

Kapuściński, R. (1983). *The Emperor: Downfall of an autocrat* (W. R. Brand & K. Mroczkowska-Brand, Trans.). Harcourt Brace Jovanovich, Publishers.

Karl, T. L. (1997). *The paradox of plenty: Oil booms and petrol-states*. University of California Press.

Kotkin, J. (2020). *The coming of neo-feudalism: A warning to the global middle class*. Encounter Books.

Lankov, A. (2007, December 13). (481) Dictating sex. *The Korea Times*. http://www.koreatimes.co.kr/www/news/opinon/2007/12/137_15479.html

Lee, S.-U., Park, J.-I., Lee, S., Oh I.-H., Choi, J.-M., & Oh, C.-M. (2018). Changing trends in suicide rates in South Korea from 1993 to 2016: A descriptive study. *BMJ Open, 8*(9): e023144. https://doi.org/10.1136/bmjopen-2018-023144; https://pubmed.ncbi.nlm.nih.gov/30269071/

Levine, Y. (2018). *Surveillance valley: The secret military history of the Internet*. Public Affairs / Hachette Book Group.

Levinson, M. (2006). *The box: How the shipping container made the world smaller and the world economy bigger*. Princeton University Press.

Lucas, R. E., Jr. (1993, March). Making a miracle. *Econometrica, 61*(2), 251–272. http://links.jstor.org/sici?sici=0012-9682%28199303%2961%3A2%3C251%3AMAM%3E2.0.CO%3B2-Mby

McGowan, D. (2014). *Weird scenes inside the Canyon: Laurel Canyon, covert ops and the dark heart of the hippie dream* (Illustrated ed.). Headpress.

Moore, K., & Lewis, D. (2000). *Foundations of corporate empire: Is history repeating itself*. Financial Times Management.

Nation Master. (Unk). South Korea Economy Stats. Nationmaster.com/country-info/profiles/South-Korea/Economy

National Tribune. (2023, January 19). Hollywood lost over $500 billion in market value in 2022. *National Tribune*. https://nationaltribune.com/uncategorized/hollywood-lost-over-500-billion-in-market-value-in-2022_4992842-html/

OEC. (2023). *South Korea*. https://oec.world/en/profile/country/kor/OECD

Oh, M., & Larson, J. F. (2019). *Digital development in Korea: Lessons for a sustainable world* (2nd ed.). Routledge Advances in Korean Studies.

Our World in Data. (2020). *Child mortality*. Ourworldindata.org

Our World in Data. (2021). *Life expectancy*. Ourworldindata.org

Park, G. (2019). *Rethinking mobile diffusion: Explanatory analysis of factors affecting mobile diffusion in African countries in the sub-Saharan region*. Paper for the Completion of "'Part A' Exam" in the Graduate School of Stony Brook University, Department of Technology and Society, The State University of New York, Korea.

Park, S. N. 2020. 'Parasite' has a hidden backstory of middle-class failure and chicken joints. *Foreign Policy*. https://foreignpolicy.com/2020/02/21/korea-bong-oscars-parasite-hidden-backstory-middle-class-chicken-bong-joon-ho/

Passport Index. (2023). https://www.passportindex.org/byRank.php

Perkins, J. (2005). *Confessions of an economic hit man*. Penguin Group (USA), Inc.

Pew Research Center. (2014, October 3–27). Older adults most likely age group to describe their smartphone as 'freeing,' 'connecting.' In *American trends panel survey*. https://www.pewresearch.org/american-trends-panel-datasets/

Pew Research Center. (2015a). *Several groups are shifting their home internet connectivity away from broadband and toward smartphones*. Home broadband 2015. https://www.pewresearch.org/wp-content/uploads/sites/9/2015/12/Broadband-adoption-full.pdf

Pew Research Center. (2015b). *The social media age gap*. Spring 2015 global attitudes survey. https://www.pewresearch.org/global/dataset/spring-2015-survey-data/

Ritchie, H. (2021). How much energy do countries consume when we take offshoring into account?, Our World In Data. https://ourworldindata.org/energy-offshoring

Salmon, A. (2022, January 3). South Korean exports hit a record high in 2021. *Asia Times*. https://asiatimes.com/2022/01/south-korean-exports-hit-a-record-high-in-2021/

Sandbrook, R., Edelman, M., Heller, P., & Teichman, J. (2007). *Social democracy in the global periphery: Origins, challenges*. Cambridge University Press.

Sassen, S. (2001). *The global city: New York, London, Tokyo* (2nd ed.). Princeton University Press.

Savage, J. (2008). *Teenage: The Prehistory of youth culture: 1875–1945*. Penguin.

Simon, J. L. (1998). *The ultimate resource 2* (Rev. ed.). Princeton University Press.

So, A. Y. (1990). *Social change and development: Modernization, dependency, and world-systems theories*. Sage.

Son, W., & Whitaker, M. D. (2020). *The danger of a single technology: Locked into a national digital signature in a globally digital era; South Korea's attempt at standardizing a "national*

PKI" framework (1999–2015), a study in path dependence that shows the danger of mandating a single technology (Manuscript article, dissertation summary of Dr. Wonbae Son).

Tyler, D. (2023). China's ensnared in the middle-income trap. *ZeroHedge*. www.zerohedge.com/geopolitial/chinas-ensnared-middle-income-trap

U.S. News and World Report. (2023). *Power*. https://www.usnews.com/news/best-countries/rankings/power

We Are Social. (2022). Digital 2022: Another year of bumper growth. *We Are Social*. www.wearesocial.com/uk/blog/2022/digital-2022-another-year-of-bumper-growth-2/

We Are Social / Hootsuite. (2017). *January 2017: Mobile's share of web traffic*. https://datareportal.com/reports/digital-2017-global-digital-overview

Whitaker, M. D. (2005). *Toward a bioregional state: A series of letters on political theory and formal institutional design in the era of sustainability*. Iuniverse.

Whitaker, M. D. (2009). *Ecological revolution: The political origins of environmental degradation and the environmental origins of axial religions; China, Japan, Europe*. LAP Lambert Academic Publishers, AG.

Whitaker, M. D., & Pawar, P. (2020). *Commodity ecology: From smart cities to smart regions via a blockchain-based virtual community platform for ecological design in choosing all materials and wastes*. Springer.

Whitaker, M. D., & Shin, G. C. (2020, December). A circular economy for the world: The commodity ecology model for achieving all sustainable development goals. *Journal of APEC Studies, 12*(2), 77–99.

Williams, R. G. (1994). *States and social evolution: Coffee and the rise of national governments in central America*. University of North Carolina Press.

Workman, D. (2021). Car exports by country. *World's top exports*. https://www.worldstopexports.com/car-exports-country/

Yonhap. (2017, December 18). Korea's ratio of domestic demand to GDP ranks low: Report. *The Korea Herald*. https://www.koreaherald.com/view.php?ud=20171218000214

You, J.-S. (2014, June). Land reform, inequality, and corruption: A comparative historical study of Korea, Taiwan, and the Philippines. *The Korean Journal of International Studies, 12*(2). https://doi.org/10.14731/kjis.2014.06.12.1.191

Zastrow, M. (2019, September 11). South Korea's 'Nobel prize project' rocked by tough year. *Nature*. https://www.nature.com/articles/d41586-019-02363-4/

Part II
Into the Present: Before and After Lockdown

Chapter 4
The Korean Wave Before and After a More Digital Post-pandemic Era

Part II begins with this first overview chapter. It has five sections. The first section is an introduction to the Korean Wave and how it has been classified by others as it changed over time. Next, it includes our suggestion of a slightly different and more continuous classification of 'regional Hallyu blending into a more global Korean Wave.' This suggestion is based on the actual history of events, showing four stages. There has been a four-stage movement (1) from more 'singular successes' in *regional* Hallyu beginning from 1992 with the Korean drama called "What is Love?" that was popularized in then-British Hong Kong and southeastern mainland China, in a 'nameless' period before it was even called "Hallyu", to (2) more 'simultaneous successes' by the late 1990s still within only regional Hallyu encompassing Korean online video games, Korean dramas, and the start of a regional love of Korean popular music. The Korean cultural wave started to be called Hallyu only from 1999. Then, once more there are (3) 'singular successes' of a *global* Korean Wave starting in 2003 with the film *Dae Jang Geum* (*Jewel in the Palace*) or in 2012 with Psy's song and video for "Gangnam Style," and then there are (4) the 'simultaneous successes' of a global Korean Wave only recently from 2018 onward in all of the sectors of regional Hallyu before, though adding many more sectors as well. This classification is described in more detail in the second section of this chapter, which is the historical timeline of all important successful events in the Korean Wave. It recounts both its growing scale and its trajectory changes. Both these sections help explain how the Korean Wave has grown over the past thirty years in stages built from specific successful events as it moved from a regional Hallyu into a global Korean Wave. The third section compares and contrasts content and strategies of the ongoing global Americanization that took a war-destroyed world after World War II, and compares it to the rising global Korean Wave that was already becoming global by 2018 yet increasingly took a digital world by storm due to in-person entertainments being destroyed in many nations' lockdowns between 2020 and 2023. Thus, the remaining sections compare and contrast content and strategies of the ongoing global Americanization, Chinese 'inverted' and 'negative' digital power strategies, and the rising 'positive' global Korean Wave. Then, different ways that the entertainment industry is conceptualized

G.-C. Shin and M. D. Whitaker, *The Korean Wave in a Post-Pandemic World*,
https://doi.org/10.1007/978-981-99-3683-0_4

are examined between the U.S., the U.K., and South Korea. Then, the many different ways people have conceptualized Korean 'soft power' is summarized, meaning, the power to move other nations' hearts and minds to align with another country's wider goals via others' appreciation of its cultural forms.

In that second section, the large factor of a strong state-primed and state-coordinated Korean Wave is discussed as important in the *success and durability* of the Korean Wave, and yet it is seen as *equally hampering its creativity and even popularity* via a formulaic and bureaucratic approach to the Korean Wave that is self-defeating. Since the days of President Chun in the 1980s, this state cultural priming of consumption historically saw its two priorities as *aiding only specific categories* of state-approved cultural content expansion and *creating political-cultural censorship on certain individuals within or outside such categories* as ultimately more important than aiding and finding individual successes for the global Korean Wave. The political-cultural censorship weakened after 2017 with the awareness of and then dissolution of a secret cultural blacklist in operation that had filtered state funding of the Korean Wave under President Park Geun-hye (2013–2017), even though some claim it started in a smaller form under the previous President Lee Myung-bak (2008–2013) (Collman, 2020). It is argued that the end of the secret cultural blacklist in 2017 was a major catalyst why the start of the first simultaneous successes of the global Korean Wave happened for the first time in the next year of 2018. In other words, the state and the companies thought they were facilitating the Korean Wave. However, crony forces within the Korean state were exposed in late 2016 as censoring nearly 10,000 creative Koreans for years via a secret cultural blacklist. The first copy of the secret cultural blacklist that was leaked was dated 2015. So, while one part of the Korean state approached the Korean Wave with only a formulaic and bureaucratic approach to funding its future, another part of the state had been bottling up the Korean Wave with secret political-cultural censorship. However, when that state-administered secret cultural blacklist was demoted from 2018, the Korean Wave started to blossom from 2018 into its first global "simultaneous successes" once there was less *categorical* censorship and less *individual* censorship as well. By 2020, the whole idea of a secret cultural blacklist was declared an unconstitutional use of Presidential power by the Korean Constitutional Court.

Those third and fourth sections compare *different global strategies in gaining influence via cultural waves* between the United States, China, and South Korea, and then compares how *different national legal and organizational conceptualizations of the entertainment industry* itself matter in state-primed cultural waves between the United States, the United Kingdom, and South Korea. Fifth, the last section discusses various ways that people analyze the Korean 'soft power' that has accrued because of the Korean Wave, discussing how such a nebulous concept has been defined or attempted to be measured. In other words, the whole world's geopolitical dynamics have changed due to the global Korean Wave, regardless how it is measured.

Overall, this first historical chapter of Part II is a timeline of the Korean Wave. It sets the stage for later discussions in Chapters 5 through 8 about how choices of governmental lockdown policies (and not directly Covid-19 pandemic conditions) *created technical changes and cultural-economic changes* in the Korean Wave by trying to maximize its digital cultural space while trying to minimize its in-person economic and social contact between 2020 and 2023. Chapter 5 is an overview of that Korean technical innovation in digital entertainment between 2020 to 2023. It is followed by three case studies in Chapters 6 through 8 for how these greater enforced digital technical and digital cultural-economic dynamics *enhanced global capacities and scale* in the Korean Wave in three cultural sectors: in Korean music (BTS), in Korean cosmetics (Cosmax), and in Korean visual broadcasts and/or cinema (*Squid Game*). So, instead of seeing a shrinking in the global Korean Wave between 2020 to 2023 like in other countries' cultural entertainment sectors during lockdown, the Korean Wave achieved greater records in its global popularity, profit, and scale.

In South Korea, various kinds of lockdowns on in-person venues were ended only as late as January 2023. Masking pressures were removed for civilians outside by February 2023, yet maintained in select infrastructures. By March 2023, Korean citizens were slowly released from all remaining governmental lockdown conditions and pressured masking imposed by the previous administration of President Moon Jae-in (2017–2022). However, complete removal of residual masking in public transportation and imposed upon business laborers happened only from late April 2023. This was over a year after many other countries, and nearly a full year after the next Korean President Yoon assumed office on May 10, 2022. Residual pressures of masking in doctors offices and other medical venues presumably ends in July 2023 or August 2023. Of course lockdowns, forced masking, ostensibly illegal digital private tracking and coerced no-liability experimental 'vaccinations' and related discriminatory 'vaccine passports' that together ended centuries of medical privacy and common civil rights temporarily occurred in South Korea and in many countries of the world, though hardly all policies were supported in all countries. In fact, the countries that ignored those technocratic, totalitarian, and intentionally discriminatory policies and instead defended normal medical privacy and common civil rights of individual decisions like Sweden, Belarus, or many African countries, in retrospect, did better without those discriminatory policies. They now find themselves better off psychologically, economically, and medically because of ignoring outside international and internal political pressures trying to spook people via mere overstated mathematical projections and via repetitious media discussion—without the hyperbolic fears ever coming true. In retrospect, the good news is that the declared pandemic was overstated from the start. The bad news is that the governmental overkill of medical, cultural, and economic effects of untested and emergency-authorized experimental injections, lockdowns, masks, and attempts at lowered business capacities via policies of 'social distancing' wreaked cultural, physical, psychological, medical, and economic harm far more than the declared pandemic did. This was particularly seen in the large numbers of business bankruptcies that acted as a 'great reset' that shifted wealth and socialization to more digital worlds in the counties that followed the piper along. These bankruptcies happened to Korea as well—except oddly for the entertainment sector of the global Korean Wave. This Korean entertainment sector was already digitalized and only became more digitalized, so almost alone in the Korean economy it was the sector that moved upwards and onwards to ever greater successes between 2020 and 2023.

Exactly how was this digital enhancement of the global Korean Wave done after 2020? The answer to this question is explained throughout Part II. Instead of lockdowns creating an economic and cultural decline in the global Korean Wave as was seen across many other sectors in the South Korean economy or the world, *a multitude of technical and organizational innovations were created* to sell and to promulgate the Korean Wave under lockdown conditions. The technical changes in this period were toward greater online versions of music, broadcasts, and films, along with the growing use of artificial intelligence (AI) and the growing use of augmented reality (AR) in the Korean Wave. While the Korean Wave's total cultural products are a larger category than the Korean entertainment industry per se, the next chapter's empirical focus will concentrate on the Korean entertainment industry and its increasing innovations toward global, online, and digital technical transmission in the period of 2020 through 2023.

Five themes or trends are noted in Part II. *The first theme* in Part II is case study analysis, whether of the timeline of the Korean Wave itself or of particularly strong examples from different cultural industries in the Korean Wave. To introduce the latter, three short chapters of Part II focus on three case studies that delve into strong digital success stories in three different economic sectors in the global Korean Wave between 2020 and 2023. Digital technical changes during this period expanded Korean successes in global popular music (BTS), in global cosmetics (Cosmax), and in global online broadcasting/cinema (*Squid Game*). One chapter is a case study about a more ongoing Korean digital success in the entertainment industry. It focuses on music and discusses the interaction of the K-pop boy group BTS and their technical innovations from the start of their career in 2012, to their global-level digital fandom in the years afterward, and then to their world-record-breaking scales of digital concert attendance and digital viewership after 2020 to the present. Within this case study analysis, a second simultaneous digital success in the entertainment industry focuses on cinema. It discusses the beginning of a more globalized online competition between many nations' digital broadcast OTT streaming subscription services, and that is why the *American* OTT service Netflix funded (and now exclusively owns) such an exorbitantly-produced *Korean* language action/drama series of nine-episodes called *Squid Game,* starting production in 2019. The screenplay for *Squid Game* seems to have been censored and blocked from domestic Korean production in Korean culture for a full ten years. However, Netflix agreed to help its screenplay writer escape such Korean censorship to produce it instead, for a global digital audience. Once produced by Netflix and shown worldwide from September 2021, *Squid Game* escaped Korean state, corporate, and cultural censorship on this content, and it immediately became Netflix's largest global financial success so far. Plus, it became the Korean Wave's largest critically-acclaimed cinematic success so far.

Another third case study of a growing digital success beyond entertainment is in Korean cosmetics. It is epitomized by *the world's largest* cosmetics 'business to business' supplier (B2B), a Korean company named Cosmax founded in 1992. On the one hand, all Korean B2B cosmetics manufacturers have been aided synergistically by the growing popularity of cosmetics styles seen on Korean faces in the imagery of the Korean Wave. In general, Korean aesthetics have inspired Korean cosmetics. In turn, Korean cosmetics seen in the visual content of the Korean Wave inspired the desire in billions of others to purchase similar products globally. Therefore, in turn, Korean business expertise in global cosmetics manufacturing is desired internationally by other nation's cosmetics companies. On the other hand, Cosmax's greater *scaled* ability to fulfill this global desire of consumers and businesses in cosmetics depended on an already achieved global scale of research and innovation before the Korean Wave, later combining with its own digital transformation that started before 2020 yet was accelerated between 2020 and 2023. Cosmax adapted well to the online cosmetics market dynamics requiring online versions of sales, advertising, brand fulfillment, and market analysis. Online cosmetics markets are known to be faster in response to fads and changes than sales through older in-person stores, so Cosmax as the world's largest B2B cosmetics manufacturer leaned to be faster in its services to aid its client companies' research, manufacturing, and market analysis in order to follow the faster online fads in cosmetics. Cosmax has been a global leader in cultivating different online information channels compared to the past when cosmetics sales were mostly taking place in physical stores and in older one-way mass media campaigns for advertisement. As cosmetics sales started to depend on a more digital market, this kind of market's faster-changing digitally viral fads required a change in material manufacturing and fulfillment sides to be more efficient and faster. This equally made cosmetics products depend more on smaller lots combined with the expected fast-paced online fulfillment and even faster turnaround expectations of the full business process itself from cosmetics concept to cosmetics product in a few short months. Market analysis, design of different brands and products to fit trends, and material solutions for manufacturing profitably now have to happen within mere months unlike the slower processes of times past. To adapt, Cosmax expanded its digital business model and increasingly uses robotic technical innovations in physical cosmetics manufacturing itself to keep it growing well beyond its smaller (yet still global) B2B competition. In short, Cosmax's recent digital transformation gives it a more flexible and profitable way to design, manufacture, and fulfill orders internationally in a cosmetics market now based on robots, more digital market sales, smaller lots, and faster online fulfillment expectations from consumers and businesses alike.

A second theme throughout Part II is beyond the discrete technological or digital changes themselves and represents what are the major cultural-economic changes of the Korean Wave itself. Throughout all of Part II's chapters we can see the *cultural expansion* of the Korean Wave overseas that starts to dominate other nations' past cultural waves, and it increasingly starts to dominate them *economically* as well by *productive outsourcing* of other nations' companies themselves in hiring Korean companies or using Koreans in their own entertainment or cultural industries' public relations, hiring, marketing, research and development, and material production. That second theme shows foreign countries and foreign companies increasingly attempt to join and to exploit the global popularity and expertise gained by Koreans in the Korean Wave for their own countries as well. Even though this erodes other countries' autonomous cultural waves and previous national cultural production, by 2022 other countries began to find many ways to join in the Korean

Wave out of their own short term economic self-interest, in market challenges over the past few years, instead of restarting their own cultural waves with better national coordination. This cultural-economic trend of *declines* in other nations' strength of cultural production along with the cultural-economic trend of the *rise* of Korea will be illustrated mostly by reference to the decline, Koreanization, or Sinicization (meaning Chinese market reliance) of Disney, Hollywood, and Broadway itself in the United States. Arguably, unless these U.S. trends change, this could mean a long term U.S. national eclipse in its own cultural industries in a growing *multi-polar* cultural and economic globalization that nonetheless for now seems to be *recentering* globally on Korean expertise, ownership, and management behind the scenes into the mid-term future.

Like Part I, Part II continues to argue that (1) the more homogeneous Korean culture and its (2) greater access to collective innovation combine well with (3) Korea's high dedication to a globalized export-led national economy. This virtuous cycle described before in the economic Korean Miracle continues to be seen and continues to help in the expansion of the global Korean Wave as well. These three interactive factors arguably matter a lot for explaining why Koreans more than others have durably been able to make the quick technical changes described later that has repositioned their cultural wave in the global economy better than other nations with a cultural wave over the past few years. Simply put, other countries with cultural waves generally have less access to all three of these factors. Generally, they have been doing more poorly than the Korean entertainment industry in the past few years. In short, even foreign entertainment companies agree to join the Korean Wave instead of fight it now by hiring Korean stars and using Korean company services.

Technically, digital innovations in many economic sectors supported this expanded cultural scale of a global Korean Wave. This makes it hard for the Korean Wave to be beat at this point. Part II as a whole attempts to show this claim of the difficulty of beating South Korea is hardly bluster or blinding patriotic pride. It is the same two trends that explain it: technical changes and cultural-economic changes. Culturally and economically, Korea already has achieved global market aggregation and the global marketing skill for priming the digital realities of a digitally saturated global economy. Korea has created as well global buyouts and consolidations in other nations' intellectual property content ownership and their online platforms during the period after 2020 that are described later as well.

When judging cultural wave trends comparatively from many countries, whether before 2020 or after 2020, other nations show a growing difficulty in innovating technically for a digital entertainment world unlike South Korea. Therefore, instead, other countries start to hire and to join in partnerships with successful Korean platform companies or Korean content creators to profit from the global Korean Wave themselves. In short, South Korea has a global Korean Wave, though *Korea starts to be the place for outsourcing other countries' attempts at global cultural production* as well.

This is shown in *two more trends or themes* seen throughout the case studies about the Korean Wave. *The third theme* and trend of Part II is the continued growth of the Korean Wave *even because of*, during, or after state lockdown conditions from 2020 to 2023. *The fourth theme* or trend is *the slow decline* of autonomous national cultural waves of all countries, *including Korea in the Korea Wave, into a more globalized Koreanization of culture.* The 'national soft power' of many already developed Western or Japanese core nations' in this period began to lose ability to prime their own autonomous digital markets or to make profit from their past autonomous national cultural waves, as Koreans begin to displace many nations' top spots in their national entertainment markets. However, even Korean culture in Korea is being displaced by the more globalized outlook of its Korean managers, like in cases of larger Korean holding companies of global intellectual property (like HYBE, manager of BTS) instead of only managing or owning Korean talent anymore though buying up American talent and their back catalogues as well. Both trends should worry Koreans as well as countries competing with Korea since the idea of a national cultural wave itself seems to be dissolving into a global cultural sphere or global soup without clear national origins or clear singular national representativeness or management. This potential future scenario is discussed more in Part III, which looks at the trends of this global cultural soup for its future implications on any nation's cultural survival. However, as said above, many countries' leaderships right now seem content or ambivalent enough to join Koreans and to hire them for their own cultural waves, instead of seeing it as a question of competing with the Korean Wave or even as a question of national cultural survival versus dissolution in the near future.

Throughout Part II, another *fifth theme* is the ongoing deep synergy seen in "public state, private profit, and Korean culture" from its tentative beginnings in regional Hallyu to now the global Korean Wave *and how it has interfered with Korean individual and cultural innovation* instead of only sponsoring it.

On the one hand, these three synergistic factors and their links *work well toward* the popularity of the Korean Wave. These three factors now are larger, more blurred, and seamless because they have been involved in a Korean virtuous cycle of the deep practice of successful global-level cultural priming for the world market, for decades. This is clear even the earliest examples of regional Hallyu in the 1990s, discussed later. South Korea, by being dominated by its export-led economy and by its state planning and priming in that economic export, increasingly sees Korean culture and the value of cultural production only in terms of global export instead of national cultural transmission that has its own localized purposes. In this way, the two organizational actors of state and companies priming the Korean Wave and Korean culture are more prone to treat national cultural production with the same cool economic rationality and bureaucratic calculus that compares its 'worth' and 'value' as only global level economic profit when compared to all other state-led export sectors like automobiles, computer chips, or cargo ships. Nowadays, after decades of practice in Korean state planning and the Korean corporate training of cultural talent, in the repeated priming and training of talent to corporate order in the Korean culture, this has created a Korean culture increasingly mass manufactured only for the global market instead of for Koreans themselves. Human talent and cultural expression is being treated as just another rationalized mass-market manufactured commodity like any other Korean mass-market manufactured product. Koreans out of collective patriotic duty, competition with other Koreans, or out of desire for fame, put themselves through a well-organized cultural industry grinder to become vetted well-trained K-idols. This is a repeatable success formula guided by subsidies from the Korean state or Korean companies in the Korean Wave. This means instead of the Korean Wave randomly waiting for rare national lightning bolts of talent or success to be harnessed, talent itself is now pre-planted and harvested as part of a growing rationalized production (Adams, 2022). Thus, the Korean Wave has become equally successful and equally dehumanizing, equally global in expanse and yet equally formulaic and thin in content.

On the other hand, we can see how this triple synergy equally works *against* both popularity and innovation in Korean Wave. Exceptions prove the rule with the rare idiosyncratic talented Korean stars that somehow keep bucking the system and *selling more or being lauded more than the state-based Korean Wave*—and thus altering the Korean Wave sponsorship patterns preferred by the Korean entertainment corporations and the Korean state. The K-pop star "Psy" is addressed as one case study of this. World-champion female figure skater Kim Yuna is another. *Squid Game* is yet another example discussed in its own chapter later. To only discuss Psy for a moment in this introduction, the more formulaic Korean Wave felt forced to adapt to Psy's more individualistic innovation that it always disliked and left unsponsored—before Psy's autonomous global success in 2012. After Psy's 'unplanned singular success' occurred in the global Korean Wave, Psy begrudgingly was back-integrated by the Korean state into the Korean Wave pantheon. Plus, when framing the Korean Wave as 'pre-Psy' and 'post-Psy' after 2012, from 2013, there was a large growing trend of far more repression of individualistic and cultural innovation in the Korean Wave, instead of appreciation of it, due to years of President Park Geun-hye's secret cultural blacklist between 2013 to 2017. However, after 2017, with the end of the cultural blacklist, there has been a trend of more tolerated individualistic innovation and even a higher cultural quality in the Korean Wave. Immediately after the blacklist was ended in 2017, this began the first documented 'simultaneous successes' of the global Korean Wave from 2018. These major successes of 2018 are argued to occur greatly because of the end of the Korean state's secret cultural blacklist that had blocked nearly 10,000 creative Koreans illegally from state funding in the Korean Wave. President Park Geun-hye (2013–2017) took a page from her father President Park's and President Chun's repressive cultural authoritarianism for a time—until she was exposed for the blacklist in 2016 and then impeached in 2017—after which her cultural blacklist ended.

Thus, within the Korean Wave there is always this fight between the more *individualistic innovation or cultural innovation* of thousands of idiosyncratic Korean artists versus the more homogeneous cultural, crony, and state-bureaucratic *collective innovation* that only wants to reward duty and teamwork in the Korean Wave. The latter drives this more homogeneous culture to judge success mostly on status competition, scale of profit, and extrinsic awards, instead of to judge cultural success mostly on memorable or intrinsic quality of the experience that is incomparable. Plus, the financial irony is that so far the most intrinsically-motivated and idiosyncratic works of art and accomplishment in the Korean Wave (with more examples recounted later) still have more sales and global lauding than those produced exclusively by the 'star-maker machinery' behind the Korean popular song. After 2018 with the sudden end of the secret cultural blacklist, there seems to be so far a better balance increasingly between individual, cultural, and collective innovation in the Korean Wave as thousands of idiosyncratic dissidents of the Korean Wave were released in exchange for the jailing of President Park. Once this politicized cultural censorship was banned in the Korean Wave after 2017, there were by default more allowances for this 'more natural' combination of the three kinds of innovations in the Korean Wave's production from 2018. It is argued that it is hardly coincidental that finally the first simultaneous successes of the global Korean Wave began in 2018 only when nearly 10,000 more individualistic and culturally innovative artists and producers were 'released' from a secret cultural blacklist run by the state, once its orchestrator President Park Geun-hye was impeached and then jailed, and once her administrative team animating such illegal censorship and bias in the Korean Wave were jailed as well.

These five themes together will be clearer as the timeline of the Korean Wave is described. Plus, once the investments and strategies of the past few years of the Korean Wave under lockdowns is known, it should be clear how a newfound less restrictive cultural freedom in Korea from 2018 combined mutually with technical successes after 2020 to try to take advantage of wider digital and online economies of scale for such individual and cultural innovation instead of only collective innovation within Korea. So this is hardly just a story of technological enhancements of the Korean Wave's scale between 2020 to 2023. It is a story of the wider and more balanced cultural freedoms for different kinds of innovation allowed in the Korean Wave itself from 2018 onward that could take advantage of those technical innovations.

In conclusion, Part II has both a general technical, cultural, and economic analysis as well as technical case studies of how this *greater digital global positioning* was done by BTS, Cosmax, and *Squid Game*. It makes it difficult to dismiss the Korean Wave as a temporary nationalist fad when the Korean Wave has gone on for over thirty years and when it is now starting to be a more multi-national holding company of cultural management enterprises or global cultural production in league with other foreign companies.

4.1 A Short Introduction to Hallyu or the Korean Wave

Hallyu is a phenomenon that people now yearn for around the world. The Standard Korean Dictionary defines Hallyu or the Korean Wave, as "a phenomenon in which elements of Korean popular culture are prevalent in foreign countries." Hallyu here refers to all genres of entertainment production such as movies, games, broadcasting, music, webtoons, aesthetics and other non-entertainment products like foods, clothing, and cosmetics of Korean popular culture enjoyed by people worldwide across national borders. Recently, as the scope and delivery methods of Hallyu have diversified, new terms such as Korean Wave, K-Culture, and New Hallyu have appeared. In short, the Korean Wave can be understood as a flow of the 'soft power' of cultural appreciation of Korean *cultural aesthetics* spreading around the world along with the flow of the *material artifacts carrying that cultural aesthetics* spreading around the world.

However, the chosen terminology to describe or to categorize a phenomenon like a cultural expression is always contentious because culture can be evanescent, changing, interpretive, and shared. As noted by social theorists of cultural and technical diffusion over 120 years ago like Tarde, culture and its transmissions can be without clear boundaries or without commonly agreed upon names or even clear origins. For instance, there are several theories even about the etymology of the basic terms 'Korean Wave' or 'Hallyu.' All may be wrong, one may be right, or even all may be right if cultural transmissions are indeed without clear boundaries and fail to require singular origins.

First of all, there is an argument that the term "Hallyu" started to be used in Korea. This is the view based on the idea that the Korean Ministry of Culture, Sports and Tourism has been using the term "Hallyu" since 1999 when distributing Korean music albums to other countries to prime markets and to promote K-pop. To promote Korean popular music, albums were intentionally designed to be sold to Chinese, English, and Japanese markets that were *different* than the versions of the Korean domestic albums. These were distributed to overseas broadcasters, magazines, universities, and Korean missions. The English and Japanese versions were labeled "Korea Pop Music," and the Chinese version was labeled "Korean: Song from Korea." It is theorized that the word "Hallyu," which was used exclusively in the Chinese version, became the origin of the first term used for the later wider term "the Korean Wave." Plus, Korean dramas first gained popularity in Hong Kong and mainland China from 1992 to the late 1990s, respectively. The representative Chinese newspaper *People's Daily* first mentioned the term "Hallyu" in an article entitled "After the Han Wind Passed," dealing with Korean pop culture. There is a theory about double meanings as well in Chinese script here. While expressed in Chinese script as 'Korean Wave,' to a Chinese audience, the Chinese sounds and characters had a double meaning since a synonym of 'Hallyu (寒流)' means in Chinese "other cultures are penetrating fiercely." It is argued that this double Chinese meaning of "Hallyu" was meant as both label and criticism in the Chinese media sphere—the place where the term Hallyu was used widely first. However, now the Chinese media uses the term 'Korean Wave' as well. However, non-Chinese speakers are unlikely to be aware of this critical Chinese double meaning behind popularizing the term "Hallyu" at the start.

There is a separate claim about the origin of the term 'Korean Wave': that it originated in the equally Chinese-speaking Taiwan instead of in mainland China. It is said to have started with popularity of Korean singers in Taiwan in the late 1990s. As Korean music and dramas became popular in Chinese-speaking Taiwan before 2000, it equally spread to China and other places after that. In response, Taiwanese media first used the term 'Korean wave fever,' and some argue that this is how a shorter and less critical phrase 'Korean Wave' appeared in Taiwan for the first time. What is our view? We follow Hong in noting the first success of any Korean cultural artifact overseas was in British Hong Kong in 1992 (Hong, 2014), so for us, that is when and where "regional Hallyu" starts in East Asia, even if it was still a 'nameless period' of regional Hallyu without using that term per se, as we note in the timeline in the next section.

Summarizing the several ideas of origin above, the East Asian regional term "Hallyu" can be seen as a neologism and double meaning for both a *positively* fun and regionally 'feverish' Korean Wave and a *negatively* 'penetrating' spread of Korean culture seen from the perspective of the more historically dominant Chinese culture in East Asia. For millennia, China has always tried to frame a metageography of the mind in which China was the only possible central civilization, whether in conceptualizing only East Asia to make Korea, Japan, and Vietnam as smaller and junior derivative partners, or in a more megalomaniacal sense of central China versus the rest of the whole marginalized and less civilized world. (The Greeks were equal to the Chinese in their metageographical views—in calling the whole non-Greek world as barbarians.)

However, truly now in the Korean Wave, it is the Korean tail that is wagging the Chinese dog. This is upsetting the Chinese with a very different metageography of mind that is widely supported globally, centering itself on South Korea alone. Equally, this is upsetting European/Americans who have their own *ancient* Grecian-inspired metageography of mind about their own global centralism now combined with a more *modern* metageography of mind about a central Atlanticist/Eurocentric world-system. This fresh mental model of geography in the global Korean Wave starts to erode away the exclusive soft power of a Eurocentric modern world-system, and it effectively blasts away the importance of East Asia conceptually as unit in culture at all, and instead makes Japan and China into just two of many less important global peripheries, in a more global geography that focuses on and orbits around Korea (Lewis & Wigen, 1997). There is actually a hubristic map showing this Korean-centric world-system, built into concrete of Seoul for all to see. Where is it? It is in the literal core of downtown modern Gangnam, in Seoul, directly across from the Supreme Court of Korea. This Korean-centric *metageographic statement* is appropriately placed—as it is both in front of the Supreme Court of Korea and on the floor surface of the open quad of the 60,000-member strong Korean Presbyterian megachurch called Sarang Community Church. This places the Korean-centric world map directly above the world's largest (physically) underground religious structure for worship as well. That record size is according to Guinness World Records, that measured the underground space for worship at 8,418 square meters in 2015—another Korean world first.

In short, the Korean Wave is when Korean cultural contents started to be enjoyed outside of Korea and began a fresh metageography of mind in the world. When culture crosses borders, it is transmitted in the language of original content and yet transmitted across language or cultural barriers at the same moment. In this case, it transferred the Korean language and equally Korean sensibilities of proper aesthetics or proper cultural forms of all kinds into another cultural zone that already has its own proper sensibilities and proper cultural forms. Hallyu can be defined as the process by which this new diffusing Korean cultural expression was enjoyed by people in East Asia first and then increasingly around the world. Through this process, Korean contents gain repetition in other's minds and behaviors, and thus spread sympathy and Korean 'soft power' in the short term and yet envy or worry in the long term at the same moment.

According to past typologies, the 'development stages of Hallyu' were argued to be divided into three temporal periods, with the three periods taking place only *after* the originating and early period of Hallyu in Taiwan and/or China as Korean cultural products began to be known abroad there first (Jeon et al., 2012). This interpretation of 'three periods only after 1999' is similar to the classification created by the Korean President Lee Myung-bak's administration (2008–2013). After discussion of these three typologies by the Korean State, we offer our own different understanding and interpretation in the later 'timeline' section based on starting the Korean wave from either *its actual attempts or actual successes* at popularizing Korean cultural events, and thus starting far earlier than 1999, given there is evidence of an attempt at Korean cultural popularization overseas from the 1980s and its first major success in 1992 in British Hong Kong. Our updated attempt at a more accurate historical typology then is based on noting discrete changes of the organic growth and scale expansion in the popularity of the Korean Wave, instead of trying artificially to typologize it based on discrete changing 'leadership sectors' that are seldom as clean in their transitions as the earlier typologies claim. We prefer a typology based on the ongoing scale expansions of 'singular successes' into 'simultaneous successes' instead of a typology based on sectoral content leadership changes in the Korean Wave. However, the other typologies are still useful as ways to discuss overall trends of the Korean Wave and because these other typologies counterpoint how the Korean state's managerial view of the Korean Wave is prominently involved in observing as well as guiding the Korean Wave by funding what it wants to see the Korean wave become—or starving different sectors to fit as well, based on its analysis.

Thinking mostly of only nebulous and questionable 'content leadership changes' as their way to categorize the Korean Wave, the Lee Administration divided Hallyu into Hallyu 1.0, 2.0, and 3.0 (Lee Myung-bak Government White Papers, 2013). The Lee administration itself only focused on its contemporary Hallyu 3.0, which it felt connected Hallyu to the entire Korean culture instead of only to K-pop. By 2020, the Korean Government created another typology used by the Korean Ministry of Culture, Sports and Tourism that includes an added fourth category called "New Hallyu" (Table 4.1).

Given the subjective quality of all typologies, it is clear that any attempt at Hallyu typology is pattern fitting that artificially forces it into a Procrustean bed. After all, *What is Love* is actually popular overseas from 1992. *Winter Sonata* is actually popular overseas in Japan from 2002. Thus, in the next section, we argue that there is a different real first period, that might be named 'Hallyu before it was called Hallyu' or the 'nameless period.' This part of regional Hallyu came long before the term Hallyu was even in use since the first Korean cultural product to have a large singular success was as early as 1992 in Hong Kong and Southern China. We might extend this period of 'nameless Hallyu' even earlier if judged from when the first mere attempts at foreign dubbed Korean cultural exports in TV dramas started to be produced intentionally for foreign markets in the Chun Administration (1981–1988). Plus, noted in the timeline section to follow, if we categorize based on either 'singular

Table 4.1 Development of Hallyu and New Hallyu

Division	Hallyu 1.0	Hallyu 2.0	Hallyu 3.0	New Hallyu (K-Culture)
Period	1997 ~ Mid 2000s	Mid 2000s ~ Early 2010s	Early 2010s ~ 2019	2020 ~
Characteristic	Birth of the Korean Wave; Focus on Only Video Content	Spread of the Korean Wave; Focus on Only Idols/Stars	Globalization of the Korean Wave; Global Star Products	Diversification of the Korean Wave;**** Globalization (online communication)
Key Areas	Drama	Popular Music	Popular Culture	Korean Culture + Related Industries
Representative Contents	'*What is Love*' (Drama, 1997*) 'Boa' (K-Pop, 2001) '*Winter Sonata*'/ (Drama, 2004*)	Idol Groups 'TVXQ, Girls' Generation, Big Bang, Kara', etc. (K-Pop, mid 2000s) '*Dae Jang Geum*' (meaning, 'Great Jang Geum'; English title: '*Jewel in the Palace*') (Drama, 2005)**	'Gangnam Style' (K-Pop, 2012) '*My Love from the Star*' (Drama, 2014) '*The Vegetarian*' (Book, 2016)*** '*Running Man*' (TV entertainment, 2014)	'BTS' (K-Pop, 2016****–present) 'Blackpink' (K-Pop, 2017-present) '*Parasite*' (Film, 2019) Plus: characters, webtoons, and many TV programs
Destination Country	Asia	Asia, Central and South America, Middle East, and parts of Europe, etc.	Worldwide	Worldwide (Strategic Diffusion)
Consumer	Teen Mania	Teens to Twentysomethings (10 s–20 s)	World Citizens	World Citizens (Custom Approach)

Source: Table constructed from a typology of the Korean Ministry of Culture, Sports and Tourism (2020), p. 2.

* Note the Moon administration lied about dates in 'Hallyu 1.0' to make their typology start from 1997 and end in 2002, even though the Korean Drama *What is Love* started its popularity overseas in Hong Kong in 1992—far earlier than 1997; and given the Korean Drama *Winter Sonata* was popular earlier from 2002 in Japan—instead of later in 2004; ** Note in the column of Hallyu 2.0, that '*Dae Jang Geum'* actually was started earlier in a *global* popularity from 2003—instead of from 2005; *** Note in the column of Hallyu 3.0 that the author of the award winning book *The Vegetarian* was on the secret cultural blacklist of President Park Geun-hye; **** Note in the column of New Hallyu, that "diversification" begins as early as 2018 (see timeline of the next section), and note BTS actually was started earlier in 2013 and started to win international acclaim and awards from 2013 as well—instead of from 2016.

successes' or 'simultaneous successes,' we get different answers for the 'worldwide' start of Hallyu 3.0. If we classify based on more global singular successes, a worldwide Korean Wave started much earlier with singular global successes in a Korean historical drama called *Dae Jang Geum* (English non-literal title: *Jewel in the Palace*) (2003) or other singular global successes like Psy's song and video for "Gangnam Style" (2012). If we classify based on more global simultaneous successes, it still starts before 2020. The first simultaneous successes actually started earlier in 2018 as shown in the timeline in the next section. Plus, the 'world citizens' of Hallyu 3.0 could be said to start much earlier with more 'singular successes' from 2003 or 2012, and with other singular successes like BTS from 2013 which started with a more international fandom instead of from a more Korean-dominated fandom.

Note the term Hallyu 3.0 shows the Korean government felt that the scope of Hallyu policy has been diversified and expanded to cover all aspects of Korean culture by this point, instead of only popular culture. This was framed in order to try to sell Korean cultural products from wider economic sectors in association with the entertainment sectors of the Korean Wave. In particular, the 'Hallyu Culture Promotion Group' that was launched on January 30, 2012, played a big role in providing comprehensive and systematic support so that the K-pop craze, which was strong at the time, could continue after 2012 to be framed to encompass the entire Korean culture. However, as the timeline shows, there were zero globally successful events in the Korean Wave immediately after Psy despite this 'Hallyu Culture Promotion Group.' Instead, there was a "global Korean Wave desert" between 2013 and 2017, when the Korean Wave went back to mostly only regional successes so the typology above is quite artificial. Understanding why there was such a pause after 2012 that ended by 2018 with the first global simultaneous successes of the Korean Wave is explained in the timeline section later.

The Korean President Moon Jae-in's Administration (2017–2022) attempted to solve problems that they felt hindered the spread of a global Korean Wave. Through his administration's 'New Hallyu Promotion Policy Implementation Plan' of 2020, Moon's Administration divided the temporal characteristics of Hallyu into four stages as shown in the above table, and the present period after 2020 was defined as the 'new Hallyu' (K-Culture)'—even though many of the examples of his category "after 2020" all came oddly before 2020 in just the expectation that these would continue.

In the above merged classification from both the Lee and Moon Presidential administrations, the Hallyu 1.0 era was kept as what was after 1997, which they felt was the period in which Korean popular culture became more known to the world in earnest. However, far earlier, a wide array of Korean cultural products began to appear around Southern China, Hong Kong, Vietnam, and the Philippines after 1992 and only later in the Greater China mainland region. However, Korean popularity in mainland China was still centered on Korean family dramas. In addition to dramas, early K-pop music albums by Korean singers or groups such as H.O.T., Ahn Jae-wook, Yoo Seung-jun, NRG, and Clone were distributed throughout China. All these began to gain popularity after 1997 as well (Yang, 2012).

Next, the Hallyu 2.0 era is said to be in the "mid-2000s," which was a period of widening Hallyu in many types of Korean cultural industries being shared outside of Korea. Sometimes this was actually a nascent global Korean Wave unlike what the typology above implies, even if it was a more spotty global spread. If Hallyu 1.0 is said to be a beachhead created by Korean dramas and K-pop groups centered in popularity on the Greater China region until the early 2000s, 'Hallyu 2.0' spread is said to be mainly in the other direction, into Japan. When a Korean drama entitled "Winter Sonata" aired on the Japanese TV channel NHK in 2002, it caused a huge sensation in Japan. From this point the Korean Wave began to flow across to Japan. In addition, Korean dramas were exported spottily to Singapore, Thailand, Indonesia, the Middle East, and Central/South America. So, the Korean Wave spread and accelerated worldwide after first spilling into select countries in East Asia and Southeast Asia as a group. Equally in Hallyu 2.0, the reigning theme became more K-pop instead of only more Korean dramas, even though Korean dramas remained very popular.

The growing K-pop craze from Hallyu 2.0 expanded outside of the regions of East Asia and Southeast Asia, and soon came into the entire world. K-pop first appeared regionally in only East Asia from around 1997 to around 2003, since the first Korean idol groups gained popularity only in Japan, China, and Taiwan. This was a period before wide digital cultural saturation: before Facebook (2004), before the first video sharing social media of YouTube (2005), before Twitter (2006), before the invention of smartphones (2007), or before Instagram (2010). Only later, other regions were added in K-pop popularity like the United States, Europe, and Central/South America. In Hallyu 2.0, scale of exports in the Korean cultural industries increased dramatically. This was due to the growing scale of the craze of Korean popular culture now dually centered on Korean dramas and K-pop. This duality was increasingly globalized instead of only being popular in one main region of the East Asian and Southeast Asian neighbors to Korea. The economic ripple effect of Hallyu went beyond into other industries. It created sales and added value in other industries (Jeon et al., 2012).

Since then, the Hallyu craze went beyond the early dual center of synergy in K-pop and Korean dramas. The government typology of Hallyu 3.0 adds the popularity of traditional Korean cultural arts such as the martial art of Taekwondo. However, it ignores that K-pop/dance groups that were using Taekwondo like the K-Tigers existed far earlier than the government report, yet were hardly globalized themselves. Plus, the Korean government argues that the traditional song Arirang and Korean cuisine was now spreading worldwide in Hallyu 3.0, even though Arirang was known long before, though indeed seems to have become emblematic in association with the Korean Wave instead of only in the past in association with Korean nationalism or the era of the Korean War (1950–1953) per se. The government launch of more funding aid for the Korean Wave in January 2012, from the beginning of the 'Hallyu Culture Promotion Group' in the Lee Myung-bak administration supported globalizing the K-pop export craze with state subsidies. This would soon encompass support of the entire gamut of Korean culture and products instead of only entertainment. These directed state subsidies would come to be both beneficial (in aiding) and pernicious (in politically biased denial and a secret cultural blacklist) by the next the Presidential administration of Park Geun-hye (2013–2017). This is discussed later in the timeline section and the comparative section as a slowing down of the Korean Wave between 2013 and 2017, where any potential for earlier 'simultaneous successes' in the Korean Wave literally stopped in the first year that President Park was inaugurated in 2013 and returned immediately in 2018, the year after Park was impeached in 2017. Thus, the first simultaneous successes in the global Korean Wave took off tremendously only from 2018 despite intermittent global level singular successes before that date in 2003 and 2012.

The Korean government declared the era of Hallyu 3.0 by calling it either the 'K-Culture Project' or 'Han Style,' with the aim of expanding the Korean wave to other sectors that were earlier led only by TV dramas (the 1.0 era) or by K-pop (the 2.0 era) (Jeon et al., 2012). In this typology, Hallyu 3.0 is interpreted here to spread rapidly around the world only with the increasing diffusion of ever cheaper Internet and smartphone devices. This gave rise to an innately mobile, social-media-based, and viral kind of media regime for the first time around the era of Hallyu 3.0. The first example of this synergy of Korean Wave content combining with technology of a globally-distributed smartphone culture was Psy's 'Gangnam Style' viral video hit in 2012. Psy's video for "Gangnam Style" became the first YouTube video in world history to garner 1 billion views. This was an unexpected success from a 'black sheep' of the domestic K-pop field without state sponsorship. It showed the power of the Internet and mobile networks as a growing rerouted distribution channel of the Korean Wave in Hallyu 3.0 that was starting to transcend or even veto the ability of the Korean state's preferential treatment and/or blacklisting of stars and themes in 'its' Korean Wave. Thus the Korean Wave, from 2012 with Psy and from 2013 with BTS, was the first time K-pop idols themselves started to have an autonomous way to communicate with the world via a global digital telecommunications architecture and its global platforms without relying on Korean government approval as much or the priming from appearances on centralized one-way broadcast media as much. This two-way and peer-to-peer decentralized digital media regime change by 2012 showed itself as more powerful than the past one-way mass media priming and funding of the Korean state and Korean corporate sponsorship. From 2013, BTS started in the midst of this media regime change, managed from a small music label named Big Hit Entertainment and using only the route of online popularization entirely, following up Psy's strategies.

In addition, Korean drama still played a significant role in the global spread of Korean popular culture in Hallyu 3.0. For example, the drama "My Love from the Star" (2014) gained popularity not only in Korea but throughout Asia. It rekindled the drama craze in the Korean Wave. In particular, in China, this Korean drama was referred to as Xingni (Chinese meaning, 'my love from the star'), and it caused a huge sensation. Within this drama, many different Korean culinary items were used as other 'placed advertizing' in the show. As the show gained great popularity, as expected, Korean food equally gained great popularity like the Korean love of "chimaek" (Korean abbreviated slang for "*chi*cken" and beer ("*maek*chu")) that was eaten by the female protagonist in the drama. Other placed advertisements in this Korean drama for export were the various props worn and used by actors in the drama like certain Korean publications, Korean fashion items, and Korean beauty products. The craze around the show built the regional popularity of the Korean love of 'chimaek' across all of East Asia. This food combination started to spread in restaurants founded in Hong Kong, China, and Taiwan to capitalize on the sudden popularity of Korean 'chimaek.' The wider craze of 'food Hallyu' arose from this point. Korean restaurants started to appear in other East Asian countries for the first time—even without a Korean diaspora of any scale to service them in many countries of the world, something typically associated with the past spread of 'foreign ethnic restaurants'. However, it was a digital diaspora instead: the popularity of a Korean TV drama got there first overseas, and started to make a desire to see 'surrogate Koreatowns' and their Korean food as accessible locations across all of East Asia. In this way the Korean Wave started to consume more areas of foreigners' lives beyond entertainment at this point.

Psy's 'Gangnam Style' and the K-dramas in the era of Hallyu 3.0 evoked different responses than in the earlier eras of Hallyu 1.0 and 2.0. In Hallyu 3.0, for instance, Psy's virally popular video for 'Gangnam Style' in 2012 increased interest in the Korean language for the first time, globally. From this point, people around the world started to learn his Korean lyrics directly rather than trying to translate the song into a foreign language. In this way, a lot of people became curious to know what they were singing. In addition, it caused curiosity about the Gangnam district in metropolitan Seoul. The term 'Gangnam' literally means in Korean "South ('*nam*' of the (Han) River ('*gang*'), i.e., in Korean, directly meaning "River South." The Gangnam district of Seoul was once an empty agricultural area with marshes and mountains across the river to the south. This area was outside of Seoul's walls which encompassed only the capital city north of the river historically. However, in the 1970s through the 1990s, bridges started to be built in the dozens to link the city of Seoul on the north bank to the open agricultural land on the south bank of the river for growth of the city. Gangnam soon was a "New Core" and a "New World" (both names of modern Gangnam department stores, in fact) with the largest conspicuous consumption in Seoul and the most exclusive and highest priced real estate in Seoul, compared to all other parts of older Seoul to the north of the Han River. It is said that the video for "Gangnam Style" in 2012 had a great impact on international tourism to Seoul since after 2012 many foreign tourists now wanted to see hypermodern Gangnam and shop there when they visited Korea, instead of only see and shop around historic ancient sites of open markets around a few of the old city gates of northern Seoul like near Namdaemun ("South Great Gate") and Seodaemun ("West Great Gate").

In other words, the era of Hallyu 3.0 widened the Korean cultural spread in content and in scope. This was unlike the previous 'eras' in this governmental interpretation of Hallyu. Earlier, Hallyu was tied to more singular success of temporary media phenomena like only one singular TV drama or one singular K-pop star at a time. Now, by Hallyu 3.0, a multi-wave tsunami of Food Hallyu, Fashion Hallyu, Sports Hallyu, Medical Hallyu, Tourism Hallyu, Publication Hallyu, Broadcast Hallyu, Manga, Animation, Character Hallyu, and IT Electronics Hallyu showed the Korean Wave encompassed almost all Korean cultural industries and began to be associated with basic Korean material production industries like food and electronics as well. Hallyu thus became diversified, synergistic, overlapping, and complex. In addition, as different kinds of Hallyu product waves spread together worldwide, Korea's economic profit expanded as well.

Because of this, the next Moon Jae-in Administration (2017–2022) also tried to prime the spread of Hallyu globally even further than the earlier Lee administration from 2012. In 2020, its 'New Hallyu Promotion Policy Working Implementation Plan' was established. The year 2020 was heralded as some kind of (artificial) inflection point for a 'new Hallyu (K-Culture)', interpreted as a fourth stage of Hallyu. This 'New Hallyu' aimed to discover and harvest more Hallyu contents from the wider Korean culture, and it tried to strengthen their linkages with related industries such as consumer goods and services. By 2020, the Ministry of Culture, Sports and Tourism officially announced the term 'K-Culture' would be its recommended English phrase for the 'New Hallyu.' A related international promotional brand was recommended by the government under the 'New Hallyu Promotion Policy.' Therefore, this term 'New Hallyu' or Hallyu 4.0 refers more to the latest round of promotion policies in the Korean Wave instead of some background 'organic' and autonomous Korean Wave, if that ever even existed in the first place. The Moon Administration was signaling that it wanted various Korean industries to go around the world in league with each other, in the synergistic plural, instead of seeing Hallyu 4.0 as just being a history of the Korean Wave. Plus, beyond the state priming, this 'New Hallyu' or Hallyu 4.0 is characterized more by voluntary spread of a digital fandom beyond the organizational acts of major government agencies, for-profit corporate businessmen (entertainment agencies), or Korean cultural disseminators like media companies and broadcasting stations. YouTube, which has the most expandability among internet platforms, was the first to highlight and prime K-pop idol stars since it was the 'main media' in this global music market.

With the development of youth cultures of wider saturated digital technology in many billions of mobile phones worldwide, there have come changes in the myriad paths for the global networking of the Korean Wave. Thus, K-pop represented by idol stars could be consumed digitally in real time anywhere in the world, and could be reproduced, forwarded, shared, bought, or downloaded at the same time. As a result, the fan base of the New Hallyu or Hallyu 4.0 rapidly increased to younger teenagers in their teens and twenties who are more natively familiar with a mobile digital environment. In fact, before social media spread to the public starting in the first decade of the twenty-first century, for an idol group to officially debut as a popular singer, they had no choice but to use older one-way mass media broadcasters such as TV and radio. Gradually however, through social media such as YouTube, many K-pop stars and their digital fandoms from all over the world can easily meet in a virtual space without the expense of a one-way, centralized, mass market campaign. The manager of the Korean boy group BTS chose such a digital viral strategy for popularizing BTS from the start in 2013, eschewing the mass media entirely and encouraging digital fans to view BTS as a 'daily reality TV show' that they could watch and even interact with daily if they wanted as they watched the group practice and interact via content posted the group's own personal video channels, instead of the group only publishing polished commercial videos and songs online. As such, with the advent of the smartphone and other digital media, the popularity of the Korean Wave could spread to the world in this more digital and viral way much more cheaply. From this point, the Korean Wave began to have its *primary medium* as the world's many billions of smartphones as a mobile multi-media technology. Korean content was now globally distributed easily on demand anywhere in the world more cheaply.

As such, once cheaply and digitally distributed, the intangible culture of the Korean Wave created huge global economic power and raised the image of Korea and the image of other Korean tangible products as well. This created a positive effect on Korean 'soft power' and its 'national branding.' National branding can be defined as the level of trustworthiness of any nation based on the world's media stereotypes about any of its products in global markets. National branding is close to the meaning of a country's 'soft power,' meaning a cultural power that moves hearts and minds to sympathy with a country's goals instead of a country relying on coercion ('hard power') to achieve their goals. There are at least three ways to interpret the Korean Wave's soft power and national branding: in one sense it is historically added 'on top' of the past global Americanization of the world as an update that is unable to be understood without past Americanization; yet in another sense the Korean Wave is its own 'national brand' and 'soft power' in competition with the past 'national brand' of Americanization in the world; and in another sense the Korean Wave is merging with Americanization in one global blurred morass.

This combined re-centering on Korean soft power and yet its blurring with past Americanization is due to the Korean Wave's success being greater in four areas: greater cross-sector national synergy, greater non-military pressure from Korea compared to the USA, greater cross-cultural business collaboration between American and Korean cultural production for the Korean Wave, and due to Korea being more innovative in taking earlier advantage of billions of mobile phone users in our fresh global media regime for primary distribution of the Korean Wave.

4.2 A Timeline How Regional Hallyu Became the Global Korean Wave

This section explores why four periods of the Korean Wave make sense when viewed from the actual history and growing scale of global events in the Korean Wave, instead of letting our views of history be guided only by government documents designed for planning or justifying cultural sectors of future promotion. As said in the introduction, our classification ranges from a "nameless regional Hallyu" into a "regional Hallyu by name," and then into a more "global Korean Wave." This is based on the actual history of events showing four stages of ever larger organic growth over 30 years or more. In this timeline of the Korean Wave, key inflection points are actual events in a sequence showing trends of scale in their more synergistic rise that can show without artificial demarcations how the original East Asian regional 'Hallyu' turned into the global 'Korean Wave'. Though many factors are involved in making the Korean Wave work in practice, if we focus on select product sectors and on particular events, as said above, the history of the Korean Wave first started with its *attempts* in the mid-1980s as the Chun administration intentionally started to produce dubbed TV dramas that were simultaneously both for domestic viewers and potentially foreign East Asian audiences as an export potential (National Public Radio, 2022). These four growing scales in this export expansion are a movement (1) from 'nameless' mere failed attempts at regional Hallyu in the 1980s to 'singular successes' beginning from 1992 to (2) more 'simultaneous successes' by the late 1990s within a named regional Hallyu from 1999. Then, once more on top of those regional 'simultaneous successes' by the late 1990s are more (3) 'singular successes' of a *global* Korean Wave, whether noted from 2003 or 2012. These only become (4) 'simultaneous successes' of a global Korean Wave from 2018 onward influenced by the ending of the secret cultural blacklist in 2017. This framework is illustrated in Fig. 4.1, below.

After a short introduction about the changing images of Korea that the Korean Wave has helped to created in world media about Korea, then each of these four stages of growth from regional Hallyu to the global Korean Wave are detailed with the events that made them.

The Korean Wave brought worldwide curiosity about what has been happening already for a long time from the fast economic development in South Korea, literally since 1961. However, only a few were aware of the long term Korean success at economic aggregation before the Korean Wave brought it to fuller global awareness mostly after 2012 to the present. These modern self-generated images of a very strong South Korean development and its equally strong cultural Korean Wave are in stark contrast to past Western media projections from the 1950s upon the whole Korean Peninsula. From a Western-dominated media view, Korea remained a far periphery, with only a few older stereotypical images available that were increasingly showing a mistaken and un-updated view that provided the wrong view of a static Korea. Therefore, it is unsurprising that the Korean Wave's global images of the early twenty-first century seemed to appear suddenly from nowhere in the mind of the quotidian world. However, in reality, Korea depended on over 50 years of

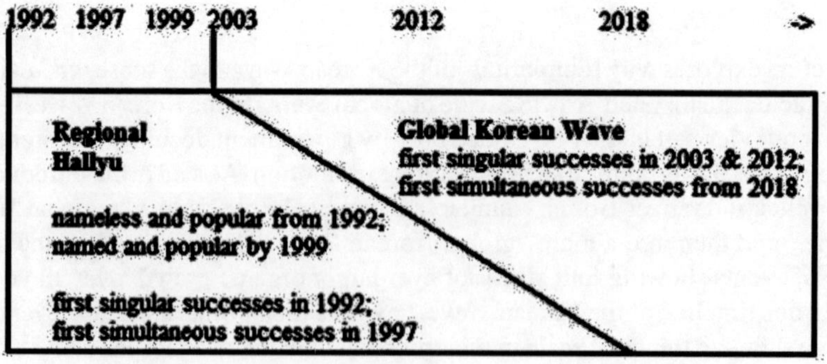

Fig. 4.1 Timeline of important dates as regional Hallyu became the global Korean Wave

economic development to achieve those different dynamic images. For much of this time, South Korea was without a wide 'national brand recognition' of what Koreans had been doing. Their brand for a long time had been what the world had done to them instead. Thus there was a past-harkening and patronizing view trying to interpret South Korea permanently only through filters of a past geopolitical Cold War, past dependent poverty, or its modern cultural derivativeness. Even reviewing images chosen by Korea itself for their hosting of the opening ceremony of the Summer Olympics of 1988 show entirely past-harkening ancient Chinese/Korean-style junks on the waters of the Han River, or old Joseon style synchronized drum presentations. For the global Western media, this meant mostly only reinforcement of dark and past-harkening or backward images existed when thinking of the past or the present in the Korean Peninsula.

Until recently, first, the global media projected only images of North Korea—an impoverished, dystopian, totalitarian, and militarized state of fear, torture, and state mind control via propaganda and surveillance that is a seeming real life fantasy warning straight from George Orwell's *1984*. Second, the global Western media regularly reduced the Korean Peninsula to grainy black and white images of the past tragic Korean War (1950–1953) as a trope for all that happened in Korea in the past 70 years after that war as well. With both major images, it became easy to hide South Korea in these categories of the past as a 'slightly less impoverished North Korea.'

However, these images were blind to the radically different present and the future that South Koreans had built for themselves. The better image to share with the world about South Korea is its economic "Korean Miracle," a successful ongoing economic aggregation and political development after 1961 to the present without stopping. This economic 'miracle' was a name attached to Korea by the 1990s as people puzzled how Korea grew so fast by that decade. However, now Korea has a 'second miracle' in how it *kept growing* while almost all other developing countries generally did stop growing economically at some point and never reached the core industrial potentials they dreamed of in the first place. South Korea at this point of 2023 has probably transcended even its own dreams in the minds of most Koreans or even Korean state planners of the past if they think about how different their country was in its earlier low economic status in the 1960s compared to now.

Until the popularity of the Korean Wave, seldom was Western academic or journalistic interest given to explaining and updating a view of South Korea beyond the tropes about its totalitarian enemy North Korea, the old Korean War, or a 'mystifying economic miracle' in a developing country. However, this book is about the 'second economic miracle' that should equally be explained, the story of Korea's choices to get to be *more* than just a 'fast developing country' though now a core state in the world-system, in the OECD from 1997, that now innovates better than other *core industrial states* instead of only better than other *developing states*. This book is equally about the 'third economic miracle'—the Korean Wave itself as a cultural wave starting to eclipse past Eurocentric global cultural principles themselves that are hundreds of years old in their hegemony. As mentioned earlier, the hybrid policies and hybrid culture of Korea seem paramount in explaining all of this in how these contexts created two virtuous cycles in politics and economics in league with a traditional more homogeneous culture instead of against it. This has led to very durable and very flexible economics and a very high-scale mass production. It has led to quickly technological innovation in applied knowledge. It has led to a hybrid culture that has a strong future economic image and hard-working orientation still *combined with a past-harkening timeless cultural reproduction.* This culture remains a strength. Equally, these two other 'economic miracles' mentioned above have a great deal to do with a fresh digital media regime that Koreans instead of Westerners were able to capitalize on first at a saturated scale (See Appendices 1 and 4). Koreans were living and projecting this hybrid digital future for decades in their strong technological mass production for export markets yet within their intentionally-preserved stable timeless cultural forms without much international attention of how oddly successful this hybrid recipe and its chosen digital recipe of development kept being, compared to other countries. The conundrums of Korea in these second and third economic miracles began to be noticed more widely when this odd hybrid package of a digital futuristic and yet traditionalist cultural mix was seen in the images of the Korean Wave.

Unfortunately, it is common to simply use one or the other term 'Hallyu' or 'Korean Wave' randomly or interchangeably into discussion as a colorful phrase without clear definitions or clear historical analysis. Unlike the typology of earlier phrases of "Hallyu 1.0 through 4.0," instead, this section promotes a more detailed historical view of the events of the Korean Wave and a steady blending from "a regional Hallyu into a more global Korean Wave." This method reveals three sometimes overlapping historical periods. Names are only suggested to demarcate any real lived experience changes in the 'Korean Wave.' First, there was the 'brandless' or nameless period of regional Hallyu from the mid-1980s to before 1999, with a few singularly successful East Asian regional attempts at a cultural wave. So, if the truer history of the Korean cultural wave with its first *attempts* instead of only its later successes or labels, then, *attempts* at Korean cultural exports start in the 1980s. This was a 'nameless' or 'brandless' period of regional Hallyu around Korean TV dramas dubbed in foreign languages. So the term "Hallyu" will be used only for this nameless period into the named period of this *earlier Chinese-centric or East Asian and Southeast Asian regional expression* of the Korean Wave. Second or continuing from this, there was the named period of the same regional 'Hallyu' period starting from 1999—the year "Hallyu" as a term was popularized from a still-debated parentage. This lasts to 2012 or even as late as 2018, as regional Hallyu continues to dominate yet overlaps with the third more global Korean Wave period from at least 2003 to 2017. On the one hand, the official branding of Korean cultural products for export to China were named 'Hallyu' from 1999. 'Hallyu' as a term did start to appear at this point in Taiwan and China. So even though there was period of 'brandless' Korean cultural products from the late 1980s through the early 1990s, it was later given the name of 'Hallyu.' However, this was still only a new regional word in East Asia from around 1999 (Salmon, 2012) giving a name to the growing 'nameless' regional Korean cultural sphere, instead of it only starting from 1999. It was given a Chinese term originally since it was a Korean expansion happening first only across regional East Asia at the time, and since Korea was aiming intentionally for the largest markets from the start, that were in China (Hong, 2014). The other double meaning of 'Hallyu' in Chinese as 'other countries fiercely penetrating' noted critically how China's smaller neighbor of South Korea with less than 50 million people was in the late 1990s having a huge and growing influence on China's larger culture of over 1 billion people despite South Korea having only approximately 5% of China's size demographically. If the concept of "East Asia" historically has been an old metageographic category that represented the geographic idea of the ancient cultural hegemony of China with its culturally peripheral nations like Korea, Japan, Mongolia, Taiwan, and Vietnam, this was additionally the way traditional or modern Chinese saw themselves. Whether past or present, the Chinese geographic ideas viewed themselves as the 'middle civilization' or a central civilization surrounded by a wider world of barbarians. Nowadays however, *a different metageography of regional East Asian penetration by Korean culture, and then global levels of penetration of Korean culture and products* has created a global re-centering. There is a global desire to learn the Korean language. In the United States, this desire is stronger now than the desire to learn Chinese and Japanese. This shows that regional Hallyu and then the global Korean Wave became an object of interest to people around the world instead of only in regional East Asia. The Korean Wave is creating a fresh metageography in world history, meaning a fresh mental map of the world in people's minds. This fresh mental map of South Korea as a geographic center conceptualizes the unexpected hegemony of smaller South Korea and its very oversized global cultural, material, and digital influence upon both larger and smaller countries *worldwide* in orbit around it (Lewis & Wigan, 1997).

The third term or period will be given the name "Korean Wave", and this term will be used only for the later more *global* expansion. Third, this period of the 'global Korean Wave' started with singular successes either judged from 2003 or 2012. The earlier date of 2003 is because the first more global success of the Korean Wave was with the Korean drama *Dae Jang Geum* (*The Jewel in the Palace*) (2003). The latter date of 2012 is another singular global success yet at a much larger scale in the "year of Psy" and his "Gangnam Style" song and video that popularized K-pop as well as popularized dozens of frenetic images of modern Seoul in his fast-paced video. However, intermittent global singular successes petered out between 2013 and 2017 in an era that will be called the "global Korean Wave desert." Only in 2018 did the Korean Wave truly leave behind its era of wandering in the global desert and become a more global simultaneous success instead of only a regional simultaneous success as before. This globalization of the Korean Wave after 2018 recatalyzed repeatedly from this date beyond a single global star like Psy, and started be known for multiple simultaneous Korean cultural offerings of film, acting, music, and dance groups across the world. So these overlapping two or three categories are how the following history is organized. It is argued that if we end the use of typologies created by Korean governments trying to frame their own current policy intervention and instead try to understand the iterative history of particular iterative events as they really happened, it follows the history of the Korean Wave more accurately.

First, the 'nameless' attempts at regional Hallyu started from the early 1980s, as the Korean state started to centralize Korea's media sphere, that was used for priming official Korean cultural events domestically even while continuing to censor other topics and people as before. This soon was turned into a cultural export *attempt* by the mid-1980s by producing Korean TV dramas that were designed from the start of production to be easily dubbed for other foreign languages (National Public Radio, 2022). Hong Kong cinema pioneered such an idea of fast and cheap film production without originally recording sound that Koreans seemed to use: filming scenes without any microphones or actors' dialogue recorded at first, with actors just using their mouths to make up words or sounds for the camera that was unrecorded. Later, in the editing studio, a voice actor would dub the words of the script while watching the film reel. It is suggested that the success and popularity at this time of the huge production of Hong Kong cinema in the 1980s influenced the attempt to use the same kind of easy and cheaper production ideas for dubbed Korean TV dramas.

The first Korean attempt to make cultural products for foreign audiences was different than the earlier Korean export economy that was entirely about inert materials in economic sectors like clothing textiles, steel, chemicals, shipbuilding, building/infrastructure construction, and automobiles. These continued in parallel to attempts at more cultural exports. Only later would cultural production seem a nice collaboration with the material products of digital telecommunications that were expanding in South Korea in the same decade of the 1980s (Oh & Larson, 2019). Thus, the growing 'nameless' Korean Wave from the start in the mid 1980s was a planned Korean state-coordinated and private-company-coordinated marketing phenomenon of Korean culture and products combined. It was unsuccessful, though Koreans attempting these synergies were already brainstorming how to export Korean culture for profit.

By the early 1990s, a still 'nameless' regional Hallyu had its earliest success when an already popular Korean drama was reshown on foreign television in British Hong Kong in 1992 (Hong, 2014). It was a large cultural product 'break' using a popular Korean TV drama at the time called "What is Love." The Korean drama "tells the story of two middle-class, middle-aged housewives who've been friends since high school, [and it] enjoyed a 50% audience share for its time slot in Korea." However, "[i]n those days, there was no demand for Korean television shows, not even in Asia" (Hong, 2014).

What happened in Hong Kong in 1992 to catalyze this 'nameless' regional Hallyu there reads like an international spy novel. A single broadcast production-quality recording of "What Is Love" in Betamax VCR format was "exported secretly" to Hong Kong in a Korean state diplomatic package in order to avoid it potentially being seized by British customs. A diplomatic pouch was used because "protocols…made it a logistical nightmare to ship broadcast-quality videos between borders" (Hong, 2014). Two Korean state civil servants used diplomatic pouches to send copies of Korean dramas like "What Is Love" surreptitiously between themselves, to get the Korean drama covertly into then-British Hong Kong. "The intention was not personal watching: it was always to seed Korean cultural products abroad to create a larger market....Their mission: to get this show on Hong Kong television by any means necessary" (Hong, 2014).

The sender was Chung Injoon, a Korean civil servant and cultural attaché who was then serving as a visiting fellow at the Korea Culture and Tourism Institute, another Korean governmental organization. The receiver was another Korean civil servant in the Korean embassy in Hong Kong. "Chung told [Hong], "I witnessed the first signs of the Korean Wave." [He] not only witnessed it, but [he] set it in motion" (Hong, 2014). Korean-based Chung and his Korean civil service partners at the Korean embassy in Hong Kong realized that by airing the show on a single network—Hong Kong's ATV—it could reach not just Hong Kong but also neighboring Guangdong Province in mainland China with a combined audience of 50 million. "It was going to be an uphill battle to convince a Hong Kong station to pick up the show. In order to ensure the network would not have an excuse to say no, Chung and the consulate's office *convinced Korean companies in Hong Kong* to buy ad time during the shows and *used Korean government funds* [italics added] to dub it into Cantonese, at no small expense. Their efforts paid off: ATV started airing the show. It became so popular in the region that during the time slots that it aired on Thursday and Saturday evening, "there were no people or cars on the street," according to Chung. Everyone in Hong Kong was at home watching the Korean drama. Furthermore, the series caused a cultural ripple in Hong Kong society, said Chung, introducing more traditional Korean Confucian concepts of spousal roles and inequality. "In those days in Hong Kong, the husband cooked dinner after work. But the show sabotaged this, displaying the father as a superpower. When they watched the show, they saw the wife cooking, which caused kind of a syndrome."...[T]he seeds of an addiction were planted. The show got picked up by mainland China's CCTV. A slew of other Korean dramas followed; their popularity spread throughout Asia Japan, Vietnam, Malaysia, and the Philippines" (Hong, 2014). This 'nameless Hallyu' period of the 1990s already features Korean industrial, consumer, or culinary product placements within the cultural vehicles themselves and in association with paid Korean advertising in commercial breaks.

After the broadcast of "What is Love," interest and curiosity in many other Korean cultural products exploded after 1992, as intended, in both British Hong Kong and in mainland Communist China. In short, the Korean government civil servants plotted and orchestrated the priming of the wider Chinese market for Korean products of all kinds from the start (Hong, 2014). Thus the Korean TV drama "What is Love" started to prime an exclusively East Asian and Southeast Asian cultural mayhem around wider Korean cultural and material products. The mayhem we are accustomed to see today as a more global cultural mayhem was catalyzed by Korean civil servant intrigue. This 'nameless Hallyu' period was originally confined to Hong Kong, Southern China, Vietnam and several Southeast Asian countries like Vietnam, Malaysia, and the Philippines.

There was another inflection point to this growing yet still 'nameless' Hallyu in 1997 into 1998. This is the year of much larger state pressure of and subsidies toward Korean cultural production due to an economic downturn and liquidity crisis in the world and in Korea particularly. Korean cultural exports were expedited from 1998 as one of many different fresh export-led economic sectors instituted during this year.

From this point, there is a dual oddity to the Korean cultural wave. The first oddity is that Korea in 1998, when faced with a similar economic setback as Japan had already experienced in 1990, decided it would be a good idea even more to facilitate the export of its own insular and ancient culture to 'fellow East Asians.' Japan in 1990 had done the inverse: it used in its own economic downturn to retrench and to stop its own budding Japanese cultural wave that was regrouped toward more national priorities. The second oddity is that the much smaller Korean state had already at this point been working for almost fifteen years in calculated state-facilitated cultural exports of some kind, unlike far wealthier and larger Japan. These points are brought up once more in Part III.

So this short sharp shock of economic downturn in 1998 in South Korea led the Korean state to *prioritize* its native cultural industries as a potentially cheaper sector for economic export growth. President Kim Dae-jung (1998–2003) reportedly was fascinated that profits from one American film like *Jurassic Park* (1993) in the world market could make as much profit with far less overhead than the production of a fleet of thousands of Hyundai cars for the same world market (Hong, 2014).

These more generous state subsidies for cultural production after 1998 started to combine with South Korea becoming the world's most thoroughly 'saturated' and digitalized economy by the first decade of the twenty-first century (See Appendices 1 and 4). So, both the Korean culture and the Korean digital technological platforms started to contribute to South Korea turning itself into a 'digital test bed' for how to market and hype digital cultural productions well. It was an era where the major Korean cultural export profit started to become online games. South Korea became at least ten years ahead of the United States in scale of general cultural digitalization, as argued earlier. It was the Korean Wave combined with viral-based mobile phone networks of distributed computing and entertainment that fully spread the Korean Wave digitally throughout South Korea first. As the rest of the world caught up to South Korean levels of digital saturation, the earlier South Korean expertise in digital marketing and production for its own nationally distributed medium gave the South Korean state, companies, and culture greater expertise in marketing Korean cultural productions across the Internet to the world of other countries as they became more digitalized as well. As noted later, South Korea retains and even sharpens this edge into the present, particularly after 2023 as post-lockdown digitalization keeps the global Korean Wave's culture and technology far ahead of the curve compared to global offerings of other countries in both.

In this period, two themes are mentioned. One theme is how Koreans alone turned private computer gaming into a collective innovation and a kind of *computerized digital spectator sports* as a cultural industry, now known as e-sports, in which digital gamers were both online stars and important real world Korean idols seen in public events on stage. These collective gaming events were held online yet were simultaneously held in large venues as international competitions first in Korea. They started to be so popular they were held in Korean stadiums. Korean spectators by the thousands sat, physically watched, and cheered as Korean 'gamer idols' played computer games online together in a virtual world, projected on screens for the stadium audiences, so the audiences could marvel at their digital gamesmanship. Huge prizes could be won by these 'K-gamer idols,' that heightened the competition and professionalism of the sport. From the year 2000 to the present, Korea began the world's first World Cyber Games. It remains an international e-sports competition of countries' best digital game players, competing against each other in online video games. Originally created by Oh Yoonseop, the Korean CEO of International Cyber Marketing, it was financially supported by Samsung. The first event was held between October 7-15, 2000, and was called the "World Cyber Game Challenge." It was sponsored by the Korean Ministry of Culture and Tourism, the Korean Ministry of Information and Communications, and Samsung as well. Seventeen countries competed for Olympic-style gold, silver, and bronze medals. In the first WCG 2000, there were only 174 competitors within 17 countries to find the best national players who came to South Korea to play each other. The prize pool was originally $20,000. Next, on December 5-9, 2001, the World Cyber Games held a larger world event in Seoul, Korea, with a total purse prize of $300,000 to attract global players to Korea. In 2001, now 24 countries participated with fully 430 players in the final tournament in Seoul with an astounding 389,000 players worldwide though participating in the national preliminaries. By 2002, it was held in Korea once more with a prize pool of US $1,300,000. In 2002, approximately 450,000 preliminary players worldwide played to find the 450 final tournament players. Next, the 2003 tournament had a total prize pool of US $2,000,000, and was the first to feature console-based competition as well. This WCG went around the world after starting in Korea. By 2014, the WCG was closed, due to personal differences of members with leadership. However, in 2017, the Samsung trademark was transferred to Korean publisher Smilegate, which revived the WGC by 2019 with its first event in Xi'an, China, held between July 18-21, 2019. The WCG competition in 2020 was held online between the two host sites of Shanghai and Seoul, and gained approximately *650 million viewers worldwide.* Korea nowadays even has special "e-sports stadiums" designed exclusively for the purpose of hosting regularly scheduled personal/online video game competitions. One of these is the venue in Seoul named LoL Park, with "LoL" being the abbreviation for the American multi-player game League of Legends made by Riot Games yet now owned by the Chinese conglomerate Tencent. Seoul in 2023 still is widely known as the "capital city of Esports."

In short, computer games as collective online games and as a digital spectator sports industry in South Korea is something Korea pioneered and dominated, starting it over twenty years ago in the late 1990s. Korea dominated because the digital sport fit well the combined technical and cultural Korean cultural wave by the late 1990s due to huge Korean state investments in faster internet connections per capita than any other nation in the world at the time. First, the speed differential between a fast bandwidth for South Korea versus a slow bandwidth for all other nations of the world (except for a few smaller exceptions easier to rollout in city states of Singapore or Hong Kong) helped this gaming environment. The greater Korean high bandwidth of its Internet began then and continues today (See Appendix 1). Second, Korean esports become more collective an event because Korean youth culture avoided the play of video games upon home consoles under the watchful eye of their parents like the American market. Korean youth preferred to play outside of the home on dedicated personal computer (PC) game sets, among friends. Plus of course the online play was faster at those "PC bangs" (PC gaming rooms) that were the first business locations purchasing high speed bandwidth connections that the Korean government was building throughout the country. Third, Koreans could dominate in this sport at the beginning because of the growing amount of free time and desperation from the late 1990s as Korean unemployment surged and many small business owners and even regular salarymen were decimated after a global financial liquidity crisis in 1996 into 1997. The economy recovered by 1999, yet Koreans did not. Koreans from this time to the present became more behaviorally addicted to living in virtual internet worlds to cope, and Korea during this period as saw itself holding the record for suicides per capita as well in the OECD. Even into the second decade of the twenty-first century, the largest profit sector of the Korean entertainment industry remained video games (See Appendix 1). This of course made Koreans great in video gamesmanship more than other nations who failed to have such a fast internet bandwidth to practice within or the 'free time' to practice, or the desperation to escape their depressing lives and win big, or a collective culture that valued the pleasure of being among peer players sharing the experience together. So, this period of 1998 onward is the sad social background of the origin of the behavioral addictions to video games or the Internet that remain a concern of the Korean government today, yet it is equally a happy social place for others with its own tight culture of competition among peers. When individual addictive desires for escapism merged with the world's fastest internet per capita for a larger country within a very competitive collective culture that enjoys togetherness, it was a recipe for 'gamer heaven' that nonetheless was catalyzed by the real world economic hell and desperation of Korean youth and adults at that time. In other words, one of the secrets to Korean desperation to be a success in the Korean cultural wave in video game competitions was the slow shrinking of the Korean middle class from this same period. More people turned to Internet games, to dance practice, to music practice, to singing practice, and to dreams of lottery-like winnings from any future stardom—to escape increasingly unstable job tenures and low-quality lives as they tried to refocus energies on addictions to excellence instead of ruminations on depression or suicide. Nowadays, professional gamers like "Faker" (Lee Sang-hyeok, born 1996) have estimated annual salaries of around $5 million dollars, earning more than the top professional baseball players in Korea.

Another big event in regional Hallyu happened in 1999 when the first expensive 'blockbuster' film came out of the Korean film industry, trying to move into the world market. The film was named *Shiri* for the world market, and named *Swiri* in South Korea. The name refers to a fish *Coreoleuciscus splendidus* found equally in Korean fresh-water streams commonly across North and South Korea. *Shiri* was the first 'Hollywood-style big-budget film' by the state-assisted Korean film industry in an era when a quickly recovered Korean economy by 1999 started to show once more nearly 10% annual growth.

Once more, the homogeneous culture of Korea preferred to use collective innovation, instead of more individualistic or cultural innovation. Thus, the film *Shiri* attempted to copy every successful action film theme ever made, and tried to put it in one film. *Shiri* had themes from the popular American action films of the 1980s through the 1990s, to themes from James Bond films, to having it merge with Asian or Hong Kong 'kung fu' action cinema and a strong romantic, nationalistic, and patriotic Korean sentimentalism. The drama focused on a star-crossed romance between North and South Korean spy agents combined with wider sleeper cells of spies, assassins, and terrorists from North Korea infiltrating and living in South Korea. If it had any politics, it was toward Korean reunification, like the fish named *Shiri*.

Shiri/Swiri was at the time the biggest budget for a South Korean film, costing approximately US $8.5 million. Connected with the triple production themes mentioned earlier of tight links between public state, private profit, and Korean culture, the Korean industrial and electronics conglomerate Samsung even financed part of the film—just as Samsung would help subsidize the first Korean e-sports competition in the next year of 2000. *Shiri/Swiri* was both a critical and financial success, breaking South Korean box office records. *Shiri/Swiri* was seen in South Korean cinemas by more than 6.5 million people, beating for the first time records held by only American produced films like *Titanic* that received 4.3 million tickets. Additionally, it was very popular in the now Chinese-jurisdiction of Hong Kong, similar to how the earlier Korean TV drama "What is Love" was very popular in Hong Kong from 1992 onward. Plus, *Shiri/Swiri* was so popular a recipe of success that it became Korea's first formulaic media franchise. The movie's story continued ten years later in 2009 in the Korean TV series *Iris*, equally popular in South Korea.

Maturing and expanding by the early 2000s, this regional Hallyu grew beyond the singular success of TV dramas into the simultaneous successes of many different regional Korean exports. Korea started to learn how to sell itself in a calculated synergy of selling whole economic sectors linked to each other, instead of just betting on singular cultural events to win profit. In turn, regional Hallyu soon became an accepted common 'brand' for many different earlier Korean products that previously suffered (or even benefited) from a lack of Korean company brand recognition. This was still an era in which Samsung was more unknown as a brand, making very bad electric fans for instance (Hong, 2014). This was far earlier than its push into global digital electronics and semiconductors. So by the 2000s, Hallyu came to associate symbolically many general images of Korean optimism, wealth, happiness, cultural polish, beauty, and technological futurism to many previously non-evocative inert Korean products. A positive symbolism of Hallyu after 1999 began to displace older tragic and pessimistic images of South Korea's poverty from the era of the Korean War (1950–1953) or products from the 1980s onward. This modern image of Korea started to be a commercial mix of TV dramas, blockbuster movies, the growing popularity of K-pop music, Korean esports, and Korean material products as the same phenomena.

The next important major event in regional Hallyu that had an equally large amount of ancillary Korean 'product placements' and Korean 'place branding' in it was the Japanese popularity of the Korean soap opera called *Winter Sonata*, produced in 2002. It represented these multiple levels of Korean product placement very well. It was partially filmed in modern Seoul and in Namiseom (Nami Island) in the remote, snowy, and mountainous Korean northwest in Gangwon Province. *Winter Sonata* created Hallyu's first 'pan-Asian' international Korean sex symbol and heartthrob, the Korean actor Bae Yong-joon. After *Winter Sonata*, Bae could command up to US $5 million per film, making him the highest paid actor in South Korea at the time even though that high paying rate is much eclipsed now by the larger Korean Wave of today (Salmon, 2012).

If much of earlier regional Hallyu gained popularity first in Chinese zones, *Winter Sonata* pivoted to the east and was the first 'Korean cultural invasion of Japan.' It was an authentic and welcomed love affair by millions of Japanese female fans for Bae, particularly middle-aged housewives. Bae in Japan was commonly referred to with the Japanese honorific "Yonsama" ("Prince Yong", after the actor's first name).

Similar to *Shiri/Swiri* in 1999, the narrative of *Winter Sonata* was formulaic. In this case it was a typical Korean "'no-sex-please, this-is-pure-love' romance that plays out to the tune of syrupy ballads and features only drop-dead gorgeous actors and dreamy locations, [and] romantic fantasy" (Salmon, 2012). Winter Sonata was so popular in Japan that the whole soap opera series was repeated twice on Japanese TV broadcaster NHK in 2002. For the first time, a Korean had become a sex symbol in Japan.

Plus, Japanese tourists started to pour into South Korea for the first time en masse. Extra flights were reportedly scheduled. Korean tour companies profited by arranging package deals to bring Japanese tourists to the Korean filming locations and, of course, to shop at select Korean stores that had hired stars from *Winter Sonata* so the popular soap opera would be associated with their outlets and brands.

As Japanese tourists flowed into South Korea, Koreans started to be accepted readily in Japanese culture for the first time as openly Korean. Reportedly, crowds surged so strongly to see Bae at one Japanese airport that fans were injured, yet Bae "sportingly paid their medical costs" (Salmon, 2012). Bae was a regular host on Japanese television—the first time a Korean was ever featured so much in Japanese media. Bae himself was asked to "endorse products, open restaurants, [and] pen books" (Salmon, 2012). In the fresh and historically odd common regional fellow feeling, both Japanese and Korean politicians started to mention Bae in their speeches as a sign of goodwill, as well as trying to associate Bae and regional Hallyu with perhaps their less popular personas.

Winter Sonata was the first wide regional popularity outside of China for a Korean soap opera, so it was attempted to be copied by future formulaic Korean melodramas. The next large hit in this genre would be 2003's *Dae Jang Geum* (literally in Korean, "Great Jang Geum"; English title: "The Jewel in the Palace"). Eventually, *Dae Jang Geum* was so successful it was broadcast in 91 countries worldwide. It was a historical costume drama about the female court physician Seo Jang Geum (family name Seo), who was originally a "Uinyeo," a female commoner maidservant trained to be an attending female physician of the court. Seo Jang Geum, despite being female and despite being of the commoner/cheonmin class, became the first female Royal Physician in Korean history. According to the Annals of the Joseon Dynasty, King Jungjong (1488–1544; r., 1506–1544) recognized Jang Geum's medical knowledge and uniquely gave her the right to use the title "Dae" (in Korean, meaning "great"), and he entrusted her to care for all royal family members instead of only the female side of the court as expected of a Uinyeo. King Jungjong promoted Dae

Jang Geum to become the third highest-ranking officer in the Court as well. Since Jang Geum was reputed to treat sickness with Korean cuisine, this drama's storyline could feature ancient Korean clothing styles, modern Korean cosmetics, Korea architectural fantasy, and traditional Korean cuisine as multiple product placements since the storyline followed a Joseon-era royal medical doctor who doubled as a chef. As mentioned earlier, you can call this a blur of regional Hallyu and the first singular success of the global Korean Wave. It was so popular that it was aired in places as far distant from each other as Iran and East Asia (Hong, 2014). It was so popular that a whole Korean historical theme park developed because tourists wanted to see the Korean buildings of the film set of *Dae Jang Geum* to bask in the show's beautiful Korean historical ambiance.

Back to the simultaneous success story of Bae and *Winter Sonata*, Bae was a professional actor before appearing in *Winter Sonata*. He hated to be typecast. So, after 2002, Bae repeatedly tried to break the formulaic and typecast mold that Japanese popularity in *Winter Sonata* had placed on himself like a yoke. In 2003, Bae next appeared in another Joseon-era historical costume drama similar to *Dae Jang Geum*. It was another formulaic attempt to make a Korean version of the very popular American Hollywood historical film called *Dangerous Liaisons* (1988), though now in the Korean historical version it was entitled "Untold Scandal." However, in attempting to escape being typecast, Bae only shocked his fan base instead of impressed them by his acting flexibility. In "Untold Scandal," Bae played a parasitical, lecherous, and seductive aristocrat—a very different part than the "romantic gentleman" and professional architect of *Winter Sonata*.

However, after experimenting with other parts for a few years, Bae resignedly returned to being typecast, adored, and well paid in the movie "*April Snow*" (2005). This was another formulaic "Sonata"-style love story that set box office records for a Korean film in Japan. By 2006, Bae had become one of the wealthiest Korean celebrities yet, by his part ownership in a talent/management agency called KeyEast. By 2015, Bae was estimated to be worth \$128 million. After *April Snow*, Bae continued starring in other Korean historical costume dramas like the Korean TV epic *The Legend* (2007) where Bae played King Gwanggaeto the Great of Goguryo. However, Bae would soon quit acting altogether in the next year, though did continue as an unseen voice actor in Japan for the *Winter Sonata Anime* (2009) and then between 2009 and 2010 he was the star of a Japanese Nintendo 'edutainment' game series for "Learning Korean with Bae Yong-Joon." However, the killing of his visual acting career had a great deal to do with trying to kill his undesired popularity that haunted him wherever he went.

Given this massive and enduring fame after 2002, Bae is perhaps the first Korean to have to worry about being *so inescapably popular* because of the Korean cultural wave. He increasingly rejected acting because of this popularity. He became someone in the background with his management agency KeyEast as well as his dabbling in health restaurant ownership. This stress of fame is a common problem for Korean idols today, though Bae seems the first modern Korean to feel such fame horribly. Bae openly admitted to reporters he felt a personal crisis in his fame since it blocked his normal life and made it impossible for him to move anonymously around Korea.

He was followed by throngs of crowds everywhere he went, making media stories just by existing. In response, Bae chose to not exist as much as possible—to become partially an urban hermit to get peace. He restricted his activities and events in public. He rarely went out of his house except to an office to work or to a gym to exercise. Bae retired from acting after 2007 to try to cope with (or kill) his fame. He was said always to have a violent temper in real life, and enjoyed practicing violent martial arts like kendo (battles with sticks). His temper was said to become worse by being typecast after 2002 in kindly and romantic roles that he found hard to live up to as an image in real life. One of his similarly popular co-stars from *Winter Sonata* did commit suicide in 2010, though Bae survived Hallyu by retiring from acting and choosing another kind of life to escape fame. He banned all media from his wedding to K-Pop idol/actress Park Soo-jin in 2015 as well.

However, these frenetic fads of regional Hallyu in the first decade of the twenty-first century were still opaque though to most of the world outside East Asia. Korean artist Gwon Osang remembers his solo exhibition at Manchester Art Gallery in 2008, in the U.K. He said he was "seen mainly as an Asian artist rather than a Korean artist... " At the time, nobody knew about K-pop and K-culture at all," he says. "However these days [by 2022], people in western culture have started to separate out Asian countries" (Cha et al., 2022).

The year 2009 was another important inflection point for regional Hallyu, because the Korean cultural wave at this point was so strong regionally that it could start to be a simulacrum of itself, i.e., start to carry itself alone on its own previous regional popularity instead of chase random popularity by being formulaic or derivative of whatever American movies were doing at the time, one after another. For instance, the Korean TV series *Iris* was a Korean action and spy drama that relied on a continuing story and characters already featured in the blockbuster film of *Shiri/Swiri* (1999), revived a decade later for Korean TV. The first scenes of *Iris* were filmed in northern Japan, in Akita, in March 2009. The Korean main actor Lee Byung-hun's popularity in Japan (and continuing popularity as he would a decade later be an actor in the Korean Netflix film *Squid Game*) caused problems of production in Japan. Lee's travels and filming was shadowed by fans, like when many thousands of Japanese greeted him upon his arrival at Akita Airport. Next, even Koreans started to flock to Akita on organized tours during filming, an accelerated inverse of what happened when Japanese tourists descended upon South Korean filming locations due to the success of Korean soap opera *Winter Sonata* (2002). At least Japanese tourists waited until after filming was done. Koreans started to fly to Japan to visit during the filming of *Iris* as it happened in select areas of Akita. Filming in Akita only lasted three weeks however.

Another trajectory change of Hallyu in the production of *Iris* was that it was the next unprecedently large film budget and combined many international locations instead of only Korean locations. As a result of a much bigger budget, *Iris* had long and large scale action sequences, and it was filmed in many beautiful locations worldwide. Plus, actors often did their own stunts and dangerous action sequences, like when Lee Byung-hun himself had to jump from a 130 m-tall dam in Akita. After several weeks of filming in Japan, *Iris* moved to Hungary and filmed in Budapest.

As another important marker of Hallyu success, Hallyu was judged for the first time more important than the economy of Seoul. *Iris* was the first time that the Seoul Metropolitan Government agreed to close any part of the central city for a mere filming event. So, *Iris* held hostage the city of Seoul, and even held hostage the whole national economy of Korea, in order to have a nice urban soundstage. This shows a growing political pull to the Korean Wave. In November 2009, for a full 12 hours, five lanes of roads in one of the world's busiest central city zones of Seoul around Gwanghwamun Plaza on Sejong-ro was closed to traffic and to pedestrians, in order merely to film a complicated gunfight scene. It was a Korean Wave 'place branding' as well, since the Seoul city government hoped the filming of *Iris* would bring more international tourism to Seoul. Within a decade, even American Hollywood would be requesting to hire and to close Seoul temporarily. Seoul was the soundstage for the Avengers/Captain America franchise film *Age of Ultron* (2015), making Seoul's spiraling exits of Han River bridges and its tangerine-orange taxis famous in film.

Starting in 2009, despite the ongoing strong regionality of Hallyu, other trends showed the slowly growing global Korean Wave. From 2009, for instance, U.S. college enrollment in Korean language courses started to rise, growing 78% between 2009 to 2016, to reach 15,000 annually by that later year. In the past, U.S. regional studies departments in East Asian Studies and their language programs were only focused on Mandarin Chinese and Japanese, so a growing desire to learn Korean was historically very odd. It was the pull of a growing global Korean Wave upon non-Koreans wanting to learn Korean for the first time. Dr. Victor Cha, a professor of government at Georgetown University, took Korean courses at Georgetown in Washington, D.C., in the 1980s. At that time, he remembers his entire class was only ethnic Korean 'heritage speakers' like himself who wanted to improve their 'missed' Korean fluency beyond their childhood or home Korean experience in the English-dominant culture of the USA. However, after 2009 "[n]ow half or more of Korean language students are made up of non-Korean students who discovered the Korean language through K-pop, he said" (Ahn, 2022).

In 2012, another major trajectory change and even watershed event started to end mere regional Hallyu and to expand a global Korean Wave. This was the optimistic change of views about South Korea that came after the unexpected global viral video of the Korean pop star named "Psy." Psy was outside the Korean cultural wave complex at the time. He only was known as a national cultural phenomenon in South Korea yet of middle-level quirky popularity. His albums generally were adored, yet regularly were banned for sale to the younger categories of youth in Korea by the Korean government, due to 'immoral lyrics'. However, his music video for his song "Gangnam Style" broke all records of global popularity in the Korean Wave to that date. The state-orchestrated Korean Wave suddenly was faced with something it disliked and had always done its best to muffle: a true individualist and cultural innovator. Psy would be so popular globally soon that he would be a government-undesired 'tail that could wag the dog' that changed the direction of the Korean cultural wave forever toward zany irony, clownish or bawdy humor, taboo breaking, and sheer fun. Previously there was mostly one template for mass manufacturing a Korean pop idol: a sexy chiseled marbled statue of pretentious cold aloofness anticipating being worshiped. Thus, Psy's autonomous global popularity started to wreck the vetted, state-approved, and state-coordinated image of the Korean Wave.

In 2012, Psy's "Gangnam Style" was the first song and video release from his sixth album. All Psy's previous albums were only domestic Korean hits, and Psy had been lacking Korean governmental priming overseas as hardly a cultural image that a conservative Korean government wanted to project. Psy's real name is Park Jae-sang. He adopted 'Psy' as a stage name meant to convey "psycho", he related to the BBC soon after his sudden global stardom: "What I thought was, you know, crazy about music, dancing, performance, so that kind of psycho" (BBC, 2012).

Psy's take on South Korea showed a far more boisterous, zany, humorous, satirical, and polished music video than the Korean Wave had produced to date. Psy was lampooning the lifestyle of conspicuous consumption of the top Korean rich zone of Seoul, called "Gangnam", hence "Gangnam Style." It was surprising it was eventually allowed into the state pantheon of the Korean Wave because Psy's more individualistic innovation and even his self-satirical clownish image of South Korea had to be reckoned with for the first time in any future success in the Korean Wave. "Gangnam" (pronounced closer to "Kong Nom", in English) literally means "River South," i.e., city districts South of the Han River. The Han River now flows through the middle of Seoul, yet historically the Han River was the protective boundary moat of the city to its south. Even into the 1970s, Seoul was mostly only a city north of the Han River, and still behind ancient city walls. However, starting in late 1970s, "River South" or Gangnam changed from a poor, oxen-plowed rural farmland into pricy real estate for the newest, wealthiest, and most modern district in the capital city of Seoul. Even the Supreme Court of Korea moved in next decades to Gangnam.

Even earlier than when featured in Psy's video in 2012, Seoul was already *demographically larger than New York City*. Plus, Seoul by 2012 was the *fourth largest metropolitan economy in the world* after Tokyo, New York City, and Los Angeles. Thus, "Gangnam" and "Gangnam Style" in Seoul is likened to the lifestyle and economic power of New York City's Manhattan 'Billionaires Row,' built against Central Park South, where the Trump Tower, internationally known hotels like the Plaza and the Pierre, international banks, Russian caviar restaurants, and American Hollywood stars live in proximity to each other overlooking a long green expanse of Central Park in New York City. To compare, New York's Billionaire's Row at Central Park South and Seoul's Gangnam are both zones of wealthy elites and conspicuous consumption. However, in 2012, everyone in the world had heard of New York, Central Park, and U.S. billionaires. Few people worldwide ever had seen something comparable in South Korea. The incredibly wealthy life and culture polish of "Gangnam Style" was proudly advertized and critically satirized by Psy's music video.

Seeing this image of South Korea's "Gangnam Style" was a shock to the world. Interest in the video, song, Seoul, and South Korea was explosive. Typically the West likes to think it has a monopoly on irony, and yet here in Psy's video was an ironic presentation of Korean success as well. Month by month in 2012, Psy started to break popularity records for the Korean Wave. He frankly soon broke records soon for *any* nation's past cultural wave, worldwide. This video helped widen interest in the Korean Wave as a more global phenomenon outside of regional East Asia in a more durable way by changing stereotypes.

However, Psy was only a singular success in 2012 despite his massive success in making a more global Korean Wave. By August 2012, "Gangnam Style" was #1 on the *global* iTunes Music Video Charts, displacing both American acts of Justin Bieber and Katy Perry—another first for a Korean artist. By September 2012, Psy was in New York City, appearing on NBC News TV to perform the song and its humorous clownish 'horse riding' dance to throngs of New Yorkers. Reviewing this NBC News segment, it is clear how happy yet uncomfortably confused and shocked the American TV hosts are by being upstaged by foreign acts on the streets of New York City. They seem unsure of how to coordinate being an American host to Psy who clearly was upstaging them with his unabashed Korean patriotism and energetic and even crazed appearance on their network. NBC producers seem to have given up on an earlier script where they tried to be the host. They just relented and let Psy take over as host. NBC let Psy perform the same song "Gangnam Style" *twice* on live television within a matter of 10 minutes. Psy taught his American TV hosts to act as happy trained seals as he taught them the 'horse riding dance.' By the next month of October 2012, Psy was hosted in New York at the United Nations, and he was appointed as goodwill ambassador of the United Nations Children's Fund (UNICEF). This is the theme seen from before around *Winter Sonata* where all manner of canny politicians try to insinuate themselves symbolically into the Korean Wave to try to make their organizations more popular. By November 2012, Psy was in England, giving a speech to the Oxford Union, where he said he interpreted his viral success as helped by going to his roots of trying to make an audience participate and laugh, as well as helped by digital 'retweets' and 'reblogging' by many already famous global American stars sending the video of Psy (that he posted at YouTube on July 15, 2012) to their own millions of followers.

This was the first example of the true great potential of digital virality in the global Korean Wave, in contrast to past one-way mass media campaigns. By December 2012, the video for "Gangnam Style" became the first YouTube video to reach 1 billion views—displacing Justin Bieber once more. By 2014, the video for "Gangnam Style" was so popular that it broke the counter at YouTube that started to display negative numbers. YouTube's computer programmers never thought a single video would ever reach over 2.14 billion views, so they had to update the whole platform to allow more views simply because Psy broke the algorithm first. In June 2023, the video now has 4.83 billion views.

Psy was given an award by the Korean Government for his services to the Korean Wave. He previously was considered an undesired 'black sheep' in the collective family of Korean (family) entertainments by upstanding 'moral artists.' Psy admitted to the Oxford Union that he was an odd Korean star because he was not very "moral." Thus Psy moved from having an intentional lack of state support or even block on youth sales in the Korean Wave, into being its perfumed clown prince. Psy's individualistic innovation and public past problems with addiction and drugs worked against the moral image attempted to be fostered for Korean entertainments worldwide to be a collective, highly-managed, clean, neutral, 'family image' inculcated by the Korean government's lead and Korean cultural production companies that followed. That collective image still mattered, yet Psy's outsized success warped the whole Korean Wave. He was officially 'back-integrated' in the Korean Wave's pantheon despite not fitting the Korean state's past highly 'regulated' moral behavior or normal beautiful visuals of state-supported K-pop idols that are predictable, boring, formulaic, cookie-cutter Adonis-or-Venus-style personas. However, instead of a plastic-surgery-enhanced Korean Adonis or Aphrodite, Psy as he would be the first to admit in 2012, was a chubby, goofy, middle aged man. At the time, he made a self-depreciating joke that if he got really popular overseas he would celebrate by holding a free concert in Seoul and perform shirtless to poke fun at himself as well as to shock or to mock Koreans' aesthetic sense even more, which he subsequently did. Psy since then has lost some weight yet his quirky individual innovations and cultural innovations, to his credit in Korea and internationally, show Psy fails to fit a teamwork-based collective innovation for success. The latter was the normal (only) way the Korean Wave was programmed to work, which makes success visible only as a team or as a national success instead of even requiring an individual's success at all. There was a lot of collective innovation and work to make the video and design its choreographed 'horse dance,' he has remarked, though the individualized comical package around Psy was uniquely at odds with the past Korean Wave.

A theme throughout this book is the conflict between different kinds of innovation inherently because of Korea's more homogeneous culture or how the Korean Wave is hampered financially as much as helped by the formulaic and bureaucratic state or corporate direction in subsidies and in star-making power. Koreans are very good at collective innovation and teamwork. This was earlier interpreted to be one of the unique cultural keys that unlocked the economic Korean Miracle from the 1960s onward and now keeps unlocking innovation into the later cultural Korean Wave. Other countries with more cultural divisions could learn from this, for how a clear collective ethos or group drive seems very important in starting and in keeping a singular economic aggregation in national development. It is clearly so in the history of the economic Korean Miracle and the cultural Korean Wave. However, equally there are costs to an exclusive collective innovation with a state-approved singular track. These costs are because Koreans in their more homogeneous culture try to avoid economic or social risks of individual innovation or cultural innovation per se, and the state coordination compounds it. This is both a modern economic strategy and a deep cultural principle, formed from an ethnic homogeneity for over 1,300 years that is rarely matched in the world, combined later with how a Confucian culture operates only by rote learning, adherence to respectable older forms, and age hierarchies inculcated into Koreans for over 600 years.

Thus in the Korean context, first, collective innovation is a deep-set *internal* principle in those two ways via a homogeneous ethnic culture and an added stable Confucian cultural form that self-reinforces each other. Second, it is a safer economic strategy as well for a fast developing country to copy other developed countries' successful global products in (to coin a phrase) Korea's "export substitution" economy. This means collective innovation has been supercharged in South Korea in the choice of an export-led economy as an *external* principle of cultural and economic extension as the basis of the success of modern South Korea since 1961. This collective innovation and an economic focus on export-led development leads South Koreans to compete only in already-established and derivative markets to please an existing world at the largest scales possible, instead of trying to change the world with nationalistic, military, individualistic, or cultural innovations. Thus, South Korea culturally is very good in projects of selling what others already globally desire a little bit better and cheaper in steel, smartphones, washing machines, computer hardware, or popular entertainment—while calling on Koreans' duty to the national interest to extend that internationally, for the good of all Koreans instead of only the interest of some particular individual's wealth or the interest of a singular company. Externally, this supercharged Korean collective innovation tries to do something established, conservative, and derivative just a little bit better than everyone else worldwide instead of aiming to break the mold entirely by pioneering fresh markets by individual innovation or cultural innovation—like by Psy, for instance.

Therefore, Psy's individualistic innovations in music and in a more participation-based performance with an audience failed to fit the mold of the deeper collective innovation and state-administered practice of minting the same kind of repeated K-pop idols from the same mold pushed on the world year after year, ad nauseum. For instance, after the "year of Psy" in 2012 with his non-state approved global breakthrough in the Korean Wave, Park Geun-hye became Korean President in 2013. She was impeached in 2017. During this period of 2013 to 2017, it was revealed by 2017 that from 2013 she immediately started elaborating a "secret cultural and arts blacklist" blocking state aid to select Korean creatives in the Korean Wave on her Presidential order, if they annoyed her or opposed her policies. Her team supplied thousands of secretly blacklisted names, and they delivered the list to the official subsidizer of the Korean Wave in the Ministry of Culture, Sports and Tourism.

One version of this list with the date of May 2015 revealed already "[a]lmost 10,000 artists (9,473) were banned under Park in the mid 2010s" (Steger, 2018). The 2015 document, revealed to the Korean public in late 2016, showed the Park Administration assembled a secret cultural blacklist of thousands Korean artists banned from receiving state support in the Korean Wave—and banned from knowing they were banned. "The exposed version of the blacklist dated May 2015 was just months before the start of a year-long cultural exchange program between Korea and France….[T]he [Park] government had ordered certain artists to be excluded from being featured in the project, for example Han Kang…author of [the] 2016 Man Booker International Prize winner *The Vegetarian*" (Steger, 2018). "This suspicion [about a secret cultural blacklist in the Korean Wave] was specifically confirmed through the contents of a complaint indicted by a special prosecutor Park Young-soo, who investigated the case of Gukjeong Nongdan, indicting former secretary chief Kim." Park's chief secretary Kim had been instructing others to take "penal measures for cultural artists who had political tendencies against the regime or had a history of expressing such political expressions," and it was claimed that Kim "established a database to exclude support."

The Park Administration's secret cultural blacklist was managed secretly by the Ministry of Culture, Sports and Tourism. Park's administration "collected and retained information on political propensities such as whether cultural artists participated in the declaration of support for specific politicians, and whether or not they participated in the declaration calling for the abolition of the Enforcement Decree of the Sewol ferry" (Aju News Desk, 2020). The tragedy of the Korean ferry *MV Sewol* (English meaning/translation, "Beyond the World") was a ship that capsized and sank in April 2014. As many as 306 passengers and crew drowned and died, many trapped in the overturned ship alive and in mobile-phone communication with the outside world as they sank and slowly drowned over many hours. The main group of dead was hundreds of Incheon teenage high school students and their teachers taking a school-based field trip from Incheon to Jeju via the ferry *MV Sewol.* Instead of arriving in sunny Jeju, nearly all died at sea after the ferry capsized due to a combination of poor management policy of the ferry company, bad piloting, and compounded by even worse management of governmental rescue response from the Park Administration. Park was presumably getting her hair done and/or taking placenta injections to remove facial wrinkles in the Presidential palace between 1 to 3 p.m. with two army nurses found to be on staff that day, and presumably Park did not want to be disturbed or they were afraid to disturb her. "[C]hief of Cheong Wa Dae's [Presidential palace's] medical office conceded that he prescribed such shots for the President, during a National Assembly investigation…." Plus, the "de-facto owner of the ferry was Yoo Byung-eun,…a cult leader who was believed to have connections with Chung Yoon-hoi, ex-husband of Choi Soon-sil" (Kim & Chung, 2016). Choi Soon-sil was a close friend of Park Geun-hye for decades, was involved in much corruption around the Park administration, and is the daughter of another cult leader Choi Tae-min (died in 1994), who was the leader of a crony religious cult of Yongsaenggyo, or the Church of Eternal Life that combined Buddhism, Christianity, and a native Korean half-shamanist religion named Cheondogyo (or Tonghak) by the 1970s. The elder Choi Tae-min himself had been strongly connected to (later President) Park Geun-hye since her youth in the 1970s (Kim & Chung, 2016). There could be many examples of how this religious cult-like environment around Park Geun-hye and this growing secret cultural blacklist elaborated from 2013 worked to create corruption and a decline of the global Korean Wave through 2017. However, for brevity, what will be discussed are only one cultural act put on the blacklist as early as 2013 and one organization put on the blacklist in 2014. A discussion of other examples of earlier cultural blacklists in Korean culture and their importance is saved for the next comparative section.

For the cultural act, the K-pop boy group called 24K was blacklisted by the Park Administration from 2013 for singing for the losing leftist Presidential opposition candidate Moon Jae-in. "24K had assisted Moon Jae-in by taking part in singing the theme song for his campaign, which was composed by Kim Hyung Suk. They also participated in a performance and appeared in a video for the song. It appears that their participation in the campaign was the reason that five out of the six members of the group at the time and their manager were included on the list." A source from their agency Choeun Entertainment said, "It's true that they were almost unable to appear on certain network shows, maybe because of the blacklist….Perhaps it's because of the blacklist, they were unable to appear on almost any show" (J.K., 2018; Koreaboo, 2018). So, Korean artists were placed on this blacklist and singled out immediately out of spite from 2013. Overall, almost 10,000 Korean artists, producers, and managers were blacklisted, though 24K was the only established K-pop group that had all its members, except one, including its manager, added to the cultural blacklist. The group 24K was successful only in promoting themselves outside of Korea between 2013 and 2018.

For an organizational example showing how the Park administration frustrated the whole priming of Korean Wave, it spitefully withdrew state funding from the entire Pusan Film Festival (abbreviated in Korean as BIFF) after it aired a critical documentary about the ferry *MV Sewol*. "So extensive and damaging was the blacklist [under President Park Geun-hye] that it managed to diminish one of Asia's biggest film festivals for years….Busan mayor and BIFF chairman Suh Byung-soo, a politician close to Park, tried to pull the film from the festival. BIFF later suffered massive cuts to its funding and its then-director was charged with embezzlement, which the festival alleged was politically motivated" (Steger, 2018). Thus, Park's administration hampered and stalled growth of the visual side of the global Korean Wave between 2013 and 2017.

The Korean media and state prosecutors started to find other connections of President Park to a "shady female confidante [Choi Soon-sil] and their involvement in a vast bribery and influence-peddling scheme that implicated many of the country's biggest companies" (Steger, 2018). After long and massive national protests against her on many above issues, on December 9, 2016, President Park was impeached from the Presidency by the National Assembly. Running true to form, Park refused to vacate the Presidency. She appealed to the Korean Constitutional Court that the National Assembly had no right to impeach her, even though it did. Therefore, on March 10, 2017, however, the Constitutional Court voted unanimously with a vote of 8–0 to maintain the legal right of the National Assembly to impeach her on the grounds that it chose. Weeks later, on March 26, 2017, state prosecutors announced they would seek ex-President Park's arrest warrant. The arrest warrant was granted by Seoul Central District Court within a week on March 31, 2017. The same day, Park was arrested. She was later tried and convicted for many crimes. She was originally sentenced to 24 years in prison on 16 charges, "including abuse of power and coercion for planning and ordering the blacklist." Seven of Park's aides were arrested, convicted, and jailed for creating the blacklist as well. About a year later, on March 22, 2018, another previous Korean President Lee Myung-bak (2008–2013) was arrested on claims of bribery, embezzlement, and tax evasion during his Presidency. His stolen funds from state coffers during his Presidency was claimed by later state prosecutors to total 11 billion won and to include moving 35 billion won more to a slush fund. Convicted on October 5, 2018, Lee was sentenced to 15 years in jail. Like ex-President Park, he appealed as well. On October 29, 2020, the Supreme Court of Korea upheld Lee's sentence.

Running true to form, Korea is sadly a land of durable Presidential corruption with many examples of Korean Presidents being jailed. However, equally running true to form, Korea is equally a land with many Presidential pardons. President Moon announced on December 24, 2021, that only ex-President Park would be pardoned and released from jail due to her deteriorating health and for "national unity." Park was released from jail a week later on December 31, 2021. Next year, on December 27, 2022, the next Korean President Yoon Suk-yeol granted ex-President Lee a pardon, ending his potential remaining 15 years of jail. This has become a crony Korean pattern as well. Running true to form, top criminal Korean Presidents or chaebol leadership regularly go free in the interests of a nebulous alibi of "national unity" even as the underlings in the case of President Park that did her bidding on the blacklist remain in jail. The late Samsung Chairman Lee Kun-hee (1942–2020) was convicted twice of corruption and tax evasion, in 1996 and in 2008, and respectively President Kim Young-sam (1993-1998) and then President Lee Myung-bak (2008–2013) both pardoned Lee Kun-hee from jail. Surely national unity is better served by following the law, by keeping them unified in jail? National unity is hardly served by unequal punishments or by creating an overlord criminal class of 'gapjil' pampered Presidential daughters of ex-Presidents, other Presidents, or chaebeol family elite that escape jail after creating nationwide cultural blacklists, large public financial fraud, or interrupting national airline service to rage about macadamia nuts being served in plastic bags. Instead, given so many Korean Presidents being jailed and then pardoned in the modern history of South Korea (Chun Doo-hwan, Lee Myung-bak, and Park Geun-hye), or given repeated recidivist chaebol families, perhaps national unity under the law means Korea should create a Presidential/Chaebol prison wing where convicted Presidents and chaebol families are imprisoned together to ruminate on the unfortunate national unity of their crimes?

In conclusion, however, for better or for worse, let us be less naïve about *this positive way that a politically divided South Korea has held itself and its fast development drive together over decades* via such repeated high level pardons, particularly where the less legitimate Left has repeatedly pardoned the widely-supported conservative Right, instead of leading into civil wars. Equally, let us be less naïve about secret cultural blacklists as only existing under Park Geun-hye as President. South Korea has a long modern history of dictatorships, corruption, and state-based cultural steering and repression. Some claim "Park's" blacklist actually was like a relay race baton, started under the previous President Lee Myung-bak and only passed to President Park Geun-hye, even if it was widely expanded by her (Collman, 2020). Even earlier though, whether under President Park Chung-hee from 1963 to 1979, or accelerating under President Chun from 1980 to 1988, there was a deep state coordination and corporate sponsorship of culture for decades before the rise of Hallyu (Kang, 2019). Plus, in the 1990s with the rise of the regional Hallyu, continuing state cultural direction and priming was behind the first major success in international Korean cultural production in that decade, starting in Hong Kong in 1992 (Hong, 2014). The Korean state has tried to prime every major trajectory change and scale expansion of the Korean cultural wave, despite rare exceptions of talents like Psy that burst on the world scene in 2012. However, even Psy was honored by the Korean state afterward.

Only from 2016 with the exposure of the secret cultural blacklist did Koreans start to see openly how the state sponsorship of culture innately and unavoidably has lighter sides of cultural promotion and darker sides of "network subversion" in this homogeneous culture where 'connectionism' is king (Kim & Whitaker, 2013). The lighter side is that state planning, subsidies, and Korean collective innovation in culture have been crucial in the creation of the export-led economy of the Korean Wave itself. The darker side is that any time you accept political administration of a culture with state money or perks in a 'star-maker machinery,' this can be biased subversively toward cultural friends, against cultural and political enemies, or even against mere neutrals of a reigning government. Subsidies can be turned on or off, promised and denied, as a way of political control of both friends and enemies alike with the same policy. Plus, direction and expression of culture and the arts can be changed by the state by putting in place biased incentive structures around artists or organizations. This innately makes any subsidies into a blacklist even if *merely* administrated fairly on a first come, first serve basis—i.e., even if a formal blacklist fails to exist. However, in this case, a formal cultural blacklist did exist and was exposed by 2016 with the names of nearly ten thousand Korean music artists, writers, producers, mangers, writers, and filmmakers. The scale of this secret cultural blacklist on the Korean arts is breathtaking—even horrifying, in how rapidly it grew to this scale in simply a matter of two years from 2013 to 2015, the date shown on the first copies that were leaked. It certainly hampered the growth of the whole global Korean Wave after Psy in 2012 by blocking thousands of individual acts and talents and by hampering whole organizations tasked with priming the Korean Wave.

It is naïve to assume that such casual power of suppression failed to exist before 2013 on still-undisclosed lists. This is for four rationales: given how subsidies by definition innately have lighter and darker sides of the same policy, given long-term and widespread Korean actions of "network subversion," given proof of people and organizations culturally blacklisted long before 2013 that predated President Park Geun-hye, and given Korea's long-term state orchestration of cultural events increasing from President Chun and all Presidents thereafter interested in aiding the Korean Wave. So, is it naïve to think a blacklist of nearly ten thousand Korean artists was invented suddenly only from 2013 to 2016 when exposed? Perhaps some form of blacklist on the Korean Wave developed long before being exposed by prosecutorial investigations in 2016 of only President Park's administration?

Koreans themselves report being skeptical of the cleanness or transparency of their own government for decades instead of becoming skeptical of it only under President Park Geun-hye. As reported by Transparency International, there has been little change in Korean opinion of their government for decades: Koreans feel their country has not gotten more transparent or less corrupt compared to the 1970s despite greater democratization from 1987 to the present (Kim & Whitaker, 2013). Thus, the issue of "network subversion" is high in South Korea. In short, it is argued that the innately lighter and darker sides of subsidy networks for Korean cultural promotion inseparately existed for decades and were only exposed in 2016 under President Park Geun-hye, impeached by the National Assembly in December of that same year for this secret cultural blacklist and for other crimes.

Second, however there is another rationale why it is hard to simply scapegoat President Park. This is because *years later* (and *not* immediately in 2016 as she was impeached, or *not* in 2017, as she was confirmed impeached) that a cultural blacklist was judged unanimously by the Korean Constitutional Court *as late as 2020* as an unconstitutional abuse of Presidential power. Thus, confusingly, despite President Park being impeached and jailed for this blacklist among other crimes, the idea of a Presidential cultural blacklist remained constitutionally legal in South Korea well into President Moon until 2020 even as Park was put in jail for that crime and others (Stenger, 2018). In the way it was phrased, only in 2020 did the Constitutional Court finally call the very existence of a Presidential cultural blacklist an "arbitrary discrimination" and that "collecting [such blacklist] information was for an unconstitutional order to block support to artists who are critical of the government...[This] was judged...[as] an exercise of public power that could not be permitted under the constitution" (Stenger, 2018).

In conclusion to this important section about cultural blacklists in the Korean Wave, it has been argued that a 'pause' in the nascent global level Korean Wave was created after Psy in 2012, and this pause continued through 2017 until President Park was confirmed impeached. It is not a surprise that the autonomously popular Psy and his video for "Gangnam Style" remade the Korean Wave in the eyes of the world in ways the Korean government may have disliked, in a country with long-term crony financial largesse before Psy, and secret state cultural blacklists immediately after Psy. Nothing of comparable global scale of popularity in Korea was facilitated after Psy in 2012 in the Korean Wave during this period from 2013 to 2017. Even if you are a devil's advocate who believes talent and success is always more random, removing nearly 10,000 Korean cultural creators between 2013 and 2017 hampered even randomness from working properly in the global Korean Wave. Director Bong Joon-ho says that only through rare private funding was he able to make both *Snowpiercer* (2013) and *Okja* (2017) (Collman, 2020).

Next comes the most recent period of "simultaneous successes" in the global Korean Wave, only from 2018 and beyond. From 2018 Korean talent started to spread as a group, and a group of different talents truly became as globally popular as Psy was individually popular in 2012.

The global Korean Wave can be divided into two sections that seem quite similar to an earlier two phases of regional Hallyu, in its full progress of evolution of scale. For instance, earlier, *regional* Hallyu had two phases: a regional first phase of 'singular successes' intermittently raising up Hallyu for a while, until it was replaced with the second phase of more regional 'simultaneous successes' of many different Korean cultural products that only under that condition could synergistically start to have positive feedback on each other and thus keep accelerating the regional Hallyu durably. The same phenomenon of two phases on the *global* level of the Korean Wave is seen as well. Including the drama *Dae Jang Geum* from 2003 and later Psy from 2012, both are examples of this first phase of a more intermittently global 'singular success' in the global Korean Wave. This phase 'lasts' or was artificially extended by cultural blacklists well into 2018. Only from 2018 does this second phase of more "simultaneous successes" of the global Korean Wave start to be seen. This is described below.

A few examples will suffice to show how this second phase of a more 'simultaneous success' from 2018 shows a more group-based, thus synergistic, and thus accelerated climb of the global Korean Wave in playlists and popularity that we still see today in 2023. Only from 2018 did the Korean Wave start to displace many top categories of cultural awards simultaneously and globally.

For instance as late as 2017, a New York musical called KPOP flopped. It was reshown in 2022 to wide acclaim, yet in 2017 no one cared. Originally in 2017, the New York musical KPOP was shown as an "immersive off-Broadway piece." This meant that audiences moved from room to room, watching disconnected scenes of rehearsals, auditions and recording sessions. Later, there was one large space for an audience to watch a simulated K-Pop concert that was part of the musical's scenes as well. So in 2017, the Korean Wave still had yet to "crack" global or American awareness beyond Psy's "Gangnam Style" of 2012 (Lunden, 2022). Further proof that this 'simultaneous success' of the global Korean Wave only started in 2018 is found in the 'big data' of Google's 'Year in Review' website. It summarizes in tables the global searches annually. The topics of North Korean dictators and Samsung products were the only two Korean topics with a large global search interest in 2017. So, in 2017, there was a complete lack of major recorded global interest in the Korean Wave at least measured by top searches on Google. In 2017, the dictator in North Korea, Kim Jong Un, was the second most searched for person in the world. In the same year, North Korea was the fourth largest search in all global news. In the same year of 2017, South Korea's Samsung Galaxy 8 smartphone was the fourth most web search in consumer tech in the world mostly because of an explosive technological disaster with its battery design and production that led to its ban on global airlines and then eventually a complete recall by Samsung in the millions of units. This severe recall was to maintain Samsung's growing global trustworthiness as an electronics brand.

However, in the next year of 2018, this second phase of more simultaneous successes of the global Korean Wave started to happen. This started to change global cultural habits durably as well. For instance, 2018 was the first year that the Korean male dance-and-singing group BTS (founded in 2013) became the first Korean popular music act to hit No.1 on the U.S.'s Billboard 200 albums chart. In that same year of 2018, BTS became the first Korean act to win at the American Music Awards, taking the coveted prize of Favorite Social Artist. In the same year of 2018, Korean films started to gain global acclaim as well. The director Bora Kim's debut *House of Hummingbird* became one of most acclaimed independent Korean films of all time. It went on to win more than 50 film festival awards. The young lead, a Korean female teen named Park Ji-hu, said she was lucky to attend a casting call for this soon critically-acclaimed Korean film. "'Filming that made me want to pursue acting with absolute certainty,' she says....At just 14, this would be her first leading role in a film. Her performance as Eunhee gained her international recognition, including an award for best new actress at the [New York City-based] Tribeca film festival" (Cha et al., 2022). This film is an excellent ethnographic overview of the social, economic, and family stresses and triumphs common to many Korean youth. The Korean director Bora Kim based this film on her previous shorter acclaimed film called *The Recorder Exam*, made while she was a student at New York's Columbia University. That film had won a prize from the Directors Guild of America (Cha et al., 2022).

By the next year of 2019, the Korean group BLACKPINK was added to this simultaneous success. They became the first K-pop girl group to perform at the American multi-weekend concert event called Coachella. It has been held annually every year from 1999 in Indio, California. This was a large scale event that gave huge American exposure for the global Korean Wave since from 2017 Coachella began to gather approximately 250,000 people in attendance for its two-weekend event.

After March 2020, because of growing global governmental lockdowns of live concerts and other entertainment venues in many nations, online digital entertainment that could be viewed from home soared in popularity, globally. The same three factors of the public state, private profit, and Korean culture got into the act in the global Korean Wave for their finest synergistic influence so far.

For the first factor, the Korean state orchestrated into existence an odd legal overlord class for the Korean Wave. The Korean government from 2020 gave a legal preferment to only major participants in the global Korean Wave over other citizens to postpone their military service. It is legally questionable because in 2020 the South Korean parliament made a special law that created two kinds of Korean citizens: normal citizens and K-culture idols. The law says *only K-culture idols*, phrased as those who "excel in popular culture and art", *can defer national military service* until the age of 30. Truly so, the obsessive fight for global cultural recognition and global profit in the Korean Wave began to chip away at Korean national legal equality, chip away at defending the nation, and even chip away at defending a common equal citizenship. So, from 2020, K-pop idols became a special citizen class. K-pop idols (perhaps extended later to film or music video producers?) have been turned into modern 'living cultural treasures' with special subsidies and rights to be kept from physical danger to maintain their cultural transmission. So far, this law of 2020 has only been applied to K-pop idols that are to be saved for global uses in the Korean Wave instead of having nearly two years of their golden youth, good looks, or performance life impaired by a "too early" national military training. Legally, it seems more important to the Korean state to defend the global Korean Wave by preserving K-pop idols' grueling cultural schedule throughout their 20's than to defend equality of the Korean nation. Like a real world *Logan's Run* (1976), once K-pop idols get old at age 30, only then do they serve at a lesser capacity in the military carousel of the nation instead of serve in the higher global Korean Wave and the export-led economy. It is an odd law that implies patriotic Korean males should aim first to be K-pop idols to defend their nation and reap its top rewards, instead of by default defending their nation as brothers in arms against other brothers across the border at the DMZ. Therefore, if a Korean male can become a K-pop idol, he can win military deferments for his whole youth and young adulthood (Seo, 2022).

However, legal preferment and subsidies to Korean cultural creators as the more important citizens hardly began in 2020. It is part of the hybrid developmental model of Korea itself from 1963. There are two older examples of this. First, from 1963 rare and typically older Koreans began to be designated as 'living treasures' given unique state subsidies to help them carry on teaching others their ancient traditional Korean cultural arts, crafts, and design skills. This was in order that beloved ancient Korean arts and crafts would have a balanced continuity in modern Korea instead of be neglected and left to be destroyed by the greater revolutionary policies of the Korean state, its urban-based industrialization drive, and its drive for mass market products at home or abroad. Japan has had a similar policy of its own for 'living treasures' from the 1950s to assure a similar balanced ancient cultural continuity in its modern development stress on reindustrializing after World War II. Second, the top "Korean Wave" subsidy institution of the Ministry of Culture, Sports and Tourism pays generous stipends of 1 million Korean won a month (approximately $1,000) *for life to only gold-medal winning athletes* of the international Olympics. Plus, the top three medal winners are additionally paid a lump sum of 63 million won for gold ($53,800), 35 million won for silver ($28,310), and 25 million won ($20,220) for bronze. However, only Korean gold medalists get the lifelong stipend. Plus, the Korean state equally lets any Korean Olympian postpone military service if they are competing or if have previously won the gold medal before the age of 28. This was instituted in 1973 (Duerden, 2021). Korean gold-medal winners are greatly rewarded when culturally carrying the *global* Korean Wave instead of only militarily carrying the *national* Korean flag, so both military deferments and lifelong subsidies are only for those who can bring home the gold. This is because the Korean state wants to give incentives to only the best, and equally because Koreans culturally are somewhat disappointed in 'failures' of silver and bronze medalists. They are interpreted as having 'failed' to win the gold instead of succeeding at winning the silver or bronze by being the best Olympians at the top of the world as they truly are. Therefore, silver and bronze medalists in Korea fail to get lifelong stipends.

As said in earlier chapters, archery was the signature cultural skill for ancient Koreans and remains the signature sport for modern Koreans, so the Korea Sports Promotion Foundation pays even more than the Ministry of Culture, Sports and Tourism for gold medals in archery. It pays 200 million won to any individual gold medalists in archery and 150 million won to all gold medalists in archery team events (Kwak, 2021) In short, the Korean state has been priming the dream of a global Korean Wave for a very long time, since at least 1973. Therefore, it is hardly very odd for the Korean state after 1963 to give cultural preferments to and even bend rules for people of excellence—whether traditional cultural artisans, Olympic stars, or now even K-pop idols.

The second factor of *Korean for-profit companies* was strong in 2020 as well. In 2020, the year of growing national lockdowns worldwide, it takes a lot of faith in the Korean Wave for a Korean digital entertainment company like Nexon to start a comprehensive global entertainment buyout strategy years in advance. This shows Nexon's faith in the Korean Wave's future or at least their desire to have their Korean company profit from culture globally whoever makes it. Nexon "announced its plan to invest a total of $1.5 billion in global entertainment companies in 2020, and [in 2021] it [started to invest]…$874 million…in Japanese entertainment holding companies

Konami, Sega, Bandai, and Hasbro, an American toy maker." By 2022, the Korean company Nexon made another purchase. It became the largest shareholder of AGBO, which is the production company of the American movie series *The Avengers*. By 2022, Nexon held an already controlling 49.12% stake and expected to purchase an additional investment of $100 million in 2022 to take their ownership of AGBO over the 50% mark of true control (Lee, 2022). Many other examples of Korean companies moving strongly to support the global Korean Wave after 2020 are mentioned in the next chapter.

For the third factor of *Korean culture itself*, from February 2020, the cast and crew of the highly acclaimed Korean film *Parasite* (2019) were heralded at the American Oscars movie awards, winning a tremendous number of awards. *Parasite* was the first *fully* foreign language film to win Best Picture. By 2022, the Korean online production of *Squid Game* became Netflix's most-watched show of all time. By September 2022, *Squid Game* won a record six Emmys in the American TV awards. It was so popular an image and theme that only one month after it started to show on Netflix in September 2021, on October 20, 2021, Korean labor protestors in Seoul from the Korean Confederation of Trade Unions dressed up in Squid Game's ominous faceless black masks and colorful body overalls for their march to a rally at Seoul City Hall against the Korean government's exploitive labor policies. Thus, real life Korean workers donned clothing of a Korean fantasy world of *Squid Game* to make a point about their similar competitive 'life or death' problems that they faced in increasing economic bankruptcies under the Moon administration's state lockdowns and its increasing neoliberal Korean political economy with lessened labor rights. It is sadly poignant that Korean laborers thought they would get far more attention and understanding only if their real world problems referenced people's sympathy for actors in a dystopian fantasy TV show about a real competition to the death, produced by the Korean Wave.

Plus, only from 2020, the culture of the Korean Wave was globally searched for online more thoroughly because of 'simultaneous successes.' In the midst of growing governmental-forced lockdowns in 2020, global searches showed the world started to seek out the cultural Korean Wave instead of explosive North Korean dictators or explosive South Korean battery technology. From 2020, for the first time, the Korean Wave was searched for avidly in multiple categories. In 2020, BTS's song "Dynamite" was the fifth most searched for song lyric. Plus, this Korean boy group of BTS (later discussed as a chapter) had a multi-country, digitally-simultaneous concert that filled movie theaters worldwide with the live internet presence of the group. It was like a big one-way Zoom meeting held on movie theater screens worldwide, though obviously more fun. This BTS concert was the fifth most searched for concert in *world* searches in 2020. BTS's global online 'virtual yet live and real' concert beat out other searches that year for concert offerings by Europe's Andrea Bocelli, the UK's Elton John, and the US's Metallica—among others. In the same year of 2020, the top movie searched for in the whole world was Korea's *Parasite*, as said above, the first fully foreign language film (and fully Korean-language and non-dubbed film) ever to win a U.S. Academy Award for Best Picture. (The French film called *The Artist* (2011) was really the first foreign film to win a U.S. Academy Award for Best Picture, though it was mostly a silent film—without a language barrier. So indeed *Parasite* can claim to be the first fully foreign *language* film to win a U.S. Academy Award, though hardly the first foreign film to do so, per se.)

By 2020, there were two Korean albums on the U.S. Billboard 200, both from BTS: their "Map of the Soul: 7" and "Be". In April 2020, BTS became the top album-selling Korean artists in South Korean history with over 20 million albums sold. In that same month, BTS held a two-day globally transmitted digital concert called *Bang Bang Con* assembled from past concert videos. The response was so great that by June 2020, it was the inspiration of the fresh 'virtual yet live and real' concert called *Bang Bang Con: The Live.* With approximately 756,000 live paying viewers at one point, BTS held the world's largest paying virtual concert in world history. It was watched from 107 countries simultaneously.

By the next year of 2021, despite original disastrous projections of viral pandemic never creating any excess deaths in 2020 or in early 2021 and despite never filling empty temporary triage zones or empty hospitals that led to many bored hospital nurses spending their empty hours practicing choreography and filming it for online viral dance videos, the world culture and economy was still widely held in the stasis of governmental lockdown. This was combined with media-led fear supporting continued destructive governmental lockdowns and attempts to push a 'digital vaccine passport' regime that started almost simultaneously in many countries of the world. A lot of people particularly in developed countries lost their jobs, their businesses (California alone lost 40% of its small businesses), stayed at home, drank heavily (as some countries' alcohol stores curiously were ordered to stay open while churches were ordered closed), abused their spouses and children (since family abuse rates went up tremendously), and of course ordered a lot of products online while watching a lot of dark satirical comedy on Netflix. For instance, the Korean-produced Netflix production of *Squid Game* (later discussed in another chapter) was the topmost search in global TV shows in 2021, similar to how another Korean Wave movie *Parasite* was the topmost movie search in the previous year of 2020. Plus, in 2021, Korea's "True Beauty" was ninth among the top 10 global searches for TV shows (Google, 2021). In music searches for 2021, BTS remained as prominent in 2021 as in 2020. In 2021, among all global searches for song lyrics, "Butter" by BTS was the seventh most globally-searched-for song.

By 2022, the Korean Wave accelerated its global presence with even wider simultaneous successes. For just a few highlights of that year, it was announced in April 2022 that BTS's star performer Jung Kook would perform at the 2022 global soccer event, the FIFA World Cup, held in Doha, Qatar. In November of 2022, he did perform at the opening ceremony and participated in the accompanying soundtrack to the World Cup, singing a song called "Dreamers" (Legaspi, 2022). By May 2022, Korean director Park Chan-wook was named Best Director at the Cannes film festival. His Palme d'Or winner was named *Decision to Leave.* In the same year of 2022, the already Emmy-winning *Squid Game* of 2021 *remained* the most watched season ever on Netflix. In 2022, *Squid Game*'s main actor Jung Ho-yeon became the first solo East Asian cover star on the American style magazine *Vogue.* In the same year of 2022, K-pop groups BLACKPINK and BTS held world record numbers of subscribers on their YouTube channels, and soon BTS once more won Favorite Pop Duo or Group *for the fourth time* at the American Music Awards. This made BTS the most awarded group in the history of that category.

Taking cynical advantage of this fresh height of BTS's popularity, in May 2022, the U.S. Biden Administration was happy to curtail its press question time and tried to distract Americans from a growing U.S. recession and near historic levels of U.S. inflation by oddly parading all seven members of world-famous Korean BTS in front of U.S. media at an official White House press conference. This was a low moment of media distraction in the Biden Administration. In the same month, Disney reported financial disaster. An 'anti-woke' backlash began to build across the United States in 2021, and by 2022 nearly all Disney movies of the past year were failures in profit. Disney reported over $180 million dollars in lost profits by May 2022, and missing its expected targets or revenue by $1 billion dollars by November 2022. Disney's board of directors then fired its CEO. It only got worse for Disney. By June 2023, movie box office analysts reported Disney had lost over $890 million dollars total on its last eight studio releases. Meanwhile, in general, "Hollywood studios, streamers, cable providers, and other [American] media giants lost a combined $542 billion in market value in 2022, with left-wing Disney, Netflix, and Comcast accounting for the bulk of the bloodshed" (Ng, 2022). It was the worst year for Disney stock since 1974 as it shares dropped 44% in 2022, while it had the worst opening autumn September movie season in 25 years (Nolte, 2022). This was more than a full fiscal year after U.S. theaters had reopened after lockdowns as well.

Meanwhile, the Korean Wave continued to rise, so, even American entertainment companies started to join the global Korean Wave out of desperation for profit. By September 2022, the financially failing online competition to Netflix, called Disney+, lost $1.5 billion itself in online streaming compared to the previous year. Since Disney now owns the *Star Wars* movie franchise series, it attempted to exploit global Korean Wave popularity to build a fan base for *Star Wars* once more after its movie flops in the same series after they purchased it. After announcing terrible financial losses in May 2022, Disney+ announced by September 2022 that it had hired *Squid Game's* lead Korean actor Lee Jung-Jae to be a main lead in a freshly written *Star Wars* series for Disney+ called 'The Acolyte.' (Kulkarni, 2022) So as U.S.'s Hollywood and Disney try to regain lost popularity by associating themselves with the Korean Wave in 2022, the same strategy was exploited by the equally poorly-performing Biden Administration that preferred to parade BTS instead of answer questions at press conferences.

In 2021, there was a one-year hiatus in Korean acts being #1 on the Billboard 200, yet by 2022 the Korean Wave returned with a vengeance *with four #1 albums* on the Billboard 200. Two of them were even by the same Korean group, and this time it was a different group than BTS. For details, between April and October 2022, another Korean male K-pop group called Stray Kids achieved their first #1 album, and then a few months later, their second #1 album on the Billboard 200. Their earlier #1 album in 2022 was ODDINARY, and their later #1 album in the same year was named MAXIDENT. Both were released via JYP/Imperial/Republic Records. By October 2022, *MAXIDENT became the fourth album by a South Korean group in 2022 alone* to top the Billboard 200. Stray Kids album MAXIDENT followed BLACKPINK's album Born Pink, BTS' album Proof, and Stray Kids' previous own album ODDINARY. As said, this was *four* top spots on the Billboard 200 *in the year 2022 alone* (Caulfield, 2022).

You would be correct to think that was enough for one amazing year in the global Korean Wave under mostly digital lockdowns. However, it was only October. There were three full months left in 2022. By November 2022, Korean K-pop group BTS beat American acts Taylor Swift, Drake and Ariana Grande to have the most #1 hits on the Billboard Hot 100 as well *in the past decade*. BTS scored six top hits in the past decade while U.S. rap superstar Drake was one hit behind them with five. Below that were American pop idols Taylor Swift and Ariana Grande with four top hits apiece. American acts Justin Bieber and Nicki Minaj were below them with only three top hits in the past decade. BTS' six top hits in the past decade were 'Savage Love' with Jason Derulo, 'Dynamite', 'Life Goes On', 'Butter', 'Permission To Dance' and their Coldplay collaboration called 'My Universe'.

Equally in November 2022, BTS once more won the Favorite Pop Duo or Group at the American Music Awards. This made *five years in a row*. BTS beat other American or British nominees such as Coldplay, Imagine Dragons, Måneskin and One Republic (Lim, 2022b).

Coming full circle, the U.S. Broadway musical called KPOP, the one that failed in 2017, was tried once more in 2022. Now it became a huge success. It featured as lead actor the now-autonomously popular Korean pop star Luna, in order to give it more Korean credibility and verisimilitude. Therefore, even the U.S. theater scene of Broadway started to exploit the Korean Wave, hiring Korean talent for achieving popularity in America and New York City. Adopting the collectivist theme of the global Korean Wave, it was reported in reviews that "KPOP is an unconventional musical—there are no traditional solos or duets where characters sing their emotions directly to the audience or to each other." There is only group dancing, giving it the appearance of a concert of two different fake K-pop groups in the musical: one male group called F8 (pronounced "Fate") and one female group called RTMIS (pronounced "Artemis").

In the same month, on November 28, 2022, the Korea Minting Corporation, the Korean state's public-owned corporation that mints gold and silver bars, and prints all South Korean paper banknotes, metal coins, and official passports, announced it will cast an official commemorative medal to celebrate the upcoming 10th year anniversary of BTS's debut in 2013. Therefore, by 2022 even the Korean mint is an agency of the global Korean Wave, which should be unsurprising as BTS by 2021 was bringing over $4 billion dollars to the Korean economy, every year (Duerden, 2021). It is said that from late 2022, the first commemorative medal would be released in advance, and it will have the BTS logo and the number 10. In 2023, another commemorative medal is planned to be minted with a group portrait of each of the seven members of BTS.

This "BTS Korean coin" shows once more the three factors mentioned earlier in the Korean Wave stamped tightly together: the coordination of the Korean state, Korean private company profit, and Korean culture. "The first official commemorative medal for the 10th anniversary of BTS's debut will be released through Korea Minting Corporation's shopping mall and [the group's management company] HYBE's official SNS channel" (Lim, 2022a). It is appropriate that the Korean state mint teams with BTS's manager HYBE to mint money, literally and figuratively, backed by nothing else except Korean culture, particularly if that culture is bankable and bringing in trillions of Korean won to the Korean economy annually (Lim, 2022a).

Appropriately, even the world soccer organization FIFA minted money figuratively by the end of 2022 in the stamp of the global Korean Wave. In November 2022, FIFA hired Jung Kook of BTS to sing at their opening ceremony in Qatar. After this live performance of the BTS/Jung Kook song called "Dreamers," the recording of the song quickly topped the U.S. Billboard Digital Song Sales Chart in the same month. As global soccer spectators saw Jung Kook on TV perform live in Qatar for FIFA, they searched online and immediately started buying and downloading a digital copy of this FIFA song for themselves. The song became the top downloaded song in the world on iTunes, reached ninth on the Global Billboard 200 Chart, and reached fourth on the U.S. Charts of Global Exclusive. In this way, BTS and the Korean Wave made the first ever FIFA song to find any place in the Billboard charts. In short, FIFA equally can bank on BTS and the global Korean Wave to gain popularity and profit after years of corruption scandals (Entertainment Tonight, 2022). Equally in November 2022, the Korean Wave's girl group BLACKPINK and the boy group Seventeen won two prizes each at the MTV Entertainment Music Awards 2022. "BLACKPINK was named Best Metaverse Performance for its virtual in-game concert, "The Virtual," held in August, and its member Lisa won Best K-pop" (Shim, 2022).

Does the year 2023 portend more awards for the Korean Wave? Yes, the year 2023 has barely started yet the Korean Wave already is breaking world records—twice. First, by November 2022, it was announced that BLACKPINK will be top of the bill in the British Summer Time (BST) Hyde Park festival in London in 2023. BLACKPINK will be the first Korean artists to perform at the British event. Equally by November 2022, "BTS has [already] been nominated in multiple categories of the 2023 Grammy Awards, becoming the first K-pop act to receive a Grammy nomination for three consecutive years." The details are that BTS was nominated for two Grammy awards in 2023: one for the best pop duo or group performance once more, this time for the song "My Universe" in collaboration with the British rock band Coldplay; and another for the best music video for the song "Yet to Come" (Shim, 2022). The 65th Grammy Awards were held on February, 5th, 2023, in Los Angeles. However, BTS were snubbed for the third consecutive year as well, losing to Taylor Swift in music videos and to Sam Smith and Kim Petras for pop/duo group performance (Brown, 2023). Does this show perhaps a kind of American resurgence or protectionism? That theme is addressed later. However, equally in 2023, at least three individual members of BTS reached the top spots on global music charts by July 2023, separately as individuals, even as BTS the group takes a hiatus for two years as one of its members goes to his delayed, yet still required, two-years in the Korean military. (There is more about these three wins in 2023 for individual BTS members in Chapter 6, about BTS.)

4.3 Comparing Cultural Waves of the U.S.A., China, and South Korea

From 2018 to 2023 in the present, the Korean Wave became a simultaneous success and spread globally. No longer is Hallyu centered on merely trying to sell intermittent singular successes of Korean TV dramas or K-pop songs to regional East Asian populations. However, it is still the same state-coordinated, export-led, and state-primed economic drive as the early 1960s. After the 2010s, the global Korean Wave is now supercharged in a third virtuous cycle with a wider global digital culture, by being joined with volunteer 'foreign' armies of millions of adoring international online fans from a hundred countries or more—all sharing, using, admiring, and buying Korean products and Korean culture. Korean Wave products increasingly spread beyond entertainment—beyond music, film, or drama—into tangible items like clothing, food, drink, smartphones, cosmetics, medical tourism, plastic surgery, computer games, and even massive foreign attendance at Korean-themed festivals held in foreign countries (Hong, 2014). The Korean Wave after 2020 even spread through the first Korean-orchestrated *global virtual reality events.* For over two days, a round of live yet virtual reality concerts by BTS (and earlier that year, in other related online events of BTS) reached tens of millions of people—simultaneously performing live and online, with the latter online audiences watching in repurposed movie theaters worldwide. The idea of 'global virtual reality concerts during lockdown' ushered in a fresh cultural form of synchronous digital concert events. These moved far beyond the original 'Korean-primed' events by BTS. Even American acts like Ariana Grande attempted to copy this tactic of the Korean Wave by hosting a concert within the shared virtual space of the online game Fortnite.

However, following the theme mentioned earlier, other nations' acts, their technological prowess, or their state governments have failed to achieve so far the same level of triple coordination of state, companies, and culture that primes the Korean Wave that renders large polish to Korean-staged cultural events. This leads to the following comparative observations about current differences between a highly coordinated and digital Korean Wave and a less coordinated and more mass-media based Americanization or in the inverted and threatening way that China is attempting to gain cultural influence around the world.

Of course to the present there is a continuing larger output of American cultural titles in all categories of 'web searched' cultural productions or awards. This is an 'old trend' because it began in the early twentieth century from the budding global popularity of cultural innovations of American's music of ragtime, blues, jazz, and swing music from the 1900s through World War II in the 1940s—carried via mostly American media innovations as well. After World War II, the American wave globalized even more with its optimistic swing music style continuing from the 1930s through the 1940s in an era that moved from a global Great Depression, through a global hot war, and then a global Cold War. Swing was soon replaced in popularity by American rock'n'roll acts touring a war-torn Europe still living in culture shock in the early 1950s and in that growing cultural Cold War between the United States and the Soviet Union.

The current Korean Wave is a *digital synergy* of the hardware production of digital communications and a cultural production of digital content both made in South Korea. This is a very united combination due to the digital convergence of information and the fact that it can reach all age groups easily. In the past and the present, all global Americanization was originally a synergy in a sense as well, though around synergy around a domestic American 'teenage product marketing' category and one-way mass media innovations during the same period. Thus, this teenage marketing category was carried simultaneously via the media artifacts themselves, yet in a more disjointed cultural production without any informational convergence due to many different parallel mass media that were simultaneously their own separate media productions and cultural productions in magazines, films, radio/records, etc. These fragmented and parallel mass media products of media hardware and culture were sent globally out after World War II, yet were primarily aimed at a teenage audience only. Over decades from the 1870s through the 1940s, the United States invented this teenage synergy, generation after generation. It repeatedly primed a marketing category to adolescent buyers and media entertainment consumers so much that it became a real ongoing manufactured commercial culture, with its own simultaneous successes. This commercialized culture turned the United States into a 'teen culture' of media/cultural consumption—the world's first. The U.S. pioneered the invention of this teen culture from the late 1800s stemming from its mixed immigrant youth living in polyglot multi-ethnic cities and cultures who could work and earn money of their own without mandatory forced schooling in many states. The raw mass market power of these teenage workers/buyers in a consumer culture of those cities, and youth's desire to differentiate themselves as an American group distinct from their multiple and divided "Old World" families, and America's many fresh mass media technological innovations were tied together in a common adolescent cultural, media, and consumptive experience. American teenage culture was consumption, i.e., was made on that commercial mass media consumption. The repeated group consumption and sharing of American movies, records, and wireless radio reached millions of people daily. A teenage culture based on consumption of mass media products and dance/movie crazes fit well with a growing mass society of an urban, individualist, consumerist culture. What held this teen culture together and gave it common cultural identity was an ongoing faddish and primed product line of fresh music, bands, events, clothing, sheet music, color magazines, cartoons, music recordings, cinema, movie actors, and radio broadcasting of songs. Imagine a cultural world without all of this, and a teen culture disappears. After World War II, American companies and the American state exported this teenage synergistic cultural sales complex to the world as part of the cultural Cold War geopolitics. To counter the revolutionary Soviet Bloc, with its different youth culture ideals, the American wave's mostly optimistic feelings and images of the future conquered the world by spreading American happy tunes, movies, bands, fads, dances, and songs via a culture that followed what was happening with Hollywood films, movie stars, and the music recording industry (Savage, 2008).

This strong mass media with its strong images of America were reproduced and shared around the world. It flowed easily across the world's war-destroyed ruins and the destroyed cultural wastelands with their cultural pessimism after World War II. They were being given a rigged forced choice of American mass consumerism or Soviet mass communism—both cultural conquests. After World War II, a collectivist Communist political movement with icons of Marx and Lenin in the East faced individualist yet corporate consumerist icons like the idiosyncratic Groucho Marx or John Lennon in the West. The former were dedicated collectivists and political revolutionaries, and encouraged a youth culture in that vein. The latter were rebellious, irreverent, and individualistic figures popular in American or British mass media entertainment as the key to their iconic status, instead of being really political role models outside of their entertainment sector. However, they were *cultural* role models selling images of a future based on pleasure, irreverent rebelliousness, and individual freedom in a consumption-based and entertainment-oriented West.

However, these clear global political and cultural polarities are gone. Korea's first international success in 1992 in British Hong Kong comes directly after the collapse of the Soviet Union in 1991. So, by the early 1990s, one side of this Cold War geopolitical polarity has been totally smashed by the decline of the Soviet Union in 1991, yet now the remaining one-way mass media of globalized Americanization is somewhat being smashed in the early twenty-first century by the digital revolution of the easier sharing of a synergistic global digital sphere, exemplified by the Korean Wave. Both the United States and Korea are equally being smashed or pressured by a world in which a Communist Party-run China is running the second largest capitalist global economy at the same moment as gathering surveillance from global big data provided via a corporate global grid of surveillance by the near monopoly of Tencent's WeChat in China and its many purchased entertainment companies increasingly around the world (Magnates Media, 2023). However, instead of a positive culture of a Chinese wave, there is simply a negative Chinese wave of repressive attempts at censorship and globalist control of others' cultures via China, either by granting or denying access to its major billion-strong consumer market. China tries to control and to bring to heel any companies or talents selling cultural content of the Korean Wave or Americanization by using their own greed for Chinese markets against themselves, to get them to stay silent on any Chinese atrocities witnessed via the global media. Thus China builds a cultural wave of sorts less by exporting its own culture though by attempting to control and censor the content of all other cultures by using the greed of other cultural waves' desires to penetrate the markets of China.

Synthesizing what was said above about the Korean Wave between 2012 through 2023, it so far seems an American sunset and an Asian (and particularly Korean) dawn, yet it is a multi-polar dawn. The multi-polar dawn is coming particularly because America keeps losing the top spots to Korea from 'the year of Psy' onward and more regularly after 2018 when the global Korean wave accelerated. It is equally a world where even American basketball stars and coaches feel forced by their greed to do public kowtow to China and apologize for supporting democracy in Hong Kong otherwise the U.S. National Basketball Association (NBA) will be blocked from Chinese profits and markets.

The global Korean Wave emerges as a similar phenomenon to the post-World War II American wave, yet the destructive economic wasteland and global pessimism is in the United States and the global West at this time, added to by self-inflicted governmental lockdowns after 2020. It is joined with a global optimism of the growing markets of developing countries that are equally important to the Korean Wave as a digital fandom. Instead of only because of its positive culture, South Korean culture appears to the world as more innovative, adaptable, and larger than ever in its impact worldwide *because of* the parallel cultural crisis before 2020 in the global West as well as the damage and economic suffering of lockdown conditions after 2020. Just like earlier Americanization expanded across the shocked cultural wasteland after World War II, the Korean Wave accelerated its digital cultural expansion across a world of overzealous governmental lockdowns and their terrible aftermath. Starting in 2021 with the massive printing of American money to subsidize closed businesses in lockdown, there is now growing American and global inflation, a growing global recession starting in 2022 onward, growing American bank runs from March 2023, and a worldwide de-dollarization growing from April 2023 refusing an inflated American currency and assembling a potential fresh international reserve currency based on the "BRICS+" countries, with the 'plus' meaning the many others now joining them in that project. Throughout these economic crises, this trying time still sees South Korea starting truly to outclass both Asian and Western nations alike in digital hardware and a global digital culture. South Korea is now setting global digital production standards of entertainment events and physical products that the world wants as consumers. Meanwhile, by Summer 2023, as profits plummet for the U.S.'s Hollywood productions in the past years, this now is combined with the Hollywood writers' and Hollywood actors' guilds on strike simultaneously for the first time since 1960. They are both striking over concerns about how a changing digital media regime is inventing fresh problems in their contract dynamics. Actors are losing profits to the growing streaming services globally and fail to get a cut of that profit. Actors are equally losing control of their own images to training artificial intelligence applications using their images for free that will replace them. Writers complain of losing their jobs of writing scripts to assistants of artificial intelligence as well (Roth, 2023). As noted in the discussion of media regime change in Part III, this is the 'earthquake' event that starts to raze any institutions and buildings on the surface that are already 'hollowed out' and organizationally mismatched due to media change developing such stresses for a long time underground until it erupts on the surface and looks more sudden of a collapse than it really was.

In turn, the rest of the world's nations find it hard to challenge or to produce equally high quality cultural, material, or digital media offerings as South Korea. Such synergies are possible only from a few highly digitally saturated countries like South Korea that have made fully digital production changes and digital cultural changes themselves. As related in later chapters, at this point in history it seems other waning competitors to South Korea are satisfied simply to make profitable global digital partnerships with the global Korean Wave instead of (re)develop any true cultural opposition to the Korean Wave.

In short, the Korean Wave became a global cultural tsunami by spreading in four ways: (1) by spreading far beyond regional East Asia after 2018 as a simultaneous success globally; (2) by spreading beyond the visual or audio entertainment biases and limitations of a past one-way media sphere; (3) by spreading beyond physical events and physical products into global permanent synchronous virtual reality events and virtual communities online; and (4) by perhaps the most difficult to counter, by the high production quality of Korean digital offerings and their skill in marketing asynchronous or synchronous digital events to a virtual world, compared to other countries with less experience and less state-facilitated coordination and support. For instance, let us look at the more dystopian digital competition of the global Korean Wave. The earlier Americanization still spreads globally in its ideological, military, and cultural supremacist battles—which to a point becomes a block on its own market expansion due to the polarization generated in other countries against all three aspects. Plus, earlier Americanization as a media regime used asychronous one-way mass communication mostly without many chances for convergence across media, unlike that easier digital convergence seen in the Korean Wave that is possible now, and without many chances for creating synchronous experiences en masse. Meanwhile, China is using the same digital culture and digital convergence in the inverse of Korea by building a global police state via applications like WeChat and TikTok global surveillance and purchase consolidation within Tencent's many global corporate acquisitions, and by placing repressive conditions on all other countries' cultural expressions worldwide if they want to access the markets of China. Thus, technology is hardly destiny or deterministic to uses. It depends on what you want to do with the technology. In the same digital distributed technologies as the United States and China, Korea is specializing in profiting from the technology for a more politically neutral global entertainment even as China is specializing in the technology as a negative politically-driven global surveillance and global cultural censorship and control.

Increasingly during the past several years, both China and the United States started to look like the same negative digital media sphere in this technology as well. Both showed themselves in the years after 2020 working on closed and negative uses of state coordination and (at least for the United States) illegal state-media censorship to support government propaganda for lockdowns and dangerous vaccine drives without human testing instead of allowing an open media sphere to judge risk, and instead of attempting after 2022 a positive cultural wave about themselves as South Korea is doing with the same technologies. In China, the same negativity and digital repression is seen in Chinese 'vaccine passports' and the related social credit system of cultural, consumer, and citizen censorship and surveillance judgment of all actions mediated by the Internet. In the United States, something similar to a Chinese-style social credit system is developing in piecemeal, seen in the recent exposure of the "Twitter files" in 2022 or the "Facebook files" in 2023 showing how the Biden Administration orchestrated a Chinese-style digital repression in a massive and illegal U.S. government-coordinated national and even international cultural censorship. The Biden administration even paid private companies like Twitter to censor American citizens. Plus, this has been orchestrated by putting many hundreds of previous state intelligence agents within those 'private' social media platforms to make it easier to subvert both private Twitter and Facebook to coordinate the Biden Administration's censorship policy and to rig elections through biased or censorious media coverage and by cancellation of many different opposition candidates' media presences. Thus, using the same technologies, the United States' applications of them is toward culturally repressive actions and government censorship of free speech and opposition candidates starts to look like totalitarian China. In short, the United States exhibits far more of an image of illegal state-run censorship, state repression, and heightened cultural and ethnic divisiveness than coordinating a positive image of the future in its cultural and political expression.

So, in this increasing global use of the same digital technologies in different ways and in the 'digital ebb and flow' of the marketing of the Korean Wave back and forth between online and the physical world, the success of the Korean Wave is creating its own autonomous and self-generating popularity by default given the erosion of its weakening competition from the United States or given the merely censorship-based globalization of culture from China. Meanwhile, different than South Korea, larger states like the United States and China use the same technologies to create digital surveillance states—even as both countries are filled with Korean popular culture and Korean material products. Scenarios about these separate yet interactive national trends into the future are discussed in the later chapters of Part III.

Once Korean popular culture became primed by the Korean state as a globally-shared interest to people around the world, that globally shared Korean culture, as said above, now starts to self-perpetuate itself worldwide in that fresh 'third' virtuous cycle of the Korean political economy in league with a global digital culture. Note from the above cursory descriptions of other declining or negative cultural waves, particularly those from the United States are trying simply to join the Korean Wave instead of compete anymore. This was noted in the examples mentioned in the strategies of Disney+ and the *Star Wars* franchise. This was noted in the Biden Administration. This was noted in Broadway shows relying on Korean Wave K-pop idols, now similar to how FIFA world soccer tournaments join the Korean Wave for more popularity as well. The Chinese culture is still an avid consumer of Korean products, whether dramas or cosmetics. The Chinese market is the largest market in the world for Korean-made cosmetics, and the cultural Korean Wave was primed first intentionally within the large Chinese market from 1992. Even Korean companies now direct, manufacture, and manage whole Chinese cosmetics brand lines and launch Chinese product lines and mix their recipes as noted in the later chapter on the global Korean cosmetics corporation Cosmax.

Thus, the Korean Wave now spreads laterally and virally online by consumer fans and by the willing desire of the national corporations of the also-rans that the Korean Wave is merging with in business collaborations. This is different than the Korean Wave spreading only via older, top-down, expensive, mass marketing campaigns or state/cultural industry-coordinated events alone in the earlier American wave. Now the Korean Wave spreads via digital campaigns that commandeer and take advantage of peer sharing across a global Internet and across billions of smartphone owners, and by commandeering the failing uncoordinated state and corporate leadership of even the American wave, while even taking advantage of the lesser desired content by the Chinese from their own Chinese digital and consumer sphere. The global Korean Wave reaches markets and users of up to 2.5 to 3.3 billion smartphone owners by 2019 or, reaching over 5.1 billion mobile phones of all kinds by the same year (We Are Social / Hootsuite, 2019). The visuals of the American wave still keeps a greater reliance on its past traditional channels of top-down and one-way mass media regimes like Disney and Hollywood, and yet its music and music video industry pioneered global digital examples earlier like Napster (now defunct of course), now replaced by the likes of iTunes, and with updates of visual distribution via Netflix's global OTT online broadband movie delivery service challenging the mass media of older Hollywood that finds it hard to get the celluloid out of its blood to compete on a digital global realm. However, the latter two global American platforms are open to becoming part of the global Korean Wave itself, like American iTunes making money for selling top BTS downloaded singles or American Netflix funding and then profiting greatly from the success of the Korean Wave's *Squid Game* in the interests of Netflix's market share in the whole world.

To an extent not seen before in world history or in any other's nation's culture, the Korean Wave in its earlier existence before 2018 was not spreading in more documentable ways that measured a singular cultural success before. In many countries Korean music, TV, games, etc. were for a long time not appearing originally on the surface in nations' top hit in radio, TV, movie theaters, and other playlists that summarized successful hits of the one-way mass media only. Instead, the Korean Wave appeared in fresh digital ways of measuring popularity like aggregate raw statistics like the numbers of downloads, views, comments, searches, online purchases, and the scale of digital crowds gathering to see, interact, and participate themselves in the Korean Wave. This digital flow, like an underground river, was undermining other nations' hierarchical public ways of measuring their own cultural successes and popularity on the surface. Moreover, this Korean Wave's undermining influence on other nations' cultures was being done simultaneously online, worldwide.

Only from around 2018 onward, and only from 2020 onward in the beginnings of a near global national (digital) lockdown, did South Korea unlike other countries take advantage of their digital and marketing prowess in the Korean Wave to start to dominate even older other national 'list-based' views of cultural success. Particularly from 2020 onward, these lists started to be swamped by the global Korean Wave. From this point, the Korean Wave bubbled out of, or was in league with, the global Internet in a virtuous cycle of growth that reached public critical mass, globally and simultaneously. Many nations thus were caught off guard in their own national cultural productions both by lockdown conditions economically at the same moment they were facing a sudden second global challenge of cultural irrelevance against a well-oiled machine of the Korean Wave priming its dynamics for nearly thirty years at that point. South Korea could exploit the real world disruptions of other countries' economic lockdowns with its further digital cultural success far more than other countries could.

Even though American cultural products still dominate global lists in 2023 as they have since the early twentieth century, in recent years as noted above, the top hits on American national or global lists are not American, though Korean. The ongoing growth of the Korean Wave across the world is a big sea change in culture, upending hundreds of years of unchallenged global cultural leadership from European-heritage states toward a more multi-polar global cultural world. Such older European-heritage hegemons are accustomed to using different and older centralized mass media for their media presence and agenda setting. Now they face the aggregated global simultaneity and greater digital convergence culture of the Korean Wave. Plus, older hegemons are accustomed to competing with a different economic model of country, where a competitor's exports are only a small portion of its national economies, just like them. Now much of the global West faces a Korean developmental model different on both points: where sometimes over 40% of the Korean economy is expected to be exports and where digital platforms of a two-way synchronous media are the mechanisms of cultural expression instead of centralized and one-way media broadcasting that misses half the now desired conversation and feedback. Thus, Korean market intelligence means more of a life-or-death search for finding existing markets in other countries to displace in order to grow, instead of only expanding Korean national consumption or production with its diminishing returns. That was what was said earlier that is a misnomer to simply call the South Korean economic strategy an "export-led development" when it is more a plan of a very high level of "export substitution" in other multiple countries' economies simultaneously with Korean products, whether material or cultural.

The Korean Wave is getting so durable and strong that by 2022, the United States' cultural managers seem fed up with Americans (and American products/profits) losing top spots of the American Music Awards or the American Academy Awards to Korean entertainment and movies even if it is by popular demand and by critical acclaim. The American Grammys for three years from 2020 to 2023 have nominated the Korean boy group BTS each time for multiple awards, and yet snubbed them now for three years as well. From 2022, Hollywood and the American cultural production complex, in a *cri de coeur,* started to change or to rig the American Academy rules to pre-segregate and to detour the many 'Korean entries' for music awards into a special segregated category of awards suddenly for 'Korean' popular music, for the first time. Even though it is possible for Korean acts to still win in other 'American' categories, perhaps American judges will now segregate Korean acts to the Korean category instead of allowing the Korean Wave to continue to dominate American popular music's lower popularity in general? Koreans are now making globally accessible and American-accessible music and movies, winning top spots in the American awards, being paid by Americans companies to produce more Korean culture for global online empires (like Netflix), as well topping global lists for several years when judged fairly by American audiences and judges.

On the one hand, we can interpret this as a special recognition for Korean entries as an honor to this K-Nation, since no other nation has ever had so many strong entries to even conceive of creating such a special country-based foreign category in the global American music awards. However, on the other hand, we can interpret this special recognition in a more negative way. For instance, there is no special category for France or Latvia, so why should Korea get segregated? Does the American cultural industry admire or fear the Korean Wave? Will it start to rig the American Academy Awards for cinema later? With segregation on Korean music in place in the U.S.'s award system, perhaps Korean films will be segregated in the American Academy Awards, the Grammys, or the Emmys soon, as well?

Remember, Western Europeans in general have been dominating global culture via their own pioneering media regimes for at least 300 years (See Appendix 4). Americans alone have been dominating global culture for nearly 70 years, merging with what came before with even more novel American one-way mass media technologies instead of only moving against that earlier European hegemony. Therefore, Americans understandably may be embarrassed to see their cultural wave and media investments falling apart and selling less widely. American entertainment companies even are turning slavishly Korean themselves to survive—as they start to lose economic profits to Korean winners in global music, album sales, and film entertainment at an increasing pace. Remember these Korean Wave wins and glories are by popular American audience acclaim, judge acclaim, and global audience acclaim for several years in a row.

However the global Korean Wave is not truly making 'Korean' popular films or music anymore either. Korean acts do not aim to be the best band 'in Korea.' Korean bands aim to be the best band in the digitally-distributed world. The "Korean" K-pop dance group BTS regularly has been acclaimed as 'top of American music' by American awards. Furthermore, Koreans aim to make the best movies in the world as measured by Cannes in France or Hollywood in America, instead of only making the best or most popular movies 'in Korea.' After all, the Korean movie entry *Parasite* was the first South Korean entry to ever win the Cannes film festival's top award, the Palme D'or, and another Korean director won the Grand Prix (second place) soon after. Plus, at the 92nd American Academy Awards for films in 2020, the Korean entry of *Parasite* was the first fully foreign language/Korean film to ever be the leading film of the year in the United States. It won four American academy awards—far above other American produced films that year. *Parasite* won simultaneously Best Picture, Best Director, Best Original Screenplay, and Best International Feature Film.

Therefore, even if it may be fair to say that American judges are setting up potential rigging of the "American" awards by boxing in Korean entries in music or perhaps categorically just snubbing them in the Grammys despite nominations for years, however, Koreans are not making exclusively Korean culture in a global Korean Wave. Plus, the days of an unchallenged American global cultural hegemony now seems gone since even American popular culture is either just part of the global Korean Wave increasingly itself or the American awards systems are reacting and closing themselves off to the Korean Wave after losing so many times in the top spots.

One of the major uncommented upon effects of this digital world of multi-polarity in global culture means *an ending of clear past national categories of competition in global culture* in general, instead of thinking that multi-polarity in global culture means clear national competitions like the past per se. Instead of the world simply shifting from more American dominance to a growing Korean dominance, the whole world's popular culture and multiple past nations' cultural waves are becoming shifted to digital and being Koreanized by default, at the same moment that Korea is becoming more globalized and less nationalized in its culture in turn as well.

Given Korea historically was just as guilty of this cultural censorship before the end of the secret cultural blacklists, now it is different since not all countries do a Korean-style *positive encouraging* state, private, and cultural coordination well. Increasingly both China and the United States show they do only well a more *negative repressive* coordination among these three factors instead. Plus, there is the clear decline of the U.S.'s centralized movie making complexes like Hollywood, unable to make a good digital transition or to even know what global markets want anymore. In 2022 alone, as said earlier, Hollywood reported a devaluation of $584 billion dollars in one year due to many failed films and failed investments in online streaming services. Second, it is telling that only from 2022, the huge centralized movie making conglomerate in the USA, called MGM, has just been sold to Amazon in a *very belated* attempt to catalyze some kind of greater digital cultural coordination. Such alignments of movie making and digital media have already existed in South Korea for decades though, like through the first Korean online movie review galas pioneered by Melon Media Group that hosted film events with the Kakao Corporation as early as 2005—before even smartphone culture from 2007 onward.

This much more negative and repressive cultural coordination is seen in the past few years of the United States on state, corporate and cultural levels. It is a coordination in support of creating in the USA a more divided revolutionary culture of 'woke versus unwoke', terms respectively defined as left against right, liberal against conservative, homosexuality/transgenderism against heterosexuality, atheist against religious, hate speech versus free speech, gun bans versus gun rights, abortion against child rights, drag queens versus child protection from grooming, child gender mutilation surgeries versus parental rights over children, and in general a collectivist, statist, and corporatist culture of licentiousness and biological self-destruction toward sterility on the left versus an individualist culture of limited government, traditional family-based morality, and free speech on the right. In the American context, this leftist cultural revolution has become the tactics of the state, corporations, and aligned activists popularizing 'LGBT,' transgenderism, gay marriage, gender reassignment surgery, child/adult romance and pedophilia themes, and exclusively multi-cultural marriages. This American 'cultural war' against itself is increasingly without any clear common shared future goals or allegiances. America now seethes in mutual hatreds against various factions, whether 'woke or unwoke.' The 'woke culture' is associated with the more critical term 'cancel culture,' since people are now punished in the United States' online platforms simply for expressing opinions—punished by censorious American activists, by Ukrainian governmental requests, or even by Chinese governments reaching into the United States to silence people. Americans may find themselves organizationally repressed if they step out of line with a government-supported and corporate-supported left-wing political correctness, instead of there being a common space or a common ground of civility anymore.

The U.S.'s more leftist popular culture in the media culture resembles more of a corporate-sponsored Maoist cultural revolution doing its best institutionally in that media to 'cancel' and purge people and products that disagree with them from social institutions and public spaces, real and virtual. Many public intellectuals left and right in the United States have been discriminated against and canceled from venues like public lectures by being shouted down, had their social media canceled, had their job sites canceled by political tests, or even had their bank accounts, business bank accounts, or product lines canceled in a 'social-credit-style' punishment for speaking out on a controversial issue.

Remember what was said in previous chapters about the anti-developmental aspects of letting any cultural revolution take place, that divides a nation? It is telling that despite its verbiage of diversity and openness, a cultural wokism leads to a less tolerant USA on all sides instead of a more tolerant one as it creates a heavily divided USA incapable of moving forward as a nation. How can such a negative and intimidating American culture divided upon itself expect to keep making popular films or have common cultural standards? The Chinese communist revolutionary Mao argued for a cultural revolution—a cultural defamation and cultural change as a key revolutionary tactic, since it stops cultural reproduction and leaves a people weaker and riper for revolutionary dictatorship in the cultural vacuum. Similarly, Americans are being subjected to a similar attempted cultural revolution and iconoclasm against public statues just like Maoists attempted in China and worldwide in the 1960s into the 1970s. Mao was shut down in China by other developmental revolutionaries themselves, as Mao was judged to be leading to a pointlessly self-destructive cultural revolution working against the nation's development. So, even the Chinese leadership under Deng eventually rejected revolutionary cultural Maoism. Only rejecting this cultural revolution set China on the road to actual economic though partial development in the 1980s, showing in retrospect Mao more responsible for postponing Chinese development with various violent cultural revolutions for nearly thirty years when under his leadership between 1949 and 1978. A nomenclature for the modern culture war of the United States may be the Woke Maoist Corporate Globalists versus the Conservative Nationalists. That was the actual dynamics seen in China itself, of global support for Mao (like from the Soviet Union or from Yale in China) versus only nationalist support for Deng, played out over decades in the long Chinese Civil War before 1949 and even afterwards, just like the long American cultural war that started in the 1990s.

What does this have to do with the global Korean Wave? It matters because wokism hardly exists in China, Japan, Russia, or in Korea. In July 2023, LGB and transgenderism began to be actively repressed in Chinese media. The same media blocks on it already existed in Russia. This is due to these countries' greater sense of popularizing national duty, team spirit, and common ethos of proper conservative social gender roles, yet within their top down state-led innovation in everything technological and economic—except in social relationships. Meanwhile, other places like the United States are attempting the opposite: attempting to have the state coordinate innovation in everything around cultural relationships and less using the state to coordinate innovation in economic technologies or marketable cultural products that anyone wants to experience. Thus respectively, the United States is falling apart culturally and falling behind technically in the global cultural industries at the same time. Increasingly, even successful American sequel franchises of Hollywood like *Star*

Wars or Disney, that under proper management would be 'sure things' of profit, have started to drop repeatedly bankrupt bombs of wokeness. Hollywood increasingly becomes involved in a kind of totalitarian purge toward a sexual/cultural revolution by creating 'woke' propaganda vehicles for internal or global cultural conflicts like pushing lesbian kisses in child's animation, Disney+ animations like *Pauline* about young girls falling in love with and impregnated by Satan, or even going so far as to fire popular Hollywood voice actors over their real life conservative politics even if they are only unseen voiceovers in Hollywood animated films (Bunyan, 2022).

Korean movies and music are a different planet of culture mostly. They are almost as far from 'woke' as you can get. Plus, there are clear male K-pop bands and clear female K-pop bands that avoid touching on any political or conflictual themes. Korean dramas are global trend setters by being the opposite, being depoliticized and focused on highly enervating conflicts only in patriotic, domestic family, school, dating, or in coming of age stories. This nationalist drama and low-level family and relationship drama as content appeals to the world's daily life regardless of cultural heritage. The Korean Wave is being cognizantly respectful, apolitical, or mute on points of politics and cultural divisions to the point of avoiding seeding or even mentioning conflicts of gender, ethnicity, or sexuality like woke American Hollywood airs regularly. For instance, even Korean popular dramas like *Dae Jang Geum* (2003) were so culturally respectful that even Iranian families would watch it together (Hong, 2014). How many American cultural products can you list now that are watched by a whole family?

Plus, in many Korean dramas, characters are sexually conservative with clear gender roles. Everyone is mostly fit and clean unless a failed or damaged physiognomy is meant to teach a moral lesson by stereotype of bad outcomes or sheer horror (like in the growing theme of 'K-zombie' movies). Mostly, narrative and characters are intentionally meek about kissing on screen early into a narrative, sometimes taking a year into the series. "This sexual conservativeness is very much appreciated by the more traditionalist developing world's cultures" (Hong, 2014). In other words, the Korean Wave sells cultural traditionalism to the world instead of selling cultural revolution and sexual libidinousness to the world, like the currently competing woke Americanization does now.

According to Hong's analysis, published in and from the viewpoint of 2014, she interpreted that this is driven by Korea's pragmatic cultural marketing strategy that happens to be closer to trying to addict developing countries' larger conservative markets to conservative Korean Wave cultural products, instead of trying to conquer markets of a decadent, wealthy and global West (Hong, 2014). Actually, both agreeing and disagreeing with Hong, what she said is seen as accurate though now incomplete in explaining the global cultural strategies of the Korean Wave, since it is from a view of 2014. First, in disagreement, this marketing strategy of the Korean Wave is really hardly only exclusive or framed to the Korean Wave per se. It is the continuation of older Korean strategies of technical/material marketing of "export substitution" for the world from the 1970s onward in all manner of material products as well. Korea's goals then as now were to provide cheaper and serviceable copies of some expensive First World technical product to the rest of the world beyond the expensive rarified versions of the same technical products of a global West. Selling Korean

Wave culture partially is the same rote globalist marketing strategy as Samsung TVs, mobile phones, refrigerators, and computer chips: enter an established global market with a cheaper version of whatever they are selling and do it better than the others at the same time. From discussions with a foreign-national Samsung consultant, it is reported that the internal culture of Samsung is so conservative it does not have an interest in any innovation beyond an already established global field in which it can make a slightly cheaper and better copy of a 'sure market'. The same appears to be happening in cultural production for the world in the Korean Wave mostly.

Second, Hong argues that Koreans have lacked historical 'hard power', that that led them to never really try culturally 'to colonize' others or even to displace the West in its own zones via the global Korean Wave. She says this other cultural strategy is caused by simply good business models, because as noted above the larger markets are in the developing countries themselves (Hong, 2014). Regardless of what you think about Hong's first thesis about larger conservative developing country markets for the Korean Wave or second thesis about the lack of 'hard power' of Korea that as well helps this conservative and apolitical cultural focus, both of these are *external* ideas of why the Korean Wave culturally looks like it does. This is insufficient, since it ignores three more *internal* rationales why the Korean Wave culturally looks like it does as well, discussed momentarily as due to a more homogeneous culture, solely collective innovation, as well as state censorship.

To the extent that the Korean Wave is mostly animated by this externally oriented conservative economic strategy aiming more toward less developed countries whether in selling Korean TVs or selling Korean TV dramas, it works well. However, against this analysis, which might have made sense when Hong wrote those ideas in 2014, it is different now. Now the Korean Wave is indeed wildly popular across the global West's teenage audiences, and so the popularity of the Korean Wave is evident in the global West as well. Plus, Hong was writing these external theses about the Korean Wave as if they had nothing to do with the internal culture of Korea or the state management of culture that she mentions herself. Plus, she was writing before the exposure of the secret cultural blacklist in 2016.

So, disagreeing with Hong's two 'externalist' theses, to an extent rarely seen in a modern nation there is more at work in the Korean Wave than just external economic rational analysis of what the global markets want in less developed countries or in more developed countries. Instead, there is equally an internal cultural drive in the Korean Wave that holds it there regardless, unmentioned by Hong. There is a very deep, proudly conservative, and even xenophobic core to this internationally cosmopolitan Korean Wave that is kept under control. It is argued by Hong that this lack of cultural assimilation or openness to other cultures in the Korean Wave is simply a smart or hard-nosed marketing strategy of concentrating on non-political 'micro-drama' in Korean life and selling that to the world, since it copies other apolitical and conservative cultural themes of a status quo elsewhere assumed to more resonant and less divisive to billions of people in developing countries that themselves are assumed to be traditional. However, as noted in the film *Swiri/Shiri* and others, there is a politics in the Korean Wave—it is just one of Korean ethnic unification, ethnically against the whole world, with that world seen as a shadowy group trying to keep Koreans divided against themselves or their very conservative political values.

While it is agreed that this is the modern external 'cultural business' strategy of the Korean Wave, Hong minimizes *three other internal points* about Korean culture itself that encourages this deep cultural and conservative continuity, both ancient and very modern. First, there is the classic 'collective innovation' issue that Korea's more homogeneous culture does so well that was mentioned earlier, ranged against other kinds of individual and cultural innovation. It is bound to be more internally focused on avoiding anything culturally innovative or revolutionary instead of only choosing this because of wise external marketable purposes. Second, the next ancient point is the idea that Koreans are more *internally* supportive and generally agree in their core values of duty, patriarchy, family, clear gender roles, school hierarchies of rote memorization, love of Confucian teachers as role models and coaches in life, being shy in romance, bashful in sexual relations, and having an avoidance of public conflict stressing decorum, politeness to fans, public respect, and patriotism. If it sounds like "America, baseball, and cherry pie" in the 1950s, it is, though Korean style. Even supposed cultural rebel Psy made clear during his New York NBC TV debut in 2012 that his performance was associated in his mind with Korean national patriotism above others as well. Thus it is argued here Koreans are culturally incapable internally of doing much else than appeal to nationalism, patriotism, and a global cultural conservatism with the Korean Wave as they are culturally unable to gain much internal cultural status any other way in their own culture if they were to produce anything else, instead of it simply being a neutral or Machiavellian external business strategy as Hong implies. Koreans are trapped in a Korean Wave of their own design, trying to highlight all the dutiful and proper behaviors and perfect them while trying to censor the rest and the true growing conflicts in their own culture around gender, class, wealth, and labor. The fact that most of the secret cultural blacklist was left wing political artists proves the state censorship toward this. The fact that addressing these kinds of class conflicts in something like *Squid Game* has to be done in a darkly humorous way show individuals in the series, even when down, simply compete in a pre-determined system that no one really challenges even if it is part of their contracts to end the game if the majority of players agree. This implies a tragic resignation to a status quo and once more a lack of Korean individual or cultural innovation. It shows a true lack of a positive 'innovative' improved political vision of a real world of Korea for themselves, beyond resignation. Cultural conflicts and inequalities rarely rise to awareness in South Korean media or entertainment because of this deep cultural homogeneity and the fact that the few ethnic minorities in South Korea are mostly overseas and temporary work-visa holders, and most of those are from other Asian countries. The largest 'minority' in Korea are actually other 'Koreans': Chinese-born Koreans separated more because of the modern national boundary drawing after the 1940s more than separated by cultural or political adherences. Plus, other ethnic minorities are so minuscule a demographic factor in South Korea that a (marketable) cultural industry's topics of systemic inequalities and truly different cultural ways of life in the same country, or stories of conflicts of individual friendship loyalties higher and sometimes versus cultural ethics—a common theme in more heterogeneous cultures like the United States—fails to make much market influence or political influence for that matter.

The third modern point that Hong ignores is another internal driver of the Korean Wave: that modern Korea really is a top down "leftist revolutionary state with Korean conservative characteristics," both economic and cultural. This means an export-led neoliberal capitalist economy is soldered oddly to a revolutionary nationalist state with a left-wing five-year plan and yet linked to a cultural and regional conservatism and linked to a deep national economic rural and grass roots development, development, national protectionism, and a decentralized agriculture. Korea's heritage is this dual and hybrid one: of having a truly revolutionary developmental state with all its horrors of a history of state censorship, blacklists, political murders, and cultural repression and yet how a deep cultural conservatism tempered that revolutionary development state in some ways and guided it on in others. It is a Korean state that thus fails generally to have the cultural space for a loyal opposition both because of its leftist revolutionary developmental state heritage *and* its rightist cultural heritage, so it is intolerant of dissent regardless of its origin whether left or right is in power. This is combined with a truly bullying culture that openly represses public conflict and self-represses private dissent.

These *internal* factors of a top-down revolutionary economics combined with a state censorship and a self-censorship in Korean culture from a more homogeneous culture of only collective innovation has influenced the content of the Korean Wave more than Hong would surmise about only external marketing forces as the creators of the Korean Wave's content. This internal censorship of state and culture for what works in the export-led economy of the Korean Wave winnows what is available before global external popularity kicks in to popularize only what has been winnowed to survive to reach that level. So, in the Korean Wave, as much as there is a common Korean state, corporate, consumer, and conservative cultural alliance to *prime* it into existence, there is a common state policy to *repress* it selectively into existence as well.

Five short examples taken from the 1970s through 2017 suffice to show that cultural/state censorship is a long term internal issue in Korea. It has been occurring long before the external marketing strategies of the Korean state and Korean companies began in the 1990s to choose what to popularize and what to suppress in Korean culture.

The first example comes from before the Korean Wave even existed in Korea. There were a few modern Korean cultural stars who tried to link cultural revolutionary statements, rebellious politics, individualism or just 'patriotic noncommittal neutrality' to cultural productions in Korean mass culture. They found themselves openly blacklisted or even tortured long before President Chun or President Park Geun-hye. This is seen in *the tragic yet later triumphant story* of Shin Joong-hyun (신중현), the culturally and individually innovative and very talented psychedelic soul/metal "rocker"—the term for a rock'n'roll star in Korea. Shin Joong-hyun's story is triumphant because he is now known as the Korean 'godfather of rock.' In 2010, he was the first Asian musician to receive a Fender Custom Shop Tribute Series guitar, because he used American Fender guitars in much of his long career from the 1950s through retirement in the early 2000s. The only other singer/songwriters honored by Fender have been a handful of global American or British mega-stars like Eric Clapton, Jeff Beck, or Eddie Van Halen. In 2017, Shin even received an honorary doctorate of music from Boston's Berklee College of Music.

If that is Shin's ultimate triumph, his life from 1972 through the 1990s in Korea was the earlier tragedy under open blacklists. He was blacklisted by *both* Presidents Park and Chun, and even tortured and jailed repeatedly under President Park throughout the 1970s. What was Shin's crime? It was trying to be neutral in Park's right-wing cultural revolutionary period between 1970 to 1979. Shin formed the first Korean rock group, called Add4, in 1962. By 1968, Shin produced a million-selling album called "My Dear" for the Pearl Sisters. In this era, he was the lead in Korea's psychedelic rock scene as well. He went on to write more hit songs and produce more hit records for other musicians like Kim Chu-ja. Due to Shin's popularity in the late 1960s and early 1970s, President Park's office asked Shin in 1972 to write a song that praised President Park who had just conducted an autocoup that ended the Third Republic of Korea. This made the Fourth Republic (1972-1981) which rigged one-third of the National Assembly to be appointed by Park without elections, removed open competitive presidential elections themselves, and changed the constitution so Park could be president for life on long seven-year terms.

Instead of writing a song of praise or a song of criticism, Shin composed and recorded a ten-minute psychedelic rock 'protest song', though it was a weak protest because it was simply noncommittal to Park yet very patriotic. However, it failed to mention President Park at all. Instead, Shin patriotically sang of love, peace, and how beautiful Korea was as a nation. It was called "Beautiful Rivers and Mountains," produced in 1972. It landed him in jail. Even because of a mere noncommittal yet patriotic response, instead of an outright protest, Shin's guitars still were confiscated by police. He was arrested and tortured, and his long hair was cut—a hairstyle universally banned for men by President Park's cultural revolution at the time. However, Shin was out of jail by 1974. He then wrote and produced another million-selling hit album. Then in 1975, Shin was arrested once more by Park's administration, artificially for possession of marijuana even though it was not illegal at the time of his arrest. Shin was imprisoned this time in a psychiatric hospital and tortured once more. After being released once more, Shin found himself openly blacklisted: banned from having his songs on radio, produced, or even having live performances in South Korea. The live performance ban lasted until the assassination of President Park in 1979. However, Shin remained on an open blacklist under President Chun (from his 1979 military coup, then from 1980–1988 one Presidential Term without open elections). Shin's recorded music remained banned from radio play or distribution even after Chun left the Presidency in 1988. Only in the 1990s was he culturally 'rehabilitated.' Shin is truly an individual innovator and a cultural innovator, and that was likely his equal taboo in the eyes of Korean dictatorial politics in the 1970s into the 1980s—combined with a more homogeneous culture with little love of or places for such individual or cultural innovations. How did Shin Joong-hyun become *so innovative in individual and cultural ways* that the homogeneous culture of Korea dislikes, with the culture around him only appreciating mostly the teamwork of *collective innovation*? The answer seems tragic. Shin was denied a Korean team experience for his whole life by accidents of birth and life. He was born a Korean in 1938, under Japanese occupation, and yet his Korean mother died early when he was a child. His Korean father remarried a Japanese woman during the Japanese occupation. Therefore, Shin spent his youth with his Korean father and Japanese step-mother, while even living outside of Korea—in Manchuria and in Japan. However, when they returned to what was South Korea after World War II, his father died in 1952 within the Korean War when Shin was around fourteen years of age. After that, the teenage Shin worked in a pharmaceutical factory, attended night school, and learned musical instruments in his (greater freedom of) cultural isolation. In 1957, when only nineteen, Shin debuted at a U.S. military base, where Korean musicians could find regular work in their then-poor country. Shin got inspired by the culturally innovative forms of American rock and jazz, and soon by the 1960s, was equally inspired by the psychedelic rock that he heard on the American Forces Network radio station in Korea. Shin said this cultural crossroads was where Korean rock was born, though it was equally born within himself as a rolling stone in those cultural crossroads. Shin is full ethnic Korean, yet raised entirely in non-Korean cultural contexts and mostly in non-Korean family contexts given he lost his remaining anchor of a Korean father in his very young teenage years in 1952. Unlike most Koreans, this freed him to have nothing left to lose. Musical individual innovation could become his life more easily than most Koreans, as there was nothing else Korean to fall back upon or to stop him. Thus, foreign cultural forms of music and public performance in Korea became his life. In that context in Korea, unlike so many others, Shin began to shine as an individual innovator responsible for large mass media hits, yet it seems he shone "too brightly" for the repressive state culture of the Korean 1970s. However, thc individual and cultural innovations that Shin showed that he was capable of seem set even before his U.S. military base experiences at rock'n'roll performance.

Second, a state censorship and cultural blacklist by denial of sponsorship and even blocking of album sales can be seen in the earlier career of Psy before 2012. Psy was born in 1977 as Park Jae-sang, living in the wealthy Gangnam zone of Seoul and eldest son in a wealthy family with a father who was the CEO of DI Corporation (that makes semiconductor testing equipment). Psy's early life was as a wealthy school class clown. In order to inherit his father's company position when he retired, Park's family sent the young Jae-sang to be educated in the U.S. at Boston University in business administration in the 1990s, yet Park spent his money and time on musical instruments and digital recording equipment. After dropping out of Boston University, he was accepted in nearby Berklee College of Music, equally in Boston. However, after taking the base curriculum, he dropped out as well, and he returned to Korea to make music. His debut album in 2001, called *Psy from the Psycho World!*, got him fined by Korean government over what they felt was the album's "inappropriate content". In 2002, his second album *Sa 2* was banned from being sold to teenagers under 19 years of age. His third album *3 Psy* had a song named "Champion". It was successful somewhat accidentally due to context and hype from the World Cup Games then being held in Seoul. Despite past controversy, Psy did receive songwriting awards for the first time at the annual Seoul Music Awards. By 2003, and then in his late twenties, Psy entered the Korean military only due to it being mandatory on all Korean males aged 18 through 35. However, Psy arranged a legitimate military exemption to escape military service due to finding a job at a software company—since the government gives military exemptions for certain desired technical expertise interpreted to serve the national economic interest. However, during his time at the software company his legitimate excuse became an illegitimate use in the eyes of the Korean government. While ostensibly working at a software company to maintain his military deferment, he released his fourth album *Ssajib*, which received awards at the 2006 SBS Music Awards and even internationally at the Hong Kong's Mnet Asian Music Awards. It became obvious to the Korean government that Psy was abusing his software job as a fake alibi to escape military service. In 2007, as Psy approached being 30 years old, Korean prosecutors said Psy was ignoring his legitimate military exemption as a software company employee by spending his time mostly writing songs, holding concerts, and being on TV repeatedly. So, on October 12, 2007, the Seoul Administrative Court ruled Psy would be redrafted into the military, rejecting Psy's lawsuit filed against the government in the previous month. So, Psy was re-drafted into the Korean military in late 2007. He served as a 30-year-old Private First Class and as a signalman in the 52nd Army Infantry Division. He was released from military duties in July 2009. After being released from military service, and experiencing an inability to fund his own albums anymore, he was convinced by his wife to join YG Entertainment, whose founder and head was an old friend of Psy's, Yang Hyun-suk. Once more, upon the release of his fifth album *PsyFive* in 2010, its song "Right Now" was banned from the under-19 audience once more, this time by South Korea's Ministry of Gender Equality and Family for its "obscene" lyric, "Life is like toxic alcohol." Regardless of this, Psy did receive awards at the 2011 Melon Music Awards and at Mnet Asian Music Awards. Thus, for his bucking of the moral trend or even the body type trend of what the Korean state wanted to create in 'its' cultural production for the Korean Wave, Psy winnowed himself out of state sponsorship. However, by 2011, Psy had a string of successful national hits interwoven with a string of his domestic family and governmental conflicts. However, soon, his global fame rendered this slight governmental blacklisting moot by 2012 with the success of his song and video for "Gangnam Style." Psy was back-integrated in the Korean Wave pantheon only after global fame instead of before it. The song was released in June 2012 from his sixth album *Psy 6 (Six Rules), Part 1.* Psy produced a video for this album's song "Gangnam Style," and he says he was supported by a large team that brainstormed and choreographed the 'horse dance' for the video. The rest is history and was described in the timeline section earlier. In this way, before the pop rocker Psy became the first truly *unsponsored* global success in the Korean wave in 2012 with his 'lewd comedic pop' despite being repeatedly punished by the Korean state and blocked from Korean state sponsorship.

Third, the same theme of how poorly Korea treats its individual innovators and cultural innovators is seen in the governmental blacklist and later back-integration of the 2010 Korean gold-medal winning Olympic skating star Yuna Kim (in Korean, Kim Yeon-a (김연아). Her mother says the name "Kim Yuna" (Kim Yu-Na/김유나) came originally out of her daughter's error in applying for an American visa for skate training, with her writing 'Kim Yun-a' (김윤아) instead of 'Kim Yeon-A' (김연아) on the American form. Then, this error was compounded in turn by the American governmental official who wrote the name differently as 'Kim Yu-Na' in English (which back in Korean is "김유나"). However, Yuna Kim says she likes this name, and anyway from 2010 she chose "Yuna Kim" as her official International Skating Union (ISU) registration. So, given vague hyphen/syllable rules in Korean and governmental mistakes, she really has three names. However, "as Shakespeare might have said, a Yuna by another name like Yu-Na or Yun-A would skate as great" (Hersh, 2009). Yuna Kim was born in 1990, and began skating at the age of five. Her youthful and previously unreachable high scores in female figure skating were already a Korean national and then global phenomenon long before she won the gold medal in the Winter Olympics women's ice skating in 2010 in Vancouver. By age twelve, she was the top female skater in Korea, having won first place at the South Korean Figure Skating Championships—the youngest ever winner. She continued to be the top female figure skater in Korea in subsequent years between 2003 through 2006. She won top place at her first international competition at the Triglav Trophy competitions in Jensenice, Slovenia in 2001. Then she won her second top place international title at the Golden Bear competition in Zagreb, Croatia for 2003-4. Between 2004 and 2005, she basically won top score or was second place in all remaining other global competitions. Her gold medal win in the 2010 Winter Olympics in Vancouver additionally made a world record on high scores there that remains still in place today in 2023 as her main claim to fame. Plus, her second claim to fame is that she remains the only woman to ever win all major global female skating awards in world history. However, before her gold medal win in the 2010 Winter Olympics in Vancouver and despite her whole life skating at superlative levels before that, she was ignored by the Korean state. Thus, Yuna Kim's story was earlier tragic, far more tragic than independently wealthy Psy, though not as tragic as Shin Joong-hyun. Yuna is female, and plus, female ice skating was not selected as a state priority for gold medals. For these two rationales, in patriarchal Korea she was ignored by the Korean state for her whole training life, despite and even after her incredibly early global wins and clear talent were being demonstrated from 2001. Appeals to aid her were denied. So, her family paid for expensive private Olympic-level trainers, as Koreans in general had access only to poor infrastructural support for ice skating at the time. She even had to wear ill fitting skates in Korea and practice only at some of the few Korean public skating rinks near opening or closing hours—because it was less crowded with distractions from other public customers. However, like Psy, Yuna Kim was celebrated by the Korean state only after her self-achieved fame at being an Olympic gold medalist at the Winter Olympics in 2010, since the Korean state had nothing to do with her world-renowned success and even postponed it. Due to lack of aid in Korea, she trained mostly out of Korea—in Canada or the United States. Korean state priorities in other sports surely postponed her and other female Korean ice skater successes for years. The government could have had at least a program to provide skates to fit talented rising stars like her in the 1990s and 2000s, when such skates were hard to find in Korea then. So, Yuna Kim actually in her early career had to train in Korea in poorly fitting skates that caused injuries and damaged her early career repeatedly. She learned some jumps only safely outside of Korea, in the United States where harnesses and wires similar to circus trapeze artists were available to aid less painful learning on complicated jumps. In general, the story of tragedy to triumph in Yuna Kim as well shows that the Korean state should consider basic material aids for multiple sports, *as well as should recognize when individual innovative talent or cultural innovation should change its structural equations in the Korean Wave*. However, despite her government failing earlier to consider individual female ice skating as of general importance in state Olympic priorities, instead of team sports like speed skating and team archery, Yuna Kim is still considered to be the most awarded and wealthiest individual figure skater in world history, male or female. However, her career was entirely her own making with her family support and without Korean state assistance (Binns, 2019).

Fourth, the secret cultural blacklist is seen as postponing the career success of another now famous top Korean Wave director Bong Joon-ho. He produced the famous Korean film *Snowpiercer* (2013) and *Okja* (2017) and he was the producer of the most profitable and most awarded Korean film yet, *Parasite* (2019). However, in 2016, Bong discovered he as well as several of his actors had been secretly blacklisted for years by the Korean government under President Park Geun-hye (2013–2017), which hampered his film career, funding, and festival screenings (Collman, 2020). Thus, once more the Korean state hampered its own Korean Wave's success and profitability itself, simply out of internal problems of a repressive culture, and in this case, political spite for left-wing leanings.

Fifth, as mentioned earlier, secret blacklisting is seen clearly in the Korean K-pop group 24K. They associated themselves with the left-wing candidacy of Moon Jae-in in 2012, and thus were against the future President Park Geun-hye during the election as they sang for Moon's campaign. After Park's win though, the popular K-pop group 24K found themselves secretly blacklisted from past Korean Wave funding as well as blacklisted from Korean TV appearances—once more, in political spite for left-wing leanings.

Reflecting on these five examples of state-organized censorship and blacklisting over thirty years in Korean cultural production, thus, the Korean Wave gives and taketh away. It lavishes support if artists follow the mold of state development desires, yet it denies other artists by blocking cultural innovation and talent, as it tries to cut them shorter if they fail to fit the Procrustean bed of the Korean state-developmental mold. This state blacklisting seems done on oddly capricious, emotional, petulant and spiteful rationales. This has only repeatedly self-sabotaged the Korean Wave. What does it say about the Korean culture and state *internally*, that repeatedly the very best stars of Korean culture and of the global Korean Wave (Shin Joong-hyun, Kim Yuna, Park Jae-sang (Psy), Bong Joon-ho, and 24K) have this dual theme of being far more hampered or ignored in their home country instead of helped, and yet then they are lauded and enshrined only once it later serves that more bureaucratic system to recognize them begrudgingly only after major foreign wins overseas?

The long *internal* experience of cultural censorship in Korea that is both organizational and cultural itself, first open and later covert, echoes the earlier points about collective innovation in a more homogeneous culture. It as well echoes themes of how the Korean Wave first conquered at home by conquering Korea's more open domestic culture with state-sponsored cultural productions and one-sided partisan content whether during Park I, Chun, Roh, or Park II and beyond. This is meant to be complementary to Hong's more 'external' ideas that the Korean Wave is just a neutral expression of an ancient culture or a savvy rational international business strategy for only developing countries' markets. Hong might have been able to get away with a one-sided 'external' interpretation in 2014 as her book about the Korean Wave was published then, before the massive growth of the global Korean Wave across the developed West as well as before the cultural blacklist was known from 2016. However, the fact of a secret blacklist of nearly 10,000 Korean artists should make clear that far more internal organizational and cultural problems of Korean politics designed the marketing strategies of the Korean Wave by being so far unable to accept individual innovation and cultural innovation. This caused a delayed expansion of the global Korean Wave—not the least by blocking up to 10,000 Korean artists from support categorically between 2013 to 2017—and perhaps even more even earlier on other cultural blacklists never revealed, ever. In other words, the Korean State and even the Korean culture has historically before 2017 been its own worst enemy in hampering, censoring and artificially homogenizing the profitability and advance of the Korean Wave by blocking thousands of artists from participating in it by being less adoring of individual innovation or cultural innovation. The first more 'simultaneous successes' in the Korean Wave came a quick mere year after the cultural blacklists were ended, breaking the dam of a long-term domestic cultural censorship with a flood of the global Korean Wave. However, the more homogeneous culture of the Korean Wave in the nation and government itself still is a major filter that prefers more collective innovation in safe teamwork tasks instead of more risky individual or cultural innovation that regularly makes global entertainment stars just the same—or even better.

In summary, Korea's internal cultural and organizational factors *and* external cultural market factors have to be considered together as what has made the Korean Wave unique and unlike past Americanization. American cultural products after World War II tended to expand out of the United States due to several factors: its domestic industrial success, its success in inventing and marketing a consumer culture of products exclusively for teenagers for the first time in world history, its skill at propaganda in Cold War politics, and of course by being by default the only undestroyed urban industrial economy without any competition across the Atlantic countries of North America and Europe. On that point of the sheer default scale of the United States' domestic industrial success compared to others after World War II Americanization took the world mostly by default due to this sheer scale of production versus smaller production scales of other nations, empires, and colonies that were greatly diminished in finance and in cultural shock after World War II (Mattelart, 2000). Americans created their own synergistic flow of material production in many different one-way mass media and a cultural production entirely geared toward a worldwide teenage market, to which was added a Cold War and rebellious rhetoric. Thus, Americanization tended to focus more on promoting universalist themes of proud individualist youth innovation, rebellion, and cultural revolutionary themes from renegades in a youth culture, mafias, or rebellious and intentionally culturally shocking rock-n-roll stars. Other historical rebels like Atlantic pirates, smugglers, anti-heroes, religious rebels, and brave individuals against corrupt (collectivist) systems were all common universal themes pushed by Americanization. Perhaps the best example of all of these American wave themes of heroic individual rebellion thrown together in one film (except missing a rock-and-roll star) is the Disney film *The Scarecrow of Romney Marsh* (1963), starring Patrick McGoohan, based on a popular book of the early twentieth century.

However, South Korea now is expanding its cultural wave in a more depoliticized post-Cold War environment from the 1990s. Plus it is exporting those more collectivist, more traditional, and more hierarchical images of proper gendered behaviors, formulaic beautiful men and women, admirable deferential behaviors in polite pop stars, pro-patriotic stories, and love stories that are stronger than political divisions. Stories glorifying rebellion or individual heroes fail to exist in the Korean Wave—even though the main successes of the Korean Wave as noted above have been marked by the successful rebellion of its individual heroes. Plus, there are very few Korean films or Korean popular music groups romanticizing mafias, sexual recklessness, drug addiction, and violent behavior instead of it being shown simply for the sheer horror of entertainment or as precautionary tales. Even if 'Korean black sheep' like Shin, Park, or Kim break the mold by being successful in the Korean Wave despite a lack of original approval, their adult public behavior and statements remain patriotically Korean and deferential in honor to nation and/or family. In the case of Psy, how many other cultures create a pop star like the delinquent rebel Psy, who nonetheless later wrote a famous Korean rap love song called "Aboji" (honorific term for 'father') about himself as a wayward son and his anguished regret that he neglected to love his hardworking father, who took care of his whole family, until it was almost too late in life for the son to realize it to say he loved his father. Few modern pop songs are tearful yet happy Confucian abeyances and apologies to a father, yet it Psy made it a major hit as a concert 'sing-along' song in South Korea along with its animated video. On the other side of the Pacific, American rap stars like Eminem write songs that curse his own mother Debbie or the group Veruca Salt talks about killing babies, seething volcano girls, or being less than sane 'born entertainers.'

Obviously, Korean and American cultural waves are very different in content, internally for who are the stars are and what the culture is like, and externally for who they are attempting to market toward, to reach, and why. Markets in the Korean Wave can be simpler since it is spreading out of a more homogeneous culture instead of a more heterogeneous one with different innovative preferences, and can be more politically one-dimensional since the Korean Wave was spreading regionally or globally only after 1992 which was after the end of the Cold War. Even themes of modern Korean Wave dramas that do mention Cold War dynamics like the theme of North Korea in *Shiri* or *Iris* turn it into a romantic narrative of star-crossed lovers broken by what is framed as the 'externally extruding' modern history of the two countries that really are one country at heart, thus trying to treat global geopolitics as just a factor of background noise in a romance, while implying divisions of North and South are driven only by nebulous external global unknown forces trying to break up 'naturally unified' Koreans instead of equally and truly caused by Koreans themselves in disagreements over ideal political forms. Meanwhile, Americans have always tried to do so much with their cultural wave: build a global export-led market for teen cultural product categories of mass media worldwide, while trying to connect it to making some geopolitical point about ideal and bad political systems and which political system creates a better future and culture, while encouraging other cultures to honor like themselves their own internal and psychological conflicts linked to individual rebels as heroes or anti-heroes, or cathartically celebrating self-destructive youth angst and nihilism. In short, the Korean Wave can be more simple and direct in its messaging by developing after the Cold War, coming from a very homogeneous culture, as well as suffering under long term state censorship as well.

4.4 Comparing the Entertainment Industry in the U.S.A., the U.K., and South Korea

Keep in mind there have been very few *multi-product global cultural waves* in the modern world of mass media from the 1870s onward—only a handful if we list both short term and long term cultural waves: United States, Soviet Union, German Nazi period, German modern 1970s through the 1980s, United Kingdom, France, Italy, Hong Kong, Japan, and South Korea. A wider sample might include more single product cultural waves like Brazilian music, Mexican telenovelas, or Indian Bollywood films. An even smaller sample has durability for decades as multi-product global cultural waves: only the United States, United Kingdom, Soviet Union, and South Korea. Thus, Korea has become one of these few countries to hone such a skill of exporting its culture. Others can only join it, catch up, or fail. Many countries nowadays prefer to join Korean expertise to avoid difficulties with the other two options.

When Hallyu first spread around East Asia, Korea's cultural exports changed the youth cultures of other Asian countries nearby and evoked in the elites of those nations a growing desperation at the "Korean wave fever" in their own youth. Similarly, European leaders had the same worried feeling about America after World War II as their own domestic national youth cultures were dissolving into the sharing of 'Americanized' media products and cultural images. In turn, these nations' youth were emotionally changed, increasingly noncommittal about or rebellious in rejection of their past local European national cultures. So, in the face of European cultural collapse of youth markets after World War II, European states rushed to protect and to subsidize their own failing book publishing, music cultures, and film industries from economic bankruptcy at the time—though equally protecting them from cultural content bankruptcy as well (Mattelart, 2000). However, nowadays instead of resisting, most 'competing' national entertainment industries and their past cultural waves are simply joining the global Korean Wave. The argument here is that it is hardly enough to simply protect a national political economy and culture from outside influences anymore. This is because in a world of the Internet which is based increasingly on mobile phone networks, with half of the world's Internet accessed by mobiles for the first time by 2017 (We are Social / Hootsuite, 2017), a culture that is outside a country is always inside a country's Internet access easily, and thus inside already the daily thoughts of its population. Therefore, while protectionism and national subsidies alone seemed a proper strategy after World War II against Americanization's physical one-way mass media of cultural artifacts that could be blocked at borders easily in the interests of national development and for preserving a national entertainment industry, that now seems an antiquated response like the French Maginot Line to a changed world of globally common mobile phone networks, globally common platforms, and globally common Korean wave content. Despite many countries turning off their Internet temporarily during protests, none of them conceive of turning it off permanently, and thus permanently being able to filter foreign cultures' content out of themselves as easily as in the previous media regime that had to physically travel across borders instead of simply be downloaded into minds. It is argued that the only true response is for countries to try to do what Korea is doing and raise the profile of their own global digital entertainment industry. However, many countries are poorly placed to do just that by a combination of their past and current limitations on hard power, economic power, and soft power.

Given much of the global Korean wave is now in the production of TV, cinema, video games, and multimedia K-pop music dance video songs, "entertainment" is core to the profit and interest in the Korean Wave. However, the way it is organized is different in different countries. Korea has a more extensive state-primed and prioritized entertainment industry, compared to the United States or the United Kingdom.

The etymology of the word "entertainment" that we use today is a compound word from the Latin 'inter' (in the public, in the middle) and 'tenere' (maintain, pay attention). The word's meaning thus can be interpreted as 'to draw public attention.' The term "entertainment" is a cultural concept that means to give pleasure, fun, and emotion to people. Some argue entertainment is as much drawing public attention as it is publicly and individually desired distraction and pleasurable escape of putting attention somewhere else. Thus, in stratified state societies, entertainment regularly has been both a state-organized and an individual cathartic release valve for the poor in world history so the latter ignore class dynamics. This is seen from ancient Rome's Coliseum to the fresh European and American urban industrial cities with their swelling labor underclasses of the mid-to-late 1800s—which was the period of high labor unrest as well as the period that invented mass amusement parks as modern Coliseums (Beacham, 1999; Kasson, 1978). This is seen as what some Koreans called the "3S's" (the state's propaganda and distractions framed as 'sex, screen, and sports') from President Chun's era of the 1980s (Kang, 2019). Third, entertainment is equally cathartic and serves as political propaganda sometimes. For instance, the Nazi Reich Minister of Propaganda Goebbels (1933–45) opined that political propaganda is best framed as entertainment because the watcher's guard is down.

Thus given entertainment's positive emotional meanings and negative distractive or political manipulation potential, and given varying degrees of state oversight in it, 'entertainment' is thus an organizational phenomena and a different more socially-shared concept than mere personal leisure or recreation which means to recharge or to refortify the mind and body. In Harold Vogel *Economics of the Entertainment Industry* (2014), entertainment *when it becomes an industry* starts to prime, promote, stimulate or create an *ongoing* ubiquitous situation of pleasurable diversions to the public as the industry tries to grasp the public's attention over and over without cease. Different nations have a different organization to their entertainment industry, yet regardless of whether the cultural industry has a success or a failure, if it is to survive, it has to increase its ability to seize the mind of the public and to do so with more success over time. Korea has been doing this since the 1980s by extensive state prioritizations (interventions and censorship is a better phrase) in cultural entertainments. This was long before regional Hallyu or the global Korean Wave, so there has been a lot of practice on the organizational side of the entertainment industry in Korea for decades since the 1980s.

As shown in the earlier timeline section, the growing scale the global Korean Wave itself is the evidence of an improving skill of this Korean entertainment industry to seize the world mind and to keep seizing it. The Korean state subsidized a great deal of the entertainment industry particularly after 1998 and even more after 2008. Plus in the private sector, Korean Wave promoters learned over time how to create more wins, and thus more potential for their wins to exist as a more simultaneous success over time with previous wins. This encouraged more synergistic cross-sector cultural communities and even permanent digital platforms to grow around such a durable K-culture worldwide. In the chapter on BTS, the group's popularity is a classic example of cross-product marketing savvy from its manger, around BTS in multiple kinds of products, instead of only 'managing BTS as a musical dance group.'

However, the organization and thus classification of the entertainment industry differs from country to country. As its policy environment and contents differ from country to country, an internationally standardized classification system has not been established. If we relate the entertainment industry to the cultural contents industry that has emerged as one of the best value-added industries in the twenty-first century, the cultural contents industry is the production of creative content in music, broadcasting, performance, computer games, film, video, character, animation, and spectator sports. Plus, the cultural contents industry is a *synergistic combination* of new technologies such as music, broadcasting, performances, games, movies, images, characters, and animations that are increasingly *digital*. UNESCO defines the cultural contents industry as "an industry that produces tangible or intangible artistic and creative results, which has the potential to generate wealth and generate income through the use of cultural assets and the production of knowledge-based goods and services." This includes areas like computerized games as digital spectator sports that Korea pioneered and dominated at the start over twenty years ago in the late 1990s. The creative digital side developed in the wider cultural contents industry itself. Korea was well placed earlier for merging both, perhaps because it was the earliest and the most successful example of national *digital* development that the world had seen by the early twenty-first century (See Appendix 1). While many countries attempted digital development and did it successfully for short periods before falling behind, Korea has done digital development successfully for over 40 years, defined as making both the material products of digital hardware as well as making a cultural production via digital content for that digital hardware. Doing both of these for decades, Korea is a world first for a rising ex-developing country (Oh & Larson, 2019).

The term cultural industry is not a term commonly used in all countries in the world, but a term used by some including Korea. Other similar terms for such a field include the 'entertainment industry' centered on the United States and the 'creative industry' in the United Kingdom. Thus, the cultural contents industry can be viewed as similar to 'entertainment,' and it can be collectively referred to as the 'entertainment industry.' Vogel (2014) divides the entertainment industry into two broad types: media-dependent and live events. Specifically, the former includes mainly video-related media industries such as movies, music, and broadcasting. The latter does not require media though could be aired through media simultaneously like in a broadcast live performance or experience for instance. Live entertainment includes events at particular places or how experience of place itself is enjoyed as entertainment like the tourism of visiting an amusement park, the city of Las Vegas, or Gangnam in Seoul (Table 4.2).

The first official use of the term cultural industry in Korea was in 1993, when the Cultural Industry Planning Bureau was established under the Ministry of Culture and Sports (the same Ministry that would later be the Ministry of Culture, Sports

Table 4.2 Entertainment Industry Scope (Vogel, *Entertainment Industry Economics* [2014])

	Subject	Contents
Media-dependent entertainment	Movie	Film production, Distribution, Screening, Marketing, Home video, etc.
	Music business	Composing, Publishing, Managing, Royalty, Concert, Album production
	Broadcasting	Production and Distribution of Programs
	Cable	Broadcast Operation (SO), Paid Broadcast (PPV)
	Toys and games	Characters, Game contents
Live Entertainment	Gambling	Slot machine, Casino management
	Sports	Cooperation project with Broadcasters (broadcasting rights)
	Performing arts	Commercial plays, Orchestras, Operas, Dances, etc.
	Tourism / Amusement park/ Theme park / Cities / Countryside / Natural wonders	Experiencing a place (and its crowds or its solitude) as entertainment instead of a specific staged content or predictable event

and Tourism). This planning bureau was established only one year after the first big success of starting a (then nameless) regional Hallyu in 1992. This was when many Korean businessmen overseas and many civil servants in the Korean government and in Korea's Hong Kong embassy collaborated to get a then-popular Korean TV drama called "What Is Love" to be shown on Hong Kong TV, with added Chinese dubbing for accessibility. The term cultural industry began to be used in earnest only when the Basic Act on the Promotion of Culture Industry came into effect in 1999—the first year that "Hallyu" started to be used as a term for the regional love of Korean cultural products throughout East Asia and Southeast Asia. The Act stipulates that "the cultural industry refers to an industry that provides services related to the planning, development, production, production, distribution, consumption, etc. of cultural products." By 2001, the term 'cultural contents' was used by the Ministry of Culture and Tourism in August 2001 by its Korea Cultural Content Promotion Agency. This agency since its inception has been active in priming the Korean Wave.

In the Korean case, the term 'cultural industry' is stipulated in the Culture and Arts Promotion Act and the Framework Act on the Promotion of Cultural Industries. According to the Culture and Arts Promotion Act (Article 2.2), the term 'cultural industry' refers to the production, performance, exhibition, and sale of cultural and artistic creations or cultural and artistic products by means of industry as a business, focusing on the arts industry. On the other hand, according to the Framework Act on the Promotion of Cultural Industries (Article 2.1), the 'cultural industry' is defined as an industry that provides services related to planning, development, production, production, distribution, consumption, etc., of cultural products. Here, 'cultural product' refers to tangible and intangible goods, services, and complexes (including cultural-related contents and digital cultural contents) that create economic added value by embodied cultural factors. In addition, the term 'cultural factor' refers to artistry, creativity, entertainment, and popularity. The concept of the cultural industry is more comprehensive than the provisions of the Culture and Arts Promotion Act.

However, despite all these state planning agencies in the Korean entertainment industry, it is the United States with its much less pronounced centralized planning in culture that is the most influential country in the world in this field of the cultural contents industry and with its larger content stress on individual innovation and cultural innovation. That content is hardly the only factor. The United States as well is a much larger country and market than South Korea, with much larger budgets and larger organizational history in its cultural industries. This helps in expanding American cultural exports and in cheaper production. The United States thus has a huge influence both overall in the world market and in detailed areas of competition within the global industry. In the United States, the industry in this field is called the Information or Entertainment and Media Industry. It includes film, television, radio, music, internet, games, magazine publishing, newspaper publishing, book publishing, information services, advertising, amusement parks, and sports.

After recognizing the economic and social value of this field, the United Kingdom's Ministry of Cultural Heritage was established. It was in the midst of the global economic crisis in 1997, just like in South Korea, that the U.K. expanded and reorganized the Ministry of Cultural Heritage into the Department of Culture,

Media and Sports (DCMS). DCMS's main work areas are largely divided into culture (art, museums and galleries, libraries, architecture, cultural heritage, etc.), media, sports, tourism, and creative industry. What should be noted here is the distinction between culture and creative industries in the United Kingdom. DCMS (1998) established the 'Ministerial Creative Industries Strategy Group' in 1997 and defined the creative industry as having an "origin [that] lies in individual creativity, skill and talent, and through the generation and use of intellectual property, [making an industry] that has the potential to create wealth and jobs." U.K. sub-sectors within that industry include advertising, architecture, art and antique markets, crafts, design, designer fashion, film and video, interactive leisure software, music, performing arts, publishing, software, TV and radio, etc.

In Korea however the entertainment sector is not classified as an industry per se, but nonetheless it has been defined in the Framework Act on the Promotion of Cultural Industries, which was enacted in February 1999 and amended in January 2002. According to the Framework Act, the cultural industry is a business in which cultural products such as films, records, video products, games, publications and printing, cultural assets, advertisements, performances, etc. are produced and distributed, and related services are provided up to final consumption. It is stipulated in the Promotion Act (2004) as well. Notice South Korea's version says nothing about encouraging *individual* creativity, as the U.K.'s view of the cultural industry does.

In conclusion, the development of state-specific organizations for priming cultural industries is different in different countries, as well as the different in expectations of where that cultural creativity is to be generated. However, in both South Korea and the U.K., which are about the same size demographically at around 50 million people, both nations started to accelerate state priming of their respective cultural industries in the late 1990s in the midst of a global financial downturn from 1997 over the next few years and in the rise of our present digital media regime. However, in the United States, such a state planning agency of a cultural industry hardly exists *overtly* within this much larger nation despite large *covert* U.S. military networks coordinating cultural production out of the Cold War and thus increasing having deep state connections to the U.S. entertainment industry along with starting and managing its Internet networks (McGowan, 2014; Levine, 2018). Plus, despite entertainment downturns occasionally in the United States as well, the United States has so far been more successful in the past in its cultural industry for this larger nation. On the one hand, it is perhaps expected that more 'mid-sized' nations will have more state planning in defense of their cultural industries against the globalization of the cultural industries of larger nations like the United States. However, on the other hand, situations are changing now in a fresh digital media regime. It is now expected that larger nations' cultural industries may have the harder time holding together in their cultural waves due to their greater heterogeneity and due to the influence of shifting to a digital culture that makes common wide markets in a cultural industry difficult to create anymore like Hollywood of the past, for instance. These ideas of how our current media regime change may be ending the organizational hegemony of larger nations' cultural industries in the world-system are saved for the discussion in Part III.

4.5 Different Ways to Think of the Culture and Soft Power of the Korean Wave

Beyond its contribution to the Korean economy, the global Korean Wave and its entertainment industry are contributing to Korea's 'soft power.' This section discusses the interaction of that cultural popularity and the more political concept of 'soft power' in the Korean Wave. The Korean Wave is arguably the most important cultural phenomenon in Korea in this century and has had an impact on changing the dynamics of the international community due to the growing popularity of Korean culture. This Korean 'soft power' leads to a further love for Korean products, allowing Korean companies and even the Korean state to utilize cultural marketing as a source of competitive advantage in the world. Korean 'soft power' is even repeated twice: as a powerful echo through foreign media around the world and through the viral online sharing of global consumers of the Korean Wave, as a digital fandom.

Let us define culture before defining soft power. A definition of culture is the general thinking, language, and norms of behavior agreed upon by a group of people to coexist and to accommodate in a specific time and space. The origin of the English word 'culture' is the Latin word *cultus*, which means cultivation. In other words, culture means to change or to create a new natural state, object, or way of thinking through human action. Therefore, instead of culture in natural objects themselves, there is a tendency to express culture in humanly-formed artificial objects or to project culture onto natural objects. This makes even *natural materials* or *material artifacts* carry a certain culture as a sign of shared and transmitted meaning. Culture additionally is found in more *ephemeral phenomena* like events that can carry, transmit, and thus reproduce symbolic and interpreted meanings. In 2001, the United Nations Educational, Scientific, and Cultural Organization (UNESCO) defined culture as a combination of both, as mostly something which has an *intangible* symbolic meaning and interpreted expression made *tangible*: "the distinctive spiritual and material properties of art, literature, lifestyle, living, values, traditions, and beliefs that appear in a society or social group. It was defined as an integrated and comprehensive concept of "intellectual characteristics." For a summary of this interaction of intangible culture and tangible components, Table 4.3 includes the following three interpenetrating themes of culture: artifacts, values, and basic assumptions.

To discuss these three categories without any particular order, given they are causally interactive in feedback loops, first, culture can refer to *artifacts and creations*. These are the visible and interpretable material works of art or the eventful creations expressed through either tangible techniques like craftsmanship or intangible techniques like dance, song, and speech. Respectively, this includes material art and behavioral patterns. Second, there are the concepts of *values* symbolically put in those material works or events. Each cultural group expresses, transmits, and thus reproduces a unique concept of value in this way. The third aspect of culture is the *basic assumptions* or ontological principles of what people consider the ground of their being that is real and important whether social or physical. This refers to assumptions about human-to-environmental relationships, real time-or-space relationships,

Table 4.3 Cultural elements, ranging from intangible to tangible (Adapted from Schein, 1985)

Artifacts and Creations Technology Art Visible and audible behavior patterns	Tangible and Visible, but often not decipherable
↑↓	↑
Values Testable in the physical environment Testable only by social consensus	Greater Level of Awareness
↑↓	↑
Basic Assumptions Relationship to environment Nature of reality, time, and space Nature of human activity Nature of human nature Nature of human relationships	Intangible and Invisible, taken for granted, preconscious

human behavior, human nature, and human relationships. These three components of culture are mostly noetic, taken for granted, or understood unconsciously in cultural lives, artifacts, or actions in the process of people being raised among other members of the culture and taught through its shared behaviors and intangible symbols, instead of strictly using tangible items or learning a list of formal tenets. Culture is thus both interpretive upon tangible material artifacts and interpretive upon intangible performed behaviors around social and environmental relationships.

On the one hand, this cultural matrix is reinforced daily and mostly indirectly by making material artifacts and by making events from which interpretations or reinforcements come from those actions. Thus a cultural matrix is mostly unvoiced interpretations and feelings associated with cultural elements instead of generally clear intellectual statements. *On the other hand*, a cultural matrix *can be demoted daily and directly by coming into interaction with others' cultural matrix that people feel is doing a better job of providing them those three meaningful factors desired* in Table 4.3, to give even people originally in other cultures the chance to share in another cultural transmission and reproduction of that other culture. Thus with this view of culture, reproduction and competition ensues due to multiple cultures existing in interaction in the world. This can range from *cultural appropriation* in more self-interested benefits of spreading a culture, to merely *cultural appreciation* where another person or culture becomes infused with a different culture willingly because they admire it, enjoy it, make it their own, and want to help it spread. 'Soft power' entails the latter cultural appreciation by others originally outside the culture who nonetheless want to help it to spread.

As noted in Appendix 4, another way to classify culture is to think about the different biasing influences of the media regime hegemonically used in that culture.

Thus equally cultural change is influenced by media regime change and by different cultures simultaneously in the same physical world involved in different dissonant media regimes, abutting and interacting with each other. For instance, on the first point, we innately began to live in the first media regime of oral speech only once our evolving human biophysical capacities for symbolic speech allowed for it because of increasing neural links between the brain, larynx, and mouth in an evolutionary sense to make us better language-speaking creatures and thus symbol-sharing creatures (Deacon, 1997). Living in a world once without external paper, books, writing scripts, or electronics, humans were the core biological medium of the first media regime, and out of that, extensions off our biological bodies are the more tangible artifacts and intangible symbolic behaviors created that become interpreted signs of a wider cultural matrix than merely our biological bodies. This first media regime of oral speech for the first time created lived shared symbolic behaviors among aural, visual, and tactile symbolic signs in tangible artifacts and intangible behaviors carrying such signs between each other, transmitting over generations. These ongoing shared behaviors started to be a shared mental cultural world older than anyone alive in the culture, yet which of course depend upon daily individual interpretation and our biophysical body's ongoing ability to interpret, carry, and transmit such oral speech and its non-oral symbolic body actions. In this way the shared mental world of an oral spoken language innately becomes a shared external expression, and then through that, a transmission of an internalized cultural interpretation as well. Oral speech influenced humanity more than any other media regime and can be said to even have created humanity—via our bodies becoming collected into many different cultural oral groups of the same oral speech-linked cultural animals—yet believing many different things in different abutting groups. Once it was invented, oral speech remained the main cultural transmission of humanity worldwide for perhaps the past 50,000 to 100,000 years. Plus, on the second point, in the issue of media regimes abutting each other, the whole world had the same media regime, and different versions of this identical media regime abutted each other.

In short, with the beginning of spoken language in Regime 1, we invented a complex *individually interpreted and yet socially shared* cultural world of communication of that culture, in awareness and discussion of meanings placed in material artifacts and in symbolic events whether language or rituals that expressed and transmitted that culture's values and basic assumptions. However, since different individuals may interpret the same external shared behavior or symbol in different ways, there is an innate disalignment in all shared social activities. Regardless, once speech was invented, or really once speech invented us culturally, speech remained the main cultural transmission of humanity. In a world before states or literacy, it created a world of thousands of small groups run by mostly inherited lines of shamanistic medical elites, mutually incomprehensible tongues, and culturally different values than each other, yet commonly tied to their different environments in specific ongoing regional relationships attempting optimality in particular places. When we were only oral speakers in media Regime 1, in other words, we culturally fit into particular regional ecological zones. Our populations worldwide were plural with shared language, symbols, actions, and interpretations that were sometimes very different in culture than others in other zones very close nearby. There was little 'soft power' in such a world, as there was less place for more hierarchical status of one group over other that is a part of soft power.

As we changed media regimes over time, the next media regimes of written complex scripts and then simple scripts invented states and their bureaucracies from which past political economic inequalities and past cultural hierarchies became larger and more organized—both *within* a culture (of now small numbers of literate elites over larger groups of oral illiterates) and *between* cultures that abutted each other, with now some cultures themselves coming to dominate other cultures by being in more media regimes that were more encompassing of other mere oral cultures. So, from the beginning of complex scripts in Regime 2, 'soft power' as cultural appreciation of another culture started to be easier to spread, since a script is a longer lived and potentially more easily shared means to transfer material artifacts with symbolic value to other cultures. Thus culture could start to spread even without the people of that culture having to be physically there or even physically alive to explain the culture to someone else, if others could learn to read another culture's complex script, and thus learn another language, and thus open themselves to another culture's longer heritage of writings created to express and to transmit its values of that different mental world. Thus, a world of 'soft power' potential was born from more possible regular media experiences of another culture, between cultures.

From where we are now in "Regime 7" of decentralized digital networks of mobile mass-media, we have changed a great deal about the space and time qualities of any externally shared symbols and internal individual interpretations of cultural socialization and transmission, to make a culture more potentially global and synchronous immediately at all times. On the one hand, built as this is out of and upon the past's more organized cultures and cultural inequalities between states, this allows the 'soft power' of cultural appreciation to spread very easily. On the other hand, the fresh global digital simultaneity itself can create fresh cultures entirely, yet mostly in different kinds of temporary peer-oriented ones, that dissolve past or current hierarchies of cultural appreciation quickly. However, because digital hardware production and digital cultural production still have to come from somewhere instead of come from the nebulous cultural anywhere that they create, this allows very different kinds of regions, cultures, and states to rise to the top of the global pyramid of soft power based on which zones can successfully keep reproducing that entertainment thralldom of digital hardware and digital culture despite a fast-changing global digital economy, culture, and decentralized media experience. In short, it is argued that hardly all current large hegemonic states or cultures that exist now will be successful in surviving in this competitive fresh media regime because of this, as noted in Part III. As media regimes change over world history, the three basics of cultural transmission may stay the same (see Table 4.3) but changing media regimes alter a culture's space and time orientations on that transmission, and thus change more radically the soft power locations, scales, and capacities, depending as culture does on the different dominant media regimes and how that influences socialization biases or changes the dynamics of core and periphery relations of status zones. So, countries like South Korea, with an earlier saturation in our current 'digital mobile multimedia regime,' innately had an earlier lead in socializing differently toward a more global and synchronous cultural transmission, compared to other cultural areas less digitally saturated at the time. This gave South Korea a greater head start in the soft power of such a cheapened way to influence hearts and minds of people worldwide. South Korea's ongoing success in digital hardware production, digital cultural production, and its regular ongoing cultural reproduction in a more homogeneous culture may keep that fresh global kind of digital 'soft power' centered within itself for a long time, versus other nations that seem to be falling apart without that dual digital capacity or without a strong homogeneous culture that can more easily replicate itself against the culturally eroding effects of the media regime now in existence. Thus South Korea seems to better culturally hold itself together to take advantage of this fresh (culturally eroding) digital media regime, better than other countries for these three rationales.

Another way to define culture is more functional to tasks that the culture does in adaptation. For instance, Schein defined a view of the specific 'business culture' in South Korea in terms of its capacities of long term administration of tasks that result in 'collective learning' being valued in Korea. The most important dual tasks of collective learning is how to adapt externally and to integrate internally. In any culture, various events and transactions occur in some external and ongoing mutual relationship. Opportunities and threats always exist in events or transactions at this time, and any society grows through the process of adapting to these opportunities and threats. The internal integration is as important as the external adaptation. No strong company, country, group, or organization can exert strong influence unless it is internally connected. These two characteristics are characteristic of culture. As said earlier, South Korea as a more homogenous culture, and as the earliest digitally saturated culture, respectively, means they had twice over more potential for this collective internal and external learning and faster response.

Another way to think about culture is in the degree of its homogeneity or heterogeneity, in how that influences different kinds of cultures around how that adaptation mentioned above proceeds as specific and different kinds of innovations. There are of course many other intervening influences on innovation, particularly around science and technology as described earlier in the concluding section of Chapter 2. However, just to artificially focus on this point discussed earlier, there is a tremendous resource for what Schein calls 'collective learning' in South Korea, called in earlier chapters 'collective innovation,' because Koreans can access a more homogeneous culture at large scale of around 51 million people for more lateral learning and networking that allows greater and faster learning and innovation. In other words, while culture is something commonly invented, discovered, and developed for a group to overcome and to solve problems of external adaptation and internal integration in this functionalist view, cultural transmission's characteristics are influenced by how homogeneous or heterogeneous that culture is in its human artifacts, values, and basic assumptions and the particular media regime involved. On the one hand, the more homogeneous cultures yield a culture of more collective innovation toward the present and future in material objects and yet have a more durable and less innovative cultural reproduction in intangible ideas compared to a heterogeneous culture. On the other hand, the latter more heterogeneous cultures yield a culture of learning that comes potentially from more chances of individualized innovations and culturally innovative changes themselves, though these may be slower innovations without faster collective innovation being possible due to lacking durable cultural reproduction of the past. These are weaker influences because a more heterogeneous culture learns more from individual innovation and cultural innovation toward the present and the future as stronger forces within it. Thus a heterogeneous culture creates a less durable cultural reproduction, or phrased more optimistically, creates a more durable process of individuals and separate subcultural groups themselves capable of faster cultural change and yet slower material or organizational change when different cultures are in competition.

Another way to think about culture is as a form of hierarchical power itself between cultures. The intangible and tangible elements of culture have the effect of creating both economic power and raising a cultural or national *image power* in their own minds and in the minds of others. This broaches the discussion of the many ways to understand *power differences between cultures*, and that leads now into a discussion now of soft power.

For one instance, the Korean independence activist Kim Gu (1876–1949), known under the pen name Baekbeom (백범, 白凡), meaning "ordinary person," might be interpreted as one of the earliest global 'soft power' theorists. This is despite in Korea additionally Kim Gu being one of the main 'hard power' Korean revolutionary agents against the Japanese colonial occupation of Korea, since he helped found and led from 1931 the Korean Patriotic Organization (that assassinated Japanese leadership) and from 1940 helped found the Korean Liberation Army (the armed forces of the Provisional Government of the Republic of Korea in exile, during the Japanese occupation). Kim Gu summarized 'the power of culture' in his journal: "I want our country to be the most beautiful country in the world. We don't want to be the richest country. The only thing I want infinitely is the power of high culture. This is because the power of culture makes us happy, and furthermore, it gives happiness to others. What humanity lacks now is neither military power nor economic power. The root cause of mankind's unhappiness at present is a lack of benevolence, a lack of mercy, and a lack of love. It is only culture that cultivates this spirit." RM (Kim NamJun), a BTS member, recently quoted Kim Gu at an E-Daily award ceremony, "Remember the saying, 'The only thing I want to have infinitely is the power of high culture'? I believe that culture is indeed the most powerful intangible force that breaks down all boundaries more than any other physical force. I will become a BTS member that works harder, thinking that this is an award given to spread the power of Korean culture to the world."

This view of cultural power as an "infinite" power of happiness is of course ironic, given that though Koreans may desire a culture of happiness and satisfaction, such a culture fails to exist in practice in many Korean lives except through the ideals being sold in this image of the future in the Korean Wave. This can be said because of the absurdly high suicide rates of Korea (more among men) and very high levels of depression (particularly among females). This is discussed in the concluding chapter as the odd underbelly of this country that is crafting a mostly happy cultural image of a global Korean Wave. Thus, the two Korean statements above about the power of culture and the growth of happiness are interpreted as statements of Korean national culture and teamwork in *the happiness of collective duty* to their own culture. This is because when judged directly on whether greater *individual* happiness in Korea is getting larger with the rising Korean Wave from the late 1990s as would be expected, instead Korea's levels of happiness, nuclear family cultural transmission, satisfying lives, and economic stability are falling even while the cultural export success of the Korean Wave rises. These two trends of growing national cultural and domestic unhappiness in the midst of growing global 'cultural happiness' in the global Korean Wave start to wildly diverge in the 1990s, particularly after 1998 by which time regional Hallyu started to really shine. From this year, the Korean economy began to undergo a massive economic crash and loss of investment capital. Fully half of the top thirty business conglomerates (chaebol) failed within 1997 to 1999. Unemployment was high. Even as the economic scale and rate of economic growth recovered within a year, the middle class started to shrink and has continued to shrink. Plus, subjective quality of life measured by happiness and life satisfaction is shrinking in South Korea from the same year onward measured by rising suicide, depression, and single-person households from this point. Thus, Kim Gu's view that simply more culture means more happiness of all kinds is one view of the power of culture. However, it is argued we require a view of many different origins of happiness and they all should be balanced, instead of expecting the global Korean Wave and its 'culture' to excoriate or entirely compensate for deficiencies of other missing sources of economic happiness or family-based happiness being lost in Korea—or in the world.

Another view of the power of culture and of 'soft power' comes from French sociologist Pierre Bourdieu. He felt that if economic capital is understood as income and ownership, then social or cultural capital and its power refers the power of status or hierarchies of inequality made simply by cultural knowledge awareness and consumption of culture itself, in relation to others without such cultural capital. Thus 'cultural capital' as happiness and power refers to a person's objective knowledge of art and culture, their cultural tastes and preferences, and achievements like official qualifications (university degrees, contest prizes, etc.). Cultural capital is understood though as hardly only abstract education and cultural objects, since it depends on *which schools and which objects* are consumed or known about *compared to* others. Thus Bourdieu sees culture as shared, and yet as creating hierarchies and tension in its reproduction of various kinds of cultural inequalities instead of only reproducing "infinite" shared happiness (Bourdieu, 1986). Indeed, the Korean Wave has generated a kind of Bordieuian 'status culture' worldwide since 'hip' young people nowadays increasingly are judged upon and judge themselves upon material consumption, awareness, and capacities of their digital participation in products or online platforms that are sharing Korean culture.

All of the above views of culture help us understand the power of culture in the Korean Wave as a force of intangible *national* 'soft power' as innately *versus* other national cultures. 'Soft power' is defined as how the power of culture of a nation can move the emotions of other national opponents into empathy with another country's people and goals (Nye, 2004). Unlike the traditional meaning of a "national power" or a "hard power" expressed physically in 'coercive products' such as military intervention, coercive diplomacy, or economic sanctions, Nye's power of culture in "soft power" refers to a national ability to obtain a desired thing through the power of using its culture instead, to move other nations' "hearts and minds" through positive emotional attraction rather than through the violent shock and awe of coercion or motivated by the selfish briberies of physical rewards (Nye, 2004). Therefore, national "soft power" is closer to empathy, and it has characteristics of trustworthiness and intimacy. As said earlier, soft power is cultural appreciation. It conquers the heart and emotions with love, which in turn conquers the physical body or economy of another nation through a self-desired cultural conversion—or more cynically, equally a foreign-desired cultural subversion. This is closer to the way Nye considers it given Nye was U.S. Assistant Secretary of Defense for International Security Affairs in the 1990s and additionally how he is now a more Machiavellian theorist of what he calls "smart power" which is the mutual use of hard power and soft power. When Nye first mentioned Korea's overall soft power in 2009, researchers began to pay attention to Korea, and began to illuminate the meaning of Korean culture as a resource of national soft power. In summary, Nye's idea of national "soft power" refers to the ability to achieve Korean national goals through the international cooperation born after cultural conquest—by persuading opponents until they agree with Korean national norms, institutions, and goals through sharing the enervating power of culture and attraction in the global Korean Wave.

Due to the global Korean Wave, South Korea indeed has gained a lot of national "soft power." It is a true cultural capital of status, yet it resides in the hearts and minds of others worldwide instead of resides within oneself in the Bordieuian fashion. Despite being easily defined, soft power is a nebulous concept to measure. It has been debated how to operationalize and measure this abstract idea of a nation's cultural soft power over other nations. Many measures try to track and rank people's aggregate comparative opinions of nations historically in a handful of factors below—to note ongoing rises and falls in each nation's soft power against each other. However, exactly what are those factors being measured?

For just a few examples, soft power has been attempted to be measured or classified in various ways. Soft power has been broadly measured in three empirical categories seen to contribute to patterns of international relations between nations: *culture, political values, and foreign policy* (Nye, 2004, 2008) "Ideological resources" like 'democracy,' institutions, values, and culture apply. Many scholars claim that the first section, of 'cultural acceptance outside the home country,' is core to the scale of a nation's soft power in other countries (Matlary, 2006; Nye, 2004, 2008) Plus, this kind of soft power can be seen as a kind of compensatory power for the lack of its opposite in 'hard power' outside the home country, defined in economic or military terms of coercion. According to Nye, Korea in the 1960s was economically on the same level as Ghana, a newly independent yet poor country in Africa. So while Korea then had little economic hard power, it as well as other countries may try to compensate with more cultural soft power instead. However, in over half a century, Korea has developed that economic 'hard power' by becoming the world's 10th largest economy (World Bank National Accounts Data, 2022), joining the OECD in

1996, and becoming a member of the G-20 as it was founded in 1999. The United Nations Conference on Trade and Development (UNCTAD) unanimously incorporated Korea into the group of 'developed countries' by unanimous consent in 2021, the true 'hard power' economic club. Thus as Korea gained economic 'hard power,' if the compensatory theory of soft power is true, you might expect there to be a less stress in Korea on soft power. However to the contrary, from the late 1990s, Korea has concentrated on its national soft power as much as its hard power of national economic growth. In particular, Nye himself predicted around 2009 that Korea has developed an 'outsized' national 'soft power' that lets it compete in a compensatory fashion with greater economic and military/imperial 'hard powers' such as China and the United States by battling internationally more in the field of soft power and national culture instead. Nye felt Korea's national soft power would continue to grow (Nye, 2009). Stated more strongly, Watson explained that Korea has become a *leading* state in national soft power due both to the *culture* of the Korean Wave and due to another factor of the outsized scale of Korean *foreign aid*. Both the culture of the Korean Wave and Korea's foreign aid budgets were interpreted to help Korea have a future-oriented soft power and national branding for itself in less developed nations. The Korean state's subsidies to other countries touch on the other two soft power categories (political values and foreign policy), while the Korean Wave is the extension in the category of cultural empathy. Thus, with Korea hitting all three valences of soft power, it is unsurprising that many less developed countries come to appreciate Korean culture and the global Korean Wave as well (Watson, 2012).

Korean national soft power is exemplified by growing world empathy to many Korean cultural themes expressed in the Korean Wave. Korean traditional arts, crafts and food have spread all over the world within the sharing of Korean dramas, movies, and music. In addition, Korean pop culture starting from a base in more regional Hallyu in the 1990s has increased into the global Korean Wave. This means Korean TV dramas, K-pop, and other Korean cultural artifacts helped create a wide global cultural attractiveness of Korea. The whole world now shares to some degree an appreciation of Korean tastes of fashion, music, movies, and food related to this. Hayashi and Lee (2007) said Korean melodramas created a craze in Japan, and a resulting Japanese fandom around Korean dramas and popular culture improved general Japanese sympathy to Korean culture, thereby increasing Korea's soft power. They explained the earlier regional Hallyu as a source of national soft power suggesting it could contribute to soft power by creating a digital network effect in many nations' popular culture everywhere, thus building a favorable image of Korea through influential dramas, songs, K-pop idols, and other Korean celebrities.

However, Korean soft power is interpreted to have grown mostly in only two of these three main subsections of soft power: in cultural power and in foreign policy power, instead of in political values. For instance, in *cultural power*, this is seen in the global coverage and scale of the Korean Wave. In *foreign policy*, this is seen via the scale of Korean foreign aid, and even the high 'passport power' of South Korea in having more visa free travel for its own citizens worldwide into other countries than almost any other country (This was described earlier in Chapter 3, Sect. 2). This is a sign of this more empathetic Korean power in other countries already, given they are willing to allow easy access for Koreans into their countries. It shows they are already wanting to inculcate more connections to Korean foreign policy and Korean cultural power—as well as showing desires for attracting Korean investments or consumer spending in their country from Korea's more classic economic 'hard power' of course.

The lesser used category of Korean soft power spreading its *political values* is evident so far, on the one hand, because of many people's interpretation (including Koreans) of inveterate corruption in their nation (Kim & Whitaker, 2013). However, on the other hand, there are highlighted three kinds of political values that Korea should be admired on nonetheless that have been increasing in recent years. These three kinds of political values are theorized as added ways to measure the soft power that comes from political values of a nation: *its institutional/developmental political values, its ethnic political values, and its more 'internalized hard power.'* The latter is a kind of soft power from political values that shows a county is prepared for war and yet chooses to avoid war. Political values of military brinksmanship and choosing peace despite being prepared for war is widely admired in the world, far more admired than the military hard power of imperialism and jingoism that destroys a country's soft power.

So, while Korean national soft power has been interpreted to be earlier weak in the remaining category of 'political values' it is potentially growing stronger, particularly after 2017. For instance, even though it was noted earlier that a more hybrid dictatorial past was rejected from 1988, yet there remained in Korea a long time a strong statist culture culturally and in political values that approved of either open or secretive state-controlled blacklists that seemed to remain a very legitimate tool to organize culture from the 1970s onward among Koreans until found unconstitutional by the Korean Constitutional Court only from 2020. The exposure from 2016 about extensive secret cultural blacklists and the wide desire of Koreans to remove it, instead of simply to fear being put on it, allows greater political and cultural participation in the civil sphere. It surely should create greater global admiration of Korean political values after 2017 for impeaching President Park Geun-hye for creating such a secret dictatorial political and cultural management—and for other points. Other points about increasingly admirable Korean political values can be gleaned from Appendix 1. For instance, Koreans have increasingly rejected an imposed authoritarian past, durably over time. Plus, Koreans have even more strongly rejected a renewal of a digital authoritarianism in the past 20 years, via ending many policies of online surveillance over the years and for defending a free online civic space from governmental repression or retribution. These are strongly admired political values of "digital democracy" that fall into the category of 'developmental/institutional' political values.

Nonetheless, there is always a risk in Korea of having a *more homogeneous culture*, with its strong sense of 'nunchi' (described earlier as being a proud follower anticipating how to make a leader happy without asking) that can combine in wide acceptance for a strongly dictatorial culture (or at least as described earlier, a more hybrid 'authoritarian parliamentarianism'). These three factors can be mutually encouraging factors that create bad political values that passively accept or openly justify repression. However, in reflecting on the above positive and negative political values, two different kinds of political values are really being discussed here. Thus, it is argued that two kinds of political values can be disaggregated: 'developmental/institutional' political values and 'ethnic political' values. First, for ethnic political values, it is argued that the homogeneous culture of Korea remains only about their ethnically autonomous or supremacist political values of Ilminism in South Korea and Juche in North Korea. However, as mentioned earlier about the hybrid politics of this nation, Korea's more 'developmental/institutional' political values work against its ethnic political values happily, and seem to check and balance that darker side of its own homogeneous culture because of slight amounts of 'good accidents' of some kinds of cultural heterogeneity that exists to animate Korea's republican multi-party political institutions making these political institutions into deliberative and more civil-rights protecting institutions over time, 'despite themselves.' Nonetheless, despite this, Korean ethnic political values remain domestically more of a barrier to foreign nationals in sharing in the politics and culture in Korea. This is despite ethnic political values after 2010 finally becoming more accepting of plural cultural origins in Korean culture itself with greater allowances for married foreign nationals to become Korean citizens or long-term visa holders instead of denying it before. This is despite 'institutional/developmental' political values now protecting wider common civil rights against an authoritarian government as well as putting foreign nationals into the same universal/national 'Korean' welfare and pension systems even despite the lack of Korean citizenship of most foreign nationals.

So if we note the *trends* of these widening political values in 'ethnic political' and 'developmental/institutional' issues shown in the aforementioned ongoing compromises in procedures, processes, and goals, these are unlike Korean political values of the past that more valued respectively *ethnic exclusivity* and *justified authoritarianism*. Given these changing historical trends in Korean political values toward more openness in both categories can be seen, this should generate more Korean soft power even from its political values in time. Thus, optimistically *maybe this book can contribute to people being aware of these changing trends in Korean political values* that should increase Korean soft power if more people—including Koreans—are aware of the interesting changes in both their ethnic and developmental/institutional political values over time. This seems to follow the earlier mentioned hybrid solutions of compromise that now are even being applied to Korean political values. Over the decades of modern Korean history, we can see these more admirable developmental/institutional and ethnic political values at work: toward more consensus, greater collective innovation, modern development, traditional culture (yet increasingly accepting of foreign nationals in Korea), land distributions, export-led neoliberal economics yet with a strong universalistic welfare state (that is inclusive of non-Korean ethnic guest workers), good public transportation, and public hospitals (inclusive even of non-Korean ethnic guest workers put equally on the national hospital insurance plans). These and other factors mentioned in Appendix 2 and 3 represent a trend of more admirably inclusive political values of Koreans over time. These increasingly consensus-based processes, that seem to be opening even

Korean political values over time, express the country's winning durable, flexible, and fast development drive that has made it the envy of the developing world. More people should know that Korea is starting to win the combined hard power and soft power 'trifecta': becoming the envy of *economically developed world*, the *global cultural world* in the Korean Wave, and even somewhat the *political world* given its greater and growing protections for digital democracy in its political values, and for its widening political values of its social democratic welfare state (in pensions and health insurance access).

Another Korean political value that can be admired, and thus which can generate soft power, is Korea's ability to be *prepared* for war and yet to *avoid* war and to choose peace. This is a mix of both hard power and soft power. On the one hand, Korea's combination of soft power and a positive national brand image can be said to be a compensatory strategy because Korea's 'hard power' dimensions of external military pressure have been weak in modern history—as well as weak in ancient history even if Korean defense technologies have been historically innovative, strong, and admired or feared widely among its neighbors in ancient Korean history (See Chapter 2). It is argued here that Korean military 'hard power' has thankfully been weak, because as said earlier, getting into a foreign war either with North Korea or another country would have surely destroyed South Korea's economic aggregation. If that had happened, Korean national potential down the development gauntlet would be lost, compared to where it stands today in 2023. Thus it is an admirable political value of South Korea to continue to choose peace. In this political value a Korean lack of external foreign warfare exists in the ancient past or the present because Korea for centuries has had a kind of military brinksmanship of 'hard power' that it seldom and only used within the Korean Peninsula alone instead of truly against foreign enemies. This idea of military brinksmanship as a political value and a successful kind of 'internal hard power' strategy (to coin a phrase) that becomes a soft power of political values is distinct from regular violent 'external hard power.' This kind of internal hard power can be seen in the equally heavily-armed Switzerland, that nonetheless has been at peace and uninvaded for hundreds of years. Similar to Switzerland, Korea's more 'internal hard power' creates an odd tension because despite being able to avoid war after 1953, both South and North Korea are the two most militarized cultures per capita in the world according to American data mentioned earlier. Nonetheless, they both exhibit political values that avoid war with each other and with other countries despite or even because of a great deal of bluster and brinksmanship with each other. Thus, we hypothesize that South Korea does have 'hard power' though of the Swiss kind, a more 'internal hard power,' that uses a military more in a manner of brinkmanship and only as a defensive threat that converts this 'internal hard power' into a statement of political values for a "prepared peace" and thus is a form of soft power as well. So, Korea does have a kind of compensatory strategy that creates pressures for more Korean soft power due to Korea lacking much external hard power that has been judged rightfully to be "too destructive" of the Korean main goal of export-led economic development since 1961 to the present. So, the global admiration that the world gives to a country with political values that avoids war or chooses peace might be said to be another source of political values that encourages its soft power.

National soft power has been measured over time using ongoing global indices in both soft power and 'national branding.' First, for the soft power indices, the 'Global Soft Power Index' by Brand Finance, a British brand consulting firm, feels Korea ranked 12th in 2022 and 11th in 2021—both though showing a slight rise from being 14th in 2020. Recently, *Fortune Magazine* created another typology of soft power. From it, the magazine ranked South Korea as 'second' in the "World Cup of Soft Power." This is only partially to do with excellence of sportsmanship and athletic skill in world soccer competitions. It is their interpretation of how a country's members were viewed or behaved at the 2022 World Cup in Qatar. *Fortune* writes with alliteration of "three criteria: 'brilliant' soft power, which comes from high performance levels and generates feelings of admiration; 'beautiful' soft power, which inspires hope and a sense of togetherness; and 'benign' soft power, which is found in positive attitudes and altruism" (Yoo, 2022). Actually, Korea received a similar award for a similar kind of soft power after it co-hosted the Olympic Games in 1988, winning the Olympic award that year for having the most enthusiastic and welcoming crowds of any nation at the Olympics. In several other measures of this nebulous national 'soft power,' Korea is ranked highly as well. It ranked 19th in Portland's Soft Power 30 Report from 2019. This was just a year before the true explosion of Korean soft power in 2020 onward, and that is reflected in a higher rank of soft power of Korea in 2020, ranking as high as 2nd in Monocle's Soft Power Survey in 2020 (Shin, 2022).

Similar to the concept of "soft power" is the idea of a 'national brand.' A national brand is the *interaction* of greater soft power and greater economic hard power. It either means how greater soft power aids greater economic hard power, or even visa versa, i.e., how a country's more trusted material products, quality, and workmanship act as another factor in greater soft power as well. Nations nowadays are said to get 'positive brand images' or to get 'bad brand images' that bias any future symbolic communication and any economic purchases they have with global consumers. In general, a positive national brand image is formed through positive feelings about the culture of a specific country or about its products as well. Both in turn influence consumers to purchase more economic products and services from that country. A good country brand image also reduces or makes more ambivalent any negative feelings in the patriotic consumers of other countries about buying certain products from foreign countries. For instance, even Koreans love Japanese cameras. So, a growth in good quality products from a country can influence a growth in that country's soft power as well.

A growing national brand image for Korea, derived partially from the soft power of the global Korean Wave, has had a positive effect on increasing purchases of all kinds of Korean products in the global market. By an analysis using the terms of Fig. 4.2 below, Korean commercialization increasingly relies on cultural factors of soft power in the global Korean Wave and of course increasing high material product quality to reach a positive national brand image in global trade. This in turn improves Korean economic "hard power."

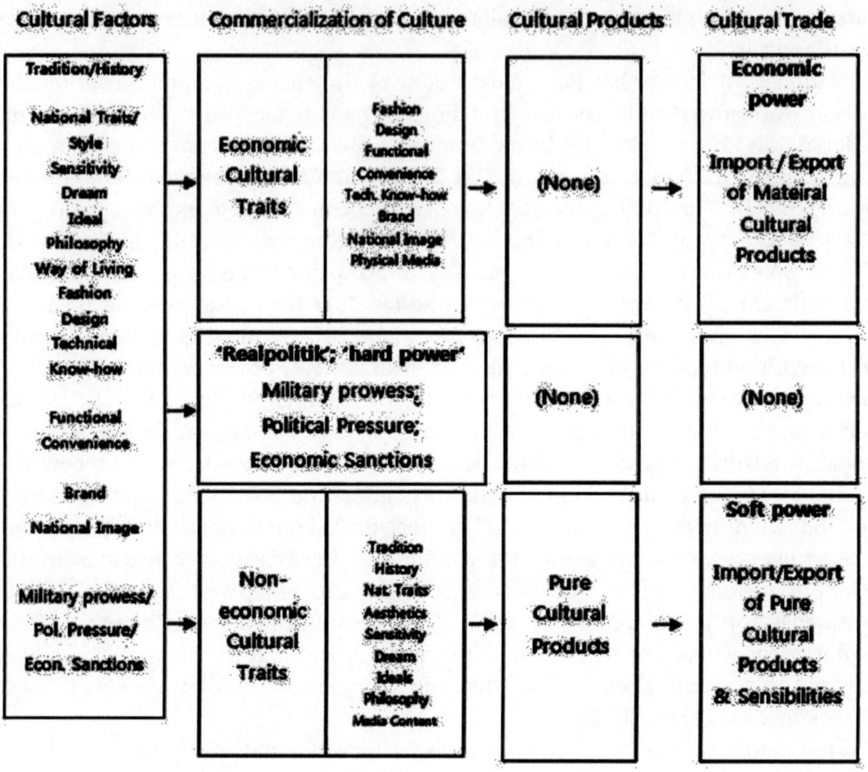

Fig. 4.2 Economic cultural traits and non-economic cultural traits are equal factors in expansion of hard power, economic power, and soft power (Adapted from McCracken, 1998)

What are these 'pure' cultural products of trade mentioned in the figure that are analytically separated from military prowess and economic/material functionality of items in the market? For a start, 'pure' cultural products would include symbolism from traditional history, identity, ethnicity, technological know-how, brand image, and national image. In order to commercialize a 'pure' cultural product, we can think about a range of items deriving their power either from the material functionality of items (the economic cultural factors) or about their more (pure) non-economic cultural factors mentioned above (like songs, dances, music, etc.). The more economic power factors include fashion, design, functional convenience, technological know-how, brands, and national image. The more non-economic cultural factors include traditional history, ethnicity, fashion, sensibility, dreams, ideals, values, identities, preferences, and lifestyle. Cultural trade refers to exporting or importing economical cultural products as culturally-utilized products, and promoting exports and imports by making pure cultural products that have non-economic purposes. That contributes to a country's soft power as well.

Plus, for other ways of thinking about the interaction of cultural soft power, national brand, and economic hard power, one foreign nation's interpretation of the first two can be different than other foreign nations' opinions. For instance, it is not uncommon for the same product to have high or low purchases depending on different countries' interpretations of another nation's national brand. This is a case where a consumer's purchase is influenced by the society's history, values, and traditional differences.

In summary of this discussion about soft power, the global Korean Wave has emerged as a major resource in Korea's national soft power and national branding. However, the Korean Wave is hardly the only source of Korean soft power. For instance, Korea's historically strong foreign policy in foreign aid donations along with its growing strength in defining itself with more open political values (in those three ways mentioned earlier), including 'internal hard power' of military brinksmanship instead of external war as a political value toward peace as another source of soft power, all matter for Korean soft power. Nonetheless, the Korean Wave is the most visible source of Korean soft power right now. It has contributed to making a global powerhouse out of South Korea from its originally being a minor-level political, economic, and cultural player in the world. The Korean Wave thus gives the Korean nation an outsized global influence in cultural soft power. The Korean Wave has had a positive impact on Korea's international cultural capital, while of course equally generating enormous economic power and other political leverages for the country in global politics. South Korea now is positioned culturally and economically as *the only major twenty-first century cultural rival* that confronts *a mostly European/Western twentieth century's heritage* in global popular culture. In the past, global popular culture was represented mostly only by European cultural forms combined with the American entertainment industry that comprises Hollywood films, Broadway stages, and the U.S. music industry. Now that previous global focus on the Transatlanticism of European and American soft power is more blurred by the rise of Korean soft power as the strongest entry yet in the rise of a more multi-polar world culture.

Korea's soft power helps the country have a compensatory strategy in international relations because its economic 'hard power' by itself has been weak in the past or intermittent globally, as Korea repeatedly has suffered many short yet major setbacks in the years of the late 1970s, in 1997–1998, or in 2008–2009. Thus, to smooth out perhaps the innate ups and downs of participating more greatly in the global economy than most countries, South Korea can paper over any short-term economic instability in its economic power by the buffer of this greater "soft power" strategy and by its positive national brand image. Both can be relied upon to maintain global consumer desire for Korean products through any bad times economically.

Once the global Korean Wave spread around the world in the past decade, Korea has benefitted from having multiple different kinds of 'soft power' as well as a raised 'national brand'. This has catalyzed Korea's greater economic hard power that is hard to separate from the soft power of its culture or from the concept of a national brand. This power of national culture as influential on the power of a nation's economics will be analyzed later in three case studies about BTS, Cosmax, and *Squid Game*.

However, before this is done, it is important to explain how a growth in soft power and a growth in economics both have been involved in the accelerated digital transformation of South Korea between 2020 and 2023. Economically, this digital transformation was required due to South Korea being a country that depends greatly on export-led economic sectors yet its buyers after 2020 increasingly were forced into different levels of government lockdowns worldwide with few exceptions. This meant that South Koreans more than others had a much stronger incentive to reposition themselves in both general economics and in their entertainment industry to create more online digital technical solutions to continue to export Korean products in the Korean Wave and in the Korean economy to continue to have the same access to the same global customers. Those digital technical solutions are discussed in the next chapter.

References

Adams, T. (2022, September 4). K-everything: the rise and rise of Korean culture. *UK Guardian*. https://www.theguardian.com/world/2022/sep/04/korea-culture-k-pop-music-film-tv-hallyu-v-and-a

Ahn, A. (2022, October 19). Enrollment in Korean classes has shot up. Thank K-pop. *National Public Radio*. https://www.npr.org/2022/10/19/1129380984/korean-language-classes-us-colleges-k-pop-parasite-squid-game

Aju News Desk (2020, December 22). Constitutional Park Geun-hye Government's 'Culture and Arts Black List' was prepared and the support excluded was unconstitutional. *Aju News*. https://aju.news/en/constitutional-jae-park-geun-hye-governmentculture-and-arts-black-list-was-prepared-and-the-support-excluded-was-unconstitutional.html

Anon. (2022). Hollywood just lost a whopping $500 billion in value this year alone. *Freedom Beacon*. https://freedombeacon.com/hollywood-just-lost-a-whopping-500-billion-in-value-this-year-alone/

BBC (2012, December 4). Video: Psy explains his name to the BBC. *BBC*. https://www.bbc.com/news/av/business-20590170

Beacham, R. C. (1999). *Spectacle entertainments of early imperial Rome*. Yale University Press.

Binns, M. (2019). The 10 highest-paid figure skaters in the world. *The Richest* October 15th. https://www.therichest.com/rich-powerful/highest-paid-figure-skaters/

Bourdieu, P. (1986). The Forms of Capital. In J. Richardson (Ed.), *Handbook of theory and research for the sociology of education* (pp. 241–258). New York Greenwood Press.

Brown, A. (2023, February 5). BTS gets snubbed, again, at 2023 Grammys. *Los Angeles Times*. https://www.latimes.com/entertainment-arts/music/story/2023-02-5/bts-gets-snubbed-again-grammys-2023

——— (2022, November 16). BTS receives multiple 2023 Grammy nominations. *Yonhap News Agency*. https://m-en.yna.co.kr/view/AEN20221116000751315

Bunyan, R. (2022). Disney's Lightyear FLOPS in opening weekend that saw it fail to topple Jurassic Park at box office after controversy over lesbian kiss and decision to ax conservative star Tim Allen as voice of Buzz. *Daily Mail: Mail Online* June 19th. https://www.dailymail.co.uk/news/article-10932399/Jurassic-draw-N-American-theaters.html

Caulfield, K. (2022, October 16). Stray kids notch second no. 1 on Billboard 200 With 'Maxident'. *Billboard*. https://www.billboard.com/music/chart-beat/stray-kids-number-one-billboard-200-chart-maxident-album-1235156753/

Cha, F., H. Farah, K. Goh, R. Liu & L. Benson (2022, September 17). Meet the stars riding the crest of Hallyu, the Korean wave in fashion, art, film and music. *UK Guardian*. https://www.theguardian.com/culture/2022/sep/17/hallyu-south-korean-wave-fashion-art-film-television-music

Collman, A. (2020, February 13). The Oscar-award winning director of 'Parasite' was once blacklisted in his own country for being too liberal. *Insider*. https://www.insider.com/parasite-director-bong-joon-ho-blacklisted-south-korea-2020-2

Deacon, T. W. (1997). *The symbolic species: The co-evolution of language and the brain*. W W Norton & Co Inc.

Duerden, J. (2021). South Korean athletes seek Olympic gold to avoid military service. *Nikkei Asia* June 29th. https://asia.nikkei.com/Spotlight/Tokyo-2020-Olympics/South-Korean-athletes-seek-Olympic-gold-to-avoid-military-service

——— (2022, September 28). Woke movies drive September box office to lowest in 25 years. *Breitbart*. https://www.breitbart.com/entertainment/2022/09/28/nolte-woke-movies-drive-september-box-office-lowest-25-years/

Entertainment Tonight (2022, November 30). 'Congratulations Jungkook': Dreamers tops billboard digital songs chart. *Entertainment Tonight*. https://m.economictimes.com/news/international/us/congratulations-jungkook-dreamers-tops-billboard-digital-songs-chart-see-details/amp_articleshow/95865322.cms

Google (2021). Google Year in Review, 2021. https://trends.google.com/trends/yis/2021/GLOBAL/

Hayashi, K., & Lee, E.-J. (2007). The potential of fandom and the limits of soft power: Media representations on the popularity of a Korean melodrama in Japan. *Social Science Japan Journal, 10*(2), 197–216.

Hersh, P. (2009, March 30). No matter how you write it, Kim spells greatness, *Chicago Tribune News Blogs*. https://newsblogs.chicagotribune.com/sports_globetrotting/2009/03/by-philip-hershi-had-a-nice-email-from-a-korean-reader-who-suggested-that-the-phonetic----or-transliterated----spelling-being.html

Hong, E. (2014). *The birth of Korean cool: How one nation is conquering the world through pop culture*. Picador.

J.K. (2018, May 11). 24K Included on blacklist of Former President Park Geun Hye's Government. *Soompi*. https://www.soompi.com/article/1168083wpp/24k-included-blacklist-former-president-park-geun-hyes-government.

Jeon, B.-J., et al. (2012). 한류본색: 아시아를 넘어 세계로, 문화강국 코리아 프로젝트. Maekyung Press.

Kang, H.-k. (2019, October 21). Three S's in 1980s—a left-wing conspiracy? *The Korea Times*. https://www.koreatimes.co.kr/www/nation/2021/05/356_277394.html

Kasson, J. F. (1978). *Amusing the million: Coney Island at the turn of the century*. Hill and Wang.

Kim, B.-e., & Chung, H.-c. (2016, December 6). 'Park spent 90 minutes hair styling when 315 students were trapped in sinking ferry.' *The Korea Times*. https://koreatimes.co.kr/www/nation/2022/09/113_219630.html

Kim, U., & Whitaker, M. D. (2013). Network subversion: The contrasting effects of multiple networks on bribery in South Korea. *International Journal of Law, Crime and Justice, 41*, 16–35.

Koreaboo (2018, May 10). This is the only K-Pop group that was included on Former President Park Geun Hye's Cultural Blacklist. *Koreaboo*. https://www.koreaboo.com/news/kpop-group-included-former-president-park-geun-hyes-cultural-blacklist/

Kulkarni, P. (2022, September 13). Squid game's Lee Jung-Jae to lead star wars series 'The Acolyte'. *Augustman*. https://www.augustman.com/sg/culture/film-tv/squid-game-star-lee-jung-jae-bags-the-lead-role-in-star-wars-series-the-acolyte/

Kwak, Yeon-soo. (2021, August 3). "How much do Olympic medalists earn?" *The Korea Times*. https://www.koreatimes.co.kr/www/sports/2021/08/800_313251.html

Lee Myung-bak Government White Papers (2013). Government of Korea.

Lee, J.-s. (2022, November 21). Nexon has become the largest shareholder of AGBO, the production company of Avengers. *Infostock Daily*. https://www.infostockdaily.co.kr/news/articleView.html?idxno=184480

Legaspi, A. (2022, November 12). BTS' Jung Kook to perform at 2022 FIFA world cup opening ceremony; Singer will also participate in the World Cup Qatar 2022 soundtrack. *Rolling Stone*. https://www.rollingstone.com/music/music-news/bts-jung-kook-2022-fifa-world-cup-opening-ceremony-1234630048/

Levine, Y. (2018). *Surveillance valley: The secret military history of the internet*. Public Affairs / Hachette Book Group.

Lewis, M. W., & Wigen, K. E. (1997). *The Myth of continents: A critique of metageography*. University of California Press.

Lim, H.-b. (2022a, November 28). Korea Mint, releases official commemorative medal for the 10th Anniversary of BTS' Debut. *Naver News*. https://n.news.naver.com/article/015/0004780481?sid=101

Lim, J.-w. (2022b, November 21). BTS wins favorite pop duo or group at American Music Awards. *Korea JoongAng Daily*. https://koreajoongangdaily.joins.com/2022b/11/21/entertainment/kpop/Korea-AMA-American-Music-Awards/2022b1121100500329.html

Lunden, J. (2022). Korean pop star Luna comes to Broadway in 'KPOP.' *National Public Radio* November 21st. https://www.npr.org/2022/11/21/1137813095/kpop-musical-broadway-luna

Magnates Media. (2023). *The Secret Chinese Company That Owns Everything* [Tencent/WeChat] (Documentary). YouTube. https://www.youtube.com/watch?v=51fWzJ-A5w4

Matlary, Janne H. (2006). When soft power turns hard: Is an EU Strategic Culture Possible? *Security dialogue*, *37*(1), 105–121.

Mattelart, A. (2000). *Networking the World, 1794–2000*. University of Minnesota Press.

McCracken, G. (1998). *Culture and consumption: New approaches to the symbolic character of consumer goods and activities*. Indiana University Press.

McGowan, D. (2014). *Weird scenes inside the canyon: Laurel canyon, covert ops and the dark heart of the hippie dream*. Headpress; Illustrated ed.

Ministry of Culture, Sports and Tourism (2020). Homepage, Hallyu: Hallyu Development Strategies, http://www.mcst.go.kr

National Public Radio (2022, September 8). How Korean culture went global. *National Public Radio*. https://www.npr.org/transcripts/1121364712

Ng, D. (2022, December 31). Woke Fail: Disney Lost $123 Billion in market value in 2022 as Shares Drop 44 Percent—Worst Year Since 1974. *Breitbart*. https://www.breitbart.com/entertainment/2022/12/31/woke-fail-disney-lost-123-billion-in-market-value-in-2022-as-shares-drop-44-percent-worst-year-since-1974/

Nolte, J. (2022, October 1). Woke 'Bros' delivers another weekend box office bust, the worst September in 25 years. *Breitbart*. https://www.breitbart.com/entertainment/2022/10/01/nolte-woke-bros-delivers-another-weekend-box-office-bust/

Nye, J. S. (2004). Soft power and American foreign policy. *Political Science Quarterly, 119*(2), 255–270.

Nye, J. S. (2008). Public diplomacy and soft power. *The Annals of the American Academy of Political and Social Science, 616*(1), 94-109.

Nye, J. S. (2009, November 11). South Korea's growing soft power, *Foreign Affairs*.

Oh, M., & Larson, J. F. (2019). *Digital development in Korea: Lessons for a sustainable world*, 2nd Edition (Routledge Advances in Korean Studies).

Roth, E. (2023, July 17). Hollywood's writers and actors are on strike. *The Verge*. https://www.theverge.com/2023/7/17/23798246/strike-hollywoods-writers-actors-wga-sag-aftra

Salmon, A. (2012, May 30). 'Yonsama': Korean love god captures Japanese hearts. *The Korea Times*. http://www.koreatimes.co.kr/www/news/nation/2012/05/113_112054.html.

Savage, J. (2008). *Teenage: The prehistory of youth culture: 1875–1945*. Penguin.

Schein, E. H. (1985). *Organizational culture and leadership: A dynamic view*. Jossey-Bass.

Seo, Y. (2022, November 25). BTS singer Jin set to begin South Korea military service, source says. *CNN*. https://www.cnn.com/2022/11/25/entertainment/bts-jin-south-korea-military-intl-hnk/index.html

Shim, S. (2022, October 22). BLACKPINK to headline BST Hyde Park festival next year. *Yonhap News Agency*. https://m-en.yna.co.kr/view/AEN20221022000700315

Shin, J.-h. (2022, August 15). What is behind South Korea's growth in soft power? The Korea Herald. *Asia News Network*. https://asianews.network/what-is-behind-south-koreas-growth-in-soft-power/

Steger, I. (2018, April 10). Counting the damage: Former Korean president Park Geun-hye's blacklist of artists filled 60 pages with 9,473 names. *Quartz*. https://qz.com/1248581/former-korean-president-park-geun-hyes-blacklist-of-artists-filled-60-pages-with-9473-names

Vogel, Harold L. (2014) *Entertainment industry economics: A guide for financial analysis*, 9th ed., Cambridge University Press.

Watson, I. (2012). South Korea's State-led soft power strategies: Limits on Inter-Korean Relations, *Asian Journal of Political Science* 20(3).

We Are Social / Hootsuite (2017). January 2017: Mobile's share of web traffic. https://datareportal.com/reports/digital-2017-global-digital-overview

We Are Social / Hootsuite (2019). Digital 2019: Global internet use accelerates. https://wearesocial.com/blog/2019/01/digital-2019-global-internet-use-accelerates

World Bank (2022) National Accounts Data.

Yang, H.-R. (2012). Cultural Exchange, Hallyu Culture, and Future of Hallyu: Focused on Capitalization and Post-Commercialism. *The Journal of Humanities Studies, 39*(1), 381–406.

Yoo, Y. G. (2022, December 21). Fortune ranks Korea 2nd in 'World cup of soft power.' *Korea.Net*. https://www.korea.net/NewsFocus/Culture/view?articleId=226199

Chapter 5
Korea's Entertainment Industry: Lockdown as Opportunity for Technical Innovation

This chapter describes discrete technical and organizational changes toward wider global markets in the Korean Wave between 2020 and 2023. Many technical changes happened to facilitate the already deeply export-led economy of Korea to continue to connect more digitally online with its entertainment buyers, since many of its previous consumers were now under many different national lockdowns. This is a fascinating story because so much happened so quickly between 2020 and 2023 in South Korea that may reverberate throughout the world for a decade or more. This is because these changes of digital infrastructure and business organization are still there to influence the future. It put South Korea far ahead once more compared to other countries in technical changes and economic reorganizational changes in the global entertainment industry. This makes South Korea ever more of an outlier instead of a harbinger because it will be even harder for other countries now to achieve a cultural wave on their own, particularly as Koreans and Korean platforms of all kinds start to be relied upon in other countries for expertise and experience in globally managing or even globally owning other countries' digital content, making other countries' digital content, or delivering other countries' content for the global entertainment industry.

The effects of a declared Covid-19 pandemic more directly means many countries' *chosen* governmental strategies of social and economic lockdowns in *lockstep* following totalitarian China. These choices of response were economically catastrophic and historically unheard of in the modern world for abridgement of human rights of all kinds. It was dystopian to have so many human, civil, political-legal, and medical rights attempted to be revoked by governments all at once across plural nations uniformly. Human rights were replaced with unapproachable televised technocratic politicians announcing rules on basic socialization, trying to keep citizens in apoplectic fear intentionally, for example, like shown by U.K.'s Health Minister Matt Hancock's private message leaks in early 2023, showing he was texting in 2020 "when do we release the next variant?" to media colleagues. The attempt was to try to push and to keep everyone in digital surveillance based on mere 'projected cases' in 2020 that failed to come true, and then use a series of 'variants' long after

G.-C. Shin and M. D. Whitaker, *The Korean Wave in a Post-Pandemic World*,
https://doi.org/10.1007/978-981-99-3683-0_5

it was well known that it was not a dangerous pandemic, given death and survival rates common to a regular flu season, and given examples like U.K.'s Prime Minister Boris Johnson caught holding after-hours drinking parties with governmental staff without masks or without social distancing rules secretly in governmental buildings while making such events and behaviors illegal for his whole nation. Before 2020, the Orwellian euphemism of "lockdown" would have been called for what it was: an illegal attempt to institute a 'national house arrest' or national martial law. It was opportunistically combined with a crony capitalist 'great reset' of economic and social life of many nations globally at the same moment toward being forced into investing in surveillance and technocratic management of basic behaviors from a political center. It was in many countries well into 2023 a situation where previously non-revocable and permanent human, civil, and medical rights were indeed revoked by politicians in many cases. Some permanent common human rights like freedom of movement within a country and freedom of access to public places and public accommodations were attempted to be turned into temporary passports and licenses for governmental-approved behaviors, expirable, altered at will, or removed unpredictably on mere government emergency announcements or media announcements instead of via laws. Other permanent human rights like medical privacy or doctor-patient confidentiality that help avoid human rights discriminations and medical discriminations, were instead attempted to be inverted into weaponized doctors, hospitals, universities, and private businesses all deputized as agents of a totalitarian state as a wider police force of intentional medical discrimination that included denial of public accommodations and denial of schooling, jobs, medical services, or even scheduled life-saving surgeries unless the proper 'credentials' were presented. In voiding all human rights, governments tried to turn private medical decisions, individual travel plans, and personal mobile phone geolocation services into one public digitally-convergent database, making countries into tracked open-air prisons—that is, if your country let you outside without arresting you in some cases like Italy or if it let you travel beyond your local province without arresting you, unlike Australia.

South Korea as well as other Western nations worldwide literally took coercive policy advice from totalitarian China—which began these policies in early 2020. However, Koreans protested, sued, and the Seoul Court and Korean Constitutional Court eventually blocked by early 2022 the extension of coercive rules about 'vaccine passports' to younger teenage groups—with Koreans remembering a history of opposing their own past dictatorships still in living memory. The result in Korea was a milder lockdown than most countries. South Korea never chose a policy of full forced lockdown in homes in 2020 unlike other countries like Italy, though Korea did start with the same global spiel of a promised "two-week period only" of full business closures—that were like elsewhere continued off and on for over three years in Korea instead, unless of course the businesses had gone bankrupt earlier. As said, the milder result in Korea came eventually from a lawsuit taken to the Korean Constitutional Court which blocked President Moon's desired extension of mandated adult rules on forced experimental injections to include all teenagers (that were never a risk group) to access public accommodations.

Though Korean citizen protests, court cases, and eventually the Korean Constitutional Court made lockdowns milder or optional in formal ways, Koreans are a very homogeneous culture of peer pressure with a strong culture of physical bullying by people in authority and a fear of being singled out. Therefore, Koreans repress themselves and police each other, living as they do in a homogeneous culture without much legitimate individual innovation or oppositional cultural innovation. However, the Korean economy is very global, so even if internally Korea was in a mild lockdown dissembled between January 2022 to March 2023, many of Korea's trading partners and consumers were placed under more Chinese-inspired lockdown from 2020 of various kinds. Therefore this still had a catastrophic impact on all economic and cultural sectors of Korea.

5.1 Global Organizational Innovation in Korean Content and Distribution Industries After 2020

The Korean entertainment industry was no exception to this shock doctrine (Klein, 2007) around lockdowns institutionalized across many countries beginning from March 2020. Like in other countries, in Korea there was a sharp decline in face-to-face content consumption and a growth in overall digitally distributed 'non-face-to-face' consumption and behavior. However, unlike other countries, Koreans innovated many businesses' organization and digital communications to maintain a national and global market scale and even to enhance it in the entertainment industry. This innovative change to digital online markets and events created even further economic shakeout of many remaining in-person businesses, leading more into bankruptcy the more they depended upon markets of face-to-face economic and cultural relationships. This created a durable *digital deflection point* in the Korean economy and culture—even though Korea was already very digitally saturated. (See Appendix 1). It is expected that this added digitized globalization to the whole Korean entertainment industry compared to other nations will continue to have ripple effects long afterwards.

So while the Korean entertainment industry did have early chaos in 2020, it adapted well compared to other Korean economic sectors and definitely better compared to other countries. For instance, exports of the Korean entertainment industry increased from 2019 to the beginning of 2020, the period before the announcement of the aforementioned comparatively mild lockdown policies. Trends such as greater non-face-to-face and home consumption and the greater spread of global OTT (Over The Top) online broadcast/streaming distribution networks are factors of opportunity for video content industries (entertainment, drama, etc.) and the online game industries. These home-delivery sectors of the Korean Wave *saw a significant growth from 2020 beyond the level of compensating for the loss of the music industry* in 2020 which was hit hard by the suspension of live concerts. In the music industry, K-pop's already large online content adapted to enforced non-face-to-face culture well. Actually, the number of simultaneous viewings of BTS's online performances *continued to set new records under lockdown conditions.* Plus, Korean dramas that can be easily viewed anywhere in the world through an online video service continued their success story after 2020. In 2020 alone, Korean dramas called "Kingdom", "Crash Landing on You" and "Secret Forest" were highly watched in Hong Kong, Singapore, Vietnam, and Japan. Plus, this globally-uneven lockdown period was when the Korean-created online broadcast series *Squid Game* was produced from late 2019 through 2021. It was exorbitantly funded by Netflix and then distributed as Netflix-exclusive content in September 2021. *Squid Game* soon took first place in the world on that online streaming service within a week.

Looking at change in the proportion of overseas consumers who use Korean video content through online and mobile platforms, Korean drama watchers surged from 47.4% in 2016 to 76.9% in 2020, *and it also increased by 8% in 2020 compared to 2019*. Korean entertainment, movies, and animation consumption also increased by around 30% compared to 2016 and from *5–7% in 2020 compared to 2019*. This demonstrates the expansion of OTT's influence on digital video content of the Korean Wave.

Among online broadcast OTT services, Netflix's global usage rate *increased* by 15% on average, while YouTube's global usage rate *decreased* by 2–8% by genre compared to 2019. In particular, Netflix usage rate for watching Korean dramas and movies was about 63–64% which was larger than that entertainment shows (56.8%) and animation (53.2%). Global OTT services like Netflix through its multinational distribution networks and its original Korean content production have greatly expanded access to and watching of Korean video content for consumers of the global Korean Wave. If you look at the Netflix ranking of the most preferred of all dramas in 2020, Korea's "Crash Landing on You" was in first place and "The King" was in sixth place. Both were Korean-made content either exclusively only distributed through Netflix or both produced and distributed through Netflix contracts with Korean producers and their companies. Compared to a Netflix survey from 2019, the scale of Netflix watchers in 2020 was *double* that of the three main Korean dramas seen in the earlier survey of 2019, with 2019's top Korean Wave content being "Hotel Del Luna", "Kingdom", and "Goblin." Working more in tandem instead of in competition, this shows the influence of the global American Netflix priming the global Korean Wave, and it shows the influence of the loved content of the Korean Wave behind Netflix's own massive success after 2020. *Squid Game* was Korean content exclusively produced for American Netflix. Squid Game was so popular a Korean offering that it achieved *the first place in viewership ratings in every country where Netflix is a service worldwide by October 2021* just a month after release.

This confirms a fundamental global and digital change in the video content industry. There are an interactive *four keys* to this change in the video content industry: the globalization of all past national entertainment industries hardly just in the Korean Wave, story intellectual property (IP)-centric videos, the importance of IP businesses in general in owning exclusive content, and a worldwide digital fandom loyalty that is more likely to keep its global market scale returning over time if achieved in the first instance. The Korean video content industry thus is being reorganized in a way that is closer to a global market compared to the past. The recent trend in Korea is video using story IP such as webtoons and web novels. The synergistic practice of linking fresh video concert production to already-popular story IP like webtoons is being strengthened as well. Plus, the strength of value-added businesses in sales of products using IP is also expanding, secured by the same global-scale digital fandom. This shows that past national video content industries will expand their character into a global content IP business through connection with the growing global digital-based fandom. (KOFICE, 2022).

The extension of IP content in a wider global market instead of only a singular national market is in full swing. To elaborate what was mentioned above, this is confirmed from the fact that among the content receiving attention, a lot of fresh Korean Wave content is increasingly this kind of 'extended IP content,' for example, based on already successful and popular stories from webtoons. For example, Korean works such as "Along with the God" (literal Korean title of 신과함께: 죄와 벌 would be closer to "Together with God: Sin and Punishment") was produced as a series, or similarly there was "Hell" in Netflix, then "Moving" in Disney+, and then "Doctor Brain" in Apple TV+. These are representative examples of extended IP markets of webtoons of the Korean Wave becoming bigger than their original media of webtoons. This idea of extended content is referred to as 'story IP.' The reason why story IP is used is because there are three advantages. First, *since it is a story already well known*, it has advantage of reducing the box office risk of a fresh movie story that requires a lot of production money to develop as content as well as requires more advertising costs to prime the market for an unknown story. Plus, most of these 'webtoon Story IP' derivative works on video already have a strong digital fandom formed through the webtoons in advance—so, second, *even its fans are already well known*. This reduces the content production costs and contributes to an easier free spread of publicity in an online environment since advocates and spreaders of past webtoon content will advocate and spread the video when it is later released as well. Third, in reverse, wider market scale can be achieved when a video work is released, and *it serves doubly as synergistic advertising for the original webtoons*. Thus additional revenue can be expected through people who later want to buy the original webtoon work in connection with the video production, if they were unaware of the webtoon earlier.

The global Korean Wave has been moving strongly in globalizing webtoon story IP. In early 2021, the top Korean online portal and search engine company Naver acquired Canada's 'Wattpad,' making *Naver the world's largest distributor* both *in webtoons* via Naver Webtoon *and next in web novels* via Naver's acquisition of Wattpad, the former Canadian web novel platform website. Plus, the desire of other Korean companies to profit from global story IP was seen. In the middle of global lockdowns in May 2021, Kakao Entertainment, an affiliate of the top Korean social media platform company Kakao, acquired another North American web novel service for itself, called 'Radish.' Thus these double acquisitions by major Korean entertainment and social media platform companies like Naver (buying Wattpad) and Kakao (buying Radish) provide a double opportunity for any earlier 'nationality' of a webtoon Story IP to expand globally to the world in the future, managed by two major

Korean companies. Third, more story IP can be seen in how some Korean movies now are TV series as well. For example, director Bong Joon-ho's once singular movies of *Snowpiercer* (2013) and later *Parasite* (2019) have been expanded into their own global drama series as well. The TV Series for *Snowpiercer* first appeared on TNT in May 2020. The HBO TV movie adaptation of *Parasite* was announced to be in development in 2020.

Also, in the first half of 2021 there was an important change in the Korean entertainment industry: many fresh globally-oriented platforms quickly developed in just two years. Big Hit Entertainment, a leader in the industry, changed its name to HYBE and converted its national platform 'Weverse' into a more globally accessible platform using multiple language/script translation. So HYBE, a once-national entertainment company based on the music business management (and BTS) in the Korean Wave is changing into a global platform company that wants to lead as a global lifestyle brand and through owning global content IP from other nations for wider competitiveness. Above, Naver's Wattpad and Kakao's Radish were already mentioned as other examples that made their past Korean national platforms into Korean global platforms in the same short period of time. So, another current trend in South Korea is for Korean companies that used to be *different and separate* national talent management agencies, national Internet portals, and national telecommunication companies now *aim to become the same kind of comprehensive global entertainment platforms* gradually expanding their stake in same global markets and using the same '*four keys*' mentioned above as the same strategy around global IP business models.

Thus, the content production business is shifting mainly to the global IP management business. Even the current entertainment industry as a content business is not limited to content. It has become important to make a global platform to commercialize the intangible value derived from content and to increase the number of people it can connect with worldwide. In other words, a global digital fandom anywhere in the world now becomes a core asset and value for everyone who develops a platform, a service, and a content business. These changes are brought about by the huge global smartphone networking environment and its daily delivery of media content individualized to anyone, anywhere. It calls for changes in the industry's profit structure and inventing better ways to harness this new way of combining mass media and yet an individualized media for accessing economic value. This is different than the past 'shotgun style' delivery of the one-way mass media or advertising that hoped to hit a few individual customers at best. Now such digital and global content delivery can be a mass media that additionally can be tailored individually, to continue the analogy, in which every 'shot' of expensive production and distribution potentially can land a tailored and individualized consumer hit anywhere in the world. Shotgun fire in a nation has been exchanged for multiple laser-sighted targets over the whole globe from satellites in space and from undersea cables. More global and digital opportunities are being created both offline and online, respectively, whether in physical reality or in virtual reality.

Thus, a very important factor is the global level of digital fandom in the Korean Wave. Fandom activities get reinforced with positive psychology such as trust, charm, and friendliness felt from interaction with Korean stars, as well as a sense of self-reliance and belonging felt in the fan club community. Both interactions with Korean stars and a fan club community are easier to make as a permanent daily experience in a platform that hosts a virtual community from all over the world. Thus, there is a synergy of content, platform, and fandom that provides new business opportunities when globalized and digitized into a platform environment. This will fundamentally change the structure of the industry. A global IP-based platform businesses will emerge as a major business model in the entertainment industry.

In this regard, another entertainment industry leader, Korea's CJ ENM, which is the top player in the Korean OTT industry as well, is attracting attention by its large dreams of being the 'Korean Disney' of content creation as well as distribution. For background, in July 2018, CJ O Shopping absorbed CJ E&M and changed its name to the current CJ ENM. CJ ENM's business areas are largely composed of media, commerce, movies, and music. Excluding the commerce area, all three business areas are in content production and distribution. CJ Group began its dream of becoming 'Korea's Disney' with establishment of 'Studio Dragon' in 2016. At that time in 2016, Studio Dragon was established as a spin-off of CJ E&M's drama business before the name change to CJ ENM in 2018. Studio Dragon itself then grew by acquiring a large number of movie and drama production companies with its abundant cash assets. These many production companies soon became creative wings that could expand CJ ENM globally, with other plans to establish overseas networks with business alliances with other major entertainment producers and distributors in the United States and Japan connected to the many creative producer companies owned by Studio Dragon. In fact, Studio Dragon has signed a cooperation contract with Skydance, the American production company that made the movies *Terminator* and *Mission Impossible.* CJ ENM declared an investment of 5 trillion won (approximately US $4 billion) by 2025. It started with an investment of 800 billion won in its own OTT content production in 2021 alone. This is a larger Korean investment on OTT and content production by CJ ENM than by the already massive Korean investment in OTT and content production by Netflix, which said it would invest 'only' approximately 550 billion won in Korean content production in 2021. However, the Korean CJ ENM faces a serious challenge due to attacks from other global OTT dinosaurs such as Netflix, which is already dominant in the Korean market, and Disney+ , which entered Korea in October 2021. Both of these are the same business model of OTT services that produce and distribute their own content, globally.

In conclusion, the above 'four keys' explain the recent organizational changes in major Korean content producers and distributors as they now are going global and becoming the same kind of global IP content management empires, using when possible the 'extended' markets of story IP due to its many benefits. Next, associated market shifts from technical changes are discussed that make this growing global organizational scale possible and profitable for Korean companies.

5.2 Global Technical Innovation in Korean and American Entertainment Industries After 2020

If the previous section dealt with the more global reorganization of businesses in the Korean entertainment industry after 2020 that will keep influencing the future, this section deals with related technical innovation of the same industry that makes that organizational scale possible. All technical changes aimed for the same strategy: to more effectively participate in, manage, gather data from, and profit from a global cultural market. That is how the earlier mentioned global reorganizations will work with the technological innovations to continue to influence a more global entertainment future, instead of only influence a national Korean cultural wave.

Entering the twenty-first century, as new technologies are introduced around the world, the entertainment industry faces a new *global* competition. In fact, technological innovation in the media and entertainment industry becomes a means of competition itself. In this industry, innovation is directly related to competitive advantage, so it is very active in introducing and utilizing new technologies. In particular, the 'first mover' advantage has a decisive effect on market share. A pursuit of innovation to use new technologies for comparative advantage over global competitors became a core strategy of Korean entertainment companies particularly between 2020 and 2022.

After an introduction, the technologies innovated in this short period are summarized (1) in Korean global music sales and delivery, (2) in Korean film broadcasting, and (3) in many increasing Korean uses of artificial intelligence (AI) in four applications of music, music composition, broadcasting, and the 'metaverse.' Even though four different applications of the 'metaverse' exist (described later), generally the term 'metaverse' means a virtual reality construct, half real and half part augmented reality (AR) meant to be a parallel 'digital city' for real world meetings and businesses. There virtual backgrounds are like shops or concerts, and virtual people in these virtual spaces meet in real time for coordination worldwide in culture and sales. It is based on a mutually shared telepresence of 'digital face-to-face' avatars from all over the world seeing and interacting with each other's avatars in one virtual space in real time. Between 2020 and 2022, the Korean entertainment industry applied all of these, in experiments for how to keep hosting and to keep coordinating global level cultural events of the Korean Wave under lockdown conditions across many countries.

As an increasingly globalized entertainment industry utilizes new technologies, global consumers are also changing in their main technological use as well. In particular, a digital content consumption in entertainment is becoming the epitome of consumption today. Technological innovations have led the entertainment industry over the past decade to interact with consumer preferences of platforms, social media, and mobile phone networks. As the use of the Internet and mobile devices becomes more common and the multimedia of mobile digital devices become easier to use, the consumption of digital content has been extended to all generations. It is interesting that more 'generation gaps' existed in the use of mobile phones in more developed countries by 2015, while greater 'digital parity' across all generations in the use of mobile phones existed from that year in the less developed countries which are central to the expansion of the markets of the global Korean Wave. (Pew Research Center, 2015) In the past decade, the advent of ever more miniaturized and mobile content delivery and communication devices (smartphones, tablets, smartwatches, etc.) means digital consumption experiences become seamless and ubiquitous throughout the user's day with market opportunities and data mining possibilities increasing. Combining these trends of digitalization, the mobile revolution, the smart era, big data, and social media, the entire global entertainment industry is converging into a form of surveillance capitalism. (Zuboff, 2019) Through this, it creates a mismatch for how people consume that is increasingly against older media ecologies based on analog technology and one-way mass media broadcasting. The cheaper and more efficient digital distribution of content via two-way media in our mobile revolution has capacities of mass yet individually tailored content. This is slowly neutralizing and dissolving the past's default profitability and market power of legacy media companies optimized to earlier analogue and one-way mass media regimes with their more expensive, random, and scattershot approach to finding individual consumers.

In the process of this media regime change (Appendix 4), even originally non-media information technology companies such as Google, Facebook, Amazon, and Apple emerge as new powerhouses in entertainment delivery, data mining, and advertisement placement services combined. Currently, they are leading a technological innovation in globalizing the entertainment industry through intelligent information technologies such as artificial intelligence, big data, cloud-based distribution/storage of data, and the data monitoring possible through the Internet of Things (IoT).

PwC, a global accounting and consulting network, has been publishing a report every year since 1999 that contains information about the profits of the media industry in 53 countries and 14 industries over the next five years. Major organizations around the world cite the PwC report which forecasts the global content market every year. From 2020, this global media and entertainment market was about $2 trillion. (PwC, 2020) For comparative reference, as of 2018, the global food market was worth about $6.291 trillion, the IT market $3.581 trillion, the automobile market $2.15 trillion, the steel market $1.357 trillion, and the semiconductor market $478 billion. So, as consumption of digital content accelerates worldwide, the global content market including entertainment grew at a CAGR of 4.3% during 2019–2023. This entertainment expansion *was estimated to exceed the overall economic growth rate* of 3.7% from 2016 to 2020. According to PwC statistics, the global entertainment media industry revenue was expected to reach $2.6 trillion in 2023 up from $2.1 trillion in 2018. Through this, it can be seen that the global entertainment media industry is similar in economic scale to the global automobile industry, smaller than the IT industry, and far ahead of the semiconductor industry. However, given the global entertainment industry is increasingly a digitally distributed network, it would be appropriate to consider its merged hardware requirements (the IT and semiconductor industries) with the content of the entertainment industry. This yields an approximate total of $6.659 trillion for this 'digital entertainment industry' simply by adding the above revenue numbers. Thus these three linked *digital hardware and digital content entertainment industries* have a larger estimated revenue than the global food market at this point by 2023. However, what really happened? Instead of rising to $2.6 trillion by 2023, total global entertainment and media revenue was only $2.32 trillion in 2022, according to PwC, and growth was shrinking instead. In 2022, the global entertainment growth kept declining, to a growth of only 5.4%, which was an abrupt deceleration from a strong 10.6% growth globally in 2021 in a rebound from lockdowns worldwide. Now PwC projects the opposite: that the next five years of entertainment revenue growth will continue to decline, expecting by 2027 just a 2.8% annual growth above 2026. That is now *estimated to be slower than the overall economic growth rate* of 3.1% projected by the International Monetary Fund for 2027.

The U.S. entertainment industry by itself is the largest in the world and accounts for nearly one-third of the global total revenue, recorded at about $660 billion in 2020. The U.S. entertainment market has been greatly affected by U.S. lockdown policies. The International Trade Administration predicted it would have reached about $71.3 million more in revenue in 2020 without the impact of the lockdowns. "After falling 2.3% in 2020, total global entertainment and media (E&M) revenue rose a strong 10.4% in 2021, resuming its trend of outpacing global growth." (PwC, 2022) According to PwC, the 'cable' pay TV subscription market in the United States has continued to decline in recent years. The number of cable subscriptions was about 97.9 million in 2016, and the number decreased by 23% to about 75.6 million in 2020. As this downward trend is expected to continue for some time, the number of subscriptions is expected to decrease to approximately only 25 million in as little as five years.

The large and fast economic decline of cable TV subscription markets in the USA results from both the growing demand for more online video subscriptions in 'Subscription Video on Demand (SVOD)' and competition from 'Virtual Multi-Channel Video Programming Distributor (vMVPD). To define these terms, Subscription Video On Demand (SVOD) is a type of 'over-the-top' (OTT) platform, and refers to a service that provides online video on demand through a subscription method. Examples include Netflix, Amazon Prime Video, Hulu, Apple TV+ , Disney+ , HBO Max, and more. Virtual Multichannel Video Programming Distributor (vMVPD) is a term that refers to a service that aggregates live video and video on-demand (VOD) television content, equally provided over the Internet. Representative service providers in the United States are DIRECTV NOW, Hulu Live, fubo TV, Roku, Apple TV, Amazon Fire TV, and YouTube Live. Traditional cable pay TV broadcasting providers in the United States are trying to reduce as much as possible their service fee, which is interpreted as a key factor to maintain the declining loyalty of the existing consumer base amid a shift toward more online video on demand. Plus, their investments in other related cable technologies such as broadband service, 5G, and IoT is also continuing.

Meanwhile, according to Statista, a global research institute, the total music market in the United States is recorded at about $8 billion in 2020. As noted in Chapter 6, the Korean group BTS was pulling over $4 billion into the Korean economy alone by 2020—thus with BTS comparable in scale to one group pulling half of the whole U.S. music market. The largest profit sector within the total music market in the United States is coming from the continued growth of the digital music market such as music subscription and streaming. In addition, the American film market represented by Hollywood is one of the sectors hit the hardest by American policies of lockdown instituted in 2020. By 2022, many movie theaters in the United States had yet to recover from their pre-lockdown situation. The data show that American movie theater box office sales totals in 2019 were $2.1 billion, and sales fell by as much as 80% in 2020. By March 2021, 23% of all theaters in the United States still were closed. In the future, American movie box office sales are expected to grow at a CAGR of 37.3% over the next five years, gradually recovering. Sales are predicted to increase to about $10.4 billion in 2025. This seems overly optimistic for a 500% growth in five years compared to 2019. This is because Hollywood movie content in 2021 through 2023 was mostly a failure in popularity and profit, because the global Korean Wave is on the rise, and because global subscription video on demand (SVOD) is growing instead of movie theater attendance. This is due to prolonged state policies pushing lockdowns, how existing movie consumers gradually moved to the OTT video platform field, and due to Hollywood mistakes in pushing movie content and stories that less people wanted to pay to see. As a result, the U.S. movie theater market seems to be continuously losing demand. A 'perfect storm' is developing in Hollywood by mid-July 2023 as on top of massive profit losses over the past few years in Hollywood now both the Hollywood writers and actors are on strike together for the first time since 1960. Hollywood writers via their union, the Writers Guild of America (WGA), went on strike from May 2, 2023, and the union of Hollywood actors, the Screen Actors Guild—American Federation of Television and Radio Artists (SAG-AFTRA), joined on July 14, 2023 after their contracts expired as well with the Alliance of Motion Picture and Television Producers (AMPTP) which represents media producers like Netflix, Disney, Paramount, and Universal. Therefore, the future outlook of the U.S. movie market in general is really more uncertain than the estimates above. "Both writers and actors are fighting for contracts that prevent an AI from replacing them at their jobs, whether it's writing scripts or appearing as a background actor. They're also looking for better pay when working on shows for streaming services." The actors' strike joined the writers' strike when "major studios' refus[ed] to meet [actors'] demands for a two percent cut of streaming revenue and a 230 percent increase in foreign streaming residuals...[and, the producers refused]...to require that a performer has to consent to any use of their performance to train an AI system...[as]...the AMPTP [wants to] give studios carte blanche to train AI systems to create 'synthetic' performers, or for other purposes." (Roth, 2023)

Meanwhile, the more global over-the-top (OTT) video market provides video streaming services over the Internet. It is *the fastest growing segment even in the US entertainment and media industry.* This OTT market rapidly emerged as core to the U.S. entertainment industry, reaching its heyday due to the surge in consumer demand due simply to the policy of lockdowns forcing the issue. The United States, which already is considered the world's largest OTT video market both in terms of subscribers and in transaction volume, recorded an OTT video market size of about

$22.8 billion in 2020—already more than ten times the profit of U.S. movie theaters in pre-lockdown conditions of 2019 at $2.1 billion.

In 2021, the related 'Transactional Video On Demand (TVOD)', a concept different from SVOD, is also growing significantly. Nonetheless, the SVOD service is about 3.4 times larger than the TVOD service. In particular, the SVOD market competition is intensifying due to new players entering the market in 2020 in competition with existing leading American companies like Netflix. Now OTT consumers have a wider range of platform choices, allowing them to access a more diverse content. The overall U.S. OTT video market is expected to grow steadily at a CAGR of about 6.9% over the next five years. In 2025, it is expected to reach about $31.9 billion in sales, a huge increase of about $9.1 billion from 2020.

5.2.1 The Korean Wave's Innovation in Global Music

Today, the Korean entertainment market is growing with the rapid development of ever more distributed, wireless, and mobile technology applied to this media market. Under lockdowns, Korean streaming viewership for performances was increasing rapidly. In this context, in August 2020, in the midst of various national lockdowns, BTS reached the number one spot on Billboard's U.S.-national based 'Hot 100' for the song and video for 'Dynamite.' This video combined English lyrics with K-pop sensibility. Just one month later in September 2020, Billboard in the United States started to rank musical hits on a 'Global 200 Chart' as well. This was a major break away from the U.S.'s past exclusive national focus. By the end of 2020, the number of concurrent viewers of BTS's online performances started to set global records, with the group sweeping seven nominations in Billboard's year-end accounts as well.

It is argued that the success of K-pop on the global stage is largely attributable to technological innovation and how music is now less broadcast and more shared in more multi-node friendship contacts across multiple platforms instead of being centrally distributed from a single source. This is particularly strong in Korea and worldwide in the twenty-first century, thanks to the spread of social network service (SNS) and its usage by consumers. Korean content has been shared this way and expanded to the global market. For example, Psy's speech to the Oxford Union in 2012 indicated that in his analysis that SNS sharing of his video for "Gangnam Style" by other major American stars, sent to their own millions of SNS followers, was crucial in his massive popularity boost that neglected old broadcast mediums. Similarly, the Korean boy group BTS, formed in 2013 which was one year after Psy's viral success, has a manager that seemed to have learned from Psy's success. BTS has eschewed old one-way media appearances from this group's formation in 2013. Instead, BTS depended on from the start on the cultivation of a large and durable digital fandom by sharing regular daily and weekly updates to that fandom. BTS operates like an ongoing digital reality show or group based 'vlogging' with weekly updates about dance practice, other commentary, etc. This facilitates ongoing synchronous communication with fans that see them grow over the years, instead of

BTS operating as a distant professional music and dance group only occasionally advertising music videos or concerts.

This global digital entertainment market shares content without time and space restrictions. Plus, it is unable to filter or compile a discrete national popularity playlist to national citizens anymore even if they wanted it, because national popularity is becoming global popularity as well. To the contrary, in the past, with the lack of digital SNS and digital platforms in the 1990s and due to an earlier poor music contract market, Korean singers in the regional Hallyu period fell short of expectations. They were unable to reach any global market given how a centralized distribution within each nation still reigned supreme. However, with the recent growth of global social media platforms of free viewing and commenting like Facebook (from 2004), YouTube (from 2005), Twitter (from 2006), and Instagram (from 2010), Korean K-pop only from the first decade of the twenty-first century can be shared globally in a short period of time. By 2022, these platforms sometimes reach as much as over 2 billion people potentially at once (like in Facebook or in YouTube) to around a still massive scale of other platforms reaching 430 million people (like Twitter). This makes the largest of these platforms the main arenas of world culture since they are far larger than any nations and because they cross all nations easily. This is combined with the growing user base of ever cheaper Internet-accessible smartphone markets. These developed after the first flat glass touchscreen smartphones were released in 2007 nearly simultaneously by Korea's LG (the LG Prada phone) and by the United States' Apple (the iPhone). (See Appendix 1.) These designs were widely copied around the world by other brands in the years afterward and cheapened in turn.

So, there is an endless global ripple effect in world culture from SNS sharing. It occurs around the world all the time due to platforms having billions of users accessed by a growing mobile phone user base of over 5 billion by 2019, and within that statistic, with smartphones owners being between 2.5 to 3.3 billion of those owners in 2019. Smartphones were distributed rather evenly around the world. Earlier, this was called a 'digital parity' to contrast it with the term 'digital divide' that indeed was suffered by much past technical diffusion of telecommunications equipment. Since Korea as a nation was more saturated first in this version of digital telecommunications (Appendix 1), a wider and equitable 'digital parity' in the same technologies globally later made it possible for the global Korean Wave to 'share' itself into a durable virtual community fandom all over the world from the second decade of the twenty-first century without worrying about paying for expensive past national one-way media sponsorship in other countries and without other national cultural waves being as digitally ready as Korea. However, it is hardly argued that a nation's digital readiness, a digital network, and digital users are the only factors in success of a K-pop group or a national cultural wave. Certainly, the Korean Wave has huge talent, hard work, stunning visuals, charisma, catchy songs and lyrics, cinema, drama, and a host of other sectors. However, it increasingly became a global Korean Wave by its global ripple effect across these global digital networks—and because digital Korea got there first. This fresh recipe for true global entertainment success in the twenty-first century remains a talent's internal capabilities yet it is now magnified at scales unseen in world history and transmitted at the speed of light around the world very cheaply compared to past distribution models in previous media regimes. The Korean public state, Korean profit-based companies, and Korean cultural talent combine with this fresh media regime of globalized mobile multimedia networks of smartphones, SNS texts, videos, and links shared between fans and shared between major stars and their fans. With Korea being more digitally saturated earlier than other countries, and thus given Korea has been priming a digital Korean Wave for over a decade, this has given Koreans more experience in digitally *marketing* to this more saturated digital culture, more than any other nation. Koreans in their digitally saturated nation first learned how to do this digital marketing *domestically* before other nations, and that helped Koreans do digital marketing *globally* before others. (See Appendix 1). Plus, the larger scale of export-led economics in Korea compared to other countries gives Koreans more economic incentives to do that global sharing, while their more homogeneous culture gives them greater access to a faster collective innovation to do so.

Thus, in combination, the Korean businesses digital marketing expertise, the Korean cultural capacities, the Korean saturated digital consumer habits, and the growing more globalized digital cultural context have interacted in the Korean Wave for years longer than other nations' cultural waves. So, the national experimentation of Korean marketers, Korean bands, and a national public were already primed with more saturated networks of digital technology in South Korea far earlier in excess than other nations. This national expertise in their own digital marketing and digital culture was preparatory for the global spillover, once the same Korean expertise in marketing and selling nationally could move wider once the world's scale of aggregate smartphones and platforms were accessible to the Korean earlier digital marketing expertise.

Other external factors of the Korean wave have to be discussed in global music. In 2011, even YouTube opened a "K-pop-only" zone in its music category for the first time, by country. This surely primed a Korean Wave through this global platform, because *the most representative example is the fact that the very next year on YouTube, in 2012, Psy's Gangnam Style was able to attract worldwide attention.* By SNS sharing and platform-based sharing, Psy was able to outflank national radio-play markets entirely that surely would have blocked him. Instead, the song spread by an entertaining video, itself spread largely by social media viewing and sharing from SNS platforms. That is even Psy's own analysis of what happened mentioned in his speech to the Oxford Union in late 2012. Upon Psy's video release in July 2012 on YouTube, Psy's video for "Gangnam Style" received an explosive response. Psy's video became the first video in YouTube history to break 1 billion views, and then the first video to break the YouTube counter, hitting over 2.14 billion views by 2014, after which the algorithm started to display broken negative numbers. The code had to be rewritten because the original programmers thought no one would ever hit that many views. As of January 2023, the video for Gangnam Style now has surpassed 4.6 billion views on YouTube in a little over ten years, and it is still growing. By July 2023, the video has 4.832 billion views. However, keep in mind as of July 1, 2023, the main audience for viral videos has settled on the audience of music videos for young children and animations for young children. By 2023, the majority of the top ten most viewed YouTube videos are children's nursery rhymes and related children's animations with fully three of the top five and six of the top ten. Eight of the top twenty are the same. Psy's "Gangnam Style" is ranked currently at #11, in between "Learning Colors–Colorful Eggs on a Farm" by Miroshka TV and "Masha and the Bear–Recipe for Disaster." Both of those are Russian children's animations. The true top viral video in the world is "Baby Shark Dance" by Pinkfong released in 2016. The song is an adaption of a late twentieth century American children's folk/camp song in the public domain, yet similar to an arrangement of it created by professional children's entertainer Johnny Only, who released his version online in 2011. Pinkfong is a *Korean* children's educational company focusing on the age group of between 1 to 5 years of age. Pingfong was founded in Seoul in 2010, and it has additionally designed and released over 170 mobile video apps for children. Pinkfong mobile apps have over 400 million downloads in total in 2023, and Pinkfong has been a four time winner of the Best Family App, awarded by Google Play. Therefore, even the global online young children's market is part of the global Korean Wave. However, "Gangnam Style" remains untouchably unique in its sonic and visual popularity, perhaps immortalized forever because of one statistic. "Gangnam Style" *is the only example of a top viral video hit staying so long as the global #1 at YouTube*: for over 1,689 days or about 4.63 years. This is only slightly approached by the next highest of "Despacito" by Luis Fonsi (1,186 days), then another Korean entry of "Baby Shark Dance" by Pingfong (971 days), then "Baby" by Justin Bieber (862 days), and then "Evolution of Dance" by Judson Laipply (652 days).

Immediately following the world-record-shattering success of Psy's "Gangnam Style" in 2012, the management group HYBE (renamed from Big Hit Entertainment in 2021) formed the K-pop boy group BTS in 2013 with its manager from the start having a similar digital virality in mind for BTS, like Psy's success. Plus, over the past ten years, Big Hit Entertainment/HYBE succeeded with more general Korean-style content in a differentiated innovation strategy. Surprisingly, HYBE and BTS have grown and succeeded with this other strategy, breaking away from trying to be an imitation of global West/Japanese-wave musicians of the 1980s that Korean musicians and entertainers before were regularly copying as the recipe for a major hit. Besides the digital virality designed around BTS from the start, it can be said that BTS's secret is casting unnoticed locals in Korea and nurturing them into K-pop idols through very long-term professional star-training programs. In other words, the Korean Wave is based on deep capacity training as much as digital networks. Taking a cue from Psy's strategies of global popularity, HYBE utilized YouTube (just like Psy) from the beginning of BTS's career almost exclusively. HYBE went further than Psy though and almost continuously shared mere activities and daily life of the fresh BTS boy group to its earliest fans around the world, priming a digital fan base. At that time, Korean talent agencies still depended on broadcasting platforms. Therefore, this strategy around BTS was a radical innovation closer to the dynamic of a 'reality TV show' around the band's media image. Plus, in the same year that BTS was founded in 2013, this was the first year that the Korean domestic culture was nearly 100% saturated with mobile phone ownership from teenagers through adult ages of

35. In the same year of 2013, the United States only had around 50% of its teenager demographic owning smartphones. (See Appendix 1) So, with this deeper and earlier digital cultural saturation of Korea, combined with HYBE's deep personalization that primed global BTS fans, BTS entered a Korean national market and a global market immediately from 2013 at very low cost and in a short time without relying on wooing other national or global talent agencies first. It was an excellent choice for BTS to utilize platform digital technology such as YouTube and Twitter, following Psy's strategy, rather than trying to book meetings with broadcasters to try to get BTS on established entertainment and music programs.

In 2019, Big Hit Entertainment/HYBE changed the base of its marketing of its managed musicians and artists from the US's YouTube and from Korea's Naver to its own independent platform, called "Weverse." Aiming to become the world's best entertainment distribution platform company as well as hosting its own music groups, HYBE used Weverse as an optimal tool. In only its first month of October 2020, Weverse as an independent community platform exceeded 300,000 unique users in the midst of growing levels of many nations' lockdowns. In less than two years, Weverse had an astounding global growth and became *the world's largest fandom platform with over 10 million users registered in 100 countries by 2022.* So by 2020, HYBE no longer uploads its musicians' performances or music videos to platforms of YouTube or Naver first. Now, it is expanding the Weverse platform's influence by uploading video content and producing and selling related products on Weverse where the music is launched directly with co-branded products. In other words, in operating Weverse, HYBE is able to promote BTS without giving money or editorial control to US platforms such as YouTube or even to other Korean platforms like Kakao or Naver, respectively, the owners of a nearly monopolistic Korean SNS platform and a Korean search engine almost exclusively used in Korea by Koreans and yet with both rarely used in any other countries of the world. Thus, Kakao or Naver were hardly optimal global platforms for popularizing a global Korean Wave given both having an almost exclusive use only inside the South Korean nation. Instead, a more global Weverse is expected to maximize economies of scale considering the global fandom effect. In short, from 2020, entertainment programs like BTS get distributed and produced by Weverse first.

So as performances of music concerts, movies, and even dance studios were attempted to be forcibly closed around Korea and the world, HYBE kept growing and achieving higher global user platform levels than before. An integrated performance business model has been established. It enables non-stop online performance payment, viewing, and purchase of related products through Weverse. By April 2020, HYBE held a concert in a situation when performances were canceled across many countries, yet HYBE succeeded in creating a virtual community of *more than 2 million fans simultaneously around the world for the event.* In two days of BTS's performances, the number of *total views exceeded 50 million*, and the *number of simultaneous users recorded the highest number at 2.24 million.* This set a record in the performance industry.

Such online and non-face-to-face live concerts in the global Korean Wave from 2020 have been recognized as a representative case of innovation in the performance industry around the world. Since then, numerous singers, broadcasters, and agencies have tried to hold similar online and non-face-to-face live concerts. BTS repeated this online live concert tactic in 2022 merged with a more traditional in-person concert. This is another good example of Korean innovation in a 'virtual reality' *extension* of the global Korean Wave around the band BTS. The event in 2022 was called 'BTS Permission to Dance on Stage-Seoul.' Actually, it was part of a 12-run show that began in Seoul on October 24th, 2021, and which would conclude in Las Vegas, Nevada on April 16th, 2022. The three more digital events of BTS discussed below were held at the Jamsil Sports Complex in Seoul on March 10th, 12th, and 13th in 2022. All three performances from March 10th and 13th were indeed face-to-face concerts with the group BTS, yet with government-reduced fans in the audience in Korea. All singing and cheering were banned in the government-enforced limited audience of 15,000 people. Showing how unscientific, fake, and merely political were any numerical claims of 'safe scales' of crowds, previously the Korean government had claimed that a maximum of 4,000 was the upward bound limit on public concerts, yet they threw out that rule for these BTS concerts. Despite this artificial limitation on fans, ticket sales alone recorded 40 billion won (approximately $40 million dollars). All three concerts were streamed online, though only the second concert held on March 12th at the BTS concert stage was broadcast *live in real-time through 'Live Viewing' at 3,711 movie theaters in 75 countries around the world simultaneously.* Tickets for this concert were $35, four times the average price of a movie theater ticket in North America at $9. However, these hybrid 'BTS live online-concert movie tickets' were sold out in Los Angeles and several other U.S. cities' venues. Due to the enthusiasm of BTS fans, this BTS concert even ranked third at the weekend box office in North America. The Hollywood review magazine *Variety* reported: "The live broadcast of the BTS concert was a blockbuster performance, which is rare for a one-night movie theater event." (Jem & Rubin, 2022) *Variety* reported that on March 12th, 2022, the single-night BTS 'global online movie theater concert' recorded a global box office profit of $32.6 million (40.3 billion Korean won). According to BTS's agency HYBE, the number of people who watched the concert online and offline for three days reached 2.5 million viewers. In total, the maximum government-limited crowed of 45,000 people came to the concerts at the Jamsil Sports Complex in Seoul from March 10th through 13th, 2022, yet 1.02 million were online streaming the concert on March 10th and 13th. Even more were watching on March 12th, the global 'concert movie theater night' for BTS when there were 1.4 million in-person live viewings in theaters around the world for that one night only. (Kim, 2022c).

In summary, BTS's concert in Seoul broadcast in theaters around the world on March 12th, 2022 was the first time this innovative 'hybrid real/virtual event' had been created in world media history. It was a successful in-person movie theater box office hit and an (online) live concert combined. It 'simply' took place in 75 countries at once across 3,711 movie theaters for 1.4 million people. Before 2022, it was assumed that online live performances were difficult make work because it is difficult to satisfy fans who want to experience live performances. However, HYBE was successful in selling 1.4 million 'online live' movie theater tickets cheaper than the 'physical live' concert. HYBE sold these tickets exclusively at the Weverse shop on the Weverse platform. This added synergy brought more users to the Weverse platform that were BTS fans, and some surely would stay for the wider platform experience of Weverse for the first time as well. As an example of music innovation, the fact is that the very first paid 'online live' yet virtual *global* theater performance immediately set a world record in profit from concert sales and in concert attendance for one night, and nearly set movie theater box office records for one night. This was a fan base and a profit base well beyond past 'physical live' concerts of one night. Although most agencies canceled world tour performances during government orders of lockdown between 2020 through 2022, HYBE showed it was possible and profitable to interact with, communicate with, and generate interest with fans via online live performances. The 'one-stop shop' entertainment service organized via Weverse owned by HYBE showed innovative results in this entertainment service field like selling related items centering on the fresh platform Weverse.

HYBE's innovation in global music maximized emotional rapport with fans through storytelling and messages, and created revenue and value through its own online platform. Five points of innovation here are important, and it shows the same story IP content ownership and management business model via online platforms, as mentioned earlier. First, HYBE opted for telling 'reality show'-style stories about BTS in the beginning that could spread virally via smartphone and SNS sharing instead of taking out global deals for broadcast time. This is an example of innovation in the performance industry of the global Korean Wave. A second innovation is based on the original intellectual property rights (IP) of music and artists, with HYBE maximizing profits by providing services that organically combine and converge three business areas once institutionally quite separate: performances, intellectual property, and online platforms. In other words, the innovation is the method of digital synergy that increases added value by expanding the original work in various forms. This expands the innovation of customer experience and the value chain through 'One Source Multi Uses' (OSMU), which captures this digital synergy well. The goal has been to create a circulation in the value chain by introducing more content and products to the fandom of BTS's music. The BTS fans who commercialize value derived from content and connect to it in their lives become the core asset of the platform, because their ongoing sharing of the content is the main marketing strategy in lieu of centralized distribution costs. A third innovation seen here in the global Korean Wave is improving the recording and transmission picture quality that will encourage more attendance for online performances. A fourth innovation is great levels of direct participation in two-way communication between the groups and the digital fandom. There is sometimes a more intimate a communication in a virtual community than in real life since the depth of having virtual yet emotionally real connections always on hand in daily life on a mobile phone in synchronous communication with BTS can grow tighter in a virtual space than simply seeing them live from a distance one time at hundreds of meters. This seems as much a personalized SNS communication with a group of friends as much as a K-pop boy band of BTS simultaneously. Fifth, the fact that it is easier to stream live video with technological innovations such as 5G was also helpful in South Korea first, since Korea rolled out the first 5G in the world hours before Verizon in the United States (See Appendix 1).

However, South Korea already had the highest density of 4G coverage before, and that helped as well in priming the domestic base of the global Korean Wave. Plus, the hype around 5G can be overstated in South Korea since moving from 4G to 5G requires a very different and closer infrastructure being rolled out without tests for health effects, and Korea was already a country offering the fastest average internet speeds for a large country in 4G and even a short-lived '4.5G' in many cities before 5G developments.

In short, the main theme in this innovation in global music is the digital synergy of various new viewing technologies, changes in organization, and how that content is both produced and distributed differently. This digital synergy is providing a new window of opportunity for HYBE and the global Korean Wave in general toward a common global online digital content and platform management model. Beyond limits of live music that has historically only been enjoyed in physical proximity and face-to-face, a new world without boundaries between reality and virtuality in synchronous 'two-way mass communication' instead of only asynchronous one-way mass communication has arrived in global music.

It is likely most countries are unable to compete technically against the global Korean Wave given many nations' dominance still in older one-way mass media broadcast regimes and single venue unrecorded/unstreamed live concerts. It is argued this only further emphasizes Korea's outlier status. Korea seems to be an outlier even further ahead digitally compared to other nations as the latter fall back, instead of Korea being a harbinger of what is to come in other countries.

5.2.2 The Korean Wave's Innovation in Broadcasting and Film

The next infrastructure to analyze for digital innovations in the global Korean Wave is in the visual production and distribution for online broadcasting for OTT markets, showing a changed broadcasting and changed way of funding filmed content creation. The OTT service market has a typical two-sided market structure. In the OTT business, operators store the content provided by content providers digitally on a computer server and then supply that stored content in a video on demand (VOD)/streaming method to generate revenue from either subscriptions or specific event fees. Thus, OTT assumes a stable digital platform and with distributed digital consumers in the millions to make it profitable. Basically, a platform is a virtual environment arranged so that multiple global groups of suppliers and consumers participate and exchange value that each group wants through transactions. Depending on the business strategy, a platform operator receives usage fees from either both groups or from only one group to generate profits that maintains and services the ongoing transactions or interactions of both groups in a two-sided market composed of independent producers and consumer groups. Unlike traditional marketing-oriented businesses such as a supply chain and distribution, a platform business has open characteristics with participants ideally having voluntary participation and ideally equal rights of communication and sales.

In practice however, there are two caveats. First, because of market shakeout and lack of many places for sellers to go except on a handful of global platform services, OTT platform providers can set market terms in their favor *over* the sellers or the consumers like exorbitant fees on consumers or exploitative exclusive contracts on the content providers. Plus, OTT platform providers can take the data transactions of their content's *competition* (available to analyze on the platform) to minimize market sales of their competition on their own platform. (George, 2001; Waldfogel, 2007) Second, platform service suppliers may bias the whole world's conversation and content particularly in league with covert government censorship on culture and in the politics around hiding factual election information as revealed in the 'Twitter files' in 2022 or the 'Facebook files' in 2023. Equally, making content that is legal and yet is content that the 'powers that be' dislike, can get you 'demonetized' or labeled as 'misinformation' on YouTube, or your whole channel can be canceled and deleted across many SNS services. Supply-side biases in platforms under the first caveat have happened widely on Amazon, and governmental-side biases in platforms under the second caveat have happened clearly on Twitter and likely OTT services.

In short, perfect markets are honored more in the breach than the observance in global platform services, because platform providers can do more than simply provide a neutral platform service. They can innately compete with providers on their own platform as well and try to minimize visibility and sales of their own competitors on their own platform by priming their own content and sales instead, based on market intelligence of their competitors assembled from their own platform. Can Korean Wave OTT content providers break this pernicious biased trend in global platform sales and distribution, or will they just perpetuate and participate in it?

It is important to know that the OTT service market acts as a platform for OTT operators *ideally* to mediate content providers and users with this two-sided market structure. Therefore, in a two-sided market environment, how much an OTT service provider (like American Netflix or Korean Wavve) as a platform operator will *allow* users to use content depends on the content supply price signed with the content provider to be supplied as well as the two caveats above. A platform strategy can be very effective if successful, but it is not easy to secure a critical mass.

However, as said, nowadays platform companies make their own intellectual property (IP) content, competing with other sellers that they attract to their own platforms. Plus, vice versa, content companies now make their own platforms as well, desiring the same tight business of priming and self-preferment of their own content in the platform market. Thus, it is common now that OTT platform operators, represented by Netflix, spend tremendously high sums to develop competitive original series to host content exclusively by contract on Netflix in order to draw consumers and other sellers to the platforms. Another typical example is the content provider Disney which supplies the movies that it puts on its own now exclusive global OTT platform called Disney+, in the process withdrawing past agreements with Netflix for all Disney distribution, as a consequence.

The history of this biased and synergistic global market organization of OTT platforms and their own self-generated content is very recent. Given requirements of having millions of distributed digital consumers as its foundation, the rise of OTT is hypothesized to be connected deeply to potentials of digital saturation that only started to existed after the first year of ever cheaper global smartphone access from 2007 through the first year of 'smart TVs' with similar internet connections manufactured from 2015. As a result, note Netflix first pioneered the OTT/online video streaming services as a business to millions of digital consumers in the United States only in the same year as the birth of the smartphone, in 2007. By 2019, smartphone users were "more than 45% of the total OTT content streaming audience" in the United States. (Johnson, 2019) It was only around 2015 with the beginning of mass manufactured smart TV's did similar OTT services competitively spread around the world—even with several OTTs now being created out of traditional TV broadcasting companies. So now by 2023, in addition to Netflix (from 2007), various OTT services based in the US are like Amazon Fire TV (from 2014), AT&T (acquisition of DirecTV from 2015, now separately managed from 2021 yet still 70% owned by AT&T), Disney+ (from 2019), Apple + (from 2019), and Comcast (from 2020). There are of course many more, and these are mentioned in Chapter 8 later in the context of the case study of *Squid Game*. All OTT services entered the global media market with divisions providing global-level services mostly after the invention of the smart TV in 2015. These major global OTT providers are pay-TV operators, content providers, and media operators of various classes like Internet hosting/server operators as well.

These OTT companies provide a variety of services with a focus on either free or paid revenue models. For examples of these services, SVOD (Subscription Video On Demand) is a service with a monthly flat rate. SVOD models are stand-alone companies or are company subdivisions. These include Netflix, Disney+, Apple TV+, CBS All Access, YouTube Premium, Hulu, and HBO Max. Advertising-based Video on Demand (AVOD) is a service operated by hosting of advertisement revenue. YouTube and Hulu are platforms that employ the AVOD model where mass users have content and services for free only by watching advertisements where these are sold by the AVOD service provider themselves, placed on the user's freely hosted videos.

By 2021, less than fifteen years after the first OTT platform of Netflix in 2007, OTT is available in 190 countries. Measured from October 8, 2021, it had a global total of 140 million paid members and a market capitalization of $280 billion. This makes OTT rank 30th when comparing all industries' global market capitalization.

What is happening in the similar OTT 'platformization' of the Korean entertainment industry? In Korea, existing broadcasting companies such as Wavve, Tving, Seezn, and native streaming services such as Watcha Play are competing successfully with the American global services for SVOD and AVOD. This is thanks to these Korean platforms' solid content, Korea being the earliest and most digitally saturated culture in world history so far for a large country, and of course given Korea has the fastest bandwidth in network infrastructure in the world for well over a decade for a large populous country. (See Appendix 1.) Plus, Korean streaming services have much greater market dominance within Korea compared to most global OTTs in Korea, except for Netflix which does dominate the Korean market. However, even Korean companies are establishing strong relationships with the American OTT giants. This seems necessary since if Korean content producers do not secure a priming alliance of production and distribution with global OTTs, the global Korean Wave may suffer from production contraction instead of further growth.

As suggested by Eisenmann and others, we can frame OTT platforms in terms of six kinds of market strategies. (Eisenmann et al., 2006) Eisenmann's team suggests six market strategies for two-sided market relationships like OTT. So, in order to create a successful two-sided market structure on OTT services, a platform should check for all six strategic elements and reflect on how to achieve all of them in a business strategy. The first element of OTT success is the cross-sided network effect. This refers to the effect that the subsidized group (in this case, the consumers) also receives the same subsidies from other platforms competing with the platforms at the same time. However, most platform suppliers try to block consumers from choosing to operate in an ideal market, because platforms dislike open markets and try to maintain some kind of encouraged easy habit or monopolistic use of consumer data or exclusive content on their platforms. The second market strategy element is the same-sided network effect. Instead of the platform as a service provider trying to force or to arrange contracts to create exclusive hosting of content by specific sellers on their platform alone, instead the platform attempts to charge a cost of hosting which can be adjusted competitively over time to encourage the same exclusive outcome. However, obviously hardly all OTT providers follow this open platform rule. The third market strategy element is finding ways to reduce the platform's production costs. Since the initial production cost of content on the platform is high, a strategy that can be taken without subsidizing both producers and consumers of the two-sided market is to establish a pricing policy that reflects the needs of both users or using the previously mentioned "story IP" of an already established market like popular webtoons. This is being done widely in Korean OTT services already. The fourth market strategy element is the user's price sensitivity, which usually refers to the price sensitivity of the end user. The platform seeks to subsidize only the more price-sensitive groups to keep them on the platform, while others less sensitive are judged more likely to remain. Using story IP in a more exclusive viewing on a single platform is one way to inculcate more habitual users to a particular platform who are less likely requiring subsidization to remain, it is conjectured. This is being done as well in Korean OTT. The fifth strategy would be the user's sensitivity to quality. The quality sensitivity of different groups of customers determines which groups should be subsidized or prioritized to encourage their use of the platform. Both American and Korean OTT have spent tremendously on original Korean content creation, so it seems a common judgment that higher quality is one way to retain users. The last and sixth strategy is to take into account the user's brand value, so the platform tries to subsidize a group in order to secure a popular or loyal user group. This is being done with Korean OTT platforms like Weverse using global fandom empires around BTS or other Korean platforms that are exclusive places to see story IP or various movie and TV drama franchises.

If we look at the current status of this market of global OTTs including Netflix and Disney+, the OTTs as a group are expected to invest in 2022 about 137 trillion won (US $111.35 billion), and this is not content though simply infrastructural investment. With scales of cash like this, competition is expected to intensify. Generally, while the global OTT platform market has entered a cutthroat context of a 'red ocean strategy' (meaning, 'how to survive in a very competitive market by cutting costs') given the advent of multiple global OTTs, equally many are attempting a 'blue ocean strategy' at the same time (meaning, 'develop fresh products that no one else has') in order to remove others' competition entirely. The *Financial Times* announced for 2022 that the business of eight major US companies such as Netflix and Disney+ had an estimated investment cost for new 'blue ocean' content creation of an astoundingly large $115 billion in that year. The company expected to invest the most was Disney. Investment bank Morgan Stanley expects Disney to invest $23 billion in new movies and TV shows in 2023. This is an increase of 35–40% compared to 2022. In the industry, Disney+ was mentioned as a rival to Netflix before its beginning, yet after movie market losses of 2022, Disney may seek a rebound by a more 'blue ocean' strategy of securing unique new content of something already popular, like the global Korean Wave. Disney+ has indeed done this by hiring Korean stars made popular in *Squid Game* to star in a specially made *Star Wars* franchise film (that Disney bought all rights to now) called "The Acolyte."

As for other related OTT investments in content creation, streaming investments in content by U.S. major OTT platform services reached $200 billion in 2021. Even more was expected to be spent in 2022. It was estimated to be around $238 billion in 2022, yet in January 2022 it was announced they would only spend collectively around $140 billion on content in 2022. (Forristal, 2022) From January 2023, global content expenditure saw "the lowest growth in a decade," and increased only by 2% from 2022 to 2023. (IBC, 2023) In a growing global recession, both Apple and Amazon reported losing a huge $800 billion in market capitalization in 2022 alone. Therefore their content delivery seems impeded as well. (Harring, 2023) For 2023, it is expected that the top eight global major investors in content will remain in this order: the movie productions of Disney, Warner Brothers, Discovery, Paramount, and only after them the OTT providers of Comcast, Netflix, Apple, and Amazon. (IBC, 2023) So, even though Netflix is already ranked the largest OTT provider in the global industry, with about 25% of all global content investments, it is still increasing its investments. Morgan Stanley predicted that Netflix will spend $17 billion (about 20.23 trillion won) on investment in new content, up 25% from the previous year. These predictions came true when Netflix announced it would maintain $17 billion content budgets through 2023, even as the streaming market grows is expected to grow more slowly in 2023. (Satin, 2023).

Netflix obviously remains keen on producing its own content because it succeeded so wildly and globally with only Korean-produced films like *Squid Game*, *D.P.*., and *Sweet Home*, among others in 2021. For example, Netflix invested 550 billion won (approximately $443 million) in Korean content alone in 2021. So, Netflix builds on its success with original Korean content in 2021 with plans to continue making large-scale investments in 2022.

Korean companies are not missing out on opportunities in such tight competition for creating more global OTT platform streaming services. The Korean company Tving plans to enter the Japanese and Taiwanese markets, marking 2022 as the first year of its more global expansion as a streaming platform. CJ ENM, the parent company of Tving, announced in 2021 that it would invest a total of 5 trillion won ($4.03 billion) in Korean content production over five years. In particular, CJ ENM acquired the American production studio Endeavor Contents in 2021. After Tving's planned entry into Japan and Taiwan as its first targets for global expansion of its SVOD (Subscription Video on Demand), Tving later plans to take its streaming platform market expansion into North American and Southeast Asian markets after 2024. After 2025, Tving says it will target markets in more than 10 countries including more European and Latin American countries as well. Additionally, Tving is concentrating on strengthening its global competitiveness by establishing partnerships with ViacomCBS, a major American media company. ViacomCBS seems to be having trouble, and thus is keen on a relationship with the global Korean Wave. For example, in November 2021, ViacomCBS started to sell off non-essential older studio lots of CBS studios in Los Angeles for $1.8 billion. These ViacomCBS sales of soundstages are interpreted as selling off "non-core assets in order [for ViacomCBS] to invest more heavily in creating shows and movies for the burgeoning streaming platforms." (Steigrad, 2021) In addition to shedding its old skin of broadcast studios for more digital content funding, ViacomCBS changed its name by February 2022 to Paramount as well. Thus, digital platform content is the mechanism through which many old TV broadcast companies like ViacomCBS are trying to be reborn as more paramount OTT players in the digital twenty-first century.

5.2.3 The Korean Wave's Innovation in Artificial Intelligence

Another way the global Korean Wave grew even during lockdowns in many countries of the world was because the Korean entertainment industry applied the latest in artificial intelligence (AI) technology. It was applied across various fields in the past few years. As demand for non-face-to-face services increased due to government lockdowns, and as time spent indoors increased with many offline meetings, events, and even concerts moved online, AI adaptations were added to the Korean entertainment industry. The advent of artificial intelligence (AI) or human–machine communication has had a tremendous impact on the Korean entertainment industry. Entertainment is an odd route to add AI applications in any nation's economy, as explained below, though it did happen in the Korean Wave in the past few years.

To introduce what artificial intelligence is, there are two schools of thought about how artificial intelligence would develop, the extrinsic or the intrinsic view. Both are now being employed in the Korean Wave. The extrinsic view of AI is how to make it appear that a machine is a human being. This follows the definition and ideas of Alan Turing in 1950. He felt that a true test of an AI would be whether it could trick a human being into believing it was another human being. This is an extrinsic model of AI that encourages applications like development of passable robotic men and women along with conversational chat bots that interact with human beings effectively and seamlessly. Companies spent a huge amount of money starting in the 1950s to the 1970s, attempting to create these kinds of extrinsic, human-imitative, machine intelligences. However, by the 1970s, without much success after 30 years of effort, funding dried up for this route.

Another route to AI was the more intrinsic view of AI. This means encouraging AI applications that concentrate on improving the thinking processes of machines. The term artificial intelligence was first used by John McCarthy at Dartmouth College in 1955, which indicates a more intrinsic definition of AI. According to McCarthy, artificial intelligence means "the science and engineering of making intelligent machines, especially intelligent computer programs." Note he said nothing about tricking people into believing it was a human. It was instead an approach to artificial intelligence from the point of view of formalization and reasoning, implemented as a high-level algorithmic system at the level of a computer program. However, progress was slow.

Only when those advanced algorithms were combined with pattern recognition upon big data did the scale of these intrinsic kinds of AIs develop far more quickly than the extrinsic AIs. This is because from the 1980s, intrinsic AI developed because of a novel source of funding for AI developed. Originally, there was less money in *tricking* humans into believing machines were intelligent and far more money in *actually making machines more intelligent* in pattern recognition from 'big data' and thus capable of making faster decision making than people, particularly in finding patterns in troves of sales data. This intrinsic AI was in league with machine learning applications built to analyze big data to find patterns or make decisions upon it that humans would be unable to find or to do unassisted. This intrinsic view of AI from machine learning in the 1980s onward has been more successful because of other parallel advances in computers that allowed more searchable 'big data' to exist because of improvements in the scale of data storage, data recall trends, more powerful computer processors, and the very wiring and processing of machine learning taking inspiration from neuroscience as well.

This became a trend of powerful intrinsic AIs once *global online industries were funding AI, since global online platforms had the big data and had deep financial funding to give to AI companies* to look for online industry patterns. Recognizing patterns in big data could becoming further profits in their own data streams for the interest of better targeted advertising, digital authentication of online security to access platforms, or could allow authenticated purchases on platforms online. These three main tasks funded more machine learning applications to solve daily business problems with global platforms and their access or use. First, there are the endless online advertisements that try to tempt us with tailored demographic factors or even advertisements based on our personal search string records. How can AI make advertisements more targeted and profitable instead of just information randomly thrown at a mass audience in the hopes that a few would buy the product? That was its task. Advertising soon became an online industry, with companies like Google and Facebook making billions from AI-placed advertisements—while they funded further intrinsic AI development greatly for this task. Second, AI automated website security tools were created for the same global platforms. From the 1990s, online companies with millions of users funded AIs to find ways to create digital authentication, combing through millions of access routes of their global users to determine when their websites' access experienced unusual access routes for its users—which can be a sign of hacking or stolen credentials. This could block access or influence whether purchase decisions on platforms were blocked. Third, digital authentication by platforms or banking platforms for purchases and transactions has been another route of funding. Facebook and Google had huge amounts of data on their users for both the first two tasks, while banks and online currency exchanges like PayPal had incentives for the other. Everyone profited from digital security. Private online global platforms became the major companies funding machine learning tools to monetize their own big data to find patterns of the information in their own aggregate users to make more money with better targeted ads, better targeted search results, as well as to global levels of online security.

Thus, we have 'backed into' an AI era from an unexpected route of massive piles of big data and big cash from global online platform's seeing actionable intelligence and surveillance about their own users. In an era of ever more powerful computing, the global companies recruited and built these more intrinsic AIs to make sense of big data patterns for them for greater profits and lesser losses in turn.

Intrinsic artificial intelligence usually goes through the following steps. First, data input from humans or objects is converted into a computer-comprehensible method. Next is analytics, which learns patterns for judgment from data using techniques such as machine learning and deep learning. The third is the inference stage, which judges the meaning of data or predicts the result through the learned pattern. In the final performance stage, actual work is performed based on the inference result.

For a comparison, the largest funders of AI applications are not Korea, and instead are places like China and the United States. Korea is not in the top ten funders of AI at all, and the top ten companies of AI are all from the United States or China, despite Korea having a far earlier digitally saturated culture requiring more digital authentication earlier than these other countries. How did this mismatch happen? This is mainly due to decisions that the Korean state made around the years 1997 to 2000, that in retrospect, may have made sense then though had bad outcomes on the 'normal' funding cycles of AI comparatively seen in China or the United States. These other two countries funded AI from online private companies making AIs useful for online advertisements or for private digital authentication. Instead, from the 2000s, the Korean state sabotaged this private funding path of AI investments because the Korean state killed all privatized digital authentication markets in technological innovation, even killing it for websites of banks or e-commerce. Instead, between 2000 and 2015, the Korean state mandated its own state-run monopoly using a unique national digital authentication certificate and a single technology employing a 'National Public Key Infrastructure' (NPKI). It was a technology mandated to be used by all Koreans for increasingly all kinds of online transactions. Users held one half of the encrypted key while the state held the other—and thus the state could monitor all digital transactions as well in Korea increasingly after 2000 through 2015. This NPKI system voluntarily still has many users today in Korea, particularly in many major banks, despite now the legal mandate to use it removed by 2015. So, while Korea regularly innovated technically in many areas over the past twenty years, there was a long conspicuous absence of deep private funding cycles for AI in Korea. This was because the Korean state managed the only system legally accepted for digital authentication of online transactions in Korea. Thus, private e-commerce, private banks, and other private platform companies with the big data lacked the financial incentives or legal requirements to secure their own platforms at all. It was the state's responsibility and the consumer's responsibility instead. Meanwhile, other countries like China or the United States seeded much AI funding cycles from private and competitive digital authentication markets where it was legal to have plural options for legal digital authentication. (Son & Whitaker, 2020).

So, now it should be understood why there is an odd route that AI development has taken by being expanded in the Korean *entertainment* industry, instead of mostly funded or created by private banks or other kinds of private Korean online platforms. The Korean entertainment industry *is that online platform,* with the big data and incentives to mine it for further profits with AI or for digital authentication on the digital fandom and their purchases. In this 'stunted AI' funding in Korea, globally, the year 2017 was the start of the world's increased funding in AI applications into multiple billions of dollars each year according to Venture Scanner. This soon led only the Chinese or American companies in AI being top of the world. Soon after that was the period of many state lockdowns, commencing in 2020. So, under these conditions after 2020, the point is that even the Korean entertainment industry started to undergo a new paradigm shift because the global *Korean Wave's entertainment 'information' is now the same kind of global private big data,* housed in equally large databases due to increased digitalization of a platform-based experience.

As a result, Korea is developing a comparatively odd path for AI utilization in the global big data in its entertainment industry. Thus "Korean AI" has found its desired application and funding niche in *entertainment* unlike in other countries that embedded AI into a competitive financial, corporate, or media website security, bank security, digital authentication, search engine recommendation engines, or advertising monetization. In Korea, AI's even get built around popular K-pop acts themselves. It is globally odd for entertainment to absorb AI innovation. When judged by the whole world's investments, entertainment is not even in the top nine global industries expected to use AI applications which are healthcare, automotive, financial services, transportation, technology, media communications, retail and consumer, energy, and manufacturing. However, as said in earlier chapters, "Planet Korea" is a unique political economy in the world. It is hard to compare the development path of South Korea to other developing or developed countries for many rationales whether in terms of Korean speed of development, or its very successful path of development, or in its many 'world firsts' in the digital world, or here—in the odd hole historically in its digital authentication and in its private AI funding cycles despite its early digital saturation. (See Appendix 1.) Thus, a strong AI-based entertainment world is another 'world first' digital feature that is developing in Korea.

5.2.3.1 Use of AI in Music and Global Fan Platforms

For the first of *eleven examples* of AI applied to the Korean entertainment industry, there is the company "MyCelebs." This is a Korean artificial intelligence (AI) application group that in November 2021 signed a consulting contract with SM Entertainment. My Celebs was charged to create a "SM TOWN AI" to advance SM's digital innovation and service advancement to the whole world. This was designed to enhance communication of Korean Wave entertainment companies and their managed music groups with their fans. The company MyCelebs provided consulting on web homepage reorganization of each individual fan, based on an AI that can search through various SM contents and give personalized homepages based on their content preferences. It was considered already a Global Best Case. Plus, the Korean company MyCelebs was also selected as an Amazon 'Advanced Technology Partner,' the highest rating in the Amazon Partner Network. The Korean company MyCelebs is thus twice recognized for its (comparatively odd) service expertise in entertainment while being general software solutions developer for applications in the Amazon Web Services (AWS) platform. MyCelebs is so extensive in its AI solutions that it has 20 separate AI services in fully 16 categories including movies, broadcasting, and beauty. MyCelebs supports AI digital innovation in partnership with other leading Korean companies equally in the Korean Wave, such as Kakao 'in country', as Kakao is the only social media that Koreans uniformly use, or 'outside of country' with MyCeleb's association with French global cosmetics company Sephora. In short, based on the know-how gained from its own fandom AI service, SM TOWN offers its original content as personalized and arranged based on individual fan tastes. Then, the ongoing rearranged and prioritized contents are gathered together to support marketing and investment decisions of the SM web presence itself. This is evolving into a personalized 'SM contents navigator.' (Choi, 2021c).

Another Korean Wave AI application from MyCelebs is MyCelebs Star, described as a 'celeb finder and ranking service, by star style.' It is used by advertisers and casting directors looking for Korean celebrities to hire like a sort of glorified matchmaking service for companies looking to hire people who fit their criteria, as already Korean celebrities with certain style characteristics for their own marketing campaigns. Another related task of this Korean Wave AI application from MyCelebs (at mycelebs.ai) is described as a 'fandom image voting portal.' According to their Twitter page, it is a "fan powered celebs ranking and casting" service. It serves its users with relevant rankings by taking the 'big data' of aggregate fans of Korean Wave celebrities along with industry and product insights from data, and lets fans contribute to the rankings.

Another example of Korean AI success is how SM Entertainment, one of Korea's leading entertainment companies, decorates its online stages with AI-based augmented reality and virtual reality. It also uses artificial intelligence to analyze music.

Next, HYBE/Big Hit Entertainment (the management company of BTS) announced its transformation into a synergistic 'label', 'software solution', and 'platform hosting' company. Big Hit Entertainment established its platform-based

Weverse Company in 2018. Through this Weverse platform, various entertainment contents and services connect fans to groups, and it has been very successful. It started as a service for managing the global fandom of BTS, but now is expanding its business with the goal of becoming the world's best entertainment lifestyle platform company based on music. It has a great deal of big data to analyze for serving AI recommendations for further purchases to global fans as well as specializing in managing the big data of other groups that take up 'residence' in Weverse to manage their own digital fandoms, connect with their fans, and analyze the data seamlessly. As a result, the platform 'Weverse' is more than a Korean Wave platform. It has become a Korean consolidation of global entertainment services for both consumers and for groups/talents as well. Plus, Weverse has deftly established itself as one of the largest global music entertainment content platforms by owning the intellectual property of even major American entertainment acts. When HYBE acquired a 100% stake in Ithaca Holdings and spent 1.184 trillion won on it, HYBE purchased the comprehensive media company of American giant called Scooter Brown. Thus BTS became the Korean member of a wider global family of artists and their intellectual property now owned by HYBE that includes ownership of American acts Justin Bieber, Black Eyed Peas, and Ariana Grande. This is hardly an example of AI though it is an example of the potential of big data that an AI could use in the future to expand profits of the management company of BTS via its Weverse's big data.

A slew of chatbots or abilities to chat with K-pop avatars now support the global Korean Wave as well. Fourth, Naver Z's social platform called Zepeto held a virtual fan signing event for the BLACKPINK avatars. Fifth, Super Junior's global fans regularly chat with Super Junior's chatbot anytime and anywhere sharing their thoughts and lives. Sixth, already four years ago, in 2019, SM introduced another artificial intelligence chatting service 'Celebbot' in collaboration with the AI entrepreneurial startup Scatter Lab. Seventh, CJ ENM also collaborated with the launch of NCsoft's 'Universe,' a media platform based on AI technology that serves tailored daily exclusive content to users such as artist music videos, pictorials, radio, and entertainment.

Eighth, yet another example is how Korea's SM Entertainment has jointly invested with the USA's OBEN, an artificial intelligence company that since 2017 has been creating virtual characters based on deep learning. Through this, they established a company named 'AI Stars' in Hong Kong and hired 'artificial intelligence artists.' Ninth, Korea's YG Entertainment created a subsidiary named 'YG Plus' to make content by using Korean Naver's artificial intelligence and big data technology along with maximizing marketing while respecting intellectual property rights of musicians and artists.

Tenth, another example is how SK's AI not only help bands to communicate freely with fans, or organize concerts, yet SK is now creating *hybrid real/virtual reality bands as content* for the Korean Wave—a concept that has never existed before. The first "hybrid AI K-pop group" was introduced by SM Entertainment as a four-member girl group called 'Aespa' in November 2020 as lockdowns expanded around the world in varying degrees and in varying places. There are four real women members of Aespa yet there are four respective virtual avatars as well connected via an AI. The plural avatars are themselves in a virtual world created through an AI. SM Entertainment debuted Aespa to try to pioneer a new future entertainment market that incorporates AI and virtual into K-pop groups themselves. Through Aespa, a variety of contents will be unfolded as an extension of technology and culture. If this particular future is found popular, it will be a world where real music celebrities and their AI music avatars coexist and are co-branded as one group. In short, thus four real people and their four digital AI avatars already converge in one K-pop girl group. A fresh future of entertainment is opening up, yet it remains to be seen if it becomes popular, duplicated, or a believable substitute or hybrid experience for real people and their fans.

The reason why development of such digital human entertainers attracts attention is because suppliers like SK want to prime such a market to succeed more than the users. For suppliers of entertainment like SK who hire, train, and manage a lot of real people, much investment and time are consumed. The risk is high for ultimate failure in a few years and thus a wasted investment. On the other hand, a digital avatar requires relatively low management cost and risk management after an initial cost is incurred, and can dance and sing perfectly as programmed virtually forever. Moreover, Generation Z consumers already have familiarity with digital human and virtual influencers. In short, a potential market change is being primed here hoping consumers start to enjoy communication with K-pop avatars as much as real world K-pop groups. Thus, entertainment companies' existing management strategies such as nurturing talent and recruiting stars expand into an easier strategy of developing digital assets as avatars of human K-pop idols. Without irony, the true manufacture of K-pop idols is being attempted by reducing the human element with AI-enhanced K-pop groups.

Eleventh, the Korean Wave is pioneering the entertainment uses of 'digital humans' as well. A "digital human" is said to be a "supercharged customer experience" in the form of a online "avatar that can produce a whole range of human body language….[b]acked by artificial intelligence that can interpret clients' input and give back to them not just the facts they need but the appropriate non-verbal response as well." (Deloitte, 2023; UneeQ, 2003) Digital humans are created from the physical world by digital scanning technology that can analyze 'reproduce' a real human body structure and movement as data that an AI reproduces as digital movements in a virtually-generated 3D space. A digital human is not only capable of transferring knowledge when the AI is connected to an online database or encyclopedia, but also capable of emotional dialogue with realistic facial expression changes. In line with the non-face-to-face trend, it has emerged as an alternative to non-face-to-face services. It has been developed to a level where it can react and talk like a real person by using the synergy of many different AI technologies of voice recognition, natural language processing, video scanning, and speech synthesis. For effective communication as close to real face-to-face situations in a virtual space, it is necessary to upgrade the virtual character in a form similar to the face, expression, and behavior of a real person. This is because it is estimated that language accounts for only 7% of people's communication, and the remaining 93% is voice (38%) and non-verbal parts (55%) such as gestures, facial expressions, and postures. (Pease & Pease, 2006) Of course different cultures have different expected ratios of each in their communication styles and proxemics that may belie such an idea of statistical global universality in communication. Therefore, getting a 'digital human' that is acceptable to different cultural audiences (like Korean, American, Thai, etc., or different regions within a country as well) may be more difficult than people imagine, though equally a digital human may be more programmable than people imagine with an algorithm that will adapt to different cultural expectations.

5.2.3.2 Use of AI in Music Composition

Beyond the eleven AI examples from Korea already, many companies and developers today around the world, not just in Korea, are using artificial intelligence to compose music as well. In 2016, Google unveiled an artificial intelligence project for songwriting called 'Magenta.' Based on the machine learning model Coconet, Google learned more than 300 of Bach's works and created notes that fit Bach's style. OpenAI, a non-profit artificial intelligence organization, introduced a music-generating artificial intelligence called Jukebox in April 2020. Jukebox, which learned data from 1.2 million songs, learned the artist and sound source data to artificially synthesize voices of dead singers like Elvis Presley and Frank Sinatra to make them sing 'new songs.' Amazon also unveiled AWS DeepComposer at the end of 2019 and introduced a music program based on an AI machine learning technique called a Generative Adversarial Network (GAN). The melody must be entered by a human, but sounds such as guitar and drums are applied to the melody through the machine learning algorithm called MuseGAN. Microsoft also created an artificial intelligence-based music program with Icelandic singer Björk.

In Korea, SM Entertainment is once more a major player in the AI conversion of the Korean Wave, as mentioned in the previous section. SM Entertainment is researching AI-based sound separation and extraction technology in cooperation with SK Telecom. (Yeo, 2019) Thus artificial intelligence has already been used widely in music composition and music data analysis. Today however, artificial intelligence is getting closer to the realm of music and melody creation. Of course, prevailing opinion is that it still does not reach the level of music produced by humans. Of course, that depreciating opinion of an innately 'uncreative AI' was accepted until a Google AI named AlphaGo started to play the ancient Asian game of 'go' (called 'Baduk' in Korea) creating its own strategies that no one had ever used or taught it before. It has revolutionized the game which people thought before only had very stable and predictable strategies to win. With its creative and unorthodox strategies, Google's AlphaGo won all Baduk games except one against Korean Baduk grandmaster Lee Sedol. So, if more data is learned over time about music instead of only Baduk, and if new algorithms continue to appear, perhaps better AI-generated musical hits can be created based on knowledge of all past (human-created) pop star hits or using melodic patterns that no one has ever invented before? Plus, it is not far away that the voice of a famous dead singer from the past is blended with the voice of a popular singer of today to release a 'new' duet. Doubling the AI potential, perhaps we shall see a popular song hit someday with an 'AI singer' that never existed yet with a voice based on fan-designed input and/or analysis of famous popular singers, combined or weighted, singing a song that it created by artificial intelligence based on a similar analysis all top hits and past famous melodies.

If or when that scenario happens, before we go over that event horizon to reach that singularity, AI likely is more simply to set the stage for only easier human input in music and melody interactions, as well as making it easier to create the virtual worlds in which real fans and real groups meet. Particularly in the latter, this use of AI applications of virtual reality and augmented reality is already providing Korean fans enjoyment in virtually joining their favorite singers' performances and events. That is discussed in the section below on use of the metaverse in the Korean Wave.

In summary of the past two sections, changes toward using AI in the Korean music entertainment industry and in its fandom interaction are surprising, such as various contents and user experiences provided online and even music duets with fans and stars created by artificial intelligence. This is the 'AI platforming' of the Korean wave entertainment companies themselves. Many Korean entertainment companies are rapidly converting themselves into something beyond companies that hire and nurture entertainers and develop contents. They are turning themselves into global platforms of AI-based fan services tailored for any individual or any demographic. After all, a Korean platform service as a business based on popular content in the global Korean Wave is increasingly becoming a necessity rather than an option in order to manage such a global scale. Thus, the Korean entertainment industry collaboration with IT and AI companies truly expands the global M&A for content expansion. This trend is expected to continue. (Kim, 2021a) They are in 'Korean entertainment' yet are making generalized AI software solutions even for American online retailer giants like Amazon. They know that AI-enhanced platforms give them greater access to profits, users, and more easily managed global business models with various regional or individual differentiations far easier to administer. In short, the global Korean Wave has created a Korean-owned consolidation of global level AI platforms for managing digital fan services and intellectual property worldwide.

5.2.3.3 Use of AI in Broadcasting

With the development of artificial intelligence to handle a global scale of the Korean Wave more effectively and profitably, the value of personalized data is gradually increasing. This is because in order to create a sophisticated personalized recommendation algorithm for the global masses and all their regional or individual differentiations, it is necessary to analyze and quickly serve very detailed personal information parsed by recommendation software engines. Companies record and store all kinds of personal information of users of their content, services, and devices in various ways. However, where AI comes into play is utilizing this big data on demand by quickly making decisions on formatting depending on the audience viewing the platform.

For a counterfactual, without AI it is fair to say that growing global scale of many of the Korean Wave entertainment platforms would be a business model that would be "too expensive" to run effectively. For example, recently, Netflix uses an algorithm itself to try to predict a user's preferred movies or TV series as it tries to maximize profit of its millions of subscribers worldwide with their very different personalizations. YouTube also provides a personalized video recommendation algorithm for every user via AI that allows different watchers to have a pre-queued video series based on their assumed past preferences, ready to watch. Of course, this personalized video queue is full of related lucrative AI-personalized commercials that by 2022 got more obtrusive. Thus, YouTube's AI-based broadcast advertising makes money pushing ever more ads, and cynically that is the strategy of YouTube to get users to accept subscription to YouTube SVOD which is sold with only one perk of stopping annoying advertisements that YouTube serves themselves. This is the same principles as a mafia racketeering operation: extorting money with an annoyance with a promise to stop that annoyance that they provide themselves. So while more advertisements may be an annoyance for the users of YouTube, the company knows that annoyed users make money for YouTube if they feel pushed into YouTube's SVOD payments simply to stop advertisements disrupting their watching. Either path is a financial win for YouTube, monetizing advertisements and user frustration with advertisements in one piece.

However, AI can go beyond personalized predictions that create content, amplify a music repertoire, unfold new stories, and bring you your favorite actors on a screen. In recent years, artificial intelligence researchers have greatly improved the *motion transfer function* and *computer-generated image (CGI) technology*. Such artificial intelligence systems have been trained on countless hours of video data. The AI 'revises' recorded facial movements and expressions and synthesizes fresh images on demand. Thus, a user could clone an older image of an actor into an AI-computer-generated image to create a new face or to create the face of your favorite actor. In the end, you would be able to cast and to direct this AI-imagined person into your own movie. These technologies open the possibility of more AI generated images for broadcasting based on easier text commands or even voice commands in the studio to direct actors that are avatars. Producers of the future may dispense with a slow writer, or with a pesky narcissistic movie star unable to follow orders, if AI can write and produce everything from the actors' data *at the same moment*: the script lines written and then spoken, the acting (expressions, voice delivery, etc., without many takes) and the broadcast-ready edited images instead of these being three separate steps of production now. Producers finally will be in command of writers and actors if writers become AIs and if actors become digital avatars that act exactly as programmed on command. This is the basis of the first double strike of Hollywood actors and writers since 1960, a strike that started in July 2023 as both their contracts with the broadcast producers expired. Both labor groups see themselves potentially outmoded in their acting or writing jobs from such AIs owned by broadcast producers. Another scenario of the broadcast future with AI may be a computer hybrid. For example, visual effects specialists at companies like the recently established Digital Domain already integrate human and computer-generated images together efficiently using artificial intelligence systems. As such, ready or not, the broadcasting industry as a content production industry starts to focus on the use of artificial intelligence in various applications.

Plus, AI can indeed already pick or write a script for you as well. Since the first step in creating content in the entertainment industry is to develop and secure storytelling content with a high potential for popularity and thus financial success, artificial intelligence technology now is used even to determine the 'future popularity' of the story. For example, during the planning and production of *House of Cards*, Netflix referred to usage behavior of viewers analyzed through artificial intelligence. Similarly in recent years in Hollywood, artificial intelligence services are used to predict box office success by judging movie scenarios. Companies and software programs that that analyze future movie narrative popularity—with names like Cinelytic, Scriptbook, Vault, and Pilot—were launched in recent years, one after another. (Vincent, 2019) The reason AI can be used in the monitoring and evaluation (M&E) industry is because all content is being digitized without hesitation. As years go by, digital revenue has taken on a greater proportion in the M&E industry.

Other examples of artificial intelligence in broadcasting are tools like Adobe Sensei that help creators and editors work more efficiency and faster in the traditional video production process. The ability to quickly match a scene relieves the pain of color grading, allowing colorists to reflect on various image attributes such as contrast, hue, saturation, black label, and white point in a moving image, video, or still image. Thus the slow human processing of editing and assembling broadcast video can be improved a great deal with AI applications.

Even broadcasting of news programs now has greater AI applications. The main features currently required for AI in the field of news broadcast editing are the enhancement of automatic metadata to provide more context to existing content such as text conversion of commentary or interview voices, facial recognition, sentiment analysis, and place recognition. It would be very expensive to hire people to record all this information particularly if they were required to watch and add metadata in real time. However, automating image and sound analysis is possible because these are repetitive and yet complex tasks that artificial intelligence can learn to perform well over time. This frees the human production team in news broadcasting to focus more on creating content value rather than on tedious editing tasks like tagging, dubbing, captioning, and translation. Changing the perception of how to use artificial intelligence is important. For example, in the early stages of producing digital news broadcast content, applying artificial intelligence to tasks that truly require a lot of human time and resources like master control, a technology hub for over-the-air television stations, or recording and collecting metadata for broadcast content can be more effective for operators using AI. By using AI, tasks like preparing a video for anchors in a newsroom can be done dramatically faster. In addition, AI is being introduced not only for strengthening metadata, but also for adjusting business procedures, predicting errors, and managing consumer statistics and advertisements. Therefore, artificial intelligence continues to grow in the automation of the value chain in news broadcasting.

5.2.3.4 Use of AI in the Metaverse

A virtual reality game called Oasis was the background of the movie *Ready Player One*, released in 2018. That film contained an image of the metaverse—a hybrid place where moving across virtual and real worlds without boundaries is possible. The game called Oasis was a virtual reality space where any character can connect as a desired character and engage in any desired activity. Technologies of artificial intelligence are used to create the virtual reality (VR) and the augmented reality (AR). Such technologies are becoming another driving force in growth of the music entertainment industry of the global Korean Wave. These VR/AR worlds are called the metaverse.

The metaverse is not a game though in its most extreme versions is an AI-based platform of immersive virtual reality where people gather, work real jobs, and attend real events, yet do it online via meeting each other's live-generated avatars in a VR space. It is a three-dimensional imaginary space realized by computer technology that is designed to be a platform of 'primary life' instead of a 'second (fantasy) life.' The metaverse is where people gather to experience 'real life online' however paradoxical that sounds because it is a *parallel and permanent* virtual community something like a virtual city infrastructure. For instance, imagine if you could live your entire day in a Zoom meeting, walking around in a Zoom universe, buying items, walking into different rooms, watching a concert, going to a museum, holding a business or school meeting of people from all over the world without travelling anywhere, and of course meeting other avatars since you are an avatar yourself traversing this permanent virtual city. That is one application of the metaverse.

To what extent is the global Korean Wave employing technology of the metaverse? Despite massive layoffs of Mark Zuckerberg's Facebook/Meta company announced in November 2022 and once more in March 2023 showing ongoing mistrust or lack of interest in at least his company's version of the metaverse, it is expected that the concept of the metaverse in other company's arrangements may affect our lifestyles and economies deeply someday. For instance, in June 2023, Apple revealed its first model of the Apple Vision Pro, almost a decade in the making, and available by early 2024. It is a more comfortable, lighter, quieter, immersive metaverse VR/AR goggles with combined eye and hand tracking (that becomes a virtual mouse tool) and voice control. For those who wear glasses, it will serve as your pair of correction glasses as well, courtesy of collaboration with Zeiss so people wearing glasses will have a clear experience. Disney has already started to collaborate with Apple to work on building immersive metaverse worlds of entertainment designed for the Apple Vision Pro. This goes full circle between Apple and Disney. Apple already has rescued Disney from declining movie sales before, through how the late Apple CEO Steve Jobs in January 2006 coordinated the Disney buyout of (Jobs' majority ownership of) Pixar digital animation studios. Perhaps Apple will rescue Disney a second time from its declining box office sales via mutual metaverse applications? More than entertainment however, particularly the World Economic Forum (WEF) is keen on pushing the daily life of people and businesses into the metaverse. Keep in mind the interest and use of technologies for creating a metaverse has been accelerated due to government lockdowns in many countries between 2020 to 2023, instead of exclusively invented because of these policies.

For background, the metaverse is a compound word of 'meta' meaning transcendence and 'universe' meaning the real world. It can be interpreted as an expanded concept beyond virtual reality. Metaverse as a term was coined in 1992 by the American science fiction writer Neil Stevenson in his novel *Snow Crash.* By 2007, ASF (Acceleration Studies Foundation), an American technology research group, viewed the metaverse as a phenomenon in which the real world and the virtual world converge through the four application zones of the "Metaverse Roadmap." They defined the metaverse as a more advanced concept from the previous virtual world.

In Fig. 5.1, the ARF divides upper to lower parts of the metaverse respectively from merely partial augmented worlds to pure virtual simulations, and divides left to right in metaverse applications that are either externally and socially shared or intimately personal, respectively. This creates four major application zones for the metaverse, reading from the top left, clockwise: augmented reality, life logging, virtual worlds, and mirror worlds. (Smart et al., 2007) Thus, ASF defines these four applications for the metaverse from weak versions of hybrid real/virtual worlds in Augmented Reality and Life Logging, to strong versions like immersive complete Mirror Worlds and Virtual Worlds. Regardless of any of these four applications, a common principle of a metaverse world is that it is a virtual space where multiple advanced technologies such as artificial intelligence (AI), virtual reality (VR), augmented reality (AR), three-dimensional (3D) rendering technologies, and live generated avatars from real people can be rendered digitally in real time, whether just for individuals or for socializing in avatar-based virtual groups.

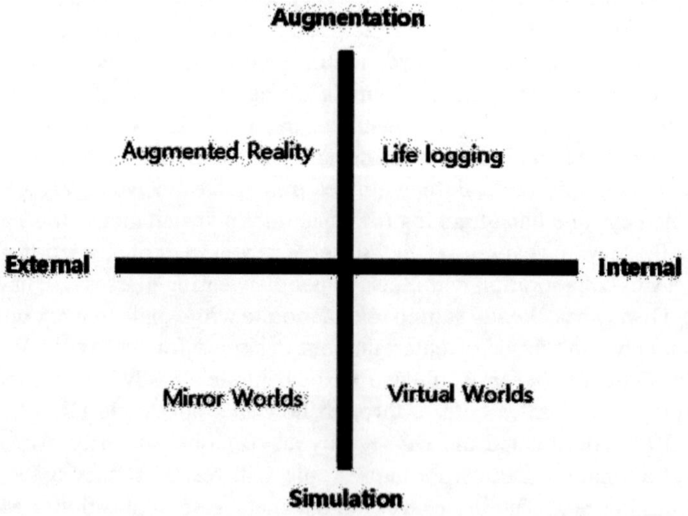

Fig. 5.1 Four quadrants of the metaverse (Smart et al., 2007)

Augmentation and virtualization are spatially-oriented classifications. Augmentation refers to the technology of accumulating added information placed on top of your visual reality. Virtualization refers to the technology of creating a completely separate immersive virtual world with the 'real world' entirely blocked out of one's senses. The other axes of 'External' and 'Intimate' are more of a content classification. Those that represent user identity, such as avatars and profiles, are used internally, and technologies that provide information or control about the world are used externally. It is the difference between whether the metaverse focuses on revealing the individual user or on revealing the world.

Lockdowns in many countries were associated with greater investment all four kinds of metaverse applications because the metaverse provides users with a variety of differentiated user experiences. Below are a handful of examples reviewed just from the past few years in Korea.

Various cases of real/virtual digital convergence have appeared recently in Korea. They are mostly cases of partnerships between metaverse platforms and entertainment, cosmetics, and even educational companies involved in the Korean Wave. Entertainment applications range from a dedicated virtual space specialized for celebrities for arranging their 'affiliated' celebrity avatars, to holding virtual metaverse events such as autograph sessions and performances with the avatars of fans, to digitally demonstrated wares for real life purchases. Many Korean entertainment companies centered on music performances now are combining with lifelogging versions of the metaverse to try to curate performance contents. As a result, entertainment companies now promote and generate additional revenue in a virtual space without time and space constraints. What are some examples of each of the four metaverse applications, whether globally or in Korea?

First, there are augmented reality (AR) applications. These refer to a technology that synthesizes and displays virtual information as an overlay screen seen in the real world. Pokemon Go, popular from its release in 2016, is a prime example of an AR game environment. Similarly, second, life logging is the process of digitally recording, storing, and/or sharing a user's real world information in a digital form for access later. These metaverse applications involve everything from social network services such as Facebook that people use *actively and consciously* as an open diary to their personal feelings and thoughts, to smart 'health watches' like FitBit that *passively and unconsciously in the background* gather your body's personal biological health information to store it or even send it to others in real time for monitoring or diagnosis. Third, virtual worlds refer to entirely artificial digital spaces realized through computer graphics like Fortnite or other multi-player online games from Korea, in which real people see each other only as digital avatars and meet there. Even though the ASF classifies a virtual world as an 'internal' and personal application of the metaverse, it can be a mutual personal space nonetheless for such applications or simply a virtual world for an individual experience only. Fourth, mirror worlds are virtual worlds yet are meant to replicate the real world and look like it as a more convenient permanent and parallel substitution for a real world. A typical example of a mirror world application that simulates reality is Google Earth.

The metaverse concept blurs the boundaries between all four application types of virtual realities by digital convergence instead of by making four separate applications. The metaverse has spread first among the 'MZ' generation (Millennials and Generation Z) because they are more familiar with the pull of participating in an immersive digital culture of the Internet and smart devices from their early childhood—long before any lockdowns of 2020–2023 exacerbated this trend of trying to push a virtual reality upon them. In particular, the youth of Generation Z are the 'experimental animals' of the metaverse. This demographic seems to like to embody themselves in fantasy whether in online avatars or in real world cosplay. Thus, they enjoy performative fantasies whether in a virtual public space or a real public space. It is an interesting hypothesis that the MZ generation's early experience with the novel media of an online private fantasy world or public fantasy world for millions of youth has been crucial in spilling out that fantasy into performative fantasies in the real world.

Representative examples of the current metaverse include America's Roblox, America's Fortnite, and Korea's Zepeto. Roblox is an online gaming platform launched in 2006. It is gaining popularity mainly among those in their early teens, to the extent that American teenagers under the age of 13 are said to spend more time sitting in this virtual reality than sitting watching YouTube. In Roblox, not only can you enjoy games, but users can also create and play games by communicating through avatars. Users can also engage in economic activities such as earning Robux, a virtual asset in the game, as well as conduct currency exchange for buying and selling goods.

Next, Fortnite is a Battle Royale game released by American-headquartered Epic Games in 2017, yet Chinese company Tencent acquired a 48.4% stake in Epic Games in 2012. Epic Games designed the world's most utilized video game rendering engine, called the Unreal Engine, which is the software behind many other online video games. Epic Games' gaming platform Fortnite has 350 million global virtual users for its metaverse world, which is more than the real population of the United States. So, if we compare the scale of real nations with virtual worlds, and since the United States is the fourth largest country in the world, then Fortnite really is the fourth largest (virtual metaverse) country in the world, placing the United States now at fifth. Given the scale of potential (virtual) crowds in Fortnite, many famous singers like Travis Scott and Ariana Grande have experimented with holding online concerts in Fortnite's already established 'Party Royal' mode of the metaverse after many lockdown governments banned real world concerts, or after lockdown governments or promotion companies made normal participation in crowds medically coercive from 2020 onward. These American stars' concerts in 'Party Royal' mode were held around a singer's Fortnite avatar while other Fortnite avatar 'participants' watched the avatar's performance in the guise of their own Fortnite game characters in a collective virtual world. In 2021, an avatar resembling the American pop star Ariana Grande performed 5 times over 3 days within the Fortnite platform. Surprisingly, 78 million avatars from Fortnite users (meaning, real live fans somewhere in the world showing their avatars) participated. (Liao, 2021).

The representative metaverse platform in Korea is Naver's Zepeto. Zepeto is a service operated by Naver Jet, a subsidiary of Korea's main search engine company named Naver. Zepeto is an augmented reality (AR) based 3D avatar application. It allows users to create their own avatars and virtual worlds using facial recognition technology combined with AR. More than 80% of all Zepeto users are teenagers. However, showing the global culture of it more than 90% of the users of this "Korean platform" are non-Korean. By the close of 2021, the number of global subscribers of Zepeto exceeded 250 million—making Zepeto rank just below Fortnite in (virtual metaverse) country scale in the world. Showing the large draw to the metaverse, Zepeto has more users than Netflix's total global paid subscribers of 213.6 million in 2022. (Kim, 2022a) Zepeto operates two other platforms: Build-It (which comprises a map as the virtual space in which the user's avatar is active) and Zepeto Studio (which can be used to assemble and to make an avatar's costume items). Using the terms of Fig. 5.1 above, this metaverse platform is divided into an official map where a user can make a virtual world, and a map that Build-It created for all Zepeto users for their shared areas of that virtual world. In the official map, game elements are provided for avatars such as jumping, shooting, escape, riding, and adventure. Zepeto is focusing on the ability to communicate with avatars in virtual space by selecting real-life themes and is attempting to enter the market using its own cyber virtual currency as a commercialization strategy for the ecosystem of the metaverse platform. As a result, the main areas of the Zepeto service are 'play activities' like 'café' or 'party' where you can sit together in the same virtual world to meet other avatars; or, there is 'photo spot' and 'performance' zones there where you can take pictures buy luxury goods, and make (and pay for) phone calls and text messages.

Korea's SM Entertainment is active in the metaverse world along with other AI applications already mentioned. In June 2021, SM Entertainment signed a Memorandum of Understanding (MOU) for metaverse research with KAIST, the top-ranked science and engineering university in Korea. This agreement took place in the middle of Korea's comparatively mild lockdowns. The MOU provided cutting-edge technologies from KAIST to be transferred to SM to operate applications optimized to reproduce accurately a virtual world. This will include collaborative innovation toward the design of artificial intelligence (AI), technologies for 'digital twins', the Internet of Things (IoT), and network compatibility in general. SM Entertainment plans to focus though on joint research with KAIST's College of Culture and Technology toward metaverse performance technology using digital avatars. The collaboration pursues technological advancement in virtualization technologies for online performance perfection. KAIST and SM Entertainment additionally will cooperate in areas like technology related to contents, robots, and academic research related to technology in culture. "The goal of this cooperation is to take the lead in the metaverse field in Korea which is considered to be a major growth engine in the future, by fusing the production and content planning capabilities of SM Entertainment" which is already a company leader in the global Korean Wave. Thus, this collaborative research "will be to build a giant virtual world in which avatars can establish relationships and communicate with better abilities than they do now." (Lee, 2021b).

In addition, and not to be confused with SM Entertainment, Korea's SK Telecom is promoting a new 'K-Pop Metaverse Project' using mixed reality technology and K-Pop stars. This project is capitalizing on the global K-pop craze by building a new exclusive venue in which to enjoy K-pop under a changing entertainment industry trend toward non-face-to-face virtual worlds. The main purpose of a telecommunications company investing in a metaverse project is to expand their technological expertise with mixed reality experiences in general, ultimately beyond the K-pop application. The first to be featured in SK Telecom's K-pop metaverse project was the idol group Weekly, currently gaining attention as a rising K-pop group. SK Telecom has produced various 'digital humans' as content of the group's members with technology of volumetric capture from the Korean company Jump Studio, which is actually Asia's first mixed reality production company, opened in April 2020 and created via close collaboration with SK Telecom and Microsoft. Jump Studio itself recently released its volumetric capture technology through its wider 'Jump AR' platform launched in 2019 that was originally optimized for volumetric capturing for e-sports instead of later for K-pop. In the K-pop application, the choreography of the K-pop group Weekly's song named 'After School' was scanned, reproduced, and recorded as digital human content, instead of just recorded for a filmed video. This is so online fans could enjoy a fresh experience of creating their own AR music video with Weekly, in their own space. The high quality digital human content of the company Jump AR is attracting attention as a new communication method between stars and fans since it embodies various 'real' (volumetrically scanned) aspects of a star or celebrity in AR content that fans like. Of course fans can save their own productions with the K-pop group Weekly and enjoy it later. Plus, as part of this, SK Telecom is also preparing to hold concerts and fan meetings of K-pop stars such as 'Weekly' in a metaverse space within the updated version of the application called 'Jump Virtual Meetup.' By July 2021, SK updated its older Jump Virtual Meetup to a metaverse application called 'ifland', directly in competition with Naver's Zepeto. In short, with the official launch of SK's 'K-Pop Metaverse Project' global K-pop fans will soon be able to enjoy new K-pop contents of all kinds based on mixed reality at any time. In addition, NCsoft Korea jointly with CJ ENM launched Universe, another K-Pop online entertainment platform. This is another Korean metaverse platform that enables direct communication between fans and stars. It also enables peer-to-peer avatar communication between fans themselves. (Choi, 2021d).

There are even two other metaverse applications recently from Korea that deserve mention. The first is mentioned in more detail in the later chapter on "K-Beauty", featuring the mostly unknown global Korean business-to-business (B2B) cosmetics empire of Cosmax. Cosmax already has a large international clientele of hundreds of other nations' cosmetics businesses interested in its Korean cosmetics research, development, and expertise in manufacturing for their companies' cosmetics, via Cosmax's business-to-business (B2B) model. Recently, Cosmax opened a metaverse store featuring its B2B cosmetics expertise for a global audience. So, Cosmax is already the world's largest B2B cosmetics product and services provider, and now it will have its own metaverse store and applications as well.

Another example is Korea's first metaverse university, Taejae University. It has equally digital global pretentions just like the already established global Korean Wave. The Korean Ministry of Education in April 2023 announced it gave its final approval to this metaverse university to recruit its first cohort of students both in Korea and internationally for the Fall 2023 semester. It is oddly funded mostly by Cho Chang-geol, founder of the Korean modern furniture company Hanssem instead of founded by someone involved in education. However Cho has recruited as President of Taejae University an ex-President of Korea University, Yeom Jaeho, who graduated from Stanford University, historically linked to California's Silicon Valley, as well as recruited Professor Emeritus administrators from Harvard University like Dr. Stephen Kosslyn who designed the curriculum for San Francisco's Minerva University from 2013 as its first Dean. Dr. Kosslyn has Stanford University links himself given he was a past director of the Center for Advanced Study in the Behavioral Sciences at Stanford University in 2010. The Board of Trustees of Taejae University is a Korean all-star cast like President Yeom Jaeho (past president, Korea University, and tellingly currently the Chairman of the Board of Directors of SK Inc., which is the second largest Korean chaebol company after Samsung, being a large information technology and holding company of which includes SK Telecom and other economic branches) and Board of Trustees members like Kim Doh-Yeon (past Korean Minister of Education, Science and Technology; university president of POSTECH); Kim Yong-hak (Chairman of the Board of directors of SK Telecom; ex-president, Yonsei University); Kim Myung-hee (Senior Vice President, SK Telecom; Deputy President and Chief Digital Officer, Shinhan Financial Group—one of Korea's Big Five financial groups); Min Kyungchan (Chairman of Scientific Advisory Board, Institute for Basic Science—the organization aided by the Korean Government to try to 'manufacture' Nobel Prize winners); and Roe Jung-hye (past president of the Korean National Research Foundation), among others. Plus, Cho Chang-geol as both Chairman of the Board of Trustees of Taejae and still Honorary Chairman of Hanssem has arranged that 'Hanssem DBEW Design Center' building will double as Taejae University's 'headquarters' in Korea.

However, Taejae is a metaverse university. Taejae *lacks* all university buildings, *only* offers online courses, *only* in English, and *only* has students living in five dormitories in five cities as they internationally travel between them, semester to semester. Taejae students are said to be working on group projects with other students in real world situations in those five different cities, while collaborating and living in all five cities for their degree. This follows two ideas from Dr. Kosslyn: first, the hybrid residential model identical to Minerva University, designed by him, in which students together rotate through various major cities of the world (one of them is Seoul); second, the fact that it is an online college, similar to two other entirely online colleges that he helped create that are both headquartered in San Francisco like Foundry College (where he is both President and Chief Academic Officer from 2020 overseeing its proprietary learning platform called the Forge) or Minerva University (where he helped create another proprietary learning platform called the Forum—yet combined with a multi-city rotation program for students). So, Taejae University is just the "Korean" Minerva University, given the entire campus experience of Taejae University for students, professors, and administrators alike is a virtual metaverse with its own online private and proprietary platform called Engageli. Thus, Taejae University is a collaboration with the company Engageli, the latter started by Daphne Koller in 2020, who previously co-founded the now large online course instruction website Coursera in 2012 with Andrew Ng. Both Koller and Ng have Stanford University links to computer science as well. While the following comments are partially critical of this metaverse model of education so far, solutions offered are for a more 'hybrid metaverse' application by the conclusion. Since Taejae professors and administrators can live anywhere in the world, and since students are split across five global cities, professors and students by design are kept from coordinating or seeing each other in the flesh, while virtual administrators are in charge of everything real. So equally by design, this leaves this metaverse university by default to the dreams of distant globalist administrators and profit-minded platform entrepreneurs alone, lording over professors and students alike from management citadels of a virtual space, harvesting their data. This keeps students in five dormitories in the five cities equally alienated and moving about globally while keeping professors equally alienated and scattered intentionally around the world and only meeting once a year in Seoul for a very short time. Thus, students are somewhat on a world tour between those five cities over the course of their degree, and yet always in the same private online metaverse 'application' of their university wherever they go instead of really 'in' those cities per se. The five real cities only serve as ever changing (perhaps dissociated and virtualized?) backdrops for their metaverse university. "Students will spend their first three semesters in Seoul…then live in Tokyo for their fourth semester, New York for the fifth semester, Hong Kong for the sixth semester, and Moscow for the seventh semester. The final eighth semester will be spent back in Seoul. Apart from [the entirely online professors and] academics, students will have to participate in study tours and visit various historic sites in each country." (Lee, 2023) The background funder of this venue, furniture magnate Cho Chang-geol, writes ominously as the Chairman of the Board of Trustees of the university: "Future universities should teach leaders how to discern the social transformation incurred by the digitalization [that he ratiocinates and creates, instead of is happening due to 'digitalization'] and to think strategically while in crisis. Now, we (sic) should break away from the traditional lecture-based education in which professors unilaterally [instead of unilateral furniture magnates and proprietary platforms?] supply knowledge." (TaeJae University, 2023) Granted that the Korean Confucian educational heritage creates this impression of rote knowledge that simply had to be learned from a central source, however, has Taejae looked in the mirror? Has any university ever "unilaterally" supplied knowledge more centrally, inflexibly, and tightly than this concept of Taejae University? In the ultimate inversion and psychological projection, isn't Taejae the one so far truly more centrally and more "unilaterally" controlling its students and professors alike in the below four ways? There are ways to fix this however.

First, Taejae is doing far more than "breaking away from the traditional lecture-based education," it is breaking away from any democratic collective or regional feedback from students or professors alike, by voiding entirely a campus physical environment as an unobserved meeting place for making their own goals and by keeping everyone divided and separated intentionally behind a screen. Second, Taejae is breaking away from physically meeting one's professors directly, and says students can only meet them in other online arrangements or in the "ten minutes before class or after class" in surveilled virtual spaces that are being monitored, judged, and recorded by the hierarchy itself on various metrics. Taejae is breaking away from having a place for students and professors to meet offline because there is a conflict of interest in these metaverse university models so far of whether it is really an educational experience for students based on innovative curricula or only a market enclosure experience set up to make money via a proprietary learning platform setting up whole universities under permanent digital lockdowns just to monopolize student and professor time to force use of that educational technology to gain a monopoly on pedagogy. In all metaverse universities so far, the privatized learning platform as a profit venture seems the main priority regardless of its buttressing innovative curricula, because instructional options against the online platform are categorically banned. Taejae and other online universities so far like to try to push digitalization to kill other forms of instruction and socialization that go against it. However, as noted by urbanist Saskia Sassen decades ago, people used to think that digitalization would automatically end the desire or requirement to live in cities or to congregate physically. However, with rising digitalization, contrary to what Chairman Cho says, management of global companies or endeavors have hardly only dispersed to a virtual world with digitalization. Equally, what has been occurring is the desire to have physically real open places to meet, to create networks of actual trust between those more digitalized people, and these have generally happened in a handful of real urban areas worldwide. Castells would call the metaverse phenomenon of Taejae as the 'space of flows.' However, Taejae is additionally in particular places, and Sassen called these globally digitized yet real geographic places the 'global city.' This occurs in particular real urban places over time whether for business trust or for trust in academic settings despite and even against growing digitalization. In other words, Taejae is trying to be a hybrid already of the space of flows and the global city. Third, Taejae University and others like it are breaking away from the whole idea of a university serving any particular people and place for a long time by breaking away from a campus location and thus breaking away from the idea that a university should serve a particular nation, culture, or economy for the long term instead of just serve nebulous 'group goals and problems' unilaterally set by its globalist founders in an ever-changing series of nearly identical global cities that they choose. In this way Taejae is very similar to the criticisms Sassen had of the 'global city' experience itself, defined by her as an alienating elite's required and desired financial services and living services around that "centralized command and control" in only a handful of urban sites, to enhance privatized and globalized financial management and digitalization that still has to exist somewhere physically to manage that decentralized and underdeveloping world of ever-shifting and digitally-managed production. Another of her critiques was that such networked situations of a global city innately underdevelop, and thus damage, any past developed national economies and democracy, while over-inflating the global city's financial management power. Plus, fourth, even Taejae will be continuing traditional centralized lecture-based education anyway, regardless, by having solely online education guided at all steps by a centralized virtual professor, a centralized virtual administrative hierarchy, and a centralized privately-owned platform. So far, what Taejae is doing is creating an *intentional* "social transformation" while blocking all other options of socialization—so it is better to call it *social engineering*. This social engineering is an enclosure of education onto private platforms, and so this social engineering hardly is being created accidentally by a mystified "digitalization" though is being created intentionally by its human founders—in this case by administrators from the second largest information technology chaebol in Korea—SK, Inc., and its SK Telecom. Taejae could be euphemistically called SK University—a telecommunications chaebol's attempt to get into the educational market of global platform profits. The main question becomes will Taejae contribute to more 'globalist citizens' and 'problem solving' or only contribute to more problem creation by its cult-like separation of its educated elites (administrators, professors, and students alike) from a particular country's problems, by teaching students always in a different alienating non-native language and by always being somewhat alienated from the cities that their dorms are in by escaping entirely to the metaverse and by constantly shuffling through different cities? Do any other kind of universities have a more cult-like centralized control and surveillance of all students and professors by omniscient administrators who record video of all instruction simply to monitor and to judge every tiny 'deviation from plan'? Tellingly, Taejae University's website by July 2023 (months before the first students presumably arrive) addresses the question "why is everything online?" by giving only a one-sided perspective of the *administrative goals being maximized* over students and professors alike, instead of being honest about drawbacks of student or professor alienation online from these other points of view. Taejae says putting everything online gives its university "flexibility (sic), advanced pedagogy [i.e., ability to sell and to use only a single private platform, which is the opposite of flexibility], and the utilization of educational data [for administrative surveillance of all transactions]"—all of which managers find hard to get in unmonitored physical spaces with real people. In this way, they bluster through the downsides of a totally online education and fail to address the current downsides because they know people may hate this surveillance-based educational model of a "permanent pandemic Zoom school without a pandemic"—which is what the world tried already between 2020–2023 with many dismal outcomes on educational attainment or student mental well-being. Will globalist Taejae be a permanently alienating elitist "Zoom school," or will it contribute to that problem solving that it desires? Like Minerva University, Taejae University is a hybrid of older by-mail or online correspondence schools and the old "Semester at Sea" model of educational outreach and broadening of student horizons. However, Taejae will be always at sea—both in the metaverse and moving physically around—and thus never fully or clearly focused in any one port, place, or durable problem at all. In short, its outreach immersion in other cultures will be very thin given the university experience is mostly immersion in the metaverse and given that 80% of the time students will be taught in an English language that will be a foreign language to the five global cities of their dormitories.

In conclusion, the development of mixed reality technology such as the metaverse is expected to act as a great opportunity in the Korean entertainment, cosmetics, and perhaps even educational industry. In the past, to meet their favorite stars live, fans had to go to concerts or use media platforms like live YouTube sessions. However, it is now possible for K-pop idols and their global fans to coexist in the same shared virtual space. In the past, to shop for cosmetics or hear a business spiel about company services, you went to a company directly. Now you may go to the metaverse. Plus, in the past, to meet professors and to take classes, students had to go to a campus. Taejae just wants everybody to log in online permanently for their whole degree on a global proprietary learning platform. For students, Taejae tries to make this educational enclosure, digital alienation, and surveillance more palatable in two ways by rooming students together physically and moving them around globally. For professors and administrators, Taejae tries to make the same educational enclosure, digital alienation, and surveillance more palatable to them by letting them live anywhere in the world they want. However, this leaves administrators literally as unchallengeable Tayloristic technocratic dictators in charge of the only social reality, thus allowing, denying, and monitoring everyone's socialization via a digital platform that will record, analyze, and judge every second of online classrooms and other interactions based on centrally-designed curricular goals for "performativity." Taejae is a split experience similar to Dr. Jeckyll and Mr. Hyde, respectively, a friendly and open group of problem solvers innovating education yet involved in trying to force people into an educational panopticon that has nothing to do with that educational goal. Hopefully, Taejae (or Minerva) will be only the first, instead of the last, attempt at a metaverse university. For a prediction, like other Minerva University styled universities, Taejae in its current platform will be unable to grow beyond a boutique market for those who want or require distance education. However, metaverse-enhanced education can be much larger and more influential if it gives up the attempt to corral all students and professors exclusively on a metaverse platform and instead uses the metaverse in a truly more flexible way. Regardless, the main question of the future will be "who will control reality" because there is an "online civil war over who controls our information flow and how they get to do it." (Robb, 2023) Taejae wants to enclose and privatize the educational experience and control it all. However, there should be more open-ended, participative, and truly more "flexible" uses of metaverse technology, since flexible really means digital activities that are optional and complimentary, instead of inflexibly mandated and required as Taejae does. The other way to use metaverse and digital technology in education is as a flexible complement to real daily life, in an information commons and in wider geographic spaces than a mere handful of global cities in an information enclosure. This other way to use digital technology for education is possible due to our world's developing "smart regions" of saturated digital media in everyone's hand worldwide. For example, to interface with these already established smart regions, other kinds of online platforms have been invented for education and for global problem solving in the circular economy that take advantage of this information commons across all the world's decentralized smart regions at once. This helps people via digital technology *to coordinate better on solving real world problems for the long-term in a particular place*—for all regions, all students, and all professors alike—in any region of the world instead of making the digital experience as alienating as Taejae or Minerva Universities in only five similar global cities of the world (Whitaker and Pawar, 2020). This use of digital technology as an information commons is very different than the inflexible, enclosed, and privatized platform of Taejae. As said, Taejae only goes to a handful of very similar wealthy global cities worldwide and ignores the majority of the world's population and its problems—despite problem solving required there just as much, and despite that wider world now having its 'digital parity' in telecommunications technology and being a smart region with just as much digital capacity as the digital zones of global cities. Thus, a better model of the future of digital education would either be, first, an online virtual platform that only coordinates an informational commons, with lateral learning between multiple real geographic communities in all particular regions, worldwide. This is contrasted with Taejae currently trying to enclose education upon a privatized platform itself and trying to enclose students in just a handful of very similar global cities while endlessly shuffling them around the world. That peripatetic enclosure of education denies students and professors alike a stable location and thus denies them a honed ability to work on solving problems well in any location, and denies them the ability to understand any particular place for the long term. What is required for education and any real world problem solving in the future is a more fine-grained and permanently regionalized social and geographic knowledge in that education to have any developmental improvements, instead of trying to ignore it. (Whitaker, 2012) The prediction for Taejae is that an educational process that only temporarily learns about a handful of very similar global cities on an enclosed online platform alienates people from any long-term experience of place or regional culture, and thus will hardly lead to the educational or innovative breakthroughs in problem solving that Taejae seeks out of its curriculum. However, for the second better model of the future of digital education, a hybrid of the Minerva/Taejae model would be the 'smart regions' model of educational outreach across all world ecoregions (instead of just a handful of cities), utilizing in parallel an information commons, and accrediting educational degrees around a circular economy for different regions of the world. This would be a good hybrid use of the metaverse and digital technology that could bring education both the benefits of the connections of digital technology and the groundedness of actual real world problems, worldwide in all ecoregions, instead of only an education in a handful of global cities.

In short, the metaverse is being actively used already in the Korean Wave, in Korean telecommunications companies, in the Korean online gaming industry, in Korean cosmetics, and now in Korean education as noted from examples above. Alliances between older software companies, entertainment companies, telecommunications companies, and top Korean universities like KAIST or fresh organizations like Taejae University see a future market for mostly teenagers and twentysomethings in the metaverse. However, large Korean digital telecommunications companies like SK Telecom see a future market for *everyone* in the metaverse. So while the current main demographics using most metaverse applications are youth related, the involvement of general Korean telecommunications companies like SK Telecom potent a future where a common telecommunications carrier provides common metaverse applications for all people, anywhere in the world, instead of only limited to one nation, one entertainment sector, and one adolescent demographic. However, for the time being, adolescents and young adults are most of the fan base of K-pop stars and the music in the Korean Wave—or potentially the students of Taejae University. Therefore, metaverse applications made exclusively for this demographic are a match made either in heaven or hell depending on your point of view of virtualization trends. It may be a heaven scenario since such developments bring further fresh content and metaverse expertise to the entire world. It may be a hell scenario since it could potentially create even greater economic shakeout, consolidation, and decline of a non-virtual (real) economy and its real live events, real stores, real universities, and real lives with or even without lockdown conditions. This would impoverish life by putting everything online that serves as an economic force that undermines real world economies and lives in particular places, instead of enriching life by putting everything online.

However, which will occur, digital heaven or digital hell, and to what extent? Some might argue let us avoid worrying about social impact trends since it could be a rising tide raising all boats, i.e., that metaverse developments could aid the real economy of live events as much as metaverse events. However, the events of the past few years are bad for that rosy assessment since actual data leans toward the hell scenario of a rising lava burning all boats, i.e., of a more-primed global level of virtual surveillance capitalism causing ever more economic shakeout of a less-primed 'real reality' of past national economies or regional economies. This is a trend moving toward a global level political panopticon of everyone sharing the same platforms and thus toward a global level of social credit system. Over the next few years, it remains to be seen which digital path is stronger than the other—digital global enclosure or permanent regional digital commons, or whether it will be a moot issue if the metaverse becomes a mutual development that strengthens all venues of culture instead of only being a parasitical "Matrix-like" culture that encourages permanent lives of escapism and erosion of reality whether in Korea or the wider world.

Regardless, one theme in all metaverse applications above so far is a common *denationalized global virtuality* controlled by major companies as 'suppliers of reality' instead of simply suppliers of entertainment. With global virtual reality platforms being controlled by distant people, will particular geographical regions like nations where we all live economically and which still require a regional economic stability and a regionally stable cultural transmission to exist, be losing more ability to prime their own autonomous culture, economic durability, and cultural transmission at all? Will there be revanchist regional revolutions of parallel economies against all virtualization trends, or can the metaverse be made more regionalized in its applications instead of globally homogenizing? All scenarios are possible, and all trends mentioned above may occur to some extent simultaneously or differently at different degrees in different areas of the world. The metaverse seems truly like a 'universal technology' (Barker and Erickson, 2005), meaning it develops as a technological system that can participate in many different kinds of technical futures instead of only foreclosing and leading us into one technical future. Therefore, the problem identified here is hardly really the technology: it is the problem of trying to apply this metaverse technology to only one "super tech" application, to use Barker and Erikson's phrase, meaning the assumption that "bigger is better" and that the purpose of technology should serve only individual leisure or automation. Communciations technology can additionally serve regional "local tech" issues for educating local problem solvers to find long-term and commons-based 'smart regional' solutions of appropriate scale and ecological integration in circular economies to solve actual problems that the twenty-first century has like problems of both social integration and environmental sustainability to help us live socially sound and ecologically regional lives. (Whitaker and Shin, 2020; Whitaker and Pawar, 2020; Whitaker, 2021; Ku et al., 2023). Metaverse applications even exist to create less mental problems in depression treatment of youth and elderly populations, instead of applications that only create more mental alienation and lack of social integration. (Whitaker et al., 2023).

Admittedly, there are both economic and cultural advantages of metaverse platform technologies, such as the metaverse's scalability without time and space constraints, a sense of presence similar to the real world, accessibility to potentially universal users (currently mostly only those in their teens and 20s) and a raised community-oriented solidarity. Currently, the metaverse applications of Korea mostly encourage fans and entertainment providers to participate in the same global virtual entertainment world on a more even basis. However, Korean music fandoms seem only the first functioning global test market toward more diverse and universal applications of the metaverse later. (Lee, 2021a).

5.3 Reconstruction of the Korean Entertainment Industry

5.3.1 Lockdown Response from the Entertainment Industry

Korea was already further ahead culturally and technically on such a digitalization project than others and found itself by 2020 in a global market situation that helped it capitalize more on its already superior digital marketing skills in the Korean Wave. Considering this hypothesis, this section explores evidence for this in Korea and the world during the economic and cultural production crises from 2000 through 2023. First, the fact remains that the Korean Wave's entertainment industry could take advantage of a huge push for digitalization between 2020 and 2023 only if mostly *worldwide* governmental policies of many national lockdowns artificially and simultaneously created a more 'harmonized' and more digitally captive global market, instead of only reflecting digitalization incentives within South Korea. Second, this could only occur if there was already this earlier and saturated digitalization in South

Korea that the Korean Wave entertainment industry could build upon in a push for further digitalization.

For an overall review of the economic power of Korea's entertainment industry under lockdown, it had mixed positive and negative influences. First, these policies caused economic recession by atrophying global economic activity—including the entertainment sector. Thus, despite a great deal of digitalization and innovation, profits were down. Globally and generally, there was a decrease in media consumption expenditure, a decrease in production investment, and a decrease in advertising expenditure. By 2023, as mentioned in earlier sections, there seems to be the start of a stasis or even a decline in funding for the content creation industry, rolling back earlier projections that it would continue to grow in 2023. Regardless of whether we look at the manufacturing or service industries, the global economy is being negatively affected by increasing unemployment, thus declining incomes, thus more fiscal state priming, and thus more state-created inflation. All of this is combining in a growing global recession and even a 'stagflation' (term for economic 'stagnation and inflation') by the beginning of 2023 characterized by declining economics, rising unemployment, and high inflation that creates a vicious cycle of ongoing economic decline. Raising government interest rates to try to deal with this stagflation has seemingly contributed to some of the first banking collapses in the United States since 2008, like the collapses in 2023 of Silicon Valley Bank, Signature Bank, Silvergate Bank, and First Republic Bank. Silicon Valley Bank was the largest bank by deposits for entrepreneurial Silicon Valley and was a bank that supported nearly half of all the U.S.'s venture-capital-based companies. The first two collapsed in March 2023 within two days of each other, and when they did, they happened to be ranked as the second and third largest banking collapses in United States history at that time, ranked after the collapse of Washington Mutual in 2008. The bank run at Silicon Valley Bank was catalyzed by a handful of wealthy tech investors who attempted to withdraw billions at once and were refused their withdrawals, immediately after the bank had announced it sold its U.S Treasury bonds at a loss—showing that the bank was already having difficulty with its liquidity if it did so. However, after the collapse of First Republic Bank in late April 2023, that bank became the second largest bank to collapse in U.S. history, instead of Silicon Valley Bank. So the trend in U.S. bank collapses is getting larger. Plus, people in general prefer to invest in government bonds of higher returns (at their recently higher-set interest rates) compared to bank deposits at lower returns and lower interest rates in an economic downturn. Therefore, U.S. government policy presumably to control inflation by raising U.S. Treasury bond interest rates is only contributing to money in aggregate flowing out of banks, i.e., toward more bank deposit runs in this way given their lower interest rate returns on investment comparatively. All of this seems to be starting another global banking and liquidity crisis, similar to 1997 and to 2008, both respectively then catalyzed off Thai or American banking and currency crises as well.

In global miniature, the economic situation in export-led Korea is also deteriorating, especially for small and medium-sized businesses and for a growing 'precariat' of non-regular workers. (Standing, 2011) The resulting unemployment and income decline are likely to lead to a decrease in consumer spending in the entertainment sector and thus a decline in profitability in the domestic Korean market in the Korean Wave. As the overall advertising budget of the Korean entertainment industry is also decreasing, its capacity to invest in its own content production is shrinking. In particular, with the growth of social media, the landscape of the media and entertainment industry is changing. Social media services provide billions of social media users with more sophisticated, personalized images, video, music, news, games and shoppable media.

Meanwhile, despite all residual public transportation masking rules in Korea finally ending by March 20, 2023, and despite Korean state pressures encouraging other kinds of collective hypochondria dropped far earlier, some people's obsessive yet *voluntary* hypochondria in avoiding people now combines with other countries' weakening or continuing *involuntary* "masking" and "social distancing." In Korea, time spent socially isolated at home increased in this period of 2020 through 2022 and led to an increase in home-based entertainments in (OTT) broadcasting and other online media usage. It provided new marketing opportunities, yet in a smaller economy. Since the beginning of early 2020 when various Korean state lockdowns or whole business sectors like mass closings of PC-gaming rooms happened in Korea, the usage of more personal web video games and child-centered educational e-books and audio books increased instead. The use of non-domestic spaces for entertainment is expected to keep decreasing if lockdowns are never categorically removed and banned from all future use, because if lockdowns are endlessly added and revoked unpredictably for years onward beyond 2023, it will yield a change in the future investment potential of non-domestic spaces in general. This means that if lockdowns are used forever as a governmental tool from this point, the predictable profit required for durable real space venues and their financial investments becomes impossible to maintain in the future if lockdowns keep being unpredictably begun, stopped, and begun once more with ever changing rules and punishments. Lockdowns perpetuate a bias against non-domestic spaces as a business location, and thus non-domestic business spaces competitively in the market will be damaged perpetually unless lockdowns are banned not only from current use through banned in all future use as well.

Regardless, the acculturated attention of the MZ Generation may be more accustomed to sophisticated social, interactive and immersive experiences through smartphones, social media, and video games. The evidence for this trend of miniaturization and personalization in home content in entertainment continues since the only media devices that showed a high rate of increase in sales were *home* game consoles, *personal* video devices, *personal* smart pads, and *wearable* smart devices in the past few years to 2022. However, what has yet to miniaturize (while it indeed has personalized with AI) is production quality of such virtual reality productions. This has turned distributed media of smartphones and other decentralized and individual viewing devices into mere passive billions of clients of centralized producers. So despite the promise of a two-way technological communication media regime, it starts to be used similar to one-way mass consumption once more because of greater love of watching big-budget productions instead of only small budget productions, as billions of decentralized devices' true equal production capacities somewhat atrophy in the thralldom of big budget productions once more. Therefore, the larger combined synergistic 'video media industry' will consume or compete with smaller stand-alone social, game, and video media industries. Thus remaining separate industries will compete head-to-head for screen time with more digitally convergent and synergistic media experiences provided by companies funded at much larger scales for much larger global audiences that can underwrite and create such immersive experiences more effectively only if it is applied to the whole world as a market. This may lead to a shakeout of many whole national entertainment industries into a handful of centralized global players of producers and distributors in a homogeneous world culture, despite being primed into it by a mass culture of decentralized and mobile viewing/ production technologies and a multi-polar world cultural participation.

This is a situation akin originally to decentralized and two-way radio 'wireless' producers of music in the United States, when peer-oriented private citizen 'disc jockeys' broadcast from their homes to a mass culture of many other home wireless kit radio listeners in the early 20th century. However, first, this soon went to more centralized models of corporate-sponsored broadcasters with paid DJs, high power broadcast stations, state-run electromagnetic spectrum rules blocking a suddenly 'pirate radio', and millions of passive 'stunted' mass radio sets mass manufactured to be only one-way receivers. This is despite the wireless technology itself innately starting as a two-way medium, though the growing broadcast chaos of the then-ruleless electromagnetic spectrum began to interfere with this growing peer wireless communications regime change, as much as it was a situation that facilitated it in the beginning. So, the later production of content and the technology itself of wide area wireless broadcast required a more licensed electromagnetic spectrum and larger investment than mere local passive listening. Over time, this precluded the more generalized peer decentralization of creators and listeners that actually started wireless. As said, second, decentralized radio as peer sharing was effectively outlawed on the wireless during World War I in many Atlantic Ocean-facing countries on the alibi and reality of potential spy communications being blocked this way. Thus, the electromagnetic spectrum was seen suddenly as an issue of states and national security, and enclosed and nationalized instead of an electromagnetic commons free for everyone to use in their personal wireless sets anymore. Third, there was a real fear of global private monopolies developing in wireless technology and spectrum use by Marconi's many different wireless corporations as the first true multinationals and world-coordinated corporate technical empires. As many national wartime government spectrum regulations from World War I continued into the 1920s, states permanently took over the whole electromagnetic spectrum as a national jurisdiction against decentralized citizens and big corporations alike. National governments centrally kept that power for the whole twentieth century authorizing or denying spectrum use instead. (Raboy, 2016) By the 1950s, the same inequality in the high cost of *production and broadcast for television* compared to *the lesser costs of passively receiving television broadcasts* encouraged similar inequalities in production in television as seen in earlier corporate radio production and programming. In this way, any earlier media regime change toward two-way wireless communication was aborted. As a result, most of the twentieth century was instead a media regime of one-way electronic mass communication of powerfully-funded central voices and many millions of passive listeners/watchers in almost all media to speak of—whether in radio, movies, recorded music, newsprint, or television.

However, that media regime change inherent in wireless communications is restarting now. The same is happening once more now yet with the benefit of having more coordinated bandwidth and switching systems developed to handle such a two-way regime of mobile multimedia—a lack that ended it prematurely in the early 1900s. However, despite a two-way mass media being ever more possible technically, it is expected that the usage of decentralized passive 'home content receivers' as one-way devices will remain high as they are sunk material costs and they are sunk consumer habits of mind even if all those passive users can now be creators themselves in the innately two-way medium of networked mobile multimedia that we live within now. So, there is a similar disjoint as the early twentieth century in how two-way decentralized wireless became centralized one-way radio that we now see in the twenty-first century's digital cultural production since it could be far more 'two-way' than it is. However, a distributed mass culture of more habitual passive digital viewers have bought more and cheaper one-way digital viewing technologies while the high costs of more expensive digital production, editing, and broadcast technologies encourage this more centralized production even in virtual reality and OTT. For example, hundreds of millions of people pay Netflix to watch its paid production of *Squid Game* instead of produce their own video content, even as that latter sector of a two-way media world exists as well. This is how big companies' combined centralized platform investments and past content production expertise comes to have millions of passive participants within its thrall despite living in a wider two-way media regime where such centralization in content production is unrequired as much as it was before.

Showing this ongoing centralization, in the field of content consumption expenditure in Korea, between 2020 and 2022, revenue from *merged video and webtoon/web novel platforms themselves increased significantly while spending on stand-alone music platforms only increased slightly*. Even beyond any forced lockdown policies, consumption expenditure in order to access these video, music, and webtoon/web novel platforms is expected to remain higher than before 2020. However, a majority of users do not appear to be willing to pay for content so there is a limit to rapid expansion of a centralized global content market regardless. (Korean National Assembly, 2021).

5.3.2 Regional and Cable Broadcast to Global Online Streaming Sales

Because the entertainment subscription market model is saturated while consumers' willingness to pay is declining, and since advertising resources are shrinking, new types of global online streaming services such as "over the top" (OTT) and Multi-Channel Networks (MCNs) are revitalizing broadcasting entertainment. The media market environment thus is changing due to globalization of the media market, greater diversity and complexity of any national users' usage behavior and thus their increased selectivity. This is because OTT models or MCNs have greater global revenue from their global market access, and of course due to hardly having to develop the basic infrastructure for their global broadcast costs and only paying greatly for their digital storage costs and bandwidth within any existing national or private Internet systems.

Plus, these OTT and MCN services are possible only because it is now technically possible to have global online broadcasting. Technological changes created the ability to arrange more customized online broadcasting services to serve more individual users' tastes based on AI, big data, and of course built on the larger internet bandwidth throughputs. Whether through dedicated wired Internet cable networks to smart-televisions or to the more wireless 4G or 5G for smartphones, both infrastructures can stream online movies without interruption. Without these many technical improvements working together harmoniously to make broadcasting's global online distribution cheaper, the profit of the many global streaming services would be much less if not impossible to compete with traditional broadcasting in discrete regions or nations. Several examples of these trends that reverse a regionalized cable TV subscription to a more globalized online broadcast TV subscription are discussed.

First, we have "Over the Top" (OTT). This is the main core of online media broadcasting competition versus the older subscription-based pay TV via physical cable networks. The OTT is the only sector of online broadcasting growing rapidly around the world. To connect to OTT requires smartphones or smart-televisions. As of December 2022, it was estimated there were 665 million households globally with smart-televisions, and as of 2019 there were at least 2.5 to 3.3 billion smartphones (We are Social / Hootsuite, 2019). Both are current foundational technological infrastructures required for OTT services. Revenue from OTT online broadcast services was recorded as a huge $46.3 billion in 2019. Plus, this revenue is projected to nearly double by 2024 to $86.8 billion, and even be up to ten times larger by 2027 at $476 billion. (TechSciResearch, 2022) Plus, it is even growing more rapidly than expected. By 2022 merely the largest segment of OTT, Advertising-based Video on Demand (AVOD) already has a market volume of $180 billion, which was far more than the 2024 estimate of only $86.8 billion mentioned above. (Fields, 2022) In particular, the growth of an Internet-based *discrete video ordering* service like Subscription Video on Demand (SVOD), which mainly provides high-quality video contents via companies like Netflix and Disney+, is expected to show remarkable growth. (Sung, 2021) However, by 2023, Disney+ is hemorrhaging subscribers already, and Netflix after a slight downturn in subscribers in 2022 has recovered by early 2023 by changing some of its subscription policies to be cheaper and even to venture into AVOD to be cheaper, instead of only SVOD.

In line with this global change to OTT, leaders of the entertainment industry in Korea include broadcasters, telecommunication companies, content producers, and IT companies. These have been merging in recent years. To include all of these synergistically together in the 'content industry' now is to expand the scope of this term as once separate categories of industries now merge in buyouts or in production alliances in the context of the global Korean Wave. The restructuring under OTT of producers in the Korean entertainment industry is related to changes in consumer market preferences, declining national-exclusive entertainment markets, and entrepreneurial search for profitable global markets and competitive business models.

In particular, an earlier globalizing OTT trend is accelerating with all these many sectors' deep investment into non-face-to-face platforms after 2020. As argued throughout, Korea has been one of the earliest leaders in this media regime change toward living in a saturated culture around digital mobile multimedia. (See Appendix 1). This created in Korea first more extreme organizational mismatches with older national media empires from the fresh networked smartphone environment. Since Korea continues to live in more digitally saturated conditions, and has lived within them years longer than other countries, Korea continues to take advantage of being slightly ahead in global digital trends of content industry reorganization, particularly in delivering global content like that of the Korean Wave.

On the one hand, the digital entertainment industry can be said to be leveling due to mass entry of ordinary people who can be now creators, producers, and distributors themselves. As a result, storytellers and storytelling media are exploding. However, at the same moment, on the other hand, as said above, fresh centralized empires host this 'leveled' content on ever more hierarchical global OTT or social media platforms, as they can over-shock and overawe the leveled audiences with their larger budgets and hired production talent skills just like what happened in radio broadcasting in the early twentieth century. So, beyond the decentralized media technologies that level the economic field, known as the 'ICBM' (the abbreviation for 'IoT, Cloud, Big Data, and Mobile'), there are still hierarchical and more expensive technologies like artificial intelligence (AI), high bandwidth 5G and LiFi, augmented reality (AR), and virtual reality (VR). These high bandwidth virtual reality technologies are spreading via the one-way broadcast media market first, as it is still very expensive to own and to operate these at a good *production* quality. In other words AR/VR production remains a more centralized media, and fits into older broadcast media expertise well, while only *distribution* so far has cheapened via the ICBM. Therefore, the current equipment ecosystem is similar to older one-way broadcast technologies, and it provides 'old centralized players' fresh life to evolve into a different media regime where their earlier professional production skills in radio broadcasts, professional audio recordings, or video production remains a useful skill for an OTT operator, producer, or a curator of live performances for AR or VR users. (Song & Kerr, 2017) So, in an era of more distributed media, the mismatch of some older one-way national organization of media sees loss of profit, while other *production and content creation aspects* of past one-way national media still are quite serviceable in updated 'virtual' content delivery and AI applications that remain so expensive they are hardly leveled in production yet.

Regardless, the environment surrounding the remaining expertise in centralized national broadcasting and media markets are rapidly changing. In broadcasting service, as OTT service and personal broadcasting increase, the proportion of traditional one-way broadcast media is decreasing and the proportion of new media is increasing. As the conversion to IP-based equipment is in full swing, broadcasting equipment is going beyond the range of equipment used in existing traditional broadcasting stations. In other words, the trend is expanding to include all equipment used by IPTV operators, CDN (Content Delivery Network) for OTT service, and personal media producers. Broadcast video production using 5G technology has already begun. As Korea launched the world's first commercial 5G service on April 3, 2019, mere hours before the USA, (Kim & Fang, 2019), even non-entertainment uses of 5G applications in various fields start to emerge in manufacturing, transportation, and medical care. 5G, which means 5th generation mobile wireless communication, is different from LTE (Long-Term Evolution) which is the existing 4th generation mobile wireless communication. Compared to LTE, 5G transmits massive amounts of data very quickly (eMBB, enhanced Mobile BroadBand) and connects everything in real time whether in URLLC (Ultra Reliable Low Latency Communications or mMTC (massive Machine Type Communications). It connects all things beyond voice calls and data communication and enables the creation of various convergence services. However, its major drawbacks are in human and environmental health, and in cost—given it is a completely different 'close' infrastructure of 5G with towers every few hundred meters since its higher frequencies cannot go through walls or go very far in distance. Thus the main two benefits of 4G wireless services are its greater economy of units per area and its ability to go through walls, yet these two features of cheap and moving wireless Internet are being abruptly ended, if a 5G world is in the offing. Thus 5G infrastructures are doubly expensive to build as fresh infrastructure—expensive now and expensive potentially later with lawsuits in considering the huge exposure to health injuries in implementing 5G. (Firstenberg, 2020) Plus, 5G is not really 'broadcasting' like 4G either. 5G is a beam-driven application to particular users alone instead of a more mass radiated signal like traditional broadcasting. In short, there are six major drawbacks of *health, distance, cost, lesser wireless penetration of walls, lesser roaming connection when in motion (perhaps blocked by walls or other buildings while travelling) and lesser mass scale broadcasting possibilities* in 5G that keeps it from advancing.

According to PwC (2022), the average annual growth rate of the global OTT market (paid OTT market) from 2015 to 2019 was about 23.5%. A total of $58.45 billion in sales in 2020 was achieved and $79.1 billion in 2021 (PwC, 2022). According to Statista (March, 2021), the global OTT market of all types of OTT in 2021 is estimated to be about $171.772 billion dollars. It was analyzed that the growth of the Internet video market was driven by the shared growth of AVOD (advertisement-based video on demand) such as YouTube and SVOD (subscription-based video on demand) such as Netflix. Large OTT platforms are competing fiercely in the global market as well as in the United States—like among Netflix, Amazon Prime Video, Disney+, Hulu/Disney, Max (AT&T WarnerMedia), AppleTV+, Paramount/ViacomCBS, Peacock/Comcast-NBC Universal, and HBO.

Since it is predicted that the growth potential of the Asia–Pacific region including Korea is the greatest among the whole world, we should analyze both China and

Korean markets for OTT. First, for China its OTT market in 2021 is estimated to be about $43.179 billion, and China is the second largest national market for OTT subscriptions after the United States. (Hong, 2021) China's OTT services are represented by Tencent Video/WeTV, iQIYI, and Youku, which occupy the third to fifth place in the number of global subscribers after Netflix and Amazon Prime Video. It is noteworthy that China's OTT services are pushing for entry and expansion into the global market such as purchasing Korean drama rights. (Song, 2021).

Second, what about OTT in Korea? The organization of the video content industry in Korea also shows rapid changes due to growth and expansion of OTT. According to the annual survey of the Korea Communications Commission (2020), the domestic OTT service usage rate was 66.3%, and that usage rate has been increasing over the past three years. For Koreans in their 20s, the usage rate is 91.6%, and fully 8 out of 10 Koreans from their teens to their 30s use OTT. According to the Mesomedia Consumer Survey of November 2020, 88% of Korean consumers in their 20s and 40s watch OTT at least 2–3 times a week, and some heavy users (55% of users) watch 4–5 times or more a week. (Insight M, 2021) As such, the reorganization of Korean broadcasting toward the OTT platform-oriented online organization reflect changes in the viewing habits of consumers of video content. This is intensifying the competition among Korean OTT providers to secure excellent content.

This recent change in the landscape of the video content industry in Korea seems to be starting in earnest with Netflix's expansion of OTT market share in Korea. As of Q2 2021, the United States had the most Netflix subscribers (67.28 million), followed by Brazil (18.22 million), the United Kingdom (12.75 million), Germany (10.7 million), and France (8.37 million). Russia, which recently pulled out, had 18.4 million subscribers. More than 66% of Netflix users are from outside the United States. South Korea ranks thirteenth in the world in Netflix subscribers with 4.4 million. The country with the highest ratio of subscribers to population is Norway (37% of total population), followed by New Zealand (25.8%), Australia (24.9%), the United States (20.4%), and the United Kingdom (19%). (Bliss, 2022).

As can be seen in the following Table 5.1, within the Korean OTT subscriber market in 2020, Netflix recorded an overwhelmingly high market share compared to native Korean OTT operators such as Wave, Tving, and Watcha. According to the results of the 2020 Korea Media Panel Survey, when expanding the survey to users of free advertising-based (AVOD) OTTs like YouTube in addition to the paid subscriber bases of subscription video on demand in OTT (SVOD), all OTT users were distributed as follows. In the case of advertising-based 'free' users of OTT, YouTube (82.5%) was mostly used. In the case of paid users of OTT, in addition to YouTube it was apportioned mostly between Netflix (35.4%), Wavve (9.4%), and Tving (5.0%).

Thus, the reality of the current Korean OTT market is that Netflix is the top subscriber-based paid service Korean OTT market even if it only takes a plurality of 35.4%. As Disney+ and Apple TV now enter Korea, competition among OTT operators and changes in video content supply and demand are predicted to increase. However by February 2023, Disney+ reported it had lost global subscribers for the first time in any fiscal quarter since it began in 2019, losing 2.4 million subscribers

Table 5.1 Major OTT services in Korea in 2021

Service	Main Features
Netflix	American OTT that entered the domestic Korean OTT market in 2016; has top market share in Korea among OTT; based on paid subscribers (SVOD)
YouTube	Premium subscriber-based paid service launched by YouTube, the world's largest free (AVOD) OTT service; however, a subscription allows viewing without advertisements, so YouTube is both AVOD and SVOD
Wavve	OTT service following the merger of POOQ (itself once a joint project of three terrestrial broadcasters) and oksusu (SKT) in 2019
Tving	OTT service owned by CJ ENM (broadcasting channel operator)
Watcha	OTT service owned by Watcha Service, a platform company
Season	Mobile OTT service provided by KT (former Olleh TV Mobile)
U+ mobile tv	Mobile OTT service provided by LG U+
Coupang Play	OTT service launched by Coupang, an e-commerce website; specializes in sports broadcasting OTT such as the Tokyo 2020 Olympic relay and in educational content; diversification into OTT for a wider e-commerce strategy

Source Constructed with data from the Korean National Assembly Research Service (Choi, 2021)

by 2023 instead of gaining them globally, and losing up to $1.5 billion. However, this is reportedly only a 1% loss in their global subscriber base. (Barr, 2023).

In addition to Korean OTTs operators like as Wavve, Tving, and Watcha, telecommunication companies with 5G networks, Internet portal platforms such as Naver and Kakao, and consumer distributors such as Coupang also are entering the OTT market. There are Korean mergers and collaborations as well in this mix. For example, Wavve is a wide joint venture between terrestrial TV and SKT, CJ ENM, JTBC (Korean cable television operator), Naver-affiliated Tving, LG U+ 's U+ mobile TV, KT's Seezn, and Watcha, etc. Interestingly, Coupang recently launched the OTT called Coupang Play in December 2020. In this way, Coupang has started a similar global IP empire in formation like other Korean companies already mentioned like Weverse, Naver, or Kakao. Coupang started its own OTT of Coupang Play by acquiring the bankrupt Singaporian-based OTT provider called Hooq that was liquidated in April 2020. Started in 2015, Hooq had been a joint-venture OTT between Singapore Telecommunications Limited (Singtel), Sony Pictures, and Warner Brothers from 2015 when Netflix coverage in Asia was limited. However that is now untrue, so that business model collapsed in the face of growing global coverage of Netflix and other American OTT services after 2015. Will Coupang be any more successful? To its credit, it may be, given Coupang is Korea's largest "Amazon-like" online shopping platform and home delivery service, founded in 2010, with a growing annual revenue from $18 billion in 2021 to $22 billion by 2022. Coupang has chosen to compete fiercely to catch up with America's Netflix to increase Coupang's share of the OTT sales market in Korea. Plus, the Korean competition even against Coupang from other Korean OTT services are heating up. By 2022, the once separate Korean OTT services of Tving and Seezn were allowed to merge by the Korean government—with more details on this consolidation mentioned later.

Amidst fierce market competition within Korea, equally strategic alliances exist within Korea's borders and across them. Within Korea, Naver as Korea's 'national search engine' company and platform accesses the Tving service for Naver Plus members via a partnership with its owner CJ JTBC. On the other hand, internationally, there are even more examples of global OTT transformation between Korean companies *and* foreign companies. First, Netflix has already promoted cooperation with Korean content producers and telecommunication companies. Second, CJ ENM and Studio Dragon have signed a three-year partnership with Netflix. Third, KT and LG U+ entered into a partnership with Netflix by installing Netflix itself on their Korean IPTV services. Fourth, an OTT alliance between Studio Dragon, Apple TV+ (an Apple OTT service) and Skydance Media (an American production company) jointly plan to produce the American drama series 'The Big Door Prize.' Many Korean telecommunication companies seek active cooperation with global OTT. There are many examples of these alliances. As a result, fifth, Disney+ entered the Korean market in November 2021 only via alliance with KT and LG U+ , and sixth, Apple TV+ entered the Korean ma rket only through an alliance with Korea's SK Telecom from 2021 as well. Seventh, in order to survive this intensifying competition in OTT, SK Telecom as a telecommunications and video content company is implementing fierce business strategies such as seeking a paid membership service that combines e-commerce and OTT through its collaboration with Amazon from 2020 as well. (Kim & Lee, 2021) (Fig. 5.2).

These alliances among OTT operators, established Korean broadcasters, IT-based Internet operators, and content producers are responding to the same OTT platform changes in video content based on various new business strategies. For example, Netflix has succeeded in popularity worldwide via producing and exclusively showing Korean Wave content such as *Squid Game* and *Hell*. Therefore, while

NETFLIX	· In 2021, 550 billion won invested in "K-content" · KT and LG U+ partnership to provide services	Disney	· Takes advantage of large Disney content including Marvel, Pixar, etc. · In 2022, Disney+ service app launched in South Korea · Partnership with IPTV through domestic broadcasting companies
kt KT	· Virtuous cycle relating to content planning, prduction, investment, etc. · Secured more than 1,000 original IPs by 2023 · Big data predicts popular contents	wavve	· Original contents production with three broadcasting companies and three general service program providers · Securing global contents with NBC Universal · Securing original contents of Kakao TV · From 2022, Wavve serves more than 70% of HBO's works to Korean audiences via an exclusive distribution rights contract
TVING	· Strengthening cooperation with JTBC in equity investment · NaverPlus users have a benefit that provides unlimited access to TVING	coupang	· Free service through existing Coupang Wow membership (monthly fee: 2,900 won) · Broadcasting Son Heung-min's EPL match in cooperation with SPOTV

Fig. 5.2 Market strategies of major OTT platforms within and outside Korea

Netflix supports production of original Korean-produced content more aggressively, Netflix is equally taking a strategy to target the Asian market for its own OTT service expansion based on hosting and even making more content of the Korean Wave for overseas markets outside of Korea. In the case of Watcha, a more differentiated business strategy is developed by its systematic collection and analysis of consumer data for creating algorithms that offer deeper personalization, automation, and recommendations. In the case of Disney+, which was launched in Korea in 2021, its strengths include popular content such as Disney, Pixar, Marvel, and Star Wars franchise content—each with their own strong and habitual fan bases in story IP. The Korean company Wavve was earlier only a domestic host for terrestrial broadcast content. However, it recently announced that it now has an international alliance to serve more than 70% of HBO's works to Korean audiences in an exclusively distribution rights contract with HBO. (Kim, 2022b) Tving was established as a joint venture between CJ ENM and JTBC from the start. It is implementing a horizontal expansion strategy, expanding its content distribution network through alliance with Korea's Naver platform. In the case of KakaoTV, the Korean OTT producer owned by Kakao which is the top Korean social media company, secured 41 million cumulative OTT users within a year of its launch (Choi, 2021a), and by 2020 has a subscriber base of over 3 million. This is near the scale that Netflix has by 2022 at only around 4.4 million. Note all of South Korea is just around 51 million people.

5.3.2.1 Korean Wave Content Investment by Global OTT Operators

With ever more simultaneous success of Korean dramas and movies all over the world as part of the global Korean Wave, the importance of Korea is growing as an outpost for others to enter the wider Asian market and its large consumer base. Over the past five years, Netflix invested approximately $2 billion dollars in Korean video content to make or buy over 70 original Korean contents. These included *Okja, Kingdom, Sweet Home*, and *Squid Game*. In 2020 alone, Netflix invested 333.1 billion won ($268.6 million) which was up 34.3% from the previous year. By 2022, Netflix's total investment in the Korean Wave had more than doubled from 2020 to 800 billion won. It is expected that this strategy by Netflix for funding and creating Korean content for the OTT broadcast world will be maintained in the future. (Kim 2021b) The following figure shows the trend of Netflix's rising investment in Korean original content that correlates with the rising trend of its Korean subscriber base (Fig. 5.3).

Recently, the "What's on Netflix" website analyzed ranked lists of the top ten Netflix daily lists in 89 countries around the world and published the rankings by country. According to this data, South Korea is now the second most popular origin for content on Netflix, only behind the United States. Korean content on Netflix is growing in popularity with 25 titles released in 2022, most recently *Solo 2* and *The Glory*. At the end of 2022, more than 60% of global users watched Korean content, according to Netflix. Plus, three of the top ten non-English language programs on Netflix are in Korean. Of course, the most popular country for Netflix content is the

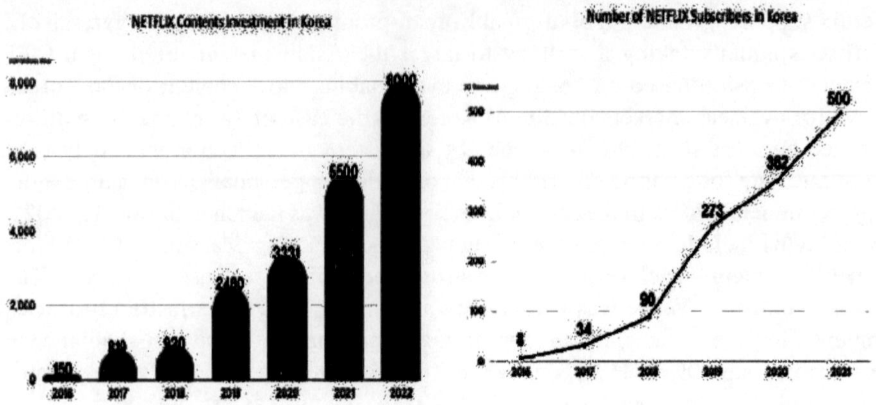

Fig. 5.3 Netflix's content investment in the Korean wave its increase in subscribers

United States. On average, 63% of the titles in the global top ten list are from the U.S. which is more than three times as much as South Korea. Nevertheless, the power of Korean content in second place is undeniable. Korean content is now a "must have" on Netflix. (What's on Netflix, 2022).

Korea's own leading domestic OTT operators like KakaoTV, Wavve, and Tving are also priming the Korean Wave by investing heavily in original Korean content. Plus, Korea's OTT operators advance themselves on the back of their own exclusive funding of content in the Korean Wave into overseas markets such as Japan and Southeast Asia. This is similar to the way that the American company Netflix created wildly popular exclusive Korean content and saw a large expansion of its own global subscriber base as well.

The following Table 5.2 shows the original IP status and investment plans of OTT operators in Korea as of 2021. It shows the plan to secure content IP by competitively investing large amounts of money by major operators. As a representative example, CJ ENM, which provides TV service, announced a plan to expand content production centered on digital platforms such as OTT and YouTube instead. This breaks away from the existing TV broadcasting-centered paradigm of content production. At the same time, CJ ENM announced a vision to build a "well-made IP mass production system and infrastructure" with huge investment plan of 5 trillion won ($4.06 billion). (Choi, 2021b).

Not only do global Korean OTT operators prime the creation of and secure exclusive use of Korean content through original content production, they sometimes exchange content between each other based on various types of partnerships and cooperation. For example, Wavve and KakaoTV exchange contents like original dramas based on cooperation between their parent companies, SK Telecom and Kakao. In the case of Tving, they are strengthening joint planning and production of contents and cooperation with Naver and JTBC. (Park, 2021) By November 2022, the Korean state approved a merger of two separate minor Korean OTT streaming

Table 5.2 Select Major Korean Domestic OTT providers (including American companies like Netflix), Their Content Partnerships, and Their Investment Plan for More Original Korean content from 2021 to 2025, with Percentage of the Subscriber Market in 2022

Company	Investment plan	Production plan 2021	Cumulative content (as of March 2021)	Masterpieces Large Hits/ Successes	Content Partnerships (2021) and Subscriber Market Percentage (2022)
Wavve (SK Telecom)	2021–2025, 1 trillion won	10 or more	16	Drama: SF8; Drama: Love Scene; Entertainment: Friends	3 terrestrial broadcasters (TV Joseon, Channel A, and MBN), plus Kakao 14%
Tving*	2021–2025, 5 trillion won	About 20	–	Entertainment: Girls' High School Mystery Class; Drama: Scripting Your Destiny; Movie: Seobok	CJ ENM, JTBC, and Naver 13%
Seezn*	2021–2023, 400 billion won	10 or so	160	Drama: Kashiriitgo; Entertainment: Eardrum Mate; Movie: My Big Mama's Crazy Ride	Open platform orientation 5%
KakaoTV	2021–2023, 300 billion won	50 or more	26	Drama: 'Myeoneuragi' (Korean translation, 'Daughter in law'; English name is "No, Thank you."); Entertainment: Should I Talk?; Drama: Not Thirty Yet	Content Wave, INISOFT (100% streaming acquisition in 2021) Netflix Unk. %** (which was 3.08 million subscribers in 2020)
Netflix	2021, 550 billion won	10 or more	80 or so	Drama: Kingdom; Drama: Sweet Home; Movie: Space Sweepers	CJ ENM, JTBC, & Studio Dragon 38% (which was 4.4 million subscribers in Korea in 2022)**

Source Reconstructed with Reference to Park (2021) and Lee and Park (2021) * Note #1: By 2022, Tving and Seezn OTT providers have merged. (Frater, 2022); ** Note #2: Reference in the conclusion of this section of over 3 million subscribers in one year for KakaoTV would seem to indicate KakaoTV pulling near to of Netflix, yet KakaoTV is in collaboration with Netflix as well, and KakaoTV shows are moving to Netflix for distribution; Note #3: This is not a full list of Korean OTT companies that would include Naver, Watcha, and Coupang Play services of Seezn and Tving (with the latter as controlled by CJ ENM yet with investments by Naver and JTBC), so they will of course be sharing content as well now. This merger joined an existing 5% and 13% of the Korean OTT market together, respectively. This put the combined Tving-Seezn company ahead of the top entirely domestic-owned Korean OTT company Wavve, with its mere 14% of the Korean OTT market. Some claim that the top OTT market provider in Korea is the American OTT operator Netflix with now a 38% market share of Korean subscribers in 2022. However, of course Netflix is priming Korean-produced broadcast content just like Korean OTT's are as noted in the above table. (Frater, 2022) Plus this claim can be challenged because from its start in 2015, KakaoTV's as a fresh OTT service has achieved a huge subscriber base of over 3.08 million in South Korea by 2020, that may soon top Netflix's 4.4 million subscribers in South Korea in 2022, even if they are collaborators as well.

5.4 Conclusion: The Korean Wave is Contributing to a General Trend of Globally Consolidated Intellectual Property Empires in Entertainment

Obviously, the importance of intellectual property (IP) that can be produced as video content is increasing in the face of intensifying competition in the OTT market. This is because as multiple platforms compete in finding original content, securing exclusive rights to that content becomes key for each global platform in order to reveal differentiation and value. Therefore, there is a frenetic competition intensifying to fund, to create, to buy, or at least temporarily to secure exclusive rights to use original content of the Korean Wave.

However, this race for intellectual property in entertainment is being done now on a global level instead of only for the Korean Wave. This is different than the past due to us living in a fresh saturated media regime of digitally networked mobile multimedia with globalizing technical and cultural characteristics. (See Appendix 4.) In the past, intellectual property was within national environs, whether in entertainment-based intellectual property or in other forms. For instance, even getting a patent registered still means mostly contacting various countries to do so.

However, by the early twenty-first century, more globalized regimes of intellectual property are being invented. The Korean Wave is encouraging this in two ways in both a 'pull' and a 'push'. It is being pulled by the Korean cultural popularly worldwide. This causes other nations' entertainment companies like Netflix to become interested in acquiring exclusive global rights to Korean content. It is being 'pushed' as well. This is being primed by the traditional well-oiled synergy between the Korean state, Korean companies, and Korean culture. This is exemplified by the recent merger of Tving and Seezn, as well as OTT content sharing between Korean companies and American companies. Koreans see yet another export-led economic sector to expand within fresh global/Korean OTT broadcasting empires carrying the content of the already global Korean Wave.

All of these mergers, sharings, and foreign investments in content for the global Korean Wave only extend Korea's export-led economic dedication. South Korean value-added exports as a percentage of GNP was earlier mentioned to be much larger than other developed or developing national economies. This means Korea is weaker domestically, if it were to be only concerned with a national economic advance of the Korean Wave alone. Therefore, Korea has a stronger internal incentive than other countries to turn its cultural wave into a global intellectual property regime and to collaborate with other global companies from other nations to make it work. Some other forms of this have been mentioned before, like how HYBE, the organization that that manages BTS, is the one that has bought the IP rights to music by American pop act Ariana Grande. Does that make HYBE a Korean company owning American IP, or does it make it a global company owning both Korean and American IP? Is Netflix really an exclusively American company if it exclusively carries and globally spreads some of the largest broadcast hits of the Korean Wave so far or if it invests in approximately 80 Korean productions, or does that make it a global company? Our analysis tends toward the latter being the ultimate effect of the Korean Wave: the creation of an infrastructure of a more merged global wave of IP management and global delivery empires, aided by AI applications, that should eventually transcend Korea and the Korean Wave itself. However, it could easily enshrine *Korean expertise globally in IP management and content production* across even other nation's OTT broadcasting and IP ownership as well.

In particular, these changes to a more globally competitive IP race suggest that the recent structural change in the OTT video content industry is equally centered on owning global rights to 'content' and the global 'platform' for the content as a combined piece of intellectual property. A more globalized distribution platform of course is required to exist if exclusive global intellectual property exists instead of letting global IP rely on various plural distributions from separate regional or national companies per se. So, behind the global OTT 'platform war' creating institutionally mismatched national broadcast arrangements based on earlier single nation media regimes, it now reveals national IP regimes of the past as institutionally mismatched as well.

Behind this OTT platform war, a second war is taking place to make and to secure original global content that can be distributed worldwide in exclusive monopolistic fashion on only one global platform. The question is how to *produce* original *global* content that guarantees this exclusivity against other global OTT services, if the world has plural national cultures, national markets, and national intellectual property regimes? How to secure source content with potential for imaging and distribution that could effectively be housed anywhere? These questions are answered in how private corporate contract rules, buyouts, and alliances are being undertaken to make a privatized and global IP regime instead of the more difficult legal regime changes of getting all nations to agree per se.

Second, the global platform war for global IP is at the same time trying to find artificial ways to limit the innately abundant and perfect copying potential of digital media. If digital IP innately can be easily copied as a digital product, exclusive platforms for exclusive IP are trying to create an artificial scarcity in digital products that in their material essence want nothing more than to be abundant and copied instead of scarce and secured. Thus a 'global digital IP regime' is trying to demote the uniquely beneficial material essence of a digital media world itself, which is free sharing and perfect copying at low or zero cost for everyone. Instead, global platforms are doing distribution as much as throttling distribution, and in the latter going against the digital essence of abundance. Media abundance is the major unique feature in world history of our current media regime, because such media abundance of perfect copies at low cost failed to exist in all previous media regimes in world history. Instead, global platforms hope to tie up this potentially abundant and copyable digital content into some kind of an artificial scarcity despite a global online access.

In this regard, the video content industry, based on both digital content and OTT, is expected to face challenges because it is trying to get global profit growth and exclusivity despite using a digital medium that desires abundance, sharing, and copying for free. Thus, because such perfect copies are materially possible, there is a synergistic dual model developing in OTT first attempting to corral cultural producers into contracts of exclusivity in distribution as well as a second strategy to diversify OTT service types and revenues to combine video content services with e-commerce and live commerce—because live commerce is more likely to have a platform's desired zero likelihood of being available as a draw to other platforms or to free digital sharing, and thus is a more innately scarce commodity product for greater profits from that scarcity.

As discussed earlier, a new value chain expansion centered on globally exclusive and exclusionary IP content management is appearing. It will lead to platforms based on global IP that will blur hosting games, serving up webtoons, movies, and TV dramas as all the same global IP arrangements. Accordingly, fresh IP-centered business strategies are based on exclusively owning source content and yet diversifying that source content. This is called either 'transmedia,' 'cross-platform,' or 'multimedia franchises.' These are expected to be developed more actively. Accordingly, it is necessary to pay attention to the expansion of newly emerging market actors such as companies planning and trading global IP or expanding new global business models based on it, or which focus even on single creators who create new types of small (IP) content to be owned exclusively as well. In addition, it is recommended to keep close watch on the investment moves of already large-scale businesses that are vertically integrated as they attempt to integrate in a new way around common IP.

In short, within the Korean Wave, the past world's more exclusively national cultural industries related to broadcasting and media, both in Korea and the world, are reorganizing now around the same globally collaborating and/or globally competing global empires of IP across any and all kinds of media and IP content for exclusive monopolistic global distribution arrangements. This is different than the past with its broadcast entertainment IP distributed only in particular countries, in singular national broadcast distributions, and in singularly discrete media. For a comparison, in the past we have seen record companies only owning recording stars and their albums as IP, or we have seen TV stations only owning and archiving their own self-produced TV productions. The change is now something like a globalized arena of producer and distributor alliances from any country, around a single global platform that will own multiple sources of IP for exclusive global distribution like owning a music star's album back catalogues now combined with multiple series of TV dramas, webtoons, live VR capacities for concerts, as well as creating and funding fresh IP simultaneously for more exclusive global distribution on only one global platform.

In this regard, such 'transmedia' mergers of many media-related companies are occurring in the Korean Wave as noted above. This is seen as well in what was mentioned earlier in this chapter about fresh content collaborations for the Korean Wave within Korea between once very different economic sectors of broadcasting companies, telecommunication companies, software companies, entertainment companies, and even major universities.

Korea is still a separate national government in its sovereignty, and yet Korea exists deeply in a world-system of commodity chains and now 'cultural production chains' of exclusive global IP empires. Thus the Korean state has divided loyalties between creating a fair and competitive environment between global operators and Korean operators, and having its own multi-decade history of priming and subsidizing exclusively Korean companies and Korean content in the Korean Wave overseas. The latter Korean export-led production development for the world has always been extreme in scale compared to the national consumption, or compared to the ratio of other countries. However, the global corporate world is now collaborating with Korean companies directly on an even larger scale that even the past Korean state is unable to facilitate, so they are hardly economic enemies per se either anymore. Thus, on the one hand, to maintain such a national bias, we expect more lenient Korean regulations may happen related to Korea's own platform operators' sharing personal information and data use, while on the other hand to facilitate a better fair and competitive system, more allowances for international collaborative mergers of Korean companies with foreign companies or at least the (already occurring) content sharing between them may continue to dominate Korean markets. Both tactics encourage the use and shared reuse of big data for the Korean Wave's synergies of sales in a more global IP. This is argued to encourage more efficient overseas expansion strategies for Korean operators, as well as for Korean-allied foreign companies in Korea and overseas.

Thus this reputed nascent more 'multi-polar global world of culture' in the global Korean Wave ironically first develops within *exclusively Korean-based global IP holding companies*, or first develops in *international* companies from past core states more *exclusively funding Korean content* for themselves. Neither trend describes well a 'multi-polar' trend, instead of showing two 'global unipolar' trends in which Koreans are simply now participating within both. In other words, what is being created in the global Korean Wave is the globalization of other countries in alliance with Korea instead of true multi-polarity of global culture of Korea versus past national cultural waves from other core countries.

This is the globalization of Korean skills *within* global content producers and *within* global IP management as other countries' companies attempt to join and to utilize the Korean Wave itself. The next few chapters explore three case studies of how this 'global Korean Wave' is increasingly becoming a 'globalization of Korean skill and talent.' This is a nascent global ruling class of the homogeneous culture of Koreans and their faster-moving collective innovation toward *global* IP content production, *global* material product production, and *global* IP content management.

References

Barker, J. A., & Erickson, S. (2005). *Five regions of the future: Preparing your business for tomorrow's technology revolution.* Portfolio, Penguin Group.

Barr, K. (2023). Disney flinches as 2.4 million subscribers abandon Disney+. *Gismodo.* Gismodo.com/disney-espn-hulu-layoffs-marvel-bob-iger-1850083319.

Bliss (2022, July 9). Top 10 countries with the most Netflix subscribers, where is South Korea? *CaTalk.* https://catalk.kr/information/netflix-subscriber.html

Choi, D. (2021a). 1 year anniversary of KakaoTV. ZD Net Korea. https://zdnet.co.kr/view/?no=2021a0906095347

Choi, J. (2021b, May 31). '5 trillion investment in 5 years' CJ ENM "Tving" to become Korea's No. 1 OTT. *BizFact.*

Choi, K. (2021c, November 15). SM contents navigator. *Artificial Intelligence Times.* https://www.aitimes.kr/news/articleView.html?idxno=23035

Choi, M. (2021d, January 5). Synergizing NC's technology with CJ ENM's content and K-pop business. *The Hankyoreh.* https://www.hani.co.kr/arti/economy/economy_general/977370.html

Deloitte (2023). Digital Human. https://www2.deloitte.com/nl/nl/pages/publieke-sector/solutions/digital-human.html

Eisenmann, T. R., Parker, G. G., & Van Alstyne, M. W. (2006, October). Strategies for two-sided markets. *Harvard Business Review.* https://hbr.org/2006/10/strategies-for-two-sided-markets

Fields, A. (2022, August 1). Top 130+ Mind-Blowing OTT statistics you need to know in 2023. *WebFX.* https://www.webfx.com/blog/pcc/ott-statistics/

Firstenberg, A. (2020). *The invisible rainbow: A history of electricity and life.* Chelsea Green Publishing.

Forristal, L. (2022, January 18). Report: Top streaming companies will spend $140.5 Billion on content in 2022. *The Streamable.* https://thestreamable.com/news/new-data-shows-top-9-media-and-tech-companies-will-spend-140-5-billion-on-content-in-2022

Frater, P. (2022, October 31). Korean regulator approves merge of Streamers Tving and Seezn. *Variety.* Variety.com/2022/biz/asia/korean-regulator-approves-merger-streamers-tving-seezn-1235419301/.

George, D. (2001). *Preference pollution: How markets create the desires we dislike.* Economics, Cognition and Society. University of Michigan Press.

Harring, A. (2023, January 3). Apple, Amazon lost a 'staggering' $800 billion in market cap in 2022. *CNBC.Com.* https://www.cnbc.com/2023/01/03/apple-and-amazon-lost-a-staggering-800-billion-in-market-cap-in-2022.html

Hong, Jin-Soo. (2021, April 25). OTT Market to Top $3 Trillion this year for the first time ever. *Kyunghyang Shinmun.* https://www.khan.co.kr/it/it-general/article/202104252127005

Hong, E. (2014). *The birth of Korean cool: How one nation is conquering the world through pop culture.* Picador.

IBC (2023). Growth in Content Investment Set to Dip in 2023. https://www.ibc.org/news/growth-in-content-investment-set-to-dip-in-2023/9381.article

Insight, M. (2021, March 12). Consumer Trend Report. *MezzoMedia.* https://www.mezzomedia.co.kr/; https://www.mezzomedia.co.kr/data/insight_m_file/insight_m_file_1102.pdf

Jem, A. & Rubin, R. (2022, March 13). 'BTS permission to dance on stage' concert scores blockbuster $32 million at global box office. *Variety*. https://variety.com/2022/film/news/bts-permission-to-dance-on-stage-seoul-llive-viewing-gross-1235203444/

Johnson, J. (2019, January 24). OTT content: What we learned from 1.1 million subscribers. *Unscreen*. http://www.uscreen.tv/blog/ott-content-trends/

Kim, J., & Fang, A. (2019, April 4). World's first 5G? South Korea and US battle over title; Seoul drives speedy launch as Verizon accuses Korean carriers of PR stunt. *Nikkei Asia*. https://asia.nikkei.com/Spotlight/5G-networks/World-s-first-5G-South-Korea-and-US-battle-over-title

Kim, H. & Lee, J. (2021, November 10). Contents, the beginning of the 4th wave. *Daeshin Securities*. http://money2.daishin.com/PDF/Out/intranet_data/product/researchcenter/report/2021/11/42635_211111_contents_4th_wave.pdf

Kim, B. (2021a). The entertainment industry enriched by AI. *Technology and Innovation* 5.

Kim, H.-k. (2021b, January 11). 5 Years After Netflix, Disney, Apple.. The global OTT Race is on. *Hankyung TV*. https://www.wowtv.co.kr/NewsCenter/News/Read?articleId=2021b01110699i

Kim, J.-W. (2022a, March 4). Metaverse platform Zepeto user base exceeds 300 million. *The Korea Economic Daily*.

Kim, J.-h. (2022b, January 6). HBO Max prepares to enter Korea with 'Game of Thrones' and 'Friends'. *News 1*. https://m.news1.kr/election/2022b0309/news/articles/?4545650

Kim, H. (2022c, March 14). Entertainment stocks jumped at the BTS concert, which ended in success with 2.5 million viewers worldwide, both online and offline. *JoseonBiz*. Biz.Joseon.com/stock/stock_general/2022a/03/14/N25RPY2PTZEZ3K4AT36EQKH464/.

Klein, N. (2007). *The shock doctrine: The rise of disaster capitalism*. Metropolitan Books/Henry Holt.

KOFICE. (2022). *Hallyu White Paper 2021*. Korean Foundation for International Cultural Exchange.

Korean National Assembly (2021). OTT utilization of cultural content and policy measures.

Ku, S., Kim, S., You, M., Whitaker, M. D. (2023). Building the Groundwork for a Natural Search, to Make Accurate and Trustworthy Filtered Searches: The Case of a New Educational Platform with a Global Heat Map to Geolocate Innovations in Renewable Energy. H. Zaynidinov et al. (Eds.), *IHCI 2022*, LNCS 13741, pp. 239–250. https://doi.org/10.1007/978-3-031-27199-1_25.

Lee, C.-h. (2021a, June 9). Is it really a new world? Real and virtual meet to conquer the metaverse. *Smart PC Love*. https://news.zum.com/articles/68669409

Lee, J.-w. (2021b, June 24). KAIST, Partnering with SM Entertainment for Metaverse Research. *Maeil Business Newspaper*. https://www.mk.co.kr/economy/view/2021b/612001.

Lee, S. & H. Park (2021). A comparative study on the key success factors of over-the-tops in South Korea. *Journal of the Korea Industrial Information Systems Research* 26(6), December, 135–54.

Lee, T.-h. (2023, April 21). Global Cyber College Taejae University to Open in September, *Korea JoongAng Daily* https://koreajoongangdaily.joins.com/2023/04/21/national/kcampus/korea-university-taejae/20230421103618060.html

Liao, S. (2021, August 6). Ariana Grande performs in concert in 'Fortnite'. *The Washington Post*. https://www.washingtonpost.com/video-games/2021/08/06/ariana-grande-performs-concert-fortnite/.

Park, J.-J. (2021, March 10). More OTT original content, more genre and format diversity. *ET News*. https://v.daum.net/v/20210310160114331

Pease, B., & Pease, A. (2006). *The definitive book of body language: The hidden meaning behind people's gestures and expressions*. Bantam Dell.

Pew Research Center (2015). The social media age gap. In *Spring 2015 global attitudes survey*. https://www.pewresearch.org/global/dataset/spring-2015-survey-data/

PwC (2020). Global Entertainment & Media Outlook 2021–2025: PwC Report. SlideShare. https://www.slideshare.net/SocialSamosa/global-entertainment-media-outlook-20212025-pwc-report

Pwc. (2022). Perspectives from the Global Entertainment & Media Outlook 2022–2026. *Price Waterhouse Coopers*. https://www.pwc.com/gx/en/industries/tmt/media/outlook/outlook-perspectives.html

Raboy, M. (2016). *Marconi: The man who networked the world*. Oxford University Press.

Robb, J. (2023, April 22). Who Will Control Reality? *Global Guerrillas* https://johnrobb.substack.com/p/who-will-control-reality

Roth, E. (2023, July 17). Hollywood's writers and actors are on strike, *The Verge*https://www.theverge.com/2023/7/17/23798246/strike-hollywoods-writers-actors-wga-sag-aftra

Satin, D. (2023, January 3). Analysis: Content spending will slow in 2023 as streamers pivot to profitability; Disney, Netflix to Lead Way. *The Streamable.* https://thestreamable.com/news/analysis-content-spending-will-slow-in-2023-as-streamers-pivot-to-profitability-disney-netflix-to-lead-way

Smart, J., Cascio, J., & Paffendorf, J. (2007). *Metaverse roadmap overview.* https://www.metaverseroadmap.org/overview/

Son, W. & Whitaker, M. D. (2020). The danger of a single technology: locked into a national digital signature in a globally digital era; South Korea's attempt at standardizing a "national PKI" framework (1999–2015), a study in path dependence that shows the danger of mandating a single technology (Manuscript article, dissertation summary of Dr. Wonbae Son).

Song, D. & Kerr, E. (2017). *Conference: The Industrial Revolution 4.0: Preparing for Disruptive Technologies in a 21st Century Asia, October 26–27, 2017.* National University of Singapore. https://ari.nus.edu.sg/events/the-industrial-revolution-4-0-preparing-for-disruptive-technologies-in-21st-century-asia/ ; https://networks.h-net.org/node/22055/discussions/177600/cfp-industrial-revolution-40-preparing-disruptive-technologies

Song, M. (2021). OTT market revenue and subscribers in Korea, Japan, and China. *KISDI Perspectives, 2*(October), 1–11. https://kisdi.re.kr/report/view.do?key=m2102058837181&masterId=4334696&arrMasterId=4334696&artId=639096

Standing, G. (2011). *The precariat: The new dangerous class.* London, UK: Bloomsbury.

Steigrad, A. (2021, November 16). ViacomCBS selling its CBS studio for $1.8 billion: report. *New York Post.* https://nypost.com/2021/11/16/viacomcbs-selling-its-cbs-studio-for-1-8-billion-report/.

Sung, Y.-T. (2021). Revitalizing the Korean Media Industry in Reponse to Changes in the Global Environment. Korea Broadcast Advertising Corporation (KOBACO).

Taejae University. (2023). Founder's Message. https://www.taejae.ac.kr/founders-message/ (Accessed: April 2023)

TechSciResearch (2022). OTT media services market—Global industry size, share, trends, opportunity, and forecast, 2018–2028F. *ReportLinker.* https://www.reportlinker.com/p06370190/OTT-Media-Services.

UneeQ (2023). Digital humans. https://www.digitalhumans.com/.

Vincent, J. (2019, May 29). Hollywood is quietly using AI to help decide which movies to make; AI will tell you who to cast and predict how much money you'll make. *The Verge.* https://www.theverge.com/2019/5/28/18637135/hollywood-ai-film-decision-script-analysis-data-machine-learning

Waldfogel, J. (2007). *The tyranny of the market: Why you can't always get what you want.* Harvard University Press.

We Are Social/Hootsuite. (2019). Digital 2019: Global Internet Use Accelerates. https://wearesocial.com/blog/2019/01/digital-2019-global-internet-use-accelerates

What's on Netflix (2022). What countries produce most popular content for Netflix? *What's on Netflix.* https://www.whats-on-netflix.com/news/what-countries-produce-most-popular-content-for-netflix/

Whitaker, M. D. (2012, August 28). Ecological Reformation in Science and Education: Local Knowledge, Universities, and the Professions as Checks and Balances in Practice Toward Sustainability, *Toward A Bioregional State.* https://biostate.blogspot.com/2012/08/ecological-reformation-in-science-and.html

Whitaker, M. D. (2021). The Commodity Ecology Mobile (CEM) Platform Illustrates Ten Design Points for Achieving a Deep Deliberation in Sustainable Development Goal #12. M. Singh et al. (Eds.) *IHCI 2020*, LNCS 12615, pp. 414–430. https://doi.org/10.1007/978-3-030-68449-5_41.

Whitaker, M. D. & Pawar P. (2020). Commodity ecology: From smart cities to smart regions via a blockchain-based virtual community platform for ecological design in choosing all materials and wastes. In *Blockchain Technology for Smart Cities*. Springer.

Whitaker, M. D., & Shin G.-c. (2020). A circular economy for the world: The commodity ecology model for achieving all sustainable development goals. *Journal of APEC Studies, 12*(2), 77–99.

Whitaker, M. D., Hwang, N., Usmonova, D., Cho, K., & Park, N. (2023). Case studies of mental problems in South Korea and India: Why knowing the national demographics first helps choose better medical technical interventions. *Global Medical Engineering Physics Exchanges (GMEPE) 2023*. IEEE Explore.

Yeo, J.-S. (2019, January 11). SKT partners SM Entertainment on AI-based technology for K-pop content. *The Korea Herald*. http://www.koreaherald.com/view.php?ud=20190111000628

Zuboff, S. (2019). *The age of surveillance capitalism: The fight for a human future at the new frontier of power*. PublicAffairs.

Chapter 6
BTS

K-pop group's song "Butter" got over 108 million views within the first 24 hours of its release. KIM: And so when Koreans talk about hip-hop, they don't talk about Koreans being the best Korean hip-hop; they talk about Koreans being the best hip-hop artists, period...[o]r the best dancers. They're not trying to become the best dancers in Korea. They're trying to become the best dancers in the world.

NPR (2022)

BTS contributes over $4 billion dollars to South Korea's economy every year.

Duerden (2021)

"BTS," in English, is the official abbreviation for the Korean boy group named 'Bang Tan Sonyeondan" [방탄소년단; Hanja: 防彈少年團], literally meaning 'Bulletproof Boy Group,' 'Bulletproof Boys,' or equally the popularly known translation of 'Bulletproof Boy Scouts.' Members of the group have commented upon multiple meanings of their name yet with two main themes. One meaning implies the 'bulletproof' reference: a process of blocking stereotypes and expectations fired upon on all adolescents 'like bullets'. This reflects the double meaning BTS announced about their name from 2017, claiming it equally means "Beyond the Scene." Another meaning stresses the 'boyhood' aspect, yet as a time of maturation and growth instead of perpetual youth: the art of coming of age by moving from childhood to adulthood as a process of fighting challenges and making choices in that growth. Beyond the concept and symbolism though, BTS was originally a 7-member Korean hip-hop boy group that debuted on June 13, 2013, managed by Big Hit Entertainment. Over the years, BTS evolved to show many different musical styles and influences beyond hip-hop however. Equally evolving, their manager Big Hit Entertainment itself was only founded in 2005, and it was renamed HYBE from 2020. Since the group's debut, given their growth strategy was toward an immediate global digital fandom, BTS has swept more international awards than exclusively Korean national awards—with the latter Korean national awards coming only after international recognition instead of before, similar to the stories of Psy and Kim Yuna mentioned in earlier chapters (see Table 6.2). BTS has matured into the top K-pop boy group representing the global Korean Wave. As planned from 2013, they are known by their particularly large

G.-C. Shin and M. D. Whitaker, *The Korean Wave in a Post-Pandemic World*,
https://doi.org/10.1007/978-981-99-3683-0_6

"digital fandom," yet even their manager Bang Si-hyuk has said his plans for BTS's digital popularization grew more than even he dreamed. Bang himself has said he was shocked scale of how BTS became a craze around the world as twenty-first century pop icons. That global success of BTS has made their manager Bang Si-hyuk the only billionaire in K-pop, and made Bang's management company HYBE into the operator of a global online platform named Weverse that organizes the same online services for digital fandom management and profit from it for any musical group worldwide, instead of only for Korean groups under HYBE's contract.

6.1 Fandom to Digital Fandom

There are many factors of BTS's success mentioned before attention focuses on the importance of this fresh kind of "digital fandom." Of course BTS has been supported with capital investment, human skills investment in 'idol' training, general state financial support for the Korean Wave, and of course by working very hard for years on perfecting their dancing and musicianship on top of huge talent. Reflecting on the work put into being a BTS member, one slang meaning of the abbreviation of BTS is "blood, tears, and sweat." However, more than most groups in the global Korean Wave, BTS has had success via a very loyal and very large global online "digital fandom" euphemistically called the BTS "Army." In the wake of Psy's globally viral hit "Gangnam Style" in 2012, BTS's management learned that lesson of viral popularity from Psy. Big Hit Entertainment debuted BTS in the next year of 2013 and from the beginning used a conscious strategy of trying to emulate Psy's globally viral media success of 2012 by making BTS popular via understanding the online digital route of popularization on social media and its ability for more daily two-way communications between BTS members and their fans. However a daily communication via social media with fans was hardly employed by Psy, though it was how BTS would become akin to a 'gamification' of K-pop, to encourage people incessantly to keep coming back to BTS's web presence in the addictive hook of an updated 'reality TV' show of seeing good close friends grow up and succeed, instead of only see distant pop idols. Thus this media presence of BTS has millions of spectators and interactions with their daily life instead of only the more traditional kind of intermittent group communications and intermittent fans that just occasionally watch a popular Korean boy group that shows their songs and dances online primarily.

Before 2000, the global entertainment sector was dominated by a small number of large producers and one-way mass broadcasters, making it almost impossible for small management teams like Big Hit Entertainment to 'invest' in that media market. However, even huge amounts of capital invested in the hope to prime a mass media campaign hardly always equated with true market success. Plus, this mass media discovery process was rather random, combining expensive market priming with first instances of popularization—which could fall flat. Thus, at the time there was little way to prime cheaply what was already independently popular or little way to popularize fresh groups without expensive mass market campaigns. However, nowadays an approach for priming a fresh K-pop group via a social media service (SNS) fandom seems more rational since it is less costly and is a far more durable way to prime a group's popularity in an ongoing daily way, online, instead of having to 'recharge' it regularly with vast capital of one-way mass media campaigns. So, instead of an expensive original popularization achieved via sponsorship in the mass media of TV shows or radio play in multiple national markets, BTS's fandom is based on a cheaper yet emotionally deeper virtual community of using a globally-distributed technology of personal smartphones, tablets, and Internet connections. All the factors above when combined did more than allow BTS quickly to rise to the top of the world's musical and dance acts. The ongoing communication with their online fandom has allowed BTS to perch there for many years in an ongoing way, even 'suspended' there between album releases and video releases. This is in many ways the result of BTS's "digital fandom."

Now let us focus on this factor of the distributed "digital fandom" of BTS, keeping in mind it is hardly the only factor of BTS's success. First, the term "fandom" refers to a group of people who passionately like a specific field or person as a cultural phenomenon. In other words, it is a concept defined by grouping people who are immersed in a specific subject and share tastes or preferences as a group phenomenon. John Fiske redefined the meaning of 'fandom' in 1989 to distinguish the 'active' pop culture audience from the 'ordinary' passive audience. Fiske (1992) divided the characteristics of this more active fandom into three main categories. First, the fandom has the characteristics of discrimination and distinction. Fans believe that the selection of stars not only differentiates the social identity provided by popular culture and the image of social experience, but also uses it as a mechanism for aesthetic discrimination in the dominant culture. Second, the fandom has the characteristics of productivity and participation. Fans not only simply accept the products of the cultural industry, but also produce new popular culture through active participation. Productivity is divided into semiotic productivity, verbal-actual productivity, and textual productivity. Third, the fandom has the characteristics of capital accumulation. Here, capital means cultural capital, and fans accumulate this cultural capital by collecting and owning cultural products related to stars. Fans exercise this cultural capital within their own group and form their identity through discrimination from outsiders who do not share the target of fandom. Unlike the mutual productivity of fans in the second characteristic above, this level of fan behavior is closer to passive consumption, in that they consume images and information about stars delivered by media and cultural industries even if they are more active in the second sense in that they accept and change it in their own way and satisfy their needs in the process.

However the term "digital fandom" adds a fourth category to fandom. Instead of only an asynchronous and occasional peer-to-peer relationship of shared symbolisms and shared material artifacts producing signs between fans for status and belonging, a digital fandom brings a more ongoing synchronous active relationship with the idol itself. It is a digital-distributed, peer-to-peer, intimate and active fans-to-artist relationship unlike an older asynchronous media presence bought by buying discrete blasts of airtime, by buying advertising in central agencies of mass media distribution, or by buying mass manufactured cultural products. In Fiske's definition of fandom, it meant buying or making products that became a surrogate to the relationship that fans were unable to have directly with their distant stars. If fandom is a substitutionary relationship around an idol, mostly among peers who love the idol and the cultural products of that idol, a digital fandom is a real relationship around an idol directly with more synchronous relationships with them and with other fans in synchronous relationships around them. This is a more real community from the synchronous and multimedia quality of the relationships despite its virtual community space. If fandom was a real space in a virtual relationship, digital fandom is a real relationship in a virtual space.

Plus, the three earlier factors pushing the global Korean Wave make this a more *hybrid digital fandom.* To quote a Joni Mitchell song, a centralized Korean "star maker machinery" still exists in those three factors of the Korean public state, Korean private profit from corporations, and Korean culture combining in big media and big venues that court the spark of fame, yet is hybridized with a wider fourth foundation due to a globally-distributed digital fandom possible in our fresh media regime (See Appendix 4). First, the earlier one-way mass media model within those earlier three factors began to lose its cultural hegemony once billions of digital mobile technologies like smartphones were diffused around the globe that preceded the more globalized Korean Wave. Second, the story of BTS is the epitome of a primary digital fandom merging with a secondary and older mass media distribution fandom later. Surprisingly, the spread of this digital fandom was faster originally in the United States than in South Korea, yet now this BTS "Army" has spread all over the world. However by now BTS and any top global Korean wave acts are more of a hybrid of *old centralized* media systems that are *secondarily* seeking to make money because they are now only echoing talent and popularity vetted and discovered from *the primary fresh distributed* systems, instead of a dichotomy that pits 'the media establishment' against BTS or any global Korean Wave act. The Korean Wave thus is not a rebellion by any means. It is a very conservative profit making venture that seeks the widest possible markets created as cheaply as possible. Particularly in the global Korean Wave, in short, a *primary* process of digital discovery of what is popular in the world is regularly joined *secondarily* by major big media campaigns seeking to maximize their own profits by 'outsourcing' to social media their past expensive and not-always-successful discovery process.

A discussion of the benefits of this hybrid media ecology, with its primary viral digital discovery of popularity and its merely secondary mass media popularization, shows how effective this interaction is in the rise of BTS. First, a large digital fandom is the foundation that began to raise YouTube views and rank on any popular charts anywhere in the world whenever BTS released a new song, particularly if the new song was first only available on social media channels such as Twitter or YouTube. At the same time, a digital fandom can swarm quickly and organize forcefully in more 'offline' venues as well: it can support BTS so that they can sweep the (online) votes of fans national in-person music awards as well. BTS won the top place award as Billboard's Top Social Artist award since 2017 which is decided by fans' (online) votes. At the Billboard Music Awards, the American Music Awards (AMA), and the Grammy Awards, which are the three major American popular music awards,

BTS has for the past several years won awards every time at Billboard and AMA, except for the Grammys. Plus, all four first BTS albums reached the top place on the Billboard 200 album chart. This was done only one time before by the Beatles in the British Wave of the 1960s. BTS started to receive ongoing annual awards at the American Music Awards starting from 2018. In 2018, after BTS received the Favorite Social Artist award, they won three more awards there in years to come: the most popular group in 2019, and both Favorite Pop Duo/Group and Favorite Social Artist Award for three consecutive years since then. BTS's song "Dynamite" topped the Billboard single chart for two weeks in a row in September 2020. Even more extreme, in 2021 BTS won three different awards at the AMA in a single year, including the highest honor, the 'Artist of the Year.'

Three beneficiaries of this more digital fandom can be seen. First, the digital fandom itself can be seen as one of its own biggest beneficiaries in the transformation from mass media fandom to digital fandom. The source of their adoration is now easily available with updates at any moment, instead of scarce and intermittent in its communications like a distant god. Second, another big beneficiary are consumers as a whole from a more diverse entertainment market since more entertainment acts are available for consumers due to wider, easier, and cheaper digital media entry. This creates a more competitive market with entry by smaller producers and (originally smaller sizes of) consumers whose market niches can be filled, instead of blocked as before (Waldfogel, 2007). Third, another beneficiary is that smaller and more entrepreneurial management agencies have a chance to make a global market for themselves with their greater access to the mass public in this way. For instance, it was hard in the beginning for BTS's manager of Big Hit Entertainment to convince Korean television broadcasters to put BTS on their TV shows in the early years of BTS, since Big Hit Entertainment was just a venture company starting out with its managed groups. Instead, in lieu of expensive centralized media exposure, Big Hit Entertainment turned BTS into an online 'reality TV' show as much as a boy group. Instead of through television, BTS members communicated directly with individuals or groups of fans through social platforms using SNS. In this way, BTS enabled exclusive content and direct communication between them and the digital fandom that other media outlets were unable to share. This built a very strong bond. The high solidarity was expressed by the term BTS "Army."

Unlike other idols, the way BTS uses SNS is that it communicates in two directions. A lot has changed now, but singers and idols in the past thought of SNS as literally only as another means of one-way communication of 'publicity.' The main purpose was to provide information about a new song release, a listed concert schedule, or to distribute a teaser (a short introduction video) for a new song as part of an album promotion strategy. Of course, BTS also used SNS for this one-way media purpose but in addition to that in this hybrid digital fandom they made videos of the members' daily routines, practice videos, or their thoughts, and provided them to fans from time to time, so that fans could have a more friendly feeling. In short, communication can be two way and synchronous in our fresh media regime. Previous media regimes were more akin to one-way communication or propaganda in which only one side talks about what they want to say to scaled audiences of silent receivers, without receivers as individuals capable of responding directly at the same scale. The importance of two-way communication in the digital fandom around BTS is appreciated by some BTS fans, who used to like American and Western pop stars more in the past, though now say that BTS are friendly stars rather than reigning stars as one of the reasons why they like K-pop stars instead.

Digital fandom seems to work. As of June 30, 2022, according to data analysis sites Social Blade and Wikipedia, BTS's Twitter followers reached 43.45 million. In addition, BTS's official YouTube channel 'BANGTAN TV' has 70 million subscribers. The 'Permission to Dance' music video uploaded to the BTS YouTube channel has about 400 million views. Most of the 3.43 million comments are written in English. In a keynote speech at the 2017 Mnet Asia Music Awards, Big Hit Entertainment Chairman Bang Si-hyuk said, "With the advent of SNS and the diversification of online platforms, the axis of the Western music industry, centered on traditional media, has been shaken violently. We actively communicated through SNS and changed the flow of existing media."

In this hybrid digital fandom, BTS has topped all the world's leading charts, national or digital: U.S. Billboard, the U.K. official chart, the Japanese Oricon, and various online global charts from iTunes, Spotify, and Apple Music. BTS has also broken records in album sales, music video views, and social media indexes. In particular, BTS is the first group to simultaneously conquer both the Billboard Hot 100 and Billboard 200 charts in one week, and topped the 'Billboard 200' five times and the 'Hot 100' four times. At the 63rd Grammy Awards, BTS was the first Korean group of singers and dancers to perform on a solo stage, and BTS set a record for performing at the top three American music awards ceremonies including the Billboard Music Awards, American Music Awards and Grammy Awards. BTS has solidified both its *primary digital* position as a global artist and in the *secondary global concert market* by holding stadium tours as well. BTS's digital fandom when combined with mass media now potentially has good influence around the world through their United Nations' speeches and the LOVE MYSELF campaign. In conclusion, how many groups anywhere can boast an "army" of digital fans who instead of armed with violence are armed with their love of global organized clicks and votes for the source of their adoration, sort of like a voluntary 'bot farm' of real people worldwide?

However, on June 14, 2022, the group announced a temporary cessation of activities. This was due to Korean state rules on mandatory male military service for almost two years—however delayed these two years have been in the case of BTS until it nearly hit some of their 30th birthdays. In an earlier chapter, it was discussed how the Korean state passed a law in 2020 to let "important Korean artists" (i.e., K-pop stars like BTS) delay universal national military service in their 'golden 20s' to fight for online popularity and for economic growth of the country instead of fight for their country militarily.

6.2 History of BTS's Growth as a Digital Fandom

As BTS takes a hiatus from touring and recording as a group as some of its members begin their long-delayed yet still required Korean military service, this quiet time in BTS's career is a good time to take stock of their massive popular influence in the global Korean Wave and in their digital fandom and its growth.

BTS made their debut in 2013 with the release of 2 COOL 4 SKOOL, and won the Rookie of the Year award for that year. BTS formed a fandom abroad as much as in Korea thanks to the fresh digital medium of direct communication with fans online through SNS from the beginning. BTS named their fan club "ARMY" in 2013 and formed an official fan club in 2014.

The name "Army" has double meanings. On the surface it means of course an analogy to a real army: that the singers and the fans will always be together in solidarity just as body armor on soldiers is closely attached. It means that the group will block the social oppression and prejudice firing on teenagers and 20-somethings, and the digital fandom in turn will protect the value of the music. Officially it is an acronym as well. It stands for "Adorable Representative M.C. for Youth." "The [BTS] fandom was officially established on July 9, 2013, which is considered ARMY day. This happened around a month after BTS's official debut on June 12, 2013." (Hegde, 2021).

The scale of the BTS digital fandom ARMY is estimated to be over 40.8 million people. This is measured "by subscribe[rs] to BTS's YouTube channel,...[plus]...more than 34 million follow both the member-run Twitter account and [the] official BTS Instagram account." (Ali, 2021) An official online survey or census of the large BTS ARMY was conducted in 2021. As many as 400,000 people responded in 46 languages. Assuming it is a representative sample, 50.3% of BTS's digital fandom is under 18 years of age, and 42.3% are between 18 and 29 years of age. The remaining approximately 8% of the digital fandom is over 30 years of age. This means about half of BTS's digital fandom are teenagers and half are more adult. Plus, from the survey, the most respondents came from Indonesia "at 20 percent...[which] had the most BTS fans anywhere in the world. Other represented territories included Mexico (10.6%), the United States (8.4%), Peru (5.12%), and the Philippines (4.5%). A mere 3.7%...of the fans surveyed were from...Korea." (Ali, 2021). This goes well with the previous assumption from 2020 that 90% of the BTS digital fandom was from outside of Korea (Jeong, 2020).

Other major factors of BTS's success are of course their artistic skill. All BTS members were equipped with musical talents as singer-songwriters. They did not have good educational degrees as expected in the strong educational status culture of Korea that leads even dozens of K-pop stars to have undergraduate college degrees before they try to become famous (Koreaboo, 2020; Tan, 2019), yet BTS worked hard in Big Hit Entertainment's extensive star "training program" organized by their manager (Bruner, 2019). They were coached and trained for years to be professional hip-hop idols and professional musicians. They compose now a number of songs themselves. They have announced their existence through music as much as social media—interacting with their fans through SNS as intended by their manager from the early days of their formation in 2013.

Elaborated in Table 6.1, the main music and performance roles of all BTS members are listed. BTS's dancing, singing, and rapping skills are top-notch. These skills are the result of unremitting efforts, and their huge results can be seen in many awards received around the world, listed in Table 6.2.

Compared to their earliest videos showing their practice to become a BTS member, it can be clearly seen how much effort they put into improving their skills. Digital fans are touched because they communicate based on sincere messages. Also, with fans knowing that their skills are the result of great effort, and since they get to see their progress as simply normal people that they know online who have a K-pop career, fans love them even more. The fact that all seven of them have the skills and capabilities to compose their own stories as singer-songwriters is also competitive in terms of music. BTS's dance, singing, and rapping skills are at the highest level thanks to their high musicality, in addition to their harmonious, dynamic, and sharp-timed group dance. BTS fans always emphasize that they love them not simply because they are handsome and dance well, but because they have excellent musicality. Plus, BTS has an ability to combine many global trends in music, dance, and performance while utilizing K-pop and their own unique strengths such as rapping and choreography.

In their global digital fandom, BTS gained popularity abroad in Europe and the Americas first. Their first album "Dark and Wild," was released in August 2014. It succeeded in entering Billboard's World Albums Chart and ranked third in the final tally. Thus, it is noteworthy in that only about nine months after their debut in 2013, BTS began to produce tangible results in their international popularity by 2014 already. By August 2014, BTS went on the stage at the Korea Convention (KCON) in Los Angeles where they successfully performed in front of 20,000 people in the audience and started to solidify their popularity abroad.

K-pop singer Psy had become a global top digital star in 2012 with "Gangnam Style," but Psy lacked a durably large digital fandom. However, BTS now has more than 40 million followers worldwide in their digital fandom. On the stage of the American Music Awards held on November 19, 2017, the BTS "ARMY's" shouts overwhelmed the cheers for all other American musicians who attended that day including Bruno Mars, Shawn Mendes, Beyonce, and The Chainsmokers. Generally, a fandom is born when a feeling of liking, passion, and solidarity with a star is combined. In the past, fandom was a product of liking and passion, but in the age of social media and a more digital fandom, solidarity becomes more important. Fans are in solidarity with stars, and stars are in solidarity with fans, and fans are in solidarity with each other. BTS has been narrowing the distance with their fans, constantly saying that they are ordinary people who live daily lives with their fans. For the fans, BTS shares their daily life with photos and videos many times weekly, and the lyrics contain the concerns of the fandom as peers instead of only as an audience.

Fans support the stars by collecting and reprocessing the constantly pouring information about the stars to create their own secondary content. As digital content consumers become digital creators, the sense of solidarity is strengthened. Fans who create content are in solidarity with other fans who consume the content. As the

Table 6.1 Profile of BTS members

Stagename	Jin	Suga	RM	J-hope	Jimin	V	Jungkook
Name	Kim SeokJin	Min YunKi	Kim NamJun	Jeon HoSeok	Pa Ji Min	Kim TaeHyung	Jun JungKook
Hometown	Gyeonggido	Daegu	Seoul	Gwangju	Busan	Daegu	Busan
Birthday	1992.12.04	1993.03.09	1994.09.12	1994.02.18	1995.10.13	1996.12.30	1997.09.01
Height (cm)	179	174	181	177	173	178	178
Weight (kg)	60	57	64	59	60	63	60
Position	Sub-Vocalist	Lead Rapper	Main Dancer, Lead Rapper	Leader, Main Rapper	Main Dancer, Lead Vocalist	Sub-Vocalist	Main Vocal, Sub-Rapper, Lead Dancer
Nationality	Republic of Korea						
Group	BTS (Korean abbreviation for "Bang Tan Sonyeondan" [방탄소년단], i.e., 'Bulletproof Boy Group')						
Agency	Big Hit Entertainment, later renamed HYBE						
Debut day	2013.06.13						
Debut song	2013 Single Album as 1st Album, "2 COOL 4 SKOOL"						

Table 6.2 BTS's award-winning career, from debut in 2013 to 2022

BTS's award-winning career, from debut in 2013 to 2022	
Year	Award category
2014	MTV Europe Music Awards (Best Korean Act)
2015	Japan's Golden Disc Awards (Best New Artist in Asia)
2015	Japan's Golden Disc Awards (Rookie of the Year in Asia)
2017	Brand of the Year Award
2017	Nickelodeon Mexican Kids' Choice Awards (Favorite overseas artist group)
2017	Shorty Awards Best (Music Award)
2017	Shorty Awards (Best in Music Award)
2017	Nickelodeon Mexico Kids' Choice Awards (A group of favorite international artists)
2018	BBC Radio 1 Teen Awards (Social Media Star)
2018	MTV Europe Music Awards (Best Group)
2018	Much Music Video Awards (Fan Fave Duo or Group)
2018	BBC Radio 1 Teen Awards (Best International Group)
2018	People's Choice Awards (Song of the Year)
2018	MTV Europe Music Awards (Biggest Fans)
2018	American Music Awards (Favorite Social Artist)
2018	Billboard Music Awards (Top Social Artist)
2018	People's Choice Awards (Group of the Year)
2018	People's Choice Awards (Social Celebrity of the Year)
2018	People's Choice Awards (Music Video of the Year)
2019	MTV Europe Music Awards (Best Group)
2019	MTV video music awards (Best K-pop)
2019	MTV Europe Music Awards (Biggest Fans)
2019	Billboard Music Awards (Top Social Artist)
2019	Billboard Music Awards (Top Duo/Group)
2019	MTV Europe Music Awards (Best Live)
2019	MTV video music awards (Best Group)
2019	American Music Awards (Favorite Social Artist)
2019	American Music Awards (Tour of the Year)
2019	Japanese golden disc (Asian Album of the Year)
2019	Japanese golden disc (Best 3 Albums Asia Category)
2019	Japanese golden disc (Best 3 Albums Asia Category)
2019	Japanese golden disc (Best Music Video Asia Category)
2019	Japanese golden disc (Best Asian Artist)
2019	American Music Awards (Favorite Duo or Group Pop/Rock)
2020	American Music Awards (Favorite Duo or Group Pop/Rock)

(continued)

Table 6.2 (continued)

BTS's award-winning career, from debut in 2013 to 2022	
Year	Award category
2020	MTV video music awards (Best K-pop)
2020	MTV Europe Music Awards (Best Song)
2020	People's Choice Awards (The Song of 2020)
2020	MTV video music awards (Best Group)
2020	MTV video music awards (Best Pop)
2020	MTV European Music Awards (Best Group)
2020	MTV European Music Awards (Best Virtual Live)
2020	MTV European Music Awards (Biggest Fans)
2020	People's Choice Awards (The Group of 2020)
2020	People's Choice Awards (The Album of 2020)
2020	American Music Awards (Favorite Social Artist)
2020	People's Choice Awards (The Music Video of 2020)
2020	Billboard Music Awards (Top Social Artist)
2020	MTV video music awards (Best Choreography)
2021	American Music Awards (Favorite POP Song)
2021	American Music Awards (Favorite Duo or Group)
2021	American Music Awards (Artist Of The Year)
2022	Golden Disc Awards (Grand Prize in the music category)
2022	Golden Disc Awards (Main prize in the digital sound source category)
2022	Golden Disc Awards (Seezn Golden Disc Popularity Award)
2022	Gaon Chart Music Awards (Artist of the Year in the Physical Album category)
2022	Gaon Chart Music Awards (Retail Album of the Year)
2022	Gaon Chart Music Awards (Long Run Song of the Year Award)
2022	The Fact Music Awards (Most votes for Fan & Star)
2022	Gaon Chart Music Awards (Social Hot Star of the Year Award)
2022	Seoul Music Awards (U+IDOL LIVE Best Artist Award)
2022	Seoul Music Awards (Main prize)
2022	Seoul Music Awards (World Best Artist Award)
2022	Golden Disc Awards (Main prize in the digital sound source category)
2022	The Fact Music Awards (Fan and Star Choice Award)
2022	Gaon Chart Music Awards (Mubeat Global Choice Award)
2022	Gaon Chart Music Awards (Singer of the Year in the digital music category)
2022	The Fact Music Awards (Idol Plus Popularity Award)
2022	The Fact Music Awards (Artist of the Year)

(continued)

Table 6.2 (continued)

BTS's award-winning career, from debut in 2013 to 2022	
Year	Award category
2022	The Fact Music Awards (Global Fan & Star)
2022	The Fact Music Awards (Grand Prize)
2022	Heart Dream Awards (Global Favorite Idol Popularity Award, Male Group Award)
2022	American Music Awards, AMA (Favorite Pop Duo or Group)
2022	American Music Awards, AMA (Favorite K-Pop Artist)

sense of solidarity between digital fans is strengthened, the fandom grows explosively. BTS's many online channels of communication can turn out three or four media posts a week, and digital fans say they feel a personal responsibility to spread BTS further (Jeong, 2020).

The way BTS treats their digital fandom is markedly different from that of any existing singers, groups, or entertainers. Usually when singers thank their fans they don't limit their audience to just their own fan club. This is to avoid sending an exclusive message of gratitude only to the most passionate fans that support them. However, BTS seldom uses the usual expression 'our fans' when expressing gratitude, and explicitly refers to the fan club as 'ARMY'. This has important implications, and it makes BTS fans feel that they are a specially recognized entity. Each BTS member gives BTS fans a sense of bonding and belonging, which is very important in the digital fandom. BTS is thankful to the great contributions of the loyal 'ARMY' that has been with BTS since the early days of difficult times, and BTS does not lose their gratitude.

In 2015, BTS released their second album "The Most Beautiful Lover of Life Pt.1," and began to win first place on music shows. By 2016, they released the album "WINGS" and won their first major prize. In 2017, they released the album "YOU NEVER WALK ALONE," and its title song 'Spring Day' entered Korea's major music charts for the longest period of time until 2022. Tables 6.2 and 6.3 show the extent of their awards from their debut in 2013 to 2022—and their many Guinness World Records that began to accrue after 2017.

Unlike other idol groups, BTS's music has a unique competitive advantage that can compete in the global market. The series of albums produced based on the strategy of storytelling have the characteristic of making fans voluntarily interpret BTS's music and make them more sympathetic. BTS's music contains symbolic messages about life, studies, employment, and social pressure from the perspectives of teenagers and those in their 20s. When BTS debuted, they sang about the difficulties of school life that they experienced in their own late teens and early twenties, and the dreams they were constantly pondering in the album '화양연화' in Korean, 'Hwa Yang Yeon Hwa,' released in 2015, and given the English-language translated title of "The Most Beautiful Moment In Life / In The Mode For Love / Hwa Yang Yeon Hwa, Pt. 2". Later, their musical themes dealt with overcoming temptation, progressing into adulthood in the album *Blood, Sweat, Tears* (2016) and concerns about what is

Table 6.3 Guinness world records by BTS, 2017–2020

Year	Guinness world records for the year	Guinness world records division
2017	DNA	K-pop group music video with most views on YouTube in 24 hours
	BTS	Most activities on Twitter
	BTS	The most active music group on Twitter
2018	IDOL	Music video with the most views on YouTube in 24 hours
	BTS	The first Korean artist to top the Billboard 200 chart
	BTS	The first Korean artist to win the Billboard Artist 100 chart
	BTS	The first K-pop group to make it to the top 10 on Billboard Hot 100
2019	Poems for the Little Things (Boy With Luv)	K-pop group music video with most views on YouTube in 24 hours
	Poems for the Little Things (Boy With Luv)	Music video with the most views on YouTube in 24 hours
	Poems for the Little Things (Boy With Luv)	Most viewed video on YouTube in 24 hours
	MAP OF THE SOUL: PERSONA	Korea's highest-selling album ever
	BTS	TikTok achieved 1 million followers in the shortest period of time
2020	BTS	Most winners of Mnet Asian Music Awards
	BTS	Billboard Social 50's longest-running No. 1 in history
	BANG BANG CON THE LIVE	The biggest live streaming audience of all time
	MAP OF THE SOUL: 7	Korea's highest-selling album ever
	Dynamite	K-pop group music video with most views on YouTube in 24 hours
	Dynamite	Music video with the most views on YouTube in 24 hours
	Dynamite	Most viewed video on YouTube in 24 hours

real love in the albums *DNA* (2017) and *Fake Love* (2018). During the lockdown, they sang the theme of hope in songs like 'Dynamite' (2020), 'Butter' (2021), or 'Permission to Dance' (2021). These topics related easily to young people because they spoke to their own condition of life. The *Wall Street Journal* analyzed seven success factors of BTS in an article dealing with the success story of BTS in March 2020. One of these was a 'solid worldview' across multiple albums: "It is difficult to find a song based on a solid worldview like BTS in the world." (Shah, 2020) Other factors are their digital fandom of over 40.8 million people who take it upon themselves to forward BTS digital content around the world and to vote for them in any online "people's awards" in music industry award shows.

Since Big Hit Entertainment (now renamed HYBE) started as a small agency, it must have been a combination of financial limitation and digital social media strategy as dual reasons why they intentionally avoided more traditional large-scale promotions. Since their debut, instead BTS shared daily life with fans through social media such as Twitter and YouTube. They communicated sincerely by introducing a music studio or room with their fans, asking about their well-being, and listening to their concerns. BTS is a successful musical group that worked hard to win the hearts of the public. From the very beginning, they worked tirelessly to win people's reactions and hearts, and to be recognized as performers that the audience trusts and enjoys. Reflecting their experiences, they honestly shared their daily life as artists with their fans. They made their music reach the public with hope and strength.

In collaboration with colleagues, they introduced idol-centered original hip-hop music to the Korean public and the world. They created a different kind of music with thick content layers and the evocative storytelling expected of great musicians. BTS made musical collaborations with other HYBE representatives, chief producers, and performance and visual staff. BTS members are musicians who always express gratitude for being with their fandom 'ARMY.' In fact, their feats on Billboard, the world record sales of their concerts, and the praise from global media were in part possible due to this massively loyal digital fandom worldwide. Other digital success factors of BTS are revealed below.

Between 2018 and 2021, the global level of BTS's digital fandom truly started to blur the borderlines of past national cultures and smash the idea of national media spheres. In 2018, BTS released "LOVE YOURSELF 轉 'Tear'" which reached number one on the American Billboard 200. At this point, BTS became the first Korean music group to reach number one on the Billboard 200. However, this was repeated constantly over the next few years. For instance, next, "LOVE YOURSELF 結 'Answer'" was released and reached number one on the Billboard 200 once more. In 2019, they released the album "MAP OF THE SOUL: PERSONA," which peaked at number one on the Billboard 200. By 2018, BTS started to sweep all the grand prize categories of the Korean Music Awards. BTS became a music group recognized for both musicality and commercial achievements by winning the Artist of the Year award at the Korean Popular Music Awards for the second year in a row in 2019. In 2020, BTS released the album "MAP OF THE SOUL: 7," setting a record as the first Korean album to be numbered in the first week of the year, reaching number one on the Billboard 200, and becoming the best-selling album of all time in Korea. After that, they released the single 'Dynamite.' This single stayed at the number one spot on the Billboard Hot 100 for three weeks. BTS is still the first and only Korean music group ever to reach number one on the ostensibly American Billboard Hot 100. Then, then did it once more. They released a remix of the single 'Savage Love (Laxed—Siren Beat).' As you probably guessed, it peaked at number one on the Billboard Hot 100. Next, the album *"BE"* was released. It soon reached number one on the Billboard 200. The title song of this album is 'Life Goes On.' It reached number one on the Billboard Hot 100 as well.

Plus, repeated top hits were produced. In 2020, as said, the single 'Dynamite' made a sensation by topping the Billboard Hot 100 for three weeks in a row. Then in 2021, BTS released the single 'Butter.' It peaked at number one on the Billboard Hot 100 and remained the top hit for ten non-consecutive weeks. It was followed by the release of 'Permission to Dance', which as well peaked at number one on the Billboard Hot 100. To summarize, BTS topped the US Billboard Hot 100 for weeks in a row in the summer of 2021 with 'Butter', and followed it by another second #1 single in their song 'Permission to Dance' that topped the 'Hot 100' the following week displacing only the earlier BTS top hit 'Butter.' This phenomenon is called a 'baton touch' according to Billboard. There have been only three 'baton touches' ever in Billboard's 63-year history: Puff Daddy, Drake, and BTS. In their 'baton touch' year, BTS went on to win the American Billboard Music Awards in 2021. In the same year, they won 'Artist of the Year' at the American Music Awards, the comparable top prize there as well.

The news of the suspension of BTS was announced on June 14, 2022, and fans around the world were in shock. On this day at a candid talk to commemorate the 9th anniversary of their debut, the BTS members honestly talked about their current difficulties and had time to confess to the fans about the 'second act' of BTS. Individual activities are not a true disbandment, and for the time being, they will have time to find their own identity and develop through individual activities rather than group activities. The fact is that BTS would still be together in 2023 except for requirements of universal military service of all Korean males that they should complete before age 30, instead of believing BTS's temporary disbanding is some voluntary time to find their own identity.

An anthology album called 'Proof' was released in the same month of June 2022 despite BTS's temporary pause of activities from June 2022 as some BTS members started their already postponed yet still required Korean military service. The Korean National Assembly has already warped Korean laws to accommodate BTS's global career, passing a law in 2020 just days before Kim Seok-jin's 28th birthday (the oldest BTS member) to create a special loophole for further postponing military service two more years until age 30 in certain situations of participation in the national arts (Blistein, 2020). As postponement of universal male military training in South Korea was unable to be further delayed after age 30, BTS now has a pause of activities from June 2022.

However, this has hardly slowed the other members of BTS, with many of them taking up equally strong individual projects in the interim. Unsurprisingly, the anthology album 'Proof' remained on the US Billboard main album chart, the 'Billboard 200,' for eight weeks in a row. This BTS album also ranked 5th on World Albums, 34th on Top Current Albums, and 53rd on Top Sales Albums. In addition on the full 'Billboard Global 200' chart three songs were listed: 'Dynamite' at 100th, 'Butter at 149th and 'My Universe' at 162nd. On the version of the 'Global' chart excluding the USA, 'Dynamite' was ranked 62nd, 'Butter' as 100th, 'My Universe' as 111th, and 'Yet To Come' as 161st. BTS's management company HYBE stated, "'Dynamite,' 'Butter,' and 'My Universe' have not fallen from the 'Global 200' and

'Global' charts since their announcement and have continued to be successful for a long time."

BTS started their enforced 'second act' very nicely. Their individual potential is being proven in their already successful solo activities even though it has only been a few months since the announcement as of this writing. The performance of BTS solo members continues to be amazing. J-Hope's album 'Jack in the Box,' released on July 15th 2022, is receiving favorable reviews from major media such as *NME* in the UK and *Rolling Stone* in the US. It has created a strong yet different image from his BTS group activities. For his first individual album as an artist, it even ranked 17th on the 'Billboard 200,' 2nd on 'World Album,' 4th on 'Rap Album,' and 5th on 'Top Album Sales' and 'Top Current Album.' The title song 'Banghwa' was ranked 96th on the 'Hot 100.' It even ranked 1st in 'Rap Digital Song Sales' and 'World Digital Song Sales.' It topped the Oricon weekly digital album chart as well. Within weeks of the album release on July 31, 2022, J-Hope performed in the finale of the American music festival 'Lula Falluja,' with a unique hour-long performance in front of 105,000 spectators. J-Hope filled the stage alone.

Plus, Suga and Jungkook also started producing songs separate from BTS. Suga was named as responsible for lyrics, composition, production, and arrangement of the title song 'That That' off the album 'Cheap 9' by Psy, released in April 2022. The song swept to the top of the Korean domestic music charts, and Suga drew attention by revealing a completely different musical color compared to past BTS's songs. In particular, in the case of Jungkook, he recorded 20 million monthly listeners with just two songs released on Spotify online under only the strength of his own name, even without an official album release from HYBE. The two songs are 'Stay Alive,' which is an original sound track (OST) song from BTS's webtoon 'Calling,' and a song named 'Left and Right,' which is a collaboration song with Charlie Puth. Jungkook and Charlie Puth's collaboration song 'Left and Right' soon ranked at 41st on the 'Hot 100,' and it charted for six consecutive weeks at 57th on the main single chart 'Hot 100,' followed by ranking in 'Digital Song Sales' at 28th and ranking in 'Canada Hot 100' at 44th. Jungkook's monthly Spotify listener count is currently the second highest among K-pop singers after BTS itself, and considering historical records, Jungkook by himself set the third record for a Korean at Spotify after BTS and BLACKPINK. It is also the highest number of listeners there for any Korean solo artist.

In addition, BTS's vocalists Jin, Jimin, Jungkook, and V together released 'Bad Decisions' in collaboration with Benny Blanco and Snoop Dogg. They are active as this group in addition to solo work, showing off their equal individual potential on global music charts. As all these individual activities are achieving good results, expectations are high for the synergy that will be achieved through the group activities. For instance, BTS released the 'World Cup Song' in the second half of 2022 at the 2022 FIFA World Cup in Qatar as Hyundai Motors' global ambassadors. In addition, BTS will appear in "&AUDITION - The Howling – ", a reality competition TV program in Japan that will judge who will be sponsored as the best fresh global boy group, that will then be debuted in Japan by HYBE LABELS JAPAN and go on to a wider international debut after that.

Despite being disbanded from June 2022, BTS still was nominated in four categories at the American awards ceremony of the MTV Video Music Awards (MTV VMA), showing a continuing global influence. On July 26, 2022, MTV VMA announced that BTS will be nominated for four performances including 'Best K-Pop,' 'Best Choreography,' 'Best Visual Effect' and 'Best Metaverse Performance' at the 2022 MTV VMA held on August 28th, 2022. There, BTS has been nominated for the categories 'Best K-Pop' and 'Best Choreography' for four years in a row. Plus, BTS was nominated for 'Group of the Year' for four consecutive years there as well.

Plus, in March 2023, Japanese media 'Danmee' conducted a survey of "March's Best Korean Male Celebrities." The Korean dancer, choreographer, and singer in BTS named Jimin won 13,068 out of a total of 27,047 votes in what was called an "overwhelming" vote of 48.3%. The media in Japan argued Jimin's recent solo album named 'FACE', released on March 24, helped explain this large win. Jimin's album 'FACE' has already become the first Korean solo artist ever to sell more than one million copies, and with those more than one million copies sold on the first day of the album release at that. Plus, by April 2023, Jimin has become the first non-Japanese solo singer in the history of 'Billboard Japan' to top the 'Billboard Japan Artist 100' chart (Ban, 2023). Equally in April 2023, BTS's Suga ranked first on Oricon in Japan, after only a few days of the release of his own solo album. It sold more than 110,000 copies in Japan alone and went straight to No. 1 on the Oricon chart. Equally, Suga showed off global popularity by topping the iTunes 'Top Song' chart not only in Japan, but also in 86 countries and regions around the world, including the U.K., Germany and France. Overall Suga's solo album 'D-Day' sold over 1.07 million copies on the first day of release based on the Hanteo Chart, becoming a million-seller at once. BTS's Jimin, a member of the same group, equally had surpassed the record of 1.02 million, which he set with his solo album 'FACE' in the previous month of March 2023 (Yonhap, 2023a). By July 2023, BTS member Jungkook's first solo single called "Seven" was at the top of the iTunes Top Song charts in 106 countries around the world merely one day after release. This included countries like the U.S., the U.K., Canada, Germany, and France. With such a strong performance, Jungkook became "the sixth member of the septet to debut as a soloist, after J-Hope, Jin, RM, Jimin and Suga." Even the mere instrumental versions of the song ranked highly online—sometimes "second and third on the charts in most countries." Jungkook's "Seven" equally found quickly the top spot on Melon, Genie, Bugs and other major Korean charts (Yonhap, 2023b).

Reflecting on BTS's globally stunning scale of popularity nearly a year after their temporary dispersal, the fire of their fame continues to burn. BTS as a group, or currently as a series of solo artists and collaborators, remains one of the world's most attention-grabbing acts of merged musicians, dancers, and artists. Despite temporarily disbanding as the Korean nation and its citizens are finally served more than the Korean economy or global consumers, BTS's members start to be even more popular now as individuals in the hearts and minds of its durable digital fandom.

6.3 Bang Si-Hyuk's Leadership in Leveraging New Technologies

Another major factor of BTS's success is their manager Bang Si-hyuk who recruited and synthesized them together on his preconceived concept in the first place. At the time of the mid-to-late 2010s, Big Hit Entertainment (now renamed HYBE) was a small domestic agency, but it was evaluated as having the ability to foster idols on the level of the three major Korean entertainment companies of SM, YG, and JYP. At the center of HYBE is the composer and producer Bang Si-hyuk, who has a Korean educational degree himself and who learned the music business trade by working in alliance with JYP before 2005. Bang graduated from the topmost ranked university culturally and politically in Korea, Seoul National University. This university fits someone with Bang's skills and fits well into the hierarchical expectations of Korean culture that assumes admiration and leadership should only come from and go to someone vetted already by top institutional credentials. Seoul National University has the most selective entry requirement of any university in Korea. Most graduates of Seoul National University have their life 'made' simply by entry to the school instead of the quality of their work there simply due to the tiny number of people allowed to attend university there versus the multitudes that apply, and because of the ongoing status and alumni networks of their school that goes into national political leadership of all political parties, judgeships on the Korean Supreme Court, famous medical doctors, and more. Bang decided to work with K-pop instead of within these Korean state networks. However, even though Bang is not directly working for the Korean state, by working in the global Korean Wave he is working with the Korean state on the same global project. Plus, the blurred power networks of the Korean state are the alumni of this university, giving an endless 'revolving door' and 'open door' relationship between both.

Koreans have a euphemism for the top three universities of status and power, appropriately calling them the "SKY" universities with the abbreviation standing for Seoul National University (founded 1946), Yonsei University (founded 1885), and Korea University (founded 1905). It really should be known as the "SKYE" universities, by adding to this abbreviation "a silent E" to understand the equal power and prestige of the earliest Western-inspired university in Korea exclusively for women, named Ewha Womans University (founded 1886). Ewha is always placed in this clique of the oldest, wealthiest, largest, most prestigious, and most expensive universities to attend in Korea.

Therefore, with Bang coming from Seoul National University, he comes down from the sky to join in the modern Korean networks of educational power, prestige, and credentialization here on earth. He had the early recognized meritocratic talent to even get into this university in the Korean culture. Bang graduated from the Department of Aesthetics there, one of the very few departments of Aesthetics in Korea nationally. This is because Korea's culture of modern fast-development is far more prone to value degrees in the 'hard sciences' like applied engineering and business instead of the arts and humanities. However, after graduation, Bang in a sense did a reputable 'applied aesthetics' by becoming a K-pop promoter and a visionary synergistic digital entrepreneur. After working with JYP for a few years, he founded his own Big Hit Entertainment in 2005 (now renamed HBYE). Bang's Big Hit Entertainment almost soon went bankrupt in 2007, though he said to have been saved financially by two of his most successfully made groups like '8 Eight' and '2AM.' By 2011, before BTS was formed, Bang was speaking publicly that he felt it was time to have a convergent group that could dance, compose, and play musical instruments all while being wholesome. Soon after, he started to assemble BTS and debuted them in 2013. On the strength of the global financial wealth that the success of BTS has brought his company, Bang is considered now the 16th richest Korean. His approximately $3 billion fortune comes from BTS as well as taking his music management company public in the Korean stock market in October 2020. After that, he became the only K-pop billionaire. Much of his wealth comes from his success at creating and managing BTS, combined with his business sense of how to capitalize and to monetize it in a digital world (Sunio, 2022).

Bang Si-hyuk "planned" BTS as much as produced BTS. This is because he spent much time in artist recruitment from all over the Korean nation, and then spent time in training them, in fan content production strategies, and honing their communication skills with their fans and with the press. Bang first selected rapper Namjoon Kim (RM). Centered on him, Bang discovered and trained seven total members from all over the country, including Suga, Jin, J-Hope, Jimin, Jungkook, and V.

Chairman Bang Si-hyuk emphasized originally that in order to target the global market, there was no chance of winning with mainstream music and culture centered on the U.S. at the beginning, immediately. Therefore, he emphasized the need to strengthen typical Korean lyrics and Korean culture in the songs and dances even while taking on a more global social media approach to their popularity. This Korean cultural theme is clear in many of BTS's hit songs and dances (Park & Kim, 2018). However, many K-pop groups now increasingly blur Korean traditional music, dance, and singing styles into their modern popular music performances, personae, and recordings (Scott, 2022).

Later, Bang developed HYBE's own digital fandom community platform called Weverse. It was originally not a globally-targeted social media platform like YouTube or Instagram, though had to become a global platform, Bang said, simply due to the scale of the global fandom of BTS and how that scale altered the arrangement of global commerce (Bruner, 2019). After the Weverse platform and the Weverse Shop apps were developed by Big Hit's subsidiary beNX, Big Hit was named the fourth most innovative company of 2020 worldwide by *Fast Company.* Chairman Bang also has focused on content diversification strategies by acquiring companies such as Superb, Source Music, Pledis Entertainment, KOZ Entertainment, and Ithaca Holdings. For the historical details, from July 2019, Big Hit Entertainment (as it still had this name) acquired Source Music. By August 2019, Big Hit bought the video game firm Superb. By May 2020, Big Hit became the majority shareholder of Pledis Entertainment, though the label retains independence while its signed artists receive much greater financial support and global promotions from Big Hit (now HYBE). From October 2020 with the success of the first market offering of stock in Big Hit

Entertainment, Bang was flush with cash. First, in November 2020, Big Hit bought KOZ Entertainment, a record label founded by the Korean rapper known as Zico (Woo Ji-hoo). Bang renamed Big Hit Entertainment as HYBE in March 2021, and by April 2021 Bang/HYBE acquired Ithaca Holdings though HYBE's subsidiary Hybe America. Ithaca Holdings is a very large American record label that owns the back catalogues of Justin Bieber and Ariana Grande among others. HYBE paid 1.186 trillion won (approximately US $963 million) for Ithaca Holdings. This was the largest foreign acquisition in the history of the Korean domestic entertainment industry, and the first overseas label acquisition by a Korean company. In 2023, HYBE acquired another American hip hop music label, Quality Control Music, for $300 million, to be kept as well under the subsidiary branch called Hybe America. HYBE continues to grow, in particular via owning Korean game companies like Superb or in alliance with Netmarble—the latter being the top mobile game company in Korea. Bang has refused collaboration so far with foreign game companies to prime Korean content development via a synergy between Korean game companies and Korean music companies.

Bang Si-hyuk's leadership and his innovative synergistic digital marketing strategy for BTS shone even more brightly under pressure of government-forced conditions on entertainment during lockdown from 2020 to 2022. Like all musicians, BTS's planned world concert tour had to be somewhat canceled, but Chairman Bang Si-hyuk took the lockdown as a further digital opportunity. He sold more than 1.75 million tickets for an online concert. He strengthened Big Hit Entertainment/HYBE's online dominance through his social network platform Weverse, which had already been developed in-house by HYBE's subsidiary beNX (later renamed Weverse Company in 2021). Bang has maximized profits by building the Artist Indirect Involvement Business Model and acquired related business fields. While training his K-pop idols, Chairman Bang bought other digital companies to take full synergistic advantage of all kinds of content and marketing opportunities for his newly recruited singers. He diversified into additional businesses that can make money even without singers—in activities such as games, books, characters, license businesses, cosmetics, sporting goods, special editions for smartphones, and distribution, consumer goods, and other content fields. While HYBE now directly operates all business areas surrounding BTS in particular, these many auxiliary profit centers provide an important source of revenue for HYBE overall, aiding and adding to its online business as well. This is important given the earlier lockdown condition and now the temporary suspension of BTS's activities mentioned above.

Bang realized over a decade ago that the development of digital technology and social media had changed the public's cultural consumption, so he focused on and actively utilized the new digital media instead of the legacy media. His use of open media platforms in popularizing HYBE's acts is a good example. HYBE simultaneously targeted domestic and foreign markets through open social media since the formation of BTS. As a result, BTS was able to overcome time and space constraints and form a global fandom from its very first year.

Realizing the effects of platforms like YouTube and Twitter, Chairman Bang sought to transform his entertainment company into a platform company as well.

After BTS became known to the world, Bang started to expand his business based on music and singer contents through his Weverse platform. In order to transform the base of BTS's activities from YouTube and Naver to his independent platform, Bang first introduced Weverse as a "star-fan community platform" in 2019. Instead of uploading BTS performances or music videos on YouTube, Weverse uploads HYBE's own produced video content and produces and sells related products, expanding the platform's influence and HYBE's profits combined. Through Weverse, HYBE distributes and produces the contents of various musicians beyond BTS. Plus, BTS's entertainment programs sent from broadcasting companies are *exclusively* released on Weverse and not on other platforms. After forming the platform Weverse in 2019, by July 2022 it had 40 million subscribers in over 200 countries. The number of different artists using the "star-fan community platform" of Weverse has steadily increased as well. From 2022, 56 groups of Korean domestic artists and foreign artists are active on Weverse including the groups BTS, BLACKPINK, Seventeen, Gracie Abrams, Jeremy Zucker, and the New Hope Club. By the first quarter of 2023, 83 bands or performers were using Weverse. By September 2023, it was announced that 12 more entertainment artists from SM Entertainment will open their official fanbase community on Weverse as well (Lee, 2023). Bang Si-hyuk in 2023 backed out of an attempted buyout of SM Entertainment, by the way, so the relationship between HYBE and SM Entertainment appears now to be one of mutual alliance instead of the past attempt at exclusive control.

Thanks to Weverse, HYBE was able to continue to grow globally and digitally, even when all large physical performances and music events were canceled due to many countries' government lockdowns or policies on forced scale reductions of such events that made them unprofitable to host in the first place. HYBE could continue to grow during these conditions because it made an integrated performance business model that can precede non-stop online through Weverse from payment, viewing, and purchase of related products. By allowing all activities of online performances and meetups to be streamed on Weverse, the platform provided much more convenience and usefulness to BTS fans as well as to the over 90 musical groups now using the open platform Weverse for coordination with their own digital fandoms. In April 2020, when large performances were completely and abruptly canceled by the Korean government or put under non-profitable scale conditions, on June 14, 2020, Weverse/HYBE opened 'Bang Bang Con' for BTS, the name of a concert to be enjoyed in the online room for the first time. It was a huge success with over 2 million fans joining the digital room from around the world. Over two days of performances, the number of views exceeded 50 million, and the number of concurrent users recorded 2.24 million creating a fresh record in the performance industry. An online non-face-to-face concert, once thought difficult to achieve, had by 2020 now been recognized as a representative case of performance industry innovation. It remains a benchmark of the potential of the online non-face-to-face concert format to transcend the smaller scales of past media or even live stadium concerts.

By September 2020, as Korean lockdowns continued, HYBE first established another joint venture with Kisswe, an American live streaming solution company.

Second, then HYBE *launched its own digital live streaming concert service* platform on the market called Venue Live. Third, to help HYBE improve this global platform of Weverse, Korean Naver invested 354.8 billion won ($321 million) in Big Hit's beNX in 2021, acquiring 49% of it. In return, Naver transferred its proprietary 'V Live' video streaming service to beNX to further develop the integrated fan community platform of Weverse. BeNX itself was renamed Weverse Company Inc., after HYBE's deal with Naver. Fourth, HYBE soon introduced another new platform addition via Weverse incorporating Naver's search and artificial intelligence (AI) technology by the first half of 2022. As a result, Weverse as a 'global fandom life platform' will strengthen its fan service now with what is called 'Weverse Live,' which integrates real-time video live service functions of Naver V Live. Weverse Live utilizes V Live's real-time streaming technology to enable artists and fans to communicate with each other, not only through photos and text messages, but also through live videos. The posting function has also been upgraded and allows users to upload photos, GIF images, and videos at the same time. Plus, fitting for a global platform, other Weverse posting functions have been added to give the platform the ability to translate posts into fifteen languages automatically. Another function allows a user to view feeds by filtering posts written in any one of those fifteen selected languages.

A month after the hiatus of BTS was announced in June 2022, HYBE remained busy. HYBE arranged a free live broadcast on Weverse Live of the large American music festival 'LOLLAPALOOZA' held in Chicago that year from July 28 to 31, 2022. Tomorrow X Together (TXT), a boy group affiliated with Big Hit Entertainment since 2019, and BTS member J-Hope participated in this festival. In Korea, it was possible to watch for free the American 'LOLLAPALOOZA' live, through Weverse. At the end of J-Hope's performance there, the number of simultaneously logged in users in the Weverse platform was 15 million. In this way, HYBE surely introduced many other HYBE-managed acts or affiliated artists on the Weverse platform to millions of fresh fans and to many artists of 'LOLLAPALOOZA' in turn as well.

HYBE continues to grow. By December 2021, HYBE announced that it was working with Dunamu, the operator of Upbit, the largest cryptocurrency exchange in Korea, to create a singer IP-based NFT (Non Fungible Token) product—giving artists on its Weverse platform the ability to sell NFTs to their digital fandoms. Given everything mentioned above, the HYBE plan to become the world's leading entertainment lifestyle platform company based on music and related products is gradually coming true.

6.4 Conclusion

The seven-member boy group BTS that debuted in 2013 opened a new era of Korean K-pop by taking the top of world's leading music hit charts by 2021 like the U.S.'s Billboard, the U.K.'s official chart, and Japan's Oricon. BTS raised the status of

K-pop around the world by winning world-class music awards, one after another from its very beginning. BTS greatly expanded the influence of Korean culture while being recognized for their musical achievements on the world stage. The U.S.'s *Time* magazine selected BTS as one of 'the 100 most influential people (sic) in the world in 2019,' and the U.K.'s BBC referred to BTS as 'The Beatles of the twenty-first century.'

Equally, the story of BTS is how an intentional strategy of a global digital fandom was built for years carefully, long before various national lockdowns worldwide. This could prepare BTS for a period of lockdown that brought BTS and their "ARMY" of fans ever closer together, evidenced literally by the largest concerts in world history ever staged (online) with millions in virtual attendance simultaneously.

In BTS's current disbandment, it is requested that agencies work hard to help K-pop idols emerge as world stars in the future following BTS. In fact, HYBE now promotes its five-member Korean boy group Tomorrow X Together (TXT) as a follow-up to BTS. Chairman Bang knows BTS will not last forever, and said in an interview that BTS's success even took himself by surprise in its scale. He feels many factors merged together in a perfect storm to make success of BTS globally—saying himself the factors included luck, their consistency in messaging, their sincerity, their convergent musical, dance, and composing skills, as well as his own intentional desire as their manager to make "Fiske-ian" tangible artifacts that filled a fandom's requirements to belong via products, along with the "trainee system" he designed for becoming a major artist, along with his decision (said to be disliked by much of his company at the time) that BTS from the start in 2013 should have a strong social media presence. Bang's team warned him that a permanent and incessant social media strategy for BTS could backfire if it became a permanent record of the group's youthful scandals and indiscretions. Bang instead presumed future physical album sales or in-person concerts would be less of a profit vehicle in general in a more digital era (Bruner, 2019), so Bang as their manager felt the fresh digital medium of contact might be able to make a strong digital fandom that could make up for those declining kinds of market sales.

These many factors succeeded beyond anyone's wildest dreams for BTS. Plus, nothing else so far in the global Korean Wave seems to approach the talented synergy or the digital fandom of BTS's popularity. Even the currently splintered members of BTS seem grander in the multiple fiery images of their individual successes, just like splitting a single hologram only makes more holograms. All discrete BTS members are doing well on their own separate digital fandoms and projects by 2023—with some even taking their own individual world concert tours in 2023. However, large and small entertainment agencies need to think and to work hard on what would be the expected 'follow up' to BTS to develop content that even may surpass BTS in the future of K-pop.

References

Ali, H. (2021, March 31). ARMY census 'shocking results': How big and diverse is the BTS fanbase? *The Silly TV*. https://www.thesillytv.com/bts-news-army-census-shocking-results-how-big-and-diverse-is-the-bts-fanbase/

Ban, B. (2023, April 10). BTS Jimin, 'FACE' million seller in Japan. 'March's best Korean male celebrity'. *The Viewers*. https://theviewers.co.kr/View.aspx?No=2780704

Blistein, J. (2020, December 1). South Korea passes 'BTS law' allowing K-pop stars to postpone military service; New exemption comes days before the group's oldest member, Kim Seok-Jin, Turns 28, the age able-bodied South Korean men must enlist. *Rolling Stone*. https://www.rollingstone.com/music/music-news/south-korea-bts-law-mandatory-military-service-1096796/

Bruner, R. (2019, October 8). The mastermind behind BTS opens up about making a K-pop juggernaut. *Time*. https://time.com/5681494/bts-bang-si-hyuk-interview/

Duerden, J. (2021, June 29). South Korean Athletes seek Olympic gold to avoid military service. *Nikkei Asia*. https://asia.nikkei.com/Spotlight/Tokyo-2020-Olympics/South-Korean-athletes-seek-Olympic-gold-to-avoid-military-service

Fiske, J. (1992). The cultural economy of fandom. In L. A. Lewis (Ed.), *The adoring audience: Fan culture and popular media*. Routledge.

Hegde, V. (2021, September 22). What is BTS ARMY? How to be a member of one of the biggest fandoms. *Sportskeedia/SK Pop*. https://www.sportskeeda.com/pop-culture/what-bts-army-how-member-one-biggest-fandoms

Jeong, E.-Y. (2020, November 12). Why BTS runs the world. *Wall Street Journal*. https://www.wsj.com/articles/bts-cover-story-interview-be-new-album-dynamite-11605114374

Koreaboo. (2020, March 10). 20+ K-pop Idols who are proud college graduates. *Koreaboo*. https://www.koreaboo.com/lists/20-kpop-idols-proud-college-graduates/

Lee, Y.-a. (2023, May 2). [컨콜] 에스파 이어 아리아나 그란데도?..."위버스, 하반기 美 가수 입점. *TechM*. https://www.techm.kr/news/articleView.html?idxno=109672

National Public Radio. (2022, September 8). How Korean culture went global. *National Public Radio*. https://www.npr.org/transcripts/1121364712

Park, T., & Kim, Y. (2018, September 25). How BTS's embrace of Korean tradition helped them blow up. *Vulture*. https://www.vulture.com/2018/09/how-btss-embrace-of-korean-tradition-helped-them-blow-up.html

Scott, M. (2022, July 3). 6 K-pop songs that feature elements of traditional Korean culture. *KpopStarz*. https://www.kpopstarz.com/articles/307560/20220703/6-kpop-songs-that-feature-elements-of-traditional-korean-culture.htm

Shah, N. (2020, March 6). Seven reasons why South Korea's BTS is an American phenomenon. *Wall Street Journal*. https://www.wsj.com/articles/seven-reasons-why-south-koreas-bts-is-an-american-phenomenon-11583505183

Sunio, P. (2022, April 19). Meet Bang Si-hyuk, the mastermind behind BTS and K-pop's only billionaire: Before forming the biggest boy band in the world, Hybe's founder worked with JYP. *South China Morning Post*. https://www.scmp.com/magazines/style/celebrity/article/3174756/meet-bang-si-hyuk-mastermind-behind-bts-and-k-pops-only

Tan, S. (2019, December 11). 10 K-pop idols who worked hard and graduated with a college degree. *Koreaboo*. https://www.koreaboo.com/lists/kpop-idols-college-degree/

Waldfogel, J. (2007). *The tyranny of the market: Why you can't always get what you want*. Harvard University Press.

Yonhap. (2023a, April 29). Suga ranked first on Oricon in Japan. *Yonhap News*. https://m.yonhapnewstv.co.kr/news/MYH20230429010400038

Yonhap. (2023b, July 15). BTS' Jungkook tops iTunes charts of 106 countries with first solo single 'Seven'. *Korea Herald*. https://m.koreaherald.com/view.php?ud=20230715000106

Chapter 7
Cosmax

The Korean cosmetics industry is very much a powerhouse of global production and innovation. This industry has been helped by the global Korean Wave in popularizing Korean aesthetic standards and beauty products via the visuals and product placements of the Korean Wave. This industry now brands itself as part of the Korean Wave, calling itself "K-Beauty."

However, Cosmax is an interesting case. For a long time, Cosmax (in Korean, 코스맥스) expanded without the aid of the wider Korean Wave as well as expanded *covertly.* This is because the company wanted to avoid the limelight themselves since it was a common global practice for Korean companies like Cosmax to do ODM styles of business (Original Design Manufacturing), in which larger or smaller cosmetics companies outsource their harder market research and chemical/material research in cosmetics or production to companies like Cosmax, with Cosmax thus supporting and building other brands' images behind the scenes instead of stealing their images. This means Cosmax's customers are only businesses. Generally nowadays, Cosmax's customers are already-popular global cosmetic companies or other nations' domestic cosmetic companies that want to avoid awareness in their end-use customers that they only outsource their cosmetics manufacture to a Korean global conglomerate. So, the Korean company Cosmax is a silent partner behind many Chinese, Japanese, Indonesian, and global Western cosmetic brands. This has made Cosmax *the world's largest cosmetics manufacturer*, despite few even hearing of it (Jin, 2018). Cosmax is a global giant in cosmetics market research, development, marketing, and production for many other well-known brands.

Though BTS is the current pinnacle of the *overt* globalization of the Korean Wave, Cosmax has been for decades a pinnacle of the *covert* globalization of Korean material product expertise in the lucrative field of cosmetics research and development. For instance, despite the company being the largest cosmetics manufacturer in the world and despite being founded over 30 years ago in 1992, its CEO Lee Kyung-soo has only given one public interview ever—recently in 2018—and then nothing after that (Jin, 2018). A search online for various journalistic pieces about Cosmax (obviously intentionally by design for over thirty years) turns up very little.

G.-C. Shin and M. D. Whitaker, *The Korean Wave in a Post-Pandemic World*,
https://doi.org/10.1007/978-981-99-3683-0_7

Mostly, first, there are only eye-witness testimonies about how people were treated as they applied to work for the monolithically large and silent Cosmax. These witness testimonies only relate how they were treated very well and discuss the structure of the interviews. Second, Cosmax is made more mysterious by a lack of newspaper curiosity or investigative reporting. The best investigative journalism on Cosmax and the many brands that it manufactures for other cosmetics companies happens to be merely a labor of love by a Reddit poster to "r/AsianBeauty" (PsSignature, 2018). Third, basic financial information is missing in the public domain about such a global conglomerate. Even public profit reporting is spotty, as Reuters reports: "Cosmax's revenue increased 18% last year [in 2017], the slowest growth for the company since 2007, *the last year when data is available* [Italics added]. It has consistently achieved annual growth of more than 20% over the past decade before a diplomatic row between Seoul and Beijing reduced Chinese demand for South Korean cosmetics in 2017. [The CEO of Cosmax] Lee said he expects the company to return to blockbuster growth in the current fiscal year ending in December [2018], with revenue seen rising 38% to 1.8 trillion won" (Jin, 2018). Of course the year 2018, as mentioned earlier, was the first year ever of many "simultaneous successes" in the global Korean Wave.

Lee Kyung-soo might be called the Willy Wonka of global cosmetics. He keeps both himself and his company's secrets intentionally aloof and out of sight despite being a global presence truly painted on faces everywhere worldwide. Lee's own mischievously smiling and leprechaun-like face, after remaining hidden for decades from the media between 1992 and 2018, truly makes it feel like his story of a reclusive cosmetics manufacturer and his global empire of bringing small joys and aesthetic beauty to people worldwide is the long lost companion volume to Roald Dahl's story about an equally reclusive chocolatier doing the same.

Increasingly with globalization of Korean visual aesthetics in the Korean Wave, the trend of Korean styles of cosmetics called "K-Beauty" is rising in purchases worldwide. "K-Beauty" has achieved a Korean trade surplus for ten consecutive years since 2012, which was the "Year of Psy" and "Gangnam Style" as the first truly massive "singular success" of the more global Korean Wave. "K-Beauty" has become so popular globally in the past ten years that exports of Korean cosmetics by 2021 were at 10,509.9 billion won (around $8 billion at 2023 exchange rates) and now are near the revenue scale of exports of Korean home appliances ($8.6 billion dollars), Korean pharmaceuticals ($8.4 billion dollars), and well over the export value of Korean mobile phones ($4.9 billion dollars). By the sheer scale of the Korean cosmetics markets now, covert Cosmax now starts to get pushed into the limelight despite itself, as the overt global Korean Wave encourages many more foreign companies to seek out which companies have greater expertise in "K-Beauty" cosmetics. So, on top of Cosmax's past expertise in global cosmetics ODM, many global or national cosmetics brands now go to Cosmax for alliances in order to enter the Korean market itself, or they seek Korean alliances to design and to produce cosmetics products in their own countries that can profit from the global Korean Wave via their own countries' cosmetics purchasing patterns nowadays as well.

Growing since its founding in 1992, Cosmax has become Korea's leading original design manufacturing (ODM) company for cosmetics along with a recently widening ambit extending to health food products and research for more healthy materials in pharmaceutical products. It competes with only a few other major Korean ODM cosmetics companies like Kolmar Korea (founded in 1990) and Cosmecca (founded in 1999). Starting small in 1992, in the 'brandless' and 'nameless' period of regional Hallyu as discussed in earlier chapters, Cosmax's cosmetics ODM sales have now become the largest in the world. More than 98% of Cosmax's total sales consist of ODM products, and it supplies its self-developed cosmetics *to over 600 domestic and foreign brands*. This includes Cosmax making products for many of the world's famous global cosmetics companies like L'Oreal and similar production relationships with even larger global holding companies that own many dozens of different branded products themselves like Unilever and Johnson & Johnson.

So, Cosmax does not sell products directly to customers ('B2C,' business to consumer), but rather only 'B2B' (business-to-business) is its main business model. Therefore, consumer awareness is low for how extensive a global logistical and creative empire that Cosmax's beauty products have become. Cosmax blends the cosmetic recipes, fills the boxes, fulfills the orders, and does the sales analysis and resulting future market analysis for literally hundreds of other globally or nationally famous cosmetic brand names' products simultaneously. Cosmax even does the market research to invent the advertising image for launching fresh cosmetic brands of products entirely for its company clientele as well. Because of its outstanding corporate competitiveness, and since it is listed on the Korean stock exchange KOSDAQ, it is also a company that attracts international investors' attention. Like the fictional chocolatier Willy Wonka, the real cosmetics manufacturer Lee Kyung-soo wants to remain independent and secretive. Despite discretely nameless companies that CEO Lee said have approached him to buy him out, he refuses to sell out his hard won aesthetic empire to give another single company Cosmax's entire labor expertise, its client base, and its patents now numbering in the hundreds for cosmetic manufacturing (Jin, 2018).

In short, Cosmax has expanded its business not only in Korea but around the world. It now additionally benefits from the growing demand for Korean-style cosmetics in the massive markets of China or the United States—with China being the largest market for Korean cosmetics and the United States being the largest national cosmetics market by revenue. In 2022, Cosmax celebrated its 30th anniversary by recording its highest sales ever, despite lockdown conditions in many countries. To achieve this amazing growth, instead of hiring more specialized human labor like Dahl's Oompa Loompas that had to labor and to live their whole lives in his fictional chocolate factory to keep the recipes secret, in the past several years Cosmax has hired more robots instead. Robots keep better production secrets. In turn, with these robotic investments, Cosmax has become a faster manufacturer, a more digitally global manufacturer, and a robotically-enhanced cosmetics company in its production in the past few years just to try to keep up with its fulfillment orders from hundreds of separate clients in many different national cultural markets, each built from their own distinctive market strategies, products, recipes, techniques, and brand images.

7.1 History and Growth of Cosmax

In the beginning, Lee Kyung-soo was a North Korean refugee at age five. However, he was smart enough to have graduated from Seoul National University in 1970, majoring in pharmacy. Lee then worked for companies like Dong-A Pharmaceutical Company, Oricom (an advertising agency), and then joined Daewoong Pharmaceuticals Company. Equally, Daewoong Pharmaceuticals is the company where Yoon Dong-han was trained and later became Vice President. In 1990, Yoon Dong-han left Daewoong Pharmaceuticals to found what would later become the *second largest* Korean ODM cosmetics manufacturer, Kolmar Korea. Thus, in a case of parallel lives, another Daewoong Pharmaceuticals employee, Lee Kyung-soo, would later leave it as well to found what would later become the now *largest* Korean ODM cosmetics manufacturer, Cosmax, named in 1994.

However, what became Cosmax in 1994 was founded two years earlier in 1992 as Miroto Korea, a slightly different kind of cosmetics company, yet still under CEO Lee Kyung-soo. Back in November 1992, Korean Chairman Lee Kyung-soo (who is still in charge of Cosmax in 2023) signed a technical partnership with Miroto, a Japanese cosmetics OEM company (original equipment manufacturer) in order for him to become head of Miroto Korea. Miroto was seeking to advance into Korea by establishing Miroto Korea. Instead, in retrospect, due to disagreements between CEO Lee and the Japanese management of Miroto, his Miroto Korea would soon become Korean Cosmax instead. It was in the process of establishing Japan's Miroto OEM research institute in Korea for the growth of Japanese cosmetics and technology business in Korea that their Korean Chairman Lee Kyung-soo broke with Miroto due to a difference of opinions. Lee felt that the goal of cosmetics manufacturing by Miroto Korea should be to create their own technologies and innovations in cosmetics, and thus Lee wanted more budget for research and development improvements instead of just following Japanese technical production standards only. Therefore, in January 1994, Chairman Lee Kyung-soo changed his company's name from Miroto Korea to Cosmax, and a new history began.

If Miroto Korea was originally only an OEM company that produced cosmetics parts and equipment manufacturing for one Japanese cosmetics company, the Korean Cosmax would start ODM, original design manufacturing. This made Cosmax a wider company that produces fresh products and fresh machines themselves for manufacturing many other companies' brands. This includes the equipment (OEM) as well as the research and development on improving cosmetics technologies in general. With another irony, this is the same story as the CEO Yoon of Kolmar Korea, another Korean OEM cosmetics manufacturer. Just like Miroto Korea was a joint venture with Japan's Miroto, Kolmar Korea started as another joint venture with Kolmar Japan for Japanese cosmetics technical support. Plus, as already said, both CEO Lee of Cosmax and CEO Yoon of Kolmar Korea were both at Daewoong Pharmaceuticals before venturing out in more entrepreneurial fashion, both first in OEM with a Japanese sponsor and then both generally as well expanding into the wider global ODM cosmetics sector.

Over time, comparatively speaking, Cosmax has made better decisions and avoided bad accidents of its main competitors of Kolmar Korea and Cosmecca. Cosmax has avoided the bad accidents of its Korean competitor Cosmecca like major factory fires or bad luck of a forced relocation of a factory in China that in turn caused its IPO on the stock market to fail originally. Equally, over time, Cosmax has made slightly better decisions that let the company thrive on a slightly larger scale than Kolmar Korea or Cosmecca. Cosmax came to serve a more global cosmetics clientele while Kolmar Korea is more of a Korean service to Korean cosmetics businesses despite some international brands connected to it. Plus, Cosmax was able to maneuver and to grow despite several global economic downturns because of its quite unique business strategies that went against the grain of other cosmetics OEM companies, as discussed below.

In general, global brand cosmetics companies develop their own basic products, with high added value. However, there is a loophole that Cosmax originally exploited very well. Most the color products for global brand cosmetics companies need to be produced in small batches of various types, and they are entrusted to ODMs. Therefore, global brand cosmetics companies do not invest in their own expensive large-scale facilities and equipment for small annual seasonal or faddish batches of color products. They prefer to outsource. Therefore, the color sector became a target market for Cosmax's ODM strategy. In the 1990s, Cosmax benchmarked the business strategy of Intercos, a leading global cosmetics ODM, and accumulated production capabilities focusing on cosmetic color products. By July 1996, a new Cosmax factory was operated at the Hyangnam Pharmaceutical Industrial Complex, and a full-fledged Korean cosmetics ODM business was attempted. Afterwards, Cosmax in turn entered into a technical alliance with ITC, a Japanese manufacturer of hair care products.

Although color sales plummeted during the Asian financial crisis that began at the end of 1997, Cosmax strengthened its development capabilities by trading with many much smaller brand shops. At that time, Cosmax had three policies: freezing the supply price, abolition of the minimum order quantity, and the principle of timely supply even if there was a profit loss. In this way, Cosmax gained the trust of its many business customers. This helped Cosmax weather the Asian financial crisis of that year, and even see its own market share improvement by the late 1990s. As many smaller cosmetics business customers developed trust in Cosmax, they started to ask the company to be their 'one-stop shop' for many other business services beyond production of color products. Therefore, Cosmax and its allied businesses grew together. Accordingly, Cosmax increased its research and development specialization because it was even then working with nearly one hundred different businesses for their cosmetic product development capabilities. Later in 1999, Cosmax entered a second technical alliance with Natera, an American functional cosmetics company in addition to keeping its earlier technical alliance with ITC, the Japanese manufacturer of hair care products.

In recognition of its technological prowess and due to its simultaneous Japanese and American technical alliances in ODM cosmetics markets, Cosmax started to pioneer acquiring other foreign certifications on many other national cosmetics standards. As a result Cosmax held Korea's first GMP certification from the Australian Drug Administration in 2003, Korea's first certification from the only European organic certification body, ECOCERT (Eco Cert), and held Korea's first OHSAS 18001 certification (Occupational Health and Safety Assessment Series, Occupational Health and Safety Management System).

Cosmax echoes a story noted in other chapters: how Korea's whole economy is far more dedicated to an export-led economic development strategy than other countries. So, in order to overcome the inherent national market limitations and demographic smallness of the Korean domestic market, Cosmax used overseas cosmetics events and expositions to raise awareness of itself and its global cosmetics services. Soon, Cosmax concluded a supply contract with the global Western/French cosmetics brand L'Oreal in 2004. Plus, by continuously investing in research and development in making itself a global ODM partner company, Cosmax received the 'Innovation Excellence Award' from L'Oreal—given by L'Oreal to only its best judged partner. By 2012, Cosmax was also listed within the 100 best companies out of 23,000 companies that the L'Oreal Group deals with in its global markets.

In the same year of 2004 as Cosmax was hired by French L'Oreal, Cosmax received approval from the Chinese government to establish Cosmax Shanghai (renamed Cosmax China by 2010) in the comprehensive industrial zone of Shanghai's Pingxiang District, and it started production in the following year. Cosmax provided information on global cosmetic trends to Chinese cosmetic companies that do not have a R&D (research and development) organization or lacked development capabilities of their own. Plus, Cosmax proposed new products tailored to the skin characteristics and cultural desires of the Chinese people. Cosmax even established its own cosmetics research institute in China, and dispatched Korean researchers to teach Chinese researchers how to develop cosmetic technologies, materials, techniques, and processes.

In 2011, Cosmax expanded and reorganized into an R&I (research & innovation) center, as its existing Korean-based cosmetics R&D organizations in Hwasong like its Central Research Center and its Oriental Cosmetics Research Center were moved to Pangyo which is a closer suburb/satellite city of Seoul and a city known as a technology cluster in Korea. This more consolidated Cosmax R&I Center in Pangyo now consists of: a skin care research institute for the development of basic cosmetics seeking various effects such as anti-aging and whitening; a makeup research institute seeking development of innovative makeup ingredients and new formulations in line with changing beauty trends; and an oriental medicine cosmetic research institute seeking to combine nanotech, biotechnology, and oriental medicine materials. At this point by 2011, Cosmax had six different R&D organizations. This massive scale of research and development is hardly odd in Korean ODM cosmetics manufacture. For instance, Kolmar Korea has nine different R&D organizations. Cosmecca only has two since it specializes only in cosmetics instead of many different product lines beyond cosmetics like both Cosmax and Kolmar Korea do. However, by 2021, Cosmax grew to have more R&D organizations than all its main competitors combined—having fifteen different ones.

So from around 2011, as mentioned above, the number of Cosmax's orders started to increase. Then by 2012, the global awareness of the Korean Wave in this "Year of Psy" and "Gangnam Style" started a massive growth and interest in Korean cosmetics worldwide. Thus, it became difficult for Cosmax to manufacture ever larger quantities for its ODM clients given its production facilities of the past being only rental factories. Cosmax's production capacity initially from this time was around 60 million units per year, though by 2014 Cosmax's production scale for its many clients was 150 million units per year. Plus, Cosmax China secured as business customers the first and second largest Chinese companies in China's national consumer cosmetics distribution: the home shopping company ICON and the distribution specialty store CHANDO. By 2014, Cosmax was becoming a cosmetics octopus. The number of its business partners was about 100, yet still at this time 80% to 90% of them were local Korean companies. However, Cosmax's overall sales to cosmetic businesses worldwide were growing astoundingly fast—and faster than Kolmar Korea or Cosmecca. Cosmax's sales moved from an annual 2 billion won (less than $2 million dollars) in 2006 to an astoundingly large 80 billion won (approximately $80 million dollars) *in a mere seven years.* By four years later, in January 2017, Cosmax completed a second factory in Shanghai for itself dedicated to color cosmetics with a manufacturing floor area of approximately 38,000 m^2. A decade later, measuring from 2013 to 2023, Cosmax is over ten times larger still. Its growth continued from sales of $80 million dollars annually in 2013 to sales of *over $1 billion dollars annually* by 2023. Surely the first "singular success" in the global Korean Wave in Psy's popularity from 2012 and then the first "simultaneous successes" of the global Korean Wave from 2018 both made their mark on all Korean cosmetic markets growing after 2012 and then after 2018. Given Cosmax's scale now, there has been growing desire for Korean cosmetics' manufacturing products and expertise worldwide when we consider Cosmax's almost exponentially growing annual sales measured from 2006 ($2 million), to 2013 ($80 million), to the present in 2023 (at over $1 billion dollars).

Cosmax did not stop at China, but further accelerated its overseas market penetration based on its long trusting relationship with L'Oreal since 2004. In 2013, Cosmax was trusted to take over multiple L'Oreal's factories in Indonesia and the United States. Both factories were where the L'Oreal Group made their main hair care products. This built an international production base for Cosmax as well, that could now additionally directly target the wider Southeast Asian and American ODM cosmetics markets, simultaneously. As Cosmax aimed to become more of a global cosmetics ODM company, it was natural to advance to the USA, as the country was then and remains by 2022 the world's largest cosmetics consumer. As Cosmax took over the American factory operated by L'Oreal in 2013, it expanded the consumer choices of color lines (Cosmax's strength) in a wider selection of products like powder and lipstick. By 2022, Cosmax established additional bases in French and Brazilian markets by respectively establishing fresh R&I centers in Europe and in the South American continent, truly establishing itself as a global cosmetics ODM company upon which the sun never sets.

7.2 Lockdown as an Opportunity

However back in 1997–1998, Cosmax suffered great difficulties in the earlier Asian financial crisis. This was a situation in which its major customers had withdrawn from the cosmetics business altogether in the economic downturn. At the time, Cosmax's competitor Taewoong Cosmetics nearly went bankrupt, and after the Asian financial crisis it changed its name to Cosmecca in 1999. Kolmar Korea itself rose only after this crisis time by inventing by the early 2000s high quality "BB creams" ('blemish base' for uniform skin color) with multiple functions of foundation, moisturizer, and sunscreen all at once.

At the time, Cosmax's sales fell by more than 50% by 1998. To overcome that crisis, as said earlier, Cosmax froze supply prices despite cost increases and several other policies just to keep trust in its supply chain and its company alliances. Plus, by the early 2000s, another strategy for expanding Cosmax products was decided upon that went against past cosmetics ODM and OEM practice, though Cosmax excelled brilliantly in it regardless. *Cosmax decided to supply ODM services to hundreds of rapidly growing yet innately small profit single brand shops.* At that time, brand shops were low-cost cosmetics that dealt with consumers at prices below 10,000 won ($10 dollars). In this situation, only small and medium-sized OEMs normally had agreed to supply their products to these brand shops, but large OEMs like Cosmax historically were reluctant to do business with the many tiny markets of these brand shops. However, Cosmax became the only large OEM that did increase sales with smaller brand shops. Plus, Cosmax strengthened its research and development services and capabilities for many smaller brand shops, even at the same time as it started to work for global brands like L'Oreal by 2004.

Similar to the business liquidity crisis of the Asian financial collapse of 1997, in the increasingly global economic downturn from 2020 to 2023 created by many nations' lockdowns, Cosmax responded quickly and proactively. This was despite shocking changes in markets and social life from government-imposed lockdowns in many countries from 2020 to 2023. Just as in the financial crisis of the late 1990s, between 2020 and 2022 Cosmax grew and expanded its markets instead of collapsed. There are five ways that Cosmax effectively overcame market crisis under lockdowns after 2020.

First, Cosmax did everything possible to keep its factories open by agreeing to the Korean government's imposed distance and quarantine measures, and Cosmax was even was forced to shrink the number of people attending various meetings or otherwise had to agree to delay events where many people were required in attendance. The CEOs of all affiliates met weekly on various issues regarding these rules. Plus, Cosmax established an inspection system to prevent any situations such as breakdowns in its supply chain of raw and subsidiary materials from other countries or a mere shortage of inventory in its supply chain. In particular, managers checked logistics trends of overseas customers and exporting countries in advance, and checked the status of raw material and subsidiary material suppliers by country every week. As a result, Cosmax established a global system in which their business activities were sustainable even under many different national statuses of lockdown conditions that would have wrecked international supply chains for many other companies. Plus, Cosmax researched the discovery of alternative raw materials or subsidiary materials, and it secured raw materials by increasing more 'in-house' developed raw materials. Through this diversification of raw material suppliers, Cosmax could establish a more stable product development system than many of its ODM competitors.

Second, the proportion of Cosmax's digital and online channel customers increased significantly from 2020. After many countries' lockdowns forcibly closed shops, global cosmetics markets and their contribution to e-commerce *both increased* instead of both declining. For example, in 2019, the global cosmetics market grew by 5%, yet the e-commerce channel grew by 27%. In the first half of 2020, the global cosmetics market still grew by 13%, though the e-commerce channel grew by 33% during the same period. Many countries' lockdowns accelerated this digital transformation of the cosmetics industry that had already begun earlier than 2020. In line with this, Cosmax developed a customized prescription inventory for each online channel. Plus, a unique idea of "online-only products" was launched like 3D gradation blushers, ceramide nail essences, and emulsion lipsticks. In addition, business customer participation activities were strengthened through SNS and the "By Me Project," discussed later.

In general, when offline and in-person businesses of mid-to-large brands of cosmetics enter the online market to seek out the same or more customers, these businesses regularly have to respond to a more rapidly changing online market in product popularity and style changes than these businesses would ever experience in their in-person stores. Thus, 'offline' cosmetics businesses moving 'online' have to shorten the development period for new products because they have to be more attuned to small changes in their online markets. In the Chinese online market for example, Cosmax did this by strengthening sales to Chinese online-specialized brands in line with the rapidly changing characteristics of online sales channels. Cosmax could do this well based on its already outstanding technology and R&D capabilities that even more rapidly started to develop fresh online products that could more quickly follow the changing desires of Chinese customers.

Third, Cosmax responded by increasing its market share in China—both through online channels and by more focus on the large Chinese market. This market was allowed by the Chinese government to end its lockdown relatively quickly in 2020 even while at this point much of the rest of the world's nations descended into their own Chinese-inspired government lockdowns of various severities. Thus, seeing an opening, Cosmax developed and launched more Chinese market-centered products after selecting one strategic product category that could increase sales in consideration of the market situation in China. This was its traditional expertise in the color category. So, by 2021, Cosmax's China-based color category sales recorded a huge 49% increase in year-on-year profits from 2020–2021, compared to 2019–2020. Strategic products were selected for cosmetic basics (like essence and cleansing) and cosmetic color tones (like lip and base). These were intensively developed as new products to propose to Cosmax's business customers. As a result, the overall growth rate of Cosmax's strategic products in 2021 achieved a 42% market share.

In particular, as sales of lip tint products rapidly increased in China, Cosmax established a strategy to penetrate the Chinese market with its own manufactured lip tints for Chinese companies. Unlike solid lipstick, lip tint is a thin liquid lip makeup that gives vivid color to the lips. In 2020, the cumulative production of a single lip tint product in Cosmax's Chinese subsidiary was about 80 million units. This was an increase of about 80% for one year, so the strategy of selling only after tailoring to existing trends of Chinese consumers was right. Plus, all of this information is taken as evidence of the hypothesis mentioned in earlier chapters about the innately greater and faster collective innovation in crisis that tends to come from more homogeneous cultures like Korea, while more heterogeneous cultures tend to fall apart in crisis.

Fourth, Cosmax researched and then manufactured products that *tried to make a market out of the adversity* of many countries' pushed masking policies. In the case of skin care products, cosmetics were reformulated to solve bad skin problems caused by wearing a mask overly long on now more humid faces that had applied cosmetic products under the mask. In 2020, Cosmax began to sell its 'SensiFilter', a system that develops cosmetics products specialized for people with sensitive skin. The system combined recommendations about particular raw materials of cosmetics, specific formulations, and follow-up care. Second, Cosmax became the first company in the Korean cosmetic manufacturing industry to develop and apply QSAR (Quantitative Structure Activity Relationships), which predicts not only specific personal allergies but also toxicity by analyzing the similar or different physical and chemical structures of different raw materials.

Fifth, Cosmax focused on eye makeup cosmetics in the color category, even though global demand had declined due to less in-person behavior due to many nations' polices of state-mandated lockdowns or social distancing. To try to arrest the declining sales trends in its eye cosmetics, Cosmax strengthened overall capabilities for some of its business customers (like Rom and 3CE, etc.) *by offering them products with a wider palette* of eye shadow colors to tempt consumers back into the eye cosmetics market. Furthermore, Cosmax developed a stick-type 'multi-balm' for the hypochondriac 'worried well' like 'untact' care products that do not directly touch the skin of the customer upon application—like Gahi's multi-balm. Any existing 'multi-balm' formulation was framed with fresh advertising using the keyword 'hands-free' to use hypochondriac fear as a priming tool to sell products in the "untact care market" from 2020 and beyond—once more trying to make a market out of the adversity.

7.3 Cosmax's Success Factors

Next, in analyzing the global growth of Cosmax, we find six main internal success factors. These can be summarized as: (1) reinforcement of its research capabilities and global intellectual property, (2) more efficient management advances through a digital transformation, (3) further globalization of its cosmetics markets, (4) strengthening its consumers' accessibility by expanding an Original Brand Manufacturing (OBM) business instead of only having its original ODM business model, (5) collaboration with subcontractors and outsourcing companies, and finally, (6) the further expansion of its already established online global digital business dominance. Based on these six changes that began after 2020, Cosmax started a new paradigm in the beauty industry by establishing a platform-based online sales ecosystem that connected global customers and end-users in the cosmetic market. Actually, a seventh external success factor is the icing on the cake, to be mentioned more in the conclusion. This is the growing popularity of the aesthetics of "K-Beauty" as a theme in the visuals of the global Korean Wave. It has encouraged more international companies in cosmetics to seek out alliances with Cosmax as it is already the premier ODM provider in Korean cosmetics as well.

7.3.1 Reinforcement of Research Capacity and Global Intellectual Property

In the first success factor, Cosmax shows the same theme mentioned in the chapters on BTS or on Netflix's *Squid Game*. This is how a reliance on and a participation within a global market innately creates capacities for profits and easier rents from owning exclusive global intellectual property empires. This is regardless of whether Korean-based global empires in intellectual property are in digital entertainment media as seen in the Korean entertainment management company HYBE that manages BTS, or as seen in Cosmax's equally Korean-based global empire of intellectual property that controls hundreds of patents for cosmetics technologies and proprietary raw materials. Cosmax has a financial capacity to make fresh patents annually as more intellectual property out of its large budget for research and development. Cosmax equally has the finances to buy and to consolidate other companies' patents into itself via the holding company of Cosmax named Cosmax BTI.

To elaborate this theme of global intellectual property empires in cosmetics, one major factor in Cosmax's success from the very beginning has been the interaction of its large research focus (recognizing the importance before others in owning and inventing innovative technology) and establishing its own research and training institutes around its proprietary technology and patents. About 25% of Cosmax's total workforce is personnel involved in research and development for future products, instead of in the daily tasks of manufacturing, blending raw cosmetic materials into products, or market trend research. This large capacity for research and development plays an important role in making Cosmax stand out both in Korea and in the global market. Related to this large capacity for funding research and development for themselves, as well as in service to hundreds of other companies that pay for such a service, what has developed is a global intellectual property empire in cosmetics. However, it has the least patents in the cosmetic industry, yet files more globally by percentage, and achieved 10 more patents in early 2022 alone. As of 2023, Cosmax has a total of 473 patent filings globally, out of which 186 have been granted. The largest amount at 162 of these patent filings were domestic to Korea. Kolmar Korea has the most cosmetics patents with over 1,287 patents globally, out of which 1,068 have been granted. Kolmar Korea has the largest number at 927 patent filings domestic to Korea. Cosmecca has 289 patents globally, out of which 193 have been granted. Cosmecca's largest number of 214 patent filings were domestic to Korea. Together, all three of these cosmetics conglomerates encourage Korean-centric global intellectual property empires in cosmetics regardless of which one profits (GreyB, 2023a, 2023b, 2023c).

Cosmax continues to expand its ability to create intellectual property empires through research and development for fresh cosmetic products and formulations. It has been developing products through regular overseas market research and joint research with local research institutes of its own subsidiaries in China, the United States, and Indonesia. Cosmax Group plans to maintain and even strengthen its competency in research and development to further enhance its global competitiveness. To this end, Cosmax's research organizations were significantly reorganized at the end of 2021. The Cosmax R&I Center, which already operated fifteen separate cosmetics research laboratories by that year, was streamlined into three main groups of research institutes for skin care, makeup, and site reliability engineering (SRE, meaning, using software to automate factory operations). This gives these fifteen laboratories a more coordinated upper division and team-based goal. Plus, each of these fifteen research institutes appoints a separate research director to catalyze convergence in specialized technologies for cosmetics manufacture.

Plus, even the wider Cosmax holding company of Cosmax BTI is preparing for future growth engines by already operating its own separate research and innovation center for more original technology development and more material development. The Cosmax BTI R&I Center recently added a synergy for its own four separate cosmetics research laboratories by establishing a fifth "bioconvergence research institute." With leadership at the Cosmax Digital Business Headquarters, the additional 'CAI Lab' ('Cosmax AI' Lab) was upgraded to a research center to accelerate securing future growth engines. In addition, Cosmax BTI plans to focus on developing innovative technologies through open innovation with others, like expanding collaborative research with Seoul National University and other domestic Korean universities. Plus, they decided to build a digital platform to advertise Cosmax's unique innovative materials including using the microbiome, and they actively promote development of more proprietary raw materials in collaboration with global raw material companies.

Recently, as the cosmetics and dry food markets around the world have been rapidly reorganized towards consumers in 'micro-brands' and 'brand shops' as influenced by our changing media regime, the market for cosmetics now has many more differentiated ideas and concepts for cosmetics manufacture. Cosmax Group expects that the ODM industry will continue to grow rapidly as barriers to market entry are lowered for smaller cosmetics businesses, like the ones that they have worked with for years. In the related dry food business sector, the number of individually recognized raw materials that have known parallel cosmetics uses is increasing. This enhances competitiveness and cheapness for Cosmax's material sourcing. Cosmax Group itself has so far independently developed four individually recognized materials including chazugi (red sesame leaf) extract, a functional ingredient for improving eye fatigue. Recently, it has obtained intellectual property for a complex around rosemary extract, since the spice rosemary has been recognized for its parallel cosmetics uses for how it can help maintain skin health from aging or damage by ultraviolet light from the sun.

Cosmax also has made efforts to make itself now a public 'brand' around its technological innovations and intellectual property empire, stepping out of the shadows behind the giants of the business of cosmetics that Cosmax has helped for decades in creating their products for them. Specifically, Cosmax now tries to convey its own unique technological prowess with its business buyers and its own unique ability to have far more tailored guidance for beauty technology in each sub-area of cosmetics manufacture such as skin care, sun care, and makeup.

7.3.2 Management Advancement Through Digital Transformation

Like BTS's management agency HYBE mentioned in the previous chapter, Cosmax has paid attention to its own digital transformation to create wider global markets for its services. Cosmax now has started to target online customers and an increasingly personalized cosmetics market combined. By expanding its 'electronic research notebook,' newly introduced in 2021, Cosmax attempts to accumulate more research assets like digital 'big data' of consumers for smarter research and innovation. Based on cosmetic 'big data,' Cosmax has a process under development for personalized cosmetics selection which can fulfill the growing global market and media trends for more individually-customized products ranging from cosmetics to medical interventions. This is being done by applying AI (artificial intelligence) to the big data patterns of consumers' co-toxicities and co-allergies to use in future research and utilization recommendations to create individually-tailored cosmetic prescriptions that are healthier to a specific consumer.

In addition, the establishment of more digital and robotic 'smart factories' was a key task for Cosmax under government-imposed lockdown rules and 'social distancing' in 2022. In order to flexibly and profitably respond to its historic alliances with many cosmetic business customers in the brand shops for their small-volume and cheaply-priced production, Cosmax started to automate cosmetic production processes that previously took a lot of labor time like molding, assembly, and packaging. Instead, Cosmax will intensively train its labor to operate industrial production robots and to work alongside more robots on its factory floors. As mentioned in Appendix 1, one of the 'world firsts' of South Korea is that the whole country already has the world's highest per capita use of robots in factory production, with over two times more robotic scale in production nationally than the also-ran competitors of Germany or Japan. Cosmax itself purchased a growing number of industrial robots in the past few years, owning 134 in 2018, 193 in 2019, and 205 in 2020. By using robots for dangerous or repetitive tasks, the safety of employees from repetitive strain injuries or from robot-caused injury can also be secured if labor and robots are well trained to avoid each other. Therefore, the use of robots in the right place can further increase productivity for Cosmax and make labor available for more creative endeavors.

In addition to the hardware of robots, Cosmax even is introducing a Robotic Process Automation (RPA) system, additionally known as 'software robotics,' to respond to the increasing demand for cosmetics. RPA applications watch and learn how people manage and interface with digital platforms of management in a production process over time, and then automate what it can about that human management. Cosmax's goal is to establish and analyze the data-based environment, establish a control production system, and build a production system using big data by 2024. This RPA system is intended to improve productivity while expanding the automation of tasks so that it can respond to a wide range of tasks in various fields. Efficient management of human resources and robots together in a matrix allows for greater flexibility and speed in meeting customer needs and overall business stability.

In addition, Cosmax plans to install a digital remote control system for all its manufacturing facilities worldwide and equip every one of its factories worldwide with a factory energy management system (FEMS), to reduce costs and make more efficient and conserved energy use. Plus in the business sector, a digital workflow management system using the cloud has been introduced to increase efficiency of information transfers between Cosmax's many institutes and production sites worldwide. In addition, this digital management infrastructure will be expanded by building a 'data lake' to accommodate and share the same big data across Cosmax's various R&D institutes—the fifteen institutes already established under Cosmax itself and the additional four separately managed by Cosmax BTI. All of these changes will support smooth inter-departmental collaboration and expand the potential of more centralized monitoring of factory statistics and control of robotic automation.

The future trend of the cosmetic market is to provide more personalized products to individual consumers. The market changes toward greater individuation are partially brought about by media regime changes, particularly the Internet and the billions of distributed smartphones connected to it in the same global network that gives the ongoing 'big data' from which such greater individualization can be approached by businesses. This gives global consumers and Cosmax a global e-commerce that never sleeps and which requires a speedy response to orders from around the world, daily and unpredictably, large or small. In particular, in order to respond to influencer marketing using SNS, the key is whether consumers can get the right product they want quickly and at the right price in their corner of the world. In this case, there is a way to solve this logistics problem by introducing AI so that there is less error in either legal issues or product stability per order to a wide variety of countries. In addition, Cosmax is planning to use big data for new product development in customized cosmetics, aided in its recommendations by the big data of an AI platform.

Therefore, Cosmax plans to lead the cosmetics industry by building both a deep personalization into cosmetic sales at the same time as building a larger customized smart factory with robotic production and RPA to make it cost effective and more logistically possible. In short, Cosmax aims to establish a sustainable competitive advantage by establishing a supply chain that can deliver products from smart factories that can make lines of products that range from small-scale production to mass production by more robotic factories that can handle added logistical problems of an increasingly personally-tailored and small lot-size cosmetic market.

7.3.3 Globalization of Cosmetic Markets

After its inception in 1992, Cosmax increasingly tried to emphasize more overseas markets than its original domestic Korean markets. To this end, Cosmax has for a long time supplied products to cosmetic businesses in many other countries, a specialization that other Korean domestic ODM cosmetics companies like Kolmar Korea or Cosmecca rarely do at the high scale of Cosmax even though these latter two do have their own international business alliances as well. Cosmax has supplied products to global luxury companies, local Chinese companies, and many discrete companies specializing in either the Southeast Asian markets, or the wider zone of East Asian markets, or even in North and South American markets.

First, to focus on the large markets of China, originally, Cosmax China was established in Shanghai in 2004. Later, Cosmax Guangzhou was established in 2013. The main purpose of most global cosmetics companies that are Original Equipment Manufacturers (OEMs) or Original Design Manufacturers (ODMs) in entering China is production for cheaper global exports. On the other hand, Cosmax focused inward on the massive Chinese domestic market itself, aiming for wider OEM/ODM business development and market expansion for local Chinese branded companies. Cosmax decided to enter the Chinese domestic market like this as the Chinese economy was growing rapidly in the first decade of the twenty-first century. Equally in 2013, as Cosmax established Cosmax Guangzhou, that was the same year that Cosmax was allowed to take over production and quality control at L'Oreal factories in both Indonesia and the United States.

Since 2019, in line with the progress of e-commerce, Cosmax focused more on discovering new global customers through online tools. As a result, more companies like Cosmax are doing business with online channels and indie brands like expanding business with Perfect Diary (完美日記), China's top online brand. Cosmax's high growth in the Chinese market is due to the continued strong demand for cosmetics, the high recognition of Cosmax in the country among Chinese businesses, and its proprietary high technology empire for cosmetics manufacture. In line with the online beauty market in China, a 'multi-variety small-volume production system' was introduced. It gained high trust by strengthening the other OBM (Original Brand Manufacturing) service that it provides, under which Cosmax develops even the brand itself for another company. In this way, Cosmax even invents the market *visibility and presence* of the other company's products that it is already making and selling for them anyway. Through OBM, Cosmax invents other companies' whole cosmetic lines to a degree that other company's brands start at ideas and ways Cosmax can launder its innovative skills by providing novel brands, their material production, and their marketing strategies and ongoing sales analysis in one package. In particular, in the online cosmetics market where product cycles are faster than offline, the ability quickly to respond to e-commerce trends in the huge Chinese market was shortened. Now the waiting time for Cosmax to turn a business's idea of a product request into a real market product can take place in as little as 5 months to 2–3 months.

Second, Cosmax actively is developing its business outside of China. An Indonesian subsidiary was established in 2011, given Indonesia is the fourth most populous country in the world, and given it is in the wider region of Southeast Asia with its high growth potential. Plus, Cosmax acquired Islamic food halal certification in order to develop products exclusively for the Islamic market, a major religious faith of a sizable portion of the religiously pluralistic Indonesia. In 2017, Cosmax entered Thailand and from that base concentrates on expanding production into other Southeast Asian markets.

By January 2022, coming full circle from its origins and in reverse, a Cosmax branch was established in Japan. Construction is scheduled to begin for a factory near Tokyo in the first half of 2023. Full Cosmax services and production operations are planned in Japan by 2025. This inverts what happened in the beginning of Cosmax's history from 1992, when a Japanese OEM cosmetics company Miroto set up a subsidiary arrangement in Korea that would soon become Cosmax after its CEO Lee disagreed with only being a branch of the Japanese company per se. Now, thirty years later, the Korean Cosmax sets up its own subsidiary in Japan. Cosmax plans to promote the ODM business in Japan for global cosmetics businesses wanting to enter the Japanese markets as well as for Japanese companies wanting to enter Korean markets. Plus, the demand for Korean-style cosmetics in Japan now increases with the popularity of the global Korean Wave of entertainment, therefore even many Korean cosmetic brands want to enter and profit from this Japanese-based market for the Korean Wave as well. Therefore, it is expected Cosmax will help these three very different kinds of OEM business markets enter Japan. Particularly, multiple Korean companies want to enter the Japanese markets with Cosmax's advice and production there, as well as conversely, while Cosmax provides the same services and products to help Japanese cosmetic businesses find customers in Korean markets.

In the United States, another local Cosmax corporation was established in 2013 named Cosmax USA. By 2016, Cosmax USA's factory was capable of producing 100 million units per year. In 2017, Cosmax purchased Nu-world, a separate cosmetic OEM company specializing in facial makeup. Cosmax USA even is increasing productivity and strengthening customer service by coordinating production between its two factories in Ohio and New Jersey. As the cosmetics market is not yet booming for Cosmax in the United States as a market, Cosmax aims to expand its market services to cosmetics companies across all of North America, which boasts the largest market size in the world, and to South America.

In short, Cosmax has established global production bases in China (in Shanghai and Guangzhou), Southeast Asia (Thailand and Indonesia), and the United States (Ohio and New Jersey), and continues simultaneously to develop cosmetic products that meet many different local, national, and cultural markets by entering Japan, France, and Brazil. Thus, Cosmax seems to be continuously expanding its ambit, which should not be surprising for the world's largest Korean-based yet truly global cosmetics ODM company.

7.3.4 Strengthen Consumer Accessibility by Expanding OBM Business

Cosmax has delivered new values to customers through an added Original Brand Manufacturing (OBM) business model. This provides a total solution for another brand: from brand development, to product production, to marketing. So, by adding to Cosmax's already strong ODM model, its OBM model was created to help other countries and companies create their own fresh brands instead of Cosmax only providing outsourced products and market research for pre-established brands. So, this added OBM business model can be said to be a business method that researches their "customer's customers," that is, the final consumer, via local market research to develop the most successful ODM-based products, while doing an overall OBM product that develops the fresh brand and its whole fresh lines of products. So as an ODM and now an OBM provider, Cosmax is promoted in its own original ODM market even more when its own OBM services are used by other cosmetics businesses.

Recently, Cosmax built an online portal named Cosmax Plus to sell this additional OBM model to other companies worldwide. On the platform, it is possible to request both Cosmax's original ODM (Original Development Manufacturing) product development as well as their fresh OBM (Original Brand Manufacturing) brand development. Any future business partner can browse the Cosmax OBM portal to verify Cosmax's patents, exclusive raw materials, formulations, subsidiary materials, as well as free information about global beauty market trends and consumer trends. Cosmax Plus also provides useful information like cosmetics development guides and system certification information explaining how new businesses more easily can access the cosmetics market. Via Cosmax Plus, future business partners of Cosmax can submit a request form and start their product planning with 700 Cosmax researchers around the world. Plus, another online tool called the "By Me Project" will also be expanded, as it is tailored to appeal directly to the younger more digital "Millennials and Generation Z" (MZ generation) to participate in the development of their own cosmetics if they want to create a new brand. Cosmax in this way will accumulate many more of its own dependent 'locked in' brands created through the "By Me Project" widening its OBM network. Appealing to the younger demographic of business entrepreneurs in the MZ generation, Cosmax even plans to operate a digital showroom using the metaverse.

7.3.5 *Collaboration with Subcontractors and Outsourcing Companies*

ODM companies develop by building and securing capabilities and innovation in management and technology. In order to make up for any technical elements lacking, Cosmax has created technical alliances with various companies to expand any of its deficient capabilities. With such technical alliances, Cosmax has developed innovative new products such as gel-type eyeliner, CC cream, and cushion foundation as requested by global luxury brands. As these became a large product line, it proved Cosmax's ability to create alliances of technological prowess in the global market.

A representative example of a successful customer partnership is the long relationship between Cosmax and L'Oreal. After two years of preparation in the late 2000s, Cosmax was finally able to meet the strict quality and purchasing conditions of L'Oreal, a global cosmetics company. The deeper partnership between Cosmax and L'Oreal started as a Maybelline-branded product in 2010. Since then, the technical alliance has created many market success stories over the past decade that contributed to the growth of both companies. Currently, Cosmax is maintaining a close partnership with several of the world's leading global cosmetics companies such as L'Oreal, Johnson & Johnson, Unilever, and Perfect Diary—the latter of which is rapidly growing in the Chinese online cosmetics market. Chairman Lee Kyung-soo recently said, "Competitors are meaningless. Now, there are only partners," emphasizing the win–win partnership relationship with its customers, and yet an oligarchic attitude against competitive markets that comes out of default from its currently untouchable globalized services and its globalized intellectual property empire in cosmetics. There is literally nothing in the world at the scale of Cosmax in the global cosmetic market.

Along with these global customer partnerships, Cosmax operates a Global Account Management (GAM) organization that can more efficiently support orders and promotions of global customers such as L'Oreal through close collaboration between overseas subsidiaries and specific factories spread around the world. Through this, Cosmax supports joint development and production of customized cosmetics for each country or market and reduces its global transport costs of products as well. These product lines can be tailored to the local situation and give Cosmax's allies several global sites of production to choose from flexibly. These activities ultimately drive the growth of both Cosmax and their allied global customers.

7.3.6 *Expansion of Online Business Dominance*

Unlike the past, channels of product awareness and distribution have changed rapidly due to our fresh digitally distributed media regime. (See Appendix 4). Older cosmetics businesses require adapting to the past's organizational mismatch of sales and marketing that has been created by this media change. All cosmetics businesses seek fresh digital opportunities for global markets, and want to learn how to enhance their market intelligence by the digital convergence possible in merging both on-and-offline consumer data and mobile phone data. In order to effectively respond to these market changes, and to keep leading in global digital markets, Cosmax has made many different efforts to become more digital in its services. In particular, Cosmax is developing products and brands suitable for the 'influencer'-driven online social media, and for other internet distribution channels as well. This is because most young consumers, represented by Millennials and Generation Z, use online commerce instead of offline commerce as their core purchasing and information route. In turn, the cosmetics trend is how the market is also changing, from being symbolized by a large corporate offline and mass market brand to a more online and personalized beauty brand. Though the importance of online distribution was growing before 2020, once non-face-to-face consumption forcibly was spread mainly due to many governments' policies worldwide about lockdowns between 2020 and early 2023, OBM/ODM for more online influencers and more online customers were required to survive in cosmetics markets.

In the cosmetics market, fresh online distribution channels are rapidly growing and even dominating. They generate sales and purchases through live broadcasts by individuals or social media influencers on their social media channels. This invention of markets via positive or negative reviews by social media influencers can reach millions of people. Thus, it has created a new distribution channel called 'social media commerce' or 'live commerce.' Companies directly advertise and sell their products via social media when those companies ship free products to these 'influencers' in hopes that they will review the product favorably on their channel for free whether on Facebook, Instagram, or YouTube.

Cosmetics ODM companies such as Cosmax now play a large part even in growth of this social media commerce. As such, Cosmax cooperates with online cosmetics brands in China. This is because online cosmetics brands have grown rapidly in China due to the very popular trend in China of that country's social media influencers, particularly the 'beauty influencers' on Chinese social media platforms like WeChat and Weibo that can influence hearts and minds of hundreds of millions of consumers in China, digitally. In particular, Cosmax strengthened its OBM business for exclusively online distribution to customers in China by securing as one of its Chinese customers the top online-only brand rapidly growing in China named 'Perfect Diary.'

7.4 Conclusion and the Growing Global Empire in 'K-Beauty'

Cosmax is now a combined ODM and OBM cosmetics company. It grew originally by proposing a product developed by itself to its business customers, and then producing and supplying it on demand to those businesses whenever an order was received, and later by developing the whole idea of a fresh brand for a business client. Cosmax grew as well by its early moves in getting multiple nations' various cosmetics and organic certifications. It additionally grew by successfully anticipating trends in cosmetic markets, and being trusted enough to take over existing production and quality control for major global brands. After 1997, Cosmax moved into global production simultaneously for many smaller regional brand stores and across separate 'incompatible' national beauty cultures. Thus, the company has a great array of alliances ranging from global brands of cosmetics that rely on Cosmax for much of their research and development, to small-scale beauty shops of more economical products that equally rely on Cosmax. In doing the latter, Cosmax broke an ODM industry trend of cosmetics manufacture in only big lots, and thus had to learn to be efficient enough to profit from the production, research, and development of many small lots of sales, and then had to learn how to profit from and reorganize for the more rapidly changing online markets of faster production of lots, whether large or small. Historically, smaller cosmetic brands were triaged against by larger global ODM companies until Cosmax came after 1997 to pioneer this kind of business relationship in a major ODM cosmetics company as well.

Thus, Cosmax provides industry-leading R&D capabilities, production, and quality management systems that meet global standards for even smaller companies, providing even smaller brands a global production and research infrastructure in cosmetics that they would otherwise entirely lack. In total, Cosmax now operates around twenty cosmetics and technology research organizations, when the research organizations under its holding company Cosmax BTI are included. It has nearly 200 patents on intellectual property around cosmetics and many different international certifications around quality management, environmental management, and international standard certifications for cosmetics, including certifications for national cosmetics standards set by the U.S. Food and Drug Administration (FDA) and Health Canada. As a result, it has been possible for this one Korean company of Cosmax to create a global production and quality management system that could sell to cosmetics businesses of any scale in the world, anywhere in the world, whether online or offline. Cosmax has factory infrastructures to produce and to supply products wherever customers want—not only in Korea, but also in Shanghai and Guangzhou in China, in Indonesia, in Thailand, and in the USA.

By 2022, Cosmax Group set a goal of entering an era of "sales of 3 trillion won" ($3 billion annually). Its competitor in second place, Kolmar Korea, to the contrary of Cosmax, lost almost half its business profit between 2020 and 2021 (Statista, 2023). In distant third place, Cosmecca's value is around $152 million dollars, and Cosmecca's large debt is starting to worry investors as well (Simply Wall St., 2020).

Meanwhile, Cosmax lacks such problems and aims to continue to expand revenues by expanding its cosmetic manufacturer's brand development (OBM) and original design manufacturing (ODM) businesses by expanding sales of its healthy 'functional food' business.

In short, Cosmax is a group of many research institutes and different production sites worldwide that aims to be a comprehensive beauty and health service company by maximizing future corporate value through the advancement of OEM, ODM, OBM, and now the functional food business. As the icing on the Cosmax cake, for that seventh external success factor, Korean aesthetics and Korean cosmetics blends and color palates are enjoying huge global popularity due to the 'K-Beauty' craze thanks to the influence of the visuals of the global Korean Wave. Accordingly, the number of Korean cosmetic companies is rapidly increasing. Since 2011, more than 1,000 companies that manufacture and sell beauty products have been newly registered with the Ministry of Food and Drug Safety of Korea. All can be future business partners with Cosmax potentially. According to the Ministry of Food and Drug Safety's statistics on cosmetics production for the recorded import and export statistics of 2021, the Korean cosmetics industry has grown steadily against expectations that a global economic downturn from many governmental lockdown policies from 2020 would sink all boats. However, the Korean cosmetics industries are experiencing a tide that raises all boats: they saw a 21.3% increase in exports in 2021 compared to 2020, growing to 10,509.9 billion Korean won. This is an all-time high for the collective "K-Beauty" industry. In 2021, the Korean trade balance of its cosmetics production increased by 28.6% from 2020, exceeding 9 trillion won annually (approximately $8 billion annually) for the first time. Given the rising trends of K-Beauty's popularity worldwide, it is unsurprising that more global cosmetics businesses now want to work with the premier Korean ODM cosmetics company, Cosmax, on making their own cosmetics a success whether in Korea or by taking advantage of the popularity of Korean aesthetics in their own national cultures due to the Korean Wave.

Via all the factors mentioned above, Cosmax has become the top ODM cosmetics business in the world, instead of only in Korea. Cosmax independently created its own good global business strategies from the 1990s onward. It additionally avoided the bad accidents that have plagued it two main competitors. It now additionally surfs the global Korean Wave that has primed a worldwide cultural desire and thus profit potential from foreign corporations seeking out Cosmax's long-developed Korean expertise and intellectual property empire in general cosmetics services worldwide.

References

Cosmax. https://cosmax.com/main.asp

GreyB. (2023a). Cosmax patents—Key insights and stats. *Insights by GreyB*. https://insights.greyb.com/cosmax-patents/

GreyB. (2023b). Cosmecca Korea patents—Key insights and stats. *Insights by GreyB*. https://insights.greyb.com/cosmecca-korea-patents/

GreyB. (2023c). Kolmar patents—Key insights and stats. *Insights by GreyB.* https://insights.greyb.com/kolmar-patents/

Jin, H. (2018, August 1). Exclusive: Cosmax CEO says he has rejected two takeover offers, wants to stay independent. *Reuters*. https://www.reuters.com/article/us-cosmax-m-a-exclusive-idUSKBN1KL34Q

SignaturePs. (2018). [K-Beauty Manufacturer #2] COSMAX, the biggest cosmetics manufacturer in Korea. *Reddit* r/AsianBeauty. https://www.reddit.com/r/AsianBeauty/comments/8zsw2m/kbeauty_manufacturer_2_cosmax_the_biggest/

Simply Wall St. (2020, June 21). Does Cosmecca Korea (KOSDAQ:241710) have a healthy balance sheet? *Simply Wall St*. https://simplywall.st/stocks/kr/household/kosdaq-a241710/cosmecca-korea-shares/news/does-cosmecca-korea-kosdaq241710-have-a-healthy-balance-sheet

Statista. (2023). Korea Kolmar Holdings' operating profit around the world from 2015 to 2021 (in billion South Korean won). *Statista.* https://www.statista.com/statistics/715364/south-korea-kolmar-korea-operating-profit/

Chapter 8
Squid Game Between Global OTT Services

"*Squid Game*" is the English name for the Korean series 오징어게임, pronounced 'Ojing-o Game,' literally meaning "Cuttlefish Game." *Squid Game* is an action suspense and survival drama series of nine episodes written and produced in Korea by Koreans yet exclusively made for the American global OTT broadcaster Netflix. Funded to be produced from 2019, the Korean director was given full artistic and financial freedom to produce it. *Squid Game* eventually cost an exorbitant $21.4 million dollars to make. However, as we think about the large cost of this broadcast TV production, first, keep in mind that as *Squid Game* was being produced in 2020 and early 2021, Netflix respectively invested fully $550 million dollars and then $800 million dollars in Korean Wave content exclusively for itself in those years. Second, keep in mind only one major global success pays off. *Squid Game* became Netflix's "biggest original series launch, … estimated to be worth almost $900 million for the streaming giant,…citing figures from an internal Netflix document" (Kalia, 2021).

This huge investment in online streaming TV entertainment in only two years is the budget of only one global OTT broadcaster in Korea, Netflix. Now there are at least 25 different global and/or large OTT services vying for either the Korean or the global markets, and likely with each of them with an eye to fund or to acquire content of the Korean Wave due to its current global popularity. From the United States, there is Netflix as the earliest global OTT broadcast service, from 2007. Then there are other American OTT entries: Amazon Prime Video, Google TV, DirectTV (70% AT&T owned), Disney+, Apple+, Comcast, HBO Max & Discovery+, peacock, Warner Media NBC Universal, Paramount+/Showtime, YouTube Premium, ESPN+ (Disney owned), Starz (Lionsgate+), and Curiosity Stream. From China, there are large OTT services like Le.com, Tencent Video, iQIYI (Baidu), Viu (Hong Kong), iflix (Tencent), and Youku. From Japan, its large OTT services are Aichi, AbemaTV (Aichi), Line TV, NHK+, and Rakuten VIKI. From the U.K., there is DAZN. From India, there is ALTBalaji and Eros Now. In Korea, there are domestic OTT services like Wavve, U+ Mobile TV, Watcha, Kakao TV, Naver TV, Coupang Play, and the recently merged Tving(CJ ENM)/Seezn(KT). Many of these domestic Chinese,

G.-C. Shin and M. D. Whitaker, *The Korean Wave in a Post-Pandemic World*,
https://doi.org/10.1007/978-981-99-3683-0_8

Japanese, and Korean OTT online streaming services plan to go global in the next few years as well.

Minor OTT services with more regionalized subscriber bases below 10 million subscribers and yet above 1 million subscribers are from the USA (BET+; Crunchyroll/Funimation, FuboTV; DailyWire+; HayU/NBCUniversal; Acorn TV; Shudder; RightNow Media; Noggin), the Philippines (iWantTFC), Brazil (Globoplay), Sweden (Viaplay), Canada (Crave), India (ZEE5; Aha; SonyLIV; Royal Bioscope), U.K. (NOW; BritBox; Neon; Mubi), Australia (Stan; Kayo Sports); Arab Middle East (Shahid), Mexico (Claro Video); Japan (Smash), Poland (Player/TVN Group), and the Netherlands (Videoland).

In retrospect, before 2019, it was a world where Netflix nearly dominated global OTT services, as it was the first global OTT service to have over 200 million global subscribers in 2017. Only a handful of these OTT services have over 100 million subscribers at all: Netflix, Amazon Prime Video, Disney+, ESPN+, Tencent Video, and iQIYI. Plus, the two in China are hardly entering global OTT competition. However, after 2019, global OTT broadcaster options are growing. Therefore, competition is becoming fierce between them to make or to acquire their own exclusive self-produced intellectual property as content for viewing on their own global digital platforms. This is for capturing a loyal subscriber base as their own 'digital fandom' just as HYBE tries to capture the whole digital fandom of the K-pop group BTS with exclusive BTS content on its exclusive Weverse platform, as mentioned earlier, and just as Cosmax goes more digital in making a wider global intellectual property empire in cosmetics.

Squid Game aired globally on Netflix in 2021, yet was produced by Netflix from 2019 as competition in global OTT services started to happen. Despite it being a huge task to oversee personally nine episodes, one person Hwang Dong-hyuk wrote the whole series screenplay, was in charge of the realization of the script, and was the sole director. It is perhaps the world's longest surrealist art film so far, taken as a whole. Thus, *Squid Game* is perhaps like something the late Italian director Federico Fellini would do with online cinema if he had a Netflix *carte blanche* contract without rules or without oversight, like Hwang did. Interestingly, the equally violent, metaphysical, and surrealist film *Fellini Satyricon* (1969) was equally about class inequalities—yet set in ancient Rome with a lot more sex, gluttony, and revolution defining it—and had nine episodes as well and ranged across an equally long film of more than two hours, while equally following characters' stories loosely woven together. Thus, director Hwang has made his own epic Satyricon, though it is about Korean competitive economic culture and the hidden widespread suicidal desperation of the common citizens in it to make money. Korean actors that appeared in *Squid Game* were Lee Jung-jae, Park Hae-soo, Wi Ha-jun, Jeong Ho-yeon, Oh Young-soo, Heo Seong-tae, Anupam Tripathi (an Indian national yet a Korean-resident foreign actor), Kim Joo-ryung, Lee Yu-mi, Lee Byung-hun, and Gong Yoo.

Since the story of *Squid Game* is told sympathetically through its characters' desperate situations, some of the actors and their characters' stories are mentioned in Table 8.1. After *Squid Game* was launched worldwide by Netflix on September 17, 2021, the drama became a huge hit worldwide. Merely within four days of its release, *Squid Game* became the first Korean drama to take the first place in the Netflix audience of the United States, and it took global second place in Netflix rankings. Within seven days, *Squid Game* rose to first place in Netflix viewers worldwide. Plus, it was the first rank in every country that had Netflix, which means all countries except four worldwide were watching *Squid Game* avidly. Only four countries ban Netflix: mainland China, Syria, Russia, and North Korea. (Note that some Netflix content is seen in China, on OTT operator IQiyi owned by Baidu).

From this global top position, *Squid Game* kept on top of the Netflix world rank for 52 days, the longest period so far for any show in Netflix history. It earned Netflix approximately $900 million dollars from a $21.4 million dollar investment (Kalia, 2021). In addition to being a huge financial success, *Squid Game* became the next in a growing line of top critical and artistic successes of the global Korean Wave. Comparable to the previous global sweep for the Korean Wave in *movie awards* in 2020 for the Korean movie *Parasite* (2019), *Squid Game* swept numerous top *broadcasting awards* in 2021 and 2022 at a comparable scale along with many other awards as noted in Table 8.2.

However, this chapter is more than a review of Korean cultural themes that came together to create the award-winning *Squid Game*, now a major example of the global Korean Wave. Additionally, as you can see from above, this chapter shows evidence that a real world 'squid game' is beginning after 2019 with the increased global competition for content and subscribers between many global OTT services. This is the global OTT providers' own version of a 'live-or-die' battle that will take place over future production seasons and episodes to come. This is a battle for market share to the death: for which global OTT service has the largest and most durable global subscriber base as their digital fandom. This money game or 'quid game' will play out on streaming services around the world in the next few years.

Therefore, this chapter describes two themes. First, it explores the Korean cultural themes and awards of *Squid Game* and how the drama expanded the popularity of the global Korean Wave even more. Second, it explores the growing global digital OTT competition as a 'quid game' from 2019 that now generates eye-wateringly huge and exorbitantly expensive battles for global Korean Wave content, like *Squid Game*. This global OTT competition has generated the odd dynamics that led to an American OTT streaming service of Netflix (of all services, and not a Korean OTT service) to come to produce one of the most expensive and most important financial and cultural hits of the global Korean Wave yet, *Squid Game*.

8.1 Squid Game: Korean Tragedy and Korean Success Factors

First, it is important first to know the background narrative of *Squid Game* to understand how it won many critical and artistic awards, and to know the background for how it came to be written. This series is a drama of nine episodes in which 456

Table 8.1 Characters played by the main actors in *Squid Game* (2021)

Lee Jung-jae (Seong Gi-hun in play)	Park Hae-soo (Jo Sang-woo in play)	Oh Young-soo (Oh Il-nam in play)	Wi Ha-jun (Hwang Jun-ho in play)
After losing his job, he goes back and forth between private loans and gambling. He needs a lot of money to treat his mother who is sick as well as his daughter who is going to the United States. He meets a mysterious man by chance on the subway who lets him participate in a game with a prize of 45.6 billion won.	Ki-hoon has been called a genius since childhood. After graduating from Seoul National University, he joins a large company and seems to be on the rise, but in reality, he has a huge amount of debt due to a failed investment. He is not afraid to risk his life due to this debt situation that he feels has no future or hope of improvement.	He is a 70-year-old man with a brain tumor who shows symptoms of dementia. He is not afraid of a survival game where he risks his life, that he thinks will not be long anyway. Rather, he shows a pure if suicidal enjoyment of the game.	He is a police officer who infiltrates the Squid Game after finding a business card with circles, triangles, and squares brought by Ki-hoon to his older brother's cheap hotel, who has disappeared. Disguised as a masked man running the game, he pursues Ki-hoon brother's whereabouts and the secrets of the game.
Jeong Ho-yeon (Kang Saebyeok in play)	Heo Seong-tae (Jang Deok-soo in play)	Anupam Tripathi (As Ali Abdul in play)	Kim Joo-ryung (Han Mi-nyeo in play)
She is a North Korean defector living a rough life by pickpocketing. She worked hard to save money to help her younger brother left in the orphanage and her parents who want to try to escape North Korea, but she loses all her savings after being scammed by a broker. She has bet everything on this game in the hope that her family can come together.	He is a gangster who has lost all of his mafia's money in a casino, and is being chased. He is immersed in the deadly game regardless, thinking that he will die anyway the moment he is caught by the mafia. He feels everything can be solved by winning the game even if that method is murder.	He is a foreign national who dreamed of achieving success in Korea, yet only found his body and mind overworked and hurt. He suffered due to an industrial accident, but his boss neglected him by refusing to pay for hospital expenses or travel to return home. In Korea due to his dream of trying to live well with his family, he wants to see if he can make a success one final time.	In the game field, her ability to survive shines. She tries to form a team by changing positions from time to time by approaching those who look strong or seem likely to win.

people participate in a mysterious secret survival game and advance to win a prize of 45.6 billion Korean won (around $35 million dollars) through six games and challenges—or they literally and voluntarily *agree* to die trying by being murdered for failure, as stipulated in the survival game contract. The title of this drama "*Squid Game*" is named after a real Korean child's game called 오징어게임 or 'Cuttlefish/Squid Game.' As long ago as 2008, Director Hwang Dong-hyuk conceived his idea

Table 8.2 Record of various awards of *Squid Game* (2021)

Year	Awards	Sector	Winner (work)
2021	1st Beautiful Artist Award	Film Artist Award	Hwang Dong-hyuk (Squid Game)
	The 12th Hollywood Music in Media Awards	TV Show/Limited Series Music Awards	Jeong Jae-il (Squid Game)
	The 31st Gotham Awards	Feature Series Award	Squid Game
	2021 Visionary Awards	2021 Visionary	Hwang Dong-hyuk (Squid Game)
	The 47th People's Choice Awards	Running Show of the Year	Squid Game
	2021 American Film Institute Awards	Special Award	Squid Game
	The 18th Korea Image Awards	Stepping Stone Statue Award	Hwang Dong-hyuk (Squid Game)
2022	The 79th Golden Globe Awards	Best Supporting Actor	Oh Young-soo (Squid Game)
	The 20th Proud Korean Grand Prize	Culture and Arts Division	Hwang Dong-hyuk (Squid Game)
		Director of the Year Award	Hwang Dong-hyuk (Squid Game)
	The 20th Director's Cut Awards	Screenplay of the Year	Hwang Dong-hyuk (Squid Game)
		Actress of the Year Award	Jeong Ho-yeon (Squid Game)
		Drama Actress Award	Jeong Ho-yeon (Squid Game)
	28th Screen Actors Guild Awards	Drama Actor Award	Lee Jung-jae (Squid Game)
		Stunt Ensemble Award	Squid Game
	The 26th Art Directors Guild of America Award	1 Hour Contemporary Single Camera Series Award	Chae Kyungseon (Squid Game)
	37th Independent Spirit Awards Ceremony	Best Actor Award	Lee Jung-jae (Squid Game)
	The 27th Annual Critics' Choice Awards	Drama Award for Best Actor	Lee Jung-jae (Squid Game)
		Foreign Language Series Award	Squid Game
	The 2nd Critics' Choice Super Awards	Best Action Series	Squid Game
		Best Actor in an Action Series	Lee Jung-jae (Squid Game)
		Best Actress in an Action Series	Jeong Ho-yeon (Squid Game)

(continued)

Table 8.2 (continued)

Year	Awards	Sector	Winner (work)
	2022 Visual Effects Society (VES) Awards	Category 5: Outstanding Supporting Visual Effects in a Photoreal Episode	Squid Game, Episode 7, "VIPS"
	American Hollywood Critics Association (HCA) TV Awards	Best International Series	Squid Game
		Best Actor in a Streaming Series	Lee Jung-jae (Squid Game)
	American Screen Actors Guild Award	Outstanding Performance by a Female Actor	Jeong Ho-yeon (Squid Game)
		Outstanding Performance by a Male Actor	Lee Jung-jae (Squid Game)
	74th Primetime Emmy Award ('Broadcasting Oscar')	Drama Directing Emmy	Hwang Dong-hyuk (Squid Game)
		Best Actor in a Drama	Lee Jung-jae (Squid Game)

of taking many innocent Korean children's games and turning them into horrible and deadly 'live-or-die' adult competitions. This was based on his own past economic difficulties and based on social reflection of many "unresolved" (his word, as he says) growing and extreme differences in wealth between classes in Korea. This increasingly makes a polarized 'live-or-die' Korean economy itself.

How did *Squid Game* come to be written? It is a particularly Korean cultural-themed take on growing economic inequality and the desperation people feel in such a debt-ridden hopeless situation without quality of life that goes nowhere. This declining sense of belief in the possibility for economic improvement in Korea came from greater economic inequality. It particularly started after the Asian financial crisis of 1997 into 1998. Before 1997, there was a growing middle class and almost zero unemployment for college graduates in South Korea in the 1990s. Thus, Korean college graduates could be assured of stable lifetime jobs after graduation in a booming economy.

After 1998, approximately 40% of the middle classes at that time fell into lower economic classes. Many small businesses disappeared as well. Korea became the top nation for suicide per capita in the world at this time, and this high suicide rate has only slowly declined despite being twenty-five years on. Plus, after 1998, this was the time of growing 'digital addictions' in the growing "PC Bang" culture (online video game room culture) and in a growing digital spectator e-sports culture around multi-player digital games—made in Korea as well. Unemployed youth and adults whiled away their time away in multi-player digital fantasy worlds courtesy of increasing Internet access and higher bandwidth speeds across Korea in the late 1990s. Some of these out of work digital gamers hoped to become 'digital game idols.' Some did. Many more did not. The intense training and desperation of Koreans made them almost exclusively into the whole first generation of 'global digital game idols' in the late 1990s through the early 2000s. (See Appendix 1). Few other countries beyond Korea at the time had the infrastructure for faster online/Internet gaming, combined with such a quickly dispossessed youth demographic desperate enough to pin their future on risky windfall 'lottery style' cash prizes for getting the top score in a global digital game competition with others. Many Koreans became more involved with pessimistic thinking, feeling that the past's stable job advance into the middle classes had stopped being possible to many anymore. Just as Korea manufactures so much for the global economy, Korea manufactured many desperate Koreans at home from the late 1990s as the country was thoroughly integrated and disintegrated into the unstable global economy's investment dynamics for the first time.

Equally after 1998, this desperate situation *intentionally* was kept in place. There were allowances for more structural unemployment built into Korean economic policies now. These policies were forced upon Korea by the conditions of the International Monetary Fund's bailout of the Korean economy in 1998. The IMF pressed for neoliberal 'structural adjustment' with Korean national financial openings for less global capital controls, more privatized state-own companies, and more allowances for foreign ownership control in Korean companies. These were only some of the conditions of the diktat by the IMF bailout of the Korean economy in 1998. It really was a political coup by the IMF because all major Korean political parties had to agree to support the IMF's policies and to avoid competing to reverse them or the loan would be blocked (Klein, 2007).

However, a great deal of the ongoing success and quick economic recovery of Korea after 1998 is that even the IMF was unable to alter an already globalized and export-led Korean economy, its national economic protectionism, its historically tight dynamics of solidarity in its homogeneous culture, or the continuing virtuous cycle of development between these issues discussed in earlier chapters that had already made Korea's state-primed and state-protected economy work tightly at home on an export-led economy abroad. For instance, first, Koreans in solidarity with each other by the millions voluntarily donated their gold and jewelry in the first four months of 1998 to the Korean government, so the IMF debt could be paid off early so they could be free of foreign control once more. Second, the Korean national social welfare state continued to advance instead of decline, even as more neoliberal policies were instituted. This makes South Korea one of only a handful of countries that has managed to maintain and even advance its social democracy and welfare state while combined with a neoliberal export-led economy. As said earlier, this rare policy mix is one of Korea's secrets to achieve that rarely combined durable economic development with a durable human development, and other nations can learn from this mix deeply (Sandbrook et al., 2007).

However, Korea's declining middle classes continued to shrink after 1998 despite economic recovery by 1999. There was the same economic growth as before to almost double digits in 1999, though this economic growth's organization was now different and more polarizing in the economy despite the ongoing strengthening of the social democratic welfare state. Plus, it is hypothesized that unemployment of Korean youth continued to grow because of another factor than these neoliberal policies: Korea's earlier growth in the digitalized economy and this fresh media regime started to cause digital economic shakeout with far earlier 'precariat' conditions in Korea than other countries (Standing, 2011). This was a normal aspect of the organizational mismatch created by this change of media regime, and it started to be felt in Korea earlier, and was only compounded by the aftermath of the Asian financial crisis in Korea as well as the IMF diktat (See Appendices 1 and 4 together).

There was another global financial crisis later, in 2008 into 2009. It had a similar effect in Korea as in 1997 into 1998, and even more of the middle class disappeared. The director of *Squid Game*, Hwang, says he first started to write his screenplay for what would become *Squid Game* in 2009 during this next global financial crisis starting from 2008. The financial crisis was further exacerbating the economic inequality already growing in Korea for the previous ten years after 1998. This next global financial crisis started from a mortgage lending bubble in the USA, compounded by U.S. federal government decisions. The U.S. federal government protected some major banks' bad investments and debt with bailouts, yet allowed other banks in similar situations to collapse like global-level Lehman Brothers. Millions of its mortgage lenders were unable to pay this bank. However, by unpredictably rescuing some banks with bailouts and letting others fail without them, this led to a chain reaction of many other world banks connected to Lehman Brothers being unable to service their own debts to many other banks if Lehman stopped paying them or loaning to them as well. This ended liquidity in the financial markets worldwide, with the scramble to make debt payments.

This made another global financial liquidity crisis in 2008–2009 for Korean companies, similar to the same global dynamics in 1997–1998. By the summer of 2009, Hwang would have been writing his screenplay while witnessing increasing economic bankruptcies and suffering in Korea. During this period, the Korean won lost over half its value in exchange by Summer 2009, reaching over 1,570.00 Korean won to the U.S. dollar. As recently as Fall 2007, the Korean won had been strong at nearly 900.00 Korean won to the U.S. dollar. So, by Summer 2009 as Hwang was writing, the Korean won and the economy became the lowest and weakest it had been since the Asian financial crisis of 1997–1998. After threats by then President Lee Myung-bak to major Korean banks, telling them to stop traitorously selling and abandoning their own inflating national-currency-denominated debts for their own personal profits, much of the national currency decline stopped.

Though the Korean won and economy recovered after 2009, Hwang's screenplay did not. After more than a decade, he still could not find a company to invest in his script idea. However, Netflix took an interest in production in 2019. After it was broadcast by Netflix in September 2021, by 2022, *Squid Game* won two awards at the American Hollywood Critics Association (HCA) TV Awards. At this HCA Awards ceremony held on August 14, 2022, it won Best International Series and Best Actor in a Streaming Series. On that day, director Hwang Dong-hyuk said he was currently producing the second season. His lead actor Lee Jung-jae won the Best Actor award, beating out American nominees such as Tom Hiddleston and Gary Oldman. *Squid Game* soon swept three other top awards for Best Actor in the United States: like the American Actors Guild Award for Best Actor, the American Critics' Choice Award for Best Actor, and the Independent Film Award for Best Actor. Plus, *Squid Game's* director Hwang was the first Korean to win a Primetime Emmy Award, called the 'Broadcasting Oscar', receiving the Director's Emmy. Lee Jung-jae won Best Actor in a Drama at the Primetime Emmy Awards as well. Without mentioning them all, *Squid Game* was given as many as 14 different nominations including Best Drama Series and Best Actor. See Table 8.2 for a non-exhaustive list of the many awards given to Squid Game between 2021 and 2022.

8.1.1 The Charm of the Korean Wave Leading American Netflix to Further Sell the Korean Wave

Next is a discussion of *Squid Game's* exorbitant production. It sets the stage for the later section about the real world 'squid game' or 'quid game' playing out in the heightened competition between global OTT services for the first time after 2019. The production of *Squid Game* itself was one of these major first battles or salvos between global OTT services for global intellectual property and market share.

The Netflix series *Squid Game* has only attracted further attention and funding into the global Korean Wave even as it made Netflix a lot of money out of the alliance as well. *Squid Game* was produced as original exclusive global content for the global yet American OTT broadcasting service Netflix. In fact, director Hwang Dong-hyuk, who could not find a Korean producer for ten years, said that *Squid Game* would not have been possible without Netflix. As said above, director Hwang Dong-hyuk conceived *Squid Game* in 2008 and scripted it in 2009, but was rejected by Korean investors and actors for over ten years because they felt it was an unrealistically strange work. Surrealism rarely is realistic, and Korean producers assuredly balked at the social criticism in the film. However, the main point of surrealism is that it is an *individually innovative* vision. The more homogeneous Korean culture prefers more collective innovation and discourages or punishes such individual innovation or discussion. Plus, the more homogeneous Korean culture may have desired to censor Hwang's tropes that were *culturally innovative* in conservative Korea: Hwang's screenplay critiques capitalism with negative stories of poverty instead of triumph, unapologetic violence, and showing one-sided stories that feature only a suicidal desperation and what it drives people to do ("give me lottery winnings or give me death!") instead of showing a positive happy attitude toward life that you see in a BTS video for their single "Butter," for example. Only from 2018 did Korean screenplay writer Hwang stop asking his fellow Koreans to fund his individual dream vision and suggest instead to American Netflix that it be made into a drama for them. By 2019, Netflix fully supported the idea, providing Hwang creative freedom and financial freedom without any interference. Netflix had an appreciation for an individual innovation and cultural innovation that the more homogeneous Korean culture discriminates against badly. However, Netflix drives a devil's bargain:

funding without limitations to maximize the chance of fame, yet gaining all ownership and profits for the creative work forever without any future profit sharing with the many actors or the producer/director Hwang.

8.1.2 Comedic Dystopias: Korean Cultural Content Gains a Global Sympathetic Reception

The cultural contents of many major Korean dramas and movies in the past ten years have attracted the attention of the public around the world since they are simultaneously sophisticated and contain serious social issues, while trying to be comic and entertaining to maintain the audience. As has been said, "if you want to tell people the truth, you had better make them laugh, or they will kill you" (Quote Investigator, 2016).

Both social problems and comic drama can be teased out of the absurd situation of an increasingly neo-feudal globalist world (Collier, 2007; Elliott, 2023; Kotkin, 2020; Oxfam, 2020, 2023) of an effete and luxurious 1% at the top of an increasingly inheritance-based and investment-based crony-capitalist class structure that is self-undermining future economic growth and innovation (Piketty, 2014) while creating only a billionaire group bored as hell and generally hating life (Johnson, 2007) yet who violently want to preserve their precarious inherited position over an increasingly rightless and serf-like precariat (Standing, 2011) by trying to stop them from awareness via media censorship or from organizing any opposition via vote fraud (Billings, 2023; Binder, 2023; D'Souza, 2022; Editorial Board, 2023; Hirwani, 2023; Roy, 2022; Taibbi, 2023a, 2023b).

There are two themes to be mentioned in films of the past ten years that have become global hits of the Korean Wave. First, the truly globally popular Korean Wave cinema over the past ten years is starting to form one genre, touching on an obvious sympathy for these themes of economic inequality and social injustice in a global public. To coin a phrase, Korea's developing genre or specialty is to produce popular "comedic dystopias" that are social commentaries. This is a 'comic dystopia' instead of an outright dystopia, and it is a theme of many *if not all* major globally popular Korean Wave films in the past ten years: like Bong Joon-ho's *Snowpiercer* (2013), or his Netflix-funded follow up *Okja* (2017), or his *Parasite* (2019), or Jo Sung-hee's *Space Sweepers* (2021) for Netflix (originally for the Korean theaters, yet blocked by government lockdowns for two years), or now Hwang Dong-hyuk's *Squid Game* (2021) for Netflix.

Four of these five Korean Wave films (i.e., all except *Okja*) reflect more lightheartedly upon the same more openly dystopian themes seen in Japanese films like *Battle Royale* (2000) or American films like *The Hunger Games* (2012). All these four Korean entries are dark comedies—or comedic horror films—that deal with either present or future economic inequality via a surreal fantasy world version of economic inequality. However, it was *Squid Game* that merged this Korean comedic dystopian genre with a second already globally popular cinematic genre of 'death survival games' seen in *Battle Royale* or *The Hunger Games. Squid Game* merged both genres to satirize the competitive structure of a neoliberalist society as a surreal childhood inversion of innocence lost. Adulthood becomes a brutal suicidal game without a safety net where adults are presented as so financially desperate that they voluntarily compete to do mockingly ludicrous things like playing deadly versions of childhood games simply for a financial way out, even as they know it is rarer to win the *Squid Game* and more dangerous to lose it than simply failing to win a multi-million dollar lottery, since their failure is their own murder and death. *Squid Game* shows the world as a rigged game of Russian Roulette, and the desperation people have when they know the game is rigged against them, and yet they still play on, trying to find that single way out. In this rigged game, instead of only one bullet in the gun, all chambers of the gun in life are filled with bullets except one. However, impoverished adults are presented as so desperate that they still play a rigged suicidal game even knowing most of them will be murdered, and so desperate they *refuse to use* the one rule in their contracts that a majority vote among players could end the deadly game itself.

Global platforms such as Netflix demanded content like *Squid Game* that was unique and 'differentiated' by clear 'local colors' or odd narratives which nonetheless could have global persuasiveness in terms of genres and themes. In this respect, *Squid Game* gained sympathy for a Korean cultural telling of this story, while dealing with global common issues of the human condition in the early twenty-first century in the sense that it deals with class and status differences that the whole globalizing world is experiencing instead of *Squid Game* showing a story or attribute unique to Korea (Elliott, 2023; Kotkin, 2020; Oxfam, 2020, 2023). *Squid Game* achieves that transcendent quality of art that Kant called the sublime, while additionally taking an unknown cue from the painter Botero who argued that all art that aspires to be universal has to first be thoroughly expressing a particular locality. In this case, the locality of *Squid Game* may be the Korean culture, yet it is expressed as a universal sublime.

As the title suggests, first, the *Squid Game* features traditional games with simple rules, such as 'The Flower of Mugunghwa has bloomed' (Red light/Green light), Dalgona, Marble Playing, and the 'Squid Game.' All of these are familiar to Koreans as innocent children's games played when they were young. This particularity of Korean culture though goes beyond language and cultural differences because these are common universal childhood games, and thus this harmonizes what is Korean with the universality of the world, generating interest.

Second, *Squid Game* features the primary problems of inequality (Wilkinson & Pickett, 2011) which are not only a problem in Korea, but also a problem faced by rejected adults, elderly, and unemployed youth around the world caused by an increasingly neoliberal policy model. Therefore, it seems that these two main universal themes of nostalgia for childhood games and the adult desperation of economic inequality were accepted by viewers of *Squid Game* around the world without any objection, and even with great sympathy, understanding that the Korean cultural version of childhood nostalgia and adult problems as presented in *Squid Game* are universal problems of the early twenty-first century as well.

8.1.3 Attractive Visuals Help Cross Global Language and Cultural Barriers

The *Wall Street Journal* argued that the production team of *Squid Game* chose to emphasize visuals as much as Korean cultural and universal themes. There are truly glaring and clashing colors in the series. For a few examples, the players wear uniforms of green training suits reminiscent of a Korean elementary school's gym wear, yet stamped with black-and-white numbers on their backs like jailed prisoners or professional sports stars. They players are surrounded by surreal dark-pink-suited 'game managers' or guards anonymized with full black masks yet with circles, triangles, or squares for faces. Of course, across nine episodes, there is plenty of time for a variety of surreally odd background sets and props that are sometimes reminiscent of children's playgrounds yet equally with deeply saturated and unreal colors. Like some hybrid of the Korean Wave and an Almodovar film, the visuals of scenes in *Squid Game* rely on actors' clothing, strong saturated colors, and background props to carry the story even more than the dialogue. This is because the success of a globally distributed drama had to take into consideration the language barrier of the Korean language and how much of a linguistic outlier it is. Plus, Netflix and Director Hwang had to take into account that it would be instantly broadcast globally into at least 37 language zones of the world that the Netflix online platform supports.

So in consideration for how to cross cultural barriers, more universal themes of (the Korean versions of) childhood games and adult economic inequality were merged, as argued in the previous section. Plus, in consideration for how to cross language barriers, the story is carried by saturated colors of thoroughly prepared sets, props, and costumes. The game managers wear dark pink clothes and black masks with square, circle, and triangle marks while their faces were covered, raising curiosity. Due to the masked appearance of the game managers, viewers are encouraged to focus more only on the story and eyes of the game participants, so a sense of immersion in only their human stories is heightened. Plus, a lot of research was done to preserve the Korean cultural atmosphere. Such cultural elements were used to immerse viewers in the drama.

There was no neglect to odd colorful details in any of the waiting rooms, game areas, lobbies, or 'triangle, square, circle' agents, or the clothes worn by participants. The colors of the stairs, walls, and floors of the death game and moving areas are also green, pink, and yellow, giving the illusion that you are in an amusement park or fairy tale that is of course also an abattoir. Thus, a bloody place has become an interesting place. There was no neglect either in taking advantage of the very visual 'original language' of humanity: the color of bright red blood. It splatters in copious amounts on screaming faces or is dragged across floors like a human paint brush in this violent drama.

As well, *Squid Game* reflects in its visuals the cutting-edge digital trends of Korea instead of only sensuous and fantastic colors and designs. As expected of a drama made in a country like Korea that is one the world's powerhouses of electronics, there is a digital aesthetic in *Squid Game* as well. The company that monitors the progress of the game is administrated by a computer program, and process and game results are also provided via images of digitally-generated screens. In short, drama in *Squid Game* is folded into both surreally colorful and coolly digital visuals that people all over the world can relate to in the cutting-edge materials, artistic designs, and passionate hues that are truly Korean, and yet which universally fit expected visuals of an age of dispassionate artificial intelligence.

Hwang stressed so much over details in the production of *Squid Game* that he says six of his teeth fell out before production ended. This pathos of the story of Hwang himself losing teeth over the stress of production of *Squid Game* is the ultimate testament to how much tragic pathos hides in normal workaholic Koreans when put in a position of great responsibility like being picked to produce a Netflix film. Hwang's situation has a similar 'lottery style' chance to win it all or to lose it all, similar to the story of *Squid Game* itself. Hwang played his own long-suffering 'squid game' in producing *Squid Game* itself, in other words. Both the story of *Squid Game* and the story of Hwang show the tenaciousness in Koreans—both in their personal work habits and their competitive cultural expectations to want to win big quickly even at the risk of losing it all. Plus, few other cultures expect their members to sacrifice themselves totally for team projects as much as Koreans do, since merely being good is interpreted as a failure. Koreans push each other to a level of excellence that looks like reckless and dangerous self-sacrifice—very similar to *Squid Game*.

Perhaps as a result of this depth of personal self-sacrifice and pathos that Hwang invested in *Squid Game*, it was nominated for VES (Visual Effects Society) Awards (VES). These VES Awards are the world's most prestigious awards ceremony in the CG/VFX field, and they are held in Los Angeles every year. Given by an organization of more than 4,000 industry experts from more than 40 countries, VES Awards are given to the works that show the best visual effects in the fields of film, animation, TV drama, advertisement, and video games during the year. The 20th VES Awards ceremony in 2022 consisted of a total of 25 categories, and at this ceremony *Squid Game's* Episode 7 "VIPS" was awarded in Category 5 for "Outstanding Supporting Visual Effects in a Photoreal Episode." Therefore, if *Squid Game* was awarded such a prestigious CG/VFX industry award from their more critical eye, it certainly would have amazed and been loved by public viewers even more.

8.2 Quid Game: Four Factors in Netflix's Long OTT Market Growth and the Start of Its Slight Market Decline by 2022

Turning from a comedic dystopia and its fantasy game filtered through Korean cultural visuals, now let us turn to a real world 'squid game' (or 'quid game', money game) now playing out in an even larger competitive arena after 2019. This is the financial competition between global OTT movie broadcasters. This real world money game is the cause why *Squid Game* was produced in the first place at such an exorbitant level, and is the cause why Netflix felt required to spend over $1 billion dollars on the future of Korean Wave productions alone between 2020 and 2021. By April 2023, the CEO of Netflix pledged in a meeting with Korean President Yoon Suk Yeol "to help create Korean dramas, movies, and reality shows for the next four years" by pledging to spend even more, $2.5 billion, which is "twice the total amount Netflix invested in Korea from 2016 to last year" (Lee, 2023).

This is a lot of cash simply to prime visual content in one country. It shows Netflix's trust in the profitability of the global Korean Wave. It shows Netflix's desire to win or simply to keep its leading share of the Korean OTT subscriber base watching the Korean Wave on Netflix, instead of perhaps more expectedly watching the Korean Wave on a large number of other domestic Korean OTT services that have started up in the past few years or even watching the Korean Wave other major global American OTT providers that entered the Korean and global subscriber competition after 2019 like AppleTV+ and Disney+.

Squid Game is a work that would not have been possible without Netflix's help in 2019, or without Netflix's fear of this growing global OTT market competition that is starting. From 2019, many other global OTT streaming services started to join the global arena in competition against the reigning king of Netflix, beginning an OTT version of a game to the death both in the Korean market and internationally. After 2019, fresh players globally started to fund their own massive content, given the entry of the likes of Apple TV+ and Disney+ as sudden rivals to Netflix globally and to Netflix in the Korean market from November 2019. That was the same year that *Squid Game* started to be produced for Netflix, and it was two years in production before it was released on September 17, 2021. For Netflix's competitors at this crucial time, the global OTT services of Apple TV+ were begun, funded by the wealthiest company in the world, Apple—the first trillion dollar company in the world in stock valuation. The other fresh global OTT service of Disney+ is connected to a truly massive and ancient media empire and brand as well. As Disney+ was invented as a global OTT service in 2019, Disney Corporation quickly withdrew its arrangement with Netflix to broadcast all Disney films—which was a large blow to the profits of Netflix. Plus, all global American OTT players are now in a double battle with other Korean, Japanese, and Chinese OTT providers that began to launch their own global OTT services around the world mostly after 2022.

As said above, even though Hwang Dong-hyuk conceived of the concept of an updated adult (or neoliberal) 'squid game' as long ago as 2008–2009 as the Korean economy and currency collapsed around him, he was told for a decade by domestic Korean investors and Korean actors that it was a strange story and unrealistic. Nevertheless, with the help of Netflix, the surrealistic social commentary of *Squid Game* was produced without restrictions on format or length. It was Hwang's dream come true to have the artistic and financial freedom to make it after ten years of waiting. Thus, Hwang was able to make *Squid Game* into a stellar big-budget aesthetic and dramatic success—and he made it a big online box-office grossing series of nine episodes. As said earlier, *Squid Game* eared Netflix approximately $900 million dollars from its $21.4 million dollar investment (Kalia, 2021), yet during these years of 2020 and 2021 Netflix is literally pouring money into global content—at the much larger scale of $36 billion dollars. Given Netflix's scale, imagine all capital spent in one year by all global OTT on all global content generation, for their equal desires of locking in exclusive global intellectual property in visual media!

Why was it left to Netflix though, instead of a Korean OTT operator, to prime the global Korean Wave to fresh heights of popularity and funding? This may seen a detour from describing *Squid Game* though Netflix's sponsorship of the series or the growing competitive global OTT markets are unable to be separated from the desperately high levels of aesthetics, beauty, and length seen and allowed in *Squid Game*. Plus, *Squid Game* was just one of many dozens of productions Netflix funded or bought from the Korean Wave that year alone. For example of just one of these, the Korean theater movie *Space Sweepers* (2019) was bought out by Netflix in 2021 after it had been denied theater showings due to two years of Korean governmental lockdowns. Instead, *Space Sweepers* got around the censorship on its physical audiences by selling out to Netflix to be aired exclusively there from February 2021. This was just nine months before *Squid Game* was shown on Netflix exclusively from September 2021 as well. Netflix subscribers did peak after *Space Sweepers* was released on Netflix as well, as they do for all major Netflix content productions regularly.

So we have to understand what was being attempted by Netflix and why before *Squid Game* was popular. The main aim was the long term growth of Netflix's global OTT services suffering under *changing dynamics of four factors*. It is argued that many of these factors are out of Netflix's control, yet they combine to explain both long-term growth of Netflix and global OTT, and now combine to explain the slight decline of Netflix's global OTT global market share and profits in 2022.

The four factors are: (1) the long term growth of our fresh digital multimedia regime, along with (2) the long-term growth of OTT original content, and how that (3) met lockdown conditions in many countries in 2020 and 2021 mostly removed by 2022, and now (4) how a very competitive global OTT field meets potential market saturation by 2022 onward that will require rethinking business strategies of all OTT services. Netflix really only has control over the second point, so it puts as much as it can into that success factor to fund content. We can explore all four factors using Netflix and *Squid Game* as a case study.

Netflix can show the first factor very well from the beginnings of the global rise of streamable OTT content, since Netflix was the world's first OTT subscription streaming service for movies in 2007. By 2019, it is curious how Netflix came to sponsor (far more than Korean companies or the Korean state did!) production of Korean entertainment products. The global Korean Wave became suddenly freer of past Korean national or cultural censorship—free enough to produce in Korea surrealistic social class commentary like *Squid Game* after ten years of being blocked nationally. This is because Hwang was so individually innovative and culturally innovative as a script writer and producer—types of innovation that the domestic Korean state, corporations, or culture rarely approve of to fund. Hwang's *individual innovation* seen in *Squid Game* and Hwang's *cultural innovation* of showing a form of desperate class conflict (and a bloody conflict however lightheartedly treated) are both themes that the Korean national culture rarely encourages, having blocked Hwang from producing it for ten years already. Once more, just like with the secret cultural blacklist between 2013 and 2017, the Korean state, Korean corporations, and its more homogenous culture can be the global Korean Wave's own worst enemy by censoring individual creativity or by censoring controversial social themes in the interest to hide conflict. Censoring social conflict effectively stops national cultural innovation and change as well. So, *global OTT services can generally be a force of cultural change globally in all nations simultaneously*. This is something left-wing American Netflix has repeatedly attempted to do globally by its funding patterns on content, and this is reflected in various national boycotts of Netflix as well, due to its choices of content. For good or for bad, global digital OTT services innately get around all kinds of past national censorship regimes on broadcasting, visual production, and all past national cultural settlements. This can be either good or bad depending on your point of view of the content, its goals, or the value of past national cultural settlements. Regardless, this is what global OTT does culturally in the long term. This is why Netflix has been banned in Syria, Russia, China, and North Korea: these states are making decisions on who ultimately has jurisdiction over a nation's cultural transmission, people inside the country or people outside the country, instead of simply making decisions about Netflix.

To begin on the first factor, *Squid Game* would not exist without Netflix, yet Netflix would not exist without our fresh digital media regime. Decisions to create or to expand such an Internet infrastructure are hardly only in Netflix's control. Only Netflix's later self-generated video content can be wholly in its control, while all other factors of its success are a constellation of factors that, like the stars of fate above, were organized well in Netflix's favor from 2007 to 2021, and from 2022 increasingly are organized against Netflix to hamper its own future growth. However, such situations of our global digital media regime are still well organized to expand global OTT services in general in a growing competition.

First, in the United States when Reed Hastings and Marc Bernays Randolf started Netflix in 1997, it was not an online movie 'renter' (streaming broadcaster) that could send movies over the Internet to individual homes, smartphones, and smart televisions with broadband connections or wireless services worldwide. In 1997, smartphones did not exist and would not exist in the current sense until June 2007 with the selling of the first iPhone. Even as late as 2013, only about half of the United States had a smartphone—hardly a strong market basis for streaming movies. Plus, in 1997, wireless internet did not exist. There were wireless 1G mobile phones of course though *wireless Internet* did not widely exist beyond small 'hotspot' zones of wireless local area network (wireless LAN) terminals that were expensive peripheral technologies that could be attached to the wired Internet in a building. Even though the first wireless LAN was the ALOHAnet at the University of Hawaii in 1971, with seven computers over four islands communicating without phone lines, the whole concept remained exorbitantly expensive compared to wires, and the data throughput was weak. Even as late as 2009, wireless LANs could only handle around 600 Mbit/sec at its best in that year's 802.11n standard. Thus, wireless Internet movie streaming was beyond the technology, as Netflix was formed in 1997.

So, what kind of business was Netflix, if Netflix could not stream moves across the Internet or even connect to Internet-accessible wireless mobile devices in 1997 because there were not any and because data throughput was weak? There are four caveats to that statement. First, American-made Palm Pilots were indeed introduced earlier in 1996, though by 1997 they were without Internet connection until later, and the technology was hardly designed for web-access or streaming movies. It was more about synchronous business use with desktop computer applications. In 1999, DoCoMo in Japan introduced the I-mode, a mobile phone with an internet connection. However, it only had a few major internet services like GPS, easy online payments (billed to phone bills), and email—and it was a tiny black and white screen. You could access the web on the I-mode by inputting the URL address with a keypad, yet the I-mode failed to support the full hypertext language of the World Wide Web (Hoffman, 2017). So the Palm Pilot or the I-mode would hardly do for easy online movie streaming. Third, the only possible place for streaming movies would be personal desktop computers, yet bandwidth was rather weak at the time for such a service anyway. In 1997, American broadband was not as 'broad' or powerful in throughput as it would be later, so it was useless for streaming large files like Hollywood movies in the United States to desktop computers, much less stream them globally to other desktop computers. Google did not even exist in 1997 when Netflix was founded, since Google was founded in 1998. YouTube's social media video streaming did not even exist until 2005, and even then it would be going only to desktop computers whether Ethernet-wired or wireless—the latter via personal boxes that made a wireless LAN service, yet even LAN hotspots were based economically on a wired Ethernet cable network. Fourth, as noted in Appendix 1, Korea did pioneer the world's first wireless Internet *national* network of technology in its "WiBro" infrastructure of base stations and 'personal/local' portable Internet-broadcast stations, though that was from 2006. Plus, it was left to Korea to invent the LG Prada phone, an Internet-accessible feature phone with the world's first flat-glass touchscreen announced and sold before the first iPhone was commercialized in June 2007. However, both of these Korean entries were so futuristic they were premature. The Korean national WiBro networks gave Korea *the world's first national wireless Internet by 2006*, which could connect to the first Internet-accessible wireless touchscreen feature phones like LG Prada by May 2007. This made Korea into a truly futuristic nation of wireless mobile technologies before any other nation. However, WiBro networks and LG Prada phones were both mostly deployed as services in Korea, despite being global products that did go outside of Korea to some regions of the world. Both were soon outmoded as 3G/4G standards of wireless LTE Internet developed and as Apple would come to standardize aesthetics of what the world wanted in a flatglass touchscreen smartphone with mobile apps instead of Korea's LG, even though Apple's iPhone looks suspiciously like the earlier Korean LG Prada touchscreen phone with its own mobile apps.

So, returning to our problem, what kind of video rental business was Netflix in 1997 if smartphones, fast bandwidth, wireless Internet, and smart televisions did not exist yet? Netflix was originally a DVD movie rental company and DVD movie sales company quite similar to the movie lender and U.S. market leader of Blockbuster at that time. In 1997, Netflix's main competitor in movie rental was Blockbuster, founded in 1985 as a VCR-video tape rental company for 'family friendly' Hollywood movies. By 1989, Blockbuster had 19 franchised videotape rental stores. At its height in 2004, it had over 9,000 franchised stores, some overseas. Blockbuster was the undisputed first in American home movie rental, and encouraged timely return of its physical VCR tapes back to its physical store by daily growing late fees.

However there was the growing media regime change to faster and more efficient information flows of digital video—first to magnetic-encoded VCR videotapes, then to more digital information on smaller physical DVDs, and then to even more digital information flowing through non-physical media like movies simply streamed over the Internet. Netflix by 2007 was one of the first older movie rental companies to try to start the opposite strategy of joining the digital revolution early—before they might be killed off as a physical business of DVD rentals and purchases later. Hastings says he was inspired by two ideas: how his gym made money with a monthly subscription plan from him, regardless of how many times he used the gym. Second, he said he was additionally inspired by the digital media potential shown by YouTube (founded in 2005) in streaming short videos successfully.

So Netflix, over its first decade from 1997 to 2007, started to make a slow switch from its main early business of physical rentals and even sales of DVDs. However by 2007 Netflix had set up a different kind of online service that eliminated late rental fees as a source of income as it was impossible to do that on a streaming service as nothing truly had to be rented out or returned. Instead, Netflix started to ask for regular monthly subscription fees to digitally distributed content that could be watched and streamed during that period as much as you wanted. This was a similar strategy of monthly subscriptions to channels delivered by physical cable TV infrastructures, though now the movies were going over the public-use Internet instead—with those wires ironically laid down by telecoms and cable TV companies themselves attempting to be competitive in delivering Internet services by wire in the previous decade. Soon, the merged telecoms and cable/Internet providers would realize they had outmoded their own cable TV subscription business model that they were merely trying to improve and to diversify.

So, with the development of the streaming speed of the wired Internet in the USA, a bold change of service away from movie rental on VCR tapes, on DVDs, or even on cable TV was in the offing to online OTT streaming. Actually, Blockbuster was given the chance to buy Netflix in 2000 for $50 million dollars when Netflix was still a regular DVD rental company though Blockbuster turned it down. By 2000,

Blockbuster was even ahead of Netflix at the time in its own digital conversion, trying to develop its own OTT streaming service in 2000, originally with the energy trading company Enron in mind. However, Enron turned down the Blockbuster's idea in 2001 concerned that Blockbuster would be unable to develop a large online film catalogue. Soon, Enron would file for bankruptcy anyway in 2001, at the time being the largest bankruptcy in U.S. history. By 2004, Blockbuster's main owner Viacom spun off Blockbuster. In the same year of 2004, Blockbuster itself introduced a Netflix-style store, meaning, an online-requested and then-physically mailed DVD of a movie. It was available at Blockbuster.com, known as Blockbuster Online. Netflix was doing this from 1997, far earlier than 2004. By 2007, it was Netflix's turn to fear a far larger potential of Blockbuster Online, since Netflix had a similar yet smaller online-requested and physically-mailed DVD service. This time, Netflix tried to buy Blockbuster Online in 2007. That deal almost happened though it was challenged by Wall Street stock raider Karl Icahn who owned much of Blockbuster at this point and refused to support the merger or the CEO who supported the merger. Later policies pushed by Icahn were different: fire that original Blockbuster CEO, raise the price of online DVD rentals, and end free movie deals. This unfortunately stopped Blockbuster Online's early growth between 2004 and 2007. This soon left much of both American fields of mailed DVD rentals and the growing OTT movie streaming field to the early pioneer Netflix that introduced online streaming in 2007, still in parallel to its other DVD rental services from 1997. By 2010, the empire of Blockbuster filed for bankruptcy, swamped by bad decisions in the digital conversion that made it physical VCR tapes or physical DVDs increasingly obsolete fixed costs compared to more virtual and 'lean and mean' online digital streaming services of OTT from the entirely online wing of Netflix with its far less overhead costs and far larger global market potentials.

On the one hand, Blockbuster's failure is a prime example of a company's leaders having a strategic failure in recognizing a growing media regime's organizational mismatch problem, discussed earlier, and mismanaging this media transition (See Appendix 4). On the other hand, Netflix's meteoric rise after 2007 is a prime example of a company being able to see ahead for what a media regime change would mean for ever-faster digital and ever-larger global distribution, as well soon the importance of being more in control of its own global intellectual property of self-produced video content that would be available only on its OTT service that drew subscribers as their own digital fandom. With its own produced content, Netflix could avoid sharing profit showing others' movies. Netflix started to create its own OTT content from 2013. Comparatively speaking, note this is the same story of exclusive global intellectual content empires that we have seen in HYBE's BTS/Weverse platform, in the many patents of the Cosmax ODM cosmetics empire, and now in Netflix's global strategies that started in 2013 for making its own intellectual property for global distribution in visual entertainment.

Because OTT services can be viewed over the Internet without a separate television set 'top box,' Netflix simultaneously replaced cable TV networks with their either pay-per-view or pay-per-month distribution of movies, retail franchise empires like Blockbuster, movie theaters, and even existing terrestrial analog/digital broadcasting at the same time. In May 2011, Netflix was getting so large that it became the largest source of Internet traffic in all of North America, with 30% of all Internet streaming traffic in North America in peak hours. In June 2011, Netflix split itself into two subscription plans, one for streaming movies and one for its older DVD rentals. By September 2011, Netflix was in 43 countries worldwide. By 2013, only as it started to create its own OTT content, Netflix surpassed for the first time the number of cable TV subscribers of Home Box Office (HBO), at the time the US's largest cable-based movie rental distribution.

However, markets like nature abhor a vacuum. Netflix started to see many other American/global OTT competitors after 2013 with Amazon Fire TV (from 2014), AT&T (which acquired the OTT/satellite TV service of DirecTV from 2015 yet now separately managed from 2021 while still 70% owned by AT&T), Disney+ (from 2019), Apple+ (from 2019), and Comcast (from 2020). Many of these competing American/global OTT services had the same strategy of developing exclusive content for global intellectual property empires that could be seen only on their own OTT services.

As Netflix tried to maintain its market share leadership in OTT in Korea where it was the first and only American OTT entry for many years, and where it held the largest market share even over Korean OTT services, the best solution would be to prime the global market with global Korean Wave content that would additionally help out its Korean subscriber market share. Netflix had been producing its own content from 2013, and Netflix had a goal of 50% of all content it hosted to be self-generated content. In this digital convergence, instead of film studio production and movie theater distribution being separate steps or companies, within Netflix both could be done by the same company. In this way, Netflix became a top movie producer itself along with an OTT service looking to distribute content. For instance, by 2020, Netflix was awarded 24 Academy Awards, the first time a 'streaming service' led all U.S. movie studios. This was because effectively Netflix is a movie studio—however outsourced to the whole world's directors or consumers that this manufacture or distribution of movies could be. By March 2021, Netflix pulled further ahead with 36 Academy Awards at that point. By August 2021, the self-produced "Netflix Originals" were 40% of Netflix's entire library in the United States, nearing their long term goal of hosting 50% of their content as "Netflix Originals." So, when Netflix agreed to sponsor *Squid Game* in 2019, it was of course unknown at the time how much of a gold mine of money and awards these nine episodes would be both for Netflix and for expanding the visibility of the global Korean Wave. However, given the awards listed above won by Netflix itself, it was known already at this point how much Netflix as a movie producer could pick a global winner.

At the height of Netflix fame and awards with *Squid Game* from 2021 to 2022, it was unknown by the first quarter of 2022 that Netflix would start to lose subscribers for the first time for rationales explored below. However, the whole global OTT service market was still expanding. Earlier, in 2018, Boston Consulting Group (BCG) predicted rosily that the global OTT market would grow 30% from its scale in 2018 to reach $141 billion in 2022 (Singh, 2018). In 2022, Digital TV Research predicted that the global OTT market, worth $106 billion in 2020, would more than double its scale to reach $224 billion by 2027 (Digital TV News, 2022). As said, with the success of early OTT providers like YouTube (from 2005) and Netflix (streaming from 2007) many global companies launched other OTT services after 2014. However, actual competition really only started to intensify after 2019. This was a pressure on Netflix to make even more extravagant big-budget investments in original content in the global Korean Wave that it could field exclusively on its OTT service. This was how Hwang got complete artistic and financial control to make what was once a single neglected ten-year old screenplay expanded into an epic of nine episodes. After all, Netflix was the top U.S. Academy Award winner for a movie producer already in U.S. history from 2020. Netflix hardly gave Hwang comparatively unique freedoms of production. It is common for Netflix to keep to their successful strategy of wide allowances for individual creative vision in directing, cost, scripting, and length.

This OTT market in Korea that Netflix now dominates had been growing at a remarkably high average *annual* rate of 26.3% or around 192.6 billion Korean won from as early as 2014. According to the Korea International Cultural Exchange Agency, the domestic OTT market, which was worth about 993.5 billion Korean won in 2020, was expected to grow to 1.91 trillion won in 2025, almost doubling in five years (KOFICE, 2022). Explaining this rapid growth of the OTT market in Korea there is the influence of global giant platforms like Netflix coming into the Korean market but it is also due to the entry and remarkable growth of local Korean OTT platform companies such as Tving and Seezn—now merged. As the Korean OTT market rapidly grows, reorganization of the existing Korean OTT services and OTT operators are happening. As mentioned in an earlier chapter, by November 2022 the Korean state approved a merger of these two separate minor Korean OTT streaming services of Seezn and Tving (the latter being CJ ENM controlled, yet equally having investments by Korea's Naver and JTBC). This merger joined 5% and 13% of the Korean OTT market together, respectively, putting the combined Tving-Seezn company ahead of the previous top domestic-Korean-owned OTT company Wavve, with its 14% of the Korean OTT market. Next, the OTT service 'Coupang Play' launched by Coupang has grown rapidly since its launch in January 2022, reaching results close to that of major operators. Plus, new global OTT operators are also entering the Korean market, challenging Netflix and Korean OTT operators alike. Apple TV+ and Disney+ launched themselves simultaneously in Korea in November 2021, merely one month after Netflix released *Squid Game* in September 2021. As Disney+ started in 2019, it stopped letting Netflix stream Disney films as previously agreed. Of course the actual top OTT market provider in Korea is the American OTT operator Netflix with 38% of the Korean market in 2022. However, for how long will this last with this massive competition?

Netflix's Monthly Activity Users (MAUs) in Korea exceeded 10 million by November 2021, and Netflix had around 3.85 million Korean subscribers in 2020. However, Netflix makes and delivers content to over 230 million subscribers worldwide, and they are Netflix's true audience instead of only the Korean audience. So any interest in the global Korean Wave by Netflix is a stress on that word 'global' instead of only the word 'Korean,' in the eyes of and the financial ledgers of Netflix.

Increasingly, that global audience wants to see the global Korean Wave. So, Netflix primes and delivers Korean-produced broadcast content of the global Korean Wave just like Korean OTT's do—to Korean citizens and to the world. However, priming Korean content would help Netflix keep and grow its own Korean subscriber base as well under this growing competition in this particular national situation.

Thus the OTT market competition will be getting more challenging for the leadership of Netflix over time despite its own excellent self-produced content if other major content streams break away from its distribution for their own OTT distributions like Disney features now going to Disney+ instead of Netflix from 2019. Plus, despite being an American company, Netflix keeps attracting more Korean subscribers by showing not only various original series but also unreleased Korean-produced movies such as *Space Sweepers*, the first Korean 'space-themed' blockbuster film. It was produced in Korea in 2019, yet blocked for two years from theater release due to Korean state lockdown policies. Therefore, the Korean producers sold the theater film to Netflix in 2021, and with its release on Netflix in February 2021 it became a very successful film in Netflix's global digital audience known for their love of the global Korean Wave. The film is described as Korea's first 'space western,' set in a dystopian future in 2092 where neo-feudal global elites live on orbiting platforms while remaining 'serfs' are forced to live on a degraded Earth below.

Netflix particularly and OTT platforms in general are free from Korean national censorship and have the capacity to produce specialized content targeting specific audiences, so they produce works that are difficult to see in traditional network broadcasting. As said in the introduction to this section, global OTT services effectively bypass national censorship regimes of all kinds, for good or for bad. Therefore, Netflix has been discovering new stories that could not be produced through any nation's particular *national* cable, screen, or traditional network broadcasts. The innocent Korean broadcast TV culture prefers to blur out lit cigarettes and exposed knives on television in any films, because of the immorality of showing these is interpreted as a kind of cultural approval of smoking or violence in the Korean censor's eyes. However, Netflix values storytelling, which is the basis of content, and respects the creativity of authors. It respects the intention of the creator so that the writer can express the story he or she thinks in the desired form and amount of drama. That is why, in order to increase viewership, most decisions are left to creators without pressure such as asking creators to revise the script or increase the length of a specific character, or censor a bloody scene. Netflix invests in providing original content creators with not only creative freedom, but also an unprecedented budget. Who else except Netflix can invest $36 billion dollars globally to produce dozens of examples of original content worldwide over the past several years? So, instead of providing a huge investment cost that is comparable to the terrestrial production cost, Netflix concludes a contract with the creator by monopolizing Intellectual Property (IP). This is a method in which all future profits after the release of the work belong to Netflix, excluding the production cost and down payment.

Many individual creators prefer the Netflix global contract structure, which allows them to freely present their works—particularly in works that their own cultural nations censored and denied production. In this way, by supporting the global Korean

Wave's somewhat censored Korean topics or ideas of the past like *Squid Game*, or by supporting Korean films that had been banned by government lockdowns from Korean theaters, Netflix demotes all national censorship regimes and attracts even more Korean and even global subscribers. This global Americanized cultural erosion of various local cultural standards or national broadcast capacity is certainly why North Korea, Russia, China, and Syria attempt to block the whole streaming platform of Netflix in their countries—just as European nations blocked American film production from dominating and destroying their own national cultural transmissions after World War II (Mattelart, 2000).

This is a repeating theme about the global American wave of the past in movies. It is a repeating theme in the present in Netflix creating more of a global empire in intellectual property while *undermining* Korean national organizational entertainment industries and rules, instead of only *facilitating* a Korea-centric Korean Wave. This combined undermining of national-based control yet facilitating a national political economy is a theme already seen in HYBE, the management company of BTS, and its Weverse global platform. This is a theme already seen as well as in the chapter on Cosmax and its developing global platforms for selling the expertise of its already assembled global intellectual patents and multiple kinds of global or national certifications as a true global empire in cosmetics-related technologies. Undermining national cultural control is a theme seen equally when Netflix's logo was openly booed at the Cannes film festival in May 2017 at the beginning of the-screening of Bong Joon-ho's Korean Wave film *Okja* (2017), and then denied from the whole competition for not following local French rules on screening the film in French theaters first, before screening it after it was nominated for the Palme D'Or competition in Cannes. However, by the end of the film there was a multi-minute standing ovation from the audience for *Okja*. Nonetheless, that year's Jury President, Spanish film director Pedro Almodovar, said at his press conference earlier than the screening that he categorically ruled out voting for either of the two Netflix films at Cannes that year because they broke the French rule mentioned above. Another Jury member that year, American actor Will Smith, supported Netflix's streaming movies that broke the French rule. Undermining national cultural control is seen in Netflix in general for how the global intellectual property rights of many other 'Korean' Wave films now are simply owned by another American (yet global) empire of intellectual property as well. This shows the high stakes game being invented around durable empires of global intellectual property that any corporation in any field nowadays can create and base from any country if the situations are right.

For the third factor that is out of Netflix's control, the period of its great financial and popular advance in 2020 and through its release of *Squid Game* in 2021 and afterward was in the middle of many countries' governmental lockdowns. On the one hand, due to many governments' policies on closure of theaters and other concert venues, the global OTT industry blossomed in this 'great reset' toward more singularly and digitally-distributed virtual content. India alone saw a growth in 60% more OTT subscriptions by December 2020 due to Indian lockdowns (Business Standard, 2020). On the other hand, digital convergence in entertainment blossomed only because of the governmental-forced bankruptcy of many more diverse entertainment businesses in the worldwide economy that are dependent upon physical venues, crowds, and geographic community—instead of because Netflix or others are true market winners per se. For example, in the month of the release of *Squid Game*, exclusively on Netflix, while many countries blocked other forms of live or theater entertainment as well, Netflix's MAU (monthly active users) *suddenly* exceeded 70% compared to the same month in 2020. Of course it was *Squid Game*, though it was this third factor of lockdowns in many nations as well.

Next, if you look at Chart 8.1 on Netflix's trend of WAU (weekly active users) in 2021, you can see that it rose *sharply* whenever original content was released, though you can see as well that it rose *most sharply and more durably only* as forced governmental lockdown conditions effectively closed much offline competition around December 2020 and throughout 2021. Showing this in the inverse, for example, as lockdowns ended mostly across 2022, and people went outside to previously closed public venues, Netflix faced far more *real world* competition in entertainment after several years in its Korean subscriber base. After the release of *Squid Game* in Autumn 2021 and onward, Netflix's subscriber scale was far more unstable than the past, and its WAU trends show both more rapid rises and rapid falls after this period. Plus, this time period of late 2021 in Korea equally was involved for the first time with far more big-budget Korean OTT and global OTT competition versus Netflix in the Korean market.

Therefore, by the first quarter in 2022, Netflix as the largest player in the Korean industry, announced disappointing results in subscriptions and profits. You can see this fast decline echoed in the fast declining WAU soon after *Squid Game* and its release in Chart 8.1. This raised for the first time concerns for Netflix that the Korean and global OTT market may have reached its limit of growth and/or depended "too much" on the serendipitous combination of the amazing success of producing *Squid Game*, a temporary decline in its real world competition to sustain itself at the high rates of the past few years, and (for another factor) the increasing global OTT competition or even market saturation that had yet to show in the digital world until 2022.

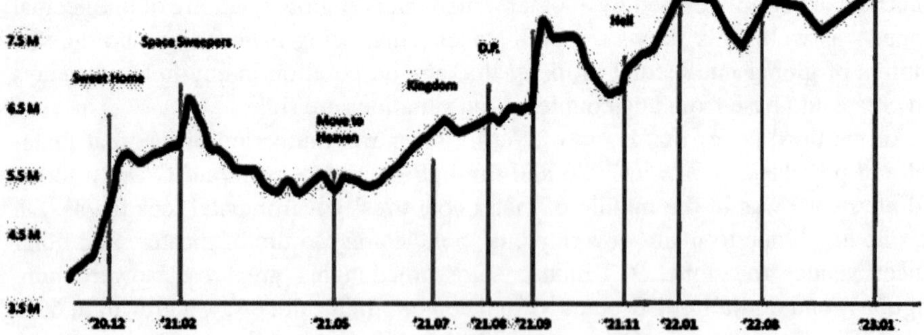

Chart 8.1 Changes in Netflix usage due to the release of OTT content, Weekly Active Users (WAU), 2020–2023

That fourth factor is discussed below. All of these factors of course combine in the real world.

The fourth factor that is out of Netflix's control as well is the growing market competition and potential market saturation of players. The results of this confluence of four factors are that both the subscribers and the revenue for Netflix started to stall and decline in the first quarter of 2022. The Netflix WAU shown in Chart 8.1 stalls in January 2022, then slowly declines, and then precipitously declines for that quarter as well. Plus, for two other data sets beyond WAU, *Netflix subscribers fell for the first time ever since 2007* by 200,000 in the first quarter of 2022, and Netflix's net income in the same quarter was $1.597 billion, which was down 6.4% from the first quarter of 2021.

It may not be a big deal for Netflix to lose only 200,000 subscribers of over 230 million globally or to have a slow quarter of a 6.4% YoY loss. Nevertheless, the market is keeping a close eye on both indicators. Both are believed to be the reason why the company's stock price per share, which was around $700 in November 2021, plummeted to around $350 a share around the time of the announcements in January 2022 about lower earnings and its first ever subscriber loss. By January 2023, the Netflix stock price recovered to comparable levels of November 2021, yet the subscriber base took over a year to rise. This was only after *radically cheaper and different subscription policies* were introduced in 2022 to try to maintain it, as indicated below.

Netflix cannot blame its subscriber/profit losses on the first factor of the weakening of the infrastructure of the Internet, which continues to advance and get faster. Netflix of course is certainly not to blame on the second factor of its incredibly innovative original content that it continues to produce at high sustained budgets that fund the cinema of the global Korean Wave and many other nations' original content at the same moment. The third factor of the ending of many governmental lockdowns on crowd-based entertainments can only be a particular factor to blame in some countries as a more 'normal' competitive market for real world entertainment returns to balance and to give more natural market choice between online and offline venues.

Thus, it is to the fourth factor that is fresh and rising that Netflix can blame. It is a factor hardly seen before in the global OTT industry: wide OTT market competition on a global scale after 2019. Just as the rise of Netflix was hardly entirely due to Netflix in three of these four factors—due to it seizing the chance in the media regime change, due to a beneficial context of a less competitive real world market on entertainment in the past few years, and due to its growing tremendously from 2007 onward by having an easier 'blue ocean' strategy without major competition for a decade or more—it is hardly Netflix's fault if this fourth factor of a more competitive market finally starts to exist as market saturation arrives.

Netflix has been a pioneer and then a rising star for a long time in the OTT industry. Netflix gathered over 200 million paid subscribers in ten years from 2007 to 2017. It became so successful that it became the object of jealousy and oligopoly by being associated in a negative way as a member of 'FAANG' (Facebook/Meta, Apple, Amazon, Netflix, and Google), an abbreviation which stands for the five largest and increasingly monopolistic global American 'big tech' companies. However, by 2023, governments increasingly look into uncompetitive practices of the FAANG, with the U.S. Department of Justice in January 2023 starting an anti-trust prosecution case against Google's near monopoly on U.S. online advertising, for instance. However, the FAANG membership of Netflix seems to be challenged first by a competitive global OTT market instead of challenged by an easily outflanked single governmental regulation. However, the future of market challenges like this is always unknown. Market challenge could just as easily turn into more global oligarchic consolidation in the global OTT market (and thus to bigger FAANGs) by mergers and alliances instead of always leading to real market competition. Only time will tell.

For details about this fourth factor of the beginning of competitive OTT markets, in the last few quarters despite spending massively more than ever in the past few years on original content, Netflix's growth still started to decelerate. Netflix secured more than 37 million new subscribers in 2020 alone, but the deceleration set in throughout 2020 into 2021. Netflix net subscriber additions even by the fourth quarter of 2020 were lower compared to the previous year. Next, into the first quarter of 2021, only 3.98 million new subscribers joined Netflix, which was a significant slowing compared to the first quarter of 2020 when there was a 15.8 million subscriber net increase only a year earlier. Next, the number of subscribers added in the second quarter of 2021 was even less at only 1.54 million, and this was only half of the already measly first quarter of 2021. Overall, the number of new subscribers fell sharply by nearly half to 18.2 million throughout 2021, since Netflix added almost double that number at 37 million subscribers in the full year before. By winter of 2021, Netflix added a few subscribers though, yet it was still slightly less than half of the year before by the last quarter of 2021, at around 8.28 million new subscribers. However, by spring 2022, Netflix recorded the first *ever* slight decline of 200,000 subscribers. Of course as the number of subscribers decline, the basis of revenue is decreased and thus earnings in the remaining subscribers can be slowed. Netflix at the time said they expected an even greater decrease in subscribers in the second quarter of 2022. This happened as predicted, with a continuing loss of 970,000 subscribers. However, this was interpreted to be positive since it was less than the 2 million subscriber loss they had been expecting. This was mostly because of fresh entertainment content in the release of the fourth season of the science fiction horror series, "Stranger Things," which was the "biggest season of English [language] TV ever" for Netflix (Pallotta, 2022). Next, in the third quarter of 2022, Netflix added more than 2.41 million subscribers once more, higher than its 1 million forecast. "Stranger Things" was said to once more help out in that third quarter advance. Equally, Netflix radically changed its subscriber model to adapt. For the first time since 2007, it began a low cost subscription plan supported by advertisements (thus, its first AVOD business model) starting in twelve countries by November 2022. Equally, Netflix is getting more surveillance-minded on its subscribers to try to stop password sharing, and thus increase actual individual paying subscribers instead of having a group of subscribers sharing the same password (Whitten, 2022). In the fourth quarter of 2022, Netflix added 7.66 million more subscribers. So by the end of 2022, despite the first declines in subscribers in 25 years in the first and second quarter of 2022, Netflix ended 2022 with a slight 4% year over year growth in subscribers after all (Maas, 2023).

However, even the relatively fresh OTT service of Disney+ started in 2019 is already reporting massive subscriber losses by February 2023 with a 2.4 million member loss, its first decline from a high of 164.2 million subscribers in the third quarter of 2022. It was originally a good assumption that the OTT market would be a 'plus-sum' game if each OTT service kept their own territory and grew the market further in various zones. However, in a saturated market, it could be a 'zero-sum' game where groups share a fixed pie or where each group goes for the whole pie. There are concerns that the existing revenue model and ecosystem theory of global OTT services cannot guarantee very much future growth per service in this very competitive global market. That growth dynamic has been broken or more aptly may have reached a ceiling of market saturation for OTT services globally among all the large players entering after 2019. For instance in addition to Netflix now Disney+, HBO Max, and Amazon Prime Video have followed their own Netflix-style growth by rapidly increasing their sales based on original content. Plus, the North American and European markets are where subscriber saturation is prominent. In this region, Netflix's competition has greatly revealed its presence. Disney+ collected 100 million subscribers within one year of its launch, and HBO Max of Warner Brothers also grew rapidly, yet Disney+ seems by 2023 to be hitting the same difficulties of expansion that Netflix had from early 2022. OTT companies in Korea are globalizing as well. This may be another factor eating into Netflix's or Disney+'s global subscriber base.

Thus Netflix and other OTT services are in this real world 'squid game' of OTT global competition where all of them cannot stop investing in content and fighting with other OTT services for market share, even though some may face losses. If investment is stopped by the fresh challengers, their gap with already reigning Netflix will widen, and Disney+ and Apple TV+ may lose instead of increase their market share in Korea. In a similar dynamic, even Korean OTT service companies have to respond to this more competitive global OTT service infrastructure now in Korea and in the world. Korean OTT services are responding in various ways: by merging like the Korean Tving and Seezn to be more powerful investors in content; by investing in more differentiated content that may be successful with a relatively small investment; by acquiring or co-producing domestic and foreign drama production companies; or by going global in the search for larger numbers of subscribers.

Although Korean OTT companies now advance into the global OTT market, it is not easy to predict what kind of impact these more globalized Korean OTT services will have in the future. In particular, Wavve is preparing to advance into the U.S. and Europe, starting with Southeast Asia. Before its merger with Seezn in November 2022, Tving was preparing to enter the U.S., starting with Japan and Taiwan in 2022. Korea's Watcha OTT has already started service in Japan, and it is aiming to advance into the U.S. and Europe. However, exporting content such as movies and webtoons abroad is different from exporting an OTT platform overseas. It is necessary to keep in mind major tasks such as marketing and content supply differ from country to country, such as partnering with local content providers in each country that they aim to enter. This is because investment strategies for not only expanding simple content but also securing distribution rights for existing content, stable service operation, and interpretation/translation work should be clearer. This is similar to how Netflix operates in Korea by in funding both the cultural production of the global Korean Wave while it moves into the Korean OTT market, as well as collaborating with existing Korean OTT players like KakaoTV. In short, even many "Korean" platforms are not only in competition in Korea, but collaborate actively in Korea with foreign OTT like Netflix and others. Plus, Korean OTT plan to move around the world themselves, just like Netflix. There are many examples of this blurring of national cultural production zones in OTT, mentioned in Fig. 5.2 in Chapter 5.

In conclusion to this 'quid game' or money game for domination of the world's global OTT markets, all OTT platforms from any country from 2019 to 2023 are now starting a more thorough global competition with each other for the first time. The online video service market was once only divided between YouTube from 2005 and Netflix from 2007, and only had a few more players after 2014. However, between 2019 and 2022, more unlimited global OTT competition starts as fresh players of already American global giants join such as Google TV, Amazon prime video, Disney+, Apple TV+, HBO Max, peacock, Warner Media NBC Universal, Hulu, and ESPN+ (with the latter two owned by Disney, respectively by 67% and 80%, in 2023). In the same period, more global OTT competition is growing from multiple countries instead of only from other global American OTT services. For example, in China and Japan, Le.com, Aichi, Tencent Video, Asahi's AbemaTV, Line TV, NHK+, and Rakuten VIKI are competing globally as well. In Korea, by 2023, native OTT services are merging like Wavve (a merger from 2019 of the three OTT of three terrestrial broadcasters of KBS, MBC, and SBS (the latter previously called 'Pooq'), and the recent merger of 2023 between CJ ENM's Tving and KT's Seezn. These larger Korean OTT services of Waave and Tving/Seezn now compete with other smaller Korean OTT services domestically and globally like U+ Mobile TV and Watcha. In addition, Kakao and Naver, those Korean IT giants, recently launched OTT services called Kakao TV and Naver TV, respectively, to participate in global OTT competition in earnest. Even Korea's Coupang, an online shopping and distribution company originally, is now participating in the OTT market by launching its own Coupang Play OTT service—taking the idea of online retailer Amazon and its success with its OTT service called Amazon Prime Video.

8.3 Conclusion

The importance of a global digital OTT platform that distributes good proprietary content versus its competitors cannot be overemphasized. *Squid Game's* worldwide success is because there was a huge global distribution platform called Netflix with 230 million subscribers worldwide which spent over $1 billion dollars total on multiple productions of Korean Wave cinema in 2020 and 2021, instead of only spent approximately $21 million dollars on *Squid Game*. Thus, *Squid Game* was just one of many global Netflix offerings, yet it has been most successful Korean offering to Netflix so far and the most popular example of the cinema of the global Korean Wave so far.

From this point of view, the success of *Squid Game* is the 'success of Netflix.' It similarly is the success of many content providers in Korea previously faced with various levels of overt or covert national censorship in a highly vetted national subsidy network around the Korean Wave of the past. For many creative Korean producers, there is no regret working for American Netflix since via Netflix they access larger markets and have less national censorship to worry about. Netflix can offer creative Koreans more individual innovation, cultural innovation, and creative control. Plus, of course there are the huge windfalls from the *global* funding of the *global* Korean Wave pumped into the Korean creative content industries for years now, that will now only get larger as well as more competitive. As said earlier, by April 2023, the CEO of Netflix pledged to spend $2.5 billion over the next four years in the Korean Wave, which is "twice the total amount Netflix invested in Korea from 2016 to last year" (Lee, 2023).

On the one hand, so, there are virtuous cycles between an artist's individual vision and a global OTT provider like Netflix, and virtuous relationships between more market competition in OTT services and consumer satisfaction. It is true that it is becoming more important for Korean companies to expand new opportunities, such as planning large-scale investments for more aggressive business expansion and overseas expansion to counter what their mostly American OTT competition is doing already in their own country.

On the other hand, there are vicious cycles of this more *global* fight between OTT producers themselves creating *the erosion of various multi-polar and thus (taken as a whole) heterogeneous national cultures in plural, with erosion of truly national cultural waves* into only one homogenized global OTT viewing audience. This includes the domestic Korean OTT market and how much the Korean OTT providers themselves may become only one among many *global* OTT providers as well. This is seen in the globalization of the Korean Wave as many global OTT services may want to homogenize and compete in "Koreanizing" the world more, instead of build a wider diversity of cultural content.

So, instead of a multi-polar world, a different world may happen similar to what we see above with Weverse by HYBE: one digital platform company owning all that multi-polar world of cultural diversity of content, in itself. For example, *Squid Game* was made by Korean producers with an exorbitant budget from American Netflix that in the final analysis could only have come at such a big budget from this high stakes 'quid game' for keeping the loyalties of a global digital fandom base on a particular global digital platform due to exclusive content, regardless of whether the digital fandom is in K-pop, cosmetics, Korean Wave film content, or exclusive content from many different countries simultaneously. The relationship between the high stakes game of making and priming fresh and competitive global intellectual property that creates exclusive global audiences, while trying to use the profits of those audiences to maintain that globally accessible OTT media platform, are two sides of the same coin. The pioneering global success of Netflix's version of this double-sided coin is in priming its increasingly original content with 40% of Netflix's content made by itself in 2021, while hosting it on its own platform with a global user base as its best asset. *This looks exactly like the story of Weverse by HYBE. It looks exactly like any other story told about global intellectual property empires throughout this book.*

There are two problems with this model of the future. First, is it actually developmental and good, or is it creating an underdevelopment and thus bad? While people think they are building and participating in a diverse multi-polar world with OTT platforms like Netflix, are they really building a more homogenized and totalitarian world simply vetted by global scale capital for what is allowed to be culture globally, i.e., without actual allowed national cultural diversity at all? Second, a more *homogeneous* culture and a common *regional/national ethos* has been a secret of all examples of national successes in multi-polar economic and human development after World War II, instead of only in South Korea. A more homogeneous national culture is a regional resource in development that encourages greater consensus potentials and collective innovation toward a nationally decided future, and allows a more durable and flexible fast development drive. However, from the twenty-first century, what will happen to encourage more regional cultural strengths of homogeneity and its greater development potential compared to more heterogeneous cultures, *given more heterogeneous cultures lack any examples of a successful fast development drive* after World War II *unless they crafted a special common regional and collective ethos out of their diversity first* like in Singapore or Mauritius? So, why are people worshipping the false god of national heterogeneity, and which minority interests or global interests does it serve to worship such a false god, given all fully and successfully developed nations after World War II are more homogeneous cultures and given more heterogeneous national cultures tend only to create tiny rarified elites and deep underclasses of inequality or fall apart under challenges, instead of rising to their challenges? Therefore, *will a deep collective, regionally sound, and economically developmental aspect of humanity disappear* under global cultural pressures of heterogeneity and disappear under global digital cultural empires that manage and fund future culture—which may censor or triage other kinds of homogeneous cultural content that challenge their business model? Will global digital platforms' thin profits across hundreds of millions scattered around the world become the only expected audience metric of what culture is, simply because it is "not profitable" to produce for smaller localized audiences of cultural transmission that do far more important things than simply entertain us, like help us come to some collective consensus for deeper regional or national purposes of how to survive well in particular regions of the world happily into the future? What about a purpose of culture in addressing, defining, and discussing real geographically shared problems, instead of a purpose of culture as a more individualistic and escapist act, vetted to only ignore problems by being distracted and entertained to death about them?

Really, the result of the "Korean" Wave seems *not* to be a more multi-polar cultural world. It seems to create a more homogenized world of singular digital platforms hosting within themselves the whole multi-polar world, managing a digital platform from anywhere, owning digital IP from the multi-polar everywhere, and maintaining a global digital multi-polar fandom from everywhere on that singular platform. Thus increasingly a more homogenizing world of global digital platforms of global intellectual property is seen as the trend more than the Korean Wave participating in a more multi-polar cultural world. From the data about the conditions of development successes and failures reviewed in this book, this more homogenized world of singular digital platforms is profoundly backwards and anti-developmental, and it is against a multi-polar world of culture. As we escape from the censorship of a particular national legal regime around cultural content, we enter an era of potential larger and more thoroughly global control and global censorship over all national cultures from a placeless global corporation. Will such corralled global consumers encourage their own nations' economic shakeout and decline, and thus encourage the decline of the development of an actually multi-polar world of many different national cultural waves? The final section called Part III discusses some of these different scenarios of the future of the Korean Wave, the future of Korea itself, as well as the future of what all nations may become under this triple global storm of globalizing economic, cultural, and media regimes. This globalizing triple context starts to separate two classes of nations: some kinds of nations likely will survive such a culturally and economically corrosive global context more than others to win in development, while many other kinds of nations more than likely will fracture and decline in that same triple global storm as they lose past national cultural identity and lose past national economic competitiveness.

References

Billings, R. (2023, February 22). Portland Press Herald: Sen. Angus King caught up in 'Twitter Files' controversy. *Spectrum News.* https://spectrumlocalnews.com/me/maine/news/2023/02/22/sen--angus-king-caught-up-in--twitter-files--controversy

Binder, M. (2023, April 7). Elon Musk apparently on the outs with Matt Taibbi over Twitter-Substack feud; Taibbi said he would no longer use Twitter after it blocked Substack. Musk then unfollowed him. *Mashable.* https://mashable.com/article/elon-musk-matt-taibbi-breakup-substack-twitter-feud

Business Standard. (2020). Covid-19 pushes up OTT subscription growth by 60%: BCG report. https://www.business-standard.com/article/companies/covid-19-pushes-up-ott-subscription-growth-by-60-bcg-report-120121601311_1.html

Collier, P. (2007). *The bottom billion: Why the poorest countries are failing and what can be done about it.* Oxford University Press.

Digital TV News. (2022, May 23). Global OTT revenues to grow to $224 billion in 2027. *Digital TV News.* https://www.digitaltvnews.net/?p=38250

D'Souza, D., prod. (2022). *2000 Mules.* Salem Media Group.

Editorial Board. (2023, March 27). The IRS makes a strange house call on Matt Taibbi; An agent shows up at the home of the Twitter files journalist who testified before Congress. *Wall Street Journal.* https://www.wsj.com/articles/irs-matt-taibbi-twitter-files-jim-jordan-daniel-werfel-lina-khan-84ee518

Elliott, L. (2023, January 16). Call for new taxes on super-rich after 1% pocket two-thirds of all new wealth; $26 trillion of new wealth created since start of pandemic went to richest, Oxfam report reveals. *UK Guardian.* https://www.theguardian.com/inequality/2023/jan/16/oxfam-calls-for-new-taxes-on-super-rich-pocket-dollar-26tn-start-of-pandemic-davos

Hirwani, P. (2023, April 8). 'Twitter Files' journalist quits 'unusable' platform after Elon Musk puts restrictions on Substack. *AOL (The Independent UK)*. https://www.aol.com/news/matt-taibbi-twitter-files-journalist-071657103.html

Hoffman, J. (2017, April 25). Before there were smartphones, there was I-mode. *The History of the Web*. https://thehistoryoftheweb.com/before-there-were-smartphones-there-was-i-mode/

Johnson, J., Dir. (2007). *The One Percent* (HBO Documentary Films) J. Johnson & N. Kurzon, prod. YouTube. https://www.youtube.com/watch?v=XpIoGgafFsE

Kalia, S. (2021, October 18). Netflix's 'Squid Game' estimated to be worth about $900 million—Bloomberg News. *Yahoo! Finance*. https://Finance.yahoo.com/news/netflixs-squid-game-estimated-worth-150422206.html

Klein, N. (2007). *The shock doctrine: The rise of disaster capitalism*. Metropolitan Books/Henry Holt.

KOFICE. (2022). Hallyu White Paper 2021. Korean Foundation for International Cultural Exchange.

Kotkin, J. (2020). *The coming of neo-feudalism: A warning to the global middle class*. Encounter Books.

Lee, G. (2023, April 25). 넷플릭스 CEO가 환하게 웃었다, 尹대통령이 보여준 영상은 *Chosun Ilbo*. https://www.chosun.com/politics/politics_general/2023/04/25/G6RDLY7AHFGO7HX7GRQVI43HMA/

Maas, J. (2023, January 19). Netflix adds more than 7 million subscribers in Q4, smashing previous target. *Variety*. https://Variety.com/2023/tv/news/Netflix-subscribers-earnings-q4-2022-1235493532/

Mattelart, A. (2000). *Networking the world, 1794–2000*. University of Minnesota Press.

Oxfam International. (2020, January 20). World's billionaires have more wealth than 4.6 billion people. *Oxfam International*. https://www.oxfam.org/en/press-releases/worlds-billionaires-have-more-wealth-46-billion-people.

Oxfam International. (2023, January 16). Richest 1% bag nearly twice as much wealth as the rest of the world put together over the past two years. *Oxfam International*. https://www.oxfam.org/en/press-releases/richest-1-bag-nearly-twice-much-wealth-rest-world-put-together-over-past-two-years

Pallotta, F. (2022, July 9). Netflix loses subscribers, but stops the bleeding. *CNN-Business*. https://edition.cnn.com/2022/07/19/media/Netflix-earnings/index.html

Piketty, T. (2014). *Capital in the twenty first century*. An Imprint of Harvard University Press.

Quote Investigator. (2016). If you want to tell people the truth, you'd better make them laugh or they'll kill you. *Quote Investigator*. https://quoteinvestigator.com/2016/03/17/truth-laugh/

Roy, B. (2022, December 5). Who is Matt Taibbi? Elon Musk Twitter files release explained. *Sportskeedia*. https://www.sportskeeda.com/pop-culture/who-matt-taibbi-elon-twitter-files-release-explained

Sandbrook, R., Edelman, M., Heller, P., & Teichman, J. (2007). *Social democracy in the global periphery: Origins, challenges*. Cambridge University Press.

Singh, D. (2018, November 22). Indian OTT market to grow 10 times to $5 bn by 2023. *Business Today*. https://www.businesstoday.in/latest/economy-politics/story/indian-ott-market-to-reach-dollar-5-billion-in-size-by-2023-says-bcg-report-117242-2018-11-21

Standing, G. (2011). *The precariat: The new dangerous class*. Bloomsbury.

Taibbi, M. (2023a, April 7). Eat Me, MSNBC: Reviewing the last six years at the network that claims now to be concerned with integrity and accuracy. *Racket News*. https://www.racket.news/p/msnbc-sucks

Taibi, M. (2023b). 1. TWITTER FILES #19: The Great Covid-19 Lie Machine; Stanford, the Virality Project, and the Censorship of "True Stories". https://twitter.com/mtaibbi/status/1636729166631432195

Whitten, S. (2022, October 18). Netflix adds more than 2.4 million subscribers, reveals details about password-sharing crackdown. *CNBC*. www.cnbc.com/2022/10/18/netflix-nflix-earnings-q3-2022.html

Wilkinson, R., & Pickett, K. (2011). *The spirit level: Why greater equality makes societies stronger* (Revised, Updated ed.). Bloomsbury Publishing.

Part III
Into the Future of the Korean Wave, Korea, and an Ever More Digital World

This research was conducted to understand precursors of the global Korean Wave and to document its incredible successes. It aims as well to be a case study for comparative insights about world development and the history of communications for what good choices and 'good accidents' help national development in general, for use in other countries, as well as for exploring choices of futures that will face all nations in the twenty-first century. One of the Korean Wave's major precursors was and remains the ongoing successful economic Korean Miracle from 1961 to the present. It started as a drive of export-led development, and then was buttressed by many other consensus policies developing out of strong Korean democratic contexts facing weakly legitimate authoritarian military coups. This consensus kept being affirmed and expanded between 1963 to 1970, yet was almost was lost to the non-consensus military forces between 1971 to 1987. However, after 1987, both forces continue to dance and to accommodate particularly with the expansion of digital capacities. Korea remained strong enough and the military wise in foresight enough to move unrepresentative authoritarian coups back toward more representative consensus, both in 1963 and in 1987. In short, President Park (1961/1963-1979) had once original and exclusive export-led development ideas to which were added many buttressed consensus policies that preserved and enhanced the Korean national culture, democratic politics, and national economy against its own self-developing inequitable problems of export-led development. Two results were a strongly durable national cultural resource and a successful economic model of "buttressed export-led development." Both were important in the economic Korean Miracle and later in the sectors of the global Korean Wave. However, a fresh digital saturation starts to provide fresh fodder for digital strategies of both tyranny and greater democratization.

Several interesting points about the Korean Wave can be summarized in Part III. In Chapter 9, first, once several selected themes of Korean culture became exports and growth sectors in themselves, only then could they synergistically interact with other past Korean material economic sectors whether they were domestic or global themselves already. Second, in this way, the Korean Wave is the product of more purely economic sector decisions unlike cultural waves of other nations that are hard to disentangle from their senses of cultural supremacism or desires of military imperialism. Third, this lends a mental coolness and calculating tenaciousness to the business sense of Koreans in their economic plans around their cultural wave that contrasts to their animation of a highly emotional and frenetic content of the Korean Wave. Plus, culturally, fourth, it seems many Koreans would just as soon be left alone, though the development drive from 1961 gave them a top-down modern revolutionary development state in long alliance with huge for-profit companies, both seeking global profit. This has put this homogeneous and conservative nation in the midst of a global cosmopolitan storm of admiration for Korean products and culture regardless.

As the product of long-term calculated decisions, the Korean Wave has been engineered to occur instead of 'naturally' or slowly blossoming by default out of urban industrial development from the virtuous development cycles mentioned earlier. However, as argued earlier how Korea is a rare case of a fast developing country finishing its 'development gauntlet' with entry into a cultural wave, it may be true that urban industrial development is a precursor of any cultural wave in existence so far, yet it is always decisions that make any path down the development gauntlet and into a cultural wave, instead of simply aggregate growth causing it automatically to spill into a global sphere of culture. The Korean public state and its private companies' decisions for coordination of certain strategies toward an attempted Korean Wave and rejection of other strategies have always been there since the 1980s. This ongoing desire for this state-based cultural tinkering and for this centralized cultural engineering started in the 1970s and has been the later Korean Wave's durability, as well as noted earlier, has been its equal danger in how state subsidies and state cultural planning are easily subverted into state censorship regimes denying common civil rights and common cultural participation itself. Despite the hopefully defunct secret state cultural blacklists from 2017, decisions by private companies for whom to put under contract or for whom to ignore have always been there as well. However, what has happened through it all so far is a widely shared Korean cultural desire to participate in and to compete to be in the Korean Wave with its rising idols, artists, singers, producers, webtoon writers, etc., instead of Korean culture rejecting it yet.

As noted in this penultimate section, will this always be true though? Thus, *what will happen to other nations and to Korea in the future*, in this growing interaction of their countries' cultures, and in the context of an increasing more mutual participation in a global digital economy, a global digital culture, and a global decentralized media?

There are two themes in this conclusion. As said above, for Chapter 9, first, important factors that make the Korean Wave uniquely synergistic in the present are discussed as what makes it successful versus other non-Western/developing countries' cultural waves since the 1980s that have shown none of the same synergy and even start to show decline under wider global competition in this eroding multi-polar global cultural space. In Chapter 10 and 11, second, the future of both Korea and the Korean Wave is discussed—not only for its implications for Korea though for implications about all nations of the world that are increasingly starting to live in a '*triple global storm*' of (1) a global digital economy, (2) a global digital culture, and (3) a global decentralized media. It is argued that the world saw this triple global storm touch down in Korea *first* in the linking of a global digital economy and a multi-polar global digital culture, mostly because Korea had the earliest best medium or mechanism for it, by being the first digitally saturated nation as described earlier with many digital 'world firsts' to its credit. (See Appendix 1.) Thus Korea could be *first* in pouring its already saturated national digital culture smoothly and virally later into a growing globally decentralized digital media, since other nations were behind Korea in digital saturation.

Though this triple global storm came calling on Korea first, it will come knocking on the door of all other nations later. For some nations, it will come like Death with a scythe. For others, it will come as an Angel, like it did to Korea, bestowing laurel wreaths to the winners to protect their hubris and excellence from the jealousy of the gods and from other nations. For all nations, this triple global storm will appear as a 'digital bottleneck' though which all countries have to pass if they wish to remain intact and if they wish to have the same "wealth of K-Nations" in the twenty-first century as Korea. However, more often, this triple global storm with its effects of creating a digital bottleneck could stop passage of and destroy many currently existing larger and smaller nations for rationales explained in Chapter 10. This digital bottleneck could reformat many countries culturally to make them unrecognizably different and tyrannical. Rarely, countries will pass through and remain intact like Korea so far. It is expected that most nations in this media regime change will have results combined with how that media regime develops in unique combinations of 'demography, geography, and culture' (and other factors) per each current nation. As a result, many nations may either be broken up or altered beyond recognition into unrepresentative digital technocracies ruled by small unchecked homogeneous cultural groups running the online platforms in league with repressive governments attempting to revoke common individual civil rights via a tyrannical social credit system based on applying digital convergence to its politics to track everyone, instead of only to apply the digital convergence to economics. Thus, the point develops that digital fragmentation of data is important to maintain as a novel 'digital check and balance' against that digital convergence in politics. We might learn from Korea here as well, as noted in Chapter 10, that its earlier applied digital convergence in politics from as early a 1995 has repeatedly seen this technocracy being reversed by its own democratic politics toward maintaining civil and political principles of data fragmentation four times between 2012 to 2022.

So, instead of just being entertained by the global Korean Wave, we can seriously learn from Korea *itself* for how to survive intact as a nation in what has been called 'general development' as well as the 'digital development' now into the future in the midst of this growing triple global storm. First, in this general development, we can learn from Korean good choices. This is because there has been a *unique stability of the formal policies of the Korean developmental model* that encouraged economic aggregation the best, and now is encouraging the same around the ever-growing global Korean Wave. This has been despite the ostensible *instability of informal politics and formal institutions* of Korea which is now on its Sixth Republic in only 75 years. What was argued in Part I was that a virtuous cycle developed with Korea's homogeneous culture in the absence of obfuscating aristocratic elites increasingly missing in all four institutional positions of social power between 1907 to 1961 (missing from military/state, economics, finance, and education/religion). This led to the culture after the military coup of 1961 to be supercharged and ever renewed in an alliance with that military coup, toward ever more representative and consensus-oriented hybrid political and economic policies. This kept the fast development drive going down the development gauntlet in Korea, while other nations were unable to have such flexibility or durability to their fast development drives in most cases. It was argued that Korea has a unique hybrid cultural mix as well: an overriding ancient more homogenous culture in the absence of an ancient aristocracy, and yet will be argued that hybrid modicum of surrogate heterogeneous divisions of regions, religious diversity, and its export-led economic orientation helped keep open more transparent democratic procedures with that modicum of dissension to check against the dangers of a more completely homogeneous culture. All this, combined with the historical power vacuum of the loss of its aristocracy, kept Korea very consensus oriented to mass concerns instead of dominated only by powerful private interests capable of vetoing or keeping the development drive more unrepresentative in its formal policy. It was argued that is why even Korean developmental dictatorships were closer to hybrid themselves. The term invented to describe Korea as an outcome of these hybrid cultural, political and economic settlements was an 'authoritarian parliamentary' system since even repeated Korean military coups were only weakly legitimate. They felt they had to always maintain parliamentarian elections of some sort, even between 1972 and 1987, and felt they had to keep running for office even after a military coup like President Park between 1963 to around 1971, or, they felt they had to redeem themselves and distance themselves like President Chun after 1980 from past abuses (between 1972 to 1979) by returning or guaranteeing even more civil freedoms to stay in power in some areas, even as other freedoms were removed. This weakly dictatorial dynamic (compared to other nations' dictatorships) kept Korea intact as a highly regionalized, multi-party republican state with growing individual civil rights, even as Korea underwent the rigors of fast development and then later in its growing 'digital development' passed through the digital bottleneck first and alone by being the world's first digital media saturated culture.

Second, in Korea's 'digital development,' we can learn from Korea's 'good accidents' as well. These good decisions to get through the digital bottleneck arguably were aided by good accidents to be described in Chapter 10 about Korea's fortunate level of being a 'mid-size' geographic and demographic nation in the world. Comparatively speaking, these national conditions seem better able to get through the digital bottleneck compared to many other smaller or larger geographic/demographic nations in which typically greater digitalization results only in a more unrepresentative technocratic censorship and central management. Plus, a second good accident of Korea has been its more homogeneous culture holds together better in such a digital triple global storm. On the contrary, more heterogeneous nations in the same triple global storm seem to have increasing cultural disintegration based upon previously hidden cultural fault lines now exposed virally and magnified emotionally in a daily way in a digital culture. Putting all three factors together—of a more 'mid-size' demography and geography in a more homogeneous culture—shows Korea has had all these three factors, and it has weathered the triple global storm well. After 2012, as Koreans became the most digitally saturated and first digitally saturated culture in the world, Koreans fought back successfully against such encroaching unrepresentative digital technocratic management and external or internal cultural erosion and dissension, as will be seen, just as they earlier fought back successfully against encroaching unrepresentative dictatorship between 1972 through 1987. Doing this, Korea has survived both its development gauntlet intact in general development, as well as survived the digital bottleneck intact in its digital development, so far. Thus, as before, both good choices of being a more saturated digital culture as well as good accidents (the latter, mostly of certain 'mid-level' national sizes of demography and geography, and certain more 'mid-level' homogeneous cultural conditions) seem to have combined to help Korea move through this digital bottleneck and remain whole and intact instead of being chewed to component cultural bits in the process. Thus, other nations with many different bad choices of less saturated media or oriented differently by many different combinations of bad accidents (of larger or smaller demography and geography, and in having a more heterogeneous culture or a "too" homogeneous culture) intersect with this fresh media regime in a bad way and may suffer a breakdown in their nation or suffer a totalitarian transmogrification of their nation in this digital triple global storm.

Nonetheless, Korea is riding the digital tiger of this triple global storm, since this is how Korea has developed since the 1980s from its development of a digital telecommunications sector. Therefore, Korea cannot get off the digital tiger and change developmental course without greatly wrecking its whole modern export-led digital political economy and digital culture that is now tightly integrated into our fresh global digital media regime. Other countries are in similar situations. However, even if they may try to resist the media regime change, they will still be surrounded by other countries that embrace it, and thus only will put themselves even further behind and in danger of national breakdown by being outclassed internationally later. So, how might we learn lessons from how Korea survived intact through the digital bottleneck, while surviving as a multi-party republic with civil rights against surveillance so far, that can be applied to other countries to help them weather this triple global storm and pass through the digital bottleneck as unscathed or even as digitally improved as Korea?

In conclusion, to address those two themes mentioned above about Korea's good decisions and good accidents that made the Korean Wave as well as how it got through the digital bottleneck of this triple global storm, Part III has three chapters. In the first, Chapter 9, we look at *the present of the Korean Wave*. It summarizes from comparative and historical analysis the present power of the global Korean Wave from its small beginnings externally in the early 1990s to the vantage point of its global soft power in 2023. It asks *why has Korea been more successful* in expanding its uncommonly large global cultural wave when only a smaller regional cultural wave was seen regularly from its peer developing countries from the 1980s onward? The answer is the tremendously greater number of synergies available to Koreans as a culture and as a political economy.

Equally comparative and historical, the second chapter of Part III in Chapter 10 looks at several scenarios *about the future of the Korean nation and the world's nations at large.* It asks where are the many trends going in our increasingly more multi-polar global digital culture and politics, and what may happen to the soft power of the Korean nation from the Korean Wave? What kinds of nations, cultures, and policies will be successful in the future digital global economy and culture, and which kinds of nations may fall behind economically or culturally without rethinking how they may participate and compete better in this fresh global level of digital economy and culture? Korea and the Korean Wave represent the 'good digital scenario' for the future of all nations sooner or later: *the "intact' or even 'improved' scenario.* It is given that all nations are increasingly pulled by the same globally distributed digital media and its economic and cultural platforms, willingly or unwillingly, into interaction, participation, and competition in a global digital economy and a global digital culture that tends to undermine past national versions of both. Other countries start to exhibit many different versions of the 'bad digital scenario': defined as either *cultural and national breakdown* with its dissolution into component cultural parts, or equally cultural and national breakdown defined as *survival only by loss of their representative governments and civil rights into a technocratic digital police state.* However, so far, Korea endures and thrives in both its general development and its digital development. How might other countries learn from this? How might other countries avoid their own national breakdown scenario and/or unrepresentative technocracy scenario that are equally seen now in current digital trends of nations?

The final third chapter of Part III in Chapter 11 discusses the *future of the Korean Wave itself*. Based on current trends, there are *four scenarios where it could go.* Plus, based on other current trends in many countries instead of only Korea, there are future problems of economic inequalities and low birth rates that may make it difficult for Korea to keep its economic development, its cultural wave, or its traditional culture. Solutions are offered how to fix Korea as well.

Chapter 9
Summarizing Past and Present Synergies in the Korean Wave

9.1 Unique High Levels of Synergy

First, it is argued that why Korea could create a *global* Korean Wave, *instead of remain a regional cultural wave like all other regional cultural waves of all other non-Western developing countries*, has a great deal to do with Korea's greater likelihood of *domestic economic synergies* and *global economic synergies* that it has as its disposal. South Korea is the fourth most 'complex' economy in the world. (OEC, 2023) Second, this was combined with greater *cultural synergies* of a more homogenous culture that allows faster collective innovation for seizing more economic chances of such an ever-changing global market situation. Third, however, this was combined with a *domestic political synergy* that provided a check and balance against the worst potentials of that kind of more homogeneous culture toward dictatorship, nationalization, xenophobia, and self-repression, and that provided a check and balance against the worst potentials of a homogeneous culture when run by a durable oligarchic aristocracy. Fourth, all of this was combined with a very saturated digital media sphere in Korea that allowed a greater *digital synergy*, unlike other regional cultural waves that equally started to appear by the 1980s still based in more analogue and one-way mass media expressions. All four points of synergy are discussed below, starting with the economic synergies unique to the later global Korean Wave that pushed it higher and wider than other regional culture waves from other developing countries that lacked such economic synergies, or in many cases lacking the cultural, political, or digital synergy of Korea as well.

First, global-level economic synergies were available for Korea almost alone among developing countries, because Korea ignored American, U.N., and World Bank development advice and chose a fast development model *of multiple export-led economic sectors*. Second, equally important beyond how Korea came to reject this bad development advice in retrospect, is how Korea had great resources of cultural synergy in its traditional homogeneous culture of great solidarity and collective innovation that could animate such an export-led urban industrialization as well as push for other buttressing policies beyond that singular developmental idea that were more

G.-C. Shin and M. D. Whitaker, *The Korean Wave in a Post-Pandemic World*,
https://doi.org/10.1007/978-981-99-3683-0_9

consensus-oriented. Both together provided great synergies with each other in the long run that were useful for globalizing the Korean Wave as well. The homogenous culture could survive to be a durable resource since Korea's regional traditional culture was respected and even enhanced in its position from the 1960s onward in the fast development model instead of taking the modernization advice of the United States and others of intentionally demoting traditional culture by direct design or by passive neglect. So, in two ways, Korea bucked the world's advice on how to develop after 1961. Korea surprised the world with how a homogeneous culture, when linked to export-led economics, instead of being only traditionalist and conservative, started to set innovative world records not only in the fast development drive itself though has received many awards in the last few years of the global Korean Wave around expanding digital businesses and technically-complicated performances beyond the capacities of other developing or even developed countries alike. South Korea first put the world in the thrall of the success of its fast economic development drive via its production of material products, and second, now has kept the world in thrall of its cultural energy, creativity, and professional production quality of a global Korean Wave.

Third, there is the oddly effective interaction of these export-led economic policies and the homogenous cultural background with a multi-party political system that protects human, civil, and property rights of individuals. This is hardly something regularly seen in a more collectivist culture anywhere, yet it does appear strongly in Korea. Thus, a home-bound, traditional, tenacious, and yet collaborative culture has been oddly *checked and balanced well by South Korean political organizational choices opposite to its cultural tenor* as well as *oddly effective in its interaction with economic organizational choices of an export-led economy opposite to its cultural tenor.* Koreans have come to fight for their national autonomy in solidarity in the export-led economy for expanding the scale of the national economy, instead of fight in an internecine way with each other within the nation over economic policies of only domestic consolidation or expansion that can only have diminishing returns and lead to divisions and recriminations. Thus, South Korean synergistic organizational choices, in an already synergistic culture, with a successful land distribution, and then toward an ever advancing export-led economic focus, and then an ever advancing multi-party state, combined with an ever advancing concern of human, civil, and property rights, led South Koreans to be more durably entrepreneurial in private investment. That now has made their nation a home for global-level technical and organizational innovations in cultural production. However, as said earlier, the global Korean Wave is hardly led by private capital. In all export-led economic sectors, there is another long and well-practiced synergy between the Korean public state, private profit, and the Korean culture.

These synergies mentioned above of *specific* hybrid choices of economic, cultural and political dynamics matter because the same homogeneous culture under different specific organizational choices of politics and economics could have become self-destructive and lacking innovation and synergy. For example, we have the 'natural experiment' that the *same* homogeneous culture in North Korea encouraged very different outcomes under *different* political and economic organizational policy choices. We can peer through a glass darkly into the same tendencies of the Korean homogeneous culture if it was everywhere under more totalitarian political organization and autarkic economic policies that frankly seem 'better aligned' to its homogeneous and collectivist culture. However, after seventy-five years of work, South Koreans with both their political institutions and economic policies counteropposed to their own collectivist and inward-facing tendencies are on top of the global economic and cultural world. Meanwhile, their cultural brothers and sisters in North Korea with both their political institutions and economic policies in league with their own collectivist and inward-facing tendencies have sunk to the bottom of the world as some of the poorest and most (self-)repressed people in the world despite enjoying a head start from Japanese Empire-era infrastructural investment in their zone well into the into the 1970s. However, North Koreans were without a virtuous cycle of greater innovation to keep improving such urban industrial infrastructures mostly given to them by earlier Japanese investment there. Thus, North Koreans show themselves in a viscous cycle without the same ongoing synergies and innovation in South Korea, despite North Koreans having the same homogeneous culture yet having different political and economic choices. North Koreans still live as in a time capsule or oubliette of the 1970s, in a land time forgot, with the same permanent one-party-state 'socialist' military dictatorship and the same old media regime of one-way mass communication. Updated two-way communication via smartphones and the internet is highly curtailed in use there. Socialist is in quotes above because of three hypocritical factors. First, North Korea is not socialist because despite the state banning all forms of private property and owning it instead, which is characteristic of a socialist regime, North Korea equally resembles more of a violent and unstable pseudo-royal court system because it is around the Kim dynasty and because it fights with an equally nepotistic neo-aristocracy of other original bloodline families of the socialist and cultural revolution still in power after 75 years. Second, North Korea is not socialist because of the lack of legal equality. The old party families gave themselves special 'legal estate' or 'caste-like' rights that has created a discriminatory hierarchy that classifies all North Koreans in different and unequal cultural levels hard to escape over generations, instead of having a socialist legal equality. Equally, North Korea is poorly described as socialist because even though nearly everything is owned by the state, the goal is hardly reducing inequality by state distribution though perpetuating inequality by state-based expropriation, denying the poorest any succor or autonomy in North Korea and requisitioning it for the party elites and the military development model. So, instead of the same homogeneous culture getting political and economic development with their choices of politics and economics, North Koreans have sunk to the bottom of the world and got nationwide family-based inherited discriminations, prison/torture camps for ideological dissidents, ongoing food scarcity, and a whole country treated as a prison camp because citizens are agricultural slaves on a tax farm where all land is owned by the state and where they see their produce planned and then confiscated by the party elite without really being shared to demote inequalities like a socialist state would reputedly do. In turn, like a prison camp, the rural agricultural laborers are surrounded by closed borders to stop them from escaping. North Koreans might as well be feudal peasants bound to the land, lorded over by a dynastic Kim family (now on Kim the Third) and hemmed in via a selfish neo-aristocracy of the original party state's bloodlines seething with inherited entitlement, strategizing for wealth and power through marriage alliances, and politically unstable against each other.

So, with the same homogeneous culture as South Korea and yet under different political and economic choices than South Korea, to the contrary North Korea is a militarized and autonomous poor economy. North Korea has the 'original social credit system' of nationalization, meaning, it is easy to control all peoples' behavior if all institutional sources of *private* property, privacy, and communication is abolished and if all land, built property, services access, and media is owned by the state and given out for only good behavior and used only for government-approved speech. North Korea is now separated in false way from the world-system by its chosen development policy of being a nation trying to be wholly autonomous—with three results only being possible from such a policy: diminishing economic returns, zero true remaining global political allies, and a black market in illegal products internationally as a way the regime makes money internationally or its citizens survive internally. By the 1990s, with the abrupt end of subsidized technical and material aid from the Soviet Union as it collapsed, North Korea started to starve as did its Caribbean twin Cuba. Given a lack of international market trading partners required in North Korea, thus little technical creativity or idea exchanges seem allowed or required in North Korea. The only innovations that seem required in North Korea are military technology improvements in its nuclear weapons industry or its massive submarine fleet that is reputed to be one of the world's largest that is useful for smuggling global contraband (or people) into and out of North Korea as if it is a nation-scale pirate enclave. Plus, when domestic talent is unable to be found in such a national autarkic system, the North Korean state further like a pirate enclave has simply kidnapped talented people it wanted from overseas, trying to get people to forcibly work for the Kim dynasty. This kidnapping of talent to North Korea happened to famous South Korean film directors in the 1960s like Shin Sang-ok and his actress wife Choi Eun-hee. It happened to dozens of random Japanese, kidnapped off their own Japanese beaches at night by the piratical North Korean navy that took them back to North Korea in boats to try to brainwash them into being spies that could be trusted enough to return to Japan.

Given the same homogeneous culture in both Koreas, what a stark happy and sad difference has happened under different institutional choices of South and North Korea. Respectively, one made a more virtuous cycle of growth and the other made a more vicious cycle of decline. In short, a theme throughout this book has been this baseline of a Korean homogeneous culture of *South Korea* interacting very well with its chosen political and economic policies in its fast development drive, contrasted to failures of *North Korea and to the many different levels of other developing countries* that all achieved far less than South Korea. It was argued that South Korea's *seemingly counteropposed political and economic policy choices in their more homogeneous culture* is a synergistic recipe that increasingly protected this homogeneous culture against itself—against similar early excesses in dictatorship and human rights violations from 1948 to 1987 that slowly fell away in South Korea and yet still tragically happen in North Korea. The policy choices of South Korea definitely have created a more durable economic development only focused globally outwards wedded to the resources of collective innovation in its homogeneous culture. So, South Koreans have been more encouraged and protected to build and to invest into that ever larger risky scale in their economy by their increasingly protected human, civil, and property rights. Plus, they are rewarded and encouraged by tremendous state financial subsidies if they follow state priorities in 'private' research and innovation. From these issues, a greater economic aggregation over time can accrue that is made possible from the civil-legal rights, from private property protections, and from the more synergistic organizational coordination—all without any obfuscating aristocratic settlement that would warp all three factors to damage the fast development drive itself or even block it from starting in the first place.

These specific hybrid organizational synergies of policies, economics, and culture are how South Korea encouraged this great economic expansion, creativity, and innovation out of the same original homogeneous culture as North Korea. However, nearly everything South Korea achieves is denied to their brothers and sisters in North Korea, and sometimes it is denied upon pain of death if North Koreans are caught with video recordings of the global Korean Wave from South Korea for instance. So we have tremendous virtuous cycles of synergies in South Korea and its economy and global Korean Wave and almost zero such synergies of economy and culture in North Korea except around military technology. The first point is noticing how the different choices of political institutions and economic policies matter in either fast development drives or ever shrinking returns that are both interactive with the same kind of homogeneous culture in different ways. The second point is that if choices of policies about political systems and economics are chosen well, that interact with a particular kind of homogeneous culture, they can supercharge that culture into great heights of synergy, creativity, and innovation, and if they are chosen poorly, it demotes all three and only supercharges cultural and economic stasis or decline.

These political, economic, and cultural synergies are responsible for pushing the regional cultural wave of South Korea more globally in scale. Just like Korea, there were many other developing countries' equal regional cultural waves. However, the latters' regional culture waves remained regional without the Korean-style synergies available to those other countries. Another kind of digital synergy was available to South Korea that interacted with all that was said above and more. It is hardly only one factor of a digital-based media sphere, because the dynamics of the exported Korean Wave are before that digital-based media regime, even if it influenced it later. To elaborate with examples, many developing countries had a regional cultural wave by the 1980s. However, they all stalled and remained known for only one entertainment sector generally and/or remained only a regional phenomenon. The 1980s thus was the beginning of our current global era of more multi-polar cultural products. Cultural products from Latin America, East Asia, and South Asia started to be enjoyed increasingly by their respective regional neighbors. This is similar to the period of then 'nameless' regional Hallyu for Korea of course. For examples beyond regional Hallyu, this was the era of Mexican and Brazilian cultural products found throughout Latin America in the proliferation of 'telenovelas' (TV dramas) only from the more urban industrialized Mexico and Brazil. Japanese animation and Japanese TV dramas were beginning to be loved throughout the less developed East Asia of that time. Even films produced in the very urban industrialized British Hong Kong were popular throughout East Asia in this period, produced in incredibly high numbers of hundreds per year. Plus, this was the era in which Indian "Bollywood" films first spread in popularity throughout South Asia. Comparatively late, a more closed South Korea, still under its 'authoritarian parliamentary' dynamics of a hybrid multi-party parliamentary government yet with a presidential dictatorship, was more concerned with *internal* state-led cultural policing and censorship until 1987, instead of concerned with *external* cultural waves like other developing countries. Despite this, South Korea in the 1980s was trying its own exportable regional cultural wave at the same time by intentionally producing Korean 'domestic' TV dramas with language dubbing in mind from the start for different international markets. Overall, in the 1980s, we can see many different non-Western developing or developed countries, or global city states like Hong Kong, making a global multi-polar mass culture. This started to interact with and to compete with the hegemonic core European or American mass cultural industries.

However, in all cases except South Korea in retrospect, many developing countries' culture industries remained only in one major cultural product and became known mostly or only in their wider local region. Only would South Korea out of all developing countries of the 1980s be able to do the "cultural triple win" later: have (1) *multiple major cultural products* that were (2) popular *worldwide in all regions*, and thus obviously touching or choosing cultural themes of (3) more *universal cultural resonance*. So, next, beyond the synergies already mentioned above, what were other successful factors that helped Korea and the Korean Wave achieve all three italicized points in its cultural wave that remained unachieved by the few other developing nations' cultural waves? This was despite many other developing countries having an earlier start with their regional cultural waves than Korea, that would presumably put them in a better position for growth of such global synergies.

There are three basic interactive answers for why only Korea has been able to exhibit a greater synergistic force in the global economy when thinking of all developing countries—with only the Korean *regional* Hallyu becoming the *global* Korean Wave, with only Korea achieving *multiple global* cultural offerings, and with only Korean culture perhaps showing a more sublime *universal cultural resonance* with people worldwide.

The first theme deals with the earlier and far more successful fast economic development of South Korea, in the economic Korean Miracle after 1961 to the present compared to other developing countries with a cultural wave. This greater economic urban industrial and technical success was based on an export-led economic policy of multiple sectors instead of only one, so it could be more easily preparatory to the later global Korean Wave. Other points about this strong Korean fast developmental drive have had many other rationales for its success, mentioned in Part 1 or in Appendices 2 and 3. The result has been how the Korean Wave could merge Korean past *technical* and *marketing* skills in *global* product sales and marketing with its later *cultural* storytelling, polished performances, and style as an export sector as well.

This means unlike other developing countries, Korea was already pinning everything on an export-led economy. Thus when it occurred, Korea's offerings in its cultural wave could be backed by the full force of an already existing global-level urban industrial production and its many different sectors offering their own globally competitive technological value and marketing experience. Other developing nations, rarely choosing such export-led economic policies, innately were unable to marshal the synergy of multiple Korean product and staffing alliances that could be a self-interested support team overseas aiding any Korea Wave in the same global-level goals. This makes Korea's later cultural products in the Korean Wave follow a well-trodden path of previous material products that *blazed the trail and were already overseas to be used to help* any regional Hallyu upon arrival. For instance, as mentioned earlier, the first major success of regional Hallyu was in 1992 in Hong Kong around ostensibly the Korean TV drama "What is Love?", yet the reality is its popularity was catalyzed by *a massive Korean synergistic team effort already established overseas*. There was a deep synergy overseas between several branches of the Korean public state, along with many different and unrelated Korean private corporate profit interests already in Hong Kong before and beyond entertainment sectors. This was aided by the homogeneous Korean cultural synergy of solidarity and teamwork for working together simultaneously at home and abroad to expand each others' sectors overseas in tandem. To summarize synergies, other developing countries are far less dedicated to an export-led development, far less culturally dedicated to each other, and far less likely to take state direction, even overseas. Thus other developing nations' cultural waves are argued to have been less likely to have as much synergistic potential for creating fellow export nationalistic allies in tandem outside their own country unlike Korean businesses.

Thus, Koreans were innately more desperate to succeed and had to use their brains and value-added products as their best resources in many different sectors because Koreans were without many raw materials to export. On the other hand, many developing countries indeed were mostly raw material exporters with a much smaller value-added sector to export than Korea as a whole by percentages of GNP. Thus, as said in earlier chapters, the 'good accident' of a lack of raw material wealth later helped Korea hold durably over time to the 'good choices' of export-led development. This export-led development drive in turn builds more synergies and grows economic aggregation by holding to the same policies instead of changing them over time. Then, once overseas, Korean cultural synergy and solidarity could be in force across many different export sectors in many different countries helping to prime regional Hallyu into a global Korean Wave, while other developing nations kept only their regional cultural waves.

The other factor of a *digital synergy* helps explain the *later* greater synergy in the global Korean Wave instead of really explains the *earlier* origin of the Korean Wave. The second answer about the greater synergy in the global Korean Wave deals with the Korean state choosing digital telecommunications from the 1980s as a priority growth sector. This media technology is innately a more synergistic industry itself in two ways—both internally in Korea and externally to Korea. See Appendix 1 for the many synergies and Korean 'world firsts' that started to come from early prioritization in a domestic sector and an export-led sector of digital telecommunications.

First, digital telecommunications as a technology and *internally* to itself as a sector is a more synergistic industry requiring expertise and collaboration ongoing in many different technical and material science fields and even Korean state funding collaborations to keep up the global competitiveness of Korean digital products. Since Korea was an export-led economy, any nascent Korean digital telecommunications technology had to be either better than then-current Japanese or Western digital telecommunications competition, or at least had to do a serviceable job cheaper than its competition. Plus, when or if something is better and cheaper, it is more likely to be bought en masse. This forms a potential synergistic loyal network effect among users as well as creates a good memory of a cultural brand. Many other non-Western countries rarely chose a sector of digital telecommunications, so they lacked this synergistic dynamic around digital telecommunications whether internal to their nation or externally as an export sector. Plus, a list of failures of many countries in their digital telecommunications industries is far longer than the shorter list of the nations with more durable successes. Even developed countries and large nations can fail at a durable export of a digital telecommunications industry given the failures of Japan, the U.K., West Germany (and Europe in general), East Germany, the USSR, Norway, India, Brazil, or China so far despite the latter trying for decades to start a semiconductor fabrication of its own. Even Japan tried to continue its lead from the 1970s into the 1990s, yet its economic recession from 1990 lasted the better part of a decade and led to less durable concerns about this sector. Hong Kong as well found it was unable to keep its early lead in digital telecommunications by a lack of state supportive synergies since a more passive British colonial state was unwilling to expend money or protective legal support on it to help it grow. This led to the passing of the digital torch to both Taiwan and Korea during this period more durably to the present in both countries, because both countries do have great resources of state, cultural, and economic synergies around digital telecommunications industries to help it grow.

However, a globally competitive sector of digital telecommunications it is a torch easier to pass to a country than to keep it alight. Therefore, what Taiwan and Korea have done in keeping it alight for decades should be celebrated and learned from for its secrets of developmental success. This sector is very hard to start, and very hard to keep durably in a country particularly in a situation of global competition and global expectations of ever changing and ever improving standards. So, even if multiple developing countries attempted digital telecommunications, the key is durably keeping it instead of only starting it, since such a fast-paced industry requires great deals of other synergistic and expensive research and development coordination. It is hard to sustain digital telecommunications as both a political priority or as a globally-competitive economic sector for decades as Korea (or Taiwan) has done. Many other states have tried and backed out of such an industry in failure.

A successful digital telecommunications industry is synergy itself. It depends on a great deal of ongoing research and investment, and it is funded from truly large scale capital. This is regularly only available for the long term in financially strong states. Only a subset of those have a more collective ideology that accepts that their state is a legitimate coordinator of long-term technical research and development of skills and infrastructures and thus legitimately choosing winners and losers in technology that keeps the whole nation competing globally and durably. So, instead of only thinking such state coordination is a cronyism in choosing winners or losers, given that the actual successful nations in such fields do this regularly, it shows there is something deeply pragmatic about it instead of it being only biasing or weakening of the sector. Many nations show they want their own digital telecommunications industries, though equally many nations have different state ideologies of less coordinated markets that hamstring them culturally from arranging help for choosing winners or losers that makes an easier state-led durable digital telecommunications as an industry. However, it is more than simply a desire to have state intervention because China with its much larger resources than Korea or Taiwan has been intervening in trying to build a semiconductor industry for decades, and still China has failed. Thus, it is ability to have more competitive and means-tested rubrics of that state support as well as checked by a global market's approval of quality instead of simply and desperately granting that state support per se.

Korea had many synergistic successes in digital telecommunications since the Chun administration in the 1980s made it a state developmental priority. This has continued in every Korean administration since as the industry remains a subsidized political priority. This has continued in every Korean administration since as the industry remains a subsidized political priority particularly clear in economic downturns like in 1997 into 1998 when the Korean state expanded many different digital sectors for promotion. By the early 2000s, Korea was *manufacturing more* digital technologies than any other country in the OECD, and was *the only country in the OECD to keep pulling ahead* by growing its share of digital global production (See Appendix 1). Very few countries manage to maintain leadership prioritization and subsidized funding for research and development in digital telecommunications over decades as Korea has.

Second, telecommunications as a final product can innately be synergistic *externally* in the world, by later *carrying cultural content* of the Korean Wave as digital information exported. This is synergistic with other Korean technical skills like digital-based transmission, recording, editing, visual production, script writing, etc. It is made easier *if the cultural medium is a common digital storage and distribution with digital convergence* instead of spread across different mass cultural industries each with their own separate recording and distribution mediums like radio, albums, films, etc. So a digital convergence of media itself is digital synergy that has helped the Korean Wave. However, as noted later in other chapters, such a digital convergence while useful for economic synergy, is toxic to maintaining an open democratic political system that relies on separation of powers and checks and balances—and thus innately relies on data of citizens being intentionally kept as fragmented instead of convergent.

In conclusion of this section about these interactive four kinds of synergies in the Korean Wave, this has touched on the factor of national cultural synergy itself for explaining why Korea has more product synergies in its cultural wave compared to other nations. There are two sub-factors here. First, there is the synergy of a more homogeneous culture particularly in its *greater solidarity and greater capacities collective innovations* in technology. As argued earlier, even the long pre-modern history of Korea's science and technology shows a long term synergistic effect on technological development across multiple fields simultaneously. When Koreans put their mind to a task together in trying to keep themselves ahead of their neighbors militarily and in other fields, greater Korean cultural synergies have given a dividend for centuries instead of only seeing a dividend in the past thirty years. It was argued earlier that a more homogeneous culture, with just a modicum of challenge and danger from outside, is a very durable and synergistic energizer of technological innovation. This can be seen in many sectors in South Korea. This can be seen even in the paucity of circumstances in North Korea, yet note still the North Korean strength in the military sectors around the scale of submarine production and their inventiveness of building nuclear bombs and intercontinental ballistic missiles despite living in such a poor economy. In historically unified Korea centuries ago, this kind of cultural innovation kept Korea together as a team and ahead of its neighbors technically in regional East Asia then. Even now it keeps South Korea ahead for decades in the global digital economy and its simultaneous successes of global Korean Wave so far.

So, transpose an ancient and ardent Korean solidarity and collective innovation in national *military* technological defense *against Chinese, Mongols, or Japanese in the last millennium* into national *economic* development *as a national defense against the whole world* in a situation where the same homogeneous culture has barely changed even as technology has around it. An ancient Korean solidarity and collective innovation now makes more modern friendly and haptic smartphones for global daily domestic uses, trying to beat its foreign enemy via technological competition, just as before. This is an ancient continuity in the modern Korean cultural resources of solidarity and greater collective innovation, and with it quicker synergistic responses than other countries that participate equally in a global economy. Particularly, other more heterogeneous cultures, whether in developing countries or in already developed countries and their more wealthy, populous, or powerful nations, have been unable to win in digital telecommunications as much as their smaller 'mid-sized' and culturally homogeneous Korean competitor over decades.

Second, there is a very durable Korean culture that is proud to share its emotions and storytelling whether about ancient dynasties or modern social problems. Such an ancient cultural pride has been transposed. Instead of only a local Korean or internal pride in regionality, this has been transposed into Korean global pride at telling more selected and sublime universalistic stories about the human condition yet made with Korean cultural color. We can see this universality of content yet regionality of color in many export films of the global Korean Wave particularly in *Snowpiercer* (2013), *Okja* (2017), *Parasite* (2019), *Squid Game* (2021), or *Space Sweepers* (2021). We can see this same universality of content yet regionality of color even in the many Korean historical costume dramas that reach a level of universality about the human condition just as if they were Shakespearian historical costume drama.

That is the four part answer to the question "why did South Korea develop a cultural wave far more global than any of its competitors in other developing countries?" It is due to the many levels of synergistic factors mentioned above. The first of these four synergistic contexts were the plural sectors of an export-led economy, that, for the second and third points, are themselves held together by the hybrid political organizational synergy mixed with the culturally homogeneous synergy of Korea. This did much to keep that export-led economy going by moving toward more consensus-based economic and cultural policies. The fourth synergy was the digital synergy, with its many innate internal and external synergies required for a durable digital telecommunications industry, and the innate material synergies of a digital medium itself. All of this synergy has placed South Korea above larger, equally homogeneous, and yet lesser export-led economies like Japan. All of this synergy has placed South Korea as well even above other smaller, equally homogeneous nations specializing in digital telecommunications and innovation like Israel. Koreans had all four synergistic factors working together in a superior way while others rarely had at most three in their global cultural wave working together. If they did, like in Japan, they only had them working together for a short time like in the earlier Japanese Wave and the Japanese international digital game industry or the Japanese electro-mechanical computer/telecommunications era that slowed under economic recession in Japan in the 1990s unable to make a stronger and more costly digital transition. Equally, the once-very popular British Hong Kong film industry for a time equally had the first three factors (missing the digital synergy) yet that changed from an earlier winnable export orientation under the British until 1997 when under an increasingly changed Chinese management and given the Asian Financial Crisis of that year. This started to cut support for Hong Kong electronics in general, and started to cut Hong Kong film production to half of the early 1990s after which it never has recovered its earlier scale so far. Other miscellaneous points about other minor synergies are addressed below.

9.2 Organizational Smallness: Handicap or Optimized?

Despite its splendid success so far, the Korean cultural contents industry still lacks in many aspects. Despite its rapid global growth in the Korean Wave, Korean cultural arts companies that lead the Korean Wave are still small compared to global content companies, and they have low corporate stability. A typical example is HYBE. Its stock price fell in vain when BTS announced the suspension of activities. Plus, HYBE by March 2023 abandoned its competitive bid war with Kakao to control SM Entertainment (Choi, 2023). Kakao is a far more financially sound Korean near monopoly of a combined Korean national social media with 53.5 million accounts by 2023 (with 47.8 million of these in Korea for approximately a 94% coverage of all Korean nationals) and a major online-bank (launched in 2017 and within that first month handled 40% of all South Korean loans totaling $1.2 billion). Instead, of outright ownership of now Kakao-dominated SM Entertainment by HYBE, it seems a networked synergy and coordination instead of a consolidation will take place, since by September 2023 twelve entertainment artists from Kakao-controlled SM Entertainment will use HYBE's Weverse platform for their official fanbase communities (Lee, 2023).

This networked coordination in the Korean entertainment industry of course is another kind of *network synergy* in the Korean Wave. So, on the other hand, given the digital mediums through which HYBE connects to its digital fandom, it may be a misnomer to compare the smaller institutions of the digital global Korean Wave to older and larger institutional size standards developed out of earlier one-way media empires from the United States. The Korean Wave has survived in the global content market despite numerous difficulties over the past 20 years at this smaller organizational scale, and indeed was the only growing cultural wave in the very difficult and challenging years between 2020 and 2023, unlike the slower moving organizational dinosaurs of Disney or other companies with Hollywood that continue to hemorrhage profits and layoff thousands of workers by February 2023. Disney actually is considering selling its ownership of ABC TV or parts of its ESPN sports TV by July 2023 to get some operating cash. So, is 'big always better' or is bigness increasingly outmoded as an organizational mismatch if network synergy will reign in the coming media regime change? Despite the comparative smallness of the more digitally-oriented organizations in the Korean Wave, the overall synergistic scope of K-content keeps expanding as it has for almost two decades. It begs the question is the utility of a large hierarchical and organizational scale a relic of a previous media regime in its older requirements of more centralized mass production and mass distribution, so much so that this large scale now fails to have a profitable purpose in a more digitally distributed media regime? Are smaller *and more networked* Korean entertainment companies a better way to organize more *synergy* in a network society for better response in a faster-paced global market situation? This is what was argued by Castells concerning the networked smaller firms of Silicon Valley that did the same over twenty years ago as they forwent large top-down hierarchies with the rise of a network society. So, it is argued that the more appropriate digital comparisons are between the smaller networked organizational scale of the Korean Wave's entertainment sector with the similar smaller and networked organizational dynamics in Silicon Valley, instead of comparing organization in digital Korean entertainment to older media regimes and their organizational dynamics in Hollywood per se. Plus, with many of these Korean (and global American) entertainment sectors networked digitally among themselves in alliances for production or distribution, the point about a more networked and smaller organization may be optimal in such a collective multi-sector Korean Wave that can form and reform various strategic alliances in the short term for collective projects and then disband later, similar to how Silicon Valley works as well (Castells, 2004).

Two opposite cases of Korean bigness surviving are within Cosmax and Kakao. However, first, Cosmax survives only by its own digital transformation and by its own network synergy—both already brought into itself. Cosmax already exhibited this network synergy for decades as an manufacturer of cosmetics for hundreds of other businesses. Cosmax may be a large organization, yet it works behind the scenes in the global cosmetics industry as an already networked form for decades. It is equally adapting now to a more digitally networked form via more robotic and digital production in order to be even more flexible to survive the faster online digital markets in cosmetics. A second opposite case of Korean bigness is Kakao, yet equally it survives by an organizationally-networked synergy and digital synergy brought into itself. Kakao is a networked empire between different synergistic digital products instead of being only one large organization producing one item. Historically, there have been Kakao subsidiaries in networked branches for entertainment called Kakao M (actually its first and core branch from Seoul Records, Inc., founded in October 1978). This entertainment section of Kakao has included KakaoMusic (a music app with sharing features), yet KakaoMusic is now merged into Kakao's other subsidiary Melon (a music streaming service), itself acquired through Kakao M itself already. Kakao's entertainment branch includes PotPlayer (a media player for Windows). In Kakao's fashion subsidiaries, there are KakaoStyle (a mobile fashion service) and KakaoHairshop (a mobile service for finding a nearby beauty salon). In finance, Kakao has KakaoPay (a mobile e-wallet networked into its social media of KakaoTalk), KakaoBank (a large mobile bank in Korea, i.e., without a physical location with over $1.2 billion in loans taken out through it within a month of its beginning in 2017), Klaytn as a consumer blockchain platform company for mobile payments (within its other subsidiary called Ground), Kakao INV (which is the way Kakao organizes investments in late stage startups), and Kakao Ventures (which is the way Kakao organizes venture capital investments for early stage startups). In transportation, Kakao has Kakao T (a mobile app for transportation services including digitally requested taxi hailing, chauffeur service, and navigation services), KakaoBus (another nationwide mobile app providing real-time ongoing locations and traffic information regarding the timing of public buses to the next stop on their scheduled line—in all cities), and KakaoMetro (which is the Korean subway lines app which lets users plan subway trips via viewing multiple Korean cities' subway maps and subway prices). Kakao has games as well via its own video game company, appropriately called Kakao Games. Of course, in social media, Kakao has a digital fandom all its own from starting Korea's largest and most successful social media, launched in March 2010, called KakaoTalk. KakaoTalk is for mobile phones and desktop applications, and it includes instant messaging, VoIP service, and built in money transfers via its own KakaoPay, mentioned earlier. Other social media branches of this large Kakao tree equally include KakaoStory (a sharing service for images, videos, and music), KakaoPage (a webtoons/comics and web-novel service), and 'Brunch' (an online publishing service for mobile contents). Still more social media subsidiaries exist in Kakao's digitally networked empire, like KakaoFriends (that includes Korean nationally known online icons/creatures used across other companies' product advertisement ranging from finance, distribution, foods, coffee, taxi livery, etc.), Kakao-Hello (a call app service for those with a Kakao account), and KakaoTV (which integrates Kakao TV Live broadcasting with KakaoTalk's open chatting at the same time, so people can watch the same TV shows online together and chat about it). The social media empire of this Kakao tree (or entangling vines) has still more branches like KakaoHome (a mobile service for managing your Smartphone home display—and thus surveillance of even more 'big data' about all users), KakaoPlace (an online service for sharing information that you know about famous places or place recommendations), and KakaoAlbum (which lets users share all pictures with their online networks of their own followers of 'Kakao friends'). *Daehan Kakao*, indeed. Nearly every event in Korea online or offline is tracked through Kakao. Koreans live in the Kakao nation. Kakao did have a U.S. social network service called Path, though it has been discontinued. To conclude, some parts of this Kakao tree were so large that pruning was done on March 2, 2021 to invent Kakao Entertainment with two main branches. These two Kakao Entertainment branches were consolidated to encourage greater synergies by putting a lot of weight on two main branches of all the webpage companies (merging KakaoPage Corp) and the music companies (under already previously consolidated Kakao M). For examples of synergies instead of scale important in the Korean Wave, Kakao Entertainment recently made good *organizational synergies* with large stock purchases of SM Entertainment throughout 2022 and into 2023 instead of simply totally absorbing it. In turn, after September 2023, it was announced that SM Entertainment will be using HYBE's digital fandom platform of Weverse for gaining more *digital synergies* in its own talents' fandom services instead of trying to make its own platform. This means SM entertainment and HYBE as well have more organizational and digital synergies, once HYBE from March 2023 gave up its own attempt to compete with Kakao for total control of SM Entertainment. Instead, HYBE will work in a more synergistic way with both Kakao and SM Entertainment. (Choi, 2023) Equally, for more organizational synergy, now that Kakao is involved with SM Entertainment as its major shareholder securely by 2023, Kakao surely will be expediting construction of its previously announced large K-pop performance venue in northern Seoul by 2025. (Yoon, 2022) The common elements here whether in a big or a small organization or whether HYBE, Cosmax, or Kakao, are the common organizationally-networked synergies and the common digitally network synergies as both crucial in growing the Korean economy and the Korean Wave.

9.3 Ongoing Synergy Now as the Vanguard Sector

For a while, first Korean TV dramas, then Korean online games, and then K-pop were seen as singular ongoing vanguards of the entertainment sectors of the growing Korean Wave, as representative leading industries for K-content. Now the K-content entertainment spectrum is broadening into theater movies, OTT broadcast films, webtoons, and web novels. This is the previous point (mentioned earlier in the timeline, in Sect. 4.2 of Chapter 4) that a durable global Korean Wave is riding on its first "simultaneous successes" from 2018, which only then could start to carry itself synergistically. Second, as well all of these different cultural sectors follow from the digital synergy of the digital convergence mentioned above, and mentioned in more detail in the next section below. In particular, Korean exports via global OTT video platforms such as Netflix continue to increase. In particular, the digitally-distributed

Korean cinema for Netflix's platform like *Squid Game*, and the global digital presence of boy bands such as BTS on HYBE's Weverse platform gave Korea's cultural and artistic copyright balance the largest surplus in history in 2021. How much higher will this go? The trend is only further up as of 2022 into 2023.

Plus, as said earlier though in a different way, in the content industry there is a synergistic effect on mere association with the Korean Wave products. Historically, an increase in export value of Korean Wave cultural products is connected with an increased export of Korean material consumer goods. For instance, when a Korean drama or movie is a hit, preference for consumer goods like Korean foods or cosmetics increases, and the number of tourists into Korea increases. According to a report by the Export–Import Bank of Korea, when K-content exports increase by $100 million, exports of synergistic consumer goods increase even more by $180 million (about 137 billion Korean won). Thus with many sectors being simultaneously successful now in the Korean Wave, as a group they become a vanguard instead, pushing each other in the global Korean Wave much easier as a durable phenomenon, like a relay race passing the baton between multiple runners in a running team.

9.4 Added Synergies of Decentralized Digital Media Networks

Mentioned above in a cursory fashion, another synergy in the global Korean Wave is its early and greater digital synergy than other nations: its spread via networks of decentralized personal digital telecommunications and online global platforms including various social network services (SNS) as mediums. From the start, this gave the greater digital content of this Korean Wave a more *intensive* and emotion-laden spread by word-of-mouth in forwarded links from friends. This equally gives the content more *extensive* global audiences immediately from posts on global platforms. By virtue of common digitalism this information has a *digital convergence* across multiple media content (sound, audio, text, letters, sound files, blog posts, etc.). This digital convergence of Korea was unavailable to earlier regional cultural waves from other developing countries in the 1980s into the 1990s that were based on more data fragmentation and segmentation in earlier media. Previous media regimes and cultural waves lacked all three factors of being more intensive, more extensive, or more digitally convergent in the ways described above. Instead in the previous media regime, popularity depended on getting specialized fame in a discrete sector of any of the one-way mass media's centralized producers and centralized distributors: whether in radio, television, movie theaters/studios, gramophone production, newspaper subscription scale, book publishing, concert venues, etc. This was the era of separate radio stars, separate movie stars, separate television stars, separate famous editorial column writers in newspapers, and separate book author stars, etc. In other words, you would be unlikely to see a newspaper columnist appear in a movie documentary or heard in a radio transmission just as you would be unlikely to see a silent film star appear on the theater stage, or a concert violinist recording star appear as a main actor in a film. Even into the 1980s, you would rarely see a radio star appear on video, and for a time, vice versa, a video star appear on the radio.

On the one hand, these separate one-way mass media technologies typically placed both production and distribution in the powerful hands of the same kind of centralized large company in a singular nation, similarly worldwide. On the other hand, there were physically different recording and playback technologies, or specialized venues, that led to a fragmented and parallel media spheres without easy physical media convergence. Think about the movie stage, the audio recording stage, the radio stage, or the live stage. In that one-way mass media world, the first media convergence was in the sound and vision of cinema. The early media convergence by the 1920s in cinema gave this medium more twentieth century universal and paramount (pun intended) power. Celluloid in movie theaters became the cultural blood of the world in the twentieth century, a weekly pseudo-religious ritual that transubstantiated dead film with projected light into real life blood and emotions in the audience once more that lived through the film.

If cinema gained such power because of early *partial* media convergence compared to less convergent other media, first, think how much more power a digital convergence has that merges everything into digital bits. Second, think how much power South Korea had gained by its comparatively earlier level of a 'saturated' decentralized digital media culture, and thus an earlier and *higher level of this media (digital) convergence* was available in Korean cultural content compared to other developing nations' cultural waves. Korea became the world's earliest and thus first example of a 'mid-sized' yet populous country with a mostly equitable fast-bandwidth and common mobile-phone ownership just as the world's media was going through a full digital convergence. (See Appendix 1). Pragmatically, given South Korean youth ownership of smartphones was near 100% in 2013, the earliest national place on record like this, and given this was extended to nearly 100% ownership through age 35 by 2015, this gave South Korean private companies involved in domestic cultural production many more years in advance over any other country in learning the pragmatic skills for marketing and selling this fully digital media convergence to a saturated national audience. That audience could be more emotionally intrinsic, more geographically extrinsic, and more digitally convergent—very useful for creating a digital synergy in Korean products compared to other countries' products.

Therefore, it is unsurprising that South Korea developed these synergistic skills at virally spreading the Korean Wave. The digital mediums of the Korean Wave from the start could wield a more emotionally enticing digital conquest first domestically on other past versions of Korean fragmented culture in other parallel media nationally. If video as a more convergent medium killed the radio star in the United States in the 1980s, in Korea, the more digitally convergent Internet killed the video star and all other media stars at once, as cultural saturation was reached around 2013 onward.

However, 'Internet stars' by being digitally convergent in their content and presentation are a much harder and rarified trick or talent to make in large numbers of such stars. The bulk number of people with such polymath entertainment skills, combined luckily with pulchritude and charisma, get inversely smaller than the much larger number of people available who could be experts in one entertainment skill and one medium. Previous music stars in the millions could concentrate on music. Actors in the millions could concentrate on visuals and vocal delivery. Producers in the thousands could concentrate on scripts and overall composition of the film. Writers could concentrate on writing. Beautiful models hardly had to be good singers or musicians or have a winning personality—that was superfluous like piano lessons for beauty queens. Actors hardly had to be friendly with their fans. Thus, cultures could be more diverse in their entertainment and more complicated or innovative in their messages due to the specialization and fragmentation of many different, parallel, and non-competing armies of excellences, instead of the fragmentation then really being noticed as a problem. As McLuhan argued, people only become aware of the cultural biases of a previous media when trying to show its content in the next media. Thus, in this case, people only became more aware of the culture of that media fragmentation once the next digital convergent medium showed up, to show it up.

Once there are *only* Internet stars however, first, everything becomes more homogeneous. No one has to be really very good in any particular discrete medium, though has to dabble in them all or has to be excellent in them all. Second, all the old excellences and skills above suddenly are seen as lacking instead of excellent at all. A really good guitar player thrown into a digitally convergent medium who is ugly or abrasive online is suddenly a fragmented digital experience instead of a famous recording star anymore. The scale of numbers of people capable of performing in a digitally convergent space shrinks, and now there is really only one Internet audience as well. Only the overall synergistic effects are what carry the content, so any fragmentation in excellence, like an *ugly, shy, yet excellent violin player* or a rude and aloof person who is only a beautiful dancer, suddenly becomes very clearly an impediment if the person is unable equally to dance, sing, play instruments, and be charismatic and polite to fans at the same time. Suddenly instead of many parallel specialized mediums of fame and culture, there was only one medium of a global digital culture seeing how to make and how to market that more digitally convergent and homogeneous experience. Past experts or specialists in one human sense or one medium seemed lesser stars on the Internet instead of becoming the brightest stars within singular mediums, with each like in enclosed glass before, that let singular senses and skills shine instead of compete. Only the overall synergistic effects are what carry the content, so any fragmentation in excellence like an ugly yet *only an excellent violin player* or a *rude and aloof person who is only a beautiful dancer,* suddenly becomes very clearly an impediment if the person is unable to equally dance, sing, play instruments, and be polite to online fans at the same time. Suddenly instead of many mediums, there was only one medium of a global digital culture seeing how to make and to market that more digitally convergent and homogeneous experience. Past experts or specialists in one human sense or one medium seemed lesser stars on the Internet instead of becoming the brightest stars within singular mediums that were each in enclosed glass before, that let singular senses shine instead of compete. Plus, the Korean nation fits well in this Internet culture world in three ways: the cultural politeness in people makes good manners for intrinsic shared content; its highly competitive cultural drive for bodily perfection and excellence makes good plural extrinsic skills; and the nation had the first saturated culture of digital convergence as well.

Thus, there were Internet stars in Korea *earlier* than other countries. Korea even has developed a whole professional industry of how to be an internet star. In Songdo, Incheon, there is even business office in a shopping mall that will teach you how to be a successful "YouTuber" in this digital medium. The same digitally convergent training occurs in various Korean famous entertainment companies, that are professional training schools manufacturing dozens of future digital K-pop idol stars with the same curricula of how to be an entertainment polymath within this digital media. It is a tough medium. Stars have to be good online personas that are friendly, polite, and interpersonal instead of distant, as well as of course good performance singers, dancers, and musicians all at once along with having technical skills of equipment use. It is gamed out with rooms for practicing digital press conferences or with rooms for planning the best ways to meet fans online in chat rooms and how to answer or initiate SNS-texted questions.

Once the rest of the world started to catch up to South Korean levels of digital saturation, the South Korean state and its private businesses more than other nations saw the digital opportunity of being inside others markets, given Korean expertise in what has been called here 'export-led substitution.' Koreans already had the export-led business experience and a decade or more of pragmatic digital marketing skills derived from their own domestic digital cultural sphere 'saturated' earlier than any other nation, practicing how to make content successful in a fresh digital convergence. So, this Internet-distributed digitalism gave the world a fresh kind of online star that (had to) mix Internet personas, visual stage presence, audio singing quality, and dance talents as a full rainbow of skills in one person. This is different as success was less possible anymore if mere 'bands' wanted to specialize in writing songs or in dance performance alone, given digital stars had to be more than mere 'dancers' on the stage with singing, musicianship, and digital diplomacy. A digitally convergent star has to be a one-person band.

Korea started to create this world of digitally convergent content in "bands" (using the term loosely) that were mostly visual dancers or singers that could play instruments, or in groups that could dance in time to their own composed songs or had songs composed for them. Meanwhile of course, Korean TV dramas remained formulaic in being produced for TV. However, it was in K-pop, distributed virally online, that felt the competition for more digitally convergent performances. This began to steal the global glow and show away from other sectors of the earlier entertainment sectors of the Korean Wave. Plus, Korea could rely on its *national digital* expertise to develop this more viral convergent content in many different kinds of *global-level digital* hardware products and convergent marketing strategies with them simultaneously.

This was a decade or more before other nations began to even be so digitally saturated (See Appendix 1). In short, Korean cultural products first digitized nationally in content orientation toward more media convergence, then that more saturated national digital environment combined with this more digitally convergent content seemed to be visually and emotionally ahead of other nations in spreading online products to the world stage. *This could occur even before the world began to be at more parity* in its own scales in its digital telecommunications to Korea. So, the way the Korean 'nation' distributed and even formulated its *national* digital cultural production was already a seed form of the current *global* digital level of production and content expectations. This allowed the Korean Wave to diffuse broader and further than the strong mobile phone densities of other countries in East Asia, and before other parts of the world caught up to the earlier levels of digital saturation found first in South Korea and more widely across East Asia.

Just like MTV starting in 1981 was once a global television underground in music, in a world of radio play, the Korean Wave became a global digital underground of digitally convergent experiences below and across dozens of other national media popularity lists for a decade or more. Thus the Korean Wave was already global yet it was demographically in the minority for a decade or more, until the rising later digital saturation in other nations would eventually cause this already global Korean viral digital underground stream to flow so much that it began to bubble up into 'national' playlists simultaneously worldwide, just like soil liquefaction in a earthquake can sink previously sturdy buildings on the surface, all at once. The Korean Wave and its digital medium began to void or at least challenge the concept of 'national playlists' that are from a previous one-way media regime broadcast in limited geographic zones.

The global digital spread of the Korean Wave did not stop when in-person culture events around the world shrank due to state-mandated lockdowns from 2020 through 2023. Despite under lockdown conditions, Korean cultural product planners reacted quickly with technological and even cultural innovations since Koreans had by this point many years of expertise in encouraging and in profiting from the spread of digitally convergent and non-face-to-facc cultural productions.

For two penultimate examples of a *globally and digitally distributed Korean live entertainment*, first, HYBE organized in 2021 a world first: a state-of-the-art, non-face-to-face 'virtual yet real' concert that mobilized millions of global spectators at once. On October 24, 2021, the online concert 'BTS PERMISSION TO DANCE ON STAGE' was seen in a record 197 countries simultaneously, as Korean cultural promoters kept expanding the size of the digital entertainment market under lockdown instead of fatalistically accepting the shrinking of in-person culture. For another example, in a *globally* and *digitally distributed Korean film*, OTT broadcast TV offerings likes *Squid Game* produced under lockdown conditions for the American company Netflix maintained the top position for the longest time in Netflix's global broadcast history so far.

In the future, the digital content market for the Korean Wave likely will keep expanding due to Non-fungible Tokens (NFTs) and even platform-specific currencies. These even higher levels of digital convergence rope in an exclusive financial medium itself into the entertainment experience. The use of the Korean metaverse may continue as well—unless a large cultural reaction against such digitally convergent virtuality proceeds. This is perhaps noted in the growing financial failure around Zuckerberg's metaverse empire project in late 2022 into early 2023, or at least the collapse of his artificial hype. Similarly, the Apple Vision Pro AR/VR goggles released as a demonstration model in June 2023 has a platform, yet similar to Meta, still lacks a cultural use or even applications for what it will do. However, to contrast, Korean metaverse projects seem to have a durable and real digital fandom base of culture to work with, while American platform offerings like Zuckerberg's Meta or the Apple Vision Pro lack it entirely so far. Korea started with the digital fandoms and built the platforms out for it later. Zuckerberg and Apple are starting with the empty platforms and just hope a digital fandom will come. Zuckerberg's earlier attempt at creating a global digital currency in 2020, called Libra and then Diem, built off his social media empire of Facebook failed as well by January 2022. It was sold to Silvergate Bank, which wrote off the investment as a failure in January 2023—right before that bank failed months later as well in March 2023. However, the already popular national Korean social media Kakao came first, and its digital KakaoBank, digital tokens, and KakaoPay came later successfully—and almost seamlessly. The lesson from Korea seems to be first establish the digital fandom, and then build extra services for them in that digitally convergent space instead of build the neutral platform devoid of users or culture first.

Despite globally choppy economic seas caused by governmental lockdowns that sank many in-person entertainment venues and which could not even create a pushed market to rescue Zuckerberg's metaverse projects, the digital 'K-content' cultural industry keeps sailing strong, fully crewed with its millions of loyal digital fans. As a result, *Korea now has the 7th largest cultural products industry in the world*. By 2021, the global number of so-called avid "Hallyu club members," meaning, the durable and habitual consumers of any kind of Korean content, is estimated to be 156.6 million across 116 countries (Korea Foundation for International Relations, 2021). So, if Korea is domestically a 'mid-size' nation of 51 million people (comparable to the 47 million in Spain, the 67 million in Great Britain, and the 68 million in France), the wider digital fandom of "Hallyu club members" is a baseline of over "three more extra Koreas" scattered around the world that can be counted upon to be habitual consumers of Korean cultural contents. This puts the full worldwide market scale and culture of this "Hallyu nation" closer to the economic size of the 215 million people in Brazil or the 218 million people in Nigeria. This makes the market scale of the full "Hallyu nation" far larger than the 124 million people in Japan or the 146 million people in Russia. Plus, the economic power of the fuller "Hallyu Nation" around the world is hardly only a one-sector entertainment and economic zone around the world for Korea. Remember what was said above from a report by the Export–Import Bank of Korea: as K-content exports increase by $100 million, exports of synergistic consumer goods increase even more—by $180 million. So the "Hallyu Nation" expands the general synergistic Korean economy around the world, instead of only expands Korea's entertainment sector worldwide.

These global synergies give huge influence to the global Korean Wave and its celebrities. These are echoed in other nations' foreign (non-Korean) media as well. First, the U.S. publication *Bloomberg Business Week* selected fifty people who led global trends in December 2021. Among them were Bang Si-hyuk (chairman of BTS's management agency HYBE) and Hwang Dong-hyuk (director of *Squid Game*). Second, another synergistic example of the large influence of the global Korean

Wave is how its durable global digital fandom as a base is making the once-isolated Korean language and its writing script Hangeul into an international language and international literature for the first time in world history. Like a popcorn kernel exploding, this has turned the tight small historical isolation of the Korean language and the Hangeul script inside out: from once being a language and script combination only used in the Korean Peninsula to suddenly and nebulously *becoming a true international (digital) lingua franca as a second language shared among the over 200 million people* who are different national fans of the full "Hallyu nation." So, thanks to this digital synergy, oddly, a language isolate and its self-reinforcing isolated script have become suddenly globally used for the first time ever. Only twenty years ago, Korean and Hangeul were marginal points of world history. However, now, in a report published by the online language learning app Duolingo, the Korean language despite still being only spoken or written widely in the Korean Peninsula has suddenly become a global (digital) language overnight. Korean is now the second fastest growing language being learned on the digital platform of Duolingo, and Korean is suddenly the seventh most popular 'second language' known. This goes well with Korea having the seventh largest cultural products industry in the world.

These historically 'inside out' changes in many facets of Korean culture are due to growing popularity of the *digital* global Korean Wave and the many unique synergies possible mentioned above. One of these factors of success is this digital synergy: how the digitally networked medium itself encourages greater *intrinsic* emotional sharing, greater *extrinsic* sharing in geographic scale, and grants greater *digital convergence* and impressiveness to any successful media content that can handle this medium's high capacities. It is argued that youth generations around the world especially in the "MZ" generations (Millennials born from 1981 to 1986 and Generation Z born after 1997) are the first global 'digital natives.' They became the first global front line of army recruits in the wider "Hallyu Nation." They have widened the Korean 'soft power' *because* they are the first global digital natives. The digital global Korean Wave, the digital MZ generation globally, and the global digital medium are one in the same.

9.5 Korea: Once Closed to Cultural Assimilation, Now Open to Global Trade

Part of the conundrum of the global Korean Wave is that with it coming out of a more homogeneous culture, much of the Korean culture remains closed to assimilation of the wider "Hallyu Nation" that has been created. This block on cultural assimilation is despite the state-developmental project being massively successful in building its own urban industrialization for global market exports and building up its global cultural projection. Korea still thinks it is a popcorn kernel, long after the popcorn has popped—similar to how many New Yorkers or Parisians hate the world's tourists descending on their cities. For example, as late as 2009 if a foreign national married a Korean national and even if they lived in Korea, the foreign partner was banned from even applying to be an equal legal citizen of Korea categorically despite married to a Korean national. However, the oddity developed anyway that if the foreigner were male, who could of course not be a Korean citizen, he nonetheless got to see his Korean wife who was a citizen transferred legally to his family's census statistics about Korean citizens—without him actually being a Korean citizen. Koreans count themselves as durable family demographic units in the Korean census, instead of counted as individuals per se—the same as the ancient Korean states counted their population by families as recorded in the ancient text of the *Samguk Sagi (ca. 1145)*. There are two kinds of citizenship generally in the world: citizenship by 'naturalization' which relates to the geography of birth (like the United States) and citizenship by bloodline links that has nothing to do with geography (like Germany, Korea, Italy, or Israel). Korea is starting to have a hybrid citizenship of both, despite scale of foreign ethnicities in Korea being truly very small. Even the largest 'foreign national' population in Korea actually is still bloodline Korean since they are 'repatriated' Chinese Koreans as temporary guest workers. This is a reflection of the wider ancient Korean homogeneous culture that extended north of the Yalu River, the current abrupt and abstract northern border between North Korea and China, yet it is hardly a cultural border per se as it is only a shallow river most people can cross very easily. However, Chinese Koreans can be discriminated against in South Korea both by their lower socioeconomic class and of course their lack of local bongwan family origins (as already described in Chapter 2). North Koreans are discriminated against in the same way in South Korea. Even if they flee illegally a dictatorship in the North at the risk of their lives in seeking freedom in the South, and even if they become South Korean citizens, they culturally remain North Koreans in the South by bongwan family designation that extends a regional/family clan location of the deep past into twenty-first century Korea.

So despite the export-led economy and the global cosmopolitanism of the Korean Wave, this is *how hard it is for even bloodline-heritage Koreans* from China or North Korea *to assimilate in South Korea*—much less non-Korean foreign nationals. Because of this, there may be other long-term curious effects in the future once millions of *more truly foreign tourists* of the Korean Wave, by definition people who are open to cultural appreciation of Korea while being dipped in Korean culture overseas, upon visiting Korea, soon find the source nation of the Korean Wave remains closed and homogeneous. Koreans are publicly friendly to foreigners at a high degree in public spaces yet are privately closed to family house visits or to business relationships generally. Plus, most collectivist Koreans have discomfort from visibly dissonant public spaces, whether caused by witnessing cultural innovation, individual innovation, or a heterogeneous culture in their own midst. This might range from a foreign face in a Korean crowd or just a different idea in a publicly dissenting mind. Even brightly colored automobiles are taboo in Korea. They stand out "too much" visually in public. Koreans prefer personal automobiles in public spaces to exude respectful collective standards. Koreans may admire what has polish and style, yet it has to remain *collective, neutral, and inconspicuous*. This results in a Korean car culture with modern eight-lane freeways filled mostly with only the three neutral 'colors' of car: white, silver grey, and black. Car windows can be so darkly tinted in Korea for privacy that no one can see inside many cars in public, furthering the uniformity and neutrality effect of public spaces while on the public roads.

However, this is the problem. Regardless of Korean discomfort with either themselves or others standing out visibly in cultural or individual diversity, the Korean public state and corporate private profit are priming that cultural innovation and individual innovation into existence just the same by pushing the global Korean Wave onto a heterogeneous world. Instead of hundreds of millions of foreigners just being content to be passive fans as consumers of the Korean Wave, millions of overseas fans become active fans, in Fiske's term. They appropriate and appreciate Korean culture by learning Korean, reading Hangeul, or visiting Korea to learn Korean modern dance or Korean traditional dance, etc. Thus the Korean state and Korean corporations are bringing the traditional Korean culture into a permanent heterogeneous world for the first time and at a global level of interaction far larger than it has experienced in thousands of years.

Even Koreans likely are unaware of the scale of this wider global "Hallyu nation" in the scale of its financial success or the scale of its entertainment personnel involved in Korean cultural production both for domestic and international audiences. For some figures, after calculating the annual estimate for 2021 based on a survey of the Korean cultural contents industry, the total Korean Wave content industry's employees was estimated to be 649,554 employees. K-content sales were estimated to be annually W136,355,900 billion won, which is *domestic and international.* This is between $95 to $100 billion dollars annually. Korean Wave *exports only* were estimated to be $13.578 billion dollars annually, or around 14% of K-content total global sales. However, it is only the Korean cultural exports that keep increasing far more, compared to domestic cultural sales that have less growth. Compared to the previous year, Korean cultural content sales as a whole increased by 6.3%, yet Korean cultural exports increased by 13.9% even while cultural content workers increased only by 1.2%. The whole Korean content industry is expected to keep growing at a CAGR of 6% until 2025. This is tremendous growth, and particularly if a large near 14% export expansion of Korean culture keeps being compounded annually for a few more years as well.

This begs the next questions: what is the percentage and what is the rising scale of the Korean Wave's cultural content export *relative to the whole world's global cultural content scale and market growth*? In other words, how much faster are Korean Wave exports growing compared to the growth of cultural content of the world at large? According to the International Economic Research Institute of the Export–Import Bank of Korea on September 5, 2022, *the global content market*, which includes broadcasts, movies, music, games, and cartoons, *increased only 6.7%* from the previous year to about $2.6 trillion as it starts to recover from the aftermath of many nations' lockdown policies. Thus, *the Korean Wave exports, at a 14% annual growth rate mentioned above, are growing at twice the rate of the total global content market's growth.* To gauge the scale of money involved, the financial size of the global cultural contents industry of $2.6 trillion is more than four times the economic size of the *global* semiconductor market of $633 billion. While the World Semiconductor Market Statistical Organization (WSTS) downgraded its growth forecast for the global semiconductor market in 2022 from 16.3 to 13.9%, on the other hand, the global content market recovered fast in 2022 compared to 2021, as face-to-face services such as movie theater screenings and music performances began to be revitalized. Thus the global Korean Wave can be expected to take an ever larger part of the 'pie' of the global cultural contents industry, given the Korean Wave's rate of growth in export of cultural content mentioned above that is double the global growth rate. Considering the total sales are out of $2.6 trillion in the global cultural contents industry, it is not a joke that the Korean Wave may revolutionize and commodify Korean culture far more than has ever happened before in the long history of cultural isolation on the Korean Peninsula.

So, in the future, the Korean Wave is inevitably going to become a more dualistic cultural tsunami: it is now more of an ebbing flow out, and yet sooner or later will be a flood back inward, inland. Just as homogeneous desert tribes of Arabian Muslims started to stream out of the once isolated Arabian Peninsula, fired with the expansion of Islam, now more heterogeneous Muslims from all over the world learn Arabic worldwide and annually come back to Mecca for the Hajj from all over the world. Similarly, as more homogeneous Korean content is streamed over the Internet out of the once isolated Korean Peninsula, more heterogeneous digital fans of the Korean Wave learn Korean and want to visit Seoul—and it is just starting. For example, according to Statista as digital fandoms join the Korean Wave and learn Korean language and culture, they now want to come to Korea to study as well. Homogeneous Seoul has become the third most popular city in the world suddenly for international students to take their 'gap year' after high school and before university, after London and Munich. However, most Koreans do not speak or use English. The stress on English in the Korean culture is only from governmental pressures in formal schooling, studying for written tests, and for status issues of job placements requiring high TOEIC scores in Korean firms or universities. It is "test English," quickly learned and soon forgotten in lack of places to use it. This contrasts to "oral English" in conversation in Korea that is rarely used as a communication medium with foreigners and is more of an internal status sign among Koreans themselves only, as a sign of documented certification and attainment of cultural capital within a Korean context. Plus, Seoul is not an ethnically diverse cosmopolitan city despite it being a large metropolitan area of 25 million people and despite it being one of the top 'digitally-wired and wireless' global cities in existence.

So, while the global Korean Wave now ebbs out and penetrates heterogeneous cultures across the world, the diverse flow back into Korea is just starting. As the Korean Wave's ebb outwards grows larger, the world's cultural penetration will flow larger back into South Korea with hundreds of millions of foreigners influenced by Korean cultural production and material products. What will be Korea's domestic response? Will the deeply homogeneous domestic Koreans find many hundreds of millions of 'non-Korean' cultural brothers and sisters that outnumber them in the world something welcomed or a nuisance? We wait and see. Korea has surprised the world with its collective innovation under pressure. However, the conundrum is that as a growing number of young people worldwide now come to know and to understand Korean culture, they are Korea's great core asset in the international community, and yet should they come to visit Korea they may remain a peripheral unintegrated group to the more homogeneous culture of Korea because deep family blood ties and deep regional ties define what is Korean instead of it being defined primarily by a more shareable language or cultural instruction.

9.6 Rapid Growth in a Cultural Empire upon Which the Sun Never Sets

Regardless of growing problems, the synergies are stronger. The global Korean Wave has made South Korea a cultural empire upon which the sun never sets. The Korean Wave created a long-sought 'national brand' and has even created an international 'empire' that it never had, simply from global consumer scale in the world. This has infused all products of Korea whether in its modern or its ancient culture with the same positive emotions of trust, high quality, and status worldwide.

In the picture book of Korea, images of *modern* Korea were limited to tragic and painful black-and-white photographs of dislocations of the Korean War (1950–1953), or images of unhappy impoverished people doing rote colorless industrial work under developmental dictatorships, whether of capitalist economic development in the South or of nationalized socialism in the North. Turning the pages of this picture book, color arrives in the 1980s—literally, as color TV was not available or broadcast before 1980. From the 1980s, ever faster-turning pages of the picture book of Korea now show jubilant color images for the first time. There is Korea's first global status victory—the hosting the Summer Olympic Games of 1988—opened by its truly first democratically elected Korean President Roh Tae-woo, since at least he passed through a more democratic multi-party procedure to be President despite a military officer background as the previous dictator-President Chun's underling. In 1988, with President Roh as host of the Olympic Games, Korea reintroduced its own ancient cultural speciality of individual and team archery to the world games, and has won almost solidly all Olympic gold medals in archery after that in an unparalleled record for over 30 years.

By 2002, the picture book of Korea shows a sea of red T-shirts. In that year, Korea was co-hosting the 2002 FIFA World Cup in soccer. In this event Korea had a double global victory: being the first non-Western (co-)hosting nation of the World Cup (with Japan), and how Korea was the first non-Western soccer team ever to enter the global semi-finals. As jubilant Korean crowds cheered throughout the streets of Seoul in Summer 2002, the Korean soccer team advanced steadily, game after game against all odds over many weeks, even though South Korea eventually lost to Turkey. In this picture book, there are many fond memories for Koreans about the 2002 World Cup. Many Koreans view the 2002 World Cup as the first truly joyous public celebration in modern Korea. Throughout the playoffs, Koreans celebrated and chanted in downtown Seoul in a moving sea of red T-shirts. Crowds were large, noisy, and dense—yet not unruly since in the Korean way, traffic rules were so respected that streets could stay open even though all sidewalks were packed, cheering, and dancing. Even whole floors of Seoul office buildings were converted into a makeshift urban stadium, with row upon row of open skyscraper windows packed with people, floor by floor, combined with packed sidewalks below, cheering as they watched the same public big screen TV from LG Electronics in downtown Seoul. Foreshadowing Korean entertainment prowess in the global Korean Wave, the 2002 Korean soccer team got the "Most Entertaining Team Award" for its jubilant crowds. At each Korean goal on the big screen TV, Seoul city shot truly massive amounts of fireworks at night or shot colored smoke rockets by day off of the tops of office buildings, as crowds below danced and even crowds above celebrated and danced within office buildings (CommOn Sound, 2006).

However at least through 2017, this picture book of South Korea historically has been upstaged on every page by their Northern brother and its missile threats. Only from 2018, judged by global Google Trends searches, did the global Korean Wave from South Korea start to drown out North Korea. The Korean Wave has changed the view of South Korea internationally into something beyond a country in a shadow of missile threats. Increasingly, South Korea is making its own images and upstaging North Korea. These images are more optimistic, stylish, energetic, creative, and even futuristic—something people want to see and be a part of worldwide. These images can be humorous and yet full of social criticism simultaneously. It is an odd dichotomy: South Korea has become famous as a cosmopolitan trendsetter of digital technology, global fashion, beauty, movies, dancing, rap music, and pop culture as much as North Korea has become infamous as a closed global pariah. However, a common Korean cultural desire for fame, excellence, and status comparison is the same. Both North and South are trying to be respected globally in their own way. Despite a rapid and wealthy modern technical change in digital South Korea and despite a slow and poor socialist modernity continuing in cult-like North Korea, much of the common Korean culture throughout the Korean Peninsula remains proudly stable and ancient by intentional design instead of by accident. Particularly in South Korea, the culture is even more of an oddly stable anchor amidst the global economic and cultural storms that South Koreans themselves created from their export-led development and then from their global Korean Wave. This culture continues to add its economic premium, raising South Korea's status in the international community while raising premium prices and cultural status for Korean products. However, for the first time the global Korean Wave is starting to have a ripple effect even on Korean popular culture. It is thought that this spread of the global Korean Wave will continue to do three main things: play an important role in raising Korea's soft power in the international community, continuing to be a major source of Korean economic growth, and of course continuing to be a source of cultural pride for Koreans that millions of non-Koreans increasingly enjoy aspects of Korean culture around the world.

References

Castells, M. (Ed.). (2004). *The network society: A cross-cultural perspective.* Edward Elgar.

Choi, H.-s. (2023, March 25). HYBE windfall. Selling SM shares bought for 120,000 won for 150,000 won, 16% stake, Kakao tender offer application. *Joseon Ilbo*. https://www.Joseon.com/economy/economy_general/2023/03/25/EIACLENLCJHHZARFIH7YPCFEME/

CommOn Sound. (2006). 2002 FIFA World Cup street cheering from Korea, Part one. *YouTube*. https://youtube.com/watch?v=HliB9VSxU28

Korea Foundation for International Relations (KF). (2021). *The status of Hallyu in the global village in 2021*. https://www.kf.or.kr/kfEng/main.do

Lee, Y.-a. (2023, May 2). [컨콜] 에스파 이어 아리아나 그란데도?…"위버스, 하반기 美 가수 입점". *TechM*. https://www.techm.kr/news/articleView.html?idxno=109672

OEC. (2023). *South Korea*. https://oec.world/en/profile/country/kor/OECD

Yoon, S.-y. (2022, April 4). Kakao to build large-scale K-pop performance venue in northern Seoul. *Korea JoongAng Daily*. https://koreajoongangdaily.joins.com/2022/04/04/business/tech/Kakao-Seoul-Arena-The-O2/20220404163256017.html

Chapter 10
The Future of Korea and the World

10.1 Future Wealth or Collapse of Nations in a Global Digital Economy and Culture?

The previous chapter discussed the internal synergies that encouraged the external expansion of the Korean Wave. This chapter reverses it and discusses our changing external digital global contexts in the early twenty-first century that encouraged the peculiar internal successes of Korea and the Korean Wave. This digital global context may dissolve and divide other past successful nations into oblivion unless they adapt well.

What images will the picture book of Korea show in the decades ahead? On the one hand, it looks like Korea will continue to take the world by storm—economically, culturally and even technically. On the other hand, it is mistaken to think that this Korean Wave is a *sudden storm*, as if it may soon pass. For instance, in September 2021, the same month Netflix released *Squid Game*, the *Oxford English Dictionary* added as many as 26 new 'English' words originating from the Korean language including the phrase "Korean Wave." By 2021, this means approximately 100 Korean words have been added to this major English dictionary. Thus, there is an external facilitating issue of the world-system that Korea participates within now that encourages the Korean Wave. This chapter discusses that *external historical context* that has made the successful Korean Wave with an eye on the future of the Korean nation in general, as well as the future of all nations participating in a global digital economy, a global digital culture, and a global decentralized media.

As mentioned in Part I, if you take an *historical internal view of Korea*, the cultural Korean Wave depended greatly on a long and slow economic Korean Miracle from 1961 onward. Instead of a sudden storm, the Korean Wave has been a *slowly building storm*, since a cultural wave from Korea has been attempted since the mid-1980s just like many other developing nations were doing by this time around the world. However, what we are seeing in the global Korean Wave is the only example so far of a developing nation with a cultural wave that has gone global. It has been having 'simultaneous successes' from 2018. This was built upon the growing 'singular

G.-C. Shin and M. D. Whitaker, *The Korean Wave in a Post-Pandemic World*,
https://doi.org/10.1007/978-981-99-3683-0_10

successes' of intentional Korean cultural exports from at least since 1992. That itself was built upon the uniquely successful and durable fast development drive. So, instead of as a trend follower, Korea is a trendbreaker that has given the world the most globally extensive, culturally successful, and economically powerful of any non-Western global cultural flows so far. Second, Korea is a trendbreaker because it has spread more than just one kind of cultural product in popular culture. Instead, it has spread Korean movies, TV dramas, K-pop music/dance, online games, cosmetics, web novels, online platforms, webtoons, metaverse applications, etc. Given this long span of time, when looking into the future, the Korean Wave is unlikely to dissipate quickly since it hardly appeared quickly either. Plus, given the statistics in the previous chapter, the growth of the Korean Wave's exports are expanding annually at 13.9% while the world's wider global cultural industries are only expanding at less than half that rate, at 6.7%. This growth has been aided by the Korean Wave being one of Korea's many collaborative, synergistic, export-led development sectors—with all of them having antecedents in the export-led economy as a national development policy, set from 1961. These policies have been maintained and conserved so long that they can take advantage of and guide the earlier synergistic growth of the economic Korean Miracle as it merges into the synergistic growth of the global Korean Wave.

While the previous chapter and even the whole book has mostly analyzed only the internal good choices and good accidents of Korea to explain its very successful fast development drive, it has somewhat discussed world-system level changes that helped these internal choices along. So, there are *more than mere internal choices* that made Korean fast paced development happen. Instead, there is a particular external global context to Korean development. That is the point of this chapter. Korea is *riding* history instead of only itself *writing* history.

It is argued that there are three major external world-system level selection factors toward success of "Korean-like digital nations" *around a particular optimized 'middle scale' recipe of 'demography, geography, and homogeneity.'* If this hypothesis is true, and if it holds true, hardly all nations will ride out this storm. Many may be smashed. All nations are being vetted in these three ways right now, which can become their national problem if they are oriented poorly. Additionally, it can become a world-system problem of stability if many older nations come to fail simultaneously as novel ones come to succeed by carving themselves out of older nations. This is because stability in the global economy of the world-system helps create such "K-Nations" in the first place. However, first, if increasing numbers of such successful 'mid-size' K-Nations start to undermine the stability of all other larger or even smaller nations in this triple way, and if these other differently oriented nations collapse older markets, may it eventually undermine "K-Nations" themselves reliant on stable global markets, global cultures, and global media participation? In other words, to have K-Nations, you require stability in all the other non-K-Nations in other words, which are the K-Nations' markets. Similarly, there was an earlier massive cross-civilizational collapse that occurred in the Mediterranean around "1177 BC" that wrecked the trade, culture, and communications of an earlier world-system that all component cultures depended upon (Cline, 2021). When that earlier network of 'ancient globalization' between cultures collapsed (Jennings, 2010), almost all component civilizations collapsed within 100 years of each other (Cline, 2021). Only a few civilizations like Egypt and Assyria made it through that bottleneck around 1177 BC to maintain their state, their economy, and a cultural transmission. Many others totally disappeared. All were challenged externally by a growing war-like context outside of them that severed all previously stable and reliable international trade and communication. All were challenged internally by a growing class warfare, inequality, and riots within themselves at the same time, toppling previously legitimated cultures and political states hundreds of years old. Many larger civilizations broke up into component parts. Many smaller city-states entirely disappeared (Cline, 2021). Now, our fresh global digital civilization and globalization seems to be headed toward a similar double global reckoning: increasing external global level war and increasing internal cultural dissension. Are we headed toward our own disastrous global reckoning—perhaps around "2077 CE," to coin a phrase? How many of our current component nations will be pulled apart by this triple global storm, as they become non-viable economically, non-viable in cultural transmission, and non-viable in producing digital technology so much so that it could unsettle the whole current world-system of global digital economics, culture, and media itself? Are we headed toward "2077 CE"?

It is argued that many nations will be unable to make it through this digital bottleneck as well as Korea has, and yet should remain stable enough to be markets nonetheless for the few growing K-Nations. That may be even more difficult than making another K-Nation, since the quicker dissolution and wrecking of a country toward greater unrepresentative arrangements or divided regional cultures can go much faster and easier than the slow economic aggregation down the development gauntlet toward urban industrial development and its slow accommodations toward unity in human civil and political development by consensus, that seem crucially involved in the former.

In the three senses of the successful "K-Nation", 'demography, geography, and homogeneity,' if Korea is the first fully digitally developed "K-Nation", will digital Korea serve as a harbinger to other nations showing them the way for their internal choices of national development strategies of what is possible, or will it serve as a warning of what is being exclusively and externally selected for in global digital conditions that fails to include them until they are broken up into pieces? Plus, will Korea remain an outlier to other nations due to its many internal good choices and many happenstance 'good accidents' (see Appendices 2 and 3) that make copying extreme Korean success at fast development as unobtainable for other countries as trying to approach an ever-receding mirage? Equally, what will happen to all nations, including Korea, as a more multi-polar and global digital culture advances with a global digital economy? Who will win and who will lose in such a situation, economically and culturally? Will larger heterogeneous cultural nations have more economic and cultural difficulties now despite the same external digital global context helping Korea? Will larger heterogeneous nations break into smaller homogeneous pieces of 'mid-sized" digital "K-Nations"? Will larger heterogeneous nations become digital police states, more repressive and unrepresentative, due to growing internal cultural dissentions and due to external economic problems of keeping up with better endless global competition from more 'optimized' and faster-responding arrangements of more mid-sized nations' 'demography, geography, and homogeneity' in a global digital economy?

Given Korea is so far *the only major 'ex'-developing* country by U.N. judgment, and given *other larger, smaller, and more heterogeneous countries are having their own difficulties* in adapting to the digital twenty-first century, the main dual question becomes, first, does a country with "the demography, geography and homogeneous culture of Korea" become the best, most durable, and most viable arrangement of development and social organization in a global digital economy? Second, will all other kinds of different arrangements of nations economically stall, culturally fail, or politically dissolve, transmogrify, or collapse *because* they are in competition with more optimized nations for a global digital economy?

This chapter is about that growing dichotomy. This would apply though only under given external conditions of what kinds of nations and cultures hold together and thrive even in a decentralized global digital economy, culture, and media regime. Both the global economy and our global digital culture are increasingly built from ever more unpredictable ebbs and flows of information and money influenced by our decentralized global digital media. For example, past powerful world culture players start to see profits and popularity diminish, and they even start to rely on the Korean Wave for their own national cultural industries' profit—like the U.S.'s Disney or Hollywood starting to bank on the profits of the Korean Wave by 2022. Plus, Disney started to lay off 7,000 workers in February 2023. It did so once more even at larger scale in March 2023. Disney+ (the fresh Disney OTT global service only from 2019) lost 2.3 million subscribers in 2022, after just launching in 2019. Even Netflix had a difficult time with subscriber loss in early 2022 for the first time ever since 2007, that was only slightly improved by the end of the year. American cultural productions start to slow down in global popularity, and even in 'national' American popularity. Plus, as many countries exit governmental enforced lockdowns on public entertainment and much else by 2023 and face wide bankrupcies in their cultural industries because of those lockdowns, the Korean Wave continues to spread without slowing down in the past few years making it harder than ever for others to catch up with Korea.

The future concern is *what characteristics of any nations will help them to prosper or to weaken in the coming twenty-first century* (1) under competitive rigors of a global digital economy, (2) within the cultural frissioning and fracturing of a global digital culture, and (3) where the ultimate test is which countries can produce distributed global digital 'media.' The definition here of 'media' means both who can produce the most trusted, engineered, *digital telecommunications hardware* and the most trusted, loved, and *profitable cultural content* in that digital hardware, more than other nations. Right now, Korea does both. The parallel global rise of digital hardware paired with the global cultural conquest of its Korean Wave represents a challenge even to the past cultural continuity of Korea, and definitely a challenge to past hegemonic world culture from Europe or the United States. At the same time, with $2.6 trillion on the line in the global cultural contents industry, this represents a high-stakes global economic game that the already developed countries of the world now start to play with Korea. However, even few developed countries have the double capacities that Korea does, to do both digital media productions. Many less developed nations do only one of these sectors. Many smaller or larger countries do neither.

So, what national characteristics will be viable in the twenty-first century, and which characteristics will lead to failure or even economic or cultural collapse as nations become unable to compete economically or become unable to preserve past national cultures in a high stakes global media game?

There are three interactive arguments. The first argument is that some *'mid-sized' geographic and demographic countries with more homogeneous cultures* give them the ability to be the next digital "K-Nation" powerhouses like Korea. This regionalization is being globally seen. It has been given academic terms like "re-traditionalization" and "re-territorialization." However, in the case of a global digital culture, this means even these more successful 'mid-size' zones can have a much larger digital public worldwide for their products. Inversely said, the related second argument is that the opposite category of *more heterogeneous countries* may increasingly be unable to compete under fast paced global digital economic and global cultural conditions. They may culturally split into pieces and fall apart, with any of their internally more 'mid-sized' and digitally homogeneous zones starting to exhibit *a politics of secession and/or of technocratic conquest* and destruction of their own past more heterogeneous cultural states. The third argument finds it concerning that *current larger and richer states as well as poorer and smaller states are both regularly the more heterogeneous countries.* In a changing media regime, these factors may combine to have these heterogeneous cultures fall apart into constituent more 'mid-sized' homogeneous regional parts. This is because the trend is how distributed two-way media developing in a past heterogeneous culture exposes older lines of internal cultural and regional divisions in such countries more clearly. This is particularly the case when there is growing economic polarization within countries between such regions which can be a 'digital polarization of regions' within richer or poorer nations alike, with one digitally rich production zone versus the masses of the digitally underserved. Plus, larger heterogeneous or larger homogeneous countries alike may fall apart into discrete smaller 'mid-sized' homogeneous zones of digital "K-Nations" similar to Korea themselves that were once within older and larger states. This may be success in a sense for these regions, and yet it represents a failure or technocratic conquest of the older nation by a highly digital homogeneous cultural region within the past nation.

10.1.1 The Triple Global Storm Building in the Korean Wave

So, if you take *a comparative and historical view of Korea*, and a view from the external world-system that is outside of Korea, what has been happening within Korea instead of a *sudden storm* is hypothesized *to be the first global touch down point of a long-building* *triple global storm.* This is starting to upend three Eurocentric global hegemonies of *economics, culture, and media* in existence for hundreds of years.

Three kinds of data already shown in this book is summarized now for how this triple global storm first triangulated well in the Korean fast *economic* development drive, given how the nation's many internal good choices and good accidents channeled that fresh global digital media context well. This triple global storm triangulated well in the *cultural* Korean Wave and due to its decentralized digital *media* production and its 'saturated' cultural use in Korea. These three issues, plus others about durable Korean consensus building from their unique hybrid political, economic, and cultural settlements, are argued to have helped Koreans get through this 'digital bottleneck' intact as a country and culture. Korea arguably has been successful in going through this digital bottleneck because it has avoided becoming a digital police state so far despite digital conditions and despite many Korean politicians attempting to do so starting from 1995. (See Appendix 1). However, Korean politics has increasingly rejected and undone five major repressive and unrepresentative digital settlements that *their government attempted to force on them in 1995, 2000, 2007, 2017, and 2021,* as discussed below. These five policies started to be undone between 2012 and 2022 in the name of preserving a more consensus-based digital republic keeping individual civil rights in Korea instead. So, Korea is more than an economic success. It is a political success in maintaining its civil rights in the face of mounting more technocratic and collectivistic digital policies. The world first example of the digital parity of a saturated mass digital politics in the Korean nation from around 2012 onward (see Appendix 1) has kept undoing technocratic policies as fast as some of its technocratic elites have tried to re-impose them. Plus, Korea is a cultural success in maintaining its more homogeneous culture despite both its successful general development and despite its successful digital development, respectively, despite its fast development drive and despite later the culturally corrosive effects of such a digitally triple global storm.

After reviewing this three-part data, then we can ask from comparative and historical views whether Korea, as the first digital "K-Nation," will be more of a harbinger that leads the way by good example to other countries or only more of a durable outlier to them. Other envious nations may be unable to follow the long-term Korean successful practices of digital economic development or digital culture simply by making bad decisions, or by having the bad accidents of being either the wrong size geographically and demographically for the future, or by having the wrong culture of more heterogeneity that may more greatly lead to the breakdown of nations under digitally saturated cultural conditions now. More detail on these points will follow. It is hoped other solutions for these more heterogeneous nations are found, as explained in another section later, so they can hold together and *continue to give their own unique six social gifts to the human condition* that, frankly, are in danger of being lost without policies to keep heterogeneous nations intact as cultures under digital conditions.

First, the three levels of this triple global storm are described. Then the problems of the digital bottleneck created by this triple global storm are described that Korea seems to have passed through already. Therefore, it is argued that Korea can show the way as a harbinger for others by its good choices and good accidents to get through the digital bottleneck durably as a nation as well to get down the development gauntlet. Next, the specific good policies and good accidents of Korean recent digital history are noted in comparative retrospect to show Korea's success through this digital bottleneck compared to other nations' upcoming greater difficulties or failures on the same factors since they are oriented differently. This will connect with an argument that Korea's good choices of unique hybrid solutions for political, economic, and even cultural development (described earlier as key to the flexible and durable Korean fast development drive toward greater economic aggregation) are better sources of consensus building available in Korea than currently in other countries. Arguably, this consensus-building helped Korea get through the development gauntlet earlier as it equally helped Korea get through the digital bottleneck intact between 2012 and 2022. Four kinds of policy movements and social movements in these years were added to the ongoing Korean hybrid political settlement to strengthen Korean's civil rights into a basic digital bill of rights of limitations on the power of their own digital database-and-surveillance state. It shows Koreans pushing back successfully in undoing unrepresentative forces in their country that have failed so far in erecting a more unrepresentative digital technocracy or digital surveillance police state in their nation. On the other hand, many other countries' citizens are ambivalent or remain divided as they watch their national elites craft more unrepresentative, technocratic, and repressive regimes of digital surveillance instead of choosing to use their digital technology for its liberating and democratizing influences like Korea has done so far.

10.1.1.1 Global Economic Storm

One part of this triple global storm is *economic*. It is toward more decentralized, multi-polar, economic development. In 2018, Korea's *economic* ranking entered the world's top 10 economies where it remains in 2022. From 2021, the status of the Korea was changed to a developed country group at the 68th United Nations Conference on Trade and Development (UNCTAD). This made Korea *the first and only case* so far of a status change from a 'developing country' to a 'developed country' since that U.N. organization was founded in 1964. This is an outrageously limited development of the world in the past 75 years, and shows very bad advice from many external international agencies and sponsors. It shows equally the huge number of internal problems and bad ideas of many countries that frustrate their own development. Korea held together durably however. Korea did not follow any major international advice. Once older Japanese and European empires started to collapse between 1945 into the 1980s, Korea could take advantage of the global economy and fresh global markets after the Military Revolutionary Committee's coup in 1961. By 1963 Korea already was making odd 'half-revolutionary' and 'half-conservative' consensus decisions, and making more compromise-based hybrid policies of the "three odd's", to coin a phrase. These "three odd's" were the ending of Korea's already-weakened informal political culture of leadership around the old Korean aristocracy yet doing this *oddly* well without a cultural revolution, while *oddly* protecting its traditional rural culture and national economy despite removing the leadership of the ancient aristocracy, and while at the same time participating in an export-led development of urban industrial mass markets in a world market yet *oddly* in the midst of policies for domestic national economic protection, traditional cultural artisan protection, and rural village-based developmental protection from that world market. Earlier, Korea avoided a totalitarian leftist cultural revolution in the late 1940s and early 1950s with several public-administered and private land distributions. Later, Korea avoided its original revolutionary statist development from 1961 via the more half-revolutionary and representative development after 1963. Later, Korea avoided another a right-wing cultural revolution between approximately 1970 to 1979 under President Park, ended by Park's assassination and somewhat adapted by Chun into what has been called the 'Proto-Korean Wave' earlier in Chapters 2 and 3. So, despite unrepresentative setbacks between 1972 through 1987, beginning in the 1980s Korea began to emerge from these consensus setbacks to have a few greater civil rights expansions even under Chun (1979/1980–1988), and more competitive party elections for all positions including the presidency after 1987. After 1987, there were finally presidents under constitutions instead of constitutions under presidents, and militaries under civilian governments instead of civilian governments under militaries. Throughout a greater power of the Korean Constitutional Court was growing as the ultimate arbiter of Korean civil rights and increasingly digital civil rights. Increasingly a greater digital economy over time and a greater saturated digital democracy with a strong digital public sphere even clawed back online anonymity in 2012 against state surveillance of all speech on the Internet—instead of clawing back all state censorship of the Internet though per se, which remains strong. The year 2012 equally saw a turnaround from state policy makers themselves, who changed their minds and stopped defending the earlier digital surveillance policy when they began to note its more dangerous economic effects due to centralized hacking and loss of Korean digital records (see Appendix 1). In short, we hope other nations follow and become developed nations in this growing global economic decentralization. We hope they learn deeply about the Korean path through the digital bottleneck as well. This analysis aims to help them.

Another way of thinking about a more decentralized global economic development is noting the erosion of past Eurocentric economic power. From 2019, the mostly Western European/Atlantacist 'G7' states (United States, Canada, U.K., France, Germany, Italy, and Japan) controlled a residual and ever-shrinking 46.3% of the world economy if measured by global GDP. If measured by purchasing power parity (PPP) in 2021, the G7 had even less global economic power with only 32% of global PPP (Calcea, 2021).

Given ongoing growth in this decentralized and multi-polar global economy, it is unlikely for a strategy of Eurocentric consolidated global control to remain possible given a high diversity of multi-polar economic interests particularly in the different interests of the world's larger and smaller countries. However, that fails to stop some Europeans from trying. There still remains a pushy Eurocentric desire to remain on top of global leadership institutions by fresh strategies, yet the Europeans/Americans lack by default the economic and demographic power to do it themselves anymore.

Therefore, the older globalist and mostly Eurocentric establishment of the G7 have been looking for a fresh block of allies to control as a group, trying to maintain their unquestioned leadership even over a multi-polar world. For example, from 1999, the idea of a 'G20' starts to be sponsored by the G8 group (as Russia was invited to join in 1998 as well) to keep the latter G7 in control of many other developing nations' economies and political agendas beyond what the G7 has ability directly to control because of a growing, decentralized, multi-polar global economy. From 2014, the trend is an ever shrinking global control by the G7. For example by 2014, Russia was temporarily suspended from meetings of the G8, moving it back to a mere G7, after the U.S. coup of the democracy in Ukraine in 2014 to end Ukraine's pro-Russian oil politics. This has led into a growing 'neo-Cold War' of the U.S./NATO versus Russia/Belarus in the proxy zone of Ukraine—despite Ukraine being outside of NATO and despite a lack of formal declaration of war by the United States. By 2018, Russia formally expressed zero interest in rejoining the G8. As noted in the next section, the growing reliance of violence by the G7, instead of compromise politics or hegemonic cultural steering, shows it is losing agenda control of this increasing multi-polar world. Plus, by 2019, there is only a weak possibility of the G7 being a global agenda-steering block of 'advanced economies' anymore because the G7's population in the G20 now is a paltry 19%, while the emerging economies in the G20 that the G7 are seeking to steer are the remaining 81% of population of the G20. An overbearing power of the G7 continues because the small number of mostly older ex-imperial European/American states (the 'G7 in the G20') rig the agenda of the meeting by continuing to have the majority of global economy of the G20 at 61.5%, while inviting a limited number of emerging or other advanced economies that are only 39.5% of the global economy. Plus, the IMF forecasted the G20 nations' total GDP to be nearly \$69 trillion, or 78% of the world total GDP of \$88 trillion in the same year. Moreover, the entire G20 is trying to control policy for 4.6 billion people, or 61% of the total world population in 2019 (MGM Research, 2019). In short, the older Eurocentric direct economic and demographic control of the world economy and a world culture is weakening so these older global powers are strategizing how to maintain their old centralized control by wider clientelism over the whole G20 and the majority of the whole world, economically and demographically—or by wider violence. However, vast national differences in sizes of geography and demography in this G20, and increasingly a multi-polar world culture, show that few are interested in shoring up a weakening European cultural or economic precedence instead of enjoying its weakening precedence into a mere peer region of the world. By April 2023, this has only accelerated as many developing countries like Brazil and even major oil exporting nations like Saudi Arabia or Russia start to dump the exclusive use of the U.S. dollar as their international reserve currency in trading with each other outside of the United States. A growing amount of global oil even before 2023 was already traded outside of the G7/U.S. 'petrodollar' exchange mechanism, starting with Venezuela in 2017 as a major oil exporter when it told the world it will stop accepting U.S. dollar payments for its oil, preferring instead to trade for oil in Euros. Russia started selling its global oil in its own rubles in 2022 as the world's second largest exporter of oil, and with China now trading for oil with Russia using its own Chinese yuan in 2022 as well. By 2023, India as the world's third largest importer of oil now trades for Middle East oil in rupees with Saudi Arabia and the United Arab Emirates (UAE). At their August 2023 meeting in South Africa, the BRICS countries plus others as a combined group are making a play for replacing the U.S. dollar as the global international reserve currency with a fresh mechanism of their own. However, in June 2023, still 88% of international transactions were conducted in U.S. dollars, with the U.S. dollar still accounting for 58% of global foreign exchange reserves, though the multi-polar world is growing (Papa, 2023). For instance, 44 countries already express interest in joining the BRICS bloc to be a "BRICS+" bloc. If all joined, it would be over 80% of the world's population against a residual Eurocentric G7 (Cocks, 2023; Richardson, 2023).

10.1.1.2 Global Cultural Storm

The second part of this global storm is *cultural*. It is toward the same kind of decentralization as the global economy, yet in a heterogeneous multi-polar world of global cultural diversity as well. For an example of the growing cultural decentralization, while the Korean economy became the 10th largest national economy in the world in 2018, this was the same year of the first global 'simultaneous successes' of the *cultural* Korean Wave. By 2021, the Korean cultural contents industry was ranked as the 7th largest in the world and even speaking and writing Korean itself is becoming a fresh global shared second-language or *lingua franca* according to analysis by the online language learning app Duolingo.

Instead of recounting the details of the Korean Wave as in earlier chapters, the point now is different and about the future. First, what will to happen to all countries now facing more global cultural diversity? How will a more permanent, heterogeneous, global digital culture from this point ebb back and forth *to undermine all future national cultural reproduction*? What are the characteristics of national cultures that have greater ability to keep culturally reproducing under this treatment, and what kinds of national cultures are more likely to be splintered by a global cultural wave in the minds' of their next generations, fracturing cultural reproduction of some nations as other nations are more immutable and immune?

Second, what will happen as the current "G7" of globalist great powers or their proxy power if the "G20" increasingly fail to make themselves believable as global cultural leaders? What if the world's opinion of the G7 or the G20 become the view that these Eurocentric cultural groups are simply selfishly out for themselves like before, trying to keep up the inequalities of an oligarchic world cultural dominance and world cultural leadership that they have enjoyed for centuries? How do you 'keep centrally controlling' innate multi-polarity if this is a contradiction in terms and a fool's errand? This is not an argument that is meant to diminish the global contributions, true beauty, and true political and cultural innovations from Western civilization to the wider human condition (discussed below in Sect. 10.3 on heterogeneous cultures' innovations and contributions to the world that are in danger of being lost if only more homogeneous cultures survive the digital bottleneck). The point here is what happens as Europeans and Americans diminish in their ability to popularize their own cultural civilization (or their globalist coordinated "G7-ilization") as the only image of the future that people want? Will they get more violent or will they acquiesce? It seems they prefer to get more violent in hard power as they are unable or unwilling to fall back on failing ideological soft power in or material subsidies to their allies. Particularly the United States and NATO as the unchained bulldogs of the G7 are getting more violent in *over twenty military invasions or blockades of other weaker countries' oceans or airspaces in the past 30 years* after the end of the Cold War in 1991 instead of getting more representative and more interested in consensus-building in a multi-polar world. However, even if they prefer to get more violent, the issue is will they have the economic capacities to follow through with that policy at all? In other words, the growing multi-polar world is hardly just the 'rise' of other national economies and cultures. It is the weakening capacities of other global powers to stop a multi-polar world as well. For instance, the U.S. military establishment is already running low on war materials and munitions in 2023 simply by trying to keep one proxy war on Russia continuing in Ukraine. Plus, it was revealed in February 2023 from many sources that the U.S. blocked a peace mediation between Russia and Ukraine in 2022, pressing Ukraine instead to continue to fight despite mutual peace overtures between Ukraine and Russia. The United States is going to fight to the last Ukrainian.

Culturally speaking, there is a slow decline in the global popularity of American cultural production as its military keeps getting more hostile abroad and at home, and as the U.S.'s global cultural revolution of 'wokism' extends to everywhere that the U.S.'s government, corporations, or even military touches. For five cultural examples of this trend, first, an 'anti-woke' backlash began to build across the United States in 2021, and by 2022 nearly all Disney movies of the past year were failures in profit (Lawson, 2022). By 2022, Disney reported over $180 million dollars in lost profits. Second, in the same year the wider associated U.S./Hollywood cultural production empire as a whole reported losing over $580 billion dollars of profit compared to the previous year. Third, by February 2023, the freshly launched OTT global service Disney+ from 2019 reported 2.3 million lost subscriptions in the year of 2022 alone, instead of an advance. American Netflix as well has been having a hard time for the first time since its start in 2007 in keeping its large global subscriber base from 2022 onward (as noted in the earlier Chapter 8 on *Squid Game*).

Fourth, American entertainment companies are starting to give up and just want to exploit the global Korean Wave themselves out of desperation for profit. By September 2022, financially failing Disney+, that now owns the *Star Wars* movie franchise series, attempted to exploit global Korean Wave popularity to build a fan base for *Star Wars* once more after its several past movie flops in the same series after they purchased it. After announcing terrible financial losses in May 2022, Disney+ announced by September 2022 that it had hired *Squid Game*'s lead Korean actor Lee Jung-Jae to be a main lead in a freshly written *Star Wars* series for Disney+ called 'The Acolyte', planned for release in 2024. However, instead of a turnaround, it seems an odd mix of conservative Korean Wave and 'woke' storyline since it is includes a popular British YouTuber and recently 'out' transgender actor Abagail Thorn, and since is set in a context without any actual wars in the *Star Wars* series, and so instead it is about more satanic Jedi exploring the 'dark side' of the Force (Copson, 2023; Maas, 2022; Trent, 2023). This fails to sound like a profitable turnaround by Disney for its failing *Star Wars* franchise that would reestablish its global sales appeal, despite incorporating popular Korean Wave stars or popular YouTubers into the mix to try to rescue Disney. Fifth, by November 2022, the Korean K-pop group BTS beat all American acts of Taylor Swift, Drake and Ariana Grande to have the most #1 hits on the U.S. Billboard Hot 100 in the past decade. BTS scored six top hits in the past decade while U.S. rap star Drake was one hit behind them with five. Below that were American pop idols Taylor Swift and Ariana Grande with four top hits apiece. Plus, now HYBE, the Korean management company over BTS, owns the back catalogues of Ariana Grande as well.

10.1.1.3 Global Communications Storm Altering How to Reach People

This third point in this triple global storm is an increasing digitally-convergent media and its increasing miniaturization and networked decentralization across the entire planet as one network. It has given us as individuals anywhere an equal global digital media access for cultural consumption, cultural distribution, and even cultural production from any country in the world. Plus, making this a true global network, now the majority of individual citizens in all regions of the world have mobile phone access. From 2019, for the first time in world history, every zone of the world has at least 50% or more of its population with powers of cultural mass production and mass distribution via a smartphone ownership and global platforms. This is an individualized communicative power and a 'smart regional' mass media cultural production in the hands of nearly anyone in any region on the planet anywhere who wants an audience globally and instantly (We Are Social/Hootsuite, 2019). This means even some of the poorest zones of the world in sub-Saharan Africa now have the majority of their citizens with mobile phone ownership as a smart region (We Are Social/Hootsuite, 2019). Three caveats of this global equitable communicative power of course are that there is still a wide array of different censorship regimes, different levels of self-censorship as well out of fear against telling the truth online, and a wide array of different costs of bandwidth and of spotty electrical service worldwide (Ang, 2020; Routley, 2019). However, with every region of the planet now having a majority of citizens and consumers with a smartphone, people will slowly get more familiar and more brave about having a permanent 'globalized yet individualized' open door for choosing any culture they want and for choosing to say anything they want. It is an open invitation to join or to build fresh virtual and digital "imagined communities" anywhere at any scale that share an image of the future.

As well, this is an open invitation to enhance various already-existing subaltern communities historically repressed from communicating their plight, as they live within other cultural nations. Equally, this is an open invitation of unrepresentative national elites to erect digital police states and technocratic social credit systems similar to China, and it is an open invitation for enemy foreign countries to try to dominate the information space of another country's population as well. The point now then is what will happen to the stability of past powerful hegemonic "imagined communities" of nations? (Anderson, 2006). If the national cultures daily-created and reinforced by the previous media regimes had a limited centralized production, and thus an easier content control due to only one-way mass publishing and then only one-way mass telecommunications, what happens to past national cultures when these centralizing forces of mass cultural production and mass distribution are gone? Alongside an *inter*national digital cultural plurality, will an *intra*-national digital cultural plurality develop, or will current national attempts on digital censorship and propaganda get worse to repress it? Will both trends happen and yet accommodate differently under different national characteristics? Which nations will break first? What will future "imagined communities" look like? Said more abruptly, will current nations even culturally exist after several generations of *saturated global digital cultural production?* Which national communities will survive in their believability and cultural legitimacy, and which will fail in their believability and cultural legitimacy?

So, the third part of this triple global storm is a media regime change. It is a world historical change of media as shown in Appendix 4. South Korea had the world's first nationally saturated version of a digital media culture of viral two-way mass communication, so the triple global storm of decentralized digital economics, culture, and media linked up in Korea first. (See Appendix 1). This helps explain why Korea is ahead and remains ahead of other nations. This explains the methods of peering at South Korea's earlier saturated digital culture for its effects, its conflicts, and its changing accommodations as a way to scry the future of other countries. Equally, it helps conceptualize how the three future trends may merge or only come to a head more in countries that are more saturated in this media.

However, some may think that some countries may try to survive the coming triple global storm and its digital bottleneck on themselves by minimizing a saturated digital culture, instead of embracing it. However, avoiding such a decentralized digital media to survive culturally may hardly be an option because if nations fail to adopt and to take advantage of this fresh media regime, they will be increasingly outclassed in communication by other nations anyway, and in this sense outclassed in the current global economic participation that follows from it even if they wish to minimize its global cultural penetration of themselves. Thus, they may increasingly fail as nations in the twenty-first century in this other way even if they may try to be stable by minimizing or repressing digital communications, while only getting dominated by nations and regions that do adopt more innovative digitally saturated arrangements. For a comparative instance from the past, the Ottoman Empire (1299–1922) successfully banned publishing technologies of European mass printing to keep its governmental and cultural stability until 1729, yet of course by that time the country for almost three centuries had been surrounded by European governments and cultures that had been using these mass publishing technologies and became faster in economic scale innovation, individual innovation, cultural innovation, and technological innovation as a consequence since the 1450s. Thus, the Ottomans were unable to avoid the world outside of them using mass printing, so they simply outclassed themselves further as a viable state and culture in competition with other states by trying to block mass printing for centuries. Adapting this story to the present, who are the modern Ottomans? Which states and national cultures are trying simply to stop playing the game of media regime change in world history, despite being unable to since all nations are immersed in common trends? The same "Ottoman-style" media suicide of a nation is happening now in countries like North Korea, India, or Ethiopia that are setting themselves back deeply. Many states like these three attempt to erect an increasingly less representative and more repressive digital surveillance model. For example, India and Ethiopia both use 'internet denial' zones or periods during protests, as these are very heterogeneous cultural nations attempting to get through the digital bottleneck. However, the second order effects of this policy in India or Ethiopia can create greater digital divides in digital economic readiness and can create even more disapproval of their regimes, instead of less disapproval. Equally, they are only teaching their citizens technically to innovate around national censorship and to regard their governments as a culturally illegitimate power and as enemies to their economic livelihoods or communicative concerns. That is a bad lesson to learn because even in an Internet world, we still live in geographic communities that require stable economics and cultures. Regularly wrecking a stable geographic nation's digital economy and digital culture while making your citizens hate you fails to serve any national interest in the long term, and such a policy only protects more unrepresentative governmental elites and their short term thinking from creating better consensus building. This is a chosen vicious cycle that ends badly for the viability of a nation in this triple global storm.

Thus, policies of Internet blocks and digital surveillance states may create political stability, though only for a short time. What it really creates for the long term is more cultural and economic instability, dropping out of the development gauntlet, or even cultural revolution—when the latter was attempted to be avoided by such digital policies in the first place when it may only catalyze it more. Digital repression makes it hard to get through the digital bottleneck or the development gauntlet at all. So, some countries in the short term that try to hold together politically with ever more detailed digital police states may be building a digital prison on their culture and economy that will catalyze only an eventual jail break by their citizens that wrecks the viability of their nation internally as well as competitively with others externally. So, like the Ottoman Empire, the modern nations of North Korea, India, and Ethiopia, other countries with this strategy can continue to try it. Even neoliberalist France under Macron is attempting it in July 2023. However, blocking this coming decentralized media communications regime marks these countries as ruled by a set of unrepresentative leaders that are making their nations more inadaptable and even further behind—economically, culturally, and in media—compared to other countries. They can be compared to more viable digital nations that keep their Internet on and censor citizens less because they chose a *different policy of learning to be more consensus-oriented instead*. Nations like France in July 2023 currently are choosing more unrepresentative digital censorship and repression against what appears to be a near Islamic jihad of civil unrest from illegal immigrants allowed into their countries or at least agent provacateurs seeded into the riots, instead of addressing the issue with more consensus of how over 70% of France wants a referendum on such illegal alien immigration. On the other hand, nations like South Korea have invented many added digital consensus mechanisms using their digital technologies instead. This is argued to help Koreans survive intact through the digital bottleneck better. However, some national governments will refuse to be more representative and consensus oriented. They will soon learn they have only themselves to blame for outclassing themselves as sites for global digital economic production and global digital cultural participation—or even leading to dropping of the general developmental gauntlet because of cultural revolution and national breakdown.

Though rare, media regime changes create powerful discontinuities in world history. Fresh media regime changes make powerful 'organizational mismatches' between older information-management institutions of a culture and its daily life. Each start to be out of sync with each other. Older core hegemonic institutions with well-practiced *procedures of cultural reproduction in the six main tasks* (like information gathering, communication/distribution/transmission, education, making decisions, selective promotion, and selective censorship) have less power to do all six tasks over time in a media regime change. This is due to the fresher ways peripheral cultural people now use other media to do these six tasks in their daily lives over time. In time, once people peripheral to core institutions develop their own daily core institutional forms around fresh media regimes that do the same for themselves, this is a different, nascent, self-perpetuating culture yet it is in parallel to older mismatched institutions that slowly fail as they are unrequired anymore. This organizational mismatch is a punishing pressure in a culture, building silently underground for many years like an earthquake. On some unexpected future conflict date in the culture, this media earthquake noisily snaps into movement and wrecks *multiple* once-stable institutions on the surface *all at once*. Only once an earthquake is felt on the surface, and only when all institutions are seen toppling all at once, will people awake to the reality of what has been happening underground in motion for a long time. The so-called 'sudden rise' of the global Korean Wave is something similar to this media earthquake. It has been building underground for over a decade, and from 2018 it began to shake other national institutions of culture to the ground around the world at once.

Underground now in many nations, this punishing pressure of media regime change is still building and being ignored—though for how long? It will someday snap, sooner or later, in other oblivious nations with their proud yet eroded and hollow institutions. As noted in Appendix 1, from 1995, Korean elites were already preparing to build a digital police state, showing how quickly they reneged on the widened journalistic freedoms of publishing arranged from 1987. However, very soon after 1995 in Korea, the media earthquake snapped and rattled an oblivious Korea to the ground in 2003 and has slowly rebuilt the nation after that. That event in 2003 was the election of President Roh Moo-hyun (2003–2008), the first 'Internet President' in South Korea, *elected without any major sponsorship of the older Korean mass media and mass party establishment*. To their impotent anger, hatred, and shock, the previous systemic power elites in Korea had lost communicative power and the 'second face of power' of agenda setting (Lukes, 2021), and thus started to lose all other kinds of social power from that. Though they lost that battle in 2003 for the institution of some parts of the state, they had yet to lose the war of control of other institutions of economics, finance, and education. So, from 1995, Korean elites were already building a digital police state. However, by 2021 in Korea, the whole project of a digital police state has been undone four times over, in the past decade between 2012 and 2022.

These five major attempts at a digital police state in Korea have all been undone by four stronger forces of digital democracy in Korea than digital dictatorship, one after the other. To explain, Korean elites by the first decade of the twenty-first century tried to build a very repressive digital surveillance state from 1995 onward. However, mostly in the second decade of the twenty-first century, Korean digital citizens aligned with their government returning to consensus dismantled it entirely between 2012 and 2022.

As noted in Appendix 1, first, from 1995, Korea developed the first internet censorship policy in the world. Second, by 2000, the Korean government built an ever expanding state monitoring and state authorization of all digital online financial transactions of all citizens. This was the state monopoly of the NPKI digital authentication system. Its growing rules required citizens to use it alone for a growing list of all kinds of online financial transactions (Son & Whitaker, 2020). Third, from 2007, the Korean government built a very repressive centralized 'real name ID net identification' for monitoring the real people behind all internet accounts, a legal requirement for major platforms to have the real names of all digital accounts, otherwise anonymous citizens were banned from use of these private/national platforms.

However, these latter two attempts to maintain state institutions of *centralized* control surveilling all financial transactions of people online by their real names and state surveillance tracking of all users' posts online by their real names started to crack and sway in the growing 'liquefaction' caused by the increasingly saturated *decentralized* digital culture. Keep in mind the year 2013 was the first year when Korea became the first nation in the world with nearly 100% smartphone ownership through age 18. Two years later, by 2015, Korea was the first nation in the world with approximately 100% smartphone ownership through age 35. The United States in 2013 only had 50% of its youth with smartphones at that point. During this period of heightened digital democracy, from 2012 the 'real name' net ID policy was revoked by the Korean Constitutional Court and even found itself unsupported by the state elites anymore as well. Korean internet anonymity was preserved in the interests of democracy and avoiding state repression, said the court (BBC, 2012). There were massive online 'netizen' protests against it, and next, the Korean state itself saw economic dangers as well and stopped pushing for the policy after more than half of the whole country's 'real name' online records of authentication was leaked from a major centralized online platform that was required by the government to keep such personal data. In 2015, an even larger dataset was leaked about the whole Korean nation's medical records. "In July 2015, medical records of more than 90% of the South Korean population were leaked to a U.S. multinational medical firm, IMS Health Korea. Records included patient data such as sex, type of disease, age, and region. A report using the collected data was sold to Korean pharmaceutical companies for \$5.2 billion" (McCart, 2022). In this context of *centralized insecurity* instead of greater security, by 2015, the centralized state monitoring and state authorization of all private financial transactions online was ended as a mandate for all citizens to use, replaced by having options of a free market in multiple private standards of digital authentication being allowed, with none of those being required to be managed by or to turn over their digital financial transaction data to the state. However, many major Korean banks still use the old technologically-outdated NPKI system regardless of it being jettisoned because of systemic ease of hacking (Kim, 2018), as it is still cheaper for them to have citizens be blamed legally for online fraud in their certificates instead of the banks, and because it is cheaper if the government does the banks' due diligence on authorizing online payment transfers instead of the banks paying to do it themselves by online fraud detection by artificial intelligence. Plus, in ongoing path dependence, the number of issued NPKI certificates—innately letting governmental agencies monitor and authorize private online purchases—continues to grow regardless that it lost its state mandate from 2015 and regardless of systemic hacking (Jang & Lim, 2021; Son & Whitaker, 2020; Statista, 2020). Moreover, this trend of financial monitoring of private transactions still continues in Korea. The country moved first to shrink the number of cryptocurrency exchanges that could have bank accounts in 2018, then began to require real name financial accounts for cryptocurrency exchanges in 2019 (Xu, 2019), and then by 2021 required real name financial accounts for all cryptocurrency account holders—though for the latter conversion was said to be very slow showing resistance (Das, 2021). This is because Korea historically has a very large underground economy, and South Korea alone was about 20% of all global cryptocurrency transactions (Xu, 2019). "The ratio of the underground economy to GDP, which stood at 24.7 percent in the 1970s, climbed to 28.7 percent in the 1980s and 35.6 percent in the 1990s before declining to 26.4 percent in the 2000s. Over the years since 2010, the figure has risen again, averaging 31.1 percent, which is about 10 percentage points higher than the average for 34 member states of the Organization for Economic Cooperation and Development. The ratio remains below 10 percent in the U.S. and most Western European countries....The study showed the size of Korea's shadow economy was much larger than calculated by a previous study, which estimated it at about 23 percent of GDP in 2013." (Kim, 2015)

Fourth, by 2017, Korean netizens and left-wing media channels exposed and then contributed to the impeachment of rightist President Park Geun-hye for building a secret cultural blacklist of nearly 10,000 Korean artists and creatives and for other scandals from 2013 onward. These other scandals started with the Park Administration in 2013 filing a winning lawsuit to dissolve an elected minor left political party, the United Progressive Party (UPP), and thus jettison them from the National Assembly. On that scandal, the Park Administration even applied for a court injunction to pre-suspend activities of the political party during the trial. That dissolution of a political party by state order was unprecedented in the whole legal history of modern Korea given it only happened once before under Rhee in 1958 without legal codification, and had never been used after being codified into the

Korean Constitution of 1960 onward (Second Republic, 1960–61) until President Park used it in 2013. In the next year of 2014, there were complaints about President Park negligently missing for seven hours, widely interpreted as dereliction of duty around a failed rescue of the sinking of the ferry *MV Sewol* in 2014—which was owned by a religious cult leader Yoo Byung-eun that had connections to Park's close female compatriot Choi Soon-sil (Kim & Chung, 2016). Over years, there was ongoing financial corruption between Park's same female confidant Choi Soon-sil and Samsung leadership. To focus on Park's secret cultural blacklist, it was compiled from 2013 from information of Korean citizen public/online statements, the content of their cultural projects, or their statements or actions of political alignments against President Park. So, while earlier in 2003 the Internet frenzy from leftist young adults simply elected a political outsider in Roh Moo-hyun (2003–2008) as Korean president in 2003, the even stronger digital democracy by 2017 would now contribute to impeach the main bloodline of the durable Korean developmental dictatorial establishment itself, in the daughter of President Park Chung-hee, who is President Park Geun-hye (2013–2017).

Park Geun-hye was previous National Representative and leader of the conservative Grand National Party (GNP) between 2004 and 2006, then, she was leader of the Liberal Korea Party from 2011 to 2012, and then, she was Korean President from 2013 to 2017. Of course she was sponsored into these positions because she was born to the 'South Korean throne' as the sole dynastic heir and daughter of the original military strong man and developmental leader—the previous President Park Chung-hee increasingly in charge from 1961 to 1963 after a group-based developmental military coup in 1961 and then President from 1963 to 1979. Many Korean citizens and netizens were enraged by President Park Geun-hye for a multitude of corrupt or incompetent points by 2016 that included educational cronyism for her friends to get into Ewha Womans University (a very hot issue given strong Korean educational competition for entry into a top university), Samsung corporate bribery through donations to a fake sports/cultural foundation run by Park's cult-connected friend Choi Soon-sil that was headquartered in wealthy Nonhyeon-dong, Gangnam-gu, Seoul, directly behind the expensive five-star hotel and restaurants in the Imperial Palace hotel. Park Geun-hye additionally was accused of theft of Korean state money placed in overseas bank accounts managed by her same friend Choi, and of course blamed for the aforementioned dereliction of Presidential duty as the *MV Sewol* sank without any governmental response in April 2014, as hundreds of high school children on a holiday trip from Incheon to Jeju instead died in that ferry accident—with the ferry line owner another rich religious cult leader and connection with Choi Soon-sil. All of this sounds like the typical human tragedy you get when an aristocracy is restored. So, on top of all this, the exposure of Park's secret cultural blacklist in 2016 was a kind of a 'straw that broke the camel's back' by showing that her administration was more than corrupt and incompetent. It was secretive and malicious. Park had been blacklisting nearly 10,000 Koreans secretly for years including very popular Korean Wave K-pop idols and producers simply for legally supporting other Presidential candidates or using their civil rights to publicly criticize her inaction during the Sewol crisis. All of these ongoing scandals catalyzed and kept a national social movement online and in the streets against her Presidency for years. However, throughout November 2016 through March 2017, pro-government media and censorship regimes were increasingly powerless with repeatedly massive protests against Park in the streets of Seoul known as the Candlelight Demonstrations or Candlelight Vigil. The largest of the early ones was on November 28, 2016, and it brought almost 2 million Koreans into the streets in protest against Park, around the nation. By December 3, 2016, an even larger estimated 2.3 million people were protesting simultaneously around the nation. In Seoul itself, an estimated 1.6 million people were protesting around the area of Seoul City Hall to Gwanghwamun Square and Gyeongbok Palace. The National Assembly eventually felt pressed with losing its own future elections or public order, and so they relented. They impeached President Park on December 9, 2016, with 234 out of 300 legislators voting for impeachment on secret ballot. However, since the total voting for impeachment was so high and far above the two-thirds requirement of only 200, it had obviously included more than half of the 128 legislators of Park's own right-wing party of the Liberty Korea Party, otherwise known as the Saenuri Party. Running true to form, Park refused to leave the Presidency in 2017. With great chutzpah, President Park in January 2017 sued a journalist and a member of the independent counsel's team for claiming Park had participated in making the secret cultural blacklist despite Park's Minister for Culture, Sports and Tourism, Cho Yoon-sun, already admitting it and already arrested herself for lying under oath about it to the National Assembly (Jung, 2017). These kind of antics started to catalyze both a constitutional crisis and other massive protests that were for Park by February 2017. However, the Constitutional Court on March 10, 2017, in a unanimous decision, confirmed the impeachment of a President is a power of the Korean National Assembly. Park was arrested a week later and charged with various crimes. She eventually went to jail for 25 years, though was released early by Presidential pardon on December 31, 2021, by the next President Moon.

Park's refusal to leave the Presidency for months after her impeachment nearly catalyzed martial law in early 2017. Showing how close Korea was to falling back into military dictatorship by March 2017, it was later revealed in July 2018 that Korea's Defense Security Command had made plans for martial law after Park's impeachment by the National Assembly during the period Park refused to accept the impeachment while the Constitutional Court was deliberating. This martial law plan was less to protect Park, and instead would have been activated only if the Constitutional Court failed to confirm her impeachment by the National Assembly, since that eventuality would have led to even larger protests both against Park and for Park clashing at the same time, with each side then being able to point to a legal rationale that they were right. For Seoul alone, the martial law plan called for 200 tanks, 550 armored vehicles, 4,800 armed military troops, and 1,400 members of the Special Forces to enforce martial law. The plan would include "1980's Chun style" military monitoring and digital censorship of national media content and even arrests of politicians involved in protests. How long that military martial law leadership and national digital censorship would last under a restored President Park Geun-hye, and on whose order it would be continued or withdrawn except hers, or what protests that the martial law or digital censorship itself would generate, or how Korea would have recovered from that to the next Presidential election or open media once more would have been unknown, since President Park Geun-hye would still be president by the (alternative) Korean Constitutional Court decision and in an ongoing martial law.

However, Korea avoided martial law under digital conditions and President Park Geun-hye in March 2017. Instead, soon after March 2017, the nearly 10,000 names were exposed and removed from Park's state censorship list that had blocked state aid of their cultural production for the Korean Wave. Perhaps unsurprisingly, once President Park's secret cultural blacklist was ended in 2017, the first simultaneous successes of the global Korean Wave began in earnest in 2018—without as much state censorship anymore at that point. In summary, ex-President Park was jailed for a time on several charges, one of which was running that secret cultural blacklist of nearly 10,000 media creatives, K-pop stars, and producers who were denied subsidies from the Korean Wave for simply voicing opinions against Park online or supporting other legal political parties. By 2020, the Korean Constitutional Court called such a state cultural blacklist an unconstitutional use of Presidential power. Thus, in this manner, the fourth attempt at state-managed digital dictatorship surveillance of the whole nation, via a secret social credit system punishing anyone for online pronouncements or public politics, was undone in Korea after 2017.

The fifth attempt at this digital police state came between 2021 to 2022. Leftist President Moon Jae-in tried to *expand* his national requirements of 'voluntary' medical vaccinations and public digital medical tracking via required 'vaccine passports' to show Koreans' private medical status *down to teenage youth* if they wanted to go into various public accommodations—despite teenagers never being in any risk group of being sick or dying. In turn, Korea's fourth democratic rebellion against a combined nationwide digital surveillance and forced injection regime merged many groups: Korean online netizens, a teenage popular YouTuber Yang Dae-rim writing and filing constitutional court battles on livestream (who had his channel censored and deleted by YouTube for popularizing it at one point), and even the Seoul Court and Constitutional Court that eventually blocked the vaccine passport requirement being extended to young teenagers. More details about this are mentioned in a later section in this chapter.

That makes four examples of Koreans, whether from the left or the right, or even together, refusing a digital police state. Korea was additionally lucky to avoid falling into martial law under digital conditions in 2017 with its unknown outcomes. All of these four digital surveillance trends have avoided and voided since the Korean government by consensus kept moving to work with their own people instead of work against them.

In short, a media regime change is an earthquake toppling institutions, agenda control, censorship, and past cultures all at once, quickly or slowly. In Korea's version of this media earthquake, it has become a stronger digital democracy because of these rejections of a digital police state, while other countries of course may experience the same media earthquake and become more like digital police states and yet more unstable and less culturally legitimate as a consequence despite themselves. However, as a consequence of combining Korea's greater consensus mechanisms, its more saturated digital culture, and even its more homogeneous culture, Korea arguably has held together and remained intact better through the digital bottleneck, while other nations may fail to get through it as a consequence, respectively, by being more unrepresentative, less saturated, and more heterogeneous cultures. Once a culture *has other, plural, and fresh media options, it still has older media-aligned institutions of power* built on trying to *monopolize, optimize, and gatekeep* content in the old media (1) for information gathering and distribution and (2) for the agenda of who gets to make the most knowledgeable decisions from processing information based on the power of having access to the best scaled information flow. Increasingly, older institutions of power in older media have less information to do either effectively. Eventually, quickly or slowly, the older media-aligned institutions' power is outclassed, undermined, and hollowed out in these two powers and in the six earlier mentioned main tasks by attrition. Increasingly in a fresh media regime, daily cultural life and information flows now outflank older institutions and start to build a culture's fresh institutions for developing coordination in the above six main tasks of these two main powers, instead of any of these tasks or powers flowing *as much* through older media-aligned institutions.

Thus, on the one hand, a media regime change creates a cultural change that impinges *similarly* upon *all* past social organizations in daily life that *similarly* exist because of their own version of these six tasks and these two powers to process information, instead of a media regime change impinging only on one area of 'media'. Plus, on the other hand, our current digital media regime change is a cultural change that impinges *differently* depending on differently oriented nations' 'demography, geography, and culture' as argued in the next section. Regardless of such differences of case context, a media regime change starts to undermine all past institutional leaderships' power to organize, command, enthrall, and delimit the information of their aggregate followers to support their particular choices and policies in those four arenas of social power in state politics, in education/religion/beliefs, in markets, and in financial currencies. *Therefore a media regime change has a simultaneous 'fourfold revolutionary potential'* for undermining agenda control and decision-making abilities of the combined and overlapping leaderships' of the four institutions of social power in states, educational institutions, market organization, and finance. The media regime change can make all four institutional accommodations *more representative only* if existing institutional leaderships' attempt to adapt to stay in power via more consensus strategies instead of by more repressive strategies. Our current digital media regime change can make all four institutional accommodations more representative equally under greater saturated digital cultures and more 'midsized' demography, geography, and a more homogeneous culture—though exactly how those three factors are defined and how they innately mix differently in different nations' saturated digital cultures is discussed in the next section.

However, there is nothing like a progressive sequence of "less representative to more representative" media regimes in history. Media regime changes are just discontinuous changes that can be used in a variety of different political and cultural ways, each time, instead of only used in only one way. There is an unsettled organizational mismatch that begins to occur during a media regime change. Despite the technologically determinist hype that claims the Internet world of communication is somehow only innately bringing democracy and greater civil rights, evidence is ambivalent for that claim given equal rising totalitarian and negative trends from the beginning of the Internet that have been forgotten that extend into the present use of it (Levine, 2018; Morozov, 2011). However, there is nothing technologically deterministic about the social organization of a media regime. A media regime change can be applied to benefit dictatorial states, global private companies, or regional civic communities alike in ongoing competition and accommodation with each other. It can be applied to affirm a wider digital democracy as well. In short, media regime changes simply provide a changing context of means through which ongoing accommodations of leaderships are exercised with aggregate followers. Regardless of how fresh media are attempted to be deployed in many different political alliances, *media regime changes and the organizational mismatches that they create are always going to be more revolutionarily discontinuous in world history* for the way we live in general, far beyond mere 'single sector' revolutionary changes like organizational changes of economic production or the organizational spread of democratic republics, for example.

See the note in Appendix 4 arguing how a primary media regime change can be interpreted as the key to the rise of Europe compared to other areas of the world in past centuries. *Europe's primary media change to mass printing seems the major cause, sooner or later, of all later 'earthquake-like' secondary power changes of organizational mismatch* that inspired the Protestant Reformation versus the Catholic Church, or inspired the European Scientific Revolution against the Catholic Church, or encouraged the consolidated Industrial Revolution and its mass printed advertising for share investors and product sales undermining delimited and localized small markets and guilds, or how it aided the spread of the (mass republished) Roman/Greek Enlightenment ideals of rational national republics and formal checks and balances against theocratic divine kings, or even aided the popular spread of mass education and mass self-education that depended on mass printing versus other kinds of previously more costly elite educational materials earlier. A lot of people think the French Revolution was the cultural break from ancient Europe to modern Europe. While this is true, it is kind of one of those media-driven earthquakes that happen on the surface only much later due to the ongoing slow underground pressures of earlier media change that all at once, it seems, collapses the already hollowed-out and organizationally mismatched surface institutions all at once. Plus, that mass printing media regime change was accelerated in 1802 with the coming of cheap paper industrially produced for the first time, that radically made the published cultural conversation more leveled for the first time in this publishing media. Comparatively, the early lead that Europeans had in living in a culture that was saturated with mass printing after the 1450s can be compared to other regions of the world with unsaturated contexts of mass printing that felt that huge pressure of scale from Europeans coming to dominance after the 1450s. Similarly, the early 'world first' lead South Korea had in the saturation of this fresh digital global media regime can be compared to all other regions of the world less saturated digitally at first, and this has made all the difference in the world for South Korea in the early twenty-first century.

In other words, a media regime change is the primary factor of this triple global storm. The two secondary factors of digital economic change and digital cultural change in this storm are the slow organizational mismatch that creates economic and cultural change, after this media regime change. So, a more global digital economy and a more global digital culture have followed from the advance of the fresh digital media regime itself. The argument is that *a global-scale institutional mismatch is happening in all nations simultaneously for the first time and happening for the first time very rapidly.* However it is happening differently in different nations by ongoing interactions of strategies and tactics of different groups and by different background conditions of the national size of demography and geography and how homogeneous or heterogeneous the country is. As first in the world, more digitally saturated, more 'mid-sized', more homogeneous, and more consensus-oriented Korea could use its own digital media storm to connect earlier than others to take advantage of this truly global economic storm and global cultural storm while weathering it and staying intact through it. The Korean Wave expansion was done first domestically in its more saturated digital culture and then increasingly internationally as the rest of the world could connect to earlier Korean saturation. When the rest of the world in many more heterogeneous and less representative countries did catch up with the digital saturation of Korea, Koreans had practice pouring their *digital content* into their own hearts and minds and then other nation's hearts and minds better than other countries could for a better part of two decades ahead of others. Koreans had developed a practice of ever greater digital consensus after 2003 that increasingly demoted from 2012 to 2022 four major unrepresentative pressures in Korea for using this fresh digital media regime as a digital police state, mentioned above.

It is unsurprising that fresh 'imagined communities' of *global* two-way virtual communities start to compete with older 'imagined communities' of *regionalized national-language* in the 'print capitalism' of one-way mass printing or now start to compete with the related 'imagined communities' of later regionalized national-language 'telecommunications capitalism' of one-way mass telecommunications of telephones, radio, movies, and television—in those same regionalized languages. Both of these more one-way mass media cultures generally held to virtuous cycles of geographic markets in a particular language region that in turn kept that same kind of 'imagined' national regional culture renewed daily for centuries (Anderson, 2006). However, our past's 'imagined communities' of national media and national power, once combined and inseparable via a national language, are being unraveled by a *global* level and *innately cross-language* digital media regime change. Korea had the first saturated digital cultural sphere making this fresh 'imagined community.' First, the early digitally saturated lead in Korea let its national regional media culture become a more global power, more readily than before. Second, the organizational mismatch that this created made the earliest series of ongoing national digital media conflicts over (1) whether a past nation would become an ever more unrepresentative digital police state, or (2) whether it would become a more consensus based digital democracy, or (3) whether it would fall apart into mutually hostile digital communities based on different homogeneous cultural and political principles as more important than common national language. The first two themes arose first in Korea and made it both a harbinger of future global digital change as well equally an even more futuristic outlier. Korea avoided the third theme by being a more homogeneous culture, as well as arguably being "not too large" demographically or geographically to set up irreconcilable spatial zones of the most digitally developed zones versus any digitally triaged zones in the same country—as well as choosing well to maintain that digital parity by good choices of direct policy instead of by sheer good accidents achieving it. Those points about why and how Korea avoided this self-destructive third theme under digital development are addressed in the next section. This means, unless Korea falters, it will be even harder for other nations' global digital economic, cultural, and media communications ever to catch up with Korean innovations now. Regardless of whether other nations can follow Korea or otherwise, Korea will remain a harbinger of this triple global storm that sooner or later will be happening within every other nation increasingly throughout the twenty-first century.

In conclusion, all nations and all citizens are facing a major choice in our current organizational mismatch (called the digital bottleneck) that Korea already has faced: do we become unrepresentative digital police states, do we become more consensus-based digital democracies, or do we fall apart into component cultural pieces? Korea has chosen the more consensus-based digital democracy so far, and Korea already has fallen apart in a sense into its component cultural piece, which leaves it unchanged, by being a more homogeneous culture. Therefore Korea remains more sturdy in this triple global storm by its greater cultural homogeneity and by that encouraging this greater consensus-based digital democracy that lacks strong geographical and culturally regional underclasses that many other nations have. Likely, some of Korea's 'good accidents' like this helped Korea maintain a digital democracy. These are discussed in the next section, like being a more homogeneous culture and being a moderate 'mid-size' in demography and geography. Korea is without other countries' challenges of being "too large", "too small", or "too diverse" as a country when facing the triple global storm that may pull those countries apart on fresh cultural and regional lines and/or lead to uneven digital development zones at the same time that pulls them apart as well. Of course, Korea has made some 'good choices' as well in this digital realm. Nonetheless, many other countries with different cultural orientations and with larger or smaller states in demography and geography, may at first choose the digital police state. However, in the long run the digital bottleneck may destroy governments that that think they will survive better as a digital police state. The digital bottleneck may destroy such countries anyway, simply by their 'bad accidents' of being oriented in culture and scale in a way that makes it very hard for them to survive the digital bottleneck intact. These ideas are now discussed in the following section.

10.2 Korea's Good Choices and Good Accidents Got It Through the Digital Bottleneck

The digital bottleneck is defined as the organizational mismatch of current economic and cultural effects facing all past nations trying economically to thrive and culturally to reproduce in a world now with this digital media regime change that has grown to become a triple global storm: a global digital *economy*, a national/global digital *culture*, and a globally distributed decentralized *media*. In short, the digital bottleneck is our current world's version of the common phenomenon in world history of an organizational mismatch that comes from a media regime change.

This gets into the questions of what are the optimal national states of the future that can remain intact past the digital bottleneck, and what are the policies and characteristics of national states that are more likely to have a breakdown or become only a dystopian shadow of their former selves? It is argued that all the world's nations will be vetted by the potential corrosive and divisive damages of this triple global storm, sooner or later. It will be a 'digital bottleneck' that may optimize *what demographic, geographic, and cultural characteristics* of nations will thrive, which may fall apart, and which will survive yet become unrepresentative digital technocracies—dystopian shadows of their former selves. This 'digital bottleneck' facing all nations, that they have to pass through successfully to survive, will be a selection factor on national success or failure in the twenty-first century.

It is argued that Korea has already passed through the digital bottleneck successfully intact, and thus Korea shows at least one way for nations to survive this coming triple storm—some of them by Korea's *good choices of more hybrid consensus policies* in politics, economics, and culture, and some sheerly by Korea's *good accidents* of *being more 'mid-sized' demographically and geographically and having a more homogeneous culture* than most. So both the good choices of more hybrid policies in Korea, that have over time encouraged consensus and greater representation, merge with good accidents. Both *minimize potential corrosive and divisive damages* of this triple global storm in Korea, and both *maximize abilities to take advantage* of such a global situation for Korean digital economic and cultural growth.

In this combination of Korea's good choices and good accidents, Korea passed through the digital bottleneck first. Nations can minimize their damages and maximize their chances of surviving intact like Korea by understanding the good choices and good accidents of Korea. Upon reflection, then those countries can try to formulate their own similar good choices of consensus policies and at least prepare for their own more unsolvable bad accidents of their different orientations of demography, geography, and culture that may require more direct policy solutions that Korea could ignore by default. In other words, there may be other ways to survive the digital bottleneck, and it is hoped there are, or it is hoped that they will be invented for smaller or larger homogeneous or heterogeneous cultural nations. Otherwise, the future may be bleak for "non-Korean" countries that are very different than Korea's good choices of policies or very different in Korea's good accidents of the three background factors of geography, demography, and culture.

As mentioned earlier, it is hypothesized that three scenarios as options arise for all nations in facing the digital bottleneck. First, if they wish to either remain the same or they wish to have the same "wealth of K-Nations" in the twenty-first century as Korea, other countries have to pass through this digital bottleneck similar to Korea: *remaining intact or even digitally improved*. We can learn from Korea in this scenario. Second, for another scenario, other countries trying to pass through this triple global storm will fail as they go through the digital bottleneck. This will perhaps lead to the *breakdown into component cultural parts* of many existing larger and smaller nations. Third, other countries will do a bit of both scenarios. They will pass through the digital bottleneck successfully, though will fail regardless to remain the same since their digital passage will alter them beyond recognition into *digital police states and unrepresentative digital technocracies* of two kinds, discussed later. Korea was developing this unrepresentative surveillance dynamic as well originally. However, between 2012 and 2021, it was undone repeatedly as Koreans and even their government itself began to reject that third digital scenario. Therefore, with Korea so far holding to the first scenario of remaining intact and even digitally improved, there are many points we can learn from Korea for how to go through the digital bottleneck well—for how to remain intact and even to thrive in a global digital economy and global digital culture.

10.2.1 Korea's Three "Good Accidents" Helped It Through the Digital "Goldilocks Zone"

This section discusses three of Korea's "good accidents" of being a demographically and geographically 'mid-sized' nation and a 'more' (yet hardly totalizing) homogeneous cultural nation. This triple middle situation is argued to better survive the economic and cultural crises of a global digital economy and global digital culture that other demographic, geographic, or cultural arrangements. A better scenario of the future for everyone is having more "K-Nations" that are intact and digitally improved, with a more equitable culture and greater representation from their digital development. This is possible, however it is hypothesized to be rare and thus come in league with two other darker scenarios. In what follows about these three different scenarios of the digital bottleneck, it is argued from four kinds of data: (1) given how rare so far has been Korea's extreme triple success in global economic, culture, and media among peer developing nations, and (2) given how rare is the durability of Korea in these policies compared to other countries with less durability in their developmental policies and a cultural wave. Therefore, from these first two kinds of data arguments, it is hypothesized that some characteristics of South Korea are more optimal and more durable for a global digital economy, global digital cultural participation, and a global digital media experience. Comparatively speaking, this means both background issues of 'good accidents' of historical happenstance in older

Korean history *and* good choices of policy in modern Korean history are considered together.

These two kinds of data about the rarity of success that is internal to Korea and comparatively judged with Korea are contrasted to two other kinds of data about growing failures of other nations in a global digital economy, culture, or media experience. The third kind of data is (3) other nations have outright failed to start this digital competition, or have tried and failed afterwards. Therefore, it is hypothesized that some characteristics of other nations as well make them more prone to have difficulties in the digital bottleneck and thus are organizationally less optimal and less durable for a triple global storm. The fourth kind of data is (4) how some nations are forming their own "internal K-Nation" zones within them, popularly called tech clusters or technological parks, yet it is hypothesized that the more successful of these will start to have similar characteristics that look like more "internal K-Nations" with less equitable regional coverages of digital development within them and thus many areas of digital triage. Some may think this is good to at least have this, yet it may be a bad trend of state failure without intervention to stop it because most nations with these "internal K-Nations" so far seek to secede to become separate "K-Nations" or attempt to have some kind of technocratic and political coup over their previous wider nation to put themselves in charge. This related scenario taking place now in many countries is how this internal K-Nation attempts *unrepresentative technically-administered coups over the whole nation's culture and politics* to gain the same control via an unrepresentative technocracy and digital police state to manage the wider nation for their own interests first. This may lead to another slower breakdown of a nation in the long run. Plus, attempts at secession or coup by this "internal K-nation" over the whole previous nation in this *slower* breakdown (scenario three) can lead to other national regions' *secession* against this internal K-nation that could lead to a *faster* breakdown of a nation (back to scenario two).

From these four kinds of data, there are three hypotheses. First, that (1) only a few other *current* nations that have the 'good accident' to be *oriented like Korea* and are expected to hold together politically, economically, and culturally to come out intact and improved on the other side of this digital bottleneck. The inverse of this means that many more breakdowns of nations may occur, and means many other fresh national forms may be invented out of those breakdowns at failing in the digital bottleneck. Some will be (2) toward the *fast breakdown* of some nations, and other nations will be (3) toward the *slow reformatting* of them to look like small internal "K-Nations within themselves" that rule over the wider nation in an unrepresentative technocracy and surveillance state that may still lead to the breakdown of the nation anyway over time. So, the argument about these three empirical trends in digital development that are occurring now and into the future is hypothesized to be related to three background or accidental factors that have large developmental consequences depending on different nations: the scale of the demography, the scale of the geography, and the quality of the culture of the country in question, whether more homogeneous or more heterogeneous. These three factors help us frame thinking about why there are different systemic digital trends and thus why there may be different future default or 'easier' scenarios of different nations.

Korea is argued to have a background situation in these three factors for the first scenario: surviving intact and even digitally improved. This means the "the best optimum K-Nation" instead of only "the first K-Nation."

For details, what economic and cultural characteristics of states may be more viable or "optimal" in the global digital future? Defining an "optimal" state under global digital conditions implies a state having the capacity to survive *durably in one geographic place by being economically, culturally, and infrastruturally updated* and maintained over decades under ongoing global crises of ever changing locations of global economic production, ever changing sources of global digital culture, ever updating global communications technology, and ever changing global flows of information and power due to a more decentralized media regime. More optimal nations will be able to keep pulling all of these into themselves, and they will keep who they are intact regardless of global flows around them. Less optimal nations will be less able to keep a competitive digital global economy, culture, hardware production, or infrastructural update of communications within themselves. Thus, they are more likely to lose their economies and identity whether in the breakdown of their nation into component pieces or into the reformatting of their larger nation into a digital police state run by their smaller and more easily updatable "internal K-Nation." Plus, such nations are more likely to become divided and conquered, and become underdeveloped client zones of other durable "K-nations" that can exhibit both greater digital economic prowess and greater ability to culturally reproduce despite the rigors of triple crises of global economic and cultural flows and ongoing globally competitive and costly requirements to keep updating technological/media hardware.

The term "K-Nation" is preferred to tech cluster zone, because of the argument that a tech cluster zone, to really durably exist in politics and economics, has to as well have *its own cultural reproduction durably over time* as well as have *control over policy priority and foreign policy for itself over other internal national competitors* who may want different priorities and policies. The term additionally represents a geographic zone that simultaneously can maintain *durably global digital cultural production and globally competitive sales of the hardware of digital telecommunications* within itself. Thus, a tech cluster can start to become a "K-Nation" when it develops both these industries, has its own separate homogeneous culture, and has its own powerful political lobby in its 'national' interest—against its previous nation. However, this is sometimes in alignment with particular kinds of current nations and sometimes in misalignment. Either way, this means an attempt to have greater control over the whole culture and policy apparatus of the past nation for the "internal K-Nation" to survive as well. So, in many cases, a tech cluster will want to become something like a K-Nation since it begins to formulate its own separate homogeneous culture and separate politics as a 'national interest in formation' against its relict nation, regardless of whether it will try to secede from or simply exploit and dominate the relict nation for its own purposes. Empirical examples of this follow in several countries outside of Korea, justifying this use of the term "internal K-Nation" since these phenomena are in formation in many larger nations now. These are particularly seen in more unrepresentative, exploitative, or parasitical relationships within their past nations. This makes the Korean model a more optimum model for the K-Nation, yet that Korean model is argued to depend on good accidents of Korean history as much as good policies.

Given the more even global playing field now in access to media communications, and given more 'national teams' playing in the two main digital games around the popularity of a *digital culture* and the competitive sales of the *digital hardware* of telecommunications, the questions become what characteristics of all nations have encouraged them to do both digital cultural production and digital telecommunications hardware production well in a competitive digital global economy, and what characteristics of all states do poorly in both, or only do one, or do none at all? Korea had done both well for decades as the first "K-Nation." Korea is a *potential harbinger and image of the future* for developed and less developed countries alike, yet the open question remains will Korea remain a *mirage* to them as well, and like a mirage always receding and going further ahead of other nations as they approach it in competition?

In an ever more digital twenty-first century, any future current nations or fresh national forms that will become these more optimal "K-Nations" are argued to have *three accidental yet useful similar characteristics* like the first "K-Nation" of South Korea. To understand this argument, it is similar in analogy to the fairy tale of 'Goldilocks and the Three Bears.' The fairy tale's story mentions a band of temperature that is "just right" in only one of the three bears' bowls of porridge for Goldilocks to eat, while the other two bowls are either "too hot" or "too cold." This analogy of a "Goldilocks zone" of optimum temperature has been used in astronomy to discuss which kinds of planets may contain life more often, and now it can be used to think similarly about what are the optimum and "just right" characteristics of states for keeping a durable digital economics and a durable digital culture in themselves so they can pass through the digital bottleneck intact and even better? Here, it is argued there are at least three Goldilocks zones of optimum and "just right" characteristics of states that will help them pass through the digital bottleneck intact and even improved. These three more optimized factors have mostly been good accidents in Korea or in other countries, instead of designable at all. Thus, the vast majority of many different national orientations in the world now make getting through the digital bottleneck alive or intact far more difficult.

So, under globally competitive conditions of a digital economy, culture and media, what three basic characteristics of national cultures are hypothesized *to be "just right" to help winners and hypothesized to harm losers in the many other orientations on the same three factors?* The three factors are 'demography, geography, and homogeneity.' In the case of Korea, it is argued that the nation is in the "just right" band of all three of these characteristics for optimizing durable digital development, while other nations are oriented in these three factors in a variety of different and less optimal ways. For Korea, these three factors are generally "good accidents," or happenstance of past history, since it is hard to design your country on these three factors centuries in advance on the outside chance that a future digital global economy is invented. So, despite Korea having *good choices* toward consensus repeatedly that have helped keep it keep together through the digital bottleneck as well, it is argued that Korea equally by its happenstance '*good accidents*' of past history has three characteristics that helped it go through the digital bottleneck as well. Other countries with less of these 'good accidents' in these three background factors thus may have to treat these factors as future 'good choices,' i.e., may have to reorient themselves with better policies to survive and to thrive in this triple global storm. All three Korean national characteristics are hypothesized to win in other countries as well, meaning, any country should pass through the digital bottleneck better is if a nation that is a similar 'mid-size' and 'more' homogeneous cultural nation like Korea.

Defining terms, "mid-size" is defined as the limited group that is both geographically and demographically mid-size, at the same time. Defining "more" homogeneous means a mid-zone as well of being a homogeneous culture though hardly "too much" homogeneity that may be a problem to creating consensus politics and hardly "too little" homogeneity toward heterogeneity that may pull the country apart through the digital bottleneck. So putting these together, mid-sized and more homogeneous cultures may be the triple "Goldilocks zone" of current and future digital nations in the global digital economy that may survive and even thrive on ongoing crises in an information society. Other kinds of nations are more likely to increasingly fall apart, quickly or slowly. The caveat is that the idea of a digital Goldilocks zone is hardly limited to these three factors. There may be other factors of course upon further analysis, one of them being the existence of a successful digital global city as defined by Sassen (2001) or greater background in digital cultural saturation itself. However, in a sense, those two factors about a global-level digital urban site and a saturated digital tech rollout throughout the nation are really the other category of 'good choices' and thus are bundled into the dual argument about 'good choices and good accidents' in these explanations already. This is a working hypothesis. We can only await the future tensely to see what happens to confirm, reject, or improve this hypothesis about a Goldilocks zone of greater stability or greater instability in current national economies and cultures as they enter the triple global storm mentioned above that puts them all through a digital bottleneck.

10.2.1.1 1 of 3: 'Mid-Size' Demography

First, for detailed definitions, what does *demographic* *'mid-size'* mean, in numbers? Given Korea has around 51 million people, that is the working hypothesis of what 'mid-size' is demographically, simply because Korea has been more successful than any other (ex-)developing country in digital development. However, it is equally a hypothesis about 'mid-size' that has developed through comparative analysis instead of only looking at Korea. As of January 2023, after reviewing successes and failures of many other nations' durable digital development, the hypothesis is that a band of around 40 to 85 million people is 'mid-sized,' with the lower bound level around the size of Poland at 40 million and the upward bound level or limitation around the size of Germany at 85 million.

This is because Poland despite having a small capital city of Warsaw at only 1 million people and a mostly rural landscape has great links to the Korean digital economy there, has large technological park developments there, and even has a very saturated digital ownership of smartphones with even better equitable and faster bandwidth access throughout its more rural nation in the past decade than its far wealthier and larger neighbor of Germany. Poland despite having a growing digital hardware and technopark economy (Czech, 2020; Trajkovska, 2019) lacks a durable digital global cultural wave of course. However, Poland is expected to be ahead of the U.K. economically per capita by the end of the 2020s mostly due to its "booming tech sector" that has "outpaced huge countries like China, India, and Brazil for growth in online services, according to the World Trade Organization." The homogeneous culture of Poland at 40 million people as well has a large educated labor pool "ranking [at] four[th] overall in STEM graduates and number one in female STEM graduates" (Jackson, 2023).

Meanwhile, Germany at 85 million is the upward bound level because it is equally and highly successful in globally competitive research and innovation in technology, though less successful in digital telecommunications, or in maintaining a top updated national equitable rollout of digital technology per se, or in having durable digital global cultural wave beyond the 1970s into the 1980s (remembering film directors Fassbinder, Wenders, Herzog, etc.) after which it became more culturally heterogeneous as well by immigration and allowed mass scale of refugees. Poland remains more homogeneous culturally and has rejected being a European site for refugee imports. (The recent influx of millions of warfare-escaping Ukrainians into Poland may start to change this, if they remain there. However, historically much of ancient Poland was territorially in control of parts of the modern Ukraine as well anyway, and the cultural distances between Poles and Ukrainians are far less extreme than the cultural distances between Catholic Polish and rejected Muslim refugees.)

Above 85 million people, any larger nation with digital development upon analysis seems really only a tiny geographic "K-Nation in formation" or "internal K-Nation" somewhere within the wider nation. For example, it is hardly the whole large and more homogenous nation of Russia's 147 million people that has digital development. It is mostly in the tech cluster around the digitally connected global city of Moscow only. Plus, to its favor, the Moscow region has over 20 million people (similar to the Seoul region at 25 million), making the zone of Moscow by far the largest urban zone in all of Europe. Plus, Moscow is in the Volga River basin which itself has about half of all the Russian population in this one zone, thus within the optimum demographic zone at approximately 73.5 million people in this "Volga nation". Russia considers itself to have 33 technology parks in 2022, with 6 of them in Moscow. Of the top five technoparks rated in 2022, two of these were in Moscow, one down the Volga from Moscow relatively close in Samara, and two further east in Perm on the Kama River, yet with this river connected to the Volga River. Perm is additionally the old industrial heart and cultural heart of the Soviet Union in the Urals (ACTP RF, 2022). Plus, Russia is involved in its own digital cultural production, having the fourth largest film market in the world from 2021 (Statisa, 2022). However, its growing film industry is not in the same geography of the "internal K-Nation" around Moscow in the Volga/ Kama River region, though mostly in the rural region of Yakutia far from Moscow in Eastern Siberia. Nonetheless, Yakutia's "Sakhawood" is admired on the international film circuit, giving Russia a slight cultural wave globally. Russia's Sakhawood films have been hosted at "special screenings dedicated to Yakut films in recent years" in Finland and in South Korea. Plus, Yakutia hosts its own International Film Festival as well (Hayes & Roache, 2020).

For another example that does have its geographic "internal K-Nation" more tightly merged than Russia, it is hardly the whole large and more heterogeneous United States that has digital development, though only one homogeneous cultural smaller "K-nation"-sized piece of geography and demographics with its northern end at the global city of San Francisco and its nearby Silicon Valley, to its southern end at the global city of Los Angeles with its Hollywood. Thus, this "internal K-Nation" zone, with its own more homogeneous culture within the United States' more heterogeneous culture, is both involved in global digital *hardware* production to the north and it includes of course Hollywood's global digital *cultural* production to the south. This zone holds about 50 million people as well, within the optimum range. Thus the United States has a clear "internal K-Nation" in the offing. Southern California is called a more homogeneous cultural zone instead of a diverse heterogeneous zone for the rationales mentioned in another section, in a moment.

The same can be said for India. It is hardly the whole large and heterogeneous nation of India that has digital development though it is mostly around the digital tech cluster in India's only 'alpha' rated global city of Bangalore (with a population of 11 milllion) that produces or houses both the global digital *hardware* and some of its digital *cultural* production. Bangalore is simultaneously one of the five regional sites for digital film production in India's "Southern Cinema." However, India's "internal K-Nation" is more dispersed like Russia, without the aggregation potential as well since India's internal K-Nation's geographic digital production zone stretches widely to the west and south given a total of five different homogeneous linguistic zones each specializing in the same digital cultural production of cinema in India. In the wider Southern Cinema, the Hindi-language digital cultural production of cinema is in the "Bollywood" of Mumbai. The Telegu-language cinema is in Hyderabad. The Tamil-language cinema is in Chennai. The Kannada-language cinema is in Bangalore itself, in the state of Karnataka. The Malayalam-language cinema is in Kochi, in Kerala. So, this entire large zone from Mumbai through all four other cities of the "Southern Cinema" mentioned above is the "K-Nation in formation" in India, yet it lacks the tight geographic aggregation in both digital economic sectors or lacks a singularly clear and strong language culture (given there are five main ones), except perhaps for the secondary common language of Hindi. The wider dispersed Southern Cinema zone which includes Bangalore additionally has a demographics that is much larger than the presumed 'optimum' zone, running into hundreds of millions of people. Plus, these digital hardware and digital cultural zones of production in the South are outside of the largest demographic zone of India which is in the North against the well-watered Southern flank of the Himalayas down the Ganges River to the Ganges Delta on the coast with about 500 million people throughout this riverine zone.

True, there are smaller examples of great digital development in demographically and geographically smaller city states like Hong Kong or Singapore, with tiny areas and with a dense population respectively of around 7 to 5 million, respectively. Though the point here is what are the contexts of more *durable* and *competitive* digital development for the twenty-first century? Smaller city states might start tech clusters or even cultural waves like Hong Kong having digital technology for export and a massive cinema industry in the 1990s, equally for export. However, both sectors in Hong Kong have shown lack of *durability* by the twenty-first century in the ongoing global technical competition for hardware, in the lack of durability of the scale of its film industry, and the lack of stability in its inability to control or optimize its own separate politics or culture for such durable digital industries once absorbed by China from 1997. So, Hong Kong has lost out so far. The same may be the case for the digital development in Israel at only around 9 million people in total. However, their tech cluster is mostly only around what is called "Silicon Wadi," and moreover, up to 20% of the Israeli population is not online by choice. Israel is thus said to be hampered by "political and structural" issues—a diplomatic way it seems of saying some people may durably value a totally offline life more than online life, as well as problems of durable political priority and small-scale 'structural' problems (Lago, 2021). Moreover, the "too small" number of Israelis as mostly Jewish (yet with a positive digital development factor of being a more homogeneous culture) is further hampered by preferring not call attention to themselves overtly in any "Jewish wave" of digital cultural production for a global digital culture anyway.

Another positive mechanism comparatively found in more 'mid-sized' demographics in a K-Nation is that it encourages *that* size of nation to seek *more* export-led markets outside of it, and thus to connect to a wider global economy in larger measure. However, for the opposite larger sense, on the one hand, Russia has a more autonomous and larger economy of 147 million people, and Japan has its larger domestic market of approximately 125 million in 2023. Both tend as a consequence to prefer technical and cultural isolation as it is still profitable in such a larger market from a larger demographic nation. For the opposite smaller sense, on the other hand, Israel, Hong Kong, or Singapore may have a size that means a greater encouragement for export-led economies, though they become hampered by another mechanism of more expensive labor costs, or an inability to scale production in a smaller country, or higher real estate costs. Thus, the hypothesis is that a 'mid-sized' demographics keeps the country 'lean and mean' in being large enough for successful urban industrialization, a domestic mass market, and a large labor pool, and cheaper real estate for expansion, yet encourages the nation to seek out global markets to maintain itself at the same time, instead of on the one side resting entirely on its domestic economic laurels digitally like Japan as any larger demographic nation regularly has the luxury of doing, or instead on the other side, of being solely dependent on an unstable global economy or its own smaller comparative capacities of capital, culture, or politics like the mere city-states of Singapore or Hong Kong. Korea seems right in the middle demographically. So, while a "too large" demographic means more national autonomy in economy, culture, and technological markets, a "too small" demographic means likely less self-control of the K-Nation's politics in a world of competitive nations, or competition between regions in a nation, as well as means a more costly and thus less durably competitive scale of technical or cultural production markets. Korea is "just right" and in the middle: "large enough" for urban industrial production, yet hardly "too large" to discourage an export-led economy of global competition in whatever digital sectors it wants and hardly "too small" in other factors that may disencourage durable global economic growth or durable culture or politics in a nation.

10.2.1.2 2 of 3: 'Mid-Size' Geography

Next, what does *geographic 'mid-size'* mean and how could that possibly encourage durable digital development? South Korea is approximately 100,210 square kilometers, making it the 107th largest country—literally almost right in the middle of the sizes of over 200 countries in the world. The hypothesized band of 'mid-size' geographies range thus from "larger Poland, to 'mid-sized' Korea, to smaller Taiwan," given Poland, Korea, and Taiwan are supremely successful in maintaining a durable digital development. Korea and Taiwan have done this for decades so far, with Poland on the rise. Poland is approximately 311,888 square kilometers in land size making it the 69th largest country, and Taiwan is approximately 36,193 square kilometers, or the 134th largest territory. Plus, it is interesting and even confirmatory that a great many other countries with *durable* digital development are within this geographic size band between Poland and Taiwan, which includes Korea, the United Kingdom, Switzerland, the Netherlands, Estonia, Costa Rica, and Ireland (with the latter more about software than hardware, historically).

On the one hand, the geographic hypothesis is that if your country is "too big," it becomes competitively expensive to keep updating your vast national infrastructure of telecommunications to be a durable competitor with other nations, in order to keep the whole world interested in collaborating with you in your country instead of encouraging the world to collaborate with others in more optimal-sized countries that can afford ongoing technological updates of their infrastructure better. For instance, consider the logistics problems of Internet architecture updates in a country of large geographic size like Russia (world's largest country) or China (3rd or 4th largest country depending how you measure it), as well think of why the "K-Nation" in formation in these countries is mostly only a digital global city area around Moscow and down the Volga to Samara or up the Kama to Perm with digital triage on the rest of the nation, or it is the three Chinese digital global cities from northern Shanghai (largest city in China and the world's largest container port), to the middle zone of Shenzhen (China's technological hardware cluster), to southernmost Hong Kong (China's international finance and still existing international cinema cultural industry) with digital triage against the rest of the nation.

On the other hand, the geographic hypothesis on the other side of the digital Goldilocks zone is that if your country is geographically "too small', on the other side of Taiwan in this geographic scale, it tends to be demographically small and exorbitantly expensive as well. So, even though it may be easier to keep updating telecommunications infrastructures in ever smaller geographic areas (since global city states like Dubai, Singapore, or Hong Kong do tend to have the most globally updated and always fastest bandwidth speeds compared to larger nations in all cases, except Korea), it may become overly costly there to do more than this in labor or real estate to create digital hardware or create digital culture. For instance, judged by the history of their failures, small global city states may have more problems in creating globally competitive digital hardware production or digital cultural production, as it may become far more costly in real estate expansion or to find a large enough demographics of skilled labor for expansion. So, despite a smaller geographic zone being better for maintaining an updated digital infrastructure attracting investment and contacts, the more costly real estate and the smaller labor market are bad compared to other more optimal places that would be cheaper in both to maintain both kinds of ongoing durable digital production.

10.2.1.3 3 of 3: More Homogeneous Culture

The third major national characteristic hypothesized to win in a more digitally global future is *a more homogeneous culture.* The homogeneity hypothesis argues that more homogeneous countries and cultures can do two main tasks better than other orientations in a global digital culture: *hold together better in traditional cultural transmission* under rigors of a fluid global digital culture, as well as being *more capable of faster collective innovation* in digital *hardware* changes or *cultural* product changes for the global market, both like Korea.

What is the Goldilocks zone argument in numbers about a more homogeneous culture though? How much is "too little" homogeneity (towards "too heterogeneous"), how much is mid-level "enough," and how much is "too much" homogeneity? Six kinds of these Goldilocks zones of "enough" homogeneity/heterogeneity are considered: ethnicity, language, religion, cultural regionality, export economic scale of total GNP, and economic stratification. Thus, it is hardly just homogeneity per se, it is how many optimal "middle zones" of interactions exist in a country between different factors of homogeneity and heterogeneity, though not overly so in either. Thus, a slight mid-level heterogeneity exists even in Korea in regional dynamics, in religious plurality, in a wider and level economic stratification (whether in land or capital), and in awareness of other cultures due to its export-led economy. All of these points have already been noted in the discussion earlier despite its 'more' ethnically and linguistically homogeneous culture.

On the one hand, this kind of analysis might take the "existing national methods" of Fearon's analysis, who disaggregated three ways to measure any current nations cultural "fragmentation" ranging from more homogeneous to more heterogeneous. From Fearon's data, the hypothesis here about the Goldilocks zone of "enough though not too much or too little" homogeneity is that the middle band of a 'more homogeneous culture' in a current nation ranges of course from 100% down to around 60% of the population sharing a more homogeneous culture. For ethnic examples, this would include Korea, Japan, Taiwan, China, to Russia (81% Russian) through the United States (61% White Europeans in 2020). However, Fearon has three separate ways to measure this homogeneity or heterogeneity. These factors Fearon calls measures of cultural "fractionalization," and these are ethnic, linguistic, and religious measures. So, sometimes the homogeneous culture might be in something else beyond ethno-linguistic homogeneity, like a religiously homogeneous culture in India with 80% Hindu yet with 415 living languages as of 2019 and with only a plurality of 43.6% speaking Hindi and thus with many different ethnolinguistic homogeneous regions making for a more heterogeneous India on that linguistic factor. The two-part argument is (1) that at least one or two of these three main cultural factors should be homogeneous enough to hold together a culture in the long term, though (2) if all three of these factors are homogeneous it is "too much"—for arguments to be saved for the next section about the benefits of slight heterogeneity in a more homogeneous culture that are seen in Korean history or Taiwanese history on some factors.

So, in this kind of triple analysis and terminology, South Korea is rated as the 27th least ethnically fractionalized nation. This means there are 26 countries above Korea that are even more ethnically homogeneous than Korea—hard to imagine—and yet these are *all tiny island nations.* This echoes what was said earlier: Korea is an odd outlier in being a very homogeneous culture oddly combined with being a 'mid-sized' country. In other words, the top 26 most homogeneous cultures are tiny island nations. By the way, Korea's big-island neighbor Japan is the next least ethnically fractionalized nation as the 28th least ethnically fractionalized nation. Japan of course is another outlier and another fast development success, and yet a less successful one in *durable* digital development which fits with the expectations of what happens in ever larger demographic and geographic hypotheses above.

Next, in linguistic fractionalization Korea is ranked as very homogeneous as well, as only the 16th lowest. Thus these are two strong factors of a homogeneous culture in Korea so far. However, Korea is rated moderately high at 42nd in religious fractionalization for a more heterogeneous culture in Korea on this point alone. That slight access to heterogeneity in the culture is a point mentioned earlier in Part I as well as a 'good accident' of happenstance in Korean history later beneficial for its modern political and economic development drive in keeping a more democratic constitution, a more multi-party state, and a growing trend of more individual and civil rights. In Korea it is religious diversity in this very homogeneous ethnic and linguistic culture that helps Korea be "just right" in the middle with enough homogeneity yet avoiding "too much" of it. So a mid-size *homogeneous* culture in Korea with some factors of *heterogeneity as well* serves to check and balance against bad political and cultural tendencies of a more purely triple homogeneous culture that was earlier argued to work to repress human rights and destroy/confiscate properties of religious minorities (i.e., revoke common individual property rights). This of course is hardly the only factor in Korea's development, though this "just right" context between homogeneity and heterogeneity is a 'good accident' that helped Korea animate its 'good choice' of a more competitive multi-party state that could have been stillborn in Korea otherwise without some actual fractionalization in the culture. Therefore, religious diversity as argued before helps save Korea from itself, with useful internal conflicts in a more homogeneous culture that helps animate a multi-party state toward more transparent human, civil, and property rights. Taiwan similarly is another doubly homogeneous ethnic and linguistic culture and durable digital development zone. However, like

Korea, Taiwan has a very high religious fractionalization of 25 recognized religions for its approximately 23 million people, making Taiwan the 30th most religiously diverse country in the world. Plus, Taiwan is like Korea in being without any clear religious collective majority at all (Alesina et al., 2003; Fearon, 2003). On the other hand, Japan is a 'triple homogeneous culture'—ethnically, linguistically and religiously—yet with a great deal of internal regional differences of culture (like the animosities of the two historical capital areas of Osaka and Tokyo, with their very different cultures, or other differences of culture across the four main islands) or with Japan's export-driven economics. All of these latter factors of heterogeneity keep the 'excessive' homogeneity of Japan somewhat in check and balanced.

As mentioned above, however, *three other kinds offractionalization* can be considered beyond Fearon's three demographic measures of it. These three other factors are a nation's geographic regionality in culture, its scale of being an export-led economy, and its economic stratification (i.e., more equitable wealth or more inequitable wealth). Korea is a very regionalized polity in the history of its ancient and modern politics and culture, and thus that is another source of its long term 'fractionalization' in its otherwise homogeneous culture. Plus, Korea is very dedicated to export-led economics, creating another source of high heterogeneity given that the Korean government, companies, and workers have to strategize as a more homogeneous cultural group about the daily concourse of ideas and materials bought and sold from a more heterogeneous cultural globe. Much of the global Korean Wave itself is an ongoing Korean version of what is already globally popular per se instead of truly only a cultural export of Korean culture autonomously per se. In the inverse sense, this is mentioned above in arguments about North Korea as only reinforcing its equally homogenous culture with even more homogeneity by choices of minimizing religious diversity, minimizing exports and minimizing a wide economic stratification by nationalizing its land and capital. This moves North Korea toward only an internal national ideological purity, economic independence, and wide differences in wealth and in respect or status between political-economic elites and common citizens that is a root of all kinds of social problems (Wilkinson & Pickett, 2011) instead of getting a slight taste of useful diversity pressures from more international trade, autonomous religious freedoms, multiple political parties, or equitable land/property ownership. This leads North Korea to miss out in adding a slight "just right" salting factor of more heterogeneity to temper the greater homogeneity there.

On the other hand, conducting an analysis of only *current* nations' "fractionalization" misses the point about the *future* national forms of K-Nations that may be only tiny *pieces* of current larger heterogeneous or homogeneous nations. These pieces of current nations may break up into more 'optimal' zones that have their own more mid-size regional homogeneous culture and greater collective innovation, greater collective action potential, and more durable cultural transmission potential. Therefore, analysis of current national patterns of fractionalization should be tempered with more *regional* analysis of the *geography and demography of internal homogeneous cultural divisions* in all current larger heterogeneous nations. This will help to understand where cultural fault lines exist geographically out of which political/economic policy fault lines may appear during this ongoing series of metaphorical cultural 'earthquakes' from our fresh media regime change. For instance, the heterogeneous regional divisions within the United States today, in decades hence, may be different homogeneous 'optimal' zones—with some of them potential K-Nations. For instance, one potential future K-Nation or tech cluster and homogeneous cultural zone in the United States may be the isolated 'tech republic' from San Francisco/Silicon Valley down to Los Angeles/Hollywood in Southern California. Southern California is a region of left-liberal and libertarian technocrat politics, and it is increasingly a *homogeneous leftist* cultural zone, gauging from election results at least. It is so different from the *equally homogeneous rightist* cultural zone in Northern California on different cultural principles and without any tech clusters. In other words, judging fractionalization based only on current nations as if they are timeless and stable may be another fool's errand if current nations start to split up in this triple global storm into more homogenous 'optimal' zones of "internal K-Nations" in formation like San Francisco to Los Angeles. Whether Northern California secedes and joins Western Oregon and Idaho as is being debated now in 2023, making an even larger "State of Jefferson" desired there by some since the mid-twentieth century, or whether Silicon Valley's homogeneous culture and politics just tries to conduct a technocratic coup over the rest of California or even the whole United States remains to be seen. That could be done by the Southern California K-Nation by having Silicon Valley corporations control the state policies and the wider national information sphere of political and cultural discourse with politically-oriented digital censorship, politically rigging Internet search engine results, and politically motivated de-platforming and censorship of journalists, true stories, or even politicians running for office. All of this is happening in the United States in the past few years (Editorial Board, 2023; Levine, 2018; Morozov, 2011; Pasquale, 2015; Roy, 2022; Taibbi, 2023; Vorhies & Heckenlively, 2021).

The issue is most people falsely consider or label a homogeneous culture as only an entirely traditional and conservative culture, when of course *a homogeneous culture is just a homogeneous culture in any factor, and that would apply to homogeneous left political zones as well.* So, what is happening in the USA particularly in its internal K-Nation in formation around California's powerful technocratic lobby of Silicon Valley and in leftist states around big cities on the East Coast in the metropolitan region from New York City to New Jersey, is a self-perpetuating homogeneous left culture instead of a classically 'liberal' or 'ethnically and sexually diverse culture' as its political rhetoric claims. All homogeneous cultures, left or right, want to police everyone in their zone to think the same homogeneous thoughts, whether they all look different or the same, and they want to repress actual minorities of thought.

Therefore, the current *actual ethnic and cultural diversity* of a wider heterogeneous cultural nation with multiple different cultures in different zones in the United States is starting to be subsumed in some zones under either a religiously conservative, collectivist, and technocratic homogeneous settlement of media control, technology regulation, and politics as it happening in some U.S. state regions from South Dakota, Idaho, Tennessee, or Florida. On the other leftist side, it is starting to be subsumed under an equally homogeneous, collectivist, and technocratic American left like between San Francisco/Silicon Valley to Los Angeles/Hollywood. The latter is replacing its zone's past true heterogeneity with an ideology of homogenous ethnic blending and even a homogenous revolutionary Maoism like China in the 1970s, now under the 'woke' label. The political, economic, and cultural power that this zone has is due to its mass production and promotion of its version of cultural revolution of 'wokism' across the rest of the United States via its two main digital industries of digital hardware production and digital cultural production that includes digital platform management. This is by definition a Maoist cultural revolutionary movement of this "internal K-Nation," in formation around Silicon Valley, given Mao argued that a strategy of revolution first is built on defaming and destroying past cultural continuity and legitimacy as a preparatory strategy for wider economic and political revolution later by first trying to delegitimize rhetorically your cultural, economic, and political opposition with a world of cultural inversions of authority. So whether in the 1970s in China, or in 2023 in the United States today, the Hollywood-to-Silicon Valley cultural revolution involves ideological public 'struggle sessions' (whether by transgender activists, Antifa, or Black Lives Matter, etc.) cultural shaming, and violent repression of actually diverse voices and other political ideas. It involves trying to emotionally shame or physically hurt an opposition and their cherished institutions and symbolic icons with street violence, arson, iconoclasm, and murder with political and ideological intent. Further showing a "internal K-Nation" in formation within the United States, some left-aligned regions of state government actually have supported such street violence and cultural revolution like the autonomous anarchistic zone that was allowed in Portland, Oregon, or how charges were dropped in Oregon against arson on U.S. federal buildings there. Such regions are now trying to enforce a homogeneous left culture across state bureaucracies, citizens, family dynamics, and corporate activities equally. This includes left-libertarian technocrats of Silicon Valley attempting to work on people's 'hearts and minds' via censored search results across the rest of the country or world that makes them effectively 'digital content police' censoring the digital platform experience and heterogeneous culture of the United States. Of course by 2023, the reaction against that is the U.S. House of Representative's Committee on Weaponization of Government subpoenaed in February 2023 many Silicon Valley CEOs to answer for their censorship of Republicans and election interference against Republicans in national politics toward aiding only the Democratic Party. When subpoenaed, the long-term CEO of YouTube (part of Google), Susan Wojecki, immediately resigned presumably to escape the Congressional subpoena inquiring into YouTube's weaponization of online content. Incidentally, Wojecki's sister runs another Silicon Valley firm called 23 and Me that is gathering the world's genomics in a database. This is how a nepotistic digital aristocracy and digital convergence merge to both endanger common civil rights—a topic discussed for Korea as well, in the below Section 10.2.2.5. By July 2023, Democratic Party members on the Committee on Weaponization of Government itself even tried to weaponize the Committee against testimony invited about government censorship itself, around government-directed censorship of Robert F. Kennedy, Jr., calling attention to people who died suddenly after the experimental vaccines like Black American baseball star Hank Aaron, or around censoring journalists online covering the Hunter Biden laptop information two days before the 2020 Presidential Election between

Donald Trump and Joe Biden, even after the U.S. FBI at the time confirmed to direct Twitter questioning that the laptop was indeed Hunter Biden's, though the FBI wanted information about it censored by Twitter anyway. Plus, Democrats on the Committee even tried to remove Presidential Democratic candidate Robert F. Kennedy, Jr. from one hearing before it even started. Fully 102 Democratic Congressional members signed a letter trying to censor RFK, Jr., from speaking on government censorship. When that failed to be allowed, another Democrat Congresswoman Wasserman-Schultz tried to move the whole hearing into an "executive session" that would be censored from being in the public view. That failed as well. Another Democrat, Plaskett, wanted assurance that RFK, Jr. would only have an introduction of less than five minutes. Later, long-term Democrat Kennedy told the Committee: "I've spent my life in this party. I've devoted my life to the values of this party—102 people signed this [letter]. This itself is evidence of the problem that this hearing was convened to address. This is an attempt to censor a censorship hearing." (Conte, 2023; Reuters, 2023) Equally, government weaponization and cultural censorship has been revealed in the illegal collusion via private online platforms that started to be exposed in the related private releases about the "Twitter files," showing illegal federal bureaucrat orders of censorship given to those running the Twitter platform to censor critics of the Biden Administration (Roy, 2022; Taibbi, 2023). Later, the Committee revealed similar "Facebook files" by July 2023 that the U.S. Surgeon General was ordering Facebook to censor truthful information about vaccine injuries.

Neutrally speaking, in the above examples, this is the way that any future homogeneous "K-Nation" may work: as an "internal K-nation" in formation within a wider country that it wants to manage. This may be from one homogeneous leftist cultural zone in one geographic area over the rest of the heterogeneous nation. This may be equally an ideological vanguard in a revolutionary ethnic or sexuality group that is a minority against a wider nation trying to dominate the latter like an imperial presence with 'diversity' commissars (or really non-diversity commissars) as political officers trying to converge, control, and exploit an older heterogeneous and diverse cultural nation's institutional life via purges to support a fresh homogenous culture. However, the dichotomy here is hardly between collectivism on the right or left here, as even right-wing zones seem to desire "K-Nations" of digital control in their own homogeneous political image. The point is that homogeneous "internal K-Nations" are in formation regardless, against each other's different kinds of homogeneity that they nonetheless both want to exert themselves upon heterogeneous others. So, it would be better to frame the politics of the future "internal K-Nation" as not left versus right, or collectivist versus individualist, though whether it is an internal K-nation in a homogeneous *digital state-collectivist* culture zone—like the zones of Silicon Valley or Shanghai-Shenzhen-Hong Kong—or an equally homogeneous '*digital state-protected-individualist and freedom-oriented culture*' somewhat developing in the U.S.'s West, upper Midwest, and South particluarly as Texas becomes one of the U.S.'s largest digital hardware manufacturing zones.

The overarching theme is that under a global digital culture, a point can be reached that all or any of the six fractionalization measures suggested above become "too much," and any basis for a common cultural ethos is lost in a more *heterogeneous* culture like the United States now torn by huge and growing economic stratification, torn by the interaction of media regime change and torn by the nearly lost ethnic homogeneity of Western European and Central European origins of many Americans. This is only partially due to the growing linguistic separation of large numbers of legal and illegal American immigrants. It is equally created by a growing unclear religious plurality, as once dominant Protestant Christianity is demographically on the decline, though becoming more regionally pronounced as well. So, there develops cultural polarization over what should be the future direction of the country culturally and what should be allowed in the public digital sphere, with a declining common or 'middle ground' ethos or 'live and let live' ethos. In such culturally divided situations, citizens can retreat culturally and civilly into private economic and media worlds or into ethnoliguistic, ideological, or religiously specific prides. So, with the United States nearing a situation without any singular or widely shared "enough" cultural hegemony on any of these six main factors anymore, what can serve as a cultural production sector in the United States except multiple, competitive, tinny, and tiny marginal revolutionary cultural ideologies and different regional ethnic supremacisms of mutual jealousies and hatreds as the wider culture?

A heterogeneous culture of the United States could more easily be held together in the older media regime, as it innately encouraged a tighter one-way mass production and cultural reproduction from such a one-way mass culture. Plus, the United States had a more homogeneous culture before the 1970s, with far higher percentages of White European Protestant Christian-heritage Americans in the country before immigration policy changes after 1964. However, *what happens from a combination of "too much" heterogeneous culture, further splintered in a media regime change,* that erodes any consolidating power of past one-way mass media by default if no one group can serve as a factor of consensus to join up or even shout down many different, homogeneous, and subaltern cultural voices anymore? What is there to take pride in, whether in petty 'woke' jealousies or in religious nationalist movements, when *both* become a common hatred of the past base of a more heterogeneous culture?

There may be two types of "internal K-Nations" to come—depending on the demographics of the larger country. Like the United States, one type may be *a smaller homogenous zone within a larger heterogeneous nation*, trying to act like a "digital cultural commissar" policing and approving the digital speech and cultural-institutional policies of all the nation from that central place and trying to change the wider culture to reflect its image alone. However, is such a divisive hatred and cultural war really a valid economic digital cultural export sector that people want to buy to experience or to see from this "K-Nation" growing in 'Silicon Valley to Hollywood', and would such a digital zone even be durable economically in the first place? In other words, some "K-Nations" like South California may develop as a technical powerhouse, though the homogeneous 'woke' culture that they exhibit and try to sell as content exclusively may hardly be 'bought' and acceptable in a competitive global digital cultural market. So it is a tricky situation to think about, given Korea has a durable balance here, dominant in both global digital technological sales durably and increasingly dominant in global cultural content sales durably.

Another kind of "internal K-Nation" in formation may have the opposite demographic situation. It may be *a smaller homogenous zone within a larger homogeneous nation,* like a "digital redoubt." Like in China, Russia, or India, it could exist within a very large geographic and common demographic nation, with the digital redoubt *sharing and protecting the stable culture of the wider homogeneous large nation, yet controlling it in digital technology and digital culture from a central location* just the same. So on the one hand while China, and Russia, and India may be "too big" geographically" to survive as their current nations as overly expensive to technically maintain in thorough digital rollouts over decades to keep it updated, on the other hand, China and Russia are more ethnically homogeneous while India is more religiously homogenous under Hinduism with much ethnic and linguistic heterogeneity instead. Therefore, some digital zones in these massive more homogeneous cultures may simply become the small fresh 'digital redoubt' capital zones from which the wider geographic and homogenous demographic nation is *surveilled and protected from change if the wider nation is given lesser technological outreach or only enough one-way technologies to do so.* A 'digital redoubt' perhaps may be exercised in the future as a technocratic management from the smaller Moscow/Volga zone in larger Russia, or from the smaller zone from Mumbai to Bangalore in larger India, or from the Shanghai-Shenzhen-Hong Kong tech and cultural zone in larger China. Meanwhile, the larger homogeneous zone is *triaged* against having a peer power by having always a less advanced two-way communication or technological capacity than the area of the 'digital redoubt.'

So there may be two kinds of future homogenous "K-Nation", one as a 'digital redoubt' existing to defend and purify an already more culturally-aligned larger nation, yet still in a repressive manner, within a *wider homogenous* nation like China, Russia, or India. The other may be a more interventionist 'digital cultural commissar' revolutionarily existing in an oppositional, exploitative, and repressive manner since it draws taxes and labor from a *wider heterogeneous* cultural nation like the United States while trying to remake it in its own homogeneous image. Whether digital redoubt or digital cultural commissar, note the wider nation's digital technologies and digital culture is made and produced in a core digital zone just the same regardless of whether the wider nation is the same homogeneous culture or a more heterogeneous culture respectively.

Does that mean *ideas of digital development for heterogeneous* cultures seem destined to be phantoms and mirages of past ideology now, or can these kinds of states and cultures work well in the digital future as well? To answer this question, we have to separate ideas of general development from digital development. This argument is only about digital development. On the one hand, there seems to be *multiple paths to fast or stable general development*. For instance, there is some evidence of this kind of extreme heterogeneity encouraging its own collective innovation and collaboration for general development, seen in small heterogeneous nations of Rwanda, Singapore, or Mauritius (Sandbrook et al., 2007) just as there is evidence that in larger more heterogeneous nations like the United States success is possible as well since the United States basically has dominated in general development, world culture, and technology development from the late 1800s to the present. However, even the United States had a core: a more homogeneous Protestant and European culture when it was very innovative from the late 1800s onward, blended with a growing more heterogeneous immigrant base. However, on the other side of this spectrum, there are fewer examples of very large homogeneous nations being very developmental outside of Japan from the 1870s onward, Russia/USSR from the 1890s onward, or China from the 1980s.

On the other hand, however, more sobering *for digital development*, there is only the "K-Nation" of Korea so far along with various other "Korea-like" nations described above. This means the three-factor "digital Goldilocks zone model" seems a good predictor of many different kinds of national locations and durability of *digital* development into the future instead of only a theory about Korea per se. Inversely, other evidence supporting hypotheses about the "triple optimums" of future K-Nations is the sobering lack of other examples so far of global/national strategies of fast development drives or digital development at all beyond the "just right" bands of these triple optimal 'mid-sized' and more homogeneous cultural nations after World War II.

On the other side, many "differently arranged" nations—bigger, smaller, or more heterogeneous—that are unlike Korea are hypothesized to have more chance of losing in a world with a global digital economy, a global digital culture, and a globally distributed media. They are more likely to fall apart into their constituent more homogeneous parts. Only some of those component regional parts may be more capable of the digital development of being good K-Nations by their good choices and by their good accidents of happenstance about their demographics, geographics, and a more homogeneous culture. This *breakdown of larger or smaller homogeneous or heterogeneous nations* may happen *unless* fresh strategies are brainstormed for how to help larger heritage nations to (1) hold together *to participate in the global digital culture without having their culture destroyed* and how they can (2) hold together *to participate in the global digital economy of hardware* without being outclassed over time by 'mid-sized' more homogenous countries of greater durable collective innovation like Poland, Korea, or Taiwan. On this point, Rwanda is interesting and should be learned from as well as finding a way to hold together in digital development seemingly outside of the Goldilocks zone hypothesis above, since it is a very small nation geographically and demographically, and with a very heterogeneous culture. Rwanda is an interesting place to see early digital development in Africa instead of only general development. For instance, Rwanda in 2007 signed a contract with Korea Telecom (KT) to build a Mobile WiMAX (or WiBro) network in Rwanda. Next in 2008, KT was under contract with Rwanda to build its whole telecommunication network. By 2012, KT was doing a national information security project in Rwanda via the Korea Internet & Security Agency (KISA). By March 2013, KT signed another contract with Rwanda to establish a joint venture to build a nationwide mobile LTE network. However, as an attentive reader can see, Rwanda's digital development really relies on being in alignment with South Korea (which is in the digital Goldilocks Zone in all three ways), since what is happening in Rwanda's digital development is hardly an example of an autonomously driven digital development at all.

On the one hand, there is the dual ability of 'mid-sized' homogeneous Korea to do both world-class digital hardware and world-class digital culture. On the other hand, there is the ongoing failure or growing failure of other larger countries to do both or either at larger scale, and yet even in their failures they are creating uncannily the same three conditions of Korea in smaller zones of "internal K-Nations" within themselves as technical clusters of success. This is the same dual ability seen in 'mid-sized' more homogeneous Southern California in the larger heterogeneous culture of the United States. This is the same dual ability seen in 'mid-sized' more homogeneous Shanghai-Shenzhen-Hong Kong in the larger homogeneous culture of China. There is the same dual ability seen in the 'mid-sized' more homogeneous five zones linked in India's dual tech hardware production and cultural production cluster between Mumbai and Bangalore, extending south only in digital cultural production in the Southern Cinema at Kochi, Chennai, and Hyderabad. There is a developing tech cluster "K-Nation" in Moscow and down the Volga for the whole more homogeneous Russian nation, yet it is split from its digital cultural production further west in Siberia. Plus, in all these cases, these larger countries have veered into ever more unrepresentative centralized technocratic control. Will of necessity the more homogeneous cultures of tech cluster zones realize different interests than their larger heritage nation (whether homogeneous or heterogeneous) under global economics, culture, and media that pushes them to survive in secession, or will they literally decide to have a technocratic coup over their whole nation to survive?

To conclude, it has been noted that a 'mid-sized' and more homogenous culture than a larger or smaller heterogeneous culture or a larger or smaller homogeneous culture seems to be selected for worldwide in the coming twenty-first century of this triple global storm. A selection for successful digital development of these mid-size more homogeneous K-Nations may mean in practice breakup of other more heterogeneous cultures and nations unable to make it through the digital bottleneck, or it means their digital domination from "an internal K-Nation." However, this internal domination from a smaller geographic homogeneous zone of digital hardware production and digital cultural production like the smaller zone of Shanghai-Shenzhen-Hong Kong can be either within a larger state with a more *homogeneous* culture like China, or it can be internal domination from a similar smaller geographic homogeneous zone like the smaller zone from San Francisco's Silicon Valley to Los Angeles' Hollywood within a larger state with a more *heterogeneous* culture like the United States. Neither of the last two versions seems very durable however, and may lead to the breakup of both larger homogeneous or heterogeneous nations regardless in a slower way instead of faster way. Meanwhile, a more homogeneous and "mid-sized" Korea seems to have mastered a threefold art: maintaining cultural continuity under a fractionalizing global digital culture while keeping competitive in a global digital economy of hardware production and digital cultural production.

In some countries, people's cultures will be pulled both ways by having characteristics of both categories like being geographically and demographically "too large" and yet more culturally homogeneous like China, India, or Russia; or, like being geographically and demographically "too large" yet being more cultural heterogeneous like the United States, Nigeria, Indonesia, Ethiopia, and India. Both kinds of geographically and demographically larger nations may segment into smaller geographic homogeneous zones dominating via their digital hardware technologies and digital cultural production in the larger peripheral homogeneous or heterogeneous nation with their technologies, given wider zones are triaged as "too expensive" to keep digitally updating with hardware as fast as the redoubt zones. It may be found much cheaper in the short term to just put wider peripheries under a repressive digital technocracy. However, in such contexts, peripheral regions could languish and/or rebel in the same countries later, simply because of that unequal digital triage against them because of our more equitable decentralized media regime now makes that rebellion against another group's enforced technical and cultural inequalities upon them more possible.

Thus the twenty-first century digital bottleneck is hardly going to be a crisis to all countries equally. This is because different countries have different starting points in 'demography, geography, and culture.' Some mid-sized nations will thrive on the ongoing crises to collectively innovate better and may enjoy their larger geopolitical enemies collapsing around them. However, on the other hand, lots of national breakdowns and civil wars through the digital bottleneck may damage the global economic markets upon which such mid-size "K-Nations" depend. Plus, three wider tasks characterize a durable K-Nation's success instead of only the two of digital hardware development and digital cultural development. The third task is cultural durability. This is crucial for the durability of the former two digital sectors over time as well.

This is why it is recommended for all larger countries and the more heterogeneous countries to find fresh recipes for a common image of the future, and to find ways to compete with possibly more 'demographically and geographically optimal' more homogeneous nations like South Korea, Taiwan, or increasingly Poland. In summary, it is the "just right" interactions between homogeneity and heterogeneity that seem to be key to durable digital development and even durable democratization anywhere instead of this being a theory only about Korea. Therefore, having some, though hardly a totalizing triple ethnic, linguistic and religious homogeneity is a way to get an interaction that is "just right" in the middle. Plus, thinking of other measures or policies like encouraging greater economic equality in stratification (versus higher levels of economic inequality), greater cultural regionality (versus a lack of it) and greater dedication to export-led economics (versus a more domestically isolated economy) are three other ways to create this durable *tango* between homogeneity and heterogeneity in a culture to get benefits of both without drawbacks of both. South Korea may be "just right" with two major sources of homogeneity (ethnicity and language) and at least three major sources of heterogeneity added into the mix despite its homogeneous culture: its religious diversity, its regional diversity of culture, and its strong export-led economics. For the other factor Korea has been losing its economic equality, its more heterogeneous driver, for some time now, and this is discussed in the later Section 10.2.2.5. However, these remaining mixed sources of heterogeneity are in interaction with its deep ethnic and linguistic homogeneity. If Japan is a more extreme 'triple homogeneous culture' as argued above—ethnically, linguistically and religiously—nonetheless, it as well does have similar high levels of regional heterogeneity and similar large external economic relations with the world and a greater economic equality internally as three major durable sources of heterogeneity interacting with its deeper 'triple homogeneous' culture to give it "enough" *between* homogeneity and heterogeneity to be durable as well. However, as a larger state, Japan has greater difficulties in upkeeping its digital infrastructures, as well as less likely to have an interest in the scale of external digital markets as a percentage of GNP as much as more 'mid-sized' Korea.

For policy recommendations, since differently oriented countries may be less likely to make it through the digital bottleneck, the point is that it is easier to more synthetically create good choices of policy than it is to address this issue with redesign of background geography, demographics, and culture per se. Creating good policies through the digital bottleneck means providing for greater consensus building, policies for real economic equality of ownership (that is more than just a centralized redistribution to achieve economic equality), and policies for greater global exports. This is because such differently oriented countries by their bad accidents of demography, geography, or culture are unable to rely on changing these three factors. Thus, more time should be spend on trying to craft solutions for more heterogeneous cultural starting points, for larger and smaller states, as well as for removing economically unequal starting points with wider shared ownership instead. Four policy suggestions follow. First, perhaps what is key to save the smaller countries is a "digital Hanseatic League" of several smaller nations and global city states networked in their regional commons with different technological clusters or cultural production clusters, and sharing across their several smaller countries in a wider information commons, a wider labor commons, a wider financial commons, a wider trading commons, and a technical production commons (Bauwens et al., 2019). Second, perhaps a "mother hen" model similar to how Rwanda and South Korea interact in their mutual digital development as mentioned above, might bring smaller poorer nations and/or more heterogeneous nations into ongoing alliances with particular other K-Nations like South Korea (or K-National internal regions of another country like in Russia, India, or China). This seems to be happening a lot in Africa between both Korea and China and many poorer African nations, particularly as China has installed 70% of Africa's 4G networks (Ersozoglu, 2020). However, this "mother hen" model of a relationship for priming digital development in other less developed countries is hardly always mutually beneficial. It simply can be used as a spying network for the developed digital country in the less developed county, as well as encourages repressed civil rights in the less developed country that uses the spying technologies on their own people (Dahir, 2019; Dou, 2021; Jili, 2020; Woodhams, 2019). Plus, China, U.K, Israel, Italy, or the United States all seem to be involved in another form of digital imperialism and external surveillance control via their more developed countries' digital hardware installations spying on other smaller and poorer countries' governments and politicians. "[China's] Huawei is not the only manufacturer of surveillance [technology in African countries] being used for authoritarian ends. American, British, Italian, and Israeli firms, as well as Huawei's Chinese competitors, are also exporting surveillance software and systems" (Ersozoglu, 2020). Third, perhaps a more pragmatic solution is continuing to allow the "internal K-Nation" to form in larger countries as a regionally discrete zone within an existing nation state yet to develop a better federated system around it that gives the peripheral and triaged zones better rights and greater representative controls on the power of the digital zone. This might work for the United States, with a policy to popularize a Digital Bill of Rights curtailing private discriminating platform power of the "internal K-Nation" zone and for maintaining personal data fragmentation instead of consolidation created to monitor particular people. This could be part of an updated Constitution that the tech cluster companies and individuals in their tech zones shall avoid infringing via digital tools on the common civil right to participate as well as to gain information by their fellow citizens in peripheral zones or anywhere for that matter. Fourth, perhaps there can be a way to integrate a more stable and culturally regionalized representation, in a wider national state, for a more durable consensus of policy whether by election redistricting on stable watersheds and by redrawing state provincial borders on stable watersheds or ecoregions (Whitaker, 2005).

So, if you are outside of Korea, chances are you are reading this book in a country or culture that will not make it through the digital bottleneck intact unless you live in a country with 'good accidents' of the three "mid-zone" characteristics of the digital Goldilocks Zone. This may happen unless much future work is done on policies that can make differently-oriented nations have more consensus politics and have a better chance at digital hardware production and digital cultural production to work against having a current demography, geography, and culture of a 'less digitally optimal' nation. This is so many different orientations of 'legacy nations' can work better in the global digital future as well. In the next two sections, there are ideas for *good policies* drawn from observing Korean situations instead of just admiring Korea's three *'good accidents'* above, along with six rationales why heterogeneous cultures and nations should be saved simply to help the wider human condition in ways that only more heterogeneous cultures can save us, in ways that homogeneous cultures and nations are unable to do.

10.2.2 Korea's Good Choices and Good Accidents Combine to Get Through the Digital Bottleneck

Beyond the Korea Wave, other countries *can develop better* by learning to apply factors that explain Korea's *"triple wins"* far above other developing countries and even far above some peer 'developed' countries. The "triple wins" are how Korea has had (1) *a successful fast development drive*, how it continues (2) a *successful cultural Korean Wave*, and how it has already (3) *passed through the digital bottleneck* of the twenty-first century successfully. Respectively, these triple wins can be judged from Korea's durable and flexible world-class economic development and many 'world firsts' (Appendix 1) along with its durable (thus recovered) wider democratic procedures after 1987, its durable domestic culture and cultural wave, and its continuing digital development that keeps preserving democracy and civil rights by demoting digital police states by intentional data fragmentation even in the face of the much easier creation of surveillance and loss of civil rights out of digital convergence and out of the digital triple global storm. In short, Korea has repeatedly avoided national economic collapses by ongoing innovations, and Korea has repeatedly rejected a deepened pre-digital or post-digital police state despite having an easier and earlier digital convergence itself after 1995 by being able to keep a more consensus-based and democratic future in its civil rights. Korea in the second decade of the twenty-first century has started to create, by default of what it rejects instead of by enumeration, 'digital checks and balances' against centralized private or centralized public information/medical data creating a widened 'digital civil rights.' This repeated consensus to reject a digital police state in Korea is of course despite some Korean elites repeatedly desiring to curtail civil rights by setting up that technocratic centralized management and repression made easier by digital convergence, instead of maintaining data fragmentation, checks and balances on state power, democratic procedural arrangements, and the space for civil rights that these principles maintain.

In earlier chapters, the focus was on learning from Korea the transferrable points only about good choices and good accidents for *national general development*, instead of learning about *national survival through the digital bottleneck from Korea.* So, the focuses of this next section are *the many good choices of Korea that have interacted with its five other good accidents* (including though beyond the earlier discussion above about the three good accidents of mid-size demography and geography, and slightly more cultural homogeneity). All of this helped Korea's national survival through this digital bottleneck. Learning lessons of Korea has a lot to do with understanding origins and ongoing effects of how Korea's increasingly representative *procedures helped out in all the triple wins above.* These procedures come from Korea's unique hybrid economic, political, and cultural policies. Widening procedures of consensus over decades—and recoveries from reverse in consensus between 1972 and 1987—have made Korea more economically successful, more politically stable as a multi-party democracy, and more able to avoid cultural revolution to maintain its more homogeneous culture and civil rights as a common ethos despite all the developmental and then digital changes of Korea.

Before beginning this section, to summarize the earlier sections in Chapter 3 about interactive 'good choices' and 'good accidents' in holding a country to more successful national general development, Korea's success factors in its fast development drive from the 1960s to the present were framed as *comparable and potentially transferrable* success factors that might be learned. In that earlier chapter, all urban industrial development for any country was framed in three terms, via the idea of (1) *a common 'development gauntlet'* to become "an urban industrialized country with a cultural wave" via a particular country succeeding in its own versions of the four common challenge points down that development gauntlet. It was argued that to go down the development gauntlet (2) *good choices* matter toward keeping on track with greater economic aggregation and (3) *good accidents* of historical happenstance matter *to help keep such good choices* over time toward that greater economic aggregation. So, by observing the very successful Korean case down this development gauntlet, many comparable good choices and even comparable good accidents of historical happenstance were summarized that have helped Korea. Plus, by comparing Korea's great success to many other developing nations' lesser successes and failures in the same fast development drive, the factors found in Korea (and missing in others) can help *any country* learn to hold to a durable aggregating path in general development by starting with authoritative yet consensus-based policies in that development.

For definitions of the other two terms, *good choices* are somewhat self-explanatory, defined as choices to *hold durably to any kind of more representative and singular policies over time as that is only route that brings durable aggregated development.* This is contrasted with how many less successful development drives in other nations endlessly reset policies and conditions due to commencing general development with uncompromising and unrepresentative arrangements. That bad choice of maintaining unrepresentative policies can lead to cultural revolutions against it that in turn breaks economic aggregation and/or can lead to ongoing reverses or changes of policy that equally break economic aggregation. Both result in a subsequent loss of any durable aggregated development over time. Thus, better aggregated economic development in a fast development drive, that generally starts from nothing, means 'conserving your small winnings' and compounding them each time instead of losing it all, each time. This comes only from starting with procedures that institutionalize widening compromises that over time are ever more durable by being flexible, compromising, and consensus-oriented instead of being durable by being inflexible. This is in the interest of maintaining that durable general development toward economic aggregation since successes create their own future unknown externalities that require readjustment of policies. Failing to do that means repeatedly falling backward each time down the development gauntlet and starting over, while other countries with more consensus-oriented starting points and more compromising flexible later policies start to race ahead of yours in economic aggregation by solving those later self-generated externality problems generated out of their own success down the development gauntlet.

The latter term of *good accidents* was defined as historical happenstances that in retrospect were important background conditions encouraging particular representative and/or *good choices to be chosen from the start that would be held to* for greater economic aggregation in a durable fast development drive down the development gauntlet more by default instead of truly by freedom of choice. Good accidents were earlier likened to a 'track' pre-laid toward a fast development drive that guides good choices of decisions down more exclusive paths. Thus good choices and good accidents are concepts that are linked together. It was argued that pressures of good accidents and good choices, *when durable, dual, and interactive like this*, are great facilitators for holding to particular good choices of economic aggregation over time, instead of indecisively changing development strategies over time. The latter is a course that has more free will, yet it minimizes potential of economic aggregation to proceed over time. In other words, good accidents sometimes seem very constraining on choices. However, if the development gauntlet depends on durable advances toward economic aggregation, over time, then obviously anything that helps (or hinders) a state to hold by default durably to particular policies instead of having easier and ever changing policies will encourage durable economic aggregation. This is in contrast to less successful nations that sometimes may have many more options and thus may try many development policies simultaneously at the start or keep changing development policies over time with each incoming administration holding a different partisan ideology or base of support. This may cancel previous development drives or sectors and of course this minimizes chances of any singular economic aggregation.

In Part I, an amazing plethora of good choices and good accidents were recounted as success factors in Korea's national general development and durable economic aggregation in its fast development drive when it was a developing country. Inversely, it was argued comparatively that many other developing countries have a scant few of either (see Appendices 2 and 3). Such comparisons explain the incomparable success of South Korea in its fast development drive from 1961 onward to the present as a true outlier, yet careful study and learning from the Korean outlier can turn it into a harbinger to all other nations.

For the topic at hand, national survival through the digital bottleneck, there are both benefits and dangers of a saturated digital future that can harm general development and national survival instead of only help it, so there are fresh questions of what are the good choices and good accidents to have cultural and national survival through the digital bottleneck. The digital bottleneck was defined as how all counties face an external challenge of trying economically to thrive and culturally to reproduce in a 'triple global storm' of a global digital *economy*, a national/global digital *culture*, and a globally decentralized digital *media*. To define what it means to 'get through' the digital bottleneck, it means four basic points: (1) being able to maintain durable globally competitive *digital hardware production* in telecommunications (particularly media technologies) and (2) durable globally competitive *digital cultural production* along with (3) *maintaining instead of losing durable internal cultural transmission* in the process (4) *by keeping both digital productions centered in the country*. The stress is 'centered in the country' and how to maintain your country as a powerhouse that benefits itself instead of culturally falls apart due to the coordination and production tasks of global digital economics, culture, and media technologies for global others and for your own culture in your own country, while how to avoid watching other regions and nations displace you while losing your country's own culture whether in the process of success or of failure at such production. Many nations are now entering the digital bottleneck and may be unable to do any of these four points, since what characterizes such a triple global storm is that it endlessly allows the easier reorientation and abandonment of previous locations of global production of digital hardware and digital culture.

We can model from Korea for how any other country may get through the digital bottleneck easier, based on Korea's successes in this task so far. Framed as four factors, we can see, respectively that Korea got through the digital bottleneck in those four factors, by: (1) Korea's durable economic production of digital telecommunications technologies for decades, then (2) the global digital production of the Korean

Wave itself as a durable and ongoing aggregated policy design for decades, even while (3) Korea maintains its own cultural transmission, and (4) how Korea kept its national economy, politics, and culture together in greater consensus instead of falling into greater internal dissention in centering this digital world upon itself, at least so far. In short, Korea's success through the digital bottleneck is evinced by *keeping in its own country its durable digital hardware production and its durable digital cultural production, while doing this without losing its economics, democratic politics, or culture in national breakdown.*

The question becomes how did Korea do these four tasks durably over time, and how to learn from it to transfer to other countries? The hypothesis will be tested by looking at what chosen resources or policies that Korea has encouraged toward its global digital development while still being able to hold its culture and nation together, instead of fracturing it greatly. Many of these are similar points to what was chosen to hold Korea together similarly during its fast development drive better than other countries, yet many other points are fresh topics dealing exclusively with how Korea chooses hold together now in our current digital triple global storm.

Despite Korea *surviving as a nation* so far as this triple global storm rages around it externally, it is an open question even if Korea will survive *culturally from basic biology and demographic reproduction* from growing internal problems on shrinking families, shrinking numbers of children, and rising real estate prices. It is creating a cultural exhaustion and demographic problem as a kind of cultural revolution against participating anymore in the externalities of the fast development drive. This has yet to be solved in Korea, or in any urban industrialized country for that matter. This is such a different topic that it is discussed later in Chapter 11 about this dawning (other) quintuple problem of how (1) failing fertility combined with (2) longer lives creates (3) a failing intergenerational cultural transfer and (4) a failing intergenerational wealth transfer for the poorer Koreans even as it is amplified in richer families, that is creating (5) a cultural revolution against future participation in the fast development drive. This growing problem is framed as a dawning common 'fifth problem' in the developmental gauntlet. It is just starting in many countries in the past two decades—*and no one has solved it yet*. Therefore, this seems to be the next level of the development gauntlet to solve and to pass through, if the desire is to maintain ongoing economic development, a stable culture, and a nation instead of fall backwards in development. However, that point is saved for the last chapter.

10.2.2.1 Hybrid Politics for Consensus Kept Korean Digital Freedoms

So, instead of good choices and good accidents to get through the development gauntlet, what are other good choices and good accidents that arguably helped Korea get through the digital bottleneck?

Discussion of good choices comes first in how Korea got through both national general development and the digital bottleneck. This allows understanding these good choices before understanding how sometimes these good choices were premised on other good background conditions of undesigned and accidental pressure that encouraged those good choices to be held to over time to get through the digital bottleneck. In comparative retrospect, the theme behind many of the following good choices of Korea to get through the digital bottleneck is that Korea has many success factors in *wide hybrid consensus building in politics, economics, and culture* that were used to get through the development gauntlet in national general development as well. This kept Korea from falling apart *politically, economically, or culturally* in its fast development drive earlier. These same factors equally matter in keeping the culture and nation intact through the digital bottleneck. The many good examples of Korea's more *hybrid political policies, hybrid economic policies and hybrid cultural policies* were already discussed in Chapter 3, Sect. 3.2. This section is for those policies' further influences on getting through the digital bottleneck by maintaining civil rights in a saturated digital culture.

This growing consensus *equally* has helped Korea get through the digital bottleneck alive in one piece against refreshed or 'undead' dictatorial pretentions of Korean policy elites who have wanted repeatedly since 1995 to keep advancing Korea into a technocratic digital police state once Koreans started to live in a different media regime that challenged past censorship and/or agenda-setting models (See Appendix 1). A digital police state may unrepresentatively hold a country together slightly in the beginning of the digital bottleneck, yet over time that policy if held to may itself contribute to pulling the country apart later in a cultural revolution against it regardless. Consensus and common civil rights stop government technocracy, and Korea shows how greater consensus mechanisms did push to create greater state recognition of 'pre-digital' civil rights before and after 1987, and thus recognize state limitations at the same time. These ongoing consensus mechanisms increasingly turned Korea's consolidated civil rights into fresh digital civil rights by the second decade of the twenty-first century by the now ongoing recognition of state limitations on data convergence and surveillance, yet of course only after an incredibly strong digital surveillance state had been erected in South Korea between 1995 to around 2012—after which it began to weaken. There was one recent grasp at a total digital surveillance state, based on publicly tracking all Koreans' private geolocation from their mobile phones in real time forever and their compliance with any number of untested and forced injections. This was planned to expand from only adults in 2021 to non-risk group teenagers by early 2022 —yet even that was rejected by courts by January 2022 as well. Thus Korea can show what makes a successful path and a successful culture that keeps a country's consensus procedures alive so it can thrive through instead of die within the digital bottleneck. The hallmarks of this are argued to be keeping wide consensus policies, keeping a more homogeneous culture, and keeping an open and equitably distributed digital civil sphere.

Originally, the good choices of consensus encouraged those good choices of more equitable digital development and a more equitable digital civil sphere itself within the Korean nation, instead of Korea having a great deal of digital divide. This digital parity helped Korea be the first more evenly saturated digital culture. Even from the 1980s and 1990s, telephones were equitably distributed throughout Korean nation, even on marginal islands, instead of only servicing only the wealthier city areas. This helped Koreans later commonly defend their civil rights more prominently through the digital bottleneck as well—helped by that greater equality of a digital sphere as well as of course other factors like a more homogeneous culture. So, in interaction with other more accidental factors like a more homogeneous culture and a weak state legitimacy, this greater digital parity in Korea arguably *helped it avoid, instead of helped it become the first digitally enhanced, technocratic police state*. A more digital police state could have happened easily out of that earlier Korean digital saturation and easier digital convergence of once separate and fragmented information sources on citizens. The point here is twofold. First, typically in the digital bottleneck a cultural dissention hidden for a long time can surface in media at last. Second, a growing digital convergence of information makes unrepresentative governing elites idealize a digital police state managing citizens in a collectivistic technocracy to control widening cultural dissention and economic planning from a center, instead of maintaining a process of consensus via an open republican constitution, dissent, social movements, and individual civil and property rights. However, since the first factor has generally been weak in the more homogeneous culture of Korea, it has kept a more unified opposition against the expansion of the second factor as well.

To explain this in more detail than the introductory section about this earlier, four mass movements of Koreans appeared between 2012 and 2022 that dismantled many advancing digital technocratic police state policies of Korea that started as early as 1995. This is how Korea kept together through the digital bottleneck as the same as before—as a multi-party national state with common human rights and civil rights. Consensus was hardly the only factor, yet in less consensus-pressured nation states, it seems more likely that the digital bottleneck only converts those nations into a digital police state in the process—with an even more difficult future stability instead of an expected future stability as the result of that though. Korean governing elites, in their 'mid-size' and more homogeneous cultural nation, have *buckled* regularly to wider consensus building, or *even voluntarily joined it* after changing their minds, instead of resorting to open digital repression that we see in larger demographic or geographic states like China or the United States.

In all four examples, Koreans mounted a combination of online politics which was later combined with an acquiescing or even compromising Korean state that began to admit its citizens had been right: that digital centralization was creating more insecure outcomes to digital security or even democratic security instead of more secure outcomes. These two factors of online/public social movements for civil rights, and how Korean administrators changed their minds and joined the consensus instead of defended their earlier positions, kept combining to undo many centralized digital surveillance tools created by earlier state administrators that introduced them.

From 1995, South Korea became the first state that legalized the state to have an agency that performed 'recommendations' for internet censorship on its people. In this year, Korea passed the Telecommunications Business Act, the first Internet censorship law in the world. So, after only a few years of wider civil freedoms of speech and publishing in South Korea from 1987 through 1994, this change in 1995 revived a Korean government of very tight information and cultural control in South Korea that continued from the days of President's Park's National Security Law (that continues) and Chun's Basic Press Law about governmental censorship and direction of all media content. That had been revoked in 1987 in modern Korean democratization yet by 1995 it started to return to censor and control the messages of a growing digital cultural sphere. The Korea Internet Communications Ethics Committee (ICEC) *was tasked to monitor the whole Korean Internet* and make recommendations for content removal. Within a year, by August 1996, the ICEC had censored about 220,000 messages on Korean Internet websites. After 2002, a revised law added more internet policing of content and allowing removal of websites entirely. By 2008, a mere complaint at this point would allow the updated Korean Communication Standards Commission (KCSC) automatically to suspend any web posting or article for 30 days, as soon as a complaint was filed. This power of the Korean state still exists, yet all other digital surveillance attempts that are described below have been removed in time.

There have been positive uses of this digital space in the same period, for growing digital democracy, instead of only for growing digital surveillance. As early as 2000, for the other trend of digital democracy in Korea, there has been an online National Assembly's petition system. However over the years, it became rarely used. It started in the 16th National Assembly opening in 2000, yet it steadily decreased in use from 765 petitions to a lower 227 petitions by the 19th National Assembly of 2012. Plus, the number of petitions adopted by the National Legislature from citizens always remained very small. Only 2 of the 227 petitions were adopted by the 19th National Assembly. Plus, in most cases, citizen's petitions were totally ignored. The petitions themselves failed to be reviewed as they should be by the subcommittee of the petition screening committee within the standing committee, even if it was received. Plus, despite it being designed as a way for online citizens to appeal directly to the National Assembly, the Assembly gave itself a veto against even addressing online citizen petitions at the same time. This was because online parliamentary petitions had to be sponsored by a letter of recommendation from a lawmaker anyway. Thus, given the fakery and mere symbolic politics of this digital democracy motif, and given the other trend of digital surveillance policies between 1995 to 2012, it seemed Korea would likely become a digital police state despite rejecting such a trend after 1987. However, Koreans started to work against this negative trend, along with their elected representatives. In the process, even the Korean Constitutional Court started to defend digital civil rights from 2012 onward.

The first time digital surveillance was undone successfully in Korea was in 2012 as the country was nearing 100% of its population under the age of 18 with smartphones in 2013, and as the legislative petition system by the 19th National Assembly was seen as a weak route toward widening democratic legitimacy. In 2012, the first good break in Korea's bad trend of a growing digital technocracy was the ending of the 'real-name net ID' policies as found unconstitutional. There was a "real-name net ID" law between 2007 and 2012 that had forced all online commenters and platform users in general to share their real names with the online platform services they were using—and which could be accessed by the state as well. Thus there was a lack of online anonymity for Korean citizens on Korean platforms between 2007 and 2012. However, in 2012, the Korean Constitutional Court rejected the "real-name net ID" law of 2007 as unconstitutional on civil and *political* rights grounds that it restricted freedom of speech and endangered democracy (BBC, 2012). Second, the same real-name net-ID law by 2011 was seen as a centralized danger *economically* to the whole country as well, because it made hacking of centralized databases far more risky. This is the aforementioned centralized insecurity. For instance, immediately after 35 million real names of South Koreans (out of 51 million total Koreans) were hacked from the company SK Communications, it catalyzed the Korean government Ministry of Public Administration and Safety to reverse itself in 2011 to want to *remove* the 2007 'real ID net law' *in the name of digital security*, instead of defending it as key to digital security as before (Cooper, 2011).

The second undoing of a trend of growing digital technocracy was the ending of the state mandate on all citizens forced to use the Korean state's monopoly in monitoring their real names online through another *financial* route. The Korean state from the year 2000 monitored all private online economic transactions within the country through the one digital authentication technology and database that it authorized and which was state owned. This was the "N-PKI" system, or National Public Key Infrastructure system. This gave the Korean government a central public record of all 'real name' private online financial transactions of all its citizens as well. This was finally undone in the year of 2015 with the merging of the rising 'netizen' protests against it that had been combining with multi-party legislative pressure for years, though it at last combined with then-President Park Geun-hye's agreement that *it was frustrating the economic development and global trade of the country instead of facilitating digital security at all*. This was the first time all three of these power groups of social movements, political parties, and the Presidency were aligned in consensus on this issue in over fifteen years despite spotty alignments before that had failed to undo this mandate on all citizens to use only one national-run online financial digital authentication system. The year 2015 was probably not so incidentally the year when nearly 100% of the whole population of Korea through age 35 had a smartphone and could be even more of a nationally unified pressure group for ending the digital authentication mandate in one technology. As the mandate was removed, this allowed instead more private and plural choices of online digital authentication and thus better competitive digital security compared to the failing overall security of the monopolistic government-run system (see Appendix 1). However, the scale of the digital certificates of the now non-mandated NPKI still continue to rise, so if Korea really cares for its digital democracy or digital security, the whole NPKI operation has to be suspended next as it still encourages hacking (Jang & Lim, 2021; Kim, 2018; Son & Whitaker, 2020; Statista, 2020). The mandate is gone, though that seems hardly enough to stop this from being maintained by many major private companies and banks themselves mandating their customers use the NPKI's state surveillance regardless.

The third time a digital technocracy in Korea was undone by consensus building was during the online netizen pressure, around revelations in 2016, that President Park had been building a secret cultural blacklist of nearly 10,000 Korean citizens immediately from her election in 2013. Park's administration was secretly blocking state funding of blacklisted citizens from equal state participation (and fame) in the global Korean Wave, *on political test grounds of opposing her* on various policy issues or in criticism of her publicly in the digital cultural sphere. This cultural blacklist was a secret Korean social credit system denying equal treatment before the law and curtailing common freedoms of those on the list based on state-judged behaviors. It was only one of the rationales why President Park Geun-hye was impeached in 2017, later arrested, found guilty, and then sent to jail with a handful of her close staff. Park's secret cultural blacklist was removed in 2017, which probably equally not so incidentally was the first year of the global Korean Wave's sudden simultaneous successes. The whole concept of a cultural blacklist was found to be an illegal use of the Presidential executive function in 2020 by the Korean Constitutional Court.

For the other digital democracy trend that kept advancing, there were already two other routes of digital democracy added in Korea beyond the National Assembly's online petition portal from the year 2000. Second, there remains the Korean government's "Kookmin ShinMunGo" encouraging an online community for a citizen-based and ongoing synchronous discussion with government participation online, though it is more of an institutional and bureaucratic level of discussion instead of addressed to the National Assembly. It remains in place today, as a place for online discussion to see public opinion and to hear a response from the government bureaucrats about complaints. A third route of direct digital democracy was inaugurated to celebrate the first one-hundred days of President Moon Jae-in. On April 17, 2017, the "Kookmin CheonWon," the National Petition of Korea, began. It was a petition system directly to the Presidency as well. In the wake of the abuses of President Park Geun-hye, this was meant as a way for forcing a president legally to respond directly about policies or to reject them if the total online petitioners became 200,000 signatures in one month. By February 2019, more than 124,500 postings existed with an average of 658 daily. Im Jong-seok, the Chief Presidential Secretary for President Moon, said, "Like [the US President's] White House [in place since 2012], we should also answer the people's petitions." However, President Moon's administration set a much higher bar and thus was less democratic. President Moon's National Petition of Korea has double the requirement of the United States—which is only 100,000 petitioners online in a month in a country of approximately 330 million people to get a Presidential response. Therefore, Moon's standard was very prohibitive to get a Korean Presidential response, despite it being another framework of digital democracy in Korea. The petitions received after this could be pre-classified into 17 categories: political reform, diplomacy/unification/defense, jobs, future, growth engines, farming and fishing villages, health and welfare, child care/education, low birth/aging, low birth/aging measures, administrative, pets, transportation/building/national land, economic democratization, human rights/equality, culture/art/sports/media, political quality, and 'other.'

The irony is by May 27th, 2019, despite President Moon desiring more direct democracy online, a petition calling for him to be impeached gathered more than 217,000 signatures by this day within a month, showing Moon's shrinking approval ratings mostly over dislike about his failing economic policies in the nation as well as his failing policy interpreted as weak toward North Korea. "The author of the online petition has not been identified but says he or she is a citizen who took part in candlelight protests in 2017 that helped lead to the impeachment and ouster of

Moon's predecessor, Park Geun-hye….[The]… "petitioner said Moon has condoned North Korea's nuclear development, human right problems and illegal transshipment of North Korean coal, while 'acting nonsense' such as lowering the military guard while North Korea has its nuclear weapons" (Roh, 2019). For those signing the petition, "[a]mong those respondents, 50% expressed frustration with Moon's economic policy, while 13% criticized his focus on North Korea and his North Korea-friendly policies." Exports had been falling for five months already by April 2019 (Roh, 2019). By Wednesday, February 26th, 2020, a second separate petition had garnered over 400,000 signatures to support President Moon's impeachment mostly about Koreans feeling betrayed by Moon leaving the border open to Chinese travelers during a supposed "pandemic" (Kim, 2020). By the next day of Thursday, February 27th, 2020, it had more than doubled to over one million Koreans signing this second petition to impeach President Moon, increasingly about a mismanagement that allowed Chinese citizens to pour into the country unobstructed despite hypocritically claiming more police powers to remove Korean freedoms because of a "pandemic" (Park, 2020).

Given a wide dislike for President Moon already by early 2019 into early 2020, this dislike only grew after April 2021. On April 1st, 2021, President Moon's administration announced they planned to introduce a digital certification system to verify an adult person above the age of 18 and their COVID-19 vaccination status through a smartphone application by the end of the month (Yonhap, 2021). The three other institutions developing this COVID-19 'vaccine passport' in league with the Moon administration were KT, the Korean telecommunications company, along with Incheon International Airport, and Inha University Hospital. "South Korea's prime minister said on the same day that the government will launch an app later this month for verifying a person's COVID-19 vaccination status." President Moon planned an identical arrangement to the totalitarian Chinese digital social credit system via a national digital identification around vaccine passports, organized in the same way as already in China. Next, people further disliked President Moon within a few months for exempting only visiting Chinese nationals in Korea from this Korean digital surveillance system. Only the Chinese could skip both Korean quarantines and Western-made forced vaccines upon entering the country. "South Korea is exempting from mandatory quarantine travelers who have received China's Sinovac or Sinopharm vaccines, becoming possibly the only country to completely remove restrictions against recipients of Chinese vaccines" (Shim, 2021).

In an example of the slippery slope of any digitally totalitarian policies, by December 2021, the Moon administration said they next planned by February 2022 to expand the national digital vaccine passport system to all Koreans below the age of 18, through to age 12. "Starting February, the government plan[ned] to require not only adults but also children aged 12 to 18 to present COVID-19 vaccination or negative test certificates at multiuse facilities, including public study rooms and cram schools" or they will be denied entry to all public accommodations nationwide. However, in the same month, on December 10, 2021, a popular Korean YouTuber activist, "Yang Dae-rim [additionally spelled Yang Daelim], an 18-year-old high school student, filed a petition signed by 453 people with the Constitutional Court, claiming that the measure runs counter to the Constitution." (*Korea Times*, 2021). By December 27th, 2021, the group around Yang was publicly accusing the government of intentional murder and attempted murder, calling out particularly President Moon Jae-in, Prime Minister Kim Bu-gyeom, Minister of Health and Welfare Kwon Deok-cheol, and the Director of the Korean Centers for Disease Control and Prevention Jung Eunkyung.

The Moon Administration's announcement about denying all access to public accommodations, removing individual private medical choice, and illegally incentivizing coercion of untested medical treatments universally down to age 12 in a non-risk group gave youth or adults only one other option of being an outcast in their own nation denied entry in all institutions. This "sparked strong backlash from students and parents arguing the measure amounts to forcing vaccination upon minors.... Yang and fellow petitioners plan to file a separate injunction request against the vaccine pass system with the court as early as next week. They also plan to submit a legal complaint against top government officials, including President Moon Jae-in, with the prosecution over alleged power abuse charges next month. A separate petition against the youth vaccine pass by a parents group was also submitted to the court earlier in the day" (*Korea Times*, 2021).

On January 7th, 2022, about 1,700 citizens protested outside the Korean Constitutional Court asking for an injunction to suspend the validity of the vaccine passport. Indeed, by January 14th, 2022, the Moon Administration was blocked by an injunction issued by another Seoul court from extending Moon's digital 'vaccine passport' to adolescents down to age 12. The Seoul court's injunction additionally blocked extending the vaccine passport into President Moon's desired 'ban on food' that would have blocked all citizens' access to food and supermarkets nationwide without a forced injection, as a way to try to strong-arm and to coerce medical procedures without voluntary compliance and without an informed consent. Seoul is of course half the country's population (Shin, 2022). Three days later, on January 17th, 2022, the Korean Constitutional Court ended all obligation to show a COVID-19 vaccine passport nationally, yet only in larger stores across the whole country, following up the Seoul-based court's injunction against it on January 14th, 2022. The Korean Constitutional Court...."lifted the obligation to show a COVID-19 vaccine pass in larger stores across the country after a court last week issued an injunction against them in Seoul....'Limiting entry to unvaccinated people is an excessive restriction,' it added....The same day, another division of the same court, however, refused to reject the vaccine passport mandate, and only widened it to allow alternatives saying, '[h]alting the mandate is not necessary [as long as it is] provided [that] there are alternative ways such as a negative PCR test result' (Kim, 2022). Of course allowing for alternatives to a mandate is ending a mandate, despite the strange verbiage claiming otherwise.

In short, this was the fourth example of netizen pressure and government agreement undoing a digital technocracy attempt pushing coercive experimental injections into young teenagers that had been tried from April 2021 to January 2022. A combination of online netizen politics, a lawsuit by a famous Korean teen YouTuber activist (who livestreamed the writing and composition of his lawsuit to thousands of fans), the Seoul courts, and the Korean Constitutional Court all stopped the implementation of President Moon Jae-in's truly totalitarian desire to institute a state-forced mandatory 'Covid-19 vaccination requirement' down to age 12 that would be digitally-tracked from institution to institution in all citizens across all Korea, basically forever, given the digital pass expired automatically every six months. Durable civil rights would have ended. The whole idea of common public accommodations and public space would end because it would have created a digitally managed central police state that only gave temporary or arbitrary *individualized* access to any public venue, while tracking citizens nationally anywhere they went by reference to a national digital database of what would have been once private medical information turned into coercive and discriminatory public medical information. President Moon's policies aimed to be a functioning discriminatory Korean social credit system like China since principles of common, permanent, and free access to all institutions for all citizens would have ended forever and only from that point access to anything would be granted only temporarily by centralized government permission. This would have effectively required all Koreans down to age 12 to take state-mandated injections every six months, forever, to keep up their temporary freedoms of travel and institutional access to businesses, hospitals, restaurants, supermarkets, public transport, study zones, etc. However soon after it was announced on April 1st, 2021, by January 2022 it was blocked by that rising combination of netizen action, Seoul courts, and the Korean Constitutional Court thanks to lawsuits filed by YouTuber teenagers like Yang Dae-rim. Ultimately, the mandatory requirement of medical treatment ordered by government was rejected by the Korean Constitutional Court itself, and yet it was a digital democracy repeat of a similar consensus combination of netizen, political, legal, and court forces that blocked the "real name net-ID" law in 2012, or a different combination of consensus that ended in 2015 the mandate to use only a state-run digital authentication technology that publicly monitored and centrally recorded all private online purchases.

In conclusion, the rising trend of a saturated 'digital republic' in Korea has increasingly opposed the other ongoing trend that keeps attempting a digital surveillance police state and a centralized digital technocracy in the country. In keeping this digital democratic trend alive, the same dynamics of governmental compromise, consensus building, and preservation of civil rights can be seen in all four points from 2012 through 2022. This is why it is argued that Korea has gone through the digital bottleneck—i.e., keeping its homogeneous culture intact, keeping its republican constitution with individual civil rights intact, while even being digitally improved. Korea has seen the rejection of real name surveillance of all online social media (2012), the rejection of mandated state surveillance of all online financial transactions (2015), the rejection of a state social credit system operating as a secret cultural blacklist designed to financially punish free speech and political opinions online or offline (after 2017), and the rejection of a state jurisdiction over personal and private medical decisions or medical records and the rejection of tracked and individualized access to public venues based on an inverted authoritarian assumption that 'everyone is guilty before being proven individually innocent' (2022). All of these 'undoing' actions demoted state digital surveillance between 2012 and 2022, and doing this has kept the country together in consensus through the digital bottleneck.

So a homogeneous culture interacting with digital saturation, instead of having the sole effect in Korea of mass shaming in a repressive online bullying culture (which Korea has as well), supercharged greater resource mobilization for collective action to maintain Korean civil freedoms within an online world and in the physical world. Korean consensus with its very active netizen culture (see Appendix 1) undid four major projects of a digital surveillance state between 2012 and 2022 that if allowed to stand or to merge in digital convergence later, would have killed Korean democracy and replaced it with an unrepresentative digital technocracy and digital social credit system that would have had (1) all citizen's private financial information of online purchases, (2) their private political views from real ID use online, (3) a secret cultural blacklist financially punishing them and limiting their mass media access, and (4) their private medical status becoming a public state discrimination on Koreans. If Korea kept all four of these digital surveillance policies, South Korea would be a copy of China's digital social credit system that already has all these four points in place in China. However, in Korea, a strong drive to political consensus and civil rights in a more homogeneous culture and with a common netizen culture with a saturated digital parity supercharged Korea to go through the digital bottleneck in one piece without becoming a technocratic police state like China so far. However, despite the final foreign national travel quarantine rules relaxed on July 15, 2023, which required a digital surveillance and home quarantine address (KBS World, 2023b), and finally ending in August 2023 all remaining quarantine and masking pressures in various doctor's offices (KBS World, 2023c), the Korean government at the same time is starting to build yet another expandable national biometric digital database via facial recognition technology at Incheon International Airport as a gauntlet before boarding all airplanes (KBS World, 2023a). A national database of facial scans could late be connected in digital convergence to already existing technology that records facial scans from public CCTV cameras in public spaces—and track people around the country by their face similar to what can already happen in China now. In other words, it remains a Sisyphean task to maintain data fragmentation upon which civil rights are protected, when living in this world of easy digital convergence of all data now.

10.2.2.2 Hybrid Economics for Consensus

Next, Korea's good choices of hybrid *economic* policies built consensus as well. They held the nation together through the fast development drive earlier, and now they help get Korea through the digital bottleneck in that greater economic consensus as well. Examples of economic consensus in Korea show its government policies under President Park in the 1960s kept tempering complaints about the national externalities from the government's desired economic policies of external export-led expansion. This happened first in 1963 with more subsidization of artisan economic models, then in 1964 with the first social insurance program, then in the 1970s with more village-based economic models combined with national economic protection of agriculture from the world market despite the ongoing export-led economy.

Later by 1977, as President Park was pressured greatly by a declining support in the National Assembly, a national health care service was introduced under him though it was hardly universal at first. Equally as President Chun was pressured greatly by a similar declining support in the National Assembly by 1985 onward, a law of 1986 was passed that would establish a National Pension Service by 1988. Therefore, by 1988, the National Pension Service began and it could siphon off labor cost pressures for calls for corporate-based pensions (that exist as well) that were pushed to the state instead. Equally to aid employers, they can join the National Pension Service as well as a way to pay later their own corporate private-based worker pensions anyway. Since employers even are covered under the workplace-based pension scheme, this helps meet their employee's compulsory 9% deduction by providing the remaining 4.5%. The National Pension Service covers laborers who work in businesses employing five or more, as well as fishermen, farmers, and self-employed people in rural and urban areas.

The year of 1988 of course was one year after modern democratization in Korea from 1987, with the first open multi-party Presidential elections since the late 1960s and with the first legalization of unions in 1987. So in heightened now-legal labor union protests from 1987 onward, the pre-arranged National Pension Service began in 1988. With further pressure from labor unions and strikes, the national health care service of 1977 was expanded into a universal health care program in 1989 under President Roh. Next, the first employment insurance was introduced in 1995.

The National Pension Scheme from 1988 passed into law under Chun from 1986 is a mandated worker contribution. To receive it later, the worker should be at least 62 years old and have made ten years of contributions. However, a reduced early pension can obtained at age of 56. Later, the normal pension age disbursement will be raised to the age of 65 by 2033. Only about 29% of elderly receive these national pensions, as of data from 2013 since hardly all retirees can draw benefits from the pension without a ten year contribution requirement. Because of that, it has led to other levels of Korea's national pension scheme tailored to other means-tested pensions on top of that more universalistic pension. Over time, this has created three basic pensions in South Korea's state disbursements. First, is the National Pension Scheme from 1988 onward. However, another base pension was added only for impoverished elderly without family only, called the Basic Livelihood Security Program. It was introduced in 2000 after the 1997 Korean financial crisis. It provides cash payments and other benefits like housing and education for elderly citizens living in the worst poverty who have to prove they lack family aid. Next another Basic Old-Age Pension was started 2008, after another Korean financial crisis. Only small percentages of people get disbursements from these two secondary programs.

Currently, the overall national pension system of Korea is a universal mandate and yet divided in a corporatist welfare state model as well, based on four classifications with different pension benefits: national, military, government service, and private school teacher. Plus, there are two other means-tested pension systems for other very marginalized groups of isolated elderly, added into the mix. In short, many different consensus layers of internal economic policies of protection of individual laborers in both universal pension plans and means-tested pension plans developed along with different occupational categories splitting the national pension in the Korean growing welfare state, particularly after labor movements were legal from 1987, after the 1997-8 Korean financial crisis, and after the 2008-9 Korean financial crisis. The national pension disbursement is universal because it is based on age and residence instead of based on means-tested income like the other two later programs, and the national pension service covers people widely—between the ages of 18 to 59. Overall, a welfare state pension in South Korea was first very (cynically) strong around only governmental bureaucratic workers working around President Park instead of working for the National Assembly, yet then expanding to other governmental workers later, and then expanding to individual laborers by 1988 as the welfare state policy tried to accommodate and to make more ambivalent the ongoing more combative democratic and labor movements that were legal only after 1987.

Other examples equally show the Korean state having direct policies supporting small-scale businesses sometimes even above larger scale ones, tempering economic shakeout from its many other policies encouraging economic scale. Korea equally supports public corporations run by the state alongside larger private companies as well. All of this keeps Korea together in consensus better than other economic policies, particularly as a growing digital economy leads to domination of and economic shakeout of individual laborers or small scale businesses by online platform shopping (Standing, 2011).

To enumerate the above, first, the Korean hybrid economic policies by the 1970s were a combination of ten policies. The first three were (1) President Park's developmental state model of export-led urban industrial development supporting and picking large scale private corporate winners on competitive rubrics from 1961/1963 onward, (2) tempered by support for internal regional artisans from 1963, then (3) tempered more by internal regional grass roots democratic development from 1970 (with small villages/towns deciding their own priorities of what would be done, instead of the central state deciding). This was combined with (4) more internal national economic protection of some economic sectors from outside competition sometimes like in protecting private small-scale Korean agriculture, or protecting Korean digital authentication technology from 2000 from outside private global firms displacing it by instead in Korea creating a nation-run monopoly on it between 2000–2015, or protecting private large-scale Korean telecommunication firms in 2007 from being inundated with Apple iPhone imports for a few years till 2009. Sometimes (5) the outright nationalization of some sectors was done as well like Korea's public hospitals and their price setting of medical procedures in the national medical welfare state and national insurance plans (though there remain private hospitals out of the system as well) and in electrical markets, yet it is tempered with (7) ongoing support for the strongly-protected private professional guild-like arrangements of other sectors like pharmacies that defend themselves against both governmental or large private consolidation. (8) Protections of small businesses against larger businesses exist by closing larger franchised stores like supermarkets nationally twice every month on alternative weekends as a sop and supplicant to smaller business markets instead of seeing small food stores and 'corner store' businesses disappear as the default policy. All of this is combined with (9) five-year plans of state coordination since 1963 and with (10) state subsidies of encouragement and funding of much research and innovation to aid private transnational Korean businesses to profit and to stay ahead in a global and external export-led economy in state-decided areas. Typically in the world, these ten economic policies are implemented as if they are in a battle of ideological purity to the death with each other, or as if they are innate dichotomies or zero sum games. This hardly has been the case in Korea. These hybrid economic policies have been the result of ongoing political contention and accommodation that increasingly resolved itself in ever 'bigger tent' economic policies of consensus building that arguably remain important today in holding the nation together economically in the digital bottleneck.

Second, choosing to expand a strong internal national welfare state while expanding an export-led neoliberal economy is a synergistic policy that many other countries treat as if it is another dichotomized ideological war to the death between respective socialist- or neoliberalist-inspired total models of economic policy. However Korea and only a few other nations in the world like Chile, Mauritius, Costa Rica, and Kerala (a province in India) have hit on this hybrid economic policy by their openness to internal consensus building, their openness to external international trade, and the cultural weakness of their government elites historically at the same time. This synergy creates a national welfare state that takes care of economic and social externalities of any neoliberal economy in the country. It seems a far better hybrid model than any classic socialist or classic neoliberalist model alone, since this hybrid economic policy choice *alone* has given this handful of countries a superior quality of life, good health carc, and a social safcty net combined with an expansionary and innovative export-led economy (Sandbrook et al., 2007). So, despite choosing a global export-led economic policy from the early 1960s, Korea increasingly compromised and created consensus by expanding a strong economic welfare state as its solution for an ever expanding 'social democracy' instead of only a political democracy. Rarely do the world's countries, dominated now by the short-term ideology of American neoliberalism, either see or much less have the vocabulary to conceptualize the greater benefits of such a hybrid economic situation in which a nation has both the benefits of a growing export-led neoliberal economy and the benefits of checking and balancing against that model's social and economic externalities in a nation by matching it with an equally strong national economic policy that strengthens the universalistic advance of a domestic welfare state. It is universalistic in a dual sense that it covers everyone (even foreign nationals in the country), and in the sense that both left and right-wing parties advance the domestic welfare state. For instance, in Korea even right-wing Presidents like Park Geun-hye (2013–2017) advanced the Korean welfare state (mostly to her elderly followers) instead of thinking by definition that a welfare state is only a left-wing situation or institution. Plus, as said, Korea's welfare state, pension plans, and public hospital access are a universalistic model that leaves no one behind, even covering all foreign national laborers in the country. This is another hybrid economic policy secret of

Korean consensus building that helps to hold together the nation and culture durably, helps to keep everyone as healthy as possible for labor productivity and for quality of life, and even helps to avoid developing a foreign underclass and rightless working population (like that you see in Dubai for example).

Third, this Korean welfare state is argued to be facilitated by a very strong independent labor movement developing after 1987 when unions were legal for the first time, combined with the ongoing government's desire to undercut it in its popularity by the government expanding the *national* welfare state, in order to try to minimize support for labor movements and strikes seeking better economic policies *from companies* by substituting that economic policy advance *from the government* instead. The dynamics of the Korean welfare state are sometimes cynical like this, sometimes idealistically universal in covering even foreign workers, and even pragmatically beneficial to the economy as a whole by keeping Korean businesses far more nimble under law about their hired labor that allows Korean companies to adjust faster in the global economy. The ultimate outcome has been to expand a universalistic social democratic welfare state in Korea at the same moment it has a more flexible neoliberalist economy for exports. Given such private business freedom of when they retire older workers, the common Korean retirement age is as early as 55 years of age, giving many decades of elderly life without very stable income for many people. This has resulted in Korea having some of the poorest elderly in the OECD despite their state pension plans. This encourages a lot of elderly workers to go into low-exertion taxi service or delivery jobs. Plus, from the early 1980s, Koreans over 65 years of age are given a universal perk of free (subsidized) public transportation for the rest of their life. It now helps with elderly poverty and isolation by helping them keep mobile and active. Instead of only used for tourism and higher quality of life, this has encouraged the creation of the "silver delivery" jobs—elderly workers in delivery services that get paid little for carrying small packages in major cities, yet they can transport themselves (and their packages) free around the major cities to maximize meager profits and minimize costs. The rising costs of subsidizing a rapidly aging society in Korea, while still retiring people 'early' at age 55, are causing policy tensions. In 2023, three Korean economic debates are around a rise in adult public transportation fares, a potential rise in the retirement age to 60 years of age, and a potential rise in the free public transportation access to 70 years of age (Shin & Kim, 2023). In other words, Koreans tend to prefer to tinker and adjust their whole system all at once, instead of have clear ideologically driven singular solutions like keeping or rejecting a whole policy. This is the ongoing consensus idea mentioned above.

Fourth, Korea tries to have or at least show economic checks and balances against promoting only economic scale, however tokenistic is the policy. As said earlier, there are national rules that close larger department stores *nationally* on alternative weekends throughout the year solely to try to give consumer business in intermittent and short periods to help small and medium enterprises survive in a competitive market, instead of just letting rules by default consolidate all economic sectors into ever larger companies that wreck the ideal of competitive markets themselves with ever larger oligopolies. More examples can be found in Appendices 2 and 3.

All of these oddly-mixed hybrid cultural, political, *and even here economic policies* are built from consensus and the ongoing accommodations among plural groups trying to work out the conflicts. This is because a top-down 'half revolutionary, half traditionalist' state development model from 1961 kept buckling to stop cultural revolution and kept listening to social protests about inequality due to its weak legitimacy.

10.2.2.3 Good Choices of Digital Telecommunications Deployed in an Equitable Way

Another good choice of Korea has been *durably* prioritizing digital telecommunications from the 1980s as an export-led sector. Korea has *held to* this policy for decades, which as argued earlier is a key way that keeps a growing aggregation potential in anything contrasted to other states that keep adding and dropping sponsored sectors and thus seldom allowing any sectors to aggregate for the long term in any fast development drive. However, it is *the particular organization of digital equity and digital saturation of digital media* in Korea that is argued to be the actual good choice to get through the digital bottleneck, instead of only digital telecommunications itself per se or instead of having a digital divide as many other countries do.

As a more synergistic sector innately as discussed in Chapter 9, digital telecommunications has done three main points for Korea. First, as mentioned in Part I, digital telecommunications was one of Korea's first ways of moving further than other developing countries down the development gauntlet, by escaping its own growing 'middle income trap' of the late 1970s via telecommunications as well as via other fresh sectors in the 1980s (Gill & Kharas, 2006; Oh & Larson, 2019). Other developing countries can stall economically in the 'middle income trap' and be less inventive in creating fresh economic sectors unlike what Korea has done regularly for decades in its great collective innovation.

Second, keeping expertise in digital telecommunications defines how to get through the digital bottleneck. To pass through it means your country still has *self-determination in digital hardware* production in telecommunications and self-determination in keeping a durable *digital cultural production of content* instead of ceding both or either to other nations. Korea does both as the first "K-Nation." Many countries are unable to do both or either one, and those other nations will likely see their past industrial economy, past culture, and their modern youth digitally colonized by other nations' producers of global telecommunications hardware and global digital content that both benefit another land more as it underdevelops the laggards economically and culturally in turn. This is a triple global storm, and to ignore the storm is to surely die as an autonomous nation, dominated from outside instead. If your country is not trying to be a dually digital "K-Nation," it is led by people trying to be an "ex-nation."

Third, it is good to avoid digital divides as your nation rolls out its digital communications technology. Korea from the start had a policy of true national digital coverage, even of its rural zones and hundreds of islands. It is hard to find documentation on this point, though first, its origin is argued to have started with the politics of Korea's strong grass roots regional development policies in the 1970s in Saemaeul Undong that gave every Korean village legitimated political input on regional priorities. The village based grass roots development did have a policy of rural electrification and telephone service as well, however slow that seems to have been in practice. However, second, it joined with how earlier Korean villages saw the installation of thousands of village-based telecommunications public address systems for public announcements—for at the time, the nightly announcements about national curfew and other public announcements, for example. Third, this joins with how Korea has a common collectivist culture that likes to put public speaker address systems everywhere for group public announcements. Such systems are installed in even 'private' modern apartment buildings instead of only public university buildings or corporate office spaces. Fourth, this stress on equitable telecommunications seems a lot to do with potential invasion readiness due to facing North Korea for decades in the mere armistice. South Korean cities have military sirens that can blare deafeningly across the modern urban landscape in regularly scheduled test drills of the wartime telecommunications network. So overall, a daily rural, urban, and cross-regional familiarity with telecommunications equipment combined with ongoing state-supported collective interests in rural villages and other points above kept all of Korea involved in the telecommunications changes of the 1980s. President Chun ended the national curfew in 1982 as well as the slow and inefficient governmental monopoly on telephone installation under President Park with its long backlog of installations running into years. Instead, rules about an equitable national telecommunications rollout was built from large competitive private telecommunications companies that competed among each other for the first time. This policy of a more even geographic spread and wider inclusion of distributed digital communications—yet combined with a competitive market economy of ongoing innovation in that technology—has encouraged Korea to pass through the digital bottleneck politically intact as a multi-party democracy with consensus and inclusion of all regions as well as kept their telecommunications and computer expertise focused on what international markets want as well. In short, the ongoing decades of national telecommunications parity for various rationales and then adding to this modern competitive corporate export-led development in such telecommunications equipment kept up a digital communications parity in Korea in the last 25 years without the technology being outdated or suffering loss of markets to foreign companies. This equity and ongoing competitiveness of the organization of the telecommunications sector in Korea helps to temper an ongoing strong economic regional disparity in transportation or medical services that does exist between richer urban zones and poorer rural zones in Korea.

So, despite other kinds of rural social or governmental service triages in Korea, rural zones avoided being left behind in digital media however. One of the effects of this has surely has been greater inclusion of diverse regional voices in Korean online netizens for later consensus building, and that makes a stronger homogeneous culture online as well as encourages heterogeneous regional divisions to speak up. Korea has become a land of "smart regions" (Whitaker & Pawar, 2020). Korea's digital virtual community of netizens online mixed with its more homogeneous culture and its regional differences has kept Korean digital democracy very strong instead of only making a digitally-administrative state strong. See Appendix 1 for other examples of how Korea encouraged and now exhibits the world's greatest digital parity of access to online information for all citizens instead of supporting policies of digital inequality. As said earlier, between 2012 and 2021, online netizens of Korea contributed greatly toward protecting their common civil rights by preserving online anonymity in 2012, by ending governmental authorization and oversight on all private online transactions from 2015, by ending secret governmental cultural blacklists and thus ending secret cultural censorship between 2018 and 2020, and by blocking in 2022 a proposed law for a national digital database of all citizens down to age 12 that would have turned their private medical information and private medical decisions into public state-run databases and state coercion on all medical decisions.

10.2.2.4 Four Miscellaneous Good Accidents Behind Korean Good Policies

Four other good accidents helped Korea keep on track both in its good decisions of its fast development drive and later in helping Korea get through the digital bottleneck intact. Already in the earlier section on the "digital bottleneck" above, three other good accidental factors as a group were used to help explain the superlative digital development of Korea compared to other countries with less of these three good accidents at their disposal. Those earlier three good accidents were argued to put and to keep a country in the digital "Goldilocks zone"—defined as a 'mid-sized' demographic, geographic, and more homogeneous cultural place that yields greater interactive capacities to keep a choice of digital development centered in a country over time. In that earlier section, there was more empirical detail on the argument why Korea is lucky historically and *developmentally* on these three happenstance factors in having a 'mid-size' demography, a 'mid-size' geography, and a more homogenous culture compared to other countries. Equally in this triple digital storm, Korea by happenstance in these three factors is arguably less likely to come apart in cultural transmission due to the triple global storm. Thus, it is more optimized for the long term to have greater resources of collective innovation and resilience to keep adjusting rapidly and effectively as a national team in the midst of global digitalization compared to other countries that arguably may fail or may be challenged more regularly in their economics and culture under global digital conditions unless they find ways to reorient or reinvent on these three factors. Other less optimal scenarios were mentioned for the other countries outside this digital "Goldilocks' zone." Thus, all other countries without the luck of Korea on these three background factors still can learn from these Korean default conditions on how to craft their own creative policies to try to synthesize something similar.

Another fourth good accident of Korea is having a "singular primate yet 'global city'" of high-quality digital telecommunications in Seoul. It is considered an accident because even though it is based on the good choices of telecommunications, it is an accident since no one could have foreseen the scale of success in Korea due to other accidental factors of how Korea's historically primate city of Seoul in an era of digital telecommunications became equally a 'primate *global* city' in Korea as well (Sassen, 2001). Thus this good accident is an interactive two part good accident: having historically a primate city only in Seoul, and then having a "primate global city" of high-quality digital telecommunications in Seoul later as well.

For the digital side of this, on the one hand, Korean investment in digital telecommunications infrastructures has encouraged the world's international companies, legal firms, banks, and insurance companies to reside in global cities like Seoul for their own interests of regional command and control (Sassen, 2001). In the growing global Korean Wave, this more recently has turned Seoul into a location for much digital processing of video for other countries' advertising and other media due to the skill of digital cultural production from Seoul's advertising and film editing agencies interacting with wider world regional/international clienteles instead of only interacting with the Korean Wave. This brings global development and global capital infrastructure of financial services to Korea, as well as adds more global digital cultural and advertisement production services to Korea. On the other hand, for the 'singular primate city' side of this, comparatively, it has been argued that a useful comparative key to stable development is to have 'accidentally' less plural urban competition in a developing country. It is argued by others that if a developing country does have multiple contending urban sites for the modern sites of urban industrial development (like in Costa Rica for example), or if it had a more inter-competitive urban digitalization (like in Australia, for example), this tends to divide instead of unify national development and digital development because of different boosterish regional urban elites in these battles. This frustrates and stalls a common national development (Sandbrook et al., 2007) and frustrates and stalls a common national digitalization plan as well.

Therefore the good accident of Korea is having the singular primate global city of Seoul that has helped bring about faster and greater consensus in political and economic decisions whether in the fast development drive or later in Korea's national digital development, This is because half of Korea resides in the Seoul metropolitan region instead of, for examples, divided like in the United States between Los Angeles, San Francisco, Chicago, and New York City, or divided like several competing larger cities that exist in many Latin American countries, or divided in Australia across many cities on the coast separated by many less populated areas. There are very low chances of quick national policy decisions about either a national economy or a global digital economy in the United States, Latin America, or in Australia if a variety of equally powerful heterogeneous urban zones and/or very difficult and sparsely populated geographies to traverse between them make it easy for urban areas to compete against each other within the same nation instead of more easily collaborating with each other if there was only one major 'primate global city' like in Seoul.

This is a different argument than Sassen, the original conceptualizer of the idea of one "global city" built from global telecommunications networks with a bit of this 'city' in almost every developed country. Viewed from before 2001, she and the data showed that this global telecommunications access was mostly then only a useful digital infrastructure for big private transnational corporations and banks for their command and control in a world-system of their related global financial services. Such transnational corporate management elites want to be everywhere around the world, and yet durably be in as few as possible key minimal centralized digital areas of command and control, to manage more effectively their ever shifting and more decentralized global production. Sassen's original concern with the conceptions of the global city was the political and economic erosion of how a common past national development in already developed countries by the 1980s was ceasing to matter very much and was weakening due to privately-managed global command and control through telecommunications from a select number of plural 'global cities' acting in concert to manage the global economy privately among themselves. This 'global city' is in pieces around the trading world simultaneously, linked with telecommunications, so the same groups globally within them can manage the global economy between themselves privately from these co-capitals throughout the world around the clock without ceasing. Sassen's point of political and economic concern was that when a telecommunications-rich global city is developing in an already developed country, it dissolves a national interest into its urban self and into its global digital business networks, demoting national development capacities and democracy, and heightening national economic inequalities.

However, the more 'primate global city' of Seoul is argued to have been beneficial for Korea as a developing country instead of harming its national interest. Plus, the primate urban context of the mid-size of Korea accidentally having simultaneously most financial, industrial, cultural, political capital in this primate digital global city (which is not a situation of course found across plural global city infrastructure in Los Angeles or even New York City, for instance) meant the inverse seems to happen in a developing country particularly if it has a more consolidated and primate global city. Instead of eroding the national developmental interest like when a global city is in an already developed country, when a global city site is in a developing country and when it is in a primate city in that developing country as well, it is useful for pulling international development into the framework of its national interest. Plus, in the Korean case, this has happened without the divisiveness of plural global cities within Korea against the national interest that happens more often in other developed countries like in the United States or in other developing countries like Brazil.

Seoul in Korea is one of the few locations in any (ex-)developing country (beyond the equally primate city of Taipei in Taiwan, or Tokyo in Japan) that has generated any digital global city infrastructure within itself while in a fast development drive. This has turned its primate city situation into a digital advantage for the national interest instead of being an impediment of it. So instead of damaging a country's national sovereignty in all cases, it would be worse to be without any global city infrastructure at all. That starves a developing country of more global digital development potential being pulled into itself as those businesses flee core nations elsewhere and undermine their national interests.

Thus, we can adapt Sassen's ideas into a 'digital world-system' with various levels of nations of core, semi-periphery, and periphery now adding to this dynamic their string of plural digital global cities strung mostly through the most-developed core nations—*except in a few (ex-)developing countries at the time as well like* Korea, Taiwan, Hong Kong, and Singapore. So, once a semi-periphery nation, Korea's national sovereignty helpfully was pulled into more core nation status by arranging a 'primate global city' and its digital infrastructure in Seoul. First, Korea's general development drive was enhanced in economic aggregation by being mostly in a "Seoul-centric" urban development. Later, the digital global city infrastructure, by being Seoul-centric as well, helped pull Korea into core national status in the world-system based on plural digital global cities by the late 1990s. So, a digital global city in a semi-peripheral nation arguably can pull more core global digital networks into itself for the latter nation's own development in this context of a primate global city, instead of pulling it out of the nation in the case of other already developed core nations, or instead of it being divided across multiple plural global cities that can demote capacities of a singular national interest.

In summary, it is worth looking into this "South Korean model" of culture and development with its major intertwined factors of *good choices* of its more hybrid settlements and more consensus politics, its *good accidents* that helped Korea's general fast development drive, *as well how all this later* helped hold it together through the digital bottleneck to keep democracy, consensus, and civil rights instead of lose all three in a digital transition to a technocratic police state with dubious staying power anyway.

The caveat is Korea is hardly the only place to learn from in digital development or for getting through the digital bottleneck. Another hypothesis is that more attention should be placed on very plural heterogeneous cultures that do hold together in consensus, democracy, and civil rights well—sometimes simply because there is so much of a wide heterogeneity that it dissolves into working together instead of working against each other like in a different context of a heterogeneous culture with a singular hegemonic ethic/religious dominance and/or a larger unintegrated minority within it. Therefore, a greater focus on the very small countries that are very successful heterogeneous digital cultures, like Mauritius or Rwanda, may help the world scale up solutions to greater or lesser ethnically diverse countries that are geographically larger. Both of these countries have a degree of greater durable digital development remarkable for their small size and their very heterogeneous cultures. So, while South Korea can show a pathway for more consensus building through the digital bottleneck from the world's small number of more homogeneous 'mid-size' cultures, these other two other countries of Mauritius or Rwanda may show the way for how more heterogeneous small-size cultures may participate successfully in digital development and get through the digital bottleneck. Plus, in the conclusion to the section above about the digital "Goldilocks zone," since many countries are very different than this "Korean optimal" zone and different than heterogeneous smaller-sized Mauritius or Rwanda, other ideas were already suggested for how more heterogeneous/homogeneous larger-sized countries or more homogeneous smaller-sized countries might work on their future digital plans for their own survival. Additionally, looking at very small sized raw material export states like Kuwait or Brunei may be instructive how these very small states seem to better escape the raw material export trap with their greater development capacities for their citizens at large.

The argument here is raw material dependency may be less harsh or divisive in very small raw material export states compared to larger states, since more consensus has to be developed throughout in the smaller states, while such raw material dependency may be more dangerous for a country's survival when it is a larger geographic or demographic state where downturns may be more destabalizing in wider regionalized opposition (Karl, 1997).

In conclusion, to make it through the digital bottleneck, many other countries will have to work hard on turning lessons of Korea, Rwanda, or Mauritius and their good choices and 'good accidents' into policy for other countries. They will have to work hard to build themselves as a competitive K-Nation because the only other option may be national dissolution in our growing media regime change. Frankly, a major development problem faces the world today in how other nations' already exhibit great difficulty to catch up with the digital harbinger of Korea, even if these many enumerated and discrete points about hybrid consensus policies, or digital parity, or digitally primate global cities were learned from and applied to other countries for how they could develop their own consensus to hold together in the digital bottleneck. Nonetheless, we have hope that the above points *can be learned and transferred* to other nations to contribute to holding them together better in their fast development drives or in the digital bottleneck—whether culturally, politically, or economically. Just as before, the question remains whether Korea will be an outlier to others, a harbinger for others, or a bit of both? Only the future will tell if Korea continues its successful actions to preserve its gains. Only the future will tell if other countries can learn from those Korean gains to make useful policies for themselves as well.

10.2.2.5 Losing the Good Accident of a Hybrid Culture? Dangers of a Fresh Digital Aristocracy

Comparatively speaking, one of the best secrets of economic and political development in world history is seen in Korea. This is modern Korea's 'best foundational accident.' This is the 'hybrid cultural' format mentioned earlier: Korea *ending* its older traditional aristocratic and oligarchic families *without* a cultural revolution while oddly *keeping* and enhancing its traditional and more regionalized rural agricultural and cultural interests with land distributions. This hybrid cultural settlement in turn worked as a cultural, political, and economic check and balance against any later 'modernizing' attempts at rural agricultural industrialization and instead steered modernization only into urban-based, export-led, and value-added industrialization. Equally, this removed their aristocratic *political* vetoes or *financial* vetoes against that successful fast development drive. This made such a fast development drive possible under a consolidated military coup in that political vacuum that had wide cultural support aiming at export-led development outside the nation instead of inside the nation, as well having an effect of wide cultural protest that could press against the military coup toward more 'authoritarian parliamentarian' settlements as well over time after 1961 to the present. Without a powerful and wealthy aristocracy, there were few sources of funding to try to maintain the more unrepresentative politics of the 1970s. Therefore, both the first military coup increasingly under Park after 1961 or even the second military coup solidly under Chun in the 1980s had to adapt to be more representative over time. Plus, that hybrid cultural settlement helped maintain Korea's more homogeneous cultural transmissions, and that itself helped supercharge and maintain the collective innovation of the fast development drive. It helped first to contribute to keeping Korea's civil rights and multi-party democratic state intact despite dictatorial attempts, and second, it helped later to get Korea through the digital bottleneck without becoming a digital police state as well. The hybrid cultural settlement made all the other hybrid policies of greater consensus possible as well in politics, in economics, and in the later digital parity in Korea's digital development.

From comparative history, a secret of both ancient dynastic commercial development and modern urban industrial commercial development is the same: end your previous oligarchy and aristocracy, yet do it without a polarizing violent cultural revolution, and you will develop economically very quickly. This economic revolution happened in the commercial Song dynasty of China, built on passively losing in about 50 years in the middle 900s CE all the ancient Han/T'ang dynastic families that were about 1,000 years old at that point in power across several dynasties (Tackett, 2014). Thus, the Chinese Song dynasty's urban economic revolution has the similar secret that the commercial and modern economic fast development drive in South Korea has. Similarly, modern Korea was built on passively losing in about 50 years its ancient Korean dynastic families between 1910 through 1960 that had lasted almost 2,000 years or more at that point. Third, this economic revolution is like the United States, which never had an aristocratic landowning background in (most of) its colonies either (except Virginia), which in turn created several commercial colonies that later became civil states themselves with their own state constitutions, and in turn later became joined in the United States under a federal constitution as well.

This is not like North Korea, the Soviet Union, the People's Republic of China, or France—that did remove their aristocracies though did it by violent cultural revolutions only to see themselves uniformly have spotty commercial development. In all these cases except North Korea, instead they had decades of ongoing wars or violent coups respectively by the White Russians, the Chinese Republicans, or the French royalists supporting aristocratic returns to power. Cultural revolutions to remove an aristocracy thus only create long term simmering cultural civil wars, revolutionary dictatorships, and reactionary and equally dictatorial revanchist royalty or aristocracies that in being innately unstable regardless of who is in power may be worse and less developmental than any static and non-developmental royalist state of the past.

Equally from comparative history, another secret of world history that stops national urban industrial development is bringing back your oligarchy and aristocracy after a revolutionary settlement. For instance, in North Korea, such a neo-aristocracy redeveloped very quickly once it removed the old aristocracy and oligarchy by cultural revolution. After the rise of state socialism there, in North Korea there has been a slowed innovation and development as well as the crony return of another aristocratic settlement built from the inherited managerial dynasties of the socialist state.

In North Korea, we see the rise of the neo-dynastic family of the current ruler, "Kim the Third," along with other military families of neo-aristocrats gaining power from their socialist revolution of the 1940s. North Korean state elites are now an inherited caste literally with special legal and cultural rights based on their revolutionary heritage as families. Plus, they are now a rat's nest of intermarried socialist revolutionaries tied to or against each other's bloodlines, as they battle with lower ranked North Korean citizens as well as battle with each other or the Kim dynasty. North Korea has recreated the Joseon Dynasty, and its modern socialist aristocrats try to be different families of state control behind the Kim throne, or try to stay out of sight as modern agricultural peasants on the state plantation, because both groups know other options involve their likely capricious death or execution. *L'Ancien Regime* ou *la Nouvelle Aristocracie*? Plus ça change?

However, in South Korea now, similar unequal aristocratic dynamics are starting. Instead of North Korea's active policy to build a fresh aristocracy, or instead of South Korea's policy to rebuild an old one, a nation can passively allow a construction of a fresh aristocracy by refusing to recognize the danger of growing corruption of commercial and governmental family dynasties that both benefit from economic monopolization and crony capitalism. Commercial dynasties can come to join with each other in marriage, as well as marrying with or at least collaborating with modern state political dynasties in other growing family nepotisms and intermarriages over time. When both commercial leadership and political leadership become a caste, a modern nation is on the road to feudalization once more unless steps are taken to stop the families involved from further political economic consolidation in their management of the nation, passed from parents to children like a fiefdom.

This passive construction of a fresh 'digital aristocracy' is what is unfortunately happening in South Korea. It could undo the 'hybrid cultural' settlements and thus undo everything about (1) Korean consensus and (2) durability in its other hybrid policies and (3) in its digital development in time.

Comparatively historically, when an aristocracy is removed, it is like a dead hand being removed that allows much innovation in the economy and state to occur. So, it is bad news if it returns because it undermines any of the above three points. However, even South Korea is now experiencing two present neo-aristocratic dangers. The first is the neo-aristocracy of export-led industrial chaebol families intermarrying with each other as well as merging in alliances with fresh families involved in digital Big Tech sectors. They have equal interest in the economic empire powers and wealth possibilities of digital convergence in our fresh media regime applied to the Korean economy or to the whole world in global platforms. So, the 'neo-aristocracy' of South Korea are less involved in ancient landed wealth or even modern industrial wealth, though now exist via interlinked directorships, co-ownerships, stock trades, family networks spread out across the top management positions of ostensibly modern bureaucracies of companies, and a dozen other currently legal stratagems that make Korea's large capitalist enterprises of any kind (in manufacturing, retail, banking, or digital) marry into each other—financially, organizationally, and biologically—with increasing use of bloodlines of executive families making decisions across multiple generations.

The second present danger is seen in the 'platform-ization' of Korea whether domestic or overseas digital platform-based companies. The risk is that an increasingly stable aristocracy of families could come to control the policy of Korea's consolidated national digital platforms like Naver, Coupang, and Kakao, among others—and could join in the other neo-aristocratic dynastic powers of the chaebol families and run Korea's information sphere of culture from behind the scenes—or behind the digital screens—equally. The potentials of wealth from digital convergence could lead bigger companies into centralized digital surveillance and censorship capacities instead of only greater sales from the information.

So, the more there is global digital consolidation of platforms, whether in the nation or internationally, and the more there is an increasing corporate co-ownership organizationally or a family-based inherited executive class of intermarriage biologically, this toxic synergy of bloodlines and digital convergence endangers Korean democracy and can block its innovation and competitive economy as well.

Digital convergence of information can become a dangerous holistic 'behavioral management' platform for whole nations' citizens based on common digital identity accounts and censorship and vetting of its shared information sphere, and it becomes dystopian and abused particularly if there is parallel *'biological convergence'* of all major platforms owned or run by the same intermarried families. This kind of toxic synergy could mean a nation's private corporate digital platforms become para-state entities of civil management of behavior and access rights, while states in turn become para-platforms—equally managing civil behaviors and access rights from their own online platforms. Korea already had a handful of chaebol families running the major corporate organizations. Korea is adding many national and near monopolized platform economy companies by now. Kakao, Naver, Coupang, Baedal Minjok, and Weverse are a few good examples. The whole nation of Korea virtually uses only Kakao mobile apps to move around the country: Kakao T(axi), KakaoMetro, and KakaoBus. Plus, Korean citizens can be tracked nationally by public transportation cards. One subway card can be charged in one Korean city, and then used across the country by the same card in other cities' subways. It can even be used (surveilled) consecutively between subways and public buses that connect a user's previous trip to the next one to grant rebates if the next trip on public transportation happens within a short period. The same subway card can be used in touchless payment in taxis as well. Plus, most of Korea uses one major app called Baedal Minjok that centralizes almost all menus of takeout food and food delivery services across the whole nation. Plus, the Korean state from the 1990s has been very strong in building governmental digital platform solutions for itself as well as other nations as an export industry as well (Oh & Larson, 2019) (see Appendix 1).

It is a 'new kind of rule' now given that platform-based corporations and platform-based states now have uncannily similar ways of digitally managing and censoring real people by banning or limiting their digital world access to accounts and thus limiting their digitally-managed connections to manage their real world lives. Combine this with a handful of intermarried families in both that could use these para-state or para-platform powers to promote their own further private political power and economic consolidation against people that disagree with them and you have a recipe for weaponizing daily life as an informal private social credit system of digital censorship run by a corporate oligarchy. A handful of these 'new powers' exercised alike in this way by states and companies are: banning digital accounts, banning anonymity, spying on digital accounts, disrupting financial transactions and speech, blocking speech, censoring searches, blocking bank accounts, refusing to allow certain kinds of financial transactions, punishing protest behaviors or legal free speech with public or private digital denials later, creating a private platform-based social credit system of demerits and graduated different levels of access to the same social online services to try to coerce real world behavior, banning competition, banning travel bookings, automated censorship, and automated boosting of other pro-state or pro-corporate narratives. Is this not a digital feudal world now? There are few places online or offline defending common universal laws and legal equality, whether in a digital sphere or a civil sphere, when the information sphere has been privatized or is run by private or state-run platforms. We become digital serfs in digital nations if all we depend upon or expect is a capricious *noblesse oblige* of private billionaires running digital platforms (Binder, 2023).

In conclusion, a bad scenario would be *the digital convergence and the biological convergence merging* into a *'digital aristocracy'*. However, this is what trends show is occurring both in Korea as well as in several other highly digitally developed countries like the United States, the United Kingdom, or Sweden. This developing digital aristocracy may undo one of the great accidents of history, particularly in Korea, which is the passive destruction of long-term durable aristocracies. That passive destruction is the main factor that unleashed the fast development drive into real world actions in the first place in the political vacuum, whether in the past or in present world history.

This Korean digital aristocracy could start to erode the hard-won equitable 'digital republic' that Koreans have created from 2012 to 2021 by undoing those four separate attempts earlier that have *intentionally fragmented citizen's data in the name of protecting civil rights* against any state level digital convergence of all citizen's data. In the past, data fragmentation was just the way past media regimes worked by default. Paper in a doctor's office about your private medical information was not clearly connected to your monthly payments for your car or house, or connected to your food budget, diet, purchase behavior, genetics, your religious or political beliefs, or your online comments. However, to avoid that digital convergence in our current media regime, and to maintain civil rights now, data fragmentation has to be consciously maintained (possibly by permissioned blockchains?) to avoid the drift of digital dictatorships that will keep coming out of the background in the digital convergence. If all media and information falls like a black hole into some central point, and thus becomes a gravitational pull of corporate or governmental actions that can warp, influence or disrupt any behavior at a distance across the whole nation, online platforms public or private will *have 'new powers' of centrally mediating all different and once separated behaviors, and thus tacitly authorizing or denying all individual behaviors*. Imagine a technocracy where your individual access to digital platforms or denial of digital platform rights (which would include purchase and travel rights) whether organized by companies or states becomes a means to coerce behavioral modification in you or in all citizens, or a means to punish or reward you or all citizens. This is a digital aristocracy and a digital domestication. China is big on the latter, with automatic social credit digital financial currency deductions linked to the facial-recognition cameras in the streets of Shenzhen piloted from 2017 onward, yet missing the former. South Korea is growing strong in the former, in its many privately consolidated national private platforms yet with ongoing attempts to keep data fragmentation and preservation of civil rights after 2012. Woe to the country (or planet) that has both a digital aristocracy and a digital domestication. This This is because there is a lack of natural geography, political boundary, or any check and balance on the dreams or nightmares of global digital management due to our fresh media regime lacking all clear boundaries anymore. Thus, there is something like a global social credit system that is trying to be enforced across all peoples from China that can be seen already in how the Chinese government is leveraging the global power of the company Tencent, its many invested businesses, and its 'superapp' of WeChat (Magnates Media, 2023). The World Health Organization is attempting a global-level vaccine passport in April 2023 that would curtail all freedom of movement worldwide, managed from a global database that would outmode or outrank all national passports at once. The International Monetary Fund is attempting to create a global central bank digital currency (CBDC) that would outmode cash and made all purchases and transactions permissioned only. The World Economic Forum meeting in China in July 2023 had a talk about the 'benefits' to technocracy of central bank digital currencies that can be a permissioned digital money, banning people centrally from certain purchases with their own digital money or doing automatic 'unpermissioned' withdrawals as punishments.

Korean entertainment platforms like Weverse and others like Naver or Kakao are buying up different nations' intellectual property and platforms to combine them in similar ways. *Naver has become the world's largest distributor* both in webtoons via Naver Webtoon and in web novels via Naver's Wattpad, which was the former Canadian web novel platform website. In May 2021, Kakao Entertainment, an affiliate of the top Korean social media platform company Kakao, acquired another North American web novel service for itself, called 'Radish.' So, while Korea culturally has been building ever wider legal blocks against digital convergence and digital domestication within its nation from 2012 to 2022, yet Korea has so far ignored finding policies to end the growth of a national and global digital aristocracy that have a politics to keep pushing for that digital convergence and digital domestication globally or nationally, regardless of a national consensus against it. If allowed to continue, a fresh digital aristocracy has a permanent interest in bringing about its desired political national or global system based on digital convergence, replete with a digital technocracy and a social credit system for ensuring their ongoing centralized rule and their 'undisturbed' wealth management and profit over repressed digital masses. This is similar to China's already established state-level digital convergence of Chinese citizens' data on one integrated platform and one social credit system and one digital central bank digital currency of a 'digital yuan' tied into it.

Therefore to avoid these problems, there are two policies. First, *avoid digital convergence* in the hands of a single company, state or any agency, worldwide—whether in money, in citizen databases, in purchases and sales, or in search results and information distribution. Find a way to *create intentional digital fragmentation* of information once more on all citizens, because it used to exist as a check and balance on this kind of 'new power' (Pasquale, 2015) since older media regimes were without such information convergence though they are rapidly disappearing. Second, *avoid a digital aristocracy* that has an interest to keep ignoring the first policy. If wealthy families and big data are not *both* kept fragmented intentionally, their ensuing combined political and economic pressures over time for digital convergence could turn any country with rights of privacy, free movement, freedom of market/job participation, and open decisions into an open air prison of temporary and revocable 'permissions' of all kinds—faster than you can say 'vaccine passport' or 'central bank digital currencies.' Civil rights have rarely been more in danger globally all at once and in all countries at once than they are now with the digital convergence of data. However, on the other hand, civil rights have rarely been more powerful all at once in and all countries at once in the online digital social media and its power of peer-to-peer communication to get around state or corporate blockades on sharing information or ignoring such 'deplatforming' strategies of powerful digital aristocracies.

In conclusion, for a counterfactual about a parallel world that failed to happen, arguably keeping the aristocracy in South Korea through the 1960s as economically and politically powerful would have encouraged foreign war once more with North Korea as that was the main policy of aristocratic Syngman Rhee, who refused to sign the armistice of the Korean War after 1953, and thus would have encouraged even further economic stasis and setbacks in South Korea into the 1960s. An ongoing ancient aristocracy in South Korea in power would have later encouraged a less representative use of Korea's digital technologies in the long run toward more of a surveillance state and with less digital civil rights that require keeping data intentionally fragmented and out of the hands of the state or big companies alike. In short, Korea may have been left undeveloped without jettisoning its aristocracy first. Only with the ending of the Korean aristocracy did a useful power vacuum occur that has led to a more even consensus-building on general national development and even survival through the digital bottleneck as well. This has made Korea into a country where mass protests and now online netizens truly matter more than in other countries, due to the weakness of state legitimacy and due to a missing elite cultural control in Korea. For how long will the latter be though?

Therefore, it is argued it would be very bad news for modern development if a neo-aristocracy of oligarchic families in economics and politics were to redevelop in modern digital form—whether in Korea or in any nation. It would frustrate the many hybrid consensus mechanisms that led Korea to be so much more successful and durable in its fast development than other countries. A return to a digital aristocracy now would extinguish more meritocratic development, innovation, and universal civil rights protections. It would reignite neo-feudal fires of the old Korea that was not stable or as beautiful as a Korean historical drama, though was mostly divided, indecisive, plotless, nepotistic, repressive, inefficient, lazy, and self-destructive of their own people and each other. Oligarchy has seldom developed a nation, and only frustrated it or destroyed it, due to its lack of desire to participate in consensus building or to compromise on its private politics that are elevated above the nation without remorse in violently trying to achieve it.

How Korea or any nation handles a growing digital aristocracy and the current slow return to an unrepresentative oligarchic-based power of interactive wealth, families, and digital platforms of ownership may decide if nations continue through the digital bottleneck or collapse into a global Chinese-style social credit system administered by states as regional administrators of globally-dominant platforms and states run via nationally-dominant digital platforms. However, the power of digital democracy seems equal to and against oligarchy. More homogeneous nations may have a greater ability to coordinate that digital democracy if they have greater digital parity, yet the larger more heterogeneous nations are the only ones that gave us modern large scale democracy, even if the ideals of transparency, and the procedures of consensus came from small scale more homogeneous cultural democracy in the first place. That latter point is the topic of the last section below.

10.3 Heterogeneous Cultures' Six Innovations and Ethics May Be Lost Without Finding Policies to Keep Them

It would be inhuman to try to destroy all human cultural diversity simply on the premise that it has to be rationalized to fit only one kind of digital future or one kind of homogeneous culture. There are many futures in competition. Therefore, it would be a shame to devalue more heterogeneous cultural starting points simply because they have a harder time to develop equitably or durably over time under global digital conditions. This is *because* such towers of Babel are the source of much of the world's durable individual innovation, durable cultural innovation, and durable democratic principles despite generally their greater problems of durable inequality.

A puzzling point in the early twenty-first century is that if the world is truly selecting for homogeneous 'mid-sized' cultural zones like Korea, to be successful in working on digital development and ultimately holding together better culturally, Korea is still very dependent upon individual and cultural innovations of more heterogeneous cultures that are being devalued and breaking down.

On the one hand, on our wish list for the future, it would be nice for more heterogeneous cultures to have more access to the strengths of greater collective innovation that are more clearly found in more homogeneous cultures like Korea in order to have equal capacities of fast changes and coordination. On the other hand, equally on our wish list is that it would be nice for more homogeneous cultures to have greater individual and cultural innovations and principles of democratic ethics that are found only in more clearly in heterogeneous cultures. These are transcendent heterogeneous gifts that regularly come out of more tragic inequalities of such countries particularly in underclass cultures of ethnicity, language, or religion interacting in the wider culture. All of this is part of the human condition. Can we have a better situation? Can we get rid the different parallel tragedies of heterogeneous or homogenous cultures? Can we accentuate positives somehow of "too small", "too large", or "too diverse" nations in the digital economy? It remains to be seen.

Obviously, *a major future problem is crafting solutions to keep larger more heterogeneous nations alive* if what seems selected for in this triple global storm are three different kinds of winning hegemonies triangulating durable success mostly or only in 'mid-size' and more homogeneous cultural groups so far. To encourage solutions, the tacit virtues from more heterogeneous cultures should be more clearly stated for how such cultures improve the human condition in general while more homogeneous cultures mostly or only improve themselves. Therefore, the focus in this section is the wider point of how do we try to keep the benefits of more heterogeneous cultural conditions alive simply for a better future of the human condition instead of for their own national sakes only. Otherwise, heterogeneous cultures may be censored into non-existence worldwide by their own digital national breakdowns and by different kinds of homogeneous "internal K-nation" technocratic managements of what cultural content gets vetted, produced, or censored *internal* to them, or what cultural content is similar vetted, produced, or censored by durable *foreign external* digital control on their own cultural production from more successful 'mid-sized' homogeneous cultural groups elsewhere.

There are two interactive points here. First, there are many virtues and ethics of truly *heterogeneous* cultures worth preserving and finding solutions for in the twenty-first century because *homogenous* cultures are unable to exhibit these virtues and ethics, generally. So despite the historical moral inequalities and problems with heterogeneous nations, *more homogeneous nations can be worse if they are the sole dominant heritage of the twenty-first century.* Second, we might solve two of the durable problems of past heterogeneous cultures themselves in the process.

The first problem to solve is that many heterogeneous cultures are regularly less representative states. They are more likely ruled by very oligarchic closed groups having their own more durable homogenous culture, lording over a wider 'divided and conquered' public of groups that are poorer and more culturally or civilly marginalized in the heterogeneous cultural nation. The second common problem is many heterogeneous cultures suffer from vast regional environmental inequalities in their quality of life related to the above inequalities. This creates situations of majority or minority environmental underclasses coded on ethnicity, religion, language, occupation, etc. A *majority* environmental underclass existed (or still exists) in the heterogeneous states of Bolivia or South Africa, run historically by the same kind of apartheid system, respectively, of a tiny pureblood Spanish or Afrikaner Dutch/British ruling class both over a large (and regionally divided) underclass majority that is repressed. On the other hand, a *minority* environmental underclass can exist in a heterogeneous culture as well, and it would be the experience of many smaller demographic (divided) regions of Black American, Hispanic, or Native Americans in the United States, living among a deeply intermarried and mostly homogeneous European White wealthy ruling class. That European White ruling class lives away from immigrant industrial zones of cities and away from poorer White rural groups as well. In the United States, they live away in a handful of small zones in major cities like the Upper East Side in New York City, or in nearly private community enclaves on quiet isolated coastlines or islands ranging from the north or south shores of New York's Long Island, to Georgia's historical Jekyll Island, to currently Florida's Jupiter Island and (the island of) Palm Beach, or the 'urban island' of Beverly Hills in Los Angeles. This culture is maintained greatly by attendance at a handful of expensive private college preparatory schools in the United States and Europe that are separate from their nations' mass public compulsory education. Thus, even poorer White European stock of ethnicities in the United States might be considered mostly a majority environmental underclass in the way that it has been treated with disgust and hatred by its richer White Anglo-Saxon Protestant European-heritage ruling class (Isenberg, 2016) that was truly a closed social oligarchy of 'green, blue, and white' respectively of money, inherited family position, and ethnic/reputational status.

So, we might try to solve these two durable problems of heterogeneous cultures in order to save these kinds of heterogeneous nations from greater chances of oblivion that they face in the digital bottleneck. This is because their two main inequitable characteristics are their two main problems that are going to be responsible for pulling these heterogeneous nations apart more than ever because everyone is starting to live in a fresh media regime change towards two-way mass media. In the past, it was easier to make and to hold together a heterogeneous culture and nation despite its two kinds of massive inequalities. This was because the people who owned the mass media ignored and censored many heterogeneous national problems and refused to give voice to them. As the famous saying goes, "you have freedom of the press, only if you own one." So, in the previous two far more expensive and only one-way mass printing or mass telecommunications regimes, there was an easier centralized, managed, vetted, and censored mass cultural production.

The first saturated culture for such a one-way mass telecommunications media was invented and elaborated widely inside the United States from the late 1800s, and more strongly outside the United States on a global level only in Americanization after World War II. This previous media regime is known for its one-way centralized mass culture of big radio broadcasters, big movie theaters, big productions in movies, big broadcast television stations, big mass production of recorded music, and big newspapers from its wealthiest cities read for news and opinion nationwide and even worldwide. However, a modicum of a representative civil sphere was built from the fact that mass print and analogue mass telecommunications both were less consolidated even just fifty years ago than these same media sectors now that are very consolidated and easily co-managed by the early twenty-first century because of the digital convergence.

However, regardless of being plural or oligarchic, the cultural bigness of the one-way analogue mass telecommunications media was itself centralized or even required to be big as how all one-way mass telecommunications media technically and economically worked to be profitable. It is very different now from a more interactive two-way digital mass media culture of the twenty-first century that is decentralized and without large centralized capital organizations being required for its production or distribution except due to the 'first generation' of investments in more centralized platforms that have gone around the world. *On the one hand*, there is a growing centralized digital convergence of all those earlier kinds of media now in the common digital format that makes for easier centralized data and tracking possibilities on those centralized platforms down to tracking individual consumers and producers over time, across different media. Therefore, one issue arises that a centralized censorship based on digital convergence and a centralized distribution is ever more possible in our fresh media regime even while, *on the other hand*, cultural production itself is unable to be similarly centralized, managed, and vetted beforehand. This makes any centralized cultural censorship have to come out in the transparent open, later and after the fact now, if some groups want it in their centralized distribution, instead of in the past relying on their preferred plausible deniability or weakness of attribution by simply hiding in the background as they decide what is to be selectively produced, censored, and distributed at the same moment.

This is now a transparent and exposed conflict over cultural censorship and cultural distribution, since censorship by unrepresentative groups managing past heterogeneous cultural nations have to do this censorship after the fact on public platforms in real time, and thus now in the open in public. Thus, they have to expose themselves as repressive to keep censorship control at the very moment they are losing control over centralized cultural production—and even increasingly losing centralized distribution in many 'second generation' online platforms organized differently for enfranchising users themselves as owners and profiteers of their own data instead of the platform itself coming to own cultural producers' data that is uploaded there. At the same moment, these 'first generation' platforms are losing cultural legitimacy by mass awareness of that coordinated censorship in such centralized distribution that has to come out in the open in public to be done nowadays—which only pushes more people into migrating to those 'second generation' platforms with greater digital freedoms. All these points were much easier to bundle into a quiet censorship regime by default in a past one-way mass media regime of mass printing or of analogue telecommunications.

The argument is that these kinds of one-way mass media dynamics of the past helped by default grow the scale of heterogeneous nations by ignoring mostly their growing inequalities mentioned above, given many people were unable to produce media awareness or complaints about it. Now however they can in our fresh media regime. However, without irony, *this is the benefit of heterogeneous cultures: conflicts get exposed and made more transparent over time.* Thus dealing with conflicts is *potentially* more public, thus more ethical, and thus more representative over time. On the other hand, internal conflict is unfortunately an ethical problem in more homogeneous cultures which mostly prefer to ignore conflicts and keep them private regardless of the media regime available. Thus, ethical problems can continue unvoiced in more homogeneous cultures, because such cultures can be less transparent about their own decision making processes, and from that, have less formal institutional pressures for creating more representative procedures in the first place.

So the point of this section is that *instead of only dealing with different kinds of collective, individual, or cultural innovations between homogenous or heterogeneous cultures* as earlier mentioned, there are additionally *four very different kinds of ethical, procedural, and institutional innovations* elaborated differently in heterogeneous versus homogeneous cultures. The charm of heterogeneous cultures despite past faults of inequality is that we owe such open heterogeneous conflicts respect as the source of four ethical factors we might take for granted: (1) our common civil rights, (2) our ideals of transparency in decision making, (3) any deep thought about more institutionally-elaborated democratic procedures and republics, and in turn, (4) the combined institutional procedures and ethical principles respectively that show (4a) a desirability of *slow consensus building* toward change (4b) *and toward preservation of individual human rights* instead of the desirability of quick revolutionary change and repression of individuals and groups.

Thus, the more visible and open conflicts of a heterogeneous culture yield (1) greater potentials for a common cross-group ethics that can solve wider conflicts with its common human, civil, and individual rights, (2) that can create more transparency in decision making procedures, and thus (3) can create more representative formal institutional procedures and (4) an institutional procedure that creates slow consensus change and a respect for individual rights as legal interventions against policies of all kinds—human, civil, and property. Inversely, these four factors regularly are stunted in a homogeneous culture that instead (1) has less pressure to have common human, civil, or individual rights, thus (2) less pressure to have transparency in decision making, and thus (3) less pressure to have more representative formal institutional procedures or even multiple political parties, and (4) less checks and balances to slow quick revolutionary change and its policies that crush individuals or groups of all kinds.

Now, you may see the dangers or even horrors of what may happen if only more homogeneous cultures are selected for in the twenty-first century by the digital bottleneck. We have talked about the happy *benefits of digital development* in 'mid-sized' homogeneous cultures for their greater economic, technical, and cultural development or cultural survival through their greater and faster collective innovation. However, this section now mentions *the ethical and political dangers if digital development is only elaborated within these more 'successful' homogeneous cultural zones* of the world as it seems to be doing so far.

Now, in a world with a more decentralized global media in nearly everyone's hand for their own cultural production, distribution, reception, and response, since this media is more equalizing and representative, its content will innately catalyze more collective action on grievances previously unvoiced or censored in heterogeneous cultures that follow ethnic, religious, regional, and/or class-based fault lines. This is part of the problems of a digital bottleneck in more heterogeneous cultures as mentioned above: it will pull their slowly-developed (and sometimes only thinly developed) common universal, human, and individual civil rights and ethics apart—pulled apart into nothing durable except homogeneous group-based competition which will resolve or devolve into many different homogeneous digital groups battling each other.

In short, *if the world loses the sociological pressures of heterogeneous cultures, the world may lose six total great gifts to humanity* if such cultures become less digitally successful or even fail to pass through the digital bottleneck. As the hypothesis is that as this triple global storm selects for more success from mid-size more homogeneous K-Nations, six ethical innovations that improve the wider human condition may be lost if heterogeneous cultures become less successful or less durable. We may lose: (1) more individual innovation, (2) more cultural innovation, (3) greater potentials for a common cross-group ethics that can solve wider conflicts with inclusive religious movements or common human, civil, and individual rights, and (4) greater pressures for more public transparency in decision making procedures. Thus, we may lose (5) more representative formal institutional procedures and (6) out of that lose more institutional procedures that create slow consensus change and a respect for individual rights as legal interventions against policies of all kinds—human, civil, and property.

However, in the digital twenty-first century, instead of only mid-size homogeneous K-Nations inheriting the earth, as said earlier, perhaps the K-Nations with a bit more *hybrid homogeneous and heterogeneous gifts* merged, like Korea, may inherit the earth. In some sense, even 'more homogeneous cultures' like Korea or Taiwan do have useful "fractionalization," already discussed, in other social divisions within them that makes surrogate conflicts that keeps these more 'heterogeneous' gifts and innovations active in a more homogeneous culture. Both the more 'homogeneous' Korea and Taiwan are blessed with the 'good accident' by happenstance of having a large degree of heterogeneous religious diversity (or other diversities mentioned) as said earlier, that is useful in the modern world in keeping those six gifts alive in the human condition even in mostly homogeneous cultural nations. Korea additionally has other 'good accidents' by happenstance of a very ancient regional mutual dislike between its regions, that in modern conditions now animate into reality as more ethical, transparent, and democratic 'heterogeneous' procedures in Korea against the grain of and despite its more homogeneous culture. The greater participation in a global economy is another way that even a more homogeneous culture has to face daily the reality of a heterogeneous cultural world as well. Greater equality of wealth and property ownership in a nation is another kind of heterogeneous pressure towards greater transparency and democracy as well.

So, one hypothesis is that perhaps the more homogeneous larger nations like China will simply destroy themselves in their own political excesses and repressions of themselves without common individual human rights, since upon reflection what seems part of the recipe of durable digital success in Korea is its many 'good choices' of more *hybrid* and consensus-oriented development policies in economics, politics, and culture as mentioned earlier. These built greater ongoing consensus-building procedures into Korea *despite* its homogenous culture. Plus, these heterogeneous ethical gifts in Korea do come as well out of several deep surrogate heterogeneous factors of 'good accidents' like regional mutual animosity, religious plurality despite the homogeneous culture, the strong export-led economic dedication, and the greater equitable economic stratification historically stronger in Korean rural areas than in modern Korean urban areas though.

So, perhaps modern Korea has been so successful in modern fast development and in its now global cultural wave because it has resources of both homogeneous and heterogeneous factors in its culture, as already said, in other words. Perhaps more pure homogenous K-nations autonomously, or those "internal K-Nations" in formation in larger states are the ones that are going to self-destruct themselves and their wider states because they are "too homogeneous" on all three fractionalization factors (ethnic, linguistic, and religious), while at least Korea and Taiwan have some higher levels of religious, regional, and global economic fractionalization. This keeps their national cultures and politics involved in in 'democratically useful' internecine conflicts and thus more culturally heterogeneous despite themselves. These are 'good accidental' pressures toward all six gifts of heterogeneity as well.

What is now very risky for heterogeneous cultures and nations in this digital triple global storm is that the greater teamwork required toward common collective innovation and collective goals to get through the digital bottleneck together are very difficult to hold together in our fresh media regime, and much easier to make durable only in a more homogeneous culture. Teamwork as a national resource is starved in heterogeneous cultures via now more 'media-highlightable' deep divisions due to ethnocultural, linguistic, or religious heterogeneity. Heterogeneous cultures have always had more difficulty agreeing on any image of a common ethical future except individualism, so finding a common *collective* future much less creating it in real life or adapting nimbly to crises as a national team or in the global market seem difficult. So, the already weakened team-based collective innovation in the United States and other increasingly culturally heterogeneous countries are starting to fail. Plus, in this fresh media regime, such innate divisions in a heterogeneous cultural nation are more easily manipulated by unrepresentative actors, inside or out, who benefit from their enemy's internal divisions that further demote their enemy's national competitiveness or response. Thus other nations are trying to weaponize heterogeneous cultures against themselves. The Chinese have a saying about this method of war, "Strangle them with their own systems."

However, despite strong benefits of collective innovation in a more homogeneous culture particularly useful for fast development drives, a major drawback of a more homogeneous culture is that it can facilitate other kinds of 'collective innovation' like ingenious or systemic stratagems of networks of corruption. For example, even when polling Koreans themselves, the majority of Koreans freely admit if they were in a position of power they would happily break the law to favor only other Koreans from their own local hometown, educational, or family networks. This is likely connected to the phenomenon in Korea of the long-term and durable scale of the underground economy and thus unreported tax bases as well. This means Korea overall creates a culture with a large penchant for "network subversion" of even altruistic networks for private corrupt purposes (Kim & Whitaker, 2013). The homogeneity of the traditional cultural and regional rootedness of Korea is argued to be part of this problem of corruption, because even the widening level of democratic systems or even tremendously more wealth since 1988 has hardly changed Korea's opinion of itself as a less corrupt country since the 1970s. A change in self-perception to a less corrupt country typically happens after wider democratization or greater wealth in a nation, though this trend has stalled in Korea (Kim & Whitaker, 2013). So there is a double-edged sword in a homogeneous culture around its beneficial collective innovation. The positive side is its greater speed in catalyzing *group ethics* of collective action toward common goals. The negative side is less rewards or benefits for *personal ethics* standing up against collective ethics—which creates more private corruption, less transparency, and thus network subversion.

This helps explain another difference between more homogeneous and more heterogeneous cultures in the way they treat formal institutions. The caveat is on the word 'more,' since there is nothing like a pure version of either factor, only greater tendencies toward one or the other. A more homogenous culture like Korea repeatedly has changed three of its main formal institutions of its political life over the past 75 years: the constitution, the Presidential bureaucracies, and the formal political parties. Korea is on its Sixth Republic in 75 years. Korea regularly changes its formal institutions over the past while keeping to the same hybrid political, economic and cultural policies mentioned earlier. Korea regularly sees its whole political party system collapse and reform yet maintains similar informal political dynamics of regional clientelism and even maintains the same informal politicians in that clientelism just under different formal party names. The Korean state, particularly the President and the whole national bureaucracy, *regularly changes its formal organizational* chart of authority between divisions with each incoming Presidential administration. However, what rarely changes in Korea are cultural expectations, *formal policies*, or *informal politics*. Thus, it is argued that a more homogeneous culture and its state is hardly held together in continuity by its formal institutions, it is held together by the common virtues of cultural transmission through families and the life course of relationships of ethical and social expectations of previous anticipated hierarchies, particularly in this more Confucian cultural expectation. So, at least these three aspects of formal institutions matter less in a more homogeneous culture—allowing Korea to just keep adapting some parts of them very quickly for ongoing changes in their own administration, in export-led orientations, or in prioritized projects. Basically, many formal institutions in more homogeneous Korea become treated as just instrumentalist parts of the ongoing collective innovation of team building in a homogeneous culture, adaptable quickly to the cultural tasks at hand, instead of treated any differently or more sacrosanctly stable and separate from other team building.

This is very different than the way formal institutions are treated gingerly in more heterogeneous cultures like the United States where changing anything about the current conditions of formal institutions, formal policy, or informal political alliances can erupt in sudden violent contention. Why is this? There are obviously many factors and more than one factor. Scale may matter of course given the United States is large in geography and demographics, while Korea is 'mid-size' in both. However, to focus on this one point, it is argued in more heterogeneous cultures, of which many nations are larger in scale anyway so scale is hardly such a different issue than heterogeneity, they are more likely to be without a common background of ethics, ethnicity, or religion to hold them together as much, and are regularly colonial conquests of others already there as well, so formal institutions become the open battleground and the peace treaty at the same moment. They are the ongoing key to a temporary stability that holds together this accommodating conflict and conditional agreement to only a particular historical formal institutional, formal policy, and informal political dynamics, and they can be used and abused for the interest of any more consolidated cultural majorities for this temporary stability as well. Plus, in a more heterogeneous culture, this is why its individualistic ethics and other aspects of transparency and democratic procedures can be seen as the surrogate common cultural expectations of what formal institutional arrangements should do for all dissenting parties in a more heterogeneous culture, that has to be respected to keep the whole heterogeneous arrangement together.

The danger now for more heterogeneous cultures is that if it has more unrepresentative managers, they can try to shift away from ongoing democratic ethics and transparent procedures as the way to try to hold themselves together in power, into substituting another way of managing the same heterogeneity with a more unrepresentative and fine-grained digital surveillance police state of a social credit system that can ignore democratic ethics and transparent procedures. This is why it was said above that larger more heterogeneous cultures may not survive the digital bottleneck that culturally breaks them down into wider civil war or where some groups try to have a more digital technocratic coup over all formal institutions and culture to change them entirely. Neither option seems to lead to a durable way to preserve more heterogeneous culture. So, the tried and tested manners of the four points of democratic ethics above are argued to remain timelessly important to keep heterogeneous cultures together, despite current hubris of some of their more short-term-minded technocratic managers at present.

However, when formal institutions change in a more homogeneous culture, it is less of importance as it is just another quickly adjusted team in the wider common culture. The Korean state "does not fall apart" as many foreigners would anticipate whenever the constitution changes regularly, or when the whole Presidential bureaucracy is reorganized every five years with each incoming President, or when all political parties collapse at the same time and reformat yet with the same informal people in them with different party names. Nonetheless, what keeps Korea more stable than most, in its four points of democratic ethics as said above, has been its modicum of heterogeneity particularly in religious differences and regional animosities which gives more homogeneous Korea that nicer mixed culture of balance. It additionally gives Korea a civil location where formal institutions do rather matter, in the other manner above, around individual civil rights expansions or transparent procedures over time against the state. For instance, there is a long term formal institutional trend in Korea of an increasing part played by the Korean Constitutional Court in explicitly defining these four democratic ethics for instance—because they are hardly tacitly rewarded in a more homogeneous culture as a resource for teams in many ways. However on the other hand in more heterogeneous cultures if their constitutions, formal institutions, or political parties simultaneously collapse, all bets are off for maintaining the previous conditions of peace unless fear and brinkmanship brings everyone immediately back to the table of compromise.

In conclusion, the ancient Greek writer Polybius (c. 200–c. 118 BCE) wrote in his *Histories* a classic statement of preference for a *mixed political system* and a for a constitution with separation of powers in his analysis of the Roman Republic. Polybius's words survived to inspire the constitutional engineering of the European Enlightenment and the United States nearly 2000 years later. However, the argument here has been for the value of a '*mixed culture.*' Such a mixed culture has its own dual benefits to political science. On the one hand, cultural heterogeneity maintains the four ethical benefits of formal institutions and the two technical creative benefits or lived freedoms of individual innovations or cultural innovations. On the other hand, a more homogeneous common culture would be more innately (and beneficially) hamstrung by such six 'benefits' mentioned earlier, instead of held together by them as heterogeneous cultures are, and yet would still conserve the quicker collective innovation of a nation. Thus in a slightly mixed culture, the benefits of both can be preserved.

Thus, a culture that is a 'more homogeneous culture with some heterogeneous characteristics' balances the dangers of either extreme. The six total innovative and ethical benefits above should keep us inspired enough to keep a more heterogeneous culture alive and to find solutions to do so. Korea luckily got a modicum of a mixed culture, and thus got a slight amount of heterogeneous ethical benefits 'for free' via its religious plurality and its regional animosities as 'good accidents' that aided the slow advance of more transparent dynamics and more representative politics over time in its modern development. Policies of its export-led economics added a good choice toward more heterogeneous influences on the country as well. However, other larger and more heterogeneous nations, or larger and more homogeneous nations as well, may both have to work harder on finding policies to keep both kinds of larger states intact so they respectively avoid falling apart or avoid getting more digitally centralized censorship and repression capacities that equally could contribute to their own internal dissention and self-destruction as well. The overriding point is the potential selection pressure of a global digital economy, culture, and media for where success and failure in political, economic, and cultural survival are allocated across different modern nations indicate that high levels of heterogeneity may be toxic and divisive, and create crises in themselves in moving forward as a nation.

There is an irony here that a more heterogeneous culture is more likely to go through greater democratic pressures having greater individual ethics yet lacking the collective innovation and true civic spirit undergirding it to make it actually work. Such a bureaucratic and legalistic approach to democratization, without cultural civics, seems a hollow and standoffish republic of more court battles than compromises for consensus. Another irony is that most civic benefits come from a more homogeneous culture than from a more heterogeneous culture, yet in a more homogenous culture there is less likelihood of transparent governmental apparatuses and more likelihood of corruption to block expression of civic culture. Thus, neither greatly homogenous cultures nor greatly heterogeneous cultures seem ideal in their dichotomized and equally 'half complete' modern republics. Both have problems. Both have good features. As said above, perhaps the greater hybrid cultural qualities behind Korean developmental policies that have contributed to its stability and durability, compared to other developing countries, equally come from Korea having a equally a mixed culture of homogeneous and heterogeneous factors that benefit great collective action toward fast development drives. This helps hold together more transparent democratic procedures, individualist ethics, or regional divisions to challenge dictatorial repression during the development drive, or now, to stop repression under greater potentials for digital censorship in the twenty-first century.

At present in 2023, it seems all of the more heterogeneous cultures of the geographically larger and demographically larger nations are falling apart—resolving into multiple, hostile, and competing mid-size regional heterogeneous cultures within them when such nations are placed under digital globalization. Therefore, if we care deeply about the greater individual and cultural innovation that comes from such heterogeneous cultures, as well as if we care deeply about cultivating situations that preserve living democratic ethics of individual civil rights, public transparency, and democratic formal institutions in our modern republics, what is of paramount concern is finding ways to balance more homogeneous cultures with a modicum of more heterogeneous divisions, as well as finding ways to balance more heterogeneous cultures with a modicum of fresh common homogeneous collective ethos.

This fresh collective ethos might be like a clear image of the future to share for such heterogeneous nations so they have some way to see beyond their growing divisions to make it through the digital bottleneck to participate more successfully in digital globalization, instead of only have an image of falling apart within it. This section of the book aims to provide that image of the future of why more heterogeneous cultures should hold together instead of digitally falling apart. This would be in order to have more heterogeneous cultures continue to give us their unique innovations of carrying and reproducing a living cultural tradition that rewards a transcendent personal ethics and rewards the slow consensus of democratic ethics out of their greater heterogeneity, instead of only letting the homogeneous inherit the earth which may only reward faster responses, group ethics, repression of dissent, and corruption.

References

ACTP RF. (2022). ACTP RF announced results of the VIII National Rating of Technology Parks of Russia—2022. *Association of Clusters, Technology Parks, and SEZ of Russia.* https://akitrf.ru/en/news/actp-rf-announced-the-results-of-the-viii-national-rating-of-technology-parks-of-russia-2022

Alesina, A., et al. (2003). Fractionalization. *Journal of Economic Growth, 8*, 155–194.

Anderson, B. (2006). *Imagined communities: Reflections on the origin and spread of nationalism* (New and Rev. ed.). Verso.

Ang, C. (2020, July 3). What does 1GB of mobile data cost in every country? *Visual Capitalist.* https://www.visualcapitalist.com/cost-of-mobile-data-worldwide/

Bauwens, M., Kostakis, V., & Pazaitis, A. (2019). *Peer to peer: The commons manifesto* (Illustrated ed.). Critical, Digital and Social Media Studies. University of Westminster Press.

BBC. (2012). South Korea's real-name net law is rejected by court. www.bbc.com/news/technology-19357160

Binder, M. (2023, April 7). Elon Musk apparently on the outs with Matt Taibbi over Twitter-Substack feud; Taibbi said he would no longer use Twitter after it blocked Substack. Musk then unfollowed him. *Mashable.* https://mashable.com/article/elon-musk-matt-taibbi-breakup-substack-twitter-feud

Calcea, N. (2021, June 11). How the G7's economic power has diminished. *The New Stateman.* https://www.newstatesman.com/business/economics/2021/06/how-g7-s-economic-power-has-diminished

Castells, M (Ed.). (2004). *The network society: A cross-cultural perspective.* Edward Elgar.

Cline, E. H. (2021). *1177 B.C.: The year civilization collapsed: Revised and updated.* Princeton University Press.

Cocks, T. (2023, July 20). More than 40 nations interested in joining BRICS, South Africa says. *Reuters.* https://www.reuters.com/world/more-than-40-nations-interested-joining-brics-south-africa-2023-07-20/

Conte, L. (2023, July 21). DNC leadership tries to censor RFK, Jr. as He testifies at congressional hearing on censorship. *The Kennedy Beacon.* https://thekennedybeacon.substack.com/p/dnc-leadership-tries-to-censor-rfk

Cooper, D. (2011, August 12). South Korea plans to end "real name" web requirements. *Covington.* www.InsidePrivacy.com/international/south-korea-plans-to-end-requirements-for-internet-users-to-use-their-real-names/

Copson, J. (2023, June 29). Star Wars casts first-ever transgender star in major role for new TV series, *Metro.* https://metro.co.uk/2023/06/29/star-wars-casts-first-ever-transgender-star-in-major-role-for-new-tv-series-19036108/

Czech, P. (2020, August 18). Forget Silicon Valley: Poland is creating its own deep-tech startup hub. *Nasdaq.* https://www.nasdaq.com/articles/forget-silicon-valley%3A-poland-is-creating-its-own-deep-tech-startup-hub-2020-08-18

Dahir, A. L. (2019, September 18). Chinese firms are driving the rise of AI surveillance across Africa. *Quartz.* https://qz.com/africa/1711109/chinas-huawei-is-driving-ai-surveillance-tools-in-africa

Das, S. (2021, March 4). 8% of anon cryptocurrency accounts switch to real-names in South Korea, so far. *CCN.com.* https://www.ccn.com/8-anon-cryptocurrency-accounts-switch-real-names-south-korea-far/

Dou, E. (2021, December 14). Documents link Huawei to China's surveillance programs. *The Washington Post.* https://www.washingtonpost.com/world/2021/12/14/huawei-surveillance-china/

Editorial Board. (2023, March 27). The IRS makes a strange house call on Matt Taibbi; An agent shows up at the home of the Twitter files journalist who testified before Congress. *Wall Street Journal.* https://www.wsj.com/articles/irs-matt-taibbi-twitter-files-jim-jordan-daniel-werfel-lina-khan-84cc518

Ersozoglu, E. (2020, May 28). Huawei and the Chinese surveillance network in Africa. *SOFREP: Military Grade Content.* https://sofrep.com/news/huawei-and-the-chinese-surveillance-network-in-africa/

Fearon, J. (2003). Ethnic and cultural diversity by country. *Journal of Economic Growth, 8*, 195–222.

Gill, I., & Kharas, H. (2006). *An East Asian renaissance: Ideas for economic growth.* The World Bank. https://openknowledge.worldbank.org/bitstream/handle/10986/6798/399860REPLACEM1601OFFICAL0USE0ONLY1.pdf

Hayes, S., & Roache, M. (2020, January 31). Why the film industry is thriving in the Russian wilderness. *Time.* https://time.com/longform/film-industry-russia-yakutia/

Isenberg, N. (2016). *White trash: The 400-year untold history of class in America.* Viking.

Jackson, J. (2023, February 3). Poland's reverse brain drain: Meet the Poles returning home to work in its booming tech sector. *EuroNews.Next.* www.euronews.com/next/2023/02/03/polands-reverse-brain-drain-meet-the-poles-returning-home-to-work-in-its-booming-tech-sect

Jang, G., & Lim, J. (2021, August 17). Technologies of trust: Online authentication and data access control in Korea. *Carnegie Endowment for International Peace.* https://carnegieendowment.org/2021/08/17/technologies-of-trust-online-authentication-and-data-access-control-in-korea-pub-85163

Jennings, J. (2010). *Globalizations and the ancient world.* Cambridge University Press.
Jili, B. (2020, December 11). The spread of surveillance technology in Africa stirs security concerns. *Africa Center for Strategic Studies.* https://africacenter.org/spotlight/surveillance-technology-in-africa-security-concerns/
Jung, N.-y. (2017, January 23). Park sues reporter over blacklist. *The Chosunilbo.* http://english.chosun.com/site/data/html_dir/2017/01/23/2017012301374.html
Karl, T. L. (1997). *The paradox of plenty: Oil booms and petrol-states.* University of California Press.
KBS World. (2023a, July 10). Face registration to open for Incheon airport's 'smartpass' app. *KBS World.* https://world.kbs.co.kr/service/news_view.htm?lang=e&Seq_Code=179006
KBS World. (2023b, July 12). COVID-19 Q-code requirement for int'l arrivals to end on Saturday. *KBS World.* https://world.kbs.co.kr/service/news_view.htm?lang=e&Seq_Code=179073
KBS World. (2023c, July 23). S. Korea likely to lift remaining quarantine requirements for COVID-19 in early August. *KBS World.* https://world.kbs.co.kr/service/news_view.htm?lang=e&Seq_Code=179312
Kim, B.-e., & Chung, H.-c. (2016, December 6). Park spent 90 minutes hair styling when 315 students were trapped in sinking ferry. *The Korea Times.* https://koreatimes.co.kr/www/nation/2022/09/113_219630.html
Kim, K. (2018, October 16). Woes of government driven standard—Korean PKI implementation 1999–2018. *IEEE Standards University E-Magazine.* https://www.standardsuniversity.org/e-magazine/october-2018-volume-9-issue-3-privacy-freedom-human-rights/woes-of-government-driven-standard-korean-pki-implementation-1999-2018/
Kim, K.-e. (2022). Korea scraps vaccine pass mandate after court ruling. *Joseon Ilbo.* http://english.Joseon.com/site/data/html_dir/2022/01/17/2022011700562.html
Kim, K.-h. (2015, December 28). Underground economy still huge. *The Korea Herald.* https://www.koreaherald.com/view.php?ud=20151228000945
Kim, S.-h. (2020, February 26). Over 400,000 sign petition to impeach President Moon. *The Korea Herald.* http://www.koreaherald.com/view.php?ud=20200226000605
Kim, U., & Whitaker, M. D. (2013). Network subversion: The contrasting effects of multiple networks on bribery in South Korea. *International Journal of Law, Crime and Justice, 41*, 16–35.
Korea Times. (2021, December 10). High-school student files constitutional petition against vaccine pass expansion. *The Korea Times.* https://koreatimes.co.kr/www/nation/2023/04/251_320332.html
Lago, C. (2021, February 4). How Israel became a tech powerhouse. *The New Statesman.* www.thenewsstatesman.com/science-tech/2021/02/how-israel-became-tech-powerhouse
Lawson, J. (2022). Disney unleashes even more wokeness, ignores 'go woke go broke' lessons. *STG Report.* https://www.sgtreport.com/2022/05/disney-unleashes-even-more-wokeness-ignores-go-woke-go-broke-lessons/
Levine, Y. (2018). *Surveillance valley: The secret military history of the internet.* Public Affairs/Hachette Book Group.
Lukes, S. (2021). *Power: A radical view, third edition.* Bloomsbury Academic.
Maas, J. (2022, September 9). 'Squid Game' Star Lee Jung-Jae Joins Disney+ 'Star Wars' Series 'The Acolyte', *MSN.com* https://www.msn.com/en-us/movies/news/e2-80-98squid-game-e2-80-99-star-lee-jung-jae-joins-disney-2b-e2-80-98star-wars-e2-80-99-series-e2-80-98the-acolyte-e2-80-99/ar-AA11BSAN
Magnates Media. (2023). The secret Chinese company that owns everything [Tencent/WeChat] (Documentary). *YouTube.* https://www.youtube.com/watch?v=51fWzJ-A5w4
McCart, C. (2022, December 20). Korea cybersecurity statistics. *Comparitech.* https://www.comparitech.com/blog/information-security/korea-cybersecurity-statistics/
MGM Research. (2019). G20 GDP rankings, 2019. *MGM Research.* https://mgmresearch.com/g20-nations-gdp-rankings-2019
Morozov, E. (2011). *The net delusion: The dark side of internet freedom.* Public Affairs.

Oh, M., & Larson, J. F. (2019). *Digital development in Korea: Lessons for a sustainable world* (2nd ed.). Routledge Advances in Korean Studies. Routledge.

Papa, M. (2023, June 25). How long will the dollar last as the world's default currency? The BRICS nations are gathering in South Africa this August with it on the agenda, *Fortune,* https://fortune.com/2023/06/25/dollar-reserve-currency-brics-brazil-russia-india-china-south-africa/

Park, S.-s. (2020, February 27). Coronavirus: 1 milion sign petition calling for Moon Jae-in's impeachment. *The Korea Times.* https://www.koreatimes.co.kr/www/nation/2021/12/113_285196.html

Pasquale, F. (2015). *The black box society: The secret algorithms that control money and information.* Harvard University Press.

Reuters. (2023). *LIVE: Presidential candidate Robert F. Kennedy Jr. testifies to House* [Judiciary subcommittee on the 'Weaponization of the Federal Government.'] https://www.youtube.com/watch?v=XrWh_LtNxCA

Richardson, A. (2023, July 24). 44 countries now interested in joining BRICS as multipolar world takes shape: Report. *The Daily HODL: News and Insight for the Digital Economy.* https://dailyhodl.com/2023/07/24/44-countries-now-interested-in-joining-brics-as-multiploar-world-takes-shape-report/

Roh, J. (2019, May 27). Petition calling for impeachment of South Korea's Moon to force a response. *Reuters.* https://www.reuters.com/article/us-southkorea-moon-petition-idUSKCN1SX0XR

Routley, N. (2019, November 27). Mapped: The 1.2 billion people without access to electricity. *Visual Capitalist.* https://www.visualcapitalist.com/mapped-billion-people-without-access-to-electricity/

Roy, B. (2022, December 5). Who is Matt Taibbi? Elon Musk Twitter files release explained. *Sportskeedia.* https://www.sportskeeda.com/pop-culture/who-matt-taibbi-elon-twitter-files-release-explained.

Sandbrook, R., Edelman, M., Heller, P., & Teichman, J. (2007). *Social democracy in the global periphery: Origins, challenges.* Cambridge University Press.

Sassen, S. (2001). *The global city: New York, London, Tokyo* (2nd ed.). Princeton University Press.

Shim, E. (2021, June 17). South Korea exempts recipients of Chinese vaccines from quarantine. *United Press International.* https://www.upi.com/Top_News/World-News/2021/06/17/skorea-South-Korea-Chinese-vaccines-approve/5551623946941/

Shin, H. (2022, January 14). South Korea court exempts teens, supermarkets from vaccine passes. *Reuters.* https://www.reuters.com/business/healthcare-pharmaceuticals/skorea-extends-distancing-curbs-ahead-holidays-omicron-wave-2022-01-14/

Shin, H., & Kim, H. (2023, February 16). In South Korea, free subway rides for the elderly become a political headache. *Reuters.* http://www.reuters.com/world/asia-pacific/south-korea-free-subway-rides-elderly-become-political-headache-2023-02-16/

Son, W., & Whitaker, M. D. (2020). The danger of a single technology: locked into a national digital signature in a globally digital era; South Korea's attempt at standardizing a "National PKI" framework (1999–2015). A study in path dependence that shows the danger of mandating a single technology (Manuscript article, dissertation summary of Dr. Wonbae Son).

Standing, G. (2011). *The precariat: The new dangerous class.* Bloomsbury.

Statista. (2020). Number of NPKI certificates issued in South Korea from 2000 to 2020 (in million cases). *Statista.* https://www.statista.com/statistics/1298952/south-korea-npki-certificates-issued/

Statisa. (2022). Film industry in Russia—Statistics & facts. *Statista.Com.* https://www.statista.com/topics/6719/film-industry-in-russia/

Taibbi, M. (2023). 1. TWITTER FILES #19: The great Covid-19 Lie machine; Stanford, the Virality Project, and the censorship of "true stories". https://twitter.com/mtaibbi/status/1636729166631432195

Tackett, N. (2014). *Destruction of the medieval Chinese aristocracy.* Harvard University Asia Center, Distributed by Harvard University Press.

Trajkovska, B. (2019). Warsaw's startup ecosystem at a glance. *EU Startups*. https://www.eu-startups.com/2019/01/warsaws-startup-ecosystem-at-a-glance/

Trent, J. (2023, July 20). Leslye Headland reveals 'Star Wars: The Acolyte' does not feature an actual war, *Bounding into Comics*. https://boundingintocomics.com/2023/07/20/leslye-headland-reveals-star-wars-the-acolyte-does-not-feature-an-actual-war/

Vorhies, Z., & Heckenlively, K. (2021). *Google Leaks: A whistleblower's exposé of big tech censorship*. Skyhorse.

We Are Social/Hootsuite. (2019). *Digital 2019: Global Internet use accelerates.*. https://wearesocial.com/blog/2019/01/digital-2019-global-internet-use-accelerates

Whitaker, M. D. (2005). *Toward a bioregional state: A series of letters on political theory and formal institutional design in the era of sustainability*. Iuniverse.

Whitaker, M. D., & Pawar, P. (2020). Commodity ecology: From smart cities to smart regions via a blockchain-based virtual community platform for ecological design in choosing all materials and wastes. In *Blockchain Technology for Smart Cities*. Springer.

Wilkinson, R. & Pickett, K. (2011). *The spirit level: Why greater equality makes societies stronger* (Rev. and Updated ed.). Bloomsbury Publishing.

Woodhams, S. (2019, September 12). Huawei, Africa and the global reach of surveillance tech. *DW.com*. https://www.dw.com/en/huawei-africa-and-the-global-reach-of-surveillance-technology/a-50398869

Xu, L. (2019, December 3). Real name virtual bank accounts required for South Korean cryptocurrency exchanges. *Associated Press*. https://apnews.com/press-release/newswire/cryptocurrency-technology-business-asia-south-korea-303f99053172b8d5cd093757426e52dd

Yonhap. (2021). S. Korea to adopt 'vaccine passport' showing person's COVID-19 vaccination status: PM. *YonhapNews Agency*. https://en.yna.co.kr/view/AEN20210401002700315

Chapter 11
The Future of the Korean Wave and the World

11.1 Four Scenarios in the Future of the Korean Wave

What will happen to the global Korean Wave into the future? This is an extension of arguments about Korea as already beyond the digital bottleneck, and already working well in the triple challenges of a global digital economy, culture, and media, so how much further can Korea go? Plus, will other nations join Korea in this, or will Korea remain paramount for a while longer? The global Korean Wave may be only the first example of this kind of a fresh global cultural thrall almost exclusively aided by global digital networks. Korea is blessed in having durable 'push' factors priming it from the Korean public state, the Korean for-profit private companies, and now even global American OTT operators like Netflix, and yet a potentially less durable 'pull' factor from an innately fey global entertainment public.

Considering these questions, *four different organizational trends* of the global Korean Wave are competing for dominance. Therefore, we can project *four different scenarios of the future of global digital culture* based on each of them: (1) will it be a future with a multi-polar global culture and multi-polar global economy?; or, (2) will the future increasingly look like 'global Koreanization' as other nations' failing cultural waves simply exploit the global popularity of the Korean Wave and Korean management expertise in their own cultural production or material production?; or, (3) will the future be a centralized global digital culture managed and distributed from a mere handful of de-nationalized global platforms? Will the global future 'culture from anywhere' be only a commodity kept nowhere except in vast international 'cultural holding companies' owning global intellectual property empires with content from everywhere, de-nationalized and loyal only to themselves as private global empires, rent-seeking off a global digital fandom managed from anywhere, and hollowing out all nations (even Korea) by consolidating intellectual property and global users from all over the world into themselves? Fourth, (4) will various regional commons develop around material production by default as many larger nations may collapse or smaller nations merge, and yet share a larger globalized digital commons?

G.-C. Shin and M. D. Whitaker, *The Korean Wave in a Post-Pandemic World*,
https://doi.org/10.1007/978-981-99-3683-0_11

Scenario #1 is a durable multi-polar global culture and multi-polar global economy. The global Korea Wave will be the first of many other global cultural waves from other developing countries that have the capacity to become other digitally strong "K-Nations." The Korean Wave will thus rise and fall in the future itself with the competition of and the completion of a truly more multi-polar world that becomes more popular in its cultural offerings. The power of Americanization and of Europe in global culture will continue to recede as everyone else rises. The Chairman of HYBE that manages BTS already says he feels these three points are happening.

For now, on that last point, the economic and cultural wealth of this first K-Nation is equally confusing and worrying to existing powerful 'European heritage' nations. This is because many North American or European nations seem to be falling apart economically, demographically, and culturally in the past decades, losing their more homogenous cultural identity and economic edge. Meanwhile, South Korea does keep durably growing its economic and cultural power. This cannot simply be put down to other countries' lockdown policy choices from 2020 to 2023 and its aftermath—because South Korea locked down as well. The roots of decline seem much earlier yet definitely have accelerated during the lockdown period of the 'global West' (Western Europe, Canada, Australia, United Kingdom, New Zealand, and the United States—yet less decline for Scandinavia since Sweden avoided coercive masks, lockdowns, and injections and was just fine). One theme of this book (among many) has been the changing media regime behind all these other surface changes, with Korea ahead of the curve in its transition through the digital bottleneck. Previously powerful countries within previous media regimes are having a more difficult transition time, though of course only one factor hardly explains everything in history. In the United States, there have been heightened cultural divisions between 'woke versus conservative', growing economic collapse and inflation, major American bank runs, failures, and bailouts by April 2023, about two-dozen "BRICS +" countries (to coin a phrase) wanting de-dollarization to build their own collective international reserve currency starting at their August 2023 meeting in South Africa, and increasing totalitarian-style repressive governments and digital censorship in the global West that would make a Chinese Communist blush—or celebrate. Some ideologically leftist Westerners or minorities in the global West celebrate a digital totalitarian Maoist model taking over a global West, enforcing woke cultural change via more than state policies though from states ordering platform managers to conduct censorship in 'shadowbans' (throttling down online shares and popularity in 'deboosting' them without letting people know they are banned by making them unsearchable or making posts unable to be seen by everyone), search string hiding, 'ghost deletion' (a deletion that a user is unable to see, though it is seen as deleted for others), and 'de-platformization.' Besides, in our fresh digital media regime, people come to follow and to 'friend' (which has become a verb) only those judged in their own homogeneous cultural background online, and come to 'defriend' and hate their fellow citizens in a heterogeneous culture who think differently than they do. Just like burning books can lead to burning people, people who digitally 'deplatform' and 'de-monetize' others may find that is not enough and soon seek physically to 'de-job,' 'de-house,' 'de-child' (weaponize state child protection services against their online political enemies), 'un-bank,' unenroll, displace, and depopulate others in a cultural revolution against them.

So, a more multi-polar world equally is a global decline of the cultural power of the larger more heterogeneous cultures and nations of the global West as they break into open cultural war within themselves, and as they become just one of many cases of participants in a multi-polar world culture. Plus, in this scenario, Western zones themselves keep dividing into plural more homogeneous regional cultures against their past selves. The wider global media regime change spreads a global culture and starts to facilitate the internal breakdown of larger heterogeneous cultural principles in the global West into their own battling homogeneous cultural groups. This only accelerates openings for a wider multi-polar world of economics and culture as well by default. So, in Scenario #1, instead of only seeing the economic and cultural rise of other developing countries to participate in their own global cultural waves in a shared multi-polar world, that multi-polar world comes by default via growing economic and cultural divisions in the hegemonic global West, just as strongly.

However, there is Scenario #2 of "Global Koreanization." Despite the ultimate desirability of Scenario #1 (except for the possible failures of larger more heterogeneous cultures), for the world truly to be multi-polar, it requires a great deal of catching up from less developed countries as well as quick solutions to catch up in the failing larger and more heterogeneous cultures of developed nations that have dominated past global cultural waves. Korea's 'mid-sized' more homogeneous culture, demography, and geographic territory along with its hybrid economic development policies already described encourages Korea to specialize in a fast-paced export-led economy more than other countries, as well as encourages Korea to have more synergistic national coordination to aid a global Korean Wave and to keep doing it. That synergistic and fast-paced global market adjustment is something that the Korean collective innovation does well with all the country's good choices and 'good accidents' mentioned above. Meanwhile, both other developing countries' political economies and more developed heterogeneous cultures start to falter in providing overarching cultural innovations to stick together in their own national populations' minds or the world. Thus, *the rise of other developing countries or the cultural durability of larger Western ones now is rarely seen currently*, posing a dual problem for the multi-polar global culture of Scenario #1.

Plus, against the more multi-polar world of global culture in Scenario #1, if the United States' Hollywood, Broadway, or Netflix keeps banking on paying to produce content from the Korean Wave itself or just starts to hire already-famous Korean stars from the Korean Wave in the declining profit of its own American national entertainment industry, this will effectively stop such a cultural revivification of a multi-polar world culture if even the United States starts to rely on Korea more for discovery of popular cultural content production and Korean idol-driven profit. Next, against the more multi-polar world of global culture in Scenario #1, if less developed countries as well are unable to compete in material products, digital hardware, or digital cultural production, they will simply rely more on Korea as well. Hence we get more of the world culture run by Korean Cosmax, Korean Weverse, and Korean-produced yet OTT broadcast global cinema that is already developing now. We get more of a world culture where other countries just hire popular Koreans for 'their own' national movies, concerts, and festivals—because it makes current economic sense in the short term.

This is the big open question that only the future can know: is Korea to be remembered as a *harbinger* of what other multi-polar states and cultures can do now or will later do across these same global networks (Scenario #1), or will Korea remain an *outlier* already far ahead and only getting further ahead because of other nations' internal or external/global-level difficulties of coordinating such a competing global cultural production and distribution (Scenario #2)? This is something Korea has historically done for decades now. So, it simply makes more economic sense currently to keep hiring Korean skill in the global material economy and the global digital economy, and thus to have other countries continue their own support of Global Koreanization as well. This applies to a variety of fields already discussed whether in the global entertainment management and sales platform of HYBE's Weverse, or in Netflix's CEO promising Korean President Yoon to continue to pump billions of dollars into global Korean Wave productions for its own American corporate interests, or in the global cosmetics production and foreign brand invention by Korean Cosmax behind the scenes, inventing and serving hundreds of other 'national' (sic) and international brands. Cosmax's hard work of market intelligence for adjusting material production in cosmetics over time in all regions of the world with its already globalized production facilities on many continents is a far better and unique global Korean professional service for all nations' cosmetics companies than for them to reinvent the wheel in other countries that may fail anyway against such an established Korean durable economic and cultural player like Cosmax that has seen ups and downs of a global economy several times already and survived each time. The same can be said for the growing entertainment capacities of HYBE/Weverse as it bought the American management company of Scooter Brown and thus now owns all back catalogues of Ariana Grande and other major American entertainers in the process. HYBE then tried to buy into SK Entertainment in early 2023 and yet abandoned the idea when against much higher financed players—that happen to be Korean as well like Kakao. (Choi, 2023). However, HYBE's Weverse will be the global platform that other SK Entertainment idols will now use in more of an alliance instead of a buyout. Many American stars now use Korea/HYBE's Weverse for organizing their online digital fandoms as well. Korea's Naver and Kakao respectively have bought even more international platforms of digital content like Wattpad or Radish. All of this is only continuing a more consolidated and synergistic Global Koreanization across platform services and talent management of anyone worldwide, even if the global Korean Wave declines.

If this strategy is copied worldwide and other nations' cultural or material industries merely join in the Korean Wave, or prefer Korean global platform management and services, they will face their own declining national cultural or even material productions. Thus, the promised scenario of a multi-polar global cultural world would only resemble more of a Global Koreanization just as it represented a more global Americanization before or a global Anglo-British cultural wave before, in the Victorian era. If there is to be a multi-polar world, it may be a multi-polar world of Americanization and Koreanization only now in other words. Plus, if Korea pulls further ahead of other 'multi-polar' nations, it will keep underdeveloping the material, cultural, and digital capacities of other dependent nations and only reinforce Korea's outlier status in Global Koreanization, instead of reinforcing Korea's potential harbinger status in a more multi-polar economy and culture.

Korea's representative soft power has been spread through various media around the world thanks to information and communication technology. It has formed a durable global digital fandom that takes away even Americanized or Japanese teen images of the future and replaces them in these developed countries with Global Koreanization. Even before 2015, the top winners in Japanese pop culture already started to be K-Pop. (Hong, 2014) By April 2023, three separate members of the currently disbanded Korean boy group of BTS still top the Japanese Omicron music charts with both their solo efforts and albums as well. The same is happening in the USA from 2018 onward with the top American cultural winners becoming Korean musical groups, Korean films, and with even Korean movie stars from *Squid Game* being hired to be a lead Hollywood actor in the next *Star Wars* movie franchise in the upcoming Disney+ film "The Apprentice."

The Korean Wave though is without a jingoistic military or culturally supremacist association, as the British, Americans, or Japanese before them. This makes the global spread of the digital fandom of Global Koreanization potentially far wider in cultural acceptance because it will be a less polarizing global cultural wave. This leads to a love for Korean products, allowing companies to utilize cultural marketing as a source of competitive advantage, and allowing Korea a larger capacity now in global culture all out of proportion to its geographic or economic scale in the world-system compared to countries many times its size demographically or economically. Plus, it leads declining American or British firms to ally with Global Koreanization, further strengthening Scenario #2.

After 2020, Global Koreanization becomes a conquest beyond the world's commercial teen culture into more adult institutional recognition in other countries, as other countries' cultural offerings are being outclassed even in their own national awards. For instance, there was the historic feat that the Korean movie *Parasite* (2019) won in four *American* movie award categories including the Academy Award for Best Picture. Plus, the K-pop boy group BTS achieved the top spot on the *American* Billboard Chart and Japanese Omicron charts. This shows the global Korean Wave keeps reaching the peak in film and music culture, two major genres of world popular culture. Plus, Korean films even now regularly win in the more elitist international French Cannes Film Festival typically dominated by European art film and documentary producers. In short, with these more institutional foreign conquests now, the global Korean Wave has begun truly as a Korean Globalization instead of simply as a single part of a multi-polar world culture. It is now said that Korea is on the cusp of doing what the United States was doing by the 1940s and 1950s, showing a potential of creating a transnationally global popular culture.

For Scenario #3, it argues differently. Instead of particular countries' national cultural waves or national cultural industries mattering at all in the future, the fundamental result of the expansion of the multi-polar media market is the invention of a common globalized digital market environment. This is due to the spread of the Internet with billions of mostly evenly distributed similar access portals to it via the same smartphones worldwide in everyone's hands throughout the day. For one example, the global OTT services like the presumably "American" Netflix depend on innately global market sales instead of really coming from or relying on only one country in their business strategies or content origins. Therefore, all such OTT services come to fund intellectual property for each and all of the world's segmented cultural markets in which they want to participate within and which they come to own exclusive content from, from all over the world. For another example, this way Netflix operates is exactly how Korean Weverse or Korean Cosmax operates—with either of these respectively not really a Korean company though a global company profiting from knowing a great deal about all regional cultural variety of music management or cosmetic products desired from all over the world at the same time. So the world is now one global (digital) market in media, entertainment, and products increasingly in global platforms. The future is hardly limited to a Korean Globalization in other words. It is seen in American global Google services, or Amazon cloud hosting services worldwide, or Netflix's OTT services worldwide. It is seen in Korea's Weverse, Kakao, and Naver becoming owners of global intellectual property and global businesses—as global platforms that just started in Korea. Other Chinese, Korean, and Japanese OTT services plan to go as international as Netflix in the next few years.

So, if everyone globally is on the same global digital platforms accessing the same global markets and culture, and if most digital cultural content will be produced from a smaller number of already urban industrialized nations with that capacity, Scenario #3 will be more of a consolidated and homogeneous world instead of a multi-polar world. This will particularly be the case if the multi-polar culture will just be managed and served from the same consolidated global platforms similar to YouTube, Weverse, Cosmax, Netflix, Amazon, WeChat, AliPay, PayPal, Blackboard, Brightspace, Facebook, Instagram, TikTok, and Google today. These global homogeneous platforms come to want to have globally owned content, similar to Netflix, to create their own exclusive global digital fandoms. This can be seen in Korea's Weverse, HYBE, Naver, and Cosmax. As competition for global digital users by more urban industrial regional operators intensify, global standardizations and borderless cultural markets are being created. This erodes the concept of regional cultures served exclusively as regional cultural productions. Thus, one future value of broadcasting now includes global American platforms such as Google, Netflix, and Amazon. They are gradually increasing global broadcasting to global users, more expensive synergies in production, and global cultural purchases against more regional and nationally-protected cultural markets.

On the other hand, another future is a worldwide regional national reaction against Scenario #2 and against Scenario #3, back to Scenario #1 (or even Scenario #4, discussed momentarily). This would be similar to how the world reacted against a globalized Americanization after World War II (Mattelart, 2000). Even now there is a developing global reaction against many forms of cultural globalization, including the Korean Wave. Plus, the bigger global American FAANGs of the big tech giants of the world (an abbreviation for Facebook/Meta, Amazon, Apple, Netflix, and Google) are being filed down as we speak by anti-trust lawsuits from the U.S. federal government. Will the filing down of the fangs of other Korean digital empires be far behind? Has Kakao bitten off more than it can chew in the monopolization and consolidation of much of the digital services of Korea and now buying up other global platforms as well, similar to Naver's strategy? Even China is moving against Tencent, and has already moved against Jack Ma's Alibaba. Worldwide reactions from regional cultures in the plural or from movements toward national autonomy from the world-system are both against the 'platform globalization' of Scenario #3. This is seen in rising re-traditionalization and re-territorialization as ways to maintain and secure national cultural identity or even just compete in national markets by blocking entry of large global digital platforms.

However, the argument here is for the greater likelihood of Scenario #2 by default, at least for a while. This is because another single multi-polar K-Nation that would help flesh out Scenario #1 has yet to step up to the challenge of the deep Korean synergies of public state, private profit, and Korean culture in our fresh digital media regime in quite the same tenacious way as Korea when it started in earnest to try to globalize its regional Hallyu into a global Korean Wave in the late 1990s to the present. So, instead of a situation like after World War II in which many European national entertainment industries were gelled into existence in opposition to Americanization (toward Scenario #1), instead, by the second decade of the twenty-first century, many other countries are instead simultaneously hiring or lauding Korean stars and Korean expertise of the Korean Wave to make their declining national cultural waves or media industries more profitable (toward Scenario #2).

How long can this last? Who will mount an opposition? Will there be an opposition, or will this be the first start of how a multi-polar world culture works, having a top global Korean Wave ruling class merging into business partnerships and co-production alliances across all other past national global cultural production waves that are mostly British or American? Or will Scenario #1 merge with Scenario #3, into a '*vetted* multi-polar digital globalization' where only a handful of possible stronger global cultural players with enough capital and urban industrial markets for making such services (like the many global entries into OTT global services from China, Japan, and Korea instead of only the United States) battle it out exclusively in the big stakes money games of global digital culture, while hundreds of other multi-polar nations and their billions of users become just spectators in the global stadium seats of the global digital culture?

Regardless of the number of multi-polar global players, Scenario #3 is faceless platform globalization, i.e., global digital empires without any clear national or cultural connections at all. This kind of development simply treats all cultures as instrumental means to an end for global profits or global management instead of having any intrinsic moral value for cultural transmission or greater quality of life. Scenario #3 is a global surveillance, sponsorship, and censorship empire that could end all true cultural diversity entirely in a sea of globally-managed homogeneity despite 'competition' between similar global platforms. It could be a world of global metaverse applications centrally housed. However, few people seem to want this faceless non-national platformed future without a clear geography or identity. In 2022, the European Union threw a $400,000 metaverse party, and only six people (as avatars) showed up (Russia Today, 2022).

The argument is that we many have left a period of Scenario #1 back in the multiple regional cultural waves of the 1980s. Since then, there has been a slowly growing Scenario #2 which may lead into the globally underdevelopmental Scenario #3 of a global homogeneity. This may end major cultural innovation and change as driven by actual cultures and peoples themselves, instead of culture reflecting the same handful of global corporations' strategic funding patterns for global or segmented audiences. This may happen *unless we avoid it*. Ideally, we prefer Scenario #1 for the global level of heterogeneous (global) cultural diversity that preserves nations and will generate more national innovation and national cultural innovation in the plurality. The same has been said about the useful plurality that helped spark the Korean Wave itself. Plus, there is a durable place for everyone's national cultural production and sovereignty as a real world geographic check and balance on unchecked tyrannical powers of global level actors of Scenario #3. Development should avoid homogenizing all cultures as that would end their diversity from each other. If we are truly interested in cultural diversity, then global homogeneity and a mixing and consolidating movement of peoples worldwide into one mass homogeneous global culture is the opposite of maintaining cultural diversity. Instead, it is a global homogeneity based on having the same global heterogeneity everywhere.

A Scenario #4 that merges aspects of #1 and #3 might happen as well, in a more commons-based network that is simultaneously regional in material production while shared, digital, and global in a community based on an information commons (Bauwens et al., 2019). This kind of future scenario may be by default picking up the pieces of collapsed states or cultures, that become based on smaller durable cultural regions carved out of larger failed states as regions that survived the global digital storm themselves, and yet want the benefits of larger collaborations in digital production and digital culture as well by aligning with other regions of similar interests, like a "digital Hanseatic League." Scenario #4 may make sense as a developmental model (given the next section about Korean demographic decline and all other developed countries' demographic declines), if the Korean culture itself or many other urban industrial cultures start to come apart or be less populous over time. The economic and cultural externalities of living in an urban industrial zone for several generations start to show their common effects now as hampering basic family-based biological reproduction, and thus cultural reproduction, and thus shrinking the size of a country's past reproducible culture that wants to live in such an urban industrial dynamic at all.

In conclusion, there are four future scenarios (and some mixes of them) that we can see now happening in the Korean Wave. Which will be the stronger factor is unknown for the future. These four future scenarios are summarized. Scenario #1 was multi-polar globalization. This is a scenario of multiple strong and regionally-strong cultural waves interacting in plural without a single digitally globalized or consolidated empire. This is the breakdown of past Americanization and Europeanization. Scenario #2 was Global Koreanization, meaning all other multi-polar cultural waves voluntarily join the Korean Wave and a Korea-centric world. This is equally the breakdown of other multi-polar nations that are being underdeveloped by default due to joining the Korean Wave. Scenario #3 is a unified world with the same placeless global homogenized digital platforms of culture. Culture becomes cultural management, administrated and accessible (or censored) across the world from anywhere via the same kind of global digital platforms. Regardless of the platform's past national origin, all of these global digital platforms are streaming services, metaverse applications, homogeneous in services, and homogeneous in having the same consolidated global intellectual property on them that is multi-polar in content yet managed centrally. This is the future of Planet Google, Planet Netflix, Planet Cosmax, or Planet Weverse—different from the past's more nation-centric platforms that themselves are rapidly globalizing like global Chinese Tencent/WeChat or global Korea's Naver, Kakao, Weverse, or Coupang services. This is the breakdown of all cultural nations' own capacities instead of enhancement of them. Scenario #4 is a world of durable cultural regions, likely carved out of many larger state collapses contributed to by the effects of the media regime change and the cultural aftermath of groups on the periphery of Scenario #2 and #3, that wish to work together in alliance on digital hardware production and digital cultural production, despite sometimes being discontiguous geographically because they prefer materially local economies and yet equally prefer the competitive benefits of larger participation in a global digital information commons among themselves to maintain their autonomy from others.

11.2 A 'Fifth Gauntlet' or Just a Slowly Developing Problem with the Third Gaunlet, Undermining the Future of the Korean Miracle and Korean Wave?

This section is different than the previous sections. In previous sections, the questions asked about the future of the economic Korean Miracle or the future of the cultural Korean Wave have mostly been: "How can other nations keep up with or learn from Korea to apply its policies to their own development policies?".

In this section, the question for the future becomes soberly different. The question now is: "Can Korea keep up with itself, i.e., can Korea learn to fix its own growing internal problems of a declining birth rate combined with an increasingly alienated and isolated culture of economic exhaustion of elderly and youth alike that ultimately endangers both the durability of the economic Korean Miracle and the cultural Korean Wave?" Does a mad rush to be top of the world economically and culturally from 1997 along with growing economic inequality after that year increasingly now exhaust the past cultural transmission and thus change the spirit of the country instead of renew it as before in the virtuous cycles mentioned earlier? However, this biologically reproductive exhaustion and thus exhaustion of cultural transmission is occurring as an externality in many developed countries of the world, so it is a common problem to be solved.

Using terms mentioned before, instead of a virtuous cycle of Korea supercharging its economic development with a renewed cultural transmission each generation, Korea now starts to create its own viscous cycles of underdevelopment in creating more externalities in development than aggregate improvements. This starts to damage and even self-sabotage its previous uniquely successful virtuous cycles of development. In doing so, Korean development starts to undermine itself and undermine its own once stable internal culture, its middle class, its more equitable national economic stability, and even its demographics—instead of supercharging and strengthening all these as before. It is argued it *can* be changed back to the uniquely successful virtuous cycle of Korean development mentioned earlier that supercharges the culture in its own economic development instead of exhausts it culturally and biologically. Policy ideas for this are suggested.

First, let us look at the Korean case only and understand its growing vicious cycles of dynamics before comparisons about the same phenomena in other long-term developed cultures. What exactly is this economic and cultural problem of resilience that Korea faces? A rising two-part interactive problem is occurring 'backstage' of the global Korean economy and the cultural Korean Wave. This problem is not in the loss of an ongoing inventiveness or a loss of quick responsiveness, though a loss in durability of the Korean culture and its biological transference to the next generation itself, with fewer children, less happy families, more isolation, and more depression and suicide. Particularly after 1997, Korea seems to start to come apart into a more hopeless world for an increasing number of youth as well as elderly without a future despite the wider Korean economy and the cultural Korean Wave growing. The previous fast development drive and even the hypercompetitive Korean Wave seems to take the blame as it gets more digital. How will this potentially affect attrition later in the Korean economy and the Korean Wave?

Even the Korean Wave itself is recognizing these social problems by making a profitable market of discussing them. The lyrics or narrative of Psy's "Gangnam Style" (2012), Bong Joon-ho's film *Snowpiercer* (2013), Bong Joon-ho's film *Parasite* (2019), or Hwang Dong-hyuk's *Squid Game* (2021) all discuss social inequality issues of the gap of rich and poor. As these four are some of the most simultaneously critically award-winning and popular offerings of the global Korean Wave, note all of these have a common theme. They provide tragic-comedy about the increasing faking and lies of the poor, either desperate to become rich or to merely pretend to be rich to keep up status symbolism, or they provide tragic-comedy about the delusional isolation of the unhappy rich themselves.

One part of this interactive problem is a *concern about growing economic polarization* and lack of hope within Korea itself. This is the 'real world off-stage' in the dark beyond the bright klieg lights of production in the global Korean Wave. As the country primes a generally happy and hopeful show business of the global Korean Wave, in the real world, Koreans both young and old increasingly suffer a loss of hope with some of the greatest economic inequalities of any rich OECD country, the fastest aging society in the world, and ever larger portions of youth and elderly living alone in poverty in single-personal households self-isolated from each other, alienated in poverty, and unsure how to advance.

One way to measure this economic polarization is the suicide rate in Korea. From 1997, Korea shot up to having the highest levels of suicide in the OECD. Even though suicide has declined thankfully after 1998, the level remains far elevated above almost all other countries in the world. Another way to measure the stress of economic polarization is to track the rising behavioral addictions in Korea. The irony is rising behavioral addictions and escape into digital media in Korea started to carry a great deal of the Korean cultural transmission from the late 1990s particularly in the profitability of the online gaming industry. This started in the same period as the economic collapse of 1997 through 1998 where approximately 40% of the then-Korean middle class fell into poverty instead. The economic growth of Korea returned by 1999 to almost double digits, yet Korea failed to return the same. There is an argument that market instabilities catalyze behavioral additions, and in turn behavioral addictions become a market of addicts that can support extracting economic profit from them in a digital culture in turn. This can lead to a vicious cycle of behavior addictions, isolation, and growing economic profit from behavioral addictions that fail to provide an escape from the cycle into a more stable happiness (Anderson, 2010).

Another way to measure economic polarization is cultural. We can look at the Korean neologisms that express this emotional sadness, jadedness, and economic deprivation in Korean youth as they invent fresh terms to describe their 'stuck' lives in Korea. One of these earlier terms that started to be used in 2011 is the "Sampo sedae," or the 'three giving up generation,' which was published in the *Kyunghyang Shinmun*, a newspaper founded in 1946 by the Korean Catholic Church though still a newspaper strong with its historic Korean democratic leanings of the 1950s and 1960s since its modern CEO has to be elected by journalist employees. This term "sampo sedae" means a generation of youth who feel they have to give up 'courtship, marriage, and childbirth' due to economic constraints and the lack of ability to save for a different future that would follow a normal human course of life with these three important goals of happiness that they are forgoing. The point in the modern Korean context is now that the cultural and economic wealth transference through the normal family structure and life course is breaking down twice over: first, elders live longer and have to be taken care of financially which eats up seed capital; and second, this is seen as more of a burden which additionally postpones or dissolves wealth and real estate transfers particularly to youth in inheritance. Soon after 2011, others riffed on this theme, inventing terms for the "opo sedae" (the 'five giving up generation', adding employment and home ownership), then the "chilpo sedae" (the 'seven giving up generation,' adding interpersonal relationships and hope), then the "gupo sedae" (the 'nine giving up generation', adding health and physical appearance), then the suicidal "sippo sedae" or "wanpo sedae" (the 'ten giving up generation' that completely give up on life as well). In May 2018, an analysis of all 160,000 proposed public petitions in the Presidential National Petition of Korea for about eight months showed that the most talked about issues were "baby," "women" and "policy."

If a country and its cultural wave are held together by intergenerational family transferences of culture, wealth, and beliefs about images of the future that they give to each other, these very self-destructive family patterns and images that Koreans increasingly have dissolve their hope in basic economic and biologically normal futures, despite these critical themes themselves 'currently selling well' in the global Korean Wave. Plus, perversely in a second viscous cycle, it seems this decline in economics, health and demographics come to create even more addictive desperation for success (Anderson, 2010) that is seen now in Korea because domestic national problems continue to be unsolved. By 2015, according to the U.S. Pew Research Center, Koreans subjectively *felt* that economic inequality was the most threatening issue for them now even if other countries may have more economic inequality objectively per se than Korea of course.

Around the same year of 2015, other satirical terms like "Hell Joseon" and "Spoon class theory" were developed in Korea to reflect on feelings of a 'hellish, hopeless' society of growing up in a Korea with declining advancement, and one that misses capacities of advance on the normal ten factors of life increasingly seen as inaccessible because of the decline of intergenerational transfer. The "Spoon class theory" means a view that the 'spoon that is born in your mouth' determines everything, i.e., family wealth at birth becomes the most defining characteristic to a more stratified and 'stuck' Korean youth. Young Koreans increasingly felt that there are simply people born to different castes with the 'diamond, platinum, gold, and silver' spoons in their mouth in the top 5%, and others with only the 'bronze, steel, wooden, soil, and dirt' spoons in their mouth for the lower 95%. This is a decline in youth with a more optimistic future of meritocratic advancement for themselves, as if the ultimate value of hard work is inescapably nothing beyond a certain spoon stuck into your mouth when you are born.

Another way to measure economic polarization is more material and yet still cultural: the rising number of Koreans who are "single-person households," i.e., who live alone. Many more Koreans now both actively desire or feel forced to live alone in Korea, out of a poverty that they feel they are unable to escape or out of a poverty that they are actively adapting to by removing better material expectations of the future. It has a great deal as well to do with skyrocketing real estate prices in Korean cities as well as unstable employment in a digital economy. Some levels of the films of Bong Joon-ho's *Snowpiercer* or *Parasite* show the tragic-comedy of these key dynamics and background of this Korean slow cultural/biological collapse: desperate poor, bad one-room basement housing, skyrocketing real estate prices, and the wealth of a tiny stratospherically-rich population in conflict with the growing poor around them as they try to live together.

Instead of living in a 'Korean Wave party' and in a collective culture, many Koreans are alienated now from each other and live alone in the vastness of Korean cities—not in a "Gangnam Style" at all. Over one-third of households in Korea only have one person, and by 2021 single households were a record 40.1% of all households (Heo & Seo, 2021; Korea Times, 2020; Lee, 2022). Despite a public Confucian culture that values family-based hierarchies and traditions, now single person households are the most common household type in Korea from 2020, at 8.77 million, which was 39% of the total number of households at 22.7 million in 2020. By 2021, single households were a record 40.1% of all households. In 2020, the second most common type was two-person households at 5.26 million, or 23.1%. Only 30.6% of these people living alone owned their residence in 2019. Invert that and it means approximately 70% of people living alone did not own their residence in Korea in 2019, and of those, 47.3% lived in monthly rental that wasted their money or seed capital, and only 15.8% lived in long term leases based on large lump-sum loans in Korea called 'jeonse' apartments, with the lump-sum rent money returned to the tenant when the tenant leaves. Thus, about 50% of those who live alone have a permanent income drain on their future in rent without saving capital for something different. Plus, the income of all one-person households was only 42% of the average of all households, so even more feel unable to save for the future. Most Koreans who live along are in the major cities. Seoul has 20.8% of all single person households in Korea, and Pusan has only 6.8%.

Why are they living alone though? What do they say? One third says they live alone because of jobs, and 26.2% says because they wanted to be "independent" (Lee, 2022). However, how is this "independent" if single person homes require more instead of less state budget for their currently subsidized housing, or, how is this "independent" if there are more instead of fewer worries about greater ill health, bad diet, and medical emergency problems of people living alone without a more informal social safety net, which are the current governmental and social concerns? From another survey in 2020, there are push and pull factors why Koreans live alone. The larger number of about 42.5% said they desired voluntarily to live alone. Only 39.9% said they were pushed, driven by circumstance. Previously, two years earlier in 2018, it was reversed: fully 60.8% said then they were pushed to live along by circumstances (Chea & Moon, 2020). Thus, increasingly, youth or elderly living alone, in their 'sour grapes,' come to internalize living alone as a desirable a situation despite it being more forced on them and not of their own making entirely.

Either way, this reduces future families in Korea as well as reduces traditional Korean culture venues for transmission to the next generation. The above economic stresses impinge upon Koreans biologically and demographically. Korea now has the lowest female fertility and lowest population replacement in the world. This undermines intergenerational cultural transfer and *undermines cultural reproduction* itself in Korea that is behind the Korean Wave. By 2020, the South Korean population declined for the first time in modern history. By 2020, the number of births was down by 10% more from 2019. Though the country's fertility rate has been dropping steadily for decades, Korea by 2020 had another 'world first' of the lowest fertility rate ever recorded in any nation, at only 0.84 births per woman. This is well below a normal demographic replacement at around 2.1 births per woman (Lee & Botto, 2021). What about importing brides or husbands for more children in Korea? Foreign brides married to Korean men is the most common relationship, yet the concept of Korean mixed marriage is a very rare phenomenon and has been found to be generally unworkable, *demographically or culturally. Demographically*, it can hardly be a population replacement strategy because it so small in number. This kind of rare international marriage started to grow in Korea from 2000, with mostly only imports of other Asian countries' young females (first, mostly other Korean Chinese, and later, mostly Vietnamese) marrying typically older, rural, poorer Korean males. This was aided by marriage brokers and sometimes local rural governmental subsidies facilitating the marriage to stave off depopulation in their areas. However, in aggregate, this phenomenon peaked as long ago as 2005 with only approximately 30,000 annually receiving marriage visas, declining after that. (The Straits Times, 2014) So, this has always been a tiny amount of Korean mixed marriages, since the number of Koreans marrying foreign spouses increased from 4,710 in 1990 to only 33,300 in 2009—in a country of 51 million people now by 2023. (Kay, 2011) This has always been a miniscule number. From 2000 to 2014, only a total of 236,000 foreign women settled in South Korea via marriage, giving birth only to around 190,000 children, according to Korean state statistics. (The Straits Times, 2014) Korean governmental rules were adjusted in 2014 and in 2020 to try to minimize failed marriages and domestic violence by only allowing a marriage visa after a Korean language test or some third-language they had in common, or only allowing the marriage visa if some basic level of financial soundness existed in the Korean male, or only if the Korean male was without a history of past domestic violence (from 2020). Second, Korean mixed marriages are hardly a workable option *culturally*. This is due to such brides' or childrens' wide non-acceptance in the culture or even in their extended Korean family that values homogeneity. A survey by private Asan Institute for Policy Studies found that 32% of Koreans saw "mixed-race families as a threat to social cohesion." (The Straits Times, 2014) Plus, the school dropout rate of multi-ethnic Korean children from elementary school is said to be near 10%, likely due to peer bullying and non-acceptance. Ethnically pure Korean children have a dropout rate that is basically zero. Equally, the private Korea Women's Development Institute found in a 2012 survey that 40% of mixed-ethnic Korean marriages break down within the first five years: 48% blamed irreconcilable differences, and 21% cited low income levels. (The Straits Times, 2014) Did it improve after the added marriage visa vetting processes and rules in 2014? In a poll from 2017, it seems about the same as before 2014. Approximately 42% of foreign wives in Korea in 2017 still report domestic violence—physical, verbal, sexual, or financial—from a poll by the Korean National Human Rights Commission. By comparison, in a poll from 2016, 29% of native South Korean women said they were victims of domestic violence of various kinds—in a poll by Korea's Ministry of Gender Equality and Family. (Hollingsworth et al., 2020) Therefore, for these two rationales and many others, importing foreign women to have more mixed Korean children is hardly a workable option, demographically or culturally. Pragmatically, Korean children will have to come from Korean families in the future if there is a solution.

Plus, in addition to Korea having the world record now for the lowest population replacement ever recorded at 0.84 births per woman in 2020, Korea is a country that is said to have become the fastest "aging society" in the world as well. Plus, it has some of the highest levels of elder poverty in the world for a developed country. Plus, while a rapid aging society is seen as one cause of elderly people living alone (Heo & Seo, 2021), the core issue of that is that rapid growth of elder poverty occurs due to age discrimination by companies in Korea, since there is a very early informally-judged yet generally mandatory forced retirement for many Korean workers in companies at between 50 to 55 years of age and definitely before age 60.

On the other side, the high youth unemployment, temporary work contracts, and the high price of forming a family all are seen as the main causes for youth living alone and avoiding marriage and children. After 1997, Korea has had durable high levels of youth unemployment despite it having such a consumerist youth culture orientation in the global Korean Wave. Plus, buying a house for a future family and child as real estate prices in cities are skyrocketing under little economic advance becomes impossible for many. Therefore, for these interactive rationales, increasingly more Korean youth postpone courtship, marriage, and children ("sampo sedae") and postpone buying a house due to bad or poor employment ("opo sedae"), thus postponing or giving up on marriage and children and thus missing these domestic joys and deeper emotional lives. When asked why they remained single, 30% of single-person households in Korea said lack of money for not marrying, 14.4% said because of without job or without security in the current job in the future. Only a mere 12% said they *wanted* to remain single or without children (Lee, 2022).

In general, for Korean elderly and youth, more men live alone than women, 51.4% to 48.5%, yet the trend reverses over age 60 with more elderly women living alone. It is the more rural provinces of South Jeolla, Gangwon, and North Gyeongsang that have the highest percentage of single-person households, respectively 44.1, 42.8, and 41.8% of households being only one person. By age, people in their 20s are 19.1% of people living alone. People 70 or older are nearly the same at 18.1% of people living alone, and people in the 30s were almost the same at 16.8% of people living alone. However, the fastest growth demographic of people living alone are people in their 20s, increasing by 13.5% on the year, the highest rate of increase of all age groups in 2021 (Chae & Jeong, 2021). Overall, this means from 2020 about 12 out of 100 Koreans live alone (Chae & Moon, 2020). Therefore, more people are voluntarily living along over the last few years, giving up on family and children if they are young, and lacking an informal safety net of family or much income if they are elderly and retired in the mid 50s with expectations they might live over thirty more years.

All the information above show a future vicious cycle of biological decline and a decline of intergenerational cultural transmission has set in Korea. The culture of Korea is becoming more isolated and individualistic, endangering its past's more collectivist continuity. It is estimated at the rate of growth by 2047, the population of 30% of the cities of Korea will be people living alone unless trends change (Chae & Moon, 2020). People who live along seem to start to act more desperate financially, and start to speculate on the stock market more instead of really plan a personal future. For people living alone, they are now gambling on the stock market more. Their stock investment went up from 5.5% of their total assets before 2020, to 13.3% after 2020 (Chae & Moon, 2020). Young Koreans are additionally starting to speculate in cryptocurrency 'assets' as well, as they search for their own "all or nothing" style of solution similar to *Squid Game* out of desperation. As said earlier, does hopelessness drive the obsessive desperation to success seen in the Korean Wave even more? Regardless, it is hardly biologically or economically healthy to build your national economy on behavioral addiction problems (Anderson, 2010) like gambling on the stock market, real estate, or cryptocurrencies that are desperate quick rich schemes and substitutes for slowly growing skills for durable success itself. Fully 70% of Koreans who live alone say they are without any future plan to change this status. *More than half of people in their 20s* (53%) now plan to stay single as well (Anon, 2021).

However, Korea is not alone in living alone. Many highly developed urban industrial countries in Europe and Asia have the same vicious cycle that has set in deeply. For example, the percentage of households that are single people living alone is high in Finland (47%), Sweden (45.4%), Germany (42.1%), Korea (40.1%), Japan (38%), and France (38%). (Anon, 2021) Thus this problem is unfortunately becoming common across many supposedly 'successful' developed countries, except in the United States where only 15% of adults older than 18 years of age lived alone in 2021. This is up only 2% from 1960 (13%), and up only 1% from 2011 (14%) (U.S. Census Bureau, 2021).

In other words there is a common decline in many countries that are 'economically successful yet biologially/culturally failing.' As a common problem, it sounds like another developmental gauntlet to be solved in general development, however, it is equally now part of the social repercussions of extreme digital development and its growth of a precariat in that digital economy. (Standing, 2011) Therefore, many generally and digitally developed economies all are imploding culturally, demographically, and financially instead of consolidating or compounding their economic wealth. This has a lot to do with digitalization of the economy as well as an aging society combining. First, this does have much to do with the triple global storm mentioned earlier, since most of these countries are very digitally developed as well. For comparative examples, many countries are hampered by arriving at higher levels of an urban industrial economy yet with a culture that is shattered, alienated, or defeated in the process of achieving that increasingly digital development. Worldwide, this is now called the 'rise of the precariat.' This has come out of the intentional policies to promote a digital economy and its shrinking scale of shared economic advancement, the decline of stable jobs, the rise of smaller incomes and more part-time work, and a push toward a highly technical economy that requires endless retooling and insecurity instead of stable jobs. Second, for an aging society, this has come out of the success of economic development allowing for longer lives and better medical care to such an extent it is postponing or dissolving intergenerational transfer of wealth to the next generation—reducing their ability to start a family and reducing cultural transmission as well as biological scale of whole cultures.

On the first part about the long-term cultural and biological effects of a digital economy, this investment in an ever-changing digital economy has been done, so far, without consideration of the self-destructive cultural revolution in many developed countries that this digital development is creating (Standing, 2011). The first major example of this in East Asia happened in Japan. It helps to think about the difficulties of a continuing Japanese cultural wave in the 1990s as a cultural problem of a growing lack of desire instead of only an economic problem considering Japan's rising 'Hikikomori culture' of social withdrawal starting from Japan's economic collapses of the 1990s. Next, a related Japanese crisis is in the 'Karoshi culture' of working to death. After 2010, this Japanese generation now is known as the

Satori Generation, saying jadedly with sour grapes now their aimless Hikikomori state of isolation and zero advancement opportunities is instead a positive Buddhist enlightened state (called in Japanese 'satori'), since it is free from all material desires, travel, friends, or even hard drinking which is a characteristic of Japanese friendships, business culture, and salarymen.

Such a cultural revolution against participating in an urban industrial culture is now seen across East Asia though. The same ongoing economic stress and poverty creating a 'drop out' cultural revolution in Japan are creating a similar decline of children in Korea. As said before, this can be seen in what Koreans call the 'Sampo generation' (the 'three lacks') of youth tired of fighting to find marriage, children, or even courtship. This has been infinitely expanded into the "N-po" generation complaining of many wider 'common lacks' in life beyond these three. In Taiwan, this is the "Strawberry generation" of people who want to avoid stress as they 'bruise easily' like strawberries and want to avoid working hard or the social pressure to do so. Since the turn of the twenty-first century, the same is happening in China now in the very popular 'Tang Ping' movement of 'lying flat.' Chinese youth are happily embracing refusal to participate in the stressful Chinese economy and instead work very hard for better quality of life in poverty, instead of living for only workaholic stress, debt, and status with its materialism. By 2021, under Chinese lockdowns that saw the raw cruelty of the Chinese government weld people's apartments shut with them inside, the government additionally put most major Chinese cities under a digital martial law via smartphone geotagged QR codes that limited all movement. Their earlier unrepresentative digital social credit system became an added medical 'vaccine passport' system. It got ubiquitously turned on to the 'red/quarantine' status for millions even if healthy—just to stop citizen protests gathering against the Communist Party leadership or against large bank failures, instead of the 'vaccine passport' system really being used for 'health' at all in a false alibi for why it exists. The mask was off. Digitally managed lockdowns using digital IDs will be used for anything and everything forever, once in place. Soon in China, the passive and even positive Chinese outlook of Tang Ping escalated into the nihilistic and suicidal 'bai lan,' or 'let it rot' movement now passively refusing to participate in anything to do with the Chinese culture or the Chinese Communist Party (CCP) leadership that they feel is destroying their country and their will to live. Some segments of Chinese youth in the 'bai lan' movement simply await ongoing CCP policies they feel will collapse their state, society, and culture. Many modern urban industrial Chinese feel the best way to avoid all stress now is to 'let it rot', instead of trying to fix what many Chinese youth feel is their increasingly hopeless situation in a fast-developed and highly inequitable country with low economic stability or advancement anymore while locked into a digital police state and its social credit system.

In the UK, this is the aimless "NEET" category of youth (an abbreviation for 'not in education, employment, or training.'). In the United States, this is the slacker movement. None of these cultures above are transmitting a completely positive sharable image of the future anymore to their own youth or having many children. These subcultures that are developing are all cultural revolutions resolutely against participation in an urban industrial economy in their interpretation due to jobs of low chances of advancement that exploit them more benefit them.

Framed theoretically for commonality, the many different national contexts of this 'drop out' movement show a common lack of a positive image of the future, a lack of cultural legitimacy, and a nihilistic cultural revolution that is unable to or refuses to participate in an urban industrial economy as it is without a good future outcome for them. This triple problem will be called the 'fifth gauntlet' of the development gauntlet. In comparison, the result is a developmental 'enigma of arrival'—where a fully developed nation and its generally digital economy has led only to a common cultural rejection by the youth of a past positive image of a future urban industrial culture, itself formed by the hopes and dreams of all the previous developmental generations. Since it is common to many digitized urban industrial economies everywhere, this is really a global precariat's true cultural revolution against past unrepresentative state-driven and corporate-driven models of urban industrial development as way of life, that once digitized, is increasingly unable to deliver on its own promises of growing stability and improvement of human life, and thus increasingly is undesired and precarious (Standing, 2011).

This cultural revolution and its potential later political revolution is partially why more unrepresentative forces in industrial nations globally are trying to rush to create a digital police state. However, that route as argued above will only bring about a further inability to get through the digital bottleneck. Regardless, the fifth gauntlet is partially the result of past successes down the development gauntlet that have created more externalities over time particularly due to past success of a wealthy and aging society. Equally, it is partially an entirely novel issue of a fresh digital media regime creating an unexpectedly quick economic shakeout of past stable national economies. Either way, once development in some countries seemed baked to urban industrial perfection, its own successes of wealth and long life, combined equally now with digitalization adds a bitter icing for the next generations that makes the cake inedible and unenjoyable despite the long-term work that went into it. Instead of addressing these externalities by policy changes and greater consensus to continue down the development gauntlet, many unrepresentative governments are trying to keep leadership control over this cultural revolution of youth who refuse to be force fed this unpalatable cake and who have little chances of economic advancement as the current digitized economy expands and as their elders' golden years dissolve their inheritance transmissions. Some unrepresentative groups are trying to keep leadership control by locking down their whole nation in a digital police state, with or without a health scare as an alibi, instead of finding a representative policy course of improved routes of consensus to go forward.

On the one hand these cultural revolutions show that as countries' economic and social development of improvement in health and wealth is *successful*, a point is reached when economic development for the next generations become culturally *unsuccessful*. On the other hand, it is the effect of the digital bottleneck autonomously, creating even more economic shakeout of precarious jobs and lives. *If* cultural rot starts completely to collapse past economic desires of advancement in on itself, can current models of frenetic urban industrialization be considered a good 'development' model at all, if the ultimate common effect is to only create culture in which greater number of elderly and youth give up on the will to live and isolate themselves to solace their lack of future in durable poverty to which in their interpretation they lack any individual way out? This can give rise to a host of escapist addictions rising in these 'developed' countries that further sap strength and teamwork of individuals, nations, and cultures to make better collective alternative futures and better policies that could get them as a group through this fifth gauntlet or the digital bottleneck (Anderson, 2010).

The general point is whether this is a *common* 'fifth level' to the development gauntlet mentioned earlier: a vicious cycle from a *common* declining biological and cultural transmission in caused by rising economic growth and yet rising economic inequality that damages cultural and intergenerational transmission?

Any of the other four development gauntlets have a similar theme, characterized by fresh rising challenges created by the previous levels of development success. Thus, the same is here, justifying calling this the fifth gauntlet, as the next problem to solve to continue urban industrialization, or to lose it entirely potentially. To keep developing, a country has to solve each development gauntlet's problem created by the success of the previous level. A fifth level of the development gauntlet comes full circle in this double scissors effect of successful urban industrial development: a lack of elderly-to-youth cultural transmission as well as lack of babies raised in a culture without the future of either. The economic shakeout and lack of intergenerational transmission of wealth and culture is only being exacerbated by the changing media regime that is happening in many already developed countries around the world.

The question becomes how does any country avoid snuffing itself out, culturally and biologically, if it succeeds in maintaining long term urban industrialization and if its culture instead of being a solace shared, itself becomes just another hypercompetitive commoditized economic sector of a culture wave? So, instead of this being only a Korean problem, this vicious cycle of the 'fifth gauntlet' is a problem facing all urban industrialized countries that have achieved development for several generations instead of it being truly 'caused' only after a 'fourth level' (of a cultural wave), because many of the countries experiencing it lack a global cultural wave. Instead of a 'middle income trap,' we might call the 'fifth gauntlet' problem a "DICE trap," standing for the '*demographic intergenerational* decline, then *cultural* decline, then *economic* decline trap of triple diminishing returns.' Do we see a fifth gauntlet 'DICE trap' more clearly now as a general problem only *because so few previous countries ever had to worry about it, since the main worry had been "development at all costs?"*

Perhaps the 'fifth gauntlet' is the ultimate problem that has to be solved. It gets beyond only a 'successful' urban industrialization, beyond a competitive commoditized culture of a global cultural wave, and beyond a demographic transition, *to achieve an actually successful, happy, and durable culture of high subjective quality of life* instead of only material objective quality of life. The interpretation here is that it is hardly caused by digitalization per se though digitalization exacerbates and quickens what would be happening anyway sooner or later in time down the development gauntlet.

So, if a nation wants to keep going down the development gauntlet, as argued earlier, one of the last phenomena it wants to see is a negative cultural revolution of any kind that creates a polarized cultural opposition so mistrustful that working together as a larger national or cultural team becomes devolutionary to past large scales of community, economy, and connections of trust. Thus, in some ways this is a luxury problem, as such "N-po" problems only come up as problems if a country has been economically successful in its development. In other ways, it is an existential crisis and more serious showing the whole nation is culturally unsuccessful because more than luxuries will go away if "DICE" trends and its cultural revolution continue.

This 'DICE' cultural revolution comes from tangible problems with the past and current urban industrial development and past and current versions of unrepresentative digitalization that exacerbate it, instead of arising autonomously itself. Therefore, frankly, only past unrepresentative policies of development are to blame that have to be solved now to develop further, just like previous developmental gauntlet factors. Thus these triple declines in babies, culture, and economics are *due to externalities of the previous successful development over time.* This is joined by the more active cultural revolutionary problem that threatens many nations if their youth feel stuck enough to envision only a future support of their own biological, cultural, and economic extinction and decline despite all the troubles of their elders to get them to this economic advance.

Once a handful of countries at last do have successful economic development at all costs, their tune changes to different priorities of "babies, families, and quality of life in culture and jobs, at all costs." This is the beginning of ideas of how to fix the externalities of the fifth gauntlet because it deals effectively with the sources of the growing cultural revolution. Thus, to solve this 'fifth gauntlet' and its cultural revolution and DICE trap, *more consensus-based policies for family formation and for addressing past externalities of digital development* have to come of age, in order to continue this path of industrial development, instead of trying to repress it or ignore it out of existence.

As Korea avoided a cultural revolution in its past, it is to its credit because it developed a greater history of compromising with more oppositional movements over time to make more consensus and representative policies over time instead of *only* repressing them—which it did as well of course. This greater consensus building in the Korean political economy and its policies was mentioned in all hybrid polices of the past that were a buckling of the state to popular demands whether cultural, political, or economic. Note the same consensus building was argued to help get Korea through the digital bottleneck as well. So, obviously, if Korea is developing a drop out movement as the next cultural revolution, and if job organization is experiencing problems of personal and family stability due to the advance of the current versions of a digital economy, more consensus building with what would help isolated youth and isolated elderly live a higher quality of life and ways of addressing the precariousness and externalities of that digital economy are in order. Current state leadership itself so far is to blame for its unrepresentative solutions to the growing social externalities of its own successful economic and digital development. Korea's own success of greater health care and longer lives and its own digital development have combined to cause these externalities. Therefore, learning from their own history, Korea should add further consensus policies toward a more 'hybrid digital development' that addresses these complaints of youth and elderly that are the externalities of bad structural "DICE" outcomes of past 'good' economic policies.

Korean youth particularly hold all the cards, because when they walk away from the game, all three games are over for adults as well sooner or later. These three are the regular Korean culture and Korean economy and how they may shrink and change without policy adaptation for their youth interests as a 'political party.' Plus, third, the global Korean Wave depends on the Korean youth culture. All three of these ongoing intergenerational transmissions will be slowed, and Korean cultural desirability will be minimal if both youth and elderly increasingly live alone without families or children in a poor yet workaholic world without future economic improvement.

What will become of the culture that will be transferred in the future of the Korean Wave, if Koreans culturally exhaust themselves of globally desirable 'content'? Obviously, if Korea wants to keep an urban industrial digital economy and a cultural wave into the future, the country requires policies to reduce youth anxiety, reduce economic inequality, give hope, encourage financial saving for the future, and encourage family formation and more babies, and help deal with the rapid skill set changes and precariousness of jobs in a digital economy. Otherwise, culture and economy will snuff each other out, biologically over time. We should ask what policies will allow for more family formation, more representative urban industrial economies in digital development, higher subjective quality of life, and higher levels of capacity building, instead of only higher levels of economic precariousness and stress.

Four developing ideas from other countries tackling their own 'fifth gauntlet' issues show themes of how to fix this self-destruction. All involve building greater synergies and social integration between the problems that a country has. For instance, some states at the fifth gauntlet have found policies to help both isolated youth and elderly find higher quality of life, particular in common cultural community with themselves and others. First, in Iceland, they solved some of their 'fifth gauntlet' issues of their aimless youth and a serious youth addiction problem in the 1980s into the 1990s with a whole host of structural policies to give higher subjective quality of life, more personal senses of competence and discipline, greater social integration for youth as individuals, and greater social integration for families as teams (Natural High, 2021; Young, 2017). In a very short time, Iceland ended its growing youth alcohol and drug additions and gave past hopeless youth greater capacity building for the future and gave families greater resilience in the process. Next, modeling on New Zealand, differently alienated groups can be brought together as one solution, like how childless older Kiwi farmer families 'occupationally adopt' young farming families tired of an urban digital rat race who want to learn how to farm and yet lack all practical advice, family structure, or mentorship to do so. Thus, the childless elderly farmers let the young family inherit or buy the farm from them as they teach them the skills of farming in the process. Thus, both isolated elderly and youth groups benefit. Third, other examples of solving problems of mutual alienization are institutionally developing. Some Western European societies have a policy to link elder care facilities with orphanages to turn two social problems of isolation into their own solution of cultural transmission, acculturation, and sharing. Fourth, once more solving mutual alienation and this problem of being 'together alone,' young impoverished precariat workers with little ability to move to better housing and are living alone become live-in staff for elderly in their now 'empty nest' house. The isolated elder with little income or physical mobility uses their main fixed asset of their house to get cheap rent and elder care services/subsidies from a young tenant, while the elder provides room and shared home-cooked meals as the youth shops for them both as well. It is like a surrogate grandmother or grandfather in many situations for wayward youth.

These examples show how some nations attempt now to solve this 'fifth gauntlet' in development. Though these ideas are interesting, however Korea has a family culture by blood, and a proxemics that only allows blood relatives or in-laws in private homes. Thus, Korea has a huge taboo on engineering artificial family-based solutions to social problems like many of the above ideas. Three of these four ideas are solutions that create artificial families: like by linking elder care and orphanages, or linking elder farmers to 'adopted' non-blood farmers to teach them the 'family farm,' or linking an elder with a home asset to youth desiring a cheap place to live who provide elder services as well. Korea is a culture unlikely ever to invite alienated strangers of any kind to live in their private houses or farming properties—even if the homeowner is alienated elderly in the same situation as their alienated youth boarder, and even if no one in the immediate family wants to continue farming. So, Korea may have sadly found a level of the development gauntlet that it will fail at, in other words, by being such a homogeneous culture that dislikes such deep "cultural innovations" like the three mentioned above. These cultural innovations would break the cultural back of the deep bloodline and regional family ties of Koreans. More culturally innovative nations may adapt these solutions above, and may survive better beyond this 'fifth gauntlet.'

However, there was one idea above that might work for Korea—the idea from Iceland. Despite the homogeneous culture of Iceland, it did solve some of its fifth gauntlet issues without artificial families, and by shoring up already established real families with subsidies and using educational institutions as well. It is worth examining in detail. Iceland created more state intervention instead of cultural change, by subsidizing existing high schools and subsidizing existing real families as both units of greater social integration instead of forcing or encouraging artificial families or fresh institutional pairings. It is already being replicated in the United Kingdom. (Devlin, 2021; Society for the Study of Addiction, 2021) Similarly, more Korean-style solutions from the state, from educational institutions, and by aiding real existing families would seem politically and culturally to work better in Korea. Plus, the 'after high-school' continuing hobby programs of Iceland that kept addicted and aimless youth more socially integrated and hopeful with more skills, self-discipline, and pride may provide more culturally legitimated options for the education-conscious Koreans. This might be done in Korea with similar high school programs for aimless youth, or even with private academies (hagwons) that could subsidize aimless youth to train them in certain economic growth areas to get them out of their social and financial rut. Perhaps Korean youth could be subsidized to learn a software language, video editing, a mechanical skill, or a dying cultural artistic form, and thus could have more pride in helping their community and themselves? Equally, perhaps a policy to expand Korea's welfare state and safety net may help it through this fifth gauntlet.

A fifth idea based only on Korean observation would be to encourage in some way a special higher interest rate payment in private banks for jeonse deposits. This would encourage bank solvency by larger cash deposits, would encourage homeowners with homes to rent to convert them back to more jeonse long-term leases instead of monthly rents (since they could make more money in the bank at the higher interest rates for jeonse deposits), and this would encourage married couples to maintain their seed capital for the future instead of wasting it on monthly rents. The first step could be arranged by offering perks to the bank from the government for offering such a higher jeonse interest rate, or by subsidization of a slightly higher private bank rate by the government to the banks only in the case of jeonse deposits.

Sixth, maybe instead of only subsidizing banks to offer higher jeonse interest payments, or subsidizing single person homes directly, equally, the Korean government could subsidize after school programs of homebuilding or home repair for elders or organize construction or farming clubs that build or repair homes or gardens for the elderly or for paying isolated youth themselves for these services.

Indeed the rising tide of the Korean Wave may be some solace to Koreans, though higher quality of life and happiness has many other origins instead of culture having the only power of providing happiness. For instance, Korea requires more stable economic systems and a rising middle class to be happy as well as a powerful culture, instead of the vicarious rise of the culture in the midst of lowered fertility, cultural alienation, a declining middle class, and economic instability. Unless Korea acts quickly, in retrospect the Korean Wave may be remembered as a global supernova of Korea, a vast beautiful cultural explosion ignoring how it is leaving a burned out dead core behind with declining internal cultural transmission, instead of representing a true happy and durable cultural success.

Do Koreans really want that bad scenario? Koreans themselves see it coming. To avoid it, they have to do at least three tasks: have more pro-natal and pro-family policies to give hope to their youth particularly in easier achieved family housing, have more ways to get cheaper 'second chances' in educational attainment in some required profession particularly in a fast-paced digital economy, and have more policies of cultural continuity to demote isolation of elderly and youth alike. However, instead of the digitally saturated inheriting the earth, it may be the non-digital or less digital inheriting the earth more like Iceland or New Zealand, simply because they breed children with more cultural hope for the future and more sense of stable identity and less addictions. There are smaller and more integrated communities in these tiny nations as well. (Young, 2017) Is that the global future as well? Are we going back to a commons, toward the Scenario #4 mentioned above, yet a digital commons this time given the change of media regimes? (Bauwens et al., 2019)

11.3 Conclusion: Learning Excellence from Harbingers and Outliers

Will Korea be a harbinger leading the way to a more multi-polar global economy and cultural world, or will Korea remain an outlier—so far 'ahead' in this digital world that it is impossible to catch up unless Korea falls? Arguments for Korea as harbinger and outlier were given throughout this book. We can learn from Korea regardless of one's interpretation about it.

Many analysts focus on statistical averages about world development or industrial sector patterns. However, here, we learned by looking in depth at case studies of development outliers like Korea. This is useful particularly in comparison to those averages for how to raise those averages when possible by learning from such successful outliers because they may be harbingers slightly ahead of the curve from others, from which we can learn valuable lessons about any nation's options and better futures.

Korea is the country of many comparatively good decisions and good accidents that helped catapult it to global success in the late twentieth to early twenty-first centuries. Korea is hopefully only the first of stellar successes in a constellation of more globally-distributed digital economies and a more multi-polar global culture. We argued that comparatively odd hybrid cultural, political, economic policies and high levels of digital synergies combined with a 'mixed culture' with some elements of heterogeneity in a more homogeneous culture have made both the economic Korean Miracle and the cultural Korean Wave possible at greater heights and longer duration than other countries so far. This analysis of what Korea is doing to itself and to the world as the first and thus the oldest digitally saturated country so far, helps us peer into the future of ourselves anywhere for what possibilities or problems may happen under more "digitally networked conditions." Korea may be a study of an outlier full of world firsts, yet it is equally a harbinger by being an image of what a strong trend of saturated digital communications holds for all nations.

Not only *can* we learn from Korea, we *should* learn from Korea. It is the best example yet of how to successfully hold a culture together in a fast development drive, how to keep your democracy and civil rights by intentional data fragmentation, as well as how to become a winner in a global digital economy and a global digital culture, instead of falling apart at each step of the way there. Now Korea has to solve its growing fifth gauntlet or "DICE trap" (declining demographic intergenerational transfer, to declining culture, to declining economy) to continue to develop instead of decline. However, this is a common urban industrial problem now worldwide: a problem of declining fertility, cultural revolution, and economic inequality further exacerbated by the economic shakeout of a digital economy. However, instead of the world equally looking to Korea for answers to this yet, Koreans should start to look elsewhere in the world for answers and advice.

In the process of analyzing the Korean Wave that has shown how Koreans have been successful in adapting cultural exports for over thirty years into ever larger synergistic trends, we have analyzed equally a waning unipolar American/Western-centric global economic power and cultural hegemony. Will more synergies come from South Korea? Will more eclipsing come to the global West? Will other "K-Nations" arise to join Korea, or will Korea continue to be more of an outlier instead of a harbinger? Koreans are certainly well positioned to continue the Korean Wave as of 2023. This is because they have successfully ridden the three digital global trends mentioned above better than other countries after World War II. They have created inspiration and taken up the slack in media cultural productions from the global West during lockdown conditions. However, whether Korea remains an outlier or is a harbinger of world development *depends on others wanting to learn from Korea.* Regardless, to peer into Korea is to analyze where the whole world seems to be going in the future. Even if countries try to avoid it, they will be defined by their avoidance.

Only time will tell what History will bring the world. Will it bring more multi-polar examples of "the Wealth of K-Nations" worldwide after others learn from Korean digital, economic and cultural successes? Or, will History show differently organized states being unable to make the coming global media transition that seems to be selecting so far only for a single special kind of Goldilocks zone of 'mid-size' demographic and geographic nation with a more homogeneous culture? History and the current 'triple global storm' of a global digital economy, a global digital culture, and a globally decentralized media seems to be selecting for both "global development with Korean characteristics" and for differently oriented states receiving national breakdown, dystopian digital surveillance, police states, technocracies, and the ending of individual civil and human rights within digitally-managed social credit systems.

Either way, we *should* learn from the digital, developmental, and cultural secrets of the organization of the economic Korean Miracle and the cultural Korean Wave because it is our common future, ready or not, to compete in this way globally. It is better to be knowledgeable and prepared than to be taken unawares by this digital triple global storm that already is altering everyone's lives and leading to the breakdown and reformatting of nations. Let other countries pioneer more dystopian digital visions. Korea has pioneered the most positive and consensus-driven digital future so far. Let us learn as much as we can about the economic Korean Miracle and the global Korean Wave, because by doing so, we may be learning how to save ourselves in better and more durable national development elsewhere, instead of only lauding Korea.

References

Anderson, B. (2010). *The globalization of addiction: A study in poverty of the spirit.* Oxford University Press.

Anon. (2021, May 31). Taking care of the single people (KOR). *Korea JoongAng Daily.* https://koreajoongangdaily.joins.com/2021/05/31/englishStudy/bilingualNews/Singleperson-household/20210531191000449.html

Bauwens, M., Kostakis, V., & Pazaitis, A. (2019). *Peer to Peer: The commons manifesto* (Critical, digital and social media studies). University of Westminster Press; Illustrated edition.

Chae, S., & Moon, H.-K. (2020, November 9). For single households, pandemic has been but a blip. *Korea JoongAng Daily*. https://koreajoongangdaily.joins.com/2020/11/09/business/economy/singleperson-household-oneperson-household/20201109165200393.html

Chae, S., & Jeong, J.-h. (2021, August 3). Number of single-person households surprises even statistics Korea. *Korea JoongAng Daily*. https://koreajoongangdaily.joins.com/2021/08/03/business/economy/singleperson-household-people-living-alone-single/20210803184700342.html

Choi, H.-s. (2023, March 25). HYBE windfall. Selling SM shares bought for 120,000 won for 150,000 won, 16% stake, Kakao tender offer application. *Joseon Ilbo*. https://www.Joseon.com/economy/economy_general/2023/03/25/EIACLENLCJHHZARFIH7YPCFEME/

Devlin, L. (2021, May 11). The youth in Iceland model got teens to say no to drugs—can Dundee do the same? *The Courier*. https://www.thecourier.co.uk/fp/education/schools/2194699/the-youth-in-iceland-model-got-teens-to-say-no-to-drugs-can-dundee-do-the-same/

Heo, J.-w., & Seo, J.-E. (2021, October 6). Single household registrations hit a high of 40.1%. *Korea JoongAng Daily*. https://koreajoongangdaily.joins.com/2021/10/06/national/socialAffairs/singleperson-household-residents-registration-system-individual/20211006193209136.html

Hollingsworth, J., Seo, Y., & Bae, G. (2020, August 5). South Korean authorities encourage men to marry foreign women. But their brides often become victims of abuse. *CNN.com*. https://edition.cnn.com/2020/08/02/asia/foreign-wives-south-korea-intl-hnk-dst/index.html

Hong, E. (2014). *The birth of Korean cool: How one nation is conquering the world through pop culture*. Picador.

Kay, B. (2011, July 6). Why more South Korean men are looking for foreign brides, *The Christian Science Monitor*. https://csmonitor.com/World/Asia-Pacific/2011/0706/Why-more-South-Korean-men-are-looking-for-foreign-brides

Korea Times. (2020, July 8). Single-person households most common household type in Korea: data. *The Korea Times*. https://www.koreatimes.co.kr/www/culture/2020/08/703_292501.html

Lee, C. M., & Botto, K. (2021, June 29). Demographics and the future of South Korea. *Carnegie Endowment for International Peace*. https://www.Carnegieendowment.org/2021/06/29/demographics-and-future-of-south-korea-pub-84817

Lee, H.-j. (2022, December 7). One-third of households in Korea only have one person. *Korea JoongAng Daily*. https://koreajoongangdaily.joins.com/2022/12/07/business/economy/Oneperson--household-Singles-Statistics-Korea/20221207154301170.html

Mattelart, A. (2000). *Networking the world, 1794–2000*. University of Minnesota Press.

Natural High. (2021, January 27). Iceland's radical transformation of teen substance use. *Natural High*. https://www.naturalhigh.org/icelands-radical-transformation-of-teen-substance-use/

Russia Today. (2022, December 3). Party for €387,000 EU project attracts only six guests—media. *Russia Today*. https://www.rt.com/news/567612-eu-metaverse-party-flop-investment-neutral/

Standing, G. (2011). *The Precariat: The New Dangerous Class*. Bloomsbury.

Society for the Study of Addiction. (2021, April 27). The Youth in Iceland Model in Dundee: Tessa Parkes and Hannah Carver talk to the SSA. *Society for the Study of Addiction*. https://www.addiction-ssa.org/the-youth-in-iceland-model-in-dundee-tessa-parkes-and-hannah-carver-talk-to-the-ssa/

The Straits Times. (2014, April 10). South Korea imposes new restrictions on marriages to foreigners. *The Straits Times*. https://straitstimes.com/asia/east-asia/south-korea-imposes-new-restrictions-on-marriages-to-foreigners

U.S. Census Bureau. (2021, November 29). Census Bureau releases new estimates on America's families and living arrangements. *U.S. Census Bureau*. https://www.census.gov/newsroom/press-releases/2021/families-and-living-arrangements.html.

Young, E. (2017, January 24). Iceland knows how to stop teen substance abuse - but the rest of the world isn't listening. Originally from Mosaic funded by the Wellcome Trust. *Australian Broadcasting Company (ABC)*. https://www.abc.net.au/triplej/programs/hack/iceland-teen-substance-abuse/8208214

Appendix 1
Fifty 'World Firsts' of the Republic of Korea: South Korea as the Emerald City of Digital Development, a List and Timeline, 1984–2022

Mobile ICT Networks are a big national, global, and cultural change. Arguably, South Korea became the world's first "saturated" mobile infrastructure and culture when thinking holistically about these fifty points, from 1984 to the present.

1. 1984: South Korea's 'Korea Mobile Telecommunications Services Corporation' (coming out of what is now called Korea Telecom (KT)) was the first company outside of North America to install the Advanced Mobile Phone System (AMPS), now known as "1G" or first generation cellular network (wireless) technology, an analog mobile phone system standard by Bell Labs, later modified in joint effort by Bell Labs and Motorola. Korea Mobile Telecommunications Services Corporation was founded on March 29, 1984, as originally the state-owned carrier that introduced pagers and car phones to the Korean market. In May 1984, they launched their car phone service. In July 1984, an AMPS cellular network started in the Seoul metropolitan area. AMPS had only started in North America on October 13, 1983. However, South Korea quickly became the first country to adopt it outside of North America, doing so in 1984, after the USA first in 1983 and Canada second in 1984. (As for 1G standards though, there were three standards: the Nordic Mobile Telephone (NMT from 1981), the Advanced Mobile Phone System (AMPS from 1983) of the USA, and the Japanese Nippon Telegraph and Telephone networks (NTT from 1979). Thus, NTT gave Japan the world the first national cellular mobile phone coverage by 1984, starting from 1979 in Tokyo. However in Japan the number of cellular users was far lower than other developed economies with a penetration rate of only 0.15% by 1989. Meanwhile, the far higher scale of Korean cultural uses of mobile networks started to show. Korea achieved its first national cellular mobile phone coverage in "1G" using AMPS by 1991. (Korea Mobile Telecommunications Services Corporation was originally a spinoff of the mobile services of the larger originally state-owned Korea Telecom, KT, with this mobile telecommunications branch changing its name to SK Telecom from 1997.)

G.-C. Shin and M. D. Whitaker, *The Korean Wave in a Post-Pandemic World*,
https://doi.org/10.1007/978-981-99-3683-0

2. In 1995, *Joongang Ilbo* (Joongang Newspaper) developed the first Internet news website in Asia.
3. 1995: South Korea was the first country in the world to commercialize 'code division multiplex access' (CDMA) technology to achieve the world's first "2G" *broadband-capable* cellular mobile network, as well as conceiving of this as a technology for export later. As early as April 1993, the South Korean government adopted CDMA as the next Korean national cellular telephone system for "2G" services. By 1995, South Korea got its first commercial CDMA (IS-95A) network. Operating in Seoul from October 1995, it is considered the world's earliest commercial CDMA network.
4. 1995–2002; 2002–2008: Korea passes the Telecommunications Business Act, the first Internet censorship law in the world. It continued a government of very tight information and cultural control in South Korea from the days of President's Park's National Security Law (that continues) and Chun's Basic Press Law (revoked in 1987 in modern Korean democratization). The Korea Internet Communications Ethics Committee (ICEC) was tasked to monitor the whole Korean Internet and make recommendations for content removal. By August 1996, the ICEC had censored about 220,000 messages on Korean Internet websites. After 2002, a revised law added more internet policing of content and allowing the removal of websites entirely. By 2008, a complaint would at this point allow the updated Korean Communication Standards Commission (KCSC) to suspend any web posting or article for 30 days as soon as a complaint was filed.
5. In 1996, the Korean video game company Nexus released the world's first MMORPG—massively multiplayer online role-playing game—called *The Kingdom of the Winds*, based on a graphic novel about ancient Korea. The USA did release similar games at the same time (Hong, 2014, p. 213).
6. 1999: By this year, South Korea was the first nation to have more mobile phones than fixed telephones. This was three years before China and four years before the United States (Larson and Oh, 2011, p. 92).
7. 1999: South Korea had another world first in the area of social network services, thanks to its earlier high speed broadband networks, and a culture founded on 'connectionism' that means keeping updated with activities in one's networks. The first major nationwide social media service in the world was SK Telecom's Cyworld, launched in this year. Facebook was founded four years later. As late as 2008, nearly half of all South Korea and 90% of youth into their 20s used Cyworld. Businesses, governments, and universities had Cyworld pages as well (Oh and Larson, 2011, p. 155). Cyworld was a kind of substitutionary way to program in hypertext as well, with its 'minihomepy' that provided various digital virtual purchases with its own online coin the 'dotori' (Korean for 'acorn,' with each digital coin costing about 100 won, or around 10 U.S. cents) to 'furnish' a website as an online home for the user with visual elements. Cyworld's income stream soon came from mostly virtual purchases using dotori for the 'minihomepy', perhaps a world first for any company to have the majority of its profits from simply virtual items sold. Cyworld in Korea began to decline from

2009 with the entry of Facebook into the Korean market, as well as due to Cyworld's lack of mobile phone accessibilities and even massive data leakages from Cyworld/Nate hacking from 2011.

8. 1999–2015: South Korea was the first and the only state ever mandating its citizens and consumers to use a single nationwide and nationally-exclusive digital authentication, NPKI, in all online transactions that gave the Korean state a record of all private financial transactions of all citizens online. It failed in its ultimate purpose: South Korea became the second most hacked country in the world (Son and Whitaker, 2022). Self-defeating NPKI mandates were slowly withdrawn after 2015, yet technological path dependence remains.
9. 2000 to present: The world's first World Cyber Games started. It remains an international e-sports competition of countries' best digital game players, competing against each other in online video games. Originally created by Oh Yoonseop, the Korean CEO of International Cyber Marketing, it was financially supported by Samsung. The first event was in October 7–15, 2000, was called the "World Cyber Game Challenge," and was sponsored by the Korean Ministry of Culture and Tourism, the Korean Ministry of Information and Communications, and Samsung as well. Seventeen countries competed for gold, silver, and bronze medals. In the first WCG 2000, there were only 174 competitors from 17 countries that formed the first round to find the best national players who came to South Korea to play each other. The prize pool was originally $20,000. Next, on December 5–9, 2001, the World Cyber Games held a larger world event in Seoul, Korea, with a total purse prize of $300,000 to attract global players to Korea. In 2001, now 24 countries participated with fully 430 players in the final tournament in Seoul with an astounding 389,000 players worldwide participating in the national preliminaries. By 2002, it was held in Korea once more with a prize pool of $1,300,000. In 2002, approximately 450,000 preliminary players worldwide played to find the 450 final tournament players. Next, the 2003 tournament had a total prize pool of $2,000,000, and was the first to feature console-based competition as well. This WCG went around the world after starting in Korea. By 2014, the WCG was closed, due to personal differences of members with leadership. However, in 2017, the Samsung trademark was transferred to Korean publisher Smilegate, which revived the WCG by 2019 with its first event in Xi'an, China on July 18–21, 2019. The WCG competition in 2020 was held online between the two host sites of Shanghai and Seoul, and gained approximately 650 million viewers worldwide.
10. From 2001–2013, Korea's ICT sector accounted for the highest percentage of value-added products when comparing all OECD countries, followed by Finland, Ireland, Sweden, Japan and the U.S. As of 2013, Korea's percentage of value added stood at 10.7% compared with only 5–7% for the other leading countries. During the same period, Korea, then ranking as first within the top five exporters of ICT products in the world, was the only state economy to increase its share of the world market for such value-added products (Larson, 2017).

11. 2002: In January 2002, SK Telecom deployed world's first commercial synchronous IMT-2000 facility, the global standard for third-generation ("3G") wireless communications. This first commercial network in Korea was using the CDMA-based 1xEV-DO technology in January 2002. By May 2002, the second South Korean 3G network was by KT on EV-DO. Thus, South Koreans were the first to see even *competition* among 3G operators. The first 3G in the United States was Monet Mobile Networks, using CDMA2000 1x EV-DO technology, however this network provider later shut down. The second 3G network operator in the US was Verizon Wireless from July 2002, equally using CDMA2000 1x EV-DO.
12. 2002: In May 2002, because of competition with SK's 3G service by KT's fresh 3G service in this month, South Koreans were the first to see *competition* among 3G operators as well.
13. 2004: SK Telecom launched Hanbyul, the world's first DMB satellite. DMB is 'Digital Multimedia Broadcasting,' which is a digital radio transmission technology.
14. 2004 onward: Samsung Group (founded in 1938 as Samsung) is now a Korean conglomerate with over 60 companies currently in 2023. For only its world firsts in digital development in Korea, it started manufacturing black and white televisions in the late 1960s in Korea like several other companies at the time. However, by 1997, Samsung was manufacturing small molecule OLEDs in a group with Pioneer Corporation, followed by TDK in 2001 and Samsung-NEC Mobile Display (SNMD). By 2004, Samsung Display became the world's largest OLED manufacturer, making 40% of the world's OLED displays.
15. 2005: Samsung became the world's largest manufacturer of liquid-crystal display (LCD) panels as well.
16. 2005: South Korea becomes the first country to introduce mobile TV, or digital multi-media broadcasting (DMB). It used digital radio frequencies to send wireless radio, television, or other data to mobile phones, navigation systems and other mobile devices (Oh and Larson, 2011, p. 101).
17. 2006: The Korean government announced the U-Korea Master Plan, the world's first "ubiquitous network plan" for a nation, in which persons and objects nationwide would always be digitally connected.
18. 2006: Going cashless earliest, in South Korea the idea of using a mobile phone's monthly payment for additional other small daily purchases was used by 23 million Koreans by this year, or nearly half the population. Any Korean mobile phone subscribers could pay for online goods with authorization codes via sending a mobile SNS. Thus the mobile phone payment at the end of the month became a monthly virtual credit card payment at the end of the month as well (Oh and Larson, 2011, p. 153). Korean mobile phone operators started to have other general payment options built into their hardware, like SK Telecom's Moneta Service. A mobile phone model could have a Moneta smart card inside it, and that smart card could be linked to that virtual credit card account, and thus charges could be added to a user's mobile phone bill by 'swiping' one's mobile phone over a touchless payment location installed at hundreds of thousands

of Korean businesses that had dongles on the credit card payment system in the store that could wirelessly interface with Moneta smart cards when mobile phones were passed over them. Then, the mobile phone subscriber would be billed at the end of the month for the miscellaneous purchases they made through their mobile phone wireless touch payments in the store. Moneta mobile phone chips started in 2005, and they could be used both for online payments of goods as well as in-store touchless payments. Remember, this is before Internet-accessible smartphones are available from 2007 onward.

19. 2005–2018: From 2006, Korea pioneered the world's first nationally-installed infrastructure for wireless Internet ("4G") in its patented "WiBro" infrastructure. It was demonstrated first in Pusan in 2005, and then spread around the Korean nation from 2006, yet was demonstrated at the 2006 Winter Olympics in Turin, Italy, as well. It was developed to expand data limitations of (non-Internet) mobile phones then, and to add further distances to wireless Internet mobility than was available then from wireless Internet-based on telephone wires (ASDL) or from inherently short-range wireless LANs. It was a national infrastructure with WiBro base stations connecting to the WiBro units that had a throughput of 30 to 50 MB/s with a radius of up to 1 to 5 kilometers. As a national infrastructure, it was claimed to provide for fast moving mobility to a wireless Internet connection up to 120km/hr (~75 miles/hr) travelling around the country, moving from WiBro base station to base station, though tests in Pusan at the time showed it worked at lower travel speeds than this benchmark. Monthly subscriptions were around $30 dollars a month. This was before the first wireless flatglass smartphones like the LG Prada in May 2007 or Apple's iPhone in June 2007. The first-comparable release of 4G technology was the LTE standard—yet it was commercially deployed only several years later than WiBro—with 4G LTE starting in Oslo, Norway, and in Stockholm, Sweden in 2009. However, in retrospect, because 4G LTE standards of wireless Internet services would soon outclass it as a standard later, WiBro would in the end only be a standard deployed as a service in Korea from 2006 despite Korea doing the work to make WiBro a globally certified standard under the name mobile WiMAX (IEEE 802.16e), and despite some other nations building out regional WiMAX networks in Italy, Brazil, Venezuela, Croatia, Rwanda, and the U.S. state of Michigan. In Korea, WiBro was allocated earlier the same 2.3–2.4 GHz frequency band as later smartphones. With declining use, Korean WiBro networks were shut down in 2018. If you know what you are looking for, many buildings in Seoul still sport "WiBro" ports in their walls, where you could put your portable WiBro antenna 'egg' (it was rounded like an egg) to connect to the WiBro base stations in a major building to broadcast wireless Internet nearby to your other devices.

20. 2006: On December 16th, 2006, Korea announced the world's first Internet-accessible mobile (feature) phone with a large flatglass touchscreen: the "LG Prada" from Korean LG telecommunications, created in design collaboration with luxury clothing brand Prada. It went on sale globally in May 2007. The LG Prada touchscreen smartphone was announced on December 16th, 2006,

which was weeks before January 9th, 2007—the date when Steve Jobs of Apple announced the first iPhone would be later on sale. The iPhone of course is another Internet-accessible mobile (true operating system-based) smartphone with a large flatglass touchscreen. Thus, the Korean LG Prada was the first touchscreen smartphone as it was announced earlier on December 16th, 2006, earlier than the iPhone, and went on sale in May 2007, which was earlier than the iPhone. The iPhone was announced second, on January 9th, 2007, and went on sale second, on June 29th, 2007.

21. 2006–2010: By 2006, as active matrix OLED technology (AMOLED) was developed, Samsung SDI was one of the main investors in the technology. Even to 2023, nearly all the worlds TVs, computer monitors and smartphone screens use AMOLED screens. By 2008, AMOLED first appeared on the Nokia N85 then the Samsung i7110, and both companies were early adopters of this screen on their smartphones. By 2010, however, Samsung Display had a 98% share of the global AMOLED market.
22. 2007–2020: From 2007 onward, South Korea has the world's fastest internet bandwidth for thirteen years running (2007 to 2020) for a large country. In 2017, it was 28.6 MB/s; in the same year of 2017, the United States' average was 18.7 MB/s. (Akamai). By 2020, South Korea's average fixed internet bandwidth was 156.18MB/s, and its average mobile bandwidth was 81 MB/s. (Ookla). World-first high wireless Internet speeds continue today for a large country (see point #49).
23. 2007–2012: From 2007, Korea was the first nation to ever have a 'real name net ID' requirement from this year, ending online anonymity on major digital platforms. It was removed in 2012 by the Korean Constitutional Court as a danger to democracy among other rationales like the problem of economic damage from hacking and theft of centralized records of tens of millions of Korean's real names and identification documents.
24. 2009 onward: From 2009, online gaming exports became half of all the nation's cultural content exports, the first such digital specialization in the world in exports (Oh and Larson, 2011, p. 173). By 2012, Korea's largest cultural export was still online video games that brought in 1,200% more revenue than K-pop at the time, and it was then 58% of Korea's cultural contents industry revenue at around $2.38 billion out of a total then of approximately $4.8 billion (Hong, 2014).
25. 2012: Samsung becomes the world's largest mobile phone maker by unit sales in the first quarter of 2012, with a global market share of 25.4%, unseating Nokia as market leader since 1998.
26. 2013: SK Telecom was the world's first operator to offer a commercial LTE-Advanced network ("4G") under the brand name bandLTE. This merged with release of the smartphone called the Samsung Galaxy S4 LTE-A model, which offered CPU upgrades (Snapdragon 800 vs. Snapdragon 600 used in the regular

model) and also offered LTE-Advanced capabilities. SK Telecom supported this Samsung handset at launch.

27. By 2013, South Korea became the world's first smartphone-saturated youth culture with 97.7% ownership for ages 18–24. In 2013, the USA was only 50%.
28. By two years later, in 2015, a 100% smartphone penetration extended beyond youth culture into young adults through age 35, another world first in saturation. [Korea was #3 in social media use at 87% by 2019.]
29. From 2015 to 2019, South Korea ranked #1 in the world on cheap citizen data transparency; in 2015, it was #1 in OECD; in 2019, it was #1 in OECD. (In 'OURdata Index', "open-useful-reusable data" index, in OECD Government at a Glance, 2019.)
30. By 2015, Korea was the world's biggest manufacturer of platforms of free MMORPGs in the world, in which other pieces of the game accessories for your character are value-added and cost money (Hong, 2014, p. 214). Plus, only South Korean companies make it easy to play these Korean MMORPGs all over the world by placing servers in many different countries for it. U.S. game manufactures generally refuse to do this with thus innately slower play outside of the United States.
31. 2015: Samsung granted more U.S. patents than any other company, including IBM, Google, Sony, Microsoft, and Apple. The company received 7,679 utility patents through December 11th, 2015.
32. By 2016, 88% of Korean adults owned a smartphone, then the highest percentage in the world (Poushter, 2016).
33. From 2016 to 2019, South Korea was #1 in density of AI robots working alongside human laborers, with on average 631 AI robots per 10,000 laborers. The second highest was Singapore with much less (488/10,000), then Germany (309/10,000), and then Japan (303/10,000) (Statista, 2016). By 2017, South Korea was still #1 with an even higher density of 710/10,000. By 2019, South Korean was still #1 with an even higher density of 855/10,000. By 2019, South Korea was #1 with more than double the ratio of AI robots in manufacturing compared to the #2 Japan (364/10,000) or the #3 Germany (346/10,000) (McCarthy, 2019).
34. By 2017, another Internet access saturation plateau was reached as nearly 100% of Korean households had internet access, another world first, breaking its own previous world record of 94% in 2015. (Ramirez, 2017).
35. South Korea at one point had the cheapest bandwidth cost in the entire OECD. (OECD data) This is no longer true though.
36. 2017: Samsung Electronics becomes the world's largest information technology company, consumer electronics maker, and chipmaker measured by revenues of this year, unseating Intel as market leader since 1992. Samsung Electronics' grossed total revenue that year was $69 billion, larger than the $62.8B that Intel reported. Despite a record year for Intel, with an annual increase of 6%, it was

hardly enough to stop Samsung. Intel's chips were found in 90% percent of the world's computers then, yet Intel missed the mobile boom.

37. By 2017, Korea had the world's highest 4G LTE penetration of 96% (Sohn, 2018).
38. By 2017, South Korea was #1 in the world with the highest per capita users in m-commerce (mobile e-commerce) (Hootsuite/WeAreSocial); [By 2017, Korea was #2 in world for highest per capita e-commerce, in general.]
39. By 2017, South Korea was #1 in world for netizen internet news consumption, i.e., was the highest per capita use of Internet portal sites for news consumption (77%), far higher than the average of 30% of a total of 36 surveyed countries (Newman, 2017).
40. 2018: Samsung opens world's largest mobile phone manufacturing facility in Noida, India.
41. 2018: The United Nations ranked South Korea as tied for #1 among 193 countries' online participation sector. [South Korea then ranked #3 in the world in the e-government development category.]
42. April 3, 2019: South Korea deployed the world's first 5G networks, hours ahead of the USA. Hours later, Verizon in the United States launched its 5G services, and tried to dispute Korea's claim of being the first 5G network by saying that it was only arranged as a show for six celebrities, just to generate hype. However, the three main South Korean telecommunications companies (SK Telecom, KT, and LG U+) added more than 40,000 users to their 5G subscriptions on that first launch day (Hwang, 2019). Thus, the first country to adopt 5G on a large scale was South Korea from April 3, 2019 as well.
43. June 2019: SK Telecom announced the launching of the world's first 5G roaming service partnering with Swisscom.
44. South Korea has the first nationwide, parallel, dedicated emergency services LTE network, "FirstNet."
45. 2019: South Korea ranked #1 in world on state spending for research and development as a percentage of GNP. Israel and South Korea are the only two states spending so much. South Korea overtakes Israel for the first time in 2019 (Israel is #1 again, in 2020.) (Jamrisko and Lu, 2020).
46. 2014–21: South Korea ranked #1 in the world on innovation for seven out of nine years (Jamrisko and Lu, 2020; Jamrisko, Lu, and Tanzi, 2021). Israel ranked lower at #10 or #7, respectively, despite spending similarly per capita to South Korea. The USA's rank in this period was never above #8, despite having Silicon Valley. In 2020, Korea falls to #2 below Germany—yet only by a miniscule 0.05 in the index. By 2021, Korea back to #1, Germany to #4 and USA drops out of the top 10.
47. 2020: South Korea was the #1 cashless society among 46 countries' markets with 77% of its citizens/consumers preferring to pay without cash, i.e., preferring to use digital payments of various forms (Buchholz, 2021).
48. 2020 onward: In Korea, the development of artificial intelligence as a leading sector is in the entertainment sector of the Korean Wave. It is globally odd for entertainment to absorb AI innovation. When judged by the whole world's

investments, entertainment is not even in the top nine global industries expected to use AI applications (which are healthcare, automotive, financial services, transportation, technology, media communications, retail and consumer, energy, and manufacturing). This is another 'world first' of Korea to apply AI to its entertainment sector. It has a lot to do with the starving of typical AI funding cycles because of point #8 above.

49. 2022 onward: Average 5G download speeds in the United States have been recorded at only 186.3 Mbps by T-Mobile, while in 2022 and 2023, South Korea leads globally with average speeds of 432 megabits per second (Mbps).
50. On July 6, 2021, for another world first, the status of South Korea was changed to a 'developed country' group at the 68th United Nations Conference on Trade and Development (UNCTAD). This makes South Korea the first and only case so far of a status change from a developing country to a developed country since the establishment of UNCTAD in 1964.

References

Buchholz, K. (2021, January 22). This chart shows how preferred methods of payment differ around the world. *World Economic Forum.* https://www.weforum.org/agenda/2021/01/this-chart-shows-cash-cashless-finance-payment-methods-global-preference/

Hong, E. (2014). *The birth of Korean cool: How one nation is conquering the world through pop culture.* Picador.

Hwang, J. h. (2019, April 9). 5G 첫날부터 4만 가입자…3가지 가입포인트 [40,000 subscribers from the first day of 5G… 3 subscription points]. Asia Business Daily. http://view.asiae.co.kr/news/view.htm?idxno=2019040610062165080

Jamrisko, M. and Lu, W. (2020, January 18). Bloomberg Innovation Index 2020: Germany Breaks Korea's Six-Year Streak as Most Innovative Nation, *Altshuller Institute for Triz Studies.* https://www.aitriz.org/triz-articles/triz-features/790-bloomberg-global-innovation

Jamrisko, M., Lu, W., & Tanzi, A. (2021, February 4). South Korea leads world in innovation as U.S. exits top ten. Bloomberg Innovation Index 2021. *Bloomberg Law.* https://news.bloomberglaw.com/ip-law/south-korea-leads-world-in-innovation-as-u-s-exits-top-ten-1

Larson, J. F. (2017). Network-centric digital development in Korea: Origins, growth and prospects. *Telecommunications Policy, 41*, 916–930.

McCarthy, N. (2020, September 24). The Countries with the Highest Density of Robot Workers. *Statista.* (Data from the International Federation of Robotics) https://www.statista.com/chart/13645/the-countries-with-the-highest-density-of-robot-workers/

Newman, N. (2017). Overview and Key Findings of the 2017 Report. *Digital News Report.* https://www.digitalnewsreport.org/survey/2017/overview-key-findings-2017/

Oh, M., & Larson, J. F. (2019). *Digital development in Korea: Lessons for a sustainable world*, 2nd Edition. Routledge Advances in Korean Studies. Routlege.

Son, W., & Whitaker, M. D. (2020). *The danger of a single technology: Locked into a national digital signature in a globally digital era; South Korea's attempt at standardizing a "national PKI" framework (1999–2015), a study in path dependence that shows the danger of mandating a single technology* (Manuscript article, dissertation summary of Dr. Wonbae Son).

OECD. (2019). Government at a Glance 2019. https://www.oecd-ilibrary.org/governance/government-at-a-glance-2019_8ccf5c38-en

Poushter, J. (2016, February 22). Smartphone ownership and internet usage continues to climb in emerging economies. *Pew Research Center*. https://www.pewresearch.org/global/2016/02/22/smartphone-ownership-and-internet-usage-continues-to-climb-in-emerging-economies/

Ramirez, E. (2017, January 31). Nearly 100% of households in South Korea now have Internet access, thanks to seniors. *Forbes*. https://www.forbes.com/sites/elaineramirez/2017/01/31/nearly-100-of-households-in-south-korea-now-have-internet-access-thanks-to-seniors/

Sohn, J.-y. (2018, June 24). Korea No. 1 worldwide in smartphone ownership, Internet penetration. *Korea Herald*. http://www.koreaherald.com/view.php?ud=20180624000197

Appendix 2
Summarized Comparative Methods Chosen to Think About the Development Outlier of South Korea

With its strong economic and political development and its homogeneous culture, South Korea is an outlier without a true parallel case comparison in our world due to its large degrees of a deep cultural continuity and yet a deep and fast-paced change nearly everywhere else. South Korea is unique as well in durability and flexibility of its successes for over 60 years. This can be explained by its strong collective innovation even over economic downturns that have quick recoveries without long-term setbacks mostly due to innovations of novel economic sectors after the crisis period—particularly seen after crisis years of 1979, 1997, 2008, and 2020. Therefore, instead of comparing South Korea to other states in its own category which are lacking, strategies of comparisons range from internal comparisons, external factors of global conditions, and comparing mixed internal/external factors. Discretely, five kinds of methods are used to think about South Korea in this way: (1) comparisons of various discrete factors across all countries; (2) comparisons of past conditions, i.e., comparisons of South Korea earlier to other modern countries at earlier times when South Korea was more comparable to them; (3) comparisons of ongoing temporal trends in success, failure, or decline in fast development; (4) blocking and matching on various similar factors (like having the same originating culture as North Korea) or (5) blocking and matching on missing or available factors (whether between South Korea and North Korea, or between South Korea to the rest of the world). Without any particular order, these five kinds of comparisons are summarized in 35 different explicit comparisons considered:

1. South Korea to failed or stalled development in other countries.
2. South Korea to other Asian Tigers (Taiwan, Hong Kong, and Singapore).
3. South Korea to North Korea (blocking and matching different choices of economics and politics in the same homogeneous culture).
4. South Korea to other 'bottom billion' countries (Collier, 2007) at earlier times.
5. Comparing degree of escaping Collier's four traps of the 'bottom billion'.
6. South Korea to other countries with durable telecommunications-based development.

G.-C. Shin and M. D. Whitaker, *The Korean Wave in a Post-Pandemic World*, https://doi.org/10.1007/978-981-99-3683-0

7. Comparing geographic size.
8. Comparing demographic size.
9. Comparing South Korea to other neoliberalist policy states to discuss its variation.
10. Comparing South Korea's to all other countries scale and rank in a particular economic sector or particular material throughput.
11. Comparing South Korea to national economically-protected states.
12. Comparing South Korea to other countries blending neoliberal policies with strong welfare states and social democracy.
13. Comparing South Korea to the USA, as the only two examples of durable cultural waves after World War II to the present.
14. Comparing South Korea to other states with land reform in general, whether land distribution (like South Korea, Japan, Taiwan, and England [in 1500s]) or land nationalization (like North Korea).
15. Comparing South Korea to states lacking land reform.
16. Comparing South Korea to Japan, particularly (1) in terms of blocking and matching common homogeneous culture and how both are the world's only two highly economically-developed states with non-European-heritage status in the OECD); (2) in terms of their common fast-development after World War II, despite Japan only recovering it after the war while South Korea starting its fast development drive from in 1961.
17. Modernization theory comparisons: comparing leading sectors; comparing cultural and economic slow growth alliances and ties with other developed countries.
18. Dependency theory comparisons: South Korea's short colonialism period versus others' longer colonial periods; scale and depth of periods of foreign ethnic/cultural occupation; scale of dedication to raw material exports in the national economy.
19. World-system theory comparisons: comparisons with other states in the world in the three categories of states, either:

    a. Comparisons in the raw material periphery (raw material exporters; underdevelopment),
    b. Comparisons in the semi-periphery (top down dictatorial state-led development, in league externally with the world-system's capital imports while being internally repressive of labor movements and civil rights),
    c. Comparisons in core states (highly developed economies with many industrial value-added products, organized labor movements, a strong state, and much industrial exports and much raw material imports).

20. Comparing 'global city' infrastructural readiness or capacities: comparisons to other states with a telecommunication infrastructure availability that can be used by global financial services in the country or city; comparisons to other

states missing such global city infrastructure of telecommunications and related financial services (Sassen, 2001).

21. Comparing states as zones of hardware-based telecommunications development.
22. Comparing states as zones of software-based telecommunications development.
23. Comparisons of locations of the world's cluster-based development (technology and innovation cluster development zones).
24. Comparisons of South Korea to the rest of the OECD.
25. Comparisons of degree of dedication of national GNP to an export-led economy.
26. Comparative militarization of the country (military spending/exports/imports; national army scale).
27. Comparing the relative degree of primate urbanization (meaning, one major city in the country) to the degree of multiple cities in a country where the latter are more competitive for their own regional-to-national development or their own regional-to-international development within the country.
28. Comparing counties with cultural revolutions (like North Korea) to countries without cultural revolutions (like South Korea).
29. Comparing countries unable to keep going to war, having coups, or having refugees, to countries that have been able to avoid repeating cycles of war, coups, and refugees.
30. Past or present in world history, comparing countries that have a durable traditional aristocracy in economic, political and cultural hegemony (like Japan or some European nations) to countries that have had their traditional aristocracy purged from political, economic, and/or cultural power whether via a cultural revolution (like China or Vietnam) or purged without a cultural revolution (like North Korea and South Korea), even if North Korea had it own further cultural revolution on top of that.
31. Comparisons of South Korea's grass roots development to other countries with grass roots development.
32. Comparisons of South Korea to other countries with or without strong regional identities.
33. Comparing South Korea's earlier periods of a regional cultural wave to other developing countries' regional cultural waves.
34. Comparing South Korea's dependency on stable globalized trade in our modern world-system's dynamics to earlier Mediterranean world-system dynamics before 1177 BCE.
35. Comparing media regimes.

Appendix 3
Comparing Good Choices and Good Accidents: Summarized Comparative Methods Chosen to Think About the Development Outlier of South Korea; Organized in a Chart of Comparative Factors Between South Korea and North Korea

This is an extended list for Chapter 3's discussion about the 'good choices' and 'good accidents' (general background contexts) through which fast development has occurred in South Korea. Reading down the two comparable columns, for South Korea and for North Korea, it shows the large aggregate of both factors for South Korea. There are two ways to read this chart. First, this chart is organized to compare both Korean states explicitly on many factors. This comparison helps to think more explicitly about how only South Korea built virtuous cycles of development and how it successfully kept those virtuous cycles down the development gauntlet with these good choices and good accidents, while North Korea by the 1970s was unable to do either. Second, this chart is an argument of what helps or harms fast development more generally, for what are more general 'good choices' and general 'good accidents' that facilitate or damage fast development drives globally. Thus in this second sense the column for South Korea is symbolic and proxy for the rest of the successfully developed world, while the column for North Korea is symbolic and proxy for the rest of the less-developed world. Typically a "Y" (meaning 'yes') in the column means a positive factor of good choices or good accidents, and typically "N" (meaning 'no') means a negative or hampering effect upon developing virtuous cycles of development, except when noted in the inverse in a few rows that have editorial comments describing how a 'no' or a missing factor can be positive in a few factors as well. (Note: the abbreviation "CB on A" means "checks and balances on aristocratic," oligarchic, and/or private economics and politics.)

Factor	North Korea	South Korea
Missing Aristocracy	Y	Y

(continued)

G.-C. Shin and M. D. Whitaker, *The Korean Wave in a Post-Pandemic World*,
https://doi.org/10.1007/978-981-99-3683-0

(continued)

Factor	North Korea	South Korea
Homogeneous culture; single unchallenged cultural hegemony* (Note: As said earlier, it is possible there is another equally good factor at the other extreme: having a high very divided and heterogeneous culture that encourages such collaboration by lacking a large 'veto' group within the wider national culture. This means as long as there is not a single dominant cultural portion and not a single-heritage elite culture [like Mauritius, for example, and only somewhat for Singapore, Taiwan, or Japan, or Malaysia], then a more 'synthetic' modern collective national ethos can be developed similar to a more 'natural' or 'easier' modern developmental ethos possible from a homogeneous culture per se.)	Y CB on A	Y CB on A
Blocked external war/military leadership despite ongoing military threats (from 1953)	Y/N, partial	Y, CB on A*
Top down developmental state	Y	Y
Short colonialism	Y, yet see 2nd of Collier's traps below	Y
Authoritarian leadership (Collier's point about it being good up to a point in development to stop systemic civil war in a poor country, though bad for further development in a country growing more wealthy)	Y	Y, hybrid
Experienced leaderships	N	Y, CB on A
Degree of Escaping Collier's Four Traps of Development		
1. Cycles of coups, countercoups, & civil wars; 'the conflict trap'	N	**N/Y, partial escape**
– Civil war trap	N, escaped	N, escaped
– Coup trap	N, escaped	Y/N, yet now done?
– Military leadership trap (not one of Collier's points)	Y, trapped	Y/N, partially trapped more in the past and more escaped now; however, it is hybrid: still military networks are of major importance in civilian leadership and in political and economic life
– Catastrophic loss of allies, loans, sponsorship, 1970s–90s (not one of Collier's points)	Y	N

(continued)

(continued)

Factor	North Korea	South Korea
– International allies hold back internal/external violence (not one of Collier's points)	Y, on external N, on internal	Y, on external; Y, on internal
– Refugees	N	N/Y, partial (some NK refugees in SK)
2. Raw material wealth dedication as underdevelopment trap; 'the raw material trap'	Y	**N, escaped**; CB on A; SK zone lacks many raw materials, similar to Japan's lack
– Short colonialism (not one of Collier's points though colonialism is typically based on raw material extraction)	Y, officially; N, unofficially since NK remains a neo-colonial client state after colonialism in keeping up raw material export to USSR historically & China now, just as NK zone kept up raw material export to Japanese Empire earlier	Y
3. 'Landlocked with bad neighbors'	N, escaped	**N/Y, partial escape**
– Landlocked	N, escaped	N, escaped
– Bad neighbors	N, escaped	Y, not escaped
4. Bad Governance (Corruption) in a Small Country	Y	**N, mostly escaped;** CB on A; escape into sound administration yet with corruption nonetheless; escape in larger demography, economy, geography
– Bad governance	Y	N, escaped
– Corruption	Y	Y/N, partial escape
– Small country demographically (escape bad governance with bigger population)	Y/N, borderline, same size as Taiwan	N, escaped with bigger population
– Small country economically (escape bad governance with bigger economy)	Y, not escaped	N, escaped with bigger economy
– Small country geographically (not one of Collier's points; escape with externally owning/renting productive land, yet potentially back to growing bad governance abroad and at home)	N, not escaped	Y, escaped via land rented overseas, yet may encourage corruption abroad and at home

(continued)

(continued)

Factor	North Korea	South Korea
– Wide Culture/Status for Higher Education; can pay for it (not one of Collier's points)	N	Y, so escaped with wider higher education
5. 'the fifth trap'; Collier's addendum of either 'Seizing the Chance' of Development or 'Missing the Chance' of Development; this means that even if a country can escape all four traps, it can be pointless sometimes since global investment in a country depends on external conditions of world-system and if other countries are there first or more stable then stasis of lack of development can continue even in an 'untrapped' country, and this raises the chances of falling into a conflict trap (Collier, 2007)	N, not escaped	**Y, escaped**
The 'sixth trap'—middle income trap (not one of Collier's traps)	N, no escape; never arrived	Y, escape by 1980s; telecommunication & car exports first; plus, kept escaping to other fresh sectors in time particularly in many electronics sectors (smartphones, semiconductors, OLED TVs) and the Korean Wave, etc.
Culture: Dedication to Collective Continuity, Equity, Health, Families, Nation, Education, Participation, Transparency		
Homogeneous culture and ethnicity; clear cultural hegemony	Y, CB on A originally yet developed later its own neo-aristocracy so N/'no' later as well	Y, CB on A
Traditional culture, common social status, and 'family values' more prominent than cultural revolution	N	Y
Traditional culture, common social status, and 'family values' more prominent than individualism	Y	Y

(continued)

(continued)

Factor	North Korea	South Korea
Policies to preserve/subsidize traditional cultural heritage, artifacts, and transmission of traditional cultural skills; 'living treasures' instead of demote it	N/Y, because of cultural revolution, yet other themes supported	Y/N, deep support after 1963 and only partial repression in short period of 1970s like against shamanism in 1970's grass roots development yet recognition now; CB on A
High levels of tertiary education (Master's; PhD's)	N	Y
Universal military service or national service programs of common youth and adult acculturation	Y	Y
More transparent state/corp. finance (SK post 'IMF crisis,' 1997)	N.A.	Y/N
Universal Welfare state	N, military only	Y, tax-subsidized public health insurance & retirement accounts for Koreans and visiting foreign nationals alike
Public Hospitals	Y	Y
Low Child Mortality	Y	Y
Avoiding Child Malnutrition	N	Y
Longer Life Spans	Y/N; somewhat	Y
Growing Population	Y, later N	Y, later N
Environmental renewal/restoration; policies of reforestation	N	Y
Attempts to demote inequalities of poor rural vs. wealthy urban	N	Y
Hybrid policies		
Hybrid economic development policy (export-led economy with regional grass roots development; policies for and protections of small and medium enterprises (SMEs) versus large companies' effects on them of economic shakeout even while aiding larger companies in export sector particularly)	N	Y
Hybrid economic protectionism (national economic protectionism in certain sectors as a safer test-bed allowing for later expertise and competition in international exports instead of simply national economic protection only for its own 'non-developmental' sake	N	Y

(continued)

(continued)

Factor	North Korea	South Korea
Global participation in export-led development	N	Y, CB on A
Odd mix of export-economy, strong markets, and big companies combined with strong welfare state that is seen only in a few other countries of world like Costa Rica, Mauritius, Chile, and Kerala in India (Sandbrook et al., 2007)	N	Y
More economically dictatorial when poorer (state & /or chaebol)	Y	Y
More economically democratic when richer (demote chaebol)	N, N.A.	Y/N
Hybrid political system (hybrid dictatorial/ democratic political system flexing over time; and/or at least a history of dictatorship-republicanism merged throughout in the same constitution; this allows any informal political shifts and coups to occur within a constitutional arrangement, and even ongoingly provides formal checks on informal dictatorship (i.e., without the deep formal institutional reformatting or discontinuity often seen in dictatorships that do reformat and do create discontinuities in formal institutions)	N	Y
More politically dictatorial when poorer	Y	Y
More politically democratic when richer	N / N.A.	Y
Transitions from military leadership to civil leadership are smooth or at least smoother than other states	N / N.A.	Y, smoother than other states at least; SK transition from 1988 to 1992 was a dual military transition and a democratic transition, presumed more stabilizing as both factors got a transition instead of only one
Five year plans	Y	Y
State creating and 'curating' a competitive capitalist market economy, instead of states creating crony oligarchies in economic sectors; avoiding economic oligarchies with their lesser innovations; this is different than economic oligarchy per se; the question is whether it is a state-sponsored oligarchy within a particular sector or a state-sponsored competitive capitalist market economy	N	Y/N, partial

(continued)

(continued)

Factor	North Korea	South Korea
Having both government-owned companies and private companies competing with each other in a sector	N	Y
Having both government-owned companies and private companies with certain governmental economic sectors off limits to a competitive market economy	N	Y/N
Special rules to promote small and medium-sized businesses as a durable share of market economy whether	N	Y
– in financial perks from the state	N	Y
– or in forced closures of only large stores on certain days	N	Y
– or links between larger companies and many SMEs	N	Y
Specific Sectors of Economic and Political Development		
Cheap energy / dependable electricity	N	Y
Nationally Inclusive Electrification, w/o Marginal/Regional Triage	N	Y
Development of textiles	Y	Y
Development of export of steel/chemicals/ smelting of metals	N	Y
Development of export of construction industry and shipbuilding	N	Y
Development of export of automobiles	N	Y
Development of export of telecommunications	N	Y
– Hardware-based development	N	Y
– Software-based development	N	N/Y (games; crypto)
Development of cultural production / Cultural wave	N	Y
High level of state-led, coordinated, financial assistance in research and development	N	Y (generally top in the world)
Internationally-Recruited Innovation Cluster-based development	N	N, attempted, still failing, yet trying
Domestic-Recruited Innovation	N	Y
Capable of re-centering the global economy into themselves via growing economies of scale in cheaper transportation than competitors in the world-system (Bunker, 2005; Levinson, 2006)	N	Y

(continued)

(continued)

Factor	North Korea	South Korea
Capable of re-centering global economy into themselves via economies of scale in cheaper raw material bulk prices than competitors in the world-system (Bunker, 2005)	N	Y
Capable of re-centering global economy into themselves in economies of scale in cheaper production, lower labor costs and favorable foreign investment, etc. (So, 1990)	N	Y
Military export economy	N	Y
National public hospitals / health care system	Y	Y
Decentralized Land Redistribution	N/Y, private usufruct recently to end famine	Y
Grass roots development	N	Y, CB on A
Loss of Allies and/or Creation of Policies that Encourage Starvation and Famine by lack of Agricultural Innovation	Y, then slightly N after famine in the 1990s	N
Policies of national economic autonomy	Y	Y/N, hybrid
Global city infrastructure; global financial and corporate headquarters find the place attractive	N	Y, CB on A
Singular major national primate city (without divisions of elite purpose across different regional cities)	Y	Y
Cluster-based development / Innovation Clusters (university-industry hybrid tech spinoffs, entrepreneurship zones, special legal perks for such national/int'l zones; typically linked geographically to global city zones)	N	Y/N (homogeneous culture makes it difficult to compete in this sector and to recruit internationally & durably)
National economic protectionism	Y	Y/N partial
National autonomy policies	Y	Y/N partial, CB on A
Good Public and Private Transportation	N	Y
Saturated Mobile Phone Networks	N	Y
Follow external agents' advice and financial aid/debt	Y, in USSR and China	N/Y, only somewhat U.S.A. or IMF policy pressures; other points rejected
'Mid-size' demographically	N, maybe "too small"	Y
'Small' geographically	Y	Y
Kinds of violence, military and civil	Y	Y/N, partial
– Externally-funded guerrilla warfare	N	N

(continued)

(continued)

Factor	North Korea	South Korea
– Externally-funded/organized assassination & terrorism	Y, mutual decapitation assassination attempts of SK and NK leadership, pause by '72; assassination attempts continued by NK bombing SK airliners, & NK bombing SK's leaders in state visits abroad	Y/N, ended after 1970s; mutual decapitation assassination attempts of SK and NK leadership, yet stopped by 1972
– Curtailing freedom of movement / travel / urban curfews	Y	Y/N; yes earlier, then no later
– Curtailing freedom of speech / rel. / civil society / press	Y	Y/N; yes earlier, then no later
– Curtailing freedom of political organizing / parties / labor	Y	Y (continuing); a left wing party was banned in 2013, an act that had only been done once before in Korean history in 1958; protests broken up by police continues
– Autonomous religious pluralities and civil society spheres	N	Y, CB on A
– Civil-political plurality and civil political/ cultural rights	N	Y/N, hybrid, CB on A

Appendix 4
The Seven Regimes of Communication, a List and General Timeline Over the Last 5,000 Years

Each media regime change punctures the hegemony of the previous regime. Thus, media changes come out of and depend on the history of the previous media regime, yet that fails to mean the next regime will automatically be successful. However, it can create challenges to leadership in rearrangements of the past six well-practiced procedures of cultural reproduction like: education, communication/transmission, information gathering, making decisions, selective promotion, and selective censorship. Older institutional leaderships have less power to do all six over time in a successful media regime change.

Media regime change starts to create 'institutional mismatches': social, political, and cultural lags of older institutions compared to an updated daily life of communication in a challenging and fresh media regime. Institutions are of necessity good at using and building themselves via older technological media regimes. Thus media regimes condition how leaderships and whole cultures reproduce their own power. However, as novel media regimes are invented within past cultures, it is hypothesized that such institutional mismatch can slowly erode past leadership's power regimes. These tend both to dissolve slowly after a time when a novel media regime's saturation is reached in the wider culture for how information is flowing, and more quickly when some conflicting events facilitate a showdown between different media-using groups in the culture. Of course if it rarely reaches (or is allowed to reach) these contexts, a media regime change can fail to happen. It is historically contingent. For instance, China still uses complex scripts despite many simple scripts invented in its peripheries around it for millennia. Korea rocketed ahead in the late 1800s skipping several media regimes or getting them simultaneously, in the series below. As said, it is historically contingent.

G.-C. Shin and M. D. Whitaker, *The Korean Wave in a Post-Pandemic World*,
https://doi.org/10.1007/978-981-99-3683-0

The seven media regime inventions so far in world history are described in terms of what came before them that got interrupted, challenged, or punctured by the latter media regime's challenge.

1. Regime 1: **oral language**; 'no language' punctured by oral language itself; Ong's 'first orality'; oral communication is the first regime, taking us from animals to something closer to *homo symbolicus*, linked into particular small cultures of oral communities, oral stories, and oral poetry, and oral creation myths different than the next group in cultural transmission. It includes symbolic communication with the body directly of all kinds still, and thus includes body language-based communications like dance, song, and music that likely existed before oral language itself. Politically and culturally, this is a whole world without any state governments, yet potentially some major chiefdoms, yet with medicinal shamanic elites created by this media regime, with the human body as the medium of communication and power alone.
2. Regime 2: **complex scripts**; oral languages punctured by complex scripts; this started as tokens with symbols or as symbols by shape themselves that start to be used as 'written' memory aids before full complex scripts were elaborated. Many examples of cave art in Europe already show a common set of symbolic shapes for millennia, so it is likely oral language developed some form of symbolic picture notation as well. However, even as complex scripts were invented, still oral communication exists as well. Complex scripts become elaborated in the bureaucracies of the first territorial states around 3,500 BCE in Mesopotamia, and in many other birthplaces of urban civilization that all developed their own complex scripts built into a particular physical medium suitable for long-term storage in their local ecological situation: such as the early quipu (rope knot writing) found in early Caral, or the mud brick and cuneiform mix of Mesopotamia, etc. Complex scripts are pictorial-to-'local oral' sounds of those pictures since the origins of these scripts are as memory aids. Thus, complex scripts require a human translator, speaking that oral language, to actually understand the sometimes thousands of symbolic pictures (standing for remembering *pictures* that help remember the oral sounds), instead of the signs representing sounds directly themselves. There are several kinds of complex scripts: logographic, ideographic, and/or rebus-syllabic writing. All complex scripts required a living oral speaker of an oral language to translate the written scripts of the language (because only they know what the symbolic pictures 'sound' like), so this is why many older complex scripts were lost until 'rediscovered' from the 1800s onward by patient research, testing, and study. When complex scripts lose oral speakers, no one living knows how to translate the sound meaning of the picture symbols anymore—with even the sound-to-picture relationship itself soon lost by linguistic drift anyway in the oral language. However, most complex script civilizations only used the technology in a very small percentage of the

population, with scribal elites being the "original 1%" lording over a widely oral-only and non-literate population. Thus complex scripts were mainly used to expand an administrative and exclusionary control system of a tiny number of literate elites in a bureaucracy of states over a mass of oral speakers. Complex scripts allowed scale of such cultures and their bureaucratic states to expand, as well as to plan and to have detailed accurate data for longer than one human lifetime—data that had been otherwise changed by ongoing oral story changes in transmission. Politically and culturally, complex scripts allowed many human activities to grow in scale and to gain more detail: larger states and larger logistics for labor constructions, larger trade, wider aggregate taxation bases that could compare records of previous generations, measurements, detailed receipts, inventions of libraries, etc. This set the stage for the next media regime change within the periphery of the culture of a complex script, or even in the shared periphery between multiple cultures of different complex scripts.

3. Regime 3: **simple scripts**; complex script civilizations and/or oral language groups punctured by simple scripts. True phonetic symbols as scripts develop, thus they had far fewer signs required. With far fewer signs, simple scripts are easily learned, shared, distributed, and copied by amateurs. Cultures of shared manuscripts are easier to accomplish, and *cross-cultural* discussion and communication is easier to create for the first time. There are three main kinds of simple scripts: abjads (writing consonant sounds only—like Hebrew and Arabic), abugidas (writing combined consonant–vowel units or syllables, with each syllable having a symbol like Indian Devanagari or Japanese hiragana or katakana), and alphabets (writing all consonant sounds and vowel sounds separately like the Greek alphabet). Korean "Hangeul" is a hybrid: it is an alphabet yet it is written only as a syllable-based abugida, and it has figural principles like a complex script of being a notation of abstract line *images* trying to show the approximate proper mouth-to-tongue shapes of the sounds to make as you read.

   a. As implied above, the world of complex scripts are punctured by the invention of various mass publics of simple scripts creating peer to peer religious/scientific communities sharing widely many different texts in a plural manuscript culture without clear textual authorities or 'canonization'. As a technology, the idea of simple scripts spread rapidly through the world like an early peer-to-peer Internet.
   b. Simple scripts allow wider scales of communication, and this sets the stage for the next media regime change within the periphery of the culture of a simple script, or even in the shared periphery between multiple cultures of different simple scripts or in the periphery between simple scripts and complex scripts.

4. Regime 4: **mass printing**; simple script civilizations, complex script civilizations, and/or oral cultures punctured by mass printing. Mass printing typically begins as one carved wooden 'page' or block-based printing, then moving to wooden/clay/metal type-based printing. It requires a paper medium, an ink

medium, as well as durable harder materials to make the blocks that can stand many thousands of pressings easily without falling apart.

a. It additionally requires a lot of social dynamics for successful ongoing mass printing like: mass printing technological skills, cheap paper, ink, mass markets, and politically favorable circumstances. All are required. Thus durable mass printing requires more than 'technology', since it requires either state sponsorship and subsidization with its designs of mass population of some kind of centralized instruction, which is expensive; or, it requires an underground press and/or mass commercial markets that are now possible as well to keep it going. Some contexts show both happening at once, for instance, the invention of modern European science is based on the sharing of the same mass produced copies of texts within that generally underground press and mass commercial market, instead of always popularized by state sponsorship, religious sponsorship, or aristocratic dedications for subsidizing and aiding writing and publication that happened as well. Invention of various mass publics of religious communities share widely the exact same texts at this point, instead of sharing an earlier more plural text culture of hand-copied texts without clear authorities that are changed each time regularly with each copy.
b. Mass printing with any scripts (complex or simple) allows wider scales of communication. This set the stage for the next media regime change within the periphery of a culture of mass printing. Some of the main states or zones involved in this earlier revolutionary mass printing invent and popularize faster non-electric telecommunications—though only in contexts where state militaries start to foot the bill for the expensive fresh infrastuctures.

5. Regime 5: **two-way, non-mass-media, non-electrical telecommunications**; simple script civilizations, complex script civilizations, oral cultures, or mass printing civilizations punctured by non-electrical telecommunications. This is distant sharing of information by instantaneous 'line-of-sight' communication of symbols. This can be done in various mediums: from smoke signal towers of Joseon dynasty Korea arrayed completely across the nation to give early warning of invasion from any direction, to the 'world first' series of Chappe's semaphore towers used first by the French Revolutionary state from 1792 (that perhaps saved the French Revolution from incessant royalist invasions from all sides). The Chappe '*telegraphe*' towers were soon adapted to the British Empire next, with the first line between the British Navy's port in the city of Portsmouth on the south coast of England, directly to London's Admiralty building by 1795. The British invented a grid-based shutter-based system of optical telegraph though, with dark and white squares, instead of one based on moving arms like the original French version by Chappe. Typically since the towers are an expensive technology, it was used only by states or empires for important rapid communications to and from the center of power, particularly to and from the coasts to the capital city or directly into the royal palaces of various states. Smoke towers had a simple symbolism only. The Joeson dynasty could send only a series of simple messages depending

on the minimum of one to a maximum number of five smoke fires as 'towers' that could be seen rising separately from a distance. In France of the late 1700s through the early 1800s, Chappe's *telegraphe* towers used different flashed signs based on the orientations of two long wooden arms on the top of the tower that could be rotated by pully and chains into 96 symbolic positions relatively quickly that could flash the symbolic orientation of two arm movements that were coded for a particular phrase (with more than 8,000 possible phrases in the codebook) for complicated messages down the line to the next tower separated by 5 to 20 miles (8 to 32 kilometers). This great (and cheaper) distance between towers was possible due to *telegraphe* towers being watched through a telescope. The secrecy of state messages could be maintained by only a few towers having the codebook for what the tower arm shapes actually meant. Instead of sending a whole message all at once, particular signs were flashed down the whole line, one after another like ongoing batons in a relay race, or a wave, until the whole message was received at the destination. Invented from 1792, Chappe's *telegraphe* towers look like a larger mechanical version of the later British seaman's semaphore flags and arm orientations invented in 1866, mostly because British flag semaphore's codepoints were loosely based on mechanical arm locations of a later French electrical semaphore machine called the Foy-Breguet electrical *telegraphe* invented in 1842—that retained many codepoints/shapes from the original mechanical arms of the earlier non-electrical Chappe *telegraphe* to avoid retraining. However, by the time ocean-based or land-based flag semaphore flags as another non-electrical telecommunications had been invented in 1866, it would have been a non-electrical telecommunications message that could be given to land-based electrical telecommunications—that had replaced the optical telegraph systems already by that time.

6. Regime 6: **many *separate,* one-way, mass-media electrical telecommunications, wired and into wireless broadcasting**; civilizations of non-electrical telecommunication, simple scripts, complex scripts, and/or mass printing punctured by *mostly one-way* mass media electrical telecommunications. This started with wires of the battery-operated electrical telegraph, that were expensive and so used mostly as a non-mass communication, as a military technology, down a single temporary wire before it became commercially popularized as a line of wired electrical communication regularly more permanently installed in parallel to the growing railroad track networks between stations. The italicized phrase above of 'mostly one-way' is used because a syncopated electrical telegraph could be an almost synchronous wired two-way mass communication as well. Plus, there were early, small, two-way wireless and synchronous electrical mass telecommunications possible from the 1890s. However much it was technically possible to be two-way far earlier, in practice, it became easier first (1) to built two-way wired telephones in the late 1800s, while from the early twentieth century only (2) licensing prohibitively the potentially two-way wireless electrical mass telecommunication into a one-way mass communication network. This was due to a confluence of factors: state regulations developing on granted rights to use certain frequencies of the electromagnetic spectrum to avoid confusion between

various wireless transmitters that would interfere with each other; due to state fears of spies being able to use such surreptitious technologies to communicate in World War I; and due to fear of the Marconi corporations developing an international private monopoly on use of the electromagnetic spectrum and using it against various states or for other states. (3) A third factor why it became mostly a one-way mass communications medium was the production expense. This dynamics created expensive production studios built from a few wealthy or powerful voices that was easier to broadcast via radio or to show on a movie screen to many millions of silent receivers of radio, of movies, of recorded music, etc. This resulted in many different, parallel, and separated physical mediums and electrical technologies of storage or transmission (i.e., one mass telecommunications technology for sound broadcasting in radio music halls and for reception in many home radio units; one mass telecommunications technology for sound recordings/playback in professional recording studios and in record players; one technology for image showing/recording/playback in movie cameras and movie theater projection equipment; one technology for image recording in television studio cameras and in home televisions, etc.). These different parallel tracks of one-way mass electrical communication slowly started to merge first in sound and vision of movies by the late 1920s, even as more singular technologies of wireless mass radio and discs of mass music recordings continued. In short, broadcasting and recording mass media production was very expensive at the beginning, giving rise to vastly different big radio studios, movie studios, recording studios, TV studios, etc., each with their own parallel technologies of recording and transmission. This is despite 'radio wireless' starting as small two-way synchronous non-mass media home kits, and with a change of laws turning into 'illegal pirate radio.' Soon, a vast series of parallel one-way mass electrical telecommunication mediums were available at the same time, yet it was applied mostly in a cultural hegemony of expensive, licensed, regulated, dedicated wires or dedicated wireless frequency bands only for state-authorized mass broadcasts on particular frequencies, particular venues, or through particular technologies. This built a world of big one-way (and mostly) state-censored mass entertainment media culture/politics seen in mass telegraph/telephone exchanges, mass media, mass politics, mass movies, mass radio, and broadcast TV. Totally novel recording, (re)transmission, and (re)broadcast of word sounds and images became possible from the 1930s onward, to show 'reruns' of radio or reruns of television—keeping in mind all early radio and television was just a live performance only, done once and lost forever. Understandably, all of these many different versions of one-way mass media created a mass society, a group of people politically and culturally easier to control from a central point of information dispersal—since a mass public then was unable to talk back or produce its own mass communications.

7. Regime 7: ***digitally converging*** **two-way mass-*multi*media networked electrical telecommunications**; 'Computerized Wireless Telecommunications of Digital Electronic Mobile Mass Multi-Media', abbreviated for memory in the suggested easier phrase "Diamond Democracy" that stands for the complicated

literal abbreviation of 'CWT DEM4' (with CWT being of course 'carat weight' for diamond measurement). 'Two-way mass-multimedia' telecommunication starts to puncture other existing media regimes. Two-way mass multimedia in everyone's hand became possible as millions become makers and mass broadcasters of media more cheaply in *miniaturization* of computer equipment, then greater *mobility and cheapness* of it, and then a *network* in the former cheapened technology is possible through which media can be transferred 'virally.' Once more, the state militaries of the world are prominent in this as early media regime users sometimes: the protocols of computer-to-computer communication in the early ARPANET developed into the hypertext protocol for the later Internet, as more personal computers, then commercial traffic, and then mobile smartphones of commercial traffic merged into this medium in electronic packet switching. This electronic two-way network of increasingly civilian mass media of packet switching is different than the one-way mass media broadcasts or mass consumption of a few major producer's voices versus millions of passive consumers as listeners or watchers. Instead, the ever shifting directions of networks of such mass communication are harder to exercise any past centralized state or corporate censorship upon.

From the above contingent historical discussion, despite calling these media regimes #1 through #7, that is for simple convenience. On the one hand, there of course is *a linear development of media regimes* in that the later ones have to develop upon or within the former or in their peripheries, culturally speaking. However, on the other hand, history is contingent in particular cases of states and their media. Thus, there is *nothing like a required linear replacement of media regimes* in history or a required steady improvement or clear replacement. It is quite possible for one state or culture to embrace multiple media regimes at once, or to skip many of them at once. This is because real states and cultures are political regimes that get interrupted and punctured by media regime changes, or, they successfully fend off the challenge of the media regime change in different ways. Sometimes the puncture is healed and change stops. Sometimes the puncture keeps dissolving past power dynamics. Sometimes the puncture is embraced and adopted into the existing hierarchies, instead of required to lead to institutional mismatch and past media (and political) regime collapse. Historical contingency is important. For instance, even after simple scripts were invented, China ignored them and retained its deeper social inequality and unrepresentative management made possible via a situation for how complex scripts were known fluently only by a small percentage of people over a vast zone of only oral speakers. Only true civilizational collapses across the Mediterranean around 1000 BCE of many complex script regime civilizations at once allowed a vast political opening on their common peripheries for the expansion of simple scripts. This was originally in the Phoenicians, yet this as well came from a heritage of the shorter dictation version of 'hieratic' used in a periphery in Egypt to write quickly information by Egyptian scribes alone, wanting to avoid the complex script of hieroglyphs. Given many complex script civilizations died around '1177 BCE' to 1000 BCE, thus simple scripts in the Mediterranean could peter through into a media regime of itself without much serious political challenge. Plus, the Achaemenid Empire intentionally converted itself to simple scripts, mostly because it was a large empire of several different heritage complex scripts at once, so it made more administrative sense to adopt simple scripts at the top of administrative power in that media regime change as well. Additionally, many states and cultures are in multiple regimes at once, and states and cultures can get multiple fresh media regimes at once.

All of this is why term 'media regime' is better to describe the dynamics of past communication regimes or the inventions and challenges from other communication regimes, instead of temporal assumptions about required singular linear replacement with its faulty interpretations that some places are 'backward' laggards in 'epochs' of history, or the equally faulty idea that a culture is defined only by one media regime at a time.

There is one caveat about this linearity however: nowhere so far have people en masse ever intentionally chosen to go backwards to an earlier media regime once experiencing the next one. Indeed, they may go backwards if they lose technology over time, though that is regularly for historical accidents, state collapse, or lack of market profitability, and hardly simply via acts of choice. In that sense, people prefer the easiest media possible for information storage or transmission, and are covetous to keep such ease of transmission instead of lose it and go back to something requiring more skill or hard work to create or to share information as transmission. For instance, people may prefer to have an online video conference, and loathe when the electricity goes out or the Internet is down to go back to telephone conference calls or in-person oral meetings, or written distributed documents. Similarly, once a culture has mass printing, rarely do you see people wanting to go back to manuscript copying services or an exclusive manuscript culture. Thus we as a species are always looking for better media, and the only rationale why we used or changed to older media in the first place is that it was the top best and easiest *at the time.*

Thus, media regime is a better term for communication technologies because each fresh regime invention is an open challenge that can change us and change our organizations, even as history is still open for what happens.

A Global Media View Explaining Both European Exceptionalism and Korean Exceptionalism

There is a wide debate on the origins of Eurocentrism, i.e., the exceptional regional hegemony of Europeans around the Atlantic in the world-system over other civilizations. The same questions now puzzle the world about South Korea. To review the European arguments first, this debate about the past 500 years generally leaves out how Europe almost has always been ahead of other regions in 'saturated' revolutionary media changes that benefited them exclusively for a time—whether in Regime #4, #5, #6, and #7. First, other regions of the world may have been earlier in Regime #4 of mass print though seldom ever were as saturated culturally as Europeans within it. Second, only Europeans invented fresh media regimes that they could exclusively capitalize on like Regime #5, #6, and #7. Why this switch occurred from a weak Europe to a strong Europe is of interest to many modern world historians. Explanations are multiple instead of only the media argument here. Explanations have ranged from: views about the European/Atlantic region having regional exclusive access compared to other regions of the world to exploit the plantation and minerals of the Americas (Blaut); to being beneficiary of a 'triangle trade' of slave labor related to that plantation system, to simply being unconquered by the Mongol empire by the 1300s while all other areas of Eurasia were disrupted; to Europeans hitching a ride on the Islamic world-system of trade from the 1200s and then displacing it (AbuLughod); to the unique mass death of the Black Death in the late 1300s that killed around one-third of Europeans and encouraged greater labor saving machinery in Europe compared to other areas (Gimpel); to other unique connections between royal houses and urban bourgeoisie as a tight political alliance—something most other cultures kept at a distance; to the innate heterogeneity and lack of consolidation of Europe that caused it to war around the world on itself and to militarize oceanic trade for the first time in its insecurities at home (McNeill); to how the spread of European plants and animals disrupted the agricultural systems and cultures of their global competitors (Crosby); to how a series of strong El Nino's in the late 1800s were opportunistically used by Europeans to consolidate empires around the world on their disrupted competing civilizations (Davis); to how Europeans themselves were the first globalized area, taking all good ideas from others and merging with it to expand around the world. All of this matters. However, a point that has rarely been discussed is Europe being world first in a more saturated mass print culture compared to other regions, that allowed much of the scale of Europe mentioned above to go forward. Upon that earlier head start in mass print saturation (Regime #4) after the 1450s came other world firsts in non-electrical telecommunications (Regime #5) and then other world firsts in electrical telecommunications (Regime #6 and #7). This *series* of European media world firsts throughout the expansion of Europeans over others is like the nose on the face that no one sees to think to talk about. This is the unique feature of Europeans around the Atlantic, earlier than others, that helped to set up the inequalities of other points mentioned above as well as organize the tremendous scale that was achieved over others. That made all the difference in the past 500 years for the growing communicative strengths of Euro-Atlantic states, their citizens, their educators, their traders, and their empires versus everyone else. Plus, it was a particular organization of this mass print culture that was unique to other regions of the world with much stronger censorship and state direction in mass printing. In Europe, to the contrary, these rising media regime changes toward more centralized/decentralized and ever cheaper mass publishing from the 1450s onward, originally created out of the head institutions, in turn created a headless public sphere without past state or religious censorship required. Europe as a civilization then was without any central state anyway from which to exercise such censorship on mass printing, even if it had existed. European innovation and growth was unstoppable (even by its own states) from this generally underground public sphere of mass print publishing onward that pushed wide cultural and scientific innovations, and yet pushed a more vetted scientific/technical innovation in alliance generally with those states and investors instead of against them.

In retrospect, Europe by the 1500s was earlier in a saturated mass printing media regime change in which Europe was earlier than any other region, like Korea was earlier in our current saturated media regime change in the twenty-first century compared to any other region. What happened in Europe with saturation toward mass printing after 1450 can be interpreted as the primary media regime change that was a major cause of many later secondary power changes across European organizations of politics, religion/education/science, economics, or finance that many historians frame as autonomous changes.

Respectively, (1) in politics and religion, an earlier media change *can be seen as a major influence in the decline of the Catholic Church and the rise of the many regional Protestant Reformations* from the 1500s that utilized mass print, that continues through the present. Such mass printed rebellions could now at last coordinate the longer and unorganized widespread regional and oral opposition to the Catholic Church seen for centuries in Lollardy for example or in the earlier 'proto-Protestant' rebellion of Jan Hus (1370–1415)—both of which lacked mass printing.

Next, (2) an earlier media change that influenced *a change in education and science* can be seen as the major influence in the decline of Catholic-based science censorship toward the modern European Scientific Revolution from the 1450s that continues in the present. Europeans could now at last coordinate information spreading in older scientific 'pagan' Roman or Greek authors, or 'heathen' Islamic texts, or even 'new works' of science beyond rare secret hand-passed copies—and beyond Catholic or Protestant suppression. Europe blossomed into hundreds of years of mass underground covert publishing with a mass commercial audience, parallel to state and church sponsored-mass printing and censorship that existed yet which were increasingly powerless.

(3) An earlier media change can be seen *as the major economic influence* of the Industrial Revolution of the late 1600s that continues through the present. It accelerated the mass published sharing of innovative technical commercial information in mining, agriculture, and industry and altered technical and market information away from previous different synchronous orally-transmitted secret knowledges of various guilds or smaller regional markets into mass public asynchronous advertising calls to many thousands of readers all at once, and for calls of mass financial investment subscriptions from thousands of readers all at once.

(4) An earlier media change can be seen as the major influence in *the later spread of the ideal politics of democratic republics* that started in the early 1500s that continues through the present. They were first spread in mass publications that repopularized of older Greek and Roman texts themselves with their own state/ethical concerns or even sharing of mass printed copies of older state-centric legal codes from the Roman Empire that inspired mere regional princely states to build more centralized national sovereignties over multiple regional aristocratic or church authorities and courts.

(5) A media regime of mass printing had the power to *invent much about the daily feeling of what are the 'imagined communities' of nations* that we live within today. The previous cultural world of international Latin texts and transnational religious organizations began to regionalize as mass readers of vernacular regional scripts using whatever language and script was the major spoken language in the area as that was the only effective way to make profits in books. In turn, regionalized markets for vernacular language-based Christian Bibles and then more secular regionalized publications in the same language came to dominate and create ideational views of common nationhood, half religious and half secular, instead of previous mental attachments to only more international religious-based states over multiple oral language groups.

(6) Even *the spread of mass education and mass revolution from underclasses that started in the 1800s* that continues through the present depended on the cheapening of European paper from 1802 and the general reduction or elimination of taxes on paper and newspapers. Plus many European revolutionaries of the time preferred just like European capitalists to be in or near the cities of the earliest electronic telegraph communication cores and mass newspaper wire services, to keep an ear for what was happening in Europe and throughout the world in their similar or different secular and global plots and plans.

In summary, Europe was earlier than any other world region in being a saturated culture of mass printing (dis)organized for *large publishing freedoms*. While it seems true that Europe, Korea, and Japan seem to have been quite equally saturated in mass print, hundreds of years ago, plus with all three zones having access to simple scripts of Regime #3 for themselves for centuries that encouraged such mass literacy and peer-based communication within mass print, however both Korea and Japan *lacked large mass publishing freedoms*, i.e., lacked a large or durable underground press or cross-border press and its publishing freedoms like Europe, due to Korea's or Japan's more state-dominated cultural transmissions vetting all mass print and the linguistic isolation of their languages and scripts. However, the wider underground or cross-border publishing freedoms in Europe for hundreds of years in its saturated mass print culture, among many multi-lingual readers of Europe, made all the difference in the world for having greater freedom of individual innovation and cultural innovation in such publishing contexts. Equally, Europe was earlier than any other world region in being a saturated culture earlier in non-electrical telecommunications, and then earlier in one-way electronic telecommunications, and then earlier in two-way electronic telecommunications. This ongoing media inequality of core and periphery as a power arrangement has made all the difference in the world from the 1450s to the present in the world history of different regional hegemonies over other regions. Particularly, these plural media regime changes in electronic telecommunication from the mid-1800s through the 1990s were equally revolutionary to people living only in a world of mass print-only institutions for hundreds of years whether in Europe or in their European empires.

However, it was left to South Korea to be the first nation with a more saturated national culture of mobile smartphones in our current media regime change, instead of any European heritage national areas. That has made all the difference in the world by creating a growing very different regional hegemony over other regions unlike the past Eurocentric ones. Digitally-saturated Korea started to change even metageographical concepts of what are the core states in East Asia and the world. Here's to Korea: may she continue to be a history maker that changes the world.